Georg Simmel (1858–1918)

German social philosopher and microsociologist studied small-group interaction and how people experience the minutiae of everyday life. [Ch. 1, 6]

Émile Durkheim (1858–1917)

French sociologist established the discipline at the Sorbonne in Paris. [Ch. 1, 2, 15, 17]

Thorstein Veblen (1857–1929)

American economist and social critic attacked America's "conspicuous consumption" in *The Theory of the Leisure Class* (1899). [Ch. 1, 7]

🍁 **Herbert Brown Ames (1863–1954)**

Canadian businessman and social activist campaigned for affordable housing for Montreal's working classes. [Ch. 9]

George Herbert Mead (1863–1931)

American social psychologist and symbolic interactionist looked at how the self is constructed through personal exchanges with others. [Ch. 1, 2, 5]

Robert Park (1864–1944)

American urban sociologist was a founding member of the "Chicago School" of sociology. [Ch. 1]

Charles Horton Cooley (1864–1929)

American symbolic interactionist advanced the idea of the looking-glass self, positing that the self is created and reinforced through interactions with others. [Ch. 5, 6]

Max Weber (1864–1920)

German sociologist wrote on topics ranging from economic history to world religion, and identified a set of values ("the Protestant ethic") he considered central to the rise of capitalism. [Ch. 1, 2, 6, 9, 15]

W.E.B. Du Bois (1868–1963)

American social philosopher was among the first to document the experience of American blacks from a sociological perspective. [Ch. 1, 10]

🍁 **Emily Murphy (1868–1933)**

Canadian women's rights activist became the first woman magistrate in the British Empire and, as a journalist, wrote under the pen name "Janey Canuck." [Ch. 8, 11]

🍁 **Annie Marion MacLean (c. 1870–1934)**

PEI-born sociologist specialized in the study of working women. [Ch. 1, 17]

🍁 **Colin McKay (1876–1939)**

Self-educated "radical" sociologist and social activist defended workers' rights in Nova Scotia. [Ch. 9]

Edwin Sutherland (1883–1950)

American criminal sociologist and symbolic interactionist introduced the i... c...

E. Franklin Frazier (1894–1962)

Baltimore-born sociologist ...ioneering studies ...merican families.

...is (1894–1952)

...Toronto ...omist studied ...da's staples ...uenced social ...t. [Ch. 1]

🍁 **Carl Addington Dawson (1887–1964)**

PEI-born educator founded Canada's first sociology department at McGill University in 1922. [Ch. 1]

Antonio Gramsci (1891–1937)

Italian-born political activist developed a theory of hegemony and power. [Ch. 9]

Everett C. Hughes (1897–1983)

American sociologist helped establish the sociology department at McGill University and studied the ethnic division of labour in Quebec before returning to the US to teach at the University of Chicago. [Ch. 1, 6, 10]

Herbert Blumer (1900–1987)

American student of G.H. Mead's coined the term "symbolic interactionism." [Ch. 2]

D0742410

50 — 1860 — 1870 — 1880 — 1890 — 1900

1940 — 1950 — 1960 — 1970

🍁 **Marie Battiste (b. 1949)**

Mi'kmaq scholar wrote about the connection between Aboriginal people and Catholicism. [Ch. 15]

Patricia Hill Collins (b. 1948)

American critical sociologist is known for her work on feminist standpoint theory and intersectionality, the effect of gender discrimination when compounded by other social factors, particularly "race." [Ch. 2, 10]

🍁 **Rod Beaujot (b. 1946)**

University of Western Ontario demographer examined the causes and implications of "delayed life transitions"—the tendency to put off marriage, career, retirement, etc., till later in life. [Ch. 13, 14]

🍁 **Arthur Kroker (b. 1945)**

Canadian technology and culture theorist advanced the notion of the "virtual class," a class of people dependent for their livelihood on virtual technologies and the Internet. [Ch. 22]

Margaret Humphreys (b. 1944)

English social worker brought attention to the plight of British "home children," who were removed from their homes and forcibly relocated to orphanages overseas. [Ch. 15]

🍁 **Haroon Siddiqui (b. 1942)**

Indo-Canadian journalist has written extensively about the Muslim experience. [Ch. 15]

George Ritzer (b. 1940)

American sociologist applied Weber's theory of formal rationalization to present-day consumer capitalism, coining the term "McDonaldization" to describe the way fast-food restaurants and other businesses apply the principles of efficiency, quantification, predictability, and control. [Ch. 6, 7]

Judith Butler (b. 1956)

American feminist theorist wrote *Gender Trouble* (1990), in which she examined the way people "perform" gender roles in an effort to meet society's expectations for the biological categories of "male" and "female." [Ch. 11]

Kimberlé Crenshaw (b. 1959)

American legal theorist helped develop critical race theory and coined the term "intersectionality" to refer to the linking forms of prejudice based on "race" and gender. [Ch. 2, 10]

🍁 **Mary-Ann Kirkby (b. 1959)**

Canadian writer has written about the Hutterite experience from an insider perspective. [Ch. 15]

Manfred Steger (b. 1961)

Australian director of the Globalism Research Centre is a leading globalization theorist. [Ch. 20]

🍁 **Naomi Klein (b. 1970)**

Canadian activist and consumer critic wrote the pioneering anti-globalization work *No Logo* (1999), in which she attacked the labour practices and marketing strategies of "brand bullies" such as Nike, The Gap, and Microsoft. [Ch. 7]

This timeline highlights some of the figures whose achievements have played a significant role in bringing the discipline of sociology to its present state. While the study of social life began in the earliest civilizations, the Arab scholar Ibn Khaldûn (1332–1406) is generally seen as the first to set down formally the principles of sociology in his work of world history *Al Muqaddimah*. Sociology emerged as a subject of serious academic inquiry in Europe in the late nineteenth and early twentieth centuries, with Comte, Durkheim, and Weber often cited as being among the "founders" of modern sociology. By the mid-twentieth century, sociology had become firmly established as a formal discipline at universities and colleges across North America.

The timeline traces the history of modern sociology through a number of individuals whose work is described in this textbook—sociologists and social activists, as well as historians, culture and media theorists, political scientists, educators, and others. The numbers in brackets indicate the chapter(s) of the book where the contributions of the individual are discussed.

FOUNDATIONS *of* SOCIOLOGY

John Steckley

with Guy Letts

OXFORD
UNIVERSITY PRESS

OXFORD
UNIVERSITY PRESS

Oxford University Press is a department of the University of Oxford.
It furthers the University's objective of excellence in research, scholarship,
and education by publishing worldwide. Oxford is a registered trade mark
of Oxford University Press in the UK and in certain other countries.

Published in Canada by
Oxford University Press
8 Sampson Mews, Suite 204,
Don Mills, Ontario M3C 0H5 Canada

www.oupcanada.com

Library and Archives Canada Cataloguing in Publication

Steckley, John, 1949–
Foundations of sociology / John Steckley.

Includes bibliographical references and index.
ISBN 978-0-19-544322-6

1. Sociology—Textbooks. I. Title.

HM586.S843 2013   301   C2013-901506-X

Cover image: iStockPhoto.com/karrapa

This book is printed on permanent (acid-free) paper ∞.

Printed and bound in the United States of America

1 2 3 4 — 17 16 15 14

Contents at a Glance

Contents

3 Social Research Methods 48

8 Deviance 188

PART III • SOCIAL DIFFERENCE 213

11 Gender and Sexuality 270

12 Disability 296

PART IV • SOCIAL INSTITUTIONS   361

22 Social Change and the Future   600

Tables, Figures, and Boxed Features

Tables

Figures

Boxed Features

For Starters

Our Stories

The Point Is...

Going Global

QUICK HITS

Telling It Like It Is

POVs

Introducing . . .
Foundations of Sociology

Oxford University Press is delighted to introduce *Foundations of Sociology*, a one-of-a-kind textbook designed to be the most comprehensive and dynamic introduction to sociology for Canadian students. Building on the strengths of John Steckley's highly acclaimed *Elements of Sociology*, this new introduction delivers even more straight-talking, thought-provoking coverage of an expanded selection of topics—from research methods, social difference, and culture to consumption, disability, aging, and mass media. We hope that as you browse through the pages that follow, you will see why we believe *Foundations of Sociology* is the most exciting and innovative textbook available to Canadian sociology students today.

Six Things That Make This a One-of-a-Kind Textbook

A Canadian Textbook for Canadian Students

Written specifically for a Canadian audience, *Foundations of Sociology* brings you the stories of the figures and events at the heart of sociological inquiry in this country: Dawson and Clark, Porter and Goffman, Dorothy Smith and Daniel G. Hill, the Winnipeg General Strike and Quebec's "Quiet Revolution," and much, much more.

For Starters

A Picture of Poverty in Canada's Backyard

Situated on the west coast of James Bay in Ontario's far north, the Cree community of Attawapiskat gained international attention in October 2011, when the leaders of Attawapiskat First Nation declared a state of emergency, citing inadequate housing and poor sanitation. It was not the first time the community had resorted to this measure. Just two years earlier, in May 2008, hundreds of residents were evacuated from their tents, trailers, and shelters because of serious flood conditions. And yet, in the fall of 2011, the media seized on stories of poverty and overcrowded, substandard housing as though they were new developments, while politicians claimed to have had no idea how bad the situation was.

How bad was it? You can read statistics about lack of housing, but to me, this account tells the story much more vividly:

In a one-room, tented shack where Lisa Kiokee-Linklater is watching television with her two toddlers, two mattresses lie on the floor. Each is a bed for three. Mould is creeping across one

mattress even though Ms Kiokee-Linklater just bought it last summer. It cost her $1,000.

There is no running water, no bathroom, and cold comes through the uninsulated floor. There is little room for her four children to play. The broiling cast-iron wood stove that takes up one corner of the room represents a burn hazard and eliminates the notion of the rambunctious play that is the norm for most young kids.

Moving into the tent was Ms Kiokee-Linklater's choice. It seemed a step up from her previous home next door, where she shared a single bathroom with 20 other people until it became too much for her and her growing family.

"It's kind of better, yeah," she said, keeping a watchful eye on a son as he ate spaghetti with his fingers. "But during the winter, it's hard. I cut back on the baths because it is so cold." (Scoffield 2011)

An Inclusive, Narrative Approach

Sociology is the study of people, and in *Foundations of Sociology*, the people tell their stories. Students will read first-hand accounts of what it's like to fast during Ramadan, to come out to your family, to face barriers to physical mobility, to experience racism on campus, to confront the gender expectations of an Islamic upbringing, and to raise daughters in an era of Lingerie Barbie and La Senza Girl.

A Visual, Thought-Provoking Approach

Students are challenged on every page to adopt a sociological imagination and see the sociology in everyday life. Carefully chosen photos and captions, provocative critical thinking questions, and thoughtful end-of-chapter review questions all invite readers to apply the theory and take a stance.

Coverage of Canada's First Nations

No sociology textbook can claim more extensive coverage of the issues that have affected and that continue to affect Canada's Aboriginal peoples, from two-spirit persons, residential schools, and the Sixties Scoop to Idle No More, Attawapiskat, and Grassy Narrows.

---

14 | Family   377

Telling it Like It Is

A Student POV

Telling Your Family You're Gay

Growing up in the small town of Whitby, Ontario, I never felt the negative effects of discrimination. I am an English-speaking, Caucasian female and had never been a part of a minority group, in any sense of the word. At the age of 21, this changed and I became aware of how easily people are judged. I am a lesbian, and from the moment I became open about my sexual preferences, I felt first-hand what it feels like to be viewed based solely on one aspect of your life, and not as an entire person. When meeting someone new in my life it was as though I was wearing a sign on my forehead reading, "I am gay," and it was perceived as "I am gay . . . that is everything you need to know about me." Once I divulge this information, almost instantly people form opinions on who I am as a person and who I should be. They develop expectations that quite often are illogical and unrealistic. By writing a paper such as this one, I am being given the opportunity to address a few of these numerous stereotypes and prejudiced beliefs. Hopefully, I can educate some to stop these beliefs from spreading.

From my experience, the original thought that people tend to have when finding out that I am gay is that it is simply a phase I am going through, a time of experimentation and rebellious behaviour. My brother's reaction was as such. He believed that it was just a phase and that it would pass. He

continued to express this for an entire year after I had told him. He realizes otherwise now. . . . When telling my mother (who along with the rest of my family is extremely supportive of me), I was shocked to hear her initial reaction to what I had told her. After a moment or two of silence, she . . . said, "But I thought you wanted to get married and have kids one day." The thought of these dreams possibly fading away is what seemed to unsettle her the most. I found two things wrong and rather presumptuous about this statement. To begin with, the idea that a woman must want/need a husband and children to live a fulfilling life is old-fashioned and a step backward from the times we live in today. I figure, why can't a woman who is independent and who has a satisfying career be considered to lead a successful, happy life, despite the fact that she has no family to raise. Furthermore, my mother was correct in assuming that I did want a family, but it was not the family that she had in mind. Marriage and children are a large part of my future plans, and, with adoption, and artificial insemination, this is a very feasible option for lesbian couples. Simply because a woman falls in love with another woman, it does not mean that she didn't grow up with the same desire for nurturing children and caring for a home and family that a lot of heterosexual girls do.

Interestingly, despite the recent condo boom, we continue to build houses that are on average larger than in the past, but house fewer people in more households. Why do you think that is?

What do YOU think?

do you think is the more significant cause of statistics noted above: the aging population or the delay among people under 30? What other might help you address this question?

Family in Quebec

By just about every statistical measure the family in Quebec is sociologically distinct from the family in other parts of Canada. For a snapshot of the differences, consider that in 1996, Quebec was the province with:

- *the highest cohabitation rate:* 20.5 per cent of all families, almost twice the next highest rate in Canada (New Brunswick, at 10.9 per cent)
- *the lowest marriage rate:* 3.1 per 100,000, significantly lower than the next lowest rate (British Columbia's 5.2)

---

268   Part III | Social Difference

The Point Is...

Idle No More: A Women's Ethnic Movement

At its heart, Idle No More is an Aboriginal women's movement. After all, who else would have thought of flash mob round dances as a form of protest? More seriously, it is because it is essentially about alliance with other Canadians rather than separation that you can see that it is an Aboriginal women's movement.

Idle No More was the brainchild of four Saskatchewan women, including three Cree and a white author and lawyer, who began the movement in November 2012 and coined its famous byword. They were inspired to act by their opposition to the anti-environmental and anti-Aboriginal sections of the federal Conservative government's omnibus Bill C-45. They started their personal move from "idleness" by organizing a series of teach-ins, beginning in Saskatoon, then extending to Regina and Prince Albert. Once it hit social media with the hashtag #idlenomore, the movement grew exponentially. The movement gained further momentum in December,

when Attawapiskat chief Theresa Spence added her voice to the cause to draw attention to the hideous housing conditions in her James Bay Cree community. She went on a 43-day hunger strike, drinking only liquids while waiting for the prime minister to travel the short physical distance, but long democracy distance, to meet with her.

The women behind Idle No More are principally opposed to the one-sided dismantling of the Indian Act. All agree that the Indian Act must change, but this requires a release of power and control by the federal government. Stephen Harper's Conservative government is quite happy to give up its legal duties, but it does not want to surrender power and control. Another big goal of Idle No More, one that resonates particularly with Aboriginal women as traditional keepers of the land, is protection of our rivers, lakes, and oceans—a cause that affects all Canadians.

Idle No More protesters make their way from Victoria Island, site of Theresa Spence's hunger strike, to Parliament Hill, in January 2013. Prior to reading this box, did you think of Idle No More as a women's movement? How do you think the participation of young Aboriginal women will change their lives?

Chapters on New Areas of Sociological Research

Foundations of Sociology goes beyond the traditional scope of sociological inquiry—research methods, human difference, and social institutions and models of interaction—to deliver chapters devoted to the topics generating interest among sociologists today, including mass media, consumption, disability, globalization, and the environment.

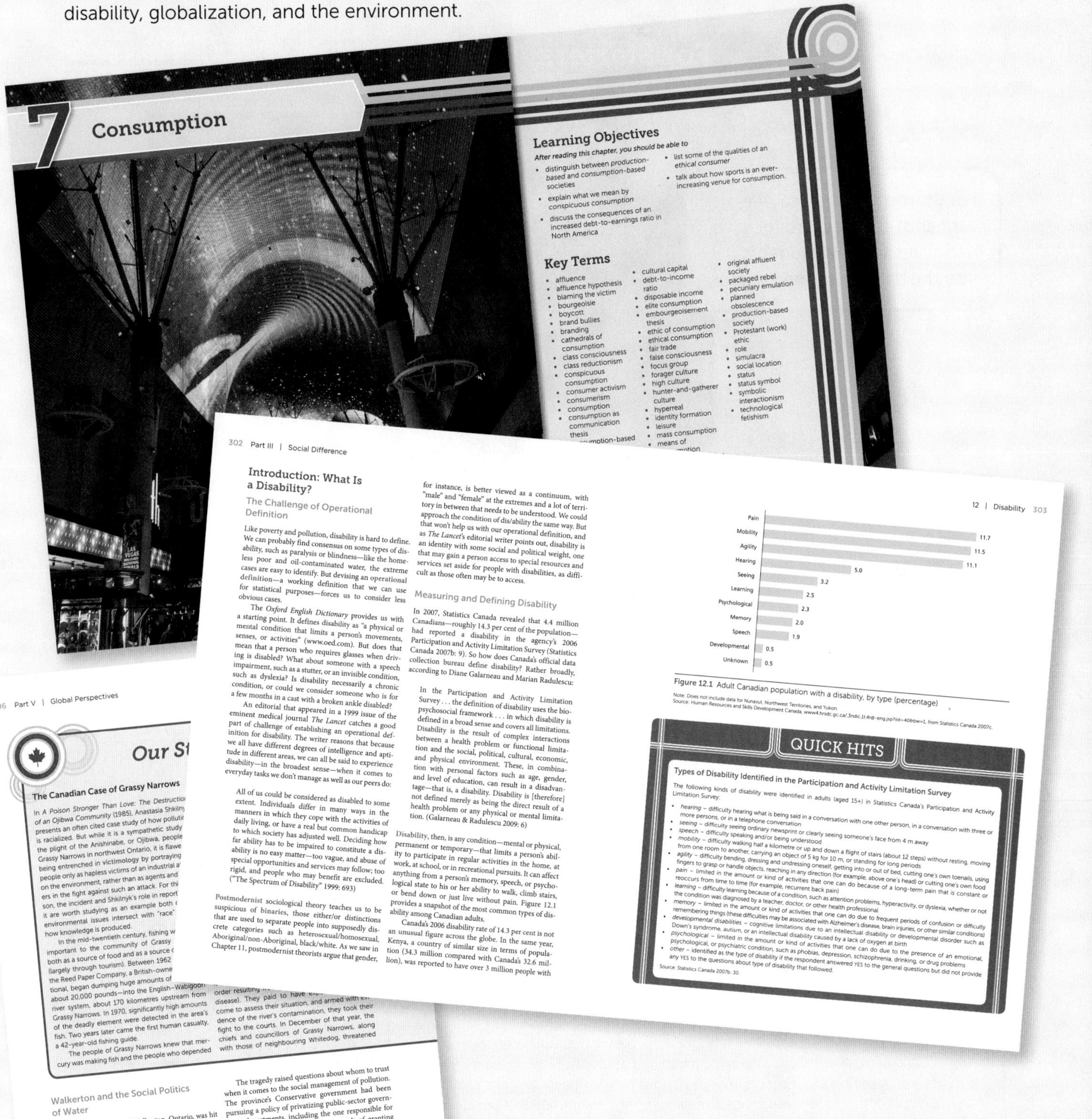

7 Consumption

Learning Objectives

After reading this chapter, you should be able to

- distinguish between production-based and consumption-based societies
- explain what we mean by conspicuous consumption
- discuss the consequences of an increased debt-to-earnings ratio in North America
- list some of the qualities of an ethical consumer
- talk about how sports is an ever-increasing venue for consumption.

Key Terms

- affluence
- affluence hypothesis
- blaming the victim
- bourgeoisie
- boycott
- brand bullies
- branding
- cathedrals of consumption
- class consciousness
- class reductionism
- conspicuous consumption
- consumer activism
- consumerism
- consumption
- consumption as communication thesis
- consumption-based
- cultural capital
- debt-to-income ratio
- disposable income
- elite consumption
- embourgeoisement thesis
- ethic of consumption
- ethical consumption
- fair trade
- false consciousness
- focus group
- forager culture
- high culture
- hunter-and-gatherer culture
- hyperreal
- identity formation
- leisure
- mass consumption
- means of
- original affluent society
- packaged rebel
- pecuniary emulation
- planned obsolescence
- production-based society
- Protestant (work) ethic
- role
- simulacra
- social location
- status
- status symbol
- symbolic interactionism
- technological fetishism

---

302 Part III | Social Difference

Introduction: What Is a Disability?

The Challenge of Operational Definition

Like poverty and pollution, disability is hard to define. We can probably find consensus on some types of disability, such as paralysis or blindness—like the homeless poor and oil-contaminated water, the extreme cases are easy to identify. But devising an operational definition—a working definition that we can use for statistical purposes—forces us to consider less obvious cases.

The *Oxford English Dictionary* provides us with a starting point. It defines disability as "a physical or mental condition that limits a person's movements, senses, or activities" (www.oed.com). But does that mean that a person who requires glasses when driving is disabled? What about someone with a speech impairment, such as a stutter, or an invisible condition, such as dyslexia? Is disability necessarily a chronic condition, or could we consider someone who is for a few months in a cast with a broken ankle disabled?

An editorial that appeared in a 1999 issue of the eminent medical journal *The Lancet* catches a good part of challenge of establishing an operational definition for disability. The writer reasons that because we all have different degrees of intelligence and aptitude in different areas, we can all be said to experience disability—in the broadest sense—when it comes to everyday tasks we don't manage as well as our peers do:

All of us could be considered as disabled to some extent. Individuals differ in many ways in the manners in which they cope with the activities of daily living, or have a real but common handicap to which society has adjusted well. Deciding how far ability has to be impaired to constitute a disability is no easy matter—too vague, and abuse of special opportunities and services may follow; too rigid, and people who may benefit can be excluded. ("The Spectrum of Disability" 1999: 693)

Postmodernist sociological theory teaches us to be suspicious of binaries, those either/or distinctions that are used to separate people into supposedly discrete categories such as heterosexual/homosexual, Aboriginal/non-Aboriginal, black/white. As we saw in Chapter 11, postmodernist theorists argue that gender,

for instance, is better viewed as a continuum, with "male" and "female" at the extremes and a lot of territory in between that needs to be understood. We could approach the condition of dis/ability the same way. But that won't help us with our operational definition, and as *The Lancet*'s editorial writer points out, disability is an identity with some social and political weight, one that may gain a person access to special resources and services set aside for people with disabilities, as difficult as those often may be to access.

Measuring and Defining Disability

In 2007, Statistics Canada revealed that 4.4 million Canadians—roughly 14.3 per cent of the population—had reported a disability in the agency's 2006 Participation and Activity Limitation Survey (Statistics Canada 2007b: 9). So how does Canada's official data collection bureau define disability? Rather broadly, according to Diane Galarneau and Marian Radulescu:

In the Participation and Activity Limitation Survey . . . the definition of disability uses the bio-psychosocial framework . . . in which disability is defined in a broad sense and covers all limitations. Disability is the result of complex interactions between a health problem or functional limitation and the social, political, cultural, economic, and physical environment. These, in combination with personal factors such as age, gender, and level of education, can result in a disadvantage—that is, a disability. Disability is [therefore] not defined merely as being the direct result of a health problem or any physical or mental limitation. (Galarneau & Radulescu 2009: 6)

Disability, then, is any condition—mental or physical, permanent or temporary—that limits a person's ability to participate in regular activities in the home, at work, at school, or in recreational pursuits. It can affect anything from a person's memory, speech, or psychological state to his or her ability to walk, climb stairs, or bend down or just live without pain. Figure 12.1 provides a snapshot of the most common types of disability among Canadian adults.

Canada's 2006 disability rate of 14.3 per cent is not an unusual figure across the globe. In the same year, Kenya, a country of similar size in terms of population (34.3 million compared with Canada's 32.6 million), was reported to have over 3 million people with

---

12 | Disability 303

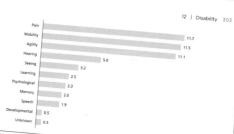

Pain
Mobility — 11.7
Agility — 11.5
Hearing — 11.1
Seeing — 5.0
Learning — 3.2
Psychological — 2.3
Memory — 2.0
Speech — 1.9
Developmental — 0.5
Unknown — 0.5

Figure 12.1 Adult Canadian population with a disability, by type (percentage)

Note: Does not include data for Nunavut, Northwest Territories, and Yukon.
Source: Human Resources and Skills Development Canada, www4.hrsdc.gc.ca/.3ndic.1t.4r@-eng.jsp?iid=40&ow=1, from Statistics Canada 2007c.

QUICK HITS

Types of Disability Identified in the Participation and Activity Limitation Survey

The following kinds of disability were identified in adults (aged 15+) in Statistics Canada's Participation and Activity Limitation Survey:

- **hearing** – difficulty hearing what is being said in a conversation with one other person, in a conversation with three or more persons, or in a telephone conversation
- **seeing** – difficulty seeing ordinary newsprint or clearly seeing someone's face from 4 m away
- **speech** – difficulty speaking and/or being understood
- **mobility** – difficulty walking half a kilometre or up and down a flight of stairs (about 12 steps) without resting, moving from one room to another, carrying an object of 5 kg for 10 m, or standing for long periods
- **agility** – difficulty bending, dressing and undressing oneself, getting into or out of bed, cutting one's own toenails, using fingers to grasp or handle objects, reaching in any direction (for example, above one's head) or cutting one's own food
- **pain** – limited in the amount or kind of activities that one can do because of a long-term pain that is constant or reoccurs from time to time for example, recurrent back pain)
- **learning** – difficulty learning because of a condition, such as attention problems, hyperactivity, or dyslexia, whether or not the condition was diagnosed by a teacher, doctor, or other health professional
- **memory** – limited in the amount or kind of activities that one can do due to frequent periods of confusion or difficulty remembering (these difficulties may be associated with Alzheimer's disease, brain injuries, or other similar conditions)
- **developmental disabilities** – cognitive limitations due to an intellectual disability or developmental disorder such as Down's syndrome, autism, or an intellectual disability caused by a lack of oxygen at birth
- **psychological** – identified as the type of disability if the respondent answered YES to the general questions about type of disability that followed.
- **other** – identified as the type of disability if the respondent answered YES to the general questions about type of disability that followed.

Source: Statistics Canada 2007b: 30.

---

596 Part V | Global Perspectives

Our St

The Canadian Case of Grassy Narrows

In *A Poison Stronger Than Love: The Destruction of an Ojibwa Community* (1985), Anastasia Shkilnyk presents an often cited case study of how pollution is racialized. But while it is a sympathetic study of the plight of the Anishinabe, or Ojibwa, people of Grassy Narrows in northwest Ontario, it is flawed by being entrenched in victimology by portraying the people only as hapless victims of an industrial attack on the environment, rather than as agents and actors in the fight against such a role. For this reason, the incident and Shkilnyk's role in reporting it are worth studying as an example both of how environmental issues intersect with "race" and how knowledge is produced.

In the mid-twentieth century, fishing was important to the community of Grassy Narrows both as a source of food and as a source of income (largely through tourism). Between 1962 and 1970 the Reed Paper Company, a British-owned multinational, began dumping huge amounts of mercury, about 20,000 pounds—into the English–Wabigoon river system, about 170 kilometres upstream from Grassy Narrows. In 1970, significantly high amounts of the deadly metal were detected in the area's fish. Two years later came the first human casualty, a 42-year-old fishing guide.

The people of Grassy Narrows knew that mercury was making fish and the people who depended

order resulting in . . .
disease). They paid to have exports . . .
come to assess their situation, and armed with evidence of the river's contamination, they took their fight to the courts. In December of that year, the chiefs and councillors of Grassy Narrows, along with those of neighbouring Whitedog, threatened

The tragedy raised questions about whom to trust when it comes to the social management of pollution. The province's Conservative government had been pursuing a policy of privatizing public-sector government departments, including the one responsible for inspecting the water supply. As a result of granting contracts for testing the water to private companies, the province had drastically reduced its funding to the Ministry of the Environment. Journalist Colin Perkel, in his thorough investigation into the Walkerton tragedy, cites this as evidence of a lack of social responsibility,

Walkerton and the Social Politics of Water

In May 2000, the town of Walkerton, Ontario, was hit by an epidemic of the bacterium *Escherichia coli*, commonly known as E. coli, that came from their main water supply. In total, an estimated 2,300 people were affected by the outbreak; just over half of them were residents of the town itself, meaning that roughly one-quarter of Walkerton's population became ill. Seven people died as a consequence of the infection.

Case Studies and Compelling Viewpoints

Foundations of Sociology features five different types of feature boxes, placed throughout every chapter to highlight issues, events, and ideas at the centre of sociological debate and investigation.

For Starters

> **For Starters boxes** use relevant and, at times, provocative narratives to draw students into the themes of the chapter.

The Cost of Religious Ignorance

Ignorance of someone else's religion is a major cause of prejudice, discrimination, and violence. The following illustration comes from Timothy J. Gianotti, a theologian and professor of Islamic studies at York University. The incident Gianotti describes surrounds an ignorant e-mail he became aware of:

Our Stories

A Minoritizing Episode: Canada's Ukrainians and the Great War

On 21 August 1914, shortly after the start of World War I, a group of Canadians was **minoritized** through the War Measures Act, which would be used as an instrument of discrimination against Japanese Canadians nearly 30 years later and then, almost another 30 years after that, against French Canadians.

As with different South Asian ethnic groups—Sikhs, Hindus, and Muslims—that were viewed as other and lumped together as "Hindoos," this minoritized group had its natural, chosen identity ignored by most Canadians, who assigned them a different, "alien" identity. Like Aboriginal people in both world wars, members of this minoritized group sometimes had to change their names and lie about their identity to pass as Canadian and join up to fight. And

like the Chinese, South Asians, Native people, and women of their time, many were denied the federal vote. During the Second World War th[...] into concentration camps, like the Jap[...]

Surprisingly, the members of [...] were white.

Britain and its allies, includ[...] were fighting Germany and the de[...] Hungarian empire. The latter was ho[...] ple who thought of themselves as [...] nationality, even though their official citizenship was Austrian. Canada's War Measures Act led to the internment of 8,579 people labelled "enemy aliens" in 24 camps across the country. More than 5,000 of them were Ukrainians. Another 80,000—most

> **Our Stories boxes** examine research and events that are especially relevant to the practice and study of sociology in Canada.

The Point Is...

David Elkind and Hurried Child Syndrome

David Elkind studies culture as an agent of socialization. One of his areas of interest is the negative effects on children whose lives have been overprogrammed by their parents, with little free time built in for spontaneous play. On this topic, Elkind's tone is dire: "[The] traditional culture of childhood is fast disappearing," he warns; "In the past two decades alone, according to several studies, children have lost 12 hours of free time a week, and eight of those lost hours were once spent in unstructured play and outdoor pastimes" (Elkind 2003).

Spontaneous play, Elkind argues, has been re-placed by a programmed schedule of organized sports and extracurricular learning. Technology is partly to blame: digital communication enables us to do more, faster, giving us a false feeling that we can accomplish much more than we used to. We extend this push for accomplishment to our children, putting pressure on them to take part in more after-school activities, play more organized sports, do more homework, and learn languages and other academic subjects at an earlier age. All of this is part of what Elkind calls the **hurried**

child syndrome, which causes kids to feel adult-like amounts of stress and guilt. It also contributes to the sometimes crippling apprehension that post-sec-ondary students feel about dea[...] reer—"I'm 21 and I don't know wh[...]

Elkind also worries about the [...] socializing children. For one thing[...] comfort with new technology is c[...] **gap** (a significant cultural and so[...] plete with an equally significant la[...] between generations). As he expla[...]

> [D]igital youth has a greater facility with technol-ogy than their parents and other adults. As a result, there is a greater disconnect between parents and children today, and some adolescents have even less respect for the knowledge, skills and values of their elders than they did a generation ago. . . .

Independence from parents and adults means greater dependence on peers for advice, guid-ance and support. The availability of cell phones and immediate access to friends through instant

> **The Point Is . . . boxes** present case studies and spotlight important contributions to sociological research, past and present.

Going Global

Al Jazeera: Media Freedom or Contextual Objectivity?

The Arab satellite news network Al Jazeera came into existence in 1996, when the emir of Qatar hired a large number of the editorial staff of the British Broadcasting Company's Arabic-language channel, [...] down several months earlier. The [...] the network's news and current [...] g would be very familiar to [...] diences accustomed to all-news [...] and the 24-hour news channels [...] ts content, Al Jazeera represents [...] ctive, but it does follow the universal journalistic credo of "getting to the truth," and the network has not been afraid to present dissenting views and criticism of Arab governments. Its broadcasting of Arab victims of war (especially in Iraq) and its coverage of the Israeli occupation of Palestine have had a very dramatic effect on its international audience.

In "The Case of al-Jazeera: An 'Arab CNN'?" German communication studies professor Kai Hafez considers the critical reception of the news network outside the Arab world. Specifically, he examines the two prevailing views of Al Jazeera in the West. Initially, he argues, it was celebrated by political commentators and media critics in western Europe and North America as a promising sign of growing democracy and media freedom in the Arab world. However, since the events of September 11, it has become a target of Western, particularly American, criticism, for its alleged bias and "soft on terror-ism" stance. Hafez places this bias in the context of "contextual objectivity," a term introduced by Arab media scholars (both based at universities in the US) Mohammed El-Nawawy and Adel Iskandar, in their work *Al-Jazeera: The Story of the Network That Is Rattling Governments and Redefining Modern*

> **Going Global boxes** shed light on international issues of interest to sociologists in Canada and around the world.

Telling it Like It Is

A Student POV

Gender Roles and Being Lesbian

People in my life in the past have tended to believe that because I am a lesbian, I automatically have more male-specific interests, ~~and that I do not enjoy typical girl-oriented~~ ... after I told my brother, he ... football game, stating, "you like ... n't you?" Although he was joking ... s an example of a very typical ... made to me. Although I may ... gs around the house, my partner ... c, and while I like to sew and knit, ... ng and romantic comedies. The ... ping, which is exactly what this comes down to, even goes so far as to include the style of clothes I wear. I remember one time that I went into work wearing a baseball cap, although I usually do not wear a hat to work, as I find it unprofessional. This particular day I was

coming from school and in a rush. Immediately after entering work I began to hear comments and mutters from my co-workers. It seemed that in their eyes because I was wearing a hat, I was portraying a male characteristic and they assumed that being a lesbian is the next closest thing to being a male.

There is a significant difference between sexual orientation and gender identity. All of the gay people that I know, including myself, are very happy with their sex. They just happen to be attracted to the same sex as well. I am proud to be a woman, and I enjoy it and would not want to change that. This leads me to my next point. For one reason or another people with little understanding of the gay population seem to need a definite clarification of "who's the man and who's the woman," which is a question that I have been asked on too many

> **Telling It Like It Is boxes** feature first-person narratives that give voice to a variety of perspectives informed by a variety of social factors—age, sex, gender, class, ethnicity, etc.

QUICK HITS

Where Do You Go When You Don't Have a Family Doctor?

According to the Canadian Community Health Survey, in 2010, 4.4 million Canadians over the age of 12 were without a regular family doctor.

- In all age groups, men were more likely than women to report not having a regular a family doctor.
- Among those who had looked for a family doctor,
  - ➢ 40.0 per cent said that doctors in their area were not taking new patients
  - ➢ 31.3 per cent said their doctor had retired or left the area
  - ➢ 27.1 per cent said that no doctors were available in their area
  - ➢ 17.5 per cent gave other reasons.

(These add up to more than 100 per cent because respondents were permitted to choose more than one option.)

- Of those without a regular family doctor, 82.2 per cent reported they had a place to go when in need of health advice; these included:
  - ➢ walk-in clinics (61.8 per cent)
  - ➢ hospital emergency rooms (12.9 per cent)
  - ➢ community health centres (8.8 per cent)
  - ➢ other facilities, including hospital out-patient clinics and telephone health lines (16.6 per cent).

Source: Statistics Canada 2011c.

> **Quick Hits sidebars** supplement the authors' narrative with relevant examples and data.

For More Information: Online Resources

Foundations of Sociology is part of a comprehensive package of learning and teaching tools that includes a vast suite of resources for both students and instructors.

For Instructors

- Carefully chosen **video clips**, matched to each chapter and streamed from our companion website, provide case studies, documentary footage, and conversations that complement themes and issues discussed in the textbook. An accompanying **viewing guide** provides a précis of each clip as well as exhaustive discussion questions and assignment topics to inspire and guide further research.
- A comprehensive **instructor's manual** provides an extensive set of pedagogical tools and teaching tips for every chapter, including overviews and summaries, concepts to emphasize in class, essay and research assignments, and links to relevant videos and online resources.
- Enhanced with graphics and tables drawn straight from the text, classroom-ready **PowerPoint slides** supplement lectures with summaries and key points for each chapter.
- A user-friendly **Test Generator** enables instructors to sort, edit, import, and distribute hundreds of questions in true–false, multiple-choice, and short-answer formats.

For Students

- The **Student Study Guide** includes chapter summaries, study questions, and self-grading quizzes, as well as explore-and-discuss exercises to help you review the textbook and classroom material.

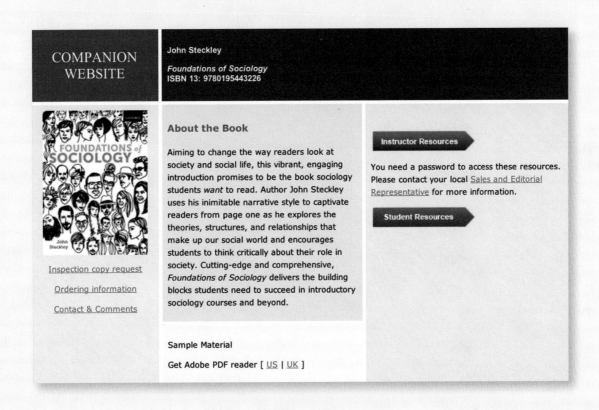

COMPANION WEBSITE

John Steckley

Foundations of Sociology
ISBN 13: 9780195443226

Inspection copy request

Ordering information

Contact & Comments

About the Book

Aiming to change the way readers look at society and social life, this vibrant, engaging introduction promises to be the book sociology students *want* to read. Author John Steckley uses his inimitable narrative style to captivate readers from page one as he explores the theories, structures, and relationships that make up our social world and encourages students to think critically about their role in society. Cutting-edge and comprehensive, *Foundations of Sociology* delivers the building blocks students need to succeed in introductory sociology courses and beyond.

Sample Material

Get Adobe PDF reader [US | UK]

Instructor Resources

You need a password to access these resources. Please contact your local Sales and Editorial Representative for more information.

Student Resources

Acknowledgements

We would like to acknowledge the following reviewers and anonymous reviewers whose thoughtful comments and suggestions have helped to shape both *Foundations of Sociology* and its predecessor *Elements of Sociology*:

- **Fiona Angus**, Grant MacEwan University
- **Tami M. Bereska**, Grant MacEwan University
- **Angela Conti-Becker**, University of Western Ontario
- **Dana Cudney**, Laurentian Univeristy
- **Howard A. Doughty**, Seneca College
- **Martha Dow**, University of the Fraser Valley
- **Janice Drodge**, Cape Breton University
- **Alison Dunwoody**, University of Alberta
- **Laurie Forbes**, Lakehead University
- **Christopher J. Fries**, University of Manitoba
- **Jane W. Haddad**, Seneca College of Applied Arts and Technology
- **Ronald Hinch**, University of Ontario Institute of Technology
- **Ron Joudrey**, Red Deer College
- **Susan Robertson**, University of Saskatchewan
- **Carolyne Willoughby**, Durham College
- **Amanda Zavitz**, University of Western Ontario

A Word or Two from the Author

Why Write This Sociology Textbook?

Textbooks are typically boring. No one, to my knowledge, has yet designed a quantitative study to demonstrate this, with scales of 1 to 10 where 1 is "really, deadly boring" and 10 is "carried it with me everywhere, couldn't put it down," but a huge amount of qualitative anecdotal evidence has given me this impression.

The thing is, a textbook doesn't have to be boring; it can be something you actually want to read, as opposed to something you have to read. The textbook assigned in the first sociology course I ever took, at Lakehead University, was so interesting that I took it along with me for years, from home to home. I would consider this book a success if students decided to keep it after the course has ended.

> "A textbook doesn't have to be boring; it can be something you actually want to read, as opposed to something you have to read."

This particular textbook has an older sibling called *Elements of Sociology*, which I designed as a shorter text than the one you're reading. Currently in its third edition, *Elements* has enjoyed some good success, and I've received a gratifying amount of positive feedback from students as well as instructors. So why would I take on the challenge of writing another introductory sociology textbook? Am I insane? I will answer only the first question, as I am not qualified to answer the second.

A perpetual frustration of college and university instructors, and certainly one of mine, is that in a 14- to 16-week "intro soc" course, the instructor really only has time to touch on certain subjects, while neglecting others that are of equal fascination and importance. The same goes for the writers of textbooks written for courses of that length. I found that there were many ideas and topics I wanted to explore but could not in *Elements of Sociology*. The book you are now reading (which I wanted to call *The Big Ass Sociology Textbook*, but was persuaded not to) gave me an opportunity to take that flight of exploration, and I hope that it takes you, the reader, on such a flight as well.

Why *Read* This Sociology Textbook?

If you are as sarcastic and cynical as I am, your immediate answer to the question above will be *Because it is a required textbook and I don't want to fail the course (duh)*. Fair enough. But I hope that as you begin to complete your required reading, you will discover other incentives to reading.

First of all, I have included in this textbook many narratives, or stories, that are funny, that are meaningful, and that will either introduce you to worlds you do not yet know or reintroduce you to a world you've seen before but from a different vantage point. Students speak in this book, and what they say is worth reading. They (and you) are good sources of sociological information. They have taught me about things I did not know.

> "Students speak in this book, and what they say is worth reading."

Second, I have tried to make this what sociologists would call an inclusive textbook. That means that there are other voices here contributing to the overall narrative, voices representing social locations other than my own. The insights of people who are Aboriginal, South Asian, and Chinese, upper-class and lower-class, homosexual, disabled, young and old, and so on, make this book far more compelling than if it featured only my own white, male, middle-class perspective.

A third reason for reading this textbook is that it practises and promotes the use of a sociological imagination. I see sociology just about everywhere there are people. I notice, for example, the way the Middle Eastern women working at the local coffee shop, some of them wearing veils and speaking to one another in Arabic, greet customers with folksy, non–Middle Eastern forms of address, such as "honey" or "hon." I wonder what socializing influences (or training seminars) have shaped the way they conduct their "front stage" interactions with clients.

Here's another example. I have long heard my students complain about working in groups. After hearing all these stories, it seems sociologically predictable to me that in a working group of five students, one never meets with the others, one is flat-out lazy, one works a bit, and two work their tails off—and they all get the same mark (again, no sociological research has been conducted demonstrating the validity of this hypothesis, but a huge amount of anecdotal evidence suggests that it is true).

I believe my greatest sociological gift is that I see patterns in social behaviour such as these. I imagine many of you do as well, but perhaps you never had a textbook

> "I see sociology just about everywhere there are people."

that supported that habit before. I also imagine that if you haven't noticed such patterns before, you will start doing so after you have finished this book. It is an addiction, but a good one (like buying baby parrots—see Acknowledgements).

I think that you will like this textbook. I have no research data of my own to back up this claim, but a huge amount of anecdotal evidence surrounding its older and smaller sibling, *Elements of Sociology*, suggests this.

Thanks

There are many people I need to thank here for helping to bring this book to the final stage. At Oxford University Press, there are Mark Thompson and Eric Sinkins. These two editors have given me a lot of direction that has led to this being a much better book than it would have been without them. They allowed me (even encouraged me) to be outrageous. I thank the readers, as well, whose critical looks at earlier versions helped me to fill gaps in my knowledge and in the breadth of information presented in each chapter. As always with my OUP books, I thank the president of

Oxford University Press Canada, David Stover, for having the idea that I could write a sociology textbook, even when I didn't believe that I could.

At home, there are the pets. Our dogs Cosmo, Egwene, Trudy, and Wiikwaas have walked through our lives and given it more meaning. The same is true for our parrots: Benji, Gus, Lime, Louis, Misha, Quigley, Sam, Stanee, and Tika. Who knew they could fill human life with so much spirit?

Finally, I would like to thank Angelika, my wife. She has taught me that happy marriage still brings the joy of new discovery.

John Steckley
June 2013

I Foundations of Sociology

THE OPENING SECTION of this textbook is like flying over a large piece of land, so that you can observe from up high what the land below is like. And we'll call this land Sociology's Contested Ground—otherwise known as "the things over which sociologists fight the most."

The first chapter of our overview may be the least controversial of the bunch, although it is bound to spark some minor disagreements about who is and isn't included among the discipline's founders. It involves a basic presentation on what sociology is about, including a very elusive definition of the subject matter and some good stuff about Canadian sociologists.

The other two chapters survey the main fault lines along which sociologists differ: theories, approaches, and perhaps most bitter of all, social research methods. If sociologists worked with Santa Claus, they would challenge him on his operational definitions of "naughty" and "nice."

It would be good for you to be aware of a topic that comes up again and again in the three chapters of this section—and, for that matter, in the chapters that follow it: a key concern of sociologists is *social location*. Your social location is your place in society, based on seven key factors: class, gender, "race"/ethnicity, age, sexual orientation, and degree of ability. You can remember them with this simple phrase:

*Can you **gen**eralize about **reaso**ns for **d**ifference?*

You will find that the borders of your social location are not as sharp as you may think. As for the question, you should have arrived at the answer by the time you've reached the end of this textbook.

1 Introduction to Sociology

Learning Objectives

After reading this chapter, you should be able to

- explain the differences and similarities between sociology and other disciplines

- describe what the sociological imagination is

- cite some key ideas of sociology's trailblazers: Marx, Durkheim, and Weber

- trace the origin and development of sociology in Europe, the United States, and Canada.

Key Terms

- capital
- communism
- cultural mosaic
- ethnography
- folk society
- Marxist
- melting pot
- narratives

- political economy
- Protestant (work) ethic
- social Darwinism
- social facts
- social gospel movement
- social location

- sociological imagination
- sociology
- staples
- structural functionalist
- vertical mosaic

Names to Know

- Helen C. Abell
- Samuel Delbert Clark
- Auguste Comte
- Confucius
- Charles Darwin
- Carl Addington Dawson
- Émile Durkheim

- Everett C. Hughes
- Ibn Khaldûn
- Harold Innis
- Annie Marion MacLean
- Thomas Malthus
- Karl Marx
- C. Wright Mills

- Horace Miner
- John Porter
- Samuel Henry Prince
- Aileen Ross
- Herbert Spencer
- Max Weber

Doughnut Shops, Drive-Throughs, and the Value of Sociology

I am a big fan of coffee-and-doughnut shops. When I go to a doughnut shop, I tend to savour the experience: I park my car, walk in, chat with the server, and generally enjoy the social aspect of the transaction. I have never used a drive-through. I feel that pulling up to the drive-through window limits the overall experience—the socializing with fellow patrons, the customer service, the ritual of surveying the assortment of doughnuts and then choosing the perfect one. For that matter, it doesn't save any time (I've done an informal study), and sitting in the rush-hour lineup with the engine idling increases the local pollution level.

I used to spend a fair bit of time contemplating why some people use the drive-through instead of parking and coming into the shop. Just who are these people who would rather interact over an intercom and receive their orders through a pickup window? I always thought it was either young men whose most significant relationships were with their cars, or else lazy, fat, older men who drive everywhere rather than walk.

My opinion changed, however, because of a student in one of my sociology classes. The student carried out his own study, in Newmarket, north of Toronto. He spent approximately an hour one morning at a doughnut shop taking notes on who was using the drive-through and who was walking in through the front door. Over that period he observed 91 people walk into the doughnut shop and 95 people use the drive-through. He did notice a gender difference in the two groups, but not the one I predicted. In terms of the counter sales, 42 of the customers were women and 49 were men—just about even numbers. But of the drive-through patrons, 70 were women and just 25 were men. He also noted that compared with middle-aged and older women, *young* women were much more likely—by a ratio of nearly 7 to 1—to use the drive-through. This was in stark contrast to the male drive-through customers, among whom there was a roughly 1 to 1 ratio of the two age-determined groups.

Another statistic enabled the student to come up with a hypothesis to account for the results of his research. He observed that the cars entering the drive-through were more likely to have child seats in them than were the parked cars of the walk-in clientele.

Further, he often identified young children among the passengers of the drive-through vehicles.

The student's hypothesis, which would apply to that time (between approximately eight and nine o'clock a.m.) and location, was that young mothers with infants and toddlers used the drive-through significantly more because it was easier than going through the complicated process of unbuckling their children and bringing them into the restaurant. To be really convincing, his hypothesis would have to be tested for other times and locations, but it presented a sociological profile that I would not otherwise have guessed, as well as a compelling example of how sociology can be used to understand everyday life.

Introduction: Why This Textbook Is a Little Different

This textbook is not like the others. It will offer candid observations, occasional humour, and lots of stories told from the perspective of the author, students, and colleagues in sociology. In keeping with contemporary sociological terminology, we will call these stories **narratives**. Narratives make up an important branch of sociological literature, one recognizing that to understand a person's situation requires input from the individual's own words, or "voice." The narrative that opened this chapter tells you something about doughnut shop customers, sure, but it also tells you some revealing things about the writer: his social position, his socioeconomic status, his social and cultural biases. For this reason, every chapter of this textbook will make use of narratives to illustrate key points and concepts.

There are two basic strategies that textbook writers can take. One is to create a kind of reference book that touches on pretty much every conceivable topic within the discipline. That sort of book can be good for students who need support outside of the classroom or away from the instructor. The other approach is to write a book that piques the curiosity of the reader as a student of the discipline, and that is what I've tried to do here. The aim is to hook you on the subject of sociology, to get you interested in reading and learning about it. I feel that—to use a baseball analogy—if you try to round the bases too quickly, you might get picked off. I'd rather see you get safely on base. You may not touch all the bases this inning, but there's a better chance you will in your next at-bat. In other words, I've tried to avoid writing a textbook you will lose interest in because it tries to introduce you to too much, too quickly.

Introduction to Sociology

Sociologists notice *social patterns*. What do we mean by a social pattern? Well, things tend to happen differently to you depending on your sex, age, class, ethnicity, "race," religion, and sexual orientation. If you are a woman, for instance, you typically pay more in Canada for a haircut and to have your shirt dry-cleaned than you would if you were a man (Dunfield 2005). It's not that you're getting more for your money—it's just that your hair and your shirt, because they are designated as "female," are more expensive to cut and to clean (respectively). If you are a young black man driving in Canada, you are more likely than a white male driver to be pulled over at night by the police—you are guilty of the offence known facetiously as "driving while black"; that's another social pattern.

What if you are a young, white, heterosexual male? If you are, you might think that all the "other groups" are ganging up on you. Insurance companies make it very expensive for you (and your parents) to pay for your driving. You read and hear that white males have privilege in terms of getting jobs, but it is often difficult for you to find the jobs that white male privilege is supposed to bring.

Sociologists also investigate and challenge the social patterns that other people perceive. For example, why do so many people, even those in the medical profession, assume that male nurses are gay? This stereotype has never been demonstrated statistically (in part because it would be unethical to ask a male nurse about his sexual preferences). Sociologists studying the subject might investigate the effects of movies like *Meet the Parents* (2000), where characters articulate their belief that male nurses are either gay or, at the very least, "sissies." Sociologists might look at how the nursing profession is thought of as "naturally feminine" because it involves caregiving and is a chronically underpaid profession involving responsibilities that we in the West consider less important than the work of (typically male) doctors. They might also look at how male nurses and nursing students might act out their heterosexuality (for instance, by boasting about how many women they've slept with) in order to combat the perception that they are gay. In short, sociologists would look carefully at the patterns of social behaviour and perceptions associated with male nurses.

Consider another example. Politicians who promote conservative social policies often talk disdainfully about the "liberal media," lumping together print, on-air, and Internet journalists who might disagree with their views. Sociologists can test assumptions about a predominantly left-leaning media by doing a statistics-based analysis of the political views expressed in the popular media on issues in which liberal and conservative positions are clearly established (gun registration and environmental policy are a couple of examples). Sociologists might conclude that the Canadian media, in fact, lean heavily to the right (see the *National Post* and the *Sun* chain of news outlets for examples). We'll talk more about statistical analysis and other kinds of quantitative and qualitative research in Chapter 2, on social research methods. For

Would you take a $20 haircut from this barber? Or would you pay considerably more to receive the same haircut from a stylist at a salon? Women typically pay more than men do to have their hair cut: how do you account for this social pattern?

now, what is important to understand is that sociologists use these kinds of tools to assess and to challenge the social perceptions that people hold, views that are sometimes accepted as "common sense."

Sociology and Issues

Sociology can help students understand issues facing society today. One of the more divisive social issues of recent years is the debate surrounding same-sex marriage. Since July 2005, same-sex marriage has been legally recognized across Canada, although many Canadians remain strongly opposed to the idea. What can sociologists tell us about this issue?

Sociology can't say what is moral, or "right." There really isn't a scientific way of measuring that. But sociology *can* tell us about who tends to be in favour of same-sex marriage: younger people, those with more education, women more than men, French Canadians more than English Canadians. As well, sociology can speak about who tends to be against same-sex marriage: older Canadians, those with fundamentalist religious views versus the more liberal members of Canada's many faiths, and people from rural rather than urban communities.

Beyond this, sociology can give us the perspectives to document and discuss the many ways that marriage is defined in contemporary cultures around the world, or in Canadian cultures over time. In this way, it can help a sociology student avoid making uninformed, generalizing statements beginning with *Marriage has always been . . .* or *Everyone knows that marriage is . . .* Sociology might also help students understand the impact that socializing influences—parents, the media, even sociology professors—have on their own opinions concerning same-sex marriage. You can have more choice in forming your own opinion when you understand what has helped to shape it in the past.

All of this relates to a question that sociology students often ask: How come I got a low mark when it's just an opinion and there are no right or wrong answers? While it is true that everyone has a right to an opinion, people owe it to themselves to become knowledgeable about issues before forming opinions on them. Sociology gives us the means to form considered opinions on social issues; in this way, sociology helps students distinguish between a well-argued, informed opinion and an uninformed viewpoint spouted off without careful thought.

Sociology as a Discipline

Academic disciplines are artificial constructions. There is nothing "natural" about the borderlines that separate sociology from other established disciplines such as anthropology, economics, history, psychology, philosophy, or political science. These various fields of interest have much in common, as Table 1.1 shows, and there is a lot of cross-referencing in the books and articles written by specialists in each discipline. Students who have taken courses in psychology, anthropology, or philosophy will notice that sociology regularly encroaches on their territory, just as those disciplines often "poach" on sociology's turf.

Still, artificial or not, the discipline of sociology does exist and is unique. It has its own history, a distinct vocabulary and set of tools, and a separate department in most colleges and universities in Canada. You'll find that people teaching such varied subjects as Canadian studies, communication, criminology, cultural studies, education, Native studies, international relations, and women's studies often have degrees in sociology. In order to understand sociology—its weaknesses and strengths, and the ways in which its perspectives have broadened over recent decades—we need to understand it as a discipline.

So, What Is Sociology?

You may have noticed that so far we have cleverly avoided defining what sociology is. That's because it's not a straightforward thing to do, and in some ways not particularly useful. Defining something is very different from understanding it. We could give you a simple (but not terribly useful) definition by saying that *sociology is the systematic or scientific study of society*. Can you imagine the multiple-choice questions that could come from that?

Sociology is:

a) the systematic study of society
b) the unsystematic study of society
c) "statistical stuff and heavy-duty theoretical bullshit" (see Mills, below)
d) all of the above.

The answer could easily be the final one, "all of the above." We could just as easily refer you to the glossary at the back of this book, where we have defined **sociology** as "the social science that studies the development, structure, and functioning of human society." Does that help?

The truth is, giving a precise, all-encompassing explanation of what sociology *is* would be much more difficult (and probably less useful) than explaining what sociology *does*. This is why we've begun our introduction to sociology by highlighting some of its uses. At this point it is enough to know that sociology involves looking for and looking at *patterns*:

- *patterns in social variables*, such as class, age, gender, "race," ethnicity, religion, degree of ability, and sexual orientation;
- *patterns in social institutions*, such as education, religion, and the family
- *patterns in social interactions*.

Table 1.1 Sociology and related disciplines

DISCIPLINE	EMPHASIS
anthropology	the comparative study of human societies and cultures and their development
economics	the production and consumption of wealth, including the distribution of goods and services among individuals and groups
philosophy	major thinkers and turns of thought in particular societies
political science	systems of government and how they serve citizens
psychology	the human mind, the social and biological influences on it, and its functions, especially those affecting behaviour
social work	the application of our understanding of society and individuals to improve people's well-being
sociology	the development, structure, and functioning of human society, especially as seen in group interaction, social relations, social institutions, and social structures

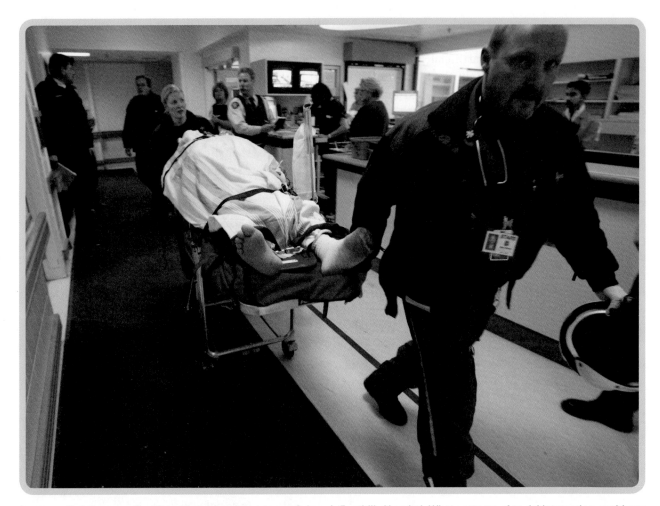

A paramedic brings a patient into the emergency room at Calgary's Foothills Hospital. What patterns of social interaction could you expect to witness at a hospital ER? How would you expect social variables such as age, ethnicity, and social class to affect those interactions? Do you think this patient would get better service if he had on a pair of expensive shoes instead of a single dirty sock? What could you learn about Canadian society by studying the hospital as a social institution?

By the time you've reached the end of this textbook, we hope that you will have formed your own idea of what sociology really *is*.

Why Study Sociology?

Studying sociology will help you obtain a greater understanding of the social world, which is essentially the social practices, attitudes, and institutions that surround us. Studying sociology will also help you to better understand yourself in terms of whether you follow or do not follow patterns of social behaviour predicted by sociological variables (think, for instance, of a young Latin woman who likes salsa dancing—quite predictable—and a black youth from the city who enjoys line dancing—not so predictable). Sociology will help you

develop an understanding about others around you in the multicultural and generally diverse social world that is Canada, as well as in the smaller social worlds of neighbourhoods, chat groups, classrooms, pubs, and workplaces. Thinking more globally, sociology can help you better understand the larger world of nations and their social institutions. You can look, for example, at how the price of oil can affect the relative presence or absence of democratic social practices in oil-producing countries such as Saudi Arabia and Iran.

During a strike by Ontario public school teachers in the 1990s, some strike sympathizers sported a bumper sticker that read: "If you think *education* is expensive, just try IGNORANCE." In a similar vein, we could say, if you think sociology is hard, try understanding society *without* it.

The Point Is...

What's *Your* Social Location?

If I were to say, "Television today does not do a good job of representing diversity," would you agree or disagree? Take a moment or two to jot down your initial thoughts on the question.

One of the aims in writing this textbook is to help you appreciate the importance of your social location to the way you experience events and interpret the experiences of others. Your **social location** is the set of social traits that informs your views on the world around you. Consider the following questions:

- Are you over or under the age of 20? 30?
- What is your sex?
- What is your gender? (Think it's the same thing? It's not, as we'll see in Chapter 11.)
- What is your ethnic background? Where are your parents from? Your parents' parents?
- Would you say you come from an upper-class, middle-class, or lower-class neighbourhood? And is that neighbourhood in the city, in the suburbs, or in a small town or rural area?
- Do you have a medical condition that affects your

everyday experience? That could be something visible like having to use a wheelchair, or something "invisible" like an anxiety disorder.
- Do you feel like you're part of the mainstream?

Your answers to these questions combine to produce your social location.

Now, look around you: how many people do you think share your social location? Not too many share your *exact* social location, although many of those around you will share certain aspects of it.

So, how do you think you might respond to the question above—the one about diversity and television—if you were a second-generation Iranian Canadian (assuming you're not Jian Ghomeshi, who is)? What if you were a member of a First Nation who grew up on a reserve in northern Saskatchewan? Or an intersex person who identifies as female? Or a wheelchair athlete? Or a female athlete who is a professional basketball player? See how your perspective changes depending on where you're "socially located"?

The Heart of Sociology: The Sociological Imagination

One of sociology's most useful instruments is the **sociological imagination**. The term was coined by **C. Wright Mills** (1916–1962), who sums it up nicely as:

> the capacity to shift from one perspective to another—from the political to the psychological; from examination of a single family to comparative assessment of the national budgets of the world. . . . It is the capacity to range from the most impersonal and remote transformations to the most intimate features of the human self—and to see the relationship between the two. (Mills 1959: 4)

Mills argues that when we create and communicate sociological knowledge, our ideas must show "how society works" in terms of our own personal lives. If you go to buy a good pair of rubber boots (as my spouse did recently), and the only ones you can get are yellow and relatively flimsy, then you are a woman, and your own frustrating shopping experience reflects the way society thinks of and treats women in general.

What happens when we fail to exercise our sociological imagination is discussed by McMaster University cultural theorist Henry Giroux in *Beyond the Spectacle of Terrorism: Global Uncertainty and the Challenge of the New Media* (2006). Commenting on the lack of sociological imagination in the post-9/11 political posturing of George W. Bush, Giroux warns

Telling It Like It Is

The Sociologist as Hero: C. Wright Mills

In my first year of university, the sociologist who captured my imagination was C. Wright Mills. He took on the rich and the powerful, and challenged his conservative colleagues and his country's government in the staid and stuffy 1950s. His public critique of American society caught the attention of the FBI, who started a file on him. He rode a motorcycle to work, dressed in plaid shirts, old jeans, and work boots. Mills became my first sociologist hero.

Mills published seven books (in addition to others that he co-authored). These include two trilogies and an important stand-alone volume that gave its name to a key characteristic of the very best sociologists and sociology students: *The Sociological Imagination* (1959). His first trilogy, a study of the three main socioeconomic classes in the United States, comprises *The New Men of Power: America's Labor Leaders* (1948), *White Collar: The American Middle Classes* (1951), and *The Power Elite* (1956). The last of these was the most influential of the three. It found a wide and varied audience that included the then young Cuban revolutionary Fidel Castro, who, after he had overthrown the American-backed dictator Fulgencio Batista, invited Mills to visit so they could discuss his ideas. After the book was translated into Russian, Mills was asked to visit Moscow.

Mills' second trilogy consists of three best-selling, mass-marketed paperbacks. The first of these was *The Causes of World War Three* (1958), an impassioned plea for an end to the nuclear arms race. The second was *Listen, Yankee: The Revolution in Cuba* (1960). The product of two weeks of interviewing in Cuba and six weeks of writing, *Listen, Yankee* was written in the style of an open letter to Americans from a Cuban revolutionary trying to communicate what life had been like under former Cuban president Fulgencio Batista, what harm American policies were having on the people of Cuba, and what accomplishments in education and healthcare

Castro had achieved during the short time he had then been in power. Of the more than 450,000 copies printed, over 370,000 were sold in Mills' lifetime. The third book of the trilogy, *The Marxists* (1962), was translated into four languages.

In the early 1950s, Mills issued a challenge to those writing sociology. Responding by letter to a question about whether sociology writing could be improved, Mills famously wrote:

> It doesn't look good. I think for two reasons: First, there is no real writing tradition in sociology, as there is, for example, in history. It just doesn't exist. Second, the field is now split into statistical stuff and heavy duty theoretical bullshit. In both cases, there's no writing but only turgid pollysyllabic (sp?) slabs of stuff. So, because that is now the field, no men get trained, have models to look up to; there is no aspiration to write well. (Mills 2000: 154–5)

While Mills himself disproved the first point, the second critique stands. Aspiring sociologists, your duty is clear. Prove him wrong!

Consider this photo of C. Wright Mills: does he look like an educator to you? Why or why not?

that "[d]emocracy begins to fall and political life becomes impoverished when society can no longer translate private problems into social issues" (Giroux 2006: 1). He spells this out in detail in the chapter "Acts of Translation":

> As the very idea of the social collapses into the private realm of the self and its fears, it becomes more difficult for people to develop a vocabulary for understanding how individual insecurity, dread, and misery could be translated into concerns of an engaged and critical citizenry. Instead, they are told that their privately held misery is a fall from grace, a flaw in character that must be suffered in isolation. Poverty, for example, is now imagined to be a problem of individual failing. Racism is rationalized and represented as simply an act of individual discrimination or prejudice. Homelessness is reduced to a freely chosen decision made by lazy people. (Giroux 2006: 4)

When we consider a gang-related gun crime that has taken place in a poor, remote part of the city and conclude that it has nothing to do with us, then we are failing to exercise our sociological imagination; it takes a sociological imagination to see that crime in the context of broader social forces affects us all and demands our attention.

The Origins of Sociology

Who Was the First Sociologist?

People since ancient times have contemplated social systems and looked for patterns in human social relationships. Perhaps the earliest person whose recorded writings reflect a true sociological imagination is the Chinese philosopher **Confucius** (*c.* 551–479 BCE). A strong proponent of role modelling—a topic discussed often in sociology today—Confucius believed it was better for leaders to engage in moral practices that modelled the principles they wanted their citizens to follow than to overuse laws to enforce morality. In his words:

> If you use laws to direct the people, and punishments to control them, they will merely try to evade the laws, and will have no sense of shame. (Kaizuka 2002: 126)

Confucius emphasized socialization over social control and stressed that a country's leaders must engage in moral practices that model the type of behaviour that would be desirable in its citizenry. Are politicians, or even celebrities and corporate CEOs, good role models?

We can all think of politicians who would have benefited from following the wise sociological advice of Confucius.

Although Confucius touched on some important sociological themes, the first person to carry out a systematic study of sociological subjects and set his thoughts down in writing is most likely the Arab scholar **Ibn Khaldûn** (1332–1406). In *Al Muqaddimah* (*An Introduction to History*), Ibn Khaldûn examined various types of societies—tribes, cities, nations, and dynasties—and their histories, cultures, and economies. Many of his ideas and much of his research are still relevant. For instance, in *Al Muqaddimah*, he provides insight into the cyclical rise and fall of power and status among desert tribes in the Middle East:

[W]hen a tribe has achieved a certain measure of superiority with the help of its group feeling, it gains control over a corresponding amount of wealth and comes to share prosperity and abundance with those who have been in possession of these things. It shares in them to the degree of its power and usefulness to the ruling dynasty. If the ruling dynasty is so strong that no one would think of depriving it of its power or of sharing [its power] with it, the tribe in question submits to its rule and is satisfied with whatever share in the dynasty's wealth and tax revenue it is permitted to enjoy. . . . Members of the tribe are merely concerned with prosperity, gain, and a life of abundance. [They are satisfied] to lead an easy, restful life in the shadow of the ruling dynasty, and to adopt royal habits in building and dress, a matter they stress and in which they take more and more pride, the more luxuries and plenty they acquire, as well as all the other things that go with luxury and plenty.

What do YOU think?

Even if you're new to sociology, you might have heard of people like Marx, Durkheim, and Weber, yet you probably hadn't heard of Ibn Khaldûn. Why do you think that Ibn Khaldûn has only recently been recognized for his contributions to the development of sociology?

As a result, the toughness of desert life is lost. Group feeling and courage weaken. . . . Their group feeling and courage decrease in the next generations. Eventually group feeling is altogether destroyed. Eventually . . . [i]t will be swallowed up by other nations. (Ibn Khaldûn 1981: 109)

Essentially, Ibn Khaldûn was arguing that as societies acquire more affluence, they also become weaker and fall into demise. Replace "tribe" with "country" and "dynasty" with "empire," and Ibn Khaldûn's observations could have been written any time in the past century. Maybe the leaders of our neighbours to the south should read his writings.

The Development of Sociology in Europe

Sociology became an area of academic interest in nineteenth-century Europe, specifically in France, Germany, and Britain. The term *sociology* itself was coined by the French philosopher **Auguste Comte** (1798–1857), who argued that the same methods used to study the natural sciences—including experiment, measurement, and systematic observation—could also be applied to the social sciences.

Sociology developed in response to the dramatic social changes taking place at that time: industrialization, urbanization, and a significant rise in population across Europe. Cities were growing rapidly, both because of the dramatic influx of people from the countryside looking for jobs in newly minted factories, and because of natural population increases. Concerned scholars like the economist **Thomas Malthus** (1766–1834), a forerunner of the modern sociologists, began to wonder whether Europe's cities

Ibn Khaldûn meets Andy Warhol: if you saw this picture in a pop art gallery and heard he was famous, what sort of individual would you think he was?

could cope with such tremendous population growth. The politics of the time were also favourable to the growth of sociology, with the French Revolution in particular providing evidence that citizens could bring about social change swiftly and on a massive scale.

What do YOU think?

1. Why do you think it was that sociology developed in Europe rather than in Africa, the Middle East, China, or South Asia?

2. How might sociology have developed differently as a discipline if the early thinkers had been African, Middle Eastern, Chinese, or South Asian?

Three Founders of Modern Sociology: Marx, Durkheim, and Weber

Karl Marx

Karl Marx (1818–1883) was an influential German economist and thinker. (*Thinker* here and elsewhere in the book is code for someone who wasn't strictly a sociologist but who made contributions to the discipline in some other capacity, such as philosopher, social critic, political commentator, historian, or journalist).

Marx's writing had and continues to have a profound effect on the social sciences. Central to his work was his belief that the capitalist system of his time created two classes of people:

1. those who owned the factories, shops, businesses, and trading companies, and who became wealthy through their control of economic activity (Marx called this class the *bourgeoisie*, also known as *capitalists*)

2. those who contributed the labour that made the owners wealthy, but who received very little in return for their work (Marx called this class the *proletariat*).

Marx believed the workers would one day rebel against the owners, and a new society would emerge in which everyone shared equally in the wealth generated by the collective economic activity of the people. He called this system **communism** (in the *Communist Manifesto*, which he co-authored with Friedrich Engels in 1848), and his work was influential in the rise of communism in the former Soviet Union and in China, and socialism in other parts of the world.

We will have much more to say on Marx in the chapters on conflict (Chapter 2), consumption (Chapter 7), social inequality (Chapter 9), religion (Chapter 15), and work (Chapter 17), but for now, we can say that the key to Marx is remembering five words beginning with *c*:

- the **c**lass **c**onflict that Marx saw operating between the class of workers and the class of owners;
- his **c**ritique of **c**apitalism, which in Marx's view enabled capitalist owners to exploit the workers; and
- **c**ommunism, the system that would result once the proletariat had risen up against the bourgeoisie.

So: *class conflict, critique of capitalism, communism*; and repeat . . .

Émile Durkheim

Unlike his predecessors, including the economist/political philosopher Marx and other "thinkers," **Émile Durkheim** (1858–1917) was a sociologist through and through. He established sociology as an academic discipline at the Sorbonne in Paris in 1913, and like Comte, he believed that a scientific approach could be taken to studying society.

With Durkheim, the letter to remember is *s*. It begins with *society*, which he saw as something that could be broken down into parts and studied the same way a botanist dissects and examines a plant. In fact, he viewed society as a kind of organic whole (like a vegetable or a moose)—a system of different parts each with its own function (for example, religion has a specific social function within society, just like the liver has a biological function within the body). This perspective made Durkheim a **structural functionalist**.

Our structural functionalist Durkheim believed that the study of society uncovered what he called **social facts**. These are well-established patterns of behaviour that are independent of the individuals that make up society but that influence the way people act. An example of a social fact, which he studied famously in a work of the same title, published in 1897, is *suicide*. Durkheim believed that the act of committing suicide was heavily influenced by one's social location, specifically whether one was married or single, male or female, an officer in the army or an

The Point Is...

Herbert Spencer: An Early Sociological Contribution

You've probably heard the phrase "survival of the fittest." Most people attribute it to biologist **Charles Darwin** (1809–1882), who, in his pioneering theory of evolution through natural selection, claimed that only those organisms "fit" enough—that is, those individuals or species that have best adapted to their particular environment—are destined to survive.

What most people don't know is that the saying itself was coined not by Darwin but by the early English sociologist **Herbert Spencer** (1820–1903). Heavily influenced by Darwin, Spencer was one of a number of scholars who tried to extend the theory of natural selection by applying it to human society as a way to describe the competitive struggle for power, wealth, and general well-being brought about by European industrialization and colonization. Using evolutionary theory in this way to describe social inequalities became known as **social Darwinism**.

Social Darwinists held up natural selection as the basis for claims of European superiority—Westerners regarded societies in Africa, Asia, and the Pacific islands as more "primitive," less evolved—and as justification for colonizing and even enslaving peoples in parts of the world outside of Europe. By the same token, they argued that governments should not intervene to help the sick and the poor in their own societies, as these people were "naturally selected" to fail. Social Darwinism was used to justify a host of discriminatory practices—sterilization, for example—against a variety of groups, including women, people of colour, and various ethnic groups. For Spencer in particular, evolution guided social change.

Poverty, as we will see later, is in fact a social problem, not a problem of one's "fitness." Notions of superiority and inferiority, and of who should have access to resources, create inequalities and are the by-products of culture and social history.

enlisted soldier, a Catholic or a member of another religious denomination.

We can add another *s* to the discussion with the word *sacred*, which Durkheim used to refer to religious items and experiences worthy of the greatest respect and reverence. These he contrasted with ordinary, everyday items and experiences, which he described as *profane*. The discussion is part of his epic and influential work *The Elementary Forms of the Religious Life* (published in French in 1912), which is discussed in Chapter 15, on religion.

Max Weber

No one better illustrates the intellectual force and impact of early sociology than German sociologist **Max Weber** (pronounced VAY-ber; 1864–1920). One of his most important and well-known contributions was his identification of a set of values embodied in early Protestantism that he believed led to the development of modern capitalism. He called this set of values the **Protestant (work) ethic**.

Weber's theory was based on a number of related ideas. One is the notion, popular among early Protestants, that there is a predestined "elect," a group of people who will be "saved" during the Second Coming of Christ. Naturally, it was important to early Protestants to be seen as part of this exclusive group. Success through hard work was considered one proof of membership. Another was the accumulation of **capital** (money and other assets, such as factories, used to generate money) through thriftiness. Working hard, making profitable use of one's time, and living a materially *ascetic* (self-denying) life by acquiring property and saving rather than spending lavishly are all principles of Weber's Protestant work ethic. As Weber himself explained:

The span of human life is infinitely short and precious to make sure of one's own election. Loss of time through sociability, idle talk, luxury, even more sleep than is necessary for health . . . is worthy of absolute moral condemnation. . . . [Time] is infinitely valuable because every hour lost is lost to labour for the glory of God. Thus inactive contemplation is also valueless, or even directly reprehensible if it is at the expense of one's daily work. For it is less pleasing to God than the active performance of His will in a calling. (Weber 1930/[1904]: 157–8)

Weber later elaborated on how demonstrating these values represents proof of being one of God's chosen few, and how these values supposedly fuelled the rise of capitalism:

> The religious valuation of restless, continuous, systematic work in a worldly calling, as the . . . surest and most evident proof of rebirth and genuine faith, must have been the most powerful conceivable lever for the expansion of . . . the spirit of capitalism. (Weber 1958/[1946]: 172)

Although the idea of the Protestant (work) ethic took hold firmly enough that it entered popular thought and speech, it was never demonstrated sociologically that capitalism developed primarily in Protestant rather than in Catholic countries, or that the work ethic Weber associated with Protestantism was somehow missing from other religions. Latin American scholars, for instance, argue that the rise of capitalism began with colonialism, a movement in which Catholic Spain and Portugal were major early players. Weber paid little attention to the role that colonialism played in the rise of capitalism as an instrument for exploiting colonized countries. Spain looted Aztec and Incan gold to become, for a time, the richest country in Europe. Weber, by attributing the development of capitalism to the strength of the Protestant will, might have been trying too hard to account for the relatively recent historical superiority of European Protestants. He did not write at all about the earlier high cultures of China and South Asia.

What do YOU think?

1. Do you think that Weber would have advanced this theory if he had been a devout Catholic, Muslim, or Buddhist, rather than a liberal Protestant?

2. Does being religious enhance one's ability to become rich?

The Spread of Sociology to North America

During the late nineteenth and early twentieth centuries in North America, the emergence of conditions similar to those that already existed in Europe—the arrival of millions of immigrants, the development of cities and urban life, and the growing impact of technology upon the daily lives of individuals—spurred the growth of sociology. In the United States, one of the country's oldest sociology departments, at the University of Chicago, arose primarily as a way of understanding the problems associated with the rapid immigration of thousands of Europeans to the city. During the 1920s and 1930s, the "Chicago School" became synonymous with both the specialized subdiscipline of urban sociology and a number of prominent sociologists including Everett C. Hughes, George Herbert Mead, Robert Park, Ruth Cavan, Edwin Sutherland, W.I. Thomas, and Florian Znaniecki.

Jane Addams (1860–1935) was a social activist associated with the Chicago School. Her sociology was more applied than theoretical: not only did she study social problems and look for remedies, but she applied practical solutions. She established Chicago's Hull House, the first settlement house in the United States, with the aim of helping newly arrived immigrant women in need. For this pioneering contribution to social activism and for her applied sociological work generally, she was awarded the Nobel Peace Prize in 1931.

What do YOU think?

Look at the list of early sociologists in Table 1.2. Why are most of them men?

The Development of Sociology in Canada

While there is no distinctly Canadian way to carry out sociological research and practice, the way the discipline developed in this country and its primary focal points are unique. The relationship between French and English, the development of the Canadian West, the connection between class and ethnicity, and a close working relationship with anthropology have all been fundamental to the development of a Canadian perspective on sociology.

Table 1.2   Some early sociologists and their contributions

SOCIOLOGIST (years, nationality)	KEY WORKS	CONTRIBUTION
Auguste Comte (1798–1857, French)	• *The Course in Positivist Philosophy (1830–42)* • *A General View of Positivism (1848)*	A proponent of positivist philosophy, he aimed to develop a social science that could be used for social reconstruction.
Harriet Martineau (1802–1876, British)	• *Illustrations of Political Economy (1834)* • *Society in America (1837)*	Widely viewed as the first woman sociologist, she wrote extensively on social, economic, and historical topics, and translated several of Comte's works.
Karl Marx (1818–1883, German)	• *The German Ideology (1846)* • *The Communist Manifesto (1848, with Friedrich Engels)* • *Capital (1867)*	The founder of modern communism, he viewed social change in terms of economic factors.
Herbert Spencer (1820–1903, British)	• *Social Statics (1851)* • *First Principles (1862)* • *The Study of Sociology (1873)*	A social evolutionist, he sought to apply Darwin's theory of natural selection to human societies and coined the term "survival of the fittest."
Friedrich Nietzsche (1844–1900, German)	• *Human, All Too Human (1878)* • *Beyond Good and Evil (1886)* • *On the Genealogy of Morals (1887)* • *The Will to Power (1901)*	A philosopher, he rejected Christianity's compassion for the weak and championed the "will to power" and the Übermensch ("superman"), who could rise above the restrictions of ordinary morality.
Thorstein Veblen (1857–1929, American)	• *The Theory of the Leisure Class (1899)* • *The Theory of the Business Enterprise (1904)*	An economist and social critic, he attacked American "conspicuous consumption."
Émile Durkheim (1858–1917, French)	• *The Division of Labour in Society (1893)* • *The Rules of the Sociological Method (1895)* • *Suicide (1897)* • *The Elementary Forms of the Religious Life (1912)*	Among the first to consider society as a legitimate subject of scientific observation, he studied society in terms of "social facts" such as ethics, occupations, and suicide.
Georg Simmel (1858–1918, German)	• *On Social Differentiation (1890)* • *The Philosophy of Money (1900)* • *Sociology: Investigations on the Forms of Sociation (1908)*	The father of microsociology, he studied the way people experience the minutiae of daily life.
George Herbert Mead (1863–1931, American)	• *Mind, Self, and Society (1934)*	The father of "symbolic interactionism," he looked at how the self is constructed through personal exchanges with others.
Max Weber (1864–1920, German)	• *The Protestant Ethic and the Spirit of Capitalism (1904–5)* • *Economy and Society (1922)*	He identified a set of values, the "Protestant (work) ethic," to which he attributed the rise of capitalism.
Robert Park (1864–1944, American)	• *Introduction to the Science of Sociology (1921)* • *The City: Suggestions for the Study of Human Nature in the Urban Environment (1925)*	An urban sociologist, he was a founding member of the "Chicago School" of sociology.
W.E.B. Du Bois (1868–1963, American)	• *The Souls of Black Folk (1903)* • *Black Reconstruction in America (1935)*	He documented the experience of American blacks from a sociological perspective.

Note: All works have been identified by their English titles, although several of these works first appeared, in the years indicated, in languages other than English.

As we will see in later chapters, sociology in this country began long before the establishment of departments of sociology at Canadian universities and colleges. However, we will begin here with Canadian sociology as it developed in post-secondary institutions across the country.

McGill University: Dawson, Hughes, and Miner

The first professional, institutionalized sociologist in Canada was **Carl Addington Dawson** (1887–1964). Born in Prince Edward Island, Dawson completed his MA and PhD at the University of Chicago. In 1922, shortly after joining the faculty at McGill University in Montreal, he founded the university's sociology department, an accomplishment not without opposition. Senior administrators worried about the left-wing political leanings of sociologists (they still do), and academics in other departments did not want their scholarly territory infringed upon. Dawson succeeded in spite of these objections. McGill's remained the only independent department of sociology in Canada until 1961.

Dawson's work reflected two elements of early Canadian sociology: the social gospel movement and hands-on social work. The **social gospel movement** developed as an attempt by people trained for the ministry to apply Christian principles of human welfare to the treatment of social, medical, and psychological ills brought on by industrialization and unregulated capitalism in Canada, the United States, Britain, Germany, and other European countries during the late nineteenth century. Out of the social gospel movement came, among other things, the Social Service Council of Canada (1912), which through various churches carried out the first sociological surveys of Canadian cities.

Dawson's affinity with the social gospel movement was natural—his first degree from the University of Chicago was in divinity—but his inspiration to become involved early on in social work came as well from the methods and philosophy of the Chicago School of sociology. The Chicago School emphasized the importance of going out into communities—what American sociologist Robert Park called "living laboratories"—to observe them. Dawson took this approach and, with his students, applied it to the living laboratory of Montreal. Their research was given a jump-start in 1929, when they were awarded a $110,000 Rockefeller Foundation grant to study unemployment in the city.

That same year, Dawson and Warren E. Gettys became the first Canadians to write a sociology textbook. The text was an instant success, adopted by over 150 colleges and universities across North America within a year. While there was not a great deal of Canadian content, it helped legitimize the study and practice of sociology in Canada.

Another figure vital to the development of sociology at McGill was **Everett C. Hughes** (1897–1983). Like Dawson a graduate of the University of Chicago, the Ohio-born Hughes joined the sociology department at McGill in 1927 a firm believer in community research.

While at McGill, Hughes focused on what he termed the "ethnic division of labour," a situation that enabled English Canadians to rise above French Canadians, creating a disparity that he wished to correct. Out of this research came *French Canada in Transition* (1943). By the time the landmark study was published, Hughes had already returned to the United States to take a position among the faculty of his alma mater.

Horace Miner (1912–1993) was another American sociologist who put the study of French Canada at the forefront of Canadian sociology. As a graduate student at the University of Chicago, he came to Quebec to study the parish of St Denis. His book *St Denis: A French-Canadian Parish* (1939) shows the blurred distinction between sociology and anthropology in Canada. His work is best described as an **ethnography**, a study of a community based on extensive fieldwork, whose primary research activities include direct observation and talking with the people observed. Ethnography is the main research method used in social anthropology. Miner described the rural peasants and farmers of his study as a **folk society**, following the model of University of Chicago anthropologist Robert Redfield, who coined the term. The close connection between sociology and anthropology can still be seen in some Canadian universities where the two disciplines are joined in the same department.

The University of King's College: Samuel Henry Prince

Another influential figure in the early days of Canadian sociology was **Samuel Henry Prince** (1886–1962), who taught from 1924 until 1955 at the University of King's College in Halifax, and was instrumental in establishing sociology as a formal academic discipline in the Nova Scotian capital. The breadth of Prince's interests and the way they guided his research are summarized nicely by his biographer, Leonard Hatfield, who wrote:

[T]he mental health movement, social planning in Halifax, housing reform, social work education, prison reform, juvenile corrections, family case work, and improved services for the mentally handicapped all became his special concerns and the centre of his activities for the most productive years of his life. The organizations which grew out of these activities were all moulded and shaped by him, and he nurtured them with personal care and attention for a quarter-century. It is difficult or impossible to imagine what the social welfare scene might have been if he had not passed this way. (Hatfield 1990: 8–9)

As sociology wasn't yet established as a distinct discipline in Canada when he was a university student, Prince earned his bachelor's degree in philosophy and his master's degree in psychology. He was also an ordained minister of the Anglican Church. His multiple specialties showed up in the fact that King's College, where he was installed as chair of the department of sociology and economics, had the only divinity school in the country where sociology was a mandatory subject (an excellent idea, in my opinion).

Prince received his PhD in sociology in 1919 from the prestigious Columbia University in New York. His doctoral dissertation was a pioneering study of social change in the wake of disaster (natural or human-made). His work was inspired by the Halifax Explosion of 1917, in which a docked naval vessel carrying explosives caught fire and blew up in Halifax Harbour, rocking the city of some 50,000 with blast, fire, and floods that killed nearly 2,000 people. Prince's thesis was that disaster created conditions that could lead to significant social change. In Halifax, he explained:

the shock resulted in disintegration of social institutions, dislocation of the usual methods of social control and dissolution of the customary. . . . [T]hrough the catastrophe the community was thrown into the state of flux which . . . is the logical and natural prerequisite for social change. . . . [T]he shock was of a character such as "to affect all individuals alike at the same time," and to induce that degree of fluidity most favorable to social change.

Prince demonstrated how this disaster had led to a variety of social changes, including the improvement of public transportation and the establishment of a building code that would see the wood-dominated architecture prevalent before the disaster gradually replaced by structures built of materials less likely to burn.

What kind of work do you think is being performed at this Montreal office *c.* 1920? Are the people you see here more likely to be anglophones or francophones?

Prince's argument that catastrophe can be viewed as a kind of social experiment capable of producing positive or negative social change is an important sociological point that we will take up in Chapter 21, on the sociology of the environment, when we look at the social effects of Hurricane Katrina in New Orleans in 2005. The Halifax Explosion was nothing like the natural event that Hurricane Katrina was, but it caused environmental devastation on a comparable scale, giving Prince's work great relevance in a sociological investigation of the hurricane's aftermath.

The University of Toronto: Innis and Clark

As sociology was developing along particular lines at McGill and King's College, the discipline was taking shape under a very different tradition, that of political economy, at the University of Toronto. **Political economy** is an interdisciplinary approach involving sociology, political science, economics, law, anthropology, and history. It looks primarily at the relationship between politics and the economics of the production, distribution, and consumption of goods. It is often **Marxist** in nature, pointing to the class tensions that arise in the extraction and distribution of goods.

A Canadian pioneer in the field of political economy was **Harold Innis** (1894–1952), who joined the University of Toronto in 1920. Innis was more an economic historian than a sociologist, but his work has exerted a strong influence on Canadian sociology. He argued that the availability of staples—resources such as fish, fur, minerals, and wheat—shaped the economic and social development of Canada.

Innis was also a mentor to the first person hired at the university specifically as a sociologist, **Samuel Delbert Clark** (1910–2003). Born in Alberta, S.D. Clark received his first two degrees from the University of Saskatchewan before joining the Department of Political Economy at U of T in 1938. Sociology remained a branch of that department until 1963, when it became a stand-alone department, with Clark as its chair. Summarizing Clark's influence, Deborah Harrison wrote:

> The importance of S.D. Clark within the development of Canadian sociology is universally recognized. Clark's publications span more than forty prolific years, with at least the first fifteen occurring when almost no other sociologists were writing in Canada; he is generally acknowledged as the father of the Canadian approach to the discipline. . . . For reasons of both his scholarly engagement and his articulation of a "Canadian" sociology, Clark is the most important sociologist Canada has yet produced. (Harrison 1999)

We could call Clark a "sociological historian": consider a selection of chapter headings in his book *The Developing Canadian Community* (1962):

- The Farming–Fur-Trade Society of New France
- The Rural Village Society of the Maritimes
- The Backwoods Society of Upper Canada
- The Gold-Rush Society of British Columbia and the Yukon
- The Prairie Wheat-Farming Frontier and the New Industrial City
- The Religious Influence in Canadian Society
- The Canadian Community and the American Continental System
- History and the Sociological Method

Social Class and Ethnicity: John Porter

Fundamentally missing from the work of both Innis and Clark are the themes of class and ethnicity, which are so persistent in much of Canadian sociology today. These themes received their definitive treatment in what is generally recognized as the best-known work of Canadian sociology, *The Vertical Mosaic: An Analysis of Social Class and Power in Canada* (1965), by **John Porter** (1921–1979). Porter joined the faculty of Carleton University in 1949, becoming the university's first full-time appointment in sociology. The title of his book plays on the term cultural mosaic, a metaphor frequently used to characterize Canada's multicultural society, especially in contrast to the melting pot image often used to portray the more assimilated society of the United States. A mosaic is a type of artwork composed of many small tiles that lend different colours to the picture. A society that is a cultural mosaic is one "in which racial, ethnic, and religious groups maintain a distinct identity, rather than being absorbed into a 'melting pot'" (Lundy & Warme 1990: 583). By contrast, a melting pot involves the "rapid assimilation of recent immigrants into their new society" (Lundy & Warme 1990: 586).

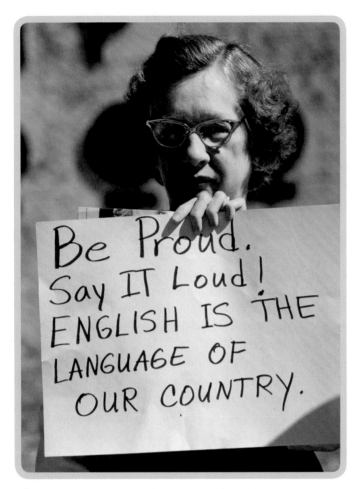

Melting pot or cultural mosaic?

degrees from Acadia University before earning her PhD at the University of Chicago. She also taught there, although, despite her excellent qualifications, in a very subordinate position.

MacLean pioneered the sociological study of working women, especially in her study *Wage-Earning Women* (1910), which was based on a survey of some 13,500 women. She conducted her research in department stores, in factory sweatshops, and among hop-pickers in rural Oregon. Though she was born in Canada, she was never hired by a Canadian university.

Aileen Ross

The first woman hired as a sociologist at a Canadian university was **Aileen Ross** (1902–1995), a native of Montreal, who taught sociology at the University of Toronto for three years before joining the faculty at McGill University. She earned her first degree at the London School of Economics, and her MA (in 1941) and PhD (in 1950) from the University of Chicago.

A founding member of the Canadian Human Rights Foundation, Ross devoted her books to two of her foremost concerns: women and India. She published *The Hindu Family in an Urban Setting* (1962) after carrying out several years of research in India. Her last book, *The Lost and the Lonely: Homeless Women in Montreal* (1982), enabled women at a shelter she helped found to tell their stories.

Helen C. Abell

Born in Medicine Hat, Alberta, **Helen C. Abell** (1917–2005) has been called the founder of rural sociology in Canada. After receiving a degree in human nutrition at the University of Toronto (1941), she worked as a nutritionist for the Ontario Department of Agriculture, then as an officer in the Canadian Women's Army Corps during World War II. She received her PhD in rural sociology (the first Canadian to do so) in 1951. She then established a rural sociology research unit in the federal Department of Agriculture. Her research, notes Jenny Kendrick:

played an important role in identifying systematically the roles women played on the farm. This was an invaluable contribution to the policy arena, virtually forcing society and policymakers to lay

Porter coined the term **vertical mosaic** to describe the situation he observed in Canadian society, in which systemic discrimination produces a hierarchy of racial, ethnic, and religious groups. To stay within the metaphor of the mosaic, we can say that Porter's study found that the different tiles were stacked and not placed evenly. White, Anglo-Saxon, Protestant tiles were on top, followed by French-Canadian tiles, the tiles of the more successful ethnic groups (e.g. Jewish, Chinese, and Italian), and finally those of everyone else, with the racially marginalized groups at the bottom. Porter concluded that ethnicity and ranking were linked.

Three Early Women Sociologists and the Writing of Gender in Canada

Annie Marion MacLean

Annie Marion MacLean (*c.* 1870–1934) was the first Canadian woman to obtain a PhD in sociology. Born in Prince Edward Island, she received her first two aside their stereotypes of the marginal contributions of farm women to agriculture. (Quoted in Eichler 2001: 382)

The Growth of Sociology in Canada

In 1958, there were fewer than 20 sociology professors in Canada, teaching in just nine universities (Clark 1976: 120). Sociology did not become a significant area of study and teaching in Canada until the 1960s and 1970s, as baby boomers entered universities and colleges. The growth of sociology during that time is astounding. Hiller and Di Luzio, for example, report that the University of Alberta "had no sociology majors in 1956–57, but a year later had nine, followed by 24 (1957–58), 44 (1959–60), and 62 (1960–61). The number of majors there reached a peak for the twentieth century at 776 in 1987" (Hiller & Di Luzio 2001: 490).

During this era of growth in sociology study and research, most of the sociologists hired to teach in Canadian post-secondary institutions were from the United States and Britain. Of those with doctorates teaching sociology and anthropology in Canada in 1967, 72 per cent had PhDs from the US, 10 per cent from Britain, and only 6 per cent from Canada (Gallagher & Lambert 1971: vii). In 1973–4, 45 per cent of the full-time sociology faculty in Canada was made up of non-Canadians (Hofley 1992: 106). This should not be surprising given that only 22 doctorates in sociology were conferred at Canadian universities between 1924 and 1967 (Gallagher & Lambert 1971: vi).

The dearth of Canadian sociologists meant that sociology textbooks lacked a Canadian perspective. John Hofley recalls that when he was hired to teach sociology at Carleton University in 1966, he saw "very little about Canada in the sociology texts that were available" (Hofley 1992: 104). It was not uncommon that a textbook used in Canada would be exclusively American. The 1970s saw a big movement to "Canadianize" sociology textbooks. Today most introductory sociology textbooks used in Canadian schools are either Canadian in origin or "Canadianized" versions of American textbooks.

What do YOU think?

How might an introductory sociology textbook written in Canada be different from a "Canadianized" one originally written in the US?

Telling It Like It Is

An Author POV

If I Were a Young Sociologist Today . . .

I don't know how many times I have said, "If I were a young sociologist today, I would love to study _____."

Just about every time I started a new chapter in this textbook, I found something—some tidbit of information, or a neglected study—that I know could lead to fascinating research that would be exciting to take on. As I write this, it is the sociology of disabilities that keeps entering my mind. It seems ideal to me because it combines an area ripe for sociological and intellectual inquiry with the chance to do work that will help society in a meaningful, practical way—one of the goals that has led a number of outstanding sociologists to enter the discipline. And there is so much that could be done in this one area—articles and articles, books and books, projects and projects, and the opportunity to change social policy. It is under-studied in Canada, like so many areas in sociology.

It was a third-year course on language and culture (1971–2) that drew me to my life's work. I was curious about Aboriginal languages in Canada, and wondered why they were so rarely used in the study of indigenous cultures. I've written five books on the subject, and with two more in the works, there are ideas I haven't touched yet; I have barely scratched the surface. And if I were a young sociologist today . . .

WRAP IT UP

Summary

In this chapter, we've tried to give you a sense of what sociology *looks like*. You likely won't have formed a really good sense of what sociology *is* until you've reached the end of the book. You've learned a bit about what my approach to writing sociology is like, and my aim of making this a textbook not like the others. You have been introduced to some of the main players that will strut the stage in the chapters that follow: Marx, Durkheim, Weber—three of the modern discipline's founders. Others have been merely mentioned here, but you will be more fully introduced to them in later chapters.

In addition to familiarizing you with some of the discipline's key figures, I have attempted to trace (admittedly briefly) the origins of sociology, examining the development of the discipline through Europe and the United States. I have also, of course, added some Canadian flavour to the overview of the discipline's history. Expect plenty more Timbits and maple syrup in the chapters to come.

THINK BACK

Questions for Critical Review

1. Outline some of the differences and similarities between sociology and other social science disciplines, such as anthropology, political science, women's studies, and Aboriginal or Indigenous studies. What are some of the places where these disciplines intersect?

2. Identify the key ideas of Marx, Durkheim, and Weber, as outlined in this chapter.

3. What has been the impact of the Chicago school on early Canadian sociology?

4. Look at the early women sociologists discussed in this chapter: Addams, MacLean, Ross, Abell. How does their work differ from the work of male sociologists in the early twentieth century?

5. What is sociology? (Just kidding, but try this: what is the value of studying sociology?)

6. Look at the chapter headings of this textbook. Which area of research would you consider most interesting? Which subject area do you think has the most potential for improving Canadian society?

READ ON

Online

C. Wright Mills [1916–1962]

www.genordell.com/stores/maison/CWMills.htm

This very useful website features a short profile of the eminent sociologist, as well as lists of works by and about Mills and links to online copies of some of his books and articles.

The Durkheim Pages

http://durkheim.uchicago.edu/

Created by University of Illinois emeritus professor Robert Alun Jones, this site contains abundant information on the French sociologist, including a biography, summaries of some of his works, and a glossary of terms important to understanding Durkheim's work.

Marx & Engels Internet Archive

www.marxists.org/archive/marx/

This is a complete guide to the works of the two fathers of socialism, complete with an image gallery and a sophisticated Google-powered search feature.

Max Weber [1864–1920]

www.sociosite.net/topics/weber.php

Created by Albert Benschop of the University of Amsterdam, this site contains links to books and articles by and about Max Weber.

In Print

Everett Hughes (1963 [orig. 1943]), *French Canada in Transition* (Chicago: University of Chicago Press).

A study of francophone Quebec by a figure associated with the Chicago School, this is a strong sociological work that is still worth reading.

Allan G. Johnson (1997), *The Blackwell Dictionary of Sociology: A User's Guide to Sociological Language* (Oxford: Blackwell).

This is a very useful reference work that outlines some of the basic terms in sociology.

Kathryn Mills, ed. (2000), *C. Wright Mills: Letters and Autobiographical Writings* (Los Angeles: University of California Press).

Gathered and edited by the daughter of C. Wright Mills, this collection makes clear connections between the famous sociologist and his life.

David Nock (2001), "Careers in Print: Canadian Sociological Books and Their Wider Impact, 1975–1992," *Canadian Journal of Sociology / Cahiers canadiens de sociologie* 26 (3), pp 469–85.

A good short look at Canadian sociology books, and the influence they have had on public policy and on the discipline generally.

2

How Sociology Works: Theories and Approaches

Learning Objectives

After reading this chapter, you should be able to

- compare and contrast the fundamental ideas of Marx, Durkheim, and Weber
- distinguish the three "functions" identified by Robert Merton
- outline the two broad categories of sociological approaches: (1) structural functionalism, conflict theory, and symbolic interactionism on the one hand; and (2) professional, critical,

- policy, and public sociology on the other
- identify the main aspects of feminist and postmodernist perspectives
- articulate the basic ideas of critical sociologists Michel Foucault and Dorothy Smith
- articulate the basic ideas of symbolic interactionist Erving Goffman.

Key Terms

- archaeology of knowledge
- bourgeoisie
- class
- conflict theory (*or* approach)
- critical sociology
- discourse
- dramaturgical approach
- egalitarian
- feminist theory
- ideological
- impression management
- interlocking matrix of domination

- intersectionality theory
- latent dysfunction
- latent function
- macrosociology
- manifest function
- microsociology
- objective
- policy sociology
- postmodern theory
- professional sociology
- proletariat
- Protestant (work) ethic
- public sociology
- social fact

- standpoint theory
- structural functionalism
- subjective
- symbolic interactionism
- theorizing
- theory
- total institution
- totalitarian discourse
- value-free
- *verstehen*

Names to Know

- Herbert Blumer
- Patricia Hill Collins
- Kimberlé Crenshaw
- Émile Durkheim
- Michel Foucault
- Erving Goffman

- Leonard Marsh
- Harriet Martineau
- Karl Marx
- George Herbert Mead
- Robert K. Merton

- Talcott Parsons
- Dorothy Smith
- Max Weber

A mural painted on grain elevators at Midland, Ontario, near the historic site of Sainte-Marie-Among-the-Hurons, depicts a meeting between a Wendat man and a Jesuit missionary. Why do you think there is no woman in this picture?

Knowing When to Take a Standpoint: Female Elders among the Wendat

My primary area of study is the Wendat First Nation, better known in textbooks as the Huron. Our main sources of information on the history of this people come from the Jesuits, a Catholic missionary order that worked and lived with the Wendat. During most of the seventeenth century and part of the eighteenth century, the Jesuits produced a series of annual reports—73 in total—called the *Jesuit Relations*. These documents provide us with clues about how the missionaries viewed the Wendat they encountered.

But you have to read them with a grain of salt.

For instance, in the *Jesuit Relations* we learn that only men had authority in Wendat society. But the Wendat were matrilineal (determining kinship along the female line), and women planted, weeded, harvested, ground, and cooked the most important food for the people: corn.

As an all-male society whose members spent most of their time with other men in a male-dominated culture, the Jesuits knew little of female authority—of female culture generally—even in their own society in Europe. Their relative lack of interaction with women and girls during their missionary work can be seen in the fact that of the 268 Wendat names they recorded in their books, only 39 of them—around 15 per cent—are female names.

Further, as Canadian sociologist Karen Anderson informs us in her beautifully titled work *Chain Her By One Foot: The Subjugation of Women in Seventeenth-Century New France* (1991), Jesuit missionaries, when they encountered a socially strong woman among Wendat, often did what they could to diminish her social strength.

Later in this chapter you will read about standpoint theory, which states that when research is done only by people of one *social location* (remember that term from last chapter?), then important aspects of the sociological study will be missed. The theory was first developed to highlight the limitations of male sociologists when it came to studying women's roles in society.

Informed by standpoint theory, I strongly suspected that women in Wendat society *did* have significant

authority—I just had to search harder for it. It was not enough to rely solely on the views of white, European, Catholic men writing about Aboriginal women in North America. I had to read between the lines, look for the hidden.

After years of searching, I finally found a relevant source, written in 1747 about to the people considered elders at that time, people who would have had a strong influence on Wendat politics. To my delight, the source referred to both "anciens" (male elders) and "anciennes" (female elders). I had never seen "anciennes" in my reading and re-reading of the *Jesuit Relations*. The source documented 60 elders, of whom 31 were men and 29 were women. I have been able to write both a scholarly article and a chapter of a book on them.

The case highlights the benefits of considering different approaches to social research. Without the insights learned from standpoint theory, and feminist theory in general, I would not have **continued** on this search, and found what I did. The bearded feminist strikes again.

Introduction: What Is (a) Social Theory?

Theory in sociology (and in other sciences) has two meanings. First, a **theory** is an attempt to explain facts or observed phenomena; **theorizing** is the activity of attempting to find explanations to account for what has been observed.

Sometimes, though, *theory* refers to a school of thought or a set of linked theories. Examples of *theory* in this second sense include Marxist theory and feminist theory, both of which are based on a body of shared assumptions, though they can still produce varying interpretations of the same phenomena. Facts do not speak to us directly, nor do they stand independently of theories. They are heavily influenced by the theory of the observer, as all theories involve choosing what aspects of the observed phenomenon are more important than others, as well as what questions are asked and not asked.

A short example will illustrate. In Chapter 10, on "race" and ethnicity, you will read about the Tutsi and the Hutu, two groups or tribes living in the neighbouring central African countries of Rwanda and Burundi. During the period of time that they were

under Belgian colonial rule, they were studied extensively by Western scholars, who seem to have focused on the differences between the peoples, not the overwhelming similarities. It appears that their basic research questions were guided by the theory that the people were fundamentally different. Differences, such as variances in average height and build, and contrasts in approach to agriculture (herding cattle versus maintaining small mixed farms), were identified and exaggerated, given primary importance. Of course, this helped the Belgian colonial authorities divide and conquer the two peoples. Had the researchers begun with the theory that the two groups were fundamentally the same, they might have asked different questions and stressed the common aspects of their lives (for example, that they spoke the same language, had the same religion, and recognized the same kinship structure). A different narrative would have been written, one less compatible with colonial rule.

What Is (a) Sociological Theory?

In the seventh edition of his influential book *Modern Sociological Theory*, George Ritzer lays down three criteria of a sociological theory is. According to Ritzer, a sociological theory must:

1. have a wide range of applicability;
2. deal with centrally important social issues; and
3. have stood the test of time. (Ritzer 2008: 2)

Of course, there is a lot of wiggle room in this definition, particularly with respect to the notion of "centrally important social issues." One sociological theorist's declaration that a particular social issue is centrally important might not find universal agreement among other theorists. And, because a sociological theory's importance can often be assessed by its staying power in the discipline, it is particularly difficult to assess the importance of more recent sociological theories (such as queer theory) that have not had the chance to stand the test of time.

You can probably tell already that a theory chapter in a sociology textbook is not easy to write. While the early theorists are relatively easy to discuss (especially the inevitable trio of Marx, Durkheim, and Weber, as they are few, their distinctive positions are relatively clear, and their influence is undeniable), the situation gets messy when we approach the present.

Writing a chapter on theory inevitably requires some judgement calls that not everyone will agree with. Simplifications and generalizations can be controversial, and invariably somebody's favourite theorist will get left out. I am choosing to err here on the side of exclusion rather than inclusion, as I want to convey just a basic idea of the kinds of theories and approaches that are applied in sociological research.

Different Kinds of Sociological Theory

As we saw in the previous chapter, sociology did not take on a uniform appearance as it grew as a discipline during the nineteenth century. Social thinkers had differing views of what sociology was, what it could do, and how it should be applied. Consequently, sociology developed into several different schools that varied according to their particular applications and the perspectives (historical, political-economical, feminist, and so on) of those who were using it.

In this chapter we will explore two ways of distinguishing the different kinds of sociological theory. The first is based on the particular approach or theory used; the second is based on the intended audience for the work and how socially critical the sociologist is. This

second method of looking at sociology is often neglected in introductory sociology textbooks and in discussions of sociological theory, but I think it provides a useful way of examining and categorizing the discipline.

These are by no means the only two ways of looking at sociology—they are simply the ones I have found the most useful.

Part 1: Sociology by Approach

The traditional way of representing different kinds of sociology in introductory textbooks is to break it down into the different approaches or theories sociologists use to pursue their inquiries:

- structural functionalism
- conflict theory
- symbolic interactionism
- feminist theory
- postmodern theory.

These terms are typically presented in the introductory chapter of a textbook and then repeated throughout most, if not all, of the subsequent chapters. The linguist Edward Sapir said, "all grammars [i.e. explanations of language] leak." We feel that this particular "grammar of sociology" leaks too much (imagine a flooded basement) to sustain using it throughout the text. Nevertheless, these distinctions do reveal some key differences, so they are worth explaining and illustrating here.

Structural Functionalism

The **structural-functionalist** approach has deep roots in sociology, especially American sociology. As the name suggests, the approach contains two dimensions. *Functionalism* focuses on how social systems, in their entirety, operate and produce consequences. The work of Émile Durkheim, Robert Merton, and Talcott Parsons represents the functionalist approach.

The functionalist approach was fused with *structuralism* (grounded in the work of anthropologists Bronisław Malinowski and A.R. Radcliffe-Brown) as a way of explaining social forms and their contributions to social cohesion. It uses an *organic*, or biological, analogy for society. How? Nursing students, when they take the dreaded Anatomy and Physiology course, have to learn all the different *structures* of the human body as well as the *functions* they perform. The structural-functionalist approach treats society in a similar way: *This is the part of society we call "organized religion," and this is what it does for society . . .*; or *This is the family, which functions like so . . .*

While the structural-functionalist approach has been popular for most of sociology's history, it has lost favour during the last few decades. It is too much of a stretch, for example, to talk about the *functions* of poverty or inequality. Poverty and inequality don't really serve the interests of society at large, just the narrow class interests of those who profit from others' misfortunes. In addition, functionalism is not usually very good at promoting an understanding of conflict or social change. While sociologists still draw on the classic works and essential concepts of structural functionalism, few contemporary sociologists are committed to the theoretical practice itself.

Émile Durkheim

To get a better sense of the functionalist approach, we'll look at the work of **Émile Durkheim** (1858–1917), who was briefly introduced in the last chapter as one of the founders of sociology. An important early sociological concept is Durkheim's **social fact**. Social facts are patterned ways of acting, thinking, and feeling that exist outside of any one individual but that exert social control over all people. Think about how social characteristics such as gender, age, religion, ethnicity, "race," sexual orientation, your role as sister or brother, or as student or teacher, exert a compelling social force over you and lead you to act in sociologically predictable ways. These ways of acting based on social characteristics are social facts.

Every social fact has three essential characteristics:

1. It was developed prior to and separate from any individual (in other words, *you* didn't invent it).
2. It can be seen as being characteristic of a particular group (young Canadian men, for instance, like to watch sports while drinking beer—a social fact that explains why so many beer commercials feature young men watching sports).
3. It involves a constraining or coercing force that pushes individuals into acting in a particular way

Vancouver's Downtown Eastside is one of the poorest urban neighbourhoods in North America. A functionalist might argue that homelessness is a social consequence naturally produced by our economic system. Would you agree?

(like when young men watching sports succumb to "beer pressure" and begin yelling, high-fiving, and displaying other behaviour associated with this social fact).

You can see how looking for social facts would be a useful way for a sociologist to get beyond focusing on individuals to examine larger social forms and how different parts of society function.

In *Suicide* (1897), Durkheim examined suicide as a social fact. You might find this strange, given the intensely personal nature of the act. But Durkheim found that in late nineteenth-century France, certain groups were more likely to commit suicide than others: military officers more than enlisted men, Protestants more than Catholics, and unmarried more than married people. He drew a correlation between suicide and the degree to which individuals were connected or committed to society, finding that those with a very strong dedication to society were more likely

to commit suicide than those with a weaker commitment. Think about it: officers are responsible for the soldiers in their charge—it makes sense that a heightened sense of honour might make them suicidal when they make mistakes that result in death. On the other hand, Durkheim also concluded that having too weak a connection to society could produce suicide as well. Protestants were in the minority in France and thus had weaker bonds to both the country in which they lived and its culture.

In Canada today, men commit suicide more often than women do. This is a social fact. Why men commit suicide more often than women do is a complicated matter. It has to do in part with the fact that women are more likely to share their problems with other people than to "suck it up" and remain silent. Women are more likely to have a network of friends with whom they can communicate about serious matters, and they are more likely to go to a therapist with an emotional problem, which lowers their likelihood of committing

The relationship between a teacher and his or her students is a social fact. What patterned ways of acting influence this teacher's behaviour towards her students? How might the teacher, should she not conform to the behaviour expected of her, be punished, either in some formal way (e.g. by law or by the school board) or in some informal way (i.e. by her peers) depending on the nature of the transgression? What are some of the patterned ways of acting that influence students' behaviour?

suicide. Women attempting suicide are also more likely to use less efficient means: pills and slashed wrists over the more deadly male choice of guns.

What do YOU think?

The author of this textbook considers himself a fairly enlightened, "bearded" feminist. Yet a woman reader commented that it was obvious this commentary was written by a man: women, she pointed out, are less likely to commit suicide because of their childcare responsibilities, not because they are incapable or more likely to "share their feelings." Do you agree?

Talcott Parsons and Robert Merton

Talcott Parsons (1902–1979) exerted a major influence on American sociology both in his writing and in his teaching. His first epic work, *The Structure of Social Action* (1937), theorized about society on a grand scale. The International Sociological Association honoured it by naming it the ninth most important book on sociology of the twentieth century. As a structural functionalist, Parsons' main approach—exhibited notably in his classic work *The Social System* (1951)—was to look at society's principal institutions (education, religion, government, the economy, etc.) in order to map out the fundamentally supportive relationships that each one had to the others.

A good example of Parsons' kind of analysis is found in an article he wrote called "An Analytical Approach to the Theory of Social Stratification" (Parsons 1940). With respect to gender roles and status he wrote the following, which might be termed, somewhat sarcastically, his "adornment theory":

The separation of the sex roles in our society is such as, for the most part, to remove women from the kind of occupational status which is important for the determination of the status of a family. Where married women are employed outside the home, it is, for the great majority, in occupations which are not in direct competition for status with those of men of their own class.

Women's interests, and the standards of judgment applied to them, run, in our society, far more in the direction of personal adornment and the related qualities of personal charm than is the case with men. Men's dress is practically a uniform, admitting of very slight play for differentiating taste, in marked contrast with that of women. This serves to concentrate the judgment and valuation of men on their occupational achievements, while the valuation of women is diverted into realms outside the occupationally relevant sphere. This difference appears particularly conspicuous in the urban middle classes where competition for class status is most severe. It is suggested that this phenomenon is functionally related to maintaining family solidarity in our class structure. (Parsons 1940: 853)

We can snicker now at Parsons' suggestion that a working woman would have to wear a bland business suit to have her accomplishments on the job taken seriously (or not—maybe the argument holds even today?). The important point here is that his analysis represents an attempt to show how gender *functions* naturally to strengthen the family unit within the overall *structure* of society. Women's preoccupation with fashion and social charm keeps them outside of the boardroom, where they might otherwise be competing for jobs with their husbands, thereby threatening the cohesion of the family.

Robert K. Merton (1910–2003), one of several of Parsons' students who became noteworthy

What do YOU think?

1. Parsons was writing in 1940, shortly after the Great Depression had ended and a year before the United States would enter the Second World War. Do you think his argument would have had the same relevance if it had been written at a time when American society was less conservative (for instance, during the war years, when the US would come to depend on women's labour)?

2. How does this analysis fit with the structural-functionalist approach?

3. Later in this chapter we will examine some feminist approaches to sociology. Keep Parsons' analysis in your pocket till then, and then make a feminist critique of it.

sociologists, contributed to the structural-functionalist approach by identifying and describing three types of functions:

1. **Manifest functions** are both intended and readily recognized, or "manifest" (i.e. easily seen).
2. **Latent functions** are largely unintended and unrecognized.
3. **Latent dysfunctions** are unintended and produce socially negative consequences.

This last group is often studied using the conflict approach, making Merton's brand of functionalism something of a bridge to conflict theory. The three examples in Table 2.1 illustrate the differences among Merton's three functions.

Do you think Parsons' argument about the division of gender roles has any relevance to the role of the American first lady, or to the women associated with high-ranking politicians generally? Consider how Michelle Obama's professional accomplishments gave way to her fashion choices, with the media debating whether bangs suit her or if she should ever wear yellow. Would a greater celebration of her occupational achievements count for something in the evaluation of the president, or would it create conflict and discord?

Conflict Theory

Conflict theory (sometimes called the **conflict approach**) is based on the four "*C*'s":

- *conflict*
- *class*
- *contestation*
- *change.*

The approach is predicated, first, on the idea that *conflict* exists in all large societies. The stress lines are major sociological factors, such as gender, "race" and ethnicity, religion, age, and class. Second, it asserts that *class* is a factor in all large societies. Third, it contends that the functions of society, as laid out in traditional structural-functionalist theory, can be *contested*, or challenged, based on the question, *What group does this function best serve?* Finally, the approach involves the assumption that society either will or should be *changed*. One of conflict theory's leading early exponents was Karl Marx.

Karl Marx

For **Karl Marx** (1818–1883), conflict was all about **class**: the division of society into a hierarchy of groups, with each group's position determined by its role in the production of wealth. This was the only aspect of social location that Marx saw as being of primary significance: not gender, or ethnicity, or sexual orientation, or level of ability—just class.

Marx saw class conflict as the driving force behind all major socio-historical change. He believed that conflict between the class of capitalists (the **bourgeoisie**) and the class of workers (the **proletariat**) would initiate a socialist revolution that would produce a classless, or **egalitarian**, society. A classless society has never really existed in more complex societies, but many of Marx's insights about class conflict and capitalist production are still valid. This is particularly true on a global scale, if you think of transnational corporations headquartered in Western societies as the capitalist "owning class" and underpaid workers in poorer countries as the ultimate "working class."

The territory of conflict theory now stretches well beyond Marxism and incorporates applications in feminist sociology, international political science, personal relations and interaction, and many other fields of study that fit rather neatly into the category of "critical sociology," which we'll encounter shortly.

Table 2.1 Examples of Robert Merton's three functions

DISCIPLINE	EMPHASIS
EXAMPLE 1	**POST-SECONDARY EDUCATION**
manifest function	Post-secondary education provides students with the skills and knowledge to find a profitable career in order to become productive, self-sufficient citizens.
latent function	It also provides a social network that will make the search for employment and a marriage partner easier.
latent dysfunction	From a left-wing perspective, post-secondary education reinforces class distinctions; from a right-wing perspective, it exposes students to socialist ideas.
EXAMPLE 2	**RELIGION**
manifest function	Religion fulfills spiritual and emotional needs, and answers important existential questions that many people have.
latent function	Religion creates a social network and marriage market.
latent dysfunction	Religion provides justification for judging outsiders ("non-believers") negatively.
EXAMPLE 3	**CANADIAN DOUGHNUT SHOPS**
manifest function	Doughnut shops provide customers with coffee, snacks, and light meals, served quickly and conveniently.
latent function	Doughnut shops serve as places to meet and socialize with others.
latent dysfunction	Doughnut shops provide late-night venues for drug dealing.

What do YOU think?

1. Could you challenge, amend, or add to any of the functions presented in Table 2.1? How?

2. Try to identify the three different functions for each of the following:

   a) children's organized sports in Canada

   b) garage sales

   c) labour unions.

Symbolic Interactionism

Symbolic interactionism is an approach that looks at the meaning (the symbolic part) of the daily social interaction of individuals. For example, two male students approach each other and say, "'Sup, yo?" lightly bringing their fists together in greeting. What are they communicating to each other about their relationship, their shared interests, and the role models that they identify with?

Max Weber

While Durkheim made his mark in the theoretical area of structural functionalism, and Marx in conflict theory, **Max Weber** (1864–1920) was an early proponent of symbolic interactionism. How individuals and societies *interpreted* the social world around them was key to his sociology. This can be seen in his description of sociology, in which he raised **subjective** meaning above the goal of discovering purely empirical and **objective** "truth" in sociological work. Weber felt that disciplines such as sociology and history were different to the natural sciences (biology, physics, chemistry, etc.) in this way. He recognized that the objects of study acted according to their subjectivity, their own interpretation of what was going on—something you can't say of genes or rocks or molecules. In *The Nature of Social Action* (1922), he described the discipline of sociology as being:

the science whose object is to interpret the meaning of social action and thereby give a causal explanation of the way in which the action proceeds and the effects which it produces. By "action" in this definition is meant the human behaviour when and to the extent that the agent or agents see it as subjectively meaningful. . . . [T]he meaning to which we refer may be either (a) the meaning actually intended either by an individual agent on a particular historical occasion or by a number of agents on an approximate average in a given set of cases, or (b) the meaning attributed to the agent

The Point Is...

Conflict Theory in Action: Party, Party, Party!

You now have a sense of what conflict theory *is*, but how would you actually *use* it?

Let's say you wanted to do a critical sociological analysis of Canada's political party system. What would you look at, and what would you look for? What aspects of social location would you involve?

You might begin with gender. First, find a list of the members of Parliament for each party, both at the federal level and the provincial/territorial level. Then, see who has the smallest proportion of women representatives. As a critical sociologist, I would suggest that you could expect to find two things. The first is that the Conservatives would have the smallest proportion of women representatives, followed in order by the Liberals, the NDP, the Bloc Québécois/Parti Québécois, and the Green Party. The second is that where the Liberals are in power, they would have a smaller proportion of female representatives than in those provinces and territories where they are not in power.

Now, let's apply the four "*C*'s" of conflict theory:

1.   Is there *conflict*? Yes: politics is all about political ideals, but in terms of gender, we can say that there are issues that are of greater importance to women, and that these issues may not enter the political discussion when women are underrepresented in our legislative assemblies.

2.   Is *class* involved? Yes: many of the biggest political campaign contributions come from wealthy business leaders. Are they more likely to support male over female candidates?

3.   Are the functions *contested*? Yes: the fact that women are underrepresented in legislative assemblies across the country is proof that the current parliamentary system does not function in a way that fairly serves all Canadians.

4.   Is there call for *change*? Yes, certainly: the underrepresentation of women has been noted, and there have been efforts to encourage more women to get involved in politics at all levels.

You could perform the same kind of analysis with some other groups that are minoritized in Canadian society: Aboriginal people, homosexuals, and black people, for instance.

---

or agents, as types, in a pure type constructed in the abstract. In neither case is the "meaning" to be thought of as somehow objectively "correct" or "true" by some metaphysical criterion. (as quoted in Runciman 1991:7)

This does not mean that Weber believed that objectivity was not an important goal in sociological research. In fact, he believed, unlike conflict theorists, that research could be **value-free**. But he recognized that the people he was studying behaved according to their own subjective interpretations of the world around them, making their actions somewhat unpredictable.

A key term that Weber introduced to sociology is the German word **verstehen**, which in ordinary German usage is quite like the English word "understand." As used by Weber it referred to the capacity of the sociologist as outside observer to comprehend how the people being studied understand or think of a particular social phenomenon within the context of their culture. Think of the concept of the **Protestant work ethic**, discussed in Chapter 1. What Weber was doing was trying to understand how Protestants saw work and monetary success in terms of their religion.

Weber's thinking exemplifies symbolic interactionism as he was dealing with meaning as the individuals he was studying perceived it (or at least, how he thought they perceived it). Standpoint theory might be used to question to what extent this is possible, although we could also say that it represents an admirable attempt at applying a sociological imagination to view a matter from another's perspective.

When we use the expression "to walk a mile (kilometre?) in someone's shoes," we're talking about gaining the kind of understanding represented by *verstehen*. Once thought to be Aboriginal, and discriminated against accordingly, when my skin was deeply tanned, my hair long and straight, I achieved a slight taste of *verstehen*. Three months on crutches took me a long way towards understanding life with a disability. Weber was arguing that the outside observer could gain such understanding by a kind of intellectual compassion, by mentally changing shoes.

George Herbert Mead and Herbert Blumer

Although we consider Weber an early symbolic interactionist, the symbolic-interactionist method is most closely associated with American social psychologist **George Herbert Mead** (1863–1931), who examined the way the self is constructed as we interact with others and how the self allows us to take on social roles, reflect on ourselves, and internalize social expectations. Another important figure in the movement was **Herbert Blumer** (1900–1987), a pupil of Mead's, who coined the term *symbolic interaction*. Blumer (1969) argued that social systems are simply abstractions that do not exist independently of individual relations and interactions. In other words, social systems (things like friendship, education, the economy) are simply by-products of our personal dealings with one another.

Sociological Theory: Macro- and Micro-

You may have noticed that the symbolic-interactionist approach, with its focus on individuals rather than larger social structures, differs from the approaches described earlier in the chapter. In this way it represents one part of another distinction used to differentiate various kinds of sociology: the distinction between **macrosociology** and **microsociology**. When sociologists engage in research and writing that focus primarily on the "big picture" of society and its institutions, then they are engaging in macrosociology. Durkheim, Merton, and Marx were all primarily macrosociologists. When our focus is, instead, more on the plans, motivations, and actions of the individual or a specific group, then we are taking a microsociological approach (see Table 2.2).

In this conversation, how is meaning being generated? Words are simply one aspect of constructing meaning in our day-to-day interactions.

Table 2.2 **Three microsociologists and their ideas**

THEORIST	KEY CONCEPTS	AREAS OF MICROSOCIOLOGICAL INQUIRY
George H. Mead	significant other, generalized other	Who plays a role in socializing this person? What group matters most to this person?
Charles H. Cooley	looking-glass self	How does the individual think he/she is viewed by others?
Erving Goffman	dramaturgical approach	How does this social actor conceptualize his/her social performance?

Our Stories

Applying Goffman to Research

I'm a fan of Goffman's research and writing. His books are readable, and his concepts are readily adaptable to research, as I discovered in 1972, when I spent a year studying a religious group in downtown Toronto for my honours thesis. I needed a theoretical base for my research, and so I turned to Goffman's *The Presentation of Self in Everyday Life* (1959). This is the book in which he famously introduced the **dramaturgical approach**, a way of conducting research as if everyday life were taking place on the stage of a theatre. According to a frequently told anecdote, Goffman was on the Hebrides Islands, off the coast of Scotland, looking for a topic for his doctoral dissertation. While sitting in a restaurant, he noticed that the wait staff acted differently when they were on the "front stage"—that is, in the public eye—than when they were "backstage" in the kitchen, away from the dining customers. They presented themselves differently depending on which stage they were on, an example of what Goffman called **impression management**. Impression management refers to the ways in which people present themselves in specific roles and social situations. His doctoral thesis and bestselling book were born that day—or so the story goes.

The religious group I was studying was managing their impressions for two different audiences. One included street kids and other youthful lost souls who might be in need of spiritual guidance. For this audience, representatives of the religious group put on a hip, anti-establishment face. However, in order to obtain food donations from supermarket chains to feed their flock, and to achieve respectability in the

eyes of both corporate sponsors and the neighbouring businesses in their rather exclusive downtown area, they had to present a more conservative face.

I predicted that the group would split according to the two "stages," divided by the two audiences to which they were presenting themselves. This happened just a year later, when the organization developed two distinct branches, one dealing with youth outreach and the other handling charitable donations. Thanks, Erving.

Can you apply Goffman's dramaturgical approach to the work of a flight attendant? Who makes up the "front stage" audience? Where is the "backstage"? Which audience are the pilots part of?

A good example of how microsociology is used, as part of a symbolic-interactionist approach, to understand people's actions, comes from the work of **Erving Goffman** (1922–1982). Born in Alberta, Goffman received his BA from the University of Toronto and his MA and PhD from the University of Chicago. Goffman was a pioneer of microsociology. His work regularly bore the stamp of originality, as evidenced by the many terms he introduced to the discipline of sociology. One example is *total institution*, an expression he coined in his book *Asylums* (1961). A **total institution** is any one of "a range of institutions in which whole blocks of people are bureaucratically processed, whilst being physically isolated from the normal round of activities, by being required to sleep, work, and play within the confines of the same institution" (Marshall 1998: 669–70). The term is used to describe psychiatric hospitals, prisons, army barracks, boarding schools, concentration camps, monasteries, and convents—institutions whose residents are regulated, controlled, or manipulated by those in charge.

Goffman carried out his research for *Asylums* in 1955–6, when he engaged in fieldwork at a mental hospital in Washington, DC. He wanted to learn about the day-to-day social world of the inmates. He did this by pretending to be an assistant to the athletic director, passing his days with the patients. In his work Goffman stressed the importance of learning the subjectivity of people, the views and feelings they have, and he denied both objectivity and neutrality in his research methodology. He unequivocally sided with the patients rather than the professionals who managed them in the hospital.

Feminist Theory

Two branches of conflict theory now comprise such an extensive collection of research and literature that they demand to be considered in their own right. These two branches are **feminist theory** and **postmodern theory**.

Feminism, it could be argued, began with Mary Wollstonecraft's *A Vindication of the Rights of Women* (1792), and like anything that has existed for well over two hundred years, and evolved over that time, it is incredibly difficult to pin down with a tidy, hard-and-fast definition. What we can say is that feminism involves correcting centuries of discrimination and male-dominated conceptions of gender roles in order to gain and present an accurate view of the social condition of women. Contrary to what some male students

believe, you don't have to be a woman to be a feminist, but you do have to accept that recognizing a female perspective (or "standpoint") is absolutely critical to forming an accurate appraisal of the roles women play in society (or so say I, the bearded feminist).

One of the first sociologists to carry out a careful examination of women's roles in society was the British writer **Harriet Martineau** (1802–1876), who wrote over 6,000 articles, many of them on the social condition of women. In 1834 she began a two-year study of the United States, which she documented in the three-volume *Society in America* (1837) and in *Retrospect of Western Travel* (1838). Her feminist thinking can be seen in her comparison of women to slaves in a chapter of the former work revealingly called "The Political Non-Existence of Women." After travelling to the Middle East, she published *Eastern Life: Present and Past* (1848), in which she briefly departed from her intended sociological spirit of impartiality to condemn the practice of polygyny (one husband with more than one wife). The work of Canadian sociologists Annie Marion MacLean and Aileen Ross, who were profiled later in the previous chapter, exemplify the feminist approach pioneered by Harriet Martineau.

Dorothy Smith: Standpoint Theory

Martineau's goal of remaining impartial was in keeping with sociology as it was practised during her time. But as we noted earlier, most feminist theorists today believe that the best way to understand the social condition of women is by trying to view life through the eyes of the women they're studying. It sounds obvious, but it was a revolutionary idea, and a foundational figure in the movement was a Canadian sociologist, **Dorothy Smith** (b. 1926). While doing graduate work at the University of California, Berkeley, Smith experienced first-hand the kind of systemic sexist discrimination that would become the subject of her first work. She moved to Canada in the late 1960s, when she earned a rare (for a woman) teaching opportunity at the University of British Columbia. (Fortunately, she once joked, departments of sociology in this country were "scraping the bottom of the barrel.") It was the start of a remarkable and distinguished academic career that also includes a tenure of more than 20 years at the University of Toronto's Ontario Institute for Studies in Education.

Smith developed a feminist **standpoint theory** directly out of her own experience as a woman discriminated against by male colleagues in the academic community. Her standpoint theory challenged traditional sociology on two fronts, both relating to sociology's preference for **objective** (depersonalized and distanced from everyday life) as opposed to **subjective** (personalized and connected to everyday life) research and analysis. Her first criticism attacked the traditional position that the objective approach to research is more scientific and therefore truthful, while the subjective position is **ideological**, based on biases and prejudices, and therefore distorted. According to Smith, knowledge is developed from a particular lived position, or "standpoint." Sociology, having developed from a male standpoint, had long denied the validity of the female standpoint and overlooked the everyday lives of women—an oversight that feminist researchers today are still working to correct.

Postmodern Theory

A good way to think of postmodern theory is to consider the concept of *voices*. In all societies, there are different voices that speak, and together they represent a diversity of life experiences and social locations. Postmodern theory is concerned with recognizing that there are many such voices, and that they should not be drowned out by the powerful voice of those who are dominant in society (traditionally, white heterosexual men from middle- and upper-class backgrounds).

Totalitarian Discourse: Michel Foucault

A leading figure in what came to be known as postmodern theory was the French philosopher and historian **Michel Foucault** (1926–1984). In his groundbreaking article "Two Lectures" (1980), Foucault talked about the misleading nature of what he termed **totalitarian discourse**. A totalitarian discourse is any universal claim about how knowledge or understanding is achieved. Western science, for example, is at the centre of a totalitarian discourse used by those who claim that it is the only legitimate path to discovering the "truth" about the causes and cures for different diseases, while dismissing alternative forms of medicine that are popular and trusted in many non-Western cultures.

"Totalitarian" in this context should be easy enough to understand: it describes a set of beliefs or ideas that dominates ("totally") all others. The other part of this term, "discourse," is not as easily understood. A **discourse** can be defined as follows:

> A conceptual framework with its own internal logic and underlying assumptions that may be readily recognizable to the audience. A discourse involves a distinct way of speaking about some aspect of reality. [Use of the term] also suggests that the item under discussion is not a natural attribute of reality but socially constructed and defined. (Fleras & Elliott 1999: 433)

A discourse is not necessarily wrong or false. It's really just a way of describing the particular treatment of a topic that has been created through a given set of assumptions, a vocabulary, rules, logic, and so on. However, to call something a *totalizing* (or *totalitarian*) discourse is to condemn it as overly ambitious and narrow-minded. Consider the common observation that the brain is like a computer. We can create a discourse comparing the functions and capabilities of the brain to those of a computer. Both store memories—sounds, images, video—and both acquire and process "data." We can all relate to a time when we felt that our brains had "crashed." But the discourse fails when we consider how poorly computers handle translation. Computers cannot translate well—not as well as humans—since they cannot deal with the input of social and cultural context. Very few words or phrases from any given language can be translated directly and perfectly into another. Our discourse, then, is problematic: the brain may be *similar* to a computer *in certain ways*, but it would be wrong to say that the human brain is *just like* a computer. A discourse becomes totalitarian when it is promoted by those with power and influence until it becomes widely accepted as the only "right" interpretation.

The Archaeology of Knowledge

In *The Archaeology of Knowledge* (1972), Foucault wrote about the importance of discovering how individual discourses developed as a way of examining their strengths, weaknesses, and limitations. He called this process of discovery the **archaeology of knowledge**. The sociologist must dig through the layers of presented information considered to be factual (a discourse) in order to discover how the supposed fact or truth was established or constructed. Through this process of excavation, the sociologist may find that some parts of the discourse have been distorted along the way, which affects how people interpret and act upon the discourse. The "Our Stories" feature on page 42 presents an example of how an archaeology of knowledge can lead us to reassess our understanding of a supposed historical fact.

Foucault's challenge to students of sociology is to understand that knowledge is constructed, and that it is important to investigate the question, *How do we know that?* Because there are conceptual constraints that both determine and limit our thinking in ways that we are not aware of, there may be alternative constructions of knowledge on a particular subject that are just as valid as—or even more valid than—our own.

Tahani (left), who was married at the age of 6, and her former classmate Ghada, also a child bride, stand with their husbands outside their home in Hajjah, Yemen. Every year, millions of girls under 18 enter arranged marriages. The tradition spans continents, religion, and class. Girls who marry early often abandon their education, and the incidence of maternal and infant death is high for women under 18 who give birth. How important are the factors of "race" and gender in telling the story of these girls? What might a Western, white, male sociologist miss? What might a female counterpart trained as a journalist miss? What insights might a female academic who had been raised with child marriage as part of her culture add that could otherwise be missing?

The Point Is...

From Standpoint to Intersectionality: Feminism and "Race"

While the early feminism of the 1960s and 1970s emphasized gender and the importance of adopting a female standpoint in social analysis, women of colour began to feel that race was wrongly being left out of the discussion. Their experience, they argued, was different to the experience of their "white sisters." In the late 1980s, **Kimberlé Crenshaw** (b. 1959) coined the term **intersectionality theory** to refer to the study of the intersecting or linking forms of discrimination and prejudice that come with being both female and a member of a minoritized, racialized group. Crenshaw developed this theory in the context of black feminist thought, and it was taken up by American critical sociologist **Patricia Hill Collins** (b. 1948) in her aptly entitled *Black Feminist Thought: Knowledge, Consciousness and the Politics of Empowerment* (1990).

Patricia Collins is an important figure in the development of feminist theory from a standpoint perspective, and well positioned to construct ideas in intersectionality, as she is a black woman from a working-class background. She interweaves the three social locations of gender, race, and class in her research and writing. Her work on intersectionality has extended recently (2005) to examine the intersection between male and as well as female gender for black people in the United States, demonstrating (as others have also) that being feminist does not mean being "anti-male." Men and women stand to gain from feminism.

Intersectionality theory argues against the early white liberal feminist notion that the experience of "female" is the same for all women. Rather, it states that gender is experienced differently with unique forms of oppression when combined with negatively valued social locations such as those of minoritized ethnicities to create an *interlocking matrix of domination* significantly more powerful than gender alone.

We can illustrate this important theoretical idea by looking at how the intersection of "race" and gender has adversely affected Aboriginal women in Canada. Journalist Heather Robertson spent some time in 1967 in the northern Manitoba town of The Pas. In *Reservations Are for Indians*, she describes the plight of young Aboriginal women who seemed unwelcome both in their own community and in the town, where they had only one function. The description is brutal, and is difficult to forget (I last read it 40 years ago and the images were not forgotten):

> They are the mudlarks. They linger on the fringe waiting, watching. If one of them is lucky, some man will come along, buy her a beer or two inside and take her to a flophouse around the corner for the night. She might stay with this man for a week or a year; she might be beaten and thrown out on the street in the morning. The mudlarks live on the streets of The Pas, scavenging what they can. They have no homes, their families have disintegrated or don't want them because they cost too much to feed.
>
> These pathetic little dark girls are not seductive, bundled up against the cold in ski pants and ugly nylon jackets, shivering. They

Part 2: Sociology by Audience

Another way of looking at sociology is based on the *audience* and how reflexive or critical the sociologist is. We borrow here from Michael Burawoy (2004), who divided sociology into four types:

- professional
- critical
- policy
- public.

We will consider each of these in turn.

Professional Sociology

Professional sociology has as its audience the academic world of sociology departments, scholarly are hardly noticeable, all dressed in drab black, hiding in the shadows. Skinny and bony, their faces are hard and lined already, dry and dull-eyed. Their hair is lank, dirty, and their efforts at soliciting clumsy and childish. Many men, I think, take them in out of pity. Their sickness and hunger are real but much of their pathos is fake. They feel white people are more ready to pity them than to admire them. (Robertson 1970: 145)

The continuing profoundly negative experience of Aboriginal women, their interlocking matrix of domination, can be seen in the growing number of websites dedicate to Aboriginal women who have either been murdered or gone missing. One of these is the website of Amnesty International Canada, which has a page calling for government action to change the way crimes against Aboriginal women are investigated, tried, and prevented. Under the banner "Stolen Sisters: No more Indigenous women lost to violence" are reader comments that have been posted to the site. They say much about the interlocking matrix of domination experienced by Aboriginal women.

We can say, then, that intersectionality has a cumulative effect with respect to Aboriginal women in Canada, adding one form of oppression—racism—on top of another—sexism—to put Aboriginal women in a situation that is worse than the situation experienced by both their male counterparts and their white counterparts, literally the worst of both worlds.

A Native drum circle supports the families of missing women as they make their way in to hear the findings of the Missing Women Commission of Inquiry in Vancouver, December 2012. Why do you think we have chosen a photo that shows Aboriginal men as well as women?

journals, professional associations, and conferences. The research carried out by professional sociologists is typically designed to generate very specific information, often with the aim of applying it to a particular problem or intellectual question. Consider the following partial list of articles that appeared in a 2012 edition of the *Canadian Review of Sociology*:

- "Policy Legitimacy, Rhetorical Politics, and the Evaluation of City-Street Video Surveillance Monitoring Programs in Canada"
- "Risk, Resiliency, and Urban Governance: The Case of the 2010 Winter Olympic Games"
- "Subject Positioning, Fear, and Insecurity in South Asian Muslim Communities in the War on Terror Context"
- "Policing Social Media" (*Canadian Review of Sociology* 49 [4], November)

These articles address specific sociological questions. Written in technical or specialized language, they target an academic or professional readership, but can usually be read by interested students. These can be looked upon as exercises in "tool sharpening." Intellectual tools that are not sharpened in these ways become dull, lacking in relevant meaning. Science progresses through such exercises. The way we come to understand human societies progresses more often in small pieces like this than in theory writ large.

Critical Sociology

The main role of **critical sociology**, according to Burawoy (2004), is to be "the conscience of professional sociology." It performs this role in two ways:

Critical sociology reminds professional sociology of its raison d'être, of its value premises and its guiding questions. It also proposes alternative foundations upon which to erect sociological research. In other words, critical sociology is critical in two senses, first in bringing professional sociology into alignment with its historical mission and second in shifting the direction of that mission. (Burawoy 2004)

Critical sociology, then, addresses the same audience that professional sociology does, but with a different purpose. Its aim is to make sure that professional sociologists do not lose sight of important social issues by focusing on statistics while overlooking the individuals behind them.

Our Stories

Abandoning Inuit Elders: An Archaeology of Knowledge

Several introductory sociology textbooks assert that among Inuit populations, it was once customary to abandon the elders when times got tough, such as during shortages of food. The discourse of abandoning elders, presented as fact, has been reinforced and perpetuated through the disciplines of sociology and anthropology, and internalized within popular culture. By conducting an archeological excavation of this discourse, we are able to see how this "fact" was constructed.

The first step is to check the relevant footnotes and the bibliographies contained in the textbooks. Most of the sociology textbooks studied obtained their information from three earlier studies: one on Inuit (Weyer 1962/[1932]), one on suicide (Cavan 1965/[1928]), and one on primitive law (Hoebel 1965/[1954]). When you look at these studies, you discover that none of the writers actually did their own research on Inuit—they themselves were merely citing even earlier works.

The next step is to track down the works written by those earlier scholars to find out what they actually said. Some researchers studying the Inuit merely assumed that the practice occurred, even though they didn't actually observe it. A few mentioned times when elders were temporarily left behind while others who were more fit went ahead to look for food before returning to feed and resume travel with the elders. In fact, there is no direct observation or ethnographic account of the practice of elder abandonment. The reported custom never really existed.

We could take a further step by questioning who benefited from this particular discourse of elder abandonment (and who, therefore, might have helped to promote it). This line of inquiry might lead us to large and celebrated Canadian institutions, such as mining companies, the Hudson's Bay Company, and the RCMP—all of which moved into Inuit territory without respecting their Aboriginal rights—and to sociologists and anthropologists in need of sensational examples to illustrate cultural differences between the Inuit and mainstream North American society.

As we stated earlier, much of what we call "conflict theory" would fit into this category. Two of the giants of critical sociology, Michel Foucault and Dorothy Smith, are known for having examined the production of knowledge in relation to power. Foucault discussed the conflict between "scientific experts" and other producers of knowledge, whose voices tended to be drowned out by the former group. He conceived of "madness" this way, with psychiatrists and other doctors on one side, and the individuals they were diagnosing on the other. Smith discussed conflict in terms of gender relations. Women have sociological insights into society that can and often conflict with those of men.

Policy Sociology

A relatively new branch of research and inquiry, **policy sociology** is about generating sociological data for governments and large corporations, to be used in developing laws, rules, and long- and short-term plans. A government might commission a study on crime prevention to see if tougher sentences or better rehabilitation programs are more likely to reduce the rate of criminals reoffending: this would be an example of policy sociology. Education, health, and social welfare are three main areas that policy sociology serves.

A classic work of Canadian policy sociology is the *Report on Social Security for Canada*, prepared by **Leonard Marsh** (1906–1982). Based on research Marsh had done in the 1930s while acting as research director for the McGill Social Science Research Project, it set the stage for a number of major social policy initiatives that we now take for granted. The report offered:

> a dense and detailed plan for comprehensive social programs, constructed around the idea of a social minimum and the eradication of poverty. The realization of this ideal, according to Marsh, meant the recognition that individual risks were part of modern industrial society, and that they could be met by collective benefits throughout the lifecycle. . . . "Employment risks" were to be met through income-maintenance programs, such as unemployment insurance and assistance, accident and disability benefits, plus paid maternity leave. . . . "Universal risks" were addressed through national health insurance, children's allowances, and pensions for old age, permanent disability, and widows and orphans. (Maioni 2004: 21)

Keep in mind that none of these social policies existed in Canada at the time. A particularly notable aspect of Marsh's report, as Antonia Maioni points out, was his "holistic view of social security that considered health as a central part of the welfare state, rather than a separate item and expense" (2004: 21). Our system of health insurance can be traced to this important piece of policy sociology.

Public Sociology

Public sociology addresses an audience outside of the academy (i.e. universities and colleges). Herbert Gans (1989) has identified three key traits of public sociologists:

> One is their ability to discuss even sociological concepts and theories in the English of the college-educated reader. . . . Their second trait is the breadth of their sociological interests, which covers much of society even if their research is restricted to a few fields. That breadth also extends to their conception of sociology, which extends beyond research reporting to commentary and in many cases social criticism. . . . [T]heir work is intellectual as well as scientific. A third, not unrelated, trait is the ability to avoid the pitfalls of undue professionalism. (Gans 1989: 7)

By "undue professionalism" Gans is referring to professional sociology's overly cautious style, its tendency to footnote everything, and its inclination to bury analysis in statistics. Our nominee, as the consummate public sociologist, is C. Wright Mills, whom we introduced earlier in this chapter.

Professional, Critical, Policy, and Public Sociology: A Review

Distinctions among the four types of sociology we've been discussing are not watertight. It is common for individual sociologists to engage in more than one area, even on a single piece of work. Criticisms can flow easily from people who see themselves as practitioners of one form only. Professional sociologists criticize critical sociologists for low professional standards and for being "troublemaking radicals." Critical sociologists accuse professional sociologists of being far too conservative, and of taking small bites of data

Outspoken and controversial American filmmaker Michael Moore, shown here in *Capitalism: A Love Story*, has tackled topics including healthcare, gun control, the US manufacturing sector, and the recent economic meltdown in his documentary films. Based on Gans's description of public sociology, do Moore's documentaries fall within that category?

and overanalyzing them, dazzling their reading audience with statistical science while actually saying little. Public sociologists could accuse professional sociologists of speaking only to a very small audience made up exclusively of peers; at the same time they accuse the policy sociologists of selling out to corporate and government "pimps." But policy and professional sociologists can counter-accuse the public sociologists of being in it just for the fame, of being no more than "pop sociologists" or simply "popularizers"—a dirty term among many in the academy.

What do YOU think?

1. Consider the four types of sociology we've just discussed. Where do you imagine your sociology instructor would fall in this scheme? Where would you place the author of this textbook?

2. Have you ever seen or heard a broadcast interview with a sociologist? If you haven't, why do you think this is so? Is "popular" sociology—sociology for the masses—any more or less important than the other kinds (professional, critical, policy)?

WRAP IT UP

Summary

In this chapter, we've shown you two different ways of looking at and categorizing sociology: by approach (the trichotomy of structural functionalism, conflict theory, and symbolic interactionism, plus the growing perspectives of feminism and postmodernism) and by audience (professional, critical, policy, and public sociology). References to these categories turn up frequently throughout the book.

But wait, you might be saying: *aren't these the same categories you criticized early on as "leaking too much"?* The theories and approaches introduced in this chapter are the "tools of the trade." They are useful at least some of the time, and you'll need to be acquainted with them to work with the material to come in the chapters that follow. You will find, however, that the theories overlap: a particular sociologist's work may incorporate several different approaches, and some research doesn't fit neatly under the banner of any particular theory. In addition, sometimes it is not particularly enlightening to rely on any particular theoretical approach, especially if you want to help develop social change. In other words, it's good to be familiar with these theories, but don't regard them as rigid and mutually exclusive categories—they are flexible, and they do leak, and that isn't a bad thing if several are used together.

THINK BACK

Questions for Critical Review

1. Distinguish between the structural-functional, conflict, and symbolic-interactionist approaches to sociology.

2. What do the "newer" perspectives of feminism and postmodernism add to the discipline?

3. Distinguish between professional, critical, policy-based, and public sociology. Under what circumstances might each one be useful?

4. Articulate the basic ideas of Erving Goffman, Michel Foucault, and Dorothy Smith, as outlined in this chapter.

READ ON

Online

Social Theory Pages

www.socialtheory.info

A brilliant summary of social theories by sociologist Jim Spickard of the University of Redlands in California

WWW Virtual Library: Sociology (Sociological Theory and Theorists)

www.mcmaster.ca/socscidocs/w3virtsoclib/theories.htm

A good collection of brief statements of key sociological theorists.

Sociological Theories: "The Movie"

www.youtube.com/watch?v=4IsdPlQMrRo

This short animated video by Angus MacLennan neatly summarizes a number of the theories discussed in this chapter.

In Print

CJS (2009), *Canadian Journal of Sociology* **34 (3); also online at https://ejournals.library. ualberta.ca/index.php/CJS.**

This special issue of CJS devoted to professional, critical, policy, and public sociology features articles by and about Michael Burawoy, as well as features on sociological practice in French Quebec and what public sociologists do.

Gary Gutting (2005), *Foucault: A Very Short Introduction* **(Oxford: Oxford University Press).**

This is a reasonable and concise introduction to Foucault's life and ideas. It's not for every reader, though, as it is a fairly heavy read and dense in terminology.

Michael Hviid Jacobsen, ed. (2009), *The Contemporary Goffman* **(New York: Routledge).**

This collection of readings by various authors imagines what kind of research Goffman might be involved in if he were living today.

Dorothy Smith (1989), *The Everyday World as Problematic: A Feminist Sociology* **(Boston: Northeastern University Press).**

This is probably the most often read work by the (adopted) Canadian pioneer of standpoint theory.

Learning Objectives

After reading this chapter, you should be able to

- understand the difference between fact, theory, and hypothesis
- distinguish between qualitative and quantitative social research
- recognize the defining features of the various qualitative research methods
- discuss the importance of identifying the individual informant in ethnographic research
- outline the importance of narratives to sociological research
- state the significance of operational definitions in quantitative research
- explain and give examples of spurious reasoning.

Key Terms

- absolute poverty
- anomie
- best practices
- case study approach
- causation
- content analysis
- correlation
- dependent variable
- direct correlation
- discourse analysis
- disjuncture
- ethnography
- fact
- genealogy
- hypothesis
- independent variable
- informant
- insider perspective
- institutional ethnography
- inverse correlation
- Low Income Cut-Offs
- Low Income Measure
- Market Basket Measure (MBM)
- narrative
- negative correlation
- operational definition
- Orientalism
- outsider perspective
- participant observation
- positive correlation
- positivism
- poverty
- poverty line
- qualitative research
- quantitative research
- relative poverty
- research methodology
- ruling interests
- ruling relations
- semi-structured interview
- spurious reasoning
- statistics
- theory
- third variable
- triangulation
- variable
- voice

Names to Know

- Auguste Comte
- Edward Said

Fact, Theory, Hypothesis, and Wondering Why People Speed Up When I Pass Them

It's easier to *observe* than it is to *explain*. I can observe that people speed up on the highway when I pass them, but I can't really explain why they do it. Is it because the bee-like buzz of my engine wakes them up from a semi-sleeping state? Or is it their competitive spirit that awakens when I—an aging hippie in a Toyota Corolla—pass them in their shiny, high-priced, high-powered vehicles?

I believe the idea that people speed up when I pass them is a **fact**: an observation that, as far as can be known, is true. This doesn't mean it happens all the time, though I have observed it often enough to call it at least a *tentative* fact. But if I want to use important qualifiers such as "almost all of the time," or "most of the time," or the easier to prove "often" or "frequently," then I have to find a way to *quantify* (i.e. measure) this fact—for example, by saying: "I passed 100 vehicles and 37 were observed to speed up." I should also be more specific about the situation involved, by adding

"on Highway 50, northwest of Toronto"; "while driving in the slow lane, passing someone who is in the passing lane"; "while driving home from work, travelling north." This is how I quantify and qualify my fact: by giving details about how often it occurs and under what conditions.

Now I need a theory. A **theory** is an attempt to explain a fact or observed phenomenon. My theory of why people speed up when I pass them is that I make them aware that they are travelling more slowly than they thought they were. My theory becomes a **hypothesis** when I set out to verify it by providing some kind of concrete test of its validity. What kind of test can I provide for my theory? Obviously I can't pull people over on the highway and ask them why they sped up when I passed them (although I would love to have the power to do that). However, I could develop a questionnaire that depends on people's self-knowledge. First, I might ask a question such as, "Do you frequently speed up when people pass you on a highway?" I might follow up with a multiple-choice question such as the following:

- What is your best explanation for speeding up when people pass you on a highway?
    a) Being passed makes me realize that I am driving more slowly than I thought.
    b) I do not like people passing me.
    c) I am very competitive.
    d) Other (explain).

Then I would proceed to test the hypothesis.

What steps would you take? Try jotting down some ideas now, then review the question once you've finished reading the chapter. I'll bet your perspective will have changed. Then again, that's just a hypothesis . . .

Introduction: Research Methodology Is No Joking Matter

Nothing is more contentious in sociology than **research methodology**, the system of methods a researcher uses to gather data on a particular question, hence the following joke:

Question: How many sociologists does it take to change a light bulb?

Answer: Twenty—one to change the light bulb and nineteen to question that person's methodology.

There is no single best way to do sociological research, and in fact researchers will often combine several research methods in their work. In this chapter we'll take a look at some of the different methods used in sociological research, pointing out the pluses and pitfalls of each one as we go. We begin, though, with a few prefatory comments about the history of sociology research and some challenges to be aware of.

Insider versus Outsider Perspective: Challenging Sociology's Positivist Tradition

It was French philosopher **Auguste Comte** (1798–1857) who coined the word *sociology*. The basis of Comte's sociology was **positivism** (later called *logical positivism*), which involves a belief that the methods used to study the natural sciences (including experiment, measurement, and systematic observation) and the supposed objectivity of these methods can be applied just as well to the social sciences with no accommodation made for the biases or social location of the social scientist.

Although the positivist mode of thinking had a long run, many sociologists today do not believe it's possible for an "outsider" to study a group objectively. Indeed, one way to contrast the different methods of sociology research is to look at how researchers treat **insider** and **outsider perspectives**. In Comte's view, the outsider was the "expert" and occupied a privileged position over those he or she (usually he) was studying. Most of sociology's history reflects this privileging of the outsider perspective. Of the four audience-based types of sociology discussed in the previous chapter—professional, critical, policy-based, and public—policy sociology is the one tied most closely to the outside expert ideal.

By contrast, critical sociology, particularly feminist sociology, rates the insider view highly while questioning the presumed objectivity of positivism. Dorothy Smith's standpoint theory, introduced last chapter, states that such social characteristics as gender, "race," ethnicity, age, and sexual orientation will strongly condition both the questions a sociologist asks and the answers he or she will receive. Michel Foucault, in the first volume of *The History of Sexuality* (1978), criticized the outsider approach in his discussion of the "sexual confession," an approach to treating sexual deviance in which the patient would admit to "impure" thoughts, fantasies, and taboo sexual practices in the presence of a doctor or psychotherapist. According to this model, the subject being studied provides information that comes from his or her subjective experience. But this information is marginalized: it is not recognized as authentic knowledge until it has been interpreted by an "objective" outsider who, by virtue of being an expert, is in the privileged position of deciding which parts of the account are true and which are fabricated or imagined. The subject is therefore not allowed to have a voice that is heard without translation from the outsider/expert. That means that important socio-logical messages get lost.

To get a better sense of how an outsider perspective can be flawed, imagine yourself as a non-Aboriginal sociologist studying a First Nation reserve. Taking an outsider approach, you conduct your study by look-ing only at various statistics, covering subjects such as unemployment, housing, and crime rates. Not includ-ing the voice of the people who live there means that you will miss key elements of interpretation. First, some definitions could be problematic. For instance, is a person who provides for his family when he hunts, traps, fishes, gathers plants for food and medicine, and cuts wood for home heating and cooking "unem-ployed"? Technically he is, as he does not have a "job" that pays money. Second, typical statistical surveys of Aboriginal reserves leave unanswered the question of why so many people choose to live on reserves if there is so much more unemployment, crime, and overcrowding than in non-Native communities of

comparable size. You need to hear the people's voices to answer this question.

Brian Maracle is a Mohawk who left his home reserve when he was five years old but returned as an adult. *Back on the Rez: Finding the Way Back Home* (1996) is his account of the first year of his return to the Six Nations reserve near Brantford, Ontario. This reserve is very different in certain respects from the more troubled Aboriginal communities—Davis Inlet and Grassy Narrows, for example—that are commonly cited in sociology textbooks. The people of the Six Nations reserve have lived there for over 220 years, since the land was granted to them for siding with the British during the American Revolution. In the intro-duction to *Back on the Rez*, Maracle points out that reserves can be considered homelands because they function as refuges from non-Aboriginal society:

The reserves mean many things. . . . On one level, these postage-stamp remnants of our original

Schoolchildren wait for the bus on the Membertou reserve near Sydney, Nova Scotia. Is this how you picture life on reserve? What does your answer tell you about the dangers of approaching the topic with an outsider perspective?

territories are nagging reminders of the echoing vastness of what we have lost. On another, they are the legacy and bastion of our being. They are a refuge, a prison, a madhouse, a fortress, a birth-place, a Mecca, a resting-place, Home-Sweet-Home, Fatherland and Motherland rolled into one. (Maracle 1996: 3)

Maracle writes of the importance of the reserve as the home of the Mohawk elders, who interpret past tra-ditions and adapt them to the present. In this way, he emphasizes that the reserve is very much the home of Aboriginal culture. However, it is important to see that reserves are not always homeland to everyone. They can be places where men with physical strength and political power can oppress women and sexually abuse children. While recognizing the insider's view is key to effective sociological research, it's important to remember that a variety of voices have to be heard.

Our position here is that complete objectivity is impossible whenever one human being studies others. On the other hand, complete subjectivity can be blind. A judicious balance of insider and outsider vision is the ideal.

What do YOU think?

Think of a community that you are particularly involved in—a club or team, a religious organization, your college or university residence, or some other group. How easily could it be studied by an outsider looking only at statistics? Which insider voices from your community would an outsider need to listen to in order to get an accurate picture of it?

Qualitative versus Quantitative Research

An ongoing debate in sociology concerns the relative merits of *qualitative* research and *quantitative* research. **Quantitative research** focuses on social elements that can be counted or measured, which can therefore be used to generate statistics. It often involves working with questionnaires and polls. **Qualitative research** involves the close examination of characteristics that cannot be counted or measured. Unlike quantitative research, which is typically used to find the patterns governing whole structures or systems, communi-ties, and so on, qualitative research may be used to

study those individual cases that don't fit into the larger model.

And so the debate begins. Proponents of quantita-tive research accuse qualitative researchers of relying on data that are "soft," "anecdotal," "too subjective," or "merely literary." In turn, champions of the qualitative approach dismiss quantitative researchers as soulless "number crunchers" operating under the delusion that it is possible for humans to study other humans with complete objectivity.

Of course, it's wrong to think that the two methods are mutually exclusive. Good quantitative research-ers know that, despite its close historical connection with positivism, their research always has a subjective component to it and always involves choice and some personal bias. Qualitative researchers, similarly, often benefit from using quantitative data occasionally. We'll now take a closer look at different methods of qualitative and quantitative research to see how they measure up.

Qualitative Research

Qualitative research permits—in fact, often encour-ages—subjectivity on the part of both researcher and research subject in a way that "hard" data-oriented quantitative research does not. Among the various qualitative methods are **ethnography** and the **case study approach**, which differ mainly in their breadth of focus. The former takes a broader view by attempt-ing to describe the entirety of a culture, while the lat-ter adopts a narrower focus to study individual cases.

Ethnography

Robert Gephart teaches organizational research meth-ods at the University of Alberta's School of Business. He captures the essence of ethnography when he describes it as relying on

direct observation and extended field research to produce a thick, naturalistic description of a people and their culture. Ethnography seeks to uncover the symbols and categories members of the given culture use to interpret their world. . . . (Gephart 1988: 16)

A classic example of the ethnographic approach in sociology is William Whyte's *Street-Corner Society:*

The Social Structure of an Italian Slum. Beginning early in 1937, Whyte spent three-and-a-half years living in the neighbourhood of Boston that he called "Cornerville," following a standard research practice of assigning a fictitious name to the community studied in order to preserve the anonymity of the subjects. Whyte spent 18 months of that time living with an Italian-American family. His research methodology involved **semi-structured interviews**—informal, face-to-face interviews designed to cover specific topics without the rigid structure of a questionnaire but with more structure than an open interview—and **participant observation**, which entails both observing people as an outsider would and actively participating in the various activities of the studied people's lives. Participant observation enables the researcher to achieve something resembling an insider's perspective.

Researchers engaged in ethnography typically depend as well on **informants**, insiders who act as interpreters or intermediaries while helping the researcher become accepted by the community studied. Whyte's informant was a gang leader in his late twenties who went by the name "Doc." Whyte was introduced to Doc by the latter's social worker during a meeting he describes in the book:

> I began by asking him ["Doc"] if the social worker had told him about what I was trying to do.
>
> "No, she just told me that you wanted to meet me and that I should like to meet you."
>
> Then I went into a long explanation. . . . I said that I had been interested in congested city districts in my college study but had felt very remote from them. I hoped to study the problems in such a district. I felt I could do very little as an outsider. Only if I could get to know the people and learn their problems first hand would I be able to gain the understanding I needed. (Whyte 1955: 291)

When Whyte stated his research needs, Doc replied:

> "Well, any nights you want to see anything, I'll take you around. I can take you to the joints—gambling joints—I can take you around to the street corners. Just remember that you're my friend. That's all they need to know. I know these places, and, if I

A soup kitchen in the basement of a Montreal church in the 1930s, around the time of William Whyte's study of Italian slums in Boston. How would you engage in ethnographic research in this kind of setting?

tell them that you're my friend, nobody will bother you. You just tell me what you want to see, and we'll arrange it." (Whyte 1955: 291)

Doc and Whyte would discuss Whyte's research interests and findings to the point where Doc became "in a very real sense, a collaborator in the research" (Whyte 1955: 301). Whyte, meanwhile, learned to speak Italian so that he could talk directly to the older generation from Italy. He participated in the second generation's activities of going to "gambling joints," bowling, and playing baseball and cards. He called his work "participatory action research" because he wanted his research to lead to actions that would improve the lives of the people studied.

Whyte's ethnography was typical of the sociology work then being done at the University of Chicago (where Whyte earned his PhD). In Canada, Whyte's study influenced Carl Dawson's work with Prairie communities, as well as the Quebec community studies of Everett Hughes (*French Canada in Transition*, 1943) and Horace Miner (*St Denis: A French-Canadian Parish*, 1939).

Institutional Ethnography

Institutional ethnography is a relatively new method of research, based on the theories of Dorothy Smith. This method of research differs from traditional sociological research in that it does not reflect the view that a neutral stance is necessarily more scientific than an approach that explicitly involves "taking sides" (Campbell & Gregor 2002: 48).

Institutional ethnography recognizes that any institution or organization can be seen as having two sides, each associated with a different kind of data. One side represents **ruling interests**: the interests of the organization, particularly its administration, and/or the interests of those who are dominant in society. The data associated with this side are text-based, comprising the written rules and practices of the institution. When the workers in the institution follow these rules and practices, they are activating **ruling relations**—that is, they are helping to serve the needs of the organization, often at the cost of their clients and/or themselves.

The other side of an organization is that of the informant. In this context, an informant is someone

A common subject for institutional ethnography is the hospital. Who represents the ruling interests in a hospital? Who is responsible for ensuring that those ruling interests are met? Who gets caught in the middle?

who works in the institution outside of management or the administration, the upholders of ruling interests. The data associated with the informant's side are *experiential*, based on the experience of the informant. Institutional ethnography recognizes that there is a **disjuncture**, or separation, between the knowledge produced from the perspectives of these two sides. In pointing out this disjuncture, institutional ethnographers generate information that they hope will lead to institutional change.

Schools offer a good example of the kind of organization that institutional ethnographers study. York University professor Alison Griffith asserts that teachers rely on parents (typically mothers) to get schoolchildren to do the work and acquire the skills necessary to succeed at school. Campbell and Gregor refer to this reliance on parents as "downloading educational work" (2002: 43), a practice that serves the ruling interests of boards of education and provincial governments, who can then spend less on schools and teachers. Teachers and parents, by complying with the demands of school administrators, are activating ruling relations. At the same time, they are also biasing the system in favour of students from middle-class households, whose parents are more likely to have the resources (including books, computers and Internet access, a good study space, and time) to best serve this end. Lower-class students are poorly served by the system, as they are more dependent on the school and its resources alone. The problem is made worse in provinces like Ontario, where it has become illegal for school boards to pass deficit budgets. Local boards, meeting the ruling interests of the provincial government, have been forced to consider closing pools and cutting music and athletic programs, putting the onus for children's health

and enrichment onto the parents. So there's a second disjuncture—between the provincial government and its boards—in addition to the one between boards and administrators and parents/children. This is the kind of useful finding that institutional ethnography can produce.

The Case Study Approach

British sociologist Gordon Marshall describes the case study approach as:

> [a] research design that takes as its subject a single case or a few selected examples of a social entity—such as communities, social groups, employers, events, life-histories, families, work teams, roles, or relationships—and employs a variety of methods to study them. . . . Case-studies include descriptive reports on typical, illustrative, or deviant examples; descriptions of good practice in policy research; evaluations of policies after implementation in an organization; studies that focus on extreme or strategic cases; the rigorous test of a well-defined hypothesis through the use of carefully selected contrasting cases; and studies of natural experiments. (Marshall 1998: 56)

The case study approach is often used to identify and describe **best practices**—strategies with a proven history of achieving desired results more effectively or consistently than similar methods used in the past by a particular organization or currently by other organizations in the same industry. The case study typically begins by introducing an organization or department that exemplifies the best practices under review, before describing the practices in terms of the organization's success. The case study is often geared to finding out whether certain best practices can be applied with comparable success elsewhere in the organization or industry.

The case study presented in the feature box on pages 57–58 describes policing in a First Nation community. Aboriginal communities generally did not police themselves until the early 1990s, when the federal government put enabling legislation in place to allow band councils of individual Aboriginal communities to establish their own police services, once they had signed a tripartite agreement with the federal and provincial or territorial governments.

What do YOU think?

1. Consider the "sides" involved in institutional ethnography. Which side do you think institutional researchers typically take?

2. Who should be responsible for ensuring that children get the exercise they need: school boards and the province, or parents?

3. How might institutional ethnography represent the different standpoints of teachers, parents, and students regarding homework?

Our Stories

Case Study of a Best Practice: Kitigan Zibi Anishinabeg First Nation Policing

Located about 130 kilometres north of Ottawa, Kitigan Zibi, with a registered population of 2,746 (as of May 2009), is the largest of the nine communities that make up the Algonquin Nation in Quebec. The community first had its own policing services in 1981, when, like other Quebec First Nations, it began operating a community police force under the auspices of the Amerindian Police Service (the APS). The APS is usually seen as a failure by First Nations in Quebec, owing mainly to the fact that Aboriginal officers were given limited, second-class roles as "special constables." In 1985, the Kitigan Zibi community moved ahead of other Aboriginal communities by transferring police services to its own independent force.

Following the introduction of the federal First Nation Policing Policy in April 1992, the community entered into a three-year tripartite agreement that allowed the Kitigan Zibi Anishinabeg Police Department (KZAPD) to become a fully functional force, with powers equivalent to those of any non-Native force in Canada. By 2002, the KZAPD had a chief of police, five full-time officers, and one part-time officer. Community satisfaction with the department's work has been high. In a survey conducted in 2002, 91 per cent of the members of the community surveyed felt that the KZAPD was the best police organization to meet the needs of the community. This compares favourably to the 55 per cent of community stakeholders who, in a First Nation Chiefs of Police Association survey, felt the self-administered police services in their communities were effective.

There are four keys to the success of the KZAPD. Unfortunately, two of these keys are unique to the Kitigan Zibi community and cannot be replicated in most other First Nation communities. First, Kitigan Zibi has a very stable political environment. At the time of the study, the chief councillor of the band had been in the position for over 20 years. During that time there had been few changes in the makeup of the band council. Further, there were no apparent political factions within the community, making it unlike many First Nation communities. Second, there have been no major clashes between the provincial government and Kitigan Zibi, putting it in the minority in Quebec. Largely because of this lack of conflict, the KZAPD has a reasonably harmonious relationship with the Quebec provincial police, a rarity for a First Nation force in Quebec.

Two remaining keys to the KZAPD's success offer lessons for other police forces operating in Native (and non-Native) communities to learn from. One is the strong relationship between the KZAPD and the youth of the community. In 1995, the KZAPD took part in a pilot project with Aboriginal youths aged between 12 and 24, who were paired with police officers to ride in cruisers, observe police duties first-hand, and visit the homes of their police mentors. Commenting on the mentoring experience, one officer said, "I took great pride in seeing the barriers fall and the sense of openness that developed in our communication" (First Nations Policing Update, July 1995, #3). In 1996, Chief of Police Gordon MacGregor stressed:

> [t]he importance of being among the people, being visible and approachable especially to the youth and young children. . . . [P]eople see you as being human and as a father, not just as a police figure. (Stewart 1996)

The final key is the KZAPD's dedication to training. One condition of the 1992 tripartite agreement signed with federal and provincial governments was that constables already in the force would earn the basic training equivalency diploma. This would enable the officers to assume powers equal

Continued

to those of any other officer in Quebec. All of the KZAPD's officers successfully completed the training. The chief of police even went beyond the qualifications required in the agreement, taking managerial courses for senior officers and additional courses offered at the Canadian Police College in Ottawa. When the Quebec Police Act was amended to include more training for provincial officers, the chief of police prepared a five-year forecast of the training needs of his force.

What do YOU think?

1. What indicates that the KZAPD is a good choice for a best practice case study?

2. What factors in the KZAPD's success cannot be readily replicated in other First Nation communities in Quebec? Which ones can?

3. The case study approach combines quantitative and qualitative research. How is that evident in the case presented here?

Narratives

The **narrative** is perhaps the purest form of the insider view. Narratives are the stories peoples tell about themselves, their situations, and the others around them. They have long been part of sociology. Narratives figured prominently in W.I. Thomas and Florian Znaniecki's five-volume work *The Polish Peasant in Europe and America* (1918–20): of its 2,200 pages, 800 were dedicated to letters, autobiographical accounts, and other narrative documents.

Still, the positivism of early sociology and the discipline's more recent emphasis on statistical evidence kept narrative study in a minor role in sociological research until the last 20 years. In 1993, D.R. Maines referred to the growing interest in narratives among sociologists as "narrative's moment." He saw in this trend a dual focus for sociological study, aimed at both examining the narratives of the usual subjects of study and at the same time "viewing sociologists as narrators and thereby inquiring into what they do to and with their and other people's narratives" (Maines 1993: 17). He suggested 10 propositions on which to base a new narrative sociology:

1. Since all socialized humans are story-tellers, they are always in a potential story-telling situation when interacting with or encountering others.

2. The vast majority of all speech acts and self-representations contain at least some elements of narratives.

3. Variation in situation, audience, individual perspective, and power/authority relations will produce the universal condition of multiple versions of narrated events.

4. Narratives and narrative occasions are always potential sites of conflict and competition as well as of co-operation and consensus.

5. All narratives are potentially rational accounts, but because of inherent human ambiguity and variation in linguistic competence, all narratives are ultimately incomplete.

6. Narratives exist at various levels of scale, ranging from the personal to the institutional to the cultural; they exist for varying lengths of time; and they inevitably change.

7. All social science data are already interpreted data; the uninterpreted datum does not exist.

8. All sociological facts are narrated facts insofar as they have been processed through some form of story structure that renders events as factual.

9. The act of data collection is an act of entering respondents' lives that are partly formed by still unfolding stories. Therefore, in the name of honesty, research subjects will likely tell different stories about the same thing at different times and to different people.

10. A major implication of the above nine propositions is that sociology can only be a science of interpretations and to some extent must constitute itself as an interpretive science. (Maines 1993)

Since arriving in Toronto, this young man has been working at his brother's convenience store, which sells Burmese and Thai groceries. What factors make up his social location? What could you learn from a narrative account of his life that you might not get from an article on the challenges facing immigrants to Canada?

Telling It Like It Is

A Student POV

Fasting

"Hey Moe, come join us for lunch."
"I can't, guys. I'm fasting."
"Fasting, what's that?"

This passage is quite normal and may be heard every year, asked by anyone and almost everyone. It bothers me to consider that the average person doesn't know what fasting for Muslims is. Fasting is an Islamic tradition practised for centuries, where a Muslim is subjected to no food or drink from sunrise to sunset. This is done to remind Muslims where we came from, to remind us that we started with nothing. It teaches us to value what we have and to value our gracious religion. There is fasting in almost every religion, yet the people who know the basic term of fasting don't know what type of fasting Muslims commit to. Many people [I

have spoken to] were shocked to hear that during Ramadan [fasting month] you cannot only eat, but also drink. Many people thought that water was allowed in any fasting, but it isn't for the Muslim type of fasting.

When someone asks me what fasting is for Muslims, I reply with such fatigue from saying it over and over that I simply reply, "Well, we (Muslims) basically can't eat or drink anything when the sun is up." I know that my reply may offend many Muslims since I have not included any significance or talked about the reward given for performing the fast. I simply gave a quick answer because I get that question asked every year, by anyone and almost everyone."

—Mohamed Abseh

Telling It Like It Is

Canadian by Birth, Palestinian by Culture

My name is Nadine and I am Canadian-born, but Palestinian by culture. My father was born in Palestine and my mother was born in Egypt to Palestinian refugees. Nowadays, being a Palestinian or of Palestinian origin is quite difficult, especially when you're living in a so-called multicultural nation. I guess it's not as hard for me as it has been for my parents because I am Canadian-born and my parents came to Canada knowing little about the country. However, the difficult aspect in my life was that I grew up in a one-cultured town [the predominantly Italian-Canadian town of Woodbridge, in southern Ontario] which made it extremely difficult for my brothers and I to fit in. As far as I am concerned, I have never been able to have any close relationship with anyone. Why? I guess that children needed a common ground in order to establish a relationship, and not possessing the same culture as those around me made my assimilation even more difficult. Within homogeneous groups one can be easily singled out and that happened to me. Furthermore, as I grew up it became harder for me to engage in any real relationship with boys or girls because my culture became stronger for me and as well for them, which made us even grow farther apart. Maybe it was because I didn't speak or dress like them, or because I was darker than them, it didn't matter—basically I was just different.

Entering college, it was a bit easier for me to make acquaintances, though I realized how uneducated and ignorant people could really be. It was particularly difficult for me after the events of 9/11 because, automatically, the Arab world would get blamed for it and most people, ignorant as they are, believed everything that the media's propaganda has been telling them. I was in college at that time, and explaining to people my point of view was tremendously challenging. Media brainwash had its toll on the majority of those around me. Furthermore getting into debates with individuals about what's occurring in Palestine and my views as a Palestinian was almost impossible. Right now my oppressed and displaced people who have been legitimately resisting occupation since 1948 are the bad guys. Maybe in a couple of years it will be another group, but for me now it's hard because I'm still singled out by my friends and the media. Maybe it would be a little bit easier if individuals would become open-minded about what goes on in the world. Then people could understand who we are and who I am. Knowledge is responsibility and to most, responsibility is a heavy burden to take. It is pretty sad what's going on in the twenty-first century is that people like me, Canadian-born, have difficulties growing up because of who they are and where they're from!

—Nadine Dahdah

The use of narratives in research is important because it can give voice to people who do not usually get to speak directly in research. **Voice** is the expression of *a* (not *the*) viewpoint that comes from occupying a particular social location (determined by factors including gender, "race" or ethnicity, sexual orientation, class, professional or academic status, and so on).

Consider the narrative presented on page 59 and the one above. Both give voice to viewpoints that are not often heard. In the first, a young Muslim college student talks about life in Canada. His voice is different to the voice of an older person or the voice of someone of a different ethnic or religious background. It is also different to the voices of other Muslims—those of young women, for instance, or of local religious leaders. It is not "the official view," normal or abnormal, representative or strange, but it speaks a truth because it is what the speaker thinks, and it does reflect his life's experience. We value it because it gives the non-Muslim reader a sense of what it is like to be a young Muslim living in Canada—a bit of what Weber called *verstehen*, to use a term introduced last chapter.

In the second narrative, we hear the voice of a young Canadian of Palestinian background. We are all aware of the longstanding struggles involving Palestinians in the Middle East, but we hear considerably less about Palestinians living in Canada. Consider the factors that shape her point of view: her age, her gender, her ethnic background, her nationality, the site of her upbringing, her current status as a student, even the political climate at the time of writing—all of these contribute to her unique perspective.

If you wanted a more detailed picture of what it's like to be a young Muslim or Palestinian living in Canada, you could gather additional narratives and tie them together through a process known as **triangulation**, which involves the use of at least three narratives, theoretical perspectives, or investigators to examine the same phenomenon.

No matter what your political stripe is, listening to the opinions of those whose views you don't share can be uncomfortable at best. For the person who holds opinions that are outside the political or cultural mainstream, expressing those views can be a very difficult and isolating experience. It's important to recognize that setting down a view you think may be unpopular requires courage. At the same time, recording and publishing the narratives of peoples whose political positions you don't agree with doesn't mean you accept what they say as "right." But whether you're expressing what you think is an unpopular view or recording a view you don't agree with, making such views known is an important step in generating understanding among others who might not agree with the position.

What do YOU think?

Consider an issue raised in one of the two narratives you've just read. How do you think triangulation—the use of at least three narratives—would help you gain a different understanding of the issue?

Alternative Qualitative Research Methods

Content Analysis

Content analysis involves studying a set of cultural artifacts or events by systematically counting them (to show which ones dominate) and then interpreting the themes they reflect. Cultural artifacts include children's books, billboards, novels, newspaper articles, advertisements, artwork, articles of clothing, clinical records—even textbooks. These items all have two distinct properties not normally found in the subjects studied using other types of qualitative methodology. First, they have a natural or "found" quality because they are not created specifically to be studied. Second, they are *non-interactive*, in that there are no interviews used or behaviours observed to gather the data (Reinharz 1992: 146–8).

Feminist approaches to content analysis attempt to expose pervasive patriarchal ("male-dominated") and misogynist ("woman-hating") culture. Elaine Hall, in her article "One Week for Women? The Structure of Inclusion of Gender Issues in Introductory Textbooks" (1988), demonstrated how women's issues are treated as an afterthought in introductory-level texts. Judith Dilorio, in a paper presented in 1980, used content analysis to examine scholarly articles on gender role research and found that their methods *naturalized*, or normalized, social facts that diminished women and promoted male-oriented conservatism (as analyzed in Reinharz 1992: 147, 361).

In *Gender Advertisements* (1976), Goffman undertook a content analysis of commercial pictures depicting gender in print media. He demonstrated that women in the magazine ads he examined were overwhelmingly depicted as subordinate and submissive. The magazines Goffman used represented both mass media and popular culture, having been selected on the basis of their availability and the size of their circulation. Taken together, these magazines (available in every supermarket, drugstore, and bookstore) act as cultural artifacts, reflecting or mirroring the social world. This relationship, however, is not unidirectional but bidirectional: cultural objects like magazines reflect the social world, and the social world, in turn, is influenced by cultural objects (Griswold 1994: 22–3). With their wide circulation, popular magazines give us both a snapshot of the social world and also, if we look carefully, an indication of how the social world is being constructed through mass media.

Sut Jhally, in his discussion of gender (1990), argues that magazine ads are neither completely true nor completely false reflections of social reality; they are partial truths and falsehoods. Ads depicting gender do not truly or falsely represent "real" gender

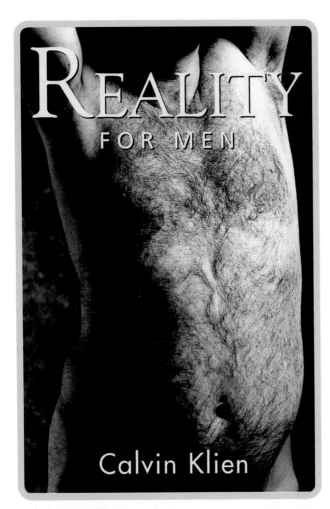

REALITY
FOR MEN

Calvin Klien

Ritualized displays of gender in advertising often assert stereo-types, exaggerating certain aspects of our social reality while de-emphasizing others. What gender stereotypes, promoted in advertising, are critiqued in this spoof ad from Adbusters? Note that the misspelling is deliberate.

relations or **ritualized** gender displays. Rather, for Jhally, they are "hyper-ritualizations" or exaggerations that emphasize certain aspects of gender display and de-emphasize others (1990: 135).

Discourse Analysis

There are two types or levels of **discourse analysis** used by sociologists. The first analyzes discourse as it is traditionally defined—that is, as a conversation, a speech, or a written text. Sociologists may examine the "discourse" found in a given ethnography, in an open-ended interview, or in a narrative. They might also focus on "texts" such as court transcripts,

newspaper stories, movie trailers, and advertise-ments. Foucault's work on totalitarian discourse, touched on in Chapter 2, can be considered in terms of this definition of discourse. Recall that he defined discourse as "a conceptual framework with its own internal logic and underlying assumptions that are generally recognizable."

The second level of discourse analysis looks at a broader definition of "text" that goes beyond individ-ual works and authors to include large "fields" of pre-sentation of information over a certain period of time: movies in general or in the early twenty-first century, for instance, reality shows, introductory sociology textbooks, Canadian historical writing, and so on. A "field," then, would comprise all known discourse on a particular cultural concept or idea—"masculinity," for instance. It is the role of the researcher to trace the discourse through time and space, looking at the rep-resentation, naturalization, change, and influence of the discursive field. An example of this kind of study would be a discourse analysis of changing popular cultural representations of masculinity in Hollywood films over the past 50 years.

Genealogy

Genealogy in its everyday use refers to the study of heredity for the purposes of genetic or social history, or the study of pedigree and lineage. In the context of dis-course analysis, **genealogy** is a method of examining the history of the second type of discourse, as defined above. Foucault, in his later works, used a genealogical method to study the "heredity" of discourses, to trace the origins and histories of modern discourses as they collide, fragment, and adhere to other cultural prac-tices and discourses over time. Foucault's genealogical work captures the dynamic nature of such discourses as mental illness (1961), the penal system (1975), and sexuality (1978).

Edward Said's classic study of Western atti-tudes towards Eastern culture, *Orientalism* (1979), offers another example of genealogical research. In the book, the Palestinian-born Said (1935–2003) acknowledged Foucault's influence, particularly his notion of discourse, which allowed Said to conceive of the genealogy of Orientalism, broadly defined as a Western fascination with or romanticization of the "exotic" culture and art of Middle and Far Eastern societies. For him, Orientalism could not be studied or understood without the concept of discourse:

> My contention is that without examining Orientalism as a discourse one cannot possibly understand the enormously systematic discipline by which European culture was able to manage—and even produce—the Orient politically, sociologically, militarily, ideologically, scientifically, and imaginatively during the post-Enlightenment period. (1979: 3)

Orientalism, in this sense, refers to "a corporate institution for dealing with the Orient—dealing with it by making statements about it, authorising views of it, describing it, by teaching it, settling it, ruling over it: in short, Orientalism as a Western style for dominating, restructuring, and having authority over the Orient"

What does this postcard from Turkey, dated 1904, tell you about how Westerners thought of "the Orient" at this time? In what sense would you call this a form of "romanticism"?

(Said, 1979: 3). As well as being a form of academic discourse, Orientalism is a style of thought based on the presumed philosophical distinctions between East and West, the Orient and the Occident respectively. Here, we take Orientalism to mean the process by which the "Orient" was, and continues to be, constructed in western European thinking.

What do YOU think?

Now decidedly old-fashioned, "Oriental" was once the common term for what many people today consider "Asian." But what does "Asian" mean to you? If you're North American, it likely refers mostly to China and Japan. If you're British, you probably associate it with India and Pakistan (countries we in Canada might refer to as "South Asian"). What countries do the terms "Southeast Asian" and "East Asian" suggest to you? What term might you use for someone from Siberia or Mongolia?

Quantitative Research

Statistics

Sociologists have mixed feelings about **statistics**, a science that, in sociology, involves the use of numbers to map social behaviour and beliefs. Social scientists, like politicians, relish the opportunity to show off by quoting facts and figures. And yet, we are also suspicious of statistics (particularly other people's statistics). There are more jokes about the science of statistics than there are about any other kind of sociological research method—and we can prove that statistically. But here is some anecdotal evidence:

- "It shames me some to hear the statistics about us in class. The shame burns holes in whatever sympathy I may have for Indians, not my mom though." – the Native protagonist of Aboriginal writer Lee Maracle's novel *Sun Dogs*, on how sociological statistics portray her people (Maracle 1992: 3)
- "There are three kinds of lies: lies, damned lies, and statistics." – Benjamin Disraeli
- "*USA Today* has come out with a new survey: apparently, three out of every four people make up 75 per cent of the population." – David Letterman
- "There are two kinds of statistics: the kind you look up, and the kind you make up." – Rex Stout

- "An unsophisticated forecaster uses statistics as a drunk man uses lamp-posts—for support rather than illumination." – Andrew Lang
- "Smoking is one of the leading causes of statistics." – Fletcher Knebel
- "Statistician: A man who believes figures don't lie, but admits that under analysis some of them won't stand up either." – Evan Esar, *Esar's Comic Dictionary*
- "Statistics: The only science that enables different experts using the same figures to draw different conclusions." – Esar

Operational Definitions

A key area of quantifiable research, and one in which a sociology student can learn to challenge the research of professionals, is that of **operational definitions**. These are definitions that take abstract or theoretical concepts—"poverty," "abuse," or "working class," for example—and transform them into concepts that are concrete, observable, measurable, and countable. This is difficult to do well.

The *Handbook for Sociology Teachers* (1982), by British sociologists Roger Gomm and Patrick McNeill, contains a brilliant exercise that illustrates one of the difficulties of using operational definitions. Students are presented with a table showing the number of thefts that have occurred at each of a number of schools. Included in the table are the following factors that may or may not have some bearing on the number of thefts at each school:

- size of school
- social class of the students
- gender makeup of the school (i.e. single-sex or co-educational).

QUICK HITS

So You Think You Know What a Single Parent Is?

Whenever you're gathering or interpreting data from questionnaires, it's critical that you understand the exact meaning—the *operational definition*—of key terms being used. Take a category as seemingly self-evident as "single parent." In this exercise, identify which of the following you would count as a single parent, then address the questions below.

		Yes	No
a)	a mother whose husband is dead	☐	☐
b)	a 41-year-old separated mother who lives with her 22-year-old son	☐	☐
c)	a father whose 4-year-old daughter sees her mother every weekend	☐	☐
d)	a mother whose 10-year-old son lives with his father every summer	☐	☐
e)	a father whose two daughters live with their mother every other week	☐	☐
f)	a mother whose husband lives in the same house but contributes nothing financially or in services to the raising of her children from a previous marriage	☐	☐
g)	a gay man who, along with his live-in partner, is raising his two sons without any assistance from the children's mother	☐	☐
h)	a mother who, along with her son, is completely supported by her ex-husband	☐	☐
i)	a mother whose husband is away at work most of the year	☐	☐

What do YOU think?

1. How would you define "single parent"?
2. Do you think that "single-parent family" is a category that would be easy to do research with? Why or why not?

Students are asked to try to determine whether there is a cause-and-effect relationship between any of these factors and the number of thefts at each school. Once they have arrived at some tentative conclusions, the teacher gives them an additional handout showing that each school defined "theft" differently. With no consistency in the operational definition, their efforts to compare schools were sociologically worthless (although pedagogically rewarding).

To get a sense of how operational definitions are used, let's consider **poverty**. There is no standard definition for "poverty" or "poor." Definitions of these terms vary across the globe. There are, however, various conventional methods of defining poverty. One is to establish a **poverty line**, an income level below which a household is defined (for statistical or governmental purposes) as being "poor."

How is a poverty line established? Again, there is no universally accepted procedure, though a few methods are prevalent. One is to link it to the availability of basic material needs: food, clothing, and shelter.

Anything below the minimum income level needed to secure these necessities is considered **absolute poverty**. But this, too, will vary, even within countries. Consider, for example, how housing costs vary across Canada. It costs more for a resident of Vancouver to pay rent on an apartment than it costs a citizen of Halifax living in a comparable dwelling.

Since 1997 Statistics Canada has used the **Market Basket Measure** (MBM) to establish a poverty line for different regions across the country. As Giles explains:

> The MBM estimates the cost of a specific basket of goods and services for the reference year, assuming that all items in the basket were entirely provided for out of the spending of the household [i.e. that none of the items were purchased for the householders by family or friends]. Any household with a level of income lower than the cost of the basket is considered to be living in low income. (Giles 2004)

The Market Basket Measure (MBM) establishes a regional poverty line for Canada. How would you define poverty? What clues in this picture suggest that this family is not poor?

The "basket" includes five types of expenditures for a reference family of two adults and two children:

- food
- clothing
- shelter
- transportation
- "other" (school supplies, furniture, newspapers, recreation and family entertainment, personal care products, and phone).

Different levels are calculated for 48 different geographical areas in Canada (HRSDC 2003).

Another way to define "poor" is to use a **relative poverty** scale, which defines poverty relative to average, median, or mean household incomes. One kind of poverty scale used in Canada involves **Low Income Cut-Offs** (LICOs), which are calculated based on the percentage of a family's income spent on food, clothing, and shelter. So, for instance, according to Statistics Canada, in 1992 the average Canadian family spent 43 per cent of their total household income (after income tax) on these three items (Statistics Canada 2011a). Statistics Canada sets the cutoff at 20 percentage points beyond the average. Thus, any family spending greater than 63 per cent of its total

The Point Is...

The Market Basket Measure: Two Different Versions

The typical method of forming an operational definition of poverty using the Market Basket Measure entails calculating how much it would cost to purchase adequate food, clothing, and transportation for a family of four (two adults and two children) living in a medium-sized city for one year. The figures are sometimes adjusted higher for families living in larger cities and lower for those living in rural areas.

While this may sound straightforward and objective, it's important to note that different agencies may calculate the Market Basket Measure differently, especially when politics are involved. For our purposes, we will compare two measures, calculated by Statistics Canada and the Fraser Institute.

Statistics Canada is a public organization that gathers and supplies statistics based on the federal census and other means. The Fraser Institute is a private think tank appealing to conservative policy-makers with policy recommendations that promote free enterprise and limit social programs. Its studies often appear in right-leaning newspapers such as the *National Post* and the *Sun* chain, and their findings are frequently cited by the federal and provincial Conservative parties. Why? In the case of the Market Basket Measure, the way the Fraser Institute's researchers calculate poverty makes the poverty line much lower than the one calculated by

Statistics Canada (see Table 3.1). The lower the poverty line, the lower the number of people considered poor in the analysis of statistics, and the lower the need for social programs like welfare.

Table 3.1 Poverty in Canada as calculated by Statistics Canada and the Fraser Institute, by province (2000)

PROVINCE	STATISTICS CANADA'S MBM	FRASER INSTITUTE'S MBM	DIFFERENCE
Newfoundland and Labrador	$21,339	$17,619	$3,721
Prince Edward Island	21,433	17,181	4,252
Nova Scotia	22,899	17,502	5,397
New Brunswick	19,724	15,995	3,729
Quebec	19,920	15,681	4,239
Ontario	23,876	18,603	5,273
Manitoba	21,322	17,585	3,717
Saskatchewan	21,527	16,098	5,429
Alberta	21,087	16,010	5,077
British Columbia	23,634	19,759	3,875

Table 3.4 Inverse correlation of independent and dependent variables: Three examples

INDEPENDENT VARIABLE		DEPENDENT VARIABLE
average temperature	⇨	average amount of clothes worn
woman's education	⇨	number of children she will have
age (of an adult)	⇨	support for same-sex marriage

relationship exists based on correlation alone, without sufficient evidence, is known as *spurious reasoning*. Spurious reasoning is one of those concepts that's hard to grasp with just the definition, and sociology instructors are challenged to explain and identify it. It usually takes lots of examples. So we'll begin here with the definition, then move on to examples.

Spurious reasoning, as we mentioned, exists when someone sees *correlation* and falsely assumes *causation*. Remember that a correlation is easy to determine; causation is not. The journey from one to the other is long and difficult. It involves proving—or else disproving—the existence of the critical **third variable**, the outside factor that influences both correlating variables.

Here are the examples. Some of them are silly, some serious.

Example #1: Birds and Leaves

There is a correlation in Canada between birds flying south and leaves falling. We can see both phenomena occurring roughly at the same time, but it would be spurious reasoning to say that the birds see the leaves falling and therefore decide to migrate. If we look for a third factor, we'll find that the angle of the sun's rays affects both dependent variables.

Example #2: Fire Trucks and Fire Damage

This is perhaps the most often taught example of spurious reasoning. There is a direct correlation between the number of fire trucks that go to a fire and the amount of damage that takes place at the fire. The greater the number of fire trucks, the greater the damage the fire *causes*. It would be spurious reasoning to say that a large number of fire trucks *causes* the extensive damage done at the site of the fire (though some budget-conscious municipal politicians might want us to believe this—they could save a lot of money on fire trucks). Seek out the third variable: the seriousness of the fire affects both the number of fire trucks that appear and the amount of damage that is caused.

Example #3: Older Men and Younger Wives

Older men who marry significantly younger women tend to live longer than the cohort of jealous men their own age. Spurious reasoning would lead us to conclude that marrying frolicsome young women keeps old men active and healthy. But before declaring that we've found the solution for men who want to live long and happy lives, we must look for a third variable. That's when we discover that if the older man is already relatively strong and healthy for his age, then

Spurious reasoning might lead us to conclude that this man will live long because he is married to this young woman. What do you think?

he is both more likely to attract and keep a younger bride and also more likely to live longer.

Example #4: Cohabitation and Divorce

There is a direct (but not strong) correlation between a couple's living together prior to marriage and the likelihood of divorce. People who live together first are more likely to divorce than those who go from living apart to living together in marriage. It would be spurious reasoning to say that a couple's greater likelihood of divorce comes from the fact that they lived together first (for example, they are disillusioned because they find no greater bliss in lawful marriage than they enjoyed in mere cohabitation). Seek out the third variable and you will find it in social liberalism and social conservatism (the latter possibly a cause or effect of that difficult-to-pin-down social factor "religiosity"). People who are socially liberal are more likely *both* to live together *and* to leave a marriage if they feel it is a bad one. People who are more socially conservative are *both* more likely to begin living together with marriage *and* more likely to stay in a marriage, even if it is horrible (our sympathies).

Example #5: Divorce and Suicide

Durkheim detected a direct correlation between divorce rates and suicide rates during a 10-year period from 1870 to 1880; some of his findings are recorded in Table 3.5.

There was, indeed, a positive correlation between divorce rates and suicide rates over this period. However, it would be spurious reasoning to say that greater rates of divorce produced higher suicide rates. For Durkheim, the third variable was **anomie**, a societal state of breakdown or confusion, or a more personal one based on an individual's lack of connection to or contact with society. Anomie, concluded

Durkheim, was the real cause of increases in both divorce and suicide rates.

What do YOU think?

Read the footnote at the end of Table 3.2. Are we guilty of spurious reasoning if we assume (because it hasn't been proven) a cause-and-effect relationship between officers' commitment to training and their increase in competency? Can you think of any third variable that might account for the correlation?

Critical Thinking and Statistics

Sociologist Joel Best, author of *Damned Lies and Statistics: Untangling Numbers from the Media, Politicians, and Activists* (2001), likes to use the following example that illustrates why we should approach statistics with a critical mind. He was on the PhD dissertation committee of a graduate student who began the prospectus of his dissertation with a questionable statistic meant to grab the attention of the reader. The student cited the following stat from an article published in 1995:

"Every year since 1950, the number of American children gunned down has doubled."

This certainly gains the reader's attention. But wait a minute, said Best: do the math. Say the 1950 figure was the unbelievably low figure of 1. Here is how it would add up from 1950 to 1995:

1950	1
1951	2
1952	4
1955	32
1957	128
1959	512
1960	1,012
1961	2,058
1965	32,768 (there were 9,960 homicides in total that year)
1970	1 million +
1980	1 billion (approximately; that's more than four times the total population of the United States at the time)
1983	8.6 billion (nearly one-and-a-half times the world's population)

Table 3.5 Correlation between divorce and suicide rates in four countries, 1870–1889

COUNTRY	DIVORCE RATE (PER 1,000 MARRIAGES)	SUICIDE RATE (PER 1 MILLION PEOPLE)
Italy	3.1	31.0
Sweden	6.4	81.0
France	7.5	150.0
Switzerland	47.0	216.0

What the author of the original article—the one cited by the PhD student—had done was misquote a 1994 document stating (accurately) that the number of American children killed each year by guns had doubled since 1950; the number itself had not doubled *each year*. If the original number had been one, that would make the 1994 figure two.

After presenting us this cautionary tale, Best warns the reader that bad statistics come to support all political stripes, from the political right wing (our Conservative Party) to the left wing (the NDP), from wealthy corporations to advocates for the poor, the sick, and the powerless. To cite an extreme Canadian example, the Mike Harris Conservative government of Ontario, in the late 1990s, officially stated that the number of people on social assistance in the province had gone down, implying that the situation for poor people had improved under their administration. It hadn't. The numbers were down because the government had changed the criteria for programs like employment insurance, lowering the number of successful applicants; as a result, government-run agencies had closed the "welfare door" on a number of people. The statistic was presented as though all the people no longer collecting social assistance had obtained jobs and were, as a result, better off. Lost behind the statistic were the people who didn't apply for social assistance because they had committed suicide (in part because of their poverty), had become homeless, had moved out of the province (to find work, family support, or better provincial assistance programs), had moved in with family members or friends, or had resorted to criminal activity for a living because they were no longer eligible for Ontario's welfare programs.

Best advises us to approach statistics critically. To be critical is to recognize that all statistics are flawed to some extent, and that some flaws are more significant than others. While Best admits that no checklist of critical questions is complete, he does present the following useful series of questions for sociology students to consider when encountering a statistic in a news report, magazine, newspaper, or conversation:

What might be the sources for this number? How could one go about producing the figure? Who produced the number, and what interests might they have? What are the different ways key terms might have been defined, and which definitions have been chosen? How might the phenomena be measured, and which measurement choices have been made? What sort of sample was gathered, and how might that sample affect the result? Is the statistic properly interpreted? Are comparisons being made, and if so, are the comparisons appropriate? Are there competing statistics? If so, what stakes do the opponents have in the issue, and how are those stakes likely to affect their use of statistics? And is it possible to figure out why the statistics seem to disagree, what the differences are in the ways the competing sides are using figures? (Best 2001)

Social Research Methods: A Final Word

In this chapter we've introduced a number of ways to carry out sociological research. In all the talk about quantitative and qualitative methods, independent and dependent variables, correlation and statistics, it's easy to lose sight of an important point: the subjects under investigation are people, and the moment you begin to study them, you start a relationship that will not always be equal. Students, soldiers, and inmates of prisons and asylums are often studied because they have little power to say no. If I can ask questions about your life but you can't ask questions about mine, then I have a kind of power over you that you do not have over me. People who are poor, who belong to racialized (e.g. black), or colonized (e.g. Aboriginal) groups when studied by white middle-class researchers have often been studied for purposes that serve more to control or exploit the subjects of research than to give them power over their lives. The Maori of New Zealand have been through that experience. Maori researcher Linda Tuhiwai Smith, in an important work called *Decolonizing Methodologies: Research and Indigenous Peoples* (1999), writes the following:

From the vantage point of the colonized . . . the term "research" is inextricably linked to European imperialism and colonialism. The word itself, "research," is probably one of the dirtiest words in the indigenous world's vocabulary. When mentioned in many indigenous contexts, it stirs up silence, it conjures up bad memories, it raises a smile that is knowing and distrustful. . . . The ways in which scientific research is implicated in the worst excesses of colonialism remains a powerful remembered history for many of the world's colonized peoples. . . . It galls us that Western researchers and intellectuals can assume to know all that it is possible to know of us, on the basis of their brief encounters with some of us. It appalls us that the West can desire, extract and claim ownership of ways of knowing, our imagery, the things we create and produce, and then simultaneously reject the people who created and developed those ideas and seek to deny them further opportunities to be creators of their own culture and own nations. (Tuhiwai Smith 1999: 1)

If your interest in sociology comes from a desire to effect positive social change, the bitter tone of this statement might shock you. Let it serve as a reminder: treat research subjects with respect and represent the data fairly, and you will go a long way towards sociology's goal of bringing clarity to social issues.

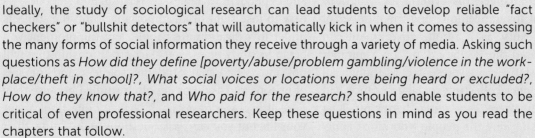

WRAP IT UP

Summary

Ideally, the study of sociological research can lead students to develop reliable "fact checkers" or "bullshit detectors" that will automatically kick in when it comes to assessing the many forms of social information they receive through a variety of media. Asking such questions as *How did they define [poverty/abuse/problem gambling/violence in the workplace/theft in school]?*, *What social voices or locations were being heard or excluded?*, *How do they know that?*, and *Who paid for the research?* should enable students to be critical of even professional researchers. Keep these questions in mind as you read the chapters that follow.

I hope that as you encountered all the diverse and, at times, opposing research strategies presented here it became increasingly clear that the facts do *not* speak for themselves. Knowledge is created, and social "facts" and hypotheses are tested by human researchers with human biases who occasionally (and perhaps unintentionally) allow these biases to manufacture distortions rather than the ever-elusive "facts" or "proof." In short, be critical.

THINK BACK

Questions for Critical Review

1. Distinguish between qualitative and quantitative research. Give examples of each.

2. Explain the importance of narratives to sociological research.

3. Explain spurious reasoning. Furnish some examples of your own.

4. Outline the different methods of sociological research.

5. Identify the importance of operational definitions in quantitative research.

READ ON

Online

Canadian Sociological Association

www.csa-scs.ca/files/webapps/csapress/student/

> The CSA's website has a separate page for student members, with news on events and workshops, student work, and employment opportunities.

Sociology and Legal Studies

http://129.97.58.10/discipline/sociology/research.html

> Maintained by the University of Waterloo, this site features a useful guide to conducting effective research, outlining the key steps from defining your topic to citing your sources.

Statistics Canada

www.statcan.ca/start.html

> We're fortunate to have a wealth of data, derived from censuses and other polls, on all kinds of information relevant to Canadians, from where we live and where we're from to how we spend our money.

In Print

Joel Best (2001), *Damned Lies and Statistics: Untangling Numbers from the Media, Politicians, and Activists* **(Berkeley and Los Angeles: University of California Press).**

> This relatively lighthearted but helpful sociological guide to understanding the manipulation of statistics was so popular that it spawned a sequel, *More Damned List and Statistics: How Numbers Confuse Public Issues* (2004).

Michael Blastland & Andrew Dilnot (2007), *The Tiger That Isn't: Seeing through a World of Numbers* **(London: Profile Books).**

> A Scottish journalist and an English economist teamed up to produce this useful guide to interpreting statistics used by politicians and other manipulators of information.

Marie Campbell & Frances Gregor (2002), *Mapping Social Relations: A Primer in Doing Institutional Ethnography* **(Aurora, ON: Garamond).**

> The insights of Dorothy Smith inform this informative work on institutional ethnography.

James Paul Gee (2010), *How to Do Discourse Analysis: A Toolkit* **(London: Routledge).**

> A relatively accessible introduction to discourse analysis by a professor of literature.

John L. Steckley (2008), *White Lies About the Inuit* **(Toronto: University of Toronto Press).**

This genealogical work puts to rest three discourse myths about the historic Inuit: that Inuit elders are sometimes abandoned on ice floes, that there are blond, blue-eyed Inuit descended from Norse ancestors, and that the Inuit have 52 (or more) words for snow.

Helen Thornham (2011), *Ethnographies of the Videogame: Gender, Narrative and Praxis* **(Farnham, UK: Ashgate).**

This work presents a British sociologist's innovative use of several methods of research to investigate standard sociological issues such as gender, power, identity, and relationships to media.

II

Social Life

PART I OF THIS TEXTBOOK provided an introduction to the discipline of sociology in general and to some of the particular theories, theorists, and theoretical approaches it is known for. Part II affords us our first opportunity to see how the practice of sociology plays out when applied to some of the discipline's principal concerns, including culture, socialization, social roles, consumption, and deviance. There will still be theory (there is always theory), but it will turn up in the context of real-life situations we have all experienced. Among the questions we will tackle in this part are the following:

- What makes up a person's culture? And how did that person come by it? (Spoiler alert: *socialization*.)
- What positions (or *statuses*) do we hold in society (e.g. mother, daughter, employee of a big company, sociology instructor)? How are these positions ranked, both by the individual who holds them (I consider myself a sociologist above all things) and by society as a whole (the college's sociology professors are valued less than the IT instructors—how wrong is that!)?
- How do people holding differently ranked positions interact? ("John, I heard that in your sociology class today you were taking shots at the college's IT instructors. Am I right?" "Yes, you certainly are, boss. But let me explain . . ."
- What do our patterns of consumption say about us and the positions we hold (or would like to hold) in society? What do patterns of consumption say about our culture in comparison with others? We in North America are great consumers of fast food; people in other parts of the world are not—what does that say about us?
- What if you feel excluded from your culture, as though you were different to what the rest of your culture considers "normal" (e.g. you don't own a cellphone, you don't watch reality TV shows, and you harbour suspicions of white men who drive black BMWs)? Does that make you "deviant"? And if so, does that make you bad? Would these same factors make you deviant in other cultures also?

The answer is yes—I think I would be a deviant in every culture. But then, who wants to be part of the mainstream anyway? Why be a sheep when you can be a coyote?

4 Culture

Learning Objectives

After reading this chapter, you should be able to

- distinguish between (a) *dominant cultures*, *subcultures*, and *countercultures*, and (b) *high culture*, *popular culture*, and *mass culture*
- explain the difference between *reading* and *decipherment*
- define and give examples of *folkways*, *mores*, and *taboos*
- identify the intellectual traps of Eurocentrism, victimology, exoticism, and the biases of Western medicine

- explain what it means for culture to be "contested"
- discuss how ethnocentrism has affected mainstream sociology's interpretation of the potlatch
- cite some of the reasons that Muslim women in Canada choose to wear the hijab
- contrast the linguistic expectations of speakers of Algonquian and Indo-European languages.

Key Terms

- agency
- Algonquian
- authenticity
- contested
- counterculture
- cultural capital
- cultural relativism
- cultural studies
- culture
- decipherment
- dialect
- dominant culture
- dominants
- ethnocentrism
- Eurocentrism

- folkways
- high culture
- hijab
- Indo-European
- linguistic determinism (*or* causation)
- mass culture
- mores
- negative sanction
- noble savage
- norms
- patriarchy
- popular culture
- positive sanction

- potlatch
- reading
- reverse ethnocentrism
- Sapir-Whorf hypothesis
- simulacra
- sociolinguistics
- subculture
- symbol
- taboos
- values
- victimology

Names to Know

- Jean Baudrillard
- Pierre Bourdieu
- William Graham Sumner

Culture and Claiming Space

I saw the conflict coming, but I could do nothing to stop it. It was all about culture.

It was 1981, and I was in Edinburgh, Scotland, in one of the few decent (according to my refined North American palate) hamburger joints in the city. It was a popular spot, both for locals and for tourists, commanding a beautiful full view of the famed castle on the top of the hill across the street. I was waiting in line with my Scottish friends when I saw the incident that would precipitate the conflict.

A pair of American tourists set their jackets on two of four chairs attached to a table, and then slowly proceeded the short distance to the lineup. I sensed that trouble was coming. As I stood in line I saw a Scottish couple looking for a place to sit with their meals. Their eyes fixed on the chairs opposite the ones the tourists had laid claim to with their jackets. The couple went over, sat down at the unoccupied chairs, and innocently began to eat.

The tourists had been distracted by the view of the castle. When then turned around and saw the couple at the table, they reacted instantly.

"What are you doing?! That's our table! Didn't you see the jackets???" The Scots looked up at them, dumbfounded, and unprepared to move. This was their country, after all, and they weren't prepared to be booted from their seats.

Looking on with interest, my Scottish friends asked me (as a Canadian, an obvious expert in all things North American): "What's wrong with them? Do they think they bought the table? Bloody tourists!"

The tourists continued to argue with the Scots before storming out of the place.

A few months earlier, I might have sided with the tourists, sympathizing with their typically North American sense of space. But having spent time in Scotland, I understood why the Scots were surprised. In Canada, when two people in a bar are sitting at a table with four chairs, and someone asks them, "Are these seats taken?", the unseated patrons will take the two extra chairs and sit at a vacant table. In Scotland, they will sit down right at "your" table, perhaps joining you in conversation or else ignoring you altogether.

It's all about culture.

Introduction: What We Mean by Culture and Why It's Contested

The word *culture* has a lot of different meanings. Some people equate it with a sophistication of manners and tastes, something you either have (if you enjoy, say, the opera, ballet, and fine dining) or are sadly lacking (if your idea of a good breakfast is cheap domestic beer and leftover pizza, eaten straight out of the box). But that's really just one kind of culture, *high culture*, which we'll get to a bit later on.

More broadly, **culture** is a system of behaviour, beliefs, knowledge, practices, values, and concrete materials including buildings, tools, and sacred items. In this sense, everyone has a culture—in fact, many people can lay claim to more than one. But although we've described culture as a system, we don't mean to suggest that there is total agreement concerning any one culture and its constituent parts. Even those who belong to a particular culture may disagree about what it does or should include.

Let's talk about hockey. Just about everybody would agree that hockey is part of Canadian culture— but that's where agreement ends. Does success by Canada's national teams in international hockey mean we've succeeded as a culture? Not everyone would agree. Is fighting an integral part of the Canadian game? You don't have to be Don Cherry to get into an argument on that point. Does the sport's long history in this country make it more culturally important than soccer, even though the latter has higher youth participation rates and tends to be played by boys and girls in more equal numbers, representing a far broader range of ethnic and socioeconomic backgrounds? Hockey, as part of our national culture, is **contested**.

In more serious cases, aspects of a culture may be contested when they become instruments of oppression. Anne McGillivray and Brenda Comaskey, in *Black Eyes All of the Time: Intimate Violence, Aboriginal Women and the Justice System*, argue that we should not assume that Aboriginal women who have suffered spousal abuse "will view 'cultural' solutions in the same way as Aboriginal men" (McGillivray & Comaskey 1999: 18). Aboriginal justice typically calls for forgiving offenders and reintegrating them into the community; this is part of Aboriginal culture. However, many of the women McGillivray and Comaskey interviewed said that they would prefer to have their male abusers spend time in jail to give the abused time to feel safe again. Under these circumstances, these aspects of Aboriginal justice—forgiveness and keeping offenders in the community—become contested.

Culture often becomes contested over the question of **authenticity**. Culture involves traditions but is not confined by them. It is dynamic, changing over time. Authenticity carries the idea of being true to a particular culture, yet think of how broadly the word "authentic" can be applied and understood. For some, an "authentic Italian meal" may be something you'd have to fly to Tuscany to experience; for others, it comes from the pizzeria down the street. Authenticity becomes a problem when a colonial society studies a colonized culture and claims to know the secret of its authenticity. Edward Said, in *Orientalism*, criticized Western intellectuals for forming their impressions of the Middle East and central Asia from historical accounts written by nineteenth- and twentieth-century Western scholars. Once they had formed an idea of what "the Orient" was, these intellectuals negatively compared their rather romanticized (think Aladdin) notions of the Eastern world's traditions to their negative perceptions of its present. In effect, they said: "You are a corruption of what you used to be." That would be like someone saying to you: "I understand you better than you do, and you were better before."

It is a common mistake to view one's own culture as being contested, in a way that makes it dynamic and complex, while holding a narrow view of other cultures as somehow simple and fixed. This leads to unhealthy cultural stereotypes—"All Americans are ethnocentric, warmongering bullies; we Canadians are far more tolerant and diverse." It is important to appreciate that all cultures are contested and subject to change.

How authentic do you imagine this Mexican restaurant in Bucks County, Pennsylvania, is? Would you expect the proprietors to be Mexican? To have lived in Mexico? To have studied Mexican cooking at a US-based culinary arts school? How should authenticity be judged?

What do YOU think?

Who is the greatest Canadian athlete? Wayne Gretzky? Donovan Bailey? Christine Sinclair? Terry Fox? Ryder Hesjedal? Clara Hughes? Patrick Chan? What does your answer tell you about how you view sport and Canadian culture?

What Kinds of Culture Are There?

As we noted at the outset, there are different kinds of culture, apart from culture in the general sense that we've just outlined. The different kinds of cultures can be seen in terms of two oppositions:

1. dominant culture *versus* subculture and counterculture
2. high culture *versus* popular culture and mass culture

As we examine each of these oppositions, you will gain a better idea of why we say that culture is contested.

Dominant Culture versus Subculture and Counterculture

Look around and it isn't hard to see the signs of the dominant culture in Canada. The **dominant culture** is the one that, through its political and economic power, is able to impose its values, language, and ways of behaving and interpreting behaviour on a given society. The people most closely linked with the cultural mainstream are sometimes referred to as **dominants**. Although statistically their share of the overall population has dropped significantly in the last 20 years, it is fairly safe to say that white, English-speaking people of Christian and European stock make up the dominant culture in Canada. It is also fair to say that the dominant culture is middle-class. How do we know what the dominant culture looks like? Think of what culture is typically represented in Canadian morning shows like *Breakfast Television*, in commercials played on Canadian airwaves, and in television programs generally. Think of the expectations they express about what people own, what their concerns are, and how they live.

We can narrow our picture of Canada's dominant culture by taking a regionalist perspective. People living in the Atlantic provinces have good reason to suspect that the dominant culture lies in central or western Canada, where most big companies have their head offices, and where the greatest share of the national population is situated. But western Canada has several times produced political parties (the Social Credit, Reform, and, most recently, Wildrose parties, for instance) to protest the West's exclusion from the dominant political culture and its unfair treatment at the hands of institutions dominated by and situated in central Canada (like the big banks and the agencies of the federal government). Power and wealth tend to be concentrated in large cities, and central Canada is home to the country's two largest metropolitan areas, Toronto and Montreal.

Feminists argue that Canada's dominant culture is male. Let's look at our House of Commons for an example. Of the 308 members of Parliament elected in the May 2011 federal election, 74 (roughly 24 per cent) were women. Just 17 per cent of the ruling Conservative Party's elected MPs were women; in contrast, the NDP had more than twice that share, with 38 per cent of their MPs being women. Meanwhile, as of May 2013, six of the country's 13 provincial and territorial leaders are women—that's more than ever before, but a small number nevertheless. It seems, then, that the closer you are to power, the fewer women there are.

We could add age to our portrait of Canada's dominant culture as well. Those who are just starting or have just ended their careers often feel peripheral to the dominant culture. Other factors to consider are sexual orientation, level of education, and overall health (since those with disabilities or chronic medical conditions might feel outside the dominant culture). To summarize, our portrait of Canada's dominant culture looks something like this: white, English-speaking, heterosexual, male university graduate of European background between the ages of 25 and 55, in good health, who owns a home in a middle-class neighbourhood of a city in Ontario or Quebec. (I came *so* close—but I'm too old, and my Ontario town is too small for "city" status.)

Minority Cultures: Subcultures and Countercultures

Minority cultures are those that fall outside the cultural mainstream. These may be **countercultures**, which are groups that feel the power of the dominant culture and

What do YOU think?

Television both reflects and contributes to our sense of culture. Pick a sitcom you're familiar with (it's probably American). In your opinion, does is reflect the dominant culture we've just described? What are the principal attitudes, concerns, and occupations of its main characters? What sexualities and ethnic backgrounds do they represent (and represent positively, not just as the subject of jokes)? How much are the main characters like you? If you're familiar with recent Canadian sitcoms such as *Mr D, Corner Gas*, and *Little Mosque on the Prairie*, do you think they do a better job than their American counterparts of presenting characters outside the dominant culture?

exist in opposition to it, or **subcultures**, which differ in some way from the dominant culture but don't directly oppose it. Subcultures are typically characterized by a more neutral cultural contrast than countercultures are. Examples include computer nerds, lawyers, sociologists, stamp collectors, and so on. A subculture, then, is defined in terms of the minor cultural differences possessed by certain groups organized around occupations or hobbies, engaged in no significant opposition or challenge to the dominant culture.

Countercultures, as we noted, are defined oppositionally. They are characterized as groups that reject

QUICK HITS

Mind Traps in Understanding Culture

Try to avoid these common mind traps in understanding culture:

- thinking that "culture" refers only to high culture
- thinking that total agreement on what defines a culture can ever exist
- thinking that culture is synonymous with tradition and doesn't change over time
- thinking that "our" culture is contested whereas other cultures are comparably simple and fixed (for instance, the false but popular notion that Christians around the globe are quite different but that all Muslims, Hindus, Jews, Sikhs, or Buddhists essentially think alike).

Corner Gas producer/director Brent Butt (left) checks the monitor as Lorne Cardinal plays a scene from the sitcom's last season. During the show's six seasons it was never pointed out that Cardinal's character, Davis Quinton, was Aboriginal. Does that surprise you? Do you think an American show would have handled a Native American character the same way?

What are Goths? Most people will be able to summon a rough image: dyed black (or, less often, blue) hair, dark clothes, with white makeup that contrasts sharply with clothing and hair colour. When we think of Goths we may think of a fascination with death and with art—especially music and film—that reflects this fascination. But who are the people who belong to this counter-culture? What can we add to this picture?

First, they tend to be young. The Goth lifestyle seems to be a phenomenon that is invented and re-invented by the youth cohort of the time. Some bloggers claim that there are three generations of Goths, each not so aware of its predecessors or reincar-nations; the "generation gap" seems a perpet-ual feature. Second, they are typically white. There are Internet references to black and Asian Goths, but it appears their numbers are smaller. Third, although there has been, to the best of our knowledge, no significant sociological study done of this, they seem to come mostly from middle-class families.

Oral/Internet history places the origins of the Goth subculture in the late 1970s. The Goth of that period is associated with the song "Bela Lugosi's Dead," released in 1979 by Bauhaus, and with the look and music of bands such as The Cure and Siouxsie and the Banshees.

The opposition of Goths to domi-nant culture is expressed most clearly in their dress and overall appearance, but it goes beyond this visual aspect. The early Goths rejected the yuppie world of finan-cial self-indulgence and the conservative politics of Margaret Thatcher, Ronald Reagan, and, here at home, Brian Mulroney. They pursued a life concerned with less world-exploitive politics and cultish small-mar-ket arts. Succeeding generations of Goths have taken up different causes, but they carry on the traditional appearance and connection to the arts that their predecessors established.

High Culture versus Popular Culture

High culture is the culture of the elite, a distinct minority. It is associated with theatre, opera, classical

certain elements of the dominant culture (for instance, clothing styles or sexual norms). Examples of coun-terculture range from the relatively harmless hippies of the 1960s and early 1970s to the dangerous biker gangs, such as the Hell's Angels, that have flourished since the 1960s. "Alternative" was a watchword of the 1990s, used to describe a culture of music and fash-ion that defined itself in contrast to what was then the mainstream.

A counterculture still in evidence today is that of the Goths. Descriptions of this counterculture abound on the Internet, from which the following brief descrip-tion is summarized.

LARPers don elaborate costumes to engage in live action role play, reenacting battles from history or fantasy. Subculture or counterculture?

QUICK HITS

Are You Excluded from the Dominant Culture?

Here is a simple, informal test.

1. How likely is it that political leaders (your prime minister, premier, local federal or provincial representative, mayor, etc.) are like you in gender, religion, clothing style, language, and ethnic background?
2. How likely is it that the homes portrayed in most television series look like your home?
3. How likely is it that the lead character in a movie lives a life like yours?
4. How likely is it that your boss is of the same gender, ethnicity, and age as you?
5. How likely is it that the people who get arrested on reality-based police shows look like you and your neighbours?
6. How likely is it that people like you are seen demonstrating or protesting something on the TV news or the front page of an online newspaper?
7. How likely is it that there are a lot of derogatory slang terms that refer to people like you?
8. How likely are people like you to be called a "special interest" group?
9. How often are people like you told they're "too sensitive" or "too pushy"?
10. How likely are you to be asked, "So where do you come from?"

For questions 1–4, "not very likely" and "not at all likely" equal exclusion from the dominant culture; for questions 5–10, "somewhat likely" and "very likely" equal exclusion from the dominant culture.

A counterculture, if it becomes popular, may have to reinvent itself or "push the envelope" to keep from going mainstream. What does this cartoon suggest about how and why culture is contested?

music and ballet, "serious" works of literary fiction and non-fiction, serious documentaries and "artsy" films (note: *films*, not *movies*) that may be difficult to appreciate without having taken courses on the subject, and a "cultivated palate" for certain high-priced foods and alcoholic beverages. High culture is sometimes referred to as "elite culture," which Canadian sociologist Karen Anderson defines as follows:

> Elite culture is produced for and appreciated by a limited number of people with specialized interests. It tends to be evaluated in terms of "universal" criteria of artistic merit and to be seen as a sign of prestige. Appreciation of elite culture usually entails a process of learning and the acquisition of specific tastes. (Anderson 1996: 471)

French sociologist **Pierre Bourdieu** (1930–2002) coined the term **cultural capital** to refer to the knowledge and skills needed to acquire the sophisticated tastes that mark someone as a person of high culture. The more cultural capital you have, the "higher" your cultural class.

Popular culture, on the other hand, is the culture of the majority, particularly of those people who do not have power (the working class, the less educated, women, and racialized minorities). Serious academic discussion of popular culture has grown with the recent rise of **cultural studies** courses and programs. Cultural studies draws on both the social sciences (primarily sociology) and the humanities (primarily literature and media studies) to cast light on the significance of, and meanings expressed in, popular culture, a topic that previously had been mostly neglected by academics.

Popular Culture and Mass Culture

There is a crucial distinction to be made between popular culture and mass culture. The two differ in terms of **agency**, the ability of "the people" to be creative or productive with what a colonial power, a dominant culture, or an instrument of mass media has given them. Sociologists disagree on how much agency people have. Those who believe that people take an active role in shaping the culture they consume (e.g. the clothing they buy, the music they listen to, the Internet sites they visit, the TV shows and movies they watch) use the term "popular culture" to describe the majority of those cultural products that fall outside the world of the cultural elite. Those who believe people have little or no agency in the culture they consume are more likely to use the term **mass culture**. They tend to believe that big companies (e.g. Walmart, McDonald's, Disney, and Microsoft) and powerful governments dictate what people buy, watch, value, and believe. Many see the Internet as a boon for popular culture, enabling people to get their stories, social commentaries, photos, and so on, seen by an enormous audience without any sponsorship by big companies; critics argue that the charming video of cat tricks or dancing babies doesn't go viral without a powerful plug from a celebrity tweeting about it or a news agency reporting on it. They also see it as mindless escapism distracting people from real social issues and political manipulation by governments. These differing viewpoints highlight the difference between popular culture and mass culture.

One feature of mass culture is what French sociologist **Jean Baudrillard** (1929–2007) calls **simulacra**. Simulacra are stereotypical cultural images produced and reproduced like material goods or commodities by the media and sometimes by scholars. For example, the Inuit are often represented by simulacra of described practices (e.g. rubbing noses, abandoning elders, and wife-sharing) and physical objects (e.g. igloos, kayaks). These images tend to distort contemporary Inuit "reality."

Consider the way the inukshuk, the Inuit stone figure, has become a Canadian cultural symbol, with models of these stone figures sold in tourist shops across the country. It has such cultural currency that it was incorporated into the logo for the 2010 Winter Olympics held in BC—a province with no Inuit community.

Baudrillard describes simulacra as being "hyperreal"—that is, likely to be considered more real than what actually exists or existed. He illustrates the principle with an analogy of a map, but we will use a GPS system instead. Imagine you were driving down a country road on a winter's night. Your GPS system told you to turn right ahead onto a major road that would lead you straight home, yet all your eyes saw was a narrow dirt road covered in snow. If you followed that road and got stuck at a dead-end street, the GPS system was hyperreal to you: you believed the information it was giving you was more real than what your eyes detected. This information is thus a simulacrum.

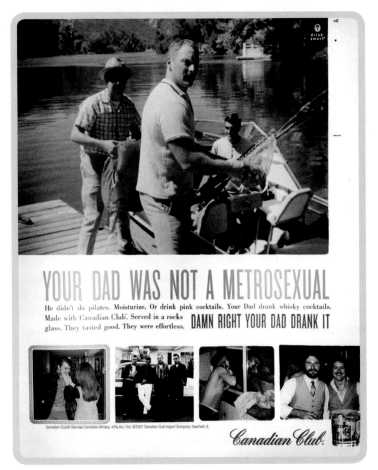

Advertisers often promote simulacra in order to manufacture a need or desire for the products they're trying to sell. What simulacra are being presented here? How persuasive is the message?

When sociologists encourage their students to be critical of what the media present, they are hoping their students will be able to detect simulacra. The famous "weapons of mass destruction" never found in Iraq are a classic example: governments operated as though these weapons actually existed. The weapons were hyperreal.

British sociologist John Fiske takes the popular culture position. He does not believe that people are brainless consumers of mass culture; rather, he believes that the power bloc—the political and cultural institutions with the greatest influence on society—merely supplies people with resources that they resist, evade, or turn to their own ends. He recognizes agency and warns about the dangers of sociologists presenting people as mere dupes of mass media. And without using the word, he expresses his concern about the dangers of **victimology**, in this context referring to an outlook that inaccurately diminishes groups by portraying them as unable to help themselves, to exercise agency.

An important distinction between the two positions involves the contrast, identified by de Certeau (1984), between *decipherment* and *reading*. **Decipherment** is the process of looking in a text for the definitive interpretation, for the intent (conscious or unconscious) of the culture industry in creating the text. For sociologists who believe that mass culture predominates, decipherment is about looking for the message that mass media presents people with, without allowing them to challenge or reject it by substituting their own.

Sociologists who believe that popular rather than mass culture predominates tend to use the term *reading*. **Reading** is the process in which people treat what is provided by the culture industry as a resource, a text to be interpreted as they see fit, in ways not necessarily intended by the creators of the text. The sociological technique of reading involves analyzing the narratives of those using the text in this way.

Eric Michaels (1986), describing the way the Australian Aborigines received the classic "shoot-'em-up" movie *First Blood* (starring Sylvester Stallone as the Vietnam War vet turned vigilante Rambo), offers a good example of the difference between decipherment and reading. A mass culture interpretation of the movie would be that it delivers a propaganda message about the triumph of the good capitalist West over the evil communist East. But the Australian Aborigines had their own reading of the film, as Michaels explains:

[T]hey understood the major conflict to be that between Rambo, whom they saw as a representative of the Third World, and the white officer class—a set of meanings that were clearly relevant to their experience of white, postcolonial paternalism and that may well have been functional in helping them to make a resistant sense of their interracial relationships. . . . The Aborigines also produced tribal or kinship relations between Rambo and the prisoners he was rescuing that were more relevant to their social experience than any nationalistic relationships structured around the East–West axis. . . . (Michaels 1986)

What do YOU think?

Reality TV has grown enormously over the past decade, with shows like *America's Got Talent* and *The Voice* giving off-the-street entrants the chance to realize a dream and achieve national celebrity (thanks to voter viewing). Do you think this is evidence of popular culture, or is the notion that the people are the real stars just a media manipulation?

Norms

Norms are rules or standards of behaviour that are expected of members of a group, society, or culture. There isn't always consensus concerning these standards: norms may be contested along the sociological lines of ethnicity, "race," gender, and age. A quick illustration: I remember, as a young child, being embarrassed when my grandmother refused to pick up after her poodle. Although stoop-and-scoop laws weren't yet in effect, it had become common custom, as far as I was aware, and yet my grandmother was completely unselfconscious, even as the neighbours eyed her and her poodle with annoyance. Many years later, when I was engaged to be married, my grandmother reprimanded me for failing to write out the invitations individually, by hand. "It is bad form," she said, "to send printed invitations unless you are inviting more than one hundred guests." Coming from different generations, the norms we recognized were very different.

Norms are expressed in a culture through various means, from ceremonies that reflect cultural mores or customs (a wedding, for example) to symbolic articles of dress (the white dress worn by the bride). In the following sections, we'll have a look at the different ways in which norms are expressed and enforced.

Sanctions

People react to how others follow or do not follow norms. If the reaction is one that supports the behaviour, it is called a **positive sanction**. It is a reward for "doing the right thing." Positive sanctions range from small gestures like a smile, a high five, or a supportive comment, to larger material rewards like a bonus for hard work on the job. A hockey player who gets into a fight is positively sanctioned by teammates at the bench banging their sticks against the boards, or by the cheering crowd.

A **negative sanction** is a reaction designed to tell offenders they have violated a norm. It could be anything from a glare, an eye roll, or a sarcastic quip to a parking ticket or the fine you pay at the library for an overdue book. When someone around me says, "Hey, look—it's Santa Claus," I know that behind the apparent joke is a negative sanction about my well-proportioned frame and my bushy grey beard. Sticks and stones, right?

Folkways, Mores, and Taboos

Folkways

William Graham Sumner (1840–1910) distinguished three kinds of norms based on how seriously they are respected and sanctioned. He used the term **folkways** for those norms governing day-to-day matters. These are norms that you "*should* not" (as opposed to "*must* not") violate. They are the least respected and most weakly sanctioned. The term "etiquette" can often by applied to folkways. George Costanza, on the TV show *Seinfeld*, continually violated folkways by, for instance, double-dipping chips at a party or by fetching a chocolate pastry out of the garbage.

Mores

Mores (pronounced like the eels—*morays*) are taken much more seriously than folkways. You "*must* not" violate them. Some mores—against rape, killing, vandalism, and most forms of stealing, for example—are enshrined in the criminal code as laws. Violation of some mores, even if they are not laws, will meet with shock or severe disapproval. Booing the national anthem of the visiting team prior to a sporting event is likely to cause offence among supporters of the visitors and even anger or embarrassment among fans of the home side. Mores are complicated and may be contested. Mores of cleanliness, for instance, are in the cultural eye of the beholder. In Britain, dogs are allowed in pubs; in Canada, they are not. This does not mean that bars in Canada are more sanitary than those in Britain. Differences in mores of cleanliness can lead to serious problems when, for instance, an overdeveloped Western sense of what is hygienic jeopardizes the health of a hospital patient (see the example of the Hmong study in Chapter 18, on medical sociology).

Like folkways, mores change over time. A young woman sporting a tattoo would once have been seen as violating the mores of acceptable behaviour for a lady. Today, many women have tattoos and display them without arousing the kind of shock or condemnation generally produced when mores are violated.

The Senators' Chris Neil raises his arms to encourage the home crowd after a fight in Ottawa. Do you see any evidence of a positive sanction? What form of negative sanction should the player expect to receive for his behaviour?

Taboos

A **taboo** is a norm so deeply ingrained in our social consciousness that the mere thought or mention of it is enough to arouse disgust or revulsion. Cannibalism, incest, and child pornography immediately come to mind. Taboos affect our dietary habits. Eating dogs, cats, or other animals that might be considered family pets is taboo in North American culture. There are religious taboos surrounding the consumption of certain foods—pork by Jews and Muslims, beef by Hindus. Some cultures recognize gender taboos, such as those surrounding women who interfere with or attempt to partake in typical male activities. Like folkways and mores, taboos will differ from culture to culture.

Culture Symbols

Symbols are cultural items that come to take on tremendous meaning within a culture or subculture of a society. They can be either tangible (i.e. physical), material objects (as illustrated in the narrative on page 89) or intangible, non-material objects, such as songs or even the memory of events. Just as culture itself is contested, culture symbols are likely to be interpreted differently by people inside and outside of the culture they represent.

Symbols of nationality tend to take on tremendous cultural significance. Think of the maple leaf a

Canadian tourist stitches to the backpack she wears when travelling in Europe. It's meant to stand not just for her country of origin but for a whole set of qualities that we like to think make up the Canadian cultural identity—courtesy, tolerance, knowledgeableness, peacefulness, and so on. To the European who sees it and recognizes it as a symbol of Canadian cultural identity, the maple leaf might conjure up a very different set of qualities: our rejection of the Kyoto agreement on climate change, our tar sands, our seal hunt, our arrogant central Canadian bankers . . . Some of these are recent developments, illustrating another point: the cultural significance of symbols can change over time.

The Veil as a Symbol for Canadian Muslim Women

Few clothing symbols have a greater power to evoke emotions than the Muslim veil, or (in Arabic) *hijab*. For many in the West, it is seen as a symbol of patriarchal domination by weapons-waving misogynist young men of the Taliban or al Qaeda, similar in effect to the full-length, screen-faced *burqa* that hides Afghan women from the world of opportunities and freedom, and to the head scarves like the *roosari* that Iranian women are forced by law to wear.

It is important to understand why women of various cultures—especially in Canada—choose to wear the veil. For this information there can be no better source than the community of Canadian women of Middle Eastern background who have considered the choice themselves. Some of their narratives are presented on page 90. What stands out, as we read their views, is that for a significant number of women in Canada, as for those women in France who opposed a law that would ban the veil in French schools, the veil is a matter of choice, not command.

For the perspective of Canadian Muslim women on this subject we are drawing upon a groundbreaking study carried out in Montreal by Iranian-Canadian anthropologist Homa Hoodfar (2003). The voices Hoodfar recorded speak compellingly of their choice to wear the veil as a way of opposing restrictions placed on them (and not their brothers) as teenagers by parents concerned that their daughters would fall prey to the irreligious sex-, alcohol-, and drug-related behaviours of North American culture. Some saw veil-wearing as a step, together with Qur'anic study and banding together with Canadian Muslim women of different cultural

What do YOU think?

For Americans, the cultural significance of their flag is firmly entrenched: it is the subject of their national anthem; in schools, they pledge allegiance to it; and many support a law that makes it illegal to burn or otherwise desecrate it. But, like the maple leaf, the stars and stripes symbolizes a whole set of cultural values that make up their national identity. What cultural values do you think the American flag suggests to someone in each of these cities?

Chicago, Illinois
Austin, Texas
Tijuana, Mexico
Tel Aviv, Israel
Moscow, Russia
Hong Kong, China
Baghdad, Iraq

What does the stars and stripes mean to you?

backgrounds, down a path of opposition to some of the patriarchal mores of their specific cultures. In addition, taking the veil gave some women the opportunity to defend their faith against the ethnocentric ignorance of some of their fellow Canadians. The narratives on page 90 are instructive.

Values

Values are the standards used by a culture to describe abstract qualities such as goodness, beauty, and justice, and to assess the behaviour of others. Values have long been a topic of great interest to sociologists. Max

The Point Is...

The Jackrocks Story: A Narrative about the Power of Symbols

In the fall of 1989, I travelled through rural Virginia on a short lecture tour, having been invited by staff and students of Southwest Virginia Community College who had attended a lecture of mine during their spring break. I spent the first night of my stay at the home of the college president. It was elegant, finely furnished, with everything in its place. While there, I noticed something that surprised me. In a glass case—the kind normally used to hold curios and *objets d'art*, such as glass and china figurines—I saw two 6-pointed objects, each one made of three nails. They reminded me of the jacks I had played with as a child, but bigger, and menacing. Why had these mean-looking items been placed on display?

The next night I stayed with a coal miner's family. It was a fascinating evening. I learned about the effects of moonshine on my brain and body, and that the term "cakewalk," which we use for a surprisingly easy task, comes from an old game resembling musical chairs, in which the winner receives a cake as a prize. More seriously, I learned about the dynamics of a months-long coal miner's strike in the one-industry area. I was taken on a tour of the strike centre, where bunk beds were being built to accommodate the families of striking workers who had been thrown out of their homes for failing to pay the rent. The people I met there were friendly, but the long strike was crushing their spirit.

The mining company was owned by people from outside the area—foreigners, in the eyes of the locals. The company owners had circumvented the picket lines by trucking the coal out at night, but striking miners in camouflage had found ways to thwart their efforts. One of my cherished souvenirs of the trip is a camouflage T-shirt bearing the slogan "Holding the Line in '89." I wore it with pride during a strike at Ontario community colleges that same fall.

The next day, at the college, I spoke to a sociology class about symbols. Near the end of the class, I asked students to name some local symbols. One student shouted out "jackrocks." When I asked what "jackrocks" were, I got a description of the 6-pointed objects I had seen in the president's glass case, as well as a bag full of jackrocks handed to me by a student who went to his car to get them. I was told that one of the tactics used to keep the coal trucks from shipping out the coal was to toss these jackrocks underneath the tires. The jackrocks had become symbols of the miners' resistance. They appeared in store windows in the town nearest the mine, and I was given a pair of small, aluminum jackrock earrings. I then understood why the college president kept the two jackrocks in the glass case. He was from Florida, and therefore a "foreigner" to the area. By keeping the jackrocks in a place of honour, he was expressing solidarity with his students and their community.

What do YOU think?

1. What cultural significance did the jackrocks have for the local people of southwestern Virginia?

2. Why do you think the college president kept jackrocks in his glass case at home? Do you think he fully appreciated their significance?

Telling It Like It Is   Student POVs

The Hijab as Worn by Young Canadian Muslim Women in Montreal

The narrative of a 19-year-old Palestinian-Canadian woman

The veil has freed me from arguments and headaches. I always wanted to do many things that women normally do not do in my culture. I had thought living in Canada would give me that opportunity. But when I turned fourteen, my life changed. My parents started to limit my activities and even telephone conversations. My brothers were free to go and come as they pleased, but my sister and I were to be good Muslim girls. . . . Life became intolerable for me. The weekends were hell.

Then as a way out, I asked to go to Qur'anic classes on Saturdays. There I met with several veiled women of my age. . . . None of them seemed to face my problems. Some told me that since they took the veil, their parents know that they are not going to do anything that goes against Muslim morality. The more I hung around with them, the more convinced I was that the veil is the answer to all Muslim girls' problems here in North America. Because parents seem to be relieved and assured that you are not going to do stupid things, and your community knows that you are acting like a Muslim woman, you are much freer. (quoted in Hoodfar 2003: 20–1)

The narrative of a 17-year-old Pakistani-Canadian woman

Although we did not intermingle much with non–Indian-Canadians, I very much felt at home and part of the wider society. This, however, changed as I got older and clearly my life was different than many girls in my class. I did not talk about boyfriends and did not go out. I did not participate in extracurricular activities. Gradually, I began feeling isolated. Then my cousin and I decided together to wear the veil and made a pact to ignore people's comments; no matter how much hardship we suffered at school, we would keep our veils on. . . .

At first it was difficult. At school people joked and asked stupid questions, but after three months they took us more seriously and there was even a little bit of respect. We even got a little more respect when we talked about Islam in our classes, while before our teacher dismissed what we said if it didn't agree with her casual perceptions. (quoted in Hoodfar 2003: 28–9)

The narrative of Mona, an Egyptian-Canadian woman

I would never have taken up the veil if I lived in Egypt. Not that I disagree with that, but I see it as part of the male imposition of rules. . . . The double standard frustrates me. But since the Gulf War, seeing how my veiled friends were treated, I made a vow to wear the veil to make a point about my Muslimness and Arabness. I am delighted when people ask me about my veil and Islam, because it gives me a chance to point out their prejudices concerning Muslims. (Hoodfar 2003: 30)

A Muslim student from Montreal reacts to the examples

The young women in these articles claim that wearing the hijab, overall, brought them joy and happiness. However, look at the reason they decided to wear the hijab. In the first example, it was because her parents were not letting her go out and be free like her brothers. So she wore it to gain her own freedom, not to appreciate anything about the culture. In the second, it was because they did not talk about going out or boyfriends. Big deal! Many people do not talk about those things. It was their own minds that made them feel isolated, not the culture surrounding them. And the third example, I feel she did it for more right reasons than any of the others. Nevertheless, to prove a point???

I do not wear this "veil," but have relatives that do. It does not make me a "poor" Muslim woman. Even if a girl has this "veil" on, she can still do bad things and be persuaded to do bad things just like anyone else.

—Ferita Haque

Weber's identification of the Protestant work ethic is one early example of a sociological study of values, and many others have followed since. But in spite of these studies, values remain difficult to understand and to represent accurately. What makes the issue especially puzzling is that the values that people claim to have are not always the ones they act upon. Do we recognize, then, the value that is professed or the value that is reflected in human action? Is the person who preaches a value but fails to honour it in his or her daily life necessarily a hypocrite?

Canadian and American Values

Canadians regularly compare themselves with Americans on anything from foreign policy to curling prowess. Some Canadians like to define themselves by what an American is *not*, making statements like, "A Canadian is an unarmed American with health insurance." But how much do our two neighbouring societies really differ in their values?

Michael Adams, of the Environics Research Group, has been conducting and publishing opinion polls since the early 1980s. During the 1990s, he measured and tracked 100 "social values" of Canadians. In *Fire and Ice: The United States, Canada and the Myth of Converging Values* (2003) he contrasts the values of Canadians and Americans, aiming to demonstrate that Canadians and Americans are becoming more different rather than more alike in their values. It certainly seemed so in 2003, when the American military was heading into Iraq and Canada was not, and when a modest majority of Canadians supported gay marriage and the liberalization of marijuana laws, which a majority opposed in the US.

Adams based his findings on data from Environics polls conducted in the US and Canada in 1992, 1996, and 2000. It's always important to look at the data critically. For instance, the polls invited respondents to "talk" about their values. But you will recall that there is often a difference between the values we profess and those we act upon. Another point: is the time period—from 1992 to 2000—long enough to produce evidence of what he calls "long-term shifts"? All of this data was gathered before 11 September 2001. Adams is quick to point this out, though he argues that the events of that day would only make the differences he identified greater.

Even Canadian and American flags reflect different cultural values. The Canadian flag, handed down by the government in 1965, features a leaf that is not native to most of the country. First sewn by Betsy Ross, the American flag emerged as a powerful symbol during the American Revolution and is still the subject of the country's national anthem. Children in the US "pledge allegiance to the flag" at the beginning of the school day.

Here we will look at one of the value clusters Adams identified: **patriarchy**. We have left out his interpretation of the findings, leaving you, the reader, to put in your own. Adams used two statements to measure patriarchy:

1. "The father of the family must be master in his own home."
2. "Men are naturally superior to women."

Respondents were asked whether they agreed with these two statements. Tables 4.1 and 4.2 present the results.

Note the increase in the difference after each four-year period. Even the ranges of the two countries do not intersect: agreement with this statement among Canadian respondents ranged from a province-wide low of 15 per cent (in Quebec) to a high of 21 per cent (in the Prairie provinces) in the 2000 poll; agreement among US respondents ranged from 29 per cent in New England all the way to 71 per cent in the Deep South (Adams 2003: 87).

The percentage of difference between Canadian and American agreement on the second question was less than on the first (see Table 4.2), but notice how the difference again increased over each four-year period.

Table 4.1 Percentage of respondents agreeing with the statement "The father of the family must be master in his own home"

YEAR	CANADA	UNITED STATES	DIFFERENCE
1992	26	42	16
1996	20	44	24
2000	18	49	31

Source: Adams 2003: 50–1. Copyright © Michael Adams, 2003. Reprinted by permission of Penguin Group (Canada), a division of Pearson Education Canada.

Table 4.2 Percentage of respondents agreeing with the statement "Men are naturally superior to women"

YEAR	CANADA	UNITED STATES	DIFFERENCE
1992	26	30	4
1996	23	32	9
2000	24	38	14

Source: Adams 2003: 50–1. Copyright © Michael Adams, 2003. Reprinted by permission of Penguin Group (Canada), a division of Pearson Education Canada.

What do YOU think?

1. The findings in tables 4.1 and 4.2 appear to support Adams' thesis that American and Canadian social values are becoming less alike. How convincing do you find them?

2. What do you think the cause of the growing difference might be? What do you think a more recent poll on the same questions might show?

3. Could the difference be caused by the greater participation of Americans in organized religion? If so, do you think the use of values likely to be shaped by religion is a fair way to measure Canadian–American social difference?

Ethnocentrism

Ethnocentrism occurs when someone holds up one culture (usually the culture of the ethnocentric individual) as the standard by which all cultures are to be judged. It follows a simple formula: "All cultures like the gold-standard culture are good, praiseworthy, beautiful, moral, and modern. Those that are not are bad, ugly, immoral, and primitive." Ethnocentrism can manifest itself in many forms, but it often entails declaring that there is only one right way (the way of the cultural model) to run a business, handle finances, or manage social policy.

Ethnocentrism is often the product of ignorance, something that Hmong refugees living in the United States have experienced. The Hmong have been targeted in the US because of their supposed practice of stealing, killing, and eating dogs. Lack of evidence or truth does not deter an ethnocentric public from spreading these stories about a "foreign" culture. The false stories follow particular themes:

[Rumoured] methods of [dog] procurement vary. Some are coaxed home by Hmong children. Some were adopted from animal shelters. . . . Others are strays. The most common accusation is theft, often from backyards, sometimes leaving the head and collar as mute testimony to Rover's passing. . . . The dog is usually an expensive one, often owned by a doctor. The theft is observed, the license plate number is marked down. When the police check, the dog is already in some Hmong family's pot.

The supposed proof varies. That fixture in the urban legend, the garbage man, reports the presence of canine remains in Hmong garbage cans. Carcasses are seen hanging in the cellar by meter readers, salesmen, or whomever. Freezers are said to be full of frozen dogs. A bizarre touch is that the dogs are supposedly skinned alive to make them more tasty. (quoted in Fadiman 1997: 190–1)

On a larger scale, ethnocentrism has played a role in the colonizing efforts of powerful nations imposing their political, economic, and religious beliefs on the indigenous populations of lands they "discovered." The following discussion highlights how Canada's First Nations were forced by an ethnocentric government to abandon a traditional custom.

The Potlatch Act of 1884

The **potlatch** is a traditional ceremony of Northwest Coast Aboriginal people. It often involves the acquisition or affirmation of hereditary names. During the ceremony, the host of the potlatch demonstrates his social, economic, and spiritual worthiness to be given the hereditary name. An important aspect of the event is the telling, singing, and acting out of stories. In this way, potlatches affirm the possession of the stories, songs, dances, carved and painted images, masks, and musical instruments used by the hosting group to celebrate the cultural history of the name and those identified with it. These hereditary names carry more than just symbolic significance: they are connected with rights to fish, hunt, or forage for plants in a particular territory, and with the responsibility to conserve the living entities within that territory. Potlatches serve to maintain the strength and social unity of the group.

Another important aspect of the potlatch is the giving away of gifts and possessions. One traditional way for a high-ranking man to prove he was worthy of his position was to give away many gifts. The hierarchical nature of Northwest Coast culture made this competitive, as those holding or aspiring to high rank gave away as much as they could afford. The level of competition rose after European contact, in part because of the sudden availability of European manufactured goods, but also because of the toll European diseases took on the Native population. The population of the Kwakiutl of Vancouver Island, for example, dropped from roughly 8,000 in 1835 to around 2,000 in 1885. When diseases decimated lineages entitled to important names, more distant relatives would vie for prestigious family names. In some cases, competition could become socially divisive, and there were even incidents in which property was destroyed as a show of wealth ("I am so rich, that this property means nothing to me"). Such incidents appear to have been rare, but over-reported in the literature.

In 1884, the Government of Canada, under pressure from church leaders opposed to "pagan practices" and fearful of the Native population because of rumoured Métis, Cree, and Blackfoot hostility on the prairies, made the potlatch illegal with the following decree:

> Every Indian or other person who engages in or assists in celebrating the Indian festival known as the "Potlatch" . . . is guilty of a misdemeanour, and shall be liable to imprisonment for a term of not more than six nor less than two months in any gaol or other place of confinement, and any Indian or other person who encourages, either directly or indirectly, an Indian or Indians to get up such a festival or dance, or to celebrate the same, or who shall assist in the celebration of same, is guilty of a like offense, and shall be liable to the same punishment.

In 1921, 45 of the highest-ranking Kwakiutl were arrested. Twenty-two were sentenced to prison terms of two to three months. The people lost many sacred potlatch items that were taken as a condition for the release of community members arrested but not charged. The items became the property of the Minister of Indian Affairs, who distributed them to art collectors and museums.

In 1951, the potlatch ban was repealed. But it wasn't until 1975 that the National Museum in Ottawa declared it would return the sacred items—provided they be kept in museums. The Royal Ontario Museum returned its items in 1988, and the National Museum of the American Indian in New York repatriated some of its holdings in 1993. Some items were never recovered.

It should be noted that such incidents of ethnocentrism are not confined to the West, or to white people. When the Japanese seized control of its northern islands from the Ainu, the **indigenous** people there, they developed and implemented ethnocentric policies and laws similar to those enacted by the governments of Canada and the United States concerning their indigenous people.

Eurocentrism

Eurocentrism involves taking a broadly defined "European" (i.e. western and northern European, plus North American) position to address others, and assuming that the audience shares (or would like to share) that position. It can be seen in historical references to the "known world"—i.e. the world as it was known by Europeans—and to Christopher Columbus "discovering," in 1492, continents that were already home to millions of people. It foregrounds discoveries and contributions that are Western, and backgrounds those that are not. Did you know that our standard numbering system is known (poorly) as the Hindu–Arabic system? Did you know that corn, squash and pumpkins, most beans, peppers (hot and sweet), potatoes, tomatoes, and sunflowers—arguably the most, by volume, of all the crops currently grown—were first grown by Aboriginal people? The Eurocentric perspective of many textbooks used here in the West tends to champion advances made by people of European stock while downplaying (or altogether

Going Global
Observing Cultural Globalization in Taiwan

The impact of cultural globalization struck me when I was visiting the Taipei night market in Taiwan. As I was shopping for clothes, I turned a corner and was jolted by the sudden appearance of a tall black man. As my mind and eyes adjusted, I realized that it was none other than NBA star Michael Jordan, decked out in his Chicago Bulls uniform, circa 1996. True, It was merely a life-sized cardboard cut-out, used for promotional purposes, but it was a shock nevertheless.

A few days later, talking to a high school class in Taipei, I asked the students what their favourite sport was. I was expecting it to be baseball, given Taiwan's enviable international record in Little League Baseball. I was surprised to hear most of them answer, "Basketball!"

While writing up this narrative, I checked on some statistics, and I noticed something interesting. While Taiwan had been very successful in international Little League Baseball at all age levels (9–12, 14–16, and 16–18) throughout the 1970s and 1980s, that success was not repeated from the mid-1990s, when Michael Jordan was at the pinnacle of his career and international fame, into the early twenty-first century, when Chinese centre Yao Ming made his successful debut with the Houston Rockets. The NBA has, for some time, been very aggressive in marketing its product around the globe. I wondered: could Taiwan's baseball program be a victim of cultural globalization? Was a significant aspect of Taiwanese culture being pushed aside through the marketing efforts of a commercially successful North American sports league?

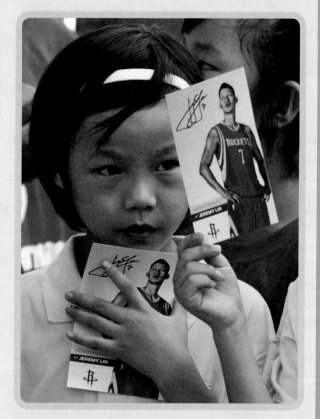

Basketball's popularity got a boost in the North American Chinese community when point guard Jeremy Lin, a second-generation American of Chinese/Taiwanese descent, was promoted to the starting lineup of the NBA's New York Knicks in 2012 (he's since moved to the Houston Rockets, where another Chinese player, Yao Ming, made his mark). Could you imagine a North American athlete gaining notoriety here at home for accomplishments abroad in a sport like soccer, cricket, or rugby?

ignoring) important non-European developments such as these.

Cultural Globalization

Manfred Steger defines cultural globalization as "the intensification and expansion of cultural flows across the globe" (2003: 69). Our concern is with the one-way flow of culture from the West, or what we might call the "Americanization" of the world. Think of the factors. First of all, English has emerged as by far the most prominent language of science, of the Internet, and of other powerful media. Second, American movies and television are seen in almost every country in the world. But to label this "American" culture is perhaps giving it too broad a scope, when you consider that it is just a small number of transnational companies—Time Warner, Comcast, Viacom, and Disney in the US, as well as the European companies Bertelsmann and Vivendi, and Sony in Japan—that control most of the media. Not only do these companies reap enormous dividends by exporting their respective brands of Western culture to consumers across the globe, but as Steger points out, they draw audiences abroad away from the culture of their own countries into a global "gossip market" that revolves around the "vacuous details of the private lives of American celebrities like Britney Spears, Jennifer Lopez, Leonardo DiCaprio, and Kobe Bryant" (Steger 2003: 77).

It's worth noting that the interpretation of globalized items of American culture are not necessarily the same abroad as they are in the US. The classic study of a cultural reading by a non-Western audience of a Western cultural item is described by anthropologist Laura Bohannan in "Shakespeare in the Bush" (1966). In it she describes her experience of telling the story of Shakespeare's *Hamlet* to the Tiv of West Africa, and the reading they put on it. The article concludes with the words of a Tiv elder. After admitting that he had enjoyed Bohannan's story, told "with very few mistakes," the elder said:

> Sometime . . . you must tell us some more stories of your country. We, who are elders, will instruct you in their true meaning, so that when you return to your own land your elders will see that you have not been sitting in the bush, but among those who know things and who have taught you wisdom. (Bohannan 1966: 47)

Reverse Ethnocentrism

Reverse ethnocentrism involves assuming that a particular culture that is not one's own is better than one's own in some way. Reverse ethnocentrism sets an absolute standard that one's own culture does not or cannot match. In the United States, liberal Americans who blame their own country's cultural values and foreign policy for terrorist attacks on Americans at home and abroad are sometimes accused of reverse ethnocentrism and anti-Americanism by more conservative thinkers.

The myth of the **noble savage** is a product of reverse ethnocentrism. The term refers to an idealized representation of primitive culture that symbolizes the innate goodness of humanity when free of the corrupting influence of civilization. The image of the noble savage, which is frequently invoked by opponents of globalization, is typically drawn by matching the perceived flaws of Western civilization—pollution, consumerism, exploitation, welfare—with their opposites: environmental balance, subsistence economy, fair trade, peace.

Prototype for New Understanding #23 (2005), by Vancouver artist Brian Jungen. What do you think the message of this art is? Is it a critique of globalization? Would the message differ depending on whether the artist is Aboriginal or not?

A strong sense of reverse ethnocentrism is sometimes felt by the children of immigrants, who may turn their backs on their parents' cultural roots in an attempt to fit into their adoptive culture. Children of families that have immigrated to the West can be bombarded by messages implying that the cultural ideal is not their own, not the one of their parents or grandparents. When these first-generation Canadian children achieve positions of linguistic power by having "better English" than their parents, and when peer pressure makes them want to be like "real Canadians," they can easily succumb to reverse ethnocentrism.

Telling It Like It Is

An Author POV

A Sociologist Sees Beauty in Taiwan: Reverse Ethnocentrism

It was my first trip to Asia. Not a moment passed when I wasn't aware I wasn't in Canada. The streets of Taipei, capital of Taiwan, buzzed with the sound of scooters; small feral dogs roamed the sidewalks; rooftop gardens crowned many of the buildings with lush greenery; and everywhere my whiteness drew stares from the locals. A group of school kids in the museum pointed to me more often than to the exhibits.

Late one evening, my companions and I decided to go to the Shilin night market, where food and clothing are sold at hundreds of stalls. (For a special price, you can have the tourist special: "freshly killed snake.") Weighing well over 200 pounds, I often find it hard to get well-fitting clothes in Canada, and at the night market, where I was something of a curiosity because of my size, it was even more difficult. It was fascinating, nevertheless, to visit the clothing vendors, to be encouraged by entire families to buy from their family stall.

During the tour I saw something strange. My sociological Spidey sense began to tingle. After noting it once I began to look for it, and I saw it repeatedly: the mannequins in the clothing stalls were modelled after Europeans. I did not see one "Chinese" mannequin, either there or anywhere I went the entire week-and-a-half I spent in Taiwan.

What does a sociologist make of this? While I was in Taipei, I read an article in one of the English-language newspapers questioning whether the Taiwanese people admired the West too much. What I had found was an example. Mannequins, which we, as prospective customers, are meant to admire for their beauty, are in Taiwanese terms "not us." Beauty is "not us." It couldn't be economics dictating this move. These couldn't be spares from the Western market. They must have been made and bought for the domestic market.

Then I remembered a beautiful young Italian-Canadian woman, a former student of mine, who made money in Japan as a model. She had remarked to me that a number of her colleagues in the Japanese modelling industry were white. I also remembered reading about how, during the Vietnam War, some South Vietnamese prostitutes underwent eye operations on their epicanthic folds (the technical term for the skin and fat tissue that makes most Asian people distinctive) to make themselves look "more white." I thought of Japanese animé characters with big eyes—Sailor Moon comes to mind.

Are these examples of "beauty is not us," of a prevailing belief that standards of beauty come from another culture, of reverse ethnocentrism? I think so, but some of my students do not agree with me (particularly the white students). What do you think?

What do YOU think?

1. Summarize the author's experience of reverse ethnocentrism in Taiwan. Do you agree with the author that the prevalence of European mannequins in Taiwan can be attributed to reverse ethnocentrism?

2. Do you think that Canadians sometimes subscribe to reverse ethnocentrism? Under what circumstances?

Cultural Relativism

Cultural relativism is an approach to studying the context of an aspect of another culture. It can be spoken of as existing at two levels. One is the level of understanding. Because of the *holistic* nature of culture—because everything is connected in a system—no single thing can be understood outside of its social, historical, and environmental context. Every aspect of culture has strings attached. Just as you can't understand a single part of a car without understanding the system of which it is a part, so you must understand individual aspects of culture within their cultural context.

Unlike what Spock used to say in the original *Star Trek*, logic (as a pure entity) does *not* dictate. Logic is a cultural construct, and every society has its own cultural logic. Any explanation of a cultural practice or belief must in some way incorporate this logic. This is especially important in medicine. Western medicine is dominated by a kind of ethnocentric logic that states that nothing worth knowing comes from non-Western traditions. Yet in order to cure or to heal, it's important to respond to the way the patient envisions the healing process. This point comes across with striking clarity in the award-winning book *The Spirit Catches You and You Fall Down: A Hmong Child, Her American Doctors and the Collision of Two Cultures*, by Anne Fadiman (1997). The book describes American doctors and nurses failing to respect, among other things, the Hmong people's spiritual connections to medicine, the importance of encouraging their belief that a cure is available, and the role this belief plays in the curing process.

The second—and more contested—level at which cultural relativism operates is that of *judging*. One viewpoint suggests that individuals should not be judged by the practices of their culture. They have relatively little choice in what they do. After all, those living today no more invented those customs that you might find objectionable than you invented customs in Canadian culture that they find strange. Consider the Maasai, an African people with a strong warrior tradition, who have a custom in which boys, at the onset of puberty, are circumcised. It is frightening and painful, but it is an important initiation ceremony: only once he has gone through the ceremony is a Maasai boy treated as a man and permitted to have sex with women. It is easy for Canadians to judge this custom negatively, to be critical of those who perpetuate what they consider a cruel and barbaric ritual. But is that right? The Maasai might identify as a sign of our cultural weakness the fact that most Canadian boys are never ritually transformed into men.

Cultural Relativism, Ethnocentrism, and Smell: Two Stories

Our senses—the way we perceive what is beautiful or ugly, pleasant or disgusting—are culturally conditioned. Think of female beauty. For many North Americans, the image that comes to mind is that of a skinny model. And, if sales and commercials are anything to judge by, North Americans set a great deal by the whiteness of a person's teeth. Do you think this is true in other cultures?

What we hear as either "music" or "noise" is conditioned by our experience—our ears are not totally our own. The same applies to our noses. Describing his experience working in the Peace Corps, an organization of volunteers working in developing countries, Tom Bissell noted how difficult he found it to share a bus in the central Asian country of Uzbekistan with people who were overdressed for the weather and, understandably, hot and sweaty. He observed:

> When I was in the Peace Corps, one of my least favorite things was when my fellow volunteers complained about Central Asian body odor. . . . But Gandhi probably smelled bad. Surely Abraham Lincoln smelled. William Shakespeare was, in all likelihood, rank. . . . Most certainly Jesus and Julius Caesar and the Buddha all smelled terrible. People have been smelly for the vast majority of human history. By gooping up our pheromonal reactors with dyed laboratory gels, could it be that we in the West are to blame for our peculiar alienation? Might not the waft from another's armpit contain crucial bioerotic code? Could it be by obscuring such code we have confused otherwise very simple matters of attraction? (Bissell 2003: 98)

In a very different setting, Emma LaRocque, a Métis writer from northeastern Alberta, came to a similar conclusion:

> Several summers ago when I was intern-teaching on a northern reserve, one of the teachers told me

how she "had to get used to" the smells of the children. She insisted it was not just stuffiness but a "peculiar odor." . . .

Oddly enough, the "peculiar" smell was a redolent mixture of spruce, moosehide, and woodsmoke. All the while this teacher was complaining about the smell of the children, the children reported a "strange" odor coming from the vicinity of some of the teachers and their chemical toilets. And it never seemed to occur to the teacher that she could be giving off odors.

More to the point, both the teacher and the children attached value judgments to the unfamiliar odors. As a friend of mine noted, "to a person whose culture evidently prefers Chanel No. 5 or pine-scented aerosol cans, mooseshide and woodsmoke can seem foreign." The converse is true, I might add. (LaRocque 1975: 37)

Going Global

Pioneer Global Village

I was taking some Indonesian science teachers on a bus trip to a few of the educational sites near my college in northwestern Toronto. We went to Crawford Lake Conservation Area, where they have reconstructed fourteenth-century Iroquoian longhouses. These were easy to explain to my visitors, who knew of cultures in their own country that had lived in similar dwellings. I was aware of this connection, and it made my explanations that much simpler.

The next site we were going to visit would, I thought, be more difficult to contextualize. We were going to Black Creek Pioneer Village, a reconstructed nineteenth-century settler community, where historical interpreters dressed in period costume demonstrate various aspects of pioneer life. As we approached the site, I was frantically searching my mind for points of connection that would make this part of the trip understandable.

I needn't have bothered. For as I entered the park with my Indonesian teachers, and they all looked out in interest, one loud voice suddenly piped up, "Hey, it's like *Little House on the Prairie.*" That television show, based on the novels by Laura Ingalls Wilder, depicting life in the American West during the 1870s, had been shown from 1975 to 1982 in North America, but had lived on in reruns around the world—including Indonesia.

My visitor's ready reference to a classic American television show caught me by surprise, but then the American Midwest of the nineteenth century has no less to do with Indonesia than turn-of-the-twentieth-century Prince Edward Island has to do with Japan, where Lucy Maud Montgomery's heroine

Anne of Green Gables flourishes as a cultural icon. Should we feel proud, as Canadians, that one of our literary figures has been embraced halfway around the globe, or unnerved that a piece of cultural property has been bought and transformed to serve the global marketplace?

Sailor Moon meets Anne of Green Gables.

As we have seen, ethnocentrism and cultural relativism are opposing ways of looking at cultures, both our own and those of others. Ethnocentrism is laden with negative judgement, while cultural relativism is characterized by a greater appreciation for context in understanding and evaluating culture. This is not to say that everything is relative, or that there are no standards, as some sociology students seem to conclude after learning about the two concepts. Some things, such as female genital mutilation, the use of land mines, and the torture of political prisoners (say, by the CIA) can be considered universally bad.

The point to take from this is that it's important to realize how easy it is to make an ethnocentric assessment of a different culture. It is important to try to understand why different cultures do what they do. And, while true appreciation of aspects of other cultures might not always be possible, it is worth the trip to take a few steps down that path.

Sociolinguistics

Sociolinguistics is the study of language as part of culture. Language exists at the centre of communication between individuals and between groups. It is a source both of understanding and of misunderstanding. It is also the main vehicle for transmitting culture, and a culture cannot be understood without some sense of the language(s) it uses and the fit of language with other aspects of culture. Sociolinguistics thus looks at language in relation to such sociological factors as "race," ethnicity, age, gender, and region.

Dialect as a Sociological Term

A **dialect** is a variety of a language, a version that is perhaps different from others in terms of pronunciation, vocabulary, and grammar. To the sociologist, the distinction between dialect and language is interesting because it can be as much a product of social factors as of linguistic ones. Dutch and German, for instance, are considered separate languages, although based strictly on linguistic criteria they could be called dialects of the same language. For some German speakers living near the Netherlands, Dutch is easier to understand than dialects of German spoken in Austria or Switzerland. Dialects, unlike languages, are often evaluated according to whether they represent proper or improper, casual or formal, even funny or serious

versions of a language. These judgements usually depend on the social status of the dialect's speakers. In Britain, the "Queen's English" is an upper-class dialect, more highly valued in written and formal communication than are regional dialects like that of the city of Manchester. The latter is often heard spoken by characters of TV shows such as *Coronation Street*, where it signifies that the characters using it are "real people" rather than aristocrats. A few years ago, a commercial for a Nissan SUV featured a voice-over spoken in a Newfoundland accent. The accent here is used to put the audience in a receptive mood by evoking the famed good nature and affability of the people of Newfoundland and Labrador. You would not hear that accent extolling the marketable features of a Lexus.

Linguistic Determinism and Relativity

The relationship between language and culture is usually discussed in terms of the **Sapir-Whorf hypothesis**, which posits the existence of **linguistic determinism** (or **causation**). The principle of linguistic determinism suggests that the way each of us views and understands the world is shaped by the language we speak. Like theories of biological or social determinism, the Sapir-Whorf hypothesis can be cast either as strongly or weakly deterministic—that is, language can be seen to exert either a strong or a weak influence on a person's worldview. We favour a weak determinism. We feel that linguistic relativity is a valid form of cultural relativity, that exact translation from one language into another is impossible, and that knowing the language of a people is important to grasping the ideas of a people.

Noun Classes and Gender

Consider linguistic determinism in the context of the following statement: the different noun classes that exist in a language can reinforce the beliefs its speakers have within their culture. English speakers in Canada have some awareness of difference in noun classes through the presence of gender exhibited by the Romance (i.e. based on Latin, the language of the Romans) languages—French, Italian, Portuguese, Spanish—to which they are exposed. Students struggling through French classes may wonder why every French noun has to be masculine or feminine. Why are the words for "tree" (*arbre*) and tree species masculine, while the parts of trees—roots, leaves, branches, bark, blossoms—are feminine?

While it does not have noun classes labelled as "masculine" or "feminine," English does have a certain degree of grammatically mandated gender, with our use of *he, him, his,* and *she, her, hers.* Take the following two sentences: *One of my sisters is called Ann. She is younger than I am, and her hair used to be the same colour as mine.* In the second sentence, the words *she* and *her* are grammatically necessary but do not add any new information. Am I assuming that you have forgotten the gender of my sister? We already know from the nouns "sister" and "Ann" that the person spoken about is female. Most **Indo-European** languages—the family of languages that includes almost all the languages of Europe plus Farsi (Iranian) and the languages of Pakistan and northern India—impose gender grammatically in some way.

Algonquian languages, which together make up the largest Aboriginal language family in Canada and the United States, have no grammatically mandated gender, in either the French or the English sense. They have no pronouns meaning "he" or "she." They are not alone in that respect. Almost every Canadian Aboriginal language does not recognize gender. Does

this mean that Algonquian speakers were traditionally more flexible about gender roles than their European contemporaries, that there was a greater degree of equality between the sexes? The latter was certainly true at the time of contact, but whether that can be related to the absence of grammatical gender in their language is difficult to determine.

A Final Thought

Sometimes the terms that a language *doesn't* have tells you something significant about the culture. Take the following case. In translating for the movie *Whispers Like Thunder,* I found that on several occasions I was required to translate concepts for which there were no corresponding words in the Aboriginal language Wendat (Huron). A few examples should provide insight into the differences between Aboriginal and European cultures. There are no Wendat terms for "guilt" or "guilty," "innocence" or "innocent." There are terms for "good" and "very good," but no terms for "better" or "best." What do you think might be the cultural implications of these "holes" in the Wendat language?

WRAP IT UP

Summary

If I could summarize this chapter in a statement or two, I would say this: not only do cultures differ, but cultures are viewed and lived differently by people according to the different social locations they occupy (based on gender, sexuality, "race," ethnicity, age, and so on). Similarly, although humans, as intensely social creatures, cannot live without culture, they can also feel oppressed by their culture, if their social location is not one of power and influence.

Remember, as well, that cultures are contested, that not everyone is in agreement concerning the rightness or goodness of every aspect of their mainstream culture. This is why there are minority versions that exist in contrast or opposition to the dominant culture. Subcultures tend to organize around preoccupations—we might call them hobbies or pastimes—not found within the dominant culture. Countercultures oppose the defining elements of the dominant culture, but there's something inherently attractive in a counterculture—people like to cast themselves as rebels—and so a counterculture sometimes must reinvent itself repeatedly to keep from becoming mainstream. Even high culture, which occupies a privileged position, is a minority culture, concerning itself with sophisticated pursuits that may be beyond the reaches of the masses. Which brings us to popular culture or mass culture: the label you use depends on whether or not you believe people create culture independent of the powerful and manipulative influence of large commercial interests.

THINK BACK

Questions for Critical Review

1. Differentiate the following:
   - high culture
   - mass culture
   - popular culture.

2. Differentiate and provide examples of the following:
   - dominant culture
   - subculture
   - counterculture.

3. Differentiate and provide examples of the following:
   - folkways
   - mores
   - taboos.

4. Explain and give examples of Eurocentrism and ethnocentrism.

5. Contrast the linguistic expectations of speakers of Algonquian and Indo-European languages.

READ ON

Online

Anishinaabemowin Learner's Grammar

http://imp.lss.wisc.edu/~jrvalent/ais301/index.html

This is an excellent introduction to the grammar and other key aspects of the Ojibwe language. Students can consider linguistic determinism as they enjoy an introduction to an Aboriginal language.

Cannabis Culture

www.cannabisculture.com

This websites reflects the viewpoints of the marijuana counterculture, particularly in Canada. Students can consider the aspects that define it as a counterculture and whether there's any chance of its going mainstream.

TED: Ideas Worth Spreading

www.ted.com/conversations/2289/pop-culture_a_subculture_tel.html

TED stands for Technology Entertainment Design, a non-profit organization dedicated (since 1984) to what it terms "ideas worth spreading." This website attempts to draw visitors into conversations about pop culture.

In Print

Sajida Alvi, Homa Hoodfar, & Sheila McDonough, eds (2003), *The Muslim Veil North America: Issues and Debates* (Toronto: Canadian Scholars' Press).

This insightful look into the cultural image of the veil focuses especially on the North American (particularly Montreal) experience of the 1990s.

John Fiske (2010), *Understanding Popular Culture*, 2nd edn (London: Routledge).

A classic sociological study of popular culture, recently updated.

Edward Said (1979), *Orientalism* (New York: Vintage Books).

Said's landmark work is a Palestinian-American's influential study of how the Middle East has been misrepresented by Western scholars.

Socialization

Learning Objectives

After reading this chapter, you should be able to

- outline and assess the basic ideas of Freud as they apply to sociology
- discuss the application of *oversocialization* to the concepts of Mead and Cooley
- discuss the similarities and differences between *social determinism* and *biological determinism*
- distinguish between *agency* and *determinism*
- explain the roles of various agents of socialization
- discuss critically the effects of television violence.

Key Terms

- agency
- agents of socialization
- bar mitzvah
- bat mitzvah
- behaviourism
- behaviour modification
- branding
- confirmation
- culture and personality
- degradation ceremony
- desensitization theory
- determinism
- ego
- eros
- game stage
- generalized others
- generation gap
- habitus
- hurried child syndrome
- id
- internalize
- law of effect
- longitudinal study
- looking-glass self
- national character
- observational learning theory
- oversocialized
- packaged rebel
- peer group
- peer pressure
- play stage
- preparatory stage
- primary socialization
- psychoanalysis
- reproduction
- resocialization
- rite of passage
- role-taking
- secondary socialization
- significant others
- superego
- swaddling hypothesis
- thanatos
- total institution
- vision quest
- XYY males

Names to Know

- Pierre Bourdieu
- Charles Horton Cooley
- Sigmund Freud
- John T. Hitchcock
- George Herbert Mead
- Ann Leigh Minturn
- Edward Thorndike
- John B. Watson

For Starters

Small-Town Socialization "in the Hood"

I live in Bolton, just north of Toronto. It's a largely white, middle-class bedroom community, inhabited by people who commute to jobs in the city. It's also home to a strangely large population of white teenage boys from middle-class homes who walk around as if they were black urban youths. They've got the loose-hanging, load-in-the-drawers pants, the brooding slouch, the rhythmic, side-to-side walk, the hoodie done up tight in even the warmest weather, the ball cap worn crooked or backwards, and the light fist-to-fist greeting reserved for peers and initiated members of the Bolton white boys' fraternity. They didn't learn that at home. No Bolton parents socialize their kids that way. Could you imagine?

"Word up, Jackson, my little homey. Let's get you into those fubus and out of this crib. And try to be cool, like. Hang your baggies down a bit so I can see your Boxers—you don't want to look like the wiggas down the street, do you?"

So if Jackson's parents didn't socialize him in the ways of African-American youth, who or what did? Well, music videos, movies, and video games are all powerful socializing agents. Friends and older teenagers who have been socialized previously and are considered cool can act as agents as well. Jackson has probably been practising his act in front of a mirror, since socialized skills and mannerisms generally need to be rehearsed before they are performed in front of an audience.

A more puzzling question: if you're a white teenager from a middle-class suburb who has never been a part of black urban culture, why act black? As *The Daily Show* host and comedian Jon Stewart quipped, musing over the question, "You might as well talk like a pirate"—you'll sound just as ridiculous.

As a sociologist, I have a few theories. For one thing, African Americans have long led the way in popular music—jazz, rock and roll, soul, reggae, rap, and hip hop all began with black musicians playing for black audiences, before non-blacks caught on and the performers became more and more white. Pop recording artists are typically "cool," and appearing cool is important to teenage boys. I know it was important to me. Just talking like a musician has a lot of cool to it. The first band I was in was a British-style rock group. We spoke with British accents too generic (and pretentious) to resemble the Liverpudlian cadences of the Beatles.

Another thing: hip hop is a recognizable identity that white, middle-class teenagers can slip into easily (unlike, say, a Scottish kilt or a pirate shirt). It's got a look that will help you fit in rather than stand out. When I was a teenager, long hair, faded jeans, old military shirts from the army surplus store, and blue pea jackets were indispensable parts of the image that I and my friends cultivated. We carefully observed what the British rocker bands wore, and we emulated their identity.

Many companies, from clothing stores to soft drink sellers, invest huge amounts of time and money trying to socialize teenagers and younger children (the all-important "tween" demographic) through branding, getting them to covet brand-name products linked, through advertising, to the cool or fashionable identity of the day. Many products today are marketed to consumers of hip hop culture. Individual performers have their own lines of jewellery, footwear, and fragrances, all designed to socialize young people concerning what to wear and what to smell like.

The walk and the gestures aren't sold with the brand, but they are part of the package deal, thrown in for free. The **packaged rebel** has long been a treasured image among Western youth: an identity that says, "I swim against the tide" is readily available for sale at any mall, making it something of a capitalist oxymoron. (An oxymoron, like "jumbo shrimp," brings together contradictory elements—in this case, a desire for nonconformity and a susceptibility to mass merchandising.) The snowboarder image, for example, is packaged as that of a rebel, but you need middle-class parent money and brand-name gear to carry off this rebel look with authenticity. Repeat after me: "We will all think for ourselves."

Will they grow out of it—the white boys of Bolton acting black? My money says they will, as they become resocialized as adult members of society, earning a living, paying their taxes, mowing the lawn, raising children, and trying to fit in where they work. Part of the package may remain. I no longer use my faux British accent, but I still have long hair.

Introduction: Socialization Is a Learning Process

Socialization is an area of sociological study that brings the discipline close to psychology. The intersection of sociology and psychology is clear from the fact that a good number of the leading socialization theorists are psychologists. Socialization is a learning process, one that involves learning how to be a social person in a given society, and it brings changes in an individual's sense of self. This applies both in the earliest socialization that an individual undergoes in childhood, generally known as **primary socialization**, and in socialization that occurs later in life, which is sometimes known as **secondary socialization**.

Determinism: Nature versus Nurture

Any discussion of socialization needs to cover the topics of *determinism versus free will* and *biological determinism versus social determinism*. When we speak of **determinism**, we are talking about the degree to which an individual's behaviour, attitudes, and other "personal" characteristics are determined, or caused, by a specific factor. There are "hard" and "soft" versions of determinism. Proponents of the former claim that we are, in essence, programmed to think and act in a particular way, either by our biology or by our culture. Champions of the latter believe there is some room for free will or the exercise of agency in one's life. **Agency** involves personal choice above and beyond the call of nature or nurture.

Biological Determinism

Biological determinism (the side of "nature" in the old "nature versus nurture" debate) states that the greater part of what we are is determined by our roughly 26,000 genes. Biological determinism has become a popular subject of discussion and debate in the mainstream media, owing in large part to the rise of human genetic research generally and, in particular, the Human Genome Project, which involves a painstaking count of the number of genes we have and investigation into what each of those genes actually codes for.

Certain abilities seem to fall into the "nature" category. We all know of people who are "naturally good" at sports, music, art, and so on. However, we have to be very careful in making even tentative statements about biological determinism. A notorious research study into the **XYY males** that began in 1962 provides a cautionary tale. The standard pattern of chromosomes in men is XY; the corresponding pattern for women is XX. During the 1960s, the atypical XYY chromosome pattern was found in some men who were being studied in hospitals for dangerous, violent, or criminal patients with emotional/intellectual problems, first in England and then in the United States and Australia (see Jacobs et al. 1965; Price & Whatmore 1967; Telfer 1968). The "criminal gene" was hastily declared.

The problem was that the researchers had neglected to study non-criminals. When the study was extended to the general population, researchers discovered that roughly the same percentage (about 1 in 1,000) were XYY (Court Brown 1968). There remain some well-documented associations of XYY males with above-average height, with a tendency to have acne, and with somewhat more impulsive and antisocial behaviour and slightly lower intelligence, but there is no evidence to conclude that XYY males are genetically determined criminals.

Softer forms of biological determinism focus on predispositions that people have (for shyness, for aggressiveness, and so on). These findings tend to have a stronger foundation and are easier to support than the more sensational claims of hard determinism—the ones beginning "*Scientists have discovered the gene for _____*"—that sometimes make the news. What we are comes from too complex a mixture, even too complex a genetic mixture, for one gene to be an absolute determinant of behaviour or personality.

Social (Cultural) Determinism: a.k.a. Behaviourism

Behaviourism is a school of thought in psychology that takes a strong cultural determinist position. In other words, it emphasizes the power of learning (or "nurture" in the "nature versus nurture" debate) in the development of behaviour.

For the behaviourist, the social environment is just about everything in the creation of personality. Biology and free will count for very little. One cautionary statement about this school of thought is that much of the research on which it is based involves nonhuman animals: Pavlov and his dogs, Thorndike and his cats, B.F. Skinner and his rats and pigeons. Critics argue that the theory disallows the existence of choice, of agency, which even a dog, pigeon, or rat can be seen as possessing (my recent attempts at training our dachshund have shown me that sometimes no amount of nurture can prevent a free-spirited dog from exercising free will).

One of the earliest principles of behaviourism is the **law of effect**, introduced by **Edward Thorndike** (1874–1949) in his book *Animal Intelligence* (1911). The law of effect has two parts. The first one says that if you do something and it is rewarded, the likelihood of your doing it again increases; the rewarded behaviour is said to be thus "reinforced." On the other hand, according to the second part, if you do something and it is punished or ignored, then the likelihood of your doing it again decreases. It boils down to the idea of the carrot (reward) and the stick (punishment). Accordingly, if the screaming child in the grocery store lineup is given a chocolate bar to be quiet, the reward reinforces the screaming—expect it to happen again.

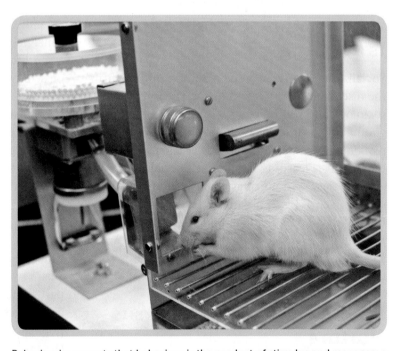

Behaviourism asserts that behaviour is the product of stimulus and response: a lab rat will develop certain patterns of behaviour (say, pressing a lever in a cage) if it produces a particular reward (like a pellet of food) even some of the time. Do you believe that human behaviour is mostly conditioned the same way?

There are debates about what constitutes a reward for an individual, and about what behaviour is or is not being rewarded. For example, if you punish a child who is acting out at school by making her sit in the corner and the objectionable behaviour persists, could it be argued that she sees the "punishment" as a reward? Is she getting attention, and is that her goal? If you pick up a baby who is crying, does that teach him that he can get anything he wants by crying? Or does it reward communication, which, once he learns to speak, becomes words and not tears? Attempting to change someone's behaviour using this kind of approach is called **behaviour modification**.

Hard social determinism claims that just about any behaviour can be taught and learned. A powerful expression of this view comes from **John B. Watson** (1878–1958), the founder of behaviourist psychology, who declared:

Give me a dozen healthy infants, well-formed, and my own specified world to bring them up in and I'll guarantee to take any one at random and train him to become any type of specialist I might select—doctor, lawyer, artist, merchant-chief and yes, even beggar-man and thief, regardless of his talents, penchants, tendencies, abilities, vocations, and race of his ancestors. There is no such thing as an inheritance of capacity, talent, temperament, mental constitution and behavioral characteristics. (Watson 1925: 82)

Sounds like it comes from a very scary science fiction movie: *Revenge of the Rat Psychologists*. Indeed, some of Watson's research methods were controversial—his most famous experiment involved conditioning fear of a white rat in an 11-month-old infant (Watson & Rayner 1920)—and it is hardly surprising that someone

The Point Is...

Parrot Socialization

If John Watson could be called a "rat psychologist," I could probably be considered a "parrot sociologist." Our parrot room (which used to be our living room) is home to seven birds that are fascinating to watch for the insights they yield into animal behaviour. I believe, like the classical behavioural psychologists, that an understanding of animal behaviour can help us to understand human behaviour. Consider this example.

Our Senegal parrot, Sammy, is a "rescue parrot," having lived in hideously dark, crowded but lonely living conditions for a year before we "saved" him and brought him home. At first, he was very antisocial—both with humans and with the other birds in his flock. During his first week with us, he bit off the toe of Stanee, the highly maternal "mother" of the flock, and got into a brutal fight with Louis, Stanee's mate, blooding the smaller bird on his beak and head.

It has been over a year now, and Stanee, together with the "father" of our flock, Quigley (Louis is just the biological mate—it's a complicated love triangle), has been socializing Sammy. The two of them do this by preening him, gently scratching the back of his neck (the way to a parrot's heart). Sammy now approaches them with his neck turned in anticipation, and it is common to see the three hanging out together, like mother, father, and child. Although they do have squabbles, with Sammy fluffing himself up and making loud clicking noises, and the other two parrots making gestures that are suitably loud but harmless, there is no violence. Sammy's parrot parents have socialized him into the flock.

What do YOU think?

1. How might some of the theorists we've encountered so far interpret this situation? How, if at all, would your interpretation differ?

2. Do you believe we can apply the lessons of animal behaviour to human behaviour?

who felt that manipulating humans was so easy would become involved in writing popular books and articles on parenting before entering a career in advertising.

How much of your own behaviour do you think is influenced by your social environment—by friends, family, your charismatic sociology professor—and how much were you simply born with?

Sigmund Freud: Balancing the Biological and the Sociocultural

The theories of **Sigmund Freud** (1856–1939), father of **psychoanalysis**, consider socialization in terms of a balance of biological and social aspects of human personality. Freud believed the mind had three parts (think of it as a team with three players):

- the id
- the superego
- the ego.

The **id** is motivated by two **i**nstinctive **d**rives that we are born with as part of our unconscious mind: they are *eros* and *thanatos*. **Eros** (related to the word *erotic*) is the drive that tends to be stressed by Freud's fans and critics (and Freud himself, to be fair). It is a "life drive" that involves pleasure—particularly, but not exclusively, sexual pleasure. **Thanatos**, the less celebrated of the two drives, is the "death drive," an instinct for aggression and violence.

The **superego**, also part of the unconscious, is your conscience. It takes in the normative messages of right and wrong that your parents, family, friends, teachers, and other socializing agents give you, and *internalizes* them—in other words, it adopts them as something like a personal code of moral behaviour. Picture a caped crusader with a big "S" on his chest, saying "Don't hit your sister or want to have sex with your mother—that's wrong!"

In Freud's thinking, the id and superego often come to blows in conflict that can take years of psychotherapy to resolve. If one is too strong, the individual is either too unrestrained or too controlled. The **ego**, meanwhile, mediates between the conscious and unconscious while trying to make sense of what the individual self does and thinks. It can interpret well if the individual is aware of what is going on in his or her unconscious with information from dream analysis, talks about childhood, inkblot tests, hypnosis, and "Freudian slips" ("Today, we'll be talking about Sigmund Fraud"). If the ego is weak or lacks self-awareness, there will be serious problems.

Agency

In "The Oversocialized Conception of Man in Modern Sociology" (1961), Canadian sociologist Dennis H. Wrong (*not* a Freudian slip) stressed that it was important not to view humans as passive recipients of socialization. In his terminology, such a view was an **oversocialized** representation of people. Wrong argued that people do not completely conform to the lessons of their socialization, automatically doing what socializing agents dictate. Rather, they can elect to resist their socialization. This was an important point to make at the end of the 1950s, a time of relatively great conformity to norms in North America. It remains important in the **branding** days of the twenty-first century, when advertisers try to socialize children at younger and younger ages into social acceptance through their products. It's also worth considering this point in terms of the debate, discussed in the last chapter, between proponents of mass culture (who see individuals as passive recipients of cultural messages) and of popular culture (who view individuals as having agency in interpreting culture).

Luis M. Aguiar, who teaches sociology at Okanagan University College in British Columbia, offers another view of the conflict between agency and socialization. Born in the Azores, off the coast of Portugal, Aguiar experienced the "working-class socialization" of his parents, who encouraged him to adopt a trade rather than pursue a post-secondary education. The idea of finding a "career" was incomprehensible to Aguiar's parents (Aguiar 2001: 187–8). They considered boys who preferred mental to physical work "sexually suspect" and "unmanly." Aguiar's father even supplied him with examples of men who "became insane as a result of too much reading and studying" (180).

Ultimately Aguiar did go to university, demonstrating agency by overcoming his parents' attempts to socialize him into entering a trade. However, he was not unaffected by their efforts, which left him with feelings of guilt, since he could not, because of the length of his schooling, help provide for the family until relatively late in life:

> Today I still feel terribly guilty because of my selfish educational pursuits that deprived my parents from owning a home or car or having some higher level of comfort in their retirement years. My parents never complained about my lack of financial contribution to the family, but my sense is that they are extremely disappointed at not achieving the immigrant dream of owning their own home. To my mind, only immigrant students of working-class background feel this heavy load of class guilt. (Aguiar 2001: 191)

Agents of Socialization

In the case of Luis Aguiar, his parents were among the most influential **agents of socialization**—the groups that had a significant impact on his socialization. There are many agents of socialization that can affect an individual, but the following seven in particular hold sway when it comes to socialization:

- family
- peer group
- neighbourhood/community
- school
- mass media
- the legal system
- culture generally.

The impact of each of these agents is severely contested, both in the sociological literature and in the day-to-day conversations of people in society. In the following sections, we'll take a closer look at some of the debates.

Significant Other, Generalized Other, and Sense of Self

The American psychologist **George Herbert Mead**, whom we introduced as a symbolic interactionist in Chapter 2, saw all agents of socialization falling into one of two categories he named "significant other" and "generalized other." He believed that children develop their sense of self from being socialized by the "others" in their lives. They **internalize** norms and values they observe, incorporating them into their way of being.

Significant others are those key individuals—primarily parents, to a lesser degree older siblings and close friends—whom young children imitate and model themselves after. Picture a mother or father doing yardwork with a young child imitating the practice (for instance, clearing leaves with a toy rake). Later on the child comes under sway of **generalized others** and begins to take into account the attitudes, viewpoints, and general expectations of the society she or he has been socialized into. Freud would say that the individual's superego had internalized the norms of society.

Mead even identified a developmental *sequence* for socialization, beginning with the **preparatory stage**, which involves more or less pure imitation. The next step is the **play stage**, where the child engages in **role-taking**, assuming the perspective of significant others and imagining what those others are thinking as they act. The third stage is the **game stage**, in which the child considers simultaneously the perspective of several roles. In terms of baseball, for example, this is when a child, fielding the ball at shortstop, might be able to consider what the runner and the first baseman are thinking and doing.

Significant others and generalized others continue to exert strong socialization influences later on in the

This is a common image in North American culture, one you've likely seen in TV commercials or in a scene from a movie. Why isn't the image of a mother and daughter shaving their legs or doing their makeup as common?

life of an individual, with significant consequences for the individual's self-concept. Mentors and other role models can become important significant others for the adolescent or adult individual. A generalized other may be a social group or "community" that has an impact on the individual's sense of self. Think of television ads. When an Old Navy commercial presents a group of young, attractive, and well-dressed people dancing and having a good time, the advertising agency is trying to tell you that this is what your cool, young community likes, and you should, too. And whenever a star athlete, the latest pop sensation, or any other celebrity is chosen to endorse a product, the marketing team behind the advertising is banking on the fact that the person will be viewed as a significant other by the group the product is being marketed to. Note, however, that when celebrity spokespeople transgress the

moral norms of a society, they lose their marketability as significant others. Evidence of this is Tiger Woods, who was quickly shunned by his corporate sponsors after details of his extramarital affairs became public.

Another symbolic interactionist, **Charles Horton Cooley** (1864–1929), put forth the idea of the **looking-glass self**. This is a self-image based on how a person thinks he or she is viewed by others. In Cooley's poetic words, "each to each a looking glass / Reflects the other that doth pass" (as quoted in Marshall 1998: 374). The looking-glass self has three components:

1. how you imagine you appear to others
2. how you imagine those others judge your appearance
3. how you feel as a result (proud, ashamed, self-confident, embarrassed).

Julia Bluhm, 14, holds up a copy of *Seventeen* magazine as she leads a protest urging the magazine to publish one spread each issue of model photos that have not been altered. Three months after Bluhm launched her campaign, in July 2012, the publisher announced it would no longer alter girls' faces or body shapes in its photos. Do you think readers will notice the difference? What effect could it have?

A good example of this is the relationship between body image and self-esteem, especially in young women. Harvard educational psychologist and respected feminist thinker Carol Gilligan noted how the self-esteem of girls declines during their teenage years (Gilligan 1990). Studies show that this happens more with girls and young women than with boys. The harsher standards of body type that we apply to women have rightly been associated with this difference in self-esteem.

Family

The family is the first agent of socialization, often the most powerful one. Significantly, just as the family is different across cultures, so are the means and goals of the family in socializing the child. Consider the narrative on page 113 which is based on research done on the Rajput of Khalapur in northern India, carried out by **John T. Hitchcock** (1917–2001) and **Ann Leigh Minturn** (1928–1999) in the early 1960s. Their work was part of a classic study of cross-cultural socialization, Beatrice Whiting's *Six Cultures: Studies of Child Rearing* (1963).

Culture and Personality

Some would argue that the impact of family socialization in its different forms has been overemphasized since it became a source of interest to sociologists. During the first half of the twentieth century, sociology, along with anthropology and psychology, was involved in what is called the **culture and personality** school of thought. The culture and personality school attempted to identify and describe an idealized personality or "personality type" for different societies, both small and large, and attach to it a particular form of family socialization. During World War II and in the early years of the Cold War standoff between the United States and the Soviet Union, the scope of these studies broadened to examine **national character**, the personality type of entire nations. These studies typically drew conclusions about how the primary socialization of child-raising is linked with a country's national character.

An example of national character research is *The People of Great Russia* (1949), in which Geoffrey Gorer and John Rickman proposed the **swaddling hypothesis**. They identified moodiness as a supposedly typical Russian character trait, citing extremes of controlled and out-of-control behaviour (evidenced, for example, in intense bouts of alcoholism), and attributed it to the

Telling It Like It Is

An Expert POV

The Rajputs: Child-Rearing and Personality in a North Indian Village

Although Rajput infants will be picked up and attended to when they are hungry or fussing, for the most part they are left in their cots, wrapped up in blankets. . . . Except for anxieties about a baby's health, it is not the centre of attention. A baby receives attention mainly when it cries. At that time, someone will try to distract it, but when it becomes quiet, the interaction will stop. Adult interaction with babies is generally aimed at producing a cessation of response, rather than stimulation of it. Infants and children of all ages are not shown off to others. . . . Children are also not praised by their parents, who fear that this will "spoil" them and make them disobedient.

Rajput children . . . are never left alone, yet neither are they the centre of interest. The child learns that moodiness will not be tolerated. Few demands are put on Rajput children; they are not pressured or even encouraged to become self-reliant. Weaning, which generally occurs without trouble, takes place at two to three years; but if the mother does not become pregnant, a child may be nursed into its sixth year. There is no pressure for toilet training. . . . Babies are not pressured, or even encouraged to walk. They learn to walk when they are ready, and mothers say they see no reason to rush this. . . .

Village women do little to guide children's behaviour by explaining or reasoning with them. There is also little direct instruction to small children. Small children learn . . . the customs and values of the group through observation and imitation. In the first five years of life, the child moves very gradually from observer to participant in village and family life. . . .

[C]hildren are not encouraged in any way to participate in adult activities. The chores a child is given are mainly directed to helping the mother. . . . There is little feeling that children should be given chores on principle in order to train them in responsibility. . . . Rajput children take little initiative in solving problems by themselves. Instead, they are taught whom they can depend on for help in the web of social relations of kin group, caste, and village. . . . Although chores increase somewhat as the child gets older, it is not a Rajput custom to require children to work if adults can do it. Children are not praised for their work, and a child's inept attempt to do an adult job is belittled. Thus children are reluctant to undertake what they cannot do well.

—J.T. Hitchcock & A.L. Minturn

What do YOU think?

1. How would this be interpreted by a behaviourist?
2. What values are being taught with this form of socialization?

Our Stories

An Exception to the "Rule" of Inuit Family Socialization

Early in his career studying Northern populations, Diamond Jenness was told by his predecessor Viljamhar Stefansson that an Inuit child was considered the reborn soul of an ancestor or recently deceased family member, and that the older soul became the infant's guardian spirit, or *atka*. According to Stefansson, this belief influenced the way Inuit raised their children. As quoted by Jenness in his diary:

> The atka protects the child, guarding it from harm. A little child is wiser than an adult person, because its actions are inspired by its atka—the wise old man or wise woman who died. Consequently a child is never scolded or refused anything—even a knife or scissors. (Stuart Jenness 1991: 7)

Perhaps as the tenth child of 14, Jenness had a hard time accepting that the latter statement could be true, because he would soon come to challenge the point. On 5 October 1913, he recorded the following observation of an Inuit child:

> The boy was allowed to play with the scissors or anything else that caught his fancy. He had his father's watch and began to hammer it on the floor; the father remonstrated very mildly. (Stuart Jenness 1991: 14)

By November, Jenness was directly criticizing Stefansson's theory:

> I noticed the children were scolded several times, and twice slaps were administered severe enough to make them cry—which contradicts what Stefansson told me. (Stuart Jenness 1991: 63)

Three days later, he expanded on his criticism:

> I have been watching their treatment of the children rather closely, in view of what Stefansson told us on September 27th. It is true that they are allowed to play with many things—scissors, watches, etc., which a European child would never be allowed; it is true too that their whims and caprices are often humoured and given way to; but it is not true—with these two families at least—that they are never scolded or slapped, nor that they are invariably allowed to have their own way. (Stuart Jenness 1991: 67)

Jenness's entry for 1 December brings more critical comment. The violence of the imagery is perhaps telling:

> Stefannson's theory about little children never being hit received its death blow as far as these families are concerned. Aksiatak's baby boy (about 15 months old) was tugging at Pungashuk's hair. . . . Aksiatak hit him lightly two or three times with the stem of his long pipe, then as he [the child] did not let go, he struck him a sharp knock, which made him run screaming to his mother. Aluk's wife Qapqana also gave her son a slap, which made him cry. (Stuart Jenness 1991: 70–1)

Even after the "death blow" there is one more hit, on 11 December. It is noteworthy that Jenness criticizes not just Stefansson with this statement but also any notion that children should be treated with a light hand. His reporting betrays some cultural bias, especially with his use of the word "deserved":

> Pungasuk received rather deserved punishment this evening—three slaps as hard as Aluk's wife could inflict. Aksiatak's little boy was worrying him so he gave him a slap which made him cry. Stefansson's dictum about little children not being punished does not apply here in the least. (Stuart Jenness 1991: 81)

Do these episodes add up to sufficient evidence to contradict Stefansson's theory?

fact that the country's people were tightly *swaddled*—as in "bundled up"—as infants. Similar theories were proposed for the Germans and the Japanese. Theories like these that attempt to generalize about such large populations are extremely difficult to prove.

Studies attempting to link child socialization practices to national character could very well be sitting on the dusty shelf of old theories that no longer affect us if it weren't for a persistent preoccupation with trying to understand overarching personality traits of certain populations. Since the September 11 attacks on the United States, there has been a great deal of focus in the media and among American political and military leaders on the "Arab mind." Raphael Patai's book of this very title, first published in 1973 and revamped in 1983, was reprinted in 2002, the year after the attacks. Each edition has sold well, and *The Arab Mind* is currently enjoying considerable influence in upper military circles in the United States. It replicates all the negative excesses of the national character study publications, both by oversimplifying the psychological makeup of very sociologically diverse peoples and by tying that broad portrait to overgeneralized child-raising practices. As one critic wrote,

It is hard to see how Patai's findings can apply equally to a Saudi prince and a Tunisian fisherman, to a Libyan Bedouin [a desert nomad] and a Kuwaiti commodities broker, to an Egyptian soldier and Moroccan "mulla," to a wealthy Palestinian businessman in Qatar and an impoverished Palestinian migrant-worker from Ghazzah, to a child who is growing up in the hills of Syria and the one doing so in coastal Yemen, to a woman who is an executive director of the Cairo museum and one who farms field in northern Iraq, to a Marxist in Aden and a Christian in Beirut, a "muadhdhin" in Marrakesh and a musician in Muscat, and so on. (www.Muslimmedia.com)

Different cultures socialize their children differently, but it is important to remember that no culture exhibits complete uniformity in its socialization practices. Think of how a practice like spanking can generate considerable debate and a variety of viewpoints when a newsworthy incident raises it in the Canadian media. This is no different to what we know about cultures generally. We seem to be aware that our own culture is not uniform, yet we easily slip into thinking that other cultures are different in that regard.

Peer Group

An important agent of socialization is the **peer group**, a social group sharing key characteristics such as age, social position, and interests. The term is usually used to talk about children and adolescents of the same age.

The term **peer pressure** refers to the social force exerted on individuals by their peers to conform in behaviour, appearance, or externally demonstrated values (e.g. not appearing excited about something that isn't deemed acceptable or "cool").

A classic sociological study that argues for the influence of the adolescent peer group is Paul E. Willis's *Learning to Labour: How Working Class Kids Get Working Class Jobs* (1977). Willis studied the informal

Can you imagine the chain of events that led to this moment? How do you think the two girls differ in their attitudes towards smoking? Do you agree with the statement that *how* a teenager smokes is almost as important as *whether* she smokes?

culture of a group of 12 teenage boys attending a working-class, all-male school in the industrial town of Hammerstown, England. Willis wanted to know why working-class boys settled for labouring jobs rather than directing their energies to getting the kinds of jobs obtained by middle-class kids in their cohort. He believed the boys were not passive recipients, through socialization, of the informal working-class culture. Rather, he speculated that, as an act of minority-culture resistance to the dominant culture, they were active participants both in the creation of this culture, with its belief and values systems and rules of behaviour, and in socializing newcomers into the culture.

Among the evidence Willis found to support his theory were vocalized disdain for and humour directed against more conformist middle-class peers, ridicule of the "effeminate" nature of the mind-centred work done in school and in offices, and denunciation of middle-class values in general. The minority-culture resistance also involved manipulating the classroom (by controlling attendance and the level of work done, for example) and educational figures of authority in ways that the youths would repeat in the "shop floor" environments of factories and warehouses and with the middle-management figures they encountered there. Their classroom behaviour prepared them for their future.

Community and Neighbourhood

Community and neighbourhood can be important agents in the socialization of a child. It's one of the reasons parents debate whether they should live in the city or move their family to a town or suburb outside

Telling It Like It Is   An Author POV

Experiencing Peer Pressure

Growing up, everyone is exposed to peer pressure. How we respond to the powerful influence exerted by our peer group helps to mould us into the adults we become.

When I was 10, I had a small group of classmates I hung out with. I felt they were "cooler" than I was, so I was susceptible to peer pressure from them. I was up for pretty much any of their hijinks, even when I knew they weren't the wisest things to do. We never did anything seriously wrong. We begged candy from a local candy manufacturer and stole chocolate bars from the neighbourhood drug store. We played "chicken" with trains on the railroad tracks. We threw snowballs at passing cars and apples at cars parked in the local lovers' lane. Peer pressure made me do things I would never have done otherwise.

But it's important to recognize that, while leading us to do some pretty silly things, peer pressure plays a vital role in forging personality. Peer pressure hits us hardest when we're insecure adolescents striving for acceptance among people outside our immediate family. By encouraging a degree of conformity, peer pressure helps children develop friendships and find acceptance among others their own age, fostering both self-confidence and independence. I belonged to a class of smart kids culled from various schools in the district, and it was easy to feel separate, different. My classmates and I formed a close circle from which we all gained a sense of belonging. It also gave us a safe place to test norms and values. I don't (often) throw snowballs at passing cars anymore. And perhaps, by remembering these stories, I will be less likely to judge younger people who do similar things.

the big city where they work. It's also why urban planners are concerned about creating mixed-class city neighbourhoods rather than ghettoizing the poor into government-assisted housing projects. Studies have shown that youths living outside large cities are at lower risk of becoming involved in crime and drug and alcohol abuse. Arnett and Balle-Jensen's cross-cultural study of adolescents in Denmark and the United States is one such study showing a correlation between risk behaviour and city size (1993). Their findings include the following:

> City size was related to adolescents' reports of sex without contraception, sex with someone known only casually, marijuana use, heavy marijuana use, shoplifting, vandalism, and cigarette dependency. For most types of risk behavior, adolescents in the larger city were more likely to report the risk behavior than adolescents in the smaller city. . . . (Arnett & Balle-Jensen 1993: 1849)

What do YOU think?

Do Arnett and Balle-Jensen's findings surprise you? How might you account for the correlation between risk behaviour and city size?

Mass Media

Questions about the role communication for the masses plays in socializing young people go back at least as far as the ancient Greek philosopher Plato, who felt that art (in his day, plays) aroused primal instincts, stimulating violence and lust. Plato's student Aristotle believed that violence depicted in art actually produced among those viewing it an experience of *catharsis*, a relief from hostile or violent emotions, leading to feelings of peace.

Does mass media today—through action movies that make heroes out of vicious criminals, video games

This isn't an ideal route for children walking to school, but what if you don't have a choice? What do you think the frequent sight of police cars and caution tape teaches these children about their neighbourhood, and about life?

Telling It Like It Is

Branding Consciousness, Selling Pretty

In an era in which feminism has made many legislative gains toward gender equity, and more women are entering into professional and non-traditional fields for their gender, the world of children's media seems unable or unwilling to keep up. Most toys are still marketed along strongly demarcated gender lines of what constitutes femininity and masculinity. Through pervasive marketing campaigns of many different toy brands, girls are compelled to obsess, and enjoy obsessing about, clothes, makeup, shopping, boys, and babies. They are also given the message that to be physically attractive you must also be sexy.

Through product lines and advertising, the gender roles young girls are frequently and repeatedly labelled with include Diva, Princess, Angel, and Pop-Star. These roles are not usually seen by parents as part of gender socialization, and girls who are labelled as such are often seen by parents as sweet, cute, and girly; however, these roles embody and encourage traits such as vanity, self-centredness, and an "all about me" attitude, while encouraging, normalizing, and rewarding girls' preoccupation with their bodies over their minds.

Marketing toward young girls is not just stuck in the past; in many ways, it is worse than in the past. The Bratz doll has emerged as a hypersexualized version of Barbie, Mattel upped the ante with "Lingerie Barbie," and there is an array of T-shirts that objectify and impose an adult sexuality on toddlers and young girls through slogans like "Future Trophy Wife," "Hot Tot," "Made You Look," and "Born to Shop." Costume stores feature many provocative costumes for pre-teen girls, one of which is "Major Flirt"—a provocative "military" uniform complete with high, black leather-look boots with a platform heel, kilt-style mini-skirt, and studded black leather belt and choker.

Everywhere they turn—family, toys, advertising, media, and school—girls learn that beauty, narrowly defined and sexualized, is of utmost importance. This definition of beauty is also dependent on the consumption of beauty aids and products. "Salon" and "spa" birthday parties aimed at little girls as young as three years old are gaining popularity, providing a venue for girls to indulge in a range of services from manicures and pedicures to full makeup and hair extensions. One website for such services (replete with descriptors such as "diva" and "little princess") suggests that such experiences "build confidence," a statement reflecting the sad reality of girls who are taught that their self-worth is dependent on validation they receive from others in response to their physical and sexual attractiveness.

—Angela Aujla

Young girls just can't wait to climb aboard this lingerie store's GIRLTRENDZ tour bus. But how young is too young?

that promote war and crime, and TV shows that glorify death and murder—socialize young people, especially adolescent males, into committing violence, or at least into being desensitized to violence and the pain of others? Or does it provide a safe outlet for pent-up hostile emotions? The two sides of this contentious debate are taken up by contemporary writers in the following excerpts. First, arguing for a link between media violence and criminal activity, are psychologists Brad Bushman and L. Rowell Huesmann:

> True, media violence is not likely to turn an otherwise fine child into a violent criminal. But, just as every cigarette one smokes increases a little bit the likelihood of a lung tumor someday, every violent show one watches increases just a little bit the likelihood of behaving more aggressively in some situation. (Bushman & Huesmann 2001: 248)

Arguing for the other side is communications professor Jib Fowles, in *The Case for Television Violence*:

> Television is not a schoolhouse for criminal behavior. . . . Viewers turn to this light entertainment for relief, not for instruction. Video action exists, and is resorted to, to get material out of minds rather than to put things into them. . . . Television violence is good for people. (Fowles 1999: 53 and 118)

Having whetted your appetite for the debate, we'll take a closer look at how Huesmann and Fowles arrived at their views.

Huesmann's Longitudinal Studies

Huesmann's pioneering work on the effects of television violence on children involved the use of **longitudinal studies**, which examined data gathered on research subjects over an extended period. His first was a 22-year study of 856 youths in New York State. At the beginning of his study the participants were all in Grade 3, about 8 years of age. Huesmann followed up by interviewing them again when they were 19, and then again at 30 (Huesmann & Eron 1986). Among male subjects, the relationship between viewing television violence and engaging in aggressive behaviour roughly 10 years later was both positive and highly significant—in other words, there was a link, and it was a strong one. These findings were consistent for males of different social classes, IQ scores, and levels of aggressiveness at the start age. When the male subjects were checked again at age 30, the relationship between violent television viewing and aggressive behaviour—both self-reported and as documented in criminal records—was just as strong.

In another major study, Huesmann and his colleagues (2003) studied 557 Chicago-area children from grade 1 to grade 4, beginning in 1977. Fifteen years later, they interviewed as many of them (and their spouses and friends) as they could, and also looked at public records and archival material. The researchers were able to gather reasonably complete data for 329—roughly 60 per cent—of the original research participants (153 men and 176 women, all then in their early twenties). The results of this study were similar to those of the earlier study, with the only difference being that the link between TV violence and aggressive behaviour was evident among women as well as among men. The researchers concluded their study with the following statement:

> Overall, these results suggest that both males and females from all social strata and all levels of initial aggressiveness are placed at increased risk for the development of adult aggressive and violent behavior when they view a high and steady diet of violent TV shows in early childhood. (Huesmann et al. 2003: 218)

Huesmann proposed two theories to explain the data. One, **observational learning theory**, states that children acquire what he termed "aggressive scripts" for solving social problems through watching violence on television. The other, **desensitization theory**, states that increased exposure to television violence desensitizes or numbs the natural negative reaction to violence.

Fowles's Defence of Television Violence

Jib Fowles, author of the second statement cited earlier on this page, argued that sociologists and others who condemn violence on television are really using TV violence as a pretext to tackle other issues: class, "race," gender, and generation. He calls television violence a "whipping boy, a stand-in for other clashes":

> The attack on television violence is, at least in part, an attack by the upper classes and their partisans on popular culture. In this interpretation, . . . the push to reform television is simply the latest

Which do you think is more likely: that this young man is becoming desensitized to violence, or that he is ridding himself of aggression?

manifestation of the struggle between the high and the low, the dominant and the dominated. (Fowles 2001: 2)

Fowles draws upon the work of **Pierre Bourdieu** (1930–2002), a French sociologist, anthropologist, and philosopher best known for his work on the connection between class and culture. Fowles applies two of Bourdieu's key concepts in particular: *habitus* and *reproduction*. **Habitus** (related in origin but somewhat different in meaning from the English word "habits") is a wide-ranging set of socially acquired characteristics, including, for example, definitions of "manners" and "good taste," leisure pursuits, ways of walking, even whether or not you spit in public. Each social class has its own habitus, its set of shared characteristics. **Reproduction**, in Bourdieu's definition, is the means by which classes, particularly the upper or dominant class, preserve status differences among classes. As Fowles phrases it, "the reproduction of habitus is the key work of a social class" (Fowles 2001: 3).

Fowles's main point, then, is that sociologists who condemn television violence are merely fighting proxy wars aimed at reproducing the habitus of the dominant class by condemning the habitus of the dominated class. It is ironic that he uses Bourdieu's writing to do this, as Bourdieu (1996) was a severe critic of television.

What do YOU think?

1. Do you think that Fowles's arguments are valid? What other criticisms of mass media might be challenged using this kind of approach?

2. Would you feel safe in a movie theatre parking lot after the release of latest instalment in the street racing action series *The Fast and the Furious*?

Education

Education can be a powerful socializing agent. For example, schools often are the first source of information that children receive about a social group other than their own. Teachers, curriculums, textbooks, and the social experience of being in the classroom and in the playground all play a part. We will focus here on the role teachers play in the socializing function of education.

What we call the *social location* of the teacher—his or her gender, age, ethnicity, and so on—can have an effect on the educational socialization of the student. The fact that the early years of schooling are dominated by women teachers will have very different effects on female and male students. The fact that science and math courses in high school are usually taught by men and English courses by women will also have different effects on girls and boys. Being of the same ethnic background as the teacher can have a positive effect on a child's socialization experience, as Kristin Klopfenstein points out in her article "Beyond Test Scores: The Impact of Black Teacher Role Models on Rigorous Math-Taking." In the introduction to her article she notes that:

> Poor [in terms of income] black students, amongst whom teachers are often the only college-educated people they know, are in particular need of role models who (a) are interested in their educational progress; (b) understand the school system as an institution [i.e. as being located in the middle class and more in "white culture" than in "black culture"]; and (c) actively encourage academic excellence and the pursuit of challenging curriculum. Culturally similar teachers may take more interest in mentoring black students and have more credibility with those students. Given the importance of a rigorous mathematics curriculum and that math is frequently a gate-keeper subject for black students [i.e. success in math determines whether or not they will advance to post-secondary education], same-race math teachers play a potentially vital role in preparing black students for their academic and working futures. (Klopfenstein 2005: 416)

Klopfenstein looked for a correlation between having a black math teacher in grade 9 and the kinds of math courses a black student would take the following year. She found that black students who had had a black math teacher in grade 9 were more likely to enrol in a more challenging math class in Grade 10. These students, she found, also had a greater chance of post-secondary entry and success than students who had not had a black math teacher.

The socialization effect of having black teachers does not end there. Klopfenstein quotes P.R. Kane and A.J. Orsini's assertion that "Teachers of color are important role models to white students, as they shape white students' images of what people of color can and do achieve" (Kane & Orsini 2003: 10). Though you probably didn't notice, the prevailing demographics of the teachers you had growing up—their age, sex, ethnic background, and so on—played a major role in your socialization.

What do YOU think?

How do you think the social location of a teacher might affect a student's socialization? Give some examples. How do you think this might differ for male and female students, especially during the early years when, typically, most of the teachers are women?

Issues of Socialization

In this section we will look closely at two issues of socialization, one involving adolescents and the other affecting children. Both cases involve a complex combination of agents of socialization.

Male Readers

Traditionally, school-aged boys do best in maths and sciences, while girls fare better in writing and reading. Sociologists and educators today recognize that this is partly a result of socialization: boys have always been encouraged more in the former area of study, girls in the latter. In fact, beyond a lack of encouragement, there has been outright discouragement, as girls struggling in the supposedly male subjects have often been told not to worry: "You aren't expected to do well in math," or "You won't need to know it."

A lot has been done to improve female performance in the "male preserve" of math, science, and technology (sometimes known as MST), including the institution of all-girl classes in these subjects and the conscious promotion of role models such as astronaut Julie Payette. On average, boys still tend to perform better in these areas, but the difference has been lessened.

The Point Is...

David Elkind and Hurried Child Syndrome

David Elkind studies culture as an agent of socialization. One of his areas of interest is the negative effects on children whose lives have been overprogrammed by their parents, with little free time built in for spontaneous play. On this topic, Elkind's tone is dire: "[The] traditional culture of childhood is fast disappearing," he warns; "In the past two decades alone, according to several studies, children have lost 12 hours of free time a week, and eight of those lost hours were once spent in unstructured play and outdoor pastimes" (Elkind 2003).

Spontaneous play, Elkind argues, has been replaced by a programmed schedule of organized sports and extracurricular learning. Technology is partly to blame: digital communication enables us to do more, faster, giving us a false feeling that we can accomplish much more than we used to. We extend this push for accomplishment to our children, putting pressure on them to take part in more after-school activities, play more organized sports, do more homework, and learn languages and other academic subjects at an earlier age. All of this is part of what Elkind calls the **hurried child syndrome**, which causes kids to feel adult-like amounts of stress and guilt. It also contributes to the sometimes crippling apprehension that post-secondary students feel about deadlines and their career—"I'm 21 and I don't know what I want to be."

Elkind also worries about the role of technology in socializing children. For one thing, the modern child's comfort with new technology is creating a **generation gap** (a significant cultural and social difference complete with an equally significant lack of understanding between generations). As he explains:

> [D]igital youth has a greater facility with technology than their parents and other adults. As a result, there is a greater disconnect between parents and children today, and some adolescents have even less respect for the knowledge, skills and values of their elders than they did a generation ago. . . .
>
> Independence from parents and adults means greater dependence on peers for advice, guidance and support. The availability of cell phones and immediate access to friends through instant messaging has only exaggerated this trend and quite possibly worsened the divide between children and their parents. (Elkind 2003)

On top of its role in creating a generation gap, today's digital culture, with its "many adult-created toys, games and amusements," is affecting childhood socialization in ways that may compromise personal autonomy and originality:

> Game Boys and other electronic games are so addictive they dissuade children from enjoying the traditional games. Yet spontaneous play allows children to use their imaginations, make and break rules, and socialize with each other to a greater extent than when they play digital games. While research shows that video games may improve visual motor coordination and dexterity, there is no evidence that it improves higher level intellectual functioning. Digital children have fewer opportunities to nurture their autonomy and originality than those engaged in free play. (Elkind 2003)

Elkind is hardly alone in voicing such concerns. In a recent editorial, *The Globe and Mail* sounded a similar note of alarm, warning:

> The loss of spontaneous play from children's lives is not quite complete. . . . But the situation is pretty dismal. . . .
>
> [C]hildren between grades 6 and 12 spend an average of 7 hours 48 minutes on various screens each day. Horrifying, if true. And not without risks, whether from the health problems associated with a sedentary life, cyberbullying or even pedophiles reaching through their screens. ("Editorial" 2012)

Parents reading all of this may nod in agreement, while younger readers shake their heads in bemusement. Can this be considered like Fowles's discussion of media violence: an attack of one generation, growing older and losing power, on the habitus of a younger generation?

The same cannot be said for male–female differences in performance when it comes to language arts, as a 1999 federal government report, based on studies done in 1994 and 1998, makes clear. The following is an excerpt:

> Girls score substantially higher than boys in language skills and this gender difference is already pronounced by the age of 13. Boys and girls do not differ in mathematics achievement at the age of 13; however a gender gap in favour of males, particularly in problem-solving skills, seems to emerge by the time students are in their last year of secondary schooling. . . . It appears nevertheless that any gender differences in numeracy are substantially smaller than such differences in literacy. Hence, with respect to skills attainment, by the end of secondary schooling, girls should be in a somewhat better competitive position than boys. (Thiessen & Nickerson 1999: 3)

More recently, Statistics Canada reported the following results from an international study of 15-year-old students carried out by the Organization for Economic Co-operation and Development as part of its Programme for International Student Assessment:

> In Canada, as well as in a majority of nations, boys outperformed girls in mathematics, but the difference was relatively small. On the other hand, there was a relatively large difference favouring girls in reading in all Canadian provinces and the vast majority of countries.
>
> There was no difference between girls and boys in mathematics in three provinces: Prince Edward Island, Quebec and Saskatchewan.
>
> Boys also performed better than girls in science in Canada overall. However, among the provinces, the difference was significant in Manitoba, Nova Scotia and Ontario. (Statistics Canada 2004)

This raises a number of questions. To what extent is socialization to blame for gender differences in learning? Which agents of socialization might be having the greatest effect? How might educators change their approach to socialization in order to diminish the gender differences in literacy skills? Are video games, played more frequently by boys than by girls, largely to blame here?

Resocialization

Resocialization takes place whenever an individual shifts into a new social environment. It typically involves both unlearning and learning. In its extreme form, the individual unlearns all of the behaviours, attitudes, and values that were appropriate to his or her previous social environment while learning those that make it possible to fit into the new situation.

British author Karen Armstrong describes a particularly explicit process of unlearning values in her book *Through the Narrow Gate* (1982). Armstrong was a teenager in the 1960s, when she joined a strict order of nuns in Britain. In the following passage she recollects what the Mother Superior said to her and others who had just joined the order as postulants:

> Novices and postulants are kept in a particularly strict seclusion. They may not speak at all to seculars [i.e. to those who are neither nuns nor priests]. If a secular speaks to you, you must never reply. It is only by severing yourself absolutely from the world that you can begin to shed some of its values. Again no novice or postulant may ever speak to the professed nuns unless she is working with them and those few necessary words are essential for the job. The professed are in contact with the world, and even that indirect contact might seriously damage your spiritual progress. . . .
>
> You have to be absolutely ruthless in your rejection of the world, you know, Sisters. So many of its attitudes, even in really good people, are permeated with selfish values that have nothing at all to do with the self-emptying love of God. You yourselves are riddled with these ideas; you can't help it—it's not your fault. (Armstrong 2005 [1982]: 92–3)

Resocialization can be voluntary or involuntary. *Voluntary resocialization* occurs when someone starts school or moves to a new school, when someone begins a job with a new company, when someone retires from work, or when someone undergoes a religious conversion (which can also, in extreme circumstances, be involuntary, as with cults). Associated with this kind of resocialization is the **rite of passage**, which is a ritual marking a life change from one status to another, typically following some form of training. A wedding is a rite of passage; so is a funeral. Other examples include the Christian practices of baptism and **confirmation**, and the Jewish **bar mitzvah** (for boys) or **bat mitzvah** (for girls), when adolescents become "adults in the faith" after a period of instruction.

Involuntary resocialization occurred in First Nation residential schools, like the one in Shubenacadie discussed in the narrative box on page 125, where the language, religion, and customs of Aboriginal children were brutally beaten out of them. Other examples of involuntary resocialization include being drafted into military service, being thrown in jail, being committed to a psychiatric hospital, and being subjected to mandatory retirement. Goffman (1961) calls institutions where involuntary resocialization takes place **total institutions**, as they regulate all aspects of an individual's life. A significant part of the unlearning process associated with involuntary resocialization is what has been termed a **degradation ceremony**, a kind of rite of passage where a person is stripped of his or her individuality. Hazing, whether of grade 9 students, first-year

college or university students, or rookies on amateur and professional sports teams, is a degradation ceremony in which being made to perform acts of minor (sometimes major) humiliation informs the initiates that they are in a new social world where they are mere beginners.

Sometimes voluntary and involuntary resocialization can occur together. Consider, for instance, programs for treating alcoholism or obesity, which begin with the sufferer's decision to change his or her lifestyle but then involve a strict and rigorous regime that is imposed for the duration of treatment.

Involuntary Resocialization and the Degradation Ceremony of Velma Demerson

From 1913 to 1964, thousands of women in Ontario were put into reformatories under the Female Refuge

The Point Is...

The Vision Quest: A Modern Aboriginal Rite of Passage

A traditional rite of passage for Aboriginal people is the **vision quest**, which once marked the passage from childhood to adulthood. After receiving months of informal instruction from elders, the individual would embark on a journey away from the home community to an isolated location. Then he or she would fast for days, and possibly go without sleep, in the process of seeking a vision. A vision could be a song that comes to mind, or the appearance in dreams of an animal or other spirit who instructs the dreamer and initiates a connection with him or her that will continue until death.

More recently, adults have used the vision quest as a way of resocializing themselves with traditional ideals following a period of difficulty. The following is a generalized example of the Ojibwa vision quest as it has been practised recently in northeastern Ontario (Steckley & Rice 1997: 226–7). It begins in a sweat lodge, a dome-shaped structure built around overlapping willow poles, covered with skins or tarpaulins and used as a kind of sauna. The participants throw sacred tobacco on a fire to thank the Creator. They are told the story of how the sweat lodge came to the people from a little boy who was taught about healing from the seven grandfather

spirits. Water is put onto the seven stones that represent those spirits. The Elder sings ceremonial songs.

After the sweat, the participants are led to their own small lodges, where they fast and meditate. The Elder visits them to ask about their spiritual experiences. The participants fast for three nights and four days. What they learn changes with each night:

The first is described as the night of doubt, where participants pray but are uncertain about what will happen. Hunger is mitigated by a feeling of excitement. The second night is one of fear, sometimes known as the dark night of the soul. Participants realize that their bodies are beginning to weaken, and they may question their resolve. The third night is the night of the spirit. It is often said that if something meaningful is going to happen, it will occur between the beginning of the spirit night until the fast is finished. (Steckley & Rice 1997: 226–7)

After the final sweat there is a feast with gift-giving to the Elder and to those who have assisted the individuals in their resocialization.

Telling It Like It Is

Resocializing the Mi'kmaq

The Shubenacadie Indian Residential School operated for 45 years, beginning in the early 1920s, under the auspices of two Roman Catholic orders in the small central Nova Scotian community of Shubenacadie. Mi'kmaq students at the school suffered terrible abuse at the hands of the staff, whose mission was to resocialize students by beating their traditional culture out of them—literally, if necessary. The abuse is illustrated graphically in the words of anthropologist and former student at the school Isabelle Knockwood, who provides the following account of a young Mi'kmaq girl caught speaking in her native language:

The nun came up from behind her and swung her around and began beating her up. . . . Then the Sister pinched her cheeks and her lips were drawn taut across her teeth and her eyes were wide with terror. . . . Then the nun picked the little girl clean off the floor by the ears or hair and the girl stood on her tiptoes with her feet dangling in the air. . . . The nun was yelling, "You bad, bad girl." Then she let go with one hand and continued slapping her in the mouth until her nose bled. (Knockwood 1992: 97)

Resocialization at the Shubenacadie Indian Residential School. Notice that the boys have more freedom in what they can wear than the girls do. Why do you think that was so?

Act. Among the "offences" for which young women would be placed in these institutions was being sexually active outside of marriage. This kind of behaviour and the women guilty of it were branded "incorrigible."

In 1939, Velma Demerson, 18 years old and white, became sexually involved with a Chinese man. They intended to get married. When she became pregnant, her parents reported to the authorities that she was being "incorrigible." Velma was arrested and sent first to a "home" for young girls, then to the Mercer Reformatory. The following is her account of her degradation ceremony:

> I can see that the girls ahead of me in line are getting large cotton dresses, aprons, underwear, white cotton stockings, and black shoes. When my turn comes, I put on a large faded old-fashioned dress. It's extremely wide and reaches my ankles. However, when I put on the full apron with its long ties I can see that it will hold the dress in, making it look like it almost fits. The thick cotton stockings are about two inches too long at the toes but are easily stuffed into the shoes, which are also several sizes too large.
>
> Each girl has quickly been handed a bundle without reference to size. We learn that we can expect to be issued standard Mercer attire in our own size later. What we've been given is the garb provided to all new inmates, to be worn for the first few weeks. In the months to come we are always able to recognize a new inmate by her initiation clothing. To girls already in a state of anxiety, the code of silence and humiliating dress further the subjugation. We are young women, aware of fashion. We know that large cotton dresses and wide aprons belong to a past era of drudgery on the farm. (Demerson 2004: 5)

Following this she was led to her cell, which was seven feet long and four feet wide, equipped with one bare light bulb, a cot, a cold water tap and basin, along with a covered enamel pail to be used as a toilet.

Hazing as Resocialization

Hazing is a particular way of resocializing new members of some group or organization, such as a high school, a university fraternity, a sports team, or a military unit. It is like a test in which the initiate must demonstrate, by successfully undergoing a demeaning or uncomfortable experience, that he or she is "tough enough" to be a member. In sports, hazing typically involves some form of ritual humiliation of the rookies, imposed by the veterans, who as first-year members had to go through the same trial themselves. Usually this kind of hazing is fairly minor: male players might have to shave their heads, or wear women's clothing or dress like a chicken in a public place. Sometimes, however,

Tampa Bay relief pitcher Brandon Gomes heads to the bullpen with a Dora the Explorer umbrella and travel case—accoutrements of his rookie hazing ritual. Hazing is common in professional sports. Do the benefits to the individual of this kind of resocialization ritual outweigh any potential harm?

it crosses the line in ways that can harm the individual being hazed, particularly when the activity involves nudity and sexualized activities. In 2005, sports hazing made national headlines when a member of the McGill University football team quit after he and other rookies were forced to participate in a hazing ritual: nude and gagged, they were made to bend over while being prodded up the backside with a broom. This was nothing less than sexual abuse. At around the same time, a 16-year-old rookie on the Windsor Spitfires of the Ontario Hockey League became the subject of media attention after refusing to go through a hazing ritual called the "sweat box." This entailed crowding, naked, with other rookies into the washroom at the back of the team bus, with the heat turned up high enough to make the participants perspire.

Traditionally hazing has been much more a male than a female activity. Establishing one's toughness has long been viewed as a manly thing to do. But this may be changing. In September 2009, the Carleton University's women's soccer team was suspended by the university for holding a rookie initiation party that ended up with a player becoming so drunk that she had to be rushed to hospital by ambulance. Interestingly, while the suspension made the national news, the ensuing decision to reduce the suspension to just two games did not.

What do YOU think?

1. Why does hazing often "cross over the line" into abusive acts?

2. Is proving toughness an inherent part of sports? Is it an inherent part of being male?

3. Do you think it's fair to draw parallels between hazing rituals in women's sports and the increasing acts of violence by girls and young women?

WRAP IT UP

Summary

Whether you're a lab rat or a domesticated parrot, a "wigga" trying to fit in in Bolton or a young teen buying her first bra, a rookie at training camp or a first-year student at frosh week, you, and everyone you know, have undergone processes of socialization and resocialization. (To see what human life without socialization would be like, check out the 1970 film *The Wild Child*, based on the true story of a young boy who grew up entirely on his own in the wilds of France.) The person you are depends significantly on the agents of socialization you've grown up around—parents and family, educators, peer groups, culture and the media. Sometimes these agents work together, but sometimes they send conflicting messages (you might have very different ideas about how to dress from your parents and your friends). How influential are these messages? Well, to a cultural determinist, who you are depends almost entirely on the messages you receive from your social environment. Others, though, like Dennis Wrong, believe you have the power to choose which messages you hear and which you block out—that you have agency, in other words.

Post-secondary educators are heavily engaged in resocialization, in preparing students for careers, and for making them think critically about how they were and are being socialized. In fact, in this chapter (and in all the others), *I* have been trying to resocialize you. Did you notice? Do you think it worked?

THINK BACK

Questions for Critical Review

1. Outline the basic ideas of Freud as they relate to socialization.

2. Outline the basic ideas of Mead and Cooley as they apply to socialization.

3. Explain the differences between social determinism, biological determinism, and agency.

4. Identify at least five different agents of socialization and outline their roles.

5. Career, clothing, hobbies: do you believe each of these is more socially or more biologically determined?

6. Consider one or two situations in which you have been resocialized (for instance, starting a new school, moving to a new neighbourhood or city, entering or leaving an intense relationship). What did you have to learn? What did you have to unlearn?

7. In terms of socialization, what do you feel has been the impact of television, video games, movies, and the Internet on your life?

READ ON

Online

Social Psychology Network

http://Huesmann.socialpsychology.org

> Maintained by Wesleyan University professor Scott Plous, the Social Psychology Network is dedicated to psychological research and teaching. This page presents an overview of the work of Rowell Huesmann, with free access to some of his articles.

National Longitudinal Survey of Children and Youth

www23.statcan.gc.ca:81/imdb/p2SV.pl?Function=getSurvey&SDDS=4450&lang=en&db=imdb&adm=8&dis=2

> Launched in 1994 by Statistics Canada and Human Resources and Development Canada, the NLSCY is a long-term study of Canadian children designed to follow their development and well-being from birth to early adulthood.

The Hurried Child

www.cbc.ca/ideas/episodes/2010/12/14/the-hurried-child

> This CBC Radio podcast from December 2010 examines the costs and consequences of the hurried child syndrome.

In Print

Karen Armstrong (1981), *Through the Narrow Gate: A Memoir of Spiritual Discovery* (New York: St Martin's Griffin).

> Karen Armstrong's recounting of her time inside a Catholic convent provides a window into religious training and spiritual life.

Ruth Benedict (1946), *The Chrysanthemum and the Sword* (Boston: Houghton Mifflin); **David Riesman (1950)**, *The Lonely Crowd: A Study of the Changing American Character* (New Haven, CT: Yale University Press).

> These two books are classic examples of national character studies.

Sigmund Freud (1953), *On Sexuality: Three Essays on the Theory of Sexuality and Other Works* (New York: Penguin).

> This collection features three of Freud's key articles on sexuality, ranging in scope from sexual abnormality to puberty.

Isabelle Knockwood (1992), *Out of the Depths: The Experiences of Mi'kmaw Children at the Indian Residential Schools at Shubenacadie* (Lockeport, NS: Roseway).

> Knockwood's work is an insightful ethnography on the residential school experience by one who survived the experience herself.

Laurie Kramer (2009, Winter), *Siblings as Agents of Socialization: New Directions for Child and Adolescent Development* 126 (Hoboken, NJ: Jossey-Bass).

> A look at how brothers and sisters act as socializing agents in ways similar and different to those of parents, and as differing in different cultures and classes.

Shirley Steinberg & Joe L. Kincheloe, eds (2011), *KinderCulture: The Corporate Construction of Childhood*, 3rd edn (Boulder, CO: Westview Press).

> An important look at how corporate marketing is socializing small children and teenagers.

6 Social Roles, Interaction, and Organization

Learning Objectives

After reading this chapter, you should be able to

- distinguish between the various kinds of statuses that an individual holds at any one time

- discuss the impact of role conflict, role exit, and role strain on the life of an individual

- discuss the impact of bureaucracy and formal rationality on the lives of Canadians.

Key Terms

- achieved
- ascribed
- back stage
- collectives
- control
- cosmology
- definition of the situation
- dramaturgical approach
- efficiency
- egalitarianism
- feminist organization
- formal rationalization (*or* rationality)
- formal social movement organizations
- front stage
- impression management

- looking-glass self
- marginalization
- master status
- matrilineal
- McDonaldization
- organizational behaviour
- organizational culture
- organizational theory
- passing
- predictability
- quantification
- role
- role conflict
- role exit
- role set
- role strain
- role-playing game
- scientific management

- secularism
- service-provider organizations
- small groups
- social mobility
- social organization
- social segregation
- status
- status consistency
- status hierarchy
- status inconsistency
- status set
- substantive rationality (*or* rationalization)
- Taylorism
- team approach
- theocracies
- Thomas theorem

Names to Know

- Howard Becker
- Charles H. Cooley
- Sir Francis Galton

- Erving Goffman
- Everett C. Hughes
- Georg Simmel

- Frederick W. Taylor
- Frederic M. Thrasher
- Max Weber

Learning to Be a Stepfather

In *David Copperfield*, Charles Dickens describes a truly evil stepfather for young David. That character was the model I hoped to avoid when I acquired the status of stepfather in the early 1990s, when I gained, through marriage, stepsons who were seven and eight. During my first years as stepfather I felt that of all the statuses I had, it was the one that caused me the most grief: I couldn't sort out what my responsibilities were, because they weren't clearly defined. I wasn't "their dad," and yet I felt I was expected to take on many of the responsibilities that go along with being a father of sons.

Much of the time I felt as though I was making up my job and status as stepfather as I went along. What do you do when a seven-year-old boy grasps your hand and walks with you in public? What do you do when a 10-year-old won't go out the front door because there's a bee outside? I wished there were a manual—*Stepfathering for Dummies*—that I could consult. At first, I was anxious to win them over by acting like the uncle I already knew how to be—the one who spoils nephews and nieces with candy, craziness,

and presents, then leaves Mom and Dad to deal with their rambunctious children now jacked up on sugar and gifts and inspired to recklessness by my very physical humour. But I didn't want to be like the stepfather I had once met whose stepson could get away with anything. I had stayed with this acquaintance's family for a few days, and the boy soon learned that I wasn't soft like his stepfather. When he wouldn't wash his face, as part of the routine I was asked to supervise, I took a cloth and gave him a good, hard scrub; next time, he did it himself. But then, I wasn't emotionally attached to him or his mother. I had nothing to lose.

In this new relationship, I had to be more like a father: strict but fair. Not an easy path to take for a "live and let live" kind of guy. It was a good thing that I loved sports, like they did. I went to all of their hockey, baseball, and lacrosse games. I coached Rob in baseball, and drove Justin all over the countryside when he made the local rep baseball team. I was glad that they weren't girls. Conjuring up a hideous stereotype, I just couldn't imagine myself going shopping in a mall with a stepdaughter. She'd have to love sports or I wouldn't know what to do.

I worried that people are sometimes suspicious of stepfathers, as though they're child abusers just waiting for the right opportunity. And when the school called or I went for parent–teacher interviews, I felt that my status was being judged, questioned. Sometimes after I'd explained the nature of my relationship to the boys, I perceived a certain knowing look in the eyes of teachers, principals, and office staff, a look that said, "Well *that* explains it."

Now that both boys are in their twenties, I am finally becoming comfortable with my stepfather status. I refer to them unselfconsciously as "my sons." When Rob had a near-fatal car accident and he asked me to drive him home, I was moved to tears. One of Justin's co-workers calls me "Justin's dad." I'm happy with that. Although I know I made lots of mistakes, I feel I finally know what it means to have the status of "stepfather."

And perhaps I can write *Stepfathering for Dummies* after all.

What do YOU think?

1. Why, according to the author, is the status of stepfather a complicated one? What does this status entail?

2. Imagine the narrative the author's stepsons might write in response to this. Do you think they would have found the status of stepson just as complicated?

Introduction: Why Small Groups Are Hard to Study

When we interact with people, and they interact with us, much of what goes on both in thoughts and in behaviour relates to the statuses we hold and the way we perform the roles attached to those statuses. The interaction may be relatively simple when the expectations are well understood by both parties. But if a status is more complex because the set of expectations attached to it is not well established, the exchange may be more difficult. Such is the case with stepparents and stepchildren, as the opening box suggests. Sometimes, too, the expectations associated with one status interfere with those of another, as we will see.

We'll have much more to say about statuses shortly. First, though, we'll consider group interaction and how it has been researched.

The study of small-group interaction came early to sociology, with the pioneering work of the microsociologist **Georg Simmel** (1858–1918), who was among the first to narrow his focus to the daily, one-on-one social interactions of individuals. He was, in this way, a forerunner of the symbolic interactionists—Mead and Blumer especially—whom we met in Chapter 1. Others working in this tradition around the turn of the twentieth century include **Charles H. Cooley** (1864–1929), whose concept of the **looking-glass self** is about how our individual selves are defined and reinforced through interpersonal interactions

with others, and **Frederic M. Thrasher** (1892–1962), whose classic study of gangs in Chicago (Thrasher 1927) represents a study of group interaction rooted in fieldwork. Thrasher's ethnographic research on gangs and small-group interaction was carried on to good effect in William Whyte's *Street Corner Society* (1955), which we examined in Chapter 2.

Another key contribution to the study of small-group interaction came from the symbolic interactionist William I. Thomas. It was in Chapter 2 that we first met Thomas, whose work with Florian Znaniecki, *The Polish Peasant in Europe and America* (1918–20), illustrates the important part that narratives play in defining situations. Thomas showed that people's own interpretations of their lives represented an important sociological element that was well worth studying. This idea eventually became the **Thomas theorem**, the notion that the "situations we define as real become real in their consequences" (Thomas 1966: 301). The Thomas theorem influenced other developments in symbolic interactionism, including a concept known as the **definition of the situation**. This states that given a particular situation, different individuals will interpret the situation differently and in contradictory ways, based on their own subjective experiences. In order to understand an individual's actions and responses to particular situations, you need first to understand how he or she defines the situation. You can see how this would be an important consideration in studying small groups.

During the 1950s, a group of researchers at Harvard, most notably Robert F. Bales, brought the study of small-group interaction to the laboratory—specifically, the Laboratory for Social Relations. Bales and his colleagues focused on such issues as the development and maintenance of leadership roles in small groups. At about the same time, **Erving Goffman** published *The Presentation of Self in Everyday Life* (1959), in which he introduced his **dramaturgical approach**. This, as you may recall from Chapter 2, is a way of approaching sociological research as if everyday life were taking place on the stage of a theatre, with a **front stage** for public display and a **back stage** for private, personal, or more intimate encounters. The strategies we adopt when presenting ourselves publicly are known, collectively, as **impression management**.

QUICK HITS

The Thomas Theorem and Arthur Kleinman's Eight Questions

The Thomas theorem is an important consideration in healthcare. Anne Fadiman's work on how Western medicine failed to properly address the situation of a young Hmong girl with epilepsy (see Chapter 18) concludes with a consideration of eight questions, first posed by Arthur Kleinman, that Western doctors should use in interactions with patients from non-Western cultures. Their purpose is to determine, from the point of view of the patient and her family, the definition of the healing situation and sickness in order to mitigate any problems that might arise around opposing situational definitions based on cultural differences:

1. What do you call your illness? What name does it have?
2. What do you think has caused the illness?
3. Why and when did it start?
4. What do you think the illness does? How does it work?
5. How severe is it? Will it have a short or long course?
6. What kind of treatment do you think the patient should receive? What are the most important results you hope she receives from this treatment?
7. What are the chief problems the illness has caused?
8. What do you fear most about the illness?

Most sociologists today are not involved in studying small-group interaction, for several reasons. First, the work was very much the product of a structural-functional perspective, which has become a minority perspective in twenty-first–century sociology. Second, small-group studies seemed to lack a proper consideration of gender, "race," ethnicity, and other sociological factors that are now considered essential to any rigorous inquiry. Imagine how the dynamics of a group of women change when a man is part of the group. Imagine how the opportunities and strategies for leadership differ in a small group of women and a small group of men. And what if the groups were mixed, or if we were to bring the various ethnic backgrounds of the group members into the discussion? Third, many contemporary sociologists view the study of small groups—especially in a lab setting—as artificial. Research on small-group interaction has found greater acceptance in psychology, especially social psychology, where it has been widely used in studies of leadership development in particular.

Social Status

Status and role: it sounds like an order for a quick take-out lunch, but these two concepts are central to sociology. A **status** is a recognized social position that an individual occupies. It contributes to the individual's social identity by imposing responsibilities and expectations that establish the individual's relationships to others. You don't have just one status; in fact, you can have several at once—daughter, mother, wife, CEO, volunteer board member, soccer coach, and on and on. The collection of statuses you have is your **status set**. If you are a man, you could have the statuses of son, brother, uncle, teacher, drummer (for your band), neighbour, citizen, white person—all at the same time and with little effort. These would make up your status set. We gain statuses as we age, and we also possess, however briefly, dozens of statuses throughout our lives.

One way of classifying our many statuses is to distinguish between statuses that are achieved and those that are ascribed. A status is considered **achieved** if you've entered into it at some stage of your life, but you weren't born into it; a professional position (assuming it's not a job in the family business), a role in a hobby or recreational activity, an academic standing ("college graduate")—all of these are achieved statuses. They assume some kind of personal ability, accomplishment,

Let's say you were studying this group of co-workers to try to find patterns in social dynamics: who assumes a leadership role, who plays peacemaker, who puts up the most objections, and so on. How might your gender, ethnicity, sexual orientation, and (dis)ability affect your results concerning individuals who do not share your social location?

or voluntary act, although very few statuses are completely achieved (for instance, an accomplished drummer has *some* natural ability).

An **ascribed** status is one that you were born into ("female" or "male," "daughter" or "son," "sister" or "brother," etc.) or one you have entered into involuntarily ("teenager," "elderly person," "diabetic"). Circumstances trump choice in ascribed statuses. For a long while there, it looked as though being president of the United States was always going to be an ascribed status—white, male; others need not apply. Of course, the degree to which a status is achieved or ascribed depends on how free a society is and how much **social mobility** exists. In a society where a small ruling elite dominates, the statuses of lawyer, politician, doctor, professor, or rich business owner can be more ascribed than achieved. There is little vertical mobility from the lower, labouring classes into the elite. On the other hand, while "race" is for the most part ascribed, a person from a racialized group who wants to avoid discrimination and whose appearance does not clearly put them into one group or another can successfully claim dominant racial status; this process is known as **passing**. It is not

unusual for Aboriginal people in Canada to "pass" for white, or at least to try, particularly in big cities.

Sexual Orientation and Status: A Problem Area

We would argue here that sexual orientation is primarily an ascribed status. Heterosexuality is natural for some, and homosexuality is natural for others. There are those who believe that homosexuality is simply a "lifestyle choice," one that can be overcome with heavy doses of therapy, drugs, religion, or conservative politics. Remember, homosexuality was against the law in Canada until 1969. The scholarly literature strongly argues that sexual orientation is a physical/psychological predisposition, which may or may not be acted upon at some point. According to this definition, regardless of whether you live in a gay or lesbian relationship, you are homosexual if your sexual fantasies are overwhelmingly about people who are of the same sex as yourself.

Of course, sexual orientation, as we will see in Chapter 11, is much more complicated than this. One problem with naming it as either an achieved or an ascribed status has to do with the way one's own sexuality is recognized by others. Someone who is gay but who marries into a heterosexual relationship because of social pressure would not be socially recognized as homosexual. In terms of statuses, that would mean the status of sexual orientation is, at least partially, achieved because it is a lifestyle choice based on what society recognizes and how it exerts pressure to conform with the norm. Status, then, lies in what you do, not in what you feel; in this case, choice can trump circumstances.

"Indian Chief" and Status

As the preceding section shows, the issue of achieved versus ascribed status isn't always cut and dried. But does it really matter whether a status is achieved or ascribed?

It does. In fact, the consequences can be quite serious when people incorrectly assign ascribed status to a position that has a strong achieved component. An illustration is the status of the word "chief" (an English word and, as applied to the head of a First Nation band

in Canada, a defined status in the eyes of the federal government). Consider, for example, the "peace chiefs," or *sachems* (from an Algonquian word for "leader"), of the Confederacy of the Haudenosaunee, or Six Nations of the Iroquois. There are 50 sachems, each member appointed, by tradition, according to lineage within a clan. Because the clans are **matrilineal** (determined along the line of the mother), the leading women in the clan have the power to suggest both who should receive the title of chief and when he might have this status removed. If you belonged to the right lineage—if, say, your mother was the sister of the previous chief or you were the brother of the previous chief—you would be eligible to become chief. However, you could not be chosen and awarded this status unless you were seen by key members of the clan as having demonstrated the abilities necessary for a sachem—abilities in listening, speaking, and compromising, for instance.

When the Canadian government disallowed the traditional government of the Iroquois—violently, in the case of the Six Nations (1924) and in the Mohawk community of Akwesasne (1898)—one of the reasons the federal government used to justify its position was that the First Nations government was undemocratic. Federal leaders assumed that being a hereditary chief meant that the position automatically went from father to son (or, more accurately in a matrilineal society, from mother's brother to sister's son), with no input from the community. In other words, they saw the status of sachem as ascribed rather than achieved. As we've just noted, there was a strong achieved component to the status. The government's misguided assumptions resulted in forcing an unwanted form of government on the Iroquois people. Ironically, they did so in the name of the British monarch, the holder of an ascribed status.

Master Status

Everett C. Hughes (1897–1983) introduced the concept of master status in "Dilemmas and Contractions of Status" (1945), published after he left McGill University for the University of Chicago. He applied the term in the context of "race" in the US:

Membership in the Negro race, as defined in American mores and/or law, may be called a

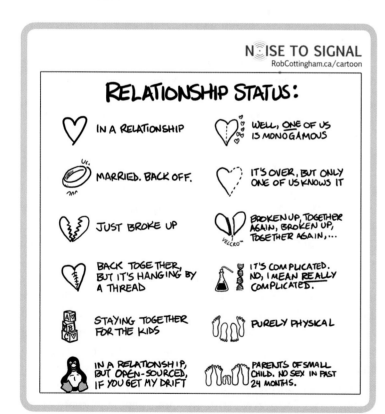

Your relationship situation is part of your status set. But human relationships can be confusing, their statuses sometimes extending over a wide range of possibilities. Wouldn't it be simpler if people could have their relationship status stitched into their clothing as well as posted on their Facebook page?

QUICK HITS

Labelling Theory

Sociologist **Howard Becker** developed labelling theory in the 1960s to explain the negative effects a label can have when applied to a group outside of the majority. Part of this theory states that when negative labels are attached to a status, a powerful master status can be created and internalized by both the individual and others. The process is well portrayed in the following excerpt from a study on drug culture:

> [I]f people who are important to Billy call him a "druggie" this name becomes a powerful label that takes precedence over any other status positions Billy may occupy. Even if Billy is also an above average biology major, an excellent musician, and a dependable and caring person, such factors become secondary because his primary status has been recast as a "druggie." Furthermore, once a powerful label is attached, it becomes much easier for the individual to uphold the image dictated by members of society, and simply to act out the role expected by significant others. (Hanson et al. 2009: 76)

A label like "druggie" thus becomes a master status that can follow a person for his or her entire life, despite efforts to change it.

Labelling theory has also been used to look at how negative, racialized statuses within education affect self-esteem, educational performance, and educational outcomes.

individual doesn't want them to be. If you met Barack Obama at a dinner party (say you crashed it) and asked him, "What do you do?", he would probably inform you, politely, of his status as leader of the most powerful nation on earth and winner of the Nobel Peace Prize. Nevertheless, during his first presidential campaign, his master status was that of a black man.

Status Hierarchy

Statuses can be ranked from high to low based on prestige and power; this ranking is referred to as **status hierarchy**. For each of the basic sociological categories of gender, "race," ethnicity, age, class, sexual orientation, and physical ability, there is a scale in which one status tends to be ranked more highly than another or others. In Canadian society we rank male over female, white over black or brown, British over eastern European, elite over middle and working class, heterosexual over homosexual, and able-bodied over disabled. Age is more complicated. Power is concentrated in the hands of those who are middle-aged, yet because we live in a society that promotes the cult of youth—the desire to look, act, and feel young—youth also has some prestige. The middle-aged often abuse their bodies, injecting poison (e.g. Botox) into their faces and fat into their buttocks, undergoing facelifts, and fighting to hold onto their youthful appearance through fitness

What statuses are displayed in this image? Which would you consider to be the master status? Could the master status be one that isn't visible in the picture?

master status–determining trait. It tends to overpower, in most crucial situations, any other characteristics [i.e. statuses] which might run counter to it. (Hughes 1945: 357)

The term **master status** signifies the status of an individual that dominates all of his or her other statuses in most social contexts, and plays the greatest role in the formation of the individual's social identity. You can learn a lot about people by asking them what they consider their master status to be. Canadians, upon being introduced to someone, will often ask: "What do you do?" This implies that a person's occupation is his or her master status. It isn't always the case, though: ethnicity and gender can be master statuses, even when an regimes and the masking effects of makeup. We could also call this a form of *passing*, as those who engage in such rejuvenating practices are trying to achieve higher status by "passing" for younger.

Status Inconsistency

Not all social statuses align in all people, creating a situation in which a person holds statuses that are seen and ranked differently. This can result in social tension. You may find yourself with a high-ranking gender or ethnic status but a lower-ranking class status. You are a WASP (a white, Anglo-Saxon Protestant), but you're working-class. As it happens, there are a fair number of people who have the complete favoured set of being male, white, of British heritage, rich, heterosexual, and able-bodied. Federal and provincial parliaments seem to be clubhouses for people with that status set—just look at the press photos from any meeting of cabinet ministers. Likewise, there are a lot of black or Aboriginal women living at or below the poverty line, and who are lowly regarded. **Status consistency** is the result when all of the social status hierarchies line up; when they do not—when one is highly ranked in

The Point Is...

Dungeons & Dragons: Virtual and Real Status

Before video games, the virtual battling worlds of Halo and World of Warcraft, and the escapism of Second Life, there was E. Gary Gygax's Dungeons & Dragons (D&D), the first worldwide **role-playing game**. During the 1970s and 1980s it sold millions of copies as a pen-and-paper, sit-at-the-table game before it joined the computer world.

D&D was set in any one of a number of fantasy worlds populated by such creatures as elves, trolls, gnomes, dreaded orcs, and wyverns, all borrowed from Tolkien's *Lord of the Rings* and the fantasy works of Michael Moorcock, H.P. Lovecraft, and Roald Dahl. Players entered these worlds as sorcerers, knights, and holy warriors, their fate in encounters with various monsters or sealed passages determined by the roll of any one of a number of different dice. As for the dungeons, they really weren't dungeons but settings invented by the person acting as the "dungeon master" (the DM). You could call the DM a sort of referee, but for author Mark Barrowcliffe, "To call the DM a referee is a bit misleading. His role is nearer to that of a god. He creates a world, sets challenges for players' characters, and rewards or punishes them according to the wisdom of their actions" (2008: 32).

Barrowcliffe's *The Elfish Gene: Dungeons, Dragons and Growing Up Strange—A Memoir* (2008) is a good introduction to D&D. Barrowcliffe grew up in working-class Coventry, England, and began playing D&D in 1976 at the age of 12. Explaining his fascination with the game, Barrowcliffe notes that he and his friends didn't aspire to their parents' simple and (from their perspective) dull lives, characterized by predictability and stability. Instead, they sought the kind of magic that was missing from their lives and their world. They were, in Barrowcliffe's estimation, intelligent (particularly in the many mathematical calculations necessary to be a successful player), but not necessarily school-smart. They certainly were not jocks or tough guys, and they weren't concerned with fashion or appearance.

What does D&D have to do with status and role? For a generation of adolescents—almost exclusively boys—their D&D characters formed a status that was recognized by other players, and that was as significant as traditional statuses such as son, brother, friend, and student. The roles played in D&D games were more engaging than those occupied in real life, though some real-life "truths" were learned through playing.

Players adopted their statuses from among a number of different character classes. Initially, these were simple: fighter (warrior), cleric (priest), and magic-user (wizard). As the game evolved, however, the number of character classes grew to include alchemists, assassins, berserkers, druids, ninjas, paladins, and female characters such as witches and the bizarrely sexual houris—"a cross between sorcerers and prostitutes" (2008: 227).

one status category but not in others—the condition is called **status inconsistency**.

Michaëlle Jean exemplified status inconsistency as governor general of Canada. She was raised in a middle-class home in Haiti, where her father, the principal of a prestigious preparatory school in Port-au-Prince, taught philosophy. However, her family was forced to emigrate to Canada after her father was imprisoned in the mid-1960s during the time of the dictatorships of François Duvalier. Shortly after coming to Canada in 1968, Jean's parents split up, and her mother was forced to work at low-income jobs. The experiences of racism and poverty that Jean faced in Canada clashed with her later achievements. Jean excelled at university, winning scholarships and eventually earning a master's degree. She taught at university and became a prize-winning journalist and social activist, honoured several times for her work with women's shelters. When she was appointed governor general in 2005, there was a significant amount of social tension surrounding her nomination. She was a black woman and an immigrant, whose first language was French. In Ms Jean's case, however, one can say, based on her accomplishments, that her status was achieved rather than ascribed.

By rolling dice and recording the results, players would determine the strength, magical ability, charisma, and intelligence of their characters, and they would speak and act as they imagined their characters would. According to Barrowcliffe:

> People . . . identified very strongly with their characters. . . . This is where it differs from a computer game. You can't reboot if your character is killed. In D&D if the character dies, he's dead, which . . . is a serious threat to his future. Losing a character that you've had for . . . years can be a major emotional experience. At fourteen years old it can be the first real grief you've known in your life. It's like having an imaginary friend but one you get to actually look at, that other people will discuss as if they're real and may even attempt to kill. (2008: 35)

The game socialized young males, giving them self-knowledge, opportunities to exercise creativity, and experience in the competitive world of adults, lessons other males might learn through their statuses as goalies, drummers, long-distance runners, or high-school students. Just as important, it allowed them to invent for themselves an alternative status set, one that gave them the control to choose a number of statuses that are typically ascribed, like sex, age, and social position.

D&D was played with dice and a map sketched on a sheet of graph paper, typically around the dining room table. How do you think that would affect the status formation of those who played? How might it differ from the experience of participants in today's online gaming community, who may never meet one another face to face?

What do YOU think?

What lessons does participating in role-playing games produce? Does it matter that they are learned while playing out fictional rather than real statuses?

Hughes noticed that when people of "lower" status moved into occupations associated with more favoured statuses, they became targets of certain strategies others used to reduce the apparent inconsistency. One strategy was to modify the stereotype surrounding the lowly regarded status. This would cause upwardly mobile individuals to be alienated both from people sharing their low ascribed status and from people defined by the more highly regarded achieved status. Referring to sociological data gathered during his research for *French Canada in Transition* (1943), Hughes wrote:

> [I]n Quebec the idea that French-Canadians were good only for unskilled industrial work was followed by the notion that they were especially good at certain kinds of skilled work but were not fit to repair machines or to supervise the work of others. In this series of modifications the structure of qualities expected for the most-favored positions remains intact. But the forces which make for mobility continue to create marginal people on new frontiers. (Hughes 1945: 356–7)

This situation, where individuals live in a kind of limbo—partly in the old world of stereotypes and prejudices assigned to one status, partly in the new world of achieved occupational status—is embodied in the figure Robert E. Park called "marginal man." The male bias implied in the term is the main reason it's no longer used; however, it is historically important and preserved in the commonly used term **marginalization**, which refers to the process by which groups are assigned into categories that set them at or beyond the margins of the dominant society.

Another strategy that Hughes identified was **social segregation**, which he illustrated as follows:

> The woman lawyer may become a lawyer to women clients, or . . . may specialize in some kind of legal service in keeping with woman's role as guardian of the home and of morals. Women physicians may find a place in those specialities of which only women and children have need. A female electrical engineer was urged by the dean of the school . . . to accept a job whose function was to give the "woman's angle" to design of household electrical appliances. The Negro professional man finds his clients among Negroes.

> The Negro sociologist generally studies race relations and teaches in a Negro college. (Hughes 1945: 358)

In this way, social segregation is both the outcome of being marginalized as well as a strategy to deal with marginalization.

What do YOU think?

In what situations do you think "race" is a master status in Canada?

Social Roles

A **role** is a set of behaviours and attitudes associated with a particular status. Roles attached to a status may differ across cultures. For example, people holding the status of elder in traditionally minded cultures of China, Africa, and certain Aboriginal communities in North America are expected to have acquired a certain level of wisdom that is then shared with younger people. The same expectations seldom exist in mainstream Canadian culture, where the status of elder has few positive role expectations attached to it; the status is more "old person" than it is elder. (Indeed, one reason that Western social scientists were slow to question the myth of Inuit elder abandonment—discussed in Chapter 2—is that Western culture lacked its own positively defined role of elder, making the myth much more credible in their eyes.)

A given status may be associated with more than one role. Robert Merton (1949) developed the idea of the **role set**, which comprises all of the roles that are attached to a particular status. As professors, we have the role of teacher to our students, but we are also colleagues to our peers, employees of our schools, and, of course, trouble-making underlings to our administrators. Students have a peer role with classmates in addition to their student role with instructors; to the college or university, they are paying customers.

Role Strain

Role strain develops when there is a conflict between roles within the role set of a particular status. For example, if a student complains to his instructor about a teacher in another class, the instructor is placed in a conflict between her role as educator, in which she has the student's best interests at heart, and her role as colleague, in which she must be loyal to the professor teaching the other class. Similarly, a student who catches a classmate cheating on an exam is at once a member of the academic community with a responsibility to report the offence and a member of the student body who wouldn't rat out a peer. Role strain can even affect a single role. Consider the parent who feels more at ease with one of his children than with the other, but tries to balance his attentions between them. It can be a very difficult game to play.

Role Conflict

Another useful concept for understanding social tensions is role conflict. **Role conflict** occurs when a person is forced to reconcile incompatible expectations generated from two or more statuses he or she holds. If you are both a mother and a student, then you know all about role conflict. Imagine: it's the night before the big exam and you need to study—part of the set of behaviour expectations attached to being a college or university student; however, your daughter needs help with her homework, your son is ill, and your husband is watching the big game—he's been looking forward to it for weeks—and so has made himself unavailable. These clashing sets of expectations illustrate role conflict. We see cases where people turn down promotions because they do not want to move into a position where they might have to reprimand peers and friends who suddenly occupy a lower position within the organization: this is role conflict.

Role Exit

Role exit is the process of disengaging from a role that has been central to one's identity, and attempting to establish a new role. Helen Rose Fuchs Ebaugh (an ex-nun turned sociologist) has studied role exit processes extensively; some of her findings are summarized in *Becoming an EX: The Process of Role Exit* (1988). According to Ebaugh, who wrote about not just ex-nuns but also ex-priests, ex-convicts, and recovering alcoholics, role exit involves shifting your master status. If you were forced to retire having always defined yourself by what you did ("I am a nurse"), you might feel uncomfortable when asked,

Imagine writing an essay with one hand, and only part of your mind on the subject. What role conflict do you think this student experiences?

A tearful Brett Favre announces his retirement from the National Football League's Green Bay Packers in 2008. Does it look to you as though he's struggling with role exit? Would it surprise you to learn that he returned to the NFL the following season with the Minnesota Vikings?

"What do you do?" If you are a stay-at-home mother and your children grow up and move away, you have lost a very important purpose in your day-to-day life that is not easily replaced by being merely a wife (and grandmother might be far away in the future). If you are a father and your parental role is reduced because your ex-wife gains primary custody of the children, then becoming a part-time dad may feel like a role exit.

The role exit of married people who become single through separation, divorce, or death of a spouse is always difficult, as it entails shifting from "we" to "I." Previous relationships with friends and family change and, in the case of divorce, people take sides. Some people you've been close to might start avoiding you, treating your divorce like something contagious and you as a carrier of the "failed relationship" virus. On the other hand, others might begin to pay you more attention, and in ways you haven't been used to. After all, if you're still reasonably young, you are expected to be "out there" meeting eligible singles, even if you have always enjoyed staying at home. Role exit, as uncomfortable as it might be, is something we will all experience throughout our lives.

Introduction to Social Organization

When we think of the term *social organization*, we might think of the way a society and its institutions—family, law, religion, polity, economy, and so on—are organized. What we seldom consider is that the basis for social organization, whether imagined or real, rests on a particular set of principles.

In the sociological literature, *social organization* is rarely defined, and when it is, it's often conflated (i.e. blended together and considered part of the same thing) with the terms *social structure* or *social institution*, as though they were all synonymous. They are not. While social institutions *are* social structures and *are* socially organized, social structures and social organization are *not* social institutions. So, what is "social organization"?

We take **social organization** to be the social and cultural *principles* around which things are structured, ordered, and categorized. In this way, we are able to speak about the social organization of cultures, social institutions, or corporations. For example, a culture may be organized around the principle of **egalitarianism** (society based on equality) or hierarchy (a system with clear, well-defined ranks or levels), and further organized in terms of the type or form that the egalitarian or hierarchal structure takes: that is its social organization.

Organizational Structure

Under the European system of feudalism, one's allegiances were first to God, then to king, and finally to country. As European societies moved from **theocracies** (religious states) to **secularism**, from monarchies to democracies, and from countries to nation-states, the nation-state became the main locus of allegiance and loyalty. When we go to war, we no longer fight for our religion or our sovereign or prime minister, but for our country. And, despite the emotional feelings—pride, loyalty, sentimentality, etc.—that are aroused when we sing the national anthem or win an Olympic gold medal, "Canada" is an imaginary geopolitical space in which a diverse population is constructed as an "imaginary community" through symbols such as the anthem and flag. Canada, then, is not a "natural" thing but rather a socially organized manifestation based on certain collectively shared principles. Culture, and the organizing principles it's based on, imposes a structure that is seen as "natural." In this way, organizing principles are upheld by shared cultural beliefs and maintained through a network of social relations.

At the heart of organizing principles are the ways in which a culture produces knowledge about the world based on a particular **cosmology**. A cosmology is an account of the origin and ruling principles of the universe, especially the role of humans in relationship to non-humans (living and non-living). Cosmologies and corresponding myths are often seen as a high form of truth.

Aboriginal cosmologies are rooted in the belief that all matter, both inanimate and animate, is interdependent: everything is connected. They emphasize the interdependence of humans and nature. Judaeo-Christian-Islamic cosmology emphasizes human dominion over nature as decreed by God. This cosmology, together with the emergence of modern science beginning in the Enlightenment, has helped control over nature to become an important organizing principle of Western culture. Consider the fact that both sides of the global warming debate in some senses believe that humans control the environment. Those who deny global warming believe that humans can control the effects of manufacturing and waste disposal, whereas those who are concerned about global warming think that we are not controlling these effects well enough and must change our behaviour to minimize the impact.

The Study of Organizations

To recap: organizational principles are based on our knowledge or understanding of the world, which is informed by our cosmology. These principles determine not just how our culture and society are organized

What principles make up the social organization of your college or university? Democracy versus hierarchy (e.g. in administration–faculty and faculty–student interaction), freedom versus strict control of discussion and debate? Commercialism? Elitism versus access? How would you detect the presence and influence of these factors?

but how other social bodies are organized, whether we're talking about social institutions like the family and education, or bureaucracies and corporations, or community-based organizations. What is important in the study of organizations is to distinguish both the level of organization and the level of analysis.

Interest in the sociological study of organizations picked up after Weber conducted his detailed work on bureaucracy, and again when the study of organizations filtered into the business sector and commerce degree programs that began to be offered at colleges and universities during the 1980s. The study of organizations shifted from the examination of social institutions to the examination of business corporations as a way to uncover more effective and efficient management practices. This led to an explosion in the fields of **organizational theory** and **organizational behaviour** (see Mills & Simmons 1995). During the last 20 years, the study of organizational behaviour has expanded by integrating approaches from other disciplines. Anthropology, for instance, has contributed to the study of organizations through its understanding of corporations as communities in which an **organizational culture**, with "organizational rituals" and "symbolic acts," is an aspect of organizational dynamics. An anthropologist may also study the informal organization of a company to determine how decisions are made or how information actually flows—processes that may not quite follow the mandated, formal structure of the organization itself.

With the spread of globalization, there has been increased study of cross-cultural organizations, which are of particular interest to businesses and those who study organizational behaviour. In the 1980s, organizational structures based on models derived from the productive corporate culture of Japan were implemented in North America. They failed, however, in part because they did not account for the organizational principles of Japanese culture, which are more collectivist than the individualist organizational principles favoured in Canada and the US. Organizational structures based on a collective model, in which employees work in teams, did not have the same success when applied to the competitive individualism found in North American business culture and society generally. Think of the TV show *The Apprentice*, where, on the one hand, competing cast members are asked to co-operate and work in teams, yet there can be only one winner in the end. There is no real commitment to the team; the commitment is only to oneself.

Much of the increase in organizational studies has been fuelled not by natural sociological interest but by Western capital, invested by companies in an effort to find ways to increase profits by managing employee behaviour and practices more efficiently. This has led to questions about the ethics of controlling worker behaviour, not to mention the inherent ethnocentric and capitalist assumptions in organizational theory given the context of global culture. These critiques have fostered the growth of critical management studies, which are critical of traditional theories of management. Two critical management theorists, Mills and Simmons (1995), have challenged the assumptions of mainstream accounts of organization. They point out that there is little in the literature of organizational theory and behaviour that deals with "race," ethnicity, class, or gender, despite the high participation rates of women and people of colour in the labour force. Even after the Royal Commission on Equity in Employment (1984) concluded that job opportunities in Canada were severely restricted because of widespread systemic discrimination against Native people, visible minorities, disabled people, and women, mainstream organizational theory continues to ignore issues of inequality within organizational structures. Mills and Simmons also note that there is little attention given in this literature to the impact organizations have on the social and psychic life of individuals and groups affected by organizations. Despite the demonstrated link between organizational life and lack of self-esteem, a sense of powerlessness, segregated work life, stress, physical injury, pay inequality, sexual harassment, and racism, organizational theory and behaviour studies continue to ignore it (Mills & Simmons 1995).

Feminist Organizations

Organizational structure and process have been a major focus for the contemporary women's movement. Whether the structure is based on networks and coalitions or at the level of individual organizations, feminists have always been concerned with the form of the organizations they create. In some instances, feminists have developed organizational forms that differ from mainstream forms as an expression of feminist politics. Because of their political and symbolic importance, issues surrounding organizational structure like the internal distribution of power and control, the division of labour, and decision-making rules

Islam and Zyphur defined the organizational ritual as "a form of social action in which a group's values and identity are publicly demonstrated or enacted in a stylized manner, within the context of a specific occasion or event" (2009: 116). The TV show *The Office* has taken aim at these organizational rituals, including the office holiday party. If you're familiar with the show, what other organizational rituals have been presented? How can they backfire?

can make it difficult for feminist coalitions to maintain their organizational cohesion.

While **feminist organizations** are generally organized around principles different to those found in traditional, patriarchal organizations based on hierarchy, it would be a mistake to think that these organizations are without internal conflict. Carol Mueller (1995) studied feminist organizational form and conflict orientation, and found that, generally speaking, the type of organization itself would either mitigate or facilitate conflict. Mueller identified three types of feminist organizational form:

1. **formal social movement organizations**, which are professionalized, bureaucratic, and inclusive, and which make few demands of their members (examples include organizations dedicated to basic women's rights)
2. **small groups** or **collectives**, which are organized informally, and which require large commitments of time, loyalty, and material resources from its members (examples include women's publishing houses)
3. **service-provider organizations**, which combine elements of both formal and small-group organizations (examples include organizations dedicated to specific women's rights, such as freedom from abuse and protection from an abuser).

Mueller found that these organizational forms varied in terms of the degree to which feminist organizational principles such as inclusivity and democratic participation were practised. She also found these forms combined in a variety of structural configurations ranging from coalitions to complex social movement communities.

Organizational conflict can also vary depending on whether it is oriented internally, toward other members, or externally, toward other organizations, the state, or civil society. When conflict is directed

The Point Is...

Feminist Organization at Work

The Teaching Support Staff Union (TSSU) represents teaching assistants, tutor markers, and sessional instructors at Vancouver's Simon Fraser University. Certified in 1978, the TSSU began as Local 6 of the Association of University and College Employees (AUCE). AUCE was a feminist trade union movement that developed out of the Vancouver Women's Caucus in the late 1960s and early 1970s. The feminist roots of the TSSU make it strikingly different from more conventional unions. From its start, the AUCE rejected the traditional form of organization found elsewhere in the Canadian union movement, which tends to be based on hierarchical structure and centralization. It successfully organized large numbers of women working in underpaid positions, mostly as clerical and teaching support staff. But since AUCE's inception, all of the AUCE locals, with the exception of Local 6, joined larger, more mainstream unions, such as the Canadian Union of Public Employees (CUPE); Local 6, now the TSSU, has continued to maintain its independent status.

The TSSU today is a grassroots union that is no longer affiliated with any other larger union or umbrella organization. All of its decisions come from the general membership. There are three salaried officers who are part of the larger executive committee and who handle the day-to-day operation of the union. The officers, as well as all members of the executive committee, are also members of the union itself, an arrangement that ensures that executives are in touch with issues of concern to the broader TSSU membership. Executive positions come up for reelection annually, and no member is allowed to occupy a position for more than two years consecutively. This practice encourages skills development among the general membership and prevents the concentration of knowledge in the hands of a few members. The executive meets every two weeks, and meetings are open to all TSSU members.

General meetings (GMs) of the membership take place three times every semester, and a minimum of 20 members must be present before decisions can be made. The membership has control of union resources and must approve the annual budget, financial statements, and most expenditures of the union. Committees and executive members make regular reports to the GM, guided by the motions put forward at these meetings. Any member can bring forward a motion at a GM.

The TSSU maintains a global vision. Not only does it fight to improve the working conditions of its own members, it also actively fights for labour rights and social justice locally, nationally, and internationally. The TSSU has supported CUPE's University Bargaining Sector, the BC Teachers' Federation, and other striking teachers from Hamilton, Ontario, to Oaxaca, Mexico. They have also initiated a Social Justice Committee to expand the scope of the union's advocacy, with a mission to fight the root causes of injustice, inequality, and poverty.

What do YOU think?

Go to the TSSU's website and look at the union's list of accomplishments: www.tssu.ca/about/our-accomplishments/. In what way do you think these reflect the TSSU's status as a feminist organization?

internally—typically around issues of identity or ideology—it can cause fracturing within the organization. When conflict is directed externally, internal divisions tend to be minimized, and there is often increased solidarity in the face of a common threat. On the other hand, external-directed conflict can create a combat-oriented climate that often legitimizes hierarchical divisions of labour. However, whether defensive or offensive, external conflict heightens participation and increases pressure for action to defend those values under attack.

Mills and Simmons (1995) believe that feminism has had a growing presence in organizational theory, where it challenges the male domination of organizations and calls attention to the absence of gender analysis in organizational theory.

Bureaucracy

The Origins of Bureaucracy

As Amitai Etzioni points out, "organizations [and bureaucracies] are not a modern invention" (1964: 1). Bureaucracies arose out of the formation of states and writing systems some 5,000 years ago. The development of a sophisticated system of administration in early Sumerian cities led to the invention of writing. The earliest bureaucrat is found in the scribe. Sumerian script was so complicated that it required scribes who had trained in the discipline of writing for their entire lives. These scribes had considerable power within Sumerian society because they held a monopoly over record-keeping and inscriptions.

As empires emerged and grew, administrative bureaucracies expanded at a pace to match imperial expansion. In the Persian empire, the central government was divided into administrative provinces: in each one, a royal secretary was posted to keep records and supervise troop recruitment. Royal inspectors were sent out to the provinces to report on the local conditions. In Han Dynasty China (fifth century BCE), the bureaucratic system developed out of Confucius's concern with creating social stability, which required a system of administrators to ensure good governance. Administrators were appointed based on the merit of examinations (i.e. written tests). What became known as the imperial examination system continued in China until the early twentieth century.

While the idea of bureaucracy has existed since ancient times, the term itself originated in eighteenth-century France and comes from the word *bureau*, meaning "writing desk" or the place where officials work. The cumbersome processes of bureaucracies is sometimes referred to as "red tape," which dates back to nineteenth-century Britain, when government officials used red tape to tie up official documents until they were needed. Red tape, then, is used to refer to the slow procedures associated with acquiring and dispensing information. Most of us have encountered bureaucratic red tape in our federal, provincial, or municipal agencies—when applying to replace a lost passport or driver's licence, for instance—but the situation is far, far worse in many developing nations that are choked by bureaucracy and red tape, a legacy of colonial administration. As we will see, despite the inefficiencies and the difficulties in changing bureaucratic organization to meet individual and societal needs, bureaucracies are necessary for the successful functioning of complex societies.

Bureaucracy and Formal Rationalization

Max Weber's extensive work on bureaucracy is still frequently cited and used today. It was part of his larger study of the process of rationalization, specifically, his examination of **formal rationalization** (or **rationality**). "Rationalization" is a term we hear frequently in business reports, where it is used as a euphemism for firing workers and cutting jobs in an effort to reduce costs and become more efficient. This is an example of formal rationalization, which, according to Weber, has four basic elements:

- efficiency
- quantification
- predictability
- control.

We will look at the implications of these terms a bit later, in the section on McDonaldization. Formal rationalization, with its emphasis on forms, differs from other models of rationality, like **substantive rationalization**, which involves the substance of values and ethical norms. Organizations governed by substantive rationalization are constantly asking themselves, *Are we reflecting our values?* By contrast, organizations governed by formal rationalization tend to ask, *Have we instituted particular forms in our organization?* Take, for example, Aboriginal organizations. Democracy, spirituality, and respect for elders are all important Aboriginal values. Forms that reflect those values are open meetings, where anyone can speak and be listened to, and prayers spoken by elders. How do you think Aboriginal organizations at opposite ends of the substantive rationalization–formal rationalization spectrum would act?

Weber was critical of both formal rationalization and bureaucracy, arguing that the former led to the "irrationality of rationality" and that the latter was dehumanizing by nature. Workers within the rational, bureaucratic organization of various companies and political bodies came to be viewed as "cogs in the wheel" or "bricks in the wall," reminded frequently that they could always be replaced. You may feel similar effects even when you're not part of the bureaucracy but are confronted by the impersonal nature of its public face.

Going Global

Economic Globalization and Formal Rationalization

One of the pillars of economic globalization is a belief in liberalizing trade by reducing or eliminating protective tariffs. The view that poor countries of the developing world will abandon inefficient industries that have been supported by protective tariffs in favour of more productive industries is heavily influenced by the principles of formal rationality. But as Joseph E. Stiglitz argues in *Globalization and Its Discontents* (2003), policies designed to enhance a country's income by forcing resources from less to more productive uses often fail in countries where, because of conditions imposed by global loan-granting agencies like the International Monetary Fund (IMF), those human and capital resources are altogether lost through diminished productivity and job loss:

> It is easy to destroy jobs, and this is often the immediate impact of trade liberalization, as inefficient industries close down under pressure from international competition. IMF ideology holds that new, more productive jobs will be created as the old, inefficient jobs that have been created behind protectionist walls are eliminated. But that is simply not the case. . . . It takes capital and entrepreneurship to create new firms and jobs, and in developing countries there is often a shortage of the latter, due to lack of education, and of the former, due to lack of bank financing. The IMF in many countries has made matters worse, because its austerity programs often also entailed such high interest rates . . . that job and enterprise creation would have been an impossibility even in a good economic environment such as the United States. The necessary capital for growth is simply too costly. (Stiglitz 2003: 59–60)

When you're told, "Your call is important to us," you know that it isn't (a point summed up nicely in the title of Laura Penny's work *Your Call is Important to Us: The Truth About Bullshit*). These examples speak to the dehumanizing feelings we experience daily through our interactions with bureaucratic organizations.

The "irrationality of rationality" involves the "disenchantment of the world," an important concept in Weber's writing. Weber believed that with the increase in formal rationalization, the West was becoming increasingly *disenchanted*—lacking in magic, fantasy, and mystery—which could only lead to further alienation. Enchantment is a quality that cannot be efficient, quantified, predicted, or controlled. Disney's "Magic Kingdom," for instance, is anything but magical: it is a rationalized system of pre-packaged enchantment commodities—there are to be no surprises. Weber worried and warned about the oncoming danger of the "iron cage of rationality," a world in which every aspect of life is controlled by the formal rationalization of bureaucracy, a world dehumanized and over-controlled. Throw away your bucket lists and your day planners. You have nothing to lose but your certainty.

The Evolution of Formal Rationalization

The Industrial Revolution, which occurred in the late eighteenth and early nineteenth centuries, was the starting point for the development of formal rationalization. **Sir Francis Galton** (1822–1911), considered the father of modern statistical analysis, was a pioneer in developing methods to measure the capabilities and productivity of individuals. He had a natural love of numbers and made formal rationalization a part of his everyday life. An example: he spent many hours getting the quantities (temperature, volume, etc.) just right for the "perfect" pot of tea (he was English, after all).

Along these same lines, **Frederick W. Taylor** (1856–1915) developed the practice he referred to as **scientific management**. Based on "time-and-motion" studies, scientific management (which became known as **Taylorism**) was designed to discover the *one best way* of doing any given job. Taylor and his team of "efficiency experts" studied the time, methods, and tools required for a proficient worker to do a particular job. His objective was to eliminate wasteful or "inefficient" (i.e. slow, non-productive) motions or movements. Frank Gilbreth, a follower of Taylor's, undertook an intensive study of a bricklayer's job and reputedly reduced the number of motions involved in laying a brick from 18 to just 5. Assembly line work also used Taylor's methods to the maximum efficiency, though Henry Ford is credited with making the assembly line an industry standard.

One of the weaknesses of Taylorism/scientific management is that it didn't allow the individual worker to develop a broad set of skills, because he or she was asked to perform a single set of actions over and over again. Workers often became alienated from their work, with little sense that they had anything to do with the overall manufactured product.

Taylorism, slightly modified, was still practised in North America during the 1980s and 1990s. At that time, the success of Japanese auto manufacturing prompted North American businesses to implement non-Tayloristic Japanese business practices in their training sessions. Among these practices was the **team approach**, which incorporated worker input and fostered the idea that workers could be involved in several stages of the manufacturing process, generating a greater sense of product ownership. (If you thought this might be an instance of substantive rationality, you'd be right.) This approach was first adopted by car manufacturer Saturn, which, until the downturn in the automotive sector in 2008, was very successful, in large part because it managed to reduce the sense of alienation among its workers.

The McDonaldization of the World

George Ritzer, in *The McDonaldization of Society* (2004), draws on Weber's concept of formal rationalization in his conception of **McDonaldization**. McDonaldization is similar to "Disneyfication," "Walmartitis," and "Microsoftening"—in Ritzer's words, "the process by which the [rationalizing] principles of the fast-food restaurant are coming to dominate more and more sectors of American society as well as the rest of the world" (2004: 1).

Do you think you would be happier performing one task in the assembly of 20 vehicles or several tasks in the assembly in 5? The first approach reflects formal rationality principles such as maintaining quotas. The second reflects the substantive rationality principle of worker ownership of the work and the product.

How do the four pillars of formal rationalization—efficiency, quantification, predictability, and control—guarantee that your experience is the same in any McDonald's restaurant around the world? Would it surprise you to know this picture was taken at a restaurant in Russia?

Ritzer applies the four fundamental elements of Weber's formal rationalization—*efficiency*, *quantification*, *predictability*, and *control*—to his examination of contemporary fast-food restaurants. To show how McDonaldization is affecting other areas of everyday life, we've applied his theory to the world of post-secondary education.

Efficiency relates to the streamlined movement in time and effort of people and things. This efficiency is achieved largely by breaking up larger organizational tasks into smaller, repeated tasks performed by individuals who are separated from each other by a division of labour. Smaller tasks are often performed later by machines rather than people. It should be noted that efficiency has different meanings in the different layers of a social organization. What is efficient for a college administrator might not be efficient for a college professor (for example, the former finds efficiency in the networking of printers, rather than allowing the prof to use his own little printer and not wait in line when print requests are heavy—personal experience

here). And being efficient in this way is not the same as being *effective*, although it's possible for a process to be both efficient and effective. Think of the potential differences between being an efficient teacher—one who teaches quickly and articulates a great number of concepts—and an effective teacher—one who successfully communicates to students all or almost all that is taught. A teacher can be one or the other, both, or none of the above. At college and university, the multiple-choice test is a classic example of bureaucratic efficiency—questions are often provided with the textbook, and they can be marked quickly using a computer. But are they the most effective means of promoting learning?

Second, formal rationalization in bureaucracy involves the **quantification** of as many elements as possible. The efficiency, or "success," of the process is measured by the completion of a large number of quantifiable tasks. For instance, the success of call centres is primarily measured by how many calls are handled rather than how many clients are actually

Telling It Like It Is

An Author POV

Little Boxes: Mass-Produced Suburban Communities

After the end of World War II, which marked the start of North America's "baby boom," there was a fairly severe housing shortage in both Canada and the United States. One response was the development of mass-produced suburban communities. The first and standard-setting effort in this regard was the series of "Levittowns" built in the eastern US. Between 1947 and 1951, Levitt and Sons built 17,447 houses on Long Island, New York, creating an instant community of about 75,000. This model would soon be reproduced in Pennsylvania and then New Jersey. The company began by building warehouses for their supplies, their own workshops for wood and plumbing manufacture, and gravel and cement plants. Ritzer describes the rationalization of the house-building process in the following excerpt:

> The actual construction of each house followed a series of rigidly defined and rationalized steps. For example, in constructing the wall framework, the workers did no measuring or cutting; each piece had been cut to fit. The siding for a wall consisted of 73 large sheets of Colorbestos, replacing the former requirement of 570 small shingles. All houses were painted under high pressure, using the same two-tone scheme—green on ivory. . . . The result, of course, was a large number of nearly identical houses produced quickly at low cost. (Ritzer 2004: 36)

The owners of the construction company knew that their employees did not enjoy many of the intrinsic rewards experienced by skilled independent tradespeople, but they felt that the *extrinsic* rewards of money would make up for that:

> The same man does the same thing every day, despite the psychologists. It is boring; it is bad; but the reward of the green stuff seems to alleviate the boredom of the work. (A. Levitt 1952, quoted in Ritzer 2004: 35–6)

Sociologists often speak of how this kind of rationalized uniformity comes at the cost of oppression of minoritized people. In the case of Levittown, the covenants (agreements signed by homeowners with the developer) included racial segregation. Blacks were not allowed. The story of how one family "conspired" to bring a black family into Levittown, and how it was resisted, sometimes violently, by neighbours and social organizations, illustrates this (see David Kushner's *Levittown: Two Families, One Tycoon, and the Fight for Civil Rights in America's Legendary Suburb*, New York: Walker and Company, 2009). This leads to the question: Does extreme rationalization of organization lead automatically to social oppression?

In the Toronto area, the suburb of Don Mills, constructed during the early 1950s, became known as Toronto's "first planned community." I grew up there beginning in 1956. It had the city's first shopping centre, the first Country Style doughnut shop, and the first Shopper's Drug Mart. As a teenager, I was a "plaza boy"—a term for someone who spent his leisure hours hanging around the mall. Famous Canadians from this community include comedian Rick Green (of *The Red Green Show*), "Martha" of the 1980s band Martha and the Muffins, and singer and writer Dan Hill. It also produced an outstanding Canadian sociologist: Neil Guppy. And yours truly, of course.

What do YOU think?

Think of a suburb you're familiar with. What aspects of it do you think reflect formal rationality or "McDonaldization"? Do you think these qualities are beneficial or not?

satisfied. When educational administrators pressure instructors to quantify the type and exact percentage of tests on a course syllabus, this is a type of formal rationalization—the logic being that if courses are equally quantified, then students are equally served. With bureaucratic education, administrators and instructors can quantify the number and length of interactions between students and professors through computer platforms that monitor such things as the number of e-mails and the number and length of "chats." In the classroom, instructors can monitor students by having them use electronic clickers to respond to questions, which is an attempt to counteract the impersonal nature of large, "efficient" lectures with increased and quantifiable electronic interaction.

Next, **predictability** means that administrators, workers, and clients all know what to expect from employees, underlings, colleagues, and companies; this is the "uniformity of rules." A Big Mac in Moscow is the same as a Big Mac in Calgary. You can wake up in a Holiday Inn anywhere in the world and not know where you are until you look out the window. Hollywood, too, is all about predictability—if you've seen one Will Ferrell movie, you've seen them all. With the advent of rationalized, bureaucratic education, teachers are replaceable in the delivery of predictable, pre-packaged courses, and creative, innovative input is minimal. Students who have already taken a course can tell others almost exactly what to expect and what will be taught. Pre-packaged online courses cut down on the time spent planning lessons, thus making class prep more "efficient," leading to what might be called the "silicon cage" of rationality. However, in a recent lecture, culture critic Henry Giroux (currently teaching at McMaster University) noted that it is the value of the indeterminate in education—in effect, the value of the unpredictable—and the free-flowing "don't know where this is going" instructor–class discussion that makes for an inspiring classroom experience. This creative process, however, is lost through formal rationality and the imposition of predictability.

Finally, **control**, for Ritzer, is always hierarchical. He characterizes the hierarchical division of labour in the following passage:

> Bureaucracies emphasize control over people through the replacement of human judgment with the dictates of rules, regulations, and structures. Employees are controlled by the division of labor, which allocates to each office a limited number of well-defined tasks. Incumbents must do the tasks, and no others, in the manner prescribed by the organization. They may not, in most cases, devise idiosyncratic ways of doing those tasks. Furthermore, by making few, if any, judgments, people begin to resemble human robots or computers. (2004: 27)

This control is exercised over both workers and clients. People who work at McDonald's are taught exactly what they have to do, while customers have their selection controlled by the menu board. Even the uncomfortable seating is part of the process, helping to control how long customers stay in the restaurant. We can see the formally rationalized, bureaucratic package at its most extreme in the following overview of material from a 1958 copy of the McDonald's operations manual, cited in John F. Love's *McDonald's: Behind the Arches* (1986):

> It told operations *exactly* how to draw milk shakes, grill hamburgers, and fry potatoes. It specified *precise* cooking times for all products and temperature settings for all equipment. It fixed *standard* portions on every food item, down to the *quarter ounce* of onions placed on each hamburger patty and the *thirty-two slices per pound* of cheese. It specified that french fries be cut at *nine thirty-seconds of an inch* thick. And it defined quality *controls* that were unique to food service, including the disposal of meat and potato products that were held more than *ten minutes* in a serving bin. (quoted in Ritzer 2004: 38)

As with people who have only ever eaten french fries from McDonald's, never real "chips" cut and prepared on site, students experiencing today's increasingly bureaucratized education might become less able to judge the quality of what they are receiving.

Social Order through Social Organization

Social organization and social stability are fundamental aspects of the human condition. We couldn't really dispense with all social organization without falling into chaos. However, the foundational principles and forms of organization themselves can have a profound effect on society and the lives of individuals, and so they deserve to be critically examined and questioned.

As we have seen, social organization impacts everything from the environment (through our relationship with nature) to the places where we work and live, where the dehumanizing effects of formal rationality sometimes prevail. Large, bureaucratized organizations, instead of serving the needs and interests of people, often dictate our values and interactions (think of your most recent shopping experience at a mall or big box store). And the perils of bureaucracy and formal rationality that Weber warned of long ago have only gotten worse, if we use Ritzer's work on McDonaldization as an indicator. The inefficiency of efficiency seems to dominate organizations from the military and businesses to hospitals and post-secondary institutions. Red tape, long lineups, quantity over quality, apathy, and even violent reactions (going "postal," road rage, fighting with the registrar's office or school board) have become the norm both within and outside of organizations and bureaucracies. In short, we need the social order that organizational structures promote, but there is evidence that bureaucracy has lost sight of the "greater good" of a greater number and a broader world. Through a perversion of means and ends, in which the means become ends in and of themselves, organizational bureaucracies become increasingly self-serving, behaving as though they were self-sustaining communities with no meaningful positive social connections to the other citizens of the planet.

WRAP IT UP

Summary

While there is a lot to learn in this chapter, a lot of terminology to remember, we would stress one basic thing. There is more choice involved in both social interaction and social organization than what might seem to be "out there." Often that choice is between oppressive forms that have been practised over years and less oppressive, and more empowering, ways that have been little tried, or that have come from groups outside the mainstream. The oppressive forms are not as "natural" as they may seem.

It is important to see that much of the frustration that we feel on a daily basis flows from the fact that we lead complicated lives. This complication arises from the increasing array of statuses we have and the many roles (including virtual roles we have online) we perform at the same time. Think of the way our master statuses change as we go through life. Shifts are not easy. At the same time, we all deal with large organizations—banks, service providers, the local motor vehicle office—that often frustrate us with their lack of flexibility and human contact. Studying organizational behaviour, as we have done in this chapter, should, hopefully, enable you to see these personal frustrations through the lens of the sociological imagination. Don't take it personally—it's not just your call that isn't important to them, but everybody's.

THINK BACK

Questions for Critical Review

1. Why and how might the status of stepmother be more complicated and difficult than that of stepfather?

2. Why do you think that the federal government disallowed the traditional Aboriginal status of "hereditary chief"?

3. Why can it be said that, generally speaking, the larger the organization, the less well it serves the needs of its customers/clients/students?

4. Do you think men or women are more likely to have virtual statuses? Why?

5. Take a social organization that you are part of—a family, business, religious organization, or school. How do formal and substantive rationality influence these organizations?

6. What do you see as the positive and negative effects of increased bureaucratization?

READ ON

Online

Erving Goffman

www.blackwood.org/Erving.htm

> A brief, readable introduction to Erving Goffman and his work, by B. Diane Blackwood.

Michaëlle Jean: A Life of "Many Possibilities"

www.cbc.ca/news/canada/story/2010/09/29/f-michaelle-jean-bio.html

> This brief CBC biography of Michaëlle Jean's life before and during her time as governor general includes a collection of photos from her term in office.

TSSU

www.tssu.ca

> The website of the Teaching Support Staff Union at Simon Fraser University shows how the organization works and reviews some of its accomplishments. The TSSU is a good example of a feminist service-provider organization; its "bargaining road map" (www .tssu.ca/2012/05/30/bargaining-road-map/), from the spring 2012 contract negotiations, is a useful graphic illustrating the collective bargaining process.

Paperland: The Bureaucrat Observed

www.nfb.ca/film/paperland

Students may enjoy this 1979 National Film Board documentary by Donald Brittain, which criticizes bureaucratic practices and their originators, but not those tasked with implementing them.

In Print

Mark Barrowcliffe (2008), *The Elfish Gene: Dungeons, Dragons and Growing Up Strange* (New York: Soho).

This memoir of how a British man spent his youth playing Dungeons and Dragons provides some insights into socialization, virtual status, and interactive role-playing games before the age of the Internet.

Amitai Etzioni (1975), *A Comparative Analysis of Complex Organizations*, rev. edn (New York: Free Press).

In this landmark text, sociologist Amitai Etzioni examines a wide range of social organizations, from prisons, hospitals, and schools to communes, churches, and businesses.

Robert Kanigel (1997), *The One Best Way: Frederick Winslow Taylor and the Enigma of Efficiency* (New York: Viking).

This readable introduction to Taylor's life and ideas gives a good account of the effects of Taylorism.

Laura Penny (2005), *Your Call Is Important to Us: The Truth About Bullshit* (Toronto: McClelland & Stewart).

Penny's work is a refreshing look at how corporate behaviour says one thing but really means another.

George Ritzer (2004), *The McDonaldization of Society* (Thousand Oaks, CA: Sage); John F. Love (1995), *McDonald's: Behind the Arches*, rev. edn (Toronto: Bantam).

Ritzer's work is a classic and readable study of how the means and methods of McDonald's are reproduced in many areas of our lives. Read it in conjunction with John F. Love's history of the fast food burger empire.

7 Consumption

Learning Objectives

After reading this chapter, you should be able to

- distinguish between *production-based* and *consumption-based* societies
- explain what we mean by *conspicuous consumption*
- discuss the consequences of an increased debt-to-earnings ratio in North America
- list some of the qualities of an *ethical consumer*
- talk about how sports is an ever-increasing venue for consumption.

Key Terms

- affluence
- affluence hypothesis
- blaming the victim
- bourgeoisie
- boycott
- brand bullies
- branding
- cathedrals of consumption
- class consciousness
- class reductionism
- conspicuous consumption
- consumer activism
- consumerism
- consumption
- consumption as communication thesis
- consumption-based societies
- consumption reductionism
- cultural capital
- debt-to-income ratio
- disposable income
- elite consumption
- embourgeoisement thesis
- ethic of consumption
- ethical consumption
- fair trade
- false consciousness
- focus group
- forager culture
- high culture
- hunter-and-gatherer culture
- hyperreal
- identity formation
- leisure
- mass consumption
- means of consumption
- means of production
- original affluent society
- packaged rebel
- pecuniary emulation
- planned obsolescence
- production-based society
- Protestant (work) ethic
- role
- simulacra
- social location
- status
- status symbol
- symbolic interactionism
- technological fetishism

Names to Know

- Jean Baudrillard
- Pierre Bourdieu
- Ronald Inglehart
- Karl Marx
- George Ritzer
- Naomi Klein
- Marshall Sahlins
- Thorstein Veblen
- Ferdynand Zweig

Doing Without?

I remember reading a cartoon in the early 1970s. It was in *Mad* magazine, that classic boomer rag that in its heyday entertained legions of fans (mostly boys) by lampooning celebrities and popular culture. Anyway, this particular cartoon featured two young adult males in conversation. Well-fed and nattily dressed, they are clearly the children of affluent parents and prosperous times—so much so, in fact, that in this snapshot they are worried about whether they will have any grim tales with which to someday lecture younger generations on the deprivations they endured during their upbringing. Says one of the lads to the other: "What will we tell *our* children that *we* did without?"

We thought we were pretty well off back in the 1970s. But as it turns out, we did without a lot of what would be considered "normal"—even essential—everyday possessions by most young people in North America today. I never had to walk to school through four feet of snow (uphill both ways), but in the year I was born (1949), there were probably fewer than 1,000 televisions in Canada. We purchased our first television when I was five, but at the time I was reading that cartoon, our family had never owned a colour TV, let alone a flat-screen, plasma, or high-def. We never used a remote to change the channel; in fact, it was a running joke in our household that *I* was the TV converter—my father would say, "John, get up and change the channel," and I did. We did subscribe to cable, which was something of a luxury in the 1970s, when television could be watched *for free*.

In the 1970s we still used a land line and a rotary-dial telephone (standard black), not a touch-tone phone, and certainly not a cellphone (which I still don't own). It was durable and impossible to lose; it didn't become dated every year—in terms either of function or of fashion—and so it hardly ever had to be replaced. Replacing it would have involved a trip to the store (if not a service call to the phone company); shopping was not then an activity that could be conducted any time of day, seven days a week. We had no microwave, and I hadn't even seen a computer, except in futuristic movies and, of course, in *Star Trek*. I listened to albums on vinyl, and scratching them was bad, not good. My music travelled with me only in my mind—there were no tapes, CDs, or MP3s, or portable devices for playing them. Bluetooth would have sounded to me like some sort of mouth disease, and blackberries came from a bush and were baked in pies. We didn't have air conditioning either—fans and open windows kept us cool in summer. And ours was an upper middle-class home— we were not possession-poor.

This long trip down memory lane does bring us to a point: it is safe to say that today, in Western society, large numbers of people are involved in the regular purchase of a greater quantity and diversity of *stuff* than the majority of people in all other societies and in all places at all other times. Perhaps that is why although the Canadian family is getter smaller, houses are getting larger. We need room for all our stuff.

Table 7.1 Items found in Canadian households, 1990–2006 (%)

ITEM	1990	2000	2006
dishwasher	41.6	51.4	57.7
microwave oven	68.2	90.8	93.9
air conditioner	24.4	34.6	48.1
home computer	16.2	55.2	75.4

Source: Adapted from Statistics Canada, www45.statcan.gc.ca/2008/ cgco_2008_006-eng.htm, Table 16: Household items.

Introduction: Shop Till We Drop?

Shop till you drop.
Born to shop.
It's not shopping—it's retail therapy.

These slogans, the kind you might find on a coffee mug, bumper sticker, or T-shirt, are statements about **consumption**, the way we purchase and use goods and services. In North American society we are practically consumed by consumption. And yet, as critics such as **George Ritzer** have observed, the sociology of consumption is underdeveloped in North American sociology. Why? According to Ritzer, consumption is a topic that many sociologists consider too "trivial" to warrant the kind of serious study that goes to what he calls "traditional sociological issues" (Ritzer 2001: 1). As he explains, "a book on a shopping mall, Disney World, or Las Vegas seems far less important to traditional sociologists than one on, say, an automobile factory. Yet, there is no inherent reason why a book on the shopping mall should be any less important than one on the factory" (1–2). In fact, he argues, sociologists could reach a much broader audience by writing about "issues that would be of interest to many readers who spend far more time in malls than they do in factories" (2).

The unequal amount of attention given by sociologists to these two topics—production and consumption—goes all the way back to **Karl Marx**. Marx spent the better part of his career studying and writing about the relationship between wealth and the means of production, and he established it as an important sociological consideration for generations of scholars since. Yet although he mentioned the means of *consumption*, he gave the topic scant attention in his writings. Fundamentally, you'll recall, Marx's **means of production** is about the main social means needed for producing wealth—namely, agricultural land in pre-industrial times and factory machinery and start-up capital since industrialization. The **means of consumption**, on the other hand, are the main social means by which people consume what is produced.

Ritzer, essentially, calls for greater balance in the way these two topics—production and consumption— are treated sociologically. Sure enough, over the last 20 years, sociologists in the West have begun to turn their attention to how we buy and use products. Specifically, a number of them have started to explore the question of whether Western societies have shifted from being **production-based societies**—in which people are defined by their work, specifically their role in providing commodities or services—to being **consumption-based societies**, in which people are defined by their purchasing practices and how they spend their free time. We're all familiar with the standard conversation starter, "So what do *you* do?" At one time, an appropriate answer would have been, "Well, I work in insurance sales," or "I own my own catering business."

Now a common answer might be, "I shop at the outlet malls most weekends," or "I spend my holidays at a resort down south." This is largely an issue of **identity formation**, the ongoing process by which an individual develops a sense of him- or herself as a unique being, but only by accumulating a set of self-ascribed labels (e.g. musician, hoops fan, college professor) that are shared with others. Later in this chapter we'll look at identity formation in greater detail, in connection with the now familiar concepts of **status** and **role**.

What do YOU think?

1. So, what do *you* do? Do you define yourself more by what you do for a living or by how you *spend* your leisure time? What do you do that makes the loudest statement about who and what you are?

2. In Newfoundland, new acquaintances are fond of asking, "Where do you belong?" It's a question about where a person was born and raised, and sometimes where the person's parents and other older relatives were born and raised. Does "where you belong" rank above or below "what you do" or "how you consume" in terms of your identity formation?

Early Theorists of the Sociology of Consumption

Thorstein Veblen

How can a sociologist evaluate consumption? In simple terms, how can we tell how "good" or "bad" consumption is for society? Clearly, the author of this textbook has some biases (reflected in the frugal lifestyle he maintains while stashing his unspent earnings in mattresses and cookie jars around the house). But the arguments surrounding the pros and cons of consumption are not all one-sided. Consumption encourages business productivity. During troubled economic times, a government will sometimes offer tax breaks while keeping interest rates low, all to encourage people to "spend their way" out of the recession. Why would a government want its citizens to spend on luxury items rather than saving? Because consumption benefits anyone who earns a living in manufacturing or retail; it creates jobs. And anyway, do we not have a

right to enjoy our hard-earned wages by spending our money however we want?

American economist and sociologist **Thorstein Veblen** (1857–1929) was an early observer—and critic—of consumption patterns. A prolific writer, he is best known for one work, *The Theory of the Leisure Class* (1899), in which he criticized not all consumption but consumption of a particular kind, which he called *conspicuous* consumption. **Conspicuous consumption**, as Veblen describes it, entails the purchase and use of possessions and services primarily for the purpose of demonstrating wealth and status. Items used this way—to show off a person's high social and economic standing—are **status symbols**. Conspicuous consumption is a practice engaged in primarily by the wealthy "leisure class," comprising businesspeople who make money from the labour of others but who do not, in Veblen's view, contribute in any meaningful way to the country's economic productivity.

At least the rich could afford these purchases. But Veblen observed patterns of conspicuous consumption among poorer people as well. They were engaged in what Veblen called **pecuniary emulation**, or copying of the expensive spending habits of their wealthy, trendsetting neighbours. Today we might describe the practice as "keeping up with the Joneses."

Veblen makes an important point—one that is not often stressed enough—that those engaged in conspicuous consumption are not necessarily motivated by a desire to "show off," or to score more consumption points that their neighbours or colleagues. More often, Veblen argues, it is about fitting in with one's peer group, specifically:

> a wish to conform to established usage, to avoid unfavourable notice and comment, to live up to the accepted canons of decency in the kind, amount, and grade of goods consumed, as well as in the decorous [i.e. socially appropriate] employment of his time and effort. (Veblen 1934: 115)

Consumption on a large scale can arguably benefit the health of a nation's economy, but it sharply increases the possibility of personal debt. Canadians today have record levels of debt (see Figure 7.1 below), and although home mortgages make up a good part of that, non-mortgage consumer debt is also on the rise. According to one credit reporting agency, consumer debt in Canada rose by over 37 per cent from 2007 to

2012 (TransUnion 2012). Given that inflation rose by just 9 per cent during that time, the increase appears to reflect consumer spending habits more than natural growth trends in the economy.

Our politicians don't always set the best example when it comes to spending within their means. Canada's national debt recently hit the $600-billion mark (Canadian Press 2012a), and a recent report of the auditor general criticized the federal government for approving the 2012 budget before the minister of finance was briefed on how details of the budget would affect the country's "long-term fiscal position" (Office of the Auditor General of Canada 2012, 7.48). Policies differ as to how to limit that situation. There are right-wing policies for reducing the debt, such as cutting social programs and getting rid of government scientists who monitor pollution, and there are left-wing policies, such as reducing tax breaks for large corporations and handouts for oil companies.

Veblen stressed that conspicuous consumption encourages waste, not to mention superficial values. Making purchases solely in order to keep pace with the latest trends means that products are not kept for the full time of their possible use (except as status symbols). If you've ever secretly hoped to lose a perfectly good cellphone just so you'd have an excuse to replace it with the latest model, you know what this is about. It certainly encourages superficial values. And when the economy suffers a downturn, those companies engaged in the production, distribution, and sale of flashy consumer goods are often the first ones to be hit. Conspicuous consumption does not provide the soundest of bases for an economy.

Veblen was unorthodox in a number of ways. Having been dismissed by the University of Chicago in 1906, he went to Stanford University in California, but soon left that prestigious institution as well. His radical ideas, combined with his utter disregard for personal and domestic cleanliness (what else would you expect from someone who opposed buying possessions for the appearance of wealth?), his conspicuous adultery (which resulted in his divorce, in 1911), and his indiscriminate rudeness made him unpopular with many more conventional academics. We might find him charming but for his uncalled for, inaccurate, and disrespectful comments about dogs (Veblen 1934: 141–2).

What objects would be recognized as status symbols among your peer group? How often do you engage in conspicuous consumption? Is it more about showing off or keeping up?

Pierre Bourdieu

In Chapter 4 we introduced you to French sociologist **Pierre Bourdieu** and his idea of **cultural capital**—essentially, the knowledge required to cultivate the sophisticated tastes associated with high culture. In his influential work *Distinction: A Social Critique of the Judgment of Taste* (1979), Bourdieu argued that how we choose to present our tastes, or "aesthetic disposition" (a pretentious phrase), is a statement of our status, one we frequently use to distance ourselves and the class we like to think we belong to from "lower" groups or classes. Think about how some people go *on* and *on* and *on* talking about different kinds of wine. While their interest may be quite genuine, on one level at least they are making a presentation concerning their membership in one of the "finer" classes—the ones that appreciate fine wine. (Me, I'm a beer drinker, and I can go *on* and *on* and *on* about my favourite brand of beer, and how little it costs when I buy it in cases of 24. That is a statement of my own, working-class cultural capital.)

People can cultivate cultural capital, but as Bourdieu explained, we are also born into it. Parents, from the very beginning of their children's lives, pass on the cultural capital of their class, encouraging their children to acquire tastes that are considered upper-class and in this way giving them a better chance to succeed in their own class aspirations later in their lives. The hierarchical ranking of tastes is established and perpetuated in processes such as this. What arts, foods, sports, and alcoholic beverages you consume have class presentation value.

Beware of politicians (a good idea generally): they can play cultural capital as a game to appeal to people of the "lower classes." They will don rodeo attire at the Calgary Stampede, play rock 'n' roll piano publicly, or eat a hot dog at a ballgame (in front of the cameras, of course) to show that they are "of the people"—the working-class people. *See*, they say: *I am really one of you (despite my massive income, expensive suits, and power).*

Jean Baudrillard

Another influential French social critic whose ideas are relevant here is **Jean Baudrillard**, whose theory that the things we buy say a lot about who we are bears a strong resemblance to Veblen's ideas about conspicuous consumption. Baudrillard saw that any object could have value in four different ways. Consider a watch, for example. It has value based on what it is used for: telling time. This is its *use value*. It also has an *exchange value*, which is what you could get for it if you wanted to sell it or trade it. Marx had already identified those two values, which were central to his own thinking. But Baudrillard went a step further by examining the symbolic value and sign value than an item might hold. Our watch's *symbolic value* is whatever sentimental significance makes it more valued than other watches of its kind—if it was received as an anniversary gift, say, or inherited from a beloved grandfather. Finally, and most important here, it has a *sign value*, which is what this watch, compared with other watches, says about the taste and social status of its owner. It's this last consideration that drives a lot of our purchasing decisions, helping to make consumption rather than production the engine of capitalist society.

Central to much of Baudrillard's work are his ideas about **simulacra** (singular **simulacrum**), which are superficial representations of life. Often drawing on and promoting stereotypes, simulacra are produced and reproduced like material goods or commodities, mostly by the media but also by other agents (including academics). Certain products that Disney creates for consumption are simulacra, including images of what little girls are supposed to be like (i.e. pouty,

What do YOU think?

For each of the following categories, describe the items or list the brands that you think convey cultural capital? What items and brands do not?

- residence (home, apartment, condo, houseboat, etc.) and location (downtown, suburb, bedroom community)
- transportation (car, bike, public transit, scooter, taxi, etc.)
- clothing
- technology (computers, cellphones, etc.)
- education (level attained and institutions attended)
- employment
- hobbies and recreational activities
- spectator events (theatre, concerts, professional sports, etc.)
- vacation destinations
- pets (breeds of dog, parrot, fish, exotic reptile, ferret, etc.).

pink-clad princesses), images of what family is supposed to be like (particularly in movies and television shows), and even images of what history and imagination are supposed to be like (in their amusement parks and resorts). In fact, Baudrillard identified the Disney fantasy theme park as the quintessential simulacrum. When we consume these simulacra we are consuming the **hyperreal**: mediated representations of real life that people relate to as though they were more real, more authentic, than what they simulate. If you've ever envied characters in a movie or TV show—*why can't my life be more like theirs?*—then you've fallen for a hyperreality, an artificial world you felt you could relate to better than to your own. Advertising promotes consumption by creating hyperreal worlds that consumers desperately want to be a part of.

Other Theories in the Sociology of Consumption

The Affluence Hypothesis

As we have been seeing, a key theme in the sociology of consumption is the extent to which we are what we consume. A related idea is the *affluence hypothesis*. **Affluence**, as it relates to individuals, can be defined as having a comfortably large **disposable income**, which is the money you have left over to spend however you wish once you've paid your taxes, rent, and other mandatory living expenses. It is "disposable" in the sense that it can be "thrown away" on whatever items or services you like without having to go without any of the basics (e.g. food, shelter, clothing, and transportation). A country or society may be described as affluent when a significant number of its citizens are affluent. We'll put an asterisk on that point and return to it shortly.

The **affluence hypothesis** states that the consumption habits of people living in Western societies, which are considered affluent, are more socially significant than those of people living in countries considered less affluent. One of the figures associated with this hypothesis is political scientist **Ronald Inglehart** (b. 1934), who observed

a change in the values and priorities of those people growing up in Europe and North America in times of relative security and economic prosperity (i.e. since the Second World War). Thanks to the rise of government social assistance programs to help the poor and unemployed, this generation, which Inglehart describes as "post-materialist," was (and is still) less concerned with meeting basic material survival needs than were the generations that came before them. As a result, it is more concerned with non-material, quality-of-life issues like human rights, gender equality, and the environment (Inglehart 1977). As it relates to the affluence hypothesis, this means that people in the prosperous West may be guided by lofty post-materialist values to make more socially responsible purchasing decisions, like paying higher prices for fair-trade coffee or locally grown produce, or replacing a functioning but outdated washing machine with a new one that uses less electricity and is therefore better for the environment.

But here's a hiccup with the affluence hypothesis: can it ever be said that the majority of citizens in any country are affluent? It may well be (and we suspect that this is more the case) that in any society considered affluent, it is only a highly influential, highly visible minority that fits that description—film and TV stars (not to mention the characters they play), high-profile athletes, and other celebrities that

One way to find out how much of a consumer you are is to see how many days there are when you *don't* buy something—either in a store or online. Can you remember the last day you didn't buy *anything*? How many days in a week or a month do you not buy anything at all?

Our Stories

The West Edmonton Mall (and other Cathedrals of Consumption)

If shopping is the new religion, then shopping malls can be considered **cathedrals of consumption**, huge constructions built primarily as places for people to gather and buy things or spend money. In the United States, the Mall of America, in Minnesota, stands out as a cathedral of consumption, but the Disney cathedrals, Disneyland and Disney World, are also prime examples.

Canada has its own shopping mecca: the West Edmonton Mall. It is huge. When it first opened, in 1981, it had over 600 stores—more than you'll find in most Canadian towns and some cities. A clear testament to Ritzer's claim that North American sociologists have not engaged to any significant extent in research on consumption is the glaring absence of sociological research on the West Edmonton Mall, or the WEM as it's fondly known to its patrons. People in other fields are studying it. The Fall 1991 edition

of *The Canadian Geographer* had several interesting articles on the WEM, but none with the critical edge that sociology can bring. Conservative western business magazines, such as the *Alberta Report*, have shed light on the politics and borrowing practices of the WEM. They have been critical of the mall's too cosy relationship with the provincial government, which may have helped its owners secure major development loans. However, they publish nothing that questions how the Canadian mega-mall has affected the social practices of its visitors.

A veritable Disneyland for shoppers, the WEM resembles an amusement park in its use of kitschy themes and gimmicks. One of these is the way various attractions are named after international sites. The mall's indoor pool and water playground, the "World Waterpark," is billed as a "tropical playground" and boasts a feature called "Caribbean Cove." Some

Bumper boats at "the WEM." Where in the mall (this one or any other large shopping centre that you're familiar with) will you find simulacra, superficial representations of life that are hyperreal or more real than real? How do they encourage consumption?

of the mall's galleries have been given themed street names, including "Chinatown," "Bourbon Street" (after the famous site in New Orleans), and "Europa Boulevard." The last of these is described in an online promotion as follows:

> Fashioned after charming streets of old European cities, Europa Boulevard is lined with a variety of designer boutiques, and specialty stores featuring fashion from some of the world's leading brands such as True Religion, Lacoste, Ed Hardy, Diesel, G-Star and more. Luxury designer brands such as Burberry, Versace, Prada, Hugo Boss, Ted Baker, and Michael Kors can also be found along Europa Boulevard.

Notice how the key words *designer* and *brands* are repeated in the description.

There are also "theme rooms" at the mall's hotel. One of these, the "Igloo Room," was amusingly described by writer Jack Hitt following a one-week stay at the WEM:

> When the bellboy took me upstairs on the "Polynesian elevator" [I hear ukuleles] to my "Igloo Room" at the Fantasyland Hotel [definitely Disney] in West Edmonton Mall, he asked me if I'd ever stayed in one of their theme rooms. I said no, and he assured me the experience would be "neat." My own choice of adjective, in hindsight, might

have been "bloody," but "neat" was everyone else's. . . . Maybe I'm no good at igloos. I smacked my hand getting out of mine, raking a couple of good strawberries on my knuckles. Then I banged my shin on a polar bear, before tripping over three huskies huddled together against an imaginary cold—distracted as I was by the seal flopping onto the icebergs behind my Jacuzzi. (Hitt 1999a: 62)

There is a long tradition of fake igloos in North America and Europe. Over a hundred years ago, styrofoam igloos were featured at fairs, often inhabited by real Inuit included, unfortunately, as "living exhibits."

The WEM's theme of "the world in a mall" provides an excellent illustration of simulacra, as described by Baudrillard. The mall offers visitors readily reproduced (i.e. manufactured, marketed, and sold) copies of actual objects and experiences—copies that are considered hyperreal, or more real than the actual. ("Buying in" to hyperreality means believing that Pizza Hut offers authentic Italian food, or that your GPS knows more about the road you're on than your very eyes.)

Modern consumers are swamped by simulacra: scripted reality shows, video games featuring actual NHL, NBA, and MLB players that you can control, online multiplayer games, cybersex, Second Life, and (we believe) "friends" on Facebook. Do we need reality detectors?

What do YOU think?

1. Although we can say that simulacra are not "real" like the objects or experiences they are designed to imitate, do they have a "reality" that needs to be given more attention than sociologists and other social commentators typically give them? For example, do Wii games actually prepare people to be better athletes on the field, in the way that driving simulators enable new drivers to learn to drive real cars? (Keep in mind the argument that violent video games are used to train soldiers to overcome resistance to shooting people.)

2. Do you think the criticism of simulacra is primarily a cohort issue reflecting the generation gap between those who have grown up surrounded by simulacra and those who did not?

populate daily entertainment shows and smile from the covers of magazines sold at supermarket checkout counters. The presence everywhere of these role models of consumption could encourage the less affluent majority to act as if they had more disposable income than they actually do (see Veblen's pecuniary emulation, above), leading to widespread debt.

North Americans do live in times of record debt, as we noted earlier. One method of measuring this, used in Canada since 1990, is the **debt-to-income ratio**, which is a measure of a household's debt from mortgages, lines of credit, credit cards, and other loans, compared with the household income after tax. It is expressed as the percentage of income that is made up of household debt. Ideally, of course, the percentage should be less than 100 per cent, signifying that household debt is less than the after-tax income. This is not the case, and hasn't been in Canada since the third *quarter* (or three-month period) of 1996, when it was 99.68 (Statistics Canada CANSIM Table 378-0123). Canada's debt-to-income ratio reached a milestone in 2010, when it reached 148.1 per cent in the third quarter, surpassing for the first time the American rate (147.2 per cent). As of the quarter ending on 30 June 2012, the average debt-to-income ratio in Canadian households was 165.8 per cent, and rising (see Figure 7.1).

What do YOU think?

1. Would you consider a large charitable donation to be an example of socially conscious spending that reflects post-materialist values, or is it really a form of conspicuous consumption? Can it be both? Consider, for instance, the effect of appearing at a gala fundraising dinner or charity ball in support of a worthy cause: it contributes to social good and perhaps encourages others to give (pecuniary emulation). It also enhances the status of the person attending the event. What about making a large donation to a hospital and having a wing or a ward named after you in return: social spending or conspicuous consumption?

2. While we're talking about charity and consumption, here's another question to consider: when companies have a special day in which a certain percentage of store revenues go to a particular charity, is the main result really increased consumption or increased charity?

Debt and Credit

While we're on the subject of debt, let's talk a little about credit cards. The following quotation comes from Terry Galanoy's *Charge It: Inside the Credit Card*

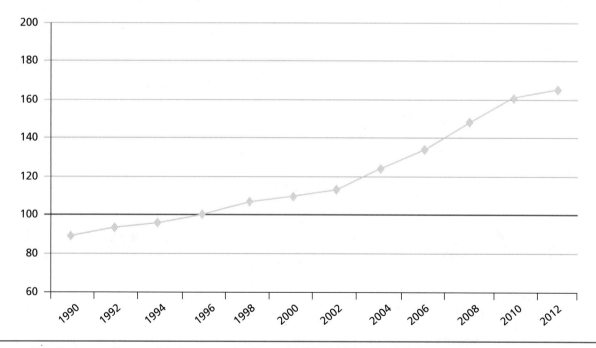

Figure 7.1 Debt to disposable income in Canada (%), 1990–2012 (4th-quarter results)

Based on data from Statistics Canada CANSIM Table 378-0123: http://www5.statcan.gc.ca/cansim/a47, CANSIM Table 378-0123, National Balance Sheet Accounts.

Conspiracy (1980); it is meant to look like the warnings on cigarette packages:

> **Caution:** Financial experts have determined that continued bank card use can lead to debt, loss of property, bankruptcy, plus unhealthful effects on long-lived standards and virtues. (Galanoy 1980: 110)

Extending credit has been a part of the Canadian economy for centuries. The oldest profession (in Canada), the fur trade, was based on extending credit to the Aboriginal producers/harvesters of furs. In fact, the name of a river a short distance west of Toronto, the Credit River, testifies to the reliability of the local Anishinabe people (living in the area now called Mississauga) in repaying their loans in beaver pelts and other furs. That was credit in an age before plastic.

In 1950, the first charge cards were issued, in the United States, by a company called Diners Club. Diners Club cards were to be used at dining and entertainment establishments only, not at stores. They differed from later credit cards in requiring the whole bill to be paid by the end of the month *or else*. Within a year, there were some 20,000 people with Diners Club cards.

In 1958, American Express, a shipping and financial services company then involved in issuing traveller's cheques, got into the charge card business, introducing the first plastic charge cards the following year. The purpose of these cards was still limited. They were designed, like traveller's cheques, to be used by people who didn't want to carry cash when travelling on business or holiday—in those days, it was difficult to withdraw money from any bank branch other than the one where you had your account. The cards were accepted primarily at restaurants and entertainment venues catering to travellers, and again, when the monthly bill came in, you paid it in full, or you were in trouble. It wasn't until 1966 that the first general-purpose credit card came out, and then you could, for the first time, keep a running tab. Different alliances of banks that year initiated the two competing cards that would eventually become Visa and MasterCard.

In Canada in 2010, there were some 72 million credit cards (Reynolds 2010). That is a staggering number when you consider that in the same year there were fewer than 35 million Canadians: it means that Canadians average more than two cards apiece. And since infants, toddlers, and primary and middle school children aren't carrying plastic—and they number roughly 6 million—that means that the average Canadian adult has approximately three cards. Long gone are the days when credit cards were reserved for big purchases and travel: credit card companies today encourage the use of credit cards for even the smallest everyday purchases by offering rewards ("points") that can be used towards consuming other items. No mention is made of the debt you're accumulating; once a major concern for credit card companies (which made their profits in the annual fees they charged to card holders), debt—or, specifically, the interest you pay on it—is now their primary source of revenue.

A significant part of Canadians' debt is tied up in home mortgages. Homes are investments, and a frequently used indicator of how well the economy is doing is how many houses are being bought. That indicator can be manipulated to an extent by governments that want to show that the economy is under strong leadership. By using the central bank (i.e. the Bank of Canada) to lower the prime borrowing rate, the government can encourage more people to enter the housing market. The government can also direct the Canada Mortgage and Housing Corporation (CMHC) to approve mortgages to higher-risk borrowers. The federal government did this in 2008, to combat the effects of the just-beginning recession. They were rewarded with a nine-point rise in their approval rating, from 33 per cent in 2007 to 42 per cent in 2008. Canada's economy has remained fairly stable when compared with national economies around the globe, and certainly the country has escaped the catastrophic collapse of the housing market that plunged the United States into economic crisis. But one of the effects of the government's lowering the lending rate has been the aforementioned rise in household debt (Dobbin 2009). One writer referred to this as a "mortgage time bomb." It hasn't exploded yet, but as Canadians fall deeper and deeper into debt, the fuse is getting shorter.

The Embourgeoisement Thesis

The interaction between class and consumption has long been discussed by sociologists under what has been called the **embourgeoisement thesis**. Marx used the term **bourgeoisie** to refer to the social class of those who owned and controlled the means of

The Point Is...

SUVs: Conundrums of Consumption

Cars have long been one of the most visible status symbols a person can own. In his foreword to the 1934 re-issue of *The Theory of the Leisure Class*, Stuart Chase, for whom Veblen was "one of my idols as a young man" (Chase 1934: xi), had this to say about the connection between cars and status:

> The motor car has provided perhaps the most obvious of example of conspicuous consumption in modern times. Cars are selected not primarily for use, comfort or transportation, but to maintain one's position in the community. The make, the model, the gadgets, the upholstery, are what count. (Chase 1934: xiv–xv)

That was 1934. What about now? Is Chase's 80-year-old observation any less true today?

Today, we have the sport-utility vehicle, or SUV, which made its dynamic, tank-like entry into the automobile market in the last decade of the twentieth century. It is a conundrum of consumption, a puzzle of purchasing. The continued high sales of gas-guzzling SUVs are baffling at a time when gasoline prices stand at a high-water mark and concerns about the environment are affecting consumers' buying decisions on everything from dish soap to vacation packages.

Recall that one of the tenets of the affluence hypothesis is that post-materialist shoppers are more inclined to make socially responsible purchasing decisions. Isn't the SUV, then, a case of "dumb and Hummer"?

So why *do* people buy SUVs? It can't be for their four-wheel drive, impressive towing capacity, and vaunted off-roading ability—it's probably safe to say that most SUV owners never drive off-road (intentionally). It could be because of the perceived roominess of these vehicles, meeting the need to carry more passengers, more purchases, more vacation "necessities," and more in-car gadgets. (It's worth noting, though, that many SUVs are still designed to carry just five passengers.)

American journalist Jack Hitt addressed the question of SUVs in terms both humorous and more purely sociological in an article that appeared in the countercultural magazine *Mother Jones*:

> Cars are not fickle fashions. They are the most expensive and visible purchases in an economy drenched in matters of status and tricked out with hidden meanings.
>
> Some people will tell you that the shift from car to truck can be explained simply: We Americans are getting, um, bigger in the beam. We aren't comfortable in those Camrys, so

production in a capitalist society. However, the term today is commonly used to refer to the middle class, especially when it's being derided for being conventional and materialistic. In fact, the word "bourgeois" is often used to insult people with tastes above their station in life, tastes they want to show off (e.g. "Her tiny loft in the club district with her stray cat and her used Toyota Corolla were perfect when she was single. Then she got married and turned all bourgeois: now she's after a four-bedroom house with the three-car garage in the suburbs for her 1.87 kids, her designer dog, and her Lexus).

"Embourgeoisement" is what happens when the working class begins to adopt the consumption patterns and tastes of the bourgeois middle class. The thesis proposes that when the working class undergoes embourgeoisement, its members experience a loss of **class consciousness**—the understanding of what is in the best interests of their class—producing a **false consciousness** that causes them to identify with the societal goals and socio-political interpretations of the bourgeoisie. In other words, they don't resent the capitalist system the way they probably should, and they lose their appetite for the kind of anti-capitalism we trade up to a vehicle we can sit in without feeling scrunched. Here's a new buzzword: . . . fatassability. (Hitt 1999b)

More seriously, Hitt believes the allure of the SUV has a lot to do with branding. Auto manufacturers bring consumers together in **focus groups** to help them learn what kinds of names will appeal to potential customers. The names given to sport-utility vehicles typically invoke the great American legend of the Wild West, as Hitt explains:

Once upon a time, Trailblazers, Explorers, and Trackers tamed the Wild West. Now, through the sorcery of focus groups, the bull-market gentry have brought the Pathfinders and Mountaineers back into their lives in the belief that they need to conquer the savage land one more time. (Hitt 1999b)

The new wilderness, of course, is mapped out by GPS on city streets, suburban cul-de-sacs, and trans-urban highways, and the new "savages" are the poor, working-class people who, if they're not riding public transit, swarm about in "their wretched Escorts and Metros," upon which the vertically superior SUV owners can literally look down.

What do YOU think?

1. Watch three television commercials for cars. Then, consider whether Chase's comment about cars and conspicuous consumption is accurate in the "modern times" of the twenty-first century. What qualities of the modern automobile do most car ads emphasize? Are they about showing off or about meeting everyday needs?

2. Elsewhere in his article Hitt points out that at the time he was writing, some 40 per cent of SUV buyers were women. Do you think that can be attributed to the reasons noted here or to something else?

3. Why do you think that so many people buy SUVs? Do you think that people who buy gas-guzzling luxury vehicles simply don't care about the environment, or is it that their eco-concerns are trumped by other considerations?

movement (like the recent Occupy movement) that Marx envisioned.

A good illustration of the embourgeoisement principle at play happened during the 1980s, when many countries in the Western world were experiencing a severe economic recession. Some of the ultra-conservative governments of the time—notably those of Margaret Thatcher in Britain and of Ronald Reagan in the United States—responded to the situation by imposing policies that benefited the upper classes and were particularly detrimental to workers (especially, in the UK, to the country's coal miners). And yet, these governments were returned to office, voted in, to a large extent, by the very people they were hurting the most. The period also saw increased levels of consumption among members of the working class who seemed not to recognize how much they were being harmed by the recession and the measures imposed to address it.

The classic work articulating the embourgeoisement hypothesis is *The Worker in an Affluent Society* (1961), by Polish economist and sociologist **Ferdynand Zweig** (1896–1988), which is based on the author's interviews with working-class employees of five British companies. Zweig's study inspired a number of other works on the subject, focused mostly on Europe, beginning in the 1960s. Not many of these entirely supported the embourgeoisement hypothesis. For example, John H. Goldthorpe et al. (1967) disputed the suggestion that affluent members of Britain's working class were voting in greater numbers for the country's Conservative Party or were becoming in any way more bourgeois. Their small study of affluent workers in Britain suggested that these people were, in a way, between classes:

> They no longer share in traditional patterns of working-class sociability [e.g. hanging out in pubs], yet few have adopted middle-class lifestyles and fewer still have become assimilated into middle-class society. (Goldthorpe et al. 1967: 11)

The subject has not been studied to a significant extent by Canadian sociologists.

The Consumption as Communication Thesis

Sociologists generally agree that acts of consumption have meaning. In fact, we can study these acts within the context of **symbolic interactionism**, the school of thought that looks at the social significance of everyday human interaction, which we first discussed in Chapter 2. The assertion that acts of consumption have socially significant symbolic meanings is sometimes termed the **consumption as communication thesis**. For instance, what is your dining companion communicating when he makes a big show of ordering the finest Cabernet Sauvignon from the restaurant's wine list, and then proceeds to make knowledgeable comments while drinking it?

Before we get too far, however, there are two cautionary statements we should issue. First, as C. Campbell wisely warns us, "it is one thing for academics to 'discover' symbolic meanings attached to products: it is another to assume that the conduct of consumers should be understood in terms of such meanings" (Campbell 1997: 350). This is the equivalent, in consumption research, of Freud's acknowledgement that sometimes a cigar is just a cigar. In this case, sometimes a purchase is just a purchase (example: I ate at that fancy new "designer hamburger" place not because I wanted to make a statement about taste, but because

I was hungry, I was craving a cheeseburger, and it was the only burger place in the neighbourhood). There is undeniably symbolism behind certain acts of conspicuous consumption as described above, and possibly meaning behind my decision to dine on a $20 hamburger at Auberge du Boucher instead of buying the value meal at the fast-food joint down the street, but other transactions are too straightforward to warrant any speculation on their deeper symbolic significance.

Second, we must avoid what may be called **consumption reductionism**. This is the practice of reducing the study of people to the study of only their consumption patterns, while failing to take account of traditionally important social factors such as class, "race," ethnicity, gender, and age. These factors have an undeniable impact on what can be and what typically is consumed (as we'll see in the discussion that follows). To overlook their role in consumption is the equivalent of **class reductionism**, in which all conditions in society are judged to arise solely from the prevailing class structure, with no regard to factors such as race, ethnicity, and gender.

Social Factors Affecting Consumption

Gender and Consumption

Early this chapter we invoked the slogan "Shop till you drop," suggesting it was the sort of thing you might see printed on a coffee mug. We didn't add—and probably didn't need to—that it's a motto associated principally with women in North American society. But why is that, and does it mean, necessarily, that women shop longer and buy more than men do?

An interesting question, and one that can lead to classroom debate, is whether there can be any way of determining whether it's men or women in contemporary Canadian society who are more engaged in conspicuous consumption. Can we say that they are both equally engaged in the practice? There isn't really a sociological literature on this, so you are going to have to think it through on your own. Here's an exercise to get you started. Think of the following items that can be considered part of conspicuous consumption, and indicate whether you would associate them more with male or with female purchasing habits; we've given you space to add any other items you can think of:

CONSUMER ITEMS	ASSOCIATED MORE WITH MEN	ASSOCIATED MORE WITH WOMEN	ASSOCIATED WITH MEN AND WOMEN EQUALLY
• home (whether a downtown condo or a hulking new house in the suburbs)	☐	☐	☐
• entertainment systems (TV, stereo equipment, gaming systems, etc.)	☐	☐	☐
• technology (cellphone, BlackBerry, iPad, etc.)	☐	☐	☐
• lawn and garden accessories ("water features," fountains, stone monuments, etc.)	☐	☐	☐
• vehicles (of all kinds—cars, boats, snowmobiles, jet skis, Vespas)	☐	☐	☐
• jewellery (don't forget watches, a common male accessory)	☐	☐	☐
• Clothing	☐	☐	☐
• footwear	☐	☐	☐
• bags (i.e. handbags and briefcases, purses and "murses," and all forms of luggage)	☐	☐	☐
• food and alcohol, whether served (i.e. at parties) or consumed (i.e. at restaurants)	☐	☐	☐
• other (specify): _____	☐	☐	☐
_____	☐	☐	☐
_____	☐	☐	☐

What other items did you think of adding? Can acquiring and maintaining a tan be considered a kind of conspicuous consumption? Can power tools and an over-stocked garage workshop be involved in conspicuous consumption?

Veblen singled out the clothing of modern women in his time as an especially good example of conspicuous consumption, arguing that most of it, from a practical standpoint, was particularly ill suited to doing physical work. In his words:

> The woman's shoe adds the so-called French heel to the evidence of enforced leisure afforded by its polish; because this high heel obviously makes any, even the simplest and most manual work extremely difficult. (Veblen 1934: 171)

Before male readers get to feeling too superior about the practicality of their clothing, consider the following. The attire worn by the typical male business executive is just as impractical in terms of physical labour. Ties can easily get stuck in machinery (like a paper shredder, or a lathe), suit jackets restrict the movement of the upper body (especially lifting), and expensive leather shoes easily slide on wet, smooth, or otherwise slippery surfaces (like the shop floor) and are not constructed to provide adequate protection against articles dropped on feet. The power suit is essentially designed to show that its wearer is above menial and manual labour.

Age and Consumption

Our consumption patterns change as we age. That probably doesn't surprise you. Just how our consumption patterns change was demonstrated in a recent study published by Statistics Canada (Lafrance & Larochelle-Côté 2011). The study was based on surveys conducted between 1982 and 2008, which generated data on a synthetic cohort of people who were in their late forties in 1982, and reached their early seventies by 2008. A cohort is a group of people who share a common statistical trait (e.g. the cohort of women born in 1992). Researchers will sometimes draw a sample of individuals from a particular cohort and track that sample over time to see how their habits change. In this case, the cohort is *synthetic* because it was not a single group of individuals studied over time, but different groups representing the same cohort (people who were in their later forties in 1982) surveyed at different times. The results should nevertheless be consistent with the data that would be

While we are on the subject of personal adornment, who do you think spends more on tattoos: men or women? Consider whose tattoos are more elaborate and more visible, and cover a larger part of the body, particularly the arms.

obtained by studying a single panel made up of the same people.

Table 7.2 shows some of findings of the StatsCan study. The amounts are given in 2002 constant dollars, which means that they have been adjusted to eliminate the effect of inflation on changes over the period, making the values much easier to compare. The data

obtained in the surveys were based on spending per household, but these figures have been adjusted to show the average amount spent annually per adult. We can see here that as the cohort aged, what they spent on property went up, both in absolute value and as a percentage of their overall spending. Most of this increase is related to shelter. Also going up are health-related costs. Spending declined on food, alcohol and tobacco, and clothing.

What do YOU think?

1. Think of someone you know who is in his or her late forties right now. Do you think that he or she will go through similar changes in consumption patterns?

2. Do you think that your cohort, once you reach your late forties, will experience similar spending changes? Why or why not?

3. If the same cohort featured in Table 7.2 had been studied in their late twenties, what do you think their spending figures in the same categories would look like?

Nationality and Consumption

Table 7.3 provides a comparison of consumption patterns in nine different countries, including Canada. The data come from household surveys conducted between 2001 and 2005 by different agencies in each country (e.g. the Consumer Expenditure Interview Survey in the US, the Household Budget Survey in Sweden, and Survey of Household Spending conducted by Statistics Canada). The spending figures, which represent the spending of an average adult, have all been converted to 2005 constant

Table 7.2 Changing consumption patterns over the life cycle, per-adult equivalent

	AMOUNT SPENT ($)			
	LATE 40s	EARLY 60s	EARLY 70s	DIFFERENCE
RESIDENCE AND PROPERTIES				
Shelter	4,900	7,000	8,000	+3,100
Other accommodation	500	500	600	+100
Household operations	1,400	1,400	1,500	+100
Furnishings & equipment	1,400	1,000	800	−600
Total	$8,200	$9,900	$10,900	+$2,700
TRANSPORTATION				
Purchased automobiles	1,500	1,700	1,700	+200
Automobile operation	2,400	2,200	2,300	−100
Public transportation	500	400	400	−100
Total	$4,400	$4,300	$4,400	$0
FOOD, CLOTHING, AND CARE				
Food	5,500	4,000	3,800	−1,700
Clothing	2,400	1,400	1,100	−1,300
Personal care	700	500	600	−100
Health	700	1,100	1,500	+800
Total	$9,300	$7,000	$7,000	−$2,300
OTHER				
Recreation	1,800	1,700	1,500	−300
Reading and printed material	200	200	200	0
Tobacco and alcohol	1,300	800	600	−700
Miscellaneous	1,500	1,100	800	−700
Total	$4,800	$3,800	$3,100	−$1,700
PERCENTAGE OF TOTAL (%)				
Residence and properties	30.7	39.6	42.9	+12.2
Transportation	16.5	17.2	17.3	+0.8
Food, clothing, and care	34.8	28.0	27.6	−7.2
Other	18.0	15.2	12.2	−5.8
	100.0%	100.0%	100.0%	0.0%

Source: Adapted from Lafrance, Amélie, & Sébastien LaRochelle-Côté (2011). "Consumption Patterns among Aging Canadians." In Perspectives on Labour and Income, Statistics Canada cat. no. 75-001-X. Retrieved: www.statcan.gc.ca/pub/75-001-x/2011002/pdf/11417-eng.pdf

Telling It Like It Is

An Author POV

Cultivating Cultural Capital at the Toby Jug in Bolton

I am a regular at the Toby Jug, a pub in my hometown of Bolton, Ontario. I go there for a number of reasons. I don't like franchise dining and drinking establishments, where the wait staff are professionally perky and adhere to a script involving highly structured interaction. The chain restaurants market an experience they guarantee will be the same for you at any of their many locations, but the familiarity I find at the Toby Jug is less about the atmosphere, the décor, and the menu than about the people I see there. The staff know me by name and by beer (Smithwicks, brewed by the fine people of Guinness), and by preferred table (a window seat by the stage). Most of the other regulars also know me by name, as well as by shared anecdotal incidents—I've hosted functions there, including a launch party for a book I wrote, and I had a heated and now legendary debate with a global warming denier that ended in colourful words not fit for printing here.

My social location is one that could predict that I would be a frequent patron of the Toby Jug. I am in my early sixties, a middle-class white male of British heritage (Scottish, Irish, and Welsh). As such, I fit the profile of the typical Toby Jug visitor, who tends to be a white man of UK ancestry between the ages of 40 and 70, a member of either the working or the lower middle class. What brings him there? What discourages women and people of other classes, ages, and ethnic backgrounds from going there?

Most of the pub's regulars live right in or around Bolton, a town that is predominantly white. Few of the town's growing Italian population make regular appearances there. All of the bartenders and serving staff are white women between the ages of 22 and 55. They wear practical, loose-fitting uniforms, nothing skimpy or revealing, and their chat with the patrons is genuine and friendly, based on personality and shared personal history with each of the regulars. There is no obvious flirting.

The bar is decorated with Canadian, British, and Scottish flags, and many pictures of Scotland. Beer, particularly British beer, is the beverage of choice; wine is available but not featured. The menu offers standard British pub fare (mushy peas, steak and kidney pie, and "crisps"—British potato chips), along with the usual bar food such as chicken wings and hamburgers. The meals are neither fancy nor expensive. The Toby Jug plays host to a darts league, and soccer and hockey are shown on the pub's big screens; no MMA, no UFC. Classic rock plays through the speakers, and the bands that play live or take part in Jam Night tend to perform the same kind of music—covers of older rock standards. Robbie Burns Night and St Patrick's Day are special occasions at the Toby Jug.

How does all of this relate to the sociology of consumption? Think of how this example of my consumption pattern fits with the social factors of gender, "race," age, my Scottish heritage on both sides, and my tendency to identify more with the working class, even though my job and income are middle-class. What does this say about my cultural capital?

international dollars and adjusted for inflation, so that they represent broadly comparable years of the early twenty-first century. The highest figure in each category is bolded.

The table shows that the Americans lead the way in total consumption, as well as in spending on health, housing, and transportation (which would include money spent on vehicle purchases and maintenance, as well as on public transit). The British spend the most on food (and that's on British food!). The Swedes spend the most on clothing, with Canada second. (Do you think this might have to do with the unique clothing requirements of people living in a cold-winter country?)

It is interesting that the highest investment in education is in South Korea. While high school isn't mandatory in South Korea, the country regularly has one of the highest secondary school graduation rates in the world. South Koreans regularly enrol in private academies to boost marks. Note, as well, that another East Asian country, Singapore, has the second highest investment in education, almost twice that of Canada

Table 7.3 International differences in consumption: Average annual spending per capita, select countries

COUNTRY	AVERAGE ANNUAL HOUSEHOLD SPENDING (IN 2005 CONSTANT INTERNATIONAL DOLLARS)						
	HEALTH	HOUSING	FOOD	CLOTHING	EDUCATION	TRANSPORTATION	TOTAL*
United States	**1,068**	**6,072**	2,543	754	372	**3,336**	15,816
Canada	575	5,613	2,271	823	387	2,886	15,094
Britain	168	5,162	**2,802**	802	223	2,463	14,786
Sweden	315	3,814	2,081	**834**	49	2,717	12,403
New Zealand	378	4,551	1,978	421	275	1,967	11,524
South Korea	476	1,117	2,362	428	**904**	1,476	8,927
Singapore	459	947	1,934	326	711	1,941	8,001
Brazil	302	1,646	962	263	189	854	4,637
Mexico	87	484	827	166	264	397	3,034

*Total for each country includes additional spending in categories not included in this table.

Source: Adapted from the International Average Salary Income Database www.worldsalaries.org/personal-consumption-expenditure.shtml

and the United States. In both countries people spend more on education than on clothing. Sweden's low score reflects not lack of interest in education, but the fact that more taxes go into funding education at all levels than in the other countries. The figure for Norway (not included here) was similar.

What do YOU think?

1. If you add up the figures given in Table 7.3 for each country, you will see that they fall short of the total given. What do you think might be missing?

2. Which country's distribution of consumption looks the most socially just to you? Why?

3. What might be misleading about comparing individual investment in education in different countries?

Examining Changing Consumption Patterns from a Historical Perspective

So far in our sociological study of consumption, we have devoted most of our attention to current trends in how people spend. We looked briefly, at the start of the chapter, at whether we in the West have moved

from being a production-based society to a consumption based society. In this section, we will consider two other ways of examining historical changes in consumption.

Becoming a Culture of Mass Consumption

In Chapter 1 we looked at German sociologist Max Weber's **Protestant work ethic**, which has to do with work having its own "religious" value ("idle hands" being "the devil's tools," according to the proverb). Wealth achieved through hard work and careful management was seen by early Protestants as a sign that one was favoured by God, and this belief, according to Weber, gave Protestants the impetus to earn and save money. It was instrumental in the rise of capitalism.

As Western society became more and more secular, the religious imperative to save money gave way to the belief that "you can't take it with you," and the Protestant ethic was gradually replaced by the **ethic of consumption**, which essentially celebrates the ability to spend. In the words of British sociologist Paul Ransome:

The new ethic of consumption decisively breaks the constraints imposed by the self-disciplines of hard work, diligence and thrift, of saving and moderation, and offers instead a new set of legit-imations based on the self-indulgences of enjoy-ment. . . . At the core of the substantive rationality of consumption-based society is a rejection of saving and moderation (but not of work), and a celebration of spending and enjoyment. Affluent consumers have trumped the work ethic with the ethic of consumption by demanding now what has been promised for so long. (Ransome 2005: 56)

No more could we say that "a penny saved is a penny earned"; now a penny earned is two pennies spent.

Accompanying this shift from work ethic to consumption ethic was a change that transformed Western society from a culture of **elite consumption** to one of **mass consumption**. Up until the twenti-eth century there were certain forms of consumption reserved almost exclusively for the rich. Employing servants, controlling large tracts of land, hunting for recreation rather than necessity, participating in some leisure sports, owning a vast and elaborate garden (maintained by one's gardeners) for beauty rather than for food or medicine, travelling to exotic places, and taking in the entertainments that make up **high cul-ture** (opera, ballet, orchestral music, etc.)—all of these forms of consumption were once exclusive privileges of the elite, or what in an earlier time was called the "idle rich" (as opposed to the working masses). The notion of **leisure**, as envisioned by Veblen when he wrote so influentially about the leisure class, was that it was a pursuit of the rich—unavailable to the less wealthy, especially those scrimping and saving in the name of Protestant values. All of that changed, of course, and luxuries once reserved for the elite became products of consumption by the masses.

Work and Leisure, and the Challenge of Becoming Time-Rich

Time and money: both can be spent, both can be wasted, and ample quantities of both characterized Veblen's leisure class. In some ways, time is intimately connected with consumption.

Societies differ in the way they consume time, in how they apportion it to work and to other pursuits. In 1972, anthropologist **Marshall Sahlins** (b. 1920) coined the term the **original affluent society** to refer to **hunter-and-gatherer** (sometimes called **forager**) **cultures**, which were not engaged in farming or in industrial manufacturing. Their material needs were few, and frequently could be met by a bountiful nature without many hours of labour. Sahlins depended for his hypothesis largely on the findings of University of Toronto anthropologist Richard Lee, who had done fieldwork in the 1960s among the Dobe Ju/'hoansi people of southern Africa's Kalahari Desert. Lee reck-oned that the people there spent on average 20 hours a week obtaining food (Lee 1993). They were affluent in the sense that they were "time-rich"—they had an abundance of what we might call "disposable time."

The advent of farming as a way of life made people richer in food, poorer in time. Agriculture is extremely labour-intensive, and it takes long days to make a farm productive. The early Industrial Revolution made many of the working people much poorer in terms of time. Prior to the introduction of laws protecting workers (such as the legislated 40-hour work week, which came at the end of an especially long and hard fight, and even then was not available to all workers), many exploited workers spent the better part of their daily lives inside factories, mills, and mines.

In Canada, during the twentieth century, many children of farmers became the first generation to leave the fields for the cities, to work in factories, ware-houses, and offices. The limited working hours gave these environments a decided advantage over life on the farm, and many wage earners learned to maximize their productivity by claiming increased pay—time-and-a-half or double time—for overtime work. Time was money—both earned and spent. Young wage and salary earners, with disposable income and time to spend it, helped fuel the rise of consumerism.

In the 1960s and 1970s, people began to envi-sion how advances in technology could produce labour-saving inventions that would further reduce work time and dramatically increase free time, making us all members of the leisure class. Sadly, it didn't turn out that way. My impression is that people work more hours today than they did a generation ago, thanks in large part to new technology—like the BlackBerry and other smartphones—that enable people to keep on top of their work when they're not in the office. These devices may make people more productive, but mostly to the extent that they steal time from non-work activ-ities. They can make you time-poor.

Interestingly, if you look at statistics on working hours, they typically document only the official "at work" or "in the office" hours, so the increasing work

Societies still differ in their consumption of time. It is generally true that North Americans work more hours in a year than western Europeans do. On average we put in more work hours per week and have shorter and fewer holidays than workers in western Europe. The two weeks of vacation time granted to many North American employees is matched by four or even six weeks in other industrialized nations. This would suggest that we in North America are generally more possession-rich but less time-rich. Given a choice, which would you want?

that we are suggesting here does not show up in the data. How would you do research on this subject? Do you think that this is more typical of employees in middle management or upper management jobs?

One of the greatest rewards of being a post-secondary educator is that you can be time-rich—by setting your own hours (in the best of teaching circumstances), by bringing your work home with you, and by adhering strictly to fixed office hours (including the virtual office hours spent replying to e-mails from students and colleagues). This time wealth affords fortunate instructors lots of time to spend with family and pets (like parrots!) and in researching and writing. Although I put in well over 50 hours a week in teaching and writing, my flexible schedule makes me feel far more time-rich than I would if I had a traditional nine-to-five job.

Branding

Generally, "branding" refers to the ways that companies market and promote their products to the public. Advertising is the main instrument of branding: it works when brand names become household names.

However, the definition of branding that we will be using here is not the business- and marketing-focused one but the more sociological, and socially critical,

What do YOU think?

1. Do you think that today's technology makes people more or less time-rich?

2. What professions or occupations might you choose to go into if you wanted to be time-rich? Which would you avoid?

definition, which relates to one part of branding in the broader sense. **Branding** in this sense is the use of marketing to establish certain brands and brand-name products as essential ingredients in the identify formation of individuals vying to establish themselves as legitimate members of certain social groups.

In Chapter 5 we introduced the idea of the **packaged rebel**, the person who tries to establish himself or herself as part of a countercultural group (e.g. skater punk, goth, hipster) by adopting the fashion (clothing, accessories, and other consumer products) associated with this image. But the products used to create the image are purchased—paradoxically—from well-known multinational stores and suppliers. They use branding to make their products appear essential to the image of the social group the consumer wishes to belong to. Canadian activist/author **Naomi Klein** called these companies **brand bullies** when she took on Nike, The Gap, Microsoft, and other major branding firms in her bestseller *No Logo: Taking Aim at the Brand Bullies* (2000). The term ably captures the aggressiveness of these companies in marketing their products, especially to younger people who are anxious to find membership and belonging in a particular social group and are therefore particularly vulnerable.

What do YOU think?

Why do you think people will pay a lot of money at a big-name retail outlet to buy a pre-ripped pair of jeans, a "distressed" army jacket, or thrift-shop fashions that have never actually been worn? Wouldn't it be cheaper to buy these items at a second-hand store? Would that make the image these consumer are trying to cultivate any more genuine?

Branded a Rebel

In the great Monty Python film *The Life of Brian*, a parody of the New Testament story of Jesus, a man called Brian is claimed by the people to be the Messiah of the Hebrew prophesies and saviour of humankind. Brian, however, is a rather reluctant messiah, and he shoos away his clingy followers, telling them, "You don't *need* to follow *me*. . . . You've got to think for yourselves! You're all individuals! . . . You're all different!"

"Yes!" they reply in unison. "We're all individuals! . . . We *are* all different!"

QUICK HITS

Hip Hop and Branding

In *Sociology as a Life or Death Issue* (2008), University of Toronto sociologist Robert Brym provides a fascinating examination of how hip hop artists very frequently refer in their music to brand-name products—particularly, very high-end, expensive products. Tables 7.4 and 7.5 illustrate the point.

Table 7.4 Brands mentioned in a selection of 20 hip hop songs

BRAND	TYPE OF PRODUCT	NUMBER OF MENTIONS
Mercedes-Benz	automobile	100
Nike	shoes and athletic wear	63
Cadillac	automobile	62
Bentley	automobile	51
Rolls-Royce	automobile	46
Hennessy	Cognac	44
Chevrolet	automobile	40
Louis Vuitton	leather goods and accessories	35
Cristal	champagne	35
AK-47	assault rifle	33
Total		**509**
Average mentions per song		**25.5**

Source: Adapted from Brym 2008: 22.

Table 7.5 Name-dropping among selected hip hop artists (2005)

ARTIST	NUMBER OF BRANDS MENTIONED PER SONG	
	BRANDS	SONGS
50 Cent	20	7
Ludacris	13	6
The Game	13	2
Ciara	10	4
Jamie Foxx	6	1
Lil Jon	6	2
Trick Daddy	6	2
Total	**80**	**25**
Average brands per song		**3.2**

Source: Adapted from Brym 2008: 23.

This response of Brian's followers comes close to capturing the paradox of the packaged rebel, which represents a kind of mass-produced, mass-consumed individuality. The packaged rebel is without a cause except to be seen as a rebel, wearing a rebel's brand; however, he is no more a rebel than a child who dresses as a cowboy on Hallowe'en is a real cowboy.

Advertising companies frequently promote products using Brian's message, "You're all different." In the summer of 2011, there were two products in particular that were aggressively marketing using the "you're a rebel" approach. One was Kraft Miracle Whip; the other, Kotex tampons. Neither product is one the average consumer is likely to associate with rebelliousness—not even a little. The Miracle Whip commercials, which aired well into 2012, feature an in-your-face troupe of dancing teenagers showing how rebellious they are by not settling for "bland alternatives." You have probably seen advertising like this yourself; whether or not you've noticed it is another matter. Most of us are so used to products being marketed to the willing rebel that we don't give the message of these ads a second thought, nor do we take the time to consider how consuming mass-marketed products is not the mark of a rebel.

It isn't easy to define precisely what a rebel is, but one of the more visible examples in recent Canadian history is former Senate page Brigette DePape. In June 2011, the 21-year-old Winnipeg native guaranteed the loss of her Senate position when she stood up during

In a song from their most recent album, Canadian rock band Billy Talent takes aim at branding and the packaged rebel, described as a "counterculture you can buy off a shelf," which has become the fashion among (in the band's words) "the target market of a corporate joke" (Billy Talent 2012). What exactly is the joke? Is the band's description of the packaged rebel apt? Does the authenticity of a "look" really come down to whether it's bought—or even available—at a big-name store?

the throne speech and displayed a placard reading "Stop Harper." Being a rebel is something you do with an act opposing stronger forces, not something you buy, along with a bunch of other people. Being a rebel comes with a social cost.

What do YOU think?

What do you think the effect of this branding would be on people who listen to this music? Specifically, what effect might it have on (a) aspiring black hip hop artists; (b) aspiring white hip hop artists; (c) young black listeners; (d) young white listeners?

Branding and Consumption among Sports Fans

I am a sports fan. My television viewing hours are mostly spent watching hockey (when there's no labour disruption), baseball, and football. Born and raised in Toronto, that makes me a fan of the Maple Leafs (sigh), Blue Jays, and Argonauts. I have a Leafs sweater and a Blue Jays cap. I don't gamble on sports, nor do I take part in fantasy drafts or rotisserie leagues. That makes me an under-consumer of sports in this day.

Teams in the NHL used to have just two hockey sweaters, one for home and one for away, and the design wouldn't change for years and years. If you were a diehard fan of a particular team, you might own one of each. Now, hockey sweaters seem to change as often as free agents change teams. As well, it has become common for teams to sport an additional "third jersey," worn on special occasions, and sometimes also vintage, or "throw-back" sweaters, worn when older franchises with longer histories face off against each other. Sports merchandisers seem eager to capitalize on the importance to sports consumers of branding. Branding in this context plays on an individual's desire to identify with a particular team and to establish him- or herself as a legitimate member of the social group made up of the team's fans (known collectively by names such as "Rider Nation" or "Habs Nation").

Professional baseball teams used to have just one style of cap, for fans and players alike. But let's consider

How else is cultural capital displayed among hip hop artists? Does this form of branding seem more prevalent in hip hop than in other kinds of popular music? Why do you think that is?

just the Jays for a moment. At the team's official online shop you can order any of the following:

- Nine different styles of Blue Jays cap for women (including the Satin Ink Mesh Cap, with embroidered logos and graphics, and the Tweeder Fidel Cap, which will have you looking like a fashionable Cuban revolutionary)
- Fifteen different styles for children (including the pink Daisy Dots Cap, the sequinned Shimmer Cap, and two styles featuring Minnie Mouse)
- Thirty-six different styles for men, including wool, mesh, denim, and regular cotton, in numerous colours and patterns divided into the categories "authentic," "replica," "Cooperstown," and "fashion."

And this is just the current line. Next year will offer a whole new assortment of fashions and colours. The numbers suggest that men are the most vulnerable consumers here, the ones most susceptible to branding.

All of this is one part of how sport is consumed by the average fan in North America. It is strangely separate from the way sport is consumed by the spectator. As a teenage hockey fan, I could get a ticket at Maple Leaf Gardens (a sacred place, unlike the Air Canada Centre, which has seen no hockey championships) in the cheapest section, the greys, where the most vocal fans were, for $4.00. I could afford that. As I was writing this, in February 2011 (before the lockout), I checked the official price of tickets for a regular-season match between the Leafs and the Carolina Hurricanes. Tickets varied from $38.50 for the "cheap" seats to the far pricier $658.50 for one of the best seats in the house (for the Leafs!). That isn't even counting the overpriced food and beverages. Instead, I'll watch the game on TV, make my own popcorn, and perhaps have a beer or two chosen from a far greater (and less expensive) selection available at the local beer store. I will place no

bets on the outcome of the match. All of this makes me an under-consumer of the game.

Needs and Wants: Necessities and Luxuries

Humans have both *needs* and *wants*. The former are intrinsic, "natural"; the latter tend to be socially manufactured. We often blur the two categories. Biologically, we really need only food, water, and sleep (despite what younger hormones say, sex is just a want). But branding, as we've seen, is about making certain consumer products essential to identity formation. *If* I'm a true Jets fan, then I *must* have the team's new sweater. *If* I'm a successful business exec, then I *must* have a BlackBerry. *If* I'm a hip teen, then I *must* have the latest smartphone. Successful advertising takes wants and turns them into these and other "manufactured needs."

One way of engaging in the sociological study of consumption is to look at these manufactured needs in terms of which ones are considered necessities and which ones are luxuries. Take, for example, the following consumer items:

- car
- TV set
- cable/satellite service
- home computer/laptop
- high-speed Internet service
- cellphone
- tablet
- air conditioning
- washing machine
- oven/stove
- microwave oven
- dishwasher.

Out of these 12 items, how many would you consider to be necessities? How many are just luxuries? If you were to add up your score and the scores of your classmates, would the results tell you anything about the nature of our consumer society?

The Pew Research Center, a US-based organization that conducts regular public opinion polls, surveyed a sample of Americans in 2009 to see which consumer items they considered necessities. Table 7.6 shows the results of their research, and how much the figures have changed since 2006. Table 7.7 looks at just

What do YOU think?

How is the author "under-consuming" sports? Let's say he had a younger colleague—a fellow sociology instructor—who was a larger consumer of sports: describe her parallel experience. Consider both the cost and the value (the benefits for the money spent) of each experience. What do the differences tell you about the way we consume sports?

one item, televisions, and how TV ownership has changed since 1975.

Table 7.6 shows a sharp decline in the perceived necessity of many of the listed items between 2006 and 2009. Does that surprise you? Bear in mind that during that period the US was suffering a major economic decline, which brought job losses, salary cuts, and house foreclosures. The more telling statistic may be which items on the list Americans were more and least willing to give up as luxuries—take away the air conditioning and the microwave, but don't take the car, the computer, or the high-speed Internet!

Table 7.7 indicates that the number of television sets per household increased steadily from 1975 to 2010, even as the size of households was decreasing. Somewhere between 2000 and 2005, the average number of TV sets per home actually surpassed the average number of people, meaning that some homes had more TVs than family members. There are several implications of this that we can consider sociologically. For instance, we know that there is a positive correlation between television viewing hours and obesity in

In September 2012, New York City's Board of Health approved a ban on the sale of sugary drinks bigger than 16 ounces (a judge invalidated the ban in March 2013). Is this an infringement on our right to consumption? What arguments could be made for and against such a ban? Do you think we could see a similar ban here in Canada?

children. With the increase in the number of TVs per household, is it possible that some children have their own television and don't even have to leave their room to watch TV?

The possible link between television sets per household and childhood obesity is a question I once put to my students. Most believed that there was a causal relationship—that having more televisions in the home produces a greater risk of obesity among the children living there. A minority of students suggested that declaring a cause-and-effect relationship here could be spurious reasoning (i.e. observing *correlation* and falsely assuming *causation*); however, they failed to come up with a viable third variable that could explain both correlating factors. Here is one possibility: if you could prove that there are fewer opportunities for unstructured after-school physical activity in the schoolyard (say, because parents, concerned about safety, pick their kids up from school at the end of the day rather than letting them make their own way home), then you could infer both that children are getting less exercise and that they are more likely to spend after-school time watching television in the home.

Some students raised a concern about the operational definition of TV viewing. Specifically, when computer game consoles (Wii, Xbox, PlayStation) are hooked up to televisions, do the hours spent playing these games count as "watching TV"? A few perceptive students even argued that Wii activities, because they

Table 7.6 Consumer items considered necessities versus luxuries, 2009 (US data)

ITEM	CONSIDERED "NECESSITY" BY (%)	CHANGE FROM 2006 (%)
Car	88	–3
clothes dryer	66	–17
home air conditioning	54	–16
television set	52	–12
home computer	50	–1
cellphone	49	0
microwave oven	47	–21
high-speed Internet	31	–2
cable/satellite TV	23	–10
dishwasher	21	–14
flat-screen TV	8	+3
iPod	4	+1

Source: Morin & Taylor, 2009 at http://www.pewsocialtrends.org/2009/04/23/luxury-or-necessity-the-public-makes-a-u-turn/.

Table 7.7 Changing television ownership in American households, 1975–2010

	1975	1980	1985	1990	1995	2000	2005	2010
PERCENTAGE OWNING								
1 set	57	49	43	35	29	24	21	17
2 sets	32	36	38	41	36	35	33	28
3+ sets	11	15	19	24	35	41	46	55
AVERAGE SETS PER HOUSEHOLD								
	1.57	1.60	1.83	2.00	2.28	2.43	2.62	2.93
NUMBER OF PEOPLE PER HOUSEHOLD								
	2.88	2.71	2.62	2.55	2.58	2.54	2.54	2.54

Source: Adapted from Nielsen Wire, *Television Audience Report* (2010), p. 4 at http://blog.nielsen.com/nielsenwire/wp-content/uploads/2010/04/TVA_2009-for-Wire.pdf

require a greater amount of physical interaction on the part of the player, should be considered exercise. This is a debatable point: Wayne Gretzky may get some exercise playing the Wii hockey game he endorses, but it's likely far from the workout he would get skating on real ice.

Hoarders: An Excess of Consumption?

If you are reading this at home—your apartment, your dorm, your bedroom—take a look around you: how many of the things you see are necessities?

An hour-long reality show on A&E, called *Hoarders*, documents the circumstances of people who, over a lifetime, have accumulated an excessive quantity of things—so many things, in some cases, that these individuals can barely make their way from one room to the next for all of the *stuff* piled in hallways and doorways. Granted, not all of the things hoarded are items acquired through retail consumption—mail, receipts, other paperwork, and garbage are all part of the hoarder's collection. Nevertheless, the show does shine a light on a crucial aspect of consumption: that apart from cultural capital and identity formation, consumption is, at its heart, about our human obsession with material things, items we can acquire, possess, and surround ourselves with.

To a sociologist, the show is also interesting in the way that it presents hoarding as a product of an individual's personality disorder. Psychologists, psychiatrists, and other expert professionals are brought onto the show to help "cure" the individual of his or her "compulsive hoarding." A sociologist might interpret

What do YOU think?

When *Hoarders* debuted in August 2009, the premiere, which aired on A&E, was watched by 2.5 million viewers, 1.8 of them aged 18 to 49. This made it the most-watched series premiere in network history among adults in that demographic. How do you account for the show's popularity? What fascinates us about people who own too much stuff? Could it be that it makes us feel our own consumption habits are, by comparison, moderate?

this as a case of **blaming the victim**. After all, given the pervasive societal influences on us to consume things, to be judged and defined by what we own, can we really lay the blame on the individual?

Technological Fetishism

The term "fetish" has long been used to refer to an object of magical power worthy of respect or fear. In modern usage it tends often to be applied to an area of the body that an individual obsesses about, typically with sexual desire, as in a foot or hair fetish.

Technological fetishism involves making recently developed technological innovations the objects of uncritical adoration. Consumers engage in it when they line up to purchase the newest in a series of barely different cellphones, smartphones, tablets, and so on, even though there is nothing objectively wrong with the older-model version of the same item purchased the year before. Technological fetishism is encouraged by advertisers on behalf of companies that can make enormous profits on sales of their "new and improved," upgraded products. These products may be part of a strategy of **planned obsolescence**, in which a product is designed not to last long so that consumers will constantly crave the newest version of a product that they "cannot live without." It is also supported by the media, which are always anxious to report on the latest trends in business and technology.

What do YOU think?

We associate technological fetishism especially with consumer electronics. However, it is interesting to take note of how many print, radio, television, and Internet ads use the magic word "technology" in promoting products we wouldn't normally think of in this context, such as deodorant and skincare products. Look and listen for the word "technology" in the advertising you encounter today. How common is it? How effective is it?

Ethical Consumption

Ethical consumption refers to the practice either of boycotting a product or service or of choosing to buy a particular product or service on the basis of one's ethics or values. Ethical considerations might include:

- the unfair (or fair) treatment of workers involved in the production of an item
- the unfair (or fair) treatment of minorities affected by the production of an item
- the environmental cost of the product, factoring in fuel required to produce, ship, or operate it, or the environmental damage caused in the item's production or disposal.

We touched on the idea of ethical consumption earlier in the chapter, in the context of Inglehart's post-materialist values. A person who is willing to pay more to buy an electronic car, or to power a home with solar energy, could be said to be engaging in ethical consumption. The **fair trade** movement claims to support workers and entrepreneurs in developing countries by promoting fair wages and safe working and living conditions for marginalized workers, equity for women, the elimination of child labour, and fair market opportunities for small-scale independent farms

and businesses. When you buy fair trade coffee, you are engaging in ethical consumption.

The Great Grape Boycott

The most famous North American boycott took place in the United States in the 1960s. It was organized by Cesar Chavez (1927–1993), Mexican–American leader of the National Farm Workers Association (renamed the United Farm Workers, or UFW, in 1974) as a way of supporting Mexican and Filipino grape pickers in California. In 1951, the US government had

QUICK HITS

The Original Boycott

The word **boycott**, which as a verb means to refrain from buying a particular service or product for ethical reasons, had a strange beginning. It is named after Englishman Charles C. Boycott (1832–1897), who was boycotted himself.

The man worked as an estate agent for the English Earl of Erne in English-controlled Ireland. The earl was an absentee landlord, meaning that he lived far from the large properties on which he received rents from poor Irish tenant farmers. Charles Stewart Parnell (1846–91), an Irish nationalist and member of Parliament, advocated a land reform policy that called for lower rents. Any landlords who refused to lower their rents, as well as any farmers who took up the lease on properties made available through the eviction of tenants who couldn't pay their rents, would have all local support taken away from them: no one would work for them, no one would deliver mail to them, no one would sell supplies to them in stores. One of Parnell's most famous quotations comes from a speech he gave in 1880:

> When a man takes a farm from which another has been evicted, you must show him . . . by leaving him severely alone, by putting him in a moral Coventry, by isolating him from his kind as if he were a leper of old—you must show him your detestation of the crimes he has committed.

Charles Boycott was one—and, it turns out, the most famous—of the agents who refused to charge lower rents.

passed a law that enabled American farmers to hire migrant Mexican farm workers to pick their grapes. The living conditions in which whole families of Mexican pickers lived were uniformly horrible. They were forced to work longer hours and for less pay (less than a dollar per family for three hours of work) than American workers.

In 1962, Chavez co-founded the National Farm Workers Association. The union began with a boycott targeting wine companies. Eventually, it broadened reach to include California grapes and raisins (and later, lettuce) sold in grocery stores. The boycott started in California but soon went national and international, and Chavez was more than once arrested and jailed for his actions. In the 1970s, contracts guaranteeing better pay (it could hardly be worse!) and safer working conditions were offered and signed. In 1978, the boycott was deemed a success, and was called off.

Consumerism and Consumer Activism

The term **consumerism** has two opposing meanings. On the one hand, it can refer to the societal promotion of the "need" to purchase goods and services in ever increasing quantities. The opposite meaning, which is better labelled **consumer activism**, refers to practices aimed at protecting consumers from being exploited by sellers. This includes promoting such features as honesty in advertising, the listing of ingredients on the labels of packaged foods (including the highly contentious "genetically modified" warning), product guarantees and recalls, and the prosecution of shady business practices. The CBC television show *Marketplace* can be considered a mainstream vehicle of consumer activism, as can Health Canada, although more radical activists would say that the latter is often more part of the problem than it is of the solution.

In 1986, the California Raisin Advisory Board created a commercial featuring anthropomorphic claymation raisins singing the R&B classic "I Heard It through the Grapevine." The commercial was a huge success, spawning a primetime television special, an animated TV series, and even a travelling "Raisins on Ice" skating spectacle. What does this tell you about the ability of advertisers to sway consumer sentiment?

WRAP IT UP

Summary

Chapter 6 ended with a discussion of George Ritzer, who recognized how elements of efficiency, predictability, and control—a model that Weber had named "formal rationality"—had been adopted by successful retail and fast-food chains such as Walmart and McDonald's. He called this McDonaldization. McDonaldization is largely about the way that goods are produced and delivered, but as Ritzer noted, sociologists have long given too little attention to the other side of the equation: the way those goods are *consumed*.

In this chapter we have taken up Ritzer's challenge by investigating this relatively uncharted territory, the sociology of consumption. It would be a fertile field for the aspiring Canadian sociologist (and just think: you can even do your research at the mall!). But while this shift from the traditional production-based look at society may be new to sociologists, it's important to recognize that our lives as consumers are being studied all the time by those who benefit most from our consumption. Market research companies, on behalf of retailers and product manufacturers, can tell us a lot about how we spend our money, how we respond to advertising, how class affects our purchasing habits, and how we feel about mass-marketed simulacra—though they might not put it in those terms. It is the role of the sociologist to examine our Canadian consuming life with a critical eye.

THINK BACK

Questions for Critical Review

1. Explain the difference between the *means of production* and the *means of consumption*. What does it mean to go from being a *production-based society* to a *consumption-based society*?

2. Why do you think that North American sociologists have generally ignored the study of consumption?

3. Explain what is meant by the following terms: *conspicuous consumption*; *pecuniary emulation*; *cultural capital*; *simulacrum*.

4. Why do you think that North Americans have an increasing debt-to-earnings ratio? Do you think that it will continue to rise in the next 10 years?

5. Explain the relationship between time and consumption. What does it mean to be *time-rich*?

6. What defines an *ethical consumer*? Do you consider yourself an ethical consumer? Why or why not?

READ ON

Online

Journal of Consumer Culture

http://joc.sagepub.com

> This free online journal features articles on consumer culture and the sociology of consumption.

Survey of Household Spending

www.statcan.gc.ca/daily-quotidien/120425/dq120425a-eng.htm

> Released in 2012, this Statistics Canada report presents the results of research on how Canadians spent their money in 2010.

Personal Consumption Expenditure—International Comparison

www.worldsalaries.org/personal-consumption-expenditure.shtml

> This is the unabridged version of the material found in Table 7.3 above.

World Values Survey: The World's Most Comprehensive Investigation of Political and Sociocultural Change

www.worldvaluessurvey.org/

> Ronald Inglehart is the director of this international organization of social scientists engaged in the study of changing social values in the post-materialist age. On the website you will find their survey questionnaires and summaries of their findings.

Surprise, Surprise

http://www.youtube.com/watch?v=ZGbNq_flErA

> Check out Billy Talent's first single from their album *Surprise, Surprise* (2012) and see if you can pick out the critique of the branded rebel.

In Print

Joseph Heath &Andrew Potter (2004), *The Rebel Sell: Why the Culture Can't Be Jammed* (Toronto: HarperCollins).

> This work by two Canadian authors looks at the image of the rebel and how it is sold as a commodity to be consumed.

Jack Hitt (1999), "The Hidden Life of SUVs," *Mother Jones* (July/August).

> Hitt takes a beautiful shot at the marketing of monster cars in an age when we are supposedly doing more to protect the environment.

Naomi Klein (2000), *No Logo: Taking Aim at the Brand Bullies* (Toronto: Vintage Canada).

> Klein's now classic work is a journalistic study of how big corporations bully consumers through branding.

George Ritzer (2009), *Enchanting a Disenchanting World*, 3rd edn (New York: Sage).

> This updated edition of one of Ritzer's classics takes the reader on a tour of such cathedrals of consumption as Las Vegas, Disney, the shopping mall, and McDonald's.

8 Deviance

Learning Objectives

After reading this chapter, you should be able to

- avoid some of the leading misunderstandings of the term *deviant*
- distinguish between *overt* and *covert* characteristics of deviance
- discuss the reasons that deviance is sometimes associated with ethnicity, culture, "race," gender, sexual orientation, and class
- talk about the contested nature of deviance.

Key Terms

- American dream
- assimilate
- bodily stigma
- conflict deviance
- contested
- corporate crimes
- covert characteristics
- delinquent subculture
- deviance
- dominant culture
- essentialism
- hallucination
- heteronormative
- ideology of fag
- impression management
- labelling theory
- marked terms
- misogyny
- moral entrepreneur
- moral stigma
- multiculturalism
- negative sanctions
- non-utilitarian
- norm
- normalized
- occupational crimes
- other
- overt characteristics
- patriarchal construct
- positive sanctions
- racializing deviance
- racial profiling
- sanctions
- social constructionism
- social resources
- status frustration
- stigma
- strain theory
- subcultural theory
- subculture
- tribal stigma
- unmarked terms
- vision quest
- white collar crimes

Names to Know

- Howard Becker
- Albert Cohen
- E. Franklin Frazier
- Erving Goffman
- Robert Merton
- Edwin Sutherland

Gordon Dias, 1985–2001

If deviance involves acting against the values of a society, then perhaps suicide is the ultimate act of deviance. It takes the gift society values most—life—and withdraws all value from it. Explaining this act of deviance has been a part of sociology since Durkheim's *Suicide* was published in 1897.

It has been over a decade since my nephew, Gordon Dias, committed suicide at the age of 16. He hanged himself from a tree in front of a local high school. As a sociologist, and as his uncle, I struggle to understand why he did this.

Gordon was a young, single man. This made him part of the social group most prone to suicide. He was on the margins of society in several ways. He was the youngest of three children, a child whose brother and sister demanded attention by their actions and by their achievements. His older brother was the first-born grandchild and nephew on both sides of the family, a position that brought him ready attention. His older sister is simply brilliant, a very hard act to follow. Both now have graduate degrees. In my earliest memory of Gordon

talking, he is straining to be heard above his siblings.

He was a person of colour, the product of a mixed South Asian and Caucasian marriage, living in the very white Canadian city of London, Ontario. He was very close to his South Asian grandmother—so much so that when he left home for a while, he went to live with her. It could not have been easy in that city to have made that choice.

Gordon was artistic. It is not easy for a young man to express himself artistically in our culture, not without presenting some counterbalancing signs of macho behaviour. Perhaps that's one reason why he sought the social company he did. According to his parents, my sister and brother-in-law, he had been hanging around with guys who regularly got into trouble. This eventually got him into trouble at school, and he was suspended. Zero-tolerance policies don't leave a lot of time for even temporary allegiances with groups of kids who act out. At some level, zero-tolerance is simply intolerance. For him, I guess, that was the final piece of the puzzle, and the picture he was left with led him to suicide. He did care enough about his education that he left his only suicide note at school.

There was nothing inevitable about Gordon's suicide, just as there was nothing inevitable about the recent suicides of Amanda Todd and Rehtaeh Parsons, victims of social exclusion whose cases gained notoriety for being tragic and senseless in equal measure. Suicide may be a personal act, but it is an act that reflects the society that alienates the victim, usually for being an outsider—a deviant.

Introduction: What Is Deviance?

Many people, when they hear the word *deviance*, think of behaviour that is immoral, illegal, perverse, or just "wrong." But **deviance** is better thought of as a neutral term. It simply means "straying from the norm or the usual." It does not mean that the deviant—the one engaging in deviance—is necessarily bad, criminal, perverted, "sick," or inferior in any way. The word is based on the Latin root *-via-*, meaning "path." To deviate is simply to go off the common path.

When looking at deviant behaviour it's also useful to distinguish between the **overt characteristics** of deviance—the actions or qualities taken as explicitly violating the cultural norm—and the **covert characteristics**, the unstated qualities that might make a particular group a target for sanctions. Covert characteristics can include age, ethnic background, and sex. In the example presented on pages 196–197, the *overt* characteristics are the "zoot suit" clothing and hairstyle—a fashion so different that it violated the cultural norm. The *covert* characteristics are age (the groups involved were mostly teens) and ethnicity (they were mostly Latino or African-American).

Deviance, then, really comes down to how we define "the norm." It's also about *who* defines the norm, and the power of those who share the norm to define and treat outsiders as inferior or dangerous. And we

Some would call this deviance, while others see it as art. What other forms of art might be considered deviant?

QUICK HITS

Getting Deviance Straight

- **Deviant** just means *different from the norm, the usual.*
- **Deviant** *does not mean bad, wrong, perverted, sick, or inferior* in any way.
- **Deviant** is a category that *changes with time, place, and culture.*
- **Deviance** is about *relative quantity*, not quality.
- Definitions of **deviance** often *reflect power.*

must recognize that just as the norm changes—over time and across cultures—so does deviance.

When we invoke "the norm," we're usually referring to what we defined in Chapter 4 as the **dominant culture**. As you read through the different sections of this chapter, keep in mind the dominant culture we asserted exists in Canada: it is white, English-speaking, of European heritage, Christian, male, middle-class, middle-aged, urban, and heterosexual. To a certain extent it is true that to differ from the dominant culture is to be deviant—to repeat, though, that doesn't make it wrong.

Another term to revisit here is **subculture**. This is a group existing within a larger culture and possessing beliefs or interests at variance with those of the dominant culture. Subculture is the focal point of one of two early theories of deviance that we'll now examine in detail.

Three Theories of Deviance: Strain Theory, Subcultural Theory, and Labelling Theory

Strain Theory: Robert Merton

Early sociological theorist **Robert Merton** developed **strain theory** (1938) to explain why, in his opinion, some individuals "chose" to be criminally deviant. The "strain" Merton identified was a disconnect between society's culturally defined goals and the uneven distribution of the means necessary to achieve those goals. Merton was describing a situation in which social reality—the real-life circumstances of some

individuals—inhibits the attainment of "the **American dream**." The American dream is essentially success, however you choose to define it (fame, wealth, social prestige—you name it), mythologized as an opportunity that any American citizen, regardless of background or circumstances, can seize provided he or she is willing to put in the hard work to get it. In reality, Merton was aware, the dream of success is most readily available to those who possess upper- and middle-class resources (capital, expensive post-secondary education, and social connections). When those without these resources find themselves prevented from achieving society's culturally achieved goals, they turn, according to Merton, to criminal deviance.

Subcultural Theory: Albert Cohen

Albert Cohen developed **subcultural theory** in an effort to challenge some aspects of Merton's work and refine others. He was also building on foundations laid by Frederick Thrasher in his studies of gangs (mentioned in Chapter 6) and by **E. Franklin Frazier** (1894–1962), who had carried out some pioneering studies of African Americans living in Chicago.

Cohen's study of teenage gangs (1955) presents a model of what he called the **delinquent subculture**, made up of young, lower-class males suffering from a **status frustration**: failing to succeed in middle-class institutions, especially school, they become socialized into an oppositional subculture in which the values of the school are inverted. For example, the youths he studied engaged in delinquent stealing that was primarily **non-utilitarian**—in other words, the objects weren't stolen because they were needed for survival but because the act of stealing was respected within the delinquent subculture. Cohen stressed that becoming a member of the delinquent subculture is like becoming a member of any culture. It does not depend on the psychology of the individual, nor is the subculture invented or created by the individual. When members of the delinquent subculture grow up and leave the gang (to join adult gangs or mainstream society), the subculture persists. Cohen asserted that:

> delinquency is neither an inborn disposition nor something the child has contrived by himself; that children *learn* to become delinquents by becoming members of groups in which delinquent conduct is already established and "the thing to do";

and that a child need not be "different" from other children, that he need not have any twists or defects of personality or intelligence in order to become a delinquent. (1955: 11–12)

We can use Cohen's model to review other ideas presented earlier in the textbook. First, the **norms** of the delinquent subculture—the rules or expectations of behaviour—would be different, at least in part, from those of the main culture. The difference, according to Cohen, comes from the inverting of norms. In Cohen's words, "The delinquent's conduct is right, by the standards of his subculture, precisely *because* it is wrong by the norms of the larger culture" (Cohen 1955: 28). Likewise, there is an inverting of the **sanctions**, the reactions to the behaviour of the individuals. The **negative sanctions** of non-gang members—negative reactions to their behaviour—can be seen as **positive sanctions** from the delinquent gang's perspective, and vice versa.

Friends attend a vigil in honour of a 14-year-old Toronto-area girl who was killed when a shootout involving rival gangs broke out at a neighbourhood block party in July 2012. Does Cohen's subcultural theory—now 60 years old—provide any clues to why young men continue to join "delinquent" gangs involved in criminal activity?

Labelling Theory: Howard Becker

One weakness of subculture theory is that it stresses subcultural values as developed in opposition to mainstream society. The theory is only partly useful (and generally inadequate) to address social situations in which the subcultural values, beliefs, and practices considered deviant by mainstream society flow in fact from the history and traditional culture of the people involved.

Consider, for instance, the way Canada's Aboriginal people have often been cast as deviant. It would be hard to argue that they have consciously shaped their customs and behaviour to oppose those of mainstream Canadian society. Certain aspects of their situation might be better explained by **Howard Becker**'s **labelling theory**.

Becker, you'll recall from Chapter 6, theorized that labels applied to individuals and groups outside the mainstream become internalized both by those cast as deviant and by the majority group. Take, for example, the image of the "Indian drunk." Cree playwright Tomson Highway described it as "our national image":

> That is the first and only way most white people see Indians. . . . In fact, the average white Canadian has seen that visual more frequently than they've seen a beaver. To my mind, you might as well put an Indian drunk on the Canadian nickel. (as quoted in York 1990: 191)

Yet when an image like this gets applied to an individual and becomes a master status, it dominates any and all other statuses, and may eventually become internalized.

A few facts are important to present here. One is that Aboriginal people, in greater percentages than any other group, abstain entirely from alcohol—they do not drink. Second, Aboriginal people who drink are more likely to be *binge drinkers* (i.e. people who have five or more drinks at a time). Third, there is no conclusive evidence that Aboriginal people have lower tolerance for alcohol than do other racialized groups. What effect do you think the image of the "Indian drunk" has on the first two statistics presented in this paragraph?

Another criticism of strain theory and subcultural theory is that while both have been used productively to address deviance in what can be termed "male culture," the research in this area falls short when applied to "female culture."

What do YOU think?

We tend to think of gangs as male, but girls and young women also band together in groups that could be considered deviant subcultures. A recent Ontario study of 9,288 students from grades 7–12 found that girls were more likely (at 28 per cent) to be cyber-bullied than were boys (15 per cent; see Canadian Press 2012b). Can Cohen's theory help to explain why girls "gang up" on other girls in this way?

The Importance of the Cultural Component in Deviance

What gets labelled "deviant" differs across cultures. Take the **vision quest** in Aboriginal culture. As noted in Chapter 5, on socialization, it is traditional for young Aboriginal people to go on a vision quest around the time of puberty. They leave on their own, they fast, and they typically go without sleep in the hopes of having a vision. In this vision, they might learn songs that will give them strength in difficult times. They might find objects that will connect them with spiritual power. And, if they are fortunate, they will identify a guardian spirit during the experience. This important rite of passage represents the major step in becoming an adult.

In the dominant culture of North America, the experiences surrounding a vision quest might be considered "normal" only among specially defined groups like artists (musicians, dancers, writers, and so on) or perhaps Olympic athletes in training. Otherwise the experience might strike members of the dominant culture as deviant. These people might be tempted to characterize the vision as a **hallucination**, an image of something that is considered to be not "objectively" there. They might want to label the person undergoing the experience mentally ill. However, it is important to recognize the long-held spiritual significance of the vision in North American Native culture.

Arthur Kleinman asks his readers to suppose that 10 sociologists have interviewed 10 different adult Aboriginal people who have experienced the death of a loved one. If they discover that 9 out of the 10 individuals interviewed reported having heard or seen the recently deceased family member in a vision, the 10 researchers can conclude that their findings are reliable. However,

> . . . if they describe this observation as a "hallucination," that is, a pathological percept indicative of mental illness, which it might be for adult non-Indian Americans, they would have an empirical finding that was reliable but not valid. Validity would require the qualifying interpretation that this percept is not pathological—in fact it is both normative and normal for American Indians since it is neither culturally inappropriate nor a predictor or sign of disease—and therefore it could not be labeled as a hallucination. (Kleinman 1995: 73–4)

Cultural differences in what is deemed deviant have unfortunate sociological effects when one of those cultures is dominant, the other a minority, in the same country. The dominant culture's definition then might condemn as deviant not just the practice of the minority culture but the minority culture itself.

The Contested Nature of Deviance

Not only will definitions of deviance differ *across* cultures, but they will vary *within* cultures. It is true that the culture defines deviance—that deviance is essentially a social or cultural construct—but it is important to remember that there is seldom total or even near total agreement within a culture as to what is deviant. In other words, deviance, like other elements in a culture, can be **contested**: not everyone agrees.

When deviance is contested in any given area, we have a situation known as **conflict deviance**. Conflict deviance is a disagreement among groups over whether or not something is deviant. The legality of marijuana is a good example. In Canada, the possession of marijuana for recreational use is against the law, and is therefore deviant. However, results of a 2002 survey conducted by the Canadian Community Health Survey suggest that 3 million people aged 15 and older use marijuana at least once a year, which goes a long way towards normalizing the practice. Further complicating the issue is the fact that possession of small amounts of marijuana for medicinal purposes *is* legal. The recurring debate over whether possession of small

Does this woman look like a pothead? In spring 2012, supporters of a Colorado ballot initiative to legalize marijuana launched an advertising campaign designed to "normalize" marijuana use. What covert characteristics of deviance do you associate with pot use? Why do you think the makers of this ad chose to avoid them?

amounts of marijuana for recreational use should be legalized is proof that smoking up, though deviant, is a focal point for conflict deviance.

Gay marriage is another issue of conflict deviance. Even though gay marriage was made legal in all provinces and territories during a two-year period from 2003 to 2005, Canadians are still far from having consensus on whether or not marriage for gays and lesbians is deviant.

Social Constructionism versus Essentialism

One of the reasons deviance is contested has to do with the differing viewpoints of *social constructionism* and *essentialism*. **Social constructionism** puts forward the idea that certain elements of social life—including deviance, but also gender, "race," and other elements— are not natural but artificial, created by society or culture. **Essentialism**, on the other hand, argues that there is something "natural," "true," "universal," and therefore "objectively determined" about these aspects of social life.

When we look at any given social element, we can see that each of these two viewpoints applies to some degree. Alcoholism, for instance, is a physical condition, so it has something of an essence or essential nature, but whom we label an alcoholic and how we as a society perceive an alcoholic (i.e. as someone who is morally weak or as someone with a medical or mental health problem) is a social construct, one that will vary from society to society.

The interplay between social constructionism and essentialism receives excellent treatment from **Erving Goffman** in his study of stigma and deviance, *Stigma: Notes on the Management of a Spoiled Identity* (1963). A **stigma** is a human attribute that is seen to discredit an individual's social identity. It might be used to label the stigmatized individual or group as deviant. Goffman identified three types of *stigmata* (the plural of *stigma*):

- **bodily stigmata**
- **moral stigmata**
- **tribal stigmata**.

The Point Is...

The "Zoot Suit Riots" of the Early 1940s: Clothes and Ethnicity as Deviant

An instructive case of deviance labelling and sanctioning surrounds the "Zoot Suit Riots" that occurred in June 1943 in Los Angeles. The targets were racialized groups—African-American and Latino males—who made convenient scapegoats for wartime tension.

In the early 1940s, Los Angeles was undergoing rapid change. The city's population was growing and its demographics were changing, with large numbers of Mexicans and African Americans coming to the city. Teenagers made up a large share of the population, as older men and women had gone off to join the war effort, and with a surplus of well-paying jobs left available by older brothers and sisters drafted into the military, the young people who remained behind made money to spend on music and clothes. These teens—black and Latino males in particular—adopted a unique style of dress, a distinctive haircut (the "duck tail," also known as the "duck's ass"), and a musical style that were countercultural. The music was jazz, rooted in the African-American experience and only slowly gaining acceptance among the conservative elements of the United States. The dancing (the jitterbug) was more sexual than dancing of the 1930s. The clothing was the zoot suit: a jacket with broad shoulders and narrow waist, ballooned pants with "reet pleats," "pegged cuffs," and striking designs. Zoot-suit culture swaggered with a distinctive bold strut and posing stance, and distinguished itself from the older set with a host of new slang words unknown to parents and other adults.

How did the zoot suit become deviant? Through the media. The main vehicle was the comic strip *Li'l Abner*, by Al Capp. In a time before television, comic strips were a major part of popular media. *Li'l Abner*, with maybe 50 million readers a day, was one of the most popular strips of the time. It's difficult to overstate its influence.

Al Capp identified the zoot suit as a target for his negative sanctioning humour. From 11 April to 23 May 1943, the strip presented the story of "Zoot-Suit Yokum," an invention of US clothing manufacturers bent on taking over the country politically and economically. These industrialists conspired to create a national folk hero, who would popularize their zoot suits by performing feats of bravery clad in this signature costume. This was the fictional start of "Zoot-Suit Mania," which was soon defeated when the conservative clothing manufacturers, determined to preserve their market share, found a Zoot-Suit Yokum doppelganger to act in a cowardly way. The triumph of conservative clothiers was proclaimed in the third frame of the 19 May strip, which displayed the mock headline: "GOVERNOR ISSUES ORDER BANNING ZOOT-SUIT WEARERS!!" (Mazón 1984: 35).

Beyond the pages of dailies carrying the *Li'l Abner* comic strip a very real hostility emerged between mainstream society and the zoot-suit counterculture. One LA newspaper ran a piece on how to "de-zoot" a zoot-suiter: "Grab a zooter. Take off his pants and frock coat and tear them up or burn them. Trim the 'Argentine ducktail' that goes with the screwy costume" (Mazón 1984: 76).

ENTIRE NATION GRIPPED BY ZOOT-SUIT MANIA!!

FROM MAINE TO CALIFORNIA A FANATICAL TYPE OF HERO WORSHIP HAS ENGULFED THIS ONCE CONSERVATIVE NATION. THE OBJECT OF ALL THIS ADULATION IS "ZOOT-SUIT YOKUM" WHO HAS, UPON INNUMERABLE OCCASIONS, RUSHED TO SCENES OF DISASTER ALL OVER THE COUNTRY—AND, WITH INCREDIBLE, FOOLHARDY COURAGE, PERFORMED AMAZING FEATS OF STRENGTH AND HEROISM. NATURALLY, "ZOOT-SUIT YOKUM" HAS BECOME THE IDOL OF ALL RED-BLOODED YOUNG AMERICANS—AND THIS IDOL-WORSHIP HAS LED MILLIONS OF MEN TO IMITATE HIS PECULIAR COSTUME, KNOWN AS THE "ZOOT SUIT." CLOTHING STORES REPORT THAT THERE HAS BEEN A MAD RUSH TO BUY "ZOOT SUITS"—WHILE THE REGULAR MEN'S CLOTHING MARKET HAS HIT ITS WORST SLUMP IN ONE HUNDRED YEARS.

ZOOT-SUIT YOKUM

Los Angeles police round up zoot-suit suspects, 11 June 1943. Do these zoot-suiters look like trouble-makers to you?

Whether it was intended with humour or not, instructions for the negative sanctioning of zoot-suiters were carried out in a very real way by some of those opposed to the counterculture. The conflict reached a climax in early June 1943, when thousands of young white men—soldiers, marines, and sailors on weekend leave from nearby military installations—launched a campaign to rid Los Angeles of zoot-suiters by capturing them, buzzing their hair down in a military style, and tearing or burning their clothing. Still, as riots go, they were relatively harmless. As Mauricio Mazón points out, "riot" is a bit of a misnomer:

> They were not about zoot-suiters rioting, and they were not, in any conventional sense of the word, "riots." No one was killed. No one sustained massive injuries. Property damage was slight. No major or minor judicial decisions stemmed from the riots. There was no pattern to arrests. Convictions were few and highly discretionary. (Mazón 1984: 1)

The conflict lasted just under a week, and was brought to an end with two acts. First, the military reined in their troops. More significant, on 9 June, Los Angeles City Council issued the following ban:

> NOW, THEREFORE, BE IT RESOLVED, that the City Council by Resolution find that wearing of Zoot Suits constitutes a public nuisance and does hereby instruct the City Attorney to prepare an ordinance declaring same a nuisance and prohibit the wearing of Zoot Suits with reet pleats within the city limits of Los Angeles. (Mazón 1984: 75)

This, the culmination of a series of increasingly explicit and punitive sanctions, shows how humour with a social edge and a large audience can be used against a particular group.

What do YOU think?

1. Why do you think the zoot-suiters were targeted?

2. Do you think there are any parallels between zoot-suiters of the 1940s and any group today?

He defined them in the following way:

> First there are abominations of the body—the various physical deformities. Next there are blemishes of individual character perceived as weak will, domineering or unnatural passions, treacherous and rigid beliefs, and dishonesty, these being inferred from a known record of, for example, mental disorder, imprisonment, addiction, alcoholism, homosexuality, unemployment, suicidal attempts, and radical political behavior. Finally there are the tribal stigma of race, nation, and religion, these being stigma that can be transmitted through lineages and equally contaminate all members of a family. (Goffman 1963: 4)

So while bodily stigmata exist physically, definitions of "deformed" can be and often are socially constructed—think of descriptions such as "too fat" or "too thin." People in a variety of societies "deform" their bodies (by dieting to extremes, by piercing and tattooing their bodies, or, in certain cultures, by putting boards on their children's heads to give them a sloping forehead) to look beautiful according to social standards. People who hear voices and see what is not physically present may be considered religious visionaries in some cultures, or just plain crazy in others. Racializing is another social process, national identity a social construct open to change over time, and different religions are privileged in different societies.

In this textbook, we have adopted a view of deviance that is more social-constructionist than essentialist. Following Howard Becker's classic work *Outsiders* (1963), we will tend not to speak of deviance as being inherently "bad," conformity to a norm being inherently "good." Instead, we will generally follow the rule that

> social groups create deviance by making the rules, whose infraction constitutes deviance, and

Canada's Mennonites are known for their belief in adult baptism, their commitment to non-violence, and the modest everyday fashion worn by the group's conservative members, all of which keep them outside of the cultural mainstream. Which type of stigma is demonstrated here?

by applying those rules to particular people and labelling them as outsiders. . . . Deviance is *not a quality* of the act the person commits, but rather a consequence of the application by others of rules and sanctions to an "offender." (Becker 1963: 8–10)

What do YOU think?

A recent trend on Facebook has people posting pictures of young female cancer patients who have gone bald because of chemotherapy treatments. Facebook members are asked whether they think these girls and women are "beautiful." Do you think this is an attempt to change the bodily stigma of having no hair, as well as the more powerful bodily stigma of having cancer? Do you think this could change the norm concerning female beauty and the way people sometimes avert their eyes from cancer patients?

The Other

An important word used in the sociological analysis of deviance is "other," or "otherness." Difficult to define and even harder to use, it intersects with such concepts as ethnocentrism, colonialism, stereotyping, essentialism, and prejudice.

The other is an image constructed by the dominant culture to characterize subcultures, or by a colonizing nation to describe the colonized. When the United States took over Haiti (between 1915 and 1934), Hollywood and the Catholic church helped to make deviant the indigenous religion of the Haitians by casting it as an element of the "other" culture. Voodoo, which combines elements of Catholic ritual with traditional African magical and religious rites, became an example of how Haitians deviated from "civilized" norms. Along with sympathy and aid for Haiti following the January 2010 earthquake came criticism of Haitians, mostly in the conservative media, for their "fatalistic" or "superstitious" views and adherence to voodoo, which, some critics argued, made the people incapable of helping themselves. The "other" label, once applied, can be extremely difficult to erase.

The image created of the other can be mysterious, mystical, or mildly dangerous, but somehow it is ultimately inferior. Edward Said, in his discussion of Orientalism, characterizes the West's treatment of the Middle East as the creation of an other. The dominant culture in Canada typically defines "Aboriginal" as other. English Canada has portrayed French Canada the same way. In "slacker movies" written and directed by men and aimed at underachieving, socially inept, young white men, "woman" seems to be constructed as an other.

Deviant behaviour, once it has been associated with otherness, is often subject to negative sanctions or punishment. But should deviant behaviour be punished? Certain acts of deviance, such as those that under our criminal justice system are considered illegal, certainly should have sanctions attached, ranging from a judge's warning to fines and jail time for more serious offences. But remember that we're using "deviance" to mean anything outside the norm. Young people trying to establish their independence and individuality will often breach societal norms when it comes to fashion and style of dress. This can make them targets of the negative sanction of *bullying*—aggressive behaviour that includes shaming, ridiculing, physical attacks, and generally drawing unwanted attention to "otherness." Should this kind of deviance be punished?

A recent study showed that children with food allergies are often targets of bullying. Children with allergies can be considered deviant in that they form a distinct minority. Although school boards are increasingly making efforts to accommodate their difference (e.g. by requiring all children to abstain from bringing certain foods, such as peanut-contaminated products, to school), these measures draw attention to the otherness of children with allergies and can actually increase the potential for the negative sanction of bullying.

An article in the October 2010 issue of the *Annals of Allergy, Asthma and Immunology* reported the results of an American study, in which 353 questionnaires were sent to and completed by parents of food-allergic children and by food-allergic teenagers and adults. Among the findings was that 24 per cent of the survey subjects reported having been "bullied, teased, or harassed" because of their allergy. Of the reported incidents, 82 per cent had occurred at school, and 80 per cent had been perpetrated by classmates.

What do YOU think?

1. Why do you think these children are being bullied?

2. What, if anything, legitimizes bullying in the minds of the bullies? How might this be changed?

Disturbingly, 21 per cent of the respondents reported having been bullied by teachers or other school staff. Also surprising is that the greater part (57 per cent) of the reported incidents were physical, including being touched with the allergen, having it thrown or waved at the individuals, and even having it used to deliberately contaminate their food.

"Race" and Deviance: To Be Non-white Is Deviant

To racialize deviance is to link particular ethnic groups with certain forms of deviance, and to treat these groups differently because of that connection. We see this in movies and television shows that portray all Italians as being involved in organized crime, and news reports that link young black men with gangs and gun violence. Part of **racializing deviance** is making ethnic background a covert characteristic of deviance, as though all people of a particular ethnic group are involved in the same supposedly deviant behaviour.

Despite the public promotion in Canada of **multiculturalism**—the set of policies and practices designed to foster respect for cultural differences—the pressure to **assimilate** (i.e. become culturally the same as the dominant culture) is persistent. Immigrants who have

experienced the embarrassment of having Canadians stumble over their names—sometimes deliberately for supposed comic effect (as when Don Cherry knowingly mispronounces French and Russian names)—may have felt pressure to anglicize their names to make themselves more "Canadian."

Racial profiling is one way in which deviance is racialized. In its report on the "human cost of racial profiling," the Ontario Human Rights Commission offers a thoroughgoing definition. It defines racial profiling as

> any action undertaken for reasons of safety, security or public protection that relies on stereotypes about race, colour, ethnicity, ancestry, religion, or place of origin rather than on reasonable suspicion, to single out an individual for greater scrutiny or different treatment. (OHRC 2003: 6)

The report notes that racial profiling can arise from a combination of these factors, and that age and gender may also "influence the experience of profiling."

Racial profiling assumes that the personal characteristics of an individual can be used to predict his or her actions, especially his or her tendency to be engaged in illegal activity. As the report notes, this is

The Point Is...

Crossing the Border While Black

I was part of an EdD (Education doctorate) cohort in a class on community college leadership. It was a high-powered group, including faculty members, middle administrators, and presidents of three colleges, and we were going on a field trip from Toronto to Monroe Community College in Rochester. It was the summer before September 11, so "home security" was not the issue it would shortly become.

The car I was in was driven by one of the administrators, who was white, as were the passengers. (I looked like an extra in a Cheech and Chong movie, but the others looked respectable.) We passed through customs with no problem. Few words were exchanged with the border guards. The same was true

for the other white travellers in our convoy: no delays, no problems.

But there was one exception. One of our cars carried two black passengers. One of the men was an upper-level administrator, well dressed and distinguished-looking, from the Caribbean. The other was a faculty member, younger, also well dressed, very articulate, with an American accent. They were stopped and asked to get out of the car. The trunk of the car was searched carefully. It would be an understatement to say that they were not treated with the respect due to people of their standing in the community. It took them over half an hour to cross the border. They were guilty of crossing the border while black.

Our Stories

Black Candle, Yellow Scare

A classic Canadian instance of racializing deviance comes from the 1922 book *Black Candle*, a collection of articles written by Emily Murphy, many of them originally published in *Maclean's* magazine. A journalist, activist, and self-taught legal expert, born of a prominent and wealthy Ontario family, Murphy was a gender heroine of first-wave feminism, becoming, in 1916, the first woman magistrate not just in Canada but in the British Empire. She would later play a role in the historic "Persons Case" (1928), in which the Supreme Court ruled that women were not "persons" eligible to hold public office; the decision was appealed to the British Privy Council and overturned the following year.

Murphy's four books of personal sketches, written under the pen name "Janey Canuck," were already well known when she published *Black Candle* to expose the insidious details of the Canadian drug trade. *Black Candle* cast Chinese Canadians as the main villains in the trafficking of illegal drugs—particularly opium, heroin, and cocaine—although blacks were also singled out for censure. The main theme was that Chinese men—those bachelors who, because of the restrictive head tax on Chinese immigrants, could not be reunited with their wives or find companionship among women "of their own race"—were corrupting white women through drug dealing, "ruining them" and making them accomplices in their dealing. The following quotation, from the chapter on "Girls as Pedlars," is typical:

> Much has been said, of late, concerning the entrapping of girls by Chinamen in order to secure their services as pedlars of narcotics. The importance of the subject is one which warrants our closest scrutiny: also, it is one we dare not evade, however painful its consideration. (Murphy 1973 [1922]: 233)

Murphy believed that the "yellow races" would use the drug trade to take over the Anglo-Saxon world, and she warned North American readers to be wary of these "visitors":

> Still, it behooves the people in Canada and the United States, to consider the desirability of these visitors . . . and to say whether or not we shall be *"at home"* to them for the future. A visitor may be polite, patient, persevering, . . . but if he carries poisoned lollypops in his pocket and feeds them to our children, it might seem wise to put him out.
>
> It is hardly credible that the average Chinese pedlar has any definite idea in his mind of bringing about the downfall of the white race, his swaying motive being probably that of greed, but in the hands of his superiors, he may become a powerful instrument to this very end. . . .
>
> Naturally, the aliens are silent on the subject, but an addict who died this year in British Columbia . . . used to relate how the Chinese pedlars taunted him with their superiority at being able to sell the dope without using it, and by telling him how the yellow race would rule the world. They were too wise, they urged, to attempt to win in battle but would win by wits; would strike at the white race through "dope" and when the time was ripe would command the world. (Murphy 1973 [1922]: 187–9)

Black Candle had a huge impact on the perception of the drug trade and on drug legislation in Canada. Chapter XXIII, "Marahuana—A New Menace," was the first work in Canada to discuss marijuana use. It contained a lot of damning half-truths and anecdotes, and led to the enactment of laws governing marijuana use.

Emily Murphy is an example of what is called, following Becker (1963), a **moral entrepreneur**. This is a person who tries to convince others of the existence of a particular social problem that he or she has identified and defined. The moral entrepreneur labours to create consensus on an issue on which no pre-existing consensus exists, trying to foster sufficient agreement among policy-makers to ensure that the action the moral entrepreneur desires takes place. Examples of moral entrepreneurs can include opposing groups, such as pro-life and pro-choice activists or the gun and the anti-gun lobbies.

not the same as criminal profiling, which "relies on actual behaviour or on information about suspected activity by someone who meets the description of a specific individual." As we saw with the example of bullying above, racial profiling uses a person's otherness as grounds to single the individual out for different treatment, often involving some sort of sanction.

Racial profiling can occur in a variety of contexts involving various agents and individuals. Examples include incidents involving:

- law enforcement personnel, such as police and border control agents
- security personnel, such as private security guards
- employers, for example, in conducting security clearances of staff
- landlords, for example, when a property owner assumes that certain applicants or tenants will be involved in criminal or other illegal activity
- service providers, for instance, a taxi driver who refuses to stop at night for certain people
- the criminal justice system, such as courts and prisons.

What do YOU think?

Read again the OHRC's definition of racial profiling. Do you believe that racial profiling is only undertaken "for reasons of safety, security, or public protection"?

Gender and Deviance: To Be Female Is Deviant

Feminists teach us that in a patriarchal society (one dominated by men), what is "male" is treated as normal, while what is "female" is treated as other and seen as inherently deviant. Male values are **normalized** (i.e. made to seem normal, right, and good), through customs, laws, and culture production. Two related concepts are important here: misogyny and patriarchal construct. **Misogyny** means literally "hating women." In a patriarchal or

male-dominated society, images of women are often constructed in ways that contain and reflect misogyny. **Patriarchal construct** refers to social conditions being thought of or structured in a way that favours men and boys over women and girls. Think, for example, of highly prized and well-paying jobs—corporate lawyer, investment banker, emergency room doctor—that have been constructed so that the job-holder is forced to place family in a distant second place to employment. This gives advantages to men, who in Canadian

This "ladies-only" train in Japan exists to protect women riders from sexual harassment. Does it seem to you as though women here are being treated as "other," singled out (and negatively sanctioned) as though protection from crime and physical violations is something only the "weaker sex" needs?

Telling It Like It Is

An Author POV

Age and Deviance: To Be Over 50 Is Deviant

"Warning," by British poet Jenny Joseph, is a poem about how many women, particularly middle-class women, spend their lives having to conform, to avoid deviance, and how they desire to be free of the pressures of conformity once they have reached older age. In the poem, the speaker longs for the day when she will no longer have to "set a good example for the children." To that end, she vows to commit a number of deviant acts once she becomes "an old woman." These acts include wearing colourful but mismatching clothes (including a "red hat which doesn't go"), spending her pension money on brandy, setting off alarms in department stores, picking the flowers from people's gardens, learning to spit, and generally "mak[ing] up for the sobriety of my youth."

So popular is the poem (which is easily found online) that there is a Red Hat Society for women over 50 that began in North America and now has thousands of members in a number of different countries. In order to give voice to the male 50+ set, I've written a poem of my own:

The Old Men's Deviant Society

When I am an old man,
I will wear any colour I want,
I will enjoy flowers, poetry,
and other unmanly pleasures
that I have secretly enjoyed for years
and maybe even talk about them
in my favourite bar.
I won't care or talk about
what car I drive
(as long as it is reliable),
whether or not I can fix it,
how fast it can go,
what my lawn looks like,
how big my barbecue is.
And I won't comment on
whether what other men wear or do
makes them look, smell, or act
like sissy boys.
It's my 50th birthday party,
and I'll cry if I want to.

What do YOU think?

1. Are there ideas here that challenge the norm for male behaviour? What signs of deviance do you find? How do they parallel to the deviant acts promised in "Warning"?

2. Do you think the existence of something as formal as a club (i.e. the Red Hat Club) undermines the deviant tendencies expressed in the poem? Or is joining the club an act of solidarity in deviance?

society are expected to fulfill fewer domestic and child-rearing duties than are women.

Casting the woman as deviant is not a new phenomenon. A particularly interesting example surrounds the witch hunts waged in Europe and, later on, in colonial America from about the fourteenth to the seventeenth centuries. Those who were identified as witches were tried and, if found guilty, executed. This for several reasons makes the witch hunts an intriguing case for the sociological study of deviance. For one, the deviance was fictitious: while the people tried may have committed criminal acts, their powers and connections with Satan were not real (although often believed to be by both accuser and some accused). Second, the vast majority of those accused were women (the figure usually cited by authorities on the subject is 85 per cent). The word "witch" itself is closely associated with women, conjuring up traditional negative images of pointed black hats, old warty faces with pointed noses, and flying broomsticks: bad clothes, bad looks, and bad use of a female-associated cleaning implement. In a patriarchal society, this image of deviance is very much associated with femaleness, its opposite—normalcy—with maleness.

Class and Deviance: To Be Poor Is Deviant

Poverty can be considered a covert characteristic of deviance. Marginally illicit activities like overindulgence in alcohol are more likely to be considered deviant in poor people than in middle-class or "rich" people. Jeffrey Reiman is a professor of philosophy who thinks like a good sociologist. In *The Rich Get Richer and the Poor Get Prison: Ideology, Class, and Criminal Justice*, he argues that the criminal justice system has a distinct class bias. This bias appears in many ways: in the way we define what constitutes a crime, and in our processes of arrest, trial, and sentencing. Each step shows bias against the poor. As Reiman explains:

> [T]he criminal justice system keeps before the public . . . the distorted image that crime is primarily the work of the poor. The value of this to those in positions of power is that it deflects the discontented and potential hostility of Middle America [the American middle class] away from the classes above them and toward the classes below them. . . . [I]t not only explains our dismal failure to make a significant dent in crime but also explains why the criminal justice system functions in a way that is biased against the poor at every stage from arrest to conviction. Indeed, even at the earlier stage, when crimes are defined in law, the system primarily concentrates on the predatory acts of the poor and tends to exclude or deemphasize the equally or more dangerous predatory acts of those who are well off. (Reiman 1998: 4)

This is how behaviours associated with poverty and criminality become synonymous with deviance while criminal activity associated with wealth and celebrity is often labelled "good business." Martha Stewart, media star and founder of a business empire aimed at aspiring home decorators and entertainers, was convicted of contempt of court for lying under oath during a probe into alleged insider trading, and yet she received a standing ovation from a mostly supportive public and press following a hearing at which she was sentenced to five months in prison.

Class bias is at the centre of what is known in the literature as the "schools-to-prison" hypothesis: the idea that in schools located in poorer, often racialized neighbourhoods, there is a biased application of practices such as "zero tolerance," which creates a misleading perception of higher crime rates. Greater rates of suspension and expulsion, higher numbers of random locker and student searches, and tough anti-violence measures like the installation of metal detectors, the hiring of security guards, and even periodical police raids characterize the schools in these poorer neighbourhoods, but these measures are greatly out of proportion to the amount of violence and crime actually occurring at the schools. But as we saw with labelling theory earlier in the chapter, when you treat people as though they are all potential criminals, they are more likely to actually become criminals.

While most of the literature and statistics relate to the American situation, the schools-to-prison hypothesis applies in urban Canada as well. In a Toronto *Star* article, "Suspended Sentences: Forging a School-to-Prison Pipeline?" (6 June 2009), authors Sandro Contenta and Jim Rankin reported that Ontario's Safe Schools Act, in force from 2001 to 2008, produced startlingly high numbers of suspensions and expulsions. The *Star*'s analysis, which examined school suspension rates for 2007–8 alongside sentences and postal code data for inmates in Ontario provincial jails, showed that the highest rates of suspension tended to be in those areas that also had the highest rates of incarceration. This is a positive correlation, which suggests that punishing youths from the city's poorest neighbourhoods with zero-tolerance measures reinforces the higher incarceration rate in those areas.

"But wait," I can hear you say; "Isn't it possible that low-income neighbourhoods naturally produce crime, and that greater rates of true crime, not increased levels of scrutiny or harsher application of zero-tolerance policies, are responsible for higher incarceration rates corresponding to these neighbourhoods?"

Indeed, lower-class people are overrepresented in the statistics on criminal convictions and admission to prison. That means that per population they are more often convicted and admitted to prison than are middle- and upper-class people, and this contributes to the idea that all lower-class people are criminally deviant. However, a closer look at the statistics helps us see why they do not give us an accurate picture of the lower classes.

"Lower class" is a designation that is often established by looking solely at recorded income, but it covers a broad and far from homogeneous set of individuals. Some are part of the working class, who labour for long hours with little financial reward. Others are on welfare. These two subgroups of the lower class are probably not significantly more involved in criminal activity than are middle-class or upper-class people. In fact, it's a separate subgroup, representing a small minority of the lower class, that is responsible for a high percentage of the crimes. These people are lumped together with the first two groups statistically because of their low reported income, giving a misleading forensic picture of the working poor.

Another reason for the overrepresentation of the lower class in crime statistics has to do with social resources. In this context, social resources refers to knowledge of the law and legal system, ability to afford a good lawyer, influential social connections, and capacity to present oneself in a way that is deemed "respectable." Lower-class individuals generally have access to fewer social resources than middle- and upper-class people do, and this makes them more likely to be convicted of charges people from the wealthier classes might be able to avoid. Tepperman and Rosenberg explain the importance of social resources:

> Social resources help people avoid labelling and punishment by the police and courts. For example, in assault or property-damage cases, the police and courts try to interpret behaviour and assess blame before taking any action. They are less likely to label people with more resources as "criminal" or "delinquent" and more likely to label them "alcoholic" or "mentally ill" for having committed a criminal act. (Tepperman and Rosenberg 1998: 118)

The authors make use of Goffman's concept of impression management, which they define as "the control of personal information flow to manipulate how other people see and treat you" (Tepperman & Rosenberg 1998: 118). The upper classes are better at managing impressions than are people who belong to the lower class. Therefore, they conclude,

> Official rule-enforcers (including police and judges, but also social workers, psychiatrists and the whole correctional and treatment establishment) define as serious the deviant acts in which poor people engage. On the other hand, they tend to "define away" the deviant acts of rich people as signs of illness, not crime. They are more likely to consider those actions morally blameless. (Tepperman and Rosenberg 1998: 118–19)

White Collar Crime

It was in a speech to the American Sociological Society in 1939 that criminologist **Edwin Sutherland** (1883–1950) introduced the term **white collar crime**. He defined it as "crime committed by a person of respectability and high social status in the course of his occupation" (1949: 9). His article "White Collar Criminality" was published the next year in the *American Sociological Review* (Sutherland 1940), and he would later devote an entire book to the subject (Sutherland 1949).

Sutherland's work was an important step in the sociological study of criminology. Previous work had focused on the poor and the crimes they committed, creating at the very least a biased sample. But Sutherland's definition is not flawless. Associating certain kinds of criminal behaviour with a particular class reflects a class bias and a misleading view of the situation. After all, you don't have to be a person of "high social status" to commit identity theft (making copies of bank or charge cards), which tends to be included in the category of white collar crime. The implication in Sutherland's original definition is that only people of the higher classes are capable of planning and carrying out crimes that are essentially non-violent. In this way it fails to recognize that industrial accidents caused by unsafe working conditions that are allowed to exist by a negligent owner are in a real sense crimes of violence. Even the term itself reflects this class bias: the addition

Table 8.1 Occupational and corporate crimes

OCCUPATIONAL CRIMES	CORPORATE CRIMES
sexual harassment	industrial accidents (sometimes called corporate manslaughter)
embezzlement	pollution
pilfering	price-fixing
expense account fraud	bribery
tax evasion	misleading advertising

of the qualifier (*white collar*) to the word *crime* suggests that most crime, ordinary crime, is not committed by people of "high social status," in much the same way that the term *white trash* carries the implication that it is unusual for whites to be "trash," unlike people of other ethnic backgrounds.

More recent works have refined the definition of white collar crime to remove the class bias associated with Sutherland's original definition. Clinard and Quinney (1973) went further, breaking white collar crime into two categories by distinguishing between what they called **occupational crimes** and **corporate crimes**. They defined the former as "offenses committed by individuals for themselves in the course of their occupations [and] offenses by employers against their employees" (1973: 188). The latter include "offenses committed by corporate officials for their corporation and the offenses of the corporation itself" (1973: 188). The difference is one of beneficiaries and victims: occupational crimes benefit the individual at the expense of other individuals who work for the company; corporate crimes benefit the corporation and its executives at the expense of other companies and the general public. This latter definition, by placing less emphasis on the individual, homes in on the negative aspects of corporate culture and the way that individuals and corporations work together to commit illegal acts against consumers and the common public.

In the spring of 2001, energy giant Enron, the seventh largest company in the United States, announced that it was declaring bankruptcy. This had devastating effects not just on the company's employees and shareholders but on the US economy as a whole. And it was only a taste of things to come, as the failure and collapse of several key financial agencies in the US between 2008 and 2010 would later contribute to a major worldwide economic downturn. The creative legal financing and letter-but-not-principle-of-the-law accounting schemes of the executives involved in the Enron affair, taken together with the multi-million-dollar salaries and perks they were paying themselves, constitute white collar crime of both varieties. Their crimes were occupational in that they took from the economic viability of the company, causing its bankruptcy; they also caused the personal bankruptcy and economic hardship of thousands of employees by encouraging them to sink their life savings into Enron stock. At the same time, their crimes were corporate in that they had a profound negative impact on the

What do YOU think?

Those who study linguistics distinguish between **marked** and **unmarked terms**. The unmarked term is the usual or standard one, while the marked term has a label added to it to distinguish it from the common term. "Field hockey" (as opposed to the usual brand of hockey played in Canada), "light beer," "white chocolate," and "decaffeinated coffee" are all marked terms. "White collar crime" is another example. By distinguishing this variety of upper-class criminal activity, are we implying that most crime is committed by the lower or working class?

American economy (particularly the financial sector) and were a major cause of the energy crisis that occurred in California.

It would be wrong to think smugly that this kind of crime is far more common in the US than in Canada, where, we like to think, we are more conservative and financially secure. Reporter Charles Davies disabused readers of this notion:

> If PriceWaterhouseCoopers' annual survey is an accurate indicator, economic or "white collar" crime in Canada is growing at a disturbing rate, and far faster than in other developed countries.
>
> The accounting giant, which has been toting crime statistics in 26 nations for the past five years, finds that in 2009, 56 per cent of Canadian companies surveyed reported instances of fraud, a 10 per cent increase since 2003. Globally, only 30 per cent of companies reported frauds this year compared to 37 per cent in 2003.
>
> The accounting firm's survey focuses on the various types of fraud—asset theft, accounting offences, money laundering, bribery, and corruption—that are either perpetrated on companies by their own employees (59 per cent of the cases in 2009) or by outsiders, including customers and suppliers (38 per cent of cases). (Davies 2009)

Sexual Orientation and Deviance: To Be Gay Is Deviant

It comes as no surprise that homosexuality is defined as deviant across the world (although not in every culture). This particular social construction of deviance does differ among cultures in terms of how and what kind of social sanctions are applied. At the beginning of 2003, sexual activity between consenting adult homosexuals was still against the law in 13 US states (Alabama, Florida, Idaho, Kansas, Louisiana, Michigan, Mississippi, Missouri, North Carolina, South Carolina, Texas, Utah, and Virginia). In June of that year, in the case *Lawrence vs Texas*, the Supreme Court voted 6–3 against the constitutionality of the Texas law. That ruling effectively rendered anti-homosexuality laws in the other 12 jurisdictions unconstitutional also. This was a big step, to be sure, although same-sex marriage remains illegal in the United States under the Defense of Marriage Act (DOMA). It's important to note that even in Canada, where same-sex marriage has been legal nationwide since 2005, the issue remains one of conflict deviance.

In Britain, homosexuality is addressed in Section 28 of the Local Government Act. It reads:

A local authority shall not:
1) intentionally promote homosexuality or publish material with the intention of promoting homosexuality;
2) promote the teaching in any maintained school of the acceptability of homosexuality as a pretended family relationship.

It would interesting to find out how accurate information about homosexuality might be conceived of as "promoting" it.

In looking at how laws concerning homosexuality differ across the globe, it is interesting to note that former British colonies or protectorates are high on the list of those countries in which male homosexuality (and in some cases female homosexuality) is against the law: Grenada, Guyana, Jamaica in the Caribbean; Botswana and Zimbabwe in Africa; and Bangladesh, Bhutan, Brunei, India, Malaysia, the Maldives, Myanmar, Nepal, Pakistan, Singapore, and Sri Lanka in Asia. Those Asian countries appear to have carried on from colonial times with different versions of an act passed in British India in 1860. They differ from Asian countries such as China, Japan, and Thailand, which were never colonized, and countries colonized by other European nations (e.g. Cambodia, Laos, and Vietnam, colonized by France; Indonesia, colonized by the Netherlands; the Philippines, colonized by Spain). In some Muslim countries—Afghanistan, Pakistan, Saudi Arabia, Uganda, the United Arab Emirates,

Do you think that, on the whole, the men in your class would react more negatively to this picture than the women would? What if the photo featured two women?

and Yemen—laws against homosexuality carry the death penalty, although in some of these jurisdictions (Afghanistan, for instance) it has rarely been applied. Ironically, it is not uncommon in Muslim countries for a young heterosexual man to have his first sexual experience with another young male, which, if it is discovered, is less likely to bring dishonour upon the families involved than would a sexual relationship with an unmarried woman.

In communities where homosexuality is regarded as deviant, negative sanctions can have a powerful influence. In Canada, young men can influence the attitudes of other young men by sanctioning behaviour perceived as effeminate or even just immature or silly with statements like, "Don't be so gay." This practice, promoting what is sometimes referred to as the **ideology of fag**, is a way of influencing people, especially young males, to behave according to gender role expectations.

The Point Is...

The Criminalization of Sexuality

Even though rights for lesbians, gays, bisexuals, and transgendered people (LGBT) in Canada are some of the most progressive in the world, the laws regarding sexual activity and sexual regulation continue to reflect a **heteronormative** bias. In Canada, acts of sodomy and buggery (which comprise any sexual activity that does not lead to procreation, such as oral sex and anal sex) were punishable by death until 1869. In 1892, any homosexual activity by men was deemed "gross indecency" under criminal law. And in 1948 and 1961, changes to the Criminal Code branded those who engaged in homosexual sexual activity as "criminal sexual psychopaths" and "dangerous sexual offenders," who could be charged with an indeterminate prison sentence. In the mid-1960s, just 50 years ago, George Klippert, after being charged and convicted of gay sexual activity, was labelled a dangerous sexual offender and sentenced to life in prison.

Today, Canadian law does not prohibit anal sex if it is between consenting parties over the age of 18 and provided there are no more than two people present. However, for all non-anal sex, the age of consent is 16 regardless of the sexuality of the participants. While both homosexuals and heterosexuals engage in sodomy and anal sex, there remains a legal double standard that continues to target gay male sexual activity over heterosexual sexual activity (Kinsman 1995).

"Bobbies Kissing," a wall mural by British graffiti artist Banksy. Why do you think certain kinds of sexual activity between consenting participants continues to be criminalized? Should they be?

It is interesting to note that the attitude towards homosexuality as deviant is, on a global scale, stricter concerning men than women. There are 30 countries in the world in which only male homosexuality is condemned (e.g. Armenia, Jamaica, Nigeria, Sri Lanka, and Uzbekistan).

Disability and Deviance: To Be Disabled Is Deviant

Society, as we have seen, punishes deviance with negative sanctions, and offers positive sanctions to those who adjust their behaviour to fall in line with the mainstream. A negative sanction can be fairly mild—a rude hand gesture from a fellow driver who didn't appreciate your sudden lane change—but we also have an institutionalized criminal justice system that exists, in part, to punish those who have been judged as deviant according to the laws of a certain jurisdiction. Punishment typically involves restriction of freedoms (e.g. of movement and residence) and an effort to diminishing the independence and self-respect of the deviant.

A reasonable sociological question to ask is whether society punishes disabled people for their disability. For example, do the ways in which we design and build houses (with steps to the front porch and narrow interior stairways), public buildings (with revolving doors), sidewalks (without sloping edges to meet the road), public transport (cramped buses too small in which to manoeuvre a wheelchair) and shelving in grocery stores essentially punish—by limiting freedom, independence, and self-respect—those who cannot walk? (An injury recently deprived me of the ability to walk for a three-month period that was as illuminating as it was terrifying.)

When it comes to "punishing" disability by failing to accommodate differences in physical ability, the sanction is typically an act of omission. It's not that disabled people have been singled out; it's actually that they haven't been taken into account at all. But there are many cases in which people with disabilities have been targeted because of their difference. A vivid example is Alberta's Sexual Sterilization Act, which was in effect from 1928 until 1972. The act was a product of the eugenics ("good genes") movement, which promoted the science of using controlled breeding to improve the population by increasing the occurrence of favourable heritable characteristics and limiting the reproduction of unfavourable ones. Essentially, the Alberta policy was designed to enact measures that would make it physically impossible for people deemed "mentally inferior" to reproduce.

It also punished racial and ethnic deviants. Many of those targeted were Aboriginal people and immigrants from eastern Europe, making this an example of how racial and cultural difference, cast as deviance, has been punished. But the act was also used against people living with mental disabilities. The signal case in this regard is that of Leilani Muir.

In 1959, Leilani Muir was confined at what was then called the Red Deer Training School of Mental Defectives. At the age of 14 she had taken an IQ test (one that reflected a number of biases concerning class, culture, and ways of evaluating intelligence) and had scored 64, earning her the official designation of "moron." ("Normal" intelligence is confirmed by any score around 100.) Muir would later take another test and score a "normal range" 87, but by then it was too late. Following the earlier test she was informed that she would be taken into surgery to have her appendix removed; instead, she was sterilized at the age of 14. This was the sanction for Leilani Muir's mental difference. In 1996, the Alberta government admitted she had been wrongfully sterilized and agreed to a court-appointed settlement of $740,280.

Lennard J. Davis is a leading figure in the sociological study of disability. In his article "Constructing Normalcy," he writes:

> To understand the disabled body, one must return to the concept of the norm, the normal body. So much of writing about disability has focused on the disabled person as the object of study, just as the study of race has focused on the person of color. But as with recent scholarship on race, which has turned its attention to whiteness, I would like to focus not so much on the construction of disability as on the construction of normalcy. I do this because the "problem" of the disabled is not the person with disabilities; the problem is the way that normalcy is constructed to create the "problem" of the disabled person. (Davis 2006: 3)

The politics of disability involves promoting respect for difference, as opposed to just respecting the "normal." For example politically militant members of the deaf community have represented cochlear implants (surgically implanted electronic devices that assist the deaf in sensing sound) as an attempt to "normalize" people with hearing disabilities while disrespecting deaf culture, with its long history of using (and respect for) sign language.

We all have different sets of mental and physical abilities; the world does not divide easily into those who are disabled and those who are not. Davis's point is that the social problem of disability is actually created by those people (typically able-bodied people) who view and treat those with a different set of abilities as "other." There is often a sense of pride and entitlement that goes with being "normal" rather than "deviant" in the context of ability. Even if it isn't mean-spirited, it shows through in even the courteous and respectful communication that may characterize interactions with those who are "differently abled." A good example of a situation in which a difference in ability is turned into the "problem" of disability is presented in the following student narrative about an incident that took place in a bookstore at Yorkdale Mall in Toronto:

> I was browsing cookbooks with my dear friend Pearl, making innocuous chit chat and the like, when all of a sudden we are interrupted by a

middle-aged soccer Mom. I assumed she wanted something standard-issue like help finding a book . . . WRONG.

"Excuse me. Are you her helper? How much do they pay you to tow her about?"

Pearl shuffled awkwardly formulating a response, while I sit with eyes blurring and feeling the sting of a slap across my cheek.

"Um, no. I'm her friend. Didn't know payment was involved but . . ."

"Oh, my, this is embarrassing. Just, I've never seen one of them out before and my son is heavily autistic. We're looking for some in-home help."

She then just walked away without contrition or even meeting my eyes once she figured we could not help her. (Mirela Todorovic)

In what ways does society punish disability? Does the failure to better accommodate people with disabilities arise simply from carelessness, or can it be taken as a negative sanction?

WRAP IT UP

Summary

Deviance can be examined from one of two positions: essentialism and social constructionism. We have taken a social-constructionist perspective in this chapter, believing that deviance is not natural but is socially constructed, artificial, and something that can vary from culture to culture and can change over time. What's more, the social construction of what is considered deviant is often contested or challenged within a culture. There is a power element found in deviance, with those who hold power in society getting to define what is deviant and what is "normal." The dominant culture's definition of deviance (in North America, a predominantly white, male, English-speaking, middle-aged, middle-class, and ablist definition) can override the definitions of deviance that come from people less powerful in the same society. People may be classified and treated as deviant not because of their behaviour, but because of their ready identification as belonging to a group outside of what makes up the dominant culture. Once branded as deviant, these groups may find themselves the targets of social sanctions designed to punish members of minority cultures and people with "alternative" lifestyles.

THINK BACK

Questions for Critical Review

1. Describe, with examples, what is meant by the term *deviant*. Is deviance always bad for society?

2. Outline how deviance can be associated with ethnicity, culture, "race," gender, sexual orientation, disability, and class.

3. Michel Foucault said that "the guilty person is only one of the targets of punishment. For punishment is directed above all at others, at all the potentially guilty." What do you think he meant by that?

4. Explain, with examples, what "conflict deviance" is.

5. Give some examples of "white collar crime." What would be the opposite of white collar crime? How would these two types of crime differ?

READ ON

Online

Albert K. Cohen

http://criminology.fsu.edu/crimtheory/cohen.htm

> This online dissertation, informative and not overly long, provides an excellent introduction to the work of Albert Cohen.

critcrim.org: Critical Criminology Information and Resources

www.critcrim.org/index.php

> Affiliated with the American Society of Criminology, this site provides a forum for organizations and individuals who are working to critically analyze, and change, the American justice system.

The SocioWeb: Criminality and Deviance

www.socioweb.com/directory/sociology-topics/criminology-and-social-deviance

The SocioWeb is a guide to sociology resources on the Internet. This page gives links to websites covering topics in criminology and deviance.

In Print

James William Coleman (2002), *The Criminal Elite: Understanding White-Collar Crime*, **5th edn (New York: Worth Publishers).**

Coleman's work offers an in-depth analysis of how white-collar crime affects society, and an evaluation of the legal remedies.

Sandro Contenta & Jim Rankin (2009, June 6), "Suspended Sentences: Forging a School-to-Prison Pipeline?" *Toronto Star*.

A readable news feature on class and criminal deviance.

Lennard J. Davis (2006), *The Disability Studies Reader,* **2nd edn (New York: Routledge).**

This volume is an updated, state-of-the-art, broadly based collection of articles pertaining to the sociological study of disability.

Erving Goffman (1963), *Stigma: Notes on the Management of Spoiled Identity* **(Englewood Hills, NJ: Prentice-Hall).**

Goffman's classic book about social stigma.

Jeffrey Reiman (2007), *The Rich Get Richer and the Poor Get Prison: Ideology, Class, and Criminal Justice*, **8th edn (Boston: Allyn & Bacon).**

Now in its eighth edition, Reiman's timeless work gives an excellent look at how class and deviance go hand in hand.

III   *Social Difference*

REMEMBER THE *mnemonic* (memory-aiding) phrase from the introduction to Part I? It went ***C****an you* ***gen****eralize about* ***reaso****ns for* ***d****ifference?* This was a way to remember the seven key sociological factors involved in social location: class, gender, "race" and ethnicity, age, sexual orientation, and degree of ability. In Part III, we will explore in detail each of these factors, and you will see what they have in common and how they are distinct in terms of the way they reinforce social difference.

A recurring theme throughout these chapters is that none of these factors is a simple binary, an either–or. Rather, each factor can be considered a continuum, or line of difference along which there are various socially defined points. That's an easy argument to grasp when it comes to factors like age and wealth (i.e. class), but when it comes to factors such as gender, sexual orientation, and ability, there is a tendency for people to believe that a clear binary exists.

We will also see that along each of these lines of difference, certain positions are more highly valued in Canadian society than others: upper class over lower classes, male over female, white and of British origin, heterosexual, and able-bodied. Age is more complicated in that while youth is highly valued, being young can be quite difficult, with older people holding onto positions of power in a way that sometimes prevents younger people from gaining a foothold on a career.

Intersectionality—the way these factors combine—is another important consideration in Part III. Although class, ethnicity, gender, disability, and age are taken up in separate chapters, it is always important to keep in mind how they operate together. Statuses of high value, when combined, can give someone considerable social power (e.g. the upper-class, heterosexual white male who drives a black BMW), while having several statuses of low value (Aboriginal and female) can place a person in a position of easier victimization.

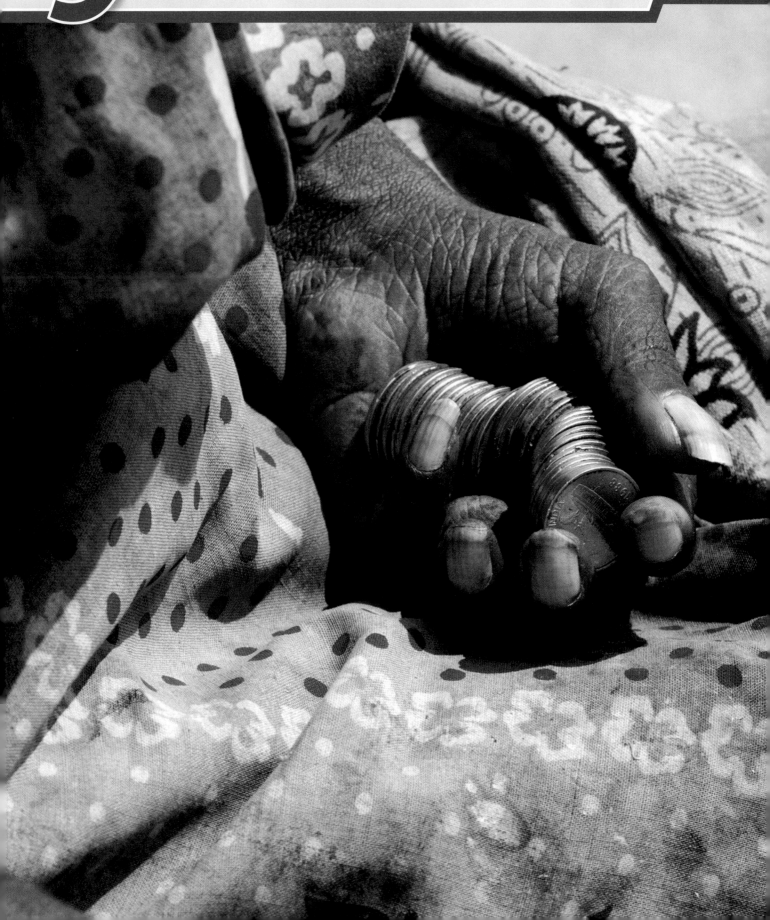

9 Social Inequality

Learning Objectives

After reading this chapter, you should be able to

- differentiate between *class* and *strata*
- discuss liberal ideology critically
- distinguish between a Marxist notion of class and one that includes a middle class
- critically discuss the history of the caste system with respect to Hinduism
- contrast the use of quintiles and deciles
- discuss the current and possible future state of food banks in Canada.

Key Terms

- American dream
- aristocrats
- blaming the victim
- bourgeoisie
- Brahmins
- capital
- capitalists
- caste
- class
- class consciousness
- class reductionism
- corporate (or organic) identity
- counter-ideology
- Dalits (Untouchables)
- deciles
- digital divide
- dominant capitalist class
- dominant ideology
- false consciousness
- food bank
- hegemony
- Highland Clearances
- ideology
- Indo-European
- Kshatriyas
- liberal ideology
- lumpenproletariat
- means of production
- middle class
- mobility sports
- peasants
- petty (*or* petite) bourgeoisie
- professionalization
- proletariat
- quintiles
- relational
- social inequality
- social mobility
- strata
- Sudras
- trickle-down theory
- Vaishyas
- varna
- workers
- working class

Names to Know

- Herbert Brown Ames
- Friedrich Engels
- Mahatma Mohandes Gandhi
- Antonio Gramsci
- Colin McKay
- Mahavira
- Karl Marx
- C. Wright Mills
- Shankara
- Siddhartha Gautama
- Max Weber

A Picture of Poverty in Canada's Backyard

Situated on the west coast of James Bay in Ontario's far north, the Cree community of Attawapiskat gained international attention in October 2011, when the leaders of Attawapiskat First Nation declared a state of emergency, citing inadequate housing and poor sanitation. It was not the first time the community had resorted to this measure. Just two years earlier, in May 2008, hundreds of residents were evacuated from their tents, trailers, and shelters because of serious flood conditions. And yet, in the fall of 2011, the media seized on stories of poverty and overcrowded, substandard housing as though they were new developments, while politicians claimed to have had no idea how bad the situation was.

How bad was it? You can read statistics about lack of housing, but to me, this account tells the story much more vividly:

In a one-room, tented shack where Lisa Kiokee-Linklater is watching television with her two toddlers, two mattresses lie on the floor. Each is a bed for three. Mould is creeping across one mattress even though Ms Kiokee-Linklater just bought it last summer. It cost her $1,000.

There is no running water, no bathroom, and cold comes through the uninsulated floor. There is little room for her four children to play. The broiling cast-iron wood stove that takes up one corner of the room represents a burn hazard and eliminates the notion of the rambunctious play that is the norm for most young kids.

Moving into the tent was Ms Kiokee-Linklater's choice. It seemed a step up from her previous home next door, where she shared a single bathroom with 20 other people until it became too much for her and her growing family.

"It's kind of better, yeah," she said, keeping a watchful eye on a son as he ate spaghetti with his fingers. "But during the winter, it's hard. I cut back on the baths because it is so cold." (Scoffield 2011)

A situation like that doesn't just develop overnight. Nor is it quickly resolved. A year later, in late 2012, Attawapiskat chief Theresa Spence began a hunger strike that would last 43 days to draw attention to the desperate circumstances of her own community and of other Aboriginal communities across the country. Unfortunately, the reaction to her protest, both in Ottawa and among more conservative members of the media, focused on the alleged mishandling of funds in her community, a "red herring" that distracted readers and viewers from the more pressing issues—specifically, the state of Aboriginal housing across Canada—that she and the leaders of the Idle No More movement were trying to address. The Conservative government's use of a third-party (i.e. independent) auditor to investigate Attawapiskat's finances, as though there was negligence or criminal wrongdoing on the part of the community, was a classic case of blaming the victim.

The plight of the residents of Attawapiskat is thrown into sharp relief by the success of its wealthy neighbour, the international mining giant DeBeers. Since the summer of 2008, De Beers has been working a diamond mine less than 100 kilometres away from the Attawapiskat settlement.

I'd learned something about Attawapiskat 20 years earlier, when I edited *Only God Can Own the Land*, a book that speaks about how extensively and positively the Attawapiskat Cree used their land—for food, for clothing, for building supplies—before the diamonds were found. The book, which was based on extensive fieldwork by the author, Bryan Cummins, is an uplifting account of the success of a community despite the exploitative effects of outside commercial enterprises and negligent governments.

So what happened? You get a different answer from different groups. Provincial and federal government officials point fingers at one another for failing to notice and address the horrifying conditions in which the people find themselves, while the conservative media start up a game of "blame the victim" for the overcrowded housing and lack of jobs—after all, the community has been receiving government financial assistance, so surely those funds are being mismanaged, right? Some of the locals recount that the mining development brought a sudden influx of outsiders, who brought, acquired, and spent big money during their short stay in Cree country, creating short-term jobs for the locals and giving a tantalizing taste of what could be. But wealth, even in the short terms, brings trouble, too—corruption, alcohol, drugs. And then there's global warming, a possible cause of the flooding that has affected the region.

As you can see, neither causes nor solutions are easy to identify. Poverty wherever it exists—in a northern Aboriginal community, a drought-stricken farming region, a once prosperous Atlantic fishing village, a rundown urban neighbourhood—is a complex problem. There is never one cause, never one solution, and it is the sociologist's job to look at each situation critically to identify causes and possible remedies. To return to the terminology introduced in Chapter 2, we need a mix of critical, policy, and public sociology.

A few years ago the CBC profiled an entrepreneur in Sudbury who was trying to start up a company in which new immigrants would be taught how to polish and cut diamonds and other gems. I wondered why that work didn't immediately go to the people of Attawapiskat. The land that bears the diamonds also bears thousands of years of their history, their sacred places, and their ancestors. A community that was once a model of social equality is now a poster child for social inequality in Canada. One can't help but wonder if it could all have been avoided.

Introduction: How Class and Social Stratification Contribute to Social Inequality

The study of social inequality has long been a part of the sociological tradition, particularly in Canada. Social inequality is a function of many factors, only some of which will be discussed in this chapter. Ethnicity and gender are discussed in their own chapters. Here we will focus mainly on two related factors: class and stratification.

Few areas are more contentious in the sociological, economic, and political study of societies than the study of social inequality, the long-term existence of significant differences in access to goods and services among social groups. The main term used to talk about social inequality is class, the definition of which has been the subject of much debate since the term was popularized by the political philosopher and economist **Karl Marx** (1818–1883). Near the beginning of *The Communist Manifesto* (1848), which Marx co-wrote with **Friedrich Engels** (1820–1895), the authors write:

The history of all hitherto existing society is the history of class struggles. Freeman and slave, patrician and plebian, lord and serf, guild-master and journeyman, in a word, oppressor and oppressed, stood in constant opposition to one another, carried on an uninterrupted, now hidden, now open fight, a fight that each time ended, either in a revolutionary reconstitution of society at large, or in the common ruin of the contending classes. . . .

The modern bourgeois society that has sprouted from the ruins of feudal society has not done away with class antagonisms. It has but established new classes, new conditions of oppression, new forms of struggle in place of the old ones.

Our epoch, the epoch of the bourgeoisie, possesses, however, this distinct feature: it has simplified class antagonisms. Society as a whole is more and more splitting up into two great hostile camps, into two great classes directly facing each other—bourgeoisie and proletariat.

There is a special language to interpreting Marx, and we apologize in advance for the large number of bold terms you will find bearing down on you as you read the following sentences.

Class, as Marx described it, was **relational**, in that it reflects a relationship to what he called the **means of production**—the resources needed to produce goods (and hence, wealth). In Europe before the Industrial Revolution, the chief means of production was land. Wealth was produced by growing food crops and raising livestock. Once Europe began to become industrialized during the nineteenth century, when Marx and Engels lived, the means of production became **capital**, the money needed to build factories, purchase raw materials, and pay labourers to turn those raw materials into manufactured products. In spite of the fact he devoted an entire book (*Das Kapital*) to the topic, the precise meaning of Marx's term "capital" has been contested. We define it here as the funds and properties necessary for typically large-scale manufacturing and trading.

Marx and Engels, along with the Marxist Soviet premier Vladimir Lenin and Chinese Communist Party founder Mao Zedong, watch over schoolchildren at a classroom in Dingri, Tibet. The portraits appear far newer than the desks, testifying to the oppression of the Tibetan peoples by the Chinese government, implemented by Mao himself.

For Marx, there were only two possible relationships to the means of production: either you owned them or you worked for those who did. In preindustrial Europe, the owners were called **aristocrats** and the workers, **peasants**. Marx called the owners of capital in industrial-era Europe **capitalists**; he referred to the members of this class collectively as the **bourgeoisie**. The class of **workers**, which succeeded the peasant class of the industrial era, made up the **proletariat**. Marx identified various sub-classes—the **petty** (or **petite**) **bourgeoisie**, made up of small-time owners with little capital, and the **lumpenproletariat**, the small-time criminals, beggars, and unemployed— but these terms do not have the significance of his two primary classes, the "two great hostile camps" referred to in the final sentence of the passage quoted above.

Marx's Historical Context

If you wonder at Marx's black-and-white view of things, remember the conditions he saw, and the context in which he lived. It was a time of laissez-faire capitalism in Britain, in which business was supposed to take care of itself without any interference by the government. The Factory Act of 1833, which targeted primarily the booming textile mills of Britain, was considered radical at the time, as it interfered with the "natural course" of business by "severely" limiting the hours that people were allowed to work. Factory owners complained that the act would ruin them financially, even drive them out of business. The act specified that the working day was to start no earlier than 5:30 a.m. and end no later than 8:30 p.m. It included the following additional provisions:

- "[N]o person under eighteen years of age shall [work] between half-past eight in the evening and half-past five in the morning, in any cotton, woollen, worsted, hemp, flax, tow, linen or silk mill. . . ."
- "[N]o person under the age of eighteen shall be employed in any such mill . . . more than twelve hours in . . . one day, nor more than sixty-nine hours in . . . one week. . . ."
- "It shall not be lawful . . . to employ in any factory . . . as aforesaid, except in mills for the manufacture of silk, any child who shall not have completed his or her ninth year."
- "It shall not be lawful for any person to employ . . . in any factory . . . for longer than forty-eight hours in one week, nor for longer than nine hours in one day, any child who shall not have completed his or her eleventh year. . . ."
- "Every child restricted to the performance of forty-eight hours of labour in any one week shall attend some school." (*Statutes of the Realm*, 3 & 4 William IV, c. 103)

Of course, such "liberal" rules would not apply to adults.

Class as a Social Identity

Another characteristic of class in Marx's view is that it has a **corporate** (or **organic**) **identity** as a real social group. There is a shared sense of common purpose among members of each class. One aspect of this is **class consciousness**, which is an awareness of what is in the best interests of one's class. Marx believed that the owner class had always possessed class consciousness, had always known what was in its best interests, and had attempted to shape society in a way that promoted those interests. Good evidence of this is seen in the **Highland Clearances** that occurred in Scotland in the late eighteenth and early nineteenth centuries. Landowning aristocrats, recognizing the increasing value of wool to the rapidly industrializing textile industry, began evicting tenant farmers from their estates to make room for sheep. The clearances caused extreme hardship among the evicted "crofters," and many were forced to emigrate, notably to North America.

The worker class, on the other hand, had not always had such an awareness. Indeed, it often has **false consciousness**, the belief that something is in its best interests when it is not. False consciousness sometimes occurs in societies that are divided by ethnicity or "race."

The Tutsi people of Rwanda provide a good example of false consciousness. When Rwanda (together with neighbouring Burundi) was a colony of Belgium, the Belgians gave this numerical minority (representing about 13 per cent of Rwanda's population) power over the numerically dominant (roughly 85 per cent) Hutu. The Tutsi suddenly enjoyed much more power than they had possessed prior to colonization. But it was only a handful of the Tutsi who held such power. The rest, the majority of the Tutsi people, were exploited by this Tutsi elite, whom they could not challenge because the elite would play the "common ethnicity" card to demand their loyalty. The exploited

Tutsi actually had class interests in common with the Hutu, who had become the most exploited group in the country during the Tutsi rise to power. However, the two groups did not share class consciousness. They did not recognize the class interests they had in common. We can argue, then, that false consciousness prevented the two exploited groups from forming a mutually beneficial alliance capable of grabbing a share of power and wealth from the Tutsi elite. The situation would later repeat itself in the reverse following the overthrow of the Tutsi monarchy by the Hutu people in 1962. The majority of the Hutu, impoverished and under the thumb of the ruling Hutu elite, could not help but think of all Tutsi as former feudal exploiters, even though many had never been any richer than the Hutu were at the time. We'll examine Rwanda's ethnic conflict further in Chapter 10.

Weber's Critique of Marx

Another early sociologist to look at social inequality was **Max Weber**, who was introduced in the opening chapter. Weber didn't quite agree with Marx's theory of class relations, and though the two men were not contemporaries (Weber came after Marx, and it is sometimes said poetically that he was engaged in a theoretical discussion with Marx's ghost), their views on the subject are frequently compared and contrasted (hint: the topic makes a good essay question on exams).

Weber did, like Marx, view society as divided into different economic classes, but he believed that Marx's materialist approach was too simplistic, that there was more to social inequality than just who owned the means of production. In particular, Weber stressed three elements—*wealth*, *prestige*, and *power*—that contributed to social inequality. For Weber, wealth, or material resources, includes not just factories and other property involved directly in making money but also properties that are highly respected by members of the society in question: in Western society, the flashy car, the expensive house, the trophy spouse, the winning good looks you seem to find so often among Super Bowl quarterbacks and sociology instructors. Prestige is the degree of respect with which individuals, their socially appropriate possessions, and their master statuses are viewed by the majority of people in a society. Prestige can be turned into various forms of social power, which is usually defined as the ability of individuals or groups to achieve their goals despite the opposition of others.

An often used example of a person embodying (literally!) wealth, prestige, and power is Arnold Schwarzenegger. As a young man, his wealth was his good looks and well-built, muscular body, which earned him prestige as a bodybuilder (his master status at the time) and winner of the Mr Universe competition. The respect accorded him for his physical appearance enabled Schwarzenegger to change careers and become an actor, which brought him further prestige, which he turned into real social and political power, first by marrying a Kennedy relative (more prestige) and then by being elected governor of California in 2004. It is interesting to note that Schwarzenegger followed a course laid out by an earlier governor of California, Ronald Reagan, who parlayed his prestige as an actor, ultimately, into presidency of the United States. From a Weberian perspective, what is important is that Schwarzenegger's membership in the dominant social class was never about controlling the means of production, in a Marxist sense.

This young man owns two gas-powered lawnmowers and, with the help of his buddy Jake (whom he pays $18 an hour) operates his own small landscaping business. Assess his class position from both a Marxist and a Weberian perspective.

Problems with Marx's Perspective

There are several problems with applying a classical Marxist model of class to societies in countries such as Canada. For one thing, there are many people who, as employees of large corporations (bank presidents, corporate lawyers, hospital administrators, high-ranking government bureaucrats, professional hockey players), are termed "workers," even though their incomes put them on a par with some owners. Likewise, there are farmers, owners of small retail stories, and other small businesses operators who have incomes and levels of control that are more like those of workers. And we can argue for the existence of a middle class with a strong sense of itself as a class.

Thus, within the Canadian context, we can apply Marx's class paradigm by arguing that there are essentially three different classes in this country. Following Curtis, Grabb, and Guppy (1999), we would identify them as follows:

1. a **dominant capitalist class** that is "composed mainly of those who own or control large-scale production"
2. a **middle class** that is "a mixed . . . middle category of small-scale business people, educated professional-technical or administrative personnel, and various salaried employees or wage earners possessing some certifiable credentials, training, or skills"
3. a **working class** "made up of people who lack resources or capacities apart from their own labour power" (Curtis, Grabb, and Guppy 1999: ix).

Marx's analysis of class may have its greatest applicability today if you add two factors: ethnicity and nation-state. When Western companies maintain non-unionized, low-wage factories with unsafe working conditions in poor countries such as Mexico, Haiti, and Thailand, employing people of particular ethnicities who are exploited in their own country, then Marx's capitalist–worker class structure exists in a true sense. Who is likely buying the softballs this Haitian factory worker is stitching? Who ultimately controls her labour?

Our Stories

Early Studies in Canadian Social Stratification

Sociology in Canada began as the study of social stratification. We get an excellent survey of stratification by examining the work of two Canadian sociology pioneers: Herbert Brown Ames and Colin McKay.

Herbert Brown Ames: A Businessman's Sociology

During the last half of the nineteenth century, the population of Montreal grew fourfold to over 270,000. With this growth came social problems—poverty, unemployment, homelessness. This led **Herbert Brown Ames** (1863–1954) to engage in Canada's first comprehensive urban sociological study, designed to promote the construction of affordable housing for the working-class people of Montreal's west end.

Montreal-born, Ames had inherited a prosperous business that would guarantee him a lifetime of financial stability. But he wanted more than to earn easy money: he wanted to improve the city of his birth. He became involved in politics at the municipal and federal levels, and he engaged in ambitious sociological research. In 1896, he and members of his research team went door to door to canvass the inhabitants of an area he called "the city below the hill." The study was very detailed for its time. Ames's fascination with statistics sometimes overwhelms even the modern reader, and at the time of the study his approach was unique. He was possibly the first person in Canada to speak of family size not in round numbers but with decimals, saying the average size of families he studied was "4.90 people," 1.41 of whom worked for wages and 1.64 being children under 16. He was keenly aware that this level of precision was key to achieving the most suitable remedy for the housing problem:

> Should the time come when capital shall be ready to be invested in the erection of improved industrial dwellings, it is evident that for its intelligent expenditure, in this or that locality, definite knowledge must be in hand as to the personnel and composition of the average family of the section selected. The number and size of the rooms to be provided, in the improved dwelling for the average

family, will depend not only upon the size of the family, but also upon its composition, since the larger the proportion of the adult or school-child element the more the amount of space and air that will need to be allowed.

> To make a success of this work of improvement we can afford to allow no facts to be overlooked. (Ames 1972 [1897]: 30)

Ames's plan was to have old, inadequate housing torn down, and then have business leaders finance construction of new housing. He led by example, bankrolling the construction of model apartments for 39 families. Unfortunately, but predictably, others were reluctant to follow his lead.

With hindsight, we can argue that Ames was naive. We can be amused by the powerful rhetoric he invoked to declare his determination to get rid of the 5,800 outhouses he reckoned there were in the city ("That the privy pit is a danger to public health and morals needs no demonstration, and yet in 'the city below the hill' *more than half the households* are dependent entirely upon such accommodation" [Ames 1972: 45]). But we must admire Ames for his concern for the lives of the working class and for his passion, shared by many Canadian sociologists that followed him.

Colin McKay: A Worker's Sociology

Nova Scotian **Colin McKay** (1876–1939) was described by Ian McKay (an unrelated namesake) as "a working-class intellectual who exemplified a widespread enthusiasm for radical sociology in turn-of-the-century Canada," and who, "drawing upon theories of Karl Marx and Herbert Spencer, . . . developed [his] own critical understanding of capitalist development" (McKay 1998: 390). Colin McKay was a self-educated man, who worked as a merchant seaman, soldier, labour organizer, and journalist. At 24, he spent a short time in jail for "defaming the reputation of a cigar factory proprietor notorious for mistreating children [workers] and discriminating against trade unionists" (McKay 1998: 401).

McKay was a prodigious writer, contributing at least 952 articles and letters-to-the-editor to union publications such as the *Canadian Railway Employees*

Monthly, the *Canadian Unionist*, *Eastern Labor News*, *Butler's Journal*, *Cotton's Weekly*, *Le Monde Ouvrier*, *Citizen and Country*, and *Western Clarion*. The scope of his work is revealed in a few selected titles:

- "Duty of the rich to the poverty-stricken: The philosophy of charity, showing it to be to the interest of the rich and strong to help the weak" (*Montreal Herald*, 21 Jan. 1899)
- "The small business man. How the capitalist system annihilates self-earned private property and reduces the small business man to the economic category of the worker" (*Eastern Labor News*, 8 June 1912)
- "The crime of low wages" (*Labor World / Le Monde Ouvrier*, 18 April 1925).

As part of a vigorous working-class press with considerable influence, Colin McKay was widely acknowledged as one of Canadian labour's leading intellectuals. It is likely that McKay's writings, which in the 1930s were reaching thousands of working-class readers in at least four major journals, probably reached far more people than ever read the works of the contemporary academic sociologists in Canada. (McKay 1998: 415)

Most Canadian sociologists today would be envious of such a large audience for their work. Ian McKay suggests that with the death of Colin McKay and the greater institutionalization (or departmentalization) of sociology, there was loss as well as gain. The drive of the well-read working-class radicals such as McKay and his peers is sorely missed in the efforts of Canadian sociologists to make a difference in the social inequality of their country.

In the early twentieth century, the more successful members of Montreal's working class moved to new homes in the suburbs, leaving poorer citizens to take up residence in abandoned houses like this one. Can you see why Ames was concerned about living conditions in "the city below the hill"?

How Class Divisions Are Reflected in Popular Sport

There is a strong connection between sport and class. The traditional association of sports like golf and tennis with the wealthy classes has been reinforced through the prohibitive cost of—and prestige surrounding—membership at golf and tennis clubs. (Weber would probably recognize a membership at an exclusive Vancouver golf club as a form of wealth.) Compare that with membership at a curling club, where players enjoy a sport generally seen as having more of a working-class appeal. Marketers and advertisers involved in professional sports will often exploit these associations to attract a particular fan base to their sport, in spite of the fact that most professional athletes earn lucrative salaries that put them squarely in the upper class.

Sports that offer people from poorer socio-economic backgrounds the chance to reap large financial rewards as professional athletes can be called **mobility sports**. Generally, any sport that is cheap to play (with low costs for equipment and enrolment in organized competition), in which opportunities to play and "be discovered" are readily available to people of all classes, and that provides middle- to upper-class incomes for the relatively few that "make it" can be considered a mobility sport. Historically, boxing has done that. It provides young men raised in poor and sometimes violent circumstances an alternative to "the streets." Professional boxers rarely come from the middle class. Boxing's decline has been hastened by the surging popularity of mixed martial arts and the Ultimate Fighting Championship, which has developed a loyal and increasingly mainstream fan base rooted in middle-class America. During the last 25 years, basketball has been a mobility sport for young black men in North America. Across the world, particularly in developing countries, soccer also provides mobility for the poor, especially the racialized poor.

Reigning two-time UFC welterweight champion Georges St-Pierre, shown here winning a title fight against Nick Diaz at Montreal's Bell Centre in March 2013, grew up in the tiny parish community of Saint-Isidore, Quebec, and worked a stint as a garbage collector before becoming a star of the Ultimate Fighting circuit. Is mixed martial arts the world's newest mobility sport?

Hockey in Canada: Mobility Sport or Elitist Sport?

Canadian hockey lore is filled with stories of poor young men from farming communities in the West or mining towns in the East rising from poverty and obscurity to achieve celebrity status playing in the NHL. Gordie Howe was one of nine children raised on a failing farm in Depression-era Floral, Saskatchewan; he became one of the greatest stars of the game. Johnny Bucyk, who grew up in a rough neighbourhood of north Edmonton, the son of parents who were Ukrainian (a group then often minoritized), recalls learning to play hockey with "road apples," without sticks, pads, or skates:

> I can remember playing street hockey when I was a kid, maybe seven or eight years old. In those days you couldn't afford to buy hockey sticks, nobody in our group could. I was from a poor family and I really didn't know what it was to own a hockey stick, so I didn't care. I played a lot of street hockey and we used brooms for sticks. We couldn't afford pucks either, so we'd follow the milk wagon which was pulled by a couple of horses, waiting until the horses did their job, dropping a good hunk of manure. Usually it would be a cold day, anytime between the start of October through the end of April, and we'd let it freeze up solid. We'd use it as a hockey puck. . . . I didn't get my first pair of skates until I was about 10 years old. It was a pair of my older brother Bill's, which he outgrew. (Quoted in Lowe, Fischler, & Fischler 1988: 43–4)

Bucyk played in the National Hockey League from 1956 to 1978, spending most of that time with the Boston Bruins. He was the fifth NHLer to score 50 goals in a season, and was inducted into the Hockey Hall of Fame in 1981.

Players like Howe and Bucyk earned decent livings playing hockey, though they came nowhere near the earnings of star players today. They also grew up at a time when the costs associated with playing organized hockey were relatively low compared to now. Over the last 20 years, the cost of raising a potential professional hockey player has risen astronomically. Beyond the price tag for the latest equipment and league fees, a player who shows skill enough to play for a rep or select team will incur travel costs and increased rink fees (both for practices and for games). Players in the elite Greater Toronto Hockey League pay between $500 and $1,600 just in annual dues. The rise in costs is a feature of the **professionalization** of elite minor hockey, which now depends more on professional coaches and trainers than on parents and volunteers.

The trend is evident not just in hockey and other sports, but in activities like music, drama, and dance. It reflects in part the changing role of schools in the extracurricular activities of young people: school boards facing tighter budgets may be forced to cut dedicated gym and music teachers, leaving athletic and music programs (if they survive at all) to be run by parent volunteers without training in these areas. It also reflects changing middle- and upper-class expectations concerning these supposed recreational activities, as parents indulge in the dream that, with the right training, their child's pastime could become a lucrative career. The result is that many lower-class families cannot provide the same experience for their children, giving middle- and upper-class families a distinct advantage and making various sports—hockey in this case—much less of a mobility sport.

Ideology

An **ideology** is a set of beliefs about society and the people in it, usually forming the basis of a particular economic or political theory. A **dominant ideology** is the set of beliefs put forward by, and generally supportive of, society's dominant culture and/or classes. In Marxist terms, it reflects the class consciousness of the ruling class. It is used to defend or justify the status quo. The **trickle-down theory** is a dominant ideology in North America. It states that if you allow the rich the freedom to generate wealth, others in society will benefit: new jobs will be created, more money will be spent on consumer goods, and a good part of the generated wealth will eventually find its way into the hands of members of the middle and lower classes. As a dominant ideology, the trickle-down theory is used to justify policies that favour wealthy business owners, such as government subsidies for certain industries and low corporate taxes.

A **counter-ideology** is one that offers a critique of the dominant ideology, challenging its justice and its universal applicability to society. Those promoting a counter-ideology are typically looking to create significant social change. Classical Marxism, which predicted

QUICK HITS

Minor Hockey, Major Cash

The cost of outfitting a child for our national sport depends on what level your child is at, where you shop, and how much you're willing to pay. The table below shows the range in the costs of equipment for a bantam-aged (13–15-year-old) player—not a goalie (that would cost even more!).

Other Basic Costs

- average registration for house league: $350
- average registration for competitive rep league: $2,500–$3,000
- ticket cost for every GTHL [Greater Toronto Hockey League] game: $5 for players and spectators older than 12
- skate sharpening: $5
- gas and fast food

- ice time for extra practices
- summer hockey schools
- power-skating lessons.

Why Gear is Dear

- **long shopping list**: No other team sport requires as much gear as hockey.
- **small market**: The number of hockey players worldwide is relatively small compared to sports such as soccer and basketball, so hockey equipment is not mass produced on the same scale as jogging shoes or baseball gloves, which affects pricing.
- **NHL influence**: For kids, the peer group isn't as important as the professionals, which means they are drawn to the best, most expensive products on the shelves.

Source: Adapted from Ormsby 2007.

	SPECIALTY STORE[a]	DEPARTMENT STORE[b]	SECOND-HAND STORE[c]
Stick	$300	$20	$20
Helmet	200	45	35 (w/ cage)
Cage	80	35	
mouth guard	60	35	10
Gloves	200	70	
shoulder pads	130	30	25
neck guard	60	12	30
practice jersey	160	70	5
Pants	200	90	30
elbow pads	80–200	20	15
Socks	40	13	10
Skates	450	80	60
shin pads	140	50	25
full undergarment	110		
shorts with cup/jill		50	
cup/jill		8	15
Bag	150	120	20
Puck	5	1	1
Total	**$2,365**	**$749**	**$301**

[a] based on new equipment available at Pro Hockey Life
[b] based on new equipment available at Canadian Tire
[c] based on new and used equipment available at Play It Again Sports

Source: Based on MacGregor 2012.

What do YOU think?

1. Do you think that hockey in Canada can still be seen as a mobility sport, or has it become solely an elitist sport? What arguments can be made for the two different positions?

2. How could you conduct a sociological study to determine which position is more true?

the overthrow of the capitalist classes by the proletariat, is the most obvious example of a counter-ideology. The Occupy movement, though it did not have what you call a well-defined ideology, is another example: its basic premise, that 99 per cent of the world's wealth is concentrated in the hands of 1 per cent of the world's population and must be subject to greater taxes in order to be distributed more equitably, challenged the dominant-ideology notion that the wealth generated by the elite will eventually trickle down to everyone else. The 2011–12 Montreal student protests represent a counter-ideology. The largest student group, CLASSE, demanded that universities cut research programs (which, they argue, benefit private interests) and advertising with an aim to making college and university tuition-free (Bruemmer & Dougherty 2012). We would argue that a counter-ideology is developing among contemporary Aboriginal people, who are drawing on traditional values and who are critical of the capitalist/materialist society that has oppressed them. The Idle No More movement is an expression of this counter-ideology. The social change they are promoting may be taking place within the Aboriginal community of Canada, but it is not without influence in mainstream society.

Liberal ideology is a dominant ideology that views the individual as a more or less independent player on the sociological scene. It reflects a belief in **social mobility**—that is, the ability of individuals to move (generally upward) from one class, or stratum, to another—and minimizes criticism of social inequality. If an individual is successful, it is because he or she has earned that success, not because he or she has benefited from the social privileges of ethnic background, class, or gender. The **American dream**—the belief that anyone can "make it" if he or she is willing to work really hard for it—reflects liberal ideology. Failure to achieve the American dream (we might call this scenario the "American nightmare" of poverty) is likewise placed solely on the back of the individual. American psychologist William Ryan referred to this as **blaming the victim**, assigning individuals more or less complete responsibility for events or circumstances that have broader social causes. The American dream, he might argue, fails to account for the notion that schools may privilege white middle-class culture over children

Egyptians in Cairo's Tahrir Square call for the resignation of president Hosni Mubarak, just hours before the leader would eventually step down on 11 February 2011. The first wave of Arab Spring protests across the Middle East were characterized by largely peaceful, largely secular calls for fairer government and economic reform. To what extent could the early days of the movement be said to represent a counter-ideology?

from non-white or poorer socioeconomic families. We can see the liberal ideology of blaming the victim in any of the following arguments:

- People become alcoholics because they lack will-power; no biological factors of genetic predisposition or sociological factors of racial or ethnic stereotypes or systematic oppression need be seriously considered.
- People receiving employment insurance are on welfare because they fail to exercise a strong work ethic, not because they come from poor families with the odds of success stacked against them.
- Criminals offend and reoffend because they have a "criminal mind," not because "the street" offered them the best chance to escape a socioeconomically disadvantaged position.

C. Wright Mills critiqued American liberal ideology in two influential studies of the middle and upper classes, *White Collar* (1951) and *The Power Elite* (1956). The excerpt below, from the former book, contains some of his criticism of the liberal ideology of the American dream, as he discusses how the upper class perpetuates its own power:

> The recent social history of American capitalism does not reveal any distinct break in the continuity of the higher capitalist class. . . . [I]n the economy as in the political order, there has been a remarkable continuity of interests, vested in the types of higher economic men who guard and advance them. The main drift of the upper classes, composed of several consistent trends, points unambiguously to the continuation of a world that is quite congenial to the continuation of the corporate rich. . . .
>
> The propertied class, in the age of corporate property, has become a corporate rich, and in becoming corporate has consolidated its power. . . . Its members have become self-conscious in terms of the corporate world they represent. As men of status they have secured their privileges and prerogatives in the most stable private institutions of American society. They are a corporate rich because they depend directly, as well as indirectly, for their money, their privileges, their securities, their advantages, their powers on the world of the big corporations. (Quoted in Horowitz 1971: 82–3)

Hegemony

Like Marx, **Antonio Gramsci** (1891–1937) was a critic of the dominant ideology. The Italian-born political theorist and activist was a co-founder and leader of the Italian Communist party and an opponent of Fascist dictator Benito Mussolini. Jailed in November 1926, he remained a political prisoner for nearly 10 years. During that time he developed the concept of hegemony.

Gramsci used **hegemony** to mean non-coercive methods of maintaining power. He believed that the ruling classes relied on something more than their military and police forces to keep society running smoothly according to a dominant ideology under which most citizens were essentially oppressed. Kate Crehan, in her study of Gramsci, defines the term as referring to all the ways by which "the power relations underpinning various forms of inequality are produced and reproduced" (Crehan 2002: 104). In other words, hegemony refers to the non-violent means by which the ruling classes get everyone else to accept the dominant ideology.

Hegemony can take many forms. It is expressed in the reproduction and celebration of the American dream—the idea that the path to prosperity is available to everyone equally, and that inequality exists not because of problems in "the system" (i.e. the dominant ideology) but because some people are willing to work harder than others. Hegemony is also reflected in the way the media present computers as bridging gaps between the world's wealthy and not-so-wealthy nations, while failing to note the ways in which technology actually widens the **digital divide** between rich and poor.

Recalling the case of Attawapiskat from this chapter's introduction, we can consider Prime Minister Stephen Harper's response to the crisis in 2011 as an instance of hegemony: he sent in an auditor to examine the community's finances. He thereby shifted blame *onto* the people and the handling of their money by the chief and council, and *off of* the inadequate measures

"5 Days for the Homeless" is a campaign encouraging Canadian university and college students to experience homelessness for five days while raising donations for local organizations supporting homeless youth. In 2013, the campaign raised over $200,000. The benefits of the campaign are obvious—can you think of any drawbacks?

taken by the federal and provincial governments and the exploitative practices of the powerful mining company. We would argue that that to a large degree that exercise of hegemony worked, as the government managed to avoid any serious backlash for failing to avert a crisis that had been building for years.

Even an introductory sociology textbook could become an instrument of hegemony, if, say, its authors portrayed Canadian society as though there were no destructive social splits based on "race," ethnicity, gender, ability, and class—in other words, as though there were no problems of social inequality that needed to be addressed.

Class Reductionism

Class reductionism occurs when a sociologist studying a situation attributes all forms of oppression to class, ignoring or downplaying the impact of such factors as colonialism, "race," ethnicity, gender, age, and sexual orientation. Social scientists in the former Soviet Union were often guilty of class reductionism when they justified the Russian oppression of Siberia's indigenous peoples in the name of class revolution against the

indigenous bourgeoisie, when in fact, in the pre-industrial world in which these peoples lived, there was no bourgeoisie. There were usually just herders who had more or fewer animals (yaks, camels, horses, etc). Calling those with more animals the "bourgeoisie" and using that as a justification for trying to get rid of private ownership of livestock was a serious distortion of Marx's analysis, and a good example of class reductionism.

Albert Memmi, who, along with Franz Fanon, was one of the founders of anti-colonialism theory, argued against class reductionism in colonial studies in his classic work *The Colonizer and the Colonized* (1957):

To observe the life of the colonizer and the colonized is to discover rapidly that the daily humiliations of the colonized, his objective subjugation, are not merely economic. Even the poorest colonizer thought himself to be—and actually was—superior to the colonized. This too was part of colonial privilege. The Marxist discovery of the importance of the economy in all oppressive relationships is not to the point. This relationship has other characteristics which I believe I have discovered in the colonial relationship. (Memmi 1991 [1957]: xii)

The failings of class reductionism are, of course, shared by anyone who reduces oppression to a single factor or fails to examine all relevant factors. This includes paying insufficient attention to the words or voices of the people affected. Edgar Dosman, in a study of Native people in Saskatoon carried out in 1968–9, rarely included Aboriginal voices at all. When he did, it was usually to criticize a comment or the individual quoted. He stressed the significance of class over the unifying experience of ethnicity among urban Aboriginal people, referring to groups with the somewhat patronizing and misleading labels of "aristocracy," "bourgeoisie," and "welfare and anomic." In so doing, he disqualified the leaders in the urban Aboriginal community from legitimately articulating a position worthy of sociological consideration.

Dosman also directly attacked two important Aboriginal leaders of the time: Métis academic Howard Adams and Cree politician Harold Cardinal, both of whom were authors of influential works published around the time of Dosman's study (Adams in 1975 and Cardinal in 1969 and 1977). Dosman criticized Adams's work for being "too flowery and intellectual for the native people; it is geared to the young students who crowd his meetings" (Dosman 1972: 162). He formed this purely speculative opinion without asking Aboriginal people of all "classes" what they thought of Adams (a well-respected figure in First Nation circles). Later on in the same study he dismissed a comment of Cardinal's with the terse remark, "What, however, does that mean in the real world?" (Dosman 1972: 183). Clearly, he was not prepared to respect the standpoint Cardinal brought to the discussion.

The Caste System

A different kind of social stratification is the caste system that exists in Hindu societies of south Asia. **Castes**, or **varnas**, are ranked classes that people are born into. Each caste is associated with certain occupations, dharmas (duties in life), rights to foods, colours of clothing (*varna* means "colour"), religious practices, and imputed personal qualities. The five castes, from highest to lowest in rank, are as follows:

- **Brahmins** (priests, political leaders, teachers)
- **Kshatriyas** (military leaders, landowners)
- **Vaishyas** (merchants, craftspeople)
- **Sudras** (manual labourers)
- **Dalits**, or "**Untouchables**" (butchers, leather-workers, street cleaners).

Members of the three highest-ranking castes are known as "twice-born," because they are expected to experience religious rebirth (similar to Christian confirmation) in addition to their original physical birth. From a historical standpoint, they are associated with Indo-European conquerors who came to the north of India/Pakistan from somewhere in the Steppes or plains area of eastern Europe and central Asia in migrations between 1500 and 1300 BCE (Keay 2000: 27). (**Indo-European** refers to speakers of a family of languages that includes almost all European languages, the main languages of Iran and Afghanistan, and northern Indian languages such as Hindi, Urdu, Bengali, and Punjabi.) The division of the three twice-born castes might be based on the class-like system of the early Celtic people, whose Druids have much in common with the Brahmins.

Hinduism and Hindu thinkers have sometimes been criticized, especially by people of Western background, for supporting the social inequality created by the caste system. This criticism often comes from a poor understanding of the history of the faith and its believers. Hinduism has at various times in its history been interpreted in egalitarian, social reformist ways. When Hinduism was first developing (around 1500 BCE), its earliest religious texts—the four Vedas and the later Brahmanas—strongly supported the social authority of the higher castes, especially that of the Brahmin priests. However, later religious texts (c. 800–300 BCE) offered what can be called a more democratic view of spirituality. During this period two high-caste spiritual leaders rejected their privileged positions to form more democratic religious/philosophical movements rooted in Hinduism. **Siddhartha Gautama** (540–480 BCE) was a Brahmin who founded Buddhism. **Mahavira** (599–27 BCE) was a Kshatriya (a member of the "warrior caste") who initiated Jainism.

In the ninth century, **Shankara** (c. 788–820), a Tamil Brahmin, went through a similar process, though he kept closer to the orthodoxy of the Hindu faith. He rejected his upper-caste life to become a travelling monk and scholar, and developed teachings based on the undifferentiated oneness of God with every individual soul. Shankara did not support the ranked division of society based on caste, as he saw no spiritual distinction between people. A famous story tells of how once, as he walked with students, a man of low caste approached from the opposite direction. One of Shankara's students told the man to get out of the way. The man, in turn, asked Shankara whether his egalitarian beliefs were just theories and not practices, given the discriminatory behaviour of his follower. Shankara felt that the man was the god Shiva, appearing in this way to teach him an important lesson about the spiritual equality of all people.

Mahatma Mohandes Gandhi (1869–1948), who led India to independence from British colonialism, is a figure from India's more recent history of social reform. He strongly opposed the social restrictions and oppression of the caste system, and worked with and fought for the rights of the low-caste "Untouchables" (so-named because their very touch was considered by many upper-caste people to be spiritually polluting).

Contemporary Caste

When India's constitution was drafted in 1950, the caste system was officially abolished, and some former Untouchables, now typically termed Dalits ("Broken People"), have benefited from India's policy of quotas in education and government jobs. However, the situation is far from resolved. Middle- and upper-caste groups have mobilized politically to fight policies and legislation that are designed to support the "scheduled castes" (a term not unlike "designated groups," the Canadian equity term referring to women, Aboriginal peoples, visible minorities, and the disabled).

There are roughly 160 million Dalits in India, making up about one-sixth of the country's population. Most of them suffer from incredible poverty and discrimination. Caste is used as an excuse to oppress them. In 1989, the Scheduled Castes and Tribes (Prevention of Atrocities) Act was passed to try to prevent the harshest of caste abuses and abusers. According to Human Rights Watch (1999), caste-related offences include

forcing members of a scheduled caste or scheduled tribe [e.g. an indigenous group] to drink or eat any inedible or obnoxious substance; dumping excreta, waste matter, carcasses or any other obnoxious substance in their premises or neighborhood; forcibly removing their clothes and parading them naked or with painted face or body; interfering with their rights to land; compelling a member of a scheduled caste or scheduled tribe into forms of forced or bonded labor; corrupting or fouling the water of any spring, reservoir or any other source ordinarily used by scheduled castes or scheduled tribes; denying right of passage to a place of public resort; and using a position of dominance

In the Chowringhee area of Calcutta a group of Dalit women sort through piles of garbage, looking for anything of value to salvage and sell. Though the caste system was officially banned in India after independence, caste still exists informally and acts as a barrier to social equality. What is the difference between a caste and a class?

to exploit a scheduled caste or scheduled tribe woman sexually. (Human Rights Watch 1999)

Between 1994 and 1996, a total of 98,349 crimes against scheduled castes were registered with the police. Of this number, 38,483 were registered under the Prevention of Atrocities Act. The actual number of offences would certainly be much higher were it not for reluctance on the part of many Dalits to report offences, as well as lack of co-operation on the part of police. The plight of Dalits has opened up a new area of sociological research in India.

What do YOU think?

What would be misleading about thinking of the Hindu caste system merely as a form of social inequality?

Strata

When we talk about social stratification, we're borrowing a geological term to describe society as though it were divided into a series of layers. In geology, a stratum is a single level or layer of rock made up of tiny particles deposited together; if you look at a cross-section of sedimentary rock, you will be able to see the different strata and note the differences.

In sociology, a stratum is a level or class to which people belong depending on their social status, education, or income. It's usually each of a number of equal groups into which a population has been divided for comparison. **Strata** are used as units of analysis in stratified sampling, an approach to statistical research in which a sample is drawn from each stratum or level of the population rather than drawn at random from the whole population. This produces a more representative sample for analysis. The following discussion will focus on two kinds of stratum used in sociological research: the quintile and the decile.

Quintiles

Most studies of social stratification in Canada examine the population in quintiles. A **quintile** is one of five equal groups into which a population is divided according to the distribution of values of a particular variable; each one represents 20 per cent of the population. Let's say, for example, that we wanted to divide

the population into quintiles according to household (family) income. Grattan (2003) offers a good explanation of how we arrive at our quintiles:

> Imagine that all families are placed in a line, a family's place being determined by its income level. The poorest family is placed at the front of the line, followed by the next poorest, and so on, until the last family, with the highest income, is placed at the end. Next, the line is split into five equal groups. The first group, or quintile, is composed of the first 20 percent of the line. Obviously, this group will consist of the poorest people. The next group consists of the next 20 percent. A similar process occurs in selecting the third, fourth, and fifth groups. The fifth group, of course, comprises those families with the highest incomes. (Grattan 2003: 64–5)

Quintiles are useful for comparative purposes, both across time periods and across countries. Look at Table 9.1. Keep in mind that if the total income for all families were distributed equally, each of the five quintiles would earn 20 per cent; however, this is not the case, as the table shows.

Table 9.1 shows that over a 60-year period, the share of the total income in Canada earned by the top 20 per cent of earners increased by almost 5 per cent, growing by nearly 3 per cent in just 15 years between 1981 and 1996. As Urmetzer and Guppy note, this last figure "may appear to be a trivial amount, but given that the total income generated in Canada surpasses half a trillion dollars a year, this increase translates into more than 14 billion dollars—enough to eliminate poverty in Canada" (1999: 59). During the same period (1981–96), the percentage earned by the three middle-income groups dropped. In fact, over the entire 60-year range, note that every quintile declined except for the fifth and the fourth (which gained only marginally). What does that tell you about inequality in Canada in the twenty-first century?

The federal government helps to even off some of these differences between the groups with transfer payments to the less wealthy provinces. Table 9.2 shows the income figures for 1995 only; two additional columns show percentages of total income per quintile before federal transfer payments are made and after taxes have been deducted from family incomes. Note here that just 20 per cent of families earned almost half

Table 9.1 Percentage of total before-tax income going to families and unattached individuals in Canada, by quintile, 1951–2010

INCOME QUINTILES	1951	1961	1971	1981	1991	1995	1996	2010
Lowest	4.4	4.2	3.6	4.6	4.7	4.7	4.6	4.2
Second	11.2	11.9	10.6	10.9	10.3	10.2	10.0	9.6
Middle	18.3	18.3	17.6	17.6	16.6	16.4	16.3	15.3
Fourth	23.3	24.3	24.9	25.1	24.7	24.5	24.7	23.6
Fifth	42.8	41.4	43.4	41.7	43.8	44.1	44.5	47.3

Source: Curtis, Grabb, & Guppy 1999. Original data from Statistics Canada, "Income in Canada," cat. no. 75-202 (1999) and "Income Distributions by Size in Canada," cat. no. 13-207 (1997).

of all income earned by Canadians before taxes and transfer payments.

After drawing our conclusions about the figures presented in Table 9.2, we can gain some added perspective by comparing the Canadian results with those of other countries. This is exactly what Urmetzer and

Table 9.2 Percentage of total 1995 income going to Canadian families before transfers and after taxes, by quintile

QUINTILES	INCOME BEFORE TRANSFERS	TOTAL INCOME	INCOME AFTER TAXES
Lowest	0.8	4.7	5.7
Second	7.5	10.2	11.5
Middle	16.1	16.4	17.2
Fourth	26.2	24.5	24.5
Fifth	49.5	44.1	41.1

Source: Curtis, Grabb, & Guppy 1999. Data from Statistics Canada.

Guppy did when they compared the Canadian results with those of 16 other countries for the years 1995–7. Table 9.3 is a shorter version; in each column, the highest and lowest extremes are represented in bold and in italics, respectively.

From the data in Table 9.3 we can draw several tentative conclusions. First, we can see that the greatest amount of equality exists in Sweden and Japan, as they score highly in the percentage of the first three quintiles and low on the last two quintiles. Conversely, Brazil and South Africa have the greatest inequality, having low scores in all but the highest quintile. Canada compares favourably with the United States (our constant comparison companion), slightly less favourably with Australia. It is interesting to see in these cases that ethnicity would appear to play a role here, as the countries with the greatest social inequality are those that have a white minority and a black (in South Africa) or a black/aboriginal (in Brazil) majority. The two least ethnically diverse countries have the greatest equality.

Table 9.3 Percentage of total after-tax income going to families, by quintile, 1995

	LOWEST	SECOND	MIDDLE	FOURTH	HIGHEST
Canada	5.7	11.8	**17.7**	24.6	40.2
United States	4.7	11.0	17.4	**25.0**	41.9
Australia	4.4	10.0	17.5	24.8	42.2
Sweden	8.0	**13.2**	17.4	24.5	36.9
Japan	**8.7**	**13.2**	17.5	23.1	37.5
Brazil	*2.1*	*4.9*	*8.9*	*16.8*	**67.5**
South Africa	3.3	5.8	9.8	17.7	63.3

Note: **Bold** indicates the highest total(s) in each column; italics indicate the lowest total(s).

Source: Adapted from The World Bank, *World Bank Development Report 1997: The State in a Changing World* (New York: Oxford University Press, 1997).

Deciles

Deciles are created with a similar methodology, but the population of census families is divided into ten, rather than five. This produces finer distinctions, with a greater capacity to detect and show inequality. There is greater distinction between the very rich, who make up the tenth or highest decile, and the very poor, who are in the first or lowest decile; the more we lump families into fewer strata, the less stark the discrepancies between extremes become. If you were a sociologist working for a provincial government that wanted to show how "things are getting better" for the poor, you would be more likely to use quintiles because they will show a narrower gap between poor and rich. If you were a working for a research institute that wanted to talk about the extremes of inequality, data tabulated in deciles would more effectively illustrate your message.

A good example of the use of deciles in Canadian sociological research comes from Armine Yalnizyan's *The Growing Gap: A Report on Growing Inequality Between the Rich and Poor in Canada* (1998). Yalnizyan (see Table 9.4) demonstrated how in the mid-1990s, CEOs of large companies were receiving huge increases in salary and stock benefits at a time when "the average worker" was experiencing minimal pay increases and fear of being "downsized" or laid off. In a series of tables comparing total family income for 1973 and 1996, tabulated in deciles, Yalnizyan drew a compelling picture of social inequality in Canada. For each of the three parts we have added, with figures for 1995, the ratio of the first and fifth quintiles to show how tabulating the data in quintiles rather than deciles gives a different impression of the results.

What do YOU think?

Look at Table 9.4. How does the 1995 quintile ratio differ from the 1996 decile ratio in each case? In what situation might it be better to use the quintile ratios for the data?

Social Inequality and Education

Post-secondary education is a major avenue of social mobility, offering people from lower-class families the opportunity to secure jobs paying middle- or upper-class salaries. But if post-secondary education becomes so expensive that low-income students either cannot attend college or university, or leave under the burden of crippling student debt, then this avenue for mobility is blocked.

In Canada, college tuition costs less and is therefore more accessible than university education. Look at the

Table 9.4 Total family income in Canada, 1st and 10th deciles compared, 1973, 1996

	1973	1996	QUINTILE RATIO (1ST:5TH), 1995
A – AVERAGE MARKET INCOME (INCLUDES EARNINGS FROM ALL SOURCES AND RETURNS ON INVESTMENTS)			
1st decile	$5,204	$435	—
10th decile	$107,253	$136,736	—
Ratio	20.61	314.34	61.875
B – AVERAGE TOTAL INCOME (INCLUDES TRANSFERS FROM GOVERNMENT INCOME SUPPORT PROGRAMS)			
1st decile	$12,913	$13,522	—
10th decile	$109,260	$138,157	—
Ratio	8.46	10.22	5.21
C – AVERAGE AFTER-TAX INCOME (INCLUDES FEDERAL AND PROVINCIAL TAX SYSTEMS)			
1st decile	$12,732	$13,353	—
10th decile	$86,196	$97,372	—
Ratio	6.77	7.24	7.21

Source: Yalnizyan 1998.

Table 9.5 University and college participation in Canada, by parental income (2001)

PARENTS' INCOME	ATTENDING UNIVERSITY (%)	ATTENDING COLLEGE (%)
Less than $25,000	19.5	29.4
$25,000–$50,000	23.3	36.5
$50,000–$75,000	25.0	38.2
$75,000–$100,000	38.2	38.1
More than $100,000	45.6	38.1
Overall	30.0	35.4

Source: Based on data from www.statcan.gc.ca/pub/11f0019m/
11f0019m2005243-eng.pdf.

figures in Table 9.5. Do you think the data point to something of a "class system" in post-secondary education?

Tuition Fees and University Education

Tuition fees for university education rose significantly during the 1990s, and have continued to climb, albeit less dramatically, since the start of the twenty-first century. Consider that the average undergraduate tuition fee in Canada has increased from $1,464 in the 1990–1 academic year to $5,366 in 2011–12, more than tripling (Statistics Canada 2010, 2011b). A drop in federal and provincial funding for post-secondary education has been a major factor contributing to the increase.

There are also significant regional differences in tuition costs (Statistics Canada 2011b). Ontario has the highest average tuition costs for both undergraduate and graduate students, at $6,640 and $7,578 respectively. Higher-than-average undergraduate tuitions are found in New Brunswick, Nova Scotia, Alberta, and Saskatchewan, while higher-than-average graduate fees are charged in Nova Scotia and British Columbia. The lowest tuitions, for both graduate and undergraduate students, are found in Newfoundland and Labrador and in Quebec, where the fees are below the average by several thousand (see Figure 9.1).

What do YOU think?

In 2012, the province with the lowest tuition, Quebec, saw massive student unrest concerning a proposed tuition increase, yet the province with the highest tuition, Ontario, has generally had no student response to this strike. Why do you think that is?

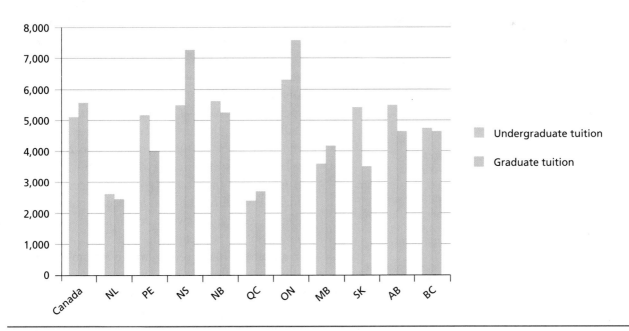

Figure 9.1 Average undergraduate and graduate tuition fees for Canadian full-time students, by province, 2011–12

Source: Based on data from Statistics Canada 2011b, Canadian Vital Statistics, Marriage Database and Demography Division (population estimates). Ottawa: Statistics Canada.

What quintile are the families of these university students most likely to be in? How would that change if this were a college library instead of a university library?

QUICK HITS

Student Employment and the Economic Meltdown

In May 2009, 18.3 per cent of students aged 20–24 who intended to go back to college or university in the fall were unemployed. This figure was up from 15.4 per cent a year earlier, in May 2008. That means that over the course of a year, roughly 59,000 full-time summer jobs were lost (www.statcan.gc.ca/subjects-sujets/labour-travail/lf-epa/lfs-epa-eng.htm).

What do YOU think?

What do you think the impact of this greater unemployment was on student life in colleges and universities in the 2009–10 academic year?

Of course, what you pay depends on not just *where* you're studying but *what* you're studying. The so-called "professional schools" of dentistry, medicine, pharmacy, and law have the highest average fees across the country, scoring $16,024, $11,345, $9,800, and $8,214 respectively in 2011–12 (Statistics Canada 2011b). Needless to say, this has affected who goes to the professional schools. A study undertaken in 2004 by the five law schools in Ontario (where the tuition is highest) found that their schools were attended by "more students from affluent homes headed by parents with a university education: two-thirds of law students come from the top 40 per cent of the family income distribution and about 10 per cent from the bottom 40 per cent of the distribution" (King, Warren, & Miklas 2004). (Think of how much greater the disparity would look if deciles or even quintiles had been reported.)

The situation at professional schools changed dramatically after 1997, when tuition fees were deregulated (meaning that governmental controls on what the universities could charge were withdrawn). The law school study reported that between 1997 and 2004

Table 9.6 Medical school tuition in Canada, 2010–11

UNIVERSITY	PROVINCE	TUITION	
		CANADIAN STUDENTS	INTERNATIONAL STUDENTS
McMaster University	Ontario	$20,831	$108,546
University of Toronto	Ontario	18,424	51,051
Queen's University	Ontario	18,228	n.a.
University of Ottawa	Ontario	18,117	n.a.
University of Western Ontario	Ontario	17,722	n.a.
Northern Ontario School of Medicine	Ontario	17,200	n.a.
University of British Columbia	British Columbia	15,547	n.a.
University of Calgary	Alberta	14,600	n.a.
Dalhousie University	Nova Scotia	13,818	21,078
University of Saskatchewan	Saskatchewan	12,276	n.a.
University of Alberta	Alberta	11,714	n.a.
University of Manitoba	Manitoba	7,499	n.a.
Memorial University	Newfoundland and Labrador	6,250	30,000
McGill University	Quebec	4,825	8,879*
Université Laval	Quebec	3,240	8,879*
Université de Sherbrooke	Quebec	3,170	9,494*
Université de Québec à Montréal	Quebec	3,102	8,501*

* Includes residents outside of Quebec and New Brunswick.

n.a. Not available.

Source: Macleans.ca 2010.

there was "an increase of 4.7 per cent in the proportion of law students' parents who earn incomes in the top 40 per cent of the average family income distribution for Canada and a decrease in the proportion of students whose parents earn incomes in the middle 20 per cent of the distribution" (King, Warren, & Miklas 2004). And, as with post-secondary tuition fees generally, there is a regional disparity in what it costs to attend a professional school. Table 9.6 shows the average cost of attending medical school at 17 different schools in eight provinces in 2010–11, presented in order of most expensive to least expensive.

Finally there is the issue of student debt. A Statistics Canada report on the impact of student loans, based on three different surveys conducted between 1995 and 2005, noted that over that 10-year period, the proportion of students graduating with outstanding debts rose from 49 per cent to 57 per cent, while the average debt rose from $15,200 to $18,800, and the percentage of those graduating with at least $25,000 of debt climbed from 17 per cent to 27 per cent (Statistics Canada 2010).

We can see, then, that post-secondary education and class (that is, parental income) relate to one another, particularly when it comes to university, especially with the professional schools. What is very Canadian about this general sociological fact is that the province in which the student lives is a factor, again especially with the professional schools, with Ontario being the most expensive and Quebec the least expensive province for university education.

What do YOU think?

Higher tuition fees are a barrier to social mobility. The universities that charge higher fees for professional schools usually justify the costs as a way of generating the revenue needed to attract "star professors" and (for medical schools) to purchase better equipment. Is it reasonable to say there's nothing wrong with students from poorer families attending cheaper universities?

Extremes

As we've seen throughout this chapter, studying social inequality is often about looking at the extremes that exist within social institutions like the family and post-secondary education. In this section we'll take a broader look at extremes of social inequality by looking first at food bank use and then at the contrast between the top 100 earners and the much maligned average Canadian earner.

Food Banks

One indicator of the social inequality that exists in Canada comes from statistics concerning the use of food banks. A **food bank**, as defined by the Canadian Association of Food Banks (2004), is a "central warehouse or clearing house, registered as a non-profit organization for the purpose of collecting, storing and distributing food, free of charge, directly or through front line agencies which may also provide meals to the hungry." Every year the Canadian Association of Food Banks (now Food Banks Canada) issues a statement called *HungerCount*, which offers statistics on food bank use. These statistics are generated from an 18-item survey distributed annually in March to food banks across the country.

The figures from the March 2011 issue of *HungerCount* are instructive, both in themselves and in how they compare with earlier figures. They show that during the preceding year (2010–11), Canadian food banks assisted 851,014 people. That figure looks good when you consider that it represents a 2 per cent decrease from the previous year (2009–10). It isn't really, though, since the food bank year beginning in March 2009 and ending in March 2010 was actually the worst year of the recession in Canada; slightly better economic circumstances led to the modest 2 per cent decline in the following year. Also, when you compare food bank use in 2010–11 with food bank use in 2008–9, you see that food bank use is up by a startling 26 per cent over that two-year period. We can comfortably predict that over the long-term trend, there will be greater and greater need for food banks.

Another telling statistic from the 2011 issue of *HungerCount* concerns the number of first-time food bank users. According to the 2011 report, 93,085 people—roughly 11 per cent of the 851,014 individuals assisted by food banks in 2010–11—were first-time

What do YOU think?

1. Which of the following social policies do you think would best stop and possibly reverse the growth of food bank dependency?
   a) issue welfare cheques as food coupons
   b) increase the minimum wage
   c) increase the age of retirement
   d) increase family allowance cheques
   e) increase the availability of low-cost housing.

2. Different statistics representing the same phenomenon can create markedly different impressions. The number of food bank users as of March 2011 is 851,014. That's 2.5 per cent of the population of Canada (up from 2.0 per cent in 2008). Which of those figures do you think sounds more negative, more damning of current socioeconomic circumstances? If you were a social activist critical of the federal government, which would you use? What if you were a cabinet minister of the federal government?

3. Do you think that food banks will always be with us? Will they increase or decrease significantly in the future?

4. Of all the provinces, Alberta had the greatest increase in food bank use (74 per cent) between 2008 to 2011. Does that surprise you? Which of these factors might have contributed significantly to the increase?
   a) migration from other provinces of people expecting high-paying jobs that they did not find
   b) migration from other countries of "temporary workers" who stayed after jobs were completed
   c) the high cost of living in oil-fuelled boom towns such as Fort McMurray
   d) the volatile nature of oil-based industries
   e) inadequate social assistance provided by the provincial government
   f) something else.

users. This supports the view that food bank use will continue to increase.

Looking at the social location of food bank users is also important. In terms of age, for example, we see that 38 per cent are under 18, while 4.4 per cent are over 65. There is relative gender balance among food bank users, 47 per cent of whom are women, compared with the 53 per cent who are men. In terms of ethnicity, 10 per cent of users self-identify as First Nation, Métis, or Inuit, a figure that is just slightly less than the 11 per cent who are recent immigrants or refugees (their numbers rise to 18.5 per cent in large cities). Then there are the college and university students: 4 per cent. Is that more or less than what you might have guessed?

Looking at household structure, we see that slightly more than 59 per cent of food bank users are families: 24 per cent are single-parent families, 23 per cent are two-parent families, and 12 per cent are couples without children. Principal sources of income for these households, in decreasing order, are social assistance (52 per cent), current or recent work (18 per cent), disability-related income (13 per cent), pensions (7 per cent), no income (5 per cent), and student loans and/or scholarships (2 per cent).

Canada's "1 per cent"

One of the key messages repeated by protesters taking part in the Occupy movement in the fall of 2011 was that 1 per cent of the world's population controlled 99 per cent of the world's wealth. Does the ratio apply in Canada?

On 3 January 2012, Canadians beginning their work year learned that by noon that day, each of the top 100 chief executive officers in Canada had already earned as much as the average Canadian makes in an entire year ("Canada's Top CEOs" 2012). The report, prepared by the non-profit Canadian Centre for Policy Alternatives, was based on figures from 2010, when the average Canadian was earning $44,300 per year, while the average annual salary for the top 100 CEOs was $8.4 million. These CEOs include the heads of such familiar companies as Canadian Tire, RONA, Air Canada, Loblaws, Rogers, Shaw, Telus, and Cineplex (no wonder the popcorn is so expensive), as well as a significant number of gold companies and the big six banks.

Reports like this are meant to shock us by sensationalizing a situation we all know exists. Issued in the early days of the calendar year—a notoriously slow

Though more economic wealth and millionaires were created in the 1990s than in any other decade in Canadian history, there were significant increases in poverty and food bank use during the same period. Why would poverty increase at the same time that overall wealth increased?

time for news—they play well in the media. As sociologists, we have to look at the statistics critically, as we learned in Chapter 2. Here, then, is some context. The figure cited as the average salary of the top 100 Canadian CEOs in 2010—$8.4 million—represents an increase of 27 per cent over the previous year, while the average Canadian salary went up by 1.1 from 2009 to 2010 (Flavelle 2013). Another way of looking at the situation: the highest salary of a Canadian CEO in 2010 was 189 times that of the average wage earner in 2010. Compare this with the situation in 1998, when the best-paid CEO made 105 times what the average Canadian earned, and in 1995, when the wealthiest CEO's salary was 85 times that of the average Canadian (Flavelle 2013). This suggests that social inequality in Canada is growing, not diminishing.

WRAP IT UP

Summary

In this chapter, we looked at social inequality from the perspective of two classic theorists, Karl Marx and Max Weber, as well as through the eyes of two early twentieth-century Canadian sociologists, Herbert Brown Ames and Colin McKay, who were engaged in investigating very specific situations.

While most of the chapter surveyed the issue of social inequality in Canada, we also examined the caste system in India, a very old, very different model of inequality.

Social inequality seems less unjust when there are good avenues for mobility, which might give someone from a lower class a decent chance to climb the socioeconomic ladder. We looked closely at two of these avenues: sports (particularly hockey, which admittedly benefits just a tiny proportion of our population, making it a pipe dream for many hockey dads and moms) and post-secondary education, which is more accessible, though perhaps not as accessible as it should be. The rising costs of hockey have helped one of our national sports creep into the elitist category, while the rising costs and student debts that come with a college or university education bring challenges of their own (as if you were unaware of them!).

We ended the chapter with a look at emblems of the extremes of social inequality in Canada: food banks, whose users don't easily fit into the stereotype of the homeless and the income-less, and the CEOs of some of our best-known companies.

THINK BACK

Questions for Critical Review

1. Distinguish between a Marxist notion of class and a system that includes a middle class.
2. Differentiate between *class* and *strata*.
3. Identify what deciles and quintiles are and demonstrate how they are used.
4. Identify what caste is and outline how it may sometimes be misunderstood.
5. Identify what liberal ideology is and outline potential weaknesses.

READ ON

Online

Is the cost keeping kids out of minor hockey? Absolutely, players and parents say

www.cbc.ca/sports/hockey/ourgame/story/2009/01/16/hockey-costs-too-much.html

> This feature article on the CBC's website gives an informative, journalistic look at the high price of hockey in Canada, which may be to blame for falling minor hockey registration numbers.

Canadian Council on Social Development

www.ccsd.ca

> The CCSD is dedicated to exploring issues of social inequality, especially poverty, with an aim to influencing social policy. The website provides current news stories and recent reports prepared by the CCSD.

Food Banks Canada

www.foodbankscanada.ca

> This website of Food Banks Canada is dedicated to documenting the hunger problems of the poor in Canada, and to addressing possible policy solutions. Its annual report, *HungerCount*, gives details of the organization's activities and findings on a yearly basis.

Canadian Centre for Policy Alternatives

www.policyalternatives.ca

> The Canadian Centre for Policy Alternatives is an independent research institute that studies inequality and creates policies addressing that inequality.

In Print

Patrizia Albanese (2009), *Child Poverty in Canada* (Toronto: Oxford).

> An important work by a Canadian sociologist on theories of and possible solutions to child poverty in Canada.

Zygmunt Bauman (2011), *Collateral Damage: Social Inequalities in a Global Age* (Malden, MA: Polity Press).

> A readable look by a prolific sociology author about how contemporary society is producing an underclass of disposable people.

Ed Grabb and Neil Guppy, eds (2008), *Social Inequality in Canada*, 5th edn (Toronto: Pearson).

> An insightful collection of articles, edited (and with some articles written) by two leading Canadian sociologists studying social inequality in Canada.

Learning Objectives

After reading this chapter, you should be able to

- discuss the extent to which "race," ethnicity, and gender are social constructs
- distinguish between different forms of racism
- explain four "mind traps" associated with studying blacks in Canada
- demonstrate how, historically, Canadian laws can be said to be racist
- contrast the social inequality in Quebec before and after the Quiet Revolution
- explain how the ethnic conflict in Rwanda was socially constructed by colonialism
- distinguish between the different legal entities that make up Aboriginal people in Canada.

Key Terms

- anti-colonialism
- colonialism
- cultural mosaic
- discrimination
- dual colonialism
- epiphenomenal
- essentialism
- ethnic class
- ethnic entrepreneurs
- friendly racism
- indirect rule
- institutional racism
- instrumentalism
- intersectionality theory
- interlocking matrix of domination
- internal colonialism
- Inuit
- master narrative
- melting pot
- Métis
- minoritized
- polite racism
- post-colonialism
- Powley test
- prejudice
- primordialism
- racial bigotry
- racialization
- registered Indian
- relational accountability
- scrip
- smiling racism
- social constructionism
- systemic racism
- vertical mosaic

Names to Know

- Patricia Hill Collins
- Kimberlé Crenshaw
- W.E.B. Du Bois
- Franz Fanon
- Daniel G. Hill
- Everett C. Hughes
- Albert Memmi
- John Porter
- Beverly Daniel Tatum

The Invisibility of Being White

Most white people living in North America are, for all intents and purposes, invisible. That invisibility affords a safety that is easily taken for granted.

In the 1960s, I—a white male—became visible for a time because of my long hair. With this new status (the countercultural hippie) I took a few baby steps down the long path of unmasked prejudice. Police, folks from small towns, and denizens of Toronto's "greaser" neighbourhoods all made me highly aware of my visibility, causing me to feel vulnerable to the emotions of others. Once, waiting for a bus in northern Ontario, dark from a summer's work in forestry, straight hair hanging well below my shoulders, one of the people working at the bus depot thought I was Native. I got a brief glimpse of what it was like to be the object of racial disdain.

My hair remains long, but age and a respectable career have made me largely invisible again. Unlike a young black male, I am not watched carefully in convenience stores, nor stopped for no apparent reason while driving. White people, even when they are visible, do not automatically lose status. On the contrary, in many cases, with greater visibility comes a rise in status. When I went to Taiwan, I had visibility, and my status brought prestige. Children watched me with respect. They would practise English with "the expert." Among school children on a trip to the museum, I became a walking exhibit of the West. They passed me with deference, their "Hi, how are you?" spoken shyly, through face-covering hands.

When I took the train south to the mid-sized city of Hualien, my visibility helped me, when the person who was supposed to meet me failed to turn up. Taxi drivers helped me use the phone (I was unsure of which coins to use), even when I told them I wouldn't be needing a ride. Would a Taiwanese visitor in a mid-sized, racially homogeneous city in Canada have been served that well?

For the first time in my life I went an entire day without seeing another white person. Far from being able to disappear anonymously into crowds, I parted the throngs like Moses through the Red Sea (the beard might have helped). I felt as though I was always on stage, but with a friendly audience.

Coming back, I needed to get a taxi from the station to the airport. I knew the name of the airport, but that didn't help me as I passed from taxi to taxi trying to communicate what I needed, each time to baffled looks. Knowing that fluency in English and administrative status often went hand in hand in Taiwan, I went to the office of the station manager, who wrote down what I wanted so that I could show it to one of the taxi drivers. Can you imagine a non–English-speaking, non-white person doing that in Canada? Imagine the response.

It was a good lesson for me to be visible, even if the experience of visibility was not a negative one. The very experience of visibility abroad helped me to imagine, in a small way, what it might be like to be not invisible at home.

What do YOU think?

It can be said, generally, that being invisible means having the freedom to act in a given situation. If you are visible in social situations—in terms of gender, ethnicity, or age, for example—how much freedom do you have? Think of different social situations, like a dance club or a concert, where a certain gender, "race," or age dominates. What would it be like to stand out?

Introduction to "Race": Why the Scare Quotes?

The term "race" was first applied to humans in the context of European colonial expansion during the sixteenth and seventeenth centuries. Use of the term reflects beliefs about biological superiority and inferiority in the context of colonial power. It does not always follow the formulas: lighter skin = good, pure; darker skin = bad, corrupt. Witness, for example, Russian racism directed at Siberian peoples speaking languages related to Finnish and Hungarian, and Japanese racism towards their indigenous people (the Ainu), and the racism of the Chinese concerning Tibetans and the Muslim Uygurs. However, white supremacy—involving discrimination against anyone not of western European ethnic background—has been the prevailing pattern since people began discussing humans in terms of different "races."

Why do we put quotation marks around "race"? Races do not exist as clear biological entities among humans. When early scientists tried to divide humans into three "races"—Caucasian, Mongoloid, and Negroid—there were always peoples left over. Where do you file the Ainu of Japan and the Aborigines of Australia, for example? Differences *within* supposed races often outnumbered those *between* races. "Negroid" people included both the tallest and shortest people in the world, and people of greatly varying skin colour. English-born anthropologist Ashley Montagu published a landmark argument against

A late nineteenth-century artist's representation of the five "human races": [*clockwise from top left*] American, Malayan, Mongolian, Ethiopian, and Caucasian (in the centre, of course). What role do you think politics and religion might have played in scientific efforts to prove the existence of different races during the eighteenth and nineteenth centuries?

the existence of separate human races in *Man's Most Dangerous Myth: The Fallacy of Race*, first printed in 1942. Since then, science has shown that there is but one human species, one race, albeit one that displays variation among its members—rather like *Ursus americanus*, the black bear, which can be black, cinnamon brown, and even white.

Racialization, though, does exist. It is a social process in which groups of people are viewed and judged as essentially different in terms of their intellect, their morality, their values, and their innate worth because of differences in physical appearance or cultural heritage. In this chapter we will examine some of the contexts in which this process plays out, and the effects it creates.

Racialization in Canada: Two Current Examples

Canada's Native People

Evidence of racialization in Canada exists in the way Aboriginal people have been and still are treated. The racialization of North America's indigenous population began in the sixteenth century in Europe, with a discussion of whether or not Aboriginal people were human and had souls. To western Europeans, they were an "other" that needed to be explained, and racialization formed part of that explanation. A few facts from the sociological profile of Canada's Native people show how this has occurred.

First, Native people have been living in what is now Canada for a very long time: a conservative estimate is 12,000 years. If you figure that the first Europeans (the Norse explorers) visited Canada's eastern shores roughly 1,000 years ago (and left shortly thereafter), we can say that roughly 92 per cent of Canadian history is Aboriginal history.

Yet from a sociological perspective, Aboriginal people have been studied primarily as social problems. Métis writer Emma LaRocque describes the impact of this kind of treatment:

> Several years ago in a sociology class on social problems, I recall wondering if anyone else was poor, because the professor repeatedly referred to Native people as statistical examples of poverty. . . . Not for one moment would I make light of the ugly effects of poverty. But if classroom groups must talk about Indians and poverty, then they must also point out the ways in which Native people are operating on this cancer. To be sure, the operations are always struggles and sometimes failures, but each new operation is faced with more experience, more skill, more confidence and more success. (LaRocque 1993: 212)

LaRocque, here, calls attention to the lack of balance in how Aboriginal people are portrayed, an example of racialization. A more productive perspective is one that Wilson and Wilson (1998) call **relational accountability**. This is an approach that shows people's strengths as well as their weaknesses, so that problems can be viewed alongside successes.

Another factor contributing to the racialization of Canada's Native people is the fact that Aboriginal voices have barely been heard in the sociological study of their people and history (Steckley 2003). Unfortunately, as Aboriginal people have only recently been able to take advantage of graduate-level work in Canadian universities, and as sociology has been tainted as an outsider-privileged research area, it will be a while yet before these voices speak loudly in Canadian sociology.

Aboriginal people are defined by a complex system of legal statuses that separates them in a number of ways from non-Aboriginal people, and from each other. The main designations, as defined in Canadian legislation, are:

- **registered Indian**
- Bill C-31 Indian
- band member
- reserve resident
- treaty Indian (a category with its own subdivisions, as each treaty is different)
- **Métis**
- Inuit.

The legal differences come from the Indian Act, which is administered by the federal Department of Indian Affairs. Passed in 1876, the Indian Act enshrined a sexist definition of "Indian" as any man of "Indian blood" reputed to belong to a particular band, any child of such a man, or any woman married to such a man. A man kept his status no matter whom he married, but a woman, if she married someone not legally an Indian, lost her status, and her children would share that fate. Ironically, a non-Native woman could gain Indian status by marrying an Indian man. This discriminatory law was in force until 1985, when Bill C-31 was passed, enabling people who had lost their Indian status through marriage or through the marriage of their mother to apply to be reinstated.

Inuit (from a word in their language meaning "people"; the singular is "Inuk") differ from "Indians," having been in Canada for a shorter time—somewhere between 5,000 and 10,000 years. It was not until 1939, when the federal government wanted to assert territorial claims in the Arctic, that Canada officially took responsibility for the Inuit. Each Inuk was given a metal disc with a number that was to be used as a token of their status. Today, about 60 per cent of Inuit have disc numbers.

The lives of Canada's Northern Aboriginal population changed on 1 April 1999, when the territory of Nunavut (meaning "Our Land") came into being. More than 80 per cent of Nunavut's 25,000 residents are Inuit. They own 18 per cent of the land, have subsurface rights to oil, gas, and other minerals for about 2 per cent of Nunavut, and will receive royalties from the extraction of those minerals from the rest of the territory. They do not require a licence to hunt or fish to meet their basic needs.

The term Métis is used in two ways. It is commonly used, often with a lowercase *m*, to refer to anyone of mixed Native and non-Native heritage. With an uppercase *M* it usually refers to the descendants of French fur traders and Cree women. Starting in the late eighteenth century, the Métis developed a culture that brought together European and Native elements. Over time, they came to regard themselves as a nation, having achieved a sense of solidarity from their shared legal struggles with the Hudson's Bay Company (HBC) over the HBC's trade monopoly. The HBC owned most of the prairies and about half of present-day Canada, thanks to a 1670 charter granted by the English King Charles II, who little knew what he was signing away. In 1867, the HBC negotiated the sale of most of its lands to the Government of Canada, which, with no regard for Métis land rights, moved to set up a colony in Manitoba. In 1869, led by 25-year-old, college-educated Louis Riel, the Métis achieved a military takeover in the colony and set up an independent government to negotiate with Ottawa. The Manitoba Act of 1870 established the province and recognized the rights of the Métis. The Métis were given scrips, certificates declaring that the bearer could receive payment in land, cash, or goods. But government officials and land speculators swindled the Métis out of their land by buying up the scrips for next to nothing. Most Métis simply moved west. In 1885, with western expansion again threatening their rights to the land, the Métis, led again by Louis Riel, set up an independent government in Saskatchewan. Federal Canadian forces attacked and defeated them, and Riel was hanged for treason.

The Métis settled in a patchwork of rural prairie communities and nearly disappeared altogether. But during the 1930s, Alberta Métis pushed for the creation of communal settlements similar to reserves. In 1938, eleven Métis "colonies" were formed (eight remain today). These colonies carry some political rights, making them more like rural municipalities. However, the Métis do not have rights to the royalties for oil and gas extracted from the land. Beyond the colonies, the Métis are represented by the Métis National Council and provincial organizations in Ontario and the Western provinces. These organizations suffer from difficulties of legal definition and lack of recognition.

In the 2006 census, 389,785 people identified themselves as Métis, representing a 91 per cent increase from 1996 and nearly doubling their overall recognized population. The Métis also upped their percentage of the Aboriginal population during that time, from 26 per cent to 34 per cent. The main reason for this increase likely is a heightened tendency to self-identify as Métis, which is due to an increase in Métis political and cultural activities.

In 1993, two Métis men, Steve Powley and his son, were charged with unlawfully hunting and possessing a moose. They fought the case on the grounds that it was their right as Aboriginal people to hunt for food. On 23 September 2003, the Supreme Court of Canada upheld Powley's right to hunt for food out of season and without a provincial licence. The case helped establish the Powley test, used to determine whether Native and Métis people can lawfully hunt without a licence. According to the test, a person must be able to show that he or she has been identified as Métis for a long time and is accepted as a member in a community that was historically and is currently Métis. Powley and his community of 900, living just outside of Sault Ste Marie in northwestern Ontario, qualified. The Powley case has been used by the Métis to obtain hunting rights in parts of British Columbia, Alberta, and Saskatchewan.

There are two views concerning the value of being racialized in terms of Aboriginal rights. Some see it as fair and right, as these rights have been earned by virtue of Aboriginal peoples' long history (over 12,000 years) of settlement in Canada, and through numerous hard-won agreements and treaties. But others see the situation as unfair, arguing that Aboriginal people are being granted special rights not available to others, based solely on their ethnicity. How do you feel? Do you think your own membership in a racialized group has a profound effect on your opinion?

What do YOU think?

Who would oppose the successful invocation of the Powley test? For what reason? How could this opposition be overcome?

Blacks in Canada

Black communities have existed in Nova Scotia since the British Proclamation of 1779 offered freedom to slaves who left their American masters to fight on the British side in the American Revolution. Over 3,000 African Americans moved north, followed 20 years later by 2,000 more, who came to the Maritime colonies when they were offered their freedom by the British government during the War of 1812, in which Britons and Canadians fought Americans (Conrad & Hiller 2001: 103, 111). They were offered significantly less land and fewer opportunities than white immigrants were, and they endured incredible hardship and prejudice.

The black population of Canada has declined several times. In 1792, nearly 1,200 black Loyalists left the Atlantic colonies for the new African colony of Sierra

Going Global

Overcoming Racialization with My Libyan Students

It was early 1983, and I was teaching English as a second language at a private school in Toronto, when a group of Libyan students arrived. I imagine they came to us because they weren't allowed into the US. Libyans were portrayed in the media as the great enemy of the West during the 1980s. "Libyan" became a kind of shorthand for "terrorist." Even the 1985 movie *Back to the Future* featured Libyan terrorists with automatic weapons to play the role of evil gunmen whose motives did not have to be explained. Libyan terrorists: story told. Then Libyan leader Mu'ammar Gaddafi was the Osama bin Laden of his day.

Despite my sociological training, I couldn't help feeling a bit suspicious of the new students. Growing up in Toronto in the 1950s and 1960s, I had encountered very few people of Arab descent—specifically, a geography teacher and two schoolmates (brother and sister) in high school. Yet somehow, for reasons I couldn't quite explain, I had this strong and mostly negative view of Libyans, which overrode any impression based on actual dealings I might have had with people of Libyan or even Arab background.

Our school was right next to the subway. One morning, as I began the long climb out of the station, I met one of my Libyan students. We greeted each other politely and walked together with few words. Then we faced the long double escalator, flanked on either side by a set of stairs that is so seldom used it seems reserved for emergencies. He turned to me and said, "Come on, we are both still young men." We took the stairs at a run, together. In that moment, my racialized view of our differences gave way to an awareness of those things we had in common—our age, our sex, our male pride—which were all that mattered just then. It was a lesson for me.

What do YOU think?

What, according to the author, contributed to his racialized view of Arabs generally and of Libyans specifically? What other racializing influences not mentioned in this narrative might have been at play?

Leone. Many more returned to the United States following the Civil War, which ended slavery in the US. Between 1871 and 1911 there was a slow decline in the black population in Canada, from 21,500 to 16,900, and a further drop—from 22,200 to 18,000—between 1941 and 1951. It wasn't until the 1970s, when the population rose from 34,400 in 1971 to 239,500 by the end of the decade, that the number of black Canadians began to increase consistently (Milan & Tran 2004: 3).

In 2006 there were an estimated 783,795 blacks living in Canada, making them the country's third highest visible minority behind Chinese people (1,216,570) and South Asians (1,262,865). In three provinces—Nova Scotia, New Brunswick, and Quebec—they are the leading visible minority. In one province—British Columbia—they rank last among the six "official" visible minorities (Chinese, South Asians, blacks, Filipinos, Latin Americans, and Southeast Asians). The high population of blacks in Nova Scotia and New Brunswick is largely a result of eighteenth- and nineteenth-century immigration, whereas in Quebec it is due to more recent immigration from former French colonies such as Haiti, Chad, and Cameroon.

Despite their long history in this country, black people are often viewed and treated as relative newcomers, recent arrivals from poor nations in Africa and the Caribbean. Canadians tend to be smug about our role in helping slaves escape the American South during the eighteenth and nineteenth centuries (although many blacks were as badly treated here as they were in the US), and yet black people today continue to be racialized by mainstream Canadian society, which views them as "other." Black people are overrepresented in our prison systems and in our homicide statistics, yet homicides occurring in black neighbourhoods tend to be viewed as a sad but inevitable consequence for those who are part of a community that (in the eyes of mainstream Canada) is drawn to gun culture and crime. Sociologists have studied the underlying causes of crime in black neighbourhoods—poverty, lack of employment opportunities, absence of strong male role models, the attraction of gangs as fostering a sense of belonging—but too little has been done to address these factors.

Then again, as with Canada's Aboriginal people, it doesn't help to view black people only in terms of

Young boys play by a CN railcar, along the railway that ran through the heart of Africville. If you didn't know where this photograph was taken, could you believe that was Canada in the mid-1960s?

What makes someone a "visible minority"? Who in this photo would count? The term is used officially in federal legislation—what does it say about us that we distinguish between visible minorities and other (invisible?) ethnic minorities?

problems. Our school systems recognize Black History Month in February, but shouldn't we make the study of black history a regular part of the year-round curriculum, rather than examining the accomplishments of black people in this country and around the world as something separate and "other"?

Racism

Four Elements of Racism

Racism can be understood as the product of four linked elements. The first is *racialization*, the construction of certain groups of people as biologically superior or inferior. This fosters ideas of relative worth and quality, which leads to the second element, **prejudice**, the "pre-judgement" of others on the basis of their group membership. The third element is **discrimination**, which includes acts by which individuals are treated differently—rewarded or punished—based on their group membership. Finally, there is *power*, which is manifested when institutionalized advantages are regularly handed to one or more groups over others. Clinical psychologist and race relations expert **Beverly Daniel Tatum** touches on the importance of power in this equation when she writes:

People of color are not racist because they do not systematically benefit from racism. And equally important, there is no systematic cultural and institutional support or sanction for the racial bigotry of people of color. In my view, reserving the term *racist* only for behaviors committed by Whites in the context of a White-dominated society is a way of acknowledging the ever-present power differential afforded Whites by the culture and institutions that make up the system of advantage and continue to reinforce notions of White superiority. (Tatum 2003: 10)

Those who share this position believe that without power, non-white people in Canada can be prejudiced, but not racist. They can perform discriminatory acts, but they cannot be racist without institutional, structural, ideological, and historical support. Certainly this is true of systemic racism, which by definition involves power.

There are different kinds of racism. **Racial bigotry** is the open, conscious expression of racist views by an individual. When racist practices, rules, and laws become institutionalized, made "part of the system," then we have **systemic** (or **institutional**) **racism**. The head tax levied in 1885 by the Canadian

The Point Is...

Mind Traps in the Study of Blacks in Canada

There are several "mind traps"—misconceptions or unsubstantiated generalizations—that you may encounter, and must avoid, when studying the history and culture of black people in Canada. Here are four to watch out for:

✗ Canada's black population consists mostly of recently arrived immigrants.
✗ Canada's black community has a relatively short history.
✗ The majority of black people living in and coming to Toronto are from Jamaica.
✗ A black student who receives a post-secondary education has just as good a chance of succeeding in Canada as a non-black student.

While there is a tendency to think of black Canadians as immigrants, almost half of Canada's black population was born in this country. The tendency of Torontonians (whose city is home to nearly half of Canada's black population) to think of all black immigrants as "Jamaicans" is also flawed. Of the roughly 139,800 black immigrants who came to Canada between 1991 and 2001, only 20 per cent came from Jamaica; 12 per cent came from French-speaking Haiti (settling mostly in Montreal),

while 23 per cent came from three African countries: Somalia (10 per cent), Ghana (8 per cent), and Ethiopia (5 per cent). It is important to appreciate that someone of, say, Sudanese background has a cultural heritage very different to that of someone whose ancestry is Jamaican, or Trinidadian, or Barbadian.

Education does not seem to produce the same benefits among black people as it does among others. In 2001, Canadian-born black people between the ages of 25 and 54 were just as likely as other Canadian-born citizens to be university graduates (21 per cent), and slightly more likely to have a college diploma (23 per cent, compared with the national average of 20 per cent: Milan & Tran 2004: 1–6). However, the average income of Canadian-born black people was substantially lower than the average for all Canadian-born citizens ($29,700 versus $37,200). Some analysts have tried to "explain away" this discrepancy by arguing that the majority of working black citizens are relatively young, earning the lower incomes typical of younger workers. Yet when the income of Canadian-born blacks is age-standardized to overcome the statistical bias, the result is an annual income of $32,000—still significantly lower than the national average.

What do YOU think?

1. How do you account for the prevalence of the four "mind traps" noted above? Do you think they are honest mistakes or myths perpetuated by certain groups that stand to benefit from the misinformation?
2. Why do you think black university graduates earn considerably less than non-white graduates?

government on immigrants from China is an example of systemic racism: the law was explicitly intended to discourage Chinese immigrants from coming to Canada. Canada's residential school system, aimed at suppressing Aboriginal culture, is another historical example. Sometimes, racism can be subtle, hidden in a way behind a smile or words that seem friendly to the perpetrator. This is called **friendly** (or **polite** or **smiling**) **racism**. Henry Martey Codjoe provides an example:

Canada's "smiling racism" was with me until the very day I left the country. The realtor who showed our house to prospective buyers quietly hinted that if I wanted my house to sell quickly, I would have to remove all traces of anything that indicated that Blacks had lived in the house: no family pictures, no African art or crafts, everything Black or African must go, and we must be out of the house before he showed the house to prospective buyers. He would call and let us know. No matter what we

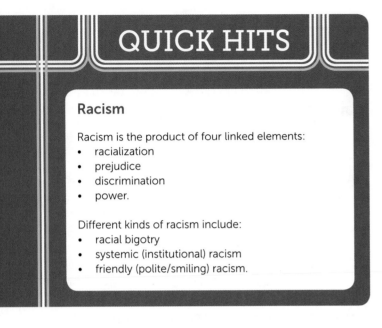

QUICK HITS

Racism

Racism is the product of four linked elements:
- racialization
- prejudice
- discrimination
- power.

Different kinds of racism include:
- racial bigotry
- systemic (institutional) racism
- friendly (polite/smiling) racism.

were doing, we must leave. One time we were late in getting out and we ended up hiding in our minivan in the garage. When he showed the garage, we ducked. It was a shameful and degrading experience. The house sold, but my wife and I never did meet the family that bought it. (Codjoe 2001: 286)

Master Narratives and Buried Knowledge

In the **master narratives** that countries construct about themselves, which get repeated in textbooks and in the stories people (especially politicians) tell about their country, racism is often downplayed or altogether omitted. Stories about the mistreatment of minorities, stories that make the dominant culture or their ancestors look bad, are often excluded. For example, the master narrative of early Canadian history describes how Native people co-operated with Europeans to make the fur trade successful, by obtaining the furs, teaching Europeans how to use canoes and snowshoes, and providing the Europeans with new foods (such as pemmican and corn). This "official" version of the story often appears in elementary and middle-school textbooks. It overlooks the exploitation and social destruction that occurred when Europeans introduced alcohol into the fur trade. To use Michel Foucault's terminology, that story is "buried knowledge."

Canada's master narrative depicts a country that is more multicultural than the United States. While there is some evidence to support this, the master narrative does not include some buried knowledge about the history of certain racial groups in Canada. The following three stories are part of that buried knowledge.

1. Defending the Women: An Act to Prevent the Employment of Female Labour

The head tax of $500 imposed on Chinese immigrants beginning in 1903 (a sizeable increase on the $50 tax levied in 1885) had a dramatic effect on immigration to Canada. For the overwhelmingly male population of Chinese immigrants who had already settled in Canada, it meant the chances of marrying a Chinese woman were greatly reduced. Many Chinese-Canadian men were forced to lead a bachelor's life, and this made them a threat to white women in the eyes of some European Canadians. This prejudice brought about Saskatchewan's Act to Prevent the Employment of Female Labour in Certain Capacities on 5 March 1912. It declared that:

> No person shall employ in any capacity any white woman or girl or permit any white woman or girl to reside or lodge in or to work in or, save as a *bona fide* customer in a public apartment thereof only, to frequent any restaurant, laundry or other place of business or amusement owned, kept or managed by any Japanese, Chinaman or other Oriental person. (Quoted in Backhouse 1999: 136)

In May 1912, Quong Wing was convicted and fined for employing two white women in his restaurant. His appeals to the supreme courts of Saskatchewan and Canada failed.

In 1924 in Regina, restaurant owner Yee Clun challenged the law. He had strong personal support in the city from members of both the Chinese and non-Chinese communities. But local newspapers were spreading poorly researched stories of Chinese men bringing opium into Saskatchewan and turning white women into "drug fiends." Clun won the case in court but found his efforts foiled by the Saskatchewan Legislature, which passed another statute authorizing any municipal council to revoke the court ruling. The Act wasn't repealed until 1969.

2. Punished for Success: Japanese-Canadian Fishers

In 1919, the Federal Department of Marine and Fisheries responded to growing concern that Japanese-Canadian gill net salmon fishers were "taking over" at the expense of white Canadian fishers. In the ironic words of Major R.J. Burde, MP for Port Alberni, reported in the Victoria *Colonist* on 22 May 1920, "they have become so arrogant in their feeling of security that many white settlers are reaching the limit of tolerance" (Adachi 1976: 105). The government reacted by drastically reducing the number of licences that Japanese-Canadian fishers could obtain (see Figure 10.1).

In just three years, white fishers gained 493 licences, an increase of 33.5 per cent; Aboriginal fishers gained 215 (up 20.8 per cent). Japanese fishers, by contrast, lost 974 licences, a drop of 48.9 per cent. Japanese-Canadian fishers in the north Skeena area were even prohibited from using power boats between 1925 and 1930. The rules had been changed, and the playing field was no longer level.

3. Not Wanted on the Voyage: The Komagata Maru

Most of the first South Asians to come to Canada were Sikhs, who had been given special status by the British as soldiers and police serving imperial purposes throughout the world. In 1904 they began to arrive in small numbers, many of them settling in Port Moody, east of Vancouver. By 1906, those small numbers had increased considerably, with as many as

5,000 Sikhs entering the country between 1905 and 1908 (Johnston 1989: 5; Burnet & Palmer 1988: 31). They were young men, most of them single, though a good number had wives back in India, and they arrived in British Columbia at a time when there was a shortage of labourers willing to work in the sawmills, on the roads, and in the bush cutting wood and clearing land. Some were greeted with a measure of respect, as many were British army veterans, and they soon earned a reputation for working hard for low wages. An October 1906 report in the Vancouver *Daily Province* quoted one employer as saying, "I would have White labourers of course if I can get them. . . . But I would rather give employment to these old soldiers who have helped fight for the British Empire than entire aliens."

BC's natural resources–based economy has long fluctuated between periods of wild success, with employers happy to hire anyone willing to work hard, and short periods of unemployment, in which newcomers are seen as taking jobs from whites. It wasn't long before the initial acceptance of the hard-working Sikh immigrants was undermined by a growing unease over their rise in numbers. The local press fuelled the simmering discord with stories about the unfamiliar cultural practices of these "Hindus" (as South Asians

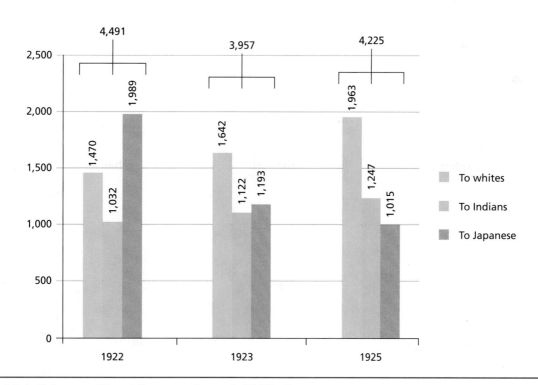

Figure 10.1 Salmon gill net licences issued, 1922–5

Source: *Report on Oriental Activities within the Province*, British Columbia Archives NW 305.895R425.

collectively were called, regardless of their religion). "Hindus Cover Dead Bodies with Butter" announced a headline in the 20 October 1906 edition of Vancouver *Daily Province* (Johnston 1989: 3).

Vancouver police began taking Sikh immigrants directly from the immigration shed to the BC interior to keep them out of the city. In spite of the deplorable accommodations in which they were placed—some were housed in an abandoned cannery with no running water and little electricity—the Sikhs showed tremendous resilience, as Johnston records:

> Two thousand had arrived during the latter half of 1906. By the end of December, with the exception of some 300 who had taken steamers for Seattle and San Francisco, all but fifty or sixty had found employment in British Columbia, most of them in saw mills. The authorities would gladly have deported any convicted of vagrancy, but there were few such cases; those who were out of work were looked after by their companions, and . . . none became a public charge. (Johnston 1989: 3)

Facing pressure both from white British Columbians disconcerted by the influx of Sikh immigrants and from British government officials in India, who wanted to curtail emigration, the Canadian government responded with clever discrimination. They passed a law requiring that all Asian immigrants entering Canada possess at least $200—a large sum for people who typically earned about 10 to 20 cents a day. They also prohibited the landing of any immigrant arriving directly from any point outside of India—significant because most Sikhs were making the journey from Punjab province by way of Hong Kong—while pressuring steamship companies not to provide India-to-Canada service or to sell tickets to Canada from Indian ports. These measures brought Sikh immigration to a halt. Unable to bring their wives and families over, denied the right to vote or hold public office, and facing open discrimination from local leaders, Canada's Sikh population became discouraged. Dr Sundar Singh, in an address at the Empire Club in Toronto on 25 January 1912, articulated the frustration many Sikhs were feeling:

Sikh passengers aboard the *Komagata Maru*. The treatment of what was called "the Hindu problem" has left a dark legacy in Canada's history. Despite that fact that Sikhs have been in Canada since 1904, their "visibility" still prompts the question: *Where are you from?*

Just at present there are two Sikh women confined on board a boat at Vancouver. . . . One is the wife of a merchant, the other is the wife of a missionary. These men have been settled in this country for five years, and are well spoken of. They went back some time ago to bring out their wives and children. . . . They came to Hong Kong, and the steamship company refused to sell them tickets; they waited there since last March and last month the CPR sold them tickets. On the 22nd, they arrived here, and the men were allowed to land, but the ladies are still confined as if they were criminals.

We have the promise of Queen Victoria that all British subjects, no matter what race or creed they belong to, shall be treated alike. . . . The Indian people are loyal British subjects. They are as loyal as anybody else. Why should there be such a difference in the treatment of these loyal people?

We appeal to you, gentlemen, to say that in any country, under any conditions, the treatment the Sikhs are receiving is not fair. . . . You may well imagine the feeling of these two men, who are suffering as I have described, for no fault at all, except that they are Sikhs. (Singh 1912)

But opposition to Sikh immigration continued to grow. On 1 December 1913, the Vancouver *Province* claimed that the "Hindu problem" had assumed "a most serious and menacing aspect" (Johnston 1989: 22), even though only 39 Sikhs had entered the area that year. The following spring, on 3 May 1914, the Japanese steamship *Komagata Maru* left Yokohama, Japan, headed for Canada. Rented by a 55-year-old Sikh, Bhai Gurdit Singh, the ship contained 376 passengers: 340 Sikhs, 24 Muslims, and 12 Hindus. News of the ship's approach was announced in headlines such as "BOAT LOADS OF HINDUS ON WAY TO VANCOUVER" and "HINDU INVASION OF CANADA" in British Columbia dailies. When the ship reached Vancouver, on 23 May 1914, the local South Asian community was ready with lawyers, funds, and food to assist the passengers. Local immigration officials, politicians, and vigilante groups were also ready. For about two months, the ship's passengers were forced to endure legal battles, severe shortages of food and water, and a confrontation with the *H.M.C.S. Rainbow*. Finally, on 23 July 1914, the *Komagata Maru* was forced to leave. Only 24 passengers were permitted to enter Canada.

On 26 September, as the ship approached Calcutta, the remaining passengers were told that they would have to be put on a special train taking them to the Punjab area. Amidst confusion and frustration, a riot ensued. Twenty of the passengers were killed; others

QUICK HITS

Who Has the Right to Vote?

1867 Confederation: Canadian federal and provincial vote is given only to white men with property.
1875 Chinese are denied the provincial vote in British Columbia.
1885 "Indians" west of Ontario are denied the vote; eastern "Indian" males are given the vote only if they own land separate from the reserve and have made at least $150 worth of improvements.
Chinese are denied the federal vote.
1895 Japanese are denied the provincial vote in BC.
1898 "Indian" males east of Manitoba are denied the federal vote regardless of property.
White males without property are given the vote federally and provincially.
1907 South Asians are denied the federal vote.
1908 Chinese are denied the provincial vote in Saskatchewan.
1917 People born in "enemy countries" (i.e. Ukrainians) are denied the vote.
Japanese-Canadian war veterans are promised the federal vote.
1931 Japanese-Canadian war veterans receive the federal vote.
1947 Chinese and South Asians get the federal vote and the provincial vote in British Columbia.
1948 Japanese Canadians get the federal vote.
1949 "Indians" are given the provincial vote in British Columbia and Newfoundland.
Japanese Canadians get the provincial vote in British Columbia.
1951 Chinese are granted the provincial vote in Saskatchewan.
1952 "Indians" get the provincial vote in Manitoba.
1954 "Indians" get the provincial vote in Ontario.
1960 "Indians" get the federal vote, and also get the territorial and provincial vote in Yukon, Northwest Territories, and Saskatchewan.
1963 "Indians" get the provincial vote in New Brunswick and Nova Scotia.
1965 "Indians" get the provincial vote in Alberta.
1969 "Indians" get the provincial vote in Quebec.

were imprisoned or became fugitives. Gurdit Singh was a fugitive for more than seven years before being captured and imprisoned for five years. In his early seventies he was elected to the All-India Congress.

Little changed afterwards. After 1918, a few of the men were able to bring over to Canada their long absent wives and children, but most could not afford such an expense. By 1941, there were no more than 1,500 South Asians in Canada. Most were men, many aged between 50 and 65. Only when India was granted its independence from British imperial control in 1947 were South Asians given the vote and full citizenship status.

On 3 August 2008, in a park in Surrey, BC—a city with a large South Asian population—Prime Minister Stephen Harper issued an apology to South Asians for the *Komagata Maru* affair. He left immediately after representatives of the South Asian community received the apology with an officially approved thank-you speech. Once the PM was gone, a South Asian leader addressed the crowd of roughly 8,000 and asked whether they accepted the apology. Most did not, and the Indian media widely condemned the apology because it had not been presented in Parliament to be written into the official record. This made it, in the eyes of its critics, a second-class apology. Some have called Harper's apology a political stunt designed to improve the Conservative Party's standing among non-white voters (see, for example, Walla 2008).

What do YOU think?

How can we evaluate official apologies by Canadian governments? Is it wrong to question the sincerity of an act that may seem staged or designed merely for political vote-gaining with a marginalized group?

Ethnicity

Everyone belongs to at least one ethnic group. But understanding ethnicity is not just a matter of collecting social traits—language, clothing, religion, foods, and so on—and applying the appropriate ethnic label. This would not help us understand conflict between closely related ethnic groups, nor would it help us understand why "ethnic pride" surfaces in certain times and situations, and not during others.

There are various ways of theorizing ethnicity. We will confine our discussion to five approaches. Political

sociologists often divide theoretical approaches to ethnicity into three categories: **social constructionism**, **instrumentalism**, and **primordialism**. Wsevolod W. Isajiw, in *Understanding Diversity: Ethnicity and Race in the Canadian Context*, discusses primordialism in relation to the **epiphenomenal** approach, which will be helpful to consider here as well. To this list we will add one more approach, **anti-colonialism**, because it is essential to understanding ethnicity in the context of the case study we are about to present.

One of the most savage and destructive ethnic conflicts of recent times—and it is still ongoing—involves rival Hutu and Tutsi tribes in Rwanda, as well as in neighbouring Burundi. The history of Rwanda since it gained independence in 1962 has been punctuated by uprisings of the disenfranchised Hutu majority against the ruling Tutsi elite, which have brought about the deaths of hundreds of thousands of civilians in both groups. The violence reached a bloody peak during the spring and summer of 1994, when Hutu military forces massacred between 500,000 and 1,000,000 of the Tutsi minority, sending more than a million destitute Hutu civilians, fearing reprisals from the surviving Tutsi population, fleeing to refugee camps in neighbouring Zaire (now the Democratic Republic of the Congo) and Tanzania. It is easy to dismiss the conflict as just another instance of tribal violence in Africa, but this is far from the truth. What happened presents a challenge of interpretation that can be facilitated by looking at it through the lens of various theories of ethnicity.

Primordialism

Primordialism (also known as **essentialism**) is the view that every ethnic group is made up of a "laundry list" of traits that have been carried down from the past to the present with little or no change. Adopting this view uncritically leads to believing that the tribal conflicts in Africa have a deep history that existed long before colonialism, and that these conflicts are reignited only once the "stabilizing influence" of the colonial power has left. It does not allow for conflicts to arise during colonization. It absolves colonial powers of any blame for regional conflicts.

Primordialism presents a static, as opposed to a dynamic, view of culture. In this view, culture does not seem to change from the inside; change is ascribed primarily or entirely to outside forces. "Modernization," for example, is credited solely to colonial outsiders. Primordialism is a kind of functionalist theory,

Our Stories

A Minoritizing Episode: Canada's Ukrainians and the Great War

On 21 August 1914, shortly after the start of World War I, a group of Canadians was **minoritized** through the War Measures Act, which would be used as an instrument of discrimination against Japanese Canadians nearly 30 years later and then, almost another 30 years after that, against French Canadians.

As with different South Asian ethnic groups—Sikhs, Hindus, and Muslims—that were viewed as other and lumped together as "Hindoos," this minoritized group had its natural, chosen identity ignored by most Canadians, who assigned them a different, "alien" identity. Like Aboriginal people in both world wars, members of this minoritized group sometimes had to change their names and lie about their identity to pass as Canadian and join up to fight. And like the Chinese, South Asians, Native people, and women of their time, many were denied the federal vote. During the Second World War they were put into concentration camps, like the Japanese.

Surprisingly, the members of this group were white.

Britain and its allies, including Canada, were fighting Germany and the decrepit Austro-Hungarian empire. The latter was home to a people who thought of themselves as Ukrainians by nationality, even though their official citizenship was Austrian. Canada's War Measures Act led to the internment of 8,579 people labelled "enemy aliens" in 24 camps across the country. More than 5,000 of them were Ukrainians. Another 80,000—most of them Ukrainians—had to register as "enemy aliens." More than 10,000 Ukrainians enlisted in the Canadian military, some by faking their names and identity to conceal their ethnicity. Among them was Filip Konoval, one of only 83 Canadians to be awarded the prestigious Victoria Cross.

Those who spent time in internment camps worked hard, developing Banff National Park, logging, working in mines and in steel mills. One hundred and seven internees died. Tuberculosis killed 26, pneumonia, 22. Six were shot to death trying to escape camp; three committed suicide. An undetermined number died due to unsafe working conditions. One hundred and six were sent to mental institutions, all but three of whom were eventually deported. Running the camps cost Canadian taxpayers $3.2 million.

The effects of the discrimination did not end with the war. Some of the land, valuables, and money possessed by Ukrainian Canadians and confiscated by the Canadian government "disappeared." Internment and suspicion killed the spirit of many who had been keen to contribute to the growth of Canada, who had nurtured high hopes for their new home.

A young "Galician" immigrant in Saint John, NB, May 1905. Ukrainians began to settle in Canada during the 1890s; today, in spite of the discriminatory and dispiriting measures they endured during World War I, Canada's Ukrainian population is among the highest in the world outside of Ukraine and Russia.

displaying one of the weaknesses of functionalism: that it poorly explains the development of conflict.

Anti-colonialism

Colonialism is the economic and political exploitation of a weaker country or people by a stronger one. Typically—historically—it involves the domination by a European state of an African, Asian, or American people; however, it is not limited to this. The Chinese have exercised and continue to wield colonial control over Tibetans and Uighurs. **Internal colonialism** is colonialism of one people by another within a single country. The history of Canada involves the internal colonialism of Aboriginal peoples by European settlers and their governments.

Anti-colonialism (or **post-colonialism**) is a theoretical framework that analyzes the destructive impact colonialism has on both the colonizer and the colonized. It was first developed by writers such as **Franz Fanon** (1925–1961) and **Albert Memmi** (b. 1920) to examine French colonies in North Africa and their fight for independence from France. Fanon, born in the French colony of Martinique in the West Indies, was radicalized by his experience as a black intellectual in France and by his work as a doctor and psychiatrist in Algeria during the fight for independence there. His influential works *Black Skin, White Masks* (1952) and *The Wretched of the Earth* (1961) deal with the psychological effects of colonization and have inspired considerable sociological study. Albert Memmi was a Jew born in the predominately Muslim country Tunisia, which gained its independence in 1956 (six years before neighbouring Algeria). His major work, *The Colonizer and the Colonized* (1957), demonstrated how the two groups negatively conditioned each other, and how no party could be "neutral" in the relationship between the two.

Anti-colonialism theory, as it applies to ethnicity, involves identifying colonialism as a factor in the development or escalation of conflict between ethnic groups. In Canada, for example, anti-colonialism theory could be used to explain the increasing conflict between the Huron and Iroquois during the 1640s in terms of the former group's connections with the French and the latter's ties with the English. In the African context, it is usefully applied to study situations involving the concept of **indirect rule**, a governance policy in which a European nation uses the members of a particular ethnic group as its intermediaries in ruling an area of Africa. (Here we prefer the term "area" to "nation" because the territorial boundaries were often defined or altered by colonizing European powers.)

One problem with anti-colonialism as a theory is that it can attribute every negative change in a colonized area to outside forces. It does not leave much room for the agency of one or more of the colonized groups. A corrective perspective is provided by **dual colonialism** theory, which is the idea that under a colonial regime, the most oppressed groups suffer both at the hands of the colonizing outsider group and at the hands of a local group that is given privilege and power by the outsider group. Political scientist Catharine Newbury applies this idea well in her discussion of Rwanda in *Cohesion of Oppression* (1988).

Primordialism, Anti-Colonialism, and Rwanda

As you read the following description of ethnic conflict in Rwanda, consider how well the theories of primordialism and anti-colonialism apply.

In Rwanda, three main ethnic groups are currently recognized: Hutu, Tutsi, and Twa. Numerically, the Hutu are by far the dominant group. The 1956 census lists 83 per cent of the population as Hutu, with 16 per cent Tutsi and 1 per cent Twa (Newbury 1993: 3). Yet from at least the eighteenth century onwards, the Tutsi have been the group with the most power. If we consider a list of typical "ethnic traits"—including physical attributes, language, religion, kinship structure, occupation, and economic circumstances—we gain some interesting findings about Rwanda prior to colonization.

PHYSICAL APPEARANCE

Tutsi and Hutu tended to differ in their physical appearance. The former were typically portrayed as being taller and thinner than the latter, with longer and thinner faces. One study (Chrétien 1967) found that the Tutsi averaged 1.75 metres in height, the Hutu 1.66 metres. We must note that before and during the colonial period, intermarriage was not uncommon. The physical differences combined with the fact that the Tutsi appear to have come later to Rwanda than the Hutu led colonial administrators and social scientists to draw otherwise unfounded conclusions about the Tutsi being a "superior, conquering race." This helped justify European colonial support of the Tutsi elite.

OCCUPATION

Concerning occupation and labour, the Tutsi were, in the pre-colonial period, primarily pastoralists—that is, they herded cattle. The Hutu, on the other hand, were primarily agriculturalists, growing crops. The division was not absolute: some Hutu, particularly those heading up the richer lineages, herded cattle, and some Tutsi were agriculturalists. Passing from one group to the other was not uncommon. But during the colonial period, the more powerful Tutsi took advantage of their enhanced privileges to gain a greater share of the cattle.

LANGUAGE

The people of Rwanda all speak the same language, with regional dialect variants. The language, belonging to the local Bantu group of languages, was likely spoken in Rwanda before the Tutsi moved into the area (probably from Ethiopia).

RELIGION

In terms of religion, the Tutsi and Hutu did not differ historically, and during the colonial period most were converted to Christianity by Catholic missionaries. However, religion would, through the education system, come to have a powerful effect on the development of a strong sense of ethnicity in Rwanda by entrenching the ethnic-based class system that placed the Tutsi at the top and the Hutu at the bottom. Established in 1932 and recognized as the best school in Rwanda, the Groupe Scolaire played a part in promoting class and ethnic divisions, as Newbury explains. One of the goals of this school was to create a "new social class,"

> and in accordance with this goal . . . very few Hutu were admitted; indeed, after World War II *the school even had a minimum height requirement for admission*. Graduates of the Groupe Scolaire considered themselves superior to other educated Rwandans, . . . and their diplomas were accorded greater value by the Belgian [colonial] administration. Thus, in theory because of their professional qualifications but in reality because they were overwhelmingly drawn from among the families of Tutsi chiefs, the graduates of the Groupe Scolaire enjoyed the benefits of both the "traditional" economic structures, and of the higher status jobs and better pay available in the "modern" sector. (Newbury 1993: 116; emphasis added)

Children in Mayange, Rwanda, a village for returning refugees of the 1994 genocide. Do you think these children are most likely Hutu or Tutsi?

IDENTITY

Identity is difficult to characterize historically. Prior to the colonial period, sense of identity was derived mainly from lineage, clan, chiefdom, or kingdom, and from a general sense of being Rwandan. Among the kin groups, the two that were of the greatest significance (and remain important today) are lineage and clan. Lineage heads were important figures, and a person's primary identity came from lineage. Clan was less important, but, interestingly, a single clan could include members of all three Rwandan ethnic groups.

Under colonialism, lineage heads lost power, being replaced by centrally appointed chiefs who were overwhelmingly Tutsi. The distinction between Tutsi and Hutu, which was of less significance in the time before the colonial period, became much more of a factor, its importance reinforced by the fact that Rwandan citizens now had to carry identification cards with "Hutu," "Tutsi," or "Twa" written on them.

The growing central authority of the king during the colonial period also helped to enhance the status of the Tutsi. During the reign of Kigeri Rwabugiri (c. 1860–1895), the king's central authority grew to encompass chiefdoms and kingdoms, some of them Hutu, that until then had been relatively independent. The colonial administration and the Tutsi elite collaborated to take away the more diverse traditional government forms through which the Hutu in particular could play one authority against another into a more simplified and powerful system. A system of taxes payable either in money or with labour was developed and exploited, with colonial support, by unscrupulous Tutsi chiefs who took advantage of free labour from Hutu civilians.

Altogether we see a situation that is not well explained by primordialism, but which fits well with dual colonialism theory. How do other theories fit into this situation?

Ethnicity as Epiphenomenal

The word *epiphenomenal* describes a secondary effect or phenomenon that arises from, but does not causally influence, a separate phenomenon. Marx was the first to apply it in a sociological context. He believed that economic structure was the main causal factor in society, and everything else was epiphenomenal, or insignificant.

When applied to ethnicity, the epiphenomenal theory suggests that any ethnic conflict is really just a byproduct of the struggle between economic classes. Thus, the strife in Rwanda stems from a situation in which the country's rich and powerful (the Tutsi elite) were exploiting its poor (the Hutu and the poorer Tutsi). Ethnicity was just a smokescreen, a false consciousness that made it impossible for poorer Hutu and Tutsi with shared class interests to overcome oppression by the Tutsi elite. This lasted through the 1950s, when Hutu of all classes shared what Newbury termed a "cohesion of oppression," until 1962, when the country became independent and witnessed a social revolution that replaced the Tutsi elite with a Hutu one. The Hutu elite used the pretense of democracy to gain broader Hutu support. There is a measure of truth in the epiphenomenal explanation, yet it fails to fully account for why the poor would identify with the rich.

Instrumentalism

Traditionally presented in direct opposition to primordialism and compatible with the epiphenomenal approach is instrumentalism, which focuses on emerging ethnicity rather than on long-established ethnic characteristics. It acknowledges that elites can mobilize others who identify with them ethnically. Ethnic identification and action come from a competition for scarce resources for and by the elite. In Newbury's words, ethnic groups are created or transformed when

> groups gain self-awareness (become "self-conscious communities") largely as the result of the activities of leaders who mobilize ethnic followings in order to compete more effectively. Improved communications and the spread of writing are important in this process; so is "ethnic learning," where groups develop ethnic awareness as a result of seeing others using ethnic solidarities to compete. The state is important, instrumentalists suggest, as an arena in which competition between these groups occurs (the state controls many of the scarce resources over which elites are competing), and also because government policies can significantly affect the strategies chosen by ethnic leaders. (Newbury 1993: 15)

Elite members who mobilize ethnicity for personal gain are called **ethnic entrepreneurs**. Examples of ethnic entrepreneurship include Adolf Hitler's construction and manipulation of the German "Aryan race," and Slobodan Milošević's use of Serb ethnic symbols to achieve and maintain dictatorial power in the former Yugoslavia. An instrumentalist approach better explains how a frustrated Hutu leadership could invoke the injustice of Tutsi elite oppression to draw poorer Hutu into their political parties and their acts of revolution.

Social Constructionism

Social constructionism is the view that ethnicity is constructed by individuals for varying social purposes. Instrumentalism can be considered a partly formed version of social constructionism in that it shows how ethnicity is constructed by the elite; however, it suffers as a theory of ethnicity and ethnic action by overstating the influence and impact of the elite. It generally fails to attribute the non-elite members any agency, any power to choose and act without being manipulated. A social constructionist theory of ethnicity would look to the motivations of the broader group.

The social constructionist approach makes sense in the case of Rwanda, where it helps to explain why the general rural population of the Hutu became so thoroughly engaged in driving off and killing local Tutsi (often neighbours). Rwanda was, for most of the twentieth century, a very crowded land, with many people, particularly Hutu, becoming regularly malnourished because their working farms were insufficient for their needs. Unlike in the nineteenth century, when there was considerably more space and people could move to new land in difficult situations, during the twentieth century people suffered through various famines and cattle diseases while the country's rise in population shrank farm size. Drive your neighbours out, and your family has an improved chance of survival.

Summary

So what can our five approaches to studying ethnicity tell us about the Hutu and Tutsi in Rwanda? We can say that by the middle of the nineteenth century, some people in the area were taller and were more likely to herd cattle, but being a member of an ethnic group was not a major part of the day-to-day lives of most Rwandans—not like lineage, region, and sometimes individual chiefdom or kingdom. First with the growth in power and widespread influence of the king (who was Tutsi) and his court working toward the development of a modern state, and then, more tellingly, from the effects of colonialism (first German, then Belgian), a dual colonialism developed in which Europeans and elite Tutsi collaborated to put social, economic, and political substance to an increasingly rigid "ethnic" divide between Hutu and Tutsi. And when, in the 1950s, European colonialism began to fade in Rwanda, the common oppression experienced by Hutu of all classes, particularly the peasant class, led to a social revolution in which the majority Hutu overthrew their oppressors, only to set up an ethnic dictatorship of their own. Ethnic violence was a not surprising effect, and an easily fanned racial hatred, combined with a powerful need for land, led in 1994 to the massacre of the Tutsi.

Ethnicity in Canada: Classic Studies

Ethnic Class: English and French in Quebec

When **Everett C. Hughes** (1897–1983) joined the sociology department at McGill in 1927, the focus of his research became the "ethnic division of labour" between the English, who held positions of power, and the French, who occupied the lowest rung of the employment ladder. This was an injustice he wished to correct.

During the 1930s, Hughes studied the small industrial city of Drummondville, summarizing the results of his research in *French Canada in Transition* (1945). In the book, he talks about two principal kinds of industries he found in Drummondville. First, there were small, local, French-Canadian–run industries, which "do not make the town grow but proliferate and grow with it" (Hughes 1963 [1945]: 47). Second, and more important, were what he called "*nos grandes industries.*" The top 9 of these 11 "big industries" had headquarters in Montreal, England, and the United States; their managers were Americans, English Canadians, and British nationals. In 1937, the largest of these industries, a textile company, employed 389 "English and Others" and 2,337 French workers. The former group occupied 24 of the 25 positions above the foreman level and 57 of the 82 foreman's jobs. The vast majority of the French-Canadian employees

(1,882) were on the "factory floor," involved directly in textile production (Hughes 1963: 55).

In a mid-century study of intergenerational (father to son) occupational mobility, Yves de Jocas and Guy Rocher (1957) found that anglophones in Quebec cities scored much higher than francophones (11.8 per cent versus 3.2 per cent) in the occupational category they called "professional, proprietor, manager," and that

Telling It Like It Is

A First-Hand POV

Ethnicity and Class in Sept-Îles during the 1960s and 1970s

Sept-Îles is located on the north shore of the Gulf of St Lawrence, in Quebec. During the 1960s and early 1970s it was often described in superlatives, thanks to a couple of American-owned mining companies. Iron ore had been discovered in the 1950s in the Quebec–Labrador peninsula. Consequently, the Iron Ore Company of Canada and Wabush Mines set up shop. The Quebec North Shore and Labrador Railway delivered the ore to Sept-Îles from the mines nearly 600 kilometres north of town. Sept-Îles was for a while the richest city in Canada in per capita income and the biggest port in terms of sheer tonnage shipped.

Originally a fishing village with a few hundred people, it grew rapidly. At its peak, it had a population of about 35,000, about 85–90 per cent French-speaking and about 10 per cent English-speaking. A small minority were Innu. They had a reserve in town and another about 15–20 kilometres east of town.

Many of the English-speaking population came from Atlantic Canada, seeking employment outside their traditionally impoverished areas. There were also many Europeans and Americans. The former brought skilled trades and professional training with them. Many of the French-speaking population were from Gaspé and the south shore of the St Lawrence.

Even as a young boy, I could discern disparities within the community. There were two better neighbourhoods in town, known locally as "Executive Point" and "the Wabush Ghetto." These areas were where the executives of the two companies lived. Although small—only a dozen or so houses in each—they were the most desirable areas of town. They were where power and money resided in the community. The residents were almost entirely English-speaking.

Within the companies, it seemed that there were unwritten rules. Unilingual French speakers could not aspire to a position above foreman, and they would be very lucky indeed to reach assistant foreman level speaking only French. The opposite was true with unilingual English speakers: the sky was the limit. The top executives, more often than not, were brought in from the parent companies in the United States.

I spent two summers working on the railroad and got to see these disparities first-hand. Most of the foremen were English-speaking; some were bilingual, and some were not. The French-speaking foremen inevitably spoke English as well as their native tongue. Unfortunately, there were many people who simply did not think they had to learn French. They believed it was up to French-speaking Québécois to learn English. I knew far too many such people.

There were a number of French-speaking schools and two English-speaking school systems: public and Catholic. There was a movement at the English-speaking public school I attended to have a school uniform. The daughters of Executive Point made monthly trips on the company plane to Montreal, a thousand kilometres away, to buy clothes. Keeping up with the daughters of the executives was a costly prospect, so a school uniform was adopted.

The uniform did have a levelling effect, with less competition over fashionable clothing. But, I cannot help but think that the school uniform, so visible as we walked home and to the shopping centre after school each day, contributed to a sense of divisiveness within the community. It was clear that the anglophones held the best jobs and, in some cases, lived in the best neighbourhoods. Here was the symbolic marker, paraded by their youths.

—Bryan Cummins

the discrepancy among their sons was even greater (17.3 per cent versus 6.8 per cent, as cited in Langlois 1999: 73). This suggested that the ethnic division of labour was increasing. John Porter, in *The Vertical Mosaic*, observed a similar growing separation (see Table 10.1). French-Canadian sociologists Jacques Dofny and Marcel Rioux (1962) described this separation as the phenomenon of **ethnic class**, in which people of a particular ethnicity belong predominantly to one class.

The balance shifted somewhat during the Quiet Revolution of the 1960s. The Quiet Revolution is the name given to a set of actions and policies that, together, represented an attempt by a growing educated, skilled, and urban middle class to overthrow three social bodies that combined to restrict the people: (1) the English-dominated large businesses; (2) the Union Nationale, a provincial political party that exerted great conservative control through the rurally supported premier Maurice Duplessis (1936–9 and 1944–59); and (3) the Catholic Church, which had a firm grip on education, the press, and the unions. In large measure, the decrease in inequality between French and English was brought about by provincial policies and practices, designed in part by sociologists, enacted as part of a concerted effort to make French Canadians *maîtres chez nous* ("masters in our own house").

John Porter and the Vertical Mosaic

The best-known book of Canadian sociology is *The Vertical Mosaic: An Analysis of Social Class and Power in Canada* (1965) by **John Porter** (1921–1979). Porter's title derives from the often-stated notion that Canadian society more closely resembles a "cultural mosaic" than a "melting pot." The term **cultural mosaic** applies to societies in which individual ethnic, cultural, and religious groups are able to maintain separate identities (a mosaic is a type of artwork made up of many tiles that lend different colours to the picture). The opposite model is the **melting pot**, where immigrating ethnic, cultural, and religious groups are encouraged to assimilate into their new society. It is the term typically used to describe American society.

Porter's **vertical mosaic** refers to a hierarchy, or ranking, of higher and lower ethnic, cultural, and religious groups. To keep with the metaphor of the mosaic, Porter found that the different tiles were stacked, not placed evenly, with the tiles representing white Anglo-Saxon Protestants on top.

Landmarks in the Sociological Study of "Race"

As we have seen earlier, standpoint theory suggests that the perspective a sociological researchers bring to her work is strongly influenced by her "social location"—her gender, age, ethnicity, and sexual orientation. This does not mean that sociologists can and should study only "their own people." But it does mean that the pioneers in the sociological study of specific groups—women, for instance, or black people—are often those who belong to the group themselves, and that they have unique and valuable insights that everyone can learn from. In this section we will look at the work of some pioneers in the sociological study of "race" and ethnicity.

W.E.B. Du Bois: First Black Sociologist

W.E.B. Du Bois (1868–1963) was the first African-American sociologist. He researched and wrote about the major problems and concerns of Africans, both those living in the United States and those living in the rest of the world. He was a "pan-Africanist," one who sees the connection between the oppression or success of Africans and that of their descendants around the world.

Du Bois's sociology had a definite applied perspective to it. He was one of the founders of the NAACP (the National Association for the Advancement of Colored People). He used his position as editor-in-chief of its magazine, *Crisis*, to advocate for such varied causes as opening up training schools for black military officers and initiating legal action against white people

Table 10.1 Percentage of francophones and anglophones in the professional and financial sectors, 1931–61

YEAR	FRANCOPHONE (%)	ANGLOPHONE (%)	DIFFERENCE (%)
1931	6.2	7.1	0.9
1951	6.0	7.2	1.2
1961	7.8	9.3	1.5

Adapted from Porter (1965). Original data taken from the following volumes of *The Census of Canada*: 1931, vol. 7, Table 49; 1951, vol. 4, Table 12; 1961, vol. 3.1–15, Table 22.

who lynched African Americans. He was a prolific writer, known for several landmark studies, including *The Suppression of the African Slave Trade in America* (1896); his comprehensive study of Philadelphia's black slums, *The Philadelphia Negro* (1896); *The Souls of Black Folks* (1903); *Black Reconstruction* (1935); and *Dusk of Dawn* (1940). The following captures the oratorical power and sense of fairness of his writing:

> [I]t is the duty of black men to judge the South discriminatingly. The present generation of Southerners are not responsible for the past, and they should not be blindly hated or blamed for it. . . . The South is not "solid"; it is a land in the ferment of social change, wherein forces of all kinds are fighting for supremacy; and to praise the ill the South is today perpetuating is just as wrong as to condemn the good. Discriminating and broadminded criticism is what the South needs—needs it for the sake of her own white sons and daughters, and for the insurance of robust, healthy mental and moral development.

Today even the attitude of the Southern whites toward the blacks is not . . . in all cases the same; the ignorant Southerner hates the Negro, the workingmen fear his competition, the money-makers wish to use him as a laborer, some of the educated see a menace in his upward development, while others . . . wish to help him to rise. National opinion has enabled this last class to maintain the Negro common schools, and to protect the Negro partially in property, life, and limb. Through the pressure of the money-makers, the Negro is in danger of being reduced to semi-slavery . . . ; the workingmen, and those of the educated who fear the Negro, have united to disfranchise him . . . while the passions of the ignorant are easily aroused to lynch and abuse any black man. To praise this intricate whirl of thought and prejudice is nonsense; to inveigh indiscriminately against "the South" is unjust. . . . (Du Bois 1903)

What do YOU think?

There is an American organization called the Association of Black Sociologists, founded in 1970 "by women and men of African descent," but which is not confined in its membership to people of African heritage.

1. Why do you think the founders of this organization felt such an organization was necessary?

2. Do you think it is important that such an organization exists today?

Daniel G. Hill: First Black Canadian Sociologist

The face of sociology in Canada has been almost exclusively a white face. Finding a South Asian, black, East Asian, or Aboriginal sociologist who has had an impact is not easy. **Daniel G. Hill** (1923–2003) is an exception. Although he was not born in Canada, he is considered the first black Canadian sociologist.

Hill studied sociology at the University of Toronto, receiving his MA in 1951 and his PhD in 1960. His primary writings include *Negroes in Toronto: A Sociological Study of a Minority Group* (1960) and *The Freedom Seekers: Blacks in Early Canada* (1981). But it is mainly in applied work that Hill's sociology is expressed. He was a researcher for the Social Planning Council of Metropolitan Toronto (1955–8), executive secretary of the North York Social Planning Council

W.E.B. Du Bois, after receiving an honorary degree from the University of Ghana, Accra, on the afternoon of his ninety-fifth birthday, 23 February 1963.

(1958–60), and assistant director of the Alcoholism and Drug Addiction Research Foundation (1960). In 1962, Hill became the first full-time director of the Ontario Human Rights Commission, and 10 years later, he became Ontario Human Rights Commissioner. He formed his own human rights consulting firm in 1973, working at various times for the Metropolitan Police Service, the Canadian Labour Congress, and the

government of British Columbia. From 1984 to 1989, he served as Ontario's ombudsman, fielding complaints from citizens concerning their treatment by provincial government agencies. In 1999 he was made a Member of the Order of Canada.

Crenshaw, Collins, and Intersectionality Theory: Tracking "Race" and Gender

Intersectionality has become an important word in current sociological research. As we saw in Chapter 2, it refers to the way different social factors—particularly ethnicity and gender, but also sexuality, class, age, and ability—combine to shape the experience of a minoritized group. It recognizes that, for instance, the discrimination and prejudice experienced by a young black woman is different to the discrimination and prejudice experienced by a man who is black.

Intersectionality theory was first developed in the context of black feminist thought by **Kimberlé Crenshaw** (b. 1959), and then elaborated shortly thereafter by critical sociologist **Patricia Hill Collins** (b. 1948) in

What do YOU think?

1. Do you think it is more likely that a black Canadian sociologist would get involved in human rights work than a white Canadian sociologist would? Why?

2. How do you balance the need to ensure that minoritized groups are well represented in citizen's groups against the perception that a black or Asian committee member is a token appointment, hired simply to give the group the appearance of diversity? What kind of appointment does Hill seem like to you?

[*left*] In his work as director of the Ontario Human Rights Commission and, later, as ombudsman of Ontario, Daniel Hill reached out to Ontarians of all ethnic and cultural backgrounds. The pamphlet shown here testifies to the importance he placed on the accessibility of his position to all citizens of the province. [*right*] Daniel G. Hill, ombudsman of Ontario, circa 1985.

The Point Is...

Idle No More: A Women's Ethnic Movement

At its heart, Idle No More is an Aboriginal *women's* movement. After all, who else would have thought of flash mob round dances as a form of protest? More seriously, it is because it is essentially about alliance with other Canadians rather than separation that you can see that it is an Aboriginal women's movement.

Idle No More was the brainchild of four Saskatchewan women, including three Cree and a white author and lawyer, who began the movement in November 2012 and coined its famous byword. They were inspired to act by their opposition to the anti-environmental and anti-Aboriginal sections of the federal Conservative government's omnibus Bill C-45. They started their personal move from "idleness" by organizing a series of teach-ins, beginning in Saskatoon, then extending to Regina and Prince Albert. Once it hit social media with the hashtag #idlenomore, the movement grew exponentially. The movement gained further momentum in December, when Attawapiskat chief Theresa Spence added her voice to the cause to draw attention to the hideous housing conditions in her James Bay Cree community. She went on a 43-day hunger strike, drinking only liquids while waiting for the prime minister to travel the short physical distance, but long democracy distance, to meet with her.

The women behind Idle No More are principally opposed to the one-sided dismantling of the Indian Act. All agree that the Indian Act must change, but this requires a release of power and control by the federal government. Stephen Harper's Conservative government is quite happy to give up its legal duties, but it does not want to surrender power and control. Another big goal of Idle No More, one that resonates particularly with Aboriginal women as traditional keepers of the land, is protection of our rivers, lakes, and oceans—a cause that affects all Canadians.

Activism in Canada's First Nation community has long been riven by a gender division. Men are overrepresented in the Assembly of First Nations, while women are underrepresented in the Aboriginal political organization. This reflects the gendering effect and loss of women's power enacted by over a century of federal legislation: until 1985, status Indian women who married non-status men lost their own official Indian status. They could not vote in band council elections until 1951. This power imbalance was not traditional: one-quarter of the Aboriginal groups in Canada were matrilineal (determining kinship on the female side). Historically, treaties were often signed not just by male chiefs but by prominent women as well. The Idle No More movement should be considered successful at least in part if it acts to redress the gender balance among the people.

her landmark work *Black Feminist Thought: Knowledge, Consciousness and the Politics of Empowerment* (1990). The theory argues against the notion, espoused by some early white liberal feminists, that all women experience prejudice and discrimination in the same way and to the same degree. Early intersectionality theorists took exception to this claim, arguing that gender is in fact experienced differently and with unique forms of oppression when combined with social locations that are negatively valued, particularly those social locations associated with "race" and class. When combined with racial prejudice, gender-based discrimination creates what intersectionality theorists call an **interlocking matrix of domination** significantly more powerful and oppressive than gender alone.

In Canada, the interlocking matrix of domination has been experienced painfully by many Aboriginal women. Amnesty International maintains an online

Idle No More protesters make their way from Victoria Island, site of Theresa Spence's hunger strike, to Parliament Hill, in January 2013. Prior to reading this box, did you think of Idle No More as a women's movement? How do you think the participation of young Aboriginal women will change their lives?

forum devoted to the topic of violence against Aboriginal women in Canada, who are "five to seven times more likely to die as the result of violence" (www .amnesty.ca/our-work/issues/indigenous-peoples/no-more-stolen-sisters). Under the heading "No More Stolen Sisters," the website chronicles the experience of families whose sisters and daughters have gone missing, likely murdered, over the past 30 years, and calls for better policing and greater funding for organizations that help First Nation women and girls. In February 2013, the American-based advocacy group Human Rights Watch released a scathing report on Canada's missing Aboriginal women, accusing the RCMP of failing to properly investigate many of the disappearances (Mackrael & Bailey 2013). The day after the report was released, the federal government announced it would consider creating a committee on missing and murdered Aboriginal women.

WRAP IT UP

Summary

There are no human "races." There is only one. From a sociological standpoint, "race" (or, rather, *racialization*) is a social process that reflects the ways in which people of different ethnic background are treated, and have been treated over time, by institutions such as our provincial and federal justice systems, our legislative bodies, our schools, and the media. It's also about how we view one another.

Racism is also a process, one that not only appears in personal biases and discrimination but is institutionalized in society as a whole; it's not just about the "rotten apples"—when it comes to racism, the whole orchard smells. Racism certainly exists at the individual level, but it requires the support of social institutions to perpetuate itself. The good news about that is that support can be withdrawn from the features of institutions that maintain the level of racism; the apple trees can be pruned, and new trees planted and encouraged to grow.

THINK BACK

Questions for Critical Review

1. Discuss the extent to which "race" and ethnicity are social constructs.

2. Explain what is meant when we say that white people are "invisible" in Canada.

3. How is institutional, or systemic, racism different from other forms of discrimination?

4. What groups have been discriminated against by voting laws in Canada?

5. How did the Quiet Revolution change the social position of francophones in Quebec?

6. How were Ukrainians minoritized during World War I? What effect do you think that had on their participation in Canadian society for the period that immediately followed? Why do you think that stories of this minoritization are not better known in Canada?

READ ON

Online

No More Stolen Sisters: Justice for the Missing and Murdered Indigenous Women of Canada

www.amnesty.ca/our-work/issues/indigenous-peoples/no-more-stolen-sisters

Amnesty International's online forum is an important source of documentation of the missing and murdered Aboriginal women who otherwise remain invisible to mainstream Canadian society.

Canadian Race Relations Foundation / Fondation Canadienne des Relations Raciales

www.crr.ca

This government-created agency is dedicated to fighting racism in Canada. The website has information on current research, diversity education and training, and anti-racism programs, as well as an extensive catalogue of resources.

Metropolis: Enhancing Policy through Research

www.canada.metropolis.net

The Metropolis project is an integrated network involved in comparative research and public policy discussions regarding diversity and the immigrant experience in cities both in Canada and in the world.

In Print

Kay J. Anderson (1991), *Vancouver's Chinatown: Racial Discourse in Canada, 1875–1980* (Montreal: McGill-Queen's University Press).

A classic study of how "Chinese" and "Chinatown" have been expressed in the Vancouver area over a little more than a century

Himani Bannerji, ed. (1993), *Returning the Gaze: Essays on Racism, Feminism and Politics* (Toronto: Sister Vision Press).

A hard, critical look at the intersection of gender, "race," and feminism.

Agnes Calliste & George J. Sefa Dei, eds (2000), *Anti-Racist Feminism: Critical Race and Gender Studies* (Halifax: Fernwood).

A collection of readings on the intersection of gender and "race," edited by two leading anti-racist theorists.

Tamari Kitossa (2012), "Criminology and Colonialism: Counter Colonial Criminology and the Canadian Context," *The Journal of Pan African Studies*, 4, 10 (January), pp. 204–26; available at: http://www.jpanafrican.com/docs/vol4no10/4.10Criminology.pdf

Brock University sociologist Tamari Kitossa looks at how criminology in the West reproduces colonial practices of racial repression. It is an excellent example of anti-colonialist/post-colonialist thinking.

Learning Objectives

After reading this chapter, you should be able to

- explain the difference between *sex* and *gender*
- compare the four different categories of feminism outlined in this chapter
- contrast the effects of biological and sociological influences on the gender of David Reimer
- explain what is meant by the "gendering" and "feminization" of work
- state the differences among the four masculinities outlined in the section on male daycare workers
- talk about the stereotyping involved in the intersection of female gender and minoritized ethnicity/"race."

Key Terms

- bisexual
- *boyat*
- complicit masculinity
- Dragon Lady
- feminist essentialism (*or* essentialist feminism)
- feminist liberalism (*or* liberal feminism)
- feminist postmodernism (*or* postmodernist feminism)
- feminist socialism (*or* socialist feminism)
- feminization
- gay
- geisha
- gender
- gendered
- gender role
- hegemonic masculinity
- heterosexual
- homosexual
- ideology of fag
- Indian princess
- intersex
- lesbian
- LGBT
- Lotus Blossom Baby
- marginalized masculinity
- metrosexual
- pay equity
- queer
- queer theory
- scientific management
- sex
- squaw
- subordinate masculinity
- tabula rasa
- Taylorism
- transgender
- transsexual

Names to Know

- Henrietta Muir Edwards
- Nellie McClung
- Louise McKinney
- Emily Murphy
- Irene Parlby

A portrait of the author as he sees himself.

A portrait of the author as he is.

What It Means to Be a Man

How flexible are we concerning gender roles?

Most of us like to think we're very flexible, both in the way we act and in the way we perceive others. But I have to be honest. Although I feel "secure in my masculinity," as they say, there are a number of things that I—a Toronto-bred white man in my early sixties—will not do because they're inconsistent with my own sense of being male, and with the sense of maleness I wish to project to others. For instance, I will not:

- carry or use an umbrella (in part from having lived in Newfoundland, where a "real man" is not afraid of getting wet)
- use a hair dryer (despite having really long hair—it seems effeminate to me to blow my hair around like I'm in a shampoo commercial)
- use one of those convenient book and file carriers on wheels, the ones that remind me of a flight attendant's suitcase (a man should carry a briefcase or a backpack)
- wear clothes that are yellow, orange, or pink

(high-school classmates of mine wearing those colours were given a hard time concerning their masculinity)
- use a snowblower instead of a shovel (real men aren't afraid of heaving snow); the same goes for leaf-blowers (rakes are easy to operate: skinny end up, wide end down)
- spend longer than five minutes getting dressed or fifteen minutes in any one clothing store
- clip favourite recipes from a magazine (man's food is that which may be fried, barbecued, or nuked in a microwave)
- shake hands in a "wimpy way" (a Canadian man is still judged by how strong his handshake is; I don't make a contest of it—as some do—but I try to meet a minimum standard)
- wear a cologne or "body spray" (women should smell good; men should try not to smell bad)
- colour my hair (or my beard)
- use the word *lovely* without being sarcastic
- have a manicure or a pedicure.

And of course, real men don't eat quiche or ask directions, so I don't do those things, either. And when I first became a stepfather and my very shy eight-year-old stepson wanted to hold my hand in public, I felt *extremely* uncomfortable (but I still did it).

It's important to note that this list reflects the perspective, or standpoint, of a mature white man. I'd like (younger) male readers to think about this list. Do you share my inflexibility on these issues? Be honest. What other things will you not do out of male pride? Women readers can set us straight. Would you be bothered if you knew the young man sitting next to you was having weekly manicures?

I was interviewed about my sense of fashion for a student newspaper last year. I referred to myself as a "rural-sexual" (because I live in a small town—it had nothing to do with livestock). I was having fun with the term **metrosexual**. What is interesting about that term is that it appears to have very different definitions, depending especially on whether a man or a woman uses it. While both male and female students can identify actors or other celebrities who can be classed as metrosexual, they are not in total agreement about what it means. It may, as some suggest, refer to "a man who takes care of himself," but for a woman that typically refers to serious mirror and clothing store time, while for a man, it often suggests taking care of his body by working out. I have found that it's still an uncomfortable label for many men, for whom, I suspect, "metrosexual" sounds a little too much like a euphemism for "gay."

Now comes the critical perspective. *Why* do we feel the way we do? And how flexible are gender roles in Canadian culture? Here are two other scenarios to consider:

1. *How would you feel if your son took an interest in figure skating?* One of my nephews, when he first learned to skate, became really interested in figure skating. He took lessons for two years before he eventually quit, in large part, I suspect, because his father didn't encourage him. To give my brother-in-law credit, he never made fun of the sport, but I don't think he gave his budding figure skater the kind of support he might have given a budding hockey player.

2. What's your reaction to women who box or who play rugby? Is your reaction more negative than it is towards female figure skaters or tennis players? Or more positive?

Compare notes on the topics above with your classmates. You're likely to find a fair bit of disagreement. That's because as inflexible as we might be when it comes to how we see gender, we all—men and women, homosexuals and heterosexuals, blacks and whites and Arabs and Asians, and so on and so on—see gender differently.

So: how do you see your own gender role? What socializing influences in your life have conditioned your view?

What do YOU think?

How long do you think it will be before young men are comfortable identifying as "metrosexual"? Will differing male and female definitions of the term come closer together?

Introduction: Gender and Sex—What's the Difference?

Gender is a highly contested area within sociology. Sociologists theorizing about gender and gender roles differ sharply, particularly on the degree to which gender is determined by either culture or biology. Even the absolute duality (male–female) of gender is contested. Not surprisingly, the greatest part of the critical work on gender has been carried out by feminist scholars, reflecting the (now) obvious fact that before the women's movement of the 1960s and 1970s, male sociologists had done an inadequate job on the subject.

Gender is different from *sex*. British sociologist Ann Oakley formally distinguished the two when she stated that **sex** refers to "the biological division into male and female," while **gender** refers to "the parallel and socially unequal division into femininity and masculinity" (Oakley 1972). *Gender*, in other words, is a sociological term that refers to the roles and characteristics society assigns to women and men; it typically carries with it notions of men and women's inequality. *Sex* refers merely to anatomical or biological characteristics of women and men. At the individual level, we could say that sex is what you're born with, but that gender is how you choose to see yourself, and how you live your life.

Another key term is **gender role**. This is a set of attitudes and expectations concerning behaviour that relates to being male or female. Think of a gender role as being similar to a movie role. It is a part we're assigned at birth, based on our sex. How we play it reflects what we understand about what it means to act as either a female or a male. Gender roles differ across cultures, both in content—in the specific expectations society holds for each gender—and in the severity or permissiveness with which society treats those whose behaviour contravenes the expectations for their gender.

In this chapter we will be looking at sex and gender, but if you think you're not getting enough sex, you

The Point Is...

Sex and Gender: A Primer

Sex refers to the differences between the categories *male* and *female*, based on biology. **Gender** refers to the social expectations that surround these biological categories. Sex categories are fairly absolute; gender categories are not—some argue that gender is better seen as a continuum extending from femaleness to maleness.

A **heterosexual** is sexually attracted to people of the opposite sex. A **homosexual** is sexually attracted to people of the same sex; **gay** and **queer** are, today, accepted (but informal) synonyms. A **lesbian** is a woman homosexual.

A **bisexual** is sexually attracted to people of both sexes. The following beliefs about bisexuality are *not accurate*:

✗ that having an early (i.e. shortly after the onset of puberty) sexual experience with someone of the same sex and then later having only heterosexual experiences makes a person, by definition, bisexual

✗ that bisexuality implies equal attraction to both sexes

✗ that bisexuals are really gays and lesbians who are in denial because of social pressure.

Concerning the last point, a longitudinal study by Rosario, et al., revealed that roughly two-thirds of youths who self-identified as bisexual maintained that self-identification over time; only a third of the youths later described themselves as gay or lesbian.

A **transgender** person is someone who either (a) does not conform to the gender role associated with his or her biological sex, or (b) does not self-identify with the biological sex assigned to him or her at birth.

The abbreviation LGBT (lesbian, gay, bisexual, transgender) is an all-encompassing term for anyone who is not heterosexual. An *I* is sometimes added to the initialism to denote intersex people (see below).

A **transsexual** is either someone with the physical characteristics of one sex and a persistent desire to belong to the other, or someone who has had surgery (or who is undergoing surgery) to have his or her sex changed surgically.

An **intersex** person is someone with both male and female sexual characteristics. It is a biological condition that may produce in an individual an atypical combination of male and female chromosomes (resulting in an XX male or an XY female, rather than the usual XY male and XX female) or both male and female genitals or secondary sexual characteristics.

What do YOU think?

1. Intersex characters have appeared in recent popular fiction, including Japanese manga (comic books, to older readers) and Jeffrey Eugenides's 2002 novel *Middlesex*, although the fascination goes all the way back to a character from Greek mythology, Hermaphroditus, who was physically joined with his lover, Salmacis, in one body that retained the characteristics of both sexes. Why do you think there is so much interest in this condition?

2. Why do you think people argue that those who identify themselves as bisexual are really homosexuals in denial?

[*Left*] Caster Semenya won the silver medal in the women's 800 m final at the 2012 summer Olympics in London. Three years earlier, the South African runner missed a year of competition while track and field's governing body, the IAAF, investigated claims that her body produced testosterone in levels far greater than those found in most women. Semenya was cleared to compete, but in April 2011, the IAAF established new gender verification guidelines, based on a maximum level of testosterone an athlete may possess in order to compete as a woman. Can gender be measured? Do you think it would be fair to make an intersex athlete who identifies as a woman compete against men because of her testosterone levels? [*Right*] Jenna Talackova appeared in the 2012 Miss Universe Canada pageant after initially being disqualified because she was born male. Do you think the transsexual beauty queen should have been allowed to take part in the women-only competition?

might be disappointed. Most of this chapter concerns gender, specifically how society views the categories "male" and "female," and how we—with considerable variation—interpret and live out our roles as "men," "women," and categories in between.

Feminism and Gender Theory: Four Categories

As we noted earlier, much of the critical work on gender theory has been carried out by feminist sociologists. In this section, we'll look at four different strains of feminist theory and how each one approaches the study of gender. We borrow here the categories laid out by Beatrice Kachuck in "Feminist Social Theories: Theme and Variations" (2003 [1995]):

- feminist liberalism
- feminist essentialism
- feminist socialism
- feminist postmodernism.

Feminist Liberalism

Feminist liberalism (or **liberal feminism**), Kachuck explains, "identifies women as a class entitled to rights as women" (Kachuck 2003: 81). In terms of gender roles, this approach values the contributions of women in the public realm of the workplace and

examines whether women receive fair pay for the work they do. In this sense, it is associated with the fight for **pay equity**, the guarantee that women in traditionally

Our Stories

David Reimer: Assigning Gender

In May 2004, 38-year-old David Reimer of Winnipeg committed suicide. His decision to take his life was likely influenced by his separation from his wife, the loss of his job, and the suicide death of his twin brother two years earlier. But there is a deeper, older cause that must be cited, too. David was the victim of a medical accident that was compounded by an unsuccessful social experiment.

As infants, David and his brother were both circumcised electronically using an experimental method. During David's circumcision, too much electricity was applied, and his penis was badly burned. There was no chance it could be even surgically repaired. Desperate for a solution, David's parents consulted numerous specialists. At the time, a psychological school of thought known as behaviourism, which emphasized the power of socialization (nurture) over biology (nature), was popular. It was held in high regard by some feminist psychologists (both male and female), as it supported the notion that gender and gender roles were not "natural" but taught. In its extreme version, behaviourism advanced the theory that each of us starts out as a **tabula rasa**, or blank slate, on which our social environment writes our lives. A proponent of this school, the psychologist Dr John Money of Johns Hopkins University in Baltimore, was one of the specialists contacted by David's parents. He persuaded them to have David castrated and

given female hormones, and to rename their child "Brenda," to be raised as a girl.

Money's articles made the "John/Joan" case study famous. They claimed that David was adapting successfully to his new gender, socially taught and hormonally enhanced. But the doctor's view of the situation was based more on wishes than on facts. In *As Nature Made Him*, John Colapinto shows that David's childhood was highly conflicted. He felt he was male, not female, and preferred to play with boys than with girls. He wasn't told he had been born male until he was 13, when his parents, under pressure from Dr Money, approached him about allowing surgeons to create a vagina. David rebelled and several times attempted suicide. He abandoned his female identity and sought out surgery, which he eventually received, to have his male sex restored. He later married and had stepchildren, but the effects of both the accident and the social experiment never left him.

David Reimer's tragic case illustrates that while gender is a social construct, it has a strong biological component. It also shows, as recent research confirms (Kruijver et al. 2000), that gender has a neurological component in addition to the biological features of genitals and hormones: the brain helps to shape our gender. It also clearly demonstrates the dangers of allowing social theory to impose itself into unthinking social practice.

What do YOU think?

1. In what way(s) can we say that David Reimer was neurologically male? How could we argue that he was not a gender "tabula rasa"?

2. How could we study individuals to determine the extent to which their gender roles are natural versus taught/learned?

female-dominated industries (nursing, childcare, library science, for instance) receive compensation similar to the salaries of those working in comparable (in terms of educational qualifications required, hours worked, and social value) professions that are typically dominated by men. Think of it this way: if we value our children so much, why do we pay so little to those in primary and early childhood education, who play such an important role in the social and educational development of our children? Feminist liberalism is credited with securing benefits for women on maternity leave, including the rights to claim employment insurance and to return to the same or an equivalent job in the same company after a fixed period of time (up to a year in Canada).

Criticism of feminist liberalism and its view of gender roles centres around the idea that it universalizes the position of white, middle-class, heterosexual, Western women. It fails to recognize that the social location of this category of women enables them to receive benefits not available to other women. White, middle-class women in Europe and North America are the main beneficiaries of the gains that feminist liberalism has obtained; it has been considerably less successful in promoting the interests of women who differ in terms of class, ethnicity, sexual orientation, and nationality.

Feminist Essentialism

While feminist liberalism concentrates essentially on making women equal to men in terms of employment opportunities and salary, **feminist essentialism** (or **essentialist feminism**) looks at differences between the way women and men *think*, and argues for equality—or female superiority—in that difference. Women's morality (Gilligan 1982) and their "maternal thinking" (Ruddick 1989) involve social norms that are more or less "natural" to them. Added to this is the idea that this morality is negatively valued in a *patriarchal* society (i.e. one dominated by and favouring male roles, views, and ideas). For Kachuck, feminist essentialism is useful in that it

generates profound questions. Should we understand women in terms of patriarchal constructions

In 2011, the story of a Toronto couple who refused to disclose to friends and family the sex of their newborn went viral. Having raised two children who were sometimes teased for failing to conform to gender stereotypes, the couple wanted their third child, Storm, to grow up without the pressure to fulfill a particular gender role. Given that contemporary Canadian society sets clear boundaries between the sexes, how far do you think that parents can go in trying to raise their children relatively free of gender scripts? Is there a point, do you think, when sex takes over?

or value their models of human ideals? How is women's sexuality to be comprehended outside of patriarchal visions? How do women resist control? (Kachuck 2003: 66–7).

Kachuck presents the criticisms of the feminist essentialist approach to gender thinking in terms of what other Western feminists think and also in terms of what feminists in India have to say. In the eyes of the first, she writes, feminist essentialism has the following shortcomings:

- It universalizes women, assuming erroneously that all experience gender alike.
- It confuses natural phenomena with women's strategies for coping with patriarchal demands.
- It invites continued perceptions of women as social housekeepers in worlds that men build. (Kachuck 2003: 66)

She adds that feminists in India have their own concerns about feminist essentialism:

The Point Is...

Patriarchy and the Bible

The holy books of the largest established religious traditions were developed in the context of specific cultures. The Judeo-Christian and Islamic sacred texts emerged out of pastoral cultures, societies engaged in the herding of animals such as sheep, goats, camels, or cows as the primary means of obtaining food. Pastoral cultures are most often patriarchal in ideology, with males significantly dominant over females. Some theorists attribute a perceived patriarchal bias concerning gender roles in the holy books to the patriarchal ideology prevalent at the time the books were written.

The Words of Paul the Apostle

"A man . . . is the image and glory of God; but woman is the glory of man. For man was not made from woman, but woman from man. Neither man created from woman, but woman for man." (1 Corinthians 11: 7–9)

"As in all the churches of the saints, the women should keep silence in the churches. For they are not permitted to speak, but should be subordinate, as even the law says. If there is anything they desire to know, let them ask their husbands at home. For it is shameful for a woman to speak in church." (1 Corinthians 14: 33–5)

"Wives, be subject to your husbands, as to the Lord. For the husband is the head of the wife as Christ is the head of the church. . . . As the church is subject to Christ, so let wives also be subject in everything to their husbands." (Ephesians 5: 22–4)

"Let a woman learn in silence with all submissiveness. I permit no woman to teach or to have authority over men; she is to keep silent. For Adam was formed first, then Eve; and Adam was not deceived, but the woman was deceived and became a transgressor. Yet woman will be saved through bearing children, if she continues in faith and love and holiness, with modesty." (1 Timothy 2: 11–15)

What do YOU think?

1. What do these statements say about the culture that Paul was part of?
2. Do you think that statements such as these have influenced the fact that the Catholic church does not allow women to hold mass or have any position of power? How else do you think statements such as these have been used to influence Western thought concerning gender roles?

Indian feminists deplore assumptions of women's inherent caring function as an ideology that impedes their full human development. Thus, essays on education critique practices that socialize girls for dedication to family service. . . . This puts them [Indian feminists] in opposition to calls for women's devotion to families as their national identity. (Kachuck 2003: 66)

In sum, then, while feminist essentialism speaks constructively about the potential for women's differences from men to be positively valued, it can fall into the trap of generalizing from the Western model—a trap that Western social scientists of all stripes have often fallen into.

Feminist Socialism

Feminist socialists (or **socialist feminists**), according to Kachuck, have to "revise their Marxism so as to account for gender, something that Marx ignored. They want sexuality and gender relations included in analyses of society" (Kachuck 2003: 67). According to this school of thought, there is insight to be gained from looking at the intersections of oppression between class and gender. The struggles faced by, and resources available to, lower-class women can be different from those of middle- and upper-class women, and feminist socialism is useful in identifying these. Still, there is the danger that factors such as "race," ethnicity, and sexual orientation get overlooked in the focus on class. Black women in North America face some of the same difficulties of prejudice and stereotyping regardless of whether they come from the upper or lower classes.

Feminist Postmodernism

Feminist postmodernism (or **postmodernist feminism**) takes the strongest social-constructionist position, a position almost diametrically opposed to that of feminist essentialism. Some postmodernists even contest the widely held view that all women are biologically *all female*, and all men are *all male*. Feminist postmodernists refer to women more as subjects than as objects of sociological study, allowing the perspective of the women studied to guide their research. Standpoint theory is an important aspect of this category of feminism.

Another methodology that fits within the broad-ranging perspective of feminist postmodernism is **queer theory**, first articulated in the book *Gender Trouble* (1990) by Judith Butler, professor of comparative literature and rhetoric at the University of California, Berkeley. Queer theory rejects the idea that male and female gender are natural binary opposites.

Serena Williams returns a shot during a match at the 2012 US Open. Although the game is becoming more and more about power rather than just strategy, women tennis players are frequently subject to negative sanctions by fans and media alike for grunting, arguing with officials, and other on-court behaviour deemed "unladylike." What does this tell you about female gender performance in a sport like tennis?

It also disputes the idea that gender identity is connected to some biological "essence," arguing instead that gender identity is related to the dramatic effect of a gender performance. Gender is seen not as each of two categories—male and female—but as a continuum with male and female at the extremes; individuals act, or perform, more one way or another along the continuum at different times and in different situations.

Telling It Like It Is   A Student POV

Gender Roles and Being Lesbian

People in my life in the past have tended to believe that because I am a lesbian, I automatically have more male-specific interests, and that I do not enjoy typical girl-oriented activities. Shortly after I told my brother, he invited me to a football game, stating, "you like football now don't you?" Although he was joking at the time, this is an example of a very typical comment often made to me. Although I may enjoy fixing things around the house, my partner is a sports fanatic, and while I like to sew and knit, she enjoys cooking and romantic comedies. The gender stereotyping, which is exactly what this comes down to, even goes so far as to include the style of clothes I wear. I remember one time that I went into work wearing a baseball cap, although I usually do not wear a hat to work, as I find it unprofessional. This particular day I was coming from school and in a rush. Immediately after entering work I began to hear comments and mutters from my co-workers. It seemed that in their eyes because I was wearing a hat, I was portraying a male characteristic and they assumed that being a lesbian is the next closest thing to being a male.

There is a significant difference between sexual orientation and gender identity. All of the gay people that I know, including myself, are very happy with their sex. They just happen to be attracted to the same sex as well. I am proud to be a woman, and I enjoy it and would not want to change that. This leads me to my next point. For one reason or another people with little understanding of the gay population seem to need a definite clarification of "who's the man and who's the woman," which is a question that I have been asked on too many occasions to count. The truth is that in many gay relationships there are no specific roles, and each individual's identity is not masculine or feminine, but it slides on a continuum. It is almost ridiculous to assume that there is a male and female figure in the relationship; after all, if I wanted a male–female partnership, I wouldn't be gay.

Another opinion that I have found many people have is that gay people, male or female, are involved in a sexual scene full of promiscuity, voyeurism, and *ménages à trois*. This is evidenced by the number of people that have made suggestive comments to me about non-committed casual sexual encounters. Although these beliefs are positive in one aspect as they break down the very untrue opinion that women cannot have the high sex drive that men are more known for, it also reflects a larger belief that being in a gay relationship is all about the sex. This leads people to believe that gay people do not commit and take part in stable, settled relationships. I remember talking with my father once about the relationship I was in and he responded, "It's alright if that's what you want, but it's unfortunate because those relationships don't last; they just don't settle." Ironically, I must say that gay relationships in fact have very little to do with sex. As a heterosexual relationship has many dimensions, so does the homosexual one, encompassing all one's needs such as emotional support, companionship, the sharing of values and spirituality, and of course, physical attraction does play its role as well. I once saw an advertisement that mocked this expectation of such extravagant sex lives. The poster was in a bookstore located in a gay community. The caption read: "What do lesbians do in bed?" and the picture had two women in bed wearing flannel pajamas, one watching television and the other reading a book. I saw this as an accurate portrayal and a clever way to challenge this opinion.

—Anonymous

Cultural configurations and norms of gender keep us from playing out a broader variety of gender performances. In this sense, gender performances are restricted by sanctions. Consider the gender performance of a male athlete crying in public, as he apologizes for having failed a drug test or having cheated on his wife. The monologue by a late-night comedian/talk-show host or the between-period comments by a former coach turned pundit might provide opportunities for popular commentators to issue negative sanctions of that kind of gender performance. Professional sport—in fact, sport in general—because it is a prominent theatre for gender performance, is a breeding ground for negative sanctions. In hockey, refusing to drop the gloves against a taunting opponent and donning a protective visor are just two actions that could incur negative sanctions drawn from what is known as the **ideology of fag**. This is a set of beliefs and sanctions that is invoked throughout society to keep people in line: if you violate a gender role, then you *must* be gay. The negative way in which this suggestion (or accusation) is presented makes it a very powerful sanction. Consider the way CBC commentator Mike Milbury, a former NHL player, coach, and general manager, invoked the ideology of fag when he characterized the movement to ban fighting from the hockey as the "pansification" of the game.

Kachuck's main criticism of feminist postmodernism (criticism that could just as easily be applied to many forms of postmodernism) is that it leads to no conclusions. It merely problematizes other people's conclusions and generates no solid criteria for judging better or worse positions, but satisfies itself with "constructing a 'feminine' space where intellectuals aggressively play out tentative ideas" (Kachuck 2003: 81).

Gendered Occupation and Education

Certain jobs, and the college and university programs preparing people to work in those jobs, are considered **gendered**. That means two things. First, one sex will be prevalent among the people employed in certain kinds of work or among the students in a particular program. When we talk about "gender prevalence" or "gender dominance," we mean that as many as 85 per cent of students or employees will be either female or male. Second, as American sociologist Paul Sargent put it, "the work itself is typically imbued with gendered meanings and defined in gendered terms"

(Sargent 2005). What this means is that, for example, the gendered profession of nursing is associated with words like "caring" and "nurturing" that are typically associated with women; nursing is thus characterized as a natural offshoot of the mother role. By contrast, the job of police officer (still often called "policeman") is described in terms of "toughness" and the "brotherhood" of officers.

In 2001, men outnumbered women by a ratio of at least 3 to 1 in the following occupations categorized by Statistics Canada:

- the primary industries of forestry, fishing, mining, and oil and gas
- utilities
- construction
- transportation and warehousing.

In the prestigious occupational fields of "professional, scientific and technical services," men outnumbered women by 14 per cent (567,800 to 431,700); in the administrative category of "business, building, and other support services," men outnumbered women by 10 per cent (352,200 to 287,000).

By comparison, women outnumbered men in the following categories:

- finance, insurance, real estate, and leasing
- educational services
- accommodation and food services
- healthcare and social assistance.

In the last of these categories, the dominance was more than 4 to 1.

Sociology students need to look at what might cause these gender specializations to occur. A place to start would be post-secondary education, where men and women typically take different routes. In both college and university, men greatly outnumber women as graduates in the engineering and applied sciences programs. For instance, in 1998–9, almost four times as many men as women received diplomas in these disciplines, and the difference grew by slightly more than 3,000 students from 1994 to 1995. In 1999–2000, men received slightly more than three times as many university degrees in the area than women did, the difference dropping slightly from 1995–6. Similarly, more than twice as many men as women received degrees in mathematics and physical sciences in 1999–2000.

On the other hand, women greatly outnumber men in college diplomas and university degrees in health professions and related occupations. This is true especially of college diplomas (where the difference is growing), which typically qualify students for less prestigious and more poorly paid occupations, such as pharmacy assistants and nursing assistants. Similarly, women dominate in fields such as social sciences and services at the community college level, and education at the university level.

In sum, there appear to be separate spheres of post-secondary education for men and women, with no sign that the trend is changing. On the contrary, in several areas—engineering and applied sciences, health sciences, and social sciences and services—the disparity seems to have grown since the early 1990s.

In Chapter 5 we looked at some of the factors that lead men and women into different programs. As Table 11.1 shows, men and women, because they typically take different routes through education, are presented with different employment opportunities once they graduate. In all age groups, there are more men than women working at full-time jobs, and more women than men working at part-time jobs. This difference is on the rise for the age groups 15–24, and 45+, especially for the latter group; only in the group aged 24–44 is the gap between the two sexes narrowing.

When looking at gender difference in occupations it is important, too, to consider relative earnings. In this area, the overall ratio does not appear to be changing. From 1992 to 2001 the earnings ratio for women to men has varied slightly from a low of 62 per cent in 1994 (when women earned 62 per cent of what men earned) to a high of 64.8 per cent in 1995. The ratio in 2001 was 64.2, slightly below the high.

The disparity in relative earnings decreases when education is taken into account. For instance, in 1993, women aged 25–34 with a university degree earned 84 per cent of what male degree-holders in the same age bracket earned. However, women aged 45–54 with university degrees earned less—just 72 per cent of what their male counterparts earned. It is interesting to note that relative earnings do not vary with age to the same degree among people holding college diplomas rather than university degrees: women diploma-holders aged 25–34 earned 75 per cent of what men earned, while those aged 45–54 earned 73 per cent.

Table 11.1 Full- and part-time gender employment, 1999–2007 (× 1,000)

AGE	FULL-TIME EMPLOYMENT			PART-TIME EMPLOYMENT		
15–24	1999	2007	CHANGE	1999	2007	CHANGE
Men	712.5	828.5	116.0	428.5	484.8	56.3
Women	510.5	606.6	96.1	554.9	669.5	114.6
Difference	202.0	221.9	**−19.9**	126.4	184.7	**+58.3**
25–44	1999	2007	CHANGE	1999	2007	CHANGE
Men	3,908.0	3,840.2	−67.8	184.3	192.5	8.2
Women	2,751.6	2,934.2	182.6	790.8	692.0	−98.8
Difference	1,156.4	906.0	**+250.4**	606.5	499.5	**−107.6**
45+	1999	2007	CHANGE	1999	2007	CHANGE
Men	2,431.7	3,241.3	803.6	200.9	301.7	100.8
Women	1,534.9	2,352.4	817.5	522.6	722.8	200.2
Difference	896.8	888.9	**+7.9**	321.7	421.1	**+99.4**

Note: The plus and minus signs denote gains and losses by women in the particular category. For instance, between 1999 and 2007, the number of 15- to 24-year-olds employed full-time rose, but the increase for men was greater (by 19,900 workers): in other words, the gap between men's and women's full-time employment increased by 19,900. Over the same span, the gap between male and female part-time workers (in which women's numbers are superior) also grew, by 58,300 workers. Overall, more women in this age category were employed part-time. How might you account for the difference?

Source: Adapted from www.statcan.ca/english/pgdb/labor and www40.statcan.ca/101/cst01/labor12.htm

Feminization of Occupations

The **feminization** of an occupational sphere occurs when a particular job, profession, or industry comes to be dominated by or predominantly associated with women. Since the start of the First World War, when women began to work outside the home in greater numbers, many occupations have become feminized, including bank teller and secretary (or, now, administrative assistant), but there are instances of job feminization occurring well before that, as the first of the two examples below describes. Typically, the feminization of an industry works to the disadvantage of those involved in it, who earn lower salaries with less job protection and fewer benefits than those enjoyed by workers outside the feminized occupational sphere.

Women's Work During the Eighteenth-Century "Gin Craze" in London

Beginning around 1720 there was a sudden rise in the sale and consumption of gin in London, England. During the so-called "gin craze," which lasted until the middle of the century, the liquor was sold not just in bars but in the streets, from wheelbarrows and baskets, in alleyway stalls, in shady one-room gin shops, and from boats floating on the Thames river.

Anyone selling gin without a licence was operating illegally. This was the case for the majority of the thousands of women involved in the gin trade, who couldn't afford the expensive licence. They operated at great risk, and were primary targets of the Gin Acts, which were passed chiefly to restrict the selling of gin to bars owned predominantly by middle-class men. Women were more likely than men to be arrested, and were more likely to be put in prison if convicted.

Why take the chance? At the time, thousands of young women were immigrating to London from Scotland, Ireland, and rural England, looking for jobs and for husbands. The quality and availability of both turned out to be greatly lacking. So why turn to hawking gin? Historian Jessica Warner gives three reasons:

[I]t required little or no capital; it did not require membership in a professional organization; and it was one of the few occupations from which women were not effectively or explicitly excluded. It was, in other words, a means of economic survival. (Warner 2002: 51)

The Gin Acts often pitted women against women. Enforcement depended heavily on the accusations of paid informants, half of whom were women. Warner describes the harsh economics that drove these women to rat out illegal gin sellers:

Consider the options of a young woman newly arrived in London in 1737 or 1738. She could work for a year as a maid and earn £5 in addition to receiving room and board, or she could inform against one gin-seller, and upon securing a conviction collect a reward of £5. There were two ways to make money, one hard, the other easy, and many people naturally chose the latter. Most did so only once, collecting their reward and then attempting to hide as best they could. (Warner 2002: 137)

This could be called danger pay, as informers were not well liked.

What do YOU think?

Did the feminization of the gin trade in eighteenth-century London benefit women or harm them? What alternatives might have been available to female immigrants to London who chose not to get involved in selling gin illegally?

Women's Clerical Work in Canada, 1891–1971

The early twentieth century saw the spectacular increase in the number of clerical workers in the Canadian labour force. It also saw the feminization of the position, along with the degradation of the position, as measured in terms of wages, skill level, and opportunity for promotion. How all three trends—growth, feminization, and degradation—mesh together is a story that gives insight on both the past and the present.

Clerical work was traditionally a man's job. The male bookkeeper's varied duties required a lot of what we now call multitasking. As companies grew in size, there was much more clerical work that needed to be done, and businesses moved towards a more rationalized and efficient approach to task management, according to the principles of **scientific management** (or **Taylorism**, which we introduced in Chapter 6). The result was a kind of assembly-line office work, in which several clerical workers were engaged in the rapid performance of repeated simple tasks, with little variety and few opportunities to move up in the company. The growing belief (based on assumptions about women's limited capabilities) that this was ideal work for women, who were supposed to be wives and mothers first and labourers second, was reinforced by discrimination that offered them few alternatives. The thinking of the time is illustrated in the following passage from a book called *Office Management, Principles and Practice*, published in 1925 by William Henry Leffingwell, a strong proponent of applying scientific management to the office setting:

> A woman is to be preferred for the secretarial position for she is not averse to doing minor tasks, work involving the handling of petty details, which would irk and irritate ambitious young men, who usually feel that the work they are doing is of no importance if it can be performed by some person with a lower salary. Most such men are also anxious to get ahead and to be promoted from position to position, and consequently if there is much work of a detail character to be done, and they are expected to perform it, they will not remain satisfied and will probably seek a position elsewhere. (1925: 116)

This job transformation got a big push during World War I (1914–18), when women seized the opportunity to enter the workforce to replace men who had gone overseas to serve in Europe. During this time the number of clerical workers in Canada jumped by 113,148—around half of them women. As an example, at the Bank of Nova Scotia's regional offices in Ontario, the percentage of clerks who were women jumped from 8.5 per cent in 1911 to 40.7 per cent in 1916. Although, overall, the number of women clerical workers in Canada fell slightly when the men returned from the war, the figure remained high and steadily grew, as Table 11.2 shows.

The secretary pool in a scene from the TV series *Mad Men*, about an advertising agency in the 1960s. What does the current popularity of the show, among both female and male viewers, say about our view of the gendered division of labour it presents? Could it be that we're a little nostalgic for a time when men's and women's roles—in the office as well as the home—were so clearly defined?

What do YOU think?

1. Where in Canada can you see evidence of the feminization of work today? What effect do you think the feminization of these workplaces has on the employees working there?

2. Is there any evidence of a reverse trend that we might call the "masculinization" of work, in which a particular type of employment dominated by men acquires greater prestige and, of course, greater pay?

Being a Gender Minority in a Gendered Occupation

When individuals find themselves in gendered jobs and they are of the minority (i.e. "wrong") sex, it can have a profound effect on their gender performance at work. Paul Sargent discusses the phenomenon with great clarity in his look at men in early childhood education (which, for Sargent's purposes, includes the lower grades of primary school as well as the daycare profession, where most ECE teaching jobs are found). Sargent incorporates Raewyn Connell's (1995) four performances of masculinity—essentially, four ways Connell identified in which men act out gender roles. These are:

1. **hegemonic masculinity**
2. **subordinate masculinity**
3. **marginalized masculinity**
4. **complicit masculinity.**

Sargent explains them this way:

> Hegemonic masculine practices are those that serve to normalize and naturalize men's dominance and women's subordination. Subordinate masculinities are those behaviors and presentations of self that could threaten the legitimacy of hegemonic masculinity. Gay men, effeminate men, and men who eschew competition or traditional definitions of success are examples frequently cited. . . . These men are vulnerable to being abused and ridiculed by others. Marginalized masculinities represent the adaptation of masculinities to such issues as race and class. For example, a Black man may enjoy certain privileges that stem from success as a small

Table 11.2 The feminization of clerical workers in Canada, 1891–1971

YEAR	TOTAL CLERICAL WORKERS	WOMEN CLERICAL WORKERS	
		NUMBER	PERCENTAGE
1891	133,017	4,710	14.3
1901	57,231	12,660	22.1
1911	103,543	33,723	32.6
1921	216,691	90,577	41.8
1931	260,674	117,637	45.1
1941	303,655	152,216	50.1
1951	563,093	319,183	56.7
1961	818,912	503,660	61.5
1971	1,310,910	903,395	68.9

Source: Statistics Canada

> business owner, yet still find himself unable to hail a cab. . . . Finally, complicit masculinities are those that do not embody hegemonic processes *per se*, but benefit from the ways in which hegemonic masculinities construct the gender order and local gender regimes. (Sargent 2005)

Using these terms, Sargent argues that men who work in early childhood education are caught up in a conflict between performing a *subordinate masculinity* (for example, by being "nurturing"), which would make them good at their job, and engaging in more stereotypical masculinity performances, which are imposed on them by the gendered nature of the job. Examples of male gender images involved in this context are "homosexual–pedophile" and "man as disciplinarian." Male ECE teachers are not allowed the caring physical contact that female teachers are encouraged to have. As one male teacher, in a narrative, explains, "Women's laps are places of love. Men's are places of danger" (Sargent 2005). This stems from the popularly reproduced image of the homosexual–pedophile, which mistakenly conflates, or links, two different sexualities. As a result, male teachers are reduced to less threatening performances of complicit masculinity, which include "high fives" and handshakes rather than hugs, and rewarding children with prizes and names written on the board rather than physical contact. This can be demoralizing for the male early childhood educator. As one male teacher wrote in a narrative, "I sometimes feel really inadequate when I watch the kids draped all over the women and all I'm doing is keeping them busy, handing out trinkets, or slapping high fives" (Sargent 2005).

The "man as disciplinarian" gender image also restricts the performance of male gender roles in the ECE environment. Because it is assumed that men more naturally perform discipline, they are assigned

Our Stories

The Famous Five and the "Persons" Case

"The Famous Five" is the name given to five Canadian women who fought for equal rights during the first half of the twentieth century. They are **Henrietta Muir Edwards** (1849–1931), **Nellie McClung** (1873–1951), **Louise McKinney** (1868–1931), **Emily Murphy** (1868–1933), and **Irene Parlby** (1868–1965). Among their distinguished achievements is their successful campaign to have women awarded the status of "persons" under British and Canadian law.

When Emily Murphy, in 1916, was named the first woman police magistrate in Alberta, her appointment was challenged on the grounds that women were not "persons" under the British North America (BNA) Act, which had officially created the Dominion of Canada in 1867. It was understood, when the BNA Act was written, that "persons" meant "men," for women were not allowed to vote or to hold public office. In 1917, the Supreme Court of Alberta ruled that women were, in fact, "persons" in that province, and Emily Murphy became officially the first woman magistrate in the British Empire. In order to advance the cause of women aspiring to hold public office at the federal level, she then had her name put forward as a candidate for the Canadian Senate, only to have the Conservative prime minister Robert Borden, invoking the BNA Act and its reference to "persons," reject her bid.

In the years that followed, the fight to have women in the Senate was taken up by numerous women's groups across the country. In 1927, Murphy and the other four members of the Famous Five, all of them prominent women's rights activists in Alberta, petitioned the Supreme Court of Canada with the question: *Does the word "persons" in Section 24, of The British North America Act, 1867, include female*

persons? The Court answered that it did not. At that time there were no women in the British House of Lords, so the notion that there might be female members in the Canadian Senate was easily dismissed.

In her popular writing, Nellie McClung often drew her readers' attention to the hard-working reality of farm women. During the early 1920s, she was a Member of the Legislative Assembly in Alberta.

greater responsibility for monitoring the behaviour of "problem kids." Classrooms occupied by male teachers then become seen as sites of discipline. No matter what the particular male's natural inclinations or teaching styles are—whether or not they are more nurturing or "female-defined"—these teachers are forced to conform to a masculinity performance that reinforces male authoritarian stereotypes.

But the Famous Five were undeterred and took their case to a higher court of appeal: the Judicial Committee of the Privy Council in Britain. On 18 October 1929, the Lord Chancellor of the Privy Council, announcing the judicial committee's decision, ruled that "women are persons . . . and eligible to be summoned and may become Members of the Senate of Canada." In their decision, the committee stated "that the exclusion of women from all public offices is a relic of days more barbarous than ours. And to those who would ask why the word 'persons' should include females, the obvious answer is, why should it not?"

The following year, 1930, Montreal-born Cairine Reay Wilson became the first woman appointed to the Senate of Canada.

QUICK HITS

Women and Canadian Politics

1867 Canadian federal and provincial vote given only to white men with property.
1916 Women in Manitoba, Saskatchewan, and Alberta get the provincial vote.
1917 World War I nurses and the female relatives of soldiers get the federal vote.
Women in British Columbia and Ontario get the provincial vote.
1918 Women in Canada get the federal vote.
Women in Nova Scotia get the provincial vote.
First woman provincial cabinet minister (Mary Ellen Smith, BC).
1919 Women in New Brunswick get the provincial vote.
1921 First woman federal cabinet minister (Mary Ellen Smith).
1922 Women in Prince Edward Island get the provincial vote.
1925 Women in the British colony of Newfoundland get the vote.
1930 First woman senator in Canada (Cairine Wilson).
1940 Women in Quebec get the provincial vote.
1951 First woman mayor in Canada (Charlotte Whitten, Ottawa).
1991 First woman provincial premier (Rita Johnson, BC).
First woman territorial premier (Nelly Cournoyea, NT)
1993 First woman prime minister (Kim Campbell).
2008 Number of women premiers in Canada: 1 (NU).
2010 Number of women premiers in Canada: 2 (NU, NL)
2011 Number of women premiers in Canada: 4 (NU, NL, BC, AB)
2013 Number of women premiers in Canada: 6 (NU, NL, BC, AB, QC, ON)

Telling It Like It Is

A First-Hand POV

On-the-Job Training: Making the Right Impression in a Male-Defined Business

I was on my very first job as a criminologist. I had gone through years of school to learn theories, statistics, research methods—everything that I *thought* was necessary before going out into the field.

I had been hired as a research assistant to make observations and conduct interviews at a law enforcement conference. This was the first time that I was actually going to be around the law enforcement community, and I was eager to make a good impression on my new colleagues.

I got to the conference a bit early and waited for the rest of the research team to arrive for our scheduled meeting. We were meeting near the entrance of the venue, where most people would be entering and exiting the premises. It was quite early, and not many people were around.

A gentleman came up and introduced himself to me as a fellow conference attendee. We chatted for a minute or so before I noticed that he was staring at the ring on my finger. Next thing I knew, he was asking me questions about whether or not I was happy in my relationship. That's when I realized that this man was not being kind or professional— he was hitting on me!

I made it very clear that I was only at the conference as a researcher, and then excused myself from the conversation. Just then, someone from my team walked through the door and I quickly went over to say hello.

I was a little thrown by the whole incident at first. While it might not seem like a big deal, I want you to consider this: imagine that you are a brand-new graduate from your field of study—who happens to be a woman. You have been given an opportunity to begin your career. On your very first day, instead of being met with professionalism, you are met with sexist attitudes that see every woman as an "available" woman.

How did I deal with this? I had brushed it off by the time the rest of the team arrived and was ready to get back to work.

As the conference continued, I started to hear that other women (researchers, attendees, and keynote speakers alike) were having similar experiences. Law enforcement is a male-dominated field, and at least 70 per cent of the people at this conference were men; women stood out.

I discussed my concerns with my supervisor and learned that my experiences were not atypical of the experiences of women criminologists. My supervisor was a wonderful source of information and support. I quickly learned how to react appropriately to inappropriateness—there's a fine line between a reaction that will enable you to work with people who have just offended you, and putting up walls that get in the way of your research objectives.

In fact, over the years, I have informally gathered similar stories from other women in the field.

Now, I do not want to paint a picture of the male law enforcement community as predators or convey any other negative stereotype. Most of the people at the conference (both men and women) were there to learn and share ideas with other professionals. However, there were a few people who made one thing very clear: the professional world is not a completely level playing field—not yet anyway. Being a woman does matter.

—Rhea Adhopia

What do YOU think?

How was the author of this narrative essentially sanctioned for being deviant?

Does this ECE's hands-off celebration of a toddler's achievement look natural to you? Why do you think we're so suspicious of men who want to be daycare workers? What societal influences have conditioned our suspicion?

Men in early childhood education are expected to want to move into occupational positions more in keeping or complicit with male hegemony: administrative positions in ECE organizations and higher grades or the principal's office in elementary schools. Sargent's study did not verify this trend, but we could argue that a longitudinal approach, looking at male teachers' careers over time, would yield evidence of men "moving up" in the system. We might find, too, that this kind of trend is as much or more the product of the gendered nature of the organizations as of the individuals' actual intent.

What do YOU think?

In some ways it's easier to examine the impact on men of working in a female-gendered occupation because it is much less common than the reverse: women working in male-dominated occupations. Think of three jobs defined as male. For each one, think of how the masculinized nature of the job might affect a female worker's gender performance.

"Race" and Gender: Intersecting Oppression

As we saw in Chapter 10, on "race" and ethnicity, "race" and gender can intersect as forms of oppression. Racial prejudice and discrimination can often reinforce gender bias, and vice versa. In some cases, opposing gender/"race" stereotypes can affect an oppressed group, as in the case of Asian women, described below.

Going Global

Boyat and Deviant Gender Performance in the Arab World

In Arab countries such as Qatar and the United Arab Emirates, there is a new pattern of deviant behaviour that cuts across gender and ethnic lines. It involves young women who adopt a masculine style of dress, including baggy jeans or military pants, aviator shades, heavy watches and other jewellery, combat boots or running shoes, and so on; many of the women keep their hair cut short. A woman dressed this way wouldn't look out of place in North America, but bear in mind that in many parts of the Arab world women in public customarily wear a *burqa* or *abaya*, a full-length, loose-fitting robe that covers the whole body from the shoulders down.

The women are known as **boyat** (singular *boyah*), an Arabic word akin to "tomboy" and sometimes translated as "transsexual." But make no mistake: the behaviour is not sexual. It is more a deviant way of acting out and exploring gender. Dressed in their male "disguise," *boyat* seem able to talk and act more aggressively and independently than they could dressed as women. It is also clear, from accounts I have read, that the women involved consider their behaviour a way of life, not just a frivolous experiment or a game, and that they find an important kind of solidarity with other women engaged in the same

behaviour (see "Cross about Cross-Dressing" 2010; "Defying Gender Expectations" 2009; Naidoo 2011).

What are the factors influencing the *boyat* phenomenon? Globalization, certainly, has played a role, by exposing girls in these countries of the Middle East to images of women acting more independently than women in the Arab world are traditionally permitted to do. Social media—e-mail, Facebook, Twitter—allow *boyat* to communicate with one another anonymously, and get together online without being seen. There are also links between the *boyat* phenomenon and higher education. For one thing, a college or university education prolongs the period of unmarried youth for young women. For another, like-minded *boyat* gathering together in colleges—especially women's colleges and campuses like those of the UAE's Higher Colleges of Technology—are less likely to arouse suspicion with their behaviour. In fact, in such settings, their increasing number makes them the majority, putting them in a position to poke fun at and even bully their more conservative female peers.

In most settings, *boyat* remain a minority, and deviant behaviour, as we saw in Chapter 6, is met

Opposing Gender/"Race" Stereotypes

There is a tendency to stereotype visible minority women into two extremes. So, for example, Renee Tajima (1989) writes about how an East Asian woman may be stereotyped either as the **Lotus Blossom Baby** or as the **Dragon Lady**. In Tania Das Gupta's words, the former stereotype "encompasses the images of the China doll, the geisha girl and shy Polynesian beauty. The latter includes prostitutes and 'devious madams'" (Das Gupta 1996: 27). Anyone who has seen reruns of the TV series *M*A*S*H* would recognize both stereotypes. Popular during the 1970s and 1980s, the show revolved around a unit of American doctors and nurses stationed near Seoul during the Korean War in the early 1950s. It featured numerous sly allusions to geisha girls and occasional appearances by Asian women who periodically became involved with the leading male characters.

It also featured characters who fit the "Dragon Lady" stereotype, including the sharp businesswoman Rosie, of Rosie's Bar and Grill, and a woman who threatens the male character Klinger with a pitchfork when she believes he is fooling around with her daughter.

The stereotype of the Lotus Blossom Baby, which gained popularity during the American occupation of Japan after World War II, has contributed to the image, prevalent in the West, of a **geisha** as an expensive prostitute. This is a narrow view, as Mineko Iwasaki makes clear in *Geisha, A Life* (2002). Born in 1949, Iwasaki was Japan's foremost geisha, having begun her training at the age of four and retired wealthy at 29. She entertained such prominent Western figures as the British royal family and the American general Douglas MacArthur. In her book, she describes her strict training in calligraphy, dance, music, serving tea, and the other hostess functions of a geisha. She dispels the stereotype

with negative sanctions. Some opponents of the *boyat* phenomenon have attempted to medicalize the "problem," by proposing rehabilitation therapy and medicine. In some jurisdictions, cross-dressing has been made illegal. It is interesting that laws of this kind, since being introduced to combat the *boyat* phenomenon, have actually been used to arrest a number of men dressed as women, showing that women are not the only ones in the Arab world acting out deviant gendered behaviour.

What do YOU think?

1. Read some additional accounts of the *boyat* phenomenon, such as those listed at the end of this chapter. Do you think this is just a social fad, or will it continue for, say, more than 10 years? Could it be a stepping stone to more independence in gender expression in Arab countries?

2. How would you compare the governmental and general institutional treatment of *boyat* to the reaction to homosexuality and lesbianism about a generation ago in the West?

of "geisha as prostitute," explaining that there were occasionally "romantic entanglements" between rich patrons and geisha artists, leading to marriage, affairs, or "heartache," but that "in the same way that a patron of the opera does not expect sexual favors from the diva," a rich and powerful man would more often support a prominent geisha "solely because of the artistic perfection that she embodied and the luster that she lent to his reputation" (Iwasaki 2002: 51–2).

Black women also face discrimination on the basis of opposing gender/"race" stereotypes. Das Gupta describes the double image as follows:

> On the one hand there was the slow, de-sexed, "cow-like" mammy, evolved into the "Aunt Jemima figure"—familiar to many from older boxes of pancake mix—a servile and contented image which brings together gender and race ideologies.

> On the other hand, there was the sexual objectification of Black women's bodies, or body parts to be more exact. (Das Gupta 1996: 27)

The sexually objectified black woman is a familiar figure in music videos, but the brief and supposedly inadvertent exposure of black singer Janet Jackson's breast on TV during the halftime show at the 2004 Super Bowl sparked an astonishing level of outrage among scandalized American viewers (not to mention all of those who had merely heard about the incident). Why the big fuss? The sudden appearance in prime time of the sexually objectified black woman experiencing a "wardrobe malfunction" seemed to have caught a largely white middle-class audience by surprise. Were these viewers right to object? Or is the North American viewing public guilty of a double standard, finding it okay for the sexually objectified woman to appear in videos on MuchMusic or MTV, but not on "family entertainment" on CBS?

The Indian Princess and the Squaw

Aboriginal women have long been subject to the opposing gender/"race" stereotypes of the "Indian princess" and the "squaw." In the United States, the **Indian princess** is a heroine that forms an integral part of the American story of how their country was built. She is the beautiful Pocahontas of Disney's worldview, saving the handsome John Smith from certain death, in the process abandoning her people to serve the interests of the incoming colonial power. She is Sacajawea, the Shoshone woman who aided the Lewis and Clark expedition from 1804 to 1806, helping to open up the West to "civilization" and the eventual reservation entrapment of her people and their Plains neighbours.

The Indian princess is not part of the founding mythology, or master narrative, of Canada. Still, she is found here and there across the country. Emily

QUICK HITS

"Two-Spirit People" and "Manly-Hearted Women": Alternative Gender Roles among North American Aboriginal People

There is evidence that some North American Aboriginal peoples have a particularly enlightened view of gender variability. One example is the *two-spirit person*, or *berdache*, who is either a man who occasionally dresses as a woman and takes part in some domestic activities traditionally associated with women, or a woman who engages in hunting and warfare and takes on leadership roles. Two-spirit people were not traditionally seen as abnormal in their communities but were, rather, respected and recognized as making up a legitimate "third gender" (Roscoe 1998).

Another example is the *Ninauposkilzipxpe*, or "manly-hearted women," found among the Peigan and described in the following passage by anthropologist Alice Kehoe:

> About a third of elderly (sixty years or older) North Piegan [*sic*] women in 1939, and a few younger women, were considered manly-hearted. . . . Such women owned property, were good managers and usually effective workers, were forthright and assertive in public, in their homes, and as sexual partners, and were active in religious rituals. They were called "manly-hearted" because boldness, aggressiveness, and a drive to amass property and social power are held to be ideal traits

for men. . . . [T]he manly-hearted woman is admired as well as feared by both men and women. (Kehoe 1995: 115)

This stereoview photograph, taken in 1877, shows "Squaw Jim" (left), a two-spirit person of the Crow Nation. How does the term *two-spirit person* compare to *transgender*?

What do YOU think?

How do we in Canadian society tend to characterize women who are bold, aggressive, and career-oriented? Can we say that we think of them as positively as the traditional Blackfoot did?

Pauline Johnson, popular Mohawk poet and novelist at the turn of the twentieth century, was frequently billed as "The Mohawk Princess" to audiences in North America and Britain, for whom she performed her poetry. Catharine Sutton, a heroic Ojibwa woman of the nineteenth century, is known in Owen Sound, Ontario, as "the Indian Princess" (see Steckley 1999).

While the stereotype of the Indian princess has been used as a metaphor for the supposed open-armed acceptance by North American Native people of European colonizers, the **squaw** is a figure that has been used by white writers (including American presidents Thomas Jefferson and Theodore Roosevelt) to characterize Aboriginal people as savages, providing ample justification for white colonial dominance (Smits 1982). The image summarizes the impressions of Aboriginal culture as brutal and barbaric, with lazy, abusive Native men overworking and generally mistreating their wives, sisters, mothers, and daughters.

The squaw figure is a familiar one in the Canadian literature on Aboriginal women (see Maclean 1970 [1889]: 148–9 and Jenness 1932: 403). The way the distorted depiction of the lives of Aboriginal women was used to justify white colonialism is evident in the following passage of a text written by a nineteenth-century missionary, Egerton R. Young:

> Marvelous were the changes wrought among these Indians when they became Christians. And in no way was the change greater or more visible than in the improved conditions of women. In paganism she has not the life of a dog. She is kicked and cuffed and maltreated continually. She is the beast of burden and has to do all the heavy work. . . . Very quickly after they become Christians does all this change. Then happy homes begin. Mother and wife and sister and daughter are loved and kindly cared for. (Young 1974 [1893]:148–9)

Gender and Immigration

There have been several instances in Canadian history when only the men or the women of a particular ethnic group were permitted or encouraged to immigrate. We have seen, in Chapter 8, that Chinese and South Asian women were effectively blocked from entering Canada for significant parts of the twentieth century. In the section that follows, we will see the difficulties Filipino women faced when they made up the majority of those allowed to immigrate to Canada from the Philippines.

Filipino Immigrants: A Second Wave of Pioneering Women

Filipino immigration to Canada is distinctive in that women have been the "pioneers"—arriving first before their husbands and other male family members, sending most of their money together with care packages of bargain-hunted goods back home to their families, sponsoring relatives and providing them with a place to stay. There have been two waves of Filipino immigration. The first wave brought nurses, mostly women, while the second wave brought nannies, who suffer more from the inequalities of gender and "race" than did the earlier generation of Filipino immigrants.

In 1981, the Canadian government instituted its Foreign Domestic Movement Program (FDMP) to address the growing need for in-house childcare that was created as more and more women began working outside the home. In 1992, the FDMP was replaced by the more restrictive Live-In Caregiver Program, which required selected immigrants to commit to 24 months of domestic work within a three-year period, during which time they were also required to "live in" with the family. Nannies came mainly from three countries: the Philippines, Jamaica, and the United Kingdom. Filipino nannies dominated the figures, the percentage of domestics coming from the Philippines rising between 1982 and 1990 from 10.6 per cent to 50.52 per cent. This trend occurred not just in Canada but in Hong Kong, Singapore, Saudi Arabia, Britain, and the United States. The political and economic unrest that surrounded the fall of the corrupt Marcos government made the Philippines a place many wanted to leave if they could.

The women of the second wave of Filipino immigration were older than their compatriots who had migrated earlier: those aged 30–34 predominated, with those aged 25–29 and 35–39 forming smaller but roughly equal groups, and those aged 20–24 and 50–54 sharing about the same low percentage. It was more difficult for this generation of Filipino immigrants. They were better educated than immigrating British and Jamaican nannies: among those receiving authorization for temporary employment as nannies between 1982 and 1990, 8 per cent held bachelor's degrees, 7 per cent had at least some university education, 17 per cent had some trade and technology training, and 12 per cent had other non-university training. Working as nannies made these women grossly underemployed, as sociologist Anita Beltran

Chen argues (1998). Yet domestic work was the only kind of work that could bring them to Canada, so they took their chances.

As women, as visible minorities, and as temporary and poorly paid employees subject to few industrial controls, the women were vulnerable to exploitation and physical, emotional, and sexual abuse. Those who had been trained in a specific field such as nursing also had to fight losing their skills through disuse. Between 15 and 20 per cent were married and had to endure separation from their husbands and, in many cases, children. Those who were single returned a large portion (estimates vary around 75 per cent) of their income to their family back home, holding onto little money to look after themselves. In short, they are restricted by the stereotypes of "race" and gender that treat Asian women as caregivers, overlooking skills that might make them productive in other areas of Western society.

WRAP IT UP

Summary

We have seen that gender and sex are different. You are born with a sex: typically male or female, although intersex people are born with both male and female sexual organs. Your gender, though, is socially constructed to a significant extent, and may not fit neatly into the binary categories "male" and "female" but may sit somewhere on the spectrum between these two points. The social construction of gender applies not just in obvious areas such as clothing and colours, but in occupations as well. You need be neither a woman nor a feminist to recognize that feminization of an occupation—in the sense of making it unrewarding in terms of pay, power, and social status—helps to create inequality between men and women. This inequality, reflected in pay ratio and in the greater likelihood of women working part-time, is changing very little. As sociologists, we need to investigate why this is so, and look for ways to address the inequity. We also must ask ourselves whether the separate paths that men and women take in post-secondary education lead to social inequality or just difference, an issue we raised in Chapter 5, on socialization.

THINK BACK

Questions for Critical Review

1. Explain, in your own words, the difference between *sex* and *gender*.

2. What does it mean to say that gender is socially constructed to a significant extent?

3. Do you think there are still common stereotypes in North America surrounding those who transgress gendered work roles (e.g. the male nurse, the woman construction worker)? If so, do you think they can be changed? What would it take?

4. Describe how gender and ethnicity intersect to create stereotypes about women of different ethnic backgrounds.

5. How do you think gender-based immigration (i.e. with immigrants of one sex entering the country in much greater numbers than the other) affects the settling experiences of different groups such as the Filipinos?

6. Do you think that the ideology of fag is used to keep men, more than women, in line with gender norms? If so, why do you think that would be?

7. To what extent can a man really be considered a feminist? How would that define his role as a sociologist?

READ ON

Online

"Cross about Cross-Dressing: Is It a Wicked Western Habit that Should be Stopped?"

http://www.economist.com/node/15403091

"Shedding Light on the 'Boyat' Phenomenon: Conference Separates Fact from Fiction on the Issue."

http://gulfnews.com/news/gulf/uae/general/shedding-light-on-the-boyat-phenomenon-1.796816

> The *Economist* article provides an account of the "debate about fashion in Qatar," and looks at both sides of the issue of cross-dressing and *boyat* in the Middle East. The second article, from GulfNews.com, reviews a conference on the topic that was held at the Sharjah Women's College in the UAE.

"Converging Gender Roles"

www.statcan.gc.ca/pub/75-001-x/10706/9268-eng.htm

> Katherine Marshall's article on the Statistics Canada website offers a stats-based view of the extent to which gender roles may be converging in Canada.

"The 'Genderless Baby' Who Caused a Storm of Controversy"

www.thestar.com/news/article/1105515--the-genderless-baby-who-caused-a-storm-of-controversy-in-2011

> This *Toronto Star* article looks at the life of Baby Storm on the eve of the infant's first birthday.

In Print

Judith Butler (1990), *Gender Trouble: Feminism and the Subversion of Identity* (New York: Routledge).

> Butler's pioneering work launched the study of queer theory.

John Colapinto (2000), *As Nature Made Him* (New York: Harper).

> Colapinto provides the definitive account of David Reimer's life and tragic death.

Andrea Medovarski & Brenda Cranney, eds (2006), *Canadian Women Studies: An Introductory Reader*, 2nd edn (Toronto: INANNA).

> This volume combines an introduction to feminist thought in general with an insightful survey of feminist theory in Canada.

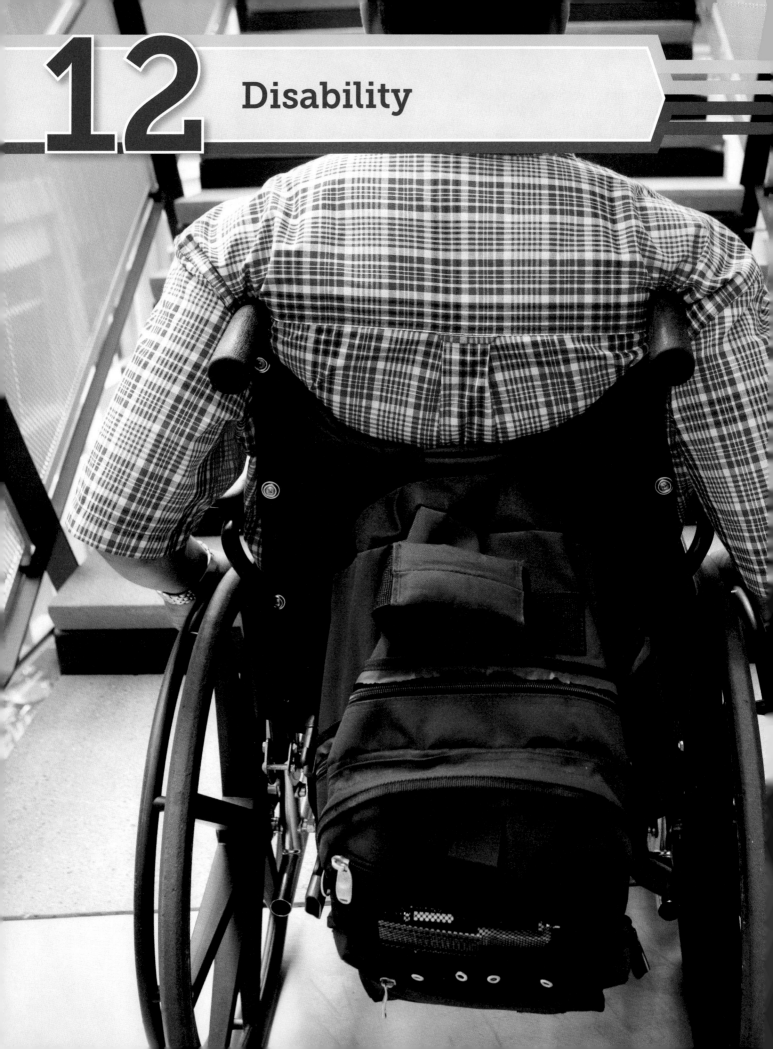

12 Disability

Learning Objectives

After reading this chapter, you should be able to

- explain why *disability* is hard to define, and why it is difficult to get statistics on people with disabilities

- comment critically on the significance of names used to categorize different disabilities

- outline the contributions of Irving Zola to the sociological study of disability

- discuss the importance of Deaf culture to people who are deaf

- differentiate between *critical disability theory* and other theories or models applied to people with disabilities

- argue the benefits of both inclusion and segregation of children with disabilities in schools

- discuss how Goffman's ideas about *stigmata* apply to people with disabilities.

Key Terms

- ablist
- agency
- American dream
- binaries
- bodily stigmata
- border crossers
- critical disability theory
- Deaf culture
- disability
- disability oppression
- disabled
- economic model of disability
- eugenics
- formal equality
- honorary members
- institutional ethnography
- intersectionality theory
- labelling theory
- master status
- medicalization
- medical model of disability
- moral stigmata
- operational definition
- oralist
- participant observation
- passing
- postmodernist theory
- positivist
- social constructionist model
- sociological imagination
- standpoint theory
- status
- stigmata
- substantive equality
- tokenism
- total institution
- tribal stigmata
- universal architecture

Names to Know

- Amitai Etzioni
- Erving Goffman
- Nora Groce
- Irving K. Zola

"Sensitive to the D-Word": A Blogger Writes on Disability and Discrimination

Monday, April 04, 2011

When you mention the "D" word (*discrimination*) in connection with people with disabilities, you get the funniest reactions. People sort of wince, they cringe, they even get angry and question your conclusions. It's as if they have accepted the concept of discrimination against other groups, like racial minorities, women, and Aboriginal people, but there's a huge stumbling block when it comes to discrimination related to disability. But why?

Is it that we cripples are usually viewed with pity, as not-quite-whole people—or "half-people," as Jerry Lewis so charmingly suggested? Does it have to do with the weird tendency to demand gratitude

from us for any service, privilege, or accommodation granted? Is it that the concept of "pitiful sick people" having equal rights is so difficult to comprehend that it is impossible to conceive that we can be discriminated against?

I don't know, and I don't get it. I especially don't get the anger. However, I *do* get why those of us who live with disabilities get angry. Some examples:

- My family and I were checked into a fancy hotel in Europe that had assured us they were wheelchair-accessible. The entire time we stayed there, I entered and exited the hotel off the loading dock and used the freight elevator.

- On another trip, we booked tickets with British Airways and were surprised when they required that I produce a doctor's note allowing me to travel (this was a long time ago; they may have smartened up by now).

- I was part of the wedding party of someone I love a lot, who had a very specific conversation about accessibility with the operators of the reception hall before reserving a date and handing over money. At the time of booking, the washrooms were not wheelchair-accessible, but the bride-to-be was given assurances that at the time of her wedding a year-and-a-half later, they would be. They weren't. When I needed to pee, I had to use a commode placed in the Manager's office, which was later emptied by a gentleman in a morning suit who left the door wide open so all the other guests could observe the procedure.

- When I applied to graduate school, I was asked to come in for an interview to discuss what it meant to go to graduate school. I was questioned on such matters as how I would manage lunch, given that there was no cafeteria in the building. When I started classes, I discovered that none of the able-bodied students had been interviewed—or asked how they were going to manage lunch.

I have a handy test to check whether situations like these are wrong. I substitute another group, such as women or a racial minority, for **disabled** people: if the substitute group would have reasonable grounds to take offence at the situation in question, then it's also discrimination when it affects people with disabilities. Because we wouldn't expect a woman or a member of a racial minority to suck it up when asked to enter a fancy hotel by the freight elevator, or gain a doctor's permission to travel (because (a) having a disability does not mean you're sick, and (b) people with invisible medical conditions are not required to do so), or pee in a pot, or submit to an interview for access to graduate school when others do not.

Disability is a protected ground in pretty much all human rights legislation. Our local one, the Ontario Human Rights Code, states that "[e]very person has a right to equal treatment with respect to services, goods and facilities, without discrimination because of race, ancestry, place of origin, colour, ethnic origin, citizenship, creed, sex, sexual orientation, age, marital status, family status or disability." Equality isn't just about getting there: it's also about getting there in a dignified manner. And it's not equal or dignified to pee in a pot; it's not equal or dignified to enter off the loading dock; and it is not equal or dignified to have to take the long way to gain entry to a facility that is accessible to others by a much shorter route.

I have another test, this one for able-bodied people to try. Rent a wheelchair for a weekend, and every time you leave your house, do so seated (most residences in North America are not accessible, so you get a pass when you're at home). Take a walk—a conceptual walk, i.e. move about in the fresh air for enjoyment, in your neighbourhood. Go downtown to a large mall. Check out a museum. Visit some friends (you're not allowed out of the chair in their homes). You get the point: participate in your community. The only time you may leave the wheelchair is when you're in a public bathroom and you have to use the accessible stall.

It's an interesting experiment, one that still has a built-in escape hatch, but it starts to give you a sense of what it's like. People I know who have tried it have reported frustration, a newfound awareness of steps and other barriers, and a curious loss of eye contact with others (before hearing this I never knew that people—strangers—made eye contact with each other in public).

If more people tried this test, maybe it wouldn't be such an uphill battle to implement universal design. And maybe the D-word would be more accepted, so we could get beyond debating whether discrimination against people with disabilities exists, and start eliminating it.

—Lene Andersen, The Seated View, http://theseatedview .blogspot.ca/2011/04/sensitive-to-d-word.html

What do YOU think?

1. According to the author of this blog post, how is discrimination against people with disabilities different to discrimination against other minoritized people?

2. What is the difference, for people with disabilities, between access and access *with dignity*? Do you believe that the former is much more often found than the latter? Explain.

Introduction: What Is a Disability?

The Challenge of Operational Definition

Like poverty and pollution, disability is hard to define. We can probably find consensus on some types of disability, such as paralysis or blindness—like the homeless poor and oil-contaminated water, the extreme cases are easy to identify. But devising an **operational definition**—a working definition that we can use for statistical purposes—forces us to consider less obvious cases.

The *Oxford English Dictionary* provides us with a starting point. It defines disability as "a physical or mental condition that limits a person's movements, senses, or activities" (www.oed.com). But does that mean that a person who requires glasses when driving is disabled? What about someone with a speech impairment, such as a stutter, or an invisible condition, such as dyslexia? Is disability necessarily a chronic condition, or could we consider someone who is for a few months in a cast with a broken ankle disabled?

An editorial that appeared in a 1999 issue of the eminent medical journal *The Lancet* catches a good part of challenge of establishing an operational definition for disability. The writer reasons that because we all have different degrees of intelligence and aptitude in different areas, we can all be said to experience disability—in the broadest sense—when it comes to everyday tasks we don't manage as well as our peers do:

> All of us could be considered as disabled to some extent. Individuals differ in many ways in the manners in which they cope with the activities of daily living, or have a real but common handicap to which society has adjusted well. Deciding how far ability has to be impaired to constitute a disability is no easy matter—too vague, and abuse of special opportunities and services may follow; too rigid, and people who may benefit are excluded. ("The Spectrum of Disability" 1999: 693)

Postmodernist sociological theory teaches us to be suspicious of **binaries**, those either/or distinctions that are used to separate people into supposedly discrete categories such as heterosexual/homosexual, Aboriginal/non-Aboriginal, black/white. As we saw in Chapter 11, postmodernist theorists argue that gender,

for instance, is better viewed as a continuum, with "male" and "female" at the extremes and a lot of territory in between that needs to be understood. We could approach the condition of (dis)ability the same way. But that won't help us with our operational definition, and as *The Lancet*'s editorial writer points out, disability is an identity with some social and political weight, one that may gain a person access to special resources and services set aside for people with disabilities, as difficult as those often may be to access.

Measuring and Defining Disability

In 2007, Statistics Canada revealed that 4.4 million Canadians—roughly 14.3 per cent of the population—had reported a disability in the agency's 2006 Participation and Activity Limitation Survey (Statistics Canada 2007b: 9). So how does Canada's official data collection bureau define disability? Rather broadly, according to Diane Galarneau and Marian Radulescu:

> In the Participation and Activity Limitation Survey . . . the definition of disability uses the bio-psychosocial framework . . . in which disability is defined in a broad sense and covers all limitations. Disability is the result of complex interactions between a health problem or functional limitation and the social, political, cultural, economic, and physical environment. These, in combination with personal factors such as age, gender, and level of education, can result in a disadvantage—that is, a disability. Disability is [therefore] not defined merely as being the direct result of a health problem or any physical or mental limitation. (Galarneau & Radulescu 2009: 6)

Disability, then, is any condition—mental or physical, permanent or temporary—that limits a person's ability to participate in regular activities in the home, at work, at school, or in recreational pursuits. It can affect anything from a person's memory, speech, or psychological state to his or her ability to walk, climb stairs, or bend down or just live without pain. Figure 12.1 provides a snapshot of the most common types of disability among Canadian adults.

Canada's 2006 disability rate of 14.3 per cent is not an unusual figure across the globe. In the same year, Kenya, a country of similar size in terms of population (34.3 million compared with Canada's 32.6 million), was reported to have over 3 million people with

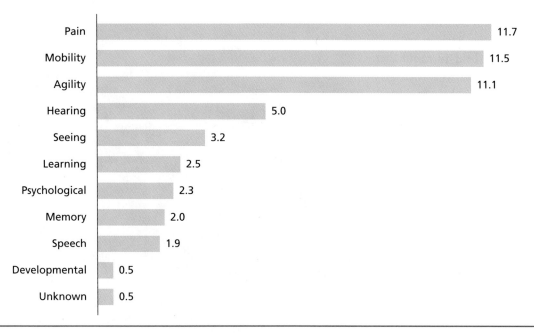

Figure 12.1 Adult Canadian population with a disability, by type (percentage)

Note: Does not include data for Nunavut, Northwest Territories, and Yukon.
Source: Statistics Canada, *Participation and Activity Limitation Survey 2006:* Tables. Ottawa: Statistics Canada, 2007 (Cat. No. 89-628-XIE - No. 003). http://www4.hrsdc.gc.ca/.3ndic.1t.4r@-eng.jsp?iid=40. Reproduced and distributed on an "as is" basis with the permission of Statistics Canada.

QUICK HITS

Types of Disability Identified in the Participation and Activity Limitation Survey

The following kinds of disability were identified in adults (aged 15+) in Statistics Canada's Participation and Activity Limitation Survey:

- *hearing* – difficulty hearing what is being said in a conversation with one other person, in a conversation with three or more persons, or in a telephone conversation
- *seeing* – difficulty seeing ordinary newsprint or clearly seeing someone's face from 4 m away
- *speech* – difficulty speaking and/or being understood
- *mobility* – difficulty walking half a kilometre or up and down a flight of stairs (about 12 steps) without resting, moving from one room to another, carrying an object of 5 kg for 10 m, or standing for long periods
- *agility* – difficulty bending, dressing and undressing oneself, getting into or out of bed, cutting one's own toenails, using fingers to grasp or handle objects, reaching in any direction (for example, above one's head) or cutting one's own food
- *pain* – limited in the amount or kind of activities that one can do because of a long-term pain that is constant or reoccurs from time to time (for example, recurrent back pain)
- *learning* – difficulty learning because of a condition, such as attention problems, hyperactivity, or dyslexia, whether or not the condition was diagnosed by a teacher, doctor, or other health professional
- *memory* – limited in the amount or kind of activities that one can do due to frequent periods of confusion or difficulty remembering things (these difficulties may be associated with Alzheimer's disease, brain injuries, or other similar conditions)
- *developmental disabilities* – cognitive limitations due to an intellectual disability or developmental disorder such as Down's syndrome, autism, or an intellectual disability caused by a lack of oxygen at birth
- *psychological* – limited in the amount or kind of activities that one can do due to the presence of an emotional, psychological, or psychiatric condition, such as phobias, depression, schizophrenia, drinking, or drug problems
- *other* – identified as the type of disability if the respondent answered YES to the general questions but did not provide any YES to the questions about type of disability that followed.

Source: Statistics Canada 2007b: 30. Reproduced and distributed on an "as is" basis with the permission of Statistics Canada.

disabilities, representing about 10 per cent of the African nation's population (and bear in mind that the techniques used to record disability in Kenya are likely to under-report the real figure). With the aging of the Canadian population, thanks to those pesky baby boomers (we'll read more about them in Chapter 13), the percentage of disabled Canadians will grow. Figure 12.2 shows the percentage of the Canadian population with a disability by age: not surprisingly, the percentage increases with advancing years.

Some statistics are encouraging. In 2006, Statistics Canada noted that 63 per cent of roughly 125,000 children aged 5 to 14 with disabilities were engaged in some sort of organized sport or other physical activity, with about 54 per cent of the same group involved in non-sport activities (e.g. dance, art, or music). Factors that increased the likelihood of participation included the

In 2010, Ontario's provincial appeal court upheld a lower-court ruling that individuals experiencing severe drug or alcohol dependence are entitled to long-term disability benefits under the Ontario Disability Support Program Act (Saint-Cyr 2010). Does it surprise you to think of drug and alcohol addiction as a disability? How does it fit with the operational definition provided above?

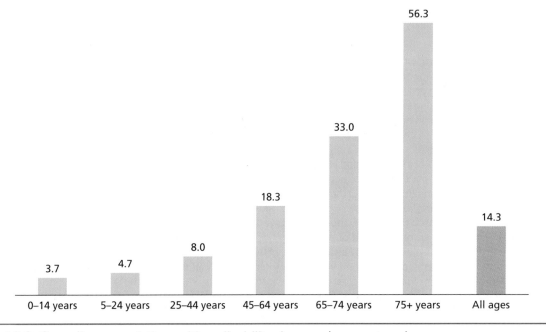

Figure 12.2 Canadian population with a disability, by age (percentage)

Source: Statistics Canada, *Participation and Activity Limitation Survey 2006: Tables.* See line 53 at http://www4.hrsdc.gc.ca/.3ndic.1t.4r@-eng.jsp?iid=40. Reproduced and distributed on an "as is" basis with the permission of Statistics Canada.

extent to which parents were involved in the school life of their disabled child, living in an urban as opposed to rural area, and higher parental income. Interestingly, the last named factor did not significantly affect non-sport interests or club memberships.

Irving Zola

Irving K. Zola (1935–1994) has been called the "father" of the sociology of disability, with good reason. He helped to establish the Society for Disability Studies, an organization promoting the study of disability as a bona fide academic discipline, and was the founding editor of the society's journal, *Disabilities Studies Quarterly*. As well as being a professor of medical sociology at Brandeis University in Massachusetts, he was an activist for disability rights and a prolific writer on the subject.

Zola published his best-known work, *Missing Pieces: A Chronicle of Living with a Disability*, in 1982. It is essentially a sociological diary of a week he had spent ten years earlier in Het Dorp ("The Village"), an institutionalized community of 400 people—almost all of them disabled—in the Netherlands. Zola's study combines **participant observation**—he lived among the people in one of the special apartments provided for residents with disabilities—and **institutional ethnography**, since he was writing from the viewpoint of the village's residents, not its administrators. This is not to say that Zola was unremittingly critical of Het Dorp, which was very progressive in a number of ways, or entirely uncritical of its patients, who themselves held some of the anti-disability prejudices Zola observed among the "normals."

Zola's approach shows parallels with the work of postmodernist feminist theorists such as Dorothy Smith, who were, at around the same time, establishing

---

Telling It Like It Is

An Athlete's POV

The Wheelchair: Good and Bad

Irving Zola experienced limitations in his everyday activities as a result of polio he developed at the age of 15 and a car accident suffered at 20. Nevertheless, his experience of disability changed dramatically when he discarded his leg brace and cane for a wheelchair.

The wheelchair provides great assistance to people who cannot walk, but it is also loaded with meaning. It is a powerful symbol that has been used to great and admirable effect by agencies promoting rights, services, and respect for disabled people. It's been used occasionally in commercials for banks and other companies trying to demonstrate their progressive, inclusive attitudes. But as a symbol, the wheelchair carries a certain ambivalence for the people who use it.

Canadian athlete, Paralympian, and "Man In Motion" Rick Hansen experienced the love–hate relationship with the wheelchair shortly after his life-changing accident at 15. The following passage of his memoir describes the exuberance he felt when he first started using a wheelchair:

The wheelchair changed everything. I had a form of transportation, I had some independence. I put miles on it, up and down the hallways and outside when I could. I learned to do a wheelie, building up speed, leaning back, and hoisting the front wheels as though I was on a motorbike. Even then, I was fooling around with a basketball. The urge to compete was there, but there was no outlet. So I just kept working. (Hansen & Taylor 2011: 18)

Later, however, he would come to feel differently about it:

I hated the chair. Just being in it told the world I was disabled. Worse, it told me. I'd use the braces and the sticks. As long as I was standing, I wasn't quite that disabled. (Hansen & Taylor 2011: 36)

standpoint theory to promote the authority of women's unique and subjective interpretations of their experiences. As a sociologist with a physical disability, Zola could readily see the need for an academic discipline devoted to the study of disability. As a researcher, he had insider insights as to what questions to ask and what answers might be trusted.

Zola was 15 when he developed polio, a viral disease that affects the central nervous system and can have a profound effect on a person's ability to walk. At 20 he was involved in a car accident. All of this meant that he had to use a heavy leg brace and a cane in order to walk. Yet because he could walk—albeit with these aids—Zola felt that he was passing, downplaying his disabled status and claiming a position in the ablist mainstream (Zola 2003: 202–5). So, for the period of time that he was at Het Dorp, Zola discarded his orthotic devices for a wheelchair, to better replicate the experience of many of the other residents. This sudden new awareness of his disability from a different vantage point was a powerful experience for Zola, and he took many important lessons from his daily experiences: soaking his clothes when he first tried to wash himself, experiencing the extreme difficulty of taking a shower, having to add to his expected travel time around the 65-acre village, and confronting his prior, unconscious avoidance of disabled people in his regular life.

What do YOU think?

In "The Country of the Blind" (1904), a short story by H.G. Wells, a mountaineer in Ecuador stumbles upon an isolated village of people who have never known sight and cannot even imagine what it is like to see. The title comes from the saying, "In the country of the blind, the one-eyed man is king," but the sighted mountaineer soon discovers that the blind villagers have come to survive quite well without the sense of sight—in fact, they interpret his own ability to see as a form of madness, a disability. What lesson does this hold about the social construction of disability?

Models of Disability

Like other areas of concern for the sociologist, disability can be examined from a number of different vantage points. In this section we will look at different models, or ways, used to represent and understand disability.

Medical Models

One model of presenting and interpreting disability can be called the medical model, which is determined and directed by doctors, specialists, and other medical practitioners. It is a positivist model in that it reflects the belief that it takes an "expert," using science, to determine the treatments, policies, and programs required to help people live with disabilities.

The medical model guides research that has led to important, life-altering advances in the way disabilities are diagnosed and treated, and its benefits are undeniable. It has been criticized, though, when used without the insights available from people outside the medical community. York University sociologist Karen Anderson outlines some potential weaknesses of research on people with disabilities carried out according to this approach:

> [B]esides being difficult for the uninitiated to understand, . . . it usually leaves out the perspective of the individual person who is being studied, and the meaning of his or her life in any discussion of the design, methods, or results of the research. It can be argued that this method of research in medicine, psychology, and sociology has been oppressive for persons with disabilities, and does not fit with a philosophy of independent living or considerations of a person's quality of life. Medical practitioners often focus on the presenting problem and its treatment without taking into account all aspects of the patient's life or considering if the treatment proposed, and its hoped-for results, will improve the person's life. (Anderson 1996: 386)

Again, this is not to say that this approach has no or little legitimacy. Rather, it is one of several paths of knowledge and causes of action that have legitimacy, and all of them need to be considered.

Economic Models

Economic models of disability are those that view people with disabilities in terms of their contributions to, or drain on, the economy. They can be either sympathetic or unsympathetic towards people with disabilities.

Favourable Economic Models

A sympathetic economic model would be one that views people living with disabilities in terms of their ability to perform meaningful labour. It looks for ways to maximize the skills of people with disabilities to enable them to become "productive" (i.e. wealth-creating) members of society. Organizations that arrange training and employment opportunities for people with disabilities, and those that fight to remove barriers to employment by promoting accessibility in the workplace, fall into this category.

The economic model has also produced some well-meaning but paternalistic approaches that reflect a limited view of how productive people with disabilities (especially those with mental disabilities) can be. A notorious case involves a program initiated in 1984 by fast-food giant McDonald's to train people with physical and mental disabilities to work in its restaurants. The McJOBS program was something like an internship, with prospective employees undergoing both classroom and on-site training under the supervision of a mentor. In television commercials that you can view for yourself on YouTube, McDonald's boasted of its success in integrating people with mental and physical disabilities into the workforce.

The program was launched at a time when the kind of employment that McDonald's had come to

---

Telling It Like It Is

An Author POV

The Visibility Factor

Already we have seen that visible and "invisible" disabilities are regarded differently. Lene Anderson, author of the narrative that opens this chapter, speculates that people with invisible disabilities do not face the same discrimination that people with visible disabilities do. On the other hand, David Onley, in the box on page 306–307, expresses his concern that people with invisible disabilities are sometimes excluded from the accessibility rights extended to people with "classically defined physical disabilities."

My wife, Angelika, and I learned a lesson about the visibility factor on a recent trip to the hospital. We were there for a medical appointment for Angelika, who suffers from two serious forms of disability: fibromyalgia, a condition that causes chronic pain in joints and soft tissues, and a neuropathy, a dysfunction of the nerves in her legs. Together, the two conditions put her in near constant pain, making it impossible for her to have a regular job (although she works to assist me in my book writing).

I had recently suffered a ruptured Achilles tendon, and at the time of our hospital visit, I was walking with the aid of crutches. I had a very visible disability, but a temporary one. Angelika's permanent disability is an invisible one.

Angelika is used to the fact that when we are together, I tend to draw more attention. I like to say that I am flashier, but it is really that I am large, loud, and outgoing. I have a big beard that attracts notice. Beside me, my quiet and introverted partner feels sometimes invisible. Normally that changes when we are at the hospital or a doctor's appointment, where Angelika is the focus of attention. On this day, however, people in the hospital reacted to the visibility of my temporary disability, opening doors for me, giving way to me in the corridors, and performing a number of other niceties that my wife did not receive. We received different treatment because my disability was flashier.

What do YOU think?

1. Would you say that the author's disability was viewed in a more positive way than his wife's was?

2. Why might it be more difficult for people with invisible disabilities to receive the care and respect they deserve?

Our Stories

An Excerpt from the Installation Speech of David C. Onley as Lieutenant Governor of Ontario, 5 September 2007

David C. Onley receives a 15-gun salute by the 7th Toronto regiment after his installation as Lieutenant Governor of Ontario.

Accessibility is that which enables people to achieve their full potential. It is inclusion. Accessibility is a human right and accessibility is right.

My dream is of a province where disability rights are advanced, not only for those with classically defined physical disabilities, but also for those so-called invisible disabilities. There are far too many people who suffer from mental health challenges, poverty, ill health; people whose psyches are so damaged that the mainstream world is just as inaccessible for them as it is for the physically disabled. While we seek to improve physical access, we must not presume that disability is only represented by a white wheelchair symbol on a blue sign.

My commitment to accessibility includes all disabilities not just the visible ones. . . .

As a child, . . . I had big dreams. The fact that I had been incapacitated by polio at age three meant that I would need more help than most to realize those dreams. I was fortunate to receive it in "full measure, pressed down, shaken together, and running over," in the words of St Luke. I was aided in ways both material and emotional, from the technical expertise of my doctors and physical therapists, to the unconditional support of my parents, brothers and sisters, and the backing of teachers, employers, and colleagues who reminded me to focus on my abilities rather than my disability.

Some of those supports were not readily apparent at the time. I remember when I was quite young, writing a letter to my hero, hockey legend Johnny Bower. Although he was not in a position to do any of the physical or medical things I needed, the autographed picture he sent me, and the letter of encouragement that he wrote, were to help me in ways no doctor or therapist could. He was, in fact, a role model.

Then almost 23 years ago Moses Znaimer hired me for the position of weather specialist on CityTV. It was only after he had hired me that he asked about my disability. Obviously, what he did was important for my career. But more importantly, it sent a message to television viewers everywhere that my physical shortcomings were irrelevant. What counted was my ability to do the job.

As one of the first visibly disabled people on television, I too have been cited as a role model for those who are disabled. But it seems to me that Moses Znaimer is a role model too. What he did for me stands as a shining example to employers, who may not realize that they have the power to change the alarmingly high level of unemployment among disabled people. I pledge to use the profile afforded by my new position to ensure that as many people as possible learn about, and are moved to do something to change, this state of affairs.

Source: Onley 2007.

Former Vancouver mayor Sam Sullivan announces his intention to bid for the BC Liberal Party nomination in the riding of Vancouver–False Creek. Sullivan is quadriplegic, having broken his neck in a skiing accident at the age of 19. Onley and Sullivan offer excellent examples of how people with disabilities can assume leadership roles in politics—but do you think it is important for a sociologist to state that their examples are exceptions to the rule concerning how people with disabilities are treated in society?

What do YOU think?

1. What does David Onley include in his definition of disability? Does his definition include anything not found among the types of disability presented in the box on page 301?

2. How, in Onley's opinion, can someone without a disability be a role model for people with disabilities?

represent—unchallenging, highly structured, low-paying work with few prospects for career advancement—was coming under scrutiny. Sociologist **Amitai Etzioni** (b. 1929) argued that "McJobs are bad for kids" in an article in which he attacked fast-food restaurants as "breeding grounds for robots working for yesterday's assembly lines, not tomorrow's high-tech posts" (Etzioni 1986). By 1991, when Canadian author Douglas Coupland popularized the term "McJob" as a "low-pay, low-prestige, low-dignity, low-benefit, no-future job in the service sector" (Coupland 1991: 5), McDonald's had abandoned the McJOBS program.

While there may be a tendency to underestimate the skills and potential productivity of people with disabilities, as illustrated by the McJOBS case, there is also a danger in setting the bar too high. In *Missing Pieces*, Irving Zola comments on how Americans' attitudes towards people with disabilities have been influenced by a version of the economic model that reflects the **American dream** (Zola 2003: 95). This is the idea that success in life is within reach for anyone simply willing to work hard enough for it. According to Zola (2003: 121), a number of American movies (he cites *The Miracle Worker* and *The Monty Stratton Story* as examples) offer a depiction of disability in which the hero or heroine with a disability "makes it" in the end, triumphing over the limitations of the disability to become successful. Zola argues that this kind of portrayal creates unrealistic expectations and reflects negatively on people whose disabilities are not as easily overcome. People in mainstream society are left with the impression that anyone who does not live up to the

The Ringer (2005) is a American comedy in which a young slacker of questionable morals attempts to pay off a significant debt by entering the Special Olympics. Despite its lowbrow humour and predictable ending (the protagonist, like the mountaineer in "The Country of the Blind," discovers he has seriously underestimated his competition), the movie won some support for its surprisingly sympathetic portrayal of people with mental disabilities, as well as its use in supporting roles of people from the disabled community. How do you think we should we assess such a film from a sociological point of view?

Hollywood image has essentially failed to realize his or her full potential and is therefore less deserving of respectful treatment. As we saw in Chapter 9 in the context of socioeconomic inequality, failing to achieve the American dream results in a situation we could call the "American nightmare."

Unfavourable Economic Models

Realistic or unrealistic, the economic models we've just seen have one thing in common: they view people with disabilities in terms of the meaningful work they can contribute to society. In contrast to these are economic models that view people with disabilities as a drain on the state. Perhaps the most extreme, and certainly the most cruel, of these involved a now discredited medical approach: eugenics.

The **eugenics** ("good genes") movement was based on the mistaken beliefs (1) that intelligence can be measured easily, and (2) that it is inherited, transferred directly, unchanged, from one generation to the next. A popular philosophy during the first half of the twentieth century, it led to efforts to have the so-called "feeble-minded" sexually sterilized so that they could not reproduce. The economic principle behind these ideas was that since people with mental disabilities received government-provided care or financial assistance, a great deal of money could be saved by ensuring that they could not bear mentally disabled children.

Among the leaders of the early eugenics movement was psychologist Henry H. Goddard, who promoted the idea that "feeble-mindedness" (then an accepted clinical term in psychology) was hereditary. In "Heredity of Feeble-Mindedness," an article published in a 1911 issue of *American Breeders Magazine*, Goddard attempted to demonstrate the inheritance of feeble-mindedness among inmates in an institution for people suffering a range of poorly diagnosed mental health conditions. He was widely considered to be the "father" of intelligence testing, having earned the reputation at Ellis Island, where he screened thousands of prospective immigrants to the United States, weeding out the feeble-minded to be sent back to their countries of origin. Yet in his research on feeble-mindedness he did not even attempt to give an operational definition of his key term "intelligence." He based his assessment on intelligence tests (which then, even more than now, had clear cultural and intellectual biases) and, we suspect, on "eyeballing" the inmates. Of course, the very fact of being in an institution or having been previously diagnosed could be enough for Goddard to conclude that an individual was a "moron" (a term he coined for clinical use, not for taunting classmates or heckling referees). He was strongly opposed to the notion that the social environment had any impact on a person's mental health—this at a time when scientists were divided squarely into two camps: the nature (i.e. biology) camp and the nurture (i.e. social environment) camp, with no middle ground.

In 1912, Goddard published his now infamous work *The Kallikak Family: A Study in the Heredity of Feeble-Mindedness*, in which he studied the genealogy of an American Revolutionary soldier, Martin Kallikak, who had fathered an illegitimate son with a feeble-minded girl he had met at a tavern. Goddard argued that this son and many of his descendants (143 out of 189 that could be assessed) showed signs of feeble-mindedness, including sexual immorality, alcoholism, criminality, epilepsy, and involvement with "houses of ill fame" (Goddard 1912: 18–19). Following his affair with the feeble-minded tavern girl, Martin Kallikak "straightened up and married a respectable girl of good family," producing a separate line of 496 descendants "all of [whom] are normal people" (29). This demonstrated conclusively, as far as Goddard was concerned, that feeble-mindedness is hereditary, and that "no amount of education or good environment can change a feeble-minded individual into a normal one, any more than it can change a red-haired stock into a black-haired stock" (53).

Influential at the time, especially among supporters of the eugenics movement, Goddard's work has since been criticized for failing to take into account social conditions such as poverty and alcoholism that might have given rise to some of the issues he detected in the line descended from Martin Kallikak's illegitimate son.

In Canada, eugenic beliefs led two provinces—Alberta in 1928 and British Columbia in 1933—to enact legislation making it legal to have mentally ill people sexually sterilized. Identifying "mental defectives" for sterilization was an inexact and controversial process, and the legislation victimized not only those with legitimate mental health conditions but also those who were marginalized by "race," ethnicity (especially new immigrants), and sex (many young women were sterilized because they were "sexually promiscuous" or involved in prostitution—two immoral tendencies that were taken as signs of mental defectiveness). The legislation was not repealed until 1972 in Alberta and 1973 in BC.

Despite the repeal of this legislation in Alberta and BC, the issue of whether individuals with mental disabilities could be sterilized without their consent remained a grey area until a 1986 Supreme Court of Canada ruling involving a girl known as Eve (not her real name). Eve had a mental disability that prevented her from communicating and understanding complex thoughts. When she was in her early twenties, her mother tried to get a court order to have Eve sexually sterilized, since she was concerned that Eve, who had developed a close relationship with a male student at the boarding school they both attended, might accidentally become pregnant. Eve's mother worried that her daughter would not be able to care for any child to which she gave birth.

The case was first heard in 1978 in the Supreme Court of Prince Edward Island, where the judge felt that he could not permit an individual to undergo sterilization via hysterectomy—a major surgical procedure—without her consent. The PEI Court of Appeal overturned the decision but did not act on it because Eve and the then-named Canadian Association for the Mentally Retarded challenged it. The Association was motivated to get involved by another incident at the time, in which a 10-year-old mentally disabled girl in BC (legally referred to as "Infant K") had been sexually sterilized in secret because, her parents explained,

she reacted hysterically to the sight of blood and was therefore likely to find menstruation emotionally difficult (Hubert 1985). The Association wanted to ensure that the reproductive rights of people with mental disabilities were preserved. In the case of *E. (Mrs) v. Eve* [1986], the Supreme Court of Canada denied Mrs E's request to have Eve sterilized, ruling against the sexual sterilization of a mentally disabled person for non-therapeutic reasons (i.e. for reasons other than the treatment of disease) without the individual's consent.

What do YOU think?

1. Are there any circumstances that would justify having a woman or man sexually sterilized without her or his consent? What if the individual were a convicted sex offender? What if the individual came from a family with a history of a disabling disorder?

2. Should the economic concerns (e.g. the potential to save taxpayers' money) ever be a consideration in deciding who has or does not have the right to have children?

Social Constructionist Models

A **social constructionist model** begins with the idea that any human social category—"race," gender, ability, and so on—is not a totally natural category, but has an important social component. **Critical disability theory** (or CDT) is a social constructionist theory that makes a distinction between a *natural impairment*, on the one hand, and *disability*, which can be understood as the barriers set up by society in dealing with that impairment. A medical condition that causes paralysis in the legs is a natural impairment until the person born with the condition is denied access to public transit because the nearest subway station has no elevator: then it's a socially constructed disability. For this reason, critical disability theorists place the emphasis on changing society rather than on "curing" or "rehabilitating" the individual.

Critical disability theory draws heavily on the **sociological imagination** in that it does not place responsibility and accountability on the individual but on society. Activism based on critical disability theory aims more at *substantive equality* than *formal equality*. A goal of **substantive equality** would be building modifications that guarantee people with natural impairments equal accessibility to and within buildings (e.g. with ramps, automatic doors, and sidewalks with no sudden drops to the road). Under the related **formal equality** model, everyone faces and must adapt to the same socially driven architecture (e.g. sidewalks with sudden drops to the road at intersections) that gives advantages to non-disabled people. Full inclusion and participation are the goals of CDT ideas and practices.

Another tenet of social constructionist theory is that each society or culture constructs its own version of social categories such as "disabled." **Nora Groce** is a medical anthropologist who specializes in looking at how different societies theorize about and treat people with disabilities. She argues that the greatest change in how we view disability is found not in how different conditions are treated clinically but "in the growing body of research that finds while disability is universal, there is marked variation in how cultures interpret disability. This research shows that the lives of individuals with disability around the world are usually far more limited by prevailing social, cultural, and economic constraints than by specific physical, sensory, psychological, or intellectual impairments" (Groce 1999: 756).

Groce identifies three main areas in which cultures differ in how they view disability:

1. causality
2. valued and devalued attributes
3. anticipated adult status.

Causality is "the cultural reason for why a disability occurs" (Groce 1999). Early Europeans, for example, attributed some disabilities (especially those involving epileptic seizures) to demon possession or witchcraft; as you can imagine, they treated people with disabilities with great suspicion and fear. Other cultures have viewed disability as the result of divine judgement, as God's punishment for some act committed by the community, or for "sins" of the parents being visited upon the children. This is an idea that seems to cross cultures and persist over time. But Groce also cites studies by medical anthropologists Benedicte Ingstad (1988) and M. Madiros (1989) showing that among the Tswana people of Botswana (in southern Africa) and among the peasant people of northern Mexico, "the birth of a disabled child is viewed as evidence of God's trust in specific parents' ability to care well for a delicate child" (Groce 1999: 756).

Groce's second point has to do with the "qualities a society finds important." In societies that value physical strength, she explains, people with physical disabilities will be at a greater disadvantage than they

QUICK HITS

But *Can They Actually . . . ? I Mean, Do They Really . . . ?*

With even a casual reading of the literature surrounding people with disabilities, you come across frequent references to the fascination among non-disabled people with whether—and how—people with physical disabilities have sex. The view that only people without disabilities are capable of (and interested in) enjoying sexual relationships proceeds from an ablist bias that assumes that certain experiences (including, also, participation in competitive sports and recreational activities) are restricted to those without disabilities.

So how do people with disabilities handle the topic when it arises? When Rick Hansen, the very athletic paraplegic wheelchair rider who travelled some 40,000 kilometres to raise awareness about disability, announced his engagement, he and his now wife, Amanda, faced the same question in different forms. Hansen explains:

> We'd already grown tired of answering The Big Question, thrown from all angles: "Uh, Amanda, we were just wondering, you know, with Rick being paraplegic and everything . . . well, um, can he . . . ? Do you . . . ? I mean . . ."
>
> It was something they wouldn't let go. The simple, truthful answers—"Yes, we do want children. No, there's no reason why we shouldn't be able to have any. Disabled people are like anyone else: some can, and some can't—and, incidentally, do you ask able-bodied people questions like that?"—apparently weren't good enough. (Hansen & Taylor 2011: 212)

What do YOU think?

Do you think that The Big Question is more about whether people with disabilities *can* have children or whether they *should* have children?

would be in a society that sets a premium on intellectual accomplishments. Likewise, a person with a speech impediment is at a disadvantage in a society that regards public speaking as a powerful means of communication.

How a society regards people with disabilities also depends on what role or status people with disabilities are expected to occupy (Groce 1999). If they are expected to participate fully in society, contributing meaningful labour and having families, then society will be willing to provide the resources to make this possible. A society that views its citizens with disabilities as a financial burden, as people in need of looking after and not in a position to contribute meaningfully,

The Point Is...

Disabling Architecture: How Mainstream Society Disables Those with Impairments

Critical disability theorists argue that impairment is a natural condition, while disability is a social one. An illustration of how mainstream society helps turn physical impairment into disability can be seen in how buildings, sidewalks, and other aspects of what we will call the "architecture of a society" are constructed. Consider the following comment from writer Nancy Mairs in her foreword to the second edition of Irving Zola's study:

> Using a power wheelchair, I grow so weary of coming abruptly to a curb without a cut, or jiggling over the brick sidewalks the city managers thought would add a touch of class to Tucson's dusty sidewalks. (in Zola 2003: ix)

But as Zola describes, in the village of Het Dorp, there were many subtle features of architecture that made homes more liveable for people with wheelchairs:

> Electric outlets were a little higher, windows a little lower, doorways a little larger—all very important to someone in a wheelchair. The bathroom was enormous by my standards. Sinks were lower, mirrors tilted, and grab bars were bolted to the walls at key points. Each home can also be fitted with electronic and mechanical devices to open and close doors, operate telephones and televisions, and reach objects. (Zola 2003:27)

Imagine what it is like to take a shower if you do not have full use of both legs. The exercise is easy if you have had the experience. When I spent three months on crutches in 2012, I had to sit on the thin edge of the bathtub and swing my legs across. My left leg was in a cast, and the cast was covered by a blue bag—which was not easy to get on—so that no water leaked into it. Then I had to have my shower while I stood on one leg. I dreaded what would happen if I dropped the soap. Zola began his lengthy description of trying to take a shower with the telling sentence: "Bathrooms are simply not designed for any but the extremely fit and stable" (Zola 2003: 133).

What do YOU think?

1. What are the benefits to society of having **universal architecture** that makes the built environment—buildings, sidewalks, parks, transit systems, ATM machines, etc.—equally accessible to people who use wheelchairs and those who do not? What do you think are the main reasons that accessibility for people who use wheelchairs has not been taken into account in the architecture of our public spaces?

2. As a learning exercise, bring a chair that will fit into your bathroom and sit on it. Then try to get into the shower. You may use only one leg. How do you think you could survive if you spent some time in a wheelchair?

will likely be stingy about the resources it allocates to help individuals overcome disability.

Master Status and Labelling Theory

In Chapter 6 we talked about the statuses that people have at any given time. Remember that a **status** is a position one holds that is recognized by society. The statuses that I hold right now are college professor, writer, drummer, husband, stepfather, brother, pet owner (especially of parrots). A person's **master status** is the one that leads the way in terms of how a person's identity is defined and how others see and interact with that person. **Labelling theory**, also presented in Chapter 6, helps us understand that sometimes a negative label that society attaches to a person can be not just an important status but a master status as well. Zola gives a very concrete example how the label "disabled" was applied to him and became, in the eyes of many people he met who noticed his cane, long leg brace, and pronounced limp, his master status:

[F]or years I have had the experience of being mistaken for someone else. Usually I was in a new place and a stranger would greet me as Tom, Dick, or Harry. After I explained that I was not he, they would usually apologize, saying "You look just like him." Inevitably I would meet this Tom, Dick, or Harry, and he would be several inches shorter or taller, forty pounds heavier or lighter, a double amputee on crutches or a paraplegic in a wheel-chair. I was annoyed and even puzzled how anyone could mistake him for the "unique me." (Zola 2003: 199)

David Morrison is a blogger and college student who has cerebral palsy. In one of his blog posts directed at people without disabilities, he provides four tips to avoid making a person's disability into a master status:

1. Speak to the person, not the wheelchair or his/her assistant.
2. Make eye contact as often as possible
3. Treat a wheelchair as part of personal space
4. Assist the person only after asking.

(Morrison 2010)

Labelling theory is fundamentally about the words we apply to people to describe them. In this photo of 23-year-old Korean pianist Hee Ah Lee, do you see a disabled musician or a musician with a disability? A four-fingered pianist/vocalist or a pianist/vocalist who has overcome a physical impairment to pursue a career in piano and vocal performance? How significant do you think the difference is?

The Point Is...

"How Lame Is That?" The Trouble with Labels

You're quitting already? That's so lame.

What a lamoid!

They won't win another game under this lame-duck coach.

She bailed—she had some lame excuse about work.

Another lame-brained idea from the geniuses at head office.

These are all phrases you could hear anywhere—around campus, at the neighbourhood coffee shop, on the Internet. Once used without judgement to describe a person who walked with difficulty because of a leg or foot injury, the word "lame" is never used in a neutral sense today: it is always derogatory. And though it has all but lost its association with disability, you can find plenty of bloggers and others online who object to the pejorative, or negative, use of the word because of the way it reflects on people with disabilities.

But should they? After all, language changes over time, and you can call a friend "lame" without intending any disrespect to people with disabilities. Think about the words that have been used for people with mental disabilities. There were once tests to distinguish, in downward fashion, a "moron" (test score of 51–70) from an "imbecile" (26–50) and an "idiot" (0–25). The scale was precise and scientific. Today we use those terms without meaning any disrespect to people with mental disabilities. And isn't that the main issue—respect?

You might be saying as you read this, *I know a person who is disabled who uses the word "lame" herself.* Writer Nancy Mairs, who wrote the foreword to Irving Zola's *Missing Pieces* and who lives with multiple sclerosis, wrote an essay titled "On Being a Cripple," in which she defended her use of the word "cripple," writing:

I choose this word to name me. . . . Perhaps I want [people] to wince. I want them to see me as a tough customer, one to whom the fates/gods/viruses have not been kind, but who can face the brutal truth of her existence squarely. As a cripple, I swagger. (Mairs 1986)

But as with the black man who uses the word *nigger* or the Aboriginal woman who uses the word *squaw*, the labels we use to describe ourselves cannot always be applied without offence to others. (I can call myself a "moron," but I wouldn't want you calling me that.)

So what is the right way to refer to people with disabilities? Outdated terms such as *crippled*, *retarded*, and *handicapped* are rightfully condemned as too negative and lacking in respect. Yet there is still disagreement among academics, people in the "disability business," and people with disabilities as to the right approach.

Here is a general rule: avoid labels that emphasize limitation. Referring to someone as "a disabled person" or "an epileptic" is like labelling the whole person with the disability, turning it into a master status. Instead, use descriptive phrases that put the person *before* the disability, and reserve labels for achievements: "a good friend of mine who has epilepsy," "a brilliant student who uses a wheelchair." Avoid pitying phrases such as "who suffers from" or "who is stricken with," and mention the disability only when it is relevant.

In *Missing Pieces*, Zola writes that he was disturbed by the use of the term *invalid* by many people he encountered in the Netherlands (Zola 2003: 3), given its implications that people with disabilities are somehow not as valid as the "normals." I was disturbed by the fact that I had never thought of that before.

Deaf Culture

The box above advises against using adjective labels (*handicapped*, *paraplegic*, *learning-disabled*, etc.) for people with disabilities. Here's an exception to that guideline.

We can speak meaningfully of there being a **Deaf culture**, or even more accurately, Deaf cultures, with historically established cultural traditions. The traditions that define Deaf culture include:

- sign language learned as a first language

- schools for Deaf people (versus integration in regular schools)
- theatre, writing (especially in magazines and journals), videos, and films for Deaf people
- social groups and organizations for people involved in Deaf culture
- a value set that integrates all of the above components.

You will notice right away the use of the capital "D," which distinguishes the term used by the people themselves to refer to the social community of Deaf people from the physical condition, for which the lowercase term "deaf" is used. Likewise "deafness" is used for the condition, while "Deafness" refers to cultural membership. Think of it in Marxian terms as a people with a consciousness of themselves as a community, like workers being aware of themselves as a group.

Many people in Deaf culture, particularly those who were born deaf as opposed to those who acquired deafness over the course of their lives (sometimes called "deafened" or "late-deafened"), object to having their deafness characterized as a disability, as they don't see themselves as disabled. For this reason, they generally prefer not to use the term "hearing-impaired," as they object to the negative connotations of the word "impaired." People with partial hearing loss who are accustomed to communicating via speech may be described as "hard of hearing" (CAD 2012a).

The social institutions key to the development of Deaf culture are primarily educational institutions, such as residential schools for the Deaf and post-secondary institutions such as Gallaudet University and the National Technical Institute for the Deaf in the United States. Located in Washington, DC, Gallaudet University is a liberal arts university that began in the mid-nineteenth century as the Columbia Institute for the Instruction of the Deaf and Dumb and Blind. It was granted the authority to grant academic degrees in 1864. Deaf clubs were instrumental to cultivating Deaf culture during the 1940s and 1950s, although their role has severely diminished over the last 40 to 50 years.

According to the Canadian Association of the Deaf (2012a), the deaf, the deafened, and the hard of hearing are distinct social groups whose differences should be respected and not lumped together collectively under the heading "hearing-impaired". What different social realities does each of these groups face? Why do you think that each would want to be seen as separate from the other two groups?

Sign Language versus Lip Reading

Central to Deaf culture is sign language. Deaf cultures are defined to a significant extent by the form of sign language that they use. There are said to be about 200 different sign languages, and these do not necessarily align themselves with the spoken languages they connect with. There is no word-to-word correspondence between, say, spoken or written English and any of the varieties of sign language commonly used in North America. Sign languages develop independently of spoken languages, with their own vocabularies and grammars; they are not merely "acted-out" versions of spoken languages. And they can be quite different from one another. American Sign Language (ASL) is used in the United States and Canada, while British Sign Language (BSL) is used in the United Kingdom—and the two are more different than North American and British varieties of English. ASL was heavily influenced by the sign language that originated in France, owing largely to the influence of French educator Laurent Clerc, who in 1817 helped establish the first long-term school for deaf children in the United States, in Hartford, Connecticut. Typically Canadian, sign languages taught in schools for the deaf in Canada in the nineteenth century were modelled on the versions first developed in Britain and in France, but now anglophones use ASL and francophones use Langue des signes québécoise (LSQ), both of which exist with regional variants.

The centrality of sign language can be seen in the battle between proponents of sign language and advocates of lip-reading. Lip-reading is essentially a passive, one-direction skill, in that it enables Deaf people to understand what hearing people are saying, but not to communicate themselves. It reflects the minoritized position of deaf (and Deaf) people. Militant Deaf people argue that it supports an **oralist** bias: *We (the Deaf) can "hear" you (the hearing), but you cannot hear us. You don't even try.* Schools have been the battlegrounds, and the trend is to favour sign language. Different jurisdictions in the United States and Canada have been introducing Deaf studies in the classroom,

and making the teaching of sign language part of the program. Since 1987, the University of Alberta has had a Chair of Deafness Studies.

Deaf Culture versus Medicalization

Deaf culture stands in opposition to what it refers to as the *medicalization of deafness*. **Medicalization** is the tendency to define a particular condition as a medical problem requiring medical intervention; it is a product of the medical model of disability that we considered earlier in the chapter. In this context, it is the view that deafness is an undesirable physical defect that must be "fixed." As Broesterhuizen and Leuven explain, "deaf people are considered as people who lack something, incapable of being fully fledged members of society, less human than others. Their language, Sign Language, is [considered] a remnant of a lower stage of evolution, an 'ape language'" (2008: 108).

Far from considering themselves disabled, many Deaf people regard themselves as part of a vibrant cultural group, with its own language, traditions, and history. Their anti-medicalization stance entails an opposition (in certain but not all circumstances) to hearing aids and cochlear implants. A cochlear implant is an electronic device that is surgically implanted in the ear to provide a sense of sound to a deaf person.

What do YOU think?

1. What is the difference between "Deaf" and "deaf?"
2. Why do Deaf communities oppose the teaching of lip-reading?

What do YOU think?

1. Is deafness a disability? Is it a cultural trait? Do you think that your position might be different if you were deaf or had a family member or friend who was deaf?
2. Some research shows that deaf children fitted with cochlear implants before the age of 2 develop spoken language skills much more quickly than children older than 2 who have had the surgery (Kral & O'Donoghue 2010). Do you think it is appropriate to have this surgery performed on children before they are old enough to be consulted? How do you think your answer might differ if you were a deaf (or Deaf) parent weighing the options?
3. Harlan Lane, distinguished professor of psychology at Northeastern University in Boston, is a champion of Deaf culture and outspoken critic of the medicalization of deafness generally and of cochlear implants in particular. Does the fact he is not deaf in any way diminish the authority of his insights?

The Blind in Canada: Border Crossers Welcome

We could argue that members of Deaf culture have used a sociological imagination to understand and define their position in society, particularly in relation to hearing people. Deaf people recognize that the challenges they face come not from their common physical condition but from the way that condition is interpreted by society at large. Their goals include community building and self-representation (rather than allowing themselves to be represented primarily by outsiders).

The position of blind people in Canada is similar. Although there is not a well-defined "blind culture" akin to Deaf culture, the blind consider blindness a cultural trait rather than a disability. Consider the following statement from the website of the Canadian Federation of the Blind (CFB):

> We believe blindness is not a handicap, but a characteristic. The high unemployment rate and lack of opportunities for blind Canadians are not due to our blindness; they are due to social and economic inequalities in society. Like the civil rights movement, we will work to establish positive and productive roles for blind people in this country. We will work to educate the public. We will work to change what it means to be blind.

Our Philosophy
* We are not an organization speaking on behalf of blind people; rather we are an organization of blind people speaking for ourselves.
* We believe that blindness is not a handicap, but a characteristic.
* We believe it is respectable to be blind.
* We believe that with training and opportunity, blind people can compete on terms of equality with their sighted peers.
* We believe the real problem of blindness is not the lack of eyesight. The real problem is the lack of positive information about blindness and the achievements of blind people.

It is important to recognize that statements such as this emphasize inclusion rather than exclusion. McMaster University cultural critic Henry Giroux uses the term **border crossers** to refer to people who do not belong

QUICK HITS

Deaf Rights

The following paragraph on the rights of Deaf Canadians comes from an entry in the *Canadian Encyclopedia* written by Clifton F. Carbin (author of the definitive work *Deaf Heritage in Canada*, 1996) and Dorothy L. Smith (no, not the sociologist). It is presented in its entirety as we cannot improve upon on it, or summarize it without cutting it too short.

For many years, deaf Canadians have had to actively fight to obtain or maintain certain human rights and privileges, such as the right to drive an automobile; to serve on juries; to have sign language interpreters present in medical and legal situations; to obtain training in their chosen careers; to keep their own schools open rather than be integrated into schools with hearing students; to be allowed to use sign language in the classroom; to have captioned programs on television; to be viewed culturally (as a linguistic and cultural group of people) rather than pathologically (as people with an audiological condition that needs to be "fixed"). Members of the Deaf community and other individuals (both deaf and hearing) who support Deaf Culture have been involved in public protests and demonstrations to make their concerns known to legislators, educators and the general public. Deaf people want to be recognized as partners in the heritage that is Canada, without having to surrender their precious language and culture. (Carbin & Smith 2012)

Opponents in the Deaf community argue that from a medical standpoint, the surgery is risky and not always completely successful. From a social standpoint, it can interfere with the identity formation of a Deaf person (especially a young Deaf person), depriving the person of membership in the cultural community into which he or she was born (Lane 1992, 1993). Other medicalized approaches to deafness include the imposition of therapies designed to teach deaf people to communicate using spoken languages, and the promotion of sign systems modelled on spoken languages (English, French, etc.) in terms of their structure and vocabulary (CAD 2012b).

Action from the 2013 Courage Canada Blind Hockey Tournament. Blind and visually impaired players use an "adapted puck that is bigger, slower, and makes noise as it travels" (Mercurio 2013). Some might argue that hockey programs are not the best place to invest in resources for blind people. What do you think?

to a group (in this case, the blind) but who are nonetheless sympathetic to the goals of the group and act in a supportive, but not primarily representative, way—in other words, they do not claim to speak *for* the group but *about* them. In the writings of Deaf culture, the term **honorary members** is used.

Topics in the Study of Disability

Inclusion/Exclusion, Integration/Segregation

Deaf culture highlights one of the tensions that arises repeatedly in the discussion of disability: inclusion versus exclusion. Deaf people want to be accepted as "fully fledged members of society" (to use Broesterhuizen and Leuven's term), no less capable than non-deaf people of contributing meaningfully to the community. They also want their difference acknowledged and respected. Are these compatible aims?

To take another example, consider the case of people with mental illness. Beginning in large numbers in the 1970s, and occurring again in the 1990s with nationwide cuts to provincial funding, many people with mental health issues such as schizophrenia were released from mental hospitals, asylums, and other large institutions (the one in Newfoundland and Labrador, on the outskirts of St John's, is known locally as "the Mental"). In some ways this is a good thing: it took people out of what **Goffman** called **total institutions**, places where all aspects of life are controlled as if the people living there were prisoners. It could potentially lead the way to independent living in group or community homes, enabling people with mental illness to integrate more completely into the larger society. But in practice, this hasn't had these desired effects. It has meant dumping people into the street to save money, without following the steps laid out in social theories on the need of people with mental/emotional disabilities for independence and integration. In major urban centres, this "downloading" has swelled the ranks of the homeless; there were simply not enough "partial institutions" to ease the integration into mainstream society of people released en masse from their total institutions.

Total institution segregation is a bad thing when it hides people with disabilities from the broader community. It does not enable people with disabilities to participate meaningfully in mainstream society, and it is especially hard on people whose relatives have relinquished their responsibility as caregivers. But segregation can also foster community development among people who share a physical condition, as is ably demonstrated in the case of the Deaf community. Schools for the Deaf—controversial because of the way they encourage segregation rather than integration—have been at the centre of the development of Deaf culture.

The Boy in the Moon: A Father's Search for His Disabled Son (2009) is journalist Ian Brown's powerful account of his relationship with his son, Walker. Walker has the rare, recently "discovered" and very disabling genetic disorder cardiofaciocutaneous ("heart-face-skin") syndrome, or CFC, which is typically associated with heart defects and some degree of learning difficulty and developmental delay. The following passage presents an argument for segregation versus integration:

At the age of five, Walker begins to attend Beverley Junior Public School—a famous local institution dedicated entirely to intellectually disabled

---

Telling It Like It Is

An Author POV

Disability and the Workplace

People with disabilities pose a challenge to employers that often results at best in their marginalization, at worst in their being "let go" (particularly when the downsizing excuse is available and there is no union to protect the outgoing employee). One employer with a documented history of marginalizing workers with disabilities is the military. In Canada, it seems, if you die in Afghanistan, then you are a hero, but if you are merely wounded or suffer emotional trauma, then you are not. You have to give all of your life to your country, not part of it. You don't return home on the Highway of Heroes. In "The Hidden Face of Our Injured Soldiers," journalists B. Campion-Smith and A. Woods (2010) identified the following problems facing Afghanistan veterans:

- The prospect of being assigned menial office work while facing long delays in career retraining.
- A paid schooling period that is too short (just two years) to complete a degree or diploma program or learn a trade.
- Exclusion from recent, non-retroactive improvements to financial assistance for soldiers injured early in the conflict.

- A one-time payout (capped at $276,000), which has replaced the lifetime disability pension.
- Inadequate resources for soldiers suffering from post-traumatic stress disorder.
- Unequal compensation for reservists, who make up 20 per cent of Canada's Afghanistan force. (Campion-Smith & Woods 2010)

Retired colonel Pat Stogran, who was the veterans' ombudsman, criticized Veterans Affairs Canada for what he called "an insurance-company culture of denial." His active advocacy for veterans lasted just one term.

The question we ask is why. Does it come down to expense? Does a dead soldier cost the system less than a wounded one? How much of this situation has to do with our lack of respect for the disabled?

We have a better understanding of the effects of post-traumatic stress, the condition that used to be called "shell shock" and which could lead to the execution of soldiers who did not recover from their emotional breakdowns during World War I. We are in a better position today to care for our veterans—but we have a long way to go.

children, where the ratio of students to teachers is a mere three-to-one. The school is a bright, airy space designed for children who can't see out of normal windows or walk easily through a standard door. Its effect on Walker's confidence is instantaneous: within a month he progresses from needing to be carried from room to room at school to walking on his own. But within a year, the [Conservative] provincial government announces its intention to close the school. The school is only for the disabled—a "segregated" facility, in the parlance of disability education—and doesn't conform to the province's policy of supporting (much cheaper) "inclusive" schools, where, theoretically, the disabled learn alongside the abled, and each gets used to the other. Inclusive schools are often excellent, and much preferred by a certain generation and political ilk of educators. But even those educators will admit integration isn't for everyone, that dedicated facilities can be more helpful for children as delayed as Walker. (Brown 2009: 87)

You should notice how using the buzzwords of inclusion—generally seen as a good thing—can be used to justify cost cutting over the welfare of people (in this case students) with disabilities. All too often the special education teachers who make the inclusive schools work are treated as "extras" by a school board looking to save money, leaving a good number of children with disabilities and their families scrambling for alternatives.

Real Inclusion versus Tokenism

The Lou Marsh Trophy is awarded annually by a panel of journalists to the most outstanding Canadian athlete. In 1983, for the first and only time since its inception in 1936, the award was given to two athletes representing different sports: Wayne Gretzky, then of the NHL's Edmonton Oilers, and marathoner Rick Hansen. Hansen's victory marked the second time the panel had awarded the Lou Marsh Trophy to an athlete with a disability—Terry Fox had won the award in 1980 for his Marathon of Hope, and track athlete

Canada's Ian Chan competes in an international rugby match. Do you think wheelchair sports should be part of the regular Olympics instead of being kept separate in the Paralympics? Should there be any difference, say, in the way athletic federations view bicycle racing and wheelchair racing, both of which involve humans trying to go as fast as they can with machines?

Chantal Petitclerc would win in 2008. But there was something about the award that Hansen did not like:

> What I actually received was an "auxiliary" award, something the Marsh committee handed out on occasions when an outstanding athlete "didn't quite fit the category."
>
> "Who does fit the category?" I asked.
>
> Well, a male or female athlete, amateur or professional.
>
> "I see. And what does that make me?" (Hansen & Taylor 2011: 70)

Hansen felt the honour was an instance of **tokenism**, a symbolic gesture of inclusion intended to give the impression that the committee respected wheelchair sports as much as mainstream sports like hockey. Hansen at first planned to hold a press conference to express his protest in public. Instead, he wrote an impassioned letter to the committee, and was happy with how they responded. To his knowledge, no one attached the word "auxiliary" to his honour in media reports announcing his award.

It's worth noting that Hansen himself did not start out with a full appreciation of wheelchair sports. These were his thoughts when he first started to compete at age 16:

> I knew there was a wheelchair basketball team in Vancouver, and a wheelchair sports organization, but I didn't have much respect for it, because I still had the same attitude that most people do: gee, look at the people in wheelchairs playing. Isn't it nice that they can have a little recreation and rehabilitation?
>
> Serious? Competitive? Don't be silly. (Hansen & Taylor 2011: 59)

He would change his opinion later, when he experienced the high level of competition in wheelchair racing, not to mention basketball and volleyball. He would later push for the inclusion of at least one wheelchair sport as a regular Olympic sport (and not just a "demonstration sport").

Disability and the Family

Parents with Disabilities

We return here to the Erving Goffman's *Stigma* (1963), which was so useful in looking at deviance. Goffman used the term **stigma** to refer to a human characteristic that is somehow discrediting. Recall how he referred to their being three types of **stigmata** (plural of *stigma*):

- bodily stigmata
- moral stigmata
- tribal stigmata.

Bodily stigmata he described as socially defined "abominations of the body"—in other words, physical features that society has judged to be undesirable. **Moral stigmata** are character blemishes, such as "weak will, domineering or unnatural passions, treacherous and rigid beliefs, and dishonesty." **Tribal stigmata** are group identities associated with "race, nation, and religion," which can be passed down from generation to generation, affecting whole families and their descendants (Goffman 1963: 4).

You might think that our concern in this chapter would be with bodily stigmata primarily. But in an insightful and pioneering work, Karen A. Blackford (1996) used case studies of 18 Ontario families with parents who had multiple sclerosis (MS) to show that a parent with a disability can be marked or discredited by all three kinds of stigma:

> That is, physical symptoms such as Mr Chapman's muscle contractures and Mrs Taylor's leg cramps can be seen as "abominations of the body," . . . while the procreation of children in spite of a chronic parental illness could be construed as "blemishes of . . . character perceived as weak will . . . or unnatural passions." . . . Finally, genetic theories of multiple sclerosis can lead to the perception of stigmatizing attributes in children that are "transmitted through lineages and equally contaminate all members of a family." . . . Thus, we can easily argue that parental multiple sclerosis has the potential to be a focus of stigma." (Blackford 1996: 185–6)

Blackford takes sociologists to task for their treatment of families with parents who have disabilities. First, she notes the general lack of research done in the area by sociologists studying family issues. Second, she finds two flaws in what she calls "mainstream rehabilitation research of families with parental disability" (Blackford 1996: 163). One is that when research turns up cases in which parents with disabilities face barriers to social relations with other family members, "there has been no exploration of the sources of that oppression. Instead, these studies leave the impression that the family system and its mere association with parental disability is somehow 'naturally' to blame" (Blackford 1996: 163). By focusing on the problem only as it exists within the household, these researchers fail to take into account the effect of systemic **disability oppression** (to borrow, as Blackford does, the term coined by leading disability researcher Michael Oliver). The term refers to all of the forms of mistreatment that people with disabilities face. Blackford argues that researchers should not ignore the way that prevailing societal attitudes towards people with disabilities can have a large impact on how parents with disabilities are treated by family members.

The second flaw Blackford notes is the failure of earlier researchers to "sensitively consider creative ways in which families have come to deal with the situation. Consideration has rarely been given to the potential for alternative definitions of family life and a parental disability that might emerge in these families" (Blackford 1996: 166). Blackford here homes in on a concept often invoked in anti-racism literature: **agency** (the ability to make choices that will affect one's situation rather than having one's circumstances decided by others). Agency is evident in a quotation she cites from a mother with a disability, commenting on parenting:

> I've come to realize that we may give our children something which is uniquely the result of our . . . disabilities. . . . To have a hand in producing emotional resilience, compassion, and the willingness to set reasonable goals for oneself is a very fine expression of parental love. (Lemaistre 1985: 291, as cited in Blackford 1996: 166)

Children with Disabilities

Being a parent of a child with a disability presents many severe challenges, including the persistent debate about whether it is better to shelter the child or encourage the child to strive for independence. Either way can produce feelings of fulfillment (being the "good parent") or guilt (being the "bad parent"). The following two quotations come from York University sociologist Karen Anderson's brilliant work on diversity. Both excerpts feature intelligent people with cerebral palsy, a much debilitating disorder, talking about the role their parents played in balancing control and independence.

What do you think should be the aims of the sociologist studying "disabled families"?

The first passage comes from "Ed Murphy" (not his real name), who as a child was wrongly labelled "mentally retarded" and put into a **total institution** at 15. Here, he speaks of his mother's over-protection:

> The doctors told my mother that I would be a burden to her. When I was growing up she never let me out of her sight. She was always there with attention. If I yelled she ran right to me. So many children who are handicapped must be in that position—they become so dependent on their mother. Looking back I don't think she ever stopped protecting me even when I was capable of being self-sufficient. I remember how hard it was to break away from that. She never really believed that after I had lived the first six months that I could be like everybody else. (Taylor & Bogdan 1984: 158–9, as cited in Anderson 1996: 387)

The second quotation comes from psychologist Sondra Diamond, from a cleverly named article entitled "Growing up with Parents of a Handicapped Child: A Handicapped Person's Perspective":

> I recall the first time I used a Kotex. My mother handed me the sanitary belt and Kotex, and said, "It's time you learned to put this on yourself." I sat on the toilet for three hours, struggling, sweating, and swearing. Every few minutes, I heard my father yelling at my mother, "Rose, go in there and give her a hand." Since it was the weekend, the usual flow of neighbours and friends were coming in and out of the house. Noticing my absence, they asked what I was doing in the bathroom so long. I remember hearing her explain, and hearing each of them say, in different ways, "Rose, how can you be so cruel?" My father was in a rage. The neighbours were outraged by my mother's treatment of me. My mother never wavered. Amid this commotion, I learned how to use a Kotex, secretly admiring my mother's fortitude, and getting a kick out of the fuss that was being made over me. (Diamond 1981: 28, as cited in Anderson 1996: 387)

Disability and Gender

In other chapters we have talked about **intersectionality theory**, which looks at the ways social factors (e.g. race and gender) combine to make an individual more minoritized and more oppressed. The same would appear to be true with gender and disability. We know, for instance, that "educated" women with disabilities are less likely than their male counterparts to find work (Fine & Asch 1988). There is a lack of good research on this topic, though, and so the two situations we will consider here are impressionistic, more in the form of untested hypotheses than something in evidence. I invite you to imagine how you might research this area to prove or disprove these hypotheses.

The first hypothesis comes from Zola, who expressed a belief that it was easier for a man with a disability to establish a lasting relationship with a non-disabled woman than for a woman with a disability to do so with a non-disabled man. Support for his belief came from Marlene, one of the residents of Het Thorp, who said:

> For handicapped men it's easier. . . . They can find a woman to care for them, but who wants a handicapped woman? Men want a woman who is whole, who can do the housework and cook and everything else. (as cited in Zola 2003: 146)

What do YOU think?

1. Do you think that what Marlene said was more true in the early 1970s, when gender roles were in some ways more traditional, than in the 2010s, when there has been a measure of change?

2. Do you believe this hypothesis would prove to be valid in twenty-first–century Canada?

3. How would you design a research study to prove or disprove this hypothesis?

The second hypothesis comes largely from my own observations as a long-time bearded feminist. Fibromyalgia (from *fibra-*, "fibre"; *myo-*, "muscle"; and *algos-*, "pain") is a disabling disorder that occurs far more frequently in women than in men (the ratio of female to male cases is 9 to 1, according to a Danish study [Bartels, et al. 2009]). It is chronic and painful.

I learned about fibromyalgia because my wife suffers from it. My impression of its treatment is that it is of the "try this and see" approach, supported by certain naturopathic "cures" without any scientific evidence behind them that I have seen, and monitored with some expensive machines "that go ping" (c.f.

Our Stories

Realizing Individual Ability through Group Action

Their ability is obvious when you see the products of their work. They are gifted artists, their work beautiful. Yet they do not draw or paint with their hands. They use their mouths; some, fewer, use one or both of their feet. They belong to an organization called the Association of Mouth and Foot Painter Artists (MFPA).

Although there had been mouth painters before (the earliest being nineteenth-century artist Sarfa Biffen), they were isolated and rare when the MFPA began in 1956. It started in Germany, when painter Erich Stegmann, who had lost the use of his arms because of childhood polio, brought artists without hands together from different countries so that they could individually and collectively gain independence, and self-esteem, by earning a living with their art. The MFPA actively markets the artists' work throughout the world. Membership extends through some 70 countries, with roughly 700 members.

Artists begin as student members, earning the right by submitting a portfolio of work for appraisal by established members. If successful, an artist will receive money for expenses and training until he or she becomes an associate, or achieves full membership.

The MFPA came to Canada in 1961. One of the most famous Canadian members is Susie Matthias, who was born in London, Ontario. Her mother, during her pregnancy, had taken Thalidomide, a drug prescribed in Canada from 1957 until 1962 as a sedative aimed at easing the effects of morning sickness. Many children of mothers who took the drug were born with serious birth defects. Susie Matthias was born without arms or legs.

Matthias was young when she began experimenting with mouth painting. It is hard to imagine the drive to art a person would have to have to want to do that, not to mention the self-awareness and confidence Matthias would have required to come to know she had talent—reaching that point is often a hard thing for any artist, writer, or musician.

With extensive training that she was able to pursue owing in part to her strong family support, Matthias rose steadily in both accomplishment and fame. In 2000, she was one of three winners of a national competition to have her art appear on a Canadian stamp. In 2008, the lieutenant governor of Ontario, David Onley, presented one of her paintings

Monty Python). Calling it a "bitterly controversial condition," rheumatologist Frederick Wolfe (2009) has written about how a large majority of doctors, sociologists, and medical historians have tended to reject fibromyalgia as a disease. Indeed, the terms "merely psychological" and "non-disease" appear in the medical literature. I suspect what Wolfe has observed is the opinion that prevails among three professions (medicine, sociology, and history) dominated by men. Mohammed Yunus, a medical specialist who wrote about the disorder in 1981, called the denial of fibromyalgia "DPS," or "disturbed physician syndrome," expressing his view that "It is the physicians who are psychologically disturbed because they ignore the

data" (Yunus, as cited in Cooper & Miller 2010: 114).

Here is my sociological hypothesis concerning the diagnosis and treatment of fibromyalgia (and other disorders that disproportionately affect women, such as chronic fatigue syndrome). No, I am not a doctor, but remember that most medical sociology in Canada is performed by medical professionals who, like me, are "visiting" a profession not their own. From my reading of the literature on the disorder, supplemented with anecdotal accounts of women who have fibromyalgia, I suggest that the condition is a symptomatic response to stress. The stress in this case (and here is where the sociology comes in) stems from situations that affect women more than men: sexual abuse, physical abuse,

Susie Matthias talks with the media at the Hockey Hall of Fame in Toronto in November 2005 after presenting a goalie mask she mouth-painted.

to Queen Elizabeth. Susie Matthias now supports herself through her art and lives independently. Of what she has gained from the MFPA she says, "You're independent in various ways and also you've proven to yourself and others the value of you, not only as an artist, but as a person. It's quite amazing. I'm so thrilled to be in the Association, I really am."

How do we assess this as sociologists? It would be misleading to frame Matthias's success in the context of the American dream, as though anyone like her who can "dream big and work hard" has just as much chance of achieving her success. It would be more realistic to observe that when people with disabilities band together as a group, as mouth artists have under MFPA (an organization owned and run by people with disabilities), they can achieve agency much more effectively than they can as individuals. What Matthias has been able to accomplish is a testament both to the talent and will of the individual, and to the strength and dedication of the group to make it work.

intense frustration at being controlled by males, working full-time and being a full-time parent, and so on. The literature gives too little attention to social causes of the condition, dwelling far more on genetics (which appears more scientific because it is lab-based).

How would I prove this hypothesis? What research would a sociologist engage in to prove or disprove this?

Disability and "Race": The Sameness of Oppression and Discrimination

Basil Johnston is a prolific Anishinabe (Ojibwa) storyteller, writer, and educator. In 1999, he published a book called *Crazy Dave*, about his uncle, David McLeod, who had played an important role in Johnston's life for five years. Dave had always had a hard time learning to do things that were easy for others to learn. It had taken him seven years to become toilet-trained. His speech was incoherent.

But Dave's learning disability did not prevent him from developing useful skills. He learned to cut and split wood so well that he earned money doing it. Later, he began salvaging and selling scrap metal. And he could roll his own cigarettes. The local Indian Agent wanted Dave placed in an institution, feeling he was a danger to society, but he wasn't.

The book contains an interesting piece in which Johnston talks about the similarity between the oppression and discrimination of people with mental disabilities and the treatment of Aboriginal people:

> The more I thought about him, the more he reminded me, in certain respects, of the place and situation of the North American Indian in Canadian society. It was assumed that Uncle David didn't know much about anything, or what he knew didn't count; what North American Indians knew didn't amount to a jar of jelly beans, and did not have any larger relevance. As long as Uncle David stayed where he belonged and didn't bother anyone or interfere with anyone's business, neighbors could put up with him; and as long as North American Indians kept the peace and didn't rock the boat, society could tolerate them. Uncle David didn't belong in the community. He wasn't one of the normal human beings; he was dumb and couldn't talk; didn't and couldn't understand.
>
> He didn't belong in the society of sensible people. He belonged in some institution where he could have learned to help himself and earn a place at the bottom of the totem pole, or the ladder.
>
> Indians didn't belong in Canadian society. They were wild. They were more at home in the forest and in the open prairies, with bears and gophers. . . . They didn't understand or practice Western European traditions. They belonged in an institution where they would be supervised, tolerated, and modified before they could be admitted into the larger civilized society. (Johnston 1999: 11)

What do YOU think?

In what ways, according to Basil Johnston, are Aboriginal people and people with mental disability viewed and treated in similar ways?

WRAP IT UP

Summary

There is an often (mis)quoted line from Matthew 26: 11 in the Bible: "the poor are always with us." The same can be said for people with disabilities. And just as people can be poor in different ways—financially, of course, but also socially, emotionally, morally—there are many forms that disability can take, some of them visible, others invisible. Defining disability is no easy feat: it can include some things we wouldn't necessarily think of right away—depression, addiction, memory loss, for instance—while the inclusion of other conditions—notably deafness—is contested by the very people who experience them. Key to the discussion is the point that while *people have impairments*, it is *society that constructs disability* as a social category. This is the underlying principle of critical disability theories. Standpoint is important to consider as well. Medical professionals generally approach disability from the standpoint of trying reverse or repair the condition; that is their job, and health professionals and researchers have made astonishing advances in treating impairments including vision and hearing loss, limited mobility, and chronic pain, to name just a few. But if we fail to consider other, non-medicalizing standpoints, we will be missing something critical. The point was developed in this chapter most completely in terms of Deaf culture and the blind, but it has relevance to other disabilities or impairments as well.

THINK BACK

Questions for Critical Reflection

1. Explain what is meant by the statement that people have impairments but societies construct disabilities.

2. What do you think the intersection between disability and "race" would look like? In what ways might the experience of disability differ among people of different ethnic backgrounds (Chinese, eastern European, Caribbean, British, Métis, etc.)? How could you study it?

3. Have you ever experienced, or do you currently experience, an impairment of some kind? Consider anything from a mobility-limiting injury (broken arm, ankle sprain) or congenital condition (muscular dystrophy) to a learning disability (dyslexia, attention-deficit disorder). How does your experience connect with what was written in this chapter? Under what circumstances did the impairment become a disability?

4. Should children with disabilities be encouraged to attend regular, mainstream schools wherever possible? Are there situations in which you think they are better off in specialized, separate schools? What criteria did you use to address this question?

READ ON

Online

Society for Disability Studies

http://disstudies.org/

> Established in part by Irving Zola, the SDS is committed to establishing disability studies as a bona fide academic discipline. The website provides information on the organization's mission and current work.

Canadian Centre on Disability Studies

http://disabilitystudies.ca

> The CCDS is dedicated to studying and developing programs with and for people with disabilities. The website has news about current projects and events, as well as published reports on research and completed community projects.

David Morrison

http://disabilities.blogs.starnewsonline.com

> David Morrison is a college student in North Carolina and chair of the Cape Fear Disability Commission. His blog provides some thought-provoking insights into the life of a person living with a disability.

Canadian Association of the Deaf

www.cad.ca/terminology_deafness.php

When it comes to disability, like other social conditions, labelling is a thorny issue. This page, from the CAD's website, gives the organization's position on a variety of terms relating to hearing impairment.

In Print

Karen Blackford (1996), "Families and Parental Disability," in Marion Lynn (Ed.), *Voices: Essays on Canadian Families*, pp. 161–94 (Toronto: Nelson).

A strong examination of the reality facing families with parents with disabilities, written by the late research chair on the Canadian Centre on Disability Studies.

Ian Brown (2009), *The Boy in the Moon: A Father's Search for his Disabled Son* (Toronto: Vintage).

A leading Canadian journalist's very moving, honest, and insightful account of a parent's relationship with a son living with a severe disability.

Erving Goffman (1963), *Stigma: Notes on the Management of Spoiled Identity* (Englewood Cliffs, NJ: Prentice Hall).

The foundational study of the nature of stigma.

Harlan L. Lane (1992), *The Mask of Benevolence: Disabling the Deaf Community* (New York: Knopf).

An important work on the social construction of disability—specifically, the medicalization of hearing impairment—by a leading advocate of Deaf culture.

Irving K. Zola (2003), *Missing Pieces: A Chronicle of Living with a Disability*, 2nd edn (Philadelphia: Temple University Press).

A first-person narrative, by a sociologist with a disability, of living in a planned community for people living with disabilities in the Netherlands.

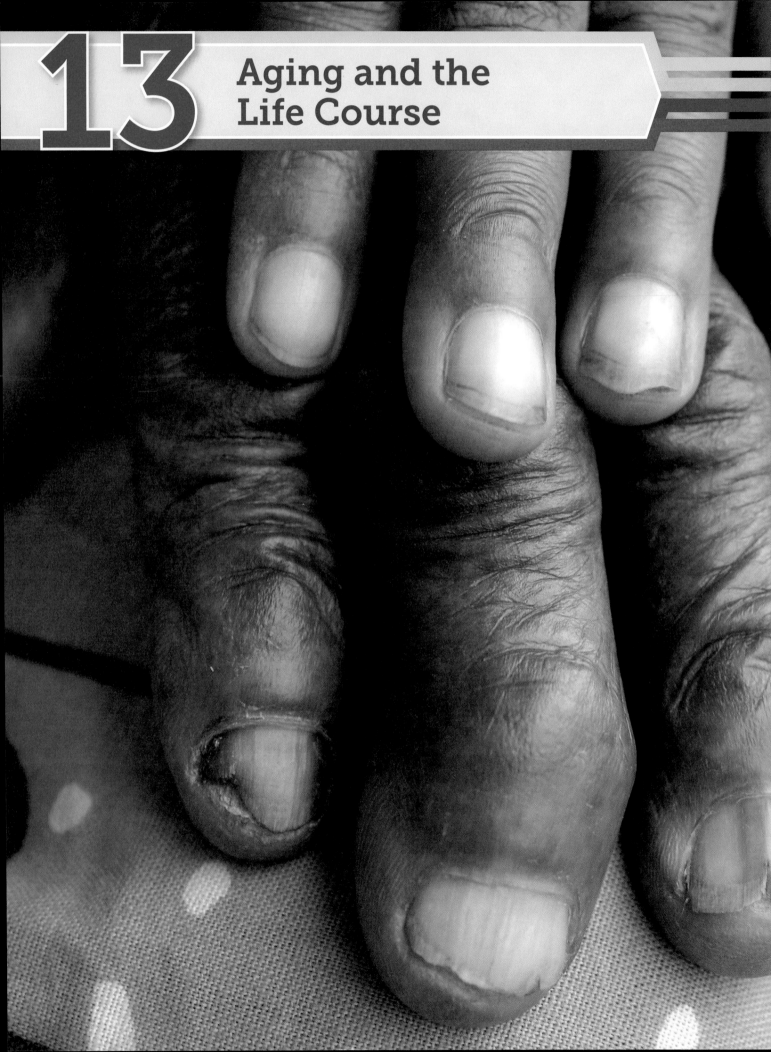

Learning Objectives

After reading this chapter, you should be able to

- explain why we can say that the Canadian population is aging

- differentiate between a *constructionist* and a *universalist* interpretation of childhood

- assess Neil Postman's statement that childhood is disappearing

- outline the impact of culture on adolescence

- discuss the role that *rites of passage* play in the process of becoming an adult

- state the difference between societies in which *elder* is a respected role and those in which it is not

- identify the causes and effects of people's decision to delay retirement.

Key Terms

- ageism
- age set
- baby boom generation
- broad socialization
- cluttered nest
- delayed life transitions
- elder
- elder abuse
- empty nest
- fertility rate
- filial piety
- honorifics
- infant mortality rate
- life course
- life expectancy at birth
- menarche
- menopause
- midlife crisis
- narrow socialization
- playing child model
- present-centred
- reincorporation
- relativist
- replacement rate
- risk behaviour
- rite of passage
- role exit
- separation
- social constructionist
- socialization
- transition
- undifferentiated accessibility
- universalist

Names to Know

- Philippe Ariès
- Rod Beaujot
- Frederick Engels
- Karl Marx
- Margaret Mead
- Talcott Parsons
- Neil Postman
- Arnold van Gennep

Growing Pains: Age Set among the Maasai

The Maasai are a pastoral people who live in Kenya and Tanzania. They number over 500,000. Prior to contact with Europeans they were a powerful people who, as they do today, maintained a semi-nomadic lifestyle with an economy dominated by cattle raising. Their traditional territory was rich in good land, but they were driven out of much of that land by successive waves of British colonialism. Known as fearsome fighters, their ideal of the warrior is reflected in the meaning of their name: "I will not beg."

A key feature of traditional Maasai culture is the **age set**, a cohort of people of similar age who experience different stages of life together. The age set helps to delineate the stages of life of Maasai males. Progression from each stage to the next is marked by a ritual. The first stage is that of childhood, typically lasting from birth to the age of 10. During the last part of this period, the male child has his lower incisors removed. This means that he is old enough to accept

the responsibility of herding cattle near his homestead. Between the ages of 10 and 12, he has his earlobes cut and stretched with progressively large implements that are inserted into the lobes. At this stage, the youth is old enough to accept the responsibility of herding cattle away from the homestead.

The big change happens next, typically between the ages of 12 and 15. During this period, the young male goes through the ritual of circumcision:

When Tepilit Ole Saitoti was just about to undergo circumcision, his father said to him:

Circumcision means a break between childhood and adulthood. For the first time in your life, you are regarded as a grownup, a complete man. . . . You will be expected to give and not just to receive. To protect the family always, not just to be protected yourself. And your wise judgement will for the first time be taken into consideration. No family affairs will be discussed without your being consulted. (Saitoti 1988: 72–3)

Before the circumcision, the initiated's head is shaved and he gives away all his possessions. He must gather food and gifts for those involved in the ceremony, and he must sharpen the knives that will be used. Just prior to the circumcision, he is doused with cold water, and held down by people assisting in the operation. After it takes place, he is led to a bed, where he lies until the bleeding has stopped. No blood is supposed to hit the ground. He is then rewarded and praised by his family, who welcome him back to society. He receives gifts of the all-important cattle. Tepilit said, in retrospect:

As long as I live I will never forget the day my head was shaved and I emerged a man, a Maasai warrior. I felt a sense of control over my destiny so great that no words can accurately describe it. I now stood with confidence, pride, and happiness of being, for all around me I was desired and loved by beautiful, sensuous Maasai maidens. I could now interact with women and even have sex with them, which I [had] not been allowed before. I was

now regarded as a responsible person. (Saitoti 1988: 72–3)

Okay, the guys who are reading this can uncross their legs now. This is an example of a **rite of passage**, enabling people socially categorized as "children" to make the transition into the stage of adulthood. Our progress through life is marked by age-related changes, some of which entail some sort of rite of passage, not all of them quite as formal (or painful) as the one described here. Birth, starting school, menarche (first period), leaving home, losing virginity, graduating, beginning a first job, marrying, retiring—such rites of passage are important milestones along the life course. Over the course of this chapter, we will encounter further examples.

What do YOU think?

What typically male rites of passage mark the move from boyhood to manhood in Canadian society (consider, for instance, drinking, getting a driver's license, and being given a stag party)? What rites of passage do girls go through on their way to becoming women (consider stagettes and baby showers)? What rites of passage are common to both sexes?

Introduction: We're All Aging

Some people thing of aging as getting old. That's not quite the case. Given that we begin aging the moment we're born, it's really the process of getting *older*. That's why this chapter, as indicated by the title, is about aging and the **life course**—the stages through which people pass between birth and death.

Giele and Elder define "life course" as "a sequence of socially defined events and roles that the individual enacts over time" (Giele & Elder 1998: 22). It is an area of study shared by sociology, psychology, and anthropology, and it's made especially interesting by comparison. Humans in all cultures go through a fairly fixed series of biological changes. Once our hormones kick in in full force we grow larger and more physically competent, until we slow down and become "old"—these things happen at roughly the same fixed biological times across all cultures. How does that similarity across the species get filed into discrete

and differently staged categories such *child*, *adolescent*, *adult* (young and middle-aged), and *elder* (or *senior*) in different societies? What characteristics do different societies associate with the different stages? How might these characteristics undergo change over the centuries? Those are some of the questions we'll explore in the pages that follow.

Population Aging

In 2011, the percentage of Canadians aged 65 and over increased to a record high of 14.8 per cent, numbering 4,945,060 (see Table 13.1). That figure had grown by 14.1 per cent since 2006—more than double the percentage increase of the Canadian population overall (5.9 per cent). Given that the fastest growing age group in Canada between 2006 and 2011 was people aged 60–64 (their total grew by 29.1 per cent), the number of over-65s is certain to continue its rise between now and the next census (Statistics Canada 2012b: 3).

Table 13.1 Canada's population by broad age groups, 1921–2011

CENSUS YEAR	AGE GROUPS			TOTAL
	0 TO 14 YEARS	15 TO 64 YEARS	65 YEARS AND OVER	
2011	5,607,345	22,924,290	4,945,060	33,476,690
2001	5,725,535	20,393,005	3,888,550	30,007,090
1991	5,692,555	18,434,335	3,169,970	27,296,855
1981	5,481,100	16,501,100	2,360,975	24,343,180
1971	6,380,900	13,443,005	1,744,405	21,568,310
1961	6,191,922	10,655,171	1,391,154	18,238,247
1951	4,250,717	8,672,439	1,086,273	14,009,429
1941	3,198,551	7,540,289	767,815	11,506,655
1931	3,281,776	6,518,934	576,076	10,376,786
1921	3,023,351	5,344,354	420,244	8,787,949

Source: Statistics Canada data at http://www12.statcan.ca/census-recensement/2011/dp-pd/hlt-fst/as-sa/Pages/highlight.cfm?TabID=1&Lang=E&PRCode =01&Asc=0&OrderBy=1&Sex=1&View=1&tableID=22. Reproduced and distributed on an "as is" basis with the permission of Statistics Canada.

Worth noting, too, is that the gap between people over 64 and people under 15 is less than a million—the narrowest it's been in a century (see Figure 13.1). There is a serious seniors boom: our population is getting older.

Why is this? It begins with the **baby boom generation**, a cohort born after World War II, between 1946 and 1964, when the return of soldiers from overseas and a more prosperous North American economy

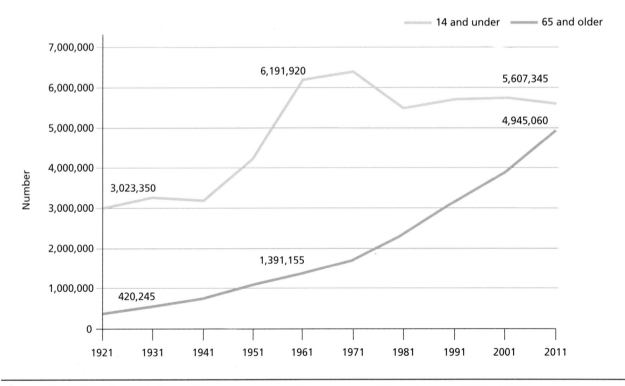

Figure 13.1 Number of Canadians aged 14 and under and 65 and over, 1921–2011

Source: Statistics Canada 2012b: 4. Reproduced and distributed on an "as is" basis with the permission of Statistics Canada.

meant that young people in greater numbers than before could afford to get married and have children. As this group aged, they regularly formed a "census bulge" in the percentage of age groups in Canada.

Another reason for the seniors boom is that people are, on average, living longer. This fact is borne out by a significant change in Canadians' **life expectancy at birth**, as documented by Statistics Canada (see Figure 13.2).

My father was born in 1920. A male born that year could expect to live to be 59 (my father actually beat the odds, living into his mid-eighties). A woman born that same year had a life expectancy that was greater by 2 years: 61.

The eldest of my two sisters was born in 1951. She has a life expectancy of 71, which is 10 years more than that of the woman born in 1920. If my sister had had a twin brother, he could be expected to live to the age of 66.

My female students born in 1992 have a life expectancy that is 10 years greater than that of my sister: 81. My male students are up by 11 years on my sister's fictitious male twin (77).

I have a grandson who was born in 2010. If we were to use the most recent Stats Can projections for him (2009), we could expect him to live to the age of 79. The girls his age at his daycare can expect to live to 83. That works out to a difference of 4 years for men and women—greater than the 2-year margin of difference in 1920, but less than the 7-year discrepancy during the 1970s and 1980s. The life expectancy for women is always greater.

There are several reasons for the growth in life expectancy. The most obvious is that medicine—including detection, diagnosis, and treatment of disease—has improved. Another is that the number of smokers is down significantly: in 1965, nearly half (49 per cent) of all people over the age of 15 were smokers—61 per cent of men (including my father and me) and 39 per cent of women smoked (CBCNews 2011). Compare the figures for that year with 2011, when just 20 per cent of Canadians aged 12 and older smoked—22 per cent of men (including my two stepsons but not me) and 17.5 per cent of women (Statistics Canada 2012c). (Keep in mind that these two data sets are perfectly comparable: the fact that one relates to people over 15 while the other relates to people over 12 will exaggerate the differences a little.) The reduction in smokers, as well as new rules about where you may and may not smoke, has helped improve the health and longevity of those who might be picking up second-hand smoke. (In the mid-1980s, you could legally smoke in the halls of my college, as well as in the cafeteria; in 1969, when I was a first-year university student, you could smoke in the classroom—in fact, I once bummed a cigarette off of one of my profs.)

Another reason for increasing life expectancy is that we have greater understanding today of nutrition,

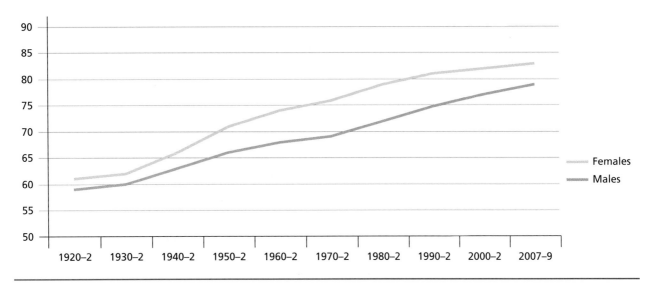

Figure 13.2 Canadians' life expectancy at birth, by sex, 1920–2 to 2007–9

Source: Statistics Canada, CANSIM, table 102-0512 and cat. no. 84-537-XIE; retrieved: www.statcan.gc.ca/tables-tableaux/sum-som/l01/cst01/ health26-eng.htm. Reproduced and distributed on an "as is" basis with the permission of Statistics Canada.

What effects could an aging population have on society? How could it affect the health-care system? Education? Religion? How could it affect the job market?

including a better sense of what is good for us and, perhaps more importantly, what is bad for us (trans-fats, for instance). Having the nutritional content displayed on packaged foods has helped us make healthier eating choices.

Another factor in the aging of the population is the **fertility rate**, the average number of children that each woman of childbearing age (15–49) will have in her lifetime. In Canada the fertility rate has fallen below the **replacement rate**, the average number of children per woman required to keep the population the same, provided there is no immigration (2.1). Declines in the number of children being born is a big part of the reason the number of Canadians over 64 appears to be on course to surpass the number of Canadians under 15 in the very near future.

Childhood

Only recently have sociologists taken a serious look into the sociology of childhood. **Karl Marx** and his research and writing partner **Frederick Engels** examined childhood in the context of child labour and its social and economic components. Specifically they

wrote about the exploitation of children, some as young as seven, working some 10 hours a day in hideous conditions in textile mills, and serving as lower-paid occasional replacement workers for adults in other kinds of work. Later sociologists confined their study of children and childhood to **socialization**, the process of learning the values and standards of behaviour of one's social group. The American structural-functionalist theorist **Talcott Parsons** was among these sociologists. In his classic work *The Social System* (1951), he described childhood socialization, in Freudian style, as the smooth, uncomplicated process whereby children internalize the norms and values of society. We know today that the process is far from uncomplicated. But consider that at the time, pediatrician C. Henry Kempe's influential investigation of child abuse (Kempe et al. 1962) was a groundbreaking revelation of one of the more serious factors that can complicate childhood socialization—one that we now take for granted, thanks to more recent work on the sociology of childhood.

Childhood: A Natural Category or a Socially Constructed One?

Talking about childhood is a great deal like talking about gender. Gender talk, as we have seen, tends to feature an intellectual dialogue between the influences of biology (which determines sex) and society (which influences gender).

When it comes to the sociology of childhood, we have, on the one hand, biology's input to consider. We could simply argue, for instance, that childhood ends with puberty, when adolescents reach sexual maturity and become capable of reproduction. Nature's role in childhood, especially the natural stages of child development, has also received notable treatment from psychologists such as Sigmund Freud, Erik Erikson, and Jean Piaget. It's the sort of material taught in courses in developmental psychology, where you might consider, for instance, at what conceptual area of life a child begins to question what is moral or "fair." We could characterize such biology-centred topics as basically **universalist**, in that they relate to experiences that all children—at all times and across all cultures—are expected to undergo.

Then, on the other hand, there is society's input. In looking at the social role in childhood, we are taking what can be called a **social constructionist** position, which argues that childhood is not just a natural category but one that has an important social ingredient, having been created or shaped by social forces. This position is more **relativist** than universalist, in that it views childhood as something that cannot be understood outside of its social, cultural, and historical context. You cannot apply the same framework to understanding childhood as it is experienced in twenty-first-century urban Canada and in fifteenth-century feudal Japan—the context is crucial.

From a social constructionist perspective, then, childhood is a socially or culturally defined stage in a person's life. It is "socially defined" because societies differ on such points as how old a child is (in medieval Europe, for example, childhood ended at the age of seven, marked by the rite-of-passage ceremony of confirmation), what behaviour and responsibilities a child should have, and how free children should be from adult control and influence.

Does All Work and No Play Make a Child an Adult?

In *Childhood and Society*, British sociologist Michael Wyness examines the social constructionist view of childhood, specifically whether "the *meaning of childhood* may be different depending on our cultural and historical backgrounds" (Wyness 2006: 9). He takes as his starting point the view that in contemporary Western society, childhood is associated with play and the absence of work: "we expect adults to provide for children economically and morally by working and earning an income. Being a child and going through the period of childhood means having no economic and moral responsibilities; it means not having to work" (Wyness 2006: 9). (Play, here, includes structured play and education.) He calls this the **playing child model** of childhood, and simplifies it in the following way:

Childhood = Play
Adulthood = Work

Yet while Wyness concedes that it is perhaps true of all cultures that "children play" (at least some of the time), he cites historical and cultural exceptions to the claim that childhood is defined by its freedom from work. During the nineteenth century, the factories of industrial Europe and North America employed legions of child workers, whose working hours were limited

Is child labour defensible? What if it involves a child helping out with the family business, like a restaurant or convenience store? What if it involves the "forced volunteerism" that's now required for credit by many Canadian high schools?

somewhat by progressive social legislation but who nevertheless were engaged in full-time labour. It isn't that parents set out to treat their children cruelly; it's simply that prior to the twentieth century, children's labour, whether in factories or on the farm, was integral to the livelihood of many families. Citing this fact, Wyness argues that "the 'playing-child' image of childhood is, therefore, a recent construction" (Wyness 2006: 10).

Likewise, even in the twenty-first century, children in many parts of Asia, Africa, and Latin America are viewed in terms of their economic value, being engaged in paid or unpaid labour that is vitally important to their families, and that pushes play and school into the margins. This applies, to a lesser degree, even in Western countries, where the universality of the playing child model is diminished by ethnic differences in how children's economic responsibilities are viewed. In a 1996 article, sociologist Miri Song wrote about the reliance on children's labour in family-run Chinese takeout restaurants in Britain (Song 1996). Here, children of the Chinese restaurant owners incorporate

QUICK HITS

Minimum Age of Work

Wyness's playing child model of childhood is based on the notion that in contemporary Western society, children play and adults work. So what are the laws concerning child labour in Canada? They vary by province. Here are a few:

Alberta

In Alberta, children under the age of 12 are prohibited from working. Children between the ages of 12 and 14 can work if they have the written consent of a parent or guardian. The hours of work for children aged 12 to 14 are limited in that they must be outside of school hours, and not between the hours of 9:00 p.m. and 6:00 a.m. There are limitations as to what kinds of work 12- to 14-year-olds can do. They are not to be engaged in factory work, for example, but they can be involved in delivery (e.g. of newspapers, flyers, pamphlets, and small retail goods—but not by car, of course!) or clerking (in an office or store).

British Columbia

In BC, children between the ages of 12 and 14 are permitted to work for up to 4 hours on a school day, 20 hours in a school week, 7 hours on a non-school day, and 35 hours in a non-school week. For this age group, there is no legal requirement of the written consent of a parent or guardian. Children under 12 can work if they receive written permission from the provincial Director of Employment Standards.

Manitoba

Manitoba can be said to have the strictest child labour laws in Canada. For someone under 16 to work, a permit from the Department of Employment Standards and a parent's or guardian's permission are required. Certain industries (e.g. logging, mining) are deemed inappropriate for people under 18. Those under 16 can work only 20 hours during a school week and may not engage in any paid work between 11:00 p.m. and 6:00 a.m. (except babysitting, provided the person under 16 is not alone). Manitoba labour law also stipulates that talent agencies must get a child performer's permit to employ children under 17.

What do YOU think?

1. Do these laws support the playing child model of childhood that prevails, according to Wyness, in Western society?

2. What kinds of child labour laws would you institute? Do you agree, in principle, with socially defined age limits, or should a child be allowed to begin work at whatever age he or she demonstrates the maturity to do so?

economically productive work into their daily lives. Thus, not only is the playing child model of childhood a recent social construction, it is not universal across all cultures today: childhood means different things to different people at different times.

In case you think that our views of childhood are shaped in ways that are largely unnoticed and uncontrolled, consider the fact that the social construction of childhood is a process occurring on a regular basis through debates in our houses of legislature and in the various media. When is a child old enough to start working, to drive, to view movies with scenes of nudity and coarse language, to watch *Girls* on HBO? Why are people in Quebec, Manitoba, and Alberta legally able to drink a year earlier (18) than youths in other parts of Canada (19)? The definition of childhood is being debated continuously.

Neil Postman and the Disappearance of Childhood

Influential American media commentator and cultural critic **Neil Postman** (1931–2003) made a significant contribution to the discussion of the social construction of childhood in his important work *The Disappearance of Childhood*. Published way back in 1982, it is just as relevant to the topic today as it was at the time of its original publication over 30 years ago.

Postman was looking at Western culture from the deep European past to the then more recent times in the United States. Essentially, he identified three distinct periods in Western history, each one characterized by a different definition of the child and childhood. Given his background as a student and critic of media, it's not surprising that he saw mass media as a key force in changing childhood, even drawing on the ideas of Canadian media theorists Harold Innis and Marshall McLuhan to state his case.

Childhood, according to Postman, was an underdeveloped social concept in medieval Europe (basically from the 1100s to the 1500s). This has been commented on by a number of social historians, including American Barbara Tuchman, who wrote: "Of all the characteristics in which the medieval age differs from the modern, none is so striking as the comparative absence of interest in children" (Tuchman 1978:50). Postman chooses a term used by French historian Philippe Ariès, among others, to describe the way children look in pictures from the time: they resemble "miniature adults," especially in their style of dress and the activities in which they are engaged.

Postman believed this was owing in part to the fact that adults and children in medieval Europe communicated exclusively in a medium—spoken language—that children were competent in by age seven. Unlike writing and print (which would come later), spoken language presented no "separation of competence"—children were just as capable as adults of understanding spoken language. This fact, combined with the circumstances in which most families lived at the time—communally, with homes being far less likely to be divided into individual rooms—meant that children of this period were not "protected" from what Postman called the "mysteries of life"—sex, birth, death, "foul language," gossip, and the like. They experienced all aspects of life more fully than children of the next period,

What caused the situation to change, according to Postman, was the advent of the printing press. As books, newspapers, pamphlets, and other print media gained in popularity, literacy as a slowly acquired skill became a way of separating children from adults: those not yet fully competent in the medium of print versus those who were. Postman does make some reference to social class, but often only indirectly. As sociologists, we would add that this new separation of childhood and adulthood would have occurred primarily among the middle and upper classes—the classes occupied by merchants, clerks, and lawyers—which benefited the most from literacy.

Postman noted that the growing importance of literacy brought a similar growth in schools, particularly in England. There had been schools in earlier days, but the students were of mixed ages, children and adults together. These new schools were based on a model of gradually acquired/revealed information and age-appropriate grades. They brought about a new way of looking at childhood. As Postman explains, the increasing importance of literacy "led to a remarkable change in the social status of the young. Because the school was designed for the preparation of a literate adult, the young came to be perceived not as miniature adults, but as something quite different altogether—unformed adults. School learning became identified with the special nature of childhood" (Postman 1982: 41). In Postman's hypothesis, this second period, from the seventeenth century through the first half of the twentieth, brought a new paradigm of childhood featuring the child as schoolboy or schoolgirl whose self and individuality must be preserved by nurturing, whose capacity for self-control, deferred gratification, and logical thought must be extended, whose knowledge of life must be under the control of adults. (Postman 1982: 63)

Childhood had been redefined, but it was not to last. According to Postman, childhood as defined in this second period began to disappear in the 1950s, with the birth and growth of television. Had he written his book in 2013, he would have added the Internet and social media to the list, for the influences are very much the same. Where Postman uses the word *television*, imagine these other, digital media as well. Television differed from print by presenting **undifferentiated accessibility**. What Postman meant by this is that television made no significant distinctions between the social categories of "child" and "adult." He offers three proofs of this claim regarding television:

1. It requires no instruction to grasp its form.
2. It does not make complex demands on either mind or behavior.
3. It does not segregate its audience. (Postman 1982: 79)

Television, in other words, erases the barrier between children and adults. A sitcom or commercial designed for an adult viewer is no different in its form to a show or an ad for children, meaning that it can be readily understood by younger viewers. And television is **present-centred**, constantly supplying information as new without requiring the viewer to be able to supply the necessary historical context or background understanding to comprehend the material. As Postman remarked, "Watching television not only requires no skills but develops no skills" (Postman 1982: 79).

Postman argued that a healthy childhood required a certain amount of secrecy concerning the ways of the world. "In the case of childhood," he wrote, "... secrecy

What kinds of television viewing are not appropriate for a child? (For the purposes of this exercise, let's consider a child to be 12 years old or younger.) Reality shows (*Real Housewives, 16 and Pregnant, The Biggest Loser*)? Crime dramas (*CSI, Bones, Criminal Minds*)? What about cult favourites *The Walking Dead* (shown above) and *The Following*? Violent sports (UFC, mixed martial arts)? Sitcoms (*The Simpsons, South Park, How I Met Your Mother*)? Would you have let a 12-year-old watch news coverage of the school shooting in Newtown, Connecticut? In each case, explain the danger of exposing children to these adult "secrets."

is practiced in order to maintain the conditions for healthy and ordered growth" (Postman 1982: 92–3). He went on to explain: "We wish to keep this knowledge from children because for all of its reality, too much of it too soon is quite likely dangerous to the well-being of a unformed mind" (Postman 1982: 93).

How is knowledge dangerous to the "unformed mind"? One of the examples that Postman presents relates to cynicism and politics. He reasons that if children are exposed to too much information about the private lives and failures of political figures, they will become pessimistic about and disengaged from the political process, and less likely to participate in election voting. The idealism of youth is a driving force in politics, one that should not allowed to become dampened by cynicism at a young age—otherwise, youth activism and the push to change things might diminish.

Ultimately, as in the first period of childhood that Postman describes, the lives of children and adults in this third period become more alike in a number of areas, including crime (with "children" committing more "adult" crimes) and fashion (with what a colleague, the mother of two little girls, calls the "pornification" of clothing for pre-pubescent girls).

What do YOU think?

To what extent do you agree with Postman that a certain amount of secrecy regarding the adult world needs to be maintained for a healthy childhood?

The Point Is...

Philippe Aries: How Attitudes Change through Centuries of Childhood

The social construction of childhood varies across different cultures, but it can also change within the same society over time. One writer who brought this phenomenon to the attention of sociologists and other readers is French family and child historian **Philippe Ariès** (1914–1984). In *Centuries of Childhood: A Social History* (1962), he used social demography—the use of population statistics to study social trends—to show that throughout European history, the **infant mortality rate** (the rate of death of children in their first year of life) has acted as an independent variable determining attitudes towards children and childhood. According to Ariès, when the infant mortality rate was high, people exhibited an emotionally practical strategy of not becoming attached to their children. Parents "could not allow themselves to become too attached to something that was regarded as a probable loss" (Ariès 1962: 38). The drop in the infant mortality rate triggered a demographic revolution that, in turn, brought about "a revolution in feeling"—an increase in the attachment that parents felt towards their children.

How would a sociologist test this hypothesis? Proving or disproving Ariès's hypothesis would involve several actions. The first would be to establish an operational definition of "increasing attachment to children." This could be gauged by the number of pictures that parents kept of their children—particularly, we would imagine, of their children alone. It could also be measured by the size and style (e.g. simple versus elaborate) of gravestones used to mark the bodies of deceased children. Among the more literate middle and upper classes, we might look for changes in how parents wrote about their children. Once we have established a measure of "increasing attachment," we would need to check the timing of the two variables, to see if the two revolutions—the demographic one and the "revolution in feeling"—actually occurred at around the same time, ideally with the independent variable preceding the dependent variable.

What do YOU think?

What other kind of evidence might supporting Ariès's hypothesis? What kind of evidence might disprove it?

Play, Sport, and the Disappearing Child

Early on in his book, Postman speaks of the disappearance of children's games. By "children's games" he means the kind of game that "requires no instructors or umpires or spectators, . . . uses whatever space and equipment are at hand, . . . [and] is played for no other reason than pleasure" (Postman 1982: 4). Examples he cites include jacks, blind man's bluff, hide-and-seek, and rhyming games played with a bouncing ball, to which I would add skipping games (which my sisters did all the time), marbles, capture-the-flag, and tag. He contrasts these kinds of games with organized sports such as Little League Baseball and peewee football, which are played by children following adult practices: maximizing adult-level competence through professional-style coaches and trainers. This leads him to the following series of questions, and a tentative conclusion:

> Why should adults encourage this possibility [i.e. adult-level competence]? Why would anyone wish to deny children the freedom, informality, and joy of spontaneous play? Why submit children to the rigors of professional-style training, concentration, tensions, media-hype? . . . What we have here is the emergence of the idea of play is not to be done for the sake of doing it but for some external purpose, such as renown, money, physical conditioning, upward mobility, national pride. For adults, play is serious business. As childhood disappears, so does the child's view of play. (Postman 1982: 131)

What do YOU think?

1. Do you think there is any connection between the disappearance of childhood games that Postman describes and (a) the apparent increase in violence in minor-league hockey, or (b) the phenomenon of aggressive parent–spectators at children's hockey games, soccer games, gymnastics competitions, etc.?

2. Does organized sport fit within the playing child model of childhood? If not, do the benefits of organized sport (to encourage fitness, to develop discipline, to be social, to keep out of trouble, etc.) outweigh the cost?

In an effort to focus on player development (and fun?), the Ontario Soccer Association recently decided not to keep score in games involving children 12 and under. Is this a move in the right direction? Do you think the introduction of relatively low-competition sports counteracts the loss of childhood that Postman describes?

The Voices of Children

Among the challenges faced in the sociological study of childhood is how to include the voices of children themselves. There is an adult bias in much of the existing research, which is not surprising given that adults write the primary documents on which historians depend, adults create the paintings that historians study for images of childhood, and, of course, adults do the research. Even accounts of childhood are overwhelmingly those of adults writing memoirs. The value of these can be seen in the opening passage of Frank McCourt's bestseller (and movie) *Angela's Ashes*, about growing up in Ireland in the 1930s and 1940s:

> When I look back on my childhood I wonder how I survived at all. It was, of course, a miserable childhood: the happy childhood is hardly worth your while. Worse than the ordinary miserable childhood is the miserable Irish childhood, and worse yet is the miserable Irish Catholic childhood. . . .
>
> [N]othing can compare with the Irish version: the poverty; the shiftless loquacious alcoholic father; the pious defeated mother moaning by the fire; pompous priests; bullying schoolmasters; the English and the terrible things they did to us for eight hundred long years. (McCourt 1996: 1)

This is good material, very useful to the sociologist, but it is still filtered through an adult's memory, experience, and knowledge of the world. Sonja Grover, advocating the involvement of children in the research process not as "objects of study" but as active participants "telling their own story in their own way," argues that "Such an approach has the potential to lead to social policy which more accurately and compassionately reflects the concerns of children" (Grover 2004: 83).

First-hand accounts, whether or not they are coloured by a grownup's perspective, are important sources of qualitative data for the sociologist. But even quantitative data can reflect an adult bias. A good case-in-point was developed by J. Qvortrup in an article called "A Voice for Children in Statistical and Social Accounting: A Plea for Children's Right to be Heard" (Qvortrup 1990). Wyness nicely summarizes his argument in the following passage:

> [Qvortrup] argues that we tend to read information about children's lives from statistics, which often concentrate on "family" as the unit of analysis. So, in Denmark, for example, there was an increase in the numbers of families with one child from 43 per cent in 1974 to 49 per cent in 1985. This is often taken to mean that almost half of all Danish children have no siblings. If we take the child as the unit of analysis, then this statistic is inaccurate, seriously underestimating the numbers of children with siblings. Counting all children rather than all families with dependent children gives us a quite different picture of family life in Denmark. The equivalent figures for the same period are 24 per cent and 30 per cent, respectively, meaning that well over two thirds of Danish children in the mid-1980s had at least one sibling. (Wyness 2006: 29–30)

In other words, if you had ten families with children, and five of them had just one child, then it's true: half of your families would be one-child families. But given that there would have to be at least two children in each of the *other* five families, the percentage of children with no siblings would be 33 per cent at most. As we saw in Chapter 3, it is always important to look critically at statistics and, in this case, to look at them from a child's-eye view.

Adolescence and Adulthood

Adolescence is an in-between or transitional stage, between the onset of puberty and full adulthood (however that is defined in a particular society). The time period varies across cultures, in part because of the difference over time of reaching puberty, but more significantly because of the different requirements of adulthood in different societies. Note that childhood and adolescence can overlap, given that childhood lasts, by some definitions, well beyond the onset of puberty.

The study of puberty varies across disciplines. Biology looks at the development of sex-related characteristics, the physical growth spurt, and brain development. Psychology stresses the cognitive developments and behavioural tendencies, fuelled by the brain and hormonal changes, through this period. Sociology looks more at the timing of the acquisition of adult roles (worker, sexual partner, soldier, voter/citizen, parent, licensed driver, etc.) and, along with anthropology, rites of passage into adulthood. There

QUICK HITS

Age of Sexual Consent

In May 2008, the age of sexual consent in Canada (sexual activity referring to everything from kissing to sexual intercourse) was changed to 16, which is a common figure in many jurisdictions (including most American states) across the world. Prior to that time, from 1890, it was 14. Earlier in the nineteenth century it was 12.

There are exceptions, though, for what are called "close in age" or "peer group" partners. Adolescents aged 14–15 can engage in sexual activity if the partner is less than five years older and there is no relationship of trust, authority, or dependency (i.e. the older partner is not a babysitter, coach, teacher, etc.). Likewise, 12- and 13-year-olds can engage in sexual activity, provided the partner is less than two years older.

What do YOU think?

1. Why do you think the age of consent changed in Canada over the years?

2. Do you think that the Canadian law is reasonable? Why or why not? (And how familiar with it were you before you read this box?)

are points of intersection where the concerns of two or more of these disciplines converge. One of these intersections is adolescent risk behaviour, which is of significance to both psychologists and sociologists.

Adolescents and Risk Behaviour

A leader in studying the socialization of adolescents is Jeffrey Arnett. A developmental psychologist, Arnett has extensively researched **risk behaviour** among adolescents. Risk behaviours include driving at unsafe speeds, engaging in unsafe sexual activities, drinking to excess, experimenting with different drugs, and so on. While he recognizes that there is a biological component to such behaviour—a genetic predisposition to certain kinds of behaviour that is present naturally in certain individuals—Arnett stresses that socialization plays a very large role in this area, too. He makes an

important distinction between **narrow socialization** and **broad socialization**, describing them as follows:

> In cultures characterized by *broad socialization*, individualism and independence are promoted, and there is relatively less restrictiveness on the various dimensions of socialization. This allows for a broad range of expression of individual differences on the developmental tendencies (such as sensation seeking) that contribute to risk behavior, and leads to higher rates of risk behavior. Cultures characterized by *narrow socialization*, in contrast, consider obedience and conformity to the standards and expectations of the community to be paramount (enforced through the parents and the school as well as through members of the community), and punish physically and/or socially any deviation from the norm. The result is greater obedience and conformity, a narrower range of expression of individual differences, and low rates of antisocial adolescent risk behavior (although risk-taking tendencies may be directed by such cultures into avenues that serve a culturally approved purpose, such as warfare). (Arnett and Balle-Jensen 1993: 1843)

In other words, young people in cultures characterized by broad socialization have greater freedom to act independently and make choices—about what they will study at school, how they will spend their time when they're not at school, where they will work, whom they will socialize with, and so on. By contrast, in cultures based on narrow socialization, there is greater pressure on young people—from families, from the authorities, and from society in general—to act a certain way and to conform to widely held expectations regarding behaviour. Adolescents in these societies, according to Arnett, are less likely to participate in risky activities.

To test his hypothesis, Arnett and Lene Balle-Jensen undertook a cross-cultural study of adolescent socialization in Denmark. While that country has a tendency towards broad socialization, the researchers noted ways in which Denmark has narrower socialization than the United States and Canada. For instance, they cite the fact that the legal driving age in Denmark is 18, reflecting, according to Arnett, narrow socialization elements in the legal system and in the cultural belief system. It reflects, too, a different cultural consensus concerning the balance between ensuring the

Growing up, you might have felt as though your parents were on your back *all the time*. Overall, would you say your upbringing was characterized by narrow socialization or broad socialization?

individual autonomy of the teenager who wants to drive a car and the good of the community, through fewer traffic fatalities and fewer cars on the road. This narrower socialization means, according to Arnett, that in Denmark fewer adolescents engage in the risk behaviour of unsafe driving than in North America.

Adolescence: Always Turbulent?

Margaret Mead (1901–1978) was a public intellectual with a profound influence on social sciences including sociology, anthropology (her own discipline), and psychology throughout much of the twentieth century. Her bestselling and perhaps most influential book is *Coming of Age in Samoa: A Psychological Study of Primitive Youth for Western Civilization* (1928). One of the major questions that she addressed in this work concerned the influences on adolescence. The 1920s were a time of social rebellion throughout the West (not unlike the 1960s), marked by the development of a major generational divide. In Mead's words:

The spectacle of a younger generation diverging ever more widely from the standards and ideals of the past, cut adrift without the anchorage of respected home standards or group religious values, terrified the cautious reactionary, tempted the radical propagandist to missionary crusades among the defenseless youth, and worried the least thoughtful among us. (Mead 1928: 1–2)

Mead believed that adolescent rebellion was not "natural," that despite the hormonal changes that all teenagers the world over experience, the tendency to rebel against authority was not biologically programmed but culturally determined. After all, she had found that there was significant cultural variance in the lives of adolescents across the world.

To illustrate her view that adolescent "coming of age" rebellion was a cultural artifact and not part of a biological imperative, Mead travelled to Samoa, a group of islands in the central Pacific, to study how girls became women in a village of just 600 people on one of the islands. She was keen to investigate what seemed to her to be a smooth transition quite unlike anything she had witnessed in the United States of that time. She looked particularly at what appeared to her to be the relatively "free" (compared to the American) attitudes toward casual sex among adolescents in the Samoan village. Mead believed that because premarital sex among the Samoan youth did not attract condemnation from the community, it actually contributed to what she saw as an easy shift to adulthood.

While her research methods and her preconceived notions of sexual freedom in Polynesia may have biased what she in fact saw—a point argued brutally by fellow anthropologist Derek Freeman (1983, 1998)— her point is well taken that cultural conditioning has a strong influence on the nature of adolescence. At the time of Mead's study in Samoa, the island community did not display the same degree of "teenage angst" that existed in North America.

What do YOU think?

Whatever . . . What factors do you think influence the cultural conditioning of adolescent rebellion in Western society? How much do television and movies play a role?

The "Children" Are Still at Home!

The term **cluttered nest** is sometimes used to describe the phenomenon in which adult children continue to live at home with their parents (the opposite, **empty nest**, describes a household in which children have moved out of the home). As Table 13.2 shows, the cluttered nest is a growing phenomenon, with an increasing percentage of young adults in their twenties living in their parents' homes. The upward trend applies both to those who are aged 20–24, where the rise is more expected, and to those aged 25–29, where it is less expected.

Causation is fairly easy to establish: it takes more time and education nowadays to establish a career. And with a higher cost of living, rising house prices, and a number of costs that earlier generations did not have to face (just think of the high costs of maintaining phone and Internet service), it is more difficult for young Canadians today to set themselves up on their own. With couples marrying later and later in life, it takes longer to set up a dual-earner household, the

only model that is financially viable for some young people who want to move out of the parental home but find the financial challenges daunting.

How do these data affect our view of adolescence, which we defined as the period between puberty and adulthood? Is a working 25-year-old college graduate who doesn't yet have the economic means to move out of his parents' home still "growing up," or is he an adult? What about the 25-year-old who could be living on his own but chooses not to because he'd prefer to save his money by continuing to live with his parents? At one time a twentysomething still living at home might have been viewed negatively as immature or irresponsible, a Peter Pan figure freeloading off of his (or her) parents and refusing to grow up. That's because our socially constructed conception of "adulthood" did not include living with parents in their home. As the situation becomes more common, with many Canadian adults simply unable to afford living on their own, how much have our attitudes about what defines an adolescent changed?

In his article "Delayed Life Transitions," University of Western Ontario demographer **Rod Beaujot** links together some of the trends we have just been discussing as part of a phenomenon he calls **delayed life transitions**. We go through a number of major life transitions in our lifetime—getting a full-time job, going out to live on our own, getting married, having children, retiring. During the prosperous

Table 13.2 Percentage of Canadians aged 20–24 and 25–29 living in the parental home, 1981–2011

YEAR	YOUNG ADULTS LIVING IN THEIR PARENTS' HOME (%)	
	AGED 20–24	AGED 25–29
1981	41.5	11.3
1986	49.1	15.2
1991	50.5	16.9
1996	55.8	21.0
2001	57.2	22.5
2006	59.5	24.7
2011	59.3	25.2

Source: Based on data from Statistics Canada, censuses of population, 1981 to 2011. Retrieved: www12.statcan.gc.ca/census-recensement/2011/as-sa/98-312-x/2011003/fig/desc/desc3_3-1-eng.cfm. Reproduced and distributed on an "as is" basis with the permission of Statistics Canada.

What kinds of problems stem from the "cluttered nest"? Are there any advantages? From a sociological standpoint, what solutions might reverse the trend of adult children living at home?

socioeconomic times of the 1950s, 1960s, and early 1970s, people went through what we could call "sped-up life transitions," making these major life changes at a relatively young age. The situation has changed considerably, and people today are making these transitions later and later in life.

Several questions arise here. To what extent is our current speed of life "delayed" and to what extent is it simply "normal"? What are the implications for today's generation of college and university students of having parents who went through life transitions at a much more advanced speed, perhaps one that was "less normal" than now? And how would you try to convince your parents that their time as young adults was less normal than yours?

Rites of Passage

It's been a long time, but I can remember it well. The 40 of us were lined up in the schoolyard on a cold day, our red "graduation" robes blowing in the wind. We were only in the fifth grade, but we were allowed to wear the robes for Confirmation—red being the color the Church uses to represent the Holy Spirit. We felt very grown-up, and very proud.

An hour later, as far as I could tell, it was over. We had been anointed (blessed with oil) on the forehead and slapped lightly on the cheek. In those days, that "slap" told us that we had to be "soldiers of Christ," ready to suffer for our faith. We had sung "Come, Holy Ghost," and the bishop had prayed over us and put his hand on our head. I felt like I had been ordained or surely something as important and official as that.

I look back on that day of years ago and ask myself, what difference did it make? It was a nice ceremony—almost like a parade or a welcome-home celebration. And of course there was the party afterwards and the Confirmation presents. But really, I didn't understand how much of a welcome it was and to what! (Martos 2000)

Confirmation, as described here by Joseph Martos, is one of the sacraments of the Catholic church. It is a rite of passage observed in other Christian churches also, and marks a greater commitment on the part of the individual to participation in the Christian faith, recognizing that the individual has achieved a certain maturity of understanding of life and church dogma necessary for that greater commitment. Centuries ago, this rite of passage took place at age seven, and signalled, in a way, the end of childhood. Now it is more likely to take place between the ages of 10 and 14.

In 1909, French ethnographer **Arnold van Gennep** (1873–1957) published *The Rites of Passage*, an influential work in which he described rites of passage as rituals in which individuals pass from childhood to adulthood, on their way to becoming more fully responsible and respected participants in the activities of society. Rites of passage take many forms around the world, ranging from religious rituals such as confirmation as described above and the bar mitzvah and bat mitzvah for Jewish boys and girls respectively, to secular ceremonies such as the traditional grade six graduation trip to Ottawa made by students in many parts of southwestern Ontario, including my home town of Bolton.

Rites of passage do not only mark the transition from childhood to adolescence; they can occur at all transitional stages of life, from bris or baptism to funeral. Van Gennep identified three basic phases of the rite of passage:

Telling It Like It Is

Parent-and-Child POVs

"Home Sweet Home"

Many twentysomethings—58 per cent—live with their parents in Toronto, more than in any other Canadian city, according to the latest census data. The early thirties crowd isn't rushing out the door, either. Across the country, a Statistics Canada study revealed, adults up to the ripe old age of 34 are delaying life transitions, such as moving out.

Is it economics or cultural dictates? A cohort of coddled kids or clingy, overprotective parents? How do the two generations—one expecting to wind down, the other eager to gear up—cope with prolonged togetherness? We asked readers for both sides of the story.

A Mother

"I am a 52-year-old married mother with two early twentysomething offspring living at home. I am not serving them cheese [there was a TV commercial at the time that said, "if you want them to leave, stop serving them cheese"], but they are not budging. They would probably tell you they're home for economic reasons only, but they would be lying. They are also here because life at home is *so* easy. Their food is on tap, their accommodation is comfortable, and they are not sharing bathrooms with strangers.

My son just started an entry-level job. After paying for TTC [public transit] and other expenses, he hardly has a penny despite five years of post-secondary education. My daughter, a university student, returned home for her final two years and plans to stay for a master's degree.

Twentysomethings remind you they are no longer teens and can do as they please. To them, that means living like pigs, coming and going at all hours, having friends around willy-nilly, and using your kitchen, laundry, whatever they want.

I love my kids dearly. I just don't want to live with them into their late twenties and beyond. I can't wait to be an empty nester."

Her Daughter

Moving back in with your parents is a lot like sending your lukewarm pasta back at a restaurant. You feel bad about it but you figure it's still within your rights. If you are thinking about returning home, be warned. Your folks are the displeased cooks and you are the penne primavera. Only this time, there won't be any cheese.

Working two jobs, I was enjoying the restful stages of sleep during my university classes. I quit one job and moved home after my second year so I could focus on my studies, not the next grocery bill. The first thing I noticed at home was that my old room had become more storage than living space. Attempts to remove said furniture were met with fierce opposition. I knew that was only the beginning.

There is a definite role-reversal. You stay home every night to study. Mom and Dad go out. They don't eat enough vegetables. They watch too much television. However, when they lodge unfounded complaints—"Your clothes have been in my (free) laundry forever!"—you let it go. What's a little squawk, when the alternative is an entire jungle of vultures, phone bills and coin laundries?

Source: "Home Sweet Home" Nancy White, *Toronto Star*, L1, October 20, 2007 at http://www.thestar.com/living/article/267486—home-sweet-home. Reprinted with permission—Torstar Syndication Services.

1. separation
2. transition
3. reincorporation.

During **separation**, the initiates (those being ushered into the new group or status) are taken from their regular places both physically in terms of space and also in terms of social position. The **transition** stage (also known as the *liminal period*, from the Latin word for "threshold") is a kind of "time out" during which the initiates are experiencing new things, learning about themselves in the process. Finally, **reincorporation**

Our Stories

Berry Fast: A Traditional (and Ongoing) Rite of Passage for Anishinabe Girls

A berry fast is a traditional rite of passage into adulthood for adolescent girls in Anishinabe culture (comprising Ojibwa, Mississauga, Odawa, Chippewa, and Saulteaux First Nations) in Canada and the United States. It begins when a girl has her first menstrual period. Around that time a ceremony is held, officiated and attended by older female relatives. Typically the berry fast lasts a year and involves not eating berries (especially blueberries, blackberries, strawberries, and raspberries), a staple food item in traditional culture. During the fasting period, the young woman-to-be receives instruction in the traditional values (e.g. generosity, selflessness) and adult female responsibilities (e.g. picking, cleaning, and preparing berries) of her Aboriginal culture.

The following excerpts of an article from *Wawatay News Online* provides an account of the berry fast of Sabrina Shawanda, a 14-year-old Anishinabe living in Sault Ste. Marie. In the first excerpt, Sabrina explains how she demonstrated the generosity she was being taught:

> "If I went to a competition powwow and won any money I didn't keep it, I gave it to people who couldn't dance—those in wheelchairs or who had been hurt or for some reason couldn't dance," she says. "When my aunt hurt her ankle and couldn't dance, I wore her outfit and gave her the money when I won." ("A Journey" 2005)

At the end of the year of her berry fast, a ceremony was held for Sabrina as she was presented as a new adult to her family:

She braided her hair while aunties and grandmothers talked to her about the past year's teachings. A blanket was placed over her head and face and she was led from her room outside and around the circle of her family.

> "We sat down and each person spoke to me from their place. Each one said to me what they'd taught me, why they were proud of me, and what they would teach me afterwards."

At the end of the ceremony she was offered berries. She refused them four times, once for the Elders, once for the children, once for family, and once for everybody else. The fifth time they were offered she ate them. A large feast followed.

> "It's an amazing feeling. I recommend young women do it. If you don't know how, get help to do it. You know you've become a young woman; you're leaving childhood behind and are joining womanhood with your aunties, grandmas, and mom. It made me stronger." ("A Journey" 2005)

What do YOU think?

What advantages does the berry fast give to Anishinabe adolescents who participate in the rite of passage over those who do not?

involves reintegrating the individuals into society, but in such a way that their new status is recognized. Upon their return they are seen as something other than what they once were.

In the narrative of confirmation presented at the beginning of this section, the children were separated into a group that lined up in the schoolyard apart from other students. They were distinguished from other students by their symbolic red robes. During the transition phase they became participants in an ancient sacred ritual in which they were anointed with oil, "slapped," and prayed over. The reincorporation back into society as changed beings was signalled by the party that followed.

Outdoor Education as a Rite of Passage

Van Gennep developed his ideas while studying small communities characterized by a relative *homogeneity*, or sameness of culture, and extensive contact among community members of all ages. How well do his ideas translate to social situations of greater complexity, such as what exists in contemporary Canada?

This question was addressed by University of Western Ontario anthropologist Pamela Cushing in a case of practical, or applied, sociology. During the 1990s Cushing studied 22 students enrolled in a high school–accredited Outward Bound course. This form of "experiential" education (sometimes called "adventure education") is dedicated to transforming adolescents into young adults by helping them develop leadership skills and greater self-awareness through a program of challenging outdoor activities such as canoeing, sea kayaking, and mountain backpacking. In Cushing's words, it is a rite of passage that helps students acquire a new skill set and a new concept of citizenship based on their "views of the world and their role in it, [developed] within socially defined parameters" (Cushing 1998: 9).

In her study, Cushing focused on the third phase of the rite of passage, reincorporation, when individuals return to their community in a new, socially recognized position or state (in this case, as "more adult" than before). Cushing felt that this was the aspect of the Outward Bound program, viewed as a rite of passage, that was the most difficult and that could best improve. The challenge of reintegration was predictable in a complex society, and she proposed six ideas for improvement:

1. the opportunity to express: getting the students to express both what they have undergone and how they feel it will have an impact on their future
2. the opportunity to perform: giving the students opportunities to apply their new learning in a situation outside the group, in which they can "succeed" or "fail" and still get help from the group
3. re-introducing the other: easing the transition by exposing the students to non-group members during the period of separation
4. planning to share: getting the individuals and the groups to communicate to family and friends in a written form what each individual has learned
5. building in rewards: rewarding the students after the program for continuing to act according to what they have learned (e.g. through awards)
6. longer-term support: keeping in touch with the students long after the program is over in order to encourage them to maintain their "new selves."

One criticism of modern North American society is that we have undeveloped—or else we lack altogether—rites of passage from adolescence to

QUICK HITS

What Marks an Adult in Contemporary Canadian Society?

Which of the following rites of passage does the most to establish an individual as an adult in contemporary Canadian society? Rank them in order from strongest to weakest declaration of a person's adulthood.

- ☐ getting a driver's licence
- ☐ getting a job
- ☐ becoming a parent
- ☐ moving into one's own place (apartment or house)
- ☐ getting married.

What do YOU think?

Consider Cushing's six recommendations to improve the reintegration phase of the Outward Bound rite of passage. How effective do you think these improvements would be? What other improvements could you recommend?

When did you first start thinking of yourself as an adult? What do you think caused that to happen? Do you feel that your parents, employers, or teachers started treating you as an adult at about the same time, or were they slower to recognize the change? Why do you think it's sometimes difficult for post-secondary students to be treated or thought of as adults?

adulthood. If you're a resident of Saskatchewan, you could get your driver's licence at the age of 16, reach voting age at 18, and be old enough to drink legally at 19—these are all milestones on the road from adolescence to adulthood, but they are separate, occurring at different times, and each one lacks the ceremony and public recognition of adulthood that should come during the reintegration phase of a rite of passage. This could account for why adolescence in North America is as conflicted as it is, with many people in their late teens and early twenties caught in a state somewhere between childhood and adulthood, ultimately to emerge as an adult but without any clear ceremony to mark the occasion and announce the new status.

Middle Age and Beyond

We've seen that when it comes to different stages of the life course—childhood, adolescence, adulthood—there are no universally accepted parameters, although

there are rites of passage, varying across cultures, that help us map out the starts and ends of some of these periods. Likewise, there is no hard-and-fast rule to help us define the period called middle age, although some people situate it roughly between the ages 40 and 60.

What rites of passage signal the shift into middle age? The one that seems to receive the greatest amount of attention is the **midlife crisis**, when an individual realizes that he or she isn't so young anymore, and that half or more of his or her life is over. The term is generally credited to Canadian-born psychoanalyst Elliott Jaques, who linked the phenomenon to a central paradox: that just as we're entering the prime of life, when "family and occupation have become established . . . and children are at the threshold of adulthood," we suddenly become aware of our own mortality, realizing that death is not "an event experienced in terms of the loss of someone else" but "a personal matter" (Jaques 1965: 506). This goes some way toward explaining why the experience of middle age varies so widely, from anxiety and depression to restlessness and a desire for new challenges.

A midlife crisis may be triggered by an event that prompts the individual to take stock of his or her life, such as a divorce, a career setback, or the death of a parent. It could also begin with that first grey hair or the experience of pain after playing sports or working out—circumstances that may force a person to consider the prospect of old age and death. The male midlife crisis is a topic given considerable attention in popular media, from cartoons to sitcoms and movies. The stereotypes of the middle-aged man buying a flashy but impractical sports car, or chasing after a much younger woman (as in the movie *American Beauty*, 2000) are common in North American culture. Less focus is placed on the experience of midlife crisis in women, but that is not too surprising, given the predominantly male-defined focus of North American movies, and the traditional male dominance in sociology and psychology departments. We tend to be more aware of the biological effects of middle age among women—notably, the hormonal changes that accompany **menopause**, the end of menstruation—than we are of the psychological and sociological effects.

Although the subject has not been researched extensively by sociologists, it has been suggested that the midlife crisis is a very Western—particularly North American—phenomenon. In "Middle Adulthood in Cultural Perspective," (2001), anthropologist Usha Menon examines what she calls the "cultural fictions" used to imagine middle age in three cultures: middle-class Anglo-America, middle-class Japan, and upper-caste rural India. She suggests that middle-age angst is not found to a significant extent in Japanese and South Asian cultures, which are not as subject to the cult of youth of the West. More cross-cultural research would be useful to investigate this situation.

We in North America live in a society that worships at the fountain of youth. Older people often try desperately to look younger than their age: botox, face lifts, and other cosmetic treatments are in vogue for those who have the money to fight the clock. When I was teaching a class of students from China, I asked them: "What do you think is the strangest thing that you have experienced in Canada?" A common, unexpected response was: "Old people who try to look young."

Part of the reason we fight so hard against the onset of old age may have to do with the way older people are treated—or mistreated—in North America. We are a society in which social change is proceeding rapidly. Consider our electronic devices, some of

When it comes to the experience of middle age, why do we tend to focus on the psychological changes among men and on the biological/hormonal changes among women? Are we oversimplifying one case or the other?

Going Global

Language and Culture: Respect for Age

One way of socially conceptualizing older people is as **elders**. In Canada this concept, which is a term of respect for a person whose wisdom and experience as the senior member of a social group are valued, is often associated with Aboriginal people. But in other parts of the world, notably Africa, and South and East Asia, the elder is a common concept.

In older cultures of the East and Far East, which tend to set store by tradition, there is a respect for age, whether it be for brothers and sisters who are older than oneself, for one's parents and grandparents, or for older people generally. This shows up readily in speech, with terms of respect known as **honorifics**, used when addressing older people. The Japanese honorific *san* is one well-known example, added after a person's name as a title of respect (as in *Karri-san*, roughly translated as "Miss Karri," or *Obasan*, a form of address for one's grandmother). The suffix *–ji*, used in South Asia after the names of respected people, is similar (*Gandhi-ji* for the Indian spiritual leader, or *Baba-ji* for one's father).

In the Huron language as it was spoken in the seventeenth century in present-day Ontario, respect for age was built into verbs referring to kinship, when the age difference was important. The older person was always made the subject of the verb, out of respect; the object was always the younger person referred to. Here are some examples:

- *Sandwen* means literally "**she** is mother to **you**" and translates to "your mother."
- *Sonywayisten* means "**he** is father to **us**" and translates to "our father."
- *Hayeniaha* means "**he** has **me** as younger brother" and translates to "my older brother."

Language and culture are engaged in a dialogue, where both speak and listen to each other. Where there is respect for age, it shows up in the grammar of the language. The grammar of the language reinforces, with honorifics, the respect that exists in the culture.

Contrast these practices with conventions observed in English as it is spoken in Canada. Titles of respect like "Sir" and "Madam" sound old-fashioned and are so rarely used that they could actually cause offence to someone who believes that a big deal is being made of his or her age. There is not enough consistency around their use for the respectful intent of the speaker to be obvious. Even the practice of using "Mister" or "Missus" to address people older than oneself appears to be diminishing—children will often use first names to address the parents of their classmates (a practice that was unheard of when I was young) and may even be on a first-name basis with some of their teachers. In our North American culture, the trend toward equality has diminished the respect for age than is evident in other cultures.

A culture well known for its respect and care for its elders is Chinese culture. Dedication to elders is a practice in keeping with the ancient Confucian virtue of **filial piety**, a lifelong respect and reverence for one's parents and ancestors, in which preserving the good image of one's parents is a major consideration in all of one's actions. These values originated in a way of life that typically could support it. The contemporary sociologist asks: What happens when filial piety meets the demographic changes (increased lifespans, urbanization, China's one-child policy, etc.) and socioeconomic pressures (increasing capitalist industry and cost of living) of twenty-first–century China? Filial piety is still strong to a certain extent, but new social forms that reflect the changing times are developing. For instance, the group home with assisted living for seniors has begun to make an appearance in a number of major Chinese cities. In Nanjing, for example, the number has risen from 27 in 1990 to 148 as of 2009 (Span 2011). A common institution here in the West, the "retirement home" was until recently unheard of in China, where filial piety would dictate that care for elders rests with the family of aged parents.

which have become almost indispensable: the technology, the names, and the buzzwords are constantly being refreshed, keeping them inaccessible to those struggling to keep up with the rapid pace of change. This is not a society in which people readily turn to elders for advice. "How did you fix your tablet, grandfather?" is not a question we hear. The anthropologist Margaret Mead, whose work on adolescence we considered earlier in the chapter, described what she called a "crisis in faith": "I believe this crisis in faith can be attributed . . . to the fact that there are now no elders who know more than the young themselves about what the young are experiencing" (Mead 1970: 64). This observation may be even truer today than it was when Mead made it, over 40 years ago.

Delayed Retirement

The age at which Canadians retire has changed significantly twice over the last 30 years. During the 1980s and most of the 1990s, there was an increase in the number of people who retired "early" (prior to age 65). This wasn't necessarily by choice, as many older workers were bought out in a wave of private- and public-sector "downsizing" in which employees who were close to but just shy of retirement age were given "an offer they couldn't refuse" (to paraphrase the Mafia expression). By 1996, only 22 per cent of Canadians 55 and older were employed, representing an 8 per cent drop from 20 years earlier (30.2 per cent in 1976). After 1996, there was a big reversal of the early retirement trend. Within just four years, by 2010, the percentage of employed Canadians over 55 had jumped to 34 per cent, including 39.4 per cent of men in that age category and 28.6 per cent of women (Statistics Canada 2011d).

A number of different factors are involved here. One of them is the law. There used to be mandatory retirement across Canada. One you reached 65, your company could let you go, and you could do nothing about it. Over the past 10 years or so, that law has been changed in every province and territory, except as it applies to jobs such as firefighting and police work, where personal fitness is a key employment requirement. Another factor is the realistic fear people have that pensions will be scaled back by governments and big companies, leaving retirees with less money to tackle rising personal debt. A final factor: 65 isn't as old as it used to be, and many people of that age just

aren't prepared for the **role exit** that comes with retiring from a position that has been an important source of status and fulfilment, not to mention income.

What do YOU think?

Do you think the social effects of later retirement are, by and large, negative and positive? Think about young people struggling to enter a work force dominated by older workers who are hanging on (in education, for example). Think about the years of experience and expertise lost when an older worker retires.

Elder Abuse

Elder abuse is a form of **ageism** that includes violence, mistreatment, or neglect inflicted on seniors. It can take place in private homes or in institutions such as retirement residences and hospitals. The perpetrators are

QUICK HITS

How Old Is "Old"?

We often hear people announce that "50 is the new 40" and "60 is the new 50." Is that what people actually think? Or is it just a marketing idea for products that make people appear younger than they actually are?

In a survey of 3,000 American adults, conducted by the Pew Research Group, the majority of respondents aged over 50 said they felt as though they were at least 10 years younger than their actual age. Respondents tended to give a different age value to "old age" depending on their own age. The average age given for the start of old age was 68. Yet interestingly, the majority of respondents over 65 moved the date up to 75. Those under 30 set the age at 60 (Arnquist 2009).

What do YOU think?

Why do you think the age of the respondent was a factor in estimating what old age is? Do you think it reflects the fact that people in today's society do not like to think of themselves as old?

usually known to the elder: they are often family members, especially spouses and adult children (the leading instigators of abuse by violence), or else people paid to take care of seniors. Strangers who abuse elders are not just robbers, as you might think, but include scam artists, often going door-to-door in the guise of a salesperson, a representative of a utility supplier (gas, hydro, water, etc.), or someone whose car has broken down and who needs to use a phone to call the CAA. There are a variety of forms of elder abuse: physical, sexual, emotional, institutional (i.e. failing to meet the basic needs of an elder in one's institutional care), economic, neglect, denial of basic rights, and spiritual (e.g., denying an elder assistance in accessing a place of worship).

Concerning elder abuse by violence, the statistics can be misleading. According to a 2007 Statistics Canada report, Canadians aged 65 or older were much less likely than those under 65 to be the victims of violent and property crime (Statistics Canada 2007d). And in 2009, the rate of violent victimization among people 55 and older was roughly one-tenth that for those 15 to 24 (Perreault & Brennan 2009). This kind of statistic has been fairly consistent over the years, even though elders tend to be more likely to report a violent attack than younger people are. A number of factors can at least partly explain the discrepancy. For one thing, elders are less likely to be found in clubs and bars, and other places where violence is possible, particularly at night. Elders may also be less likely to provoke violence by what they say and do. None of this in any way diminishes the gravity of violence against elders.

If you are looking for case studies or examples of elder abuse, you can do no better than to visit the website of the Elder Advocates of Alberta Society (EAAS). It is from this site that we obtained the following case study of an 80-year-old man named Nelson Struk.

Mr Struk's story of institutional abuse began in May 2010, when he was arrested by the Edmonton City Police, on the report of a neighbour whom Mr Struk had accused of vandalism. (Acts of vandalism carried out by the neighbour were witnessed a few days later by representatives of the EAAS.) Mr Struk had been arrested the year before under the same circumstances, and placed in the psychiatric ward, even though he had not been formally diagnosed. In the 2010 incident, he was taken to the University Hospital and detained there, under guard's supervision, even though he had not been served with legal notification

What do you think the age of old age is? Can you remember what you thought old age was when you were a child? Was the age different?

for his arrest (a human rights violation, and a breach of the Alberta Mental Health Act). He was forced into "a locked, windowless room which had no call bell. . . . Later that day . . . [he] was moved to an emergency room cubicle but continued to be held under close observation by a guard seated next to his emergency room cot." The next day he was forcibly confined by straps to a stretcher and transferred by ambulance to another hospital. Over the course of his 33-hour confinement at the University Hospital, he was not informed of why he was being held.

It wasn't until 10 days later, on 20 May, that Mr Struk was able to contact a lawyer and be informed of why he was being held. A letter from the hospital

---

Telling It Like It Is

An Author POV

The Place of the Elder in Inuit Society

Some early anthropological accounts of the Inuit spread a myth that the Inuit either abandoned or encouraged suicide among their older citizens when times got tough. In my own effort to dispel this myth, I collected a number of first-hand reports that emphasized the importance of elders in Inuit culture, and the respect that they were given. The following quoted passages should enable you to get a good sense of the importance of elders in traditional culture, and of the relationships between elders and younger people.

The first comment on Inuit elders comes from Lucien Turner's 1894 *Ethnology of the Ungava District, Hudson Bay Territory*:

> If the father live to a great age, and some of the men certainly attain the age of more than 80 years, he may have great grandchildren about him, and these never fail to show respect for their ancestor. (Turner 2001 [1894]: 190)

Next, Samuel K. Hutton, in his 1912 account *Among the Eskimos of Labrador: A Record of Five Years' Close Intercourse with the Eskimo Tribes of Labrador* (1912), remarks:

> In my visits to the Eskimo households I could not fail to be struck by the patience and devotion with which the people care for their aged ones. The old man or woman, feeble and past work, is sure of a home with a married son or daughter or other relative, and if the poor old body has

no relations, there is enough hospitality in the hearts of the poorest of the people to make them open their homes to the needy. (Hutton 1912: 111)

Ernest Hawkes published *The Labrador Eskimo* in 1916, based on time he spent among the Labrador Inuit (having spent three years earlier among the Inuit of Alaska):

> The aged are treated with great respect, and the word of the old men and women is final. The Eskimo say that they have lived a long time and understand things in general better. They also feel that in the aged is embodied the wisdom of their ancestors. (Hawkes 1916: 117)

Danish anthropologist Kaj Birket-Smith's well-known work with the Caribou Inuit, who lived just to the west of Hudson Bay, revealed to him the importance of the knowledgeable old hunter:

> An elderly, skillful hunter with great experience always enjoys great esteem as *primus inter pares* [first among equals]. When a number of families are gathered in camp, there is often an elderly *pater familias* [family father] who is tacitly looked upon as [ihumataq], i.e., he who thinks, implying: for the others. (Birket-Smith 1929: 258–9)

Then there is the work of Riley D. Moore. In 1912 he visited the Inuit (specifically the Yup'ik) of summarized the incident using the following, condescending and self-protective words:

> Privacy legislation prevents us from responding to specific details of this case but do know that the gentleman in question did receive appropriate care. (EAAS n.d.)

What do YOU think?

1. How different might this case have been if Nelson had been a 30-year-old man?

2. What similarities might there have been if Nelson had been a 15-year-old man?

St Lawrence Island, off the coast of Alaska in the Bering Sea. He tells the same story:

> The older members of the family, especially fathers and older uncles, are treated with extreme reverence and respect, accorded them because of their age and the wisdom garnered from years of experience. (Moore 1923)

This all leads to questions about why sociologists and anthropologists would spread the story that the Inuit of traditional cultures would abandon (on ice floes, in a practice jokingly called "going with the floes") or otherwise hasten the death of their elders during difficult times. Is it because these academics, coming from cultures with no elders, could not completely recognize or appreciate the significance status of the elder's roles?

In the healing and basic recovery of traditions and identity that has occurred throughout the Aboriginal community in recent decades, elders have played a crucial role. This role has been about more than the traditional one associated with knowledge of hunting, trapping, fishing, and food and clothing preparation. It has seen Aboriginal elders adapt to the contemporary needs of the people by becoming involved in education at the primary, secondary, and post-secondary levels. In 1986, Beatrice Medicine, a Lakota educator and sociologist from South Dakota, wrote an important article entitled "My Elders Tell Me," about the early development of the role of elder in education (Medicine 1986). Her concern, shared by others with similar interests, was that although Aboriginal people wanted elders to become involved in education, they were not sure how to address concrete issues such as who was an elder, and what precisely an elder should do. Telling is the following commentary by a Nakoda (Stony or Assiniboine) educator, then at the University of Calgary:

> we have misused the role of elder through our ignorance and failure to see that not all elders are teachers, not all elders are spiritual leaders, and not all old people are elders. (cited in Medicine 1986: 147)

The same article does, however, furnish two useful definitions of *elder*:

> Elders are repositories of cultural and philosophical knowledge and are the transmitters of such information. (Medicine 1986: 142)
>
> [Elders are] those people who have earned the respect of their own community and who are looked upon as elders in their own society. (as cited in Medicine 1986: 146)

We can thus establish three key criteria for the role of elder:

1. age
2. connection with traditions (stories, philosophy, crafts, and skills)
3. community recognition of this connection.

WRAP IT UP

Summary

The life course can be viewed as a natural timeline of human development through stages that are marked by certain biological milestones, including birth, puberty, menopause, and death. But the stages in the life course are not only biological: they are also social constructs, marked by rites of passage, that have different meanings for different cultures at different times. Looking at the work of Ariès and Postman, for instance, we saw that the social definition of childhood changed in Europe and in the West generally over the last 800 years. Adolescence is a stage of life often filled with conflict and turmoil both for "fact of life" reasons and also because of the way adolescence is constructed socially. Anthropologist Margaret Mead suggested that rites of passage can smooth the passage from childhood to adulthood, but is this possible only in a small community like the one she was studying, or can it be true also in a more socially complicated society such as that of twenty-first–century Canada?

Then there is old age. In societies that value traditional knowledge and wisdom, older people are regarded as elders. There is respect for them that is seen in small elements such as how they are addressed, and to a larger extent in how they are listened to and otherwise regarded. An elder in mainstream North American society is usually just an old person, or, with an attempt at politeness, a senior (there are less polite terms, too, it should be noted). The terminology says a lot about how age is viewed in our culture.

THINK BACK

Questions for Critical Review

1. In what ways do you think childhood has changed over the last 25 years? Do you think that it is better or worse than when you were under the age of 10? Explain.

2. Do you think that adolescence is a naturally stressful and turbulent time? How much has to do with cultural pressures on adolescents?

3. What is the difference between broad and narrow socialization? Select a culture (either current or historical) that represents each to illuminate the differences between the two forms of socialization.

4. The berry fast is a rite of passage for Anishinabe girls beginning around the time of **menarche** (an adolescent's first menstrual period). In what other ways is menarche observed in contemporary Canadian culture? How does this rite of passage differ among the different ethnic communities that make up Canadian society? Are there any cultural groups that do not have an established tradition surrounding this event?

5. It has been said that many North American adults are in some ways more like children than like complete adults. Why might that be true?

6. What do you think are the main social effects of the aging of Canadian society?

READ ON

Online

2011 Census Release Topics: Age and Sex

www12.statcan.gc.ca/census-recensement/2011/rt-td/index-eng.cfm#tab5

Any aspiring sociologist must become familiar with the Statistics Canada website, and what better place to start than here. This page directs you to StatsCan figures and tables concerning our aging population, but also discussions and a glossary to place those figures in context.

Brain Science, Adolescence and Secondary Schools: A Critical Disconnect

www.cea-ace.ca/education-canada/article/brain-science-adolescence-and-secondary -schools-critical-disconnect

This article from the Canadian Education Association's online journal takes an evolutionary psychological approach to adolescence that is critical of society's institutions and their expectations of adolescents.

"The Midlife Crisis is a Total Myth," by Robin Nixon

www.livescience.com/12930-midlife-crisis-total-myth.html

LiveScience is a media organization providing news on health, science, and technology for a popular audience (the kind that is also curious about the scientific evidence for ghosts and whether it really was an asteroid that killed the dinosaurs). This article, by Robin Nixon (2 Feb. 2011), presents a short critical discussion challenging the existence of the midlife crisis.

Elder Advocates of Alberta Society

http://elderadvocates.ca

The EAAS advocates on behalf of—in its own words—"the frail, dependent elderly," in the pursuit of justice for victims of elder abuse. Their website is an excellent source of case studies of elder abuse, especially institutional abuse.

In Print

Usha Menon (2001), "Middle Adulthood in Cultural Perspective: The Imagined and the Experienced in Three Cultures," in Margie E. Lachman (Ed.), *Handbook of Midlife Development*, pp. 40–74 (New York: Wiley).

A detailed cross-cultural look at how middle age is viewed in three different societies.

Roger Neustadter (2009), *The Obvious Child: Studies in the Significance of Childhood* (New York: University Press of America).

A good study of how childhood has been constructed socially across time and culture.

Neil Postman (1982), *The Disappearance of Childhood* **(New York: Delacorte).**

An insightful book about the changes in the way that childhood has been constructed in the West over the last few centuries.

S.M. Stiegelbauer (1996), "What Is an Elder? What Do Elders Do? First Nation Elders as Teachers in Culture-Based Urban Organizations," *The Canadian Journal of Native Studies* **16 (1), pp. 37–66.**

A clear presentation of the nature of the interaction between elders and the education system in Canada.

IV *Social Institutions*

TO THE SOCIOLOGIST, social institutions are subsystems of society as a whole. In fact, from a structural-functionalist perspective, they are some of society's most important building blocks: the family, organized religion, the health and education systems, and the media—essential structures performing functions that contribute meaningfully to the way society operates. As such, they are valued.

Beyond the structural-functionalist interpretation, however, there are conflicting and divisive views as to how these institutions should be structured and whether they are in certain cases more dysfunctional than functional for certain groups of individuals and for society in general.

For instance, does the family absolutely have to be heterosexual in its makeup, according to conventional belief? And are families structured in ways that might benefit males more than females?

And then look at religion and the way it can restrict the social influence of women but, at the same time, can perform a stabilizing function in society—is that, on balance, beneficial?

We can investigate how education gives even the poorest in society a chance at "success" (however that is defined), but we should also look at how it can serve to merely replicate or reproduce the pre-existing class structure, keeping people from rising above their station.

Work, of course, is necessary for the economy. But can we argue that the domination of the work world by a small minority of people (most of them white men) is harmful to the way the system operates? And do we define people too narrowly according to what they do for a living?

Next, what is the impact of gender on health and medicine? As the proportion of women doctors increases, will the social world and the delivery of healthcare change significantly? And will our hospitals open their doors to alternative medical practices, or will Western medicine become even more firmly entrenched to guard against the encroachment of these other therapies?

And as for the media, well, they colour our perceptions of everything that goes on in our culture—or do they? Are we passive recipients of mass-manufactured drivel, or do we control the cultural products we consume? Stay tuned . . .

14 Family

Learning Objectives

After reading this chapter, you should be able to

- characterize the diversity of the Canadian family
- explain the ways that family in Quebec is different from family in the rest of Canada
- discuss eight major changes taking place in the family today
- identify the different forms that *conjugal roles* can take

- describe the varying impacts of *endogamy* on different racial and ethnic groups in Canada
- identify how immigration patterns can affect family development
- outline and comment on the argument that Aboriginal families were "under attack" during the twentieth century in Canada.

Key Terms

- cluttered nest
- common-law (*or* cohabiting) union
- companionate roles
- complementary roles
- complex household
- conjugal roles
- crude marriage rate
- disabled family
- double burden (*or* ghetto)
- dynamic
- empty nest
- endogamy
- eugenics
- exogamy
- extended family
- fecundity
- gender roles
- gender strategy
- general intelligence
- genocide
- intelligences
- joint conjugal roles
- master status
- matrilineal
- nuclear family
- occupational segregation
- patrilineal
- polygamy
- polygyny
- replacement rate
- residential schools
- scientific classism
- scientific racism
- second shift
- segregated conjugal roles
- simple household
- Sixties Scoop
- total fertility rate
- work interruptions

Names to Know

- Rod Beaujot
- Sathi Dasgupta
- Ann Duffy
- Nancy Mandell
- M. Reza Nakhaie

For Starters

The cast of the popular sitcom *Modern Family*. What exactly is a "modern family"?

Family and the Negative Sanction of Humour

Wherever tension exists in a culture, there is humour. That's because humour gives us a way to address everyday issues that cause tension with an openness that doesn't come easily when the same issues are discussed more seriously. In North American culture, family life is often a target of humour, whether that humour comes from a stand-up's comedy routine, a co-worker's jocular rant about her mother-in-law, or one of the many sitcoms that revolve around family **dynamics**, from golden oldies like *The Honeymooners* and *All in the Family* to current offerings like *The Simpsons* and *Modern Family*. That's because the family is and always has been a site of tension, between people living the roles of husband and wife, parent and child, spouse and in-law.

Looking at a culture's humour can tell us where the tension is. But remember that humour is rarely sociologically "innocent." For example, it can tell us about whose perspective has power. I'll bet that if you came up with 10 jokes about husbands and wives, most

would take the perspective of the husband. Jokes can be (and often are) negative sanctions, hinting that what someone is doing is not approved of. Look at each of the following jokes and see if you can find the subtle message for husbands and wives.

Q: If a man speaks in the forest and his wife isn't there, is he still wrong?
[*subtle message, from a male perspective: don't nag your husband—he is the head of the family and should not be challenged.*]
A: Yes, unless he's talking about sports or cars.
[*subtle message, from a female perspective: men have a narrow scope of expertise; women are more broad-minded.*]

*

A woman took her husband to the doctor. After the examination, the doctor went out to talk to the wife. "How is he?" the wife asked.

"Well, it's not good. You're going to have to fix his meals three times a day, every day. You'll have to pick up after him, help him change every day, and comfort him every night, or he will die."

When the wife went in to see her husband, her husband asked, "What did the doctor say?"

a) The wife looked at him and said, "You're going to die."
   [*subtle message, from a male perspective: wives don't work hard enough to give their husbands comfort and support.*]

b) The wife looked at him and said, "Well, the good news is that we don't have to make any changes in our lifestyle."
   [*subtle message, from a female perspective: wives*

work like slaves for their husbands; husbands should do more or at least recognize how much they depend on their wives.]

I can hear you groaning over the jokes, but if you look past the humour for a moment, you will see very real sources of tension in family life that sociologists today are grappling with—issues like male patriarchy and women's "double burden." In this chapter, we will look at these and many other issues in the sociological study of family life. In the meantime, try this exercise yourself: watch an episode of your favourite family sitcom (yes, this is homework) and follow the humour to the sources of tension and the issues underlying them—we're willing to bet they've all been covered in the annals of sociology literature.

Introduction: The Modern Family Is Diverse

The opening line of Russian novelist Leo Tolstoy's famous, tragic romantic novel *Anna Karenina* reads: "Happy families are all alike; every unhappy family is unhappy in its own way." We disagree. Happy families, functional families, good families exist in many forms, and are alike only in their success at serving basic functions: providing emotional support for family members, taking care of elders, raising the next generation, and so on. In most other respects, happy families are diverse.

Family in Canada has existed in many forms historically and still does today. Before the arrival of Europeans, there was diversity among Aboriginal families. Some Native bands were **patrilineal** (determining kinship along the *male* line), some were **matrilineal** (determining kinship along the *female* line); some lived in societies structured around *clans*—like large extended families—while others did not. Based on the "family principle"—the notion that a family includes everyone related by blood—clans could include hundreds and even thousands of people. The period of European exploration and resource exploitation brought diverse and changing forms. Fur traders sometimes had European wives in New France (Quebec) and Aboriginal wives in the West. Loggers and fishers spent such long periods away from their home communities that they were like visitors when

they returned. Age at marriage has varied in Canada, rising and falling with changes to the country's economic prosperity and the availability of jobs. Women, who in the late nineteenth century worked for pay only when they were unmarried, have become more and more immersed in the workforce throughout the twentieth century and into the twenty-first, and men are taking on a greater (but still not great) share of responsibilities around the home.

It would be misleading to say that one family form is demonstrably better or worse than any other for its members. And yet newspapers, other media, and personal commentary are filled with judgemental remarks about contemporary family forms. Even traditional sociology is not free from this bias. If you were presented with the terms **nuclear family** (which includes a parent or parents and children) and **extended family** (which might include, in addition, grandparents, aunts, uncles, and cousins), you might be led to believe that the former is "normal" and the other some kind of deviation from the regular model. Such is not the case. For some cultures, historical and current, using the word "family" to mean parents and children alone would be as odd as using the term "body" to refer just to the heart.

The Huron language of the seventeenth century had no terms for either "nuclear" or "extended" family. The common way for the Huron to refer to family was through the noun root *-hwatsir-*, meaning "matrilineage," or the verb root *-yentio-*, meaning "to belong to a matrilineal clan." Matrilineage is the line of descendants that follows the mother's line. A woman, her sisters and brothers, and their mother would belong to the same matrilineage. A longhouse may be dominated by one matrilineage, with married sisters and their husbands and children forming the nucleus of the people living in one house. Thus, the most common term for "family" in the Huron language referred to a model we would probably brand with the term "extended family."

More useful, perhaps, than "nuclear family" and "extended family" are terms proposed by Frances Goldscheider and Regina Bures in their study of intergenerational living arrangements in America. They favour the terms "simple household" and "complex household." A **simple household** consists of unrelated (by blood) adults with or without children. Conversely, a **complex household** includes "two or more adults who are related but not married to each other and hence could reasonably be expected to live separately" (2003). A simple household tends to consist of a single adult or married adults living with or without children; the most common example of a complex household

today is one in which adult children live at home with a parent or parents.

We should point out that when sociologists talk of a family's diversity, they may mean one of two things. Some mean "diversity" in the sense that there are different family structures: dual-earner, single-earner/two-parent, lone-parent. We use "diversity" here and throughout this text in a broader sense that includes not just differences in structure but also cultural differences in conjugal and **gender roles**. The discussion of the family in Quebec later in this chapter highlights this broader sense of diversity.

Nine Changes in the Canadian Family

There are a number of changes occurring in the makeup and behaviour of Canadian families today. In a number of these areas where change is occurring, families in Quebec are leading the way. This is not to say that they are "further ahead" in some kind of modernist progressive model but that they offer the clearest evidence of certain general trends.

Would you call this a typical Canadian family? How many families do you know that look like this?

1. The marriage rate is decreasing while the cohabitation rate is rising.

A quick look at crude marriage rates will tell a sociologist if it's true that fewer people are getting married these days. The **crude marriage rate** is the number of marriages per 1,000 people in a population. "Crude" refers to the fact that no statistical wizardry has been used to "refine" the rate (to use an oil analogy). It doesn't mean that the marriage is crude (although one of mine was). Since the population keeps rising, the crude marriage rate will give a better indication of trends than the overall number of marriages alone. If the number of marriages were the same in 2002 and 2013, the actual rate would have to be decreasing, and a sociologist could conclude that fewer people were getting married these days.

The crude marriage rate has fluctuated over the years. In 1920, it was relatively low at 6.1 per 1,000 people, probably because so many young men had died during World War I and the Spanish flu epidemic that followed it. When I think of that statistic, I

Our Stories

The Crestwood Heights Family

Between 1948 and 1953, sociologists John Seeley, Alexander Sim, and Elizabeth Loosley studied a white, upper-middle-class neighbourhood in North Toronto, to which they gave the fictitious name "Crestwood Heights." The following is a brief introduction to their chapter on the family:

> The family of Crestwood Heights . . . consists of father, mother, and two (rarely more) children. The children are healthy, physically well developed, attractively dressed, and poised as to outward behavior. The mother, assured in manner, is as like an illustration from *Vogue* or *Harper's Bazaar* as financial means and physical appearance will allow. The father, well tailored, more or less successful in radiating an impression of prosperity and power, rounds out the family group.
>
> This small family unit is both lone and love-based. It is, more often than not, formed by the marriage of two persons from unrelated and often unacquainted families . . . who are assumed to have chosen each other because they are "in love." Other reasons for the choice (perpetuation of property within one family, the linking of business or professional interest, an unadorned urge to upward social mobility and so on), even if influential, could not reputably be admitted as grounds for marriage.
>
> This family unit is not embedded in any extended kinship system. The newly formed family is frequently isolated geographically and often socially from the parental families. It is expected that the bride and groom will maintain a separate dwelling removed by varying degrees of distance from that of each set of parents. . . . The isolation of each family acts to decrease the ability of the family to transmit traditional patterns of behavior, which might otherwise be absorbed from close contact with, for instance, grandparents. The absence of kinship bonds also tends to concentrate the emotional life of the family upon a few individuals. . . . (Seeley et al. 1956: 159–60)

What do YOU think?

1. How many families do you know that conform to the Crestwood Heights model? In what ways is it a "good" or a "bad" model?

2. In what respects does your own family differ, if at all, from the description given here? In what respects does it resemble this model?

think of two of my great-aunts who were young then—Aunt Nell the nurse, Aunt Margaret the teacher. They were gifted, intelligent women adored by the children and grandchildren of their married brothers. Neither of them ever married.

The marriage rate rose to a peak of 7.9 marriages per 1,000 people in 1950, representing a post–World War II marriage boom that would precede (and contribute to) the post-war baby boom.

After dropping a little in the years that followed, the marriage rate remained fairly high over the next three decades, peaking at 8.0 in 1980. That was just before a recession hit. Since then, the rate has dropped rather steadily, from 5.5 in 1995 to 4.7 in 2001, where it remained until 2003. After that, a directly comparable figure became harder to obtain, as laws allowing same-sex marriage were first passed in British Columbia and Ontario. They were, not surprisingly, the only two provinces that year in which the number of marriages increased. The lowest crude marriage rate was in Quebec, with 2.8 marriages per 1,000 population. It was

the only province (along with Nunavut and Northwest Territories) where the marriage rate was below the national average. The marriage rate for the other nine provinces and Yukon averaged about 5.3 in 2003.

Fewer *marriages* does not mean fewer *couples*. The number of **common-law** (or **cohabiting**) unions has risen since 1980. Precise figures are difficult to track, since society doesn't ritually mark the beginning of such relationships the way it records marriages. Still, we do know that the percentage of all couples living in common-law or cohabiting unions rose from 0.7 per cent in 1976 to 18.4 per cent as of 2006, and that between 2006 and 2011, the number of common-law couples rose by 13.9 per cent, which is more than four times the 3.1 per cent increase in the number of married couples (Statistics Canada 2012a: 3). The cohabitation rate in the United States is always lower than in Canada (for instance, the US rate in 2001 was 8.2 per cent, barely half the Canadian rate of 16.0 for that year). Can you think of why that is? Here's a hint: in 2011, the proportion of census families that included a common-law

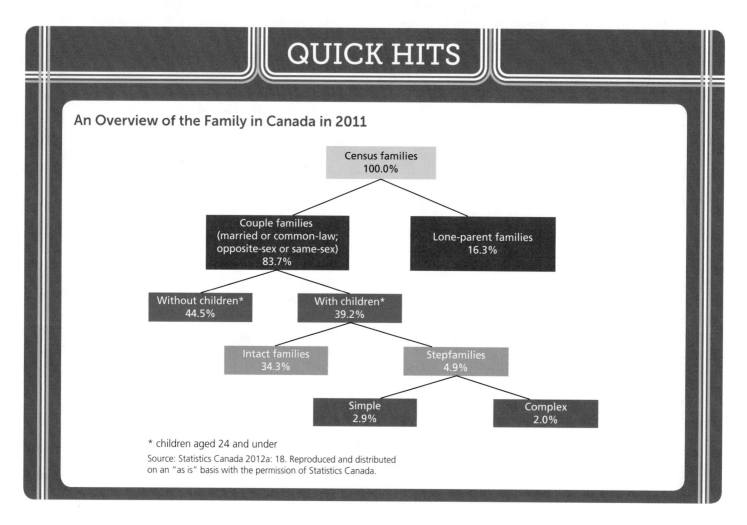

QUICK HITS

An Overview of the Family in Canada in 2011

Census families
100.0%

Couple families
(married or common-law;
opposite-sex or same-sex)
83.7%

Lone-parent families
16.3%

Without children*
44.5%

With children*
39.2%

Intact families
34.3%

Stepfamilies
4.9%

Simple
2.9%

Complex
2.0%

* children aged 24 and under

Source: Statistics Canada 2012a: 18. Reproduced and distributed on an "as is" basis with the permission of Statistics Canada.

Compare this photo with the one on page 366. Is this family any less typical of the families you know? What factors in our culture might lead us to view one family as more conventional than another?

couple was 16.7 per cent for all of Canada; Quebec, with a cohabitation rate of 31.5 per cent, skews the Canadian figures considerably (the province with the next highest cohabitation rate was New Brunswick, at just 16.0 per cent) (Statistics Canada 2012a: 6).

A number of other good questions can be addressed concerning cohabiting couples. Is cohabitation replacing marriage? Despite the dramatic increase in the number of common-law couples between 2006 and 2011, married couples still made up the predominant family structure in Canada by a wide margin (67.0 per cent, compared with just 16.7 per cent for common-law couples) (Statistics Canada 2012a: 5–6). Does cohabitation benefit men more than women? How does cohabitation, versus marriage, affect children?

One of my favourite questions concerns the following fact, which seems to generate a considerable amount of spurious reasoning: couples who cohabit prior to marriage are more likely to divorce than couples who live apart right up until the time they marry. A survey done in 1990 found that after 10 years of marriage, the breakup rate was 26 per cent for those

who had cohabited first and 16 per cent for those who had not (Le Bourdais & Marcil-Gratton 1996: 428). Think about that for a minute and see if you can come up with an explanation.

Students asked to offer hypotheses for this statistic often fall victim to false causation: something happens during cohabitation, they speculate, or else cohabiting couples, because they've already spent so much time living together, became tired of each other during marriage. A better answer, which they tend to miss, is that people with more liberal values are more likely both to enter a cohabiting union and to leave a bad marriage. Another good possibility: people who are afraid of commitment are more likely both to cohabit rather than formally wed and to leave a relationship.

2. The age of first marriage is rising.

The average age of first marriage in Canada has been rising steadily since the early 1970s, but as Table 14.1 shows, it wasn't until the 1990s that the figures really began to climb. Consider that in 1921, the average age of first marriage was 24.5 for brides and 28.0 for grooms;

Table 14.1 Average age of first marriage, by sex, 1928–2008

YEAR	1928	1938	1948	1958	1968	1978	1983	1988	1993	1998	2003	2008
Men	27.6	28.3	26.9	25.5	25.1	25.5	26.3	27.5	28.2	28.9	30.2	31.1
Women	24.2	24.9	23.9	22.7	22.6	23.2	24.1	25.2	26.2	27.0	28.2	29.1

Source: Based on Statistics Canada data.

70 years later, in 1991, the figures were 25.8 and 27.8, respectively (Statistics Canada 1992). After remaining fairly constant throughout the 1920s, the age of first marriage rose slightly during the Depression-era 1930s before dropping again, slowly, in the 1940s. The drop became more dramatic in the 1950s and 1960s: in 1965, 30.8 per cent of first-time brides were under 20 years of age (Beaujot 2000: 102).

Questions arise. Has this figure peaked, or will it continue to climb? What has contributed to the rise since the 1990s? Is this figure becoming increasingly meaningless as the cohabitation rate increases?

It's worth noting, too, that the averages differ from province to province. In 2003, the lowest average age of first marriage was in Saskatchewan, where it was 27.0 for women and 29.3 for men; the same year in Quebec, the figures were 30.4 and 31.9 respectively.

3. There are more divorces overall, but the rate is falling.

Analyzing divorce statistics can be complicated. If you ask a group of people whether they think the divorce rate is rising or falling, they will typically say that it's going up. This is not the case. The rate has jumped on several occasions over brief periods of time, but we can account for these, in part, by looking at changes to the legislation surrounding divorce.

In 1961, there were 6,563 divorces in Canada, producing a divorce rate of 36.0 per 100,000 population. In 1968, the grounds for divorce were expanded in most of Canada: no longer was adultery the sole basis to sue for divorce. Between 1968 and 1971, the number of divorces in Canada shot up from 11,343 to 29,685, representing rates of 54.8 and 137.6 per 100,000. By 1982, the numbers had peaked (at 70,346, or a rate of 285.9); in fact, they began to decline slowly. Then in 1985, the Divorce Act was changed again, allowing "marital breakdown" as legitimate grounds for divorce. By 1987, the numbers had peaked once more, this time at 90,985 (339.5 per 100,000). By 2002, the numbers

were back down to 1982 levels: 70,155 divorces for a rate of 223.7, the lowest rate since the 1970s.

In a 2012 publication, Statistics Canada reported that the number of divorce cases initiated in a sample of six provinces and territories (Ontario, Nova Scotia, BC, Nunavut, Yukon, Northwest Territories) fell by 8 per cent between 2006 and 2011, decreasing consistently each year (Kelly 2012). That's good news for marriage, right?

Not necessarily. Although it's possible that some married couples are staying together longer, it could also be that because a greater proportion of couples are living common-law rather than marrying, fewer couples require formal divorces when their relationships end. Without more detailed data, we can only speculate.

4. More women are having children in their thirties.

The number of women in their thirties giving birth for the first time is increasing. In 1987, just 4 per cent of women aged 35 and older gave birth for the first time; in 2005, the percentage rose to 11 per cent. Likewise, women in their early thirties giving birth to their first child increased from 15 to 26 per cent over the same period. An important factor to consider here is **fecundity**, the physical ability to conceive. This ability changes during a woman's fourth decade. It is estimated that 91 per cent of women at the age of 30 are physically able to become pregnant. This drops to 77 per cent for women aged 35, and just 53 per cent

What do YOU think?

Many women today want to establish themselves in a career before starting to have children. Is this a positive development in terms of the equality of women in Canadian society? Or does it indicate that society still expects women to choose between career and family? What policies might make it easier for the woman on a career path to have children earlier in life?

The Point Is...

Does Having a Disabled Family Member Mean Having a Disabled Family?

One of the lasting images of the 2010 winter Olympics in Vancouver is of Alexandre Bilodeau and his older brother, Frederic, who has cerebral palsy, hugging after Alex won the first gold medal of the games for Canada—indeed, the first Canadian gold medal ever on home soil. We remember Alex telling reporters, "My brother is my inspiration—he taught me so many things in my life." The story was inspiring, but how common is a story like that?

Wayne Hower examined the extent to which the family of a person with a disability becomes, itself, disabled in his 2006 book *Does a Disabled Child = a Disabled Family?* (spoiler alert: his answer was no). Once the politically correct replacement for earlier terms like "handicapped" and "crippled," *disabled* has now itself become a target for those who find it hideous, too close in sound and meaning to words like "dysfunctional" to be an appropriate way to characterize someone who might function at a high level in many areas of life. But Hower chose it deliberately, and a sociologist can shed some light on why he might have done so.

In Chapter 6 we examined the pitfalls of acquiring or being born with a **master status**, a trait that, in the words of Everett C. Hughes, "tends to overpower, in most crucial situations, any other characteristics" (Hughes 1945: 357). For many people, disability can be an unshakable master status that consistently overshadows or diminishes other statuses and accomplishments (older brother, musician, younger sister, mother, friend). Being viewed as "disabled"—as imperfect, less than others who are not disabled—can have a huge effect on the way one is treated by others.

Disability is also a master status that can extend beyond the individual to the family of which he or she is a part. It is clear from his comments that Hower himself feels the sting of any sanction directed at his daughter, who is developmentally delayed: "We have been asked to leave a church in which the pastor has a special education degree, and we have been turned down by a household name organization that works with the disabled in Dallas, Texas" (Hower 2006: 3). The **disabled family**, like the individual, becomes treated as other. The role of caregiver, too, can become a master status for a parent who becomes, above all else in his or her life, primarily responsible for a child with a disability. The adoption of the caregiver master status can lead the parent to neglect other children and the spouse, while blocking others from sharing the caregiver's role.

Alex Bilodeau's comments about Frederic suggest that he sees him very much as older brother and teacher—statuses that are not qualified or diminished by his cerebral palsy. But is the healthy attitude of other family members towards an individual with a disability enough to help the unit avoid the designation "disabled family"?

---

of women at 40 (Rajulton, Balakrisnhan, & Ravanera 1990). Woman in your thirties, do you hear the clock ticking? Do you think the fact that more women are waiting longer to have their first child may have a significant effect in lowering the *total fertility rate*?

5. The number of children per family has dropped below the "replacement rate."

The **total fertility rate** is an estimate of the average number of children that a woman between the ages of 15 and 49 will have in her lifetime if current age-specific fertility rates remain constant during her reproductive years. It's a projection, in other words, based on current fertility rates, even though we know that these actual rates will change.

Table 14.2 shows the total fertility rate for select years between 1941 and 2011. In 2002 the total fertility rate in Canada may have bottomed out at 1.51. How does that compare with the rate for other countries? Rates for the 100 most populous countries in the world in 2003 ranged from 3.86 to 6.98, with the top 10 fertility rates all being in Africa. Those countries with fertility rates below Canada's include the former communist countries of eastern Europe, ranging from the Czech Republic (1.18) to Georgia (1.51); some Mediterranean countries, including Italy (1.26), Greece (1.35), and Portugal (1.49); and several East Asian countries—Singapore (1.24), Hong Kong (1.32), Japan (1.38), South Korea (1.56), and Taiwan (1.57). In each of these countries, the population is expected to fall. Why do you think their fertility rates are so low? Is it just economics (at the national and family level), or is some pessimistic sense of the future involved as well?

Another way of looking at how things have changed in Canada is by considering the following. Of women born between 1927 and 1931, 31 per cent had five or more children. Compare that with women born between 1952 and 1956, of whom just 1.3 per cent had five or more children. Among the latter group, 38.3 per cent had just two children, and 33.7 per cent had one child or no children, meaning that a total of 72 per cent of women born in 1952–6 had two children or fewer, compared with 42.7 per cent of women born in 1927–31.

The **replacement rate** is the number of children that a woman must bear if the overall population is to continue at the same level. The replacement rate is 2.1, meaning that 2.1 children must be born for every woman in a population aged 15–49 in order for the population to hold constant. As Table 14.2 shows, it's been over 40 years since Canada had a total fertility rate above the replacement rate.

So what does a country do when its national fertility rate is below the replacement rate? Sociologists and politicians will answer that Canada makes up for its low fertility rate with high levels of immigration. Take note, however, that immigrants from countries with higher fertility rates soon begin to reproduce at a rate consistent with the fertility rate here in this country. Are there ways to boost the fertility rate? Would government incentives (such as those offered in Quebec) help to offset the cost of having and raising children? Would a system of universal, publicly funded daycare, similar to what exists in Quebec, change things significantly? Recent studies in the US suggest that women are willing to have more children when their husbands are willing to take a greater share of responsibility for childcare and general housework. How significant a factor do you think that could be?

What do YOU think?

How could you explain the fact that immigrants arriving in Canada from countries with high fertility rates bear children in numbers consistent with the Canadian fertility rate? What does this tell you about the factors that influence a country's fertility rate?

Table 14.2 Total fertility rate in Canada, 1921–2011

YEAR	TOTAL FERTILITY RATE	YEAR	TOTAL FERTILITY RATE
1921	3.53	1971	2.19
1926	3.36	1976	1.82
1931	3.20	1981	1.65
1936	2.70	1986	1.59
1941	2.83	1991	1.72
1946	3.37	1996	1.63
1951	3.50	2001	1.54
1956	3.86	2006	1.61
1961	3.84	2011	1.61
1966	2.81		

Source: Statistics Canada census data.

6. There are more couples without children than with.

Related to the decline in the total fertility rate is this statistic: the proportion of couples living *with* children has been surpassed by the proportion of couples living *without* children. In 2001, couples with children made up 43.6 per cent of all census families, while couples without children accounted for 40.3 per cent. In 2006, the proportion of childless couples topped the share of couples with children for the first time (42.7 per cent versus 41.4 per cent), and by 2011, the gap had spread considerably (44.5 per cent versus 39.2 per cent).

We have to be careful not to jump to hasty conclusions. This is just a 10-year trend, which is pretty short, by demographers' standards, and the next census could easily show a reversal. Still, it's worth asking: are these figures explained by the fact that women are waiting longer to have their first child? Or do they have more to do with the fact that Canada's overall population is aging, which means more couples surviving longer past the time their children leave home? If you're thinking the latter, consider the following.

7. Children are leaving home at a later age.

As we saw in Chapter 13, the term **cluttered nest** refers to the phenomenon in which adult children continue to live at home with their parents; the opposite, **empty nest**, describes a household in which children have moved out of the home. In 1981, 33.6 per cent of women aged 20–24 and 51.4 per cent of men of the same age were living with a parent or parents; by 1996, those figures had risen to 50.4 per cent and 64.3 per cent, respectively (Beaujot 2000: 98). And between 1981 and 2011, the percentage of adults aged 20–29 living with parents rose from 26.9 per cent to 42.3 per cent (Rennie 2012).

What are the reasons for the cluttered nest? For one thing, it takes more time and education nowadays to establish a career. Some adults living with parents are "boomerang kids," who have returned home after going away to college or university, prior to setting up on their own. Second, the cost of living today is higher, with higher housing prices in addition to a number of costs that earlier generations didn't have to face. (Television used to be free!) With couples marrying later and later in life, it takes that much longer to set up a dual-earner household, the only model that is financially viable for some people who want to move out of their parents' home.

8. There are more lone-parent families.

The number of lone-parent families in Canada has been increasing since 1966 (which followed a 35-year period of decrease from 13.6 per cent during the Depression year of 1931). In 1966, 8.2 per cent of all families were lone-parent families; since then, the figure has risen steadily, to 12.7 in 1986, 14.5 in 1996, 15.7 in 2001, 15.9 in 2006, and 16.3 in 2011 (Statistics Canada 2012a: 5).

People often speculate about the negative effects on children of living in lone-parent households, particularly with regard to school dropout rates and criminal activity. The critics need to be cautious here, though, as most lone-parent households began as two-parent

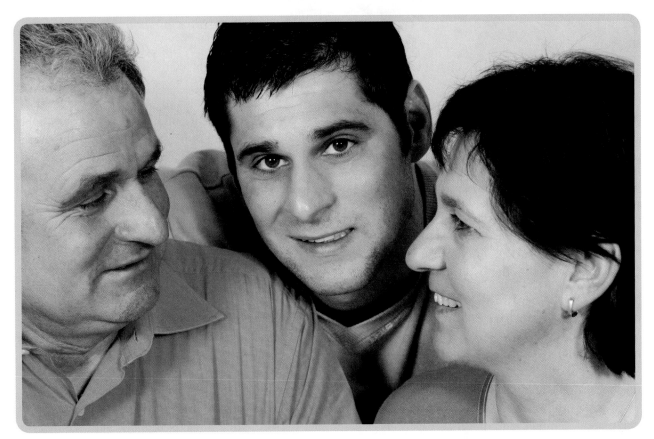

Does it surprise you that young men (20–29) are more likely than young women to be living at home with their parents? Why do you think this is the case?

Roughly 8 out of 10 lone-parent families have a female family head, although the percentage of male lone-parent families increased from 2.9 to 3.5 per cent between 2001 and 2011, while the percentage of female lone-parent families remained more or less constant (Statistics Canada 2012a: 5). Do you think the gap between male and female lone-parent families will shrink? Is it likely to be erased in your lifetime?

households. It is hard to determine if unfavourable conditions that might have existed in the pre-divorce or pre-separation family—an abusive parent perhaps, or, at least, parental fighting—could have been the real cause of a child's crime or truancy. You can't just blame the lone-parent situation.

There is, however, a strong connection between lone-parent families and poverty, especially where the mother is the family head. Beaujot (2000: 348) compared child poverty rates among lone-parent households for various countries before and after taxes have been deducted and transfer payments (social assistance) distributed. The countries include Canada, the US, Australia, Israel, and a number of European nations, all studied over a 10-year period from 1982 to 1992.

Before taxes and transfer payments, Canada has the sixth highest rate of child poverty in lone-parent households, with a 1991 pre-transfer payment rate of 68.2 per cent. What is more shocking is that Canada moves up to third on the list when the after-tax-and-transfer totals are considered. Canada, with a poverty rate in lone-parent households of 50.2 per cent, falls behind only the US (59.5 per cent) and Australia (56.2). This suggests that Canada is not doing enough—less, certainly, than the other countries studied—to help children living in poverty in lone-parent families. What do you think can be done to change this?

9. There are more people living alone.

In 1996, Beaujot (2000: 117) reported, 12 per cent of the entire Canadian population aged 15 and over were living alone; the rate was highest for those over 85 (48 per cent), and lowest for those younger than 55 (10 per cent). By 2011, the overall percentage of Canadians living alone had climbed to 13.5 per cent (Statistics Canada 2012a: 3).

A Statistics Canada publication offers an interesting comparison. In an examination of the changing percentages for 1-person and 5+-person households, the authors note:

In 2006, there were three times as many one-person households as households with five or more people. Of the 12.4 million private households, 27% were one-person households, while 9% were large households of five or more people.

In 1941, 6% of houses were comprised of one person, while 38% [N.B. *more than six times as many!*] were comprised of five or more people. (Statistics Canada 2009)

Telling It Like It Is

A Student POV

Telling Your Family You're Gay

Growing up in the small town of Whitby, Ontario, I never felt the negative effects of discrimination. I am an English-speaking, Caucasian female and had never been a part of a minority group, in any sense of the word. At the age of 21, this changed and I became aware of how easily people are judged. I am a lesbian, and from the moment I became open about my sexual preferences, I felt first-hand what it feels like to be viewed based solely on one aspect of your life, and not as an entire person. When meeting someone new in my life it was as though I was wearing a sign on my forehead reading, "I am gay," and it was perceived as "I am gay . . . that is everything you need to know about me." Once I divulge this information, almost instantly people form opinions on who I am as a person and who I should be. They develop expectations that quite often are illogical and unrealistic. By writing a paper such as this one, I am being given the opportunity to address a few of these numerous stereotypes and prejudiced beliefs. Hopefully, I can educate some to stop these beliefs from spreading.

From my experience, the original thought that people tend to have when finding out that I am gay is that it is simply a phase I am going through, a time of experimentation and rebellious behaviour. My brother's reaction was as such. He believed that it was just a phase and that it would pass. He continued to express this for an entire year after I had told him. He realizes otherwise now. . . . When telling my mother (who along with the rest of my family is extremely supportive of me), I was shocked to hear her initial reaction to what I had told her. After a moment or two of silence, she . . . said, "But I thought you wanted to get married and have kids one day." The thought of these dreams possibly fading away is what seemed to unsettle her the most. I found two things wrong and rather presumptuous about this statement. To begin with, the idea that a woman must want/ need a husband and children to live a fulfilling life is old-fashioned and a step backward from the times we live in today. I figure, why can't a woman who is independent and who has a satisfying career be considered to lead a successful, happy life, despite the fact that she has no family to raise. Furthermore, my mother was correct in assuming that I did want a family, but it was not the family that she had in mind. Marriage and children are a large part of my future plans, and, with adoption, and artificial insemination, this is a very feasible option for lesbian couples. Simply because a woman falls in love with another woman, it does not mean that she didn't grow up with the same desire for nurturing children and caring for a home and family that a lot of heterosexual girls do.

—Anonymous

Interestingly, despite the recent condo boom, we continue to build houses that are on average larger than in the past, but house fewer people in more households. Why do you think that is?

What do YOU think?

Which do you think is the more significant cause of the statistics noted on the previous page: the aging population or marriage delay among people under 30? What other figures might help you address this question?

Family in Quebec

By just about every statistical measure the family in Quebec is sociologically distinct from the family in other parts of Canada. For a snapshot of the differences, consider that in 1996, Quebec was the province with:

- *the highest cohabitation rate*: 20.5 per cent of all families, almost twice the next highest rate in Canada (New Brunswick, at 10.9 per cent)
- *the lowest marriage rate*: 3.1 per 100,000, significantly lower than the next lowest rate (British Columbia's 5.2)

- *the highest divorce rate*: 45.7 per 100 marriages, a little ahead of BC's 45.0
- *the highest number of divorces* (per 100 marriages) among couples married less than 30 years, with 47.4 in the year 2000 (Alberta's rate of 41.5 is the next highest).

In 2001, Quebec led all provinces with an abortion rate of 19.6 per 1,000 women or 421.5 per 1,000 live births (trailing only Northwest Territories in the latter statistic). In 2002, Quebec was the province with the greatest number of total births by single (never married) women; by percentage (55.3 per cent), they trailed only Nunavut. The province also had the greatest percentage of births to women who were divorced (2.1 per cent).

Another feature unique to Quebec is the province-wide support for same-sex marriage (see Table 14.3). In a poll conducted among 10,015 Canadian adults in August 2003, residents of Quebec showed the greatest support for changing the legal definition of marriage; in March 2004, it became the third province (following Ontario and BC) to legally recognize same-sex marriage.

In the 1995 Bibby Report, Quebec was also shown to have the highest rate of approval for premarital and extramarital sex (Bibby 1995: 76), with 88 per cent supporting the former (compared with 82 per cent, the next highest, in BC) and 24 per cent supporting the latter (compared with 14 per cent, the next highest, in the Prairies).

Table 14.3 Support for changing the definition of marriage to include same-sex unions, by region, 2003

	AGREE SOMEWHAT (%)	AGREE STRONGLY (%)	TOTAL (%)
Quebec	36	25	61
British Columbia	26	25	51
Atlantic Provinces	19	26	45
Ontario	19	23	42
Prairies	16	17	33

Source: Based on TNS Canadian Facts, http://www.tns-cf.com/news/03.09.05-samesex-charts.pdf, 2003.

Quebec residents also show a difference when it comes to parenting, as indicated by a *Globe and Mail*/CTV poll of 648 Canadian parents conducted by Ipsos-Reid and published in *The Globe and Mail* on 10 April 2004. The poll noted the following results:

- The percentage of parents who said they spanked their children for disciplinary reasons:
  Alberta   60%
  British Columbia   52
  Saskatchewan/Manitoba   46
  Ontario   45
  Atlantic Provinces   42
  Quebec   22

- The percentage of parents who agreed that using flashcards at an early age makes kids smarter:
  British Columbia   71%
  Saskatchewan/Manitoba   67
  Alberta   63
  Ontario   60
  Atlantic Provinces   57
  Quebec   25

What should we make of all of this? First, it is important to note that a number of the statistical indicators discussed show a major change from the situation in Quebec prior to the Quiet Revolution of the 1960s. Take divorce, for example. Prior to 1968, if you were living in Quebec and you wanted a divorce, you had to seek it through Parliament (the situation was similar in Newfoundland). A growing separation from the Catholic Church has been cited (especially by religious officials) as a possible explanation for the rising divorce rate. Yet in the 2001 census, Quebec had the third-lowest number of residents declaring they had "no religion" (a rate of 5.8 per cent, compared with the national average of 16.5 per cent). Of course, having an affiliation with the Church and being influenced by that affiliation can be two different matters. The Catholic Church considers suicide a sin, but Quebec, the most Catholic province, has the highest suicide rate in Canada, especially among men: in 1999–2001, the suicide rate for Quebec males was 30.7 per 100,000, compared with 16.1 in the provinces of Ontario, Alberta, and British Columbia.

Can we say, as more right-wing or conservative interpreters would, that family life is falling apart in Quebec? One statistic we haven't presented might be seen as supporting that view. In 2002, Quebec had the highest rate of one-person households, about 30 per cent. But from our perspective, a more likely interpretation is that Quebec went through more rapid modernization and outright change during the last 40 years than any other province. The falling away of old structures does not mean the falling apart of the institutions. Québécois are perhaps best seen as a people who are reinventing family as they are reinventing other institutions—political, religious, educational, and so on.

Conjugal Roles

Conjugal (or **marital**) **roles** are the distinctive roles of the husband and wife that result from the division of labour within the family. The first important sociological study done on this subject was a 1957 work called *Family and Social Networks*, by British sociologist Elizabeth Bott. Bott characterized conjugal roles as being either **segregated**—in which tasks, interests, and activities are clearly different—or **joint**, in which many tasks, interests, and activities are shared. The study was set against a backdrop in which men were primarily responsible for the financial support of the family, while women were primarily responsible for the housework and childcare. This was 1957, remember—how much do you think that situation has changed?

Earning and Caring: Changes in Conjugal Roles

In 2000, University of Western Ontario demographer **Rod Beaujot** published *Earning and Caring in Canadian Families* (2000). The book was the product of research Beaujot had undertaken to discover "how to better understand the changing links between earning and caring." What did he mean by that? He wanted to study how conjugal roles were changing from a situation in which they were more or less *complementary* to one in which they were *companionate*. **Complementary roles** (like Bott's model of *segregated roles*) cast men primarily as earners, breadwinners, doing paid work, with women involved primarily in the unpaid work of childcare and housework. In **companionate** relationships (like Bott's *joint* relationship) the roles overlap.

Beaujot recognized that the shift from complementary/segregated conjugal roles to companionate/joint roles is far from complete. But he also stated that complete overlap is not necessarily possible or even desired. Genders roles are different to a significant extent because, biologically, men and women are different. But there is a point at which we may be able to say that a basic fairness or justice has been reached, and we are far from that point. As Beaujot documents, married women do more total work per day than married men do, even though married women are more likely to do part-time paid work. Married women, especially those who are the mothers of small children, do much more *unpaid* work than married men do. And while women have entered new roles in the work world, men have not gone as far in entering new roles at home. This has created an imbalance in conjugal roles, leading some sociologists to use such terms as **double burden**, **double ghetto** (Armstrong & Armstrong 1978), or **second shift** (Hochschild

What does your reaction to this image tell you about our perception of the gender roles handed down by society?

& Machung 1989). The difficulty of correcting this imbalance in households with small children has led some women to conclude, pessimistically, that "childlessness is the easiest route to equality" (Beaujot 2002).

In 1995, sociologist **M. Reza Nakhaie** published "Housework in Canada: The National Picture," a summary of his study demonstrating that gender was the single most important factor—above relative income and amount of available time—in determining how much domestic labour or housework an individual did. The author's most striking discovery concerned the relationship between gender, hours of paid work, and share of the housework. Nakhaie found that there is an inverse relationship between the hours of paid work a man does and the size of his share of the housework: the more paid hours he has, the smaller his share of the housework. However, the same is not true for women. In fact, a direct, rather than inverse, relationship seems to exist over a particular number of hours of work: an increase over 30 in a woman's hours of paid work per week correlated to an *increase* in her contribution to housework.

The key to correcting the imbalance, as Beaujot and a number of other sociologists see it, is to recognize that gender roles are not carved in stone and handed down by society. Rather, they are products of what Arlie Hochschild terms a **gender strategy**, which is "a plan of action through which a person tries to solve problems at hand, given the cultural notions of gender at play" (Hochschild & Machung 1989: 15). These "problems at hand" include the fact that small children have to be taken care of. From the studies that Beaujot cites, it is clear that the typical strategy for infant care is for the mother to take time off, then to work part-time as the infant matures towards school age, and eventually to try to go back to full-time work.

The responsibility for care of children is the main reason that married women are much more likely to work part-time than are married/unmarried men or unmarried women. It is also the cause of what Beaujot calls the **occupational segregation** of men and women. Women choose occupations in fields such as education and healthcare, which have the greatest flexibility in terms of childcare-related **work interruptions** (which include staying home to care for a sick child or taking a longer-term leave to care for a newborn). Beaujot presents something of a chicken-and-egg scenario: women seek out jobs in employment areas that offer greater flexibility, but part of the reason these jobs tend to offer greater flexibility is that they are dominated by women. Is it possible, then, that if women were to enter other occupations in large numbers, a similar flexibility might develop? What do you think?

The Ethnic Factor in Conjugal Roles

One weakness of Beaujot's work is that he completely ignores the ethnic factor. The classic study looking at the division of conjugal roles among North American immigrant groups is **Sathi Dasgupta's** "Conjugal Roles and Social Network in Indian Immigrant Families: Bott Revisited" (1992). Although the article was written over 20 years ago about South Asian immigrants in the United States, its findings have a general applicability to the situation in Canada today.

Dasgupta studied 25 couples and found that *segregated* conjugal roles dominated. The men were invariably the primary breadwinners and made virtually all major decisions affecting the household, while the women, with few exceptions, were full-time homemakers and primary caretakers of the children.

Do you think Dasgupta's findings on the separation of conjugal roles among Indian families are applicable in Canada today? To what extent is the "ethnic factor" still at play?

Interestingly, however, there were aspects of joint conjugal roles among the immigrant families that would not be nearly as well accepted back in India. These include joint discussion of the children's education and of the couple's social life (with joint leisure activities the norm).

Change will come, as immigrants to North America adopt a more "Western" approach to dividing conjugal roles, but the ethnic factor still must be considered in any study of gender roles in the Canadian family.

Endogamy and Ethnicity

Endogamy means "marrying within." It is the practice of marrying someone of the same ethnic, religious, or cultural group as oneself. The opposite of endogamy, marrying *outside* of one's group, is **exogamy**. Support for exogamy, once quite low in Canada, is increasing, according to findings published by Bibby (Table 14.4). However, I believe that this set of statistics gives a picture that is more positive than it is real. It seems more an expression of ideal culture than an indication of probable practice. Contrast it with the rates of mixed common-law and marital unions from the 2006 census, shown in Table 14.5.

For all of the visible minority groups shown in Table 14.5, only people of Japanese ancestry are more likely to form a mixed union; the majority of people in

Table 14.4 Canadians' approval of intergroup marriage (%), 1975–2005

	1975	1980	1985	1990	1995	2000	2005
Whites and Aboriginal people	75	80	83	84	84	91	93
Whites and Asians	66	75	78	82	83	90	93
Whites and East Indians/Pakistanis	58	66	72	77	80	87	91
Whites and Blacks	57	64	72	79	81	88	92
Protestants and Catholics	86	88	89	90	92	93	95
Protestants and Jews	80	84	84	86	90	91	93
Roman Catholics and Jews	78	81	82	85	89	91	92

Source: Reginald Wayne Bibby, Project Canada Surveys, University of Lethbridge.

Table 14.5 Mixed couples by visible minority group, 2006

VISIBLE MINORITY GROUP	COUPLES		
	TOTAL NUMBER	MIXED UNION (%)	SAME VISIBLE MINORITY GROUP (%)
Japanese	29,700	74.7	25.3
Latin American	85,200	47.0	53.0
Black	136,000	40.6	59.4
Filipino	107,400	33.1	66.9
Southeast Asian	58,100	31.1	68.9
Arab/West Asian	105,700	25.0	74.9
Korean	34,800	19.5	80.5
Chinese	321,700	17.4	82.6
South Asian	327,200	12.7	87.3
Multiple groups or other	50,400	58.4	41.6
All visible minority groups	**1,214,400**	**23.8**	**76.2**

Note: A mixed couple is any common-law or marital relationship (opposite-sex or same-sex) comprising one spouse or partner who is a member of a visible minority group and one who is not, as well as couples comprising two members of different visible minority groups.

Source: Statistics Canada, Census of Population, 2006. Reproduced and distributed on an "as is" basis with the permission of Statistics Canada.

Telling It Like It Is

A Student POV

Italian Families and Conjugal Roles: Four Generations

When I think of the topic of gender in an Italian family, I laugh. The struggles between what it means to be male and what it means to be female arise so very often in my family, at every dinner and almost every conversation. The discussions are always split between the three generations because my grandmother lives with my parents and she never misses an opportunity to include her views. It goes like this: the eldest generation undeniably believes that the female's role in life is to be a complement to her husband; everything she does is based on his needs and his demands. All domestic duties and child-rearing except for punishment are her responsibility. Working outside the home is secondary to household work. The husband makes all decisions, although she can make suggestions. It is the male's responsibility to take care of the family financially.

My parents (second generation) feel similarly, the main difference being that the father should be very involved with the children, not solely in areas concerning punishment. Where my grandmother would discourage my father from helping around the house, my mother would welcome the help though not demand nor expect it. In this generation, family decisions are made together; however, household duties are still very divided, even with my mother working full-time outside the home. For the

female, post-secondary education and career are second to marriage and family. The main female role in life is keeping a clean house, cooking good homemade food, and keeping everyone happy and healthy. The main male role is to keep the food on the table by providing the family with its main source of income.

The third generation around the dinner table changed things a little. This generation in my family consists of my husband and I, the middle brother and his wife and the "baby brother." Most of us are in agreement that gender roles in the new Italian family have changed. No longer is the female solely responsible for all household duties. Husbands cook, clean, and are physically able to change diapers, something my father had never done even with having three children! The females have post-secondary education and careers and are not a complement to their husbands, but an equal.

I also grew up with a huge double standard that affected me immensely in all areas of my life. It goes something like this: "This is what boys can do and this is what girls cannot do" (my father's infamous words). Boys can play all day and not help their mothers (girls can't), boys can fight and play rough (girls can't), boys have to do well in school (girls don't have to), boys can go out whenever they

all other groups—including the two largest visible minority groups in Canada: Chinese and South Asians—marry or co-habit within their own group. Remember, though, that this survey includes people born outside of Canada, who might have been married when they immigrated. It also includes groups whose immigration might have been weighted in favour of one sex (consider the pattern of early immigration among Filipino women, who came to Canada to obtain jobs in the health sciences and childcare). What influence could factors like these have on the data in Table 14.5?

What do YOU think?

1. Consider Table 14.4. Do you think that Canadians' attitudes towards exogamy are different to what they were 10 years ago?

2. Have you ever been involved in a relationship with someone from a different ethnic or cultural group? If so, what kinds of challenges did you face? If not, could you imagine yourself in such a relationship?

want (girls can't), boys have to play sports (girls don't have to), boys can stay out late (girls have to come home early).

"This is what girls must do and this is what boys do not have to do." Girls must cook and clean (boys do not), girls must learn the traditions (boys do not), girls must be good always (boys do not), girls must stay home to take care of the family (boys do not), girls must not be left alone with their boyfriends (boys can live with their girlfriends). I fought with my younger brothers fairly consistently growing up. The words, "that is not fair" were spoken often. I disliked one of my brothers for years and it was not until he got a family of his own that we began to grow closer together. We even talked about the jealousy we felt for one another over different family issues and how the double standards we grew up with had a great deal to do with it.

[M]y family's views on gender have had a great impact on my life. It has carved me into the woman I am today. Much to my parents' chagrin, I cannot cook, I hate house cleaning, run away from tradition whenever I can. I am constantly in school working on a career, and even though I am married, I frequently go out with my friends and stay out late! Being married has been difficult at times also. I always have

an intense instinct to run from the gender roles that surround me, and yet I realize that in many circumstances they are needed to preserve peace in a family. I now have many concerns for my daughter. I know she will not be faced with an obvious double standard, as I do not have any sons and I am fully aware that being completely opposite of the Martha Stewart–like woman is not anything to be proud of. Something in the middle would be nice. Since little girls are greatly influenced by their mothers, I know I must be really careful to set a positive female role in our family. I truly hope the difference for my daughter will be the ability for her to choose the woman she wants to be instead of madly running away from what I demand her to become.

—Alina Mucci

What do YOU think?

1. Do you think the narrative writer's brothers would write a different story about conjugal roles?

2. Do you foresee any gender role conflict concerning the writer and her daughter?

Family and Ethnicity

As we saw in Chapter 10, on "race" and ethnicity, there is a history in Canada of the federal government policies designed to deprive racialized minorities of family. The prohibitively expensive head tax levied on immigrants from China and South Asia in the late nineteenth and early twentieth centuries made it impossible in many cases for married couples or their families to reunite in Canada. Canadian sociologists **Nancy Mandell** and **Ann Duffy**, in *Canadian Families: Diversity, Conflict and Change* (1995), noted a similar connection between government immigration policy and the denial of family for women of colour, claiming:

[I]t has been a policy of the government not to encourage the possibility of developing families among women of colour who came as domestic workers. Thus, their status as "single" and as "temporary" is deliberately organized by immigration policies. (1995: 157).

Telling It Like It Is

A First-Hand POV

The Religious Factor in Conjugal Roles: Polygamy and the Case of Bountiful, BC

In the aptly named commune village of Bountiful, British Columbia, **polygamy** (many-marriages) or **polygyny** (many wives) is practised by the leaders of the Fundamentalist Church of Latter Day Saints, an offshoot of the Mormon Church. The commune has, over the years, attracted attention and criticism, stemming mainly from reports of forced and underage marriage and the abuse of women and children. There have also been attempts to enforce Canada's anti-polygamy laws on the commune, the most recent coming in 2011.

The following quotations are taken from the testimony of a woman in her forties, given in a BC Supreme Court case examining the constitutionality of Canada's laws against plural marriages. The mother of nine children married one of the leaders when she was 16; her husband was already married to her older sister. She herself has nearly 30 siblings; her father had five wives. The woman is well educated, with six years of post-secondary training in nursing, elder care, and midwifery.

> I did not know him well, I knew he was in good standing in the church. . . .
>
> He (my father) told me, "You do not have to marry him if you don't want to." I felt good about him, and I married him. My sister wife and I have lived at times in the same

home, we've lived in different homes. I feel that we are both very committed in having a good relationship with each other. . . .

> I feel my husband really supported me through my years of education and he really has been a life-long friend to me, as well as watched my children when I went to school. . . .
>
> I believe that there's so many people in mainstream society that make so many assumptions about us that we are treated with bias and prejudice, and that affects my everyday life. If I wanted to go anywhere and get any sort of counselling in mainstream society, I feel like I would not be accepted. . . .
>
> My beliefs are that living plural marriage isn't for everyone. . . . ("Plural Wife Describes Life in Bountiful Commune" 2011)

In November 2011, BC Supreme Court Chief Justice Robert Bauman ruled that the ban against polygamy was constitutional, even though it violated the religious freedom of the fundamentalist Mormons. Protecting the rights of the women and the children, he ruled, was of greater importance than protecting the religious freedom of the commune's residents.

The policy they refer to was initiated in 1910–11, during one of the country's greatest periods of immigration. About 100 black women from the Caribbean islands of Guadeloupe came to Canada to work as domestic servants, but when authorities discovered that many of the women were not as "unattached" as they had claimed to be—many had children they had been forced to leave behind—they were sent back.

Between 1955 and 1967, a number of women from the Caribbean—primarily Jamaica—were allowed to come to Canada to work as domestics. They had to be young, of "good character," and single (in other words, not married or in a common-law relationship). They

were given the status of landed immigrants, but they could not seek other work until they had served at least a year of domestic duty. Roughly 300 Caribbean women came to Canada each year between 1955 and 1960, the number rising to about 1,000 a year during the 1960s (Bolaria & Li 1985: 178). Many of them agreed to work as domestics, even though they were trained as teachers or secretaries. Many, in order to be "single," left family behind, all because it was the only way they could enter the country.

Naturally, those immigrants who had left husbands and children in the Caribbean wanted to sponsor their families to join them in Canada, but their

Students play an afternoon game of basketball at Bountiful Elementary Secondary School. What relationship between these women does the photo appear to convey?

What do YOU think?

1. If you had been a government lawyer, what kinds of questions would you have asked this witness? What concerns would you voice about plural marriage?

2. Do you think that individuals who are legally polygamous (i.e. their marriages were performed legally in another country) should be allowed to immigrate to Canada? What conditions might you put on their entry into this country?

efforts were blocked by immigration officials. In 1976, seven Jamaican women applied to sponsor their children to come to Canada. They were ordered to be deported for having failed to report their children on their applications to come to Canada (Leah & Morgan 1979). After an intense struggle that involved community and labour groups, the seven women won their appeals and were allowed to stay in Canada.

Attacks on the Aboriginal Family

Immigrant families are not the only ones that have been touched by restrictive Canadian legislation. The Aboriginal family also has long been a target of federal policy. The following passage describes how, during the early twentieth century, an Indian Agent used the Blackfoot community's need for food rations as a tool to ensure that the people remained monogamous:

[I]n my last report, I expressed thankfulness that there had been no plural marriages during the preceding year. That report was barely out of my hand when I learned that three members of the band were dissatisfied with one wife each and had taken another. I immediately directed that the rations of these families be withheld until such time as they

According to the 2006 census, people in mixed unions "were younger, did better socio-economically, and were more likely to live in large CMAs [census metropolitan areas]" than couples who were not in mixed unions (Milan, Maheux, & Chui 2010). How could you account for these facts?

saw fit to obey the rules in this respect. One family missed one ration, and then decided that it was better to abide by the rules. The other two families held out for several rations, and then they succumbed and put away wife No. 2. (Dosman 1972: 52–3)

As outrageous as it sounds, this incident, in which food rations were withheld to control marriage choices, is not atypical of the kind of treatment Native families suffered at the hands of government agents.

It's important to point out that actions like this were often products of well-meaning agencies and their representatives. With the benefit of modern perspective, we can see just how misguided—and racist—these policies were. The following section looks closely at three policies aimed at controlling Native families. In some cases, as we will see, the same strategies have targeted other groups that governments have felt

they needed to manage, including certain cultural and ethnic groups as well as people with physical or mental disabilities.

Residential Schools

Among the institutionalized instruments of control devised to manage the lives of Canada's Native populations, the establishment of residential schools tops the list for the devastating effects it has had on Aboriginal families. Officially started in 1910 but existing as "industrial" and "boarding" schools before then in the nineteenth century, **residential schools** were created with the almost explicit objective of keeping Aboriginal children away from the harmful influences of their parents and their home communities. Families were ripped apart as parents reluctantly signed over legal guardianship of their children to school principals, then watched their children leave for the state- and church-run boarding schools, where they would live for most, if not all, of the year. Parents were discouraged from visiting, and those who did were closely monitored. Brothers and sisters were kept apart, sometimes not seeing each other for months on end. Many families were never reunited.

Historian J.R. Miller tells the story of a Cree woman who went to a residential school that was just 19 kilometres from her reserve. For hours on end, she would stand at the corner of a fence that surrounded the school property:

> She would put her hand through the fence, because that meant she was closer to her home and family by the length of her arm and watch for her parents. She would say to herself, "the next black horse that comes along" will be drawing her parents' wagon on a visit. Disappointment only led to repetitions of the childlike incantation, a wish and a prayer that never seemed to come true. (Miller 1996: 338–9)

Physical, emotional, and sexual abuse by residential school employees demoralized the students. And as those who have been abused so often become abusers, many Aboriginal children grew up to bring the abuse they learned at school to their home community.

Sexual Sterilization

In its definition of genocide, the United Nations includes attempts to destroy a people by imposing measures designed to prevent births within the group. This describes certain policies aimed at Canada's Native population during much of the twentieth century. For instance, in 1928, the United Farmers Party of Alberta passed the Sexual Sterilization Act, with the intent of sterilizing "mental defectives" so that their "bad genes" would not be passed on. The act reflects the early twentieth-century belief in eugenics, the flawed notion that a single gene responsible for intelligence was absent in "stupid people," who would be capable of having only "stupid children"—in other words, children inheriting their parents' genetically defective intellect. We know now that there is a complex relationship between a number of yet-unidentified genes and the various aptitudes that make up the biological potential known as intelligence. It would be more accurate to say that we have intelligences of various kinds and levels (for instance, I have a talent for writing, but I am inept in

drawing). This complexity makes the degree to which intelligence is inherited uncertain. We just don't know.

Eugenics has rightly been called a kind of scientific racism, as it was used to justify prejudices based on the supposed genetic inferiority or "feeble-mindedness" of certain groups of immigrants to North America—particularly those coming from eastern Europe—as well as of black people and Native people. Since it was used to support prejudice against the poor and homeless, it could also be held up as an example of scientific classism. The traditional yardstick for measuring intelligence is the intelligence quotient test. We're all aware that a high IQ suggests a high degree of intelligence, but the test has been criticized for its bias against people representing certain language and culture groups. As well, the test perpetuates a myth that we have a general intelligence to which a single number can be assigned.

During the history of Alberta's Sexual Sterilization Act, which lasted from 1928 to 1972, some 2,832 people were sterilized, most of them women. Sterilizations of Métis and First Nation people account for a disproportionately high number of the total, an estimated 25 per cent (roughly 10 times their percentage of the total population). Eastern European immigrants (Ukrainians, Russians, etc.)—people whose English language skills and cultural capital were low—were also represented in high numbers in the sterilized group.

British Columbia passed an act similar to Alberta's Sexual Sterilization Act in 1933, the same year that the notorious Law for the Prevention of Genetically Diseased Offspring was passed in Nazi Germany. Recently there have been accusations that, following both racial and religious prejudice, hundreds of non-Christian Aboriginal people were sterilized by a United Church missionary doctor in a church-run hospital in the BC coastal community of Bella Bella, and that a good number of young Aboriginal women made pregnant by residential school staff, clergy, and visiting officials were coerced into having abortions.

The Sixties Scoop

The UN's definition of genocide also includes attempts to destroy a people by forcibly transferring children of the group to another group. This characterizes what has been referred to as the Sixties Scoop, a program, which began in the 1960s, of removing large numbers of Aboriginal children from their families, their communities, and the Aboriginal world. Children could be taken from their families by government-affiliated agencies for a variety of reasons: some were children of parents judged to be alcoholics, some were newborns needing hospital care taken to the nearest city (and in many cases never returned), some were living in crowded or "sub-standard" homes. In 1964, the number of children of all backgrounds removed from their families was 4,228; roughly 34 per cent of those (1,446) were Aboriginal children.

Between 1971 and 1981 in Manitoba, where Aboriginal families were hardest hit, over 3,400 Aboriginal children were removed from their homes.

Many were taken from the province, and more than 1,000 of them were sent to the United States, where American child welfare agencies could get as much as $4,000 for each child placed. The province later launched an investigation into the practice, led by Justice Edwin Kimelman. In his summary of the investigation, *No Quiet Place* (1985), he stated:

> [C]ultural genocide has been taking place in a systematic routine manner. One gets an image of children stacked in foster homes as used cars are stacked on corner lots, just waiting for the right

First Nation artist Joseph Tisiga's painting *With Friends* "re-imagines the moment of my mother's removal from her birth family by authorities as a child of the 'sixties scoop'" (http://www.our-story.ca/joseph-tisiga.html). Can you interpret it? What might the image of the tall white man in the hall mean to an Aboriginal person who was "scooped" as a child?

"buyer" to stroll by. (cited in Fournier & Crey 1997: 88)

But statistics and judges' reports do not give a real sense of the suffering of those affected. The following statement comes from a research report on the emotional return of children to their families, communities, and people:

> I was sixteen years old when my daughter was taken from me. My partner at the time was drinking and at eighteen he went to prison. I had no way of looking after her and felt very alone. The social worker told me that my daughter would be better off with a "nice, normal family." I thought that I would at least be able to visit her sometimes, but she was placed in Pennsylvania and we did not meet her again until she was 20 years old. I took a bus to Windsor and that is where we met. I was alone and scared. She looked just like me when I was twenty, but with a very different attitude. She had suffered sexual abuse in her adopted home and she blamed it on me. She had a little girl of her own, but she would not let me meet her. I wish there was someone who could help us get past this pain. (Budgell 1999: 6)

WRAP IT UP

Summary

Family in Canada today is a diverse and complex form, and long has been so. This diversity expresses itself in family size and structure, in age of marriage and of having children, in qualifications for family membership, in who is and is not considered eligible for marriage into the family, in the expectations and practices of gender roles, and in the relationship between children (of all ages) and their parents. And this diversity works—the "good" family takes many forms. Why is there such diversity in the history, present, and, doubtless, the future of the Canadian family? The main reason is that family adapts: it evolves in the sense that it is flexible enough to change to best fit changing social circumstances.

THINK BACK

Questions for Critical Review

1. Describe the diversity of the Canadian family, both culturally and historically.
2. Describe how family in Quebec is different from family in the rest of Canada. Give some examples as well as possible explanations.
3. Outline nine major changes taking place in the Canadian family today.
4. Identify the different forms that conjugal roles can take.
5. Outline the measures used to place Canadian Aboriginal families "under attack" during the twentieth century.

READ ON

Online

Marriage & Family Processes

www.trinity.edu/~mkearl/family.html

Michael Kearl's website provides useful material on the study of the American family, including information on the cultural factors that shape family structures and data on Americans' relationship preferences.

Stats & Facts—Families: A Canadian Profile

www.ccsd.ca/factsheets/family

Maintained by the Canadian Council of Social Development, this website provides data on the distribution of families by type across Canada, on single-parent families, and on marriage and divorce rates.

The Vanier Institute of the Family

www.vifamily.ca

This Ottawa-based organization researches and publishes on issues affecting the Canadian family. You can read their recent publications on such topics as family vacations, the changing role of fathers, and young people who become responsible for the care of older family members.

In Print

Rod Beaujot (2000), *Earning and Caring in Canadian Families* (Peterborough: Broadview Press).

One of this country's preeminent social demographers, Rod Beaujot, draws sociological conclusions about the Canadian family based on an analysis of statistical data.

Elizabeth Bott (1957), *Family and Social Networks: Roles, Norms, and External Relationships in Ordinary Urban Families* (London, UK: Tavistock).

This classic work introduced and developed much of the terminology and ideas used by social scientists studying the sociology of the family today.

Wayne Hower (2006), *Does a Disabled Child = a Disabled Family?* (Authorhouse).

This is a self-published work that combines the author's personal experience raising a disabled child with an academic and professional approach.

Nancy Mandell and Ann Duffy (2011), *Canadian Families: Diversity, Conflict, and Change*, 3rd edn (Toronto: Thompson Nelson).

This edited collection features articles that outline a number of ways in which family operates in Canada.

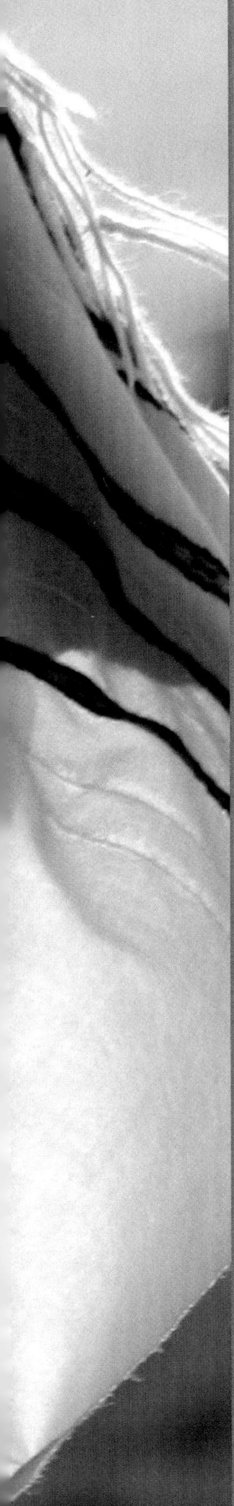

Learning Objectives

After reading this chapter, you should be able to

- outline Émile Durkheim's sociological approach to religion

- discuss the relationship between organized religion and gender roles

- talk about how the sociological profile of religion is changing in Canada

- analyze the relationship between organized religion and family

- describe the impact of religion on the lives of Hutterites in Canada

- detail the impact of Christian religious colonialism upon the Aboriginal people of Canada.

Key Terms

- Abrahamic religions
- age group
- agency
- aid evangelism
- androcentrism
- Catholic-Traditionalist
- cohort
- collective consciousness
- false consciousness
- haram
- hegemony
- Islamophobia
- liberation theology
- misogynistic
- moral community
- neo-traditionalism
- nuclear family
- Orientalism
- phantom aid
- profane
- Protestant work ethic
- sacred
- social Darwinist
- social gospel
- survival of the fittest
- tied aid
- totem

Names to Know

- Marie Battiste
- Émile Durkheim
- Margaret Humphreys
- Mary-Ann Kirkby
- Haroon Siddiqui
- Max Weber
- James S. Woodsworth

The Cost of Religious Ignorance

Ignorance of someone else's religion is a major cause of prejudice, discrimination, and violence. The following illustration comes from Timothy J. Gianotti, a theologian and professor of Islamic studies at York University. The incident Gianotti describes surrounds an ignorant e-mail he became aware of:

> Beginning with the message, "THIS IS REALITY!!!" the email takes us to a shop in a mall in Houston, Texas, where a sign was posted (and photographed) stating: "We will be closed on Friday, September 11, 2009, to commemorate the martyrdom of Imam Ali (A.S.)." The specific address of the shop is provided immediately under the picture. The email then goes on to say in bold lettering: "Imam Ali flew one of the planes into the twin towers! Nice, huh? Try telling me we're not in a religious war! This has not been around . . . so make sure it does!"

What the average recipient of this alarming message will not know is that Imam Ali has been dead for nearly one thousand, four hundred years. . . . He was the prophet Muhammad's first cousin and son-in-law, and he is revered by Shi'i Muslims as the first of the blessed Imams, or divinely guided spiritual leaders of the Muslims following the death of the Prophet in 632 CE. The "A.S." following his name means "peace be upon him" and would never be used for any other Ali in Islamic history.

The average reader will also not know that, in the solar year 2009, the anniversary of Imam Ali's death in the Islamic lunar calendar happened to fall on September 11, and so this Shi'i-owned shop closed in remembrance of that anniversary. . . . [T]his . . . had nothing to do with the atrocities of September 11, 2001. (Gianotti 2011: 14–15)

If you are looking for a fight, everything is an insult. And when it comes to religion, we do fight. Religion has been used as a justification for war for centuries. As powerfully unifying as religion is, ranking only with blood ties and nationality for its capacity to foster community, it can be just as divisive—even, as this incident shows, in the increasingly secular West. As religion is linked to so many of our enduring and most important moral codes, words or actions coming from people of religions other than ours can so easily be misunderstood; they come to be viewed as "fighting words," and they provoke powerful responses.

So does religion matter in the twenty-first century? Is it gaining ground or losing influence? How do we measure its impact on our everyday lives? What do our attitudes towards religion tell us about the society in which we live? These questions trace some of the key lines of inquiry in the sociology of religion. We hope that this chapter will get you thinking like a sociologist about topics such as these, while we attempt to offer some of sociology's best answers.

What do YOU think?

1. Why did the e-mail writer provide the address of the Shi'i-owned shop? What do you think the writer wanted to happen?

2. Would you expect the shop's owners to have been aware of the dual significance of the date their shop was closed? Do you think they would have seen any connection between their faith and the events of 11 September 2001?

Introduction: The Sociocultural Elements of Religion

One of the earliest sociological insights into religion came from the Greek philosopher Aristotle, who wrote:

> All people say that the gods also had a king because they themselves had kings either formerly or now; for men create the gods after their own image, not only with regard to form, but also with regard to their manner of life. (*Politics* i.2.7)

In part, Aristotle was suggesting that a society with a powerful king or emperor would likely have, in its religion, a commanding authority figure. On the other hand, a less hierarchical society would likely have a spiritual society of gods that is more egalitarian, in their relationships both with one another and with human beings. People are likely to use the same language they use to describe human relationships to describe their relationship with their god or gods. In this way, according to Aristotle, the gods we worship are a mirror, reflecting our own social conditions and our own cultural beliefs, values, and ideals. Aristotle, it's worth noting, spent over 20 years in Athens, the birthplace of democracy, where the Greeks worshipped a host of gods who, according to their mythology, would frequently interact with humans and be influenced by them.

You can see something of Aristotle's insight by comparing the religious and social practices of the French Jesuit priests and the Huron (or Wendat) with whom they lived and did missionary work during the seventeenth century. The Jesuits had a powerful king and, likewise, an omnipotent God. The language they used when speaking of either political or spiritual figures was one of great respect, with frequent reference to "masters" and to commanding and obeying. By contrast, the Huron nation had formed as an alliance of four member nations, or tribes. Each of the separate nations had a tribal leader who could recommend actions but not give orders. The Huron word used to refer to the leader can be translated as "we cause him to be a principle to imitate"—in essence, "he who is our role model." There were no words in the Huron vocabulary that meant "order" or "command." As for religion, the Huron recognized a series of spiritual figures, including Yaatayentsik, the first woman on earth, who had fallen from the sky, and her twin grandsons, Ioskeha and Tawiskaron, who had transformed the earth, which was built on the shell of the Great Turtle. These and other spirits did not *command* people; rather, they *inspired* them through visions or plagued them with curses. This isn't meant to suggest that the Huron or other societies without strong political hierarchy had no sense of a creator or god above all other gods. It simply means that the relationship between people and spirits was more in line with the relatively egalitarian relationships between humans in these societies.

Of course, by the late nineteenth century, the idea of a link between social and spiritual relationships became set in a **social Darwinist**, or evolutionary, model. According to this model, the "primitive" people had pesky spirits; "barbarians" had nasty but ultimately impotent gods. Only "civilized" people had a Supreme Ruler. Herbert Spencer, the early sociologist who coined the expression **survival of the fittest**, articulated such a position.

What do YOU think?

How do you think a social Darwinist would have characterized the gods and level of civilization of the seventeenth-century Huron?

How Religion and Class Intersect

Religion and class intersect. For example, if you are an Anglican in Canada, your income is likely to be higher than if you are a Catholic or a Baptist, and certainly higher than if you are a Pentecostal. Why so? One explanation is the **Protestant (work) ethic**. This theory, which we touched on in Chapter 1, was developed by **Max Weber** as part of his attempt to explain the rise of modern capitalism. Weber was familiar with the Protestant belief in a predestined "elect" who would be saved during the second coming of Christ. A person demonstrated membership in this elect group by achieving material success through hard work. According to Weber, this religious/cultural influence spurred people to accumulate wealth, making this set of values, associated with Protestantism, a key factor in the rise of capitalism. Although the religious origins of the phrase have been undermined by the rise of a consumer society bent on immediate gratification, the legacy of the Protestant ethic as Weber described it survives in the general prosperity of some religious groups over others.

But this is only part of the story. The Anglican church (a.k.a. the Church of England) is a socially conservative church with a long, historical connection to power, both in Britain and its former colonies. One of the issues that led to the 1837–8 rebellions in what are now Ontario and Quebec was the set of privileges that the Anglican church enjoyed in British North America. By contrast, the Baptist church in Canada has long welcomed members of Canada's black community, typically those of lower-than-average income. The Pentecostal church is likewise racialized, and has a connection to poor people living in rural areas. The Catholic church in Canada has been home to many racialized groups that have experienced discrimination. The earliest Catholics were the French, who, living within a British colony, never had the power that the English did. During the nineteenth century, many poor Catholic Irish immigrants came to Canada, only to find "No Irish Need Apply" on signs for jobs. Subsequent waves of immigration brought Italians, Croatians, Poles, and other working-class immigrant groups, whose presence affected the class standing of Catholics in Canada. All of this is evidence of how religion and class intersect.

On the other side of things, religion, according to Karl Marx, is an instrument of **hegemony** that serves ruling-class interests by dissuading the working class from organizing around their own self-interests to challenge the inherent inequality of class-based society. Marx used the term **false consciousness** to describe the belief that class-based hierarchy was justified on religious grounds—in other words, that God planned society to be this way—and that by simply toiling away, even under oppressive conditions, members of the lower class were really acting in the best interests of their class. They would be rewarded in the "next life." A classic example of how religion supported the class system comes from the Christian hymn "All Things Bright and Beautiful":

> The rich man in his castle
> The poor man at his gate.
> God made them high or lowly
> And ordered their estate. . . .

That last line means, literally, that it was God who determined the appropriate positions within the class system for the poor and the rich.

Yet religion in other circumstances does bring a kind of "revolutionary possibility." This is exemplified in Canada by the **social gospel** movement and the progressive politics of people such as J.S. Woodsworth, Stanley Knowles, and Tommy Douglas, who were trained as ministers and who became involved in the development of policies, such as socialized medicine, that dramatically improved the lives of working-class people. They paved the way for Canadian faith-based social organizations working today to improve the condition of the poor and working classes in this country and around the world.

Durkheim and the Elementary Forms of Religious Life

Despite the fact that he was not a particularly religious man, **Émile Durkheim** (1858–1917) has had a profound effect on how sociologists view religion. His father and grandfather were both rabbis, yet he felt no religious call himself. His great work in the area of religion is *Les Formes élémentaires de la vie religieuse: Le système totémique en Australie*, published in 1912. In 1915 it was published in English as *The Elementary Forms of the Religious Life*.

Durkheim is famous for having taken sociology into areas where at first glance it did not belong—areas such as suicide (surely the realm of psychology) and religion (certainly the realm of theology). Both suicide and religion were seen as being firmly rooted in the individual, not in the group or society, and there was strong resistance to his ideas by people studying religion at the time.

Durkheim's aim was to identify the basic elements of religion. He believed he could do this by studying the religion of the most basic society then being discussed by sociologists and ethnographers of the time: the Aborigines of Australia. Through this study he hoped to develop a sociological model of religion that would apply universally to all religions.

What Is Religion?

Here is how Durkheim defined religion:

> A religion is a unified system of beliefs and practices relative to sacred things, that is to say, things set apart and forbidden—beliefs and practices which unite into one single moral community called a Church, all those who adhere to them. (Durkheim 1995: 44)

As Fields puts it, Durkheim's view was that "religion is social, social, social" (Fields 1995: xxxiv). In using the term **moral community**, Durkheim was recognizing that religious groups are "made up of individuals who have mutually recognized and recognizable identities that set them, cognitively and normatively, on shared human terrain" (Fields 1995: xxxiv). It's clear from this how dramatically Durkheim deviated from his contemporaries, who considered religion something experienced by the individual rather than the larger community.

Three Key Elements of Religion

There are three key elements in Durkheim's analysis of religion. The first is the equation *god = society*. Durkheim formulated this idea in the context of the totems of the Australian Aborigines. To understand what Durkheim meant, we need to look first at the significance of totems.

Totem is a word that came into English in the late eighteenth century from the language of the Anishinabe or Ojibwa people of Canada and the United States. Its origin is the word *ndotem*, meaning "my clan" in the Ojibwa language. In contemporary usage, when Anishinabe people introduce themselves in formal situations, they often follow the statement of their name by saying something such as *waawaashkesh ndotem*, meaning "deer is my clan." In this way, they are telling something about their identity and who they are.

Edward Benton-Banai, a respected Anishinabe elder and the author of *The Mishomis Book: The Voice of the Ojibway*, identified seven original clans of the Anishinabe (Benton-Banai 1988: 75–7). Traditionally, he explains in the book, each clan was associated with a specific function and certain ideal characteristics of the people belonging to the clan; these characteristics connect with the clan's totem animal:

CLAN/TOTEM	ASSOCIATED FUNCTIONS/AREAS OF EXPERTISE
Crane Clan Loon Clan	leadership, chieftainship
Fish Clan	mediation, settling disputes; philosophy
Bear Clan	protecting the community; medicinal plants
Marten Clan	warfare and war strategy
Deer Clan	Poetry
Bird Clan	spiritual leadership

If you're familiar with the word *totem* from the totem poles found on the Pacific coast of North America, you can appreciate how the carved structures represent different clans connected to the villages where the poles were erected.

Having some sense, then, of what *totem* means, we can look at Durkheim's famous explanation of the god = society equation:

The images in this totem pole are culturally stylized versions of the totem animals of clans of the artist's First Nation. What impression do you think these totem poles made on the Christian missionaries arriving in villages on the Pacific coast? What impression do they make on you?

[The totem] . . . symbolizes two different . . . things. [I]t is the outward and visible form of . . . the totemic principle or god; and . . . it is also the symbol of a particular society that is called the clan. It is . . . the sign by which each clan is distinguished from the others, the visible mark of its distinctiveness, and a mark that is borne by everything that in any way belongs to the clan: men, animals, and things. *Thus if the totem is the symbol of both the god and the society, is this not because the god and the society are one and the same?* How could the emblem of the group have taken the form of that quasi-divinity if the group and the divinity were two distinct realities? Thus the god of the clan, the totemic principle, can be none other than the clan itself, but the clan transfigured and imagined in the physical form of the plant or animal that serves as totem. (Durkheim 1995 [1912]: 208)

In other words, the totem is a symbolic representation both of a god or divinity and of the society that reveres it. Another way of looking at it is that societies fashion deities represented as having characteristics like the people themselves. These characteristics are then projected back onto both the culture and individuals. The god and the people are therefore one and the same.

Collective Consciousness and the Sacred and Profane

Durkheim in his analysis focused primarily on the collective or group experiences and rituals of people belonging to a particular religion; these sacred experiences foster what Durkheim called a **collective consciousness**. In Muslim countries, the cry of the Muzzin (the religious caller) over the loudspeaker calling the faithful to early morning prayer, followed by the collective deep bowing of people who are similarly dressed, is a very compelling example of collective religious experience.

Durkheim distinguished between experiences, acts, and objects that are *sacred* and those that are *profane*. **Sacred** objects and acts are set apart from more ordinary (**profane**) ones as being positively regarded, holy, and therefore deserving of reverence or respect. Sacred objects include prayer beads, crosses, flags, and items in the medicine bundle of

Muslims pray at a mosque in Turkey. How do you think this kind of communal prayer generates a sense of collective consciousness?

an Aboriginal shaman; sacred acts include prayer and keeping kosher. But Durkheim used the term *sacred* also for those objects and acts that are forbidden or taboo. The Arabic term used in Islam, *haram*, applies here. Canadian writer **Haroon Siddiqui**, in *Being Muslim*, lists the following prohibited objects and practices:

Haram Foods: Pork and its byproducts, carnivorous animals (those that tear their food apart with claws, such as lions), almost all reptiles and insects, animals that died before being properly slaughtered, blood, and all alcoholic or intoxicating drinks.

Haram Lifestyle: Gambling, including lotteries; all drugs that cause intoxication, alter sensory perception (hallucinogens) or affect one's ability to reason and make sound judgments; and paying and accepting interest. (Siddiqui 2006: 80)

Durkheim argued that objects were not sacred by nature, but acquired the status of "sacred" as they were either set apart or forbidden by social groups.

What do YOU think?

Consider the totemic principle equating god and society. Do you think this is similar to the connection of the cross, Christ, and Christians?

The Kandariya Mahadeva temple, a Hindu holy site at Khajuraho, in Madhya Pradesh, India. Close inspection reveals its erotic reliefs. Sacred or profane?

Going Global

A Christmas Story: Christians and Muslims Standing Together in Egypt

The Arab Spring protests that brought about social and political change across the Middle East beginning in early 2011 offer innumerable topics of interest to sociologists. My sociological attention was caught by an incident that happened in Egypt in early 2011—a human interest story that was significant but relatively small in the scope of everything that would happen in that country over the ensuing months.

The protests that led to the ouster of Egyptian leader Hosni Mubarak on 11 February 2011 began in Cairo's Tahrir Square on 25 January, but this incident occurred a few weeks earlier, on 6 January, the date when Coptic Christians celebrate Christmas. Encouraged by Mohamed El-Sawy, an Egyptian Muslim arts entrepreneur with a history of trying to unite Egypt's various communities, and discouraged by the killing of 21 parishioners in a Coptic church a short time before that, thousands of Egyptian Muslims, including celebrities and prominent members of the Muslim community, stood as "human shields" around Coptic churches during the celebration of Christmas mass. It was an important show of solidarity between Coptic Christians and Muslims, two groups with a history of non-conflict in Egypt, and it set the tone for the largely secular protests that followed. During the February overthrow of the Mubarak regime, Copts and Muslims swore to protect each other. It's different to the kind of religious animosity we've come to expect in countries of the Middle East. What social factors make the situation in Egypt so different?

The Coptic faith runs deep in the history of Egypt. The word *Coptic* literally means "Egyptian," and the Coptic church is one of the oldest Christian churches. According to tradition, it was formed in the first century CE, when St Mark, one of the disciples of Jesus, came to Egypt to preach. The Coptic church broke from the Western (i.e. Protestant and Catholic) and Orthodox churches in 451 CE. It has its own pope and hierarchy and had strong historic ties with former emperors of Egypt. It has stronger elements of fasting than any other branch of Christianity, with 210 days in which strict adherents are not to eat animal by-products from sunrise to sunset. The Copts were persecuted following the Muslim Arab conquest of Egypt in the seventh century, but they now make up between 8 and 12 per cent of the Egyptian population.

Egypt's minority Copt population continues to suffer persecution, but the Christmas 2011 incident represents a promising effort to bridge the religious divide in that country. Is it an isolated symbolic gesture or something to build on? Only time will show. For now, for the sociologist, it raises interesting questions about how religious differences differ from country to country, and what are the best hopes—from laws to celebrity leadership—to remedy them.

An Egyptian woman walks past a shop selling Christmas decorations in Cairo's Shubra neighbourhood. Does the display of Western Christmas symbols in a Middle Eastern country surprise you at all?

Canadian Society and Religion

The last year that questions about religion were asked in the Canadian census was 2001. Table 15.1 summarizes some of the data from that census.

Trends in the Data

The trends in the data worth noting in particular are the categories that show the greatest increase and decrease. Those with the largest increases by percentage

Table 15.1 Canada's population by religion, 2001

		PERCENTAGE	CHANGE FROM 1991 (%)	MEDIAN AGE
Total population	26,639,030	100.0	9.8	37.3
No religion	4,900,090	16.2	43.9	31.1
Pagan	21,080	0.1	281.2	30.4
Roman Catholic	12,639,035	43.2	4.8	37.8
Protestant	8,654,850			
United Church	2,839,125	9.6	−8.2	44.1
Anglican	2,035,500	6.9	−7.0	43.8
Christian not included elsewhere	780,450	2.6	121.1	30.2
Baptist	729,470	2.5	10.0	39.3
Lutheran	606,590	2.0	−4.7	43.3
Protestant not included elsewhere	549,205	1.9	−12.7	40.4
Presbyterian	409,830	1.4	−35.6	46.0
Pentecostal	369,475	1.2	−15.3	33.5
Mennonite	215,175	0.6	−7.9	32.0
Jehovah's Witnesses	154,750	0.5	−8.1	38.7
Mormon	101,805	0.3	8.4	28.7
Salvation Army	87,790	0.3	−21.9	39.3
Christian Reformed Church	76,670	0.3	−9.5	32.3
Adventist	62,880	0.2	20.1	35.5
Hutterite	26,295	0.1	22.3	22.2
Methodist	25,730	0.1	6.1	43.9
Brethren in Christ	20,590	0.1	−22.0	38.2
Christian Orthodox	479,620			
Greek Orthodox	215,175	0.7	−7.1	40.7
Orthodox not included elsewhere	165,420	0.6	79.9	35.4
Ukrainian Orthodox	32,720	0.1	−5.1	45.8
Serbian Orthodox	20,520	0.1	109.5	34.8
Ukrainian Catholic	126,200	0.4	−1.7	45.0
Muslim	579,640	2.0	128.9	28.1
Jewish	329,955	1.1	3.7	41.5
Buddhist	300,345	1.0	83.8	38.0
Hindu	297,200	1.0	89.3	31.9
Sikh	278,410	0.9	88.8	29.7

Source: Statistics Canada.

are Pagan (281.2 per cent), Muslim (128.9), "Christian not included elsewhere" (121.1), Serbian Orthodox (109.5), Hindu (89.3), Sikh (88.8), and Buddhist (83.8). There are several points to observe. First, Canada is not "going Pagan." The respondents giving that answer are going from a low number to another low number. That is one reason why a good sociologist—professional or student—does not go by percentage alone when looking at change. The raw numbers themselves are also important. Immigration from countries in South Asia is a major factor in the increase of Muslims (primarily from Pakistan), Hindus, and Sikhs. War refugees have increased the numbers for some religions, notably Serbian Orthodox (from the former Yugoslavia) and Islam (from Somalia). The growth of Canada's Tibetan population, owing to the oppression of Tibetans by the Chinese government, is correlated with the increase in the number of Buddhists. The number of "Christian not included elsewhere" rose in part because of people from the West Indies joining local independent churches in relatively large numbers.

The decreases in percentage are also important sociologically. One important correlation to observe is that between median age and decrease in percentage. Immigration, or lack of it, is also a factor in the decreases. For example, the Presbyterian population has the highest median age and the highest decrease in percentage. Presbyterianism is a long-established religion in Canada, one connected with Scotland, which is no longer a major source of Canadian immigration. The decrease would be even sharper were it not for immigration from Korea, which for decades was a major centre of Presbyterian missionary work. The Anglican church is also an old religion in Canada, connected with Britain, a country of decreased immigration to this country.

Age Group versus Cohort

Statistical studies consistently demonstrate that young people (teens and those in their early twenties) are less religious than older people are. The danger with looking at a study like this in isolation is that we may take it to mean that overall levels of participation in organized religion are falling, that as these young people age, there will be fewer and fewer religious people in Canada. The mistake here is seeing an **age group** difference (i.e. a consistent difference between old and young) and assuming that it is a **cohort** difference (i.e. a difference between people born in two different periods). Young people may not go to temple because they are too busy. They may reject religion if they feel it has been forced upon them by parents and other members of the older generation. However, they may very well take up religion later in life—for instance, when they reach marrying age and decide to have a formal religious wedding, or when they become older still and turn to the local church as a way to become more involved in the community, either through charity work or through one of the many social clubs typically situated in churches.

Old and Established Churches

The Canadian census data presented in Table 15.1 shows the median age for each religious group in 2001 and the increase or decrease in the number of followers, by percentage, since 1991. By combining the two numbers we can verify that the religious groups with the highest median ages are also those that are dropping the fastest in numbers, and that the religious groups with the lowest median ages are those that are growing the fastest in numbers. Among the former group are the long-established Protestant churches that, despite their declining participation rates, continue to have the highest overall numbers (e.g. the United, Anglican, Lutheran, and Presbyterian churches). An exception to this trend is the Baptist church, which has a long history in Canada and a relatively high median age (39.3), but which experienced a 10 per cent increase in followers between 1991 and 2001. These gains occurred in the provinces where the median age is lower, especially Quebec (median age 33.1), which saw a 28.9 per cent jump in Baptist following between 1991 and 2001. Similar increases occurred in Manitoba and Alberta. Only British Columbia bucks the trend of a lower median age of Baptists translating into growing participation rates.

Based on these statistics, you might guess what is happening. The "Christian not included elsewhere" group is relatively young (median age 28.2) and growing rapidly (156.9 per cent). It includes evangelical and fundamentalist Christian groups. Some Baptist groups

What do YOU think?

Which religions do you think will continue to show significant increases or declines? Are there any religions you think may show a reversal of the 1991–2001 trend? Why?

call themselves evangelical or fundamentalist, so they may be gaining in numbers and, as a result, lowering the median age.

What do YOU think?

1. Why do you think younger people are turning to less established Christian denominations?

2. Why else do you think people might identify themselves as "Christian not included elsewhere"?

Religion and the Family

Religion and the Marginalized Family

Religion is often applauded for promoting "family values." We would say that it usually does. Indeed, revisiting Merton's three kinds of function from Chapter 1, we could reasonably identify "strengthening the family" as a manifest (i.e. intended and recognized) or at least latent (largely unintended and unrecognized) function of religion. Yet throughout history, there have been times when family and religion have been set in opposition to each other, particularly in situations where a family situation has been deemed bad or harmful by officials enforcing state policy shaped by religious considerations.

During the nineteenth century, beginning in Ireland, evangelical church groups established institutions to rehabilitate prostitutes and unmarried mothers. They were called "Magdalene asylums" (with reference to Mary Magdalene, the classic "fallen woman" of the Bible), or sometimes "Magdalene laundries," since the women were often forced into hard labour laundering clothes in order to support the institution. Many of the unwed mothers had their children taken away from them and put up for adoption, according to the policy of these church-run institutions, which were sanctioned by the government. Magdalene asylums were established throughout Ireland and Britain, and parts of the British Empire (including Canada), some of them surviving until the late twentieth century (see J.M. Smith 2007).

An example from Canadian history involves the church-run residential schools that many Aboriginal children were sent to throughout the twentieth century. Consider the conditions:

> Children were taken from their parents and extended families for periods of time that often lasted the entire school year, even when the residential schools were located in the students' own communities. Parental visits, when they were permitted, were typically closely monitored in a special "visiting room." Brothers and sisters were often kept apart in strict sexual separation, meaning that siblings in many cases could communicate with each other only by waving from one building to another or through secretly arranged meetings. (Steckley & Cummins 2008: 194)

Residential schools had a strong detrimental effect on Aboriginal parenting skills. Raised under the strict and often abusive authority of underpaid, under-qualified, and poorly screened teachers and administrators, described by historian J.R. Miller as the "devoted and the deviant" (1996: 321), three generations of Aboriginal parents had only these harsh role models on which to base their own parenting techniques.

Imports from Britain

In *Empty Cradles*, British social worker **Margaret Humphreys** describes how thousands of British children—the vast majority of them born to parents who were either poor or socially marginalized as single parents—were shipped to Australia to live in church-run orphanages. Certainly, some of these children benefited from their change in circumstances. Yet as Humphreys relates, many of the children were told that their parents were dead, and were subjected to the same degree of hard labour and abuse that Aboriginal children experienced in Canadian residential schools. The following questions come from a woman who was shipped out to Perth in Western Australia when she was just eight:

> Do you think I've got any family? Cousins, anybody. I'm not fussy. Anybody. They told me that my parents were dead. Do you think that's true? . . . I don't know anything about myself. Until I married, I didn't even have a birth certificate. I felt ashamed . . . Can you find out why they sent me? What did I do wrong? . . . (Humphreys 1995: 14)

Humphreys collected a story of a five-year-old girl who had long, curly, blonde hair when she entered the Australian Catholic orphanage named Goodwood:

> After being at Goodwood a few days, she packed all her possessions in a bag and ran down the drive

Telling It Like It Is

Religion and "Family Values"

While it is true that religion has been an agent of change throughout history, it is also true that institutional religion is conservative by its very nature. Witness, for example, the reluctance of the Anglican church to allow the ordination of women priests, and the Catholic church's steadfast opposition to homosexuality and birth control. These policies have become a source of conflict within their respective churches, where longstanding tradition runs counter to progressive social forces outside of organized religion.

But the battle over the traditional religious value system is not limited to the church setting. At times, deeply held religious convictions fuel a socio-political agenda to shape social policy in the image of church doctrine. Such is the case with recent campaigns to preserve "family values."

As we saw last chapter, family takes many forms and changes over generations. If there are abiding values associated with the family, they would include support for all family members, care for elders, and the socialization and education of children. Yet talk of family values today tends to emanate particularly from fundamentalist Christian groups that define the term very narrowly within a conservative, right-wing ideology. Typically, these groups privilege the **nuclear family** over other forms. They tend to oppose gay marriage and gay adoption, quoting chapter and verse from the Bible concerning sodomy, but not referring to any of Christ's own teachings on the subject. They oppose abortion, even in the case of rape, and have been known to characterize rape as an instance of "God's will" (when they're not laying the blame at the feet of the victim). They tend to oppose cohabiting unions, believing that sex is appropriate only among legally married adults. In terms of sex education, they believe that abstinence and chastity should be taught, not contraception and sexual health. They believe that instruction on these subjects will not lead to the avoidance of unwanted pregnancy and sexually transmitted disease, but to an increased desire among teenagers for sex. I've always found that a strange line of reasoning; I know that very little could have made me want sex more than I already did when I was a teenage boy.

Members of the Westboro Baptist Church protest at the funeral of an American soldier killed in combat in Iraq. The protesters believe that God is punishing American soldiers for protecting a country that harbours homosexuals. Can you reconcile such strong social views with a Christian world view?

in her nightie. The nuns followed her and dragged her back. The next morning, all the girls were made to line up in the yard and watch her being punished. . . . Two of the nuns held the little girl down, while another started cutting off her hair with garden shears. . . .

When they had finished, there was just an inch or two of hair left on her head. "God wants her punished more than that," one of the nuns said, and she produced a pair of secateurs [small pruning shears]. She started cutting again and didn't stop until the young girl's hair was gone completely and her scalp was bloody with cuts. (Humphreys 1995: 125)

In looking at the treatment of British and Irish orphans and North American Aboriginal children, we can see several common themes that characterize this discontinuity between religion and family:

- the marginalized (in terms of "race," class, and sexual behaviour) backgrounds of the families from which the children were taken
- the statistically deviant choice made by religious workers such as missionaries, priests, and nuns to opt for "religious life" over "normal" family life in their own society
- the strict hierarchical nature of religion operating in institutions such as religious orders, residential schools, and church-run orphanages
- the strict codes of discipline that are associated with religious-based institutions
- the ease with which religious concepts such as "sin" can be associated with negative judgement and used to justify harsh punishment.

Hutterites: Religion and Family

The preceding sections illustrate some of the situations in which religion and family come into conflict, with damaging results. In contrast to these accounts is the strong positive connection between religion and family found in Canada's Hutterite communities. The Hutterites are the Canadian religious group with the youngest median age (22.2). Children aged 0–14 make up 37 per cent of their population, while young people aged 0–24 make up 54 per cent—well over half—of their total population. Their fertility rate, even though it has declined somewhat in recent decades, approaches the maximum fertility rate possible for a single community and is famous in the sociological literature (see, for instance, Nonaka, Miura, & Peter 1993). The high fertility rate is attributed to several sociological factors, including the following:

- cultural/religious norms opposing contraception
- farming as the main industry, requiring a large population of strong, young farmhands
- the practice of communal living, which ensures that childcare, a shared responsibility, is always available.

We must also consider that it is when young people are aged 19–25 that they must decide whether or not to become baptized as full members of the community, a decision that involves a very critical testing of the individual (Kirkby 2007: 184). Young adults in their mid-twenties electing to leave the fold could keep the median age down.

The Hutterites are named after Jacob Hutter, the leader of a radical Christian movement started during the 1520s and 1530s. Along with Mennonites, they were part of the Anabaptist religious movement, which advocated that baptism should be administered only to believing adults. What made them radicals? They opposed the class linkages between the established church, the state, and the rich. They were also pacifists, who adhered strictly to the commandment *Thou shalt not kill*. Their belief that people should be baptized as adults, when they're old enough to make a mature choice, ran counter to the rules of the Catholic church, and the law in Austria, where the Hutterites first formed. Hutter was tortured and killed for his ideas.

The Hutterites were driven from one European country after another until they immigrated to the United States during the 1870s. In 1889, the Canadian government, wanting sturdy farmers to exploit the agricultural potential of the prairie West, offered them exemption from military service if they moved to Canada. During the First World War, many Hutterite communities, fearing persecution in the US, moved from the American plains to the Canadian prairies.

The social organization of the Hutterites involves three communal groups (called "Leuts," meaning "people"): Lehrerleut, Dariusleut, and Schmiedeleut. Each forms a moral community in Durkheim's sense. In Canada, the Lehrerleut and Dariusleut are found mainly in Alberta, Saskatchewan, and BC, while the Schmiedeleut are in Manitoba. The differences between them are slight, a measure of how conservative or liberal each is.

The three groups exist among roughly 300 farming colonies in Canada, each comprising 60 to 150 people who share a "community of goods," except for small personal possessions. They have frequently encountered opposition to their communal farming practices from other farmers and, in the past, from provincial governments as well. The Hutterite system gave them several advantages over single-family farms in ways similar to those of contemporary "factory farms." By pooling their resources, they could

Telling It Like It Is | A First-Hand POV

The Minister's Role in a Hutterite Community

The following passage comes from a study of the Hutterite community of Pincher Creek, Alberta, published by historian David Flint in 1975.

Hutterites look to their religion when making both small decisions, such as how to dress, and large ones, such as the election of their minister, who is the single most important member of the community. Not only does he attend to the spiritual needs of the colony, but his advice is often asked on everything from when the pigs should be marketed to the price that should be charged for eggs. He is the colony leader, and his election is the most vital decision the colony makes in affecting its future nature. . . .

Hutterites expect the minister, even though he has been closely identified with them all their lives, to set standards and demand conformity, and to guard the traditions and values of their religion, and they readily obey him. If the minister is easy-going about slight deviations in dress, the colony will reflect his attitude. On one new colony there was not yet a minister in residence. Dress became sloppy—women went around in summer without kerchiefs and shoes and socks. When asked about this, one embarrassed man replied, "When the cat's away, the mice will play." He admitted that there was laxity and confessed that this would change when the minister arrived. . . .

In the week-by-week, year-by-year operation of the colony, group consensus and Sunday-evening meetings play a vital role in maintaining solidarity and discipline. It is an accepted practice to bring pressure to bear on those adults who do not conform to the will of the community. It is considered ethical and necessary to report an individual's misdoings to the colony meeting, and this is accepted for the common good and in recognition of the weakness of human nature. Usually the minister will first caution any person who is stretching the colony regulations too far—for instance by showing too much interest in photographs or pictures (considered to be vain), by being overly concerned with one's flower garden (over-watering taxes the limited water supply), or by frequent outbursts of anger. If change is not evident in the person's behaviour, then the preacher and the elders will decide on a punishment. The commonly accepted practice is to have the guilty party stand during church service, or kneel in front of the entire congregation and confess guilt, or sit with the children. . . . In cases of minor transgressions against colony rules, the minister, as the elected official responsible for maintaining colony discipline, needs deep human understanding to know when and where to draw the line.

—David Flint (1975)

Three boys from the Hutterite colony near Moose Jaw cool off with some frozen treats after apple picking. More than a third of Canadian Hutterites are below the age of 15. Do you think this means their population is on the rise?

amass greater funds for equipment and supplies, and secure large contracts for their agricultural products, supplied by a large, well-trained, and comparatively cheap workforce.

Other characteristics separate the Hutterites from the general population. The primary language of the community is an Austrian dialect of German, which is taught in schools along with a more useful and widely used form of High German and English. They live an austere and conservative lifestyle. They wear dark clothing—black headscarves with white polka dots, long-sleeved blouses and dresses, and long skirts (never pants) for the women. They are not permitted televisions, radios, snowmobiles (for recreational rather than work use), jewellery, makeup, dancing, or swimming (nakedness is an issue). They have a strong sense of spiritual superiority over the mainstream that appears in such phrases as the following, posted on churches: "Whoever cannot give up his private property as well as his own self will cannot become a disciple and follower of Christ. The ungodly go each their own egotistical way of greed and profit. To such we should not be conformed" (Kirkby 2007: 5).

Religion and Gender

Organized world religions are generally characterized by patriarchal power structures. Women tend to have subordinate roles that marginalize their participation. During the second wave of feminism in the 1960s and early 1970s, women in North America and western Europe became increasingly critical of Christianity and Christian practices. They viewed Christianity's embedded patriarchy as an influential cultural factor in the reproduction of gender inequality. Consider, they said, just a few examples from the Bible:

- "Man" was created in God's image, while "woman" was created from spare parts (a rib, we are told) to be his companion. (Male and female humans have the same number of ribs.)
- The first woman, Eve, is blamed for having all humans banished from the paradise Eden after she succumbed to temptation by eating an apple supplied to her by the devil.
- The most memorable female characters in the Bible are associated with sin and destruction;

among them are Mary Magdalene, who is customarily identified as a prostitute; Delilah, who brought about Samson's downfall; and Jezebel, who was denounced for introducing the worship of rival gods into Israel, and whose name is synonymous with immorality.

Add to these points the Christian tradition of a wife's obedience, subservience, and even belonging to her husband, and you have some powerful examples that inform, transmit, and reproduce patriarchal structures of inequality, including **androcentrism** (from *andro* meaning "man") and sexism. This same patriarchal inequality is blamed for numerous instances of women's oppression in society, from the denial of voting privileges and work opportunities to sexual objectification and male violence. In this sense, Christianity—in fact, all **Abrahamic religions** (including Islam and Judaism)—has much to answer for from a feminist perspective.

Gender Construction among the Hutterites

Mary-Ann Kirkby's *I Am Hutterite* (2007) gives a good sense of what it was like to be a young girl growing up as a Hutterite in the 1960s. As in other strong religious societies, gender roles were (and continue to be) clearly delimited. Girls and women cook, sew, and take care of children and aging elders. Girls between the ages of 11 and 14 may be chosen by a new mother to take on the role of *Luckela* ("baby holder") for the first year of the child's life. It is a society in which the "community raises a child," though "community" in this case means "female community." If a woman in her prime childbearing years is pregnant and finds the care of her toddler difficult, that child can be shared out for a while to another mother in the community.

Boys and men, meanwhile, learn their traditional roles of raising crops, managing livestock, running and repairing engines, and exercising primary decision-making for the colony. The colony is led by a male head minister, who guides the *Stübel*, or men's meeting, to make community decisions. The connection between male authority and strong religion, aided by the absence of alternative models of authority from mainstream society, can foster dictatorial patriarchal power. Kirkby describes how such power was exercised in her colony:

In spiritual terms, [the Head Minister] . . . was "shepherd of the flock," providing doctrinal guidance, administering discipline, and settling disagreements. He was . . . involved in every aspect of community life. No purchase was made without his knowledge or the approval of the council which he headed. . . .

If you were out of favour with him, he had the authority to prevent you from leaving the colony to go to the doctor, to town on business, or for a Sunday visit. [His] . . . sweeping powers were enough to keep most of the men in line and agreeable, but his political manoeuvrings did not impress my father. He often found himself . . . at odds with [the minister's] . . . tactics. (Kirkby 2007: 62–3)

Women Priests in the Anglican Church

The Church of England (otherwise known as the Anglican Church or, in the US, the Episcopal Church) is the largest Protestant denomination in the world, with an estimated membership of between 76 and 84 million. Over the past half-century the battle for women to take on the orders of deacons, priests, and bishops has been long, hard, and accompanied by very emotional dialogue that has at times seriously divided the church. Of the 38 individual provinces that make up the Anglican Church, the first two to be permitted to ordain female priests were the United States and Canada, in 1976. In Canada, on 30 November 1976, six women were ordained almost simultaneously (so that no one would be considered the first), in four different dioceses.

The situation in the United States is not as clear. While the General Convention passed a resolution stating that "no one shall be denied access" of ordination into the three orders (deacons, priests, bishops) on the basis of their sex, another resolution protects bishops who oppose women priests in their dioceses. As late as 2004, there were still three (of one hundred) dioceses whose bishops would not allow the ordination of women. One opposed bishop, Bishop Jack Iker, of Fort Worth, Texas, expresses his resistance in the following question:

Are we a culturally conditioned church, trying to keep up with the times, and changing practices and teachings to conform with the times, or are we a part of the historic biblical church of the ages? (Iker 2003)

The bishop's rhetorical question raises a conundrum that is central to organized religion today: how to preserve time-honoured values that are central the church while remaining relevant to a society whose values change over time.

It wasn't until 1998, when the Japanese province voted to ordain women priests, that most Anglican provinces accepted female clergy. The "mother church" in England began permitting ordination of women only in 1993, four years after the first female bishop was ordained, in New Zealand. The first female Anglican bishop in Canada was Victoria Matthews, who was consecrated in her Edmonton diocese in 1994. She had been made a deacon in 1979 and a priest the next year.

In 1998, the thirteenth Lambeth Conference, a convention of Anglican bishops worldwide held every 10 years, was attended by 11 women bishops, all of whom had been ordained as priests between 1978 and 1984. In the words of Louie Crew, a powerful champion of acceptance within the US Episcopal Church:

> Nearly all can tell tales of painful marginalization, even, in a few cases, of being spat upon, shouted at, verbally abused. . . . With each bishop, however, such tales are told only rarely and then reluctantly, and usually, only to illustrate how much progress has been made. (Louie Crew)

As of 2013, only 15 Anglican provinces allowed the ordination of women bishops, with just 5—Canada, the US, Australia, New Zealand/Polynesia, and Southern Africa—actually having any. Parishes that have reluctantly accepted women bishops have what are termed "flying bishops," men who can step in as needed to serve in place of the woman bishop.

The resistance to women holding positions of authority within the church is not restricted to Anglicans. It remains the official position of the Roman Catholic Church, as well as some fundamentalist Christian groups in Canada and the US, that women should not be ordained as ministers or priests.

Why is there such opposition? Much of it comes back to Christianity's embedded patriarchy, which is extremely difficult to overcome in an institution that derives much of its meaning from its history and traditions. Many church leaders still justify their opposition to the ordination of women

Members of the Women's Ordination Conference group stage protest the Catholic ban on women priests in front of St Peter's Basilica, Rome, in June 2010. Can a church that bars women from positions of authority represent all of its members equally?

on the grounds that Jesus had no female disciples. Of course, in the patriarchal culture in which Jesus lived, there would have been strong social opposition to his having female disciples. He was revolutionary enough in the respectful way in which he treated women. And he did have a good number of women followers who dedicated their lives to learning from him, with his approval (see, for instance, his attitude towards Mary, sister of Martha, in Luke 10: 38–42).

The negative attitude of the disciple Paul, as expressed in his letters to the Corinthians, is another reason given for opposing women in authority, and reflects the cultural attitude towards women at that time:

> As in all the churches of the saints, the women should keep silence in the churches. For they are not permitted to speak, but should be subordinate, as even the law says. If there is anything they desire to know, let them ask their husbands at home. For it is shameful for a woman to speak in church. (1 Cor. 14: 33–35)

A similar attitude is expressed in Paul's correspondence with Timothy:

> Let a woman learn in silence with all submissiveness. I permit no woman to teach or to have authority over men; she is to keep silent. For Adam was formed first, then Eve; and Adam was not deceived, but the woman was deceived and became a transgressor. Yet woman will be saved through bearing children, if she continues in faith and love and holiness, with modesty. (1 Tim. 2: 11–15)

What do YOU think?

1. Do you think it's fair to say that Paul's statements were (to use Bishop Iker's phrase) "culturally conditioned"?

2. Why do you think that the "innovations" of female priests and bishops came not from the centre of the Anglican church in England (where the church head, the Archbishop of Canterbury is housed) but from the fringe or periphery areas of New Zealand, Africa, and North America?

3. What should the role of sociological analysis be in discussing the position of women in the social structure of religions in Canada?

Paul's historical role was to take the ideas of Jesus and organize them into a structure. That the role itself was patriarchal reflects the culture of his upbringing and experience.

QUICK HITS

The Myth about Islam and Women

While it can be argued that there is a tendency in all countries where organized religion is strong for women to be oppressed, the countries of the Middle East, where Islam is the dominant religion, have been singled out as especially oppressive and **misogynistic**. It is part of a generalized and uncritical targeting of Islam by the conservative Western media, a targeting that is related to deeper Eurocentric cultural beliefs that reproduce **Orientalism** and **Islamophobia**. When examining Islam and the rights of women, it is important to separate those anti-female practices that are specifically Muslim from those practices that happen to occur in Muslim countries but that are not supported by the faith. We have used Haroon Siddiqui's book *Being Muslim* (2006) to compile the following list.

- The practice of honour killings (killing female relatives for alleged sexual misconduct that brings dishonour upon the family) in countries such as Pakistan, Turkey, and Jordan is *not* an Islamic tradition.
- The practice of female genital cutting (FGC) in North and Central Africa is *not* condoned by Islam. (At the First Islamic Ministerial Conference on The Child, held in Morocco in 2005, FGC was condemned as un-Islamic.)
- The number of cases of polygyny (one man having more than one wife) in Muslim families in Western and Muslim countries is greatly exaggerated. Most Muslim marriages involve couples.
- Most Muslim women around the world do not wear a hijab or head-covering. (Siddiqui 2006: 96-125).

What do YOU think?

What contributes to the distorted view that prevails in the West of the way women are treated under Islamic law and tradition?

Religion and Social Change

Religion has been a primary agent of change throughout history. Both the emergence and spread of new religions—like Islam—and the loss of indigenous religions have brought about and reflected significant social and cultural change. Examples that we have already touched on include the Protestant ethic, which influenced cultural normative structures, and the European missionary movement, which was used to convert and subjugate populations as part of the broader aims of colonialism. And while religion has been used to submit populations to the will of authority, it has been used to emancipate populations as well. Take, for instance, figures like Mahatma Gandhi, Mother Teresa, Martin Luther King, Malcolm X, and Desmond Tutu, and the aforementioned Canadians Stanley Knowles, J.S. Woodsworth, and Tommy Douglas, all of whom used religion as a mechanism to carry out social change for the purposes of social justice. Marx, you will recall, claimed that religion pacifies people and stifles movements for change, as it encourages citizens to put up with their worldly hardships because of the promise of better fortunes that await in heaven. However, religion has been a driving force behind anti-colonial liberation movements, anti-racism and anti-discrimination movements, struggles against poverty, and democratic reform throughout the nineteenth and twentieth centuries.

Christian Religious Colonialism and Its Impact among Canada's Aboriginal People

When missionaries brought Christianity to Canada's Native people, their actions were an integral part of colonization, designed to make the people more like Europeans, not just in beliefs but in other social areas such as gender roles (see Karen Anderson's *Chain Her by One Foot*), and in their obedience to the Crown. But the people also had **agency**—that is, they were not merely victims of colonially imposed religions. As Native prophets reacted to the new world of Christian beliefs and ensuing political turmoil, they began to promote innovative religious beliefs. For example, the early nineteenth-century Seneca prophet Handsome Lake (*c*. 1735–1815) combined elements of traditional belief with what his people had learned from Quakers who had spent time among the Seneca. What

was known in English as the Code of Handsome Lake combined traditional aspects of the Great Law of Peace, which had brought the initially five nations (Mohawk, Oneida, Onondaga, Cayuga, and Seneca) of the Iroquois together into one confederacy, with Quaker elements such as a strong opposition to witchcraft, sexual promiscuity, and gambling.

Indigenous people developed new forms of Christianity by integrating European-based religion into their own belief system and practices. In many instances, these adapted forms of Christianity enabled the people to preserve or return to the cohesiveness of Durkheim's moral community that had existed in pre-contact times. In *"Ta'n Teliktlamsitasit* ('Ways of Believing'): Mi'kmaw Religion in Eskasoni, Nova Scotia"* (2002), Angela Robinson uses the term **Catholic-Traditionalists** to refer to Mi'kmaq who adopted Catholicism but incorporated non-Christian elements into their religious practices (2002: 143). Mi'kmaq scholar **Marie Battiste** (1997) offers the following description of how her people claimed Catholicism as their own to give strength to their community:

> In 1610 the Mi'kmaq people entered into a compact with the Holy Roman Empire when our Chief Membertou and 140 others were first baptized. While our alliance with the Church was more political than spiritual, it was solidified in daily rituals when the French priest Father Antoine Maillard learned Mi'kmaq and began addressing the spiritual questions of the people. . . . Following the expulsion of the French priests [by the English] . . . [the] Mi'kmaq people held to their strong spiritual rituals in the Catholic church by conducting their own services. They had prayer leaders who led Sunday prayers, baptized children, accepted promises of marriage, and provided last rites for the dying. . . . These Catholic rituals continue today in many communities, and elders still play an important role in them, although a priest in the community offers the primary services. (157–8)

During the late nineteenth and early twentieth centuries, Christian missionaries along with federal officials in Canada and the US took aim at important Aboriginal ceremonies that were conducted, in part, to nourish a strong, cohesive sense of community. These ceremonies were the heart and soul of "religious

In March 2007, Mark L. MacDonald, shown here with Archbishop Andrew Hutchinson, became the Anglican Church's first National Indigenous Bishop, responsible for providing ministry to Anglican Aboriginal people across Canada. How do you think his role will be different from that of other bishops in Canada?

competition" for missionaries, and a form of resistance to political domination for the government officials. In Chapter 3 we examined the potlatch and the circumstances surrounding its banning. Here we will look briefly at the Sun Dance, the main ceremony for indigenous groups living in the Prairies. "Sun Dance" is an English term. The Blackfoot, who live in southern Alberta, termed the ceremony *Okan*, after the pole at the centre of the ceremony. The Okan was initiated, sponsored, and presided over by a woman:

> The decision to hold a Sun Dance was made by a pure woman . . . who had a male relative in danger of losing his life. A husband might be ill or a son may not have returned from a raid. The woman made a public vow that if the person's life was spared, she would sponsor a Sun Dance. Then, if her prayer was answered, she began preparations for the summer festival. (Dempsey 1995: 392)

This ceremony was quite different from anything found in Christian religions. The following statement from Montana governor John Rickard, speaking in 1894, illustrates the typical sentiments of Christian culture to non-Christian religious practices:

> Investigation . . . convinces me that it is not only inhuman and brutalizing, unnatural and indecent, and therefore abhorrent to Christian civilization, but that its aims and purposes are a menace to the peace and welfare of communities. My information . . . leads me to regard the proposed exhibition as wholly inconsistent with Christian civilization. (Quoted in Dusenberry 1998: 219)

One aspect of the ceremony gave Canadian government officials an excuse for issuing a complete ban on the Sun Dance in 1895. Sometimes, as a spiritual offering, young men inserted leather thongs through their chest or back muscles, attaching the other end either to a pole or to the skull of a buffalo. They would then dance until the thongs ripped free—a painful process. Section 114 of the Indian Act was amended to include a provision making it an indictable offence to take part in any ceremony "of which the wounding or mutilation of the dead or living body of any human being or animal forms a part or is a feature." Technically, this would have made the "mortification of the flesh" (self-flagellation, or whipping oneself) illegal, even though it was associated with Christian religious dedication and was practised throughout most of Christianity's history (and is still practised in parts of Latin America and the Philippines). Little Bear, a Cree leader who had moved with his band to Montana, is reported to have stated that he was willing to remove that part of the ceremony in the spirit of getting along with colonial authorities (Dusenberry 1998: 220). However, the entire ceremony was deemed uncivilized, with no room for negotiation. This prompted the following response by one Blackfoot:

> We know that there is nothing injurious to our people in the Sun-dance. . . . It has been our custom, during many years, to assemble once every summer for this festival. . . . We fast and pray that we may be able to lead good lives and to act more kindly towards each other.
>
> I do not understand why the white men desire to put an end to our religious ceremonials. What harm can they do our people? If they deprive us of our religion, we will have nothing left, for we know of no other that can take its place. (Quoted in McClintock 1910: 378)

The ceremony continued to be held in secret, and participants who were discovered were arrested. The Sun Dance did not return publicly in Canada until 1951. However, the damage to traditional religious beliefs had already taken its toll. The ceremony never recovered its former prominence.

More recently, religious revival among Aboriginal people has gained popularity. Termed **neo-traditionalism** by some observers, it involves the reinterpretation of traditional beliefs and practices in ways that incorporate elements unique to one's own culture and others borrowed from Native cultures elsewhere. The sweat lodge, the drum, and the medicine wheel are examples of elements used in neo-traditionalist practice. The recovery of traditional customs has been very important in helping Aboriginal peoples find and strengthen their identity. Neo-traditionalist practices are often used in the rehabilitation of people in prison or in treatment for substance abuse. In this regard, Aboriginal religious leaders in some communities have finally achieved status equal to that of prison chaplains and addiction counsellors.

QUICK HITS

So How Multicultural Are We?

You have just read that Aboriginal spiritual leaders have earned the right to use neo-traditionalist rehabilitation practices to help people in prisons, where Aboriginal people are overrepresented within the general population. Until the fall of 2012, federal inmates of other faiths were likewise able to receive religious counselling from Muslim imams, Jewish rabbis, and other religious functionaries. Unfortunately, it was seen as "going over the top" when in British Columbia someone requested a Wiccan shaman. Wicca is a modern nature religion based largely on the old Celtic Druid religion. In September 2012, the Conservative minister of Public Safety, Vic Toews, cancelled the contract for the Wiccan priest, and a month later, he announced that all part-time non-Christian chaplains would be let go as of 2013. An e-mail from Toews' office to the CBC explained that while "The minister strongly supports the freedom of religion for all Canadians, including prisoners, . . . the government . . . is not in the business of picking and choosing which religions will be given preferential status through government funding" (CBC News 2012b). According to the CBC report, 57 per cent of all federal prison inmates are Christian; 4.5 per cent are Muslim; 4.0 per cent practise Aboriginal spirituality; and 2 per cent are Buddhist. Jews and Sikhs each make up less than 1 per cent of the prison population.

What do YOU think?

1. What principles of representation do you think should be applied in terms of prison chaplains? Is it enough to guarantee non-Christian prison inmates nondenominational services and counselling?

2. Do you think this was strictly a political move on the government's part, or does it reflect the diminishing role of religion in society as a whole?

The Missionary Position

The primary role of missionaries is to change people, to make them leave the religious path they are on and walk a new one, one that often bears the mark of a different culture. But it is also important that missionaries exemplify the values that are at the core of the religion they represent, particularly the principle of charity. Here the sociologist needs to ask, do the two aims clash? Can there be a kind of role strain between conversion and charity?

The practice of sending missionaries into developing countries in need of financial assistance is sometimes called **aid evangelism**. The financial assistance is a kind of **tied aid**—money that comes with purse strings attached. Often when countries in the developed world (including Canada) spend money on aid, it is given with the condition that the people receiving the assistance must spend at least some of the money on products and services that come from the donor country. Another term for this is **phantom aid**, which captures the idea that the aid is not real but rather a form of investment.

So, do religious-based aid workers and the religious communities that sponsor them sometimes see aid as a form of investment in conversion? Aid evangelism has taken various forms over the last few decades. Some American fundamentalist groups delivered thousands of 70-pound food packages to starving people in Iraq. The packages were covered with biblical verses written in Arabic. Following the disastrous tsunami that hit southern Asia on 26 December 2004, the 2,000-member Antioch Community Church, based in Waco, Texas, sent "aid workers" to Sri Lanka to stage children's plays about Jesus and hold Christian prayer services for those suffering from the devastating effects of the flood. Sri Lanka is primarily a Buddhist country, though Hinduism and Islam are also practised; the Christian element is small. Backlash to perceived aid evangelism caused vandalism and threats to local Christian groups, even to the point of attacking the offices of the Christian aid agency World Vision, which had no apparent connection with the questionable missionary practices here mentioned. In Indonesia, the world's largest Muslim country, the government blocked the move of American religious-based aid agency World Help to settle 50 Muslim children from the flooded Aceh province to a Christian orphanage, as they suspected that conversion was the cost of the aid.

What do YOU think?

What do you think is the motivation behind attacks on Christian aid agencies and government intervention against Christian charities?

Liberation Theology

Liberation theology is a progressive school of Christian thought that advocates social justice for the poor. It takes as its model the life of Jesus as being politically opposed to privilege. It is very much like the **social gospel** movement put forward by Protestant ministers of the late nineteenth and early twentieth centuries, except that it is rooted almost exclusively in the Catholic Church, particularly in Latin America, and especially among members of the Jesuit and Maryknoll religious orders. Liberation theology opposes the oppression of the poor by the corrupt, ruling class in developing and underdeveloped countries. Its proponents emphasize social practices that improve the situation for the poor. These practices are devised based on input received from the poor, not from the rich who, historically, have supported the "monarchic and pyramidic" system of hierarchical authority of the Catholic Church (Russell 2001). There has been strong opposition from conservatives within the hierarchy of the Catholic Church, particularly those bishops in Latin American countries who had been appointed from the elite class. Marxist advocates for the poor argue that these bishops are conscious of their own class interests, and act upon these interests over those of the poor.

The Sandinista National Liberation Front (known by its Spanish initials FSLN) was a Marxist revolutionary group in Nicaragua that began in the 1960s and overthrew the US-backed right-wing dictator Anastasio Somoza in 1979. The Sandinistas stayed in political power until 1990 despite an ongoing battle with the counter-insurgency Contras, who were backed by the US Central Intelligence Agency. The Sandinistas supported priests who worked to benefit the poor. The Catholic hierarchy in Nicaragua had supported the dictatorship of Somoza. In an official statement made in 1950, Nicaragua's conservative bishops said:

> [A]ll authority comes from God. God is the Author of all that exists, and from the Author comes Authority; [faithful Catholics] should remember that when they obey the Political Authority, they do not dishonor themselves, but rather they act in a way that basically constitutes obeisance to God. (Quoted in Gilbert 1988: 131)

Priests working with the poor and who believed in liberation theology became members of the FSLN.

When the Sandinistas came to power, some priests took political office, but were quickly reprimanded by Pope John Paul II and the Vatican hierarchy. One such priest was Father Miguel D'Escoto, who became the Foreign Minister for the Nicaraguan government. In 2008, he was elected president of the General Assembly of the United Nations.

Brazil is the largest Catholic country in the world, with well over 130 million people, yet it has a chronic shortage of priests. It has been estimated that in Latin America, there is one priest for every 7,000 Catholics, versus one for every 880 in the United States (Russell 2001). One strategy to overcome this shortage supported and implemented by liberation theologians is the establishment of "base communities," estimated to number as many as about 75,000 in Brazil alone (Russell 2001). Within the base communities, which average 10 to 30 members each, the focus is on shared religious instruction and prayer as well as communal self-help. Though local priests provide guidance to community leaders, the principal focus of the groups is on relating the lessons of the Bible to the day-to-day activities of their members, whether they are urbanites, slum-dwellers, or rural *campesinos*.

At a typical base community in the town of Campos Eliseos, 14 miles northwest of Rio de Janeiro, 30 local residents meet every Friday night in a cinderblock home to read the Bible and discuss their problems. Antonio Joinhas, a 44-year-old railroad signalman, relates how one study session inspired a local public health centre:

> After reading how one biblical community helped another to overcome a problem, we decided to work together too. We all supplied the manpower and raised money for materials from the community. Now we've got a health center, and it came from the Bible. (Quoted in Russell 2001)

Charitable Organizations

> And though I have the gift of prophecy, and understand all mysteries, and all knowledge; and though I have all faith, so that I could remove mountains, and have not charity, I am nothing. (1 Corinthians 13: 2)

All religions teach and practise charity. "Charity," here, is used in its original sense, which is simply

A small service at a Christian base community in São João de Meriti, Brazil. Compare the photo of Muslims praying in Turkey (p. 397). Do you think this setting is better suited to what Durkheim called the collective consciousness of religious experience?

"love," specifically "love of one's fellow humans." That meaning of charity evolved, with the concept itself, to eventually refer to the groups that provide material assistance to relieve the suffering of those in distress.

Before there was a government-funded social safety net in Canada, church-founded charities served a vital role, especially in cities, where they took care of the homeless, the new arrivals, and those generally "down on their luck." Canadian churches produced some of the first people engaged in sociological work in the name of the *social gospel*. The movement, which lasted in Canada from about the 1890s to the 1930s, developed as an attempt to apply the human welfare principles of Christianity to address the social, medical, and psychological ills brought on by the industrialization and uncontrolled capitalism of North America and Europe during the late nineteenth century. One of its great achievements in this country was the Social Service Council of Canada (1912), which, through churches, conducted the earliest sociological surveys of Canadian cities and, in 1914, sponsored the first national meeting in Canada to address social problems. One of the most influential figures to come out of this tradition in Canada was **James S. Woodsworth** (1874–1942), a Methodist minister who became one of the founding members of the Canadian Commonwealth Federation (CCF), a precursor to the New Democratic Party.

The social gospel movement was instrumental in the establishment of missions, or Christian-based, walk-in refuges, where the poor and the homeless could come in off the street and be served a warm meal. Toronto's Yonge Street Mission, formed in the poor downtown region in

Telling It Like It Is | An Author POV

The Golden Compass and Religious Censorship

Around Christmas 2008, I saw the television premiere of *The Golden Compass*, based on the first novel of Philip Pullman's bestselling *His Dark Materials* trilogy. I knew that a sequel had been planned, so I did a search online to find out when it was scheduled to come out. It wasn't. The movie had been the target of a strong religious-based boycott in the US, which had limited its American profits to just $70 million, although it had grossed a solid $300 million worldwide. The reason for the religious opposition to the movie was that the "bad guys" in the film, the evil Magisterium, were suspected to have been modelled on the Catholic Church and its hierarchical organization. I didn't pick up on that in the film, but then I wasn't looking for it—all I saw was a big evil, over-controlling administration (something I see a lot of places). The books, I've been told, are fiercely anti-religion and anti–church establishment. The author is both a declared atheist and a social anarchist.

If my reading of the religious criticism is correct, it is not so much that the movie supports an atheistic or anti-Christian position, but that it poses a threat to children who, if they enjoy the movie, will want to read the books and in turn may be turned off of religion to a life of atheism. I am of two minds about the boycott. I hate that the sequel will not appear because of religious opposition to the original. However, it is a democratic right to boycott a film, and I could not oppose that action without being a hypocrite. I, too, read into the meanings of movies that I don't like—such as *The Fast and the Furious* franchise and all the bloody *Saw* films—and consider the damaging effects such movies may have on young people. I'm concerned about the mindless Disney movies, which I fear will turn little girls into pouty, pink-clad princesses. Is there any real difference between my stance and the position taken by opponents of *The Golden Compass*?

In my mind, the difference is that *The Golden Compass*, and the books it is based on, encourage young people to think. It encourages people to challenge convention and, hopefully, be creative and original in the worlds they create as adults. Religion is often, in my opinion, overly concerned with conformity and blindly following the paths of the past. I believe that a rich religious life involves addressing the big questions of life, and perhaps answering a few of them. The movies I don't like are typically those that I believe don't encourage people to really think at all.

1896, was supported by churches of several denominations. It began as a horse-drawn "gospel wagon," and over its 110-year history it has had several locations. In 1929 at the beginning of the Great Depression, it served an estimated 5,600 beef sandwiches, 80 gallons of tea, and 26 gallons of milk every day. In recent decades it has expanded its role, advocating for low-income housing, engaging in youth work, and assisting people to receive medical, dental, and vision care.

What do YOU think?

1. How many religious-based charities are you aware of? What do you see as their role today? Is it growing, diminishing, or evolving?

2. Religious-based charities will often—though not always—try at least gently to "convert" those who come to them for food, clothing, and shelter. Do you see this as negative or positive?

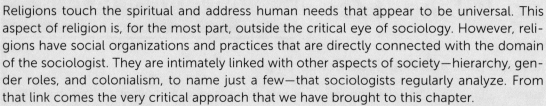

WRAP IT UP

Summary

Religions touch the spiritual and address human needs that appear to be universal. This aspect of religion is, for the most part, outside the critical eye of sociology. However, religions have social organizations and practices that are directly connected with the domain of the sociologist. They are intimately linked with other aspects of society—hierarchy, gender roles, and colonialism, to name just a few—that sociologists regularly analyze. From that link comes the very critical approach that we have brought to this chapter.

Some readers might think that we have bent over backwards to praise and promote Islam while criticizing Christianity. That is a legitimate impression, but it is not what we have set out to do. What we have tried to do is to highlight the social benefits of organized religion, while casting a light on some of areas of sociological concern, such as religious intolerance and the abuse of power. In Canada, Islam is often a target of ignorant and intolerant views, while Christian values and practices that are socially beneficial in most context have been used on some occasions as instruments of power by government and religious officials (even, occasionally, well-meaning ones). A critical sociology textbook written in a country where Islam, Buddhism, Judaism, or Hinduism are abused as tools of power (and they are so abused) would offer a different perspective by taking a closer examining of the abuse of power within those religions.

THINK BACK

Questions for Critical Review

1. What is the social tension that exists between hierarchy and egalitarianism in organized religion?

2. What would a feminist critique of organized religion look like?

3. How does religion link with colonialism?

4. Why do you think that there is such a misunderstanding about the Muslim faith in the West?

5. Why are many sociologists critical of organized religion?

READ ON

Online

The Immanent Frame: Secularism, Religion, and the Public Sphere

http://blogs.ssrc.org/tif/category/sociology-of-religion

> Founded in conjunction with the Social Science Research Council's program on religion and the public sphere, this sites provides intelligently written blogs and useful articles on the sociology of religion, written by a number of contributors representing a range of disciplines.

Marx, Weber and Durkheim on Religion

www.jeramyt.org/papers/sociology-of-religion.html

> Jeramy Townsley's very useful (and often plagiarized) article compares the three main sociological theorists of religion.

The Sociological Study of Religion

http://hirr.hartsem.edu/sociology/about_the_field.html

> Maintained by the Hartford Institute for Religion Research, this site presents a good overview of topics and current researchers in the sociological study of religion.

In Print

Timothy J. Gianotti, Jr (2011), *In the Light of a Blessed Tree: Illuminations of Islamic Belief, Practice, and History* **(Eugene, OR: Wipf & Stock).**

> This is an excellent, readable work explaining the basic beliefs and practices of Islam.

Margaret Humphreys (1995), *Empty Cradles: A Shameful Secret, a Miscarriage of Justice, and a Woman Who Wouldn't Give Up* **(London: Corgi Books).**

> This book introduces the reader to the story of over 150,000 English children from marginalized families who were deported to Australian orphanages and similar institutions.

Isabelle Knockwood (2001), *Out of the Depths: The Experiences of Mi'kmaw Children at the Indian Residential School in Shubenacadie, Nova Scotia* **(Halifax: Fernwood Publishing).**

> This classic work by a First Nation writer examines life at a residential school for Mi'kmaq children.

Haroon Siddiqui (2006), *Being Muslim* **(Toronto: Groundwood Books).**

> This well-written work is designed to inform non-Muslim readers on what Islam is and is not about.

Education

Learning Objectives

After reading this chapter, you should be able to

- outline the advantages and disadvantages of "streaming" (or "tracking") in elementary and secondary education

- discuss the positive and negative effects on post-secondary education of becoming reliant on (a) adjunct instructors, (b) online education, and (c) corporate sponsorship of research and infrastructure

- state your view, from a sociologist's standpoint, of plagiarism occurring today in post-secondary institutions

- assess the social value of having schools run by and for marginalized groups such as Aboriginal and African-Canadian students

- discuss how education can reproduce the class structure of society.

Key Terms

- access
- access without mobility
- adjunct professor
- alienation
- anomie
- assimilation
- commodification
- credentialism
- critical education
- cultural capital
- cultural reproduction theory
- cultures of education
- disqualified knowledges
- docile body
- Eurocentric
- (the) examination
- hidden curriculum
- hierarchical observation
- human capital thesis
- institution
- institutional racism
- instrumental education
- intellectual property
- legitimization of inequality
- McJob
- meritocratic
- monoculturalism
- normalizing judgement
- plagiarism
- relative deprivation
- reproduction of social structure
- role models
- social distance
- tracking
- underemployment

Names to Know

- Jean Anyon
- Jeannie Oakes

Exploit U and the Academic Underclass:
Take a Good Look at Your Professor

Take a good look at your sociology professor or TA—quick, right now, while she or he isn't looking. Is she relatively young? Does she always seem to be running late, to be hurrying in or out, to be distracted before or after class? When your instructor tells stories of her teaching experience, are these stories about some other college or university? Does your prof also teach at another school? Does the department secretary know who you're speaking about when you say your instructor's name?

If your instructor is teaching an intro soc course, chances are he's been hired only for a session, a semester, or a year. He probably isn't a full-time, tenured member of the department. He likely falls into the category of "contract faculty" or "sessional staff." Or maybe he's an "adjunct professor," which sounds a bit loftier but still means that he's teaching courses and students—particularly lower-level ones—that permanent staff members don't want to deal with. Technically he's permanent part-time, but even that sounds better than it is—my *Canadian Oxford Dictionary* (product placement for our publisher) defines *adjunct* as "an assistant or a subordinate person, esp. one with a temporary appointment only."

In other words, the person teaching you may well be fully qualified but an academic gypsy, part of a growing post-secondary underclass that get paid less for teaching you and often don't receive any benefits. It's just one of the changes taking place in education today. In this chapter we'll look at what else is changing, and why—and, most important, how it's affecting students and society today.

What do YOU think?

1. Do you think you can tell the difference between a full-time professor and an adjunct? Do you know what percentage of your instructors fit the latter category?

2. What are some of the positive and negative aspects of being taught by an adjunct professor?

Introduction: Yes, Education Is Important

Education is vitally important—few people would deny that. To a sociologist, the social institution of education is important because of the multiple influences it has on everything from socialization and status formation to social order and economic productivity. When we refer to the **institution** of education, we're using the word in the sense introduced in Chapter 6: an enduring set of ideas about how to accomplish goals that are deemed important within a society or culture. Education is an extremely powerful tool for promoting ideas among impressionable young people. Children spend more time at school than they do with their parents. Your child, if you are a parent, is raised by strangers, and simultaneously, your child becomes in some senses a stranger. This is a consequence of modern societies and their institutional structure, one that reflects elements of Durkheim's **anomie**. Anomie, you'll recall, is a state of confusion caused when the bond between individuals and social institutions break down. In the context of education, consider the sense of disconnect from the school system that many parents experience, and how this influences their children.

Education also has a significant impact on the sociability and socialization of children, one that depends greatly on the time and duration of schooling. At school, behaviours are modified, skills are developed for future employment, social interaction and conflict are negotiated, notions of social reality are defined, and structures of inequality (classism, sexism, heterosexism, and racism) are verbally discouraged even as they are reproduced. Schools prepare children to be productive citizens and obedient subjects. How they do in school plays a significant role in determining their potential social mobility, as we will see in this chapter.

The Rise of Public Education in Canada

Before the Industrial Revolution in Europe and the United States, there was little interest in educating the masses. On the contrary, it was in the best interest of the ruling elite to keep the population ignorant and illiterate so its authority could not be challenged. But beginning with the rise of industrial capitalism, companies started to demand more from their labour force. Specifically, as industry became more complex, it required a more disciplined, trainable, and literate workforce that would be more economically productive. Industrialization and public education, then, became interdependent in the same way that labour is dependent on capital and capital on labour. This symbiotic relationship still exists, and is seen in the correlation between industrial development and an educated population. For instance, one of the main functions of developing nations is to establish an educational base that ensures increased economic and social stability by producing a broader, middle-class foundation; this requires a literate, educated population.

In Canada, education was seen as an important means of achieving economic modernization as early as 1846. That's when education reformer Egerton Ryerson (after whom Ryerson University is named) began promoting the idea of a school system that would be universal, free, and compulsory. According to Schecter (1977), Ryerson's public education model was not simply a method of producing social *order* but one that procured social *control* by subverting potential social conflict and animosity from incoming Irish labourers. Speaking of the unskilled, famine-afflicted Irish Catholic migrants, Ryerson warned: "the physical disease and death which have accompanied their influx among us may be the precursor of the worst pestilence of social insubordination and disorder" (quoted in Schecter 1977: 373). Education could avert the threat of discontent from these "alien" labourers by assimilating them into the dominant Protestant culture.

Schecter (1977) argues that education has never contributed as much to prosperity and social mobility as it has legitimized social inequality. State-run education, he explains, is premised on centralization and uniformity, instruments of social control to be used on the emerging working class. To ensure the uniformity of education—from textbooks to teachers—it became necessary to establish provincial boards that could act as executive bodies to set up and maintain large systems of "normal schools" (the old and sociologically significant name for teacher's colleges). School boards were able to enforce codes of discipline and enact hierarchical authority relations that placed both students and parents in positions subordinate to the place of the teacher. Such practices, according to Schecter, were used to cover up the hidden agenda of subordinating the working class.

It may sound cynical to suggest that the state-run school system was born of a need to discipline the growing labour force for industrial capitalism and to legitimize the social order. Bear in mind, though, that at the time public education systems were established, in the latter half of the nineteenth century, many social reformers were warning of the civil disorder that might result from an unhappy working class. This perpetuated pre-existing middle-class fears of their own downward mobility, of the loss of property, and of the "lower" classes themselves. Even the ruling classes were uneasy with the ambiguity surrounding the emerging capitalist society, which promised wealth but not without the possibility of social conflict. With the newly solicited support of Canada's middle class, reformers were able to instill the need for school reform and, after numerous debates, several reversals, and considerable time, implement a public school system.

Post-war Expansion and the Human Capital Thesis

The Canadian economy after World War II required a workforce that was better educated than it had ever been before, fuelling an unprecedented expansion of colleges and universities across Canada to match the economic boom that peaked during the 1960s. Government officials may have loudly championed the expansion of post-secondary institutions as increasing access to education to all classes, but historians Newson and Buchbinder (1988) maintain that economic considerations were the driving force.

The perceived relationship between the expansion of education and economic growth is part of the **human capital thesis**, which asserts that just as industrial societies invest in factories and equipment to attain greater efficiency, so they invest in schools to enhance the knowledge and skills of their workers. When applied to social inequality, the human capital thesis is used to argue that marginalized groups earn less money than dominant groups because they possess less human capital in the form of education, skill, and experience.

Since the early 1970s, decreases in the taxes charged to corporations (but not to individuals) have contributed to cuts in governmental funding of post-secondary institutions. This has allowed the corporate sector to form stronger ties with cash-hungry colleges and universities that, in return for corporate finance, have made concessions to corporate capital. This is most evident in increased advertising on campus, visible everywhere but in the classrooms (coming soon?).

Academic research has become more closely tied into corporate agendas and control, especially in such areas as medical/pharmaceutical and agricultural product research. How long, we wonder, before your nutrition science class is brought to you by Gatorade®?

Models of Public Education in Canada

The Assimilation Model

Education in Canada has historically been based on a monocultural model that emphasizes **assimilation into the dominant culture**. English Canada was viewed as a white Protestant nation, and it was seen as natural that people arriving from outside this dominant culture had to assimilate in order to "fit in." The flaw in the assimilation model is that it failed to recognize that racial bias and discrimination—both inside and outside the school system—makes the level playing field on which the assimilation model is premised virtually impossible. According to Henry and Tator (2006), the emphasis on **monoculturalism** (the promotion of just one culture, as opposed to multiculturalism) formed a pervasive ideology that in their words "influenced the training of educators, the practices of teaching, the content and context of learning, the hiring and promotion practices of boards, and the cultural values and norms underpinning all areas of school life" (Henry & Tator 2006: 213). Students were expected to simply leave their cultural, religious, and ethnic identities at the door.

The assimilationist approach continues to influence Canadian public education, as sociologists like George Dei and Agnes Calliste observe (Dei 1996; Dei & Calliste 2000). The experience of one of our own daughters is typical: after two years of kindergarten, she had become well versed in European fairy tales and folklore, and Judeo-Christian traditions and values. Guy Letts notes that: "The experience continues throughout primary school, into secondary and post-secondary education, where literature courses are often really courses in *English* literature, which typically does not include works translated from other languages and cultures." Under these circumstances, English literature is really English cultural studies, despite the fact that only 10 to 15 per cent of Canada's population is of British ancestry. As a discipline, it represents an assimilationist and monocultural perspective. Implicit in this is the notion that British culture is somehow superior, the only thing worth learning.

In September 2006, the Ted Rogers School of Management, part of Ryerson University, moved into this state-of-the-art facility in downtown Toronto. Corporate funding made the facility possible. What are the drawbacks to this kind of corporate–university relationship? How might it affect research funding and the way courses are designed? Do you think a history of the labour movement in Canada would be taught at that facility?

Multicultural Education

The federal government implemented its official policy of multiculturalism in 1971 to preserve and promote cultural diversity while removing the barriers that denied certain groups full participation within Canadian society. With a new objective of creating a learning environment that would respect all learners, school boards launched initiatives to study and celebrate the lifestyles, traditions, and histories of diverse cultures (Henry & Tator 2006). These initiatives were based on three fundamental assumptions drawn from a study of multicultural education in six countries:

1. learning about one's culture will improve educational achievement
2. learning about one's culture will promote quality of opportunity
3. learning about other cultures will reduce prejudice and discrimination.

After two decades of multicultural education in Canada, these untested assumptions began to be undermined. Not only did teachers often have little knowledge of the cultures they were presenting, but the classroom focus tended to favour a museum approach that overlooked the complexity and vitality of these different cultures (Dei 1996). Educators focused on historical material and the "exotic" aspects of different cultures—food, festivals, and folklore; they omitted the values and beliefs that are fundamental to shaping cultural identity (Dei 1996).

Anti-racism and Anti-oppression Education

Henry and Tator argue that a glaring weakness of multicultural education is its failure to acknowledge that racism is systemic in Canadian society (2006: 213–14). While the superficial aspects of "other" cultures were being studied, the problem of racial inequality was being ignored, which made multicultural education, in this respect, little better than the assimilationist model.

Anti-racism and anti-oppression education is meant to eliminate institutional and individual barriers to equity. It is intended to create a classroom environment where:

- stereotypes and racist ideas can be exposed
- sources of information can be critically examined
- alternative and missing information can be provided
- students can become equipped to look critically at the accuracy of the information they receive
- the reasons for the continued unequal social status of different group can be explored.

The aim of this model is to change institutional policies and practices, as well as individual attitudes and behaviours that reproduce social inequality.

QUICK HITS

Does Your Knowledge of Geography Reflect a Monocultural Education?

Here is a short test to determine how monocultural your education has been. Match each of the Canadian place names in the left-hand column to its origin in the right-hand column. Two hints: you won't find "Indian" in any of the answers in the right-hand column, and the answer to number 10 is not "the centre of the universe" in any language.

We predict you'll have an easier time with the odd-numbered questions (the answers to some of the even-numbered ones are difficult to find at all, even online, much less to guess). See how you do—the answers are provided at the end of the chapter.

1.	Vancouver	(a)	Cree and Ojibwa, "murky water"
2.	Kelowna	(b)	Mi'kmaq, "flowing through broken marsh"
3.	Alberta	(c)	Name of the English navigator who charted the region
4.	Athabasca River	(d)	Surname of the British royal family
5.	Regina	(e)	Mohawk, "trees standing in the water"
6.	Saskatchewan	(f)	Cree, "swift current"
7.	Churchill	(g)	Name of a daughter of Queen Victoria
8.	Winnipeg	(h)	Cree, "there are reeds here and there"
9.	Windsor	(i)	French, after the nationality of early European whalers
10.	Toronto	(j)	Mi'kmaq and Abenaki, "where the river narrows"
11.	Sherbrooke	(k)	Latin, "Queen," in honour of Queen Victoria
12.	Quebec	(l)	Montagnais (Innu), "Mi'kmaq land"
13.	Moncton	(m)	Mi'kmaq, "straight across"
14.	Miramichi	(n)	Latin, "New Scotland"
15.	Nova Scotia	(o)	Name of the wife of George III
16.	Antigonish	(p)	Legendary island in Arthurian England
17.	Charlottetown	(q)	Name of the English-born governor-in-chief of British North America 1816–18
18.	Tignish	(r)	Okanagan, "female grizzly bear"
19.	Avalon Peninsula	(s)	Name of the British army officer who oversaw the deportation of Acadians in 1755
20.	Port aux Basques	(t)	Name of the 1st Duke of Marlborough, an ancestor of the 20th-century British prime minister of the same name

Students sit with their teacher during the opening assembly at Canada's first Africentric public school, which opened in Toronto in September 2009. Three years later, the city's first Africentric high school opened. Is it realistic to expect schools to cover all cultures in equal depth, or are ethnocentric schools the only answer for students who feel left out of the mainstream curriculum?

Anti-racism and anti-oppression education first appeared in Canada in the 1980s, when some school boards introduced new policies to promote the model. These policies included changes to teacher education, new criteria for reviewing and evaluating the practices of educators, greater analysis of teacher placement procedures, employment equity strategies, and resource and curriculum development (Henry & Tator 2006). The policy has seen gains and setbacks. As Henry and Tator explain:

> While lip service is paid to . . . ensure equality of opportunity for all students in the classroom, in reality, individuals, organizations, and institutions are far more committed to maintaining the status-quo, that is the cultural hegemony of the dominant culture with which most educators identify. (Henry & Tator 2006: 223)

What do YOU think?

What would you say are the biggest obstacles (e.g. gaps in teacher training, lack of source materials, lack of political will) to designing and implementing a public school curriculum that reflects the diversity of Canadian students while tackling racism in a meaningful way? How might these obstacles be overcome?

Topics in the Sociology of Education

The Hidden Curriculum

The hidden curriculum is a hot topic in the sociology of education, though its definition varies depending

Telling It Like It Is

An Expert POV

Eurocentric Curriculum and the University

Despite Canada's multicultural character and state-legislated multicultural policy, a **Eurocentric** curriculum still dominates our institutions of "higher learning." Such a curriculum offers a narrow view of the world. I fail to see an excuse for the exclusion of other points of view when there is a wealth of literature about non-European cultures by non-European academics. These works are not inferior to those of Europeans, but are works that are integral to the attainment of a fuller, more encompassing education in which knowledge and ideas are derived from a wider, culturally diverse range of sources and perspectives. They are particularly useful in dispelling the racist assumptions and myths placed upon "others" by Western society.

In their inadequate attempts to be more inclusive, many of the professors I have encountered take a "just add and stir" approach to the inclusion of Native people, women, and "otherized" groups which simply does not work. A professor of mine once commented that this approach is "like throwing a bunch of radishes into a salad." Just as they are treated as asides or special interest groups in society at large, women, Native people, and ethnic groups are often merely added on to Week 13 readings—if, that is, they are included at all. It was not until I experienced a course taught by a progressive, culturally sensitive anthropology professor who incorporated a multitude of perspectives that I became aware of the partial and limited view of the world to which I had previously been subjected. Those who perpetuate the mainstream academic curriculum seem to have fallen into a state of historical amnesia, whereby the contributions and, indeed, the very presence of non-Europeans have been omitted from Canadian history. Though Chinese, Japanese,

and Indian immigrants arrived in Canada at the same time as most European immigrants, one could pass through the entire school system from kindergarten to university without being aware of the fact. Many students emerge from the school system rightfully well versed in the works of Shakespeare, Plato, and Marx, but how many students come out of university knowing anything about feminist theory, the cultural genocide of Native peoples, or slavery in Canada?

I am concerned that the exclusion from post-secondary curricula of minority groups, their perspectives, and their writings perpetuates a view of the world taken through a Eurocentric lens. This exclusion is also dangerous because it may lead some students to believe that since little is studied from "other" cultures, then perhaps those cultures have nothing of benefit to offer, or else they are inferior to European thought.

The courses I have found the most valuable and educational are those that, though not designated as courses specifically about multiculturalism, women, or Native people, still managed to incorporate a variety of cultural perspectives into the reading materials, films, and seminars. A culturally diverse curriculum and alternative critical forms of pedagogy can also have a positive effect on the academic achievement of minority students, whose experiences and interests are not validated but are typically marginalized or excluded from the existing curriculum.

The education of all students and faculty would be deeply enriched through a more culturally diverse and inclusive curriculum, one that reflects the multicultural society in which we live.

—A.R. Aujla, sociology instructor, 1996

upon the specific issue being discussed and the vantage point of the sociologist doing the discussing. Using Robert Merton's three functions, as introduced in the Chapter 2, we could say that the hidden curriculum serves the latent—not openly stated on a course

outline or syllabus—function of a course, institution, or education system; it could also serve a latent *dys*function. A structural-functionalist sociologist might say that the hidden curriculum performs a positive function by helping to teach the norms of society—the value of work, or the need to respect authority and to use one's time efficiently. A conflict sociologist might argue that the hidden curriculum reproduces the class system, hindering class mobility and therefore performing a negative function, or dysfunction.

Often mentioned in discussions of the hidden curriculum is Pierre Bourdieu's concept of **cultural capital**, which we touched on in Chapter 4. The term is used to refer to the way class divisions are reproduced through differences in consumption patterns and taste (in the arts, in fashion, in food, and so on). According to Bourdieu, the "taste culture" (or "symbolic culture") of the upper classes gives them advantages in education that benefit them in their subsequent careers (Bourdieu & Passeron 1977).

Consider the way cultural capital is evident among British youths in just two areas: speech patterns and sports. A student who uses the "more educated" speech associated with the upper class may be treated with greater respect by teachers as well as employers. Having a "posh" or "BBC" accent can further a person's career in the executive boardrooms of Britain. Having

gone to an exclusive "public school" (in Britain, those are actually very expensive private schools) can also help, especially for the student who shares the "old school tie" with a potential employer. Likewise, the sports played in British schools have tended to reflect and reinforce class divisions. Soccer, played mostly in working-class schools, has been called a gentlemanly game played by hooligans, while rugby (played mostly in "public schools") is a ruffian's game played by gentlemen.

What's the result? For two candidates with identical marks and qualifications vying for an entry-level position, the decision could come down to which of them possesses the greater cultural capital. Our conflict sociologist might attribute this to the education system, which, as part of its hidden curriculum, reinforces class inequality by encouraging upper-class consumption patterns among certain students at certain schools. Consider such items in the résumé as opportunities for experiences made available by expensive schools (e.g. class trips abroad). Consider also such interview elements as the ability to chat

Parents voted in favour of school uniforms at this primary school in Abbotsford, BC, beginning in September 2012. Does a dress code take cultural capital out of the equation for students from different socioeconomic backgrounds?

The Point Is...

Discipline, Punishment, and Evaluation

Discipline is a large part of education and often forms part of the **hidden curriculum**, the unstated, unofficial agenda of school system authorities. In primary school, discipline is focused on the body, restricting movement, impeding interaction, and normalizing confinement. Children are encouraged to use their "inside voices," to raise their hands before they speak or ask permission to go to the bathroom, to sit quietly in their seats, to keep their hands to themselves, to line up, to be punctual, and so on. Secondary school continues to encourage physical discipline, though disciplining the mind, more than the body, becomes the main goal as this stage.

What is common at all levels of education is the external and internal "routinization" of the individual. Punishment is enacted if the rules are not followed—it may be a "time-out," a trip to the principal's office, a detention, or a poor mark on a report card. Grades are sanctions, designed to either negatively or positively reinforce norms that are ignored or obeyed.

While discipline can be enabling as well as inhibiting—many young students require and indeed thrive on a formalized structure of rules and routines—much of the discipline within the public school system can be considered repressive. It is not simply the body that is curtailed in its movement but also the mind. Children are naturally curious. Curiosity is the basis for asking questions, which is essential in the process of learning. Educators may learn at teacher's college that there are no "stupid questions," but when they have to stick to a strict schedule and a state-mandated curriculum, and when they are under pressure to see their students succeed on province-wide standardized tests that are used to measure the achievements of individual schools and teachers, they may respond negatively to student questions that deviate from the prescribed lesson plan. By the time they reach college and university, students have often lost much of their curiosity. Post-secondary students, too, rarely ask questions with respect to ideas (other than "Is this on the exam?").

In many respects, public education creates what Foucault termed the **docile body**, a group that has been conditioned, through a specific set of procedures and practices, to behave precisely the way administrators want it to (Foucault 1977). Docile bodies are produced through three, decisively modern forms of disciplinary control:

1. hierarchical observation
2. normalizing judgement
3. the examination.

The idea behind **hierarchical observation** is that people are controlled through observation and surveillance. While Foucault used prisons as an example, the principle applies as well to schools, offices, and malls—places where our movements and activities are under constant surveillance within a setting based on hierarchical configurations. Educational institutions are based on a hierarchical structure in which authority figures—instructors and administrators—scrutinize the behaviour of students through observational surveillance. For Foucault, hierarchical observation works on the psychology of the observed individual as much as it governs his or her specific movements. When people assume that they are always being watched, it induces in them an awareness of their permanent visibility, which enhances the power of the authority (Foucault, 1977: 172).

Normalizing judgement is another instrument of disciplinary control that produces docile bodies. Under this model, individuals are judged not on the intrinsic rightness or wrongness of their actions but on how their actions rank when compared with the performance of others. Children are ranked at school, schools are ranked against one another, provincial education is ranked, and the level of education among countries is ranked. Ranking is a cultural artifact that we in Western society take for granted. (Remember: the Huron language has no way of expressing "better" or "worse," "best" or "worst.") Normalizing judgement is a pervasive means of control because regardless of how one succeeds, a higher level of achievement is always possible.

The **examination** combines hierarchical observation with normalizing judgement. Foucault described it as "a normalizing gaze [that] establishes over individuals a visibility through which one differentiates them and judges them" (1977: 184). It is for him, the locus of power and knowledge, because it combines and unifies both "the deployment of force and the establishment of truth" (1977: 184). How? Exam and test scores are documented and recorded, and provide detailed information about those individuals examined. Based on these records, various categories, averages, and norms are formulated by those in control, and these become the basis of knowledge. Power remains invisible, while those constructed as deviant become highly visible: those students with the thickest files are scrutinized by scores of anonymous, invisible functionaries (Foucault 1977: 189). Remember that deviance reflects difference from the norm. Both Lisa and Bart Simpson have the thickest files at school, but for different reasons.

Students from a New York high school line up to leave their cellphones and other electronic devices—for a dollar a day per item—at the truck of an enterprising businessman parked a short distance from the school. The public school ban on cellphones is largely ignored except in schools with metal detectors at the door. Some public schools in Ontario were considering metal detectors after high-profile knife and gun crimes on school premises. Does this create a safe and secure environment or a "docile" one?

knowledgeably about the artwork on display in the interview room, or to engage in small talk about other topics that might show cultural capital (music, film, fashion, and so on).

Cultural Reproduction Theory

Jeannie Oakes and the Hidden Curriculum of Tracking

Does the education system, as part of its hidden curriculum, really reproduce class divisions, as our conflict sociologist might argue? **Jeannie Oakes** put this idea, also known as **cultural reproduction theory**, to the test in an influential study of tracking (or "streaming") in junior and senior high schools; her findings are published in *Keeping Track: How Schools Structure Inequality* (2005). Oakes defines **tracking** as "the process whereby students are divided into categories so that they can be assigned in groups to various kinds of classes" (Oakes 2005: 3). Both classes and students are ranked according to different levels of aptitude and projected outcomes, such as whether or not students are expected to pursue a post-secondary degree. Oakes studied 297 classrooms in 25 schools in the late 1970s and early 1980s. Her work demonstrated that sorting is based at least as much on class, "race," and ethnicity as it is on perceived ability. She also showed that lower tracks often offer lower quality of education than the higher tracks do. As a consequence, the American tracking system reproduces inequality.

Oakes argued that the disproportionate representation of lower-class and non-white students in the lower track reflects the cultural biases of testing and the prejudices of counsellors and teachers. The inferior quality of lower-track education came partly from the reduced expectations for the students in the lower track. Lower-track English courses emphasized basic punctuation and form-filling as opposed to great works of literature. Lower-track math courses emphasized basic computational skills rather than problem solving, critical thinking, and abstract logic. Lower-track vocational courses focused on clerical skills, not the managerial and financial skills taught in the higher-track courses.

Another important finding relates to differences in classroom time spent on instruction and learning activities versus administrative routines and discipline. The average amounts of classroom time spent on instruction in English and math courses in the higher track were 82 per cent and 77 per cent, respectively; the comparable figures for lower-track instruction time were 71 per cent and 63 per cent.

From a cultural reproduction standpoint, it is also important to look at relationship differences between teachers and students, among students, and between students and the institution generally. Samuel Bowles and Harold Gintis point to the "close correspondence between the social relationships which govern personal interaction in the work place and the social relationships of the educational system" (1976: 12). In other words, in terms of social relationships, the education system trains students in the lower track to become lower-class workers. Oakes summarized their position as follows:

> These [lower-class] workers will be subordinate to external control and alienated from the institutions but willing to conform to the needs of the work place, to a large extent because of the way they were treated in school. . . . Bowles and Gintis suggest that the absence of close interpersonal relationships is characteristic of both lower-class work environments and classroom environments for lower-class children. In contrast, upper- and middle-class students, destined for upper-status and middle-level positions in the economic hierarchy, are more likely to experience social relationships and interactions that promote active involvement, affiliation with others, and the internalization of rules and behavioral standards. Self-regulation is the goal here rather than the coercive authority and control seen as appropriate for the lower class. (Oakes 2005: 119–20)

Oakes found that teachers were more punitive in lower-track classes, while higher-track classes fostered more trusting teacher–student relationships. In her words, "[t]rust, cooperation, and even good will among students were far less characteristic of low-track classes than of high. More student time and energy were spent in hostile and disruptive interchanges in these classes" (2005: 132).

Key to cultural reproduction theory is the **legitimization of inequality**. If students accept that their differential tracking placement is fair, this legitimizes the inequality reproduced by the education system. Oakes found that "students in low-track classes tended to be saying that school's all right, but I'm not so good.

QUICK HITS

Student Examples from Oakes's Study

What is the most important thing you have learned or done so far in the class (in terms of subject matter)?

Answers from the High Track

- "We've talked about stocks/bonds and the stock market and about business in the USA." (student in junior high vocational education)
- "Learned to analyze famous writings by famous people, and we have learned to understand people's different viewpoints on general ideas." (student in junior high English)
- "The most important thing is the way other countries and places govern themselves economically, socially, and politically. Also different philosophers and their theories on government and man and how their theories relate to us and now." (student in junior high social studies)

Answers from the Low Track

- "Learns to fill out checks and other banking business." (student in junior high English)
- "to spell words you don't know, to fill out things where you get a job." (student in junior high English)
- "I learned that English is boring." (student in senior high school English)

Source: Oakes 2005: 68–71.

What do YOU think?

1. The strongest opposition to de-tracking comes from those involved with education of the "gifted." Why do you think they are more opposed to de-tracking than those involved with low-track education?

2. Imagine that you're the principal of a high school that is considering a tracking or streaming program. Come up with a list of pros and cons. How might your list change depending on such social factors as the class, ethnicity, and overall demographics of your school?

In contrast, students in high-track classes were feeling pretty good about both their schools *and* themselves" (2005: 143–4).

Overall, Oakes believes that with the deep class, ethnic, and racial distinctions existing in mainstream American society, a tracking system can only reproduce inequality. She argues for more of a common curriculum shared by all students, and for more mixing of students of different ability levels.

Jean Anyon: Cultural Reproduction Theory in Five New Jersey Schools

An important aspect of cultural reproduction theory is the **reproduction of the social structure**, whereby institutions such as education help upper-class children grow up to be upper-class adults, middle-class children become middle-class adults, and so on. A useful study demonstrating this aspect of cultural reproduction theory is **Jean Anyon**'s "Social Class and the Hidden Curriculum of Work" (1980), based on an ethnographic study of five elementary schools in New Jersey she carried out in 1978–9. Two of the schools she identified as working class. Here, most of the fathers had semi-skilled or unskilled jobs (assembly line work, auto repair or assembly, maintenance work); 15 per cent of the fathers were unemployed, and less than 30 per cent of the mothers worked. According to Anyon, schoolwork in these schools

> . . . is following the steps of a procedure. The procedure is usually mechanical, involving rote behavior [i.e. drilled memorization] and very little decision making or choice. The teachers rarely explain why the work is being assigned, how it might connect to other assignments, or what the idea is that lies behind the procedure or gives it coherence and perhaps meaning or significance. . . . Most of the rules regarding work are designations of what the children are to do; the rules are steps to follow. . . . The children are usually told to copy the steps as notes. These notes are to be studied. Work is often evaluated not according to whether it is right or wrong but according to whether the children followed the right steps. (Anyon 1980)

Students at a third school, identified as middle class, had parents working in skilled, well-paid trades (such as carpentry, plumbing, or electrical work), working as professionals (fire fighting, teaching, accounting, etc.), or owning small businesses. Schoolwork here was all about "getting the right answer":

One must follow the directions in order to get the right answers, but the directions often call for some figuring, some choice, some decision making. For example, the children must figure out by themselves what the directions ask them to do and how to get the answer: what do you do first, second, and perhaps third? Answers are usually found in books or by listening to the teacher. Answers are usually words, sentences, numbers, or facts and dates; one writes them on paper, and one should be neat. Answers must be given in the right order, and one cannot make them up. (Anyon 1980)

A fourth school, identified as "affluent professional," had students whose parents were employed as corporate lawyers, engineers, and advertising executives. At this school, the work involved

. . . creative activity carried out independently. The students are continually asked to express and apply ideas and concepts. Work involves individual thought and expressiveness, expansion and illustration of ideas, and choice of appropriate method and material. . . . The products of work in this class are often written stories, editorials, and essays, or representations of ideas in mural, graph, or craft form. The products of work should not be like anybody else's and should show individuality. . . . One's product is usually evaluated for the quality of its expression and for the appropriateness of its conception to the task. (Anyon 1980)

The fifth school Anyon called "executive elite," as most of the students' fathers held positions as presidents and vice-presidents of major corporations (it was 1979, remember, so most of the mothers would not have been working). In this school, work involved

. . . developing one's analytical intellectual powers. Children are continually asked to reason through a problem, to produce intellectual products that are both logically sound and of top academic quality. A primary goal of thought is to conceptualize rules by which elements may fit together in systems and then to apply these rules in solving a problem. (Anyon 1980)

QUICK HITS

Social Mobility: Meritocracy versus Cultural Reproduction

During the 1960s, John Porter wrote:

No society in the modern period can afford to ignore the ability which lies in the lower social strata. Whatever may be said about average intelligence and social class, the fact remains that in absolute numbers there is more of the highly intelligent in lower classes than in the higher. If the principles of efficiency and equality are to be upheld, Canada must be prepared to put a great deal more money into education and educational research than it has. . . . Without such policies, intergenerational continuity of class will remain [and] mobility deprivation will continue. (cited in Helmes-Hayes 2010: 137–8)

There are two fundamentally opposing positions concerning education and social mobility. One is that education is **meritocratic**: academic performance reflects natural ability (i.e. merit), and the system provides mobility for those lower-class and minoritized students who work hard to succeed. Cultural reproduction theory, by contrast, argues that the education system reproduces and reinforces the inequality of the surrounding society. See if you can flesh out the argument for each side. Which one has more merit to you as an accurate statement about education in Canada as you have experienced it?

If there were a sociology class offered at this school level, daily activities in each category might look like this:

working-class school	copying down and memorizing the instructor's notes from the board
middle-class school	reading the textbook and finding the right answer
affluent professional school	finding information on an assigned topic and writing it up in one's own words
executive elite school	analyzing social systems and looking for strengths and weaknesses

Homework and Its Sociological Effects

Sociologists study homework for a number of reasons. One is to gauge the extent to which homework helps to reproduce class structure (if you're beginning to see that this is a recurring theme in the sociology of education, you're right). Children raised by educated, middle- and upper middle-class parents have a number of advantages with respect to homework. Their parents are typically better able to understand the instructions for an assignment and so are in a better position to help their children (sometimes to the point of doing the entire project themselves). The children of better-off parents also tend to live in larger homes, where they have a quiet, dedicated space for doing homework, as well as a good-quality computer, high-speed Internet access, a colour printer, and other aids to completing their work. As a result, the more a course depends on homework as opposed to classwork, the more it favours children from middle- and upper middle-class households.

The amount of homework a child receives can also have a profound effect on family life, regardless of the socioeconomic situation of the child's family. In 2008, Linda Cameron and Lee Bartel published the findings of a study on the impact of homework on Canadian households. Their research was based on an online questionnaire completed by over 1,000 parents, the vast majority of them from Ontario. Of the 10 main conclusions drawn from the qualitative part of the questionnaire, two related to family life. The first was that homework "reduces family time":

> Homework is often seen as an incursion on what should be discretionary family time. . . . One parent stated it this way: "My children are in the educational institution for 6.5 hours per day. I feel this should be sufficient time to complete any school-related tasks. I am with them for significantly less time and would prefer to use this time engaging in activities to promote our relationship and increase bonding in order to reduce their stress levels." Consequently, parents often expressed feelings of resentment toward homework and the effect it has on family balance. (Cameron & Bartel 2008: 53)

The second finding related to family life was that homework "affects family relationships." According to the authors, homework was found to be "a primary source of arguments, power struggles, and disruptive to building a strong family." In the words of one respondent cited by the report's authors, "Fights over homework with my children are common and very upsetting" (Cameron & Bartel 2008: 54).

What do YOU think?

1. If you were the principal of an elementary school, what reasons might you give for "banning homework"?

2. What would you need to study sociologically before you could make such a decision?

Issues in Aboriginal Education

The Politics of Representation in Textbooks

Textbooks form an important and influential part of education, and yet they remain an understudied topic in the sociology of education. For my doctoral dissertation, I examined the representation of Aboriginal people in 77 Canadian introductory sociology textbooks. What I discovered was a serious and progressive lack of Aboriginal voice. Aboriginal writers were not represented as a significant source of information on their own people. In Michel Foucault's terminology, theirs were **disqualified knowledges**—"knowledges that have been disqualified as inadequate to their task" (Foucault 1980: 82). Foucault might have argued that Aboriginal writers were not included because they were not scientific or objective enough for the writers of sociology textbooks. Yet their viewpoints offer a legitimate alternative to standard sociology knowledge.

Early Canadian introductory sociology textbooks entailed collections of readings. As sociologists were not studying Aboriginal people then, contributions written about Aboriginal people were typically authored by outsiders to sociology, including Inuit leader Abraham Okpik, Ojibwa author Wilfred Pelletier, and Cree politician and scholar Harold Cardinal. When sociologists began studying Aboriginal people in urban settings in the early 1970s, the Aboriginal voice was lost from sociology textbooks: the only coverage of Aboriginal people came from non-Aboriginal sociologist writers. Since then, the "disqualification" of the Aboriginal voice has been a growing, not diminishing, trend.

Credentialism

Credentialism often blocks Aboriginal attempts to improve education. It is the practice of valuing credentials—degrees, diplomas, certificates—over actual knowledge and ability in the hiring and promotion of staff. In many Aboriginal communities, elders are deeply involved in educating children and young adults. However, elders do not typically carry paper credentials; their qualification comes primarily from community recognition. Elders are people recognized in Aboriginal communities as being experts in traditional knowledge, such as hunting, fishing, spirituality, healing, childcare, and crafts. Most teachers coming from non-Aboriginal communities are not familiar with elders because the role of elder is not assigned significant status in mainstream Canadian society.

Best Practices in British Columbia

Sociological discussions of Aboriginal education tend to focus only on the horrific stories of the residential schools, and the poor academic performance of Aboriginal students since. An alternative perspective comes from a report published by the C.D. Howe Institute (Richards, Hove, & Afolabi 2008). Summarizing the results of a study that examined Aboriginal student performance in non-Aboriginal public schools, the authors identified five "best practices" that are key to student success:

1. collaboration between school district personnel at all levels and local Aboriginal communities
2. commitment by administrators and teachers to incorporating Aboriginal content into the curriculum
3. creation of influential positions (such as full-time teachers and school trustees) dedicated to Aboriginal education
4. relationship building between Aboriginal and non-Aboriginal communities in the district
5. willingness of school district authorities to share responsibility for making decisions with Aboriginal communities.

Interviews revealed that non-Aboriginal teachers often presented obstacles to Aboriginal involvement in their classrooms. While it is easy to say that personal racism is involved, sociologists look primarily for institutional barriers. The Canadian education system teaches very little about Aboriginal people. Most Canadian teachers are ill prepared to work with an Aboriginal curriculum—they are poorly acquainted with Aboriginal history, language, and culture generally because they are products of a school system that

What do you think are the best strategies to ensure that the Aboriginal voice is heard in Canada's classroom?

has failed to adequately cover these subjects. The result is a self-perpetuating form of **institutional racism**.

What do YOU think?

What obstacles might there be to adopting the best practices referred to in this study?

Issues in Post-secondary Education

Post-secondary education in Canada has changed dramatically over the last 30 years. Many of the changes, driven primarily by shifts in economic policies, have not been positive. In spite of the fact that more students than ever are enrolled in post-secondary institutions, tuition fees have risen, while funding of public education has been steadily cut back. There has been an increase in part-time faculty, and in some areas a rapid move away from actual in-class instruction towards online programs and virtual colleges and universities. Grade inflation and plagiarism are both on the rise. Despite this, there has been very little informed public dialogue about how these trends are affecting schools, students, and society. In the sections that follow we will take a close and critical look at these issues and how they affect the quality of post-secondary education in Canada.

Long-Term Adjunct Instructors: An Educational Underclass

The growing ranks of long-term adjunct instructors in post-secondary institutions is the product of several economic and social factors, including the increasing number of post-secondary students, the reduction of government investment in post-secondary education, the increasing levels of private corporate funding, and the rising influence of a corporate culture that regards education just like any other business. The trend of turning full-time teaching positions into long-term adjunct posts is not unlike contracting out skilled jobs to avoid having to grant the benefits or long-term commitment that come with full-time work.

Names for this class of education workers differ. They are commonly referred to as **adjunct professors**, following the American convention, but you may have heard them called "sessionals," "contract staff," or "part-time instructors" (a misleading term, since many put in more hours than full-time instructors do). In Canada, the term "adjunct" is used to refer specifically to an experienced instructor who, because of seniority, is the first in line to take the courses full-time instructors can't or don't want to take on. Originally, adjuncts were professionals who had careers elsewhere—usually in business or in law—and who taught for the prestige and the extra money. This group still exists, but they are now greatly outnumbered by those whose intended career is teaching. Contract teaching used to be a first step on the path towards a full-time job or a tenure-track position. Now that path is narrower and longer.

Ghosts in the Classroom: Stories of College Adjunct Faculty—and the Price We All Pay, edited by Michael Dubson, is a collection of narratives from adjunct professors working at American colleges and universities. Almost all of the contributors are English instructors—not surprising, given that many of them teach writing for a living, and English departments are large, with lots of temporary work for adjuncts. There is a lot of competition for jobs in this area, illustrated in the writers' frequent use of the phrase "dime a dozen" to refer to their competitive position. One of the topics raised repeatedly is the low pay, which is especially tough to swallow given that salaries for full-time staff are well over double what adjunct instructors are paid. One of the collection's contributors speaks eloquently of the sense of **relative deprivation** felt by many adjuncts:

If I teach eight courses in an academic year, I make approximately $16,000. They teach eight to ten courses during an academic year and make, on the average, $40,000. I must horde my money and pinch my pennies for I must live on it during the semester breaks. Full-time teachers get paid all year long, whether they work or not.

Because the pay is so poor, . . . I must string together collections of adjunct course assignments from several different schools. I have taught six, seven, eight classes a semester at three or four different schools. . . . I have worked other jobs and taught on the side. I have split my time between teaching four or five courses, a full-time load, and another job. (M. Theodore Swift, cited in Dubson 2001: 2–3)

Many contributors to the collection comment on their working conditions, which might involve sharing a desk (or not even having a desk) and having restricted use of facilities and equipment like the departmental photocopiers. Jody Lannen Brady's description is typical:

> I shared a dingy office with twenty other instructors, and some semesters I was lucky to find a chair to perch on during my office hours. I often met with students in the hallway because it was quieter than the office. I had one file cabinet drawer I could call my own, but I hauled all my papers and books back and forth from home to office and back each day because I couldn't work in the office, never knowing how many times I would have to jump up and answer the phone, and if I would have a desk to sit at. (cited in Dubson 2001: 147)

What might surprise full-time professors is the extent to which the adjunct instructors feel they are engaged in a "class war" with full-timers. Two excerpts illustrate the point:

At one college, I share office space one day a week with one of the full-time instructors. He put a sign with my name by the door as a sort of welcoming gesture. The next week, the secretary of the English Department wrote me a note. Two of the full-time teachers were in a fury at the arrogance of my putting up a nameplate. (Gale, cited in Dubson 2001: 13)

Once, in a heated personal discussion with a full-time colleague, she blurted out, "Who the hell do you think you are? You're only an adjunct here!" (Werner, cited in Dubson 2001: 37)

Strained relations with colleagues are compounded by trying relationships with the students. Student evaluations are more important to the employment status of adjuncts than they are to the positions of full-time staff members. A poor evaluation won't get a full-timer

Have you been to this site? What do you think are some of the consequences of rating your instructors online? How are these consequences different for adjuncts and full-time professors?

fired, but it could cause an adjunct not to be hired back once the contract has ended. One writer explains:

> If I have poor course evaluations, I will be out. . . . If my students complain about me, legitimately or otherwise, I will be out. If a full-time faculty member faces any of this, he or she will be supported, worked with, helped. Full-time tenured faculty may not even be evaluated, and . . . if their students complain about them, nothing affecting their employment or job security will be done. (Swift, cited in Dubson 2001:3)

It should not be surprising that adjunct professors have been organizing. The kinds of conditions described above were a flashpoint in the strike by graduate student tutorial assistants and part-time instructors at York University in 2008–9.

Online Teaching: A Critical Sociological Approach

During the late 1990s and early 2000s, there was a push throughout North American colleges and universities to offer dramatically more online courses, even to the point of offering online diplomas and degrees, in some cases through "virtual" colleges based entirely online. This was driven by technological improvements, certainly, and by a desire to make education more accessible. But it was also spurred by cuts to post-secondary education funding. The online movement was hyped with the allure of change as progress, and played well to the susceptibility of educators to changes in intellectual fashion. It was also driven by private organizations specializing in delivering educational packages over the Internet, who coined or co-opted sexy terms like "advanced learning" and "open learning," in spite of their yet unproven ability to provide education that is either more advanced or more open. They invest heavily in hosting or attending "educational" conferences (popular perks among post-secondary instructors), where they offer product demonstrations, aided by their "pet" instructors.

The success of online education providers has come at a time when many colleges and universities, feeling the financial pinch, have turned to the private sector as a partial solution to an underfunded public system. The boosters of online education are more often administrators and educational companies looking for the government dollars that flow to public institutions than actual instructors, though the latter group does include believers. Student demand for these courses is more unsupported myth than documented fact.

In post-secondary education, a magic word is **access**. Online courses promise access to education for those who would find it difficult to attend college or university otherwise, the so-called "non-traditional students" (a group that supposedly includes working parents, who have traditionally made good use of night-school courses). As we have seen, **access without mobility** can readily reproduce the class system, while seeming to improve the lot of the more marginalized social groups.

From a sociological standpoint, how do online courses differ from in-class courses? Before addressing this question, it's worth noting that another flawed feature of many a North American university is the large lecture hall, which shares some weaknesses with online courses. The teacher–student relationship that is possible in smaller classes is replaced by a student's relationship with a teaching assistant (or TA), someone who may be at the university only temporarily and is paid significantly less than a full-time, tenured lecturer. This arrangement that features massive classes supported by smaller tutorials is, like the online movement, driven by the perceived economics of post-secondary education. When we talk in this chapter about in-class teaching, we are referring to classes held in the more intimate classroom setting, not the lecture hall or theatre.

Critics of the online movement fear that it is driven mainly by economics rather than access to education. Interestingly, though, the savings supposedly achieved by online education may be more apparent than real: acquiring and upgrading expensive technical equipment combined with hiring of additional technical and administrative staff can drastically reduce the profit margin.

When boosting revenue becomes the main objective, it leads to the **commodification** of education. Noble (2002) describes this as

> the disintegration and distillation of the educational experience into discrete, reified, and ultimately saleable things or packages of things. In the first step toward commodification, attention is shifted from the experience of the people involved in the educational process to the production and inventorying of an assortment of "course materials"; syllabi, lectures, lessons, exams. . . . As anyone

familiar with higher education knows, these common instruments of instruction barely reflect what actually takes place in the educational experience, and lend an illusion of order and predictability to what is, at its best, an essentially unscripted and undetermined process. Second, these fragments are removed or "alienated" from their original context, the actual educational process itself, and from their producers, the teachers, and are assembled as "courses," which take on an existence independent of and apart from those who created and gave flesh to them. (Noble 2002: 3)

Important here is the Marxist concept of **alienation**, which entails the separation or disconnect between people and the work that they are paid to do. People working on assembly lines are disconnected from what they do. The workers have no say in what they do or how they do it, and there is no personal fingerprint on their labour. Chefs who have signature dishes are closely connected with their work; people working the fry counter at McDonald's are not. In a similar way, instructors can become disconnected from their **intellectual property** when it is used as part of an online course. Noble elaborates:

> Once faculty put their course material online, . . . the knowledge and course design skill embodied in that material is taken out of their possession. . . . The administration is now in a position to hire . . .

The Point Is...

Online Education: A New Spin on a Failed Idea?

Historian David Noble (2002) reminds us that a movement similar to the online education movement happened from the 1880s to the 1930s, when correspondence courses—which enabled students to receive lessons and submit their work by mail, became popular. The movement began with independent, privately run schools, before the universities, fearing competition and eager to benefit from a relatively easy source of profit, got involved. People marketing the correspondence courses used a language that would be familiar to educators today, as they reached out to "non-traditional students" with the promise of "working on your own time." Mostly, however, post-secondary administrators eyed not the chance to bring higher education to the masses but a good source of profit with relatively low overhead costs. Tuition was paid up front and was non-refundable, yet the dropout rate was high—the vast majority never completed their courses. Noble refers to the main source of profit as "drop-out money." At the same time, the faculty involved were underpaid, receiving between 25 and 35 cents a lesson. By the 1930s, although correspondence courses continued to be offered, the institutions involved were criticized for being "diploma mills" serving up an inferior education.

The factors that sparked the establishment of correspondence courses in the late nineteenth century are similar to the ones that have created a favourable environment for the growth of online education today:

- the rise of *credentialism* (setting value on credentials such as certificates and diplomas)
- funding cuts, sending universities and colleges in search of new sources of revenue
- the development of private training companies
- the rapid development of information technology (then, of course, advances in mail delivery services).

Noble sees online courses as suffering from the same flaws that plagued correspondence courses—profit considered over education, poorly paid staff with very little job security, and, on average, an inferior education when measured against its in-class equivalent. Historian George Santayana famously said, "Those who cannot remember the past are condemned to repeat it." Shouldn't colleges and universities learn the lessons of history here?

cheaper workers to deliver the technologically prepackaged course. It also allows the administration, . . . to peddle the course elsewhere without the original designer's involvement or even knowledge, much less financial interest. The buyers of this packaged commodity, meanwhile, . . . are able thereby to contract out . . . the work of their own employees and thus reduce their reliance upon their in-house teaching staff. (Noble 1998)

Alienation involves the hierarchical control of a product, in which the boss has ultimate say in how it is developed, used, and distributed. With online courses, the potential for administrative monitoring and control increases. Instructors can be more closely supervised through the educational products they have supplied for the course's website. Online courses also allow administrators to measure instructor interactions with students: How often are instructors logging on? How responsive are they to students' online questions? This kind of supervision is also possible with course components offered by means of packaged Web products like Blackboard (an American company that took over the University of British Columbia's WebCT software, thereby gaining a powerful foothold on post-secondary education in Canada).

Online universities such as the University of Phoenix in the US and Canada's Athabasca University are staffed with relatively few full-time instructors and many "tutors." Professors fear that this is the face of the future: part-time and limited-time contract staff dominating over full-time teachers. The following statement from Meritus University, which opened its virtual doors in September 2008, shows that they indeed have something to fear:

While others established academic programs around tradition and tenure, Apollo has built

Coursera is an education provider that has partnered up with several big North American universities—including the University of Toronto and the University of British Columbia—to offer "massive open online courses" ("MOOCs"), interactive online courses that are essentially free. Is free online learning the way of the future? What are the pros and cons of teaching in a chatroom rather than a classroom? Do you think they are more likely to be taught by adjunct or full-time staff? How do you think professors feel about this development?

programs in conjunction with the needs of business and industry—effectively translating those needs into clear and transparent learning objectives.

In its first semester, Meritus University had just four full-time teaching staff.

The online delivery of education depends, like many exploitative systems, on getting workers to do more than they are paid for, relying on dedicated teachers who improve a bad situation with their talent and their labour. But there are also those who "work to rule," who calculate exactly how much work they have to do to get paid and do no more. At that point, the system fails the student.

So what about the students? We know that these courses suffer from significant dropout rates. Students who succeed are typically highly motivated, highly disciplined people, who get through despite the flaws inherent in the method of delivery. The good marks they get represent triumphs of individuals over systems.

Online education may work better for some kinds of courses. It lends itself more to **instrumental education**, where courses are narrowly directed to particular sets of tasks, than to **critical education**, which involves analysis of ideas and, ideally, classroom discussion. With online courses, as the information flow is more one-directional than in the classroom, more controlled by the curriculum than by student–teacher interaction, students have less input into how the course proceeds. Their instructors have less input as well, since they are typically part-timers, vulnerable to administrative control.

There is reason to worry that a two-tiered, two-class system will develop, with the middle and upper classes attending in-class institutions ("brick universities") and preparing for jobs that will maintain their family's class standing, while those "attending" the digital institutions ("click universities") will be lower-class students and others for whom regular college or university attendance is impossible (including, for instance, single mothers and other working parents). They will receive lower-cost virtual vocational training that will lead them to lower-level, lower-paying service jobs. These are also the people most likely to suffer, academically as well as socially, from the isolation that comes with online courses, and the ones who would most benefit from in-class discussions. In this way, the system will reproduce rather than challenge the North American class system.

What do YOU think?

1. What arguments would supporters of online education mount to combat the arguments given here?

2. Why might a sociology instructor be more critical of online education than an instructor from another discipline (business, for example)?

3. How could you do research that would test the effectiveness or ineffectiveness of online education?

Do You Want Fries with that Degree?

Students joke about the **McJob**—the low-paying, unskilled service job—they might get with their undervalued degree once they've graduated. What the term refers to is **underemployment**, which can have two meanings relevant to our discussion of education:

- involuntary part-time work for people seeking full-time employment
- low-wage, low-skill employment for people with valuable skills, experience, or academic credentials.

Statistics Canada defines "underemployed" as "seeking full-time work but finding only part-time work." The category does not include those who have been unable to work full-time for health or other personal reasons, nor does it acknowledge the problem of an over-skilled workforce. Underemployment is the result of several factors, including:

- the rate of unemployment
- regional disparity (lack of employment opportunities and resources like training and childcare in economically depressed areas)
- discrimination based on ethnicity, gender, disability, or lack of "appropriate" credentials.

How does this apply to post-secondary students? Those who hold high-quality skills and academic credentials become underemployed when there is low marketplace demand—a demand determined not just by the strength or weakness of the Canadian or global economy but, in the case of Canada, demographics. The demographic bulge caused by the baby boomers means that access to employment is cut off for those newly entering the workforce, many of whom may be better qualified than their predecessors. Sustained underemployment also means that skills acquired from one's degree (critical and analytical thinking, writing, researching, etc.) can wither from disuse.

During the 1990s, universities produced 1.2 million graduates, but only 600,000 jobs requiring university-level credentials were created during that same period. Currently, there are about one million students in the post-secondary system. If job creation remains the same as it did in the 1990s, then several hundred thousand graduates each year will be pursuing fewer than 100,000 job openings. This could effectively increase the structural underemployment rate from the 50 per cent level found in the 1980s and 1990s to 75 per cent.

In the case of new college and university graduates, underemployment can result from a lack of practical experience, even for those who have technical training in a specific field or who are seeking employment when the job market is strong. As a result, recent graduates may be forced to work in low-paying or part-time jobs until they find work in their field. Canadian studies conducted between 1982 and 2004 suggest that while post-secondary education attainment has increased for various occupational classes, so too has the underemployment rate for those same occupational classes. The same research also shows that the rate of underemployment is greater than the underqualified rate. Forty-five per cent of those aged 18–24 see themselves as being overqualified for their current jobs as opposed to 22 per cent of those 40 and over (Livingstone 2004).

Among the solutions that have been proposed to reduce skill-based underemployment are government-imposed restrictions on enrolment in post-secondary courses and programs with low labour market demand. However, the university system would be unable to support such a proposal, as it would reduce student enrolment and, therefore, revenues.

The Sociology of Plagiarism

Ask any professor about the problems of teaching at a post-secondary institution, and he or she will talk about **plagiarism**. This is particularly true of instructors teaching courses in the social sciences and the humanities—courses with a heavy grade component based on essay writing.

Carol Thompson defines plagiarism as "the wholesale copying of another's work or the collaging of several papers (or Web sites) via the Internet." (2006). Basically it involves passing off someone else's ideas or work as your own. The ideas and words aren't yours, and the sources of those ideas and words aren't properly identified or even mentioned.

Thompson adopts a sociological approach to address why plagiarism has become such a common phenomenon. She emphasizes the influence of **role models**, asserting that students have the very patterns

A recent university graduate takes his job search to the streets of Halifax. Should governments be allowed to cap enrolment in disciplines with low labour market demand? Or is up to the student to find the educational path most likely to lead to meaningful employment? What's your plan to avoid underemployment after graduation?

of behaviour they're warned not to fall into modelled for them by professors, school administrators, and even famous writers and academics, like American historian Stephen Ambrose (historical consultant for Stephen Spielberg's *Saving Private Ryan*) and the Pulitzer Prize–winning Doris Kearns Goodwin. In Canada the list could include Prime Minister Stephen Harper, whose speech in 2003 supporting the American attack on Iraq was copied almost word for word from a speech made by Australian Prime Minister John Howard two days earlier. More influential could be parents, who have often helped students in writing and assembling their projects in high school, and who may get involved in their children's post-secondary work as well. The idea that the work submitted does not have to have been prepared entirely on one's own could stem from that experience of having received help from parents.

Plagiarism has spawned two booming industries. One is the essay industry, represented by a number of websites such as SchoolSucks, Genius Papers, and AcaDemon that sell students ready-composed or, for a higher fee, customized papers. These companies are not engaged in anything that is technically against the law, although the means they sometimes use to obtain papers do involve theft of academic property. Copyright laws are fuzzy about academic work. The fact that there are numerous companies of this kind out there, set up to accept your credit card number or payment via PayPal, might make the practice seem legitimate.

The industry can benefit graduate students, who are often desperate for money and will take cash for their writing. They are trained to write academic papers. By selling their services to Web-based essay providers, they are capitalizing on their hard-earned skills in an industry in which these skills are valued.

Another group that profits from plagiarism are businesses that claim to be able to catch the plagiarizers, which sell their services to colleges and universities. They expand their database with every post-secondary institution that pays for their services. You have to wonder how many people working on this side of the business once worked on the other side, like hackers who become computer security specialists.

A potential social factor in the willingness to plagiarize is **social distance**. If you know your instructors, and they recognize you by name or by sight, then you are less likely to submit a plagiarized essay, since it would be like cheating a friend or lying to a parent.

However, if your professor is just a blurry face at the front of a crowded lecture theatre, or an even more anonymous presence online, the social distance is far greater. Plagiarism might be like stealing from a large corporation. It appears to be a "victimless crime," since there is no identifiable injured party. This would make for interesting sociological research: Is there more plagiarism in lower-level courses than in upper-level courses (where the classes are smaller and less likely to be offered online)? Is it more common in larger institutions than in smaller ones?

Cultures of Education

It's also worth considering plagiarism in terms of **cultures of education**. In mainstream Western culture there is a tendency to emphasize the individual's competition with others. This emphasis is made stronger when, for instance, a large first-year course is known to allow a fixed number of students to graduate with A's, or is marked on a bell curve. This makes these precious marks more valuable by putting them in limited supply (rather like gold). Honours students have their names posted in front of department offices. Students receive awards primarily for individual performance.

Other cultures put a greater emphasis on the group. Aboriginal students, for example, have traditionally not wanted to be singled out in class. They whisper answers to peers who have been asked to reply to teacher questions, so that there will be no embarrassment for a classmate who doesn't know the answer. Research has shown that they are typically more likely to share answers on tests, the same way they would help their family members and friends. The cultural value of sharing is higher than in mainstream Canadian culture.

The Western culture of education also emphasizes putting what you say "in your own words." While that may seem natural to most Canadian students, think about the following parallels. Most Canadians do not program their own computers "with their own programs," or fix their cars "with their own parts" or "to their own design." They turn to experts, the masters and the patterns they have set. There are cultural traditions in which "repeating the words of the master" is more valued than personalizing an answer. When foreign students come to Canada (paying much more for their education than Canadian citizens), they are unlikely to have been told about how education in

What in this ad makes this service seem morally legitimate and socially acceptable?

Canada follows a different model. There might be a class component here as well. In Anyon's 1980 work on the class-based hidden curriculum in education, working-class schools were taught to copy steps, while the middle-class schools stressed finding the right answer; only at the affluent professional or elite executive schools were students encouraged to put things "in their own words." (For the record, we are *not* encouraging you to plagiarize, or to attempt to excuse yourself from charges of plagiarism on the basis of your class or cultural status.)

Another influential aspect of the Western culture of education is the increasingly corporate nature of post-secondary institutions, where students are viewed as customers (or "stakeholders"—a hideous term). Students may feel that it is their right as consumers to appeal grades or even to sue. As long as school administrators feel that their institutions are competing for students, they may be reluctant to cultivate an unfavourable reputation by aggressively pursuing plagiarizers, risking bad publicity. And with the increased level of credentialism—the emphasis on "getting the piece of paper," a physical consumer product—rather than on learning, students may act more like customers than like learning apprentices. Should we be surprised, then, when resourceful students buy term papers over the Internet?

The corporate culture of the post-secondary institution is also expressed and experienced internally, within the institution, and can have an influence on how plagiarism is treated and judged. Departments where students write a lot of essays (sociology, anthropology, history, literature, philosophy, and so on) are more involved in providing electives to students who are studying in different programs than in training majors in their fields of study. Pressure can be brought to bear on a department's administrator by administrators of the students' programs to "just let my student pass," rather than doggedly pursuing cases of plagiarism. The competition for students goes on within colleges and universities, as different departments attempt to draw students to take their electives. A popular course gains status for the department and can be used to justify new hires and a higher budget. A course with a high rate of catching plagiarism offenders is not popular. The increased use of temporary, sessional, or adjunct professors, who typically don't want to "rock the boat" with administrators, also weakens the impulse to take a firm stand against plagiarism. They want to be seen as "team players" so that they will get hired again. Finally, as Thompson notes, when it comes to plagiarism, word gets around. Those schools that have a clear policy of dealing strictly with plagiarism have fewer instances of the offence. Where people often "get away" with it, student culture might simply become supportive of plagiarism.

What do YOU think?

1. Why do you think that plagiarism is on the rise at post-secondary institutions in Canada?

2. Do you accept the idea that students should always be encouraged to put things "in their own words"?

WRAP IT UP

Summary

We live in a time in which there are a number of important choices to make concerning the future of our education system. The sociology of education can help make those choices truly informed and democratic. At base, the most important issue is whether the Canadian education system—from primary school all the way up to our post-secondary institutions—is fundamentally meritocratic or whether it serves more to reproduce the class system and cultural privileges of the culturally dominant. At the elementary and secondary level, we need to ensure the suitability of the curriculum so that marginalized peoples get to read and hear about people like themselves. The effects of "streaming" (or "tracking") must be seriously studied. At the post-secondary level, we need to look critically at such practices as the increasing dependence on adjuncts, on corporate sponsorship, and on online education to uncover the potential harm as well as benefits that they may bring.

THINK BACK

Questions for Critical Review

1. Summarize the factors that contribute to the growing problem of plagiarism. Which factors make plagiarism possible? Which ones encourage it? Are there any factors that legitimize it? Is it really the problem we think it is? If so, how would you address it? Consider factors outside of education, such as online music sharing and music sampling—do we live in a society where originality and authorship are less valued than they once were?

2. What do you see as the connection between the rise in online education and the growing reliance on adjunct professors? Are they both symptoms of the same factors? Which ones?

3. Have you experienced being "overqualified" for a job? Was it possible for you to "take the job seriously," as a less qualified worker might be able to do?

Answers to the Quiz on page 424: *Does your knowledge of geography reflect a monocultural education?*

1. c	6. f	11. q	16. b
2. r	7. t	12. j	17. o
3. g	8. a	13. s	18. m
4. h	9. d	14. l	19. p
5. k	10. e	15. n	20. i

READ ON

ONLINE

"In Defense of the Traditional Classroom: An Argument Against the Move to Online Classes"

www.articlemyriad.com/argument-traditional-classroom-online/

This online article defends the value of the traditional classroom. To better under-stand the other side of the argument, have a look at university webpages defending the move to Coursera, like the following, from UBC: http://ctlt.ubc.ca/2012/09/27/ubc-to-offer-free-online-courses-through-coursera/

People for Education

www.peopleforeducation.ca

This parent-led and parent-focused guide to educational issues in Ontario offers news and views, as well as research reports and survey findings.

Stop Homework

http:/stophomework.com

This website, initiated by one of the authors of *The Case Against Homework*, is now a discussion forum for parents and students concerned about homework.

IN PRINT

James Côté & Anton Allahar (2011), *Lowering Higher Education: The Rise of Corporate Universities and the Fall of Liberal Education* (Toronto: University of Toronto).

This work, from two University of Western Ontario sociologists, looks at the effects on education of universities forming closer ties with large corporations.

George Dei & Agnes Calliste (2000), *Power Knowledge and Anti-Racism Education: A Critical Reader* (Halifax: Fernwood Publishing).

An informative collection of readings on what anti-racism education entails.

Michael Dubson, ed. (2001), *Ghosts in the Classroom: Stories of College Adjunct Faculty—and the Price We All Pay* (Boston: Camel's Back Books).

This book illustrates, through examples written by adjunct professors, the experiences and perspectives of this educational underclass.

Jeannie Oakes (2005), *Keeping Track: How Schools Structure Inequality*, 2nd edn (New Haven, CT: Yale University Press).

A classic critique of the cultural reproduction function of tracking or streaming students.

John Richards, Jennifer Hove, & Kemi Afolabi (2008), *Understanding the Aboriginal/ Non-Aboriginal Gap in Student Performance: Lessons from British Columbia* (Toronto: C.D. Howe Institute).

A useful guide to strategies used to improve Aboriginal education.

17 Work

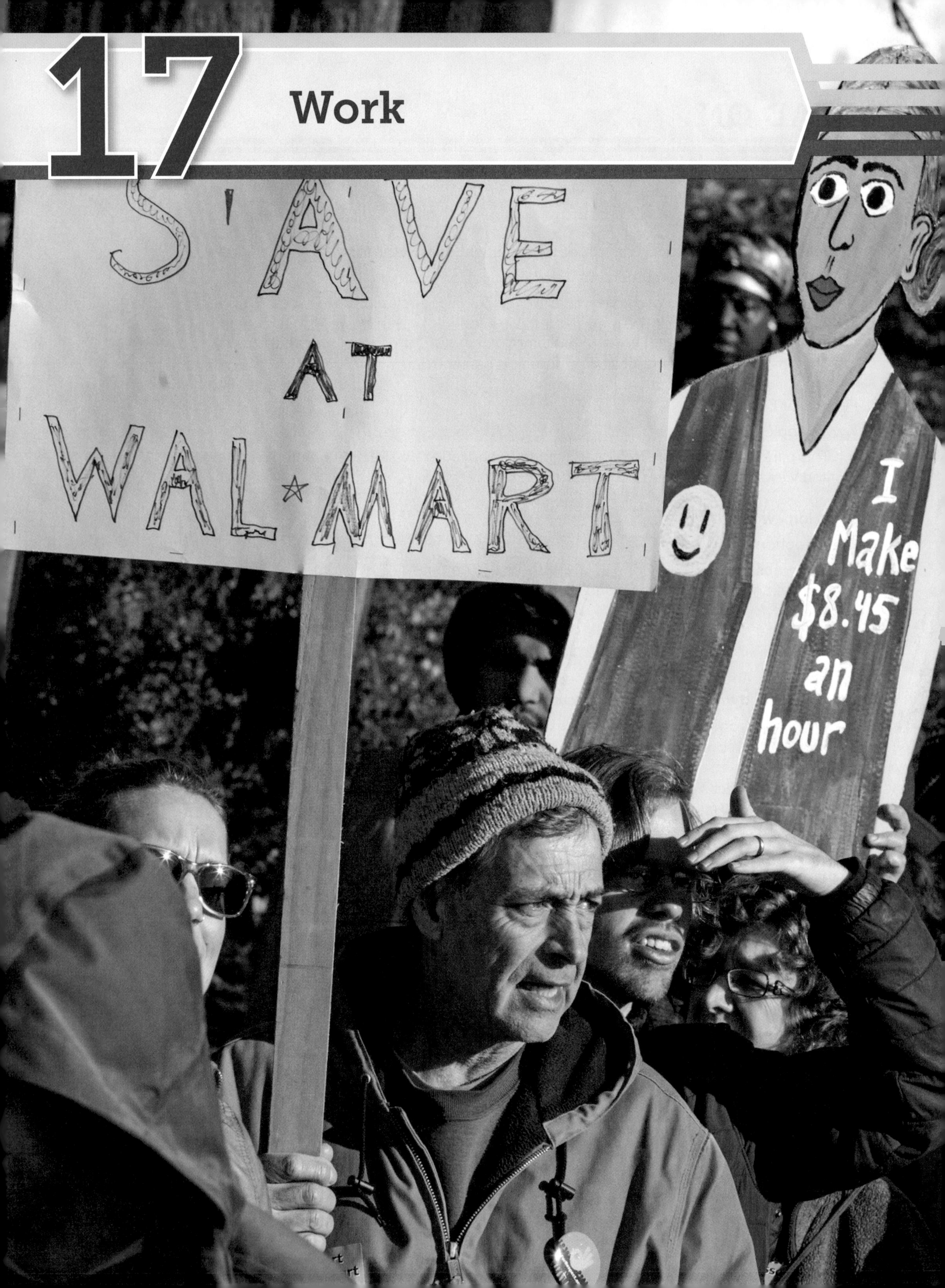

Learning Objectives

After reading this chapter, you should be able to

- distinguish between *mechanical solidarity* and *organic solidarity*, as articulated by Durkheim
- explain Marx's view of the relationship between worker and owner
- discuss the differences between left-wing and right-wing views regarding work
- outline the differences between *individual rights* and *collective rights*
- describe how the political culture of Canada differs from that of the United States in terms of union density
- talk about the connection that is often made between patriotism and anti-union sentiment, using the Winnipeg general strike and the Bienfait strike as examples
- outline C. Wright Mills' five points about mass media and unions
- talk about whether and why a gendered wage gap exists today in Canada
- suggest some possible outcomes of the globalization of labour.

Key Terms

- amalgamated unions
- aristocrats
- bourgeoisie
- class consciousness
- closed shop
- collective bargaining
- craft unions
- dictatorship of the proletariat
- disposable workers
- division of labour
- equal pay
- ethnic industries
- general strike
- guilds
- ideology
- image of limited good
- industrial unions
- left-wing
- living wage
- lockout
- means of production
- mechanical solidarity
- minimum wage
- neoliberalism
- open shop
- operational definition
- organic solidarity
- outsourcing
- owners
- paid work
- pay equity
- peasants
- pin money
- proletariat
- racial industries
- right-to-work laws
- right-wing
- solidarity
- special interest (groups)
- strike
- trickle-down theory
- union density
- unpaid work
- wildcat strike
- workers
- working poor
- work limitations

Names to Know

- Émile Durkheim
- George Foster
- Anne Marion McLean
- Karl Marx
- C. Wright Mills

Walking the Line in '89: A Canadian Observer at the Pittston Coal Miners' Strike

As a community college instructor, I have been involved in three strikes. I have felt the anxiety and the camaraderie of the picket line. I have had my spirits buoyed by rumours of imminent settlements and dashed by news of stalled talks. I have held up traffic, stopped cars, and been grazed by ones that didn't stop (one reason for my intense dislike of black BMWs). I have had sympathetic listeners (I once got on a bus to explain a strike to a supportive unionized driver), and I have had people tell me that I should get back to work, politely and not so politely (a memorable, heated exchange ended when I was told to "go f—k myself," to which I replied—cleverly, I thought—"Any love is good love," quoting a lyric from the great Winnipeg band BTO).

I believe in the right to strike, but I haven't always voted for a strike. I have been paid good wages in several jobs as a unionized worker, and paid badly as a non-unionized worker.

I got my job in 1986 because of a successful strike the year before, in which instructors won a reduction in teaching hours from 18 (teaching six classes) to 15 (five classes), leading to a large hiring of new faculty. In October 1989, I did my first picketing. Partway through the strike I flew down to rural Virginia for a four-day lecture tour at Southwest Virginia Community College. I spent a night and a day with a coal miner, his wife (a college student), and their son, who treated me like one of their own (they even gave me moonshine in a mason jar). Coal mining is an important industry in that part of the country, and at the time, there was a strike at the local coal mine (I touched on this in Chapter 3, with respect to the symbolism of jackrocks). It had been going on since April, and it gave me a feel for what a "real strike" was like.

The coal miner took me for a drive by his mine. He told me that a police officer would appear if we stopped.

Wanting to see what a southern cop looked like (were they as scary as they looked in the movies?) and being a troublemaker by nature, I asked him to stop. He did, and sure enough, a cop car appeared out of nowhere. As soon as he had driven past, we headed in the opposite direction: message received and understood.

We then took a drive to Camp Solidarity, headquarters for the striking miners. We were stopped as we turned off the road by a very serious-looking armed man, who was more intimidating than the Southern cop. When the gatekeeper saw that I was wearing a camo T-shirt with *Walking the Line in '89* stencilled on it (a gift from the miner), his face lightened up (a little) and he let us pass. The strike headquarters was a simple wooden structure, and I was greeted warmly when I said that I was on strike, too. But these men weren't quite like my unionized colleagues back at the college, picketing for modest salary increases and job security. That strike would last roughly three weeks. Here I saw several men building bunk beds for workers and their families to sleep in, for those who could not meet their rent. This was a serious strike, already well into its sixth month.

Why were they on strike? The Pittston Coal Company, claiming recent financial setbacks, had initiated several practices that were costly to miners. The mines were open 24/7, but no overtime was paid. The company was trying to save money on healthcare benefits by doubling the deductible and lowering the coverage from 100 per cent to 80 per cent while discontinuing benefits for mine workers who had retired over 15 years earlier. Around 1,500 people, including many miners' widows and disabled miners, lost their health benefits. Working miners were doing a dangerous job without health insurance.

In all, some 2,000 miners were affected by the strike, which would last until February 1990, a full 10 months after it began. The union representing the striking miners, the United Mine Workers Association, encouraged non-violent forms of civil disobedience (e.g. blocking coal-bearing trucks, forcing a shutdown of the coal preparation plant). However, some miners, mostly wildcat strikers who were not members of the UMWA, used more aggressive tactics, such as throwing the six-pointed jackrocks under the wheels of trucks carrying coal mined by replacement workers ("scabs"), and smashing the windshields of the trucks and of cars belonging to scab workers. Local support was strong. Miners' wives staged a sit-down strike in the Pittston Coal Company's headquarters. When the police asked them their names, they answered, simply: "We are the daughters of Mother Jones," invoking the name of the famous American labour organizer Mary Harris Jones (1837–1930).

What did the strike accomplish? The courts were tied up for years in million-dollar lawsuits. The Pittston Coal Company ultimately had to sell off a number of their mines. Health benefits were restored to the miners, and the Coal Act, passed in 1992, made it mandatory for mining companies to provide health and retirement benefits for its workers. The strike action produced significant changes.

When I returned to the picket line back home, wearing my *Walking the Line in '89* T-shirt, I felt that teachers were amateurs in the strike game.

I have interwoven the stories of the two strikes here for several reasons. One is to show the differences between a strike by a specialized, professional worker in a city with a mixed economy made up of many different sectors and a strike by a specialized, semi-skilled worker in a one-industry, resource-extraction town that is similar to a number of communities in Canada. Coal strikes in particular have an ugly, inglorious history. The juxtaposition also highlights some typical differences between strikes involving "white-collar," middle-class workers and "blue-collar," working-class workers.

What do YOU think?

Oil has succeeded coal as the fossil fuel of choice in the West, yet while there is a history of long-fought, acrimonious coal strikes in the United States, Canada, and Britain, there are no easy parallels in the oil industry. Why do you think that is?

Introduction: What Is Work? (And Other Not-So-Dumb Questions)

What is work?

That might seem like a dumb question, but it isn't. In fact, *work* is difficult to define. It isn't the same as employment. Ask any woman who is the primary caregiver for her children and primary cook, housekeeper, and laundrywoman for her household: she *works*, but she is not *employed*. Ask any Aboriginal hunter/trapper/fisher on a northern reserve who provides food, clothing, and building supplies for his family but does not get paid for that work. The costs to buy those supplies would be awfully high, yet he and the "stay-at-home mom" are both considered unemployed—which is misleading, because they sure are working. Nevertheless, by definition, employment entails work for pay.

Work implies that what is being done is necessary, for the good of the family, the community, or the larger group or society. But that criterion of work is a slippery concept. A sociologist could argue that just because a person gets paid to do something or *feels* it is necessary doesn't guarantee that it is, in fact, for the good of society—and how would you determine that anyway?

In this chapter we will look at many different kinds of work (and employment). We will look at how work is divided, and how it can be divi*sive*, and how it is viewed differently by people occupying different social locations. But first, a warning. The sociology of work is very political. Everyone has an **ideology**, a relatively coherent set of beliefs about society and the people in it. No one is neutral; objectivity is impossible, a balancing of arguments unlikely. Thus, it behooves me to let you know from the outset that in this area, the author of this textbook is very much in favour of workers' rights, and very suspicious of big companies and big government employers. Just so you know . . .

How do you define work? Is this woman working? Do people need to be employed and paid to be considered workers?

How Work Is Divided: Two Classic Theories

Durkheim and the Division of Labour

Émile Durkheim wrote about work (which he called *labour*) in his classic study *The Division of Labour in Society* (1893). His idea of the **division of labour** involves the way the work tasks of society are divided up or parcelled out. Durkheim viewed the division of labour in terms of **solidarity**, the social cohesion shared by groups or by an entire society. We usually use the term *solidarity* to refer to the unity shown by workers in the face of employer opposition and oppression (even among the millionaire "workers" during the NHL lockout of 2012–13), but Durkheim used it in a different sense, to distinguish between two different societies. (Hint: do you smell a quiz question here?)

Traditional societies, in which the labour is divided simply along gender lines into men's work and women's work, are characterized by **mechanical solidarity**. This is the cohesion people experience based on the similarities of their work and their lives generally: they all farm, or fish, or hunt, or gather plants, or trap to obtain their food, for example. They all face the same challenges in their work, and that helps to bring them together. This fosters a sense of the collective and the similar that is stronger than any sense of the individual and distinct innovation. Aboriginal society in Canada was this way until fairly recently. Farming communities in Canada up until about 100 years ago exhibited the same kind of mechanical solidarity.

Of course, divisiveness is bound to arise in traditional societies of this kind, particularly when there is serious competition over who is the best (at fishing, at hunting, at trapping, etc.). Many traditional societies subscribed to what anthropologist **George M. Foster** (1913–2006) called the **image of limited good**, which is the belief that there is only so much "good" (food, money, profits, success, etc.) to go around, so that when one person is more successful than the others, the others naturally lose (Foster 1965). Societies with a strong sense of mechanical solidarity typically display greater social equality in the face of concerns stemming from the image of limited good.

The attitude of this type of social equality is at the heart of an old joke told by Aboriginal people about lobster fishing. One Aboriginal fisher always managed to have a full lobster trap, while his friend's trap was empty, all of the lobsters having escaped. When asked why his lobsters don't escape, the more successful of the two fishers says, "I only catch Indian lobsters."

"How do you know that they are Indian lobsters?" the luckless companion asks.

"Because," the first fisher replies, "whenever one rises above the others to escape, the others drag him back down again."

The other kind of society is characterized by what Durkheim called **organic solidarity**. It is a society that resembles the human body in its division of labour (making it a good model for structural-functionalist thinking). In this type of society, there are many different kinds of work performed by different members of society, just as the body is made up of various organs with different functions—the brain, the heart, the kidneys, the bladder, and so on. According to Durkheim, the solidarity here comes from the fact that members of the society are dependent on each other, just as the heart is dependent on the lungs for oxygen, and the lungs are dependent on the heart for blood.

Again, of course, in this kind of society there is a divisiveness concerning the parcelling out of rewards or goods, this time based on which functions or types of work are valued more than others. Here it is much more difficult to maintain social equality, particularly when a society moves from one model of how work is divided to another. At this point, we turn it over to Karl Marx, whose pioneering study of labour provided the foundation for most investigations into the sociology of work today.

Marx and Class Conflict: Owners versus Workers

Sociological discussions of work at some point typically reference **Karl Marx**, *The Communist Manifesto*, *Das Kapital*, and his definitions of class based on relationship to work. We have already looked at Marx's theories on the division of labour in relation to conflict theory (Chapter 2), social inequality (Chapter 9), and religion (Chapter 15).

To recap, Marx saw the work world divided into two groups: **owners** and **workers**. You belonged to the first group if you owned or controlled the **means of production** (essentially, the ways by which wealth is generated); if you didn't—if you were "working for the man"—then you belonged to the second group. Marx used the terms **aristocrats** (owners) and **peasants** (workers) for the two groups in feudal Europe, up until the eighteenth century. The means of production during this time was land. During the Industrial Revolution that began in the late eighteenth century, the aristocrats evolved and became the **bourgeoisie**, also known as the capitalist class, while the peasant farmers became industrial workers, known collectively as the **proletariat**. The means of production during this time was capital, the money and assets required to operate a business involved in the manufacture and sale of goods.

In his prediction for the future of the work world, Marx imagined that the proletariat would eventually, inevitably, realize that they were getting the short end of the stick (Marx called this awareness of oppression **class consciousness**) and revolt against the control of the owners. What would follow would be called, somewhat unfortunately for those wishing to win people over to the idea of a society of worker democracy, the **dictatorship of the proletariat**.

The worker revolution Marx predicted never did take place in the industrialized countries that he studied, although somewhat distorted versions of it took place in Russia and China. In part this was because the owner–worker distinction does not neatly reflect income and power levels. NHL players are "workers," but they are also millionaires (the problem being that the owners are *billionaires*). Meanwhile, if you run a one-person consulting firm out of your home and live from contract to contract, you are technically an owner, though you may be relatively poor and powerless.

Globalization, which Marx could not have foreseen, has added a new dimension to the analysis. I am willing to guess that most of the manufactured products we buy in Canada are "made in China." The exploited workers are Chinese, but the real exploitation comes at the hands not of their direct employers—those who operate the factories and control the means of production—but of large North American retailers such as Walmart, who have an indirect but clear power-to-powerless relationship with the exploited workers.

Organizing Labour

A Short History of Workers' Organizations from Guilds to Unions

Long before Marx predicted that exploited workers would one day decide that enough was enough and wage a revolt against oppressive owners, people who work had taken steps to guard against being taken advantage of. They did this by organizing into small groups or "collectivities" based on shared interests or type of work.

The oldest known work-based organizations were **guilds**, which developed with the growth of villages and towns in medieval Europe. These guilds were typically made up of self-employed skilled craftsmen—wood carvers, stonemasons, blacksmiths, and so on—who, in Marxist terms, controlled the means of production, consisting of their materials and tools. They often set the prices their profession could charge for goods and services and in later, pre-industrial times issued patents or licences to exclusively produce certain goods. Guilds would designate the status of workers as they rose through the ranks of their trade, from apprentice to journeyman to master craftsman, and they provided a kind of insurance or pension to guild members and their families.

The earliest unions were similar to guilds, but their members, unlike guild members, were not primarily self-employed (although they could, in some circumstances, set prices for their work). These early unions were called **craft unions**, and they continue to exist today. They are made up of workers whose training and skill set are the same. In his study of the American working class, written in 1948, **C. Wright Mills** described craft unions as the oldest and smallest unions (Mills 2001). He identified a number of examples, including the diamond workers, the building trades, and certain professional fields (e.g. teachers), and explained that they accounted for the greatest number of independent (rather than affiliated) unions (Mills 2001: 59).

In contrast to craft unions are **industrial unions**. These represent entire industries, rather than specialized individual crafts, and are made up of members who tend to have a broad range of skills and training. The automotive, steel, textile, electrical equipment, and rubber industries were represented by industrial unions at the time Mills was writing. Not only are industrial unions larger than craft unions, but they are more likely to be affiliated with even larger organizations.

Somewhere between the craft union and the industrial union are **amalgamated unions**, "composed of workers from related crafts," in Mills' description (55). He offered the example of the Amalgamated Clothing Workers of America, whose members were involved in the production of different kinds or parts of clothing.

Union Membership in Canada Today

In Canada, as of 2011, there are roughly 4.3 million union members. This amounts to 29.7 per cent of the country's population of workers, or what might be called our **union density**, a measure of the proportion of unionized to non-unionized workers in the country. Although it represents a slight increase over previous years, the current union density is considerably lower than it was 30 years before. In 1981, Canada's union

This elaborate certificate of membership in the Amalgamated Society of Engineers, Machinists, Millwrights, Smiths, and Pattern Makers, designed by James Sharples in 1852, is typical of the emblems adopted by many trade unions during the mid-nineteenth century. See if you can work out the symbolism of some of the elements. Consider the laurel wreaths; the cornucopia; the portraits of James Watt, Samuel Crompton, and Richard Arkwright; Mars offering a broken sword to the smith; Clio presenting a scroll to the engineer; the locomotive and the ship; the rose, thistle, and shamrock; and the classical elements generally.

density was roughly 38 per cent. Most of the decline occurred during the 1990s, when downsizing and outsourcing were being carried out on a large scale.

Some groups have experienced more of a decline than others. Private-sector union membership represents the lower share of total union membership in Canada (most Canadian unionized workers are in the public sector), and the percentage of union members among young working men aged 25–34 dropped from 43 per cent in 1981 to roughly 24 per cent in 2004. We can see this drop mirrored in sectors that employ young men of this age group, such as forestry and mining, where the proportion of unionized workers fell from 46 per cent to just over 26 per cent during the same period. The construction and manufacturing sectors together experienced a drop of 13 percentage points. This is one of several indicators showing that the current cohort of young Canadian men will be less likely to ever belong to a union that their fathers were.

QUICK HITS

Leading Unions in Canada in 2011

In 2011, the largest two unions in Canada were:

- the Canadian Union of Public Employees (CUPE), representing 618,000 members employed in healthcare, education, municipal services, libraries, universities, social services, public utilities, transportation, emergency services, and airlines (www.cupe.ca/about)
- the National Union of Public and General Employees (NUPGE), with 320,000 members, most of whom are provincial public-sector workers employed in government services.

Just under half of the top 35 Canadian unions represent workers in the public sector, who make up the majority of unionized employees in Canada (the public sector is made up essentially of anyone employed by the government at the federal, provincial, or municipal level.) Six of the largest public-sector unions represent elementary and secondary school teachers (in Ontario, Quebec, and British Columbia).

Most Canadian unions are affiliated through the Canadian Labour Congress (CLC), an umbrella organization that represents 70 per cent of Canadian union members.

Nevertheless, the role of unions in Canada remains an important element of our political culture. The political culture of any society is a subset of its culture as a whole. It comprises the collective opinions, attitudes, and values concerning a variety of political issues, such as the rights and duties of individuals, the role of government, and the connection between religion and politics. Our union density alone indicates that unions play an important role in our political culture, and we need look no further than to our neighbours to the south to find a contrasting case.

In the United States, the union density is currently 13.1 per cent—that's the figure based on the number of workers who are represented by unions, and it's a little more than a percentage point higher than percentage of workers who are actual union members (11.9 per cent). What's the difference? In some unionized workplaces (in Canada as well as in the US), belonging to the union is not mandatory. So while the company you work for may be represented by a union, you can opt not to join it. A unionized workplace where union membership is optional is known as an **open shop**; the opposite is a **closed shop**, where all workers must belong to the union. Many US states have gone further by passing what are called **right-to-work laws** (a term that reflects a neoliberal bias when it comes to how rights are defined—we'll have more to say on neoliberalism below). This legislation essentially outlaws closed shops, by prohibiting agreements between labour unions and employers that would make membership or payment of union dues a condition of employment, either before or after the time of hiring.

Right-to-work laws are currently enforced in 24 American states, most of them in the South and the West: Alabama, Arizona, Arkansas, Florida, Georgia, Idaho, Iowa, Kansas, Louisiana, Michigan, Mississippi, Nebraska, Nevada, North Carolina, North Dakota, Oklahoma, South Carolina, South Dakota, Tennessee, Texas, Tennessee, Utah, Virginia, and Wyoming. The union density in those states (based on actual union *membership*, not *representation*) ranges from a low of 2.9 per cent in North Carolina to a high of 14.7 per cent in Nevada. Of the right-to-work states, only Nevada has a union density higher than the US national average (11.3 per cent). The highest union density overall is 23.2 per cent, in New York State, where right-to-work laws are not in effect—note that that figure is still considerably under Canada's overall union density of 29.7 per cent (Center for Labor Education & Research 2012).

What do YOU think?

1. Compare Canada's union density (29.7 per cent) with that of the US (13.1 per cent). What does it tell you about differences in the political culture of the two countries?

2. What does "right to work" mean to you? Why do you think the laws making closed shops illegal go by this name?

3. Why do you think union membership is mandatory for employees at some workplaces and in some industries? Is it reasonable, or should an employee have the right to opt out?

The Tools of Labour Disputes: Collective Bargaining, Strikes, and Lockouts

A union exists largely to negotiate fair wages and working conditions for its membership. This negotiation is known as **collective bargaining**. Collective bargaining benefits both the employer and the worker. From the employer's standpoint, it's less time-consuming to negotiate salaries across the board than to work out a deal with each and every employee individually. For the worker, it ensures that everyone is being treated equally by the employer, that no one is being taken advantage of or given preferential treatment. It also provides the employee with a powerful negotiating tool: the threat of a mass withdrawal of services. This is a **strike**, and it is one of the things that can happen when collective bargaining fails and negotiations break off.

Most strikes involve a particular union acting against the owners and management of the company that employs the union's members. A **general strike** occurs when one union's strike is supported and joined by other sympathetic unions, so that all unionized workers in a particular area are involved in the job action. This was the case during the famous Winnipeg general strike, in which 300,000 men and women of Winnipeg took up the cause of the city's builders and metalworkers. Typically, a union's decision to strike is dictated by the union head or the union executive, often following a vote by all union members on whether or not to initiate a job action. A **wildcat strike** is one that has not been authorized by the union executive through the usual process. Other forms of job action include the work slowdown, in which employees report to work but manage to reduce their output or efficiency. This can be done through a work-to-rule campaign, where

In 2011, the Liberal government of Ontario passed the Toronto Transit Commission Labour Disputes Resolution Act, which took the right to strike away from transit union workers. The move came in response to a request from Toronto's city councillors, who were concerned that with some 1.5 million commuters using the TTC every working day, a stoppage would cost the city millions of dollars. Is public transit an essential service? Would you have supported or opposed such a bill if you were a member of Ontario's Parliament?

Our Stories

The Cream Separator

Tommy Douglas—sociologist with an MA from McMaster University; democratic socialist premier of Saskatchewan, who introduced socialized medicine there; and first leader of the federal New Democratic Party—was a great sociological storyteller. Here is a story called "The Cream Separator," which he used to tell about the work situation in Canada.

I used to visit in farm homes, particularly around mealtime, and if I got in around dinner time of course, everybody in the family was busy. They were unhitching the horses. They were pumping the water. They were milking the cows. They were pitching down the hay and the oat sheaves. Somebody else was out gathering the eggs.

Somebody else was feeding the pigs and the chickens. Everybody had something to do. Even the youngsters were given a job doing something, for instance gathering the eggs or feeding the chickens.

And here I was, right off the city streets. I didn't know what to do, and I said "give me something to do." Well, nobody was going to trust this city boy with milking a good cow. They gave me the one job that anybody could do. They gave me the job of turning the handle of the cream separator.

Any of you ever turned the handle on the cream separator? Well it's quite an experience. I got to be quite good at it. I got to the place where I could tell you how many verses of "Onward Christian Soldiers" it takes to put a pan of milk through this thing. And as I was turning the handle and they were pouring in the milk, and I could see the cream come out the one spout and the skim milk coming out of the other spout, one day it finally penetrated my thick Scotch head that this cream separator is exactly like our economic system.

Here are the primary producers, the farmers and the fishermen and the loggers. They are pouring in the milk. And here are the workers, whether they work on the railroad or go down to the mines or sail ships or work in a store or a bank, or teach school, clerk in the store, work in a hospital. They are the people whose services make the economy go round, and they're turning the handle. So here you have it: primary producer puts in the milk; people who work

employees do no more than precisely what is required (refusing, for example, to stay even a minute late or to take on assignments not specified in the job description) or else follow safety procedures to the letter (e.g. subjecting every air passenger to a thorough baggage search rather than doing spot checks during peak times to reduce waiting times for travellers).

On the other side of the labour coin is the **lockout**. A lockout is an action initiated by management to prevent employees from going to work. During a contract negotiation, a lockout puts pressure on workers to accept a deal by depriving them of their regular pay. Now, there are some semantics involved in the discussion of lockouts, depending on whether you are pro-union or pro-management. In the case of the Winnipeg general strike, the city police, who were unionized, supported the strike. Because they were so badly needed to help maintain order in the city, they were required by the police commission to sign an anti-union "loyalty oath," promising not to join the strike. Only 20 signed; the remaining 210 did not, and on these grounds they were "locked out"—fired, essentially—and replaced with special constables who were anti-strike.

A more typical lockout began in March 2011, when the Canadian-based aluminum producer Alumicor locked out employees at its Toronto plant. The employees, with hand and brain turn the handle. And then I thought, but there's another fellow here somewhere. There's a fellow who owns this cream separator. And he's sitting on a stool with the cream spout in his mouth. And the primary producer and the worker take turns on the skim milk spout. And they don't like skim milk. Nobody likes skim milk. And they blame it on each other. And the worker says, "If those farmers and fishermen, you know, would work a little harder, well I wouldn't be drinking this skim milk." And the fishermen and the farmers say, "If those workers didn't demand a forty hour week, didn't want such high wages, I wouldn't have to live on this blue milk." But you know, they're both wrong.

The farmers and the fishermen have produced so much we don't know what to do with it—we've got surpluses of foodstuffs. And the workers, they've produced so well that today nearly a million of them are unemployed. The fault is not with the worker. It is not with the primary producer. The fault is with this machine. This machine was built to give skim milk to the worker and the primary producer, and to give cream to the corporate elite.

As a matter of fact, it doesn't always do that because every once in a while this little fellow sitting on the stool with the cream spout in his mouth gets indigestion. And he says, "Boys, stop this machine. We got a recession!" He says to the worker, "You're laid off, you can go on unemployment insurance. and after that on welfare." And he says to the farmers and the fishermen, "You know, we don't need your stuff. Take it back home." And then he sits for a while, indigestion gets better, burps a couple of times, says, "Alright, boys, start the machine. Happy days are here again. Cream for me and skim milk for both of you."

Now what the democratic socialist party has been saying to Canadians for a long time is that the time has come in this land of ours for the worker and the primary producer to get their hands on the regulator of the machine so that it begins to produce homogenized milk in which everybody'll get a little.

represented by the American-headquartered United Steel Workers union, were still locked out 18 months later. I would drive by the locked-out, picketing workers every day on my way to work. Here is a rare occasion in which I side with an American-based organization over a Canadian based one.

Government Involvement in Labour Disputes: Essential Services

Early in 2011, the Republican governor of Wisconsin, a state known for strong unions, caused a huge disturbance when he proposed an act that would in essence take the right to strike away from the state's public-sector employees. Democratic representatives in the state legislature fled the area so that there would not be a quorum (the number of representatives required by law to hold an official vote). Rumours began of state police being sent out to round up the runaway Democrats. Meanwhile, crowds of up to 25,000 people demonstrated in the streets of Madison, the state capital. At issue was a declaration of essential work or services.

Here are the criteria used by the federal government of Canada in determining whether or not public services are essential:

Services should be identified as essential where there are reasonable grounds for accepting the probability, or even the possibility, that human life or public safety would suffer if a work stoppage interrupted the duties of these employees.

Employees holding positions that have been deemed essential are prohibited from participating in strike activities. The issue raises a number of questions related to work. What occupations should be considered essential? When you think of safety, you might think of police officers, fire fighters, nurses, doctors, and paramedics. In a strict reading of safety, who else might be considered? Who should not be considered? How can we ensure that unionized workers who have had their services declared essential are not exploited by their right to strike being taken away?

Debating the Value of Organized Labour

Collective Rights versus Individual Rights

At the heart of the debate over the merits of right-to-work legislation is the issue of collective rights versus individual rights. Defenders of right-to-work legislation argue that it's about protecting the *individual rights* of workers to choose not to belong to a union. Opponents argue that right-to-work laws threaten the *collective rights* of workers by eroding the strength of unions and diminishing their ability to negotiate fair pay and working conditions for the people they represent. (Opponents would also argue that this, and not individual freedom, is the impetus for right-to-work legislation, particularly when its greatest supporters tend to be not individual workers forced to join a union but business leaders who stand to benefit from the weakening of organized labour.)

Collective rights are rights held by all members of a particular group of workers. They may pertain to a specific work situation (the collective rights of mill workers at the Catalyst Paper mill in Port Alberni, BC) or a more general one (the collective rights of unionized elementary school teachers). When we speak of individual rights, it's usually with reference to the rights of individual workers, typically when they are presented as being at odds with the rights of the collective (as in the case of right-to-work, or when

individual rights are supposedly being trampled by thuggish union leaders trying to keep rogue union members in line). In the context of organized labour, individual rights may also refer to the rights of individual consumers (as when they are denied access to some product or service because of a strike), or of citizens generally; the individual rights of owners are spoken of less often than they are implied. While it is true that consumers make up a collectivity, they are often individualized in the anti-union rhetoric of individual versus collective rights (as when, for instance, a news story features a single mother unable to buy milk for her children because she has been denied access to a store by striking workers).

Generally speaking, those on the left of the ideological spectrum favour collective rights (except for the collective rights of capitalists), while those on the right support individual rights (except for the individual rights of anarchists). Labour disputes between the management and owners of an organization and its workers frequently pit individual rights against collective rights, with the left-wing supporters generally championing collective rights and their right-wing counterparts defending individual rights (while quietly defending the collective class rights of owners).

Both individual and collective rights need to be respected in a democratic society, but all too often they are set in opposition to each other rather than being treated as complementary. Those who feel threatened by the expression of collective rights may attempt to diminish them by casting the collectivity (i.e. the workers) as a **special interest group** (or just a **special interest**). In this context, *special interest* is a derogatory term for a collectivity, which implies that the group is attempting to gain some kind of preferential treatment that the rest of society does not enjoy. (In fact, we could say that society abounds with special interest groups to which we all belong, based on age, ethnicity, geographical location, and so on; the class of owners, in fact, could be called a special interest, though in Canada only the NDP would call them such.)

Another strategy for opposing the rights of a collectivity involves invoking an even larger collectivity whose rights are at stake. For instance, a person might appeal to the collective rights of all citizens of the nation, who would espouse both the idealized individual rights of liberal beliefs and the idealized nation of equals. Adopting this line of reasoning, one could argue that in the interest of fairness, everyone within the larger collectivity should enjoy the same rights, without making exceptions for members of a smaller collectivity within the whole. This appeal to patriotic sentiment is sometimes referred to as "wrapping

oneself in the flag." In a *Globe and Mail* editorial entitled "Let's Embrace Michigan's 'Right to Work' Law," guest columnist Linda Hasenfratz, the CEO of a Guelph, Ontario, auto parts manufacturer, defended

The Point Is...

Competing Ideologies: Left-Wing, Right-Wing, and Neoliberal

When it comes to the sociology of work, there are two distinct political or ideological perspectives taken: left-wing and right-wing. The terms arose not from hockey but from the French Revolution in 1789, when the supporters of the monarchy sat to the right of the president in the National Assembly, while those who opposed the monarchy sat on the left. Applied to work in the contemporary setting, **left-wing** is synonymous with support for workers and the unions that represent them, while **right-wing** generally connotes a position sympathetic to employers and business owners. In political terms, the right-wing perspective is generally taken up by parties describing themselves as conservative (e.g. the Conservative Party of Canada, the Republican Party in the US), while the parties that oppose them—the ones occupying the left-wing position—are sometimes described as liberal (this includes the NDP in Canada).

Neoliberalism represents a distinct ideology relating to work. Paradoxically, it is an ideology that we would describe as politically conservative by nature—so much so that it is sometimes called neo-conservativism; *neo-* means "new," so conservativism and neo-conservativism are essentially the same thing (like flammable and inflammable). What the conservative neo**liber**als want to **liber**ate is the flow of money across countries and the ability of individuals and big companies to make as much money as possible without a lot of government restrictions or interference.

Neoliberals—who are politically *conservative*, remember—are definitely on the side of the owners, not the workers (although they claim that workers benefit from gains made by the owners—see the discussion of **trickle-down theory** in Chapter 9). They support policies that involve lowering the number of public-sector employees (i.e. people employed by the

government, such as civil servants working in a federal ministry office or sanitation workers who work for the city in which they operate); in this regard, they might make an exception for police officers and army personnel, since public safety is a principal concern for conservative-minded people (including neoliberals). While they do not favour the idea of "big government" (i.e. government characterized as too big, too expensive, and too meddling), they support the government's power to limit the wages of public servants, as well as their ability to strike.

QUICK HITS

Them's Fightin' Words: Other Terms (and Insults) for the Ideological Left and Right

Left Wing	Right Wing
liberals	conservatives, neoconservatives ("neo-cons")
social democrats	neoliberals
progressives	regressives
socialists	capitalists
communists	fascists
anarchists	libertarians
radicals	reactionaries
traitors (in the US)	patriots/flag-wavers (in the US)
pinkos (see Don Cherry and Toronto mayor Rob Ford, who are right-wing)	

Michigan's right-to-work legislation with this kind of argument:

> It's my belief that a basic right we have as free citizens is not to be forced to do something we don't want to do. That is the basic definition of oppression, something our country has long fought against, something many of our citizens fled their homelands to seek refuge from on our shores. . . .
>
> I challenge the leadership in Ontario and in Canada to embrace this change. . . . Do it for all of us, as citizens of this great country; do it because it's our basic human right to have a say and to have the right to make our own choices.

On the other side of the coin, legitimate individual rights can be trampled on by those wrapping themselves up in the banner of solidarity. Unions can be undemocratic. Union leaders can violate the rights of individual unionized workers when they do not listen to the valid concerns of their membership. Imagine a group of workers striking at a glass factory.

The management of the factory tables a new offer, but the union executive rejects it and refuses to put it to a vote of the union members, even though many of the striking workers might find the new offer acceptable. (Of course, the management side will sometimes table bogus offers that really do not deserve to be considered, just so that they can say that the workers are being bullied when the union head rightfully rejects the offer.)

Unions and Democracy

Earlier in this chapter we touched on C. Wright Mills' study of the American working class published in 1948. *The New Men of Power: America's Labor Leaders* is actually the first part of a trilogy that also dealt, in the subsequent instalments, with middle-class and upper-class workers.

A recurring theme of *The New Men of Power* is the relationship between unions and democracy. As Nelson Lichtenstein summarizes in the introduction to the 2001 edition, it was Mills' view that "[t]he

A protester makes his views known at a rally outside the state capitol building in Lansing, Michigan. A bastion of unionized industrial workers (in the automotive sector especially), Michigan became the most recent US state to pass right-to-work legislation, in December 2012. What's wrong with making union membership optional?

erosion of democratic institutions in the contemporary United States is organically linked at work and in the political arena, to the evisceration of the labor movement" (Lichenstein 2001: xxx). Mills called American labour unions "the most democratic societies of their size in the world" (Mills 2001: 5), and yet he noted that there are also undemocratic elements within unions, and things can place constraints on a union's democracy. One of these is size: he remarked that the larger the union, the less people want to actively, democratically participate (Mills 2001: 64–5). Another is closed shop/open shop status: a good argument can be made that for a union to be politically effective, the workplace in which it operates must be a closed shop. As we have seen, right-to-work laws favour individual rights and weaken the collective rights of the worker group.

According to Mills, a characteristic of an effective union is a natural tension between "the democracy of the town meeting" and the "discipline necessary for militant action" (Mills 2001: 5). In other words, a labour organization should provide a forum for dissenting views that may contribute constructively to how the union is run, but when faced with a challenge from the employer, the union must be unified with strong leadership. This is a point he returns to in a later chapter, where he warns that when it comes to labour disputes, "it takes one to fight one" (just as when hiring a personal injury lawyer to take on an insurance company: to fight a school of barracudas, you need a shark). In Mills' words:

> [I]ntra-union discipline is often essential for effective dealing with thoroughly autocratic business institutions. The managers of corporations are not democratically elected by the stockholders to represent their interest. And in this respect, the unions are often practically forced to borrow from their opponents an autocratic type of rule in order to insure unity of action. (Mills 2001: 65)

Unions must be cautious in this regard, however. If the union leadership goes too far in adopting a militaristic attitude, it can lead to unnecessary conflict when negotiation and co-operation might serve all parties better. Listening to the rank-and-file union members can often bring a fresh democratic perspective to a locked situation. Mills also pointed out that union leaders tend to have long periods of tenure at the top, outlasting opposition groups within the union. As with any government, having one party or leader remain in power for too long without serious opposition permits a movement away from democracy and towards *autocracy*, the dictatorship of a small group (see the countries of North Africa before the "Arab Spring" revolts of 2011, the federal Liberals under Jean Chrétien, and the provincial Conservative Party in Alberta for examples).

The Myth of the Foreign-Born Agitator

One long-held belief among North Americans opposed to unions is that labour organizations and job actions are led by, to quote Mills, "*Those Foreign Born Agitators*" (Mills 2001: 84). Prior to writing *The New Men of Power*, Mills did a survey among women living in what he described as a "typical Middle Western city of 80,000" (Mills 2001: 84). One of the questions he asked was this: "Do you think that most, about half, or not so many of the labor leaders in this country are foreign-born?" As Table 17.1 shows, 19 per cent of respondents believed that most union leaders were immigrants to the US, while 28 per cent put the number at around half. This is despite the fact that, as Mills determined, some 89 per cent of the union leaders he studied were American-born, with just 11 per cent "foreigners" (including some "agitating" Canadians). These figures—the roughly 9-to-1 ratio of US-born to foreign-born union leaders—reflected the American population generally at the time (Mills 2001: 86). Mills then took his analysis a step farther, noting that:

> . . . the bulk of the labor leaders are between 45 and 54 years of age; in 1940, 23 per cent of the white male population in this age group were foreign-born; among labor leaders in the same age

Table 17.1 Results of Mills' survey on whether labour leaders are foreign-born

Most are	19%
About half	28%
Not so many	25%
Don't know	27%
Total survey participants	992

Source: Mills 2001: 85.

group, only 10 per cent in the AFL [the American Federation of Labor] and 17 per cent in the CIO [the Congress of International Organizations] were foreign-born. This pattern generally holds on all levels of leadership and in all regions of the United States. (Mills 2001:86)

In other words, in the age group of most labour leaders, there was actually a greater proportion of foreign-born white men in the population overall than among union leaders, a situation that was opposite to the impression of the people surveyed.

Mills made another important point in this part of his study, linking anti-union feeling with the overestimation of foreign leadership. One of the questions he asked in his survey was: "From the standpoint of the factory workers themselves, do you think unions do a good service job or not?" Of those who said they thought unions did a good job, just 16 per cent also believed that most labour leaders were foreign-born; by contrast, 31 per cent of those who believed unions did not do a good job also believed that most labour leaders were foreign-born. So those who were most opposed to labour unions were also the most likely to believe the foreign-born myth—or at least to spread it. Mills found that the people who would cry "foreign born" in an effort to discredit labour leaders were likely to be politicians, business leaders, and others with economic reasons for opposing the practical activities of American unions (Mills 2001: 85).

It's important to recognize that Mills was writing in the immediate aftermath of the Second World War, when angst was already brewing over the spread of communism from the Soviet Union. US senator Joseph McCarthy's aggressive "witch hunt" against suspected communists on American soil would begin in earnest in 1950. It was in this political climate that suspicions around "foreign-born agitators" introducing labour practices from communist eastern Europe were negatively affecting the way people in the West viewed labour organizations. This was well over 60 years ago, but the sentiments of the time created biases that would colour the public's perception of unions for many years to come.

The Alien Agitator in Canada

The suspicion that unions were being led by "foreigners" was not unique to Americans. During significant strikes in Canadian history—notably the Winnipeg general strike (1919) and the Bienfait coal miners' strike (1931)—opposition to the strikes and to unions generally was stoked by the belief (both real and manufactured) that alien agitators were behind it all. It wasn't good, patriotic Canadian boys who were leading the strikes; it was immigrant labour leaders corrupting "our" boys with their evil, anti-Canadian and anti-British (because the two were often conflated) ways. Much of the rhetoric was wholly disingenuous—after all, many Canadian labour leaders of the first half of the twentieth century were born and raised in Britain, and had learned their union radicalism in the mines and factories of the "old country" under a Labour Party of some significance. (Such was their legacy that I grew up thinking that anyone with a Glaswegian accent interviewed on television must be a union leader.) To call the practices of Canada's labour leaders "anti-British" was a hollow claim, but an effective one, for it stirred up anti-union sentiment.

What made this union-busting tactic so effective? The first two decades of the twentieth century saw immigration numbers that would not again be matched in Canadian history. The majority of these newcomers were not the much-prized (although sometimes criticized) British immigrants of earlier decades but far less familiar and suspiciously strange people from eastern Europe. Many of the immigrants were Jewish or Russian Orthodox, or members of some other religion relatively new to Canada. Canadians were naturally leery of the new immigrants, who were seemed more foreign, less familiar than the majority of those who had previously immigrated to Canada.

The Winnipeg General Strike occurred in 1919, just after the end of World War I, at a time when the spirit of Canadian patriotism was high. The rich and powerful lawyers and businessmen who led the coalition opposing the strike, the Citizens' Committee of 1000, played to this sentiment well. In casting the strike leaders as "foreigners," they frequently invoked images of the "dreaded Hun" (i.e. Germans) and the Bolsheviks (leaders of Russia's 1917 communist revolution) to stir suspicions about the supposedly foreign-born labour organizers. Indeed, the Russian revolution, was a haunting spectre often drawn in bright colours by A.J. Andrews, the media-savvy leader of the Citizens' Committee, in the committee's newspaper (unsurprisingly named the *Citizen*), which was a major instrument of anti-strike propaganda. The presence of Russian Jews, such as Solomon Almazoff, in the hierarchy of the unions and the heavy participation in the

Our Stories

The Winnipeg General Strike of 1919

The Winnipeg general strike is considered the largest and most dramatic strike in Canadian history. It occurred in a socio-political context in which the cost of living had risen, but wages had not, and in which large companies had profited substantially from supplying the war effort, but did not seem inclined to pass the profits down to the workers. With the return of soldiers and the influx of immigrants, the unemployment rate was high. The Russian Revolution was still fresh in people's minds, and the rich and powerful feared the spread of worker-led revolts to North America.

When the general strike was called by the Winnipeg Trades and Labor Council, in May 1919, the roughly 30,000 workers who had walked off their jobs were attacked by the local media. The strike involved both private- and public-sector workers—factory workers, shop clerks, police officers, firefighters, telephone operators, trolley drivers—and so the effects of the strike on the city were widespread and immediate. The newspapers—the *Winnipeg Free Press* and *The Winnipeg Tribune*—were especially bitter as they had lost most of their employees to the strike.

Governments at the municipal, provincial, and federal level all acted to raise local tension. The army, the local militia, and the Mounties were all called onto the scene. This makeshift riot squad was supplemented with a number of specially recruited "special constables," who were given significant discretionary powers despite having had little to no training. The Citizens' Committee of 1000, formed by the city's rich and powerful to oppose the strike, had strong support from the federal government, which never met with the strike leaders.

The strike reached its climax on "Bloody Saturday," 21 June 1919, when there was a violent clash involving thousands of striking workers, strike

A rally by the Great War Veterans Association, held on 4 June 1919 during the Winnipeg general strike. How is the anti-union sentiment expressed?

opponents, and security personnel tasked with maintaining order. The day's events produced numerous injuries and arrests, the deaths of two strikers, and the deportation of two immigrants. The strike was officially called off five days later, on 26 June.

What do YOU think?

1. The strike began when negotiations between workers in the building and metal trades and their employers broke off. What does it tell you that these striking workers were joined by so many in both the private and public sectors?

2. What was the effect of the media on the strike? How might it be similar to the role of media vis-à-vis union actions today?

3. What do you think the role of patriotism was in this strike?

strike of Ukrainians, whom Canadians had suspected of being allied with Germany during the war, made these connections convenient. Moreover, a number of the most prominent union leaders had opposed the Great War and advocated for peace, adopting a stance then common among socialists in many parts of the world.

At the time of the 1931 coal miners' strike in Bienfait, Saskatchewan, the Ukrainian Labour Temple in Bienfait was gaining a reputation as a place for Ukrainian-born Canadians to reminisce about the old country, and to arrange for groups of people to visit the "workers' paradise" that the Soviet Union had by many accounts become. It all seemed too revolution-friendly to the American- and Canadian-born mine owners. References made by some of the more left-leaning leaders to the Marxist "dictatorship of the pro-letariat" (remember—we mentioned it earlier) didn't help their cause in many people's eyes. They ended up victims of changes made to the Immigration Act during the Winnipeg strike 12 years earlier. The language of the act had been revised and made suitably vague that clever prosecutors were able to successfully obtain deportation orders for the leaders of that strike, and of the Saskatchewan miners' strike.

Throughout the Cold War, for as long as the communist Soviet Union continued to exist, conservative elements in Canadian political circles and the media could always raise the phantom of socialism to delegit-imize left-wing policies and movements, including the labour movement. With the fall of the Berlin Wall in 1990, the breakup of the Soviet Union in 1991, and what one foolish American writer labelled the "end of history," eastern Europe ceased to be a source of "alien agitators" that some in the West could use as scape-goats to demonize socialist labour practices.

Mass Media and the Unions: From 1948 to the Twenty-First Century

In Chapter 2 of *New Men of Power*, Mills discussed what he called the "mass public's view," what we today might call the "mass media view." He raised five key points concerning media and unions. We would argue that these points are still true today and, if anything, are even more pertinent with television, online, and other media added to the mix.

1. Any Union News Is Bad Union News

It has been said that there's no such thing as bad publi-city, but when it comes to unions, the opposite is true, according to Mills: no news is good news. Generally speaking, the media are not kind to labour unions and their leaders. As a general rule, they ignore the peaceful and stable features of organized labour while reporting in detail the deadlocks, the strikes, and the seizures. Violence is the meat and gravy of labour news; labour peace is seldom part of the coverage, unless the media have first created the expectation of violence that never arose. The media tend to report those labour actions that seemingly indicate great and irresponsible power on the part of unions and their leaders rather than any constructive work they may do (Mills 2001: 32).

2. The Opposition Is Varied but Support Is Singular

Mills makes the point that anti-labour comments quoted in the media come from a broad and diverse range of sources, such as government officials, busi-ness leaders, the often anonymous rank-and-file union members who oppose the labour action under discus-sion, and concerned members of the general public who are worried about how the strike will affect them. However, pro-union opinions tend to come only from union leaders or representatives, the "union bosses" as a former Conservative premier of Ontario used to call them (Mills 2001: 33).

3. Union Coverage in Newspapers Is Episodic

Mills observed that the media's coverage of labour news tends to be episodic, not continual. That is, there is no regular feature in the local news dedicated to reporting on day-to-day union activities, such as peaceful con-tract negotiations (these make up the majority), equit-able workplace practices (increased hiring and training of minorities and the disabled), or charitable acts, such as when unions helped with the post–Hurricane Katrina reconstruction of New Orleans—the kinds of pieces, in other words, that are generally the stuff of union newsletters. Unions typically make headlines only when there is a strike that dramatically affects the public or when accusations of corruption among a big union's leadership become public.

Mills made the point that at the time he was writing (the mid-twentieth century), about 14 million people either belonged to unions or had household members who did (Mills 2001: 4). The figure was much greater than the number of people who owned or ran businesses, and yet there were regular business columns, sections, and pages. Labour in Canada and in the US is still without continual mainstream media coverage.

4. "I Am Generally in Favour of Unions, *but . . ."*

To Mills, the big daily newspapers of the time, no matter how ideologically left-wing or right-wing they were, all seemed to take the same position: *I am generally in favour of unions, BUT. . . in this particular case, the union is wrong.* A variation on this theme is: *Unions once played a useful and important role in society, but today they do not* (see Mills 2001: 33–4). Mills had trouble finding stories written by columnists or reporters expressing unqualified support for unions.

5. There Are No Working-Class Heroes

In world of entertainment media, Mills felt that the working-class hero, the active union member,

was essentially invisible. Speaking of mass media, he wrote:

> In their entertainment as in their news, they are anti-labor. In radio soap opera, in the comic strips,

Over the years, TV has produced its share of working-class heroes—or anti-heroes. Would you say, overall, that working-class characters are depicted favourably or unfavourably in the entertainment media?

movies, and pulp fiction, labor unions or labor leaders are almost never brought into the picture in any way. Even the factory worker is practically unknown in the dramas of popular culture. (Mills 2001: 34)

The Working Poor

Many people associate poverty with unemployment. Yet the vast majority of Canadians who are poor belong to a category known as the **working poor**. The term applies to working people and their families whose household income is below the poverty line, however that may be calculated. In Canada, you can safely say that if a household's primary breadwinner earns $20,000 per year or less (which was the case, according to Statistics Canada, for close to 7 million workers in 2001) or is paid at or below the **minimum wage** (which would not enable workers in any Canadian province to achieve $20,000 for full-time work with a 40-hour work week), then the worker and the household are among the working poor.

When you consider how many Canadians living in poverty belong to the category of working poor, the portrayal of poor people as lazy "welfare bums" not only does them a terrible disservice but is mostly inaccurate. Even poor people who are unemployed work hard to find work, which can be like a full-time job in itself. But governments benefit from the prevalent notion that the vast majority of poor people are so because they are unemployed. Unemployment is a serious issue, but most people accept that there will always be some level of unemployment. It is more difficult to accept that there are people who are living in poverty despite working full-time. The subject of the working poor forces governments to defend their inaction on other issues that contribute to poverty, such as the low minimum wage, the high cost of public transit, and the lack of affordable housing.

Defining Canada's Working Poor

A good study of the working poor in Canada was carried out by Dominique Fleury and Myriam Fortin for Social Development Canada, the federal department responsible for crafting social policies in support of families with children (it is now part of Human Resources and Skills Development Canada). In their working paper, called "When Working Is Not Enough to Escape Poverty," Fleury and Fortin address the initial challenge of arriving at an **operational definition** of working poor.

First, they had to determine who qualifies as a worker and who makes up a working family for the purpose of their study. They chose to define a worker as anyone between the ages of 18 and 64 "who is not a full-time student and who worked for pay at least 910 hours" in the year of the study (Fleury & Fortin 2006: 10). A working family is any family including at least one member who is a worker.

Next, the researchers had to establish their measure of poverty. They based their definition on two measures we considered in Chapter 3: Low Income Cut-Offs using income after tax (LICO–IAT) and the Market Basket Measure (MBM). The MBM, which measures poverty according to whether or not a family can afford to buy a fixed set of goods and services that the average family might be expected to purchase in a year, is the measure Fleury and Fortin felt was most relevant to their study; however, because it is a fairly new way of calculating poverty, it could not be used effectively for historical comparisons. For this, the researchers turned to Low Income Cut-Offs, which involve calculating the average share of total household income that a family will spend on food, clothing, and shelter—a family is considered poor if it spends above the average (i.e. a greater share of total household income) on these basics. A person is considered poor if he or she lives in a family that is poor, based either on the Market Basket Measure or the Low Income Cut-Offs.

Using their operational definition of a worker and the Market Basket Measure as their measure of poverty, Fleury and Fortin calculated that in 2001 in Canada, there were 653,300 people who were working poor, and 1.5 million Canadians (a third of them children under 18) living in a working-poor family (Fleury & Fortin 2006: 17). (By comparison, when LICOs are used as the basis for establishing poverty, the number of working-poor Canadians falls to 460,000—Fleury & Fortin 2006: 118.) When comparing the social characteristics of Canada's working-poor (WP) and working non-poor (WNP) populations, Fleury and Fortin produced a number of interesting findings including the following:

- *working hours*—nearly a quarter of all working-poor Canadians (24.3 per cent) worked 2,500 hours or more in 2001; by comparison, 13.2 per cent of working non-poor Canadians worked that many hours (p. 24, Table 3.4)

- *self-employment*—the working poor were three times as likely as the working non-poor to be self-employed (40.7 per cent vs 13.2 per cent—p. 24, Table 3.4)
- *family type*—WP Canadians were twice as likely as WNP Canadians to be living in an unattached family arrangement (28.4 per cent vs 13.8 per cent)
- *disability*—the working poor were almost twice as likely as the working non-poor to have **work limitations** resulting from a disability (11.6 per cent vs 6.2 per cent—p. 23, Table 3.4)
- *ethnicity*—the working poor were more than twice as likely (11.5 per cent vs 5.3 per cent) to be recent immigrants or Aboriginal people living off-reserve (p. 23, Table 3.4)
- *education*—the working poor were much less likely than the working non-poor to have a university degree (11.2 per cent vs 20.1 per cent), and much more likely to have less than a high school diploma (19.6 per cent vs 11.7 per cent—p. 23, Table 3.4)

Fleury and Fortin used a "myth and fact" format to summarize some of their conclusions. Here are three of their conclusions to consider:

Myth: The working poor are low paid.

Facts:

- In 2001, salaried working-poor Canadians earned on average $12 per hour. In fact, fewer than 50% of them were low-paid and less than 7% earned the minimum wage.
- Furthermore, in 2001, 88% of low-paid salaried workers (i.e. those who earned less than $10/h) were not poor.

Myth: Bad jobs are the main cause of poverty among workers.

Facts:

- Family characteristics are the most important determinants of poverty for workers. Workers who are the sole breadwinner in their families are much more vulnerable to low income.

Estimate how much you spend each year on shelter, food, and clothes (never mind non-necessities like cellphones, the Internet, gym memberships, etc.). Do you think you could live comfortably on $20,000 or less per year?

- Being low-paid is a significant risk factor but, contrary to popular belief, it is not the most important determinant.
- Self-employed workers are at greater risk of low income than low-paid salaried workers.

Myth: Working poverty is a short transition between welfare and "decent" work.

Facts:
- Although working poor Canadians are more likely than other workers to be social assistance (SA) recipients, most of them never relied on SA.
- The working poor are more likely to escape poverty in the longer run than the "welfare" poor. However, between 1996 and 2001, the

QUICK HITS

The Cost of Living in an Early Twentieth-Century Industrial City

The third edition of historian Jack Granatstein's *Nation: Canada Since Confederation* includes a fascinating table, adapted for our use below (see Table 17.2). It shows the number of hours per week individuals in four different trades would need to work to purchase selected goods and services in 1920 in the city of Hamilton, Ontario (chosen by the author as a typical industrial city of the time).

Table 17.2 Number of hours of work needed to pay for basic commodities, Hamilton, Ont., 1920

| TRADE | HOURLY WAGE | NUMBER OF HOURS OF WORK REQUIRED TO PAY FOR . . . | | | | | |
		RENT (1 MONTH)	COAL (1 TON)	COFFEE (1 POUND)	FLOUR (1 POUND)	BUTTER (1 POUND)	SIRLOIN (1 POUND)
Bricklayer	$1.03	25	14	0.5	0.07	0.6	0.4
Carpenter	$0.85	30	17	0.6	0.08	0.7	0.5
Machinist	$0.73	36	20	0.7	0.10	0.8	0.6
Factory labourer	$0.41	63	35	1.2	0.13	1.1	0.7

Source: Adapted from Granatstein 1990: 275.

Say that a family used 2 pounds of coffee, 20 pounds of flour (people were still making their own bread back then), 4 pounds of butter, and 20 pounds of sirloin. The bricklayers, here representing the skilled trades, would have their rent, heating (the coal), and food basics (without considering fruits and vegetables) paid after 52.5 hours of work. The factory labourers, representing the working poor, would need 121.4 monthly hours—over three 40-hour weeks—to buy the same. And this is without factoring in beer, fruits and vegetables, ice for the icebox, transportation, clothing, and medicine.

What do YOU think?

1. How many hours of work at your last job would pay for your rent and utilities? How does compare with the bricklayers' 39, the carpenters' 47, the machinists' 56, and the factory labourers' 98?

2. How many hours of work do you think it would take a member of the working poor to pay for rent and utilities today?

working poor spent on average three years in low income and 40% of them experienced persistent poverty.

- Furthermore, many of those who exited poverty over the same period did so mainly because of a change in their family circumstances, not because of their progression in the labour market.
- In fact, five years later, close to 50% of those who were working poor in 1996 still had low earnings and would not have been able to provide for themselves had they lived alone. (Fleury & Fortin 2006: i–ii)

What we can see, then, is that family structure—specifically, whether a family with dependent children is a sole-earner household or a dual-/multiple-earner household—is more significant than income in determining whether someone belongs to the class of working-poor Canadians.

What do YOU think?

Does it surprise you that "having low hourly wages is not the most important determinant of poverty" (Fleury & Fortin 2006: 95)? Why do you think family structure plays a greater role than wages earned in determining whether or not a person is working poor?

What It Means to Earn a Living Wage

PEI-born sociologist **Annie Marion MacLean** was a pioneer in the sociological study of working women. In 1916 she wrote about the economic hardships faced by women underpaid as factory workers:

An industry unable to pay a living wage should be crushed out; it is parasitic, and not entitled to economic consideration. No industry that preys upon another has a right to exist. (MacLean 1916: 31)

One of her main concerns was that underpaid young women who supported themselves might turn to prostitution to supplement their meagre incomes.

Labour advocates and union representatives today talk about the need for workers to be able to earn a **living wage**, meaning generally a wage on which an individual can living, maintaining a reasonable standard of living and supporting a family without suffering from poverty. It is an abstract sociological term in that it is very hard to define precisely in concrete terms; an operational definition would be difficult to generate. For this reason, it has become a term more likely to be used by people advocating for better wages and benefits generally. Maclean put the problem in these terms:

There are half a million women in the sewing trades in the United States today, and in an overwhelming majority of cases, their wages fall below seven dollars a week and frequently below six, when investigators assert that it costs from eight to nine to live respectably. (MacLean 1916: 27)

But what does it mean to "live respectably"? It is hard to draw an operational definition from that kind of language.

Women and Work

It is trite to say that women have always worked, but it is necessary in order to correct the somewhat prevalent notion that woman is a new factor in industry, a factor antedating but little the industrial revolution. (MacLean 1916: 10)

Even a brief look at women and work must point out that there is a distinction between **paid work** (which at the start of the chapter we called *employment*) and **unpaid work** (the vast amount of domestic or household work, including everything from "housekeeping" and laundry to caring for children and elderly parents). And all studies indicate that when you add the two up, on average, women do more work than men do. This is particularly the case when there are small children around the home.

Canadian sociologist Annie Marion MacLean received her post-secondary education first at Acadia College in Nova Scotia and then at the University of Chicago, where she earned her PhD in sociology in 1898. She taught at that university as well, although always in a somewhat marginalized position, teaching primarily through correspondence courses. She also worked as a sociologist researcher/educator for the YWCA. She would have seen these outside-the-mainstream sociology activities as ways to educate women who could not get away from their homes because of family duties, and to educate people about women's issues generally. Her principal area of study and advocacy was the situation of women in the workplace in the early twentieth century—a position she states clearly in her preface to *Women Workers and Society* (1916):

> This little study of women workers is offered in the hope that it will interest people at large in an important class in society, namely the eight million

or more women who go out from home daily to the various tasks that that the industrial and professional world offers to them. (MacLean 1916: i)

Her research on women workers was diverse. She engaged in and directed ethnographic field work about women working in a variety of environments, including a department store, the Pennsylvania coal fields, an Oregon hop farm, and urban sweat shops.

The Point Is...

When Home Is the Workplace

The number of people doing paid work at home instead of an outside place of employment is increasing, but not rapidly. This was documented in a research paper published in an online issue of *Canadian Social Trends* (Turcotte 2010). The Statistics Canada study looked at changes in Canada from 2000 to 2008. The number of Canadians with paid employment who worked at home at least occasionally increased during the period from about 1.4 million to 1.8 million, representing a slight rise from 10.2 per cent of all paid employees to 11.2 per cent. Somewhat coincidentally, there was a parallel increase among self-employed workers, but the percentage increase was, of course, larger: over the

same period, the percentage of self-employed people working from home rose from about 50 per cent to 60 per cent. When paid workers and self-employed workers are taken together, their share of the total workforce grew by two percentage points, from 17 per cent to 19 per cent.

The sociological face of the paid worker at home (as opposed to the unpaid but equally hard-working person responsible for domestic work and care of the family at home) is defined by a number of social characteristics, including gender, education, professional/managerial status, and family circumstances. Statistics from 2008 show that among paid employees who had

Reasons for working at home differ for women and men. In 2008, 12 per cent of self-employed women reported that they were working at home for "family reasons," while only 3 per cent of self-employed men reported the same. Why the difference?

At the time of MacLean's study, women workers were a growing group in the United States. She put their numbers at 8 million strong, based on 1910 census figures—that marked an increase of 3 million from 10 years before (MacLean 1916: 20). Those 8 million women workers represented 21.2 per cent of the country's breadwinners (MacLean 1916: 21). Most of them (80 per cent) were single, and young, their typical working period beginning between the ages of 14 and 18 and ending with marriage at around the age of 25.

MacLean recognized that women were paid less than what men were paid, but she felt that this was due mainly to the lack of skilled work available to women. And she wasn't expecting women to receive equal wages—not yet, anyway. Her main concern was that women receive a decent wage, what we called earlier in the chapter a *living wage*:

worked at home, a slight majority (54 per cent) held a university degree; by comparison, of those who had never worked at home, just 25 per cent were university degree–holders (Turcotte 2010: 4). The implication is that people with post-secondary education are more likely to have worked at home, but we would add a caveat to that last statistic: had the researchers chosen to include college diplomas of two or three years along with university degrees, they would have seen, we would argue, a significantly higher number of post-secondary graduates who hadn't worked at home.

Of those who had worked at home at least occasionally, 55 per cent were in jobs classified as professional or managerial. Just 23 per cent of employees who had not worked at home were in similar jobs. This supports the author of the report's claim that "Professionals are among the workers most likely to work at home" (Turcotte 2010: 4). However, it is worth noting that these figures vary greatly depending on the profession, from a low of 8 per cent for workers in healthcare and social assistance to highs of between 34 and 36 per cent for people employed in finance, insurance, real estate, and "culture and recreation," and 54 per cent for workers in the vaguely defined category "other services" (Turcotte 2010: Chart 2).

Not surprisingly, women and men differ in several areas with regard to working at home. While in absolute percentages there was little difference between the two groups (10 per cent of women had worked at home, compared with 12 per cent of men), among workers in the managerial/professional category there was a much greater discrepancy: 29 per cent of male professionals had worked at home, while just 19 per cent of professional women had done the same (Turcotte 2010: 5).

One of the things these statistics do not show is the number of people, usually women, who *cannot* work outside the home, who have succumbed to ads promising that you can earn "$$$ *from your own home.*" The ads are very misleading, and the jobs often require extremely long hours of tedious labour (say, stuffing envelopes) to come close to being profitable. This kind of work can be described as long-distance exploitation, a household sweatshop. The industry has grown considerably with globalization and the advertising reach of the Internet, but a century ago, in 1916, Annie Marion MacLean expressed her concerns over the early forms of these kinds of businesses, which she called "the sweated industries" being run from "sweated homes." She was especially worried about the negative effects of these industries on the young children of working mothers. Potential worker beware: these stories point to the long tradition of exploiting women in the workforce.

Another element of worker exploitation that does not show up in the StatsCan study is the 24/7 access to the mid-management employee via BlackBerry or some other smartphone. Does the unofficial work time spent responding to employer demands from home count as "working at home"?

The really vital question at present in regard to the wages of women, is not that they be made equal to men's though that will come eventually, but that they shall be made adequate to the needs of life. (MacLean 1916: 30–1)

On this point she, and women workers, had to overcome the commonly held notion that women didn't take their work that seriously, and that the pay they received wasn't very important to them either. It was just **pin money**, to be spent on trivial things, not on food and rent. In her words, employers:

> established the fiction, since maintained, that women were working for "pin money," and therefore need not receive the rate paid to men. This undoubtedly affects the economic status of women today, while, in fact, "pin money" workers are a negligible quantity. (MacLean 1916: 3)

MacLean added that despite the fact many working women were young and living at home, their earnings were often important to the family's survival. The practice among young women working and living with their families was for them to give their pay packet to their mothers, who would then dole out an allowance for them.

Equal Pay and Pay Equity

There are two basic ways of addressing the problem of the lower pay women receive for their work. One is **equal pay**, which is about making sure that women and men receive the same pay for doing the same job. As a policy, this is not as difficult to implement as is **pay equity**. Consider the definition/explanation of pay equity found on the Equal Pay Coalition website:

> Pay equity is equal pay for work of equal value. Pay equity is the fundamental human right of women workers to be paid wages that are free of the systemic gender-based discrimination that values and pays women's work less than men's work of comparable value. (www.equalpaycoalition.org/about-pay-equity/)

The principle of pay equity begins with recognizing, as sociologists long have, that there are certain jobs that can be identified as "women's jobs" and others that can be called "men's jobs," and that the "feminizing" of

a job has traditionally been accompanied by a decrease in salary and benefits. Professions associated with women include childcare, nursing, and library science. A good example of a feminized occupation is secretarial work, which in the late nineteenth century was strictly a man's job.

Implementing pay equity involves looking at the salaries and benefits awarded in a traditionally female-dominated industry (nursing, say) and making sure that these are equal to the salaries and benefits paid in a traditionally "male" occupation that is comparable in terms of its educational qualifications, hours worked, and social value (an X-ray technician, for example). To quote again the website of the Equal Pay Coalition:

> Pay equity requires that women's and men's jobs be evaluated in a non-discriminatory way by accurately identifying and valuing the skill, effort, responsibility and working conditions of the job. Pay equity requires that female jobs be paid the same as male jobs of similar value. If a female job is paid less than a male job of similar value, pay equity requires that pay to the female job be raised to . . . match the male job. (www.equalpaycoalition.org/what_is.php)

Honey, I Shrunk the Wage Gap

When it comes to the imbalance in salaries earned by men and women, there is some good news. In an excellent article entitled "Why Has the Gender Wage Gap Narrowed?" Marie Drolet, a senior research economist with Statistics Canada, demonstrated that from 1988 to 2008 the gender wage gap in Canada decreased. Using the ratio of men's to women's hourly wages as a primary measure of equality, she showed that the degree of equality increased from 0.757 in

What do YOU think?

1. Do you think that the diminishing equality with age reflects an age difference (i.e. that the decrease in equality is a product of age and stage of career) or a cohort difference (i.e. today's young workers will experience the same or even greater gender wage equality throughout their working years)?

2. Do you think that there will be a *significantly* narrowed gap in the next 20 years? Why or why not?

Telling It Like It Is

A Writer's POV

How to Get Along in a Male-Dominated Workplace

Shaunti Feldhahn is a popular author specializing in explaining the "inner lives of men" to women. In research for her book *The Male Factor: The Unwritten Rules, Misperceptions, and Secret Beliefs of Men in the Workplace*, she had 3,000 men fill out an anonymous survey asking for their thoughts on workplace interactions. The following observations are excerpted from an article that appeared in the Toronto *Star* (Nebenzahl 2011: B5).

Three Golden Rules

First, get to the point. Men want to hear the details only after the main point is made. The woman who is processing verbally may simply look scatterbrained. Second, don't overreact. Your male colleague will then be more comfortable addressing concerns or offering criticism. Third, let it go. That means don't hold grudges. Three out of four men in the survey, Feldhahn writes, "looked quite negatively at someone who did not let a conflict go, perceiving as a big problem for the company and an individual's career."

Feldhahn raised another significant point:

A worker shouldn't take things too personally. This is a troubling behaviour many

talented women exhibit, said many of the men surveyed. A woman who is asked to do better or change something sees this as disapproval, one interviewee complains. "The men may say, 'Well, I disagree with you about that,' or 'That's fine.' Then they walk away and it's over. It's not really that way with women, even senior women." In a man's mind, these interviewees said, it should be possible to be upset with a situation, but not take it personally.

What do YOU think?

1. If a similar questionnaire were developed for workplaces dominated by women, what three golden rules might the research produce?

2. It is likely that women were in the minority in many of the workplaces Feldhahn studied. Assuming that is so, could "taking things personally" have more to do with the way criticism is raised (i.e. by a male manager inexperienced in delivering feedback to a woman employee)? Could the apparent overreaction have anything to do with the uncertainty with which a woman might perceive her position, given how much harder than her male colleagues she has had to work to prove herself on the road to achieving a position in a male-dominated workplace?

1988 to 0.833 in 2008. Drolet found the greatest degree of equality in the lowest age group she studied (25- to 29-year-olds), where the ratio rose from 0.846 to 0.901 over the 20-year period. The ratio diminishes with successive age groups before bottoming out at 0.74 in the 45–49 age group (Drolet 2011: Table 1).

The Globalization of Work

Outsourcing

Outsourcing refers to the practice of sending work for a company or public service outside of the usual ranks of workers and employees to companies and individuals outside the organization. From a worker's perspective this can, in the private sector, mean the loss of a well-paying unionized job to a cheaper, non-unionized worker in another company or even another country. In the public sector, this can mean the loss of new jobs (certainly new unionized jobs), less equity hiring (i.e. hiring people from among social groups recognized as being underemployed, including women, visible minorities, Aboriginal people, and the disabled), and less freedom of access to information generated by the companies doing the outsourced work. One of the first results of free trade was the migration abroad of relatively unskilled work in domestic industries such as clothing manufacture; today, even the traditional Canadian bush jacket (popularized by comedian Red Green and sometimes known in Ontario as a Kenora dinner jacket) is made in China. Call centre jobs relocated to India and IT jobs all over the world are other examples of outsourced work. Companies have cut costs, and Canadians have lost jobs.

In March 2011, the Canadian Centre for Policy Alternatives, a recently formed think tank, published an enlightening article called "The Shadow Public Service: The Swelling Ranks of Federal Government Outsourced Workers" (Macdonald 2011). It demonstrates how unionized public service workers—civil servants working for the Canadian government—are having their numbers reduced through the outsourcing of their work to nonunionized companies. Not only have outsourcing costs ballooned while the budgets of many federal departments have been capped, the outside contractors are not held to the same hiring practices, privacy policies, and standards of transparency required within the public service.

Going Global

Migrant Workers, Disposable Workers

The Temporary Foreign Worker Program (TFWP) is not just a federal device for bringing foreign workers into Canada: it is a creature of globalization that has a profound effect on the conditions of work in Canada.

Under the program, the owner of a company initiates a hiring process by asking the federal government for a labour market opinion (LMO), which would declare that there is a need to hire workers from another country to fill a need in a particular industry here in Canada. Traditionally, the program was used primarily to bring seasonal agricultural workers (i.e. fruit pickers) and live-in caregivers (i.e. nannies) into Canada to perform work that most Canadians are not eager to accept. The program legitimizes what could in some circumstances be deemed slave labour, and often produces a supply of **disposable workers**, who are kept in the country only for as long as the work is available, with no promise of permanent residence or citizenship. Many were and are overworked, underpaid, and given inadequate housing and privacy. In practice even more than in theory, their rights are few.

More recently, and certainly since the Conservative Party came into power, the program has taken off, with the development of the Alberta tar sands fuelling a high demand for workers to take both high-skilled and low-skilled jobs. In 2007, Alberta employers applied for 100,000 temporary workers. By the end of 2008 there were 251,235 temporary foreign workers in Canada, two-and-a-half times the number of temporary foreign workers in 2005 (99,000) (Contenta & Monsebraaten 2009a, 2009b). By 2009, employers in Alberta and in British Columbia (which was absorbed in last-minute preparations for the 2010 Winter Olympics) had their LMOs fast-tracked, so that the turnaround time was just a little over a month. These requests focused on 33 job areas, including construction trade workers (such as carpenters and roofers) and low-level service jobs (hotel staff, sales clerks, residential cleaners).

The abuses of the system, and of the workers involved, are many, as we shall see. Award-winning Canadian journalist Andrew Nikiforuk reports that in his home province of Alberta:

> Abuse of guest workers is so widespread that the Alberta government handled 800 complaints in just one 3-month period in 2008. Qualified chefs hired in Fiji typically ended up sweeping floors in Alberta, while 120 Chinese construction workers at CNRL's [Canadian Natural Resources Limited's] Horizon Mine received only a fraction of their wages due to corrupt contracting practices. (Nikiforuk 2009: 203)

And yet, migrant workers desperate for jobs are in some cases so anxious to come to Canada that they

The Racialized Workplace: Working for Themselves

Like other social institutions, the Canadian workplace is racialized. We have seen, earlier in the chapter, how the myth of the alien agitator and the threat of the temporary foreign worker have been cultivated to create suspicion and anti-immigrant sentiment in the Canadian workplace. In North America, the scaremongering over foreigners "taking away our jobs" dates back to the 1840s, when the Irish potato famine sent refugees from their homeland across the Atlantic to find work. Signs reading "No Irish Need Apply" still appeared in Toronto around the end of the nineteenth century. Immigrants facing discriminatory hiring practices developed the strategy of working for themselves in what could be called **ethnic** or **racial industries**. In England, displaced Irish immigrants became the orange vendors of London—the importing of oranges came to be known as the "Irish harvest." Here in Canada, Italian workers who managed to find work building Toronto's streetcar and subway system in time began operating

are willing to pay entrance fees charged illegally by recruitment officers. Often these workers end up using the greater share of their wages to pay off the extortionists. Meanwhile, many people recruited to perform skilled labour find themselves employed in low-skill, low-pay jobs once they get here. Why? Because it is time-consuming and costly for employers to apply for a new LMO when the work they need done changes; it is simpler to shift recruited workers from well-paying and relatively skilled jobs into lower-skill jobs that pay far less, giving the workers little warning and no outlet for their complaints. And while federal governmental rules state that reasonable, affordable housing and healthcare must be provided by the employer, there is little actual monitoring of employer practices. As the supply of illegal workers in the big cities grows, employers get used (Toronto *Star* writers Sandro Contenta and Laurie Monsebraaten use the term "addicted") to treating their "guest" workers like disposable goods—wherever they were born.

It is not just the foreign workers who can suffer under this system. The TFWP can be and has been used as an instrument of collective agreement and union busting. A case in point involves Windsor Manor, a nursing home with 149 residents in Kelowna, BC, owned by Park Place Seniors Living, which runs 11 nursing homes in the province. In September 2006, Windsor Manor laid off some 70 long-serving care aides, all of them members of the British Columbia General Employees Union (BCGEU). They were earning just over $19.24 per hour, with good benefits that included a pension, generous sick leave, and paid vacation. Through a job agency, AdvoCare Health Services, Windsor Manor offered the laid-off staff the same positions at between four and five dollars an hour less, and with benefits severely cut. Not surprisingly, 40 per cent of the home's former employees refused. AdvoCare had anticipated this problem, and had applied for and received an LMO to hire temporary foreign workers from Columbia, India, the Philippines, and South Korea to replace the departed workers. They were able to do so because the provincial Liberal government had, in 2003, passed Bill 29, the ironically named Health and Social Services Delivery Improvement Act, which permitted healthcare employers to eliminate job security from signed collective agreements with health and social service workers.

The story faded as news (as C. Wright Mills would have predicted), so we had to call a union representative to find out what happened to the laid-off workers. The results were, unfortunately, predictable. A small number of employees accepted the diminished pay and benefits to stay on at Windsor Manor. Among those who left, some were able to carry their benefits into related jobs, while others, at least, were able to claim a half-decent severance package. Generally, though, the TFWP ploy worked, leaving the workers worse off than they were before.

their own house and road construction companies. Greek immigrants took over the restaurant business in the same city, while Portuguese immigrants ran drivers' education schools and office cleaning companies. More recently, Korean convenience stores and South Asian–run gas stations appear across the country, and as Figure 17.1 shows, self-employment rates among immigrants have been on the rise for some time now.

How Safe Is Work?

When I ask students what they believe are the most high-risk jobs in Canada, they typically respond with police officers and firefighters.

Not so.

Work-related deaths in other occupations are far greater in number than they are for emergency services personnel. In 2009, a year in which 939 Canadian workers died in job-related accidents, the highest on-the-job fatality rate occurred among those who fish and trap for a living (see Table 17.3).

The number of workplace fatalities in Canada has been slowly climbing (along with occasional falls) over the last 20 years, as Figure 17.2 shows. Ontario "led the way" each year, peaking at 439 workplace deaths in 2007, with Quebec and BC not far behind. If the average Canadian worker puts in 230 days of work a year, then the 2010 total for workplace fatalities in Canada

Table 17.3 High-risk jobs in Canada, 2009

INDUSTRY	FATALITIES PER 100,000
Fishing and trapping	52
Mining, quarrying, and oil wells	46.9
Logging and forestry	33.3
Construction	20.2
Transportation and storage	16

Source: www.cbc.ca/news/interactives/map-workplacesafety/cbcMap2.swf

works out to a rate of close to five per day. And these are the reported and determined deaths—slow deaths from radiation, asbestos, and other occupational hazards that may take years to take a life are not always connected with the workplace. April 28 is the National Day of Mourning for people killed at work.

What do YOU think?

Are you surprised by the number of workplace fatalities in Canada? Is it higher or lower than what you would have expected? Are you surprised by the industries in which these fatalities most commonly occur? Why do you think these figures are not well known in Canada?

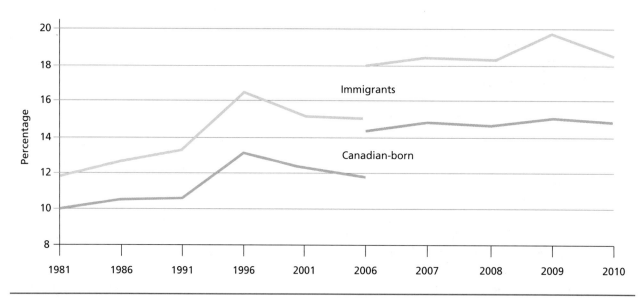

Figure 17.1 Self-employment as a percentage of total employed individuals by immigration status, 1981–2010

Source: Statistics Canada, Hou/Wang, Immigrants in self-employment, pg. 4. http://www.statcan.gc.ca/pub/75-001-x/2011003/article/11500-eng.pdf. Reproduced and distributed on an "as is" basis with the permission of Statistics Canada.

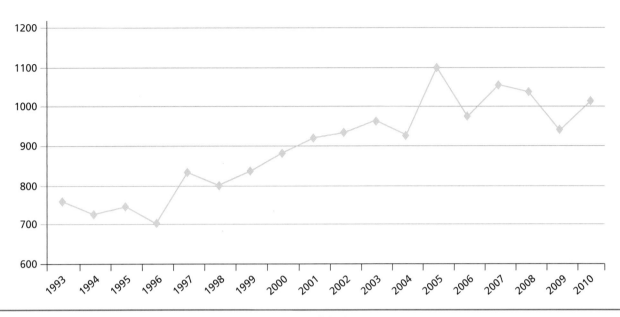

Figure 17.2 Workplace fatalities in Canada, 1993–2010

Source: Based on data from The Association of Workers' Compensation Boards of Canada at http://www.awcbc.org/common/assets/nwisptables/all_tables.pdf

Why do you think immigrants often end up working for themselves? What effect does immigrant self-employment and the growth of "ethnic industries" have on Canadian society?

WRAP IT UP

Summary

If this chapter showed anything, it is that work is a divisive topic. We started off by looking at two early sociologists whose theories about the division of labour have had a lasting influence on the way we view work. Durkheim's classification of work according to whether it promotes mechanical or organic solidarity is mainly about whether the members of a community perform the same kinds of work or different, complementary kinds of work. Organic solidarity is more characteristic of larger communities with diversified economies, and Durkheim found that these kinds of community tend to experience a greater loss of social equality. Marx, likewise, examined the ways that work creates inequality. His model was based on the relational distinction between owners and workers, the major source of class conflict.

A good portion of the chapter focused on the benefits, drawbacks, and contrasting views of unionized workers and strikes. One of our favourite sociologists, C. Wright Mills, provided us with some thoughts on union leaders and the unhappy, often adversarial relationship between organized labour and the media; it's worth asking whether his ideas, written more than half a century ago, still apply today. This discussion was followed by a look at the gender wage gap, informed in particular by the insightful studies of early Canadian sociologist Annie Marion MacLean, and then the supposed competition for jobs between domestic workers and workers abroad. Finally, as many things do, we ended with death (in the workplace).

THINK BACK

Questions for Critical Review

1. What is the difference between *work* and *employment*? Why is it important to recognize the difference?

2. How might Marx's theories on labour relate to an increasingly globalized world?

3. Do unions have a role in twenty-first–century Canada? Should they? Are they more important in either the public sector or private sector? What do you see as the future of unions in Canada?

4. Can it be said that media in Canada are not union-friendly? Scan a newspaper or online news site for stories about labour. Are there any "good-news" stories among them? What appears to be the attitude towards unions of the authors of any stories you examine?

5. What evidence is there that work is racialized in Canada? Is the racialization of labour a trend you expect to continue?

6. What is a *disposable worker*? What relationship does a disposable worker have to a *guest worker*? Do you believe that the number of disposable workers will increase in Canada?

READ ON

Online

CUPE

http://cupe.ca

> This is the main site for the Canadian Union of Public Employees; it will give you a look at the many functions of the largest union in Canada.

Why Has the Gender Wage Gap Narrowed?

www.statcan.gc.ca/pub/75-001-x/2011001/pdf/11394-eng.pdf

> This article by Statistics Canada senior research economist Marie Drolet gives a detailed and revealing look at the gender wage gap in Canada.

The Cream Separator

www.youtube.com/watch?v=IE5fOJfKRNk

> This 6-minute YouTube clip allows you to hear a brilliant analogy of work and class relationships by Tommy Douglas, an inspiring politician with degrees in sociology, set to a montage of relevant archival images.

In Print

Stephen L. Endicott (2002), *Bienfait: The Saskatchewan Miners' Struggle of '31* (Toronto: University of Toronto Press).

> Canadian resource industries were especially hard hit by the Great Depression of the 1930s and saw considerable labour unrest as employers slashed worker salaries in a desperate effort to cut costs. A strike by coal miners in Bienfait, Saskatchewan, became a flashpoint when a peaceful protest turned rowdy, and three miners were fatally shot by police. Endicott's book is an insightful look at the dynamics of this classic coal mine strike.

Reinhold Kramer & Tom Mitchell (2010), *When the State Trembled: How A.J. Andrews and the Citizens' Committee Broke the Winnipeg General Strike* (Toronto: University of Toronto Press).

> Kramer and Mitchell give a detailed and fascinating account of the largest strike in Canadian history.

C. Wright Mills (2001 [1948]), *The New Men of Power: America's Labor Leaders* (Urbana & Chicago: University of Illinois Press).

> A close study, by our favourite sociologist, of union leaders in the United States yields insights that are very useful in looking at unions today.

Learning Objectives

After reading this chapter, you should be able to

- explain what is meant by the terms *sick role* and *social course of disease*
- outline the various aspects of *biomedicine*, and contrast them with alternative medical practices, such as those found among Chinese healers and Canada's Aboriginal peoples
- discuss how the process of *medicalization* takes place
- articulate the different views surrounding the accreditation of immigrant doctors
- provide an overview of Ivan Illich's critique of modern medicine.

Key Terms

- absolutist
- alternative medicine
- Arctic hysteria
- Big Pharma
- biomedicine
- brain drain
- clinical iatrogenesis
- commodification
- complementary medicine
- critical sociology
- cultural iatrogenesis
- cultural syndromes
- cultures of medicine
- iatrogenesis
- inverse care law
- medicalization
- medical sociology
- patient role
- policy sociology
- posttraumatic stress disorder
- psychoneuroimmu-nology
- racialized
- radical monopoly
- reductionist
- sick role
- social course (of disease)
- social iatrogenesis

Names to Know

- Talcott Parsons
- Ivan Illich

A trash can for biological and infectious waste, outside a feedlot run by Granjas Carroll de Mexico Farms, one of a number of industrial pig farms in Mexico owned or partly owned by Smithfield Foods. The lake contains the excrement and urine of 1,500 pigs, as well as other waste.

Swine Flu: Big Farm Meets Big Pharma

We will remember 2009 as the year of the swine flu scare. Or, given that the H1N1 virus never quite lived up to the fear-mongering hype, maybe we won't. But the scare and the virus survive as topics of interest to medical sociologists for the way they were socially constructed by two big industries, the main players in the drama. We call them Big Farm and Big Pharma.

Big Farm

To analyze the swine flu of 2009 from a sociological perspective, we have to examine the practices—social and environmental—of the industrial farm in La Gloria, Mexico, where the H1N1 virus emerged. It was run by Smithfield Foods Inc., an American company based in Virginia. Operating in nine countries, Smithfield is the world's largest "producer and processor" of pork.

The company has a horrible environmental record. In 1997 it was fined $12.6 million for violating the US Clean Water Act. The company's industrial farm practices include keeping a high concentration of pigs (typically within the small stalls used to confine pregnant and nursing sows) and dumping hog feces into nearby rivers with little attempt at treating the material to make it less polluting. These practices have made Smithfield a target for farm workers and nearby residents, who blame the company for creating health problems. In the face of public opposition in its home country, Smithfield found Mexico, with its relative lack of environmental controls, an attractive site for its commercial farming.

A critical sociologist would suggest that swine flu and the greater danger of serious illness to workers and locals are products of the practices and attitudes of industrial farms and the environmentally lax governments they deal with. And yet, we read nothing in the mainstream media about Smithfield Foods during the H1N1 scare of 2009.

Big Pharma

The term **Big Pharma** is used to refer to the world's large pharmaceutical companies, which reap enormous annual profits from developing and manufacturing the drugs used to fight and manage disease. Take Roche, the owners of the patent for the main vaccine used against swine flu, Tamiflu (its generic name is oseltamivir). During the 2005 scare surrounding avian (bird) flu, Canada, the US, Britain, Israel, and Australia bought billions of dollars' worth of Tamiflu to stockpile "just in case" of a serious outbreak. The money was mostly wasted on a pandemic that never emerged (or, if you prefer, never lived up to the hype). Meanwhile, countries that couldn't afford the expensive patented vaccine, and companies that wanted to provide generic versions of oseltamivir, had to fight to make those cheaper versions of the vaccine available. In 2009, an Indian company (Cipla Ltd) won the right to produce an alternative version of Tamiflu, called Antiflu, for the populace of India. Canadians were not so fortunate. Big Pharma lobbies against generic drugs, which cut into their massive profits. They invest hugely in research and development, and fiercely defend their patents. Their lobby is strong in Canada, and affects policy. Big Pharma benefits when the media uncritically spreads fear over pandemics, sending concerned citizens to the nearest public health clinic for an immunization shot. Curiously, the same drug companies that market and sell anti-viral drugs seem immune to media criticism. (Big Pharma spends a lot on advertising, in print and online news media, and with their advertising dollars comes some influence.) The flu shot sold in Canada hadn't been through a complete set of clinical trials when it was distributed in the fight against H1N1. Possible side effects and risks to people with certain pre-existing conditions weren't completely known when the vaccine began to be used. Yet the Canadian government granted GlaxoSmithKline (GSK, a manufacturer of the anti–swine flu vaccine) indemnity, meaning that the government (that is, you, the taxpayer) would cover the cost of any lawsuit filed against the drug maker, in the event the drug failed to work or produced fatal side effects. GSK might have invested heavily in developing the vaccine, but the government gave the company a deal that carried no financial risk and the promise of huge profits for the drug manufacturer, which currently earns an estimated $1.66 billion (US) a year on sales of Tamiflu.

What do YOU think?

Facing an outbreak of a potentially deadly flu epidemic, the Canadian government purchased the only vaccine believed to effectively combat the virus, in quantities sufficient to immunize the entire country, even though the vaccine had not been through the full set of clinical trials. Ignoring the fact that the epidemic never really materialized (hindsight is 20/20, after all), did the government at the time make the best decision for the health of Canadians? What were the alternatives?

Introduction: The Social Side of Medicine

Medical sociology is based on the view that medical practices and beliefs are intensely social. A large part of medical sociology involves **policy sociology**, which is about generating sociological data to help governments and health professionals develop the policies that drive healthcare in this country. Thus, we can say that one of the principal aims of medical sociology is to improve the delivery of health services through sociologically informed research. **Critical sociology** contributes significantly as well, especially when the focus shifts to the practices of multinational pharmaceutical companies (as in the opening narrative), medical schools (particularly when they raise their fees), and privately run, for-profit clinics and hospitals.

Healing is achieved through social means, so it's natural that sociology has a lot to contribute to our understanding of the field of medicine. "Race," gender, ethnicity, age, and class—all social factors—can greatly affect an individual's experience of the medical professions. How? Let's say you're a middle-aged woman living outside the city, suffering from intensely sore feet. You go to your family doctor. She was born in Sri Lanka and educated in Britain, having moved to Canada just five years ago. She can't find a cause for your ailment, so she recommends a number of specialists. Which specialists she recommends will depend on her professional social network, the circle of people she knows and trusts. This network depends on such social factors as the location of her practice (outside the city) and the level of status she has a doctor (itself possibly determined by how long she has been practising and the degree to which she has been politically active in medical associations). Religion can be a factor, since certain hospitals are governed by specific religious groups. Her sex might be a factor, as men are still more prominent in medicine than women are.

Compare this scenario with that of a very successful businessperson with a prominent white male doctor who has hospital privileges at one of the best hospitals in the city. Your doctor has been head of the provincial medical association and is often asked to present papers at medical conferences around the world. Imagine how his professional social network might differ from that of the doctor discussed in the preceding paragraph, and how your treatment might differ as a result.

This is just one illustration of why sociology cannot be ignored when it comes to health, an idea we hope to reinforce over the course of this chapter with many more examples. Now you can just sit back and say, "Ah!"

The Sick Role

American sociologist **Talcott Parsons** (1902–1979) came up with perhaps the first medical sociology term when, in *The Social System* (1951), he developed the concept of the **sick** (or **patient**) **role**. Like other sociological roles, he argued, being sick came with certain expectations—four, to be exact. In his thinking, two relate to what the sick person can expect from society, two to what society should expect of the sick person. The four expectations are outlined as follows:

1. The person engaged in the sick role should expect to be granted "exemption from normal social responsibilities." In other words, a sick patient should not be expected to have to work, either at home or at his or her job, while he or she recovers.
2. The patient should expect to be "taken care of" rather than having to take care of him- or herself.
3. The patient is socially obligated to try to "get well" rather than remain in the undesirable state of being ill.
4. The sick person is socially obligated to "seek technically competent help" (in other words, the help of a qualified health professional).

The sick role, according to Parsons, gives the individual licence to be temporarily "deviant" with regards to the first two expectations, provided that he or she acts in accordance with the second two.

Parsons' work is considered the epitome of structural functionalism, in terms of both its strengths and its weaknesses. Structural functionalism presumes a social uniformity that conflict or critical sociologists would challenge. But ask yourself: is the sick role the same for everybody? The first challenge to the uniformity of the structural-functionalist model came quickly. In 1954, just three years after Parsons' work was published, Earl Koos wrote *The Health of Regionville: What the People Thought and Did About It*. It was based on research he had carried out between 1946 and 1950 on differences in what people thought and did about their health depending on their class. He learned that people in higher occupational groups were better able to afford to play the sick role, a privilege less available to those of lower occupational groups.

Similar arguments against the uniformity of the sick role can be made based on other standard sociological factors, such as gender, ethnic background, and age. Society has different expectations for, as one

This worker has just been injured at the job site. According to the sick role, what actions is he expected to take? What kind of treatment should he expect? Now, imagine he has a wife and a young child at home and is paid only for the hours he works. Why might he opt out of the social contract that goes along with the sick role?

TV commercial calls her, "Dr Mom" than for Dad. When children are sick, it is the mother who is typically expected to take time off work to look after them. And who is *least* likely to be able to play the sick role if the whole family gets sick? We can also look at people with chronic illnesses or disabilities. Are they to be considered permanently "deviant" according to Parsons' model?

When looking critically at Parsons' model of the sick role, it is hard to defend its universal applicability. In part, this is because the model changes over time. Ivan Emke (2002) has proposed that in Canada at the turn of the twenty-first century, the sick role carries five new expectations. Two of these are central. The first is that "patients in the New Economy are responsible for their own illnesses." Emke's point is that instead of looking at social and environmental causes of sickness (pollution, unsafe working and living conditions, stress through overworking, economic insecurity, and social disruption), we've become inclined to blame individual "choices" (smoking, drinking, not belonging to a health club, not making time for exercise, eating foods with trans fats). Emke notes that the bulk of cancer information currently provided in ads and public health materials focuses on individual risk factors rather than those presented by society, including polluting industries and weak anti-pollution laws. This expectation, by lowering society's sense that everyone is equally entitled to free healthcare, is borne at least in part on the search for ways to lower rising healthcare costs in Canada. Do we feel less sympathetic to smokers with lung cancer? You can see how those who buy into this expectation might use the underlying argument to justify charging "user fees" for some medical services.

The second new expectation we'd like to highlight is really a conflation of two expectations Emke identified: "the patient in the new economy is instructed to tread lightly on the system" and "patients in the new economy are not to be trusted." We could recast it, a little less subtly, as "patients are assumed to be abusing the system." Emke raises this belief in connection with the increasing public education campaign to encourage people to use as few medical services as they can. He cites as an example a 1994 pilot project by the Conservative Ontario government designed to encourage residents of the city of London to stop going to their family doctor for relatively minor complaints. No research had been done to see whether people were

Do you believe that people who smoke are fully entitled to free healthcare? What about people who eat too much junk food? People who engage in dangerous recreational activities?

actually "abusing" the system. The assumption underlying the project was clearly that escalating healthcare costs can be attributed significantly to a large number of "unnecessary" visits to family doctors. Perhaps, though, rising healthcare costs are actually the result of building huge technology-intensive hospitals that are less cost-effective than having a greater number of small-town and community-based medical centres. Perhaps nurses, who make less than doctors do, should be permitted to perform basic medical procedures (stitching wounds, for example) that doctors are normally responsible for, so that the same work can be done more efficiently and at lower cost.

The Social Course of Disease

One of the medical breakthroughs of the nineteenth century was the realization that every disease has a natural, or biological, course it goes through, a lifespan during which you catch the disease, suffer through it, and gradually get well (or, in some cases, sicker). It depends on the virus or bacteria, and the way the human body reacts to it. Think of a cold virus. Doctors can prescribe medicine to help alleviate the symptoms and speed up recovery, but they can't fundamentally change the natural course of a cold.

Our Stories

The Social Course of Tuberculosis among the Inuit

The ethnic background of a patient is a sociological factor that can greatly affect the social course of a disease. Witness the treatment of Inuit with tuberculosis. In 1949, new antibiotics, combined with improved sanitation, screening, and treatment, helped reduce the tuberculosis rate in Canada to about 33 deaths per 100,000, down from 165 per 100,000 in 1908. But at the same time, the rate among Canada's Inuit population was rising dramatically, peaking at an alarming 569 per 100,000 (then highest in the world) in 1952. In that year, there were 54 deaths among the Canadian Inuit population of roughly 10,000.

The high rate of TB among Canada's Inuit was caused by a number of factors. First, the severe cold of the Arctic—though not cold enough to kill the *tuberculosis bacillus*—made the Inuit especially susceptible to respiratory problems. The intimate closeness of the Inuit in their igloos facilitated the spread of TB from one family member to another. A more significant cause was the increasing contact with people from southern Canada. Author and researcher Pat Grygier explains that

as the Inuit adapted to accommodate the desires of the newcomers, trapping to exchange furs for store goods or working for the RCMP or on military construction sites for cash, their highly nutritious fresh-meat

or fish diet and their warm caribou-skin clothing were gradually exchanged for a diet largely of white flour, lard, tea, jam, and canned goods, and for much less warm southern clothing. When the caribou declined or the pattern of migration changed (possibly as a result of the incursions of military and mining into the North), malnutrition occurred. (Grygier 1994: 55)

Arguably as devastating as the disease itself was the way in which Inuit TB sufferers were treated. At the time, the standard treatment for tuberculosis involved a period of confinement—from six months to two years—in a hospital or sanatorium. These were not to be built in the Arctic, so the Inuit with tuberculosis were brought (or, more accurately, taken, since many were reluctant to leave their homes) to southern Canada. Grygier eloquently describes what happened once health professionals, brought north by ship, had conducted their patient examinations:

When the doctors had made their final decision on whether an individual should go to hospital for treatment or stay in the North, the evacuees were sent down to the Inuit quarters in the prow of the ship and the rest were sent ashore. The evacuees were not allowed to go ashore to collect

Likewise, we can speak of the **social course** that diseases and disorders go through, a course affected by sociological factors such as ethnic background, culture, class, age, and sex of the people most commonly affected. The following example traces the social course of an injury and illustrates how that course is affected by just one sociological factor: class.

I recently injured myself while running. I am not a runner, and it wasn't for exercise. I was running when I should have walked, and I ruptured my Achilles tendon, which wasn't prepared for the rigours of this unfamiliar activity. Here is how my social

class affected the social course of the injury and my recovery from it.

During my initial trip to the hospital, my left leg was put in a cast, so that I could move only through the use of crutches. I was billed for both the fibreglass cast and the crutches, but because I am a full-time salaried employee with benefits, my employee health plan covered the cost of both. My middle-class job does not require heavy lifting, or great physical exertion, or standing for long periods of time, so I continued to work, despite having to hobble around the campus on crutches for nine weeks. I could have

belongings, to say goodbye, or to make arrangements for their families or goods. If a mother was judged sick but her children were not infected, the children (sometimes including unweaned babies) were given to an Inuk woman going ashore. Fathers had no chance to arrange for someone to hunt for food for their families or to look after their dogs and equipment. Mothers had no chance to arrange for someone to care for their children or to sew and process the skins needed to keep the family warm. . . .

Those needing hospital treatment were kept on board, the rest sent ashore, and on sailed the ship to the next settlement. (Grygier 1994: 96)

The tuberculosis rate among the Inuit dropped during the 1950s to a low of 53 per 100,000 (amounting to just 5 actual cases) in 1959, but the effects of the separation lasted. Many families were never reunited, often because a sick loved one died, but even when the TB-suffering family member recovered.

Tuberculosis is still a problem among Canada's Inuit, as this sign at a nurses' station in Cape Dorset, Nunavut, makes clear. According to Canada's Public Health Agency, the tuberculosis rate in Canada reached an all-time low of 4.6 per 100,000 in 2010, yet there were 101 active TB cases in Nunavut that year, representing a rate of 304.0 per 100,000 (CCDIC 2012). Is it possible that ethnicity is still a factor in the social course of this disease?

decided not to work during that period, and a good disability allowance would have ensured that I lost no significant income. The injury was severe enough that there was the distinct possibility of a blood clot, which could lead to a stroke or lung failure, but my doctor persuaded me to take preventative medication to ensure that any clot wouldn't threaten my health. Fortunately, my drug plan covers almost all of the cost of this expensive drug.

My wife suffers from a disability that makes it very difficult for her to work full-time. Because I am well paid in my middle-class job, we can afford to live on one income, and so my wife was able to be at home and to take very good care of me during my recovery period. It would have been much worse for my emotional state and physical health (I would likely have tried doing things that might have brought further injury upon myself) if she had not been so diligent in helping me. I owe her a lot.

Once the cast was removed, I began to do physiotherapy, as advised by the specialist (after asking, first, whether or not I had health insurance at work). It has helped immeasurably, and my recovery has proceeded much more quickly than I had hoped.

I can only imagine with dread what the social course of my healing would have been if I had been employed instead doing unskilled work in a factory or warehouse, or if I were unemployed and looking for work at the time of my injury. Then again, how would class have affected my recovery if I were a corporate executive earning a seven-figure salary? You will likely have picked up, too, on other sociological factors that influenced the social course of my recovery, including my marital status and the fact that I work and spend much of my time in a large urban centre with abundant medical resources and facilities. What would the social course of my recovery have been like had I been living alone, or caring for young children, or living in a rural area without access to transportation? What other factors might have changed the course?

The Our Stories box on pages 486–487 provides another example of factors that affect the social course of a disease. It's good to keep in mind that the sociological factors surrounding a patient, just like physical factors such as medicine, clean living conditions, and rest, can influence the social course of recovery in either a positive or a negative way.

Biomedicine

Biomedicine involves the application of standard principles and practices of Western scientific disciplines, particularly biology, in the diagnosis and treatment of symptoms of illness and disease. It uses physical tests to find defined, purely physical entities (such as bacteria, viruses, and trauma) and then applies purely physical medicines and therapies to counteract them. It is the dominant practice in Western society.

When, suffering from migraine headaches, you visit your family doctor and she prescribes medication to reduce the severity of your symptoms, you have experienced biomedicine. If you've grown up in Canada, this is likely the approach you expected when you booked your appointment. But there are other approaches to treatment that fall outside of mainstream medical practice (sometimes described as "conventional medicine"). We refer to these approaches collectively as **alternative** (or **complementary**) **medicine**. Your doctor, for instance, might have recommended acupuncture for your migraines. Or she might have recommended massage therapy or yoga as means of reducing the stress that may have contributed to your headaches. She might have tried to discover any environmental causes—bright lights in the area where you read or study, for example—of your condition. These would all be considered alternative approaches.

Alternative approaches are used to treat many medical ailments. Recent research in **psychoneuroimmunology**—the study of the effect of the mind on health and resistance to disease—has shown links between a person's psychological state and his or her ability to fight diseases such as cancer. A study at the University of Texas monitored the spread of cancer in two groups of mice. One group was placed in small plastic chambers for several hours at a time, which caused a surge in their stress hormones. Tumours in these mice grew more quickly and in greater number than those in the mice that were not so confined, suggesting a link between stress and the spread of the disease. As *The Globe and Mail*'s Margaret Philip (2006) reports, the study is one of a number that have caused oncologists to consider more holistic approaches to treating cancer sufferers, using massage, meditation, music therapy, and support groups to help reduce tension.

A good example of divergent biomedical and alternative approaches to health is childbirth. Most

North American women choose to deliver their infants in a hospital, under the care of a team of medical professionals including an obstetrician, an anaesthesiologist, and several nurses. Increasingly, however, women are choosing to stay at home to give birth under the care of a midwife. There are good reasons to recommend the latter approach. For one thing, many people find hospitals uncomfortable. Some women do not want to be separated from their families, especially if they have other young children, and knowing they will remain at home eliminates stressful contemplation of the hurried trip to the hospital once the contractions begin. Many new mothers-to-be find that a midwife is more available to provide support and answer questions than is an obstetrician. And, it's important to point out, for thousands of years and in many parts of the world today (in developed as well as developing countries), giving birth at home was and is the only option. On the other hand, there are many advantages to having a hospital birth, including ready access to doctors and medical equipment in the event that either the mother or the infant requires immediate care for life-threatening complications. Some women choose to combine these approaches by having a hospital birth attended by the midwife who has guided them through their pregnancy. In cases such as this, the term "complementary medicine" is really more apt: biomedicine and alternative medicine do not need to be mutually exclusive.

Biomedicine remains the norm in North American society, but it is increasingly called into question by those who endorse a more holistic approach to diagnosis and treatment. Biomedicine has been criticized for looking at health from a **reductionist** perspective that attributes medical conditions to single factors treatable with single remedies. It fails to take into account the broader set of circumstances surrounding a person's health or illness. Those involved in biomedicine are

When you look at this picture, do you see a woman being treated by "health professionals"? An illegal practice less than 25 years ago, midwifery is now an integral part of the medical system. Why do you think midwives were once banned from medical practice in Canada?

QUICK HITS

Hallucinations and Visions: Two "Views"

As evidence of the distinct cultures surrounding medicine, consider the following descriptions of "hallucinations," from a biomedical perspective, and "visions," from an Aboriginal perspective. Are they really different, or is it only in how we look at them?

Hallucinations

- things that are seen but are not physically there
- associated with drug use, nervous disorders, stress
- sign of mental or emotional instability.

Visions

- pictures, words, tunes, dances coming from a quest for visions
- associated with inspiration, intuition, "sixth sense"
- sign of spiritual health, creativity.

sometimes accused of being **absolutist**, of failing to recognize that just as there are different cultures when it comes to business, policing, or clothing, there are **cultures of medicine**, each with a unique approach to interpreting medicine in ways that reflect and reinforce other aspects of the culture from which it is derived. Every patient, critics argue, should be treated in the context of his or her culture. No single treatment should be applied universally across all cultures.

In Chapter 4 we touched on Anne Fadiman's study of the Hmong people living in the United States (Fadiman 1997). Originally from China, the Hmong were forced to flee their homeland after resisting the Chinese government and encouraging the participation of the United States in the Southeast Asian wars of the 1960s and 1970s. Fadiman's study shows how Hmong refugees suffered because of narrow Western biomedical practices that did not respect their cultural beliefs. She cites, as just one example, the failure of North American doctors to take into account their fear—widespread among the Hmong people—of losing their soul. The Hmong wear (and put on their infants) neck-rings and cotton-string spirit bracelets to combat their fear of soul loss, and they rely on their spirit doctors or shamans, the *tsiv neebs*, to address and help them overcome these fears. Problems occurred when

Hmong patients arriving at a refugee camp in Thailand had their spirit strings cut by American health workers, who claimed they were unsanitary. The neck-rings thought to hold intact the souls of babies were also removed, placing this especially vulnerable group in graver danger of soul loss in the eyes of the Hmong.

Medicalization

An offshoot of the biomedical approach to medicine is a practice known as medicalization. Sociologists Chang and Christakis define **medicalization** as:

> the process by which certain behaviours or conditions are defined as medical problems (rather than, for example, as moral or legal problems), and medical intervention becomes the focus of remedy and social control. (Chang & Christakis 2002: 152)

The point of reference for Chang and Christakis's discussion of medicalization is obesity. The authors were summarizing the results of a content analysis aimed at investigating how the discussion of obesity had changed between 1927 and 2000 in a widely consulted American medical textbook, the *Cecil Textbook of Medicine*. They found that although the textbook was consistent over time in citing, as the root cause of obesity, the factor of caloric intake exceeding energy expenditure, it had medicalized obesity through its successive editions. Early editions of the textbook identified "aberrant individual activities such as habitual overeating" as being of great significance; they placed blame for the condition squarely on the individual. Later editions looked more to genetic and social environmental factors, such as the increased availability of fast food and the decreased amount of physical labour required in many jobs.

Critics of the health industry's tendency to medicalize conditions describe the practice as a form of reductionism that reduces complex medical conditions to biomedical causes without examining possible sociocultural or political factors. A second, and related, criticism is that Western health professionals are too quick to situate the problem exclusively or primarily in the individual human body, rather than, say, in an oppressive social or political system. Medicalization, by ascribing conditions like alcoholism to genetic factors, does excuse the sufferer by removing individual blame, but at the same time it portrays the sufferer as a genetic "victim" who can be saved only by an intervention engineered by the medical profession. In this way, it takes away the individual's ability to make empowering choices that will affect the outcome of his or her condition. This leads to a further criticism: that medicalization promotes the **commodification** of healthcare by identifying certain conditions that might be considered normal (though slightly regrettable) as diseases that may be treated with "commodity cures" (such as certain drugs or procedures). Part of this commodifying process involves turning conditions that might be, in medical terms, relatively normal into deviant disorders (to use sociological terms). Examples for the aging male include obesity, male pattern baldness, increasingly frequent nighttime trips to the bathroom, and erectile "dysfunction." A current advertising campaign assures men that embarrassing excess breast tissue (there's even a medical name for it: gynecomastia) can be removed. These are not diseases; they are relatively normal aspects of the aging process and do not need to be medicalized. If it ain't broke (just a little bent), don't fix it.

A social determinist might argue that the upward trend in obesity rates is a societal problem having to do with the prevalence of fast food advertising and the ready availability of cheap, unhealthy food. So if our streets were lined with healthier options, would obesity rates decline? Is obesity more a social problem or an individual one?

Government agencies and health professionals are sometimes guilty of medicalizing disorders that can be traced to complicated social or environmental factors much more difficult to address than the purely medical factors. Medical journalist Lynn Payer offers an example in her eye-opening work *Disease-Mongers: How Doctors, Drug Companies, and Insurers Are Making You Feel Sick* (1992):

> When . . . a child died of lead poisoning in Michigan, there was a call for screening for lead poisoning. But when you read the circumstances, you found that the child was homeless, living in an abandoned building. Calling for blood testing was obviously easier than calling for a policy of providing safe and low-cost shelter for the poor, but who can doubt which policy would really benefit such children more? (Payer 1992: 39)

Posttraumatic stress disorder is another condition that is often medicalized (see Kleinman 1995). Suffered especially by those who have experienced the extreme violence of warfare (as soldiers or civilians), violent political oppression, or crime, PTSD was first diagnosed by Western psychiatrists who traced its origins to bleak, unstable environments in countries such as Cambodia, El Salvador, Tibet, and the former Republic of Yugoslavia. Gradually, though, the focus of treatment has shifted from the pathology of the environment to the pathology of the individual. Patients are often treated as though their psychobiological reactions to these harrowing circumstances are not normal, as if a psychologically healthy person would not react that way. To be clear, it is not wrong to help people by recognizing that they have suffered psychological trauma, but it is misleading to remove from an individual's story the sickness of the social situation he or she has endured.

Ivan Illich: Pioneering Critic of Medicalization

Ivan Illich (1927–2002) introduced the notion of medicalization in his highly creative and popular work. Although Illich was trained as a medieval historian, theologian, and philosopher, sociologists stake claim to him as a public sociologist.

Illich developed the concept of medicalization as part of a general critique of what he called **radical monopolies** in industrial societies. He described the concept as follows:

> A radical monopoly goes deeper than that of any one corporation or any one government. It can take many forms. . . . Ordinary monopolies corner the market; radical monopolies disable people from doing or making things on their own. . . . They impose a society-wide substitution of commodities for use-values by reshaping the milieu and by "appropriating" those of its general characteristics which have enabled people so far to cope on their own. Intensive education turns autodidacts [people who teach themselves] into unemployables, intensive agriculture destroys the subsistence farmer, and the deployment of police undermines the community's self control. The malignant spread of medicine has comparable results: it turns mutual care and self-medication into misdemeanors or felonies. (1976: 42)

This passage comes from a work called *Medical Nemesis: The Limits of Medicine*, which opens with the shocking claim: "The medical establishment has become a major threat to health" (1976: 1). In the book, Illich describes a "doctor-generated epidemic"

QUICK HITS

Illich on Medicalization

What do you think Illich meant by each of the following statements? Do you agree with him?

> The fact that the doctor population is higher where certain diseases have become rare has little to do with the doctors' ability to control or eliminate them. It simply means that doctors deploy themselves as they like, more so than other professionals, and that they tend to gather where the climate is healthy, where the water is clean, and where people are employed and can pay for their services. (1976: 21–2)

> In a complex technological hospital, negligence becomes "random human error" or "system breakdown," callousness becomes "scientific detachment," and incompetence becomes "a lack of specialized equipment." The depersonalization of diagnosis and therapy has changed malpractice from an ethical into a technical problem. (1976: 30)

> In every society, medicine, like law and religion, defines what is normal, proper, or desirable. Medicine has the authority to label one man's complaint a legitimate illness, to declare a second man sick though he himself does not complain, and to refuse a third social recognition of his pain, his disability, and even his death. It is medicine which stamps some pain as "merely subjective," some impairment as malingering, and some deaths—though not others—as suicide." (1976: 45)

> Medicine always creates illness as a social state. The recognized healer transmits to individuals the social possibilities for acting sick. Each culture has its own characteristic perception of disease and thus its unique hygienic mask. Disease takes its features from the physician who casts the actors into one of the available roles. To make people legitimately sick is as implicit in the physicians power as the poisonous potential of the remedy that works. (1976: 44)

that is harming the health of citizens in industrialized society by taking away people's freedom to heal themselves or prevent their illnesses, as well as their freedom to criticize industrial society for the ills of stress, pollution, and general danger that are "sickening" (i.e. making sick) the people. Illich's term for this is **iatrogenesis**, and he distinguished three different kinds:

- clinical iatrogenesis
- social iatrogenesis
- cultural iatrogenesis.

Clinical iatrogenesis refers to the various ways in which diagnosis and cure cause problems that are as bad or worse than the health problems they are meant to resolve. This occurs, for example, when a patient enters hospital for treatment of one ailment and becomes infected with a virus originating in the hospital. **Social iatrogenesis** occurs when political conditions that "render society unhealthy" are hidden or obscured (Illich 1976: 9). Examples include lax monitoring by government agencies of laws concerning workplace safety. **Cultural iatrogenesis** takes

place when the knowledge and abilities of the medical community are extolled or mythologized to the point where the authority of the health profession "tends to mystify and to expropriate the power of the individual to heal himself and to shape his or her environment" (Illich 1976: 9). In other words, the patient is given no credit for his or her role in the recovery.

Medical Sociology and Ethnicity

Unemployed Immigrant Doctors: A Problem with Many Standpoints

The Canadian healthcare system is currently facing a shortage of doctors in some communities far from large urban centres. At the same time, the country is welcoming immigrants with medical degrees and general credentials that are considered insufficient to qualify them to practise medicine in this country. It is a perplexing issue, one that must be considered from a number of standpoints (perspectives shaped by social location). The sections that follow outline four of these differing standpoints.

In July 2012, the Charlton campus of Hamilton's St Joseph's Hospital experienced an outbreak of *Clostridium difficile* (or *C. difficile*, as it's commonly known). While relatively harmless in most people, symptoms of the bacterial infection can be quite serious among elderly patients. In Canada, nursing homes and hospitals have been particularly susceptible to outbreaks of the infection. What form of iatrogenesis does this represent?

1. Immigrant Doctors

As an immigrant doctor, you have come to a country that offers a greater financial opportunity for you and your family. On the strength of skills and experience gained in your home country, you have scored highly in the "point system," by which the worthiness of candidates for immigration is judged. It seems as though the Canadian government is encouraging you to come. As soon as you arrive in Canada, the problems hit you in the face. If you have chosen to settle in Toronto—as many do—you encounter a two-step problem. First, your skills and knowledge must be assessed through a training program. The Ontario International Medical Graduate Program takes 48 weeks—close to a year—and has limited entrance. Assuming you manage to gain entrance and do well in the program, you still face a second, even higher hurdle: you must go through a residency program of several years in which you essentially re-learn everything you needed to know to earn your medical qualifications in the first place. But like many others in your position, you accept this and are eager to get on with it. However—and this is the biggest problem you face—there are so very few residency positions available. You are one of more than 1,100 immigrant doctors in Ontario competing for just 36 spots open each year in the residency program.

In the meantime, your family must eat. If you are fortunate, you may get a job in the medical field, possibly (with training) as a lab assistant. But it is more likely you will end up working as a telemarketer, driving a taxi, delivering pizza, or doing manual labour in factories. Your dream of practising your chosen profession in this country supposedly rich in opportunity has proven elusive.

2. Rural Communities

You live in a community that is home to fewer and fewer doctors. The older ones retire; the young graduates opt to take up medical work in the big city. Your family doctor has retired and closed her practice, and you, like her other patients, are scrambling to find another doctor to take you on. But most family doctors are already seeing more patients than they can handle. The trouble is that you're older and, face it, older people have more complicated and time-consuming medical problems, so you're not the most attractive candidate even if you managed to find a doctor taking new patients. So you put up with minor complaints, knowing that anything more serious will require a trip down to the big city, where the bigger research hospitals and more lucrative practices are.

Occasionally you wonder whether there's something your town should be doing to attract doctors. You don't really care where they come from. In Ontario, 136 communities have been designated as "underserved" by the provincial ministry of health. Saskatchewan and Newfoundland and Labrador have higher percentages of foreign-trained doctors than other provinces. The reason: not as many obstacles for immigrant doctors.

3. Countries of Origin of Internationally Trained Doctors

In developing countries, especially in rural areas, there are even fewer doctors per population than there are in Canada's rural communities. The cost of educating medical professionals

Naseem Ahmed Pasha arrived in Toronto from India in 2006, having completed medical school at Mysore University and then having practised for 15 years in India and Saudi Arabia. Although he has passed the Canadian exams, he hasn't been able to get into the requisite residency and currently earns a minimum-salary wage at a home improvement store. Do you think he was prepared for this when he came to Canada? What effect do you think the 6-year wait to practise his profession in this country has had on his morale? How do you think this type of situation can be changed (without taking away from residency opportunities for Canadian students)?

is prohibitively high. It is much more likely that your country will lose trained doctors to emigration than benefit from an influx of health professionals. In post-apartheid South Africa, the government decided to block doctors immigrating from other African nations to halt the **brain drain**—the exodus of educated professionals—eroding the healthcare systems of those countries. Canada experiences a bit of that brain drain when some of its medical specialists go to the US—but it's nothing compared to the brain drain of doctors leaving developing countries for North America.

4. Doctors' Associations

Placing restrictions on internationally trained medical graduates gives Canadian-trained doctors more power as a sociopolitical body of professionals. As Linda McQuaig explains in her commentary on a doctors' strike in New Brunswick in 2004,

> Doctors have managed to maintain enormous bargaining power in Canada by threatening, from time to time, to abandon us for more prosperous climes. But these threats only have teeth because doctors can rely on the fact that there is no one here to replace them if they go—even when potential replacements are already here and desperate to get to work. (McQuaig 2004)

On the other side, consider the Ontario Medical Association's "Position Paper on Physician Workforce Policy and Planning," dated 4 April 2002. It's a document addressing the OMA's concerns about "the problem of inadequate physician human resources, and the related consequences for public access to medical treatment." One of the 18 recommendations in the report was to "Temporarily increase the number of fully qualified international medical graduate (IMG) positions." In a 2004 speech, OMA president Dr Larry Erlick, addressing the same problems, noted that:

> We . . . need more foreign-trained physicians to practise in Ontario. The fact that we have relied on foreign-trained physicians in the past should come as no surprise, as 25 per cent of physicians practising today in this province are in fact international medical graduates! Some of the red tape has to be cut.

Still, in both documents, helping foreign-trained physicians gain accreditation to practise in Canada

QUICK HITS

Where Do You Go When You Don't Have a Family Doctor?

According to the Canadian Community Health Survey, in 2010, 4.4 million Canadians over the age of 12 were without a regular family doctor.

- In all age groups, men were more likely than women to report not having a regular a family doctor.
- Among those who had looked for a family doctor,
  - ➤ 40.0 per cent said that doctors in their area were not taking new patients
  - ➤ 31.3 per cent said their doctor had retired or left the area
  - ➤ 27.1 per cent said that no doctors were available in their area
  - ➤ 17.5 per cent gave other reasons.

(These add up to more than 100 per cent because respondents were permitted to choose more than one option.)

- Of those without a regular family doctor, 82.2 per cent reported they had a place to go when in need of health advice; these included:
  - ➤ walk-in clinics (61.8 per cent)
  - ➤ hospital emergency rooms (12.9 per cent)
  - ➤ community health centres (8.8 per cent)
  - ➤ other facilities, including hospital out-patient clinics and telephone health lines (16.6 per cent).

Source: Statistics Canada 2011c. Reproduced and distributed on an "as is" basis with the permission of Statistics Canada.

was clearly viewed as a secondary solution. The words "temporarily" and "fully qualified" in the first statement leave holes in that support, and Dr Erlick's recommendation was one of a number of "short-term

What do YOU think?

1. Are there any other "stakeholders" in this issue who should be considered?
2. What do you think the position of Canadian universities with medical schools would be?
3. Why do you think the word "temporarily" was put into Dr Erlick's recommendation?
4. What is your position on the subject of immigrant doctors?

recommendations," given decidedly less priority than bringing back Ontario medical graduates now practising elsewhere.

The Intersection of "Race" and Medicine

In Canada, "race" and the medical professions intersect at a number of points. The one we've chosen to examine here, in the section that follows and in the box on page 497, is the issue of nurses who are not white.

The Filipino Nurses

Filipinos were later than other Asian immigrant groups—Chinese, Japanese, Koreans, and South Asians—to come to Canada. It wasn't until 1962, when some of the more overt forms of discrimination in Canada's immigration policy were abolished, and again in 1967, when the points system rewarding candidates with desirable skills and education was established, that Filipino immigration to this country increased significantly.

In 1967, the demand for nurses in Canada outstripped the supply of qualified nursing professionals. That year, 4,262 nurses were allowed to immigrate to Canada; 1,140 of them—roughly 27 per cent—were Filipino. (In fact, an astonishing 43.3 per cent of the 2,632 immigrants from the Philippines were nurses.) Over the next three years, 2,002 of the 8,897 immigrant nurses—22.5 per cent—were Filipinos. More than a thousand Filipino nurses entered the country over the next five years.

During the same period, the United States also accepted a large number of Filipino nurses. However, the American approach to immigration was more expansive than the Canadian one in one crucial regard: whereas Canada limited the immigration of Filipinos to those with nursing experience or training, the US welcomed all manner of Filipino health professionals, including physicians, surgeons, and dentists. In 1970, for example, 968 Filipino physicians, surgeons, and dentists entered the US, compared with 954 nurses; that same year, all but 53 of the 571 Filipino health professionals to enter Canada were nurses.

Given that most of the Filipino nurses coming to Canada were young women in their twenties, Canada's immigration policy resulted in a huge gender imbalance among the Canadian Filipino population during the early years of Filipino immigration. The sex ratio of males to females among immigrants from the Philippines between 1967 and 1969 was about 1 to 2.75, with 2,293 men and 6,380 women coming to Canada during that time. While this rate would even out over the next two decades, with the percentage of male Filipino immigrants rising to 74 per cent of the total in 1971, 90 per cent in 1975, and 86 per cent in 1979, a second wave of large-scale immigration would lower it again. By 1992 it was back down to 50 per cent.

Sociological studies suggest that because they were fluent English speakers and Christians coming from a capitalist country where they were very familiar with Western culture, the Filipino immigrants adapted more easily to life in Canada than other Asian groups did. Even so, Winn (1988), in a study of 15 ethnic groups in Canada, demonstrated that while Filipinos ranked the highest in college or university education, their ranking dropped when it came to income return on university education. Imagine, as well, the effect on women coming from a culture where family is an extremely strong social element to one where they would often have to delay marriage until eligible Filipino immigrants arrived. Others, married in their home country, had to leave their husbands behind until, years later, they could sponsor them to immigrate.

The Racialization of Disease

An illness or disease has been **racialized** when it has become strongly associated with people of a particular ethnic background, and people of this background are treated negatively because of that association. A good example is severe acute respiratory syndrome, or SARS, an ailment that, during a 2003 outbreak, afflicted Canadians of all ethnic backgrounds but became primarily associated with two.

SARS: The Racialization of Disease

Canadians began hearing about severe acute respiratory syndrome in March 2003. Throughout the spring and early summer it became the focus of widespread media attention, and over the course of this period, the disease became racialized: because it originated in China, and because members of a Catholic Filipino community were among those who had contracted it, the disease took on a racial identity. Chinese and Filipino Canadians became targets of discrimination.

In June 2004, researchers Carrianne Leung and Jian Guan noted, among other things, how the mainstream

Telling It Like It Is

A Student POV

An Account of Systemic Racism from a Black First-Year Nursing Student

I regret to say that I have had my first clinical experience in the nursing profession and I feel I have already been subjected to systemic racism. Examples of this include disciplinary actions that are different from other student nurses such as when myself and a non-Black student returned late from break. I was pulled aside and it was stated that the teacher felt sorry for the other student. When I asked "why," it was implied that I coerced her into returning late against her will. Also, vague work appraisals are given and no specific areas of improvement are suggested. Comments such as, "You seem like a very angry person," and "I have a hard time approaching you and can only imagine how the residents feel,"

or "Any monkey can be trained to take a blood pressure" are an everyday occurrence. There are many cases where my mistakes are far more noted and exaggerated than those of other students. When defending myself (as I feel I am performing equally well to everyone else), I am labelled as not being "self-aware" and not accepting feedback. Yet, when feedback is taken and changes are made, I am told I take things too literally. As a result, I can do no right.

It is sad to say that events like these are commonplace. As a result, promotions as well as workload may not be fairly distributed.

—Nadine Smith

What do YOU think?

1. In what ways might the social situation of the clinical experience lend itself to forms of systemic or personal racism? What recourse should a student nurse have to be able to address this kind of experience?

2. Why do you think a black nursing student might be more sensitive to the inequality of the relationship between the clinical supervisor and the student nurse?

media had racialized SARS by portraying Asians as carriers of disease in a way that spread fear among non-Asian Canadians. Table 18.1 summarizes Leung and Guan's findings about the content of pictures accompanying articles on the disease in four national newspapers and periodicals (Leung & Guan 2004: 9, 10).

Leung and Guan found that photographs accompanying stories about SARS tended to feature Asians, particularly Asians wearing masks to reduce the spread of the disease. The researchers noted that the exaggerated use of frightening words and unreasonable parallels drawn between SARS and the Spanish influenza

Table 18.1 Photographic treatment of SARS in the national media, 2003

NEWSPAPER / MAGAZINE	NUMBER OF SARS PHOTOS	SHOWING PEOPLE		SHOWING ASIANS		SHOWING ASIANS WITH MASKS	
		NUMBER	PERCENTAGE	NUMBER	PERCENTAGE	NUMBER	PERCENTAGE
National Post	120	95	82.0	65	54.2	60	50.0
The Globe and Mail	119	68	57.1	52	43.9	41	34.5
Maclean's	27	17	63.0	8	29.6	6	22.2
TIME (Canada)	17	15	88.2	8	47.0	6	35.3

Source: Leung & Guan 2004.

pandemic of 1918–19 (in which at least 20 million people died over an 18-month period) were also part of media fear-mongering. Fear surrounding the disease had a devastating economic impact on parts of Canada where the outbreak was prevalent, notably Toronto and, in particular, its various Chinatowns. Commentators were quick to note that many of the patrons suddenly avoiding Chinese business communities and restaurants were themselves Chinese, as though this fact somehow justified similar acts of discrimination on the part of non-Asian Canadians. But whether the economic losses can be attributed more to a drop in Chinese-Canadian patronage or to decreased patronage by non-Chinese Canadians makes little difference. The fact is that the loss of business occurred, and it did so because the disease was racialized to the point where many Canadians, of all ethnic backgrounds, temporarily changed their purchasing habits

What do YOU think?

1. Who is involved in racializing a disease like SARS? Whose role should it be to challenge the racialization of disease as it is occurring?

2. To what extent can we blame the media for exaggerating the association of SARS with Asians and spreading fear about the disease? Is it the media's responsibility to make people aware of the gravest possible outcomes of an event?

3. To what extent does blame lie with individuals, for succumbing to fear-mongering? Can regular patrons of Chinatown businesses be blamed for altering their purchasing habits if there's any chance at all that not doing so will increase their odds of contracting the virus? Should people be expected to weigh decisions about their personal health against the greater economic and social impact of their decisions?

THURSDAY, APRIL 3, 2003 ★ TORONTO STAR ★ B3

SARS Outbreak

China admits wider spread of SARS

12 more deaths reported among inland provinces

First cases found in Latin America and Israel

ANN PERRY
STAFF REPORTER

The global death toll from Severe Acute Respiratory Syndrome jumped yesterday as China broke its silence and admitted it had more cases in more provinces than it had previously revealed.

The South China Morning Post reported today that the first victims of the deadly illness were people in China's southern province of Guangdong who ate or handled wild game, confirming earlier reports linking the disease to ducks.

China said it had 1,190 suspected cases through the end of March, and 46 deaths instead of the 34 it had admitted. Cases were reported in Guangxi, Hunan and Sichuan provinces as well as Guangdong for the first time.

In total, the World Health Organization estimated that SARS has infected more than 2,200 people worldwide and killed an estimated 78.

Brazil reported its first suspected case, which, if confirmed, would be the first in Latin America. Israel also reported its first suspected case.

China agreed yesterday to let a team of WHO investigators visit the southern province of Guangdong, where the disease is believed to have started.

The four-member international team, which will leave Beijing today, will take samples from suspected patients to help identify a culprit virus and assess how infectious and virulent it is.

And, for the first time in its 55-year-history, WHO recommended that travellers avoid part of the world because of an infectious disease: Hong Kong and adjoining Guangdong province.

In the first public statement by a senior leader, Chinese Health Minister Zhang Wenkang said the outbreak was "under effective control."

He said 80 per cent of those diagnosed with SARS have recovered.

For weeks, U.N. agency officials have appealed for more cooperation from China.

With Hong Kong being the global centre of the SARS outbreak, face masks are common on the city's streets. Some residents strive for their own style amid the crisis. Chinese officials are reporting there are more cases and more deaths than they previously admitted.

REUTERS

"Because the mainland is not sharing information . . . the outbreak has been lengthened," Taiwan's Mainland Affairs Council said in a recent report.

Laboratories around the world are racing to come up with a test for SARS.

The U.S. Centers for Disease Control has issued two tests that health officials can give to patients with suspected SARS. Dr. Julie Gerberding, the director of the Atlanta-based centre, said until a large number of people are tested, no one can say whether the disease is caused by the main suspect — a coronavirus.

But she said so far 400 healthy people had been tested for the virus, a previously unknown relative of one of the common cold viruses, and all had tested negative.

Several patients with SARS have tested positive.

"It is not yet proof. There are other viruses still under investigation," she said. In Toronto, Dr. Raymond Tellier of the Hospital for Sick Children, has developed a test that detects this new species of coronavirus. It is currently being used here.

A top health expert in China told a newspaper the earliest SARS patients in Guangdong had close and continuous contact with chickens, ducks, pigeons and owls.

"We will explore further if the disease was passed to human beings from wild animals. You know, Guangdong people like eating exotic animals and I don't find it a healthy practice," said Bi Shengli, a vice-director at the Chinese Centre for Disease Control and Prevention.

The earliest cases of the disease were traced to either chefs or bird vendors, Bi said.

In Thailand yesterday, the government said it would turn back foreigners suspected of having SARS and would force those allowed in from affected countries to wear masks in public.

In the Philippines, which has no confirmed cases, President Gloria Macapagal Arroyo put in place a contingency plan — including air and seaport checks — to prevent an outbreak. Health officials in New Zealand urged indigenous Maori tribesmen to forgo their traditional "hongi" nose-rubbing greeting for visiting Chinese at a convention.

In Hong Kong, the Roman Catholic Church ordered priests to wear masks during Communion and put wafers in the hands of the faithful rather than on the tongue.

FROM STAR WIRE SERVICES

Telling It Like It Is

A Student POV

SARS and Being Chinese

Around the time of the SARS crisis, being Chinese made people look at me in a different way, whether it was at school, at work, or in public places such as the subway and buses. It did not bother me at first, but as more and more individuals died due to SARS, the more I kept my eyes open for tainted looks darting in my direction.

Around that time in school, it wasn't so much the looks, but comments made in class about the situation. What I have learned and understood in this game we call life is that everyone is entitled to his or her opinion. I have also learned and understood that not all opinions are necessarily right or wrong. Unfortunately, not all people feel that their opinions are wrong, hurtful, disrespectful, condescending, and rude.

One incident happened in my math class at college. Our class got off topic, and our focus was turned from present and future value to SARS. Our teacher was reminding us that proper hand washing helps in preventing the spread of infection. One obnoxious fellow who felt he was the class clown replied to our teacher's comment and stated that to prevent the spread of infection, we need to stay away from all those darn Chinese people. His language use and vocabulary was a little cruder. Being the only Asian person in the class, everyone turned and looked in my direction as if they were expecting me to curse at him. I was beside myself and decided to let the one and only authority figure take care of his biased opinion. However, our teacher said absolutely nothing, except to get on with the lesson. His comments offended me and our teacher not correcting him hurt my feelings. It made me pay more attention to the things that were being said in all the rest of my classes. The impact it had on my school life made me more defensive towards what my peers had to say about those of Asian descent. . . .

Ethnicity is a sociological factor that made an impact on my life within the last year. Because I have been on the end of a biased opinion at school and indirect discrimination at work, I have further learned another aspect of the game of life: the value and meaning of equality and fairness and that even though there are different ethnicities and races, we are all part of one race called the human race.

—Karin Koo

What do YOU think?

1. What do you think motivated the student to say what he did? Why might he have thought that he was "just joking"?

2. How might you have responded to the student's comment had you been the instructor in charge of this class? What is the danger in saying nothing?

as a precaution against contracting the virus in communities where it was thought to be prevalent.

Throughout their report, Leung and Guan note the effects that acts of discrimination, large and small, had on individuals of Asian ancestry. In the narrative above, one student tells her story.

Cultural Syndromes

SARS, as it was depicted in the North American media, took on the qualities of a **cultural syndrome**—a disorder believed to afflict primarily people of certain ethnicities. There are many examples of minority cultures being further marginalized through their association with cultural syndromes, which create or perpetuate strong stereotypes that can be very difficult to stamp out. In some cases, cultural syndromes have been devised in order to psychologize problems brought on by Western colonial control. A classic example is **Arctic hysteria**, a condition first identified and described by the wife of Arctic explorer

Robert Peary in 1892. In her journal, Josephine Peary described the "crazy" acts of Inuit women who would suddenly scream, tear their clothes off, imitate the sound of some bird or animal, or run in circles—apparently for no reason—to the point of collapse. White visitors to the Arctic began to record this phenomenon as *pibloktuq* (or any one of a number of linguistically challenged variations of this).

The term *pibloktuq* first entered the historical record, then the psychiatric medical record, as a form of "Arctic hysteria," via an Austrian psychiatrist, Abraham Arden Brill, who had translated several of Freud's works and was influenced by his work on hysteria (Brill 1913). It still exists as a psychological disorder legitimated by a medical name and "authenticated" by case studies. It also became enshrined in anthropology textbooks (e.g. Harris 1987: 328–9, and Barnouw 1987: 207) as one of a number of culture-specific syndromes or psychoses.

In a 1995 article entitled "'Pibloktoq' (Arctic Hysteria): A Construction of European–Inuit Relations?," historian Lyle Dick challenged the validity of the phenomenon as a part of traditional Inuit culture. He offered his opinion that it was more likely the product of the White–Inuit power imbalance embodied in such contexts as the obsessively driven Robert Peary forcing the Inuit to take unwise risks in exploration, and the sexual abuse by white men of Inuit women.

Medical Sociology and Gender

Physicians and Gender

Both the number and the percentage of women in and graduating from medical schools in Canada are increasing. In 1959, women accounted for just 6 per cent of medical school graduates. Forty years later, they made up 44 per cent of the graduating class. According to Burton and Wong, authors of a paper called "A Force to Contend With: The Gender Gap Closes in Canadian Medical Schools" (2004), Canadian medical school classes "have a range of 43%–74% women (mean 58%), compared with a range of 26%–57% men (mean 42%)." The percentage of women graduating from medical school and entering the health profession will only increase in the coming years, as the majority of doctors approaching retirement are men. Male doctors in Canada make up

74 per cent of physicians aged between 45 and 65, and 90 per cent of those over 65.

How might this trend affect the profession? How are women physicians different from their male counterparts? A number of features have been regularly noted in the literature—here are just a few examples. Women doctors are more likely to:

- screen their patients for preventable illnesses
- spend time counselling patients about psychosocial issues
- enter primary care (i.e. become family physicians)
- work fewer hours and see fewer patients
- leave the profession sooner.

Women doctors are less likely to

- become surgeons
- be sued for malpractice
- join professional organizations.

What do YOU think?

1. How much do you think this changing gender dynamic will affect the practice of medicine in Canada?

2. Do you think this could lead to a reduction in the power differential between doctors and nurses in Canadian hospitals?

Pharmacy Professors in Canada and Gender

In 1996, sociologist Linda Muzzin carried out a study of the practices of departments of pharmaceutical sciences at Canadian colleges and universities. Her research (Muzzin 2001) uncovered several gender-based patterns in the hiring practices of these departments.

To gain a proper perspective, it's important to know that there is an almost class-like distinction between the two kinds of jobs held by pharmacy professors. The first position involves molecular biology research and some teaching of basic science. This position offers a lighter teaching load and tends to be a "tenure-stream" position, making it highly valued. The second class of teaching jobs, which is less valued, is described by Muzzin as the "professional caring" or clinical and social-administrative jobs.

As Muzzin discovered, the distinction between the two kinds of teaching position fell along gender lines. Consider the following:

- In 1996, the majority (86 per cent) of the basic science jobs were tenured or tenure-stream positions; only 37 per cent of the professional caring jobs were tenured.
- That year, a substantially higher proportion of the professional caring jobs were held by women. Only in some smaller universities, where a greater percentage of the professional caring jobs were tenure-stream positions, were these jobs more likely to be held by men.
- Of the 112 tenured or tenure-stream basic science jobs that Muzzin looked at, only 15 (13 per cent) were held by women.

The picture may have changed in the 20 years since the article was published, but Muzzin's research highlights a key area of interest to medical sociologists. Not only did her work point to possible discrimination in the hiring practices of Canadian pharmacy departments, but it raised awareness of a gender imbalance in the teaching ranks that could be reproduced in the pharmacy profession itself.

Medical Sociology and Class

The Inverse Care Law

Dr Julian Tudor Hart studied medicine at Cambridge and interned at the equally prestigious St George's Hospital in London. A natural career move for a British doctor on that path would have been to serve the needs of the middle class or the rich in London or some other big city. Instead, he dedicated his life to helping the citizens of a working-class mining village in Wales. Dr Hart became famous among medical sociologists for an article he wrote in 1971. In it he introduced the idea of the **inverse care law**:

> The availability of good medical care tends to vary inversely with the need for it in the population served. This inverse care law operates more completely where medical care is most exposed to market forces, and less so where such exposure is reduced. The market distribution of medical care is a primitive and historically outdated social

form, and any return to it would further exaggerate the maldistribution of medical resources. (Hart 1971: 405)

Hart was describing a system that had, for almost 20 years, experienced socialized healthcare similar to the one that exists today in Canada, a system markedly different from the private or market-force system found in the United States. What the inverse care law meant in terms of the Britain he was describing can be seen in statistics concerning infant mortality from the years 1949–53. From Hart's perspective, these statistics:

> showed combined social classes I and II (wholly non-manual) with a standardised mortality from all causes 18% below the mean, and combined social classes IV and V (wholly manual) 5% above it. Infant mortality was 37% below the mean for social class I (professional) and 38% above it for social class V (unskilled manual). (Hart 1971: 405)

In other words, the lower classes experienced a greater likelihood of infant mortality (i.e. death of an infant during the first year of life). This, of course, would tend to reflect both the working and living conditions of the different classes, as well as differences in medical care in areas where the various classes live, work, and see doctors. Regarding doctors, the main focus of his article, Hart observed the following trends:

What do YOU think?

1. Do you think that the inverse care law holds in Canada? How would you, as a sociologist, go about trying to prove or disprove it?

2. How do you think class affects the social course of disease?

3. We know that certain classes of individuals are routinely allowed to "jump the queue" to receive medical procedures faster than most Canadians would normally be able to (when was the last time you heard of an NHL player having to wait four to six months for an MRI?). Who in your opinion is entitled to priority care? Professional athletes? High-ranking politicians, like the prime minister or a provincial premier? Emergency services professionals (paramedics, police officers, fire fighters)? Hospital workers? Spouses and families of any of the above?

In areas with most sickness and death, general practitioners have more work, larger lists [of patients], less hospital support, and inherit more clinically ineffective traditions of consultation [e.g. short visits with little listening to patients' problems] than in the healthiest areas; and hospital doctors shoulder heavier case-loads with less staff and equipment, more obsolete buildings, and suffer recurrent crises in the availability of beds and replacement staff. (Hart 1971: 412)

Rising Tuition Fees and Medical Students

Most students can relate to the effects of rising tuition fees. How does that affect medical students? A study conducted by Kwong et al. in early 2001 and published in 2002 compared tuition costs in Ontario with costs in the rest of Canada (except for Quebec, which, as is so often the case, was excluded). The reason for highlighting Ontario tuition costs is that medical students in that province had the greatest hike in tuition fees in Canada from 1997–8 to 2000–1. The cost of tuition at the University of Toronto's school of medicine, for example, nearly tripled over that period, from $4,844 per year to $14,000. (It currently sits at $18,424 for Canadian students—see Table 18.2.) The researchers contrasted people in their fourth year with those in their first, because they represented the two extremes. They found that there were three differences between the two academic cohorts that were unique to Ontario. First, the proportion of respondents with a family income of less than $40,000 declined significantly between the first-year and fourth-year students, from 22.6 per cent to 15.0 per cent respectively; the same figure among non-Ontario schools stayed just about the same (decreasing slightly from 16.0 per cent to 15.8 per cent overall). The figure of $40,000 was chosen

This student works 20 hours a week at the University of Toronto's athletic complex to supplement the student loans that pay for his education. He expects to graduate $40,000 in debt and worries rising costs will deter his younger siblings from seeking a post-secondary education. Should medical students expect to graduate with higher debts given the greater earning potential their degree confers?

to represent "low income," as it was beneath the median family income of $46,951 in Canada in 1996. Another difference between the two groups was that the median debt level anticipated upon graduation by first-year medical students in Ontario was $80,000. The debt anticipated by the graduating class was a lower, but still nasty: $57,000. No such contrast existed in the other provinces. The problem here for the sociologist is that there are no earlier studies with which to compare these findings. What if first-year medical students often project a higher figure than their more experienced graduating colleagues? Is the control group sufficient here for comparative purposes? What do you think?

Finally, first-year medical students in Ontario were more likely than fourth-year students to report that their financial situation was "very" or "extremely" stressful (20.5 per cent vs 17.5 per cent; the reverse was true in other provinces: 11.9 per cent vs 15.8 per cent). They were also more likely to cite financial considerations as having a major influence on their choice of specialty or practice location (25.4 per cent versus 13.3 per cent, compared with a reverse ratio of 21.4 per cent to 26.0 per cent in the other provinces). Again, is this a cohort problem or a stage problem somehow conditioned by being in Ontario?

Medical Sociology and Quebec

As we have seen elsewhere, Quebec, from a sociological point of view, is distinct from other provinces in Canada. Here are four areas in the sociology of health and medicine that illustrate this point:

- the relative number of male nurses
- the number of female medical students
- the number of people without regular doctors
- the cost of tuition fees for medical students.

In 2002, there were 219,161 women registered nurses (RNs) in Canada, compared with just 11,796 male registered nurses (about 5.4 per cent of the total). In Quebec, the 5,272 male RNs made up roughly 9.8 per cent of the total (59,193). The more striking statistic is that approximately 45 per cent of the male nurses in Canada were working in Quebec.

It should not be surprising, then, that there is also a non-traditional gender difference when it comes to Quebec medical students. The number of female medical students is consistently higher in Quebec than elsewhere in Canada. In 1997, 59 per cent of the students at Quebec's four medical schools were women, compared with 46 per cent in the 12 schools throughout the rest of the country. That year, the University of Sherbrooke had the highest proportion of women starting medical school—71 per cent (the lowest figure, for comparison, was just over 30 per cent, at the University of Manitoba). In the 2003–4 academic year, Laval University had the highest percentage of female first-year medical students, with 74 per cent; the University of Saskatchewan had the lowest, with 43 per cent. Overall, 68 per cent of all medical students in Quebec in 2003–4 were women.

The third factor, relating to people without regular doctors, is borne out by a 2010 study of Canadians over the age of 20. The national average for people without a regular family doctor was 15.2 per cent, while the figure for Quebec residents was 24.9 per cent—the highest of any province, and the highest total in that province in decades (Statistics Canada 2011c).

The fourth factor is the cost of a medical degree, which is much lower at universities in Quebec than in medical schools elsewhere in Canada. Compare the figures in Table 18.2, presented in order of most to least expensive. It should also be noted that with the exception of Newfoundland and Labrador, whose medical school tuition fees were frozen for four years in the early 2000s, and Manitoba, where fees dropped in 2000–1 and then held constant for the next three

Table 18.2 Average annual cost of attending medical school, by province, 2010–11

Ontario	$18,420
British Columbia	15,547
Nova Scotia	13,818
Alberta	13,157
Saskatchewan	12,276
National average	**11,319**
Manitoba	7,499
Newfoundland and Labrador	6,250
Quebec	3,584

Source: http://www2.macleans.ca/2010/09/16/how-much-they-pay-for-it/

The homepages for two Canadian schools of nursing. What messages does each convey? How do they differ?

years, Quebec has had the slowest growth rate in medical school fees.

Final Thoughts: Twelve Tips for Better Health

In 1999, British sociologist David Gordon drew up the following list of "Alternative 10 Tips for Better Health."

It was meant to present an alternative to the British Medical Officer's 10 health tips, which included the usual things about not smoking, eating healthy foods, drinking in moderation, driving safely, and so on:

1. Don't be poor. If you can, stop. If you can't, try not to be poor for long.
2. Don't have poor parents.

3. Own a car.
4. Don't work in a stressful, low-paying manual job.
5. Don't live in damp, low-quality housing.
6. Be able to afford to go on a foreign holiday and sunbathe.
7. Practise not losing your job and don't become unemployed.
8. Take up all benefits you are entitled to, if you are unemployed, retired, or sick or disabled.
9. Don't live next to a busy major road or near a polluting factory.
10. Learn how to fill in the complex housing benefit/asylum application forms before you become homeless or destitute. (Quoted in Pohlmann 2002)

This tongue-in-cheek but accurate appraisal has been adapted a number of times. In a 2003 speech, Roy Romanow, author of the Romanow Report on the state of Canada's healthcare industry, expanded this list to include two additional items:

11. Graduate from high school and then go on to college or university. Health status improves with your level of education.
12. Be sure to live in a community where you trust your neighbours and feel that you belong. A civil and trusting community promotes health and life expectancy.

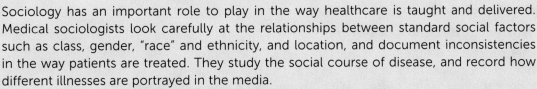

What do YOU think?

1. How do these "health tips" reflect William Ryan's idea of **blaming the victim** (see Chapter 7)"?
2. Are there any items you can think of adding to this list?

WRAP IT UP

Summary

Sociology has an important role to play in the way healthcare is taught and delivered. Medical sociologists look carefully at the relationships between standard social factors such as class, gender, "race" and ethnicity, and location, and document inconsistencies in the way patients are treated. They study the social course of disease, and record how different illnesses are portrayed in the media.

Canada has a public healthcare system, but make no mistake about it: it's a big business heavily influenced by big business interests. Hospitals grappling with barely adequate budgets make business decisions every day, deciding where best to allocate their funding, while companies ranging in size from huge multinationals selling pharmaceutical products to private clinics offering cosmetic procedures like tummy tucks have a vested interest in making us feel less healthy than we are, and incapable of improving our health without costly medical interventions. It is our firm belief that one of the best ways of improving the healthcare system in Canada, and the health of all Canadians, is to increase the amount of medical sociology being carried out in this country.

THINK BACK

Questions for Critical Review

1. Take a particular disease or injury that you have experienced and discuss the social course that you went through to get it diagnosed and treated. Where did you go? Who healed you? How were you socially processed?

2. Identify what biomedicine is and talk about its weaknesses and strengths. In what situations is biomedicine most successful? In what situations does it fail to serve the needs of patients as well as alternative medical approaches?

3. Define medicalization. How and why are certain physical conditions medicalized? When is medicalization more harmful than helpful?

4. Describe the situation that faces immigrant doctors upon arriving in Canada. What barriers do they face to practising medicine in this country? Why do these barriers exist? What would happen if they did not exist?

5. Give an overview of Ivan Illich's critique of modern medicine. Do you agree or disagree with his views? Why?

READ ON

ONLINE

"50 Years of Medical Sociology"

http://somatosphere.net/2010/12/50-years-of-medical-sociology-html

Eugene Raikhel reviews the fiftieth anniversary issue of the *Journal of Health and Social Behavior*, which looked back at a number of issues that had been tackled in the 50-year history of the journal. It is effectively an overview of issues in the history of the medical sociology in the United States. Raikhel provides titles and abstracts of the special issue's contents, and the issue itself is available online at http://hsb.sagepub.com/content/51/1_suppl.

Medical Sociology Fact Sheet

www.ndsu.edu/ndsu/academic/factsheets/ahss/medsoc.shtml

This description of the program in medical sociology at North Dakota State University is useful for its focus on the kinds of jobs that this degree can lead to for sociology students.

Medical Sociology online (MSo)

www.medicalsociologyonline.org

The British Sociology Association's free-access online journal provides its own articles, commentaries, and reviews, and acts as a portal to other news and information in the wider world of medical sociology.

IN PRINT

Tania Das Gupta (2009), *Real Nurses and Others: Racism in Nursing* (Halifax, NS: Fernwood Publishing).

> Tania Das Gupta is a professor in the Department of Equity Studies at York University. This book is her study of the racism experienced by visible-minority nurses in Canada.

Michel Foucault (1973), *The Birth of the Clinic: An Archaeology of Medical Perception*, trans. A.M.S. Smith (New York: Vintage Books).

> Foucault's work offers a good look at the social processes involving the development of roles and practices in a medical setting.

Pat Grygier (1994), *A Long Way from Home: The Tuberculosis Epidemic among the Inuit* (Montreal: McGill–Queen's).

> Grygier provides an enlightening (and alarming) examination of how Inuit with tuberculosis were treated in Canada during the 1950s.

19 Mass Media

Learning Objectives

After reading this chapter, you should be able to

- outline Marshall McLuhan's theories of mass media
- discuss the factors involved in the propaganda model of mass media
- assess the impact of embedded journalism
- describe the connection between globalization and mass media
- explain why the Internet might or might not represent a failed attempt at democracy
- break down the impact of social media
- discuss the impact of media spectacles
- define what is meant by *counter-narrative*.

Key Terms

- agency
- border crossers
- cool media
- contextual objectivity
- counter-narrative
- cyber-bullying
- demotic turn
- détournements
- digital divide
- disinformation
- dystopian
- embedded journalism
- global village
- hot media
- hyperreal
- info-elites
- junk food news
- mass culture
- media spectacles
- medium is the message
- myth of the liberal media
- oversharing
- peep culture
- popular culture
- propaganda model
- public sphere
- simulacra
- situationists
- social media
- special interests
- standpoint theory
- technological determinist
- technological fetishism

Names to Know

- Jean Baudrillard
- Noam Chomsky
- Guy Debord
- Edward S. Herman
- Marshall McLuhan
- C. Wright Mills
- Neil Postman

A View to the Future

Growing up I read a lot of science fiction. It fired my imagination and, sometimes, my nightmares, particularly when the novels were **dystopian**, or "anti-utopian," presenting fantasy worlds of a nightmarish future in which technology is a tool used for evil by controlling, authoritarian governments, and everything is terrible.

One of the most powerful and frightening sci-fi images I can remember is of the "parlour wall" in Ray Bradbury's 1953 novel *Fahrenheit 451*, set in a world the author might have imagined would exist by the end of the twentieth century. The novel's main character, Guy Montag, is a "fireman," as in someone who works for the state burning books (the title of the novel is a reference to the temperature at which paper is supposed to burn). The world of the novel is one in which people are totally hedonistic, feeding their senses however they can, but they are kept away from critical thought by their government (hence the book burning) and their technology. People listen to seashell ear radios. There are rooms in which one is surrounded on all sides by floor-to-ceiling TV screens broadcasting content designed to be interactive. With sound systems that engulf the listener, individuals become hooked on the hyperreal images of their "fourwall televisors," also known simply as the "parlour walls." They become addicted to them.

I found this scary, even scarier than the large eye-like devices that Big Brother used to spy on citizens in another dystopian work, George Orwell's *1984*. Big Brother presented a visible enemy that you could either avoid or oppose, if you chose to. But in *Fahrenheit 451*, people willingly attach themselves, long-term, to their controlling agents via the parlour walls. The enemy has become the enemy within; people choose to be connected. One of the spookiest lines for me occurs when a character who has been asked to shut off her parlour wall responds: "That's my family." But the most prescient line of the book is the following:

The televisor is "real." It is immediate, it has dimension. It tells you what to think and blasts it in. It must be right. It seems so right. It rushes you on so quickly to its own conclusions your mind hasn't time to protest, "What nonsense!" (Bradbury 1953: 84)

It's a remarkable comment when you consider when it was written: not only was reality TV a long way from being invented, but television itself had only just begun to enter people's homes and become a fixture in their living rooms.

Never before have we been so immersed in media technology as we are today. Forget fourwall televisors: the video screen follows us everywhere. If it's not in the shop or the restaurant or the classroom we're in, it's in our pockets, keeping us connected, keeping us informed, and continually redrawing the line between real life and entertainment.

What do YOU think?

1. Why do you think that dystopian novels such as *Fahrenheit 451* came out just as television began to appear in people's homes? Do you see a similar trend in movies and books developed over the past two decades, associated with the rise of new media technologies?

2. The premises of *Fahrenheit 451* and *1984* are frightening because of the link between mass media (the televisor, the big eye of Big Brother) and government power. Those same fears are sometimes expressed today in the context of government control of the Internet. Do you think that these fears are realistic?

Introduction: Becoming an Informed Consumer

It doesn't take a sociologist to tell you that mass media—the world of television, magazines, newspapers, radio, social media, and the Internet—play an enormous role in the lives of people around the world, nor that that enormous role is growing. But determining what the social effects of mass media are and whether they are primarily good or bad are important tasks for sociologists today and in the near future. (Do you hear that, sociology majors?)

You've heard of people becoming informed consumers of material items, from cars and appliances to organic vegetables. This chapter is about becoming informed consumers of the information that bombards us via the media we see, hear, and carry around with us. We will look at the views of a number of different theorists, including Canadian Marshall McLuhan, Americans Noam Chomsky and Neil Postman, and French thinker (we always seem to call them French *thinkers*) Guy Debord. Not all of them are sociologists, strictly speaking, but what they have to say is often good sociology.

First, though, we need to revisit some terms introduced in two earlier chapters, on culture (Chapter 4) and consumption (Chapter 7). The first two are *mass culture* and *popular culture*. These are sometimes used interchangeably in the literature, though they actually differ in meaning. **Popular culture** refers to the culture of the people in which the people play an active, creative role. The ability to take an active, creative role is called **agency**. By contrast, when we use the term **mass culture**, we are referring to culture for the masses, created and disseminated by those with power, particularly power in the media. People are consumers of mass media, but they don't play an active role in creating it. We take the position here that there is a strong connection between mass culture and mass media: that while mass media may be used in the creation and distribution of popular culture, they are indispensable to the spread of mass culture, that fast food for the senses.

Simulacra (singular *simulacrum*) are aspects of mass culture that draw on and promote stereotypes, and that are produced and reproduced like material goods or commodities, primarily by the mass media. Developed by French sociologist **Jean Baudrillard**, the idea refers to things that are, to use another of his terms, **hyperreal**, in that they are artificial, made-up versions of real life that people relate to as though they were "more real" than the actual things they simulate. All you have to do is think of the term "weapons of mass destruction" to understand how a simulacrum is created by mass media. To many Westerners, the media-generated idea that an Islamic state in the Middle East was building powerful weapons to be deployed from afar on its enemies was much more believable than the reality (that these weapons did not exist). The simulacrum of "WMDs" was spread through the mass media—particularly news organizations—to the point where it was hard not to have some idea about the nature of weapons of mass destruction and what they were capable of. This simulacrum formed the pretext for the invasion of Iraq. The real reasons for the attack were far more complex, but it was easier to rally public support around the idea that Americans were under threat of imminent attack. The real was very different from the hyperreal.

Two Twentieth-Century Media Critics: McLuhan and Mills

Marshall McLuhan: The Medium and the (Sometimes Unclear) Message

An early Canadian figure, indeed a giant, in media theory was Edmonton-born **Herbert Marshall McLuhan** (1911–1980). McLuhan has been described by some as a media "prophet," and there are a good number of terms and phrases he coined that continue to resonate today. But he was at times an obscure writer, which means that interpreting his thinking is not always easy. One anecdote speaks at once to that obscurity of thought and to McLuhan's "rock star status" during the 1960s and 1970s. He made a guest cameo appearance in Woody Allen's 1977 movie *Annie Hall*, which won the Academy Award for best picture that year In the scene, Allen's character is waiting in line next to, and arguing with, a pompous intellectual who is interpreting McLuhan's work. McLuhan himself then joins the line and comes to Allen's rescue, using a line he often spoke concerning people he felt mis-interpreted him: "You know nothing of my work." Indeed, *our* work is cut out for us here.

The first step to understanding McLuhan is to know that he was a **technological determinist**. Recall from Chapter 5, on socialization, what determinism is: it is the belief in a primary cause, or determinant, for human behaviour and thinking. A *biological* determinist believes that our individual natures, in terms of our abilities and psychology, are basically predestined—we have little ability to change what genetics has determined. A *social* determinist argues that our upbring-ing, our friends, and our social environment in general determine who we are and who

we become. A *technological* determinist, then, is some-one who believes that a given form of technology will determine how humans act and think, and McLuhan was indeed of this opinion. He is not, however, a truly postmodern theorist in that he did not talk signifi-cantly about how a particular technology would allow some groups to rise to power at the expense of others.

That he was a technological determinist provides a clue to understanding McLuhan's most famous, and perhaps most often misinterpreted, statement: **the medium is the message** (McLuhan 1964: 23). The thrust of the statement (and we hope Mr McLuhan isn't standing behind us right now to dismiss our interpret-ation) is that the medium—whether it be television or radio or print—has a causative effect on the way that human groups think, act, and organize socially. The

Marshall McLuhan working in his home in Toronto in 1972. Do you think that if McLuhan were alive today and still writing, the books in this picture would be replaced by a computer and some sort of e-reader? Would he embrace new technology, do you think?

importance of any medium is how it affects the way people behave, how it "shapes and controls the scale and form of human association and action," regardless of its content.

McLuhan first developed this idea in his 1962 classic *The Gutenberg Galaxy: The Making of Typographic Man*, in which he attempted to explain how European culture was fundamentally changed, or re-invented, by two developments: first, the emergence of alphabetic writing (the representation of one sound with one symbol or letter, a practice that was fully developed about 3,000 years ago); second, the invention in the mid-fifteenth century of the printing press and movable type printing by Johannes Gutenberg (used to create the first printed Bible in around 1455). McLuhan was interested in how these two new technologies had altered human patterns of thinking by making sight more important than the other senses:

> If a new technology extends one or more of our senses outside us into the social world, then new ratios among all of our senses will occur in that particular culture. It is comparable to what happens when a new note is added to a melody. And when the sense ratios alter in any culture, then what had appeared lucid [i.e. clear] before may suddenly become opaque [i.e. less clear], and what had been vague or opaque will become translucent [i.e. more clear]." (McLuhan 1962:41)

In McLuhan's thinking, alphabetic writing and the printing press had combined to alter human "sense ratios" by dramatically increasing the significance of the visual—what we could see and, specifically, what we could read—at the expense of the oral/aural (speaking/hearing). It wasn't all good, according to McLuhan. The new medium of printing had supplanted the social role of story-telling that had defined earlier oral cultures (cultures that passed values and traditions from generation to generation by word of mouth) and had thrown off the balance among the senses by making listening much less important.

Another of McLuhan's well-known coinages is **global village**. Thirty years before the Internet, which some commentators believe he predicted, McLuhan wrote and spoke about how the purely visual-based and individualistic culture of the printed page would be replaced by what he termed an "electronic interdependence," which he felt would be more orally/

aurally focused, and more "tribal." The tribal entity formed by this media technology would be the global village. In an incredibly prescient (i.e. prophetic, literally "before-knowing") observation for 1962, he wrote:

> Instead of tending towards a vast Alexandrian library [the Royal Library of Alexandria in Egypt was the largest and most significant library of the pre-Christian world] the world has become a computer, an electronic brain, exactly as an infantile piece of science fiction. And as our senses have gone outside us, Big Brother [the over-controlling government of Orwell's *1984*] goes inside. So, unless aware of this dynamic, we shall at once move into a phase of panic terrors, exactly befitting a small world of tribal drums, total interdependence, and superimposed co-existence. . . . Terror is the normal state of any oral society, for in it everything affects everything all the time. . . . In our long striving to recover for the Western world a unity of sensibility and of thought and feeling, we have no more been prepared to accept the tribal consequences of such unity than we were ready for the fragmentation of the human psyche by print culture. (McLuhan 1962: 32)

His anthropology is weak, but his predictive abilities were strong. McLuhan needed to learn how oral society could be relatively free of terror, and he really should have read more of the extensive ethnographic literature on the subject. However, it is easy to see in his writing how he predicted such features of contemporary life as the online conspiracy theory and the video that goes viral.

What do YOU think?

McLuhan believed that different media extend different human senses—for instance, print technology extended the visual sense. If he had been around to see the advent of cellphones, would he have seen this as a move from visual culture back to an oral/aural one? There is still texting and tweeting, but a line like "c u 2nite" seems governed less by the laws of writing than by the freer ways of speech. Consider this in the context of his observation that "Nobody ever made a grammatical error in non-literate [i.e. oral] society" (McLuhan 1962: 271).

C. Wright Mills and the Mass Media: A Vocal Minority and a Silent Majority

In *The Power Elite* (1956), **C. Wright Mills** identified two main sociological characteristics of mass media:

1. Very few people get to communicate to a great number of people.

2. The audience has no truly effective way to communicate back.

Wright argued that the mass media, as it was constructed back in the 1950s, were inherently undemocratic. As they exist today, they are no more democratic. Those with power—governments, media outlets, and large corporations—are still able to get their messages

The Point Is...

Hot and Cool Media

McLuhan followed up *The Gutenberg Galaxy* with his best-known work, *Understanding Media: The Extensions of Man*, in 1964. It is in this book that he developed more fully the idea that "the medium is the message," that studying a particular medium, apart from its specific content, is key to comprehending what is being communicated. If McLuhan were alive today (and waiting in line with us at a movie theatre), he might say that the message we should take from texting, tweeting, and blogging is that short, impulsive narratives are important, no matter how quickly they are developed, how little they are backed up by evidence, and how ill-qualified the writer is. But then, McLuhan was often sarcastic.

It was also in *Understanding Media* that he developed the distinction between **hot media** and **cool media**. The difference boils down to the degree to which the recipient or consumer of the medium participates actively in the interpretation or consumption of what is being communicated. *Hot* meant low effort or low intellectual participation. Hot media tend to make demands on one sense over the others and can involve total immersion in the medium. Bradbury's fourwall televisor was hot. Social media are hot. Movies, according to McLuhan, are hot (and he never saw Robert Pattinson and Kristen Stewart). Radio is hot because it places much greater demands on one sense (listening) than on others. Comics are cool because they require involvement on

the part of the reader/viewer to fill in missing details. A lecture to an auditorium full of students would be considered hotter than a seminar or an interactive lecture to a small class. He thought television was cooler (but then, he never saw reality television), and he would have considered HDTV a hot medium. Jazz was considered cool (it is cool, in all meanings of that word). Reading books is cool.

Would McLuhan have classified social networking sites such as Facebook and Twitter as hot or cool media? Would you agree with his classification? Why or why not?

heard above the rest. Tens of thousands of tweets do not make a significant contribution to media democracy.

In the hands of those with power, mass media can be a very effective dictatorial tool. The former Soviet Union's government propaganda newspaper, *Pravda* (meaning, ironically, "truth"), told its version of the truth to the people of the USSR until the Soviet empire fell in 1990. Prior to that time, contradictory information was hard to come by. In Rwanda, the government-run radio station successfully incited thousands of members of the Hutu tribe to kill hundreds of thousands of other Rwandans (most of them members of the minority Tutsi, but also many more moderate Hutu).

We tend to believe that the rise of the Internet, social media, and "user-generated content" has changed the media landscape—and it has. We can throw any topic from alien abductions to zookeeping into Google and immediately produce a spectrum of opinions and perspectives. We can connect via Twitter with our favourite athletes, actors, and politicians [?]— celebrities who were once inaccessible to common fans and observers such as us. But as we will see in the discussion that follows, mass media in the United States (and increasingly in Canada) are more commonly and readily used as an instrument of propaganda than as a means for giving more information and, ultimately, more power to the public.

The Propaganda Model of Information Delivery

The most important book of the last 30 years on the sociology of media is arguably *Manufacturing Consent: The Political Economy of the Mass Media*, published in 1988 by economist and media analyst **Edward S. Herman** (b. 1925) and noted linguist and political/ social critic **Noam Chomsky** (b. 1928). In Herman and Chomsky's view, powerful commercial and political interests pretty much control the flow of news to the people. The two authors make this clear in the introduction to the 2002 edition of their work:

> It is our view that, among their other functions, the media serve, and propagandize on behalf of, the powerful societal interests that control and finance them. The representatives of these interests have important agendas and principles that they want to advance, and they are well positioned to shape and constrain media policy. This is normally not accomplished by crude intervention, but by the selection of right-thinking personnel and by the editors' and working journalists' internalization of priorities and definitions of newsworthiness that conform to the institution's policy. (Herman & Chomsky 2002: xi)

In other words, a media company, like a cable news network, doesn't necessarily tell its journalists which stories to report and how to report them, but hires employees it knows will follow an editorial policy that promotes the organization's perspective, whether it's left-wing or right-wing, liberal or conservative, pro-union or pro-business, and so on.

Herman and Chomsky's Six Filters

To explain the social means by which news reporting is controlled, Herman and Chomsky put forward what they call the **propaganda model** of media analysis. This model identifies six main factors, or "filters," that contribute to bias in the media.

The first is the increasingly narrow concentration of ownership among media organizations, in which companies such as Disney, Time Warner, Viacom, News Corporation, Bertelsmann, Comcast, Sony, Liberty Media, and Vivendi SA rule the field. The four most powerful (and the scariest) of these are:

- Disney, whose holdings include its famed theme parks and resorts, the TV networks ABC and ESPN, movie companies Pixar Animation and Lucasfilm, and Marvel Comics
- Time Warner, which owns Warner Bros. Entertainment (producing movies, TV shows, and music), the TV networks HBO and CNN, and of course, magazines including *Time*, *People*, and *Sports Illustrated*
- Viacom, which owns Paramount Pictures, as well as cable networks MTV, Nickelodeon, BET, and Comedy Central
- News Corporation, headed by newspaper baron Rupert Murdoch, which controls *The Times* (London), *The Wall Street Journal*, and the *New York Post*, along with book publisher HarperCollins, movie and television production company 20th Century Fox, and the Fox television network.

These companies are all multimedia marketers with diverse assortments of holdings that include movies and theatre outlets, books, magazines, newspapers, television programs, cable TV stations, music, retail outlets, toys, theme parks, and an extensive online presence to represent all of the above. When a single organization can own multiple news outlets operating through different media—print, TV, and Internet—it becomes much easier to control the news message while increasing the size of the audience it will reach.

The second of Herman and Chomsky's filters involves the financial dependence of the media on powerful advertisers, who can significantly influence the nature of the news and general articles appearing in print media. Media critic Ben Bagdikian, author of *The Media Monopoly*, had the following to say about the pressure to ensure that the "mood" of magazine articles fits with advertisements appearing in the same issue:

> The influence of advertising on magazines reached a point where editors began selecting articles not only on the basis of their expected interest for readers but for their influence on advertisements. Serious articles were not always the best support for ads. An article that put the reader in an analytical frame of mind did not encourage the reader to take seriously an ad that depended on fantasy or promoted a trivial product. An article on genuine social suffering might interrupt the "buying" mood on which most ads for luxuries depend. The next step, seen often in mid-twentieth century magazines, was commissioning articles solely to attract readers who were good prospects to buy products advertised in the magazine. After that came the magazine phenomenon of the 1970s— creating magazines for an identifiable special audience and selling them to particular advertisers. (Bagdikian 2000: 136)

You can imagine how the delivery of news may be compromised when a newspaper or magazine editor is worried about harshening the mood of her readers.

The third filter has to do with how media organizations obtain the news they report. If you're a journalist, producing a news story from a slickly prepared media release you've been fed by a large public relations firm with a good reputation is much easier than engaging in time-consuming research and cobbling together a story from sources that aren't as well established. This allows major corporate and conservative

political figures who are represented by influential communications agencies favoured by the media to get their stories and their message "out there."

A fourth and related filter is the ability of special interest groups to furnish "experts" to be interviewed or quoted by the media. Think, for example, of the "security experts" who appear on newscasts and who always seem to be supporting government fears (we're tempted to say paranoia) about anything even remotely connected to terrorists or terrorism. For example, the Fox Network (jokingly dubbed the Faux Network by some) was able to mobilize a contingent of global warming deniers when they needed them during the world climate conference in Copenhagen in 2009. This was following the direction of an e-mail sent by Bill Sammon, the managing editor at Fox's Washington bureau, instructing Fox News journalists "to refrain from asserting that the planet has warmed (or cooled) in any given period without IMMEDIATELY pointing out that such theories are based upon data that critics have called into question" (Dimiero 2010). There were no serious critics, just vested commercial interests. Representatives of major polluting industries, which have the most to lose when concerns over climate change and its human causes gain momentum, could easily provide news organizations like Fox with names of *embedded* scientists (discussed below) who could be counted upon to support their corporate media position in interviews.

The fifth filter is "flak," to use the terminology of the authors. This is the negative reaction to how the media are presenting information, and can include anything from individual consumer complaints and letters to the editor, to lawsuits, organized boycotts, and the withdrawal of corporate sponsorship and advertising. If you know a particular story or opinion might generate a lot of flak, you might think twice about printing or broadcasting it.

Finally, the controlling interests have the power to preserve the status quo and perpetuate dominant ideologies. Herman and Chomsky recognized that dissent happens, that a newspaper could feature counternarratives that oppose the paper's usual political stance. However, those counter-narratives are typically kept to the margins so that they do not interfere with the official media agenda.

The authors do not comment directly on the total effect of the media on the news-consuming public, as they haven't engaged in specific research measuring

The "Disneyfication" of Star Wars (Disney acquired the rights to the movie franchise when it bought Lucasfilm in 2012) provides one example of how media concentration allows content to be repackaged for different audiences to reach a much larger and broader consumer base. Do you think this kind of packaging will "capture the imagination" of young viewers—and if so, will it be restricting their imagination?

those effects. They know that there is resistance to this kind of reporting as well.

What do YOU think?

1. Which of these filters, do you think, has the most powerful influence on restricting the "freedom of the press"?

2. Why is it that sociology textbooks are more likely to present counter-narratives than newspapers are?

3. Do you think that sociology textbooks written and published in Canada are more likely to present counter-narratives than their counterparts published in the United States, where there is more political monitoring of what is taught in secondary and post-secondary education?

Embedded Journalism

There is an old saying, usually attributed to Californian anti-war senator Hiram W. Johnson, that "the first casualty of war is truth." The idea is almost as old as war itself. It takes us to the idea of *embedded journalism*, which we can examine in the context of the propaganda model of news delivery.

Embedded journalism is not a new phenomenon, but the term and practice gained currency rather recently, during the American attack on Iraq in 2003. The US Army permitted certain reporters and photographers (close to 800 of them) to travel with the troops to document their activities. All of these embedded journalists had signed contracts promising not to report on any sensitive military information that could compromise the army's efforts. Given the risk that a

Our Stories

Media Concentration in Canada and the Myth of the Liberal Media

As in the United States, the media in Canada are increasingly coming under the control of large conglomerates—notably Bell, Rogers, Shaw, Astral, Newcap, and Québecor—each with a diverse mix of media holdings.

Technically, the rules in Canada are stricter than they are in the US. The Canadian Radio-television and Telecommunications Commission (CRTC), the regulatory body that oversees broadcasting and communications companies in this country, has the power to restrict mergers in order to guard against a situation in which one or two companies control too many of the country's print and broadcast media outlets. Since 2008, the CRTC has had the power to limit big companies to two media types (e.g. TV and radio, or radio and newspapers, or newspapers and magazines) in a given market (e.g. the Greater Toronto Area). The CRTC also imposes a television market cap share, which means that no one company may own more than 45 per cent of the total television viewership in the country. Yet consider, for example, the current television holdings of Bell Media, along with its very powerful partners (as of January 2013):

- The Sports Network, TSN (have you noticed how the network's sportscasters recently have been flogging Bell devices?), along with TSN2 and the French-language RDS (Réseau des sports), all partly owned by the American sports network ESPN, which is, in turn, owned by Disney

- MuchMusic and its spinoff station MuchMore, which are partnered with the American music network MTV, owned by Viacom

- the Discovery Channel, which has a partnership with the rising US media and entertainment firm Discovery Communications

- The Comedy Network, which is partnered with the American cable channel Comedy Central, once owned by Time Warner and now owned by Viacom

- Bravo and the celebrity-worshipping E!, which are licensed by NBC Universal, a company owned by the American giant Comcast

- and, finally, the so-far Canadian-owned CTV (with all its local affiliates), CTV News, CP24, and the Space network, for fans of old sci-fi movies.

In their work on the propaganda model, Herman and Chomsky examine the way that media organizations with ties to powerful corporate and political groups—the ones who really set the agenda for news reporting, in Herman and Chomsky's view—promote the idea that the media

journalist might unwittingly give away a strategic position or some other classified information vital to the success of the campaign, it's worth wondering why the army would allow reporters into their ranks at all. When questioned on this point, Lieutenant-Colonel Rick Long, then in charge of media relations for the US Marine Corps, replied:

> Frankly, our job is to win the war. Part of that is information warfare. So we are going to attempt to dominate the information environment. (cited in Kahn 2004)

With the army as censor, engaged in "information warfare," there can be little doubt that accuracy took second place to propaganda during the war in Iraq. It is why critics of embedded journalism sometimes refer to the reporters as "in-bedded" journalists.

Can the bias of embedded journalists be studied productively? The Pew Research Center believes it can. In a 2003 study of embedded reporters, Pew's Project for Excellence in Journalism did a content analysis of television news reports during the first six days of the war. They found that Americans were well served by embedded journalists, as seen by the "fact" are, in fact, dominated by a left-of-centre political and social perspective. Herman and Chomsky call this idea the **myth of the liberal media**. The myth of the liberal media allows journalists with a right-wing perspective to present their views as though they are in the minority and under attack by the supposedly dominant liberal media. Invoking the myth is a tactic more common in the US, where organizations like the ultra-right (and ultra-powerful) Fox News use it to rally support around their conservative positions on issues such as gun control, abortion, and gay marriage (a.k.a. "family values"), but claims of a liberal media bias are sometimes heard in Canada also. Canadian media figures who sit on the far right of the political spectrum, including Don Cherry, Claire Hoy, Margaret Wente, and Christie Blatchford, are quick to set their extreme views as running counter to the general sentiment of the left-wing, liberal media. In fact, most of the mainstream Canadian media occupy a position that is blandly centrist or moderately right-wing—albeit still to the left of the perspective taken more vociferously by the figures noted above. Ask yourself what television shows make a critique of the politically and corporately powerful in Canada. I can think of only three: CBC's *Marketplace*, *The Nature of Things*, and *This Hour Has 22 Minutes*. The last named is, of course, a comedy.

Conservative media critics often argue that the left-leaning, liberal media are controlled by, and pander to, **special-interest groups**, including unions and unionized workers (e.g. teachers), racialized groups, and other minoritized people (gays, lesbians, the poor, the disabled etc.). Evidence for such control would be hard to find.

What do YOU think?

In October 2012, the CRTC blocked an attempt by Bell Canada Enterprises (BCE) to take over Astral Media (which owns The Movie Network, HBO Canada, the Family Channel, Disney Junior, and the French-language station Super Écran) with a $3.4 billion buyout. It would have given Bell ownership of 107 radio stations, 2 national television networks, and 49 paid specialty channels (Parry 2012). The CRTC argued that the merger would put too much power in one company's hands, noting also that BCE made no commitments to local programming or the promotion of emerging local artists. For its part, BCE (which is still pursuing the deal) said that they needed the power to compete with foreign companies such as Netflix. They argued that the CRTC's decision gave more power to BCE's main competitors—Rogers, Telus, and Québecor. Do you agree with the CRTC's decision? Why or why not?

that 93.5 per cent of the reports "were primarily factual in nature"; commentary (3.7 per cent), analysis (1.9 per cent), and opinion (0.9 per cent) made up the remaining 6.5 per cent of the reports (Journalism.org 2003).

There are several sociological problems with this. One is that what the embedded reporters chose to show (or what they were permitted to show by their military masters) was already interpretively biased. The fact that only one of the reports documented in the study showed pictures of Iraqi dead is indicative of that. What is not chosen as content is always a potential weakness of content analysis. In this case it is a major weakness. What is needed for a more accurate study is to systematically compare and contrast embedded and un-embedded journalists. This was not done. The study is flawed.

What do YOU think?

Which of Herman and Chomsky's filters is in evidence in embedded journalism?

Telling It Like It Is

An Author POV

Objectivity Is Elusive—And That's a Fact

Based in Washington, DC, the Pew Research Center is a non-profit organization that uses opinion polls, demographic research, and other social science methods to gather data to inform the American public on trends and attitudes in politics, religion, technology, international events, and other research areas. It describes itself as a "non-partisan fact tank," which implies that the organization generates hard facts instead of opinions. In this way, we're meant to see it as different to the many traditional "think tanks" that use research findings to advocate a particular political position and influence policy-making on matters ranging from business and the economy to immigration and national defence. (Canadian examples of think tanks include the Centre for Policy Alternatives, the C.D. Howe Institute, the Canada West Foundation, and the Centre for Policy Studies.)

I believe that Pew is actually made up of old-time positivists who believe too much in their ability to be objective and who don't understand standpoint theory. A good illustration of what I might call unconscious interpretation at the presumed fact level can be seen in a study they released in June 2012 on "The Rise of Asian Americans" (Pew 2012). The authors of the report have been criticized for lumping together and extolling the virtues of very different groups—Chinese, Filipino, South Asian, Vietnamese, Korean, and Japanese—and for perpetuating stereotypes of the high-achieving, family-oriented Asian immigrant realizing rags-to-riches success through hard work (Hing 2012). By generalizing the findings to all Asians, the report's authors glossed over some serious problems in employment, household income, and education attainment among certain subgroups of the Asian-American population.

Junk Food News

In 1985, **Neil Postman** (1931–2003), a leading scholar of media and media abuse, whose important work on childhood we surveyed in Chapter 13, published a groundbreaking book called *Amusing Ourselves to Death: Public Discourse in the Age of Show Business*. His thesis, which relates primarily to the medium of television, is that the way information is packaged and delivered makes it more about being entertaining than about being informative, at great cultural cost to Americans (and, by implication, to others who experience the medium in the same way). The book features his most (mis)quoted observation that "Americans are the best entertained, and quite likely the least informed society in the Western world" (Postman 1985: 106—the words "quite likely" and "Western" are often left out).

Robert MacNeil is a Canadian-born journalist and TV anchor, one half of a duo that presented the long-running and very popular television news show *The MacNeil/Lehrer Report* (later *The MacNeil/Lehrer News Hour*), which aired on PBS from 1975 until 1995. A comment on television journalism, which comes from his memoir, is both frightening and instructive to those who worry about the growing ignorance of North Americans:

> The idea . . . is to keep everything brief, not to strain the attention of anyone but instead to provide constant stimulation through variety, novelty, action, and movement. You are required . . . to pay attention to no concept, no character, and no problem for more than a few seconds at a time. . . . [B]ite-sized is best, . . . complexity must be avoided, . . . nuances are dispensable, . . . qualifications impede the simple message, . . . visual stimulation is a substitute for thought, and . . . verbal precision is an anachronism. (MacNeil 1982: 2, 4, as cited in Postman 1985)

MacNeil here could be talking as well about most Hollywood movies, the vast majority of current magazine articles, and, very unfortunately, a good number of the most popular non-fiction books of our time.

According to Postman, the kind of information broadcast by the television news media is actually **disinformation**, a term he explains in the following way:

> I am using this word almost in the precise sense in which it is used by the CIA or KGB. Disinformation does not mean false information. It means misleading information—misplaced, irrelevant, fragmented or superficial information—information that creates the illusion of knowing something, but which in fact leads one away from knowing. (Postman 1985: 107)

Postman's disinformation would not be a feature of Herman and Chomsky's propaganda model of news, because disinformation is not *deliberately* misleading. It is simply an unavoidable by-product of "news . . . packaged as entertainment" (Postman 1985: 107). It is generally benign in intent, but it could be argued that it is as malignant in result as propaganda. Postman was writing about the United States, but he could well have been talking about Canada. We might be a little less entertained by our television, but we are probably only a little more informed.

Much of what Postman described as misinformation falls into a category labelled **junk food news**. This consists of media reports that do not inform the audience in ways that are useful to creating a greater understanding of socio-political issues and making them more informed citizens of their town, country, or planet. Think, for example, of how the American news media obsessed over 2008 Democratic candidate Hillary Clinton's fashion sense and personal style, giving too little attention to her progressive, feminist ideals and her thoughts on issues related to the environment and public health. Such distracting issues are the Twinkies of the media world, or, to use a Canadian analogy, the Jos. Louis of media presentations. They are sweet and delicious, but not very good for you.

The term *junk food news* is often attributed to Carl Jensen, a communications professor at Sonoma State University and founder of the media watchdog Project Censored. Junk food news contributes to censorship by using up time in the newscast or taking up space on a website or newspaper that could otherwise be given to items of far greater importance. As Project Censor editors Peter Phillips and Mickey Huff, explain:

Any interference with the free flow of information is censorship. Even if the interference is structural or not deliberate, it has the same impact of creating a lack of public awareness on critical issues. This means that when the *New York Times* chooses to cover the updates of celebrity deaths, marriages, or divorces, and ignores the ACLU's [the American Civil Liberties Union's] release of military autopsy reports proving that the US was torturing prisoners to death in Iraq and Afghanistan, . . . that is censorship. It is censorship even if most of the *New York Times* journalists didn't know about the ACLU report; they certainly should have—it was an AP [American Press news service] release! . . . For a story this important to go virtually unreported implies a degree of overt censorship. (Phillips & Huff 2010)

Jensen identified several categories of these stories that "[blur] the lines of entertainment and information while favoring the trivial and inane over the substantive and germane" (Huff & Project Censored 2012), including the following:

- *brand name news*, where the unremarkable actions and comments of people like the Royal Family, the Kardashians, and Donald Trump are considered newsworthy simply because of the celebrity status of the people involved
- *sex news*, where the breakups, makeups, and affairs of celebrities make headlines
- *yo-yo news*, which places undue importance on day-to-day or even hour-to-hour shifts in the economy, stock prices, the dollar; this also includes daily speculation and rumours about the status of, say, a person who may or may not decide to run for political office
- *crazed news*, on fads of the day, like the end of the world as predicted according to the Mayan calendar, or the short-lived debate about whether cellphone use causes cancer
- *showbiz news*—who wore what at the Oscars, what Hollywood stars do when they're off the set, and so on
- *sports news*, including the events that take place away from the game, such as Lance Armstrong's confession interview with Oprah Winfrey, the Tiger Woods scandal, and the hoax involving Notre Dame football star Manti Te'o and his fictitious girlfriend

- *political news* that focuses on polls, photo ops, and scandals that have little to do with policy-making and governance.

QUICK HITS

Top Ten Junk Food News Stories for 2008 and 2009

Project Censored publishes an annual list of the 25 most censored, or underreported, news stories of importance to Americans. In 2010, it also published a list of the top 10 junk food news stories from 2008–9:

1. Olympic Medalist Michael Phelps Hits a Bong
2. Jessica Simpson Gains Weight
3. First Lady Michelle Obama's Fashion Sense
4. The Brangelina Twins
5. Lindsay Lohan Dates a Woman
6. The Presidential First Puppy
7. Heidi Montag "Marries" Spencer Pratt
8. Barry Bonds' Steroid Trial
9. Jamie-Lynn Spears Gives Birth
10. The Woes of Amy Winehouse (Huff & Capell 2010)

That's two sports stories that have little to do with sports, two "political" stories that have nothing to do with politics, three acting stories that have nothing to do with acting, two music stories that don't talk about music, and one story about someone famous for being famous.

What do YOU think?

1. Can you identify junk food news when you see it or read it? Watch a newscast on television, and for each story tick off one of two categories:

   ☐ junk food news, presenting information that is irrelevant, superficial, and generally unimportant

   ☐ "healthy" news, presenting information that it is important to know concerning the state of the world where you live

   How many stories in the newscast fall into each category?

2. Use Jensen's categories to classify the junk food news items. Which categories do most of the junk food news items fall into? Are you surprised by the results?

When we're thinking of junk food media, we must also consider current non-fiction books (the current love of vampires, zombies, and shades of grey has made junk food fiction pretty much a given right now). Of the ten best-sellers promoted by Amazon.ca right at this moment, seven are celebrity biographies—of Shania Twain (the token Canadian), Tina Fey, Betty White, Nikki Sixx (previously unknown to me), and three "bad-boy" celebrities, Steven Tyler, Keith Richards, and Rob Lowe.

Media Spectacles

If we can consider consumerism a religion, it would need rituals, many of which would exist as media spectacles.

Media spectacles are big events that dominate the mass media. They may fall among Jensen's categories of junk food news, and they can certainly be subject to propaganda. Media spectacles often centre around annual events such as "the big game" or "the big series" (the Super Bowl, the World Series, the summer or winter Olympics) or anniversaries of important national events (Remembrance Day, the anniversary of 9/11). They can also involve singular events such as a military operation (the "Attack on Iraq"), the death of a very famous person (Diana, the Princess of Wales), or a devastating act of nature (Hurricane Katrina, the Boxing Day tsunami in South Asia, the earthquake in Haiti). These events become commodities that are force-fed to media consumers on a large scale. You know you have consumed a media spectacle when it strongly affects how you envision the world, and when it seems there is no possible **counter-narrative**, no way of seeing the event in a different light. As a media consumer you "pay" for a media spectacle by buying the products advertised during the coverage. More metaphorically, you can pay with an uncritical acceptance of the narratives surrounding the event. Newspapers and magazines, radio and television, the Internet and social networks all combine to jam people's minds full with the object of the spectacle during the limited period of time leading up to and during the event and its aftermath.

Media spectacles are very difficult to avoid. In *The Society of the Spectacle*, French theorist **Guy Debord** (1931–1994) described them as totalizing narratives, one-way communications in which those with power—especially governments and corporations—control

BREAKING NEWS: patrons of a Boston tavern watch ongoing coverage of the manhunt for the fugitive suspect in the Boston Marathon bombing, 19 April 2013. Viewers may have found the live coverage of the police investigation compelling, but was it really necessary, or was this a case of a media spectacle?

the interpretation of the events, in terms of values and beliefs represented. In Debord's interpretation, the public are mostly passive consumers of the spectacles, with few opportunities for meaningful independent input but plenty of chances to express vigorous agreement and demonstrate enthusiastic support.

Debord was the central figure in a short-lived (1957–1972) intellectual movement of a group known as the **situationists**, who were devoted to analyzing the social construction of the situations that make up everyday life. They were members of a European organization known as the Situationist International, which brought together Marxist and avant-garde artists in a kind of social constructionist media experiment. Their idea was to create situations that would serve as alternatives to the situations constructed by advanced capitalism. Their media events would be **détournements** (literally "diversions," from the French verb *détourner* meaning "to divert, turn away, or hijack"), ways of creating what sociologists would now call counter-narratives to oppose the mainstream narrative of media events controlled by governments and powerful capitalist interests.

These détournements were, in the more recent language of culture commentators like Mark Dery and Naomi Klein, instances of "culture jamming," attempts to subvert or upend mainstream media culture. The situationist movement peaked in a series of wildcat strikes waged in France in May 1968. In a way, the situationists are like the Luddites: figures of a particular time and place who did not effect any significant change against the main flow of history, but who have left us with a message that is useful for the future. Unfortunately, rather than presenting readers with a clear message, Debord's writing is difficult to follow, rooted more in philosophical speculation than in researching or presenting clear evidence of analysis. *The Society of the Spectacle* (1967) comprises a series of 221 theses or philosophical postulates. Here are two of the most often quoted ones, numbers one and four:

THE WHOLE LIFE of those societies in which modern conditions of production prevail presents itself as an immense accumulation of *spectacles*. All that once was directly lived has become mere representation. (Debord 1995: 12)

THE SPECTACLE IS NOT a collection of images; rather, it is a social relationship between people that is mediated by images. (Debord 1995: 12)

Douglas Kellner is a prominent critical media theorist, trained in philosophy, whose writings on a wide variety of subjects include intellectual biographies of left-wing social theorists Herbert Marcuse and Jean Baudrillard, revolutionary Ernesto "Che" Guevera, and American ex-president George W. Bush. While acknowledging his intellectual debt to Debord, Kellner argues that in the highly competitive world of growing media venues, producing counter-narratives as alternatives to the totalizing narratives of mainstream media is often possible. The example he uses is the American/British invasion of Iraq in 2003, a key subject in a book he wrote (Kellner 2005).

The media spectacle surrounding the invasion of Iraq serves, in a number of ways, as the perfect example of Debord's ideas concerning how such spectacles reflect the perspectives and serve the needs of governments (specifically in this case, the administrations of George W. Bush's Republican Party and, to a lesser extent, Tony Blair's Labour Party) and large corporations (private contracting firms that took part in the post-war "reconstruction" of Iraq, making millions in profits from the venture). The names given by the news media to the invasion, including "Operation Iraqi Freedom" and "the War on Terror," reflected a pro-government perspective. The more conservative American networks, such as Fox, CNN, and NBC, presented their coverage in pro-government terms of patriotism overcoming terrorism, with some news items set to patriotic American music. They also used **technological fetishism** to glorify the modern weapons of war in the American arsenal, thereby conveying a message of American superiority. (In the process, they set up future sales of video games based on the same technology.) These networks consciously avoided looking at casualties (American and Iraqi) and at the destruction of Iraqi buildings and general infrastructure. They did, however, show the burning oil wells initiated by Iraqi resistors. Generally, the networks used images consistent with the message, *We are winning. We are effecting a regime change, opposing a regime, not the Iraqi people, for whom we are creating freedom and democracy.* You could say that the American media were effectively promoting the attack the way they might advertise a consumer product. *Don't enter Iraq without it.*

The pivotal moment in coverage of the invasion of Iraq was a staged event—the toppling of the statue of deposed Iraqi leader Saddam Hussein. The destruction of the 12-foot monument was portrayed by American media as an expression of the joy of Iraqi citizens at the "regime change." But it was staged: the statue was located in Baghdad's Firdus Square, directly in front of the Palestine Hotel, where journalists from many countries happened to be staying. What looked like—and was meant to look like—a huge throng of hundreds or even thousands of jubilant Iraqis was in fact just dozens of people, shot close-up to give the impression of greater numbers. The main participants

In a 2004 article in the *Los Angeles Times*, long-time media columnist David Shaw argued that people "want pre-packaged news—news presented in small, entertaining bites and delivered with edge, with attitude" (Shaw 2004). He compared *Fox News* and *The Daily Show*, noting that, despite their dissimilarities, "you can watch either and come away feeling informed, entertained and confirmed in your world view, all with a minimum of intellectual effort." Do you agree with Shaw's statements? Why or why not?

included several American marines and an Iraqi wrester/weight-lifter who had been imprisoned after an argument with one of Saddam's sons.

Kellner identified several counter-narratives to the patriotic American media spectacle. The CBC and BBC both showed scenes of Arab (particularly Iraqi) outrage at the invasion, as well as scenes of global protest, both anti-war and anti-US. These networks presented a more balanced picture. And comedians, particularly Canadian but also some American, made good use of the Bush administration's phony excuse for going to war, the infamous nonexistent "weapons of mass destruction," which has been a catchphrase for humour ever since.

Telling It Like It Is | An Author POV

The Death of a Police Officer: A Media Spectacle

In January 2011, there was a media spectacle surrounding the funeral of a young Toronto police officer, Sergeant Ryan Russell, killed in the pursuit of a man who was recklessly driving a stolen snowplow. Note that in writing about this incident sociologically, I do not mean to diminish the tragedy or valour shown by Sergeant Russell in attempting to thwart a man who was endangering the lives of motorists and pedestrians.

Sergeant Russell received the kind of funeral befitting an officer killed in the line of duty. It included a long funeral procession thronged by thousands of people—police and civilians—who lined the city streets along the route. Several hours of coverage were given to the funeral and procession on television.

Had he been watching the coverage, Debord might have noted the repeated affirmation that all police are heroes and good guys. Debord might have seen this as a conscious, deliberate attempt to counteract the negative attention the Toronto police received during another media spectacle that occurred in the summer of 2010, the G20 conference, during which police were accused of bullying, abusing, and generally mistreating protestors. For months following the conference—right up until the week before the funeral, in fact—the media kept the story of alleged police brutality alive. And yet, during the funeral of Sergeant Russell, the networks—TV and radio—appeared to be competing over who could devote the most airtime to covering the event while expressing the most pro-police sympathy. The winner would receive the most viewers and listeners. A Debordian cynic might note

that the publicly funded CBC, a network that regularly receives criticism from conservative commentators over its presumed "left-leaning" agenda, was a leader in this respect, perhaps in an attempt to come across as being more conservative.

It would be less cynical to look at the uncritical, sometimes over-the-top pro-police media sentiment as more a latent (i.e. unintended) function of the media spectacle, with the various media not intending to deliberately counteract the negative impression of the police after the G20 protestor issue. Further, the unscripted expressions of individual citizens, and the choice of a particular set of those expressions by the interviewing media, could be seen as communicating the emotional needs of people living in Canada's largest city to create a sense of "community" (a term used by at least one interviewed spectator of the funeral procession) in a complicated society.

At the end of the portion of the evening news devoted to covering the spectacle, one CBC announcer commented that the officer "would not soon be forgotten" by the citizens of Toronto. Sadly, public memory can be short. Writers of sociology textbooks have to update the examples they use of media spectacles, especially when it comes to the public mourning of celebrities. The media spectacles surrounding the funerals of Princess Diana (1997) and Michael Jackson (2009) quickly lose resonance. We have recently witnessed the royal "marriage of the century," followed soon after by the birth of the next heir to the British throne, and the election of a new head of the Catholic church. What will the next spectacle be?

The distinction between the two approaches Kellner discusses reflects the different mindsets represented by mass culture and popular culture interpretations (as discussed in Chapter 4). Debord, a Marxist, represents a mass culture approach: he presents media spectacles as overwhelming the masses, who are passive victims forced to consume the spectacle presented to them. Kellner's own interpretation represents a popular culture approach: there are contestations of the Western or American or capitalist spectacle, available from different sources. In his deconstruction of the coverage of the invasion of Iraq, Kellner has made his point well, at least in terms of a global audience. However, counter-narratives often lack the power and reach of the mainstream narrative; they amount to a contestation so minor that Debord's portrayal is more instructive. This is particularly the case with media spectacles of public mourning, as illustrated in the box on page 525.

Two Views (Maybe Three) of Multinational Media Companies

A transnational media conglomerate can be viewed in one of two ways. The first is that it is a product of a specific national culture and thus represents a foreign influence in every country (outside of its home country) in which it operates. In this sense, it both dominates the media landscape in the countries it enters, and forces the home culture into the homes of media consumers around the world.

The second view—and the one that most transnational media companies themselves tend to hold—is that the soul of these companies is global, not national. According to this view, transnational media organization are corporate citizens of the world, without any kind of national cultural agenda. Media critic Robert W. McChesney captures this sentiment:

> The dominant media firms increasingly view themselves as global entities. Bertelsmann [one of the top ten world media conglomerates] CEO Thomas Middelhoff bristled when, in 1998, some said it was improper for a German firm to control 15 per cent of both the US book publishing and music markets. "We're not foreign. We're international," Middelhoff proclaimed. "I'm an American with a German passport." In 2000 Middelhoff proclaimed that Bertelsmann was no longer a

German company: "We are really the most global media company." Likewise, AOL–Time Warner's Gerald Levin stated, "We do not want to be viewed as an American company. We think globally." . . . (McChesney 2003: 29)

Fair enough. But can a company like Disney, say, be called a global corporate citizen when it takes stories from around the world—the Andes, the Middle East, China—and introduces American (or Americanized) characters in these foreign settings, with plotlines that cross borders? And the movie companies that profit so much in Canadian theatres by selling American stories, leaving Canadians (outside of Quebec) without the opportunity to view on the big screen the wars, sports, and "inspired-by-a-true-story" adventures of their own people: what do they prevent us from creating? And isn't it depressing that when the prime minister of Canada looks for news, he goes to the American cable news network CNN?

Perhaps a third view is most appropriate here, following a colonial model. Like the early colonial companies they resemble in other ways, the transnational media companies have become socio-political entities unto themselves, neither national (although they tend to benefit primarily the finances and cultural content of their countries of origin) nor international in the sense of operating with an awareness of what is best for the world.

What do YOU think?

1. How could you research the question of how globally a transnational media company thinks?

2. What is lost when national and local newspapers are controlled by a transnational media company?

3. Should media, sometimes referred to as a "cultural industry," be protected from transnational media companies? How should that be done?

The Shrinking of the Public Sphere in Media

Herman and Chomsky have defined the **public sphere** as "the array of places and forums in which matters important to a democratic community are debated and information relevant to intelligent citizen participation is provided" (Herman & Chomsky 2002: xvii).

Going Global

Al Jazeera: Media Freedom or Contextual Objectivity?

The Arab satellite news network Al Jazeera came into existence in 1996, when the emir of Qatar hired a large number of the editorial staff of the British Broadcasting Company's Arabic-language channel, which had closed down several months earlier. The format and style of the network's news and current affairs programming would be very familiar to North American audiences accustomed to all-news networks like CNN and the 24-hour news channels of CBC and CTV. In its content, Al Jazeera represents a pan-Arab perspective, but it does follow the universal journalistic credo of "getting to the truth," and the network has not been afraid to present dissenting views and criticism of Arab governments. Its broadcasting of Arab victims of war (especially in Iraq) and its coverage of the Israeli occupation of Palestine have had a very dramatic effect on its international audience.

In "The Case of al-Jazeera: An 'Arab CNN'?" German communication studies professor Kai Hafez considers the critical reception of the news network outside the Arab world. Specifically, he examines the two prevailing views of Al Jazeera in the West. Initially, he argues, it was celebrated by political commentators and media critics in western Europe and North America as a promising sign of growing democracy and media freedom in the Arab world. However, since the events of September 11, it has become a target of Western, particularly American,

criticism, for its alleged bias and "soft on terrorism" stance. Hafez places this bias in the context of "contextual objectivity," a term introduced by Arab media scholars (both based at universities in the US) Mohammed El-Nawawy and Adel Iskandar, in their work *Al-Jazeera: The Story of the Network That Is Rattling Governments and Redefining Modern Journalism* (2003):

> Mohammed El-Nawawy and Adel Iskandar accept that the network is biased, but call this "contextual objectivity": al-Jazeera has to be pro-Arab to make up for the pro-American and pro-Israeli tenor of Western media. Nawawy and Iskander are right to underline the sense of relief and fascination which al-Jazeera has inspired in the Arab world as partisan of the Arab cause. The West's hegemonic control of the information flow, embodied in the large news agencies and broadcasters, has been broken for the first time. (Hafez 2007: 79)

The notion of **contextual objectivity** seems to mean that in the broader context, objectivity (or at least pluralism) is served by the existence of contrasting biased views, although calling Al Jazeera an "Arab CNN" is something of a negative distortion.

What do YOU think?

1. Why would calling Al Jazeera the "Arab CNN" be something of a negative distortion? Is it reasonable to judge the Arab news network in terms of its similarity to an American cable news channel?
2. Why is it important that Al Jazeera exist? Whom does it benefit?

One of the social dangers identified by the propaganda model is the shrinking of the public sphere under the assault of powerful private interests and their relentless commercialism (University of Illinois media critic and author Robert McChesney makes this argument in *Rich Media, Poor Democracy*, 1999). Another danger

of the shrinking public sphere is a diversion of attention from the socially important to the glorified trivial (e.g. celebrity worship).

A sign of the shrinking public sphere is the decline of public broadcasting. This has happened in developing nations, where deregulating the national broadcasting networks (i.e. removing protective regulations in order to encourage competition from private broadcasters) is a typical condition of loans from the World Bank. These are the same countries that have been forced to cut government spending in response to the effects of globalization, which is championed by many of the same powerful multinational companies with ties to the media.

In contrast, developed nations have experienced what media critic James Ledbetter termed the "malling" of public broadcasting (Ledbetter 1997). This is the process in which public broadcasters avoid "hard-hitting," politically controversial programming in favour of imitating the conceptual fluffiness produced by private networks. In Canada, you need look no further for evidence of this than the CBC. Our national public broadcaster recently purchased the broadcasting rights to two North American game show franchises, *Wheel of Fortune* (with the still smiling and ever plastic-wrapped Vanna White and Pat Sajak—they are making millions of dollars every year) and *Jeopardy*, starring Canada's gift to TV game shows, Alex Trebek. There is also a trend evident in the news programming on some of the CBC's local affiliates, where the hosts have developed an apolitical and unchallenging "hosting-a-parade" style of banter that is almost identical to what we see on *Canada A.M.* (whose breezily uncritical style is beautifully parodied by CBC's *22 Minutes*), which airs on the private broadcaster CTV.

The Internet: The New Public Sphere or a Failing Attempt at Media Democracy?

So I know what you're probably thinking. So what if our national public broadcaster is now competing with private networks for big advertising dollars by adopting a lineup of silly reality programs and American game shows? *Front Page Challenge* was *so* twenty years ago. Hasn't the Internet succeeded public television broadcasting as the new public sphere?

And you'd have a point. (Except you probably didn't make that comment about *Front Page Challenge*—you're too young to have watched it.) With the growth of online chatrooms, discussion forums, and advocacy sites, as well as the emergence of independent, non-profit online news sites like openDemocracy and Wikinews, which welcome contributions from citizen journalists, the Internet looks like the pathway to opening up media democracy, globalizing knowledge

and the flow of information, and expressing the views of marginalized groups that may be ignored by the mainstream, commercial media. But is this actually happening? Or is the Internet failing in this regard as I write and you read? (Keep in mind that a video of a "talking" dog that goes viral on YouTube with millions of hits is not a case for democracy; it's more a kind of well-attended freak show.)

Foremost among the arguments for media democracy via the Internet is the lack of government and corporate control over the Web. Noted Australian activist/journalist Julian Assange has made a lot of enemies around the world with the release of sensitive political cables and other confidential documents on his WikiLeaks website; to date, however, he has not been charged with any crime related to the activities of WikiLeaks, and the website continues to broadcast. Score one for media democracy.

As for corporate control, the Internet was not primarily market-oriented in its origin or early development. This seems to be changing, however, as the Internet gets more and more inundated with ads, and as sites that were once free to browse (including news sites such as *The Globe and Mail*) are increasingly putting up paywalls, requiring visitors to pay for their content. It is worth considering also the tale of the *Huffington Post*. The independent blog and news forum launched in 2005, concentrating on American politics and presenting a primarily left-of-centre political perspective that ran counter to the conservative tenor of many big US news agencies. For five years the website grew in popularity, and then in 2011 it was purchased by American multimedia giant AOL. It now has a number of local editions, including Canadian sites in English and in French. It invites the question: how long can a website with such enormous global reach operate independently of the big multimedia organizations? There are also the sheer numbers to consider. There are millions of people worldwide who use the Internet, and that number is constantly growing. Surely that would enable people to connect more completely than ever before, allowing global citizens concerned about social justice to link with each other across borders to overcome oppressive governments and corporate giants.

But this isn't quite borne out by the evidence. For one thing, movements of this kind appear so far to be very rare—much less common, in fact, than what theorists were predicting in the 1990s. There is also the suggestion, expressed by Kai Hafez, that communications of this kind tend to be limited in scope. Internet-based communications *within* nations far outnumber those *between* countries. In an admittedly early study (published in 2000), Alexander Halavais found that some 90 per cent of hyperlinks in the United States remained there, and that in Europe, the percentage of domestic links varied from 60 to 70 per cent, with about 70 per cent of cross-border European links leading to US sites (as reported in Hafez 2007: 102–3).

A second argument against the international democratization of the Internet comes from what Hafez refers to as the "Tower of Babel" effect, with reference to the biblical story of a tower built to reach Heaven, which God thwarted by jumbling the languages of the builders so that they could not communicate with each other. English dominated the Internet in its early days, but that dominance has dramatically decreased. By 2004, the proportion of English users online had dropped from around 75.0 per cent in the late 1990s to 35.8 per cent, with Chinese second at 14.1 per cent, Japanese third at 9.6 per cent, and Spanish closely following at 9.0 per cent. Hafez interprets these figures with the following warning:

[T]he Internet threatens to disintegrate into linguistic sub-communities, which runs counter to the notion that it is helping to globalize knowledge. The "Babel" variant of the global knowledge society will do little more than create a highly compressed version of cultures anchored in their national languages, rather than promoting the exchange of global knowledge. (Hafez 2007: 105)

Figure 19.1 shows the 10 languages most commonly used online.

The main argument against the Internet as an easy route to media democracy stems from the **digital divide**, the separation in society between those *with* and those *without* ready access to computers and the Internet and the knowledge of how to use them effectively. The International Telecommunications Union, an agency of the United Nations, reports that as of 2013, just 41 per cent (estimated) of all households worldwide have Internet access, and under 40 per cent of the world's population is online (ITU 2013). This flies in the face of what many in the West believe is true, especially (in our experience) college and university

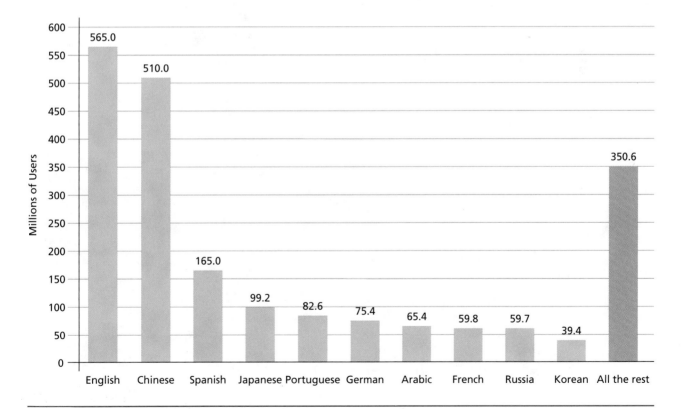

Figure 19.1 Internet users by language, 2011

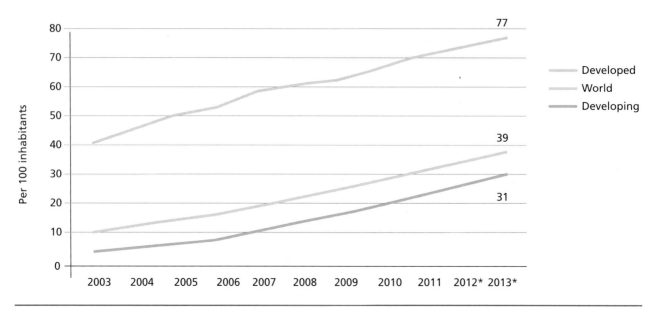

Figure 19.2 Internet users by development level, 2003–13

Note: * Estimate
Source: ITU World Telecommunication/ICT Indicators database.

In Bangladesh, *Tattahakallayani* ("Info Ladies") travel by bike to bring laptops and Internet connections to remote villages, helping tens of thousands of people—especially women—get everything from government services to contact with distant relatives. Here Info Lady Mehedi Akthar Misty (right) helps Amina Begum talk with her husband via Skype. Do *you* think that the Internet will become more of a source of media democracy than it is now? Why or why not?

students, who tend to imagine that Internet use is far more widespread globally.

The digital divide is a twofold division. First, it is a division *between* countries, with, on the positive side of the divide, the developed countries of North America, Europe, China, Japan, India, and Korea—those that Hafez and others have called the **info-elites**—and, on the other side, the developing countries of the Middle East, most of Asia, and Africa (see Figure 19.2). Second, it is a divide that exists *within* countries, even within developed countries, with the middle and upper classes (especially those who are better educated) on the one side, and the poor and the elderly on the other side, representing a lack of access and knowledge. We should worry about post-secondary students in the latter group, given that colleges and universities are relying more and more on computer-based platforms for delivering and evaluating education (so much for "learner-centredness"). It is a widely publicized myth that every kid in North America is a "computer whiz." Many are not, by mental inclination or for financial reasons, on that side of the digital divide.

What do YOU think?

How could a sociological researcher investigate the extent and nature of the digital divide in a country, a city, or even a community?

Television stations sometimes use a drop in the ratings as an excuse for laying off older female news readers. Do you think that this is more an excuse, or that television viewers on a large scale prefer to watch younger women as "eye candy" on news shows?

Gendered and Racialized Media

Gender and Mass Media

In Canada, women and girls engage more in social media than do their male counterparts. This is borne out by the results of a 2012 Ipsos Reid survey of adult Canadians with Internet access, which found that 37 per cent of women were likely to visit a social media site daily, compared with just 24 per cent of men (cited in Dewling 2013: 2). What other differences can be said to exist? Recall from Chapter 3, on research methods, that a good content analysis of television, film, and websites reveals the patriarchal and often misogynist portrayal of women in mass media. Advertising in the media would lead us to believe (erroneously) that women exclusively are obsessed with their hair and their weight, and that only skinny women (not full-figured women and certainly not men) eat yogurt. These are among the many sexist stereotypes that the media perpetuate.

The gendered division of media doesn't end there. Male and female news readers (I like the term "talking heads") have different rules applying to them. There is greater pressure on news presenters who are women to look young and attractive. Fox News (sometimes known as "Foxy News") sets the standard in this regard with young, mini-skirted, well made-up women journalists whose looks will appeal to the older male audience that is Fox's target demographic and mainstay. Are we making this up? Hardly. There is evidence to show that women who violate these sexist norms are negatively sanctioned. A notable example occurred rather recently, in 2012, when a 37-year-old news anchor for a Wisconsin television station received an e-mail from a male lawyer criticizing her for being "obese." He suggested that the news anchor, Jennifer Livingston, was an unsuitable role model for the community's young people, especially its young women, writing:

I was surprised indeed to witness that your physical condition hasn't improved for many years. Obesity is one of the worst choices a person can make and one of the most dangerous habits to maintain. I leave you this note hoping that you'll reconsider your responsibility as a local public personality to present and promote a healthy lifestyle. (cited in Irish 2012)

How likely do you think it is that a male news anchor would receive such an e-mail? Fortunately, Ms Livingston was strong and independent enough to reply to her critic publicly, in a four-minute presentation on her news show. It will be interesting to see where her career goes from here.

Age discrimination also occurs more often with women news readers than with their male counterparts. Among the many incidents that demonstrate this is a groundbreaking case that occurred in 1983, when Christine Craft sued a Kansas affiliate of the ABC network for age and sex discrimination. She had been demoted from news anchor to reporter in 1979, after a focus group panel had declared that Craft was "too old, too unattractive and wouldn't defer to men" (Acuna 2012). She was awarded $500,000 in compensation. More recently, in 2010, Karen Scott, the former news director for the New York station WPIX, filed a lawsuit against the station for wrongful dismissal, alleging age discrimination (Ms Scott was 60 when she was let go by the network in 2009).

"Race" and Mass Media

Print, TV, and online news coverage of Hurricane Katrina and its aftermath provides a striking illustration of how the media are racialized in a way that propagates racist ideologies concerning African Americans. A disproportionate amount of televised post-hurricane news coverage focused on black looters, many of whom were, indeed, scavenging for their survival. Yet the depiction of lawlessness, violence, and disorder in New Orleans was greatly exaggerated in the media. In 2011, sociologists Kirk Johnson and John Sonnett, together with journalism professor Mark Dolan, conducted a quantitative content analysis of the news coverage around Katrina, finding that "although many hurricane victims were low-income African Americans, news of looting and other activities featured disproportionate numbers of Whites,

particularly in speaking roles" (Johnson, Dolan, & Sonnett 2011: 302). Moreover, they found that the coverage was overly critical of the looters without providing the necessary context for viewers to understand the behaviour (i.e. that those who had been left with nothing after the storm were scrounging for whatever food, water, and other necessities they could find). The authors conclude that race represents a powerful filter that should be added to any consideration of Herman and Chomsky's propaganda model of news delivery.

Meanwhile, white vigilantes were seldom, if ever, mentioned in the coverage of the storm and its aftermath. In Algiers Point, a fairly isolated and predominately white area of New Orleans that was (like many white neighbourhoods) left relatively unscathed by the storm, the residents took up arms to defend their territory:

> Facing an influx of refugees, the residents of Algiers Point could have pulled together food, water, and medical supplies for the flood victims. Instead, a group of white residents, convinced that crime would arrive with the human exodus, sought to seal off the area, blocking the roads in and out of the neighborhood by dragging lumber and downed trees into the streets. They stockpiled handguns, assault rifles, shotguns and at least one Uzi, and began patrolling the streets in pickup trucks and SUVs. The newly formed militia, a loose band of about 15 to 30 residents, most of them men, all of them white, was looking for thieves, outlaws, or, as one member put it, anyone who simply "didn't belong." (Thompson 2008)

According to investigative journalist A.C. Thompson, at least 11 black people were shot, all of them by white men (Thompson 2008). Official police reports were few, and media reports even fewer, which is why Project Censored made this one of the top 25 underreported stories for that year.

Aboriginal People and the Media

With just a few notable exceptions, the mainstream media (or MSM) have a poor track record when it comes to covering Aboriginal issues. This leaves Aboriginal media with the important role of picking up the slack. We know, having learned from Dorothy Smith's **standpoint theory**, that experience and general social location play an important part in determining what questions get asked, what answers are given, and what issues are considered important. This is not to say that only Aboriginal people can write about Aboriginal issues; there are **border crossers**—outsiders who have understanding of and compassion for the issues of peoples different from themselves. It is just that it is not very likely, given the scant coverage of Inuit, First Nation, and Métis history and culture in the Canadian education system, that outsiders in the media are going to know enough about Aboriginal issues to approach news items with Aboriginal eyes.

A recent case that highlights this is the story of an 11-year-old who was tasered by the RCMP in an incident that occurred in Prince George, BC, in April 2011. It was underreported and insufficiently discussed in the mainstream media. The most comprehensive article available on the subject appears in *Windspeaker*, an Alberta-based Aboriginal monthly magazine that has been operating for over 25 years, during which it has earned a great deal of respect from Aboriginal communities (and the author of this textbook).

An editorial in a 2011 issue of *Windspeaker* provides us with the details of the case ("This Should Not Have Happened" 2011). The 11-year-old was an Aboriginal child who was a suspect in the stabbing of the 37-year-old manager of the group home in Prince George, where the boy was living. The editorial includes comments from the Union of British Columbia Indian Chiefs (UBCIC), who were pushing strongly for an inquiry into the incident. No other media report (CBC, *Vancouver Sun*, CTV, *Globe and Mail*, etc.) at the time mentioned that the child is Aboriginal, nor did they include quotations from representatives of the Aboriginal community (though some did present comments the RCMP's detachment commander in Prince George). There was little continued discussion of the case in the mainstream media prior to February 2013, when BC's representative for children and youth

The Point Is...

The OPP and the "Rock-Throwing Mob"

Christie Blatchford is a features writer and columnist for the *National Post*. She has worked as an embedded journalist with the Canadian army in Afghanistan (an experience that she turned into a book), and has been known to write articles that are biased against Aboriginal people (which she has also turned into a book, the sensationally titled *Helpless: Caledonia's Nightmare of Fear and Anarchy, and How the Law Failed All of Us*).

In August 2010, Blatchford, then writing for *The Globe and Mail*, wrote an article with the title "OPP on Remote Reserve Chased Out by Rock-Throwing Mob" (Blatchford 2010). The OPP are the Ontario Provincial Police, and the "rock-throwing mob" are Aboriginal citizens of Pikangikum First Nation, who were evicting the community's 11-member OPP detachment in protest over the way police had treated a deaf and mute Pikangikum man.

It is a classic example of one-sided reporting. The key to its one-sided nature is that the parties interviewed are all white: the details come from an OPP occurrence report, supplemented by quotes from OPP superintendant Ron van Straalen and the president of the OPP Association, Karl Walsh. No Aboriginal leaders in the community—not the chief, nor the councillors, nor the elders—were reported as having anything to say; neither were outside Aboriginal authorities, such as the Nishnawbe-Aski Police Service, a First Nation–run police service that provides policing for most of the Aboriginal communities in the area. The incident that sparked the band's anger is treated in just two paragraphs, appearing more than halfway through the 33-paragraph article, with the only details coming from the OPP's own occurrence report.

The article is written in such a manner that there is no way for the average reader to react but with shock and anger at the mob's alleged lawlessness. But there is no balance to it. Without testimony from the Aboriginal parties involved, the article cannot provide a fair account of the incident, and readers looking for the other side of the story must go to Aboriginal-run media.

issued the results of her investigation into the incident. Her finding that the BC Ministry for Children and Family Development failed to provide the boy's basic rights to safety, education, health care, socialization, and cultural identity (McKenna 2013) should have sparked a broader public discussion, but we have not seen this in the media.

There is another aspect to the media's ignorance of Aboriginal matters that is worth noting. This is an aspect I don't enjoy talking about, but it would be intellectually dishonest not to mention it. The ignorance of the mass media with respect to Aboriginal issues means that Aboriginal people can make claims that non-Aboriginal journalists and editors are simply not able to properly fact-check. To a certain extent, these journalists must simply accept the claims at face value. Yet they often do not fully realize that individual Aboriginal people and groups, like individuals and groups in all societies, have political agendas that lead them to stray from what might be called truthful or even credible. Just because, for example, a representative of a First Nation community claims that something is traditional, or that a particular place is the site of ancient burial grounds does not mean that it is. The representative may believe something is true, but may also be counting on the ignorance of the non-Aboriginal media not to know much about what is going on.

Social Media

Social media is a difficult term to define because of the speed at which the technology and fashion surrounding it are changing. In essence, social media include all of the means that enable people to be socially interactive within the virtual community supported by the Internet. Social networking sites such as Facebook, MySpace, and Twitter, which allow individuals to reach out across their entire social circle, are obvious examples. Professional networking sites such as LinkedIn and dating sites such as eHarmony and LavaLife also count, as do file-sharing sites such as Flickr and YouTube. Online gaming is considered a social medium, particularly when it involves simulated communities and stable personas or characters that participants identify with long-term. Once purely social (or, in the case of **cyber-bullying**, antisocial), social media are increasingly used in the development of professional contacts and for business generally.

Telling It Like It Is   An Author POV

Aragorn and the Arabs: The Treatment of Race in Hollywood Film

In March 2004, my wife and I saw the movie *Hidalgo*. Set in the late nineteenth century and starring Viggo Mortensen, the movie tells the supposedly true story of Frank Hopkins, an aging American cowboy and dispatch rider for the US cavalry, who rides his mustang against some of the finest Bedouin thoroughbreds in a 3,000-mile race across the Arabian Desert.

We had admired the work of the movie's lead actor in *The Lord of the Rings*, and the trailers for *Hidalgo* made it seem like the type of adventure movie we both enjoy. What we weren't prepared for was the Oriental simulacrum promoted relentlessly throughout the movie. All of the stock features of a romanticized portrait of Arabia were on display: an omnipotent sheik, the Arabs' insatiable thirst for vengeance and callousness concerning the lives of others, Islamic fanaticism and intolerance for non-Muslims, and a veiled Muslim woman willing to be threatened (and rescued) by the heroic Westerner so that she may be freed from the "oppression" of her veil. She closely resembled the stereotype—another simulacrum—of the Indian Princess discussed in Chapter 11, on gender and sexuality.

We appreciated that the hero acknowledged and drew upon his Aboriginal roots, even if his character embodied a few too many clichés. However, the movie was like an old Western, pitting cowboys against Indians—only in this case, the cowboy was part-Indian, and the Indians were really Arabs. Note to the director: Muslims, unlike Orcs, cannot be depicted, one and all, as villains without creating waves in the "real world" of contemporary politics.

In Canada, the number of people belonging to social networking sites is now greater than the number of people who do not. Facebook alone had, by 2011, over 18 million Canadian users, of whom the majority (53 per cent) were female (www.socialbakers.com/facebook-statistics/canada). Around the world, social networking is more a female than a male activity, with women spending more time than men on social networking sites (Abraham, Morn, & Vollman 2010).

Overshare and Peep Culture

Hal Niedziviecki is a Canadian novelist, broadcaster, and prolific writer. In 2009, he published *The Peep Diaries*, which introduced the term **peep culture** to a popular audience. He defines it as:

> . . . reality TV, YouTube, Twitter, Flickr, MySpace and Facebook. It's blogs, chat rooms, amateur porn sites, virally spread digital movies of a fat kid pretending to be a Jedi Knight, cell phone photos—posted online—of your drunk friend making out with her ex-boyfriend and citizen surveillance. (2009: 1)

In other words, it's the fascination with watching the often mundane behaviour of people in unguarded moments, caught on film and then broadcast to an eager audience of strangers.

Peep culture, as a media phenomenon, is nowhere near as new as the term that describes it. We could say it began in 1948 with the first television broadcast of the show *Candid Camera*, which used a hidden camera to film innocent citizens drawn into all manner of (mostly harmless) pranks and practical jokes. (The show had an undeniable influence on the very popular Quebec-produced show *Just for Laughs: Gags*, which has aired since 2000.) Print was an important medium for early peep culture, with grocery store tabloids offering candid photos of celebrities with their guard down and makeup off, captured by photographers hiding in bushes. But the Internet and improvements to digital recording technology have made it easy to take a picture or shoot a video and upload it for all the world to see. For 15 years, the only place to share that grainy, homemade video of your brother Chet wiping out on his new skateboard or your Aunt Doris's cat teasing the neighbour's dog was the immensely popular (and still running) *America's Funniest Home Videos*. Then along came YouTube and the camera phone, and peep culture was born.

There is an undeniable dark side to peep culture and reality programming. Whether it's the entertainment shows that trace the daily trajectory of falling Hollywood stars, the "competition" shows like *X-Factor*, *The Amazing Race*, *Survivor*, and *American Idol*, in which people get publicly judged and insulted, or the celebrity shows, which follow the unscripted daily-life minutiae of people like Paris Hilton, Ozzy Osborne, the Kardashians, and others (e.g. the "stars" of *Jersey Shore*), who have become famous for being exposed on television as attractive but stupid and fundamentally messed up, reality programming seems designed to play less to our need for information and enlightenment, more to our desire *Schadenfreude*. The German word, which literally means "harm-joy," refers to the pleasure we derive from watching the misfortunes of others. It is what we feel when we watch an episode of *Hoarders* or *The Biggest Loser*. These shows allow us to feel satisfied with our own lot—*my home isn't that messy, I'm not that overweight*—and in this way, it's possible they discourage the impulse for self-improvement. Reality television offers depressingly few role models to emulate.

Social networking sites and reality programming depend on our willingness to share personal, sometimes private details of our lives. At times they involve **oversharing**, which Niedziviecki defines as the tendency "to divulge excessive personal information, as in a blog or broadcast interview, prompting reactions ranging from alarmed discomfort to approval" (Niedziviecki 2009: 1). Oversharing occurs when individuals are drawn into compromising situations, knowingly or unknowingly, and have the details of these situations recorded and then broadcast, sometimes to an audience far greater than the originator intended. This can open a person up to cyber-bullying, which is the use of social media to shame or generally denigrate someone.

Cyber-bullying, like all forms of bullying, can have long-lasting and tragic consequences. The point is illustrated poignantly by two recent high-profile cases. The first involves Amanda Todd, a 15-year-old British Columbia girl who was talked into flashing her breasts for an online picture. She was already being bullied at school as an outsider, as someone who did not go along with the mainstream. This picture was used to bully her virtually, until finally, in 2012, she committed suicide. The second case is that of Rehtaeh Parsons,

R.I.P Amanda Todd
660,063 likes · 12,439 talking about this

👍 Like   Message ⚙ ▼

Cause
Memorial page for Amanda Todd and to spread awareness about the effects of bullying. Bullying is not a joke. Keep comments respectful or be banned.

About - Suggest an Edit

Photos   Likes

👍 660k

In the wake of the suicide of Amanda Todd, a number of tribute sites began to appear on the Internet. Designed to show support for the teen and her family, some of the sites attracted negative postings that essentially perpetuated the cyber-bullying after the victim's death. There were also vigilante sites determined to publicly identify Todd's tormentors. How does the case highlight the best and worst of social media?

a 17-year-old Nova Scotia girl, who was sexually assaulted in November 2011 and had a cellphone image of the assault circulated electronically. She hanged herself and was taken off life support in April 2013.

What do YOU think?

1. A person's social capital includes his or her social network. Differences in social capital are one form of class separation. Do you think that job-related social networking sites such as LinkedIn can help students develop social networks that will increase their social capital?

2. Some American research has shown that in the US, there are class and ethnic divisions in the use of social networking sites, with white, middle-class users on Facebook and lower-class African Americans and Latinos using MySpace (see, e.g., boyd 2011). Do you think that there is a class or racial divide in the use of social networking sites in Canada?

3. Why do you think there is such a passion for watching people's weaknesses and failures on television? What might it say about contemporary culture?

Social Media Fasts

A recent educational phenomenon involves social media "fasts." Dr Robert Doede is a professor of philosophy at Trinity Western University, a Christian liberal arts institution in BC. He offers students in his Philosophy 210 class a 5 per cent bonus credit (I would have made it more) if they abstain from all social, as well as more traditional, media, for an entire three-month semester, and keep a journal about their experiences. He states that out of a class of 35, only 12 might try, and usually just 4 to 6 have the stamina to complete the task of being "media abstinent."

Doede is critical of the sociological and psychological effects of the fast-paced, multiple demands of social media. He explains: "If we are not extremely careful in how we allow these sites to enter our lives, we will find our capacities to attend to other humans with the care and sensitivity they deserve subtly yet profoundly diminished" (Mussolum 2009).

The "insider's view" of this experiment comes from a student who, admittedly, was chosen by the writer of the piece as a "star example" (my term), which means that her views may not be entirely representative of

Telling It Like It Is

An Author POV

Facebook: A Newcomer's Perspective

In July 2012, I bowed to social pressure (mostly my wife's) and joined Facebook. By October I had 73 "friends." Fitting in with the gender profile of Facebook users generally, 39 of my friends are female, while 34 are male. (Only a sociologists would keep score in that way.) I will "like," but I don't share. I don't want to hear about what video games people are playing or what they had for dinner. I have come to know some of my Facebook friends better than people I see almost every day. One person joined my social network after we spoke for about two minutes at my wife's high school reunion. Now I get messages from him all the time. We have a similar sense of humour, and it has been a positive development.

Through Facebook I have re-established contact with old friends I hadn't seen in decades, with far-flung, long-lost cousins in PEI, Alberta, and Australia, and with nephews and nieces in British Columbia. I have learned not to make smart-ass comments about pictures of just-entering-teen-age-years nieces, or they will never, ever send you pictures again. From people my own age I get "Like if you know what this is," and I do well with that.

I find that former students want to keep in touch, and I find that I am more in touch with trends of the moment—the ones that go viral and then disappear—than I have been in ages. Last week, in October 2012, it is miscellaneous jokes and comments about Mitt Romney's carelessly worded reference to his "binders of women." It has been three days since the second presidential debate, and those pictures and jokes are no longer appearing.

Sometimes Facebook mystifies me. I never knew there were so many people obsessed with pictures of cats in cute and unnatural poses, and with the bumper-sticker wisdom captured in short, epigrammatic, philosophical sayings about life.

I've learned about how social media can be a social force for good. During the summer I received a substantial number of communications with titles such as "Like if you think she is beautiful," accompanying photos of female cancer survivors with chemo-induced baldness. Usually when a critical sociologist thinks about mass media and the social construction of beauty, the thoughts that come to mind are of skinny, pouty-lipped waifs, and how those images negatively influence young girls into becoming insecure about their own bodies. But here were photos of beautiful women, shared in an attempt to socially construct beauty in a much more positive way, encouraging citizens of the virtual community to accept people as they are. Mitt Romney would do well to keep binders of these brave, bald-headed women.

the majority of students who have undertaken the experiment, though I believe they may be. She wrote in her journal:

> At first when I went off Facebook I found it really difficult. . . . A big feature of it was events and when you aren't on Facebook you are disconnected from invitations. There is also a lot of anxiety around responding to people and projecting the right image of yourself. I was anxious about making sure I had the right photos up.

I think Facebook and meaningless television (which is not all television) owe a huge percentage of their success to people being dissatisfied with their lives. In our modern brilliance, we have invented ways to avoid our shortcomings instead of looking them in the eye and overcoming them. Screens are too easy, too accessible and too freeing to ignore. They offer an escape from reality but for so many people they become the reality, and the inadequacies which they were trying to escape simply mount higher.

After the mark-gaining experiment was over, she deleted some 400 of her more marginal "friends," and found that she read (offline) more often.

The Demotic Turn

In a series of works that includes *Understanding Celebrity* (2004) and *Ordinary People and the Media* (2010), Australian cultural studies professor Graeme Turner has explored a topic captured in his insightful term "the demotic turn." It is based on the Greek word *demos*, meaning "people" (just as "*democracy*" means roughly "government by the people"). But the demotic turn is not about the increasing democracy within the media, which others in the field of cultural studies (the same ones who cheerfully see popular culture in place of mass culture) have optimistically predicted. The theory of the **demotic turn** reflects a pessimistic, mass culture approach. It examines the way the "ordinary person" is increasingly elevated to the status of celebrity in contemporary media. It creates a false consciousness, akin to the unrealistic "American Dream," by promoting the belief that anyone can become a celebrity. In his introduction to *Ordinary People*, Turner discusses how he developed the term:

> I coined the term "the demotic turn" as a preferred means of referring to the increasing visibility of the "ordinary person" as they have turned themselves into media content through celebrity culture, reality TV, DIY ["do it yourself"] websites, talk radio, and the like. In the context of that book [*Understanding Celebrity*], it was used as a means of understanding the proliferation of celebrity across the media since the 1980s, as well as celebrity's colonization of the expectations of everyday life in contemporary western societies, particularly among teenagers and young adults. (Turner 2010: 2)

Celebrity has long been a source of fascination among "ordinary people," but never before have people been able to achieve celebrity status the way they can today, thanks to social media. Still, the statistics are against you. Remember, too, that a video clip can go viral, but most viruses don't live very long.

WRAP IT UP

Summary

In this chapter we have charted one of sociology's new territories, venturing beyond the discipline's usual boundaries into the newly developing fields of cultural studies and communication studies. Boundaries should be flexible, allowing for overlapping, or inter-disciplinary, studies. Some gatekeepers call this "poaching," but we believe that some tra-ditional sociological methodologies—content analysis is an example—can be applied to understanding these emerging areas of research.

Mass media have become so much a part of contemporary culture that you can see clear links between this chapter and Chapter 4, on culture. The approach taken here is one that is very critical of the new mass media, especially the Internet (which, we admit, we have used as a source of information in writing this chapter) and social media, which we have examined pretty much from an outsider's view. The role of sociology is to cri-tique, meaning to evaluate both positively and negatively the changes that affect our social worlds. Unthinking acceptance of these media is so common, and is encouraged by many with vested interests (including consultants and guest speakers at colleges and universities who make money by being creatively non-critical), that a bias in the other direction brings, we hope, a necessary balance to the discussion.

THINK BACK

Questions for Critical Review

1. Explain Marshall McLuhan's significance to the sociological study of media. Was he really the "media prophet" that some claim him to be, or do you feel that the influence of his ideas is exaggerated? Had you heard of him before?

2. Explain the propaganda model of information delivery. To what extent do you believe that contextual objectivity is possible, and beneficial?

3. Has the Internet succeeded in bringing about media democracy? Are we on the path to greater media democracy, or are we moving away from that goal?

4. What do you think the effects would be of social media abstinence as a group project in an introductory sociology class? What do you think it would show? Would it even be worthwhile?

5. Discuss why it is important to consult Aboriginal media for Aboriginal issues. Check a news media source for examples of one-sided reporting. What other groups or voices are sometimes excluded?

READ ON

Online

Age Discrimination on TV: 10 Anchors who Were Replaced by Younger Women

www.businessinsider.com/age-discrimination-on-tv-10-anchors-who-were-replaced-by-younger-women-2012-8

> This page, from the website Business Insider, presents profiles of 10 news anchors who were allegedly replaced because of their age.

Project Censored: Media Democracy in Action

www.projectcensored.org/

> This site includes discussions of stories that are excluded from mainstream media, and of the junk food news that tends to be the standard fare emanating from many media outlets.

PolitiFact

www.politifact.com/

> This online branch of the *Tampa Bay Times* attempts to cut through rhetoric and get to the "truth" concerning political issues and politicians.

Postmortem: Iraq War Media Coverage Dazzled but It Also Obscured

http://berkeley.edu/news/media/releases/2004/03/18_iraqmedia.shtml

> Jeffery Kahn's feature for University of California, Berkeley's NewsCenter offers a good look at embedded reporters and the attack on Iraq.

In Print

Guy Debord (1995), *The Society of the Spectacle* (New York: Zone Books).

> This work contains Debord's best presentation of the concept of the "spectacle" in mass media.

Edward S. Herman & Noam Chomsky (1988), *Manufacturing Consent: The Political Economy of the Mass Media* (New York: Pantheon).

> Herman and Chomsky's groundbreaking work lays out their argument for the propaganda model of news delivery, according to which the media present the news in a manner that supports a conservative political, economic, and social agenda. A biopic of the same title uses archival footage to trace the evolution of Chomsky's views on the media.

Mickey Huff & Andy Lee Roth, eds (2013), *Censored 2013: The Top Censored Stories and Media Analysis of 2011–2012* (New York: Seven Stories Press).

> This is the most recent instalment of Project Censored's brilliant look at the stories that the mainstream media ignore or neglect.

Marshall McLuhan (1962), *The Gutenberg Galaxy: The Making of Typographic Man* **(Toronto: University of Toronto Press).**

This includes McLuhan's main theories about mass media.

Neil Postman (1985), *Amusing Ourselves to Death: Public Discourse in the Age of Show Business* **(New York: Penguin Books).**

This is Postman's classic look at how entertainment is featured in American television at the cost of being informative.

V Global Perspectives

IN THIS TEXTBOOK WE have looked at *microsociology* and we have looked at *macrosociology*. Part V deals with the most macro of the macrosociologies. Here, we are broadening the scope of our thinking to the entire globe. We are also taking the macro view in terms of time: past, present, and future. It was the Spanish-born philosopher George Santayana who famously observed that "Those who cannot remember the past are doomed to repeat it." He might have been speaking to a class of sociology students preparing for final exams, but the sentiment is a good theme for the final three chapters generally. One-directional globalization (in which but a few powerful societies benefit at the expense of many other, less powerful ones) and socially caused environmental damage have taken place before, and they can offer us lessons about the best ways forward. What are the obstacles to acting on these lessons? Politics, mainly. The topics we will be surveying in the final three chapters are among the most controversial and divisive topics making news today. They are the kinds of issues by which political parties have defined themselves through the positions they take. These positions don't allow for a lot of common ground.

The discussions we will be entering into in each chapter do not provide ready answers, but they offer lines of thought and a vocabulary that can help you to critically examine the questions raised in the media. They are designed to enable you, sociology students of today, to develop an awareness that may, I hope, empower you to change the future. (I like to end on a positive note.)

Learning Objectives

After reading this chapter, you should be able to

- outline the various forms of globalization
- distinguish between *hyperglobalizers* and *skeptical globalizers*
- discuss the social effects of neoliberalism on developing nations
- recognize the problematic nature of defining and attaching the labels of "democracy" and "terrorism"
- distinguish between *universalist protectionism* and *particularist protectionism*.

Key Terms

- crusade
- cultural capital
- cultural globalization
- democracy
- developed nations
- developing nations
- economic globalization
- embedded journalist
- first law of petropolitics
- First World
- globalism
- globalists
- globality
- globalization
- globalization from above
- globalization from below

- glocalization
- government terrorism
- group formation effect
- hyperglobalizers
- inverse correlation
- Islamists
- jihad
- jihad-i-akbar
- jihad-i-asghar
- liberalism
- neoliberalism
- (the) North
- particularist protectionist
- political globalization
- positive correlation
- power elite
- preventive war

- rentier effect
- repression effect
- skeptical globalizers
- Second World
- sociological imagination
- (the) South
- spending effect
- taxation effect
- terrorism
- Third World
- transnational corporation
- tribalism
- ummaic jihad
- universalist protectionist

Names to Know

- Mukulika Banerjee
- Noam Chomsky
- Mir Zohair Husain
- Roland Robertson
- Michael L. Ross
- Alfred Sauvy
- Adam Smith
- Manfred Steger

A Canadian Breakfast: Nothing You Can Globalize

When it comes to food, Canada has definitely been a beneficiary of globalization. My small hometown of Bolton, about 14 kilometres outside of Toronto is hardly a cosmopolitan community, yet we have separate Japanese, Thai, Chinese, Greek, and Italian restaurants. The closer you get to the big city, the more likely you are to find other international offerings—Indian, Ethiopian, Caribbean, Vietnamese, Korean, Lebanese, Hungarian . . . The list goes on and on.

But is there anywhere in the world where you can find a "Canadian restaurant"? I'm talking "Canadian" in terms of food, not ownership. I really don't think so. For that matter, are there even foods that are considered genuinely Canadian? Sure, there may be a few—but are they recognized outside of Canada? In other words, are they globalized?

In Chapter 17 I gave an account of a lecture tour that took me to rural Virginia. It was on that trip that I first read the words "Canadian Breakfast" on the menu

board of an airport greasy spoon. I was fascinated. I rushed up to the counter, and asked the server what a Canadian breakfast was.

He looked at me as if I were the dumbest person he had seen that day. "It's eggs with Canadian bacon," he explained with an implied "duh."

I had to ask another question, kind of knowing the answer but anxious for confirmation. "What's Canadian bacon?"

"It's back bacon," he said, with a dismissive shake of his head.

What else is "Canadian food"? There are Nanaimo bars, delicious slabs of cookie crust and vanilla cream, covered in chocolate. I love them, but was disappointed when I arrived in Nanaimo and found no sign announcing the city's status as home of the Nanaimo bar. It turns out that the Nanaimo bar first came to be identified with the area when a local woman named Mabel Jenkins submitted a recipe to a Woman's Institute cookbook in the early 1950s. It has gone global, thanks to the American coffee company Starbucks, which has taken it to Japan and Australia—but they don't identify it as Canadian.

Another product of the 1950s, poutine has been gaining popularity lately. You can now find it in trendy bistros, high-end restaurants, and eateries that specialize in the rural Quebec dish of french fries, cheese curds, and gravy. It feels like a small cannonball in your stomach. Some American fast food companies are spreading its popularity throughout Canada, but I don't know whether they are trying to market it as Canadian food elsewhere.

Sometimes when we're struggling to identify Canadian culture—the kind that is recognized beyond our borders—we draw on our Aboriginal heritage (which we too often ignore, unless we're putting on a show for tourists). A small assortment of restaurants serving meals derived from the Aboriginal culinary tradition have opened in recent years, and it is interesting to see how they differ in what they offer. Some specialize in exotic dishes made with what we might call "pre-contact" ingredients—wild game, foraged berries and mushrooms, and other staples of the Native diet before Europeans arrived. Others feature "reserve-style" home cooking using the kinds of ingredients the Department of Indian Affairs provided, including, flour, lard, and sugar—whatever was readily available and cheap. That approach helped establish bannock, or fried bread (flour, baking powder, and salt), as a mainstay of the Aboriginal diet. Originally Scottish, it was brought over by people working for the Hudson's Bay Company and adopted by Aboriginal people. If you ever go to a pow-wow, see if they have "Indian tacos," which are made with this (it tastes much better than it sounds).

So what should my totally Canadian breakfast be made of? Timbits and a double-double? No, it would start with back bacon and bannock, or perhaps poutine. Then, to finish it off sweetly, one or two Nanaimo bars. I could definitely go for that—but would it sell globally?

What do YOU think?

1. Do you think it is unlikely that there will ever be a Canadian-style restaurant in other countries? Why do you think this is so?

2. Why are few foods identifiably Canadian? Is it a cultural weakness, a sign of our vulnerability to American tastes, or a testament to our multicultural willingness to incorporate ingredients and dishes from other countries?

Introduction: Does Globalization Make You Hyper or Skeptical?

Globalization as a social process is not unlike the sociological imagination, which was introduced way back in the opening chapter. Both are about making connections between the small and the large. With the sociological imagination, that connection is one that is made in the mind between the individual and the greater society. When it comes to globalization, the connections we're interested in are any of the various processes that link the local community with the global one.

The study of globalization draws contributions from many disciplines—political science, economics, anthropology, and cultural studies. Sociology, generally, has lagged behind these other disciplines in this area of study, but sociologists have a great deal to add, particularly on the topic of social inequality. One sociologist who has already made important contributions to globalization studies is **Roland Robertson** (b. 1938), an emeritus professor of sociology at the University of Aberdeen, Scotland, where he served as director of the university's Centre for the Study of Globalization. He has also taught in the US, Sweden, Japan, Hong Kong, the Czech Republic, and Brazil (four continents!), and his work has been translated into German, Spanish, Danish, Japanese, Mandarin, Turkish, Italian, Portuguese, and Polish, making him a very global expert on globalization. Later on in this chapter we will discuss some of his influential work.

Another expert whose work we will examine closely is **Manfred Steger**, director of the Globalism Research Centre at Australia's RMIT University. Globalization, as Steger and others have observed, is a very contested area of study, with champions and opponents in almost equal measure. The most zealous of those who promote globalization view it as something of a dream, a modernist heaven-on-earth. Steger refers to these people as **hyperglobalizers**. A hint of

QUICK HITS

Confessions of a Globalizer: American General Smedley D. Butler

I spent thirty years and four months as a member of . . . the Marine Corps. And during that period, I spent most of my time being a high-class muscle-man for Big Business, for Wall Street, and for the bankers. . . . Thus, I helped make Mexico . . . safe for American oil interests in 1914. I helped make Haiti and Cuba a decent place for the National City Bank to collect revenues. . . . I helped purify Nicaragua for the international banking house of Brown Brothers in 1909–1912. I brought light to the Dominican Republic for American sugar interests in 1916. I helped make Honduras "right" for American fruit companies in 1903. (quoted in Bellegarde-Smith 2004: 93)

What do YOU think?

Are these the words of a hyperglobalizer, skeptical globalizer, or neutral observer? Why do you rarely read words like these in contemporary news reports on modern globalization?

the fervour of their belief can be glimpsed in the following forecast issued by the American investment firm Merrill Lynch and printed in newspaper ads in 1998. It was a response to the global economic mini-crisis of the time, brought on by the collapse of several Asian economies. It is remarkable as a statement of blind faith coming from otherwise well-educated and experienced people:

The World is 10 Years Old

It was born when the [Berlin] Wall fell in 1989. It's no surprise that the world's youngest economy—the global economy—is still finding its bearings. The intricate checks and balances that stabilize economies are only incorporated with time. Many world markets are only recently freed, governed for the first time by the emotions of the people rather than the fists of the state. From where we sit [i.e. on top of an economic hierarchy] none of this diminishes the promise offered a decade ago by the demise of the walled-off world. . . . The spread of free markets and democracy around the world is permitting more people everywhere to turn their aspirations into achievements. And technology, properly harnessed and liberally distributed, has the power to erase not just geographical borders but also human ones. It seems to us that, for a 10-year-old, the world continues to hold great promise. In the meantime, no one ever said growing up was easy. (Friedman 2000: xvi)

Indeed, growing up turned out to be anything *but* easy. Just 10 years later, the subprime mortgage crisis plunged the US into a recession that dragged the global economy down with it. Merrill Lynch, which was deeply affected by the crisis, suffered heavy financial losses and was taken over by Bank of America. Hindsight, of course, is 20/20. But outside of the naive nature of the statement above, which testifies to the ignorance of social inequality held by people who stand on the top rung of the ladder, the writers show a lack of knowledge of history. Global economies have existed before, and we would do well to learn their lessons. The last one crashed with the Great Depression of the 1930s, and the current one is still recovering from that recession of 2007–9.

At the opposite end of the spectrum, and looking upon globalization as very dangerous to the global environment and to the economies and social welfare of the world's "have-not" countries, are those Steger refers to as **skeptical globalizers**. The position taken in this chapter is essentially an optimistic one, but one that occasionally bends towards the stance and concerns of this latter group. Divisive as it is, globalization is one of those areas where a sociologist cannot pretend to be neutral "in the interests of science."

Defining the Terms of Reference

Before we get started on our exploration of globalization, we need to define some key terms relating to this relatively new field of academic interest. We will be relying heavily on Manfred Steger's excellent *Globalization: A Very Short Introduction* (2003) for terms and much of the perspective taken here.

To start, it is important to think of globalization as a social *process*, not as a set of social *conditions*. For the set of globalized social conditions that exist at any one time Steger uses the term **globality** (2003: 7). These conditions include the amount of global interdependence (social, economic, cultural, and political) and the rate of exchange (or, if in one direction, flow) of social, economic, and political information and materials between global markets. Globality, like globalization itself, is contested. If you believed everything you saw in computer and cellphone commercials (generally not a good thing to do from a sociological standpoint), you would think that the state of globality is higher than it actually is. We in North America tend to have a grossly exaggerated understanding of how "connected" the world is. The vast majority of the world's people have never even seen a cellphone, and as we saw last chapter, most have never been online. One of many shocks for people of Indonesia and the smaller Pacific islands in the aftermath of the "Boxing Day" tsunami in December 2004 was their sudden exposure to strange people coming to their aid via strange technology.

Globalization, then, refers to the processes that lead the world towards a state of globality, of connectedness and interdependence. Steger explains it this way:

Globalization refers to a multidimensional set of social processes that create, multiply, stretch and intensify worldwide social interdependencies and exchanges while at the same time fostering in people a growing awareness of deepening connections between the local and the distant. (Steger 2003: 13)

The key point here is that globalization exists on several levels: social, economic, political, cultural, and ideological. It falls not just within the domain of sociologists but is relevant to a number of different disciplines: political science, economics, history, anthropology, and the newly developing cultural studies. For this reason, it will be useful to look at globalization in the context of each of these spheres. But before we get to that, we need to go over who the main "players" are in any examination of globalization.

It is also important to define the blocs of countries commonly referred to in discussions of globalization. To recap an explanation from Chapter 3, on research methods, the world's rich and poor nations were once referred to, respectively, as **First World** countries and **Third World** countries, using terms coined by French social scientist **Alfred Sauvy** (1898–1990) in 1952. The First World was seen as including the rich capitalist countries, while the Third World comprised those countries without social or economic power. The

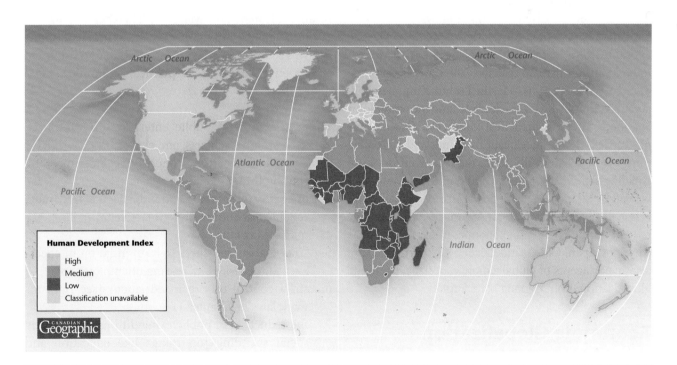

Figure 20.1 International human development, by country (high, medium, low)

Source: Based on this map of high, medium, and low development, does it make sense to you to divide the world conceptually into North and South? East and West? (www.canadiangeographic.ca/worldmap)

USSR and the eastern European countries under its power (sometimes called Soviet Bloc or Eastern Bloc) were identified as the **Second World**.

More recently, the First World–Third World designation has fallen out of favour, and more recent terminology distinguishes instead between **developed nations** and **developing nations**. One problem with this is that not all of the so-called developing nations are necessarily developing. According to the skeptical globalization position, they should really be called "underdeveloped nations," or perhaps more accurately "underdevelop*ing* nations," since they are undergoing an ongoing cycle of being exploited and running up huge debts incurred as a result of globalization.

Theorists today often divide the world conceptually into **the North** and **the South**, based on the fact that almost all of the powerful and rich nations are in the northern hemisphere, while the less powerful and poorer nations are typically found in the southern hemisphere. Of course, this has some flaws, too: Australia and New Zealand, squarely in the southern hemisphere, are not among the world's poorest nations; Brazil is emerging as a southern economic powerhouse; and a number of the northern hemisphere's central Asian countries are considerably poorer than their immediate neighbours. Nevertheless, we will use these terms in the discussion that follows.

This introduction ends with a disclaimer. Despite appearances to the contrary, this chapter is not meant to be an anti-American diatribe. The country that produced C. Wright Mills, Martin Luther King, baseball, apple pie, the blues, jazz, rock 'n' roll, and the writer John Steinbeck deserves a great deal of respect for its continuous capacity to produce beautiful minds and incredible things. It is, to use Mills' term, the **power elite**—those wielding significant financial and political power—that we will be taking issue with here. Further, globalization is not, like baseball or jazz, an American-only phenomenon. The more dynamic economies in Asia and Europe (those of Japan, China, and Germany in particular) are also major agents of globalization, especially economic globalization. Even Canada plays a role.

Economic Globalization

From Liberalism to Neoliberalism

Economic globalization is all about global markets and the flow of capital, technology, and goods (Steger 2003: 37). In order to understand economic globalization, we need to go over some other terms first. We encountered the term *neoliberalism* in Chapter 17, in the context of work. It's a term that can be confusing for students, as it is practically identical in meaning to the seemingly opposite term *neoconservativism* (rather like the way *flammable* and *inflammable* mean the same thing). But before we get to neoliberalism (which literally means "new liberalism"), we need to understand *liberalism*.

It helps to think of **liberalism** as an old idea, born and raised in the eighteenth and nineteenth centuries. As conceived by early economists such as **Adam Smith** (1723–1790), it was the idea that the market was like a living thing that needed to be free to expand and grow in a healthy way (think of the root word *liberate*, meaning "to set free"). Liberalism is related to laissez-faire capitalism, the policy of not interfering with market processes. The market, in this view, is seen as a self-regulating organism, responding to the dictates of supply and demand. Restricting forces created by government and state bureaucracies—stifling taxes, tariffs, customs duties, and the like—were considered detrimental to the growth and overall health of this organism.

Neoliberalism, an offshoot of traditional liberalism, came to the fore in the United States, Canada, and Britain during the political regimes of Ronald Reagan, Brian Mulroney, and Margaret Thatcher during the 1980s. It gained strength with the fall of communism in 1989–91. As Steger neatly summarizes it, there are 10 key elements in the political economic agenda of neoliberals:

1. privatization of public enterprises [i.e. utilities, such as like water, gas, and electricity]
2. deregulation of the economy [i.e. not imposing caps on things like tuition costs]
3. liberalization of trade and industry [i.e. free trade: reducing or eliminating protective tariffs]
4. massive tax cuts
5. "monetarist" measures to keep inflation in check, even at the risk of increasing unemployment
6. strict control on organized labour [see right-to-work laws in Chapter 17]
7. the reduction of public expenditures, particularly social spending [on things like education and healthcare]
8. the downsizing of government
9. the expansion of international markets
10. the removal of controls on global financial flows
(Steger 2003: 41)

The neoliberal agenda is typically championed by governments branding themselves "conservative" (remember that *neoliberal* and *neoconservative* mean essentially the same thing). Nearly all 10 of the measures cited above were brought into effect in Ontario during the eight-year reign (1995–2003) of the provincial Conservative Party under Mike Harris, who was neoliberal but definitely not a Liberal.

Steger uses another important term, **globalism**, to refer to "an ideology that endows the concept of globalization with neoliberal values and meanings" (Steger 2003: 94). Globalists are those who think that the only way for globalization to occur is through the implementation of neoliberal policies such as those listed above. But as we will see later, there are those who believe that globalization can take other paths.

QUICK HITS

Keeping Track of the *Global*– Words

You may by now be slightly reeling with the number of similar-sounding terms that begin with *global*–. Here they are all together, to help you keep them straight:

- *globalization* is an ongoing social process
- *globality* is a set of social conditions (at a particular time)
- *globalism* is an ideology connecting neoliberalism with globalization
- *globalist* is a proponent of globalism.

The Role of Transnational Corporations

An integral element of economic globalization is the **transnational corporation** (formerly known as either a *multinational corporation* or, simply, a *multinational*). Transnational corporations are companies that are typically based in countries in the North (over two-thirds have their head offices in the United States, Japan, or Germany) but have branches all over the world. Examples are numerous, but they include car manufacturers, such as General Motors, Honda, and Volkswagen; oil companies, such as Exxon-Mobil

A cargo ship is unloaded in Prince Rupert, BC. Maintaining production facilities abroad exempts transnational corporations from having to pay to maintain pollution standards of their home country. What kind of impact do you think shipping has on the environment?

and Royal Dutch/Shell; computer firms, such as Microsoft—whose founder and chairman is by far the richest man in the world—and IBM; high-tech companies, such as Sony, Nokia, and Apple; clothing manufacturers, such as Nike; and retailers, such as Walmart. The economic power of these companies can be seen in a statistic reported by Steger: of the world's 100 largest economies, only 49 are actual countries—the majority (51) are transnational corporations (Steger 2003: 48).

Transnational corporations are often condemned by unionists, environmentalists, and nationalists from the developed nations in which they are based for having a high percentage, if not all, of their manufacturing or production carried out in developing countries, where labour costs are much lower than they are in the North. Maintaining production facilities abroad also exempts these corporations from having to pay to maintain the pollution and safety standards of their base country.

A good example of how certain forms of economic globalization can yield unequal gains comes from an anecdotal case picked up by a number of news outlets late in 2002 (see, for example, Bezlova 2002). According to the report, if you were to buy a Barbie Doll at a Walmart store in the United States, you would pay about 10 dollars. However, the import price at the US customs office would be only about 2 dollars. Of that 2 dollars, half would be for transportation (which, of course, would include American carriers) and management fees (part of that would go back to Walmart), and 65 cents would be for raw materials (which would not have come from China, where the doll was manufactured). The manufacturing costs would be 35 cents per doll. You can imagine what that would leave to pay the workers who assembled the doll.

The Role of International Lending and Development Agencies

As Steger notes, hyperglobalizers claim, among other things, that globalization benefits everyone more or less equally (Steger 2003: 103). In terms of economic globalization, this seems like a rather spurious claim, as the beneficiaries would appear to be the rich countries of the North. In Steger's words:

> Data published in the 1999 and 2000 editions of the *UN Human Development Report* show that, before the onset of globalization in 1973, the

income ratio between the richest and poorest countries was at about 44 to 1. Twenty-five years later it had climbed to 74 to 1. (Steger 2003: 105)

One major cause of this apparently growing gap is the existence of globalizing bodies such as the World Bank, the World Trade Organization (WTO), and the International Monetary Fund (IMF). These global institutions grant loans to developing countries. However, the loans are tied to certain conditions. Often, for instance, the borrowing countries must agree to adopt certain neoliberal policies. And as Steger explains:

> Unfortunately, however, large portions of the "development loans" granted by these institutions have either been pocketed by authoritarian political leaders or have enriched local businesses and the Northern corporations they usually serve. . . . Most importantly, however, structural adjustment programmes rarely produce the desired result of "developing" debtor societies, because mandated cuts in public spending translate into fewer social programmes, reduced educational opportunities, more environmental pollution, and greater poverty for the vast majority of people. Typically, the largest share of the national budget is spent on servicing outstanding debts. For example, in 1997, developing countries paid a combined $292 billion in debt service, while receiving only $269 billion in new loans. (Steger 2003: 53–4)

In total, then, according to this 1997 statistic, the countries receiving the loans and paying the debts are losing $23 billion.

In Chapter 6, we touched on the work of Nobel Prize–winning economist Joseph E. Stiglitz, who criticized IMF programs and ideology for reducing or eliminating trade protections on local industry in countries of the South. In *Globalization and Its Discontents* (2003), he examined the way the neoliberal policy of trade liberalization fails when applied to poorer countries of the global South. In theory, trade liberalization makes a country's economy more efficient: when trade barriers are removed, those industries that can't hold their own against international competitors close down, to be replaced by new, more productive industries. The trouble, as Stiglitz explained, is that developing countries typically lack the start-up capital and entrepreneurial spirit that make the sink-or-swim principle of trade liberalization more successful in the North. Moreover, the IMF has loaned money at such high interest rates that, in Stigliz's words, "job and enterprise creation would have been an impossibility even in a good economic environment such as the United States" (Stiglitz 2003: 59–60).

Haiti, often referred to as the poorest nation in the world, provides an excellent but depressing example of how economic globalization can harm a country in the South. Haitian scholar Patrick Bellegarde-Smith explains:

> High unemployment, low wages, political repression, and high productivity—the very same factors that render the country politically unstable—make Haiti a manufacturer's paradise. Corporations "can count on a profit margin of at least 30 percent, and sometimes as much as 100 percent, from their Haitian operations." The low investment rates; the absence of restriction on profit "repatriation" [returning to the country of investment origin], a primary feature of the Haitian model; and low labor costs make these high profit margins possible. Government policy has led to foreign business opportunism and a domestic lack of opportunity. Haiti has, in a sense, become the "land of opportunism." (Bellegarde-Smith 2004: 153)

In other words, policies of economic globalization encourage poorer countries of the South to open their doors to transnational corporations of the North promising to create jobs by setting up factories in the poorer countries. But when a North American company moves its manufacturing operations from, say, a North American city to a Central American one, it pays local workers the local rate, which is considerably less than what it would pay for the work to be done in the US. This brings considerable savings to the North American company without bringing a lot of wealth to workers in the South.

A Bangladeshi woman weeps holding a picture of her missing husband at the site of an eight-storey building that collapsed in Savar, near Dhaka, in April 2013. Over 1,00 people were killed, and many of the survivors were trapped for days before they were rescued. The building, which had developed visible cracks in the days before the collapse, housed a number of garment factories, including ones that manufacturing clothing for Canadian retailers. Do you ever consider where your clothing comes from? Would you pay more to buy a shirt you knew was produced in a safe facility where the workers—whether in Canada or abroad—were being paid fair wages?

Making matters worse for Haiti was the earthquake that devastated the country in 2010. Since that time, many Northern countries have contributed to the rebuilding effort. Yet even this hasn't entirely benefited Haitian citizens. As journalist Mark Weisbrot reports:

not a single US government contract for Haiti's reconstruction in the last five months has gone to a Haitian company. In fact, out of $194 m[illion] awarded since the earthquake, just $4.8m, or $2.5m of the total, has gone to Haitian companies. USAID [the US Agency for International Development] has given our $35.5m, none of which has gone to a Haitian company; some 92% of USAID's contracts have gone to Beltway (Washington, DC, Maryland, and Virginia)

contractors. Now, isn't that a geographical oddity? About 15.5% of contracts in January 2010 were "no bid," which presumably could be justified because of the urgency; however, this proportion has increased to 42.5% over the last five months. (Weisbrot 2011)

What do YOU think?

Why do you think USAID contracted American companies instead of Haitian ones to undertake reconstruction efforts in Haiti? Do you think that it might be a case of paternalism, in which the "helping" country treats the "helped" country like a child? Would it have been better to have given the money directly to the Haitian government, even if it might mean the work might be done less effectively or less efficiently?

Going Global
Death of a Garment Worker

The following "confession" appeared in *The Globe and Mail* in January 2013, months after a fire at a garment factory outside of Dhaka, Bangladesh, killed over 100 workers.

I would like to confess to lighting the recent fire that led to the many deaths at the Tazreen Fashions Ltd factory in Bangladesh.

I am neither Bangladeshi nor a factory worker, and I have never set foot in the building that was set ablaze in late November. Nonetheless, I have ashen thoughts and blood on my hands.

As clothing designer for the Canadian arm of a multinational clothing retailer, my work consists of taking fashion styles in the marketplace and adapting them for our customers' pocketbooks. I design inexpensive clothes destined to be manufactured by the most competitive manufacturers, in what we call "offshore" factories. The company that pays my salary was a client of Tazreen until the fire, as were many Canadian retailers.

I know what the smoke smelled like as it hit the nostrils of the factory workers. I even know what the smoke looks like from synthetic fibres catching

on fire. I was in a factory in India when an electrical fire started. The clouds of smoke pushed their way up from the basement into the design studio on the third floor. As we rushed down the stairs, we had to pass the grey mist of synthetic fibres that had caught fire and were reborn in a thick and acrid cloud pushing its way out of the building.

I remember waiting for the fire trucks to come and watching as the sewers rubbed their hair with blackened hands to get out the white ash. Prematurely grey Indian faces in colourful saris with kabuki-like makeup stood silent with the circle of survivors. The shock and the sudden disconnection from work had lent a dreamlike veil over the scene. In a Canadian setting, this surrealistic silence would have been broken by a fire engine or two.

Not on this side of the planet.

On this side of the world, a senior factory worker figured out the source of the electrical fire and, with the help of his colleagues, put out the blaze in relative silence, as one would have during a yoga class. Two official cars did arrive after the fire was contained. Inside were police officers, but these officers were not there to help put out the fire—they had

Political Globalization

Steger defines **political globalization** as "the intensification and expansion of political interrelations across the globe" (Steger 2003: 56). These interrelations tend to range across whole groups of countries. They include the United Nations and its affiliated organizations as well as regional coalitions such as the European Union (EU) and NATO (the North Atlantic Treaty Organization); they also include NGOs (non-governmental organizations) such as Amnesty International and Greenpeace.

Among the concerns posed by the spread of political globalization are questions about **democracy**. According to Steger, champions of globalization argue that globalization processes further the spread of democracy around the world (Steger 2003: 110). The validity of this claim depends on how you define democracy. At the foundation of a democracy is a government elected by its citizens. But this is a rather thin definition; merely holding a vote for a leader does not guarantee true democracy. In the former Soviet Union it was not uncommon to have a single name on the ballot (people still had to vote), and democratic elections in some countries are still marred by vote-rigging and other illegal activities designed to fix the result. And how many people must be allowed to vote in order for there to be a true democracy?

A broader definition of democracy might include such features as the following:

- an electorate that reflects the diversity of the country's citizens in terms of gender, class, and ethnic background
- freedom of the press and freedom of speech

come for the customary bribe so this incident would not be officially recorded. The loudest part of the day was the sound of the officers' steps, heavy with their loot, as they left the building.

In Bangladesh, stories circulate that the Tazreen fire was arson. My point is, this fire was lit by me.

I am the one who asked our factories to make a $9 blouse, and, by default, Bangladesh is one of two countries in which clothing can be imported duty free.

My employers are happy that we will have this item on the floor en masse for next season's sales. Our customers have forced us to hack down the prices to be competitive in this market of cheap clothing and off-price bargaining that we call the Canadian clothing sector.

Popular thinking is that clothing at this level, since it is mass-produced, is automated. The truth is that most of the procedures used to make these garments that fuelled the Tazreen fire passed through the now deceased workers' hands. Perhaps one of the perished women was sewing the back neck of a garment to its collar. This operation in Bangladesh costs a fraction of a cent compared with what it would cost in Canada.

I wonder whether she was holding on to the collar that I had asked her to sew to meet my cost target when she died. I know that our shipments are sometimes rushed at the last minute to make the vessel. Maybe that's why the managers asked some of the workers to stay seated when the fire started.

We have third-party inspections and in-house compliance staff, and our company is world class. This means that factories are inspected on a routine basis. I wonder: Where were the inspectors that day? Perhaps they were at one of the other hundred factories that are officially working for us. For sure, they were not at the thousand factories that we have not asked to be used as subcontractors.

The point is clear.

I confess to the murder.

The reason is clear.

The collar that the Bangladeshi woman was holding as the smoke pushed through her lungs was destined for a killer-priced shirt next season.

Source: Sujeet Sennik, *The Globe and Mail* (18 Jan. 2013).

- freedom of association and of travel (within and between countries)
- the presence of a viable opposition (and one that does not literally fear for its life)
- a system of education in which people can teach and take courses that can be critical of society's institutions
- protection of the rights of minorities
- relative equality of men and women.

Thin democracy might be spreading, but broad democracy really is not.

The American government has a consistent record of supporting the "stable" governments of democracy-crushing dictators—Ferdinand Marcos in the Philippines (in power 1965–86); Raden Suharto in Indonesia (in power 1965–1998); Nicolae Ceaușescu in Romania (in power 1967–89, and once referred to by American secretary of state George Shultz as among the "good communists"); Jean-Claude "Baby Doc" Duvalier, like his father, "president for life" in Haiti (1971–86); Muhammad Reza Pahlavi, the shah of Iran (a title inherited from his fellow-dictator father; in power 1941–79, except for a brief period in 1953, before he was returned to power following a CIA-supported coup). Some, such as Saddam Hussein of Iraq and Manuel Noriega of Panama, were supported by Washington until they were "suddenly discovered" to be dictators, upon ceasing to be useful to Washington or opposing policies of the American power elite.

The opposition of the American government to democracy in foreign countries when it countered their neoliberal agenda was never more in evidence than during its involvement in Haiti. The United States "temporarily" took control of the country in the name of its economic interests between 1915 and 1934 (during which time Hollywood contributed to Haiti's poor image in the US by vilifying Voodoo, the island country's main religion). The US then had the nerve, as a public relations gesture, to hold a plebiscite to legalize the occupation. Only 5 per cent of eligible voters took part in the poll to rubber-stamp a policy they knew they couldn't change. After supporting dictator after dictator—particularly the Duvaliers, father and son, who ruled Haiti with ruthless but stable government—the US tried to set up another election in 1990 and failed. Haitian sociologist Alex Dupuy captures the political sense of the moment well:

[T]here was the United States, which after the fall of communism, sought to change its ugly image as the defender of dictatorship by promoting an "ersatz [cheap substitute] of democracy" in the poor countries. In Haiti, the problem for Washington was how to compel its traditional allies—the bourgeoisie and the military establishment—to accept a minimal democracy . . . while at the same time preserving Haiti as a source of cheap labor for the assembly industries and the multinational agribusinesses. The solution lay in electing a candidate who accepted the new game plan and who was supported by the local oligarchies and the United States. Unfortunately, the Haitian masses . . . spoiled it by voting for their own unexpected and unpredictable candidate [37-year-old priest Father Jean-Bertrand Aristide, who won 67.7 per cent of the vote]. (Dupuy 1997: 133)

Noam Chomsky's Skeptical Political Globalization Challenge

Noam Chomsky, although not a sociologist, has taken the place of C. Wright Mills as America's foremost public intellectual critic (a more educated and better-dressed version of subversive documentary filmmaker Michael Moore of *Fahrenheit 9/11* fame). We have already seen his ideas in connection with mass media in Chapter 19. Chomsky began his career as a linguist and revolutionized his discipline. He now teaches primarily as a philosopher of modern society and writes prolifically. In *Hegemony or Survival: America's Quest for Global Dominance* (2004), he discussed the Bush government's policy of attacking countries in the name of **preventive war** (i.e. attacking another country before that country has the chance to attack your own). He claimed that the ideal target of such a preventive war must meet three conditions:

1. It must be virtually defenseless.
2. It must be important enough to be worth the trouble [i.e. by having desirable natural resources such as oil or a strategic military position].
3. There must be a way to portray it as the ultimate evil and an imminent threat to our survival. (Chomsky 2004: 14)

The Point Is...

Authoritarianism and Oil: Hand in Slippery Hand?

In 2001, American political scientist **Michael L. Ross** wrote an important article on the relationship between democracy and globalization, focusing specifically on the oil industry. Titled "Does Oil Hinder Democracy?", the article considers the possible **inverse correlation** between a country's economic dependence on oil and the level of democracy found in that country. Ross's hypothesis was that the more dependent a country is on oil, the less democracy we are likely to find there.

Ross's article contains four main findings. The first is that "oil *does* hurt democracy" (Ross 2001: 356), especially in poor countries, for reasons we'll get to in a moment. Second, this effect is not limited to the Middle East but applies also to countries in Africa, the Pacific islands, and North and South America. Third, it is not just oil that has this effect but any mineral on which a country is economically dependent.

It is Ross's fourth finding that provides some answers to the question of the inverse correlation between oil dependency and democracy (or, if you prefer, the **positive correlation** between oil dependency and authoritarianism). Ross found that two factors contribute especially to the relationship between oil dependency and democracy: the *rentier effect* and the *repression effect*.

The **rentier effect** is actually a set of three related effects: a *taxation effect*, a *spending effect*, and a *group formation effect*. The **taxation effect** dictates that "when governments derive sufficient revenues from the sale of oil, they are likely to tax their populations less heavily or not at all, and the public in turn will be less likely to demand accountability from and representation in their government" (Ross 2001: 332). No one complains about low taxes—just ask anyone from Alberta. The only province without a sales tax has given the Progressive Conservative Party control of the provincial government since 1971. The Conservatives succeeded the even more conservative Social Credit Party, which had been in power since 1935! The **spending effect** involves "greater spending on patronage, which in turn dampens latent pressures for democratization" (Ross 2001: 333). Patronage is the power to control political appointments. The suggestion here is that if a government can afford to buy off potential opponents with well-paying jobs or positions of authority, it effectively silences its critics. Along the same lines, the **group formation effect** is about the government's use of oil revenues "to prevent the formation of social groups that are independent from the state and hence that may be inclined to demand political rights" (Ross 2001: 334).

Rentier comes from a French word for a person who lives on income from property and investments. It makes sense, then, that the three features of the rentier effect are about how an oil-rich government spends its revenues to appease its critics and maintain a comfortable hold on power. The **repression effect**, by contrast, has to do with how a government builds up its "internal security forces to ward off democratic pressures" (Ross 2001: 357). It's about quelling dissent by force, not by incentives.

Five years after Ross published his influential article, American foreign affairs journalist Thomas L. Friedman recast Ross's hypothesis as the **first law of petropolitics**, stating that that there is an inverse relationship between the price of oil and the democracy of a government, and a positive correlation between the price of oil and the degree of autocracy with which that government deals with the governments of other countries.

What do YOU think?

In *Tar Sands: Dirty Oil and the Future of a Continent*, Andrew Nikiforuk applies Ross's and Frideman's ideas to the current situation in Alberta and the province's infamous tar sands. What signs would he be looking for to suggest a lack of democracy in that province, and possibly in the Canadian federal government, related to a dependence on oil?

What do YOU think?

Consider the three conditions for preventive war identified by Chomsky (p. 556). Do you think they accurately reflect the political globalization tactics of the American government? Potential examples to try this out on include Afghanistan, Haiti, Iraq, Libya, and Nicaragua (see below).

Terrorism: A Slippery Term

No discussion of political globalization would be complete without a discussion of terrorism. The fact that the term is used so frequently in the media does not mean that we can easily define it sociologically. Who should be labelled a terrorist and who should not? Can terrorism ever be considered a legitimate form of political protest? Does terrorism act only against globalization?

A rough working definition of **terrorism** is the intentional use or threat of violence against civilians (people who are not soldiers, political leaders, or police) in order to attain political objectives (freeing "political" prisoners, establishing an independent nation, destabilizing a political regime, and so on). But it is important that there not be just one way of viewing terrorism. Colonial powers (including the US, Britain, China, and Russia, as well as Canada, Australia, and New Zealand in their relationship to their indigenous peoples) have the upper hand in defining their position and presenting it to other members of the global community. In a war between equals—either of the two world wars, for example—each side, although defaming the other, grants its opponent formal equality of status. By contrast, colonial powers downgrade the status of their subject populations with names that "outlaw" them in order to delegitimize their cause. Indian anthropologist **Mukulika Banerjee** make this important point in discussing the Warziris, a people living in the North-West Frontier Province of what was then the British colony of India:

> [V]iolent acts by such groups were categorized by colonial states as revolt, rebellion, insurrection, sedition, terrorism, banditry, brigandage, mutiny, piracy, faction fighting or murder—as anything other than legitimate wars of independence. Classified as domestic troubles requiring police action, the acts of violence by the indigenes were thereby denied any political status. Thus when the Waziris launched a guerrilla campaign against the British in the 1930s they were simultaneously denied the dignity of war's status, being condemned by the authorities as mere insurrectionists and bandits, but given full "benefit" of modern air raids and bombardment. (Banerjee 2000: 102)

The Canadian "master narrative" depicts the victories of Aboriginal people over European settlers encroaching on traditional Native territories as "massacres," which delegitimizes the victors. And when the Métis, a people that developed a unique culture and sense of identity from their mixed Aboriginal and European roots, opposed the Canadian government's attempts to deny their rights and identity on two occasions (in 1869–70 and again in 1885), they had these two moments of resistance branded "rebellions" (they remain known as the "Riel Rebellions," named for the Métis leader Louis Riel, who was executed for his efforts).

Who do we think of when we hear the word *terrorist*? In the Western media, the label *terrorist* is normally reserved for Middle Eastern Muslim fundamentalists. In fact, terrorism includes people of many religions and locations: the Muslim Chechens in Russia, the Catholic Irish Republican Army in the United Kingdom of Britain and Northern Ireland, and the Hindu Tamil Tigers in Sri Lanka. The Basques, a people who speak a language unrelated to any other in the world, and who live on both sides of the Spanish–French border, have within their number an extremist group that wants to separate from Spain; these separatists have been identified as terrorists. If you believe the Chinese government (you shouldn't), Buddhist Tibetans are terrorists, and have been since the Chinese took over their country in 1950. To complete the religious ecumenicalism of terrorism, in 1947, the Jewish terrorist group known as Lehi (from *Lohamei Herut Israel*, "Fighters for the Freedom of Israel") assassinated UN peacekeeper Count Folke Bernadette of Sweden because they felt he would favour Arabs in the creation of the Jewish state of Israel.

Government Terrorism

But are we missing any major groups in our list of terrorists? Should we include the CIA, for undermining regimes the American government did not like in

Members of the Free Syrian Army gather at their base camp in Darkoush, Syria. The rebel group took up arms when the Syrian national army was deployed to suppress (violently) Arab Spring protests demanding the resignation of Syrian president Bashar al-Assad in April 2011. Since that time, the conflict has developed into an all-out civil war. For his part, al-Assad has attempted to downplay the opposition to his rule by characterizing the rebels as armed terrorists and foreign mercenaries, going so far as to claim links between the rebel group and al-Qaeda. What do you think is the effect of branding the rebels as terrorists?

Latin America and in the Middle East? A good case to consider here is the CIA's involvement in Chile.

The CIA and Chile in the 1970s

In presidential elections held in September 1970, the Chilean people elected Salvador Allende, leader of the Popular Unity Party and a Marxist, much to the chagrin of Washington. In the midst of the Cold War with the Soviet Union, the US was suspicious of any signs that communism was gaining ground in the western hemisphere, close to American shores. In response to the election outcome, American president Richard Nixon ordered the CIA to do all it could to prevent Allende's inauguration. National security adviser to the president Henry Kissinger supervised the allocation of US$10 million to oust Allende through such means as attempting to bribe Chilean politicians and funding a coup attempt by military officers.

In 1971, Allende socialized the economy, taking it out of private hands and placing it in government control by nationalizing US-controlled copper mines and other foreign-controlled businesses and industries. He turned management of many factories over to the workers and the state, while raising salaries and stabilizing prices for basic goods.

In 1972, the Chilean economy went into decline, owing in part to some of the government's own mistakes but also to American boycotts and the withdrawal of American financial assistance and loans (except to the Chilean military). At the same time, the CIA received $7 million to fund Chilean opposition groups, and to exploit the economic weaknesses of the country. Paralyzed by economic problems, external opposition, and internal division, all influenced by the CIA, the Chilean government was forced to call another election. However, the election of March 1973 was inconclusive. This development was met with protests and strikes, some of them sparked by CIA-financed unions, others merely a reflection of the country's dissatisfaction with the political stalemate.

In September 1973, with US Navy ships on alert offshore, with 32 US observation and fighter planes landing in Argentina near the Chilean border, and beneath a US-piloted airborne communications control system, American-trained extremists in the Chilean military, led by General Augusto Pinochet, overthrew the government and assassinated Allende and several cabinet members. Opposition parties were banned, and thousands of Chileans—many of them identified as "radicals" on CIA lists—were tortured and killed. The US government officially recognized the Pinochet government and restored financial aid to the country.

From 1973 to 1990, Pinochet ruled Chile as dictator. US President Bill Clinton later apologized to the people of Chile for American intervention in the country. In 2000, Pinochet was arrested for crimes against humanity. He died in December 2006.

The CIA and Nicaragua in the 1980s

From the late 1930s to the 1970s, one family held enormous power in Nicaragua: the Somozas. Anastasio Somoza took over political control in 1966, at a time when Nicaragua was globalizing its economy by moving from subsistence farming to agriculture for export. But while aspects of the economy grew, the number of poor Nicaraguans increased. Somoza held onto political power by accepting money from the US for development and for fighting revolutionaries who opposed his dictatorship. His National Guard was an oppressive force that crushed revolutionaries and bullied those who came to the support of the guerrilla fighters of the Sandinista Front for National Liberation. During the early 1970s, Nicaragua was hit by an earthquake, and Somoza siphoned off much of the foreign aid money given to help rebuild

In June 2012, hundreds of anti-Pinochet demonstrators clashed with pro-Pinochet supporters at the premiere of a documentary casting the former dictator as a national hero who saved Chile from communism. Does it surprise you that the legacy of a man who oversaw the torture and murder of thousands of political opponents—many of whom remain missing—is still in dispute 40 years after the coup that brought him to power?

Managua, the capital, which had been hardest hit by the earthquake.

Increasing opposition from the Sandinistas brought on further oppression of the people by the National Guard. The situation grew so grave that US president Jimmy Carter in 1978 cut American aid to the country because of human rights violations. The Sandinistas soon came into power, and within a few years, they made socio-economic improvements that the conservative World Bank deemed "remarkable" (Chomsky 2004: 98). In terms of healthcare, Nicaragua witnessed "one of the most dramatic improvements in child survival in the developing world," according to a UNICEF document.

But the conservative American government took no pleasure in watching a politically independent Nicaragua, whose resources were not flowing freely into the US. In the 1980s, during the White House administrations of Ronald Reagan and George H.W. Bush, Nicaragua was plagued by a CIA-backed terrorist group known as the Contras, many of them former members of Somoza's National Guard, who made a regular practice of terrorizing the people of the countryside. In 1985, the US Congress voted to cut off aid to the Contras, but the CIA continued to fund them through secret arms sales to Iran (then officially an enemy of the US). In 1986, the International Court of Justice at The Hague ruled that the US was guilty of "unlawful use of force" in Nicaragua (Chomsky 2004: 99). The UN Security Council endorsed the world court's ruling, only to have their resolution vetoed by Washington's representatives to the international body.

In 1990, knowing that they had American guns literally pointed at their heads, the people of Nicaragua voted to turn the leadership of their country over to a US-endorsed candidate. One-sided economic globalization and wide-scale political corruption ensued. Nicaragua has become the second poorest nation in the Americas.

Episodes like the ones described here have happened both earlier (for example, the overthrow of the Iranian prime minister in favour of the Shah) and since (notably in Guatemala). This kind of involvement in foreign affairs by official government agencies can be called **government terrorism**. What is significant about government terrorism is that, contrary to the usual portrayal of terrorism as a narrow or particularist (see below) *resistance* to globalism, government terrorism is often used to *promote* globalism (albeit a narrow-visioned imperialist form of it) with one or several countries only at the controls. When political commentator Benjamin Barber famously characterized opposition to globalization as "Jihad vs McWorld" (in *The Atlantic Monthly*, 1992), he meant that globalism (McWorld) was being opposed by a new **tribalism** (a movement to promote the cause of smaller cultures rather than whole countries). Acknowledging that government terrorism is a major force in certain processes of globalization, we would perhaps do better to characterize opposition to globalization as Jihad vs McJihad, or small tribalism vs big tribalism, both of them fighting against a more equitable form of globalization.

What do YOU think?

1. Is it possible for sociologists to define and discuss "terrorism" in a textbook without showing their political biases?

2. Can terrorism be called "legitimate" when it is carried out in the name of freeing a people from oppression by the government of their own country or by an outside government (say for Tibetans against Chinese control)?

3. Would it be legitimate to call the political and economic violence of the dictatorial leaders of an undemocratic state a form of terrorism?

Jihad: A Misunderstood Term

A term often wrongly connected with terrorism is the Arabic word **jihad**. Movies, websites, 24-hour news channels, radio call-in shows, and even dictionaries and encyclopedias often lead us to believe that *jihad* means "holy war." Yet if you look in English copies of the Qu'ran, the Muslim holy book, you will find the Arabic word translated as "struggle, striving, endeavor." The following is a description of jihad taken from the Qu'ran:

> Those who believe, and emigrate
> And strive with might
> And main, in Allah's cause
> With their goods and their persons,
> Have the highest rank
> In the sight of Allah:
> They are the people
> Who will achieve [salvation]. (9: 20)

There are three types of jihad: personal, community, and martial. In his insightful book *Global Islamic Politics*, **Mir Zohair Husain** explains them in the following way:

The personal jihad, or **jihad-i-akbar**, is the greatest jihad. It represents the perpetual struggle required of all Muslims to purge their baser instincts. Greed, racism, hedonism, jealousy, revenge, hypocrisy, lying, cheating, and calumny [false and malicious accusation] must each be driven from the soul by waging jihad-i-akbar, warring against one's lower nature and leading a virtuous life. . . .

Likewise, **ummaic jihad** addresses wrongs within the community of Muslims, whether by the written word or by the spoken word. Ummaic jihad represents the nonviolent struggle for freedom, justice and truth within the dar-al-Islam [Muslim world]. . . .

Martial or violent jihad is referred to in Islam as **jihad-i-asghar** (lit., the smaller, lower, or lesser jihad). Martial jihad ideally represents a struggle against aggressors who are not practicing Muslims. . . . Martial jihad should be used to protect and to promote the integrity of Islam and to defend the umma [community] against hostile unbelievers, whether they are invading armies or un-Islamic internal despots. (Husain 1995: 37–8)

Muslim college students asked for examples of jihad in their lives have given answers as varied as the following:

- donating money to a charity rather than spending it on yourself
- studying for an exam rather than watching television
- working hard at a job you don't like because your family needs the money
- avoiding temptation in all forms (similar to the Christian avoidance of the seven deadly sins).

Mukulika Banerjee provides a good example of how the principles of jihad can guide peaceful

In December 2012, the Chicago chapter of the Council on American–Islamic Relations (CAIR) launched a multimedia campaign to reclaim the word *jihad* and educate people about its true meaning. The campaign was inspired in part by some anti-Islamic, anti-jihad ads that had appeared in New York City subways. Do you think this is a campaign that can succeed? Or is the association of jihad with terrorism (however inaccurate) simply too strong?

actions in her examination of the Khudai Khidmatgar ("Servants of God") movement of the North-West Frontier Province of British India (now part of Pakistan) between 1930 and 1947 (Banerjee 2000). The movement was led by Badshah Khan. He was Pathan, a member of a people living on both sides of the border between Pakistan and Afghanistan. The Khudai Khidmatgar movement unified a perpetually divided people against the oppression of the British and their locally powerful feudal lord. In leading the movement, Khan persuaded a people not unfairly described as warlike and subject to feuds of revenge to follow a course of non-violent civil disobedience. Their actions involved boycotting colonially controlled and corrupt courts, tax offices, schools, and police services, and setting up parallel institutions that served the Pathan people rather than their oppressors. They nearly succeeded in establishing an independent state before larger powers prevailed.

While the movement was developed more or less in tandem with the better known civil disobedience movement of Gandhi, Khan was no mere Pathan "lieutenant" of Gandhi's. He and his followers drew inspiration from Pathan custom and Islamic principles (including jihad) to create an ideology of non-violence that produced significant change in his land. Khan and Gandhi brought about similar results by similar means, but from quite different religious bases.

Crusade: A Parallel Term

Just as the term *jihad* has taken on a distorted meaning among many in the West, the word **crusade**, as it is understood by Muslims, is imbued with connotations of hatred and conflict. During the eleventh, twelfth, and thirteenth centuries, European Christians launched a series of military expeditions in an attempt to claim holy land from Muslims and Jews. These lands were no less sacred to Muslims and Jews, yet the Christians crusaders waged a bloody campaign to capture the territory. Consider the following:

- In 1096, the year after Pope Urban II called for the first Crusade, Crusaders killed French and German Jews on the way to the Holy Land.
- In 1099, Crusaders captured Jerusalem and killed some 40,000 Muslim prisoners in just two days.
- In 1187, the Muslim leader Saladin captured Jerusalem, killed no Christian prisoners, let Jews

back into the city, set ransom of prisoners at a low rate, and granted his brother the right to release 1,000 prisoners outright. Saladin afterwards declared, "Christians everywhere will remember the kindness we have done them."

Why, then, does the mostly Christian West consider holy war a uniquely Muslim element? Partly, of course, the fault lies with long-term ignorance, on the part of the West, about the Middle East in general and Islam in particular, something well documented by Edward Said. Part of the blame lies, too, with those extremists within Islam who have (literally) hijacked the term, narrowing the term from a broader context and rubbing the noses of the West in that meaning in a number of recent high-profile incidents.

What do YOU think?

1. What kind of definition do you predict you would find if you were to look up *jihad* in an English dictionary? What about if you were to look up *holy war*?

2. How free of bias would you expect an American encyclopedia to be in its discussion of the history of Islam?

3. How would you teach about the Crusades if you were an elementary school teacher in a multicultural school?

4. How would you differentiate between *jihad* and *crusade*?

Cultural Globalization

Steger defines **cultural globalization** as "the intensification and expansion of cultural flows across the globe" (Steger 2003: 69). Those who have expressed concerns about cultural globalization are typically worried about the "Americanization" of the world, or what can more broadly be termed the danger of a one-directional flow of culture. They cite the fact that English has emerged as by far the most prominent language of science and one of the dominant languages of the Internet and social media. American movies and television are seen in almost every country in the world, although labelling this "American" culture is perhaps giving it too broad a scope, given that, as we saw in Chapter 19, it is just a small number of transnational companies that control most of the media. These companies reap enormous dividends by exporting their respective brands of Western culture to consumers across the globe, while drawing audiences abroad away from the culture of their own countries into a global "gossip market" that revolves around the "vacuous details of the private lives of American celebrities like Britney Spears, Jennifer Lopez, Leonardo DiCaprio, and Kobe Bryant" (Steger 2003: 77). Global capitalism thus contributes not only to global poverty but also to cultural imperialism and the loss of cultural identity in favour of a homogeneous culture based on Western icons and values.

During the US-led invasion of Iraq, news reports introduced the term **embedded journalist** to describe the reporters stationed with American and British troops. This was a new practice, designed (according to military leaders) to protect journalists so that they could do their jobs without fear of being kidnapped by Iraqis or shot at by allies. Critics, however, argued that this was another example of a one-directional flow of information, which greatly diminished the independence and neutrality of reporters, who were presenting only what the military allowed them to see. The Qatar-based television station Al Jazeera emerged as an Arab alternative to army-controlled American journalism.

Another focus of studies of cultural globalization, because it deals with patterns of consumption, is resource use and its effect on the environment. The countries of the North consume much more than those of the South, both overall and on a per capita basis. Agricultural producers in the South, eager to supply the North with its most coveted crops (corn, coffee, and chocolate, for example), abandon their cultivation of less lucrative plants; the resulting decrease in biodiversity leaves some crops susceptible to extinction.

An Indonesian boy sleeps on a piece of cardboard in a Jakarta slum. Do you think he knows who Spiderman is? If so, how would he have been exposed to this information?

The Point Is...

Table Manners as Globalized Cultural Capital

In his brilliant memoir *In the House of the Interpreter*, author and university professor Ngũgĩ wa'Thiong'o, a Kikuyu from Kenya, describes his first year as a student at the prestigious colonially run Alliance High School. It was the mid-1950s, and Kenya was still a British colony, one with local Mau Mau "terrorists" fighting for their people's freedom. In his first English literature class, his teacher, a white man named P.R. Oades, took his students to his house in order to expose them to the way of life to which his African students should be aspiring. They should strive for more worldly, "globalized" knowledge, and that meant learning how to be English gentlemen (all the students were boys) and being able to find their place within the colonial social structure of the British Empire (above their fellow Africans at least). This message was clearly articulated in Oades's dining room, where the youths were taught how to sit properly, how to use their knives and forks, and how to make correct use of their napkins (placed on the lap, not tucked around the neck, and never, ever for blowing one's nose). Significantly, according to wa'Thiong'o:

> We learned that one placed one's knife and fork crossed or at an angle, preferably a wide angle, to show the waiter that one had not yet finished with the dish at hand, and of course, to place knife and fork together in parallel to tell the waiter that he could now take the plate. . . . It was all abstract, so different from my rural cuisine of *ugali* [a cornmeal-based porridge] and *irio* [mashed peas, potato, and corn] that I usually ate with my fingers, certainly without anybody waiting on me. Under the ideals of table manners, Oades was training us into the habit of being waited upon, or, at the very least, planting the idea in our minds. (wa'Thiong'o 2012: 20–1)

What do YOU think?

1. Do you think that acquiring the **cultural capital** that comes with having been educated in British upper-class manners (along with essentially the same British literature and Eurocentric history and geography that I learned as a Canadian high school student in the 1960s) would have significantly improved wa'Thiong'o's chances of a successful career? Would he be as likely to have written a memoir without this kind of education?

2. Were you ever taught to place your knife and fork in this way? When did it happen? Under what circumstances might this kind of knowledge benefit you?

Opposing Globalization

Particularist Protectionism

There are fundamentally two kinds of opposition to globalization: *particularist protectionism* and *universalist protectionism*. **Particularist protectionist** opponents of globalization focus on the economic, political, and cultural problems caused in their home territory by increasing processes of globalization. In Steger's words:

> Fearing the loss of national self-determination and the destruction of their cultures, they pledge to protect their traditional ways of life from those "foreign elements" they consider responsible for unleashing the forces of globalization. (Steger 2003: 114)

Particularist protectionists are a mixed group. They include **Islamists**—people like those associated with the al Qaeda network, who opposed globalization with narrow-minded and distorted fundamentalist notions of Islam. They also include European ethnic entrepreneurs, who use the arguments of particularist protectionism as a shield against the attacks of narrow-focused political parties campaigning for "racial/national purity" (such as the French National Front, which strongly opposes any manifestation of Islam in France, and the German People's Union, a neo-Nazi party). The group of particular protectionists even includes Americans who argue that skilled and unskilled trade workers are losing their jobs to citizens of the South, and are not benefiting from economic globalization the way the power elite are. While they sometimes identify "big business" as the culprit, it is often easier to blame Japanese-owned firms. Sociologist Roland Robertson, who teaches in the United States, wrote the following for a Japanese publication in 1997:

> I can assure you that the *anti*-global sentiment is very, very strong in the United States of America. It is playing a key part in the current campaign to decide which candidate should run for president from the Republican Party; the phrase "anti-globalism" is a significant one in American politics; there are numerous movements which are directed in opposition to the teaching of the subject of globalization, to so-called "international education"; there have been people protesting at school boards all over America about American children learning about other countries; they fear that if they learn about ancient Greek philosophy or about Japanese religion or French philosophy, that their minds will be destroyed, in other words, that their views will be relativized. (Robertson 1997)

But from a Canadian perspective, a certain amount of particularist protection would seem necessary. Only about 2 per cent of the movies we watch are Canadian, despite the fact that there is a relatively booming movie production business in Toronto and Vancouver. Think of how many times you have seen someone play the part of an American president in a movie. Can you ever remember seeing a movie with someone cast as the Canadian prime minister? Our stories are simply not being told on film, except in Quebec, where

Illegal loggers harvest timber from the Malaysian rainforest. Illegal logging for the export market has had a devastating effect on rainforests around the world. What economic and social impacts do you think illegal logging produces?

French-language films are being produced for the domestic market. Canadian content rules and specially funded programs have helped many of our musicians begin careers in the face of the competition from the loud voices to the south.

Glocalization

A useful, but contested, term to use in looking at resistance to globalization is **glocalization**. According to Roland Robertson (1997), this term first appeared in the 1980s in Japanese business literature, where it was used to describe the way Japanese transnational companies were tailoring their commodities to fit neatly into a local culture (rather like diseases that disguise themselves so that the immune system doesn't know they're invaders, to use a cynical analogy). More recently, the term—or the concept it describes—has come to be viewed more positively as a strategy worth adopting. One advocate of this strategy is Pulitzer Prize–winning American author Thomas Friedman. In his book *The Lexus and the Olive Tree* (2000), Friedman argues that economically weaker nations of the South must develop multiple filters when they receive the flow of cultural, political, and economic commodities from the North. In his words:

> I believe the most important filter is the ability to "glocalize." I define healthy glocalization as the ability of a culture, when it encounters other strong cultures, to absorb influences that naturally fit into and can enrich that culture, to resist those things that are truly alien and to compartmentalize those things that, while different, can nevertheless be enjoyed and celebrated as different. The whole purpose of glocalizing is to be able to assimilate aspects of globalization into your country and culture in a way that adds to your growth and diversity, without overwhelming it. (Friedman 2000: 295)

In support of his argument, he offers the example of Jewish scholars in the fourth century BC, who learned about Greek philosophical logic and incorporated it into their thinking. They succeeded in building on Greek scholarship without becoming overwhelmed by Greek culture, and without becoming heavily influenced by Greek polytheism and eroticism.

Modern examples are abundant. When, in the early 1990s, North American DJs of South Asian descent started splicing traditional Punjabi bhangra music in with electronic music, the resulting mix made its way through the urban dance clubs, and bhangra glocalization had arrived. Consider Japanese anime as another example: if a Canadian version were to develop (we could call it "Canime") featuring characters with big eyes and toques, then it could be seen as a glocalization.

Universalist Protectionism

At the outset of this discussion we noted that there are two kinds of opposition to globalization. Particularist protectionists argue that globalization causes political, cultural, and economic problems in their own countries. The second category is **universalist protectionism**. As Steger describes them, universalist protectionists promote a **globalization from below**, which represents the interests of the poor and other marginalized groups while advocating greater social, economic, environmental, political, and cultural equality worldwide (Steger 2003: 115). Globalization from below operates in opposition to what Steger calls **globalization from above**, those processes controlled by the power elite of the North. Thus, while particularist protectionists are mostly concerned with how globalization operates in their own countries, universalist protectionists take up the cause of those hurt by globalization worldwide. Amnesty International, Doctors Without Borders, World Wildlife Federation, and similar organizations can be seen as universalist protectionist in this way.

Telling It Like It Is   An Expert POV

The New Realities of Slavery and Consumerism

Does slavery exist today? Even though it is illegal in practically every country around the globe, we could say that it does. Realistic numbers are hard to come by, as there is no hard-and-fast operational definition of slavery. But from indentured brick makers in Pakistan to child prostitutes in Thailand, there are people who have become enslaved as a result of an expanding global economy. Many people around the world work and live in oppressive conditions to make it possible for us to fulfill our insatiable appetite to consume. A can of Coke, a pair of Nikes, or the latest fashions at the Gap—so many of our wants and "needs" are made abundant and affordable through the labour of those working in miserable conditions for meagre wages.

The chain of events goes something like this. Transnational corporations and their shareholders are constantly looking for ways to increase profits. The national governments of "overdeveloped" countries are, likewise, always in search of ways to encourage economic growth. Together, they rely on increases in the consumption of goods to fulfill their objectives.

In order for companies to maximize increases in consumption, their goods must be desirable, readily available, and inexpensive. The mass production of inexpensive goods and services requires the use of cheap labour—the cheaper the labour, the cheaper the good produced. Too often, this is accomplished by exploiting the poor, the desperate, and the vulnerable. Thus, the increased demand for profits demands an increase in cheap labour, which encourages the global practice of slave labour.

It is important to recognize that while cheap labour is a necessary component in this cycle, so too is the practice of consumption—for without consumption, the need for cheap goods produced by cheap labour is diminished. And just as many workers are in thrall to the transnational corporations that that demand low-cost goods, so too are consumers, in a way. Think of it this way: though it is less obvious and operates covertly, consumerism acts to enslave our minds, bodies, and identities on a daily basis. Reproducing the practices of consumption requires the corporate reformulation of desire. This is the process whereby our natural desires are redirected to conform to market commodities. Sexuality, for instance, takes the form of a shampoo, loneliness gets transfigured into online dating services, and the freedom of mobility can be found in a new car or cellphone. Advertising is the key element in the decoding and recoding of our desires. It operates by destabilizing our identities and promoting self-doubt. We are bombarded with reminders that we aren't skinny enough, good-looking enough, smart enough, popular enough, or rich enough, but products *X*, *Y*, and *Z* will magically transform us and our lives. These attacks on our personhood are not only demeaning but create deep insecurities which lead to and reinforce low self-esteem, loneliness, depression, anxiety, and eating disorders, to name just a few symptoms.

One of the pillars of our capitalist society is the belief that consumerism is a fundamentally democratic practice through which freedom, liberty, and equality are achieved. But how much freedom do we have when we are manipulated into buying products we don't need? Where is the liberty for the commuter stuck in rush-hour traffic in a new SUV? And what do we mean by *equality* if it comes at the expense of someone else's freedom?

—Adapted from Guy Letts, Canadian sociologist

McDonald's India serves dishes like Chicken Maharaja and Chicken McCurry Pan, while proudly declaring that they serve no beef and no pork products, since many Hindus will eat neither beef nor pork. But does this kind of glocalization, with the people of India accepting McDonald's on their terms, really represent resistance to globalization? Or does it represent a clever marketing strategy by a multinational corporation that is willing to tailor its product to the market it hopes to dominate?

The Anti-corporate Globalization Movement

It is not just academics and transnational non-governmental organizations (NGOs) that have actively opposed globalization. There have also been large citizens' protests directed against meetings of pro-globalization organizations, including the WTO, the IMF, the World Bank, the Summit of the Americas, the European Economic Summit, the G20 (referring to the 20 most powerful country economies in the world), and the World Economic Forum. Beginning with the "Battle of Seattle" in 1999, tens of thousands of protestors have staged their opposition to globalization outside of meetings held in the US, Canada, Switzerland, Britain, Sweden, and Italy. The Occupy protests of 2011–12 had a strong anti-globalization element.

The global social movement behind these protests is generally referred to as the anti-corporate globalization movement, a term on which both insiders and social scientists agree. In an insightful article published in 2004, sociologists Frederick Buttel and Kenneth Gould identify some key factors in the social structure of these protests, while plotting the future trajectory of the anti-corporate globalization movement.

First, they note that most of the protests have taken place not in the North but in the global South (in Argentina, Bolivia, Brazil, Ecuador, Indonesia, and Thailand), where they have garnered less international media attention though they have been "generally more radical and confrontational than their counterparts in the North" (Buttel & Gould 2004: 42–3). Second, they point to the influence of NGO supporters and affiliates, which have provided some of the more prominent intellectual leaders, among the best known of whom is Canadian social activist and writer Naomi Klein (*No Logo* [2000], and *Fences and Windows: Dispatches from the Frontlines of the Globalization Debate* [2002]). Third, they remark on the fact that the movement is "largely and consciously and intentionally acephalous" (Buttel & Gould 2004: 44), meaning that it is without a single head or leader outside of the local organizers of particular protests. Fourth, they note that young educated people make up the lion's share of the participants of the protests. Finally, they observe that the anti-corporate globalization movement has both benefited from and been hurt by coverage in the mainstream media, which has generated attention for the movement but has largely condemned the protests.

WRAP IT UP

Summary

Globalization is a major force in the world, one that isn't likely to be reversed or even slowed. Those who passionately believe that's a good thing are known as hyperglobalizers, and they typically have a financial interest in seeing transnational corporations move their manufacturing processes into cheaper labour markets while pushing their goods into untapped commercial markets of the global South. You'll find hyperglobalizers residing in the developed nations of the world, in the global North. We seldom call it the First World today; it seems too much like gloating.

There are also those we call skeptical globalizers, who challenge what they see as the one-way direction of globalization. We find them defending their interests and their cultural integrity in the developing world, the global South, although there are many young people in the global North who have not hitched their wagon to the corporate world and have taken part in anti-globalization protests. Skeptical globalizers can point to the fact that one-way attempts at globalization have been the norm for the last 10,000 years, with one empire after another dominating the globalization process. While globalization today is a more complete process (the globality of the world is greater), it still seems to be characterized by a one-way flow of globalizing influences from the North to the South. The big question is whether or not that will ever change, whether there can be a number of significant players, and whether there have to be big winners and big losers in every globalized situation.

Terrorism is a topic to be taken up together with globalization as it often features the violent actions of a group opposing cultural and political globalization. Defining who is and who is not a terrorist is a challenge for the sociologist. What one group labels "terrorism" another calls "freedom fighting" or "defending our national interests." Governments and corporations have supported terrorism. In the sixteenth century, British royalty supported British pirates who stole from, brutalized, and terrorized Spanish ships carrying gold that they, in turn, had stolen from the Incas and other Aboriginal groups. Centuries later, the CIA, who had their acts of torture legalized by George W. Bush, acted in similar ways to promote American corporate and national ends. The story continues.

THINK BACK

Questions for Critical Review

1. Distinguish the views and positions of hyperglobalizers and skeptical globalizers.

2. Outline what neoliberalism is and discuss the social effects that it has on developing nations.

3. Describe the political difficulties of defining and identifying what democracy is.

4. Describe the political difficulties of defining and identifying what terrorism is.

5. Distinguish between universalist and particularist protectionism.

READ ON

Online

Anti-Slavery: Today's Fight for Tomorrow's Freedom

http://www.antislavery.org

> The website of Anti-Slavery International, a UK-based NGO, provides an interesting take on what constitutes slavery in the modern-day, globalized world.

Introduction to Anti-Globalization: Definitions and Resources

http://www.anti-marketing.com/anti-globalization.html

> This is a very political but also insightful website representing Anti-Marketing, a group promoting economic responsibility and opposed to economic globalization.

Oxfam

http://www.oxfam.org.uk/

> The international development NGO and charitable organization has long been involved in helping reduce global poverty and in fighting against globalized injustice.

What Is Globalization?

www.cbc.ca/news/background/summitofamericas/globalization.html

> The CBC delivers a good summary of the issues involved with globalization.

In Print

Jagdish Bagwati (2007), *In Defense of Globalisation: With a New Afterword* (New York: Oxford University Press.

> An economist from Columbia University, Bagwati defends globalization against those who have blamed it for a range of social and environmental problems, and argues that if properly regulated, globalization processes can benefit the world.

Feminist Review Collective (2002), *Globalization* (London: Palgrave Macmillan).

> This volume of essays provides a look at how globalization is affecting women's lives, from several feminist perspectives.

Ray Kiely (2009), *The Clash of Globalizations: Neo-Liberalism, the Third Way and Anti-globalization* (Chicago: Haymarket Books).

> This book offers a Marxist take on both globalization and anti-globalization.

Manfred Steger (2009), *Globalization: A Very Short Introduction* (Oxford: Oxford University Press).

> A short, comprehensive, and insightful introduction to globalization and its issues.

Joseph Stiglitz (2003), *Globalization and Its Discontents* (New York: Norton).

> This enlightening work by a Noble Prize–winning economist presents an insider's critical view of pro-globalization organizations such as the International Monetary Fund.

Learning Objectives

After reading this chapter, you should be able to

- discuss the *vested interests* that come into play when "scientific judgements" are made about the health of the environment
- outline the ways in which different kinds of societies have an impact on the environment
- debate whether environmental disasters can lead to positive social change
- explain how "race," gender, and class intersect with environmental practices
- identify and analyze some current environmental issues in Canada.

Key Terms

- blaming the victim
- carbon footprint
- China price
- community of scholars
- density threshold
- ecofeminism
- environmental refugees
- epidemiology
- farming culture
- forager culture
- genetically modified
- horticultural
- hunter-and-gatherer culture
- industrial culture
- informant
- moral community
- operational definition
- organizational culture
- peer-review process
- post-industrial
- rotten apple approach
- social ecology
- sociological imagination
- standpoint
- tobacco strategy
- transgenic
- vested interests
- victimology

Names to Know

- Murray Bookchin
- Françoise d'Eaubonne
- Samuel Henry Prince
- Lloyd Tataryn

When a Natural Disaster is Sociological

WRITTEN TESTIMONY FOR THE RECORD
By Leah Hodges,
Evacuee, New Orleans, Louisiana
Select Bipartisan Committee to
Investigate the Preparation for and
Response to Hurricane Katrina
6 December 2005

I wish to thank everyone who is listening today for the chance to communicate my story. I come to Congress today representing not just myself, but hundreds, even thousands of other New Orleans residents who experienced the same or similar traumatic experiences and witnessed the same or similar events. . . .

Let me begin with a few general points.

1. I don't need to point out the failures of the President, the Governor of Louisiana and the Mayor of New Orleans, as these individuals have already claimed responsibility for everything that happened to us as the result of the hurricane and its aftermath.

2. The people of New Orleans were stranded in a flood and were allowed to die. The military had personnel stationed just 40 miles outside the city, and they could have moved in and gotten people out sooner. People were allowed to die.

3. Animals from the animal shelter and fish from the fish aquarium were evacuated before the people.

4. The President and local officials issued "shoot to kill orders" and people were shot. People who asked for help were threatened with being shot. My niece and her fiancé, they needed gas. Her fiancé asked the military for help and they told [him] "if you don't get back inside we will shoot you."

5. Bodies are still being found every day in New Orleans. Most people in New Orleans do not believe the official body counts.

6. The devastation that hit New Orleans was foreseeable and avoidable, and because it was

not avoided, New Orleans was turned into a mass grave.

7. As a hurricane survivor, I and my family were detained, not rescued.

. . . The city was flooded. Soldiers had showed up with M16s and military weapons. They had declared New Orleans and Jefferson Parish a war zone. They loaded us onto military trucks after they told us they would take us to shelters where our basic needs would be met.

We were dropped off at a site where we were fenced in, and penned in with military vehicles. The armed military personnel brought in dogs. There, we were subjected to conditions only comparable to a concentration camp. . . .

We were just three miles from an airport, but we were detained there for several days. Many of those who were there when we arrived had already been there several days. On any given day there were at least ten thousand people in the camp. On my last day there, I would estimate there were still three thousand detainees. By that time, nearly all the white people had been selected to evacuate first. They were put on buses and shipped out, leaving the remaining population 95 per cent black. . . .

The military did not bring anything to help keep any of us alive. Not even a first aid kit. But they had body bags. They were doing nothing for the pregnant women. Some women miscarried. . . .

People died in the camp. We saw the bodies lying there. . . . (Hodges 2005)

Eight years after Hurricane Katrina wreaked devastation upon the US Gulf Coast, sociologists are still analyzing the human tragedy and the environmental event that caused it. It has been described as a natural disaster—but how natural was it? If significant amounts of money had been invested in infrastructure in New Orleans (for example, in reinforcing the levees) to prevent the flooding that was clearly predictable, and if evacuation had involved equal treatment of all "races" and classes of people from the city, the number of dead would have been markedly less. As you will discover throughout the chapter, there is no such thing as a (purely) natural disaster.

As well as examining the human role in the causes of environmental disasters like Katrina, sociologists look closely at the human element in the way we respond. I don't think you have to be told that Leah Hodges is a black woman. Environmental disasters affect different social groups with varying degrees of intensity—typically, the weakest get hit the hardest and are the last to recover. Sociologists look for such patterns and the reasons behind them in an effort to see how they can or should be adjusted.

The environment: so often it comes down to, *What have we done? What are we doing? What are we doing about it?*

Introduction: Environmental Sociology— Science or *Social* Science?

Environmental sociology is a fast-growing subdiscipline within the social sciences. It examines the history of our relationship with the environment, focusing especially on where we have gone wrong and looking for ways to reverse our mistakes in the future.

There is a lot of science involved in environmental studies—in proving or disproving climate change, in tracking carbon emissions and weather patterns, in testing the safety of drinking water—but sociology teaches us that the science of the environment, like other sciences, is deeply embedded in a social context. The scientific world is political. Scientific facts cannot really "speak for themselves"—they have interpreters who are part of the social world and who cannot always be trusted to report "the facts" without a distorting bias based on their place in that world, their **standpoint**.

Lloyd Tataryn is a Canadian investigative journalist who has written about the dangers in our environment, from the formaldehyde found in home insulation to the uranium mined at Elliot Lake. His work often looks at the places where the facts of environmental science and politics collide. Consider the following passage from *Dying for a Living* (1979):

The scientific truth must first run a political gauntlet. For after the authorities give their advice, and all the technical data is in, the decision arrived at is ultimately a political verdict and merely masquerades as a purely scientific ruling.

Politicians, corporations, and unions are aware of this environmental fact of life. And since in the long run they must rely upon the combined political and scientific judgement of their technical advisors, they tend to choose as advisors scientists whose biases are similar to their own—scientists who are prone to ask the type of questions that produce answers which most often serve the interests of their employers. . . .

Unfortunately, the public is seldom informed of the political, economic, and scientific biases which scientists in environmental health conflicts bring to their investigations. Most of us have been led to believe that "science" and "scientists" are above such considerations. (Tataryn 1979:90)

This book, now over 30 years old, was written well before the "science" of global warming and climate change became a common topic in the popular media, and before the Northern Gateway pipeline was a gleam in Alberta's eye. How much do you think the situation Tataryn describes has changed?

Imagine that a large petroleum-exporting company wanted to run a natural gas pipeline through your community. Who would you trust to give you reliable information on its safety: an engineer employed by the company? An environmental regulator working for the federal government (whose job status might be affected by a negative report)? A university professor whose research is funded by a grant? An activist working for a charitable organization dedicated to saving the environment? What are the *vested interests* of each of these parties?

Assessing Environmental Arguments from a Social Scientific Perspective: Two Keys

1. Operational Definitions

In Chapter 3, on research methods, we looked at the importance of establishing clear **operational definitions** for variables in any research you are analyzing or carrying out yourself. Operational definitions are essential to the process of creating social policies concerning social issues. But as we saw, it can be difficult to take relatively abstract concepts such as poverty and abuse and turn them into concrete, countable entities. All operational definitions "leak": they are imperfect, and sociologists, as scientists, will disagree on the best definition for any given term. Scholarly debate can bring clarity to an operational definition, especially during the **peer review process**, when a draft of an article, report, or book written by an academic researcher (or team of researchers) undergoes rigorous assessment by other "experts" in the field to ensure that it is suitable for publication. The author must take into consideration any and all criticisms before the work can be published. Eventually, through this scientific social process, the best leaky term or terms win out.

The peer review and the author's follow-up work of addressing and incorporating feedback from what we call the **community of scholars** are steps in the social-intellectual process that helps to advance the discipline as a whole. This practice, which we called a "scientific social process," is a well-developed and effective method of reaching consensus on an idea. But while the process is known to most scientists, it is not as familiar to people outside the scientific community. Among the outsiders are journalists, politicians, and interest groups, who may be guided by non-scientific social processes and ideas, like the notion that there are two sides to every story, and that presenting a "balance of views" is always necessary. A classic example of this flawed notion is the persistent but as yet unsuccessful attempt by American Christian groups to provide "balance" to the debate surrounding evolution by bringing forward non-scientific arguments in support of creationism and intelligent design. Only evolution is scientific.

When it comes to the science of the study of the environment, the same elements of difficulty involving operational definitions are involved, with critical arguments hinging on abstract terms that are incredibly difficult to define. How would you begin to devise operational definitions for concepts such as "pollution" or "lung damage"? Where do you set the limits on "safe" versus "dangerous," or "acceptable" versus "unacceptable" levels of exposure to a particular toxin? The stakes are high when millions of dollars and people's lives are involved. Consider the following statement from uranium miner Gus Frobel, who later died from cancer he believed was caused by his everyday working conditions:

> When you read the scientific papers you find the really knowledgeable scientists, the experts in the field, don't use the term "safe" level of exposure. They know they can't defend it scientifically. They say that to their knowledge there is no "safe" level. Some use the term, "acceptable level." Now what's an "acceptable level?" That means some men have to die—but how many? How many deaths are acceptable? (Tataryn 1979: 100)

Pollution is like poverty. Just as you can tell when someone is very poor (a person sleeping on the street in the middle of winter is definitely poor), so you can tell when water or air is extremely polluted: it smells bad, looks horrible, and makes you sick. But extremes are easy to identify, even for non-scientists. Finding the line that separates "polluted" from "not polluted" for the purpose of definition is not so easy—it takes a scientific approach to get there. It is especially difficult when the damaging effects of pollution may not become apparent for many, many years. For instance, if it takes 20 years for an asbestos mine worker to die from exposure to an unsafe level of asbestos in the air, it could take 20 years for a hypothesis of what constitutes an "unsafe level of exposure" to be proven true, although reasonably sound predictions can be made earlier on.

Operational definition thus becomes a key aspect of environmental debates. In any discussion of the environment, look closely for abstract terms. Are they carefully defined? Do the definitions look sound? How were the definitions arrived at? Do the people presenting the information use the words *significant* or *serious* without explaining what they mean by them? The answers to these questions will tell you a lot about whether a particular argument is being fought on scientific grounds or political ones.

Ice-o-lation. How would you go about drafting an operational definition for "climate change"? Who would you consult? Who would you not consult? What vested interests might be involved in the varying answers you receive?

2. Vested Interests

Once the operational definitions of an environmental argument have been assessed, there remain certain sociological questions that are important to address. For example, who paid for any research studies cited in the argument? Who stands to benefit or lose from a particular test result? Politics are almost always involved in environmental research, especially when some social policy is being proposed, implemented, attacked, or defended. That's why it is important to identify the vested interests surrounding any argument about the environment.

A **vested interest** is any interest in the results of a scientific study—and the way those results are interpreted—that may be strong enough to override the interest of ensuring those results are accurate, or "truthful." Remember that although scientific measurement can be precise, the interpretation of data can be highly subjective. Give two scientists the same numbers, and they may come up with two very different interpretations.

The way operational definitions are derived (or not derived) may be influenced by the vested interests of the person designing the study or interpreting results. Look for the word *significant*, which is a weasel word that appears scientific but that can be very much a guess unless it is defined clearly. Another example: it is statistically predictable that if a scientist is paid by a mining company or an oil extracting company, that scientist is likely to have a higher level for "safe" and will be more likely to give workers a clean bill of health than someone who is acting independently; a scientist being paid by the union of the miners or oil workers may have a different view altogether. Take the following example. By 1960, 63 scientific papers had been published on the effects of exposure to asbestos. Eleven of those papers were sponsored by parties associated with the asbestos industry; 52 were published by hospital and medical school staff. The papers sponsored by the "industry 11" all claimed to show there was no relationship between asbestos exposure and cancer, while playing down the seriousness of asbestosis. The papers published by the "independent 52" drew connections between asbestos and cancer, and made a stronger case for the destructiveness of asbestosis on the human body. As Lloyd Tataryn concluded, "Clearly the perspectives of the doctors writing the reports were influenced by whether they were employed treating the victims of the diseases, or hired by the perpetrator" (Tataryn 1979: 31).

An important work on the subject of vested interest in environmental science is Naomi Oreskes and Erik Conway's *Merchants of Doubt: How a Handful of Scientist Obscured the Truth on Issues from Tobacco Smoke to Global Warming* (2010). They assert that the same tactics (and, in many cases, the same scientists) are deployed to manufacture and merchandise doubt about environmental concerns and health issues caused by huge multinational companies. These scientists can be considered *scientific mercenaries*, or *embedded scientists*, but their dedication to science is secondary to their dedication to the conservative, pro-business political agenda. They fight science with science in the name of industry, following the blueprint of the **tobacco strategy**, which was the first large-scale application of the tactics. It was in the 1950s that scientists began to understand how damaging cigarette smoking could be to one's health. By the 1960s, the community of scholars knew it, but the tobacco industry successfully paid teams of scientists to combat the growing evidence, forestalling the onslaught of successful lawsuits against the industry until the 1990s.

When searching for vested interests, it is always important to trace the science back to its social location. Many of the "think tanks," "institutes," and other organizations that publish policy recommendations and reports are funded by capital from large companies, so they tend to be conservative by their very nature. They generally take positions that support the big-business agenda while downplaying or dismissing potential harm to the environment or industry-related health risks. University researchers are generally more reliable concerning environmental issues, but it is necessary to see who funds their work, governments or corporations.

The tobacco strategy has been used by other deniers of science, to dispute other facts including acid rain, ozone layer depletion, and, most recently, anthropogenic (human-produced) global warming.

Different Historical Relationships to the Environment

Over time, different societies have had very different ways of looking at, interacting with, and treating the environment. These ways are shaped by the cultural ideologies that distinguish every society's relationship to the environment. To a large extent, they are conditioned by prevailing beliefs about the value of the environment, about what can be obtained from the land and the sea, and about how powerful humans are in controlling the environment.

Hunter-and-Gatherer Cultures

Traditional **hunter-and-gatherer** (or **forager**) communities survived by fishing, hunting, and harvesting wild crops. They were typically nomadic, moving from place to place according to the migration patterns of their prey and the availability of seasonal crops. Like

---

QUICK HITS

Oreskes and Conway on Two Scientific Mercenaries

In the following passage, Naomi Oreskes and Erik Conway describe the practices of two "scientific mercenaries," Frederick Seitz and Siegfried Singer. Both were scientists who had produced legitimate and well-regarded research in physics before their connections to conservative American government administrations and industry interests damaged the scientific credibility of their work:

> From 1979 to 1985, Fred Seitz directed a program for R.J. Reynolds Tobacco Company that distributed $45 million to scientists around the country for biomedical research that could generate evidence and cultivate experts to be used in court to defend the "product." In the mid-1990s, Fred Singer co-authored a major report attacking the US Environmental Protection Agency [EPA] over the health risks of secondhand smoke. Several years earlier, the US surgeon general had declared that secondhand smoke was hazardous not only to smokers' health, but to anyone exposed to it. Singer attacked this finding, claiming the work was rigged, and that the EPA review of the science—done by leading experts from around the country—was distorted by a political agenda to expand government control over all aspects of our lives. Singer's anti-EPA report was funded by the Tobacco Institute, channeled through a think tank, the Alexis de Tocqueville Institution. (Oreskes & Conway 2010: 5–6)

---

all societies, they altered their environment—by cutting down trees and killing some animals but not others—but they did so with restraint, aware that too much change could destroy their livelihood.

In Canada, some Aboriginal hunter-and-gatherer societies would stop hunting, trapping, or fishing over an area so that the species they were pursuing would have a chance to return to a viable population size. (The analogous practice in agriculture is letting a field lie fallow for a growing season to allow nutrients in the soil to be replenished.) These indigenous societies

[*Left*] Having grown up in an age where the dangers of tobacco use were well established, you might find it easy to scoff at the naiveté of magazine readers in the 1950s and 1960s who found these kinds of ads compelling. But be honest: how often do you find yourself picking up the skincare product, toothpaste, or pain-relief medication that's advertised as "clinically proven" or "doctor-recommended"? (It only takes one doctor.)

[*Far right*] The Scientific Division of the US Tobacco Institute put out this ad encouraging readers to get the whole story on second-hand smoke. Look at the way the argument is crafted. Is it effective?

regarded certain plants and animals with a spiritual reverence they expressed in religious terms, reflecting their recognition of how dependent they were on these species. This does not mean that they were natural "conservationists"—they simply understood (and many of their descendants still understand) that conservation of species meant survival.

A beautiful expression of this comes from an unnamed Innu **informant** quoted by anthropologist Frank Speck in *Naskapi: The Savage Hunters of the Labrador Peninsula* (1935). The Innu of Labrador (at one time called *Naskapi* by anthropologists) have long depended on herds of caribou for their survival. The caribou provide food, clothing, tools, and even housing (i.e. tents, made from their skins). In the passage that follows, the speaker's identification with the caribou reflects his sense of the need to conserve the species. The story of *Ati'k'wape'o*, or "Caribou Man," begins with an old man and his son:

And it happened that the son dreamed that he cohabited with the caribou. It seems that he killed a great many caribou. Once, then, it happened

that during the winter he said to his father: "I will depart. And I will kill caribou enough for the whole winter. So do not wait for me as respects anything. I will come back. For, indeed, I am going to go with the caribou." Then he sang: "The caribou walked along well like me. Then I walked as he was walking. Then I took his path. And then I walked like the caribou, my trail looking like a caribou trail where I saw my tracks. And so indeed I will take care of the caribou. I indeed will divide the caribou. I will give them to the people. I will know how many to give to the people. It will be known to me. . . . He who obeys the requirements is given caribou, and he who disobeys is not given caribou. If he wastes much caribou he cannot be given them, because he wastes too much of his food—the good things. And now, as much as I have spoken, you will know forever how it is. For so now it is as I have said. I, indeed, am Caribou Man. . . . (Speck 1977 [1935]: 81)

The Labrador Innu later fought to save the caribou in the 1980s and 1990s, when NATO proposed to

HERE'S WHAT'S NOW BEING SAID ABOUT OTHER PEOPLE'S CIGARETTE SMOKE.

Scientist disputes findings of cancer risk to nonsmokers

Smoking Test Fights Past Work

Others' cigaret smoke may not hike cancer risk

FROM CIGARETTES
2nd-Hand Smoke Risk Discounted

Study Downplays Nonsmoker Risk

Passive-smoking research disputed

Effect of smoking on others doubted

Non-smoker cancer 'risk' questioned

New study contradicts non-smokers' risk

Several months ago, headlines around the world trumpeted alarming news. A Japanese study was claiming that non-smoking wives of smokers had a higher risk of lung cancer because of their husbands' tobacco smoke. That scared a lot of people and understandably so, if this claim was the last word.

But now new headlines have appeared. First, because several apparent errors are reported to have been found in the Japanese study—raising serious questions about it.

Second, because Lawrence Garfinkel, the statistical director of the American Cancer Society who is opposed to smoking, published a report covering 17 years and nearly 200,000 people in which he indicated that "second-hand" smoke has insignificant effect on lung cancer rates in nonsmokers.

For more information on this important public issue, write Scientific Division, The Tobacco Institute, 1875 I St., N.W., Washington, D.C. 20006.

BEFORE YOU BELIEVE HALF THE STORY, GET THE WHOLE STORY.

use the Goose Bay area to test low-level jet fighters, which would have threatened the species (Steckley & Cummins 2001: 153–6).

What do YOU think?

What aspects of hunter-and-gather life might have made plant and animal species preservation easier than it is in today's industrial culture?

Farming Cultures

Hunter-and-gatherer culture gradually gave way to **farming culture** when people began to put down roots (so to speak) and settle in fixed communities, where they could grow crops and raise animals that had once been wild. Succeeding generations of farmers and agricultural technology have brought increasing amounts of control over nature, from the selective breeding of plants and animals to altering the DNA of commercial plant crops to produce **genetically modified** (or **transgenic**) food crops (notably corn, soybeans, and

canola) that are more resistant to certain insects and plant diseases.

Farming societies have a potentially more destructive relationship to the environment than hunter–gatherer societies have. Farming begins with clear-cutting forest land to create fields for planting crops, and the subsequent work required to irrigate, fertilize, and cultivate the land can do serious damage over time. Geographer Jared Diamond's *Collapse: How Societies Choose to Fail or Survive* (2005) features historical examples of how this destructive relationship pushed certain societies, like the Norse (Vikings) in Greenland, to collapse. The environmental problems they created included deforestation and soil problems such as erosion, salinization (too much salt in the soil), and a loss in soil fertility. More recent times have seen further examples. The Great Depression is still known as "the dirty thirties" because of the huge dust storms caused by the combination of wind, drought, and loose, ploughed-up soil that had once been held in place by wild plants and grasses. Around the world, deserts have been created or extended by farming peoples.

Even **horticultural** societies, which practise low-level agriculture on a much smaller scale (sometimes called *slash-and-burn agriculture*), can have a damaging impact on the environment. The Wendat (Huron) of the seventeenth century had to move their villages every 10 to 15 years as they used up resources and as the soil lost its fertility. That was a luxury that more recent generations of farmers have not enjoyed, thanks to the loss of so much good agricultural land to industrialization and urban growth.

Industrial and Post-industrial Cultures

While many parts of the developing world continue to rely on agriculture, the developed North has become a predominantly **industrial culture**, where farmland has been swallowed up by cities, and traditional farming practices have given way to large-scale manufacturing that causes pollution and draws heavily on natural resources. The factory farm, where poultry, pigs, and cattle are closely confined indoors and reared under strictly controlled conditions highly conducive to the development of new diseases (think H1N1), is what has evolved from traditional farming in the industrial age. The mining/extraction, processing, and consumption of non-renewable resources such as oil, gas, and coal are all characteristic of our industrial culture. The

This genetically modified pig, developed at the University of Guelph, provides a distinct advantage over regular pigs: its pig poo is environmentally friendly! If you're a bacon lover, would you have any reservations about eating meat from a genetically modified pig? If you're a vegetarian, how do you feel about the fact that many soy products are made with genetically modified soybeans? Overall, what are the benefits and dangers of consuming food with genetically modified ingredients?

Telling It Like It Is | An Author POV

Peer Review and Vested Interests: The Case of the Northern Gateway Pipeline

A defining characteristic of our industrial culture is our never-ending reliance on fossil fuels. It has driven the development of Alberta's oil sands, but this has not occurred without controversy, both within Canada and abroad. Among the more contentious issues domestically is the proposed Northern Gateway pipeline, which would carry oil extracted from the tar sands over 1,172 kilometres of land in Alberta and British Columbia to Kitimat on the BC coast, to be shipped out by tankers through a particularly island-riddled part of British Columbia's coastland en route to China.

Debates about the safety and risks of the pipeline pit environmentalists, Aboriginal groups, and many British Columbians (particularly those connected with the Liberal government) against the proposed developer Enbridge, many Albertans, and the Conservative federal government.

There are many issues to consider here. They include Enbridge's record of leaky pipelines that spilled 132,715 barrels' worth of oil in numerous leaks and spills between 2000 and 2010 (Nelson 2012); the company's use of maps that, whether through carelessness or deceit, omit many islands, in presentations designed to show the ease of tanker traffic; the inflation of the number of Aboriginal groups supporting the pipeline, achieved by including peoples living far enough from it that they will never feel the impact; and the question of whether any long-term jobs will really result from the development. Here, however, we will carry out a social-process-of-knowledge assessment of a relatively small part of the overall environmental picture surrounding the proposed pipeline.

One animal that appears to be threatened by the pipeline is the caribou, which has tremendous value among Aboriginal hunter–gatherer cultures. The caribou remain a source of good-quality food and clothing for northern peoples. Now scientists can baffle the untrained, unscientific reader with statistics based on concepts that have operational definitions that are hard to assess, but the sociologist can look at just a couple of factors to see what is likely to be truth and what might be a lie dressed up to look like truth.

We have already seen that vested interests come into play frequently in debates surrounding the environment and health. Remember that when someone writes a report for Enbridge, or has been hired to consult for them, the management of Enbridge has a say in how the material is interpreted and presented. This is why we favour independent reports over those prepared for the company. Specifically, we are looking for reports that have undergone the kind of peer review process discussed earlier in this chapter. Warning bells should go off whenever you are presented with a scientific report that has not been peer-reviewed.

With respect to caribou, a key biological concept is **density threshold**, which is a measure of the amount of human development that can occur in caribou habitat before a given herd will begin to experience a population decline. In Enbridge's environmental assessment of the proposed pipeline, a density threshold of 1.8 kilometres of development within a square kilometre of habitat was cited. Now you and I cannot tell just by looking at the numbers whether this is accurate or not, but we can use the social factors of vested interests and peer review to assess whether it seems reliable or not. The Enbridge presentation cited "Francis et al. (2002)" to support their position. Upon investigation, this source turned out to be not a peer-reviewed article on Caribou in British Columbia but a PowerPoint presentation on caribou in Yukon. Yukon caribou deal with a different environment to the one inhabited by the caribou of northern BC. When this point was raised, an Enbridge biologist was quick to say that that reference had been changed in the errata (comments added to a study, correcting mistakes made in the original). The "real" source was "Salmo and Diversified (2003)." The problem was that if you went to the report prepared for Salmo Consulting Inc. and Diversified Environmental Services (2003), you would see that they attributed their information on density threshold to "Francis et al. (2002)."

The problem is that a PowerPoint presentation is not considered "scientific" according to the conventions of developing a strong scientific argument. Use of this source in the Enbridge presentation on environmental sustainability and the long-term survival of caribou in northern BC is therefore problematic: it should make us question the presentation's authority, especially given that it supports the vested interests of Enbridge.

---

garbage we produce, both the by-product of commercial processes and the everyday waste of individuals, has become a subject of ongoing concern. Industrial culture is all about total human control of nature, and in the eyes of environmental sociologists (among others), that's a big problem.

Some environmental sociologists, though, see signs of better things on the smoggy horizon. They cite the fact that there has never been a time when we were more aware of the environmental damage we are causing. With that awareness comes the possibility that we can correct some of the worst habits of our industrial culture and reduce our **carbon footprint**—a measure of our impact on the environment based on the amount of greenhouse gas emissions we have caused through our reliance on transportation and industrial activities that require carbon-based fuels such as wood, coal, oil, and natural gas. This hopeful new phase of humans' relationship to the environment is sometimes called the **post-industrial** age, and leading us there is a sociological school of thought known as social ecology.

Social Ecology

As we've noted, a large part of the optimism some environmentalists feel comes from our heightened awareness of the human role in environmental issues, from the importance of household recycling to the dangers of our carbon emissions. As it's stated in so many self-help books, the first and hardest step

The Point Is...

Does Disaster Bring Positive Social Change?

Central to the social ecology viewpoint is the idea that environmental problems reproduce—and even arise from—existing social problems. But can they produce social change for the better? We can consider this idea in the context of two environmental disasters that occurred in North America nearly a century apart.

The idea that environmental disaster creates the circumstances for positive social change was first put forward by influential Canadian sociologist **Samuel Henry Prince** (1886–1962), who taught at the University of King's College from 1924 until 1955. As we saw in Chapter 1, his PhD dissertation involved pioneering work on "disaster" as a context for social change. The New Brunswick–born Prince took, as his case study, an incident that had occurred close to home: the Halifax Explosion of 1917, in which a docked ship carrying explosives caught fire and exploded, killing close to 2,000 people and causing widespread devastation. Prince showed that the catastrophe, while tragic, created the "state of flux" necessary to basically start fresh and carry out a number of improvements to the social infrastructure of Halifax (including, for instance, better public transportation and a new building code that would guarantee safer, more durable housing for the city's citizens). Prince concluded that the social change was largely positive.

The Halifax Explosion draws an obvious parallel with the situation in New Orleans following Hurricane Katrina. While the Halifax Explosion involved human causes, the two tragedies created environmental devastation on a comparable scale, giving Prince's work great relevance to any sociological consideration of Hurricane Katrina and its aftermath.

We should point out that Prince's work reflects a greater amount of positivism than one finds in most work taking the social ecology approach. Contemporary sociological studies tend to support the hypothesis that there is a direct link between social and environmental problems. All so-called natural disasters occur within a social context: they have different impacts on groups occupying different social locations based on gender, "race," ethnicity, class, age, and (dis)ability. The greatest victims of Hurricane Katrina were black, female, poor, and disabled. The greater the number of those social features you possessed, the more likely you were to suffer, or even die, from the natural effects of the storm and the social response to the storm.

So what to make of Prince's hypothesis that disaster brings positive social change? Rebuilding in New Orleans has tended to benefit large, well-connected companies that were able to obtain government reconstruction contracts. Privately run schools that cater to the wealthy have managed to secure education contracts in the city, while the public system suffers. Even though the city is better protected and better prepared for the natural aspects of a future hurricane (the damage from Hurricane Isaac in August 2012 was considerably less), it would be inaccurate to argue that Hurricane Katrina has brought only positive social change to New Orleans, or that the city is better off than it was before the storms of 2005.

What do YOU think?

Are there parallels here to the two environmental disasters of the summer of 2013, the flooding in Alberta and the rail explosion at Lac-Mégantic, Quebec? What social changes might result? Do you think the flooding will change the discussion of human-induced global warming in a province where oil interests have tried to downplay the effects and very existence of climate change? How do you think the Lac-Mégantic disaster will affect the debate surrounding the future of oil pipelines in Canada?

is acknowledging you have a problem. This is a key tenet of **social ecology**, a school of thought that was founded by American thinker and ecologist **Murray Bookchin** (1921–2006). He explained social ecology as follows:

> What literally defines social ecology as "social" is its recognition of the often overlooked fact that nearly all our present ecological problems arise from deep-seated social problems. Conversely, present ecological problems cannot be clearly understood, much less resolved, without resolutely dealing with problems within society. To make this point more concrete: economic, ethnic, cultural, and gender conflicts, among many others, lie at the core of the most serious ecological dislocations we face today. . . . (Bookchin 1996)

To get a better sense of how a social ecologist might view the relationship between social conflict and environmental issues, we will look at the role of class conflict in the context of industrial pollution.

Industrial Pollution and Social Ecology

We can adopt a social ecology approach to better understand how the exposure of workers to unsafe environmental conditions reflects larger trends in the issue of industrial pollution. First, in order for workers to be placed in this situation, it requires the complicity of the employer—the company that requires the work—and sometimes the government, which is ultimately responsible for overseeing environmental protection as well as workplace safety. As Lloyd Tataryn notes, it is not just the workers whose lives may be most under threat from the damage caused by the company's practices:

> Today, people who work and live in contaminated environments serve as early warning systems for toxic substances, much like the ancient royal food tasters and the canaries the coal miners once trundled underground to test the air. Workers and those who live in the shadow of polluting industries are the first people to encounter intense and prolonged exposure to toxic wastes. Much of what is known about environmental health and the consequences of exposure to poisonous and cancer-causing materials has been learned from examining disease patterns among workers and exposed populations. Exposure standards are usually established once an unusual pattern of disease has been detected. In this way workers and people living in industrially contaminated environments act as guinea pigs for the rest of society. (1979: 1)

There appear to be two different ways of interpreting workplace-related illness and injury. The first is the social ecology view, which sees these as essentially *social* in their origin and in the way that they are dealt with. Working conditions are set in place by a company and monitored in varying degrees by the political authorities in an area. You can see, reflected in this, C. Wright Mills' notion of the **sociological imagination**, in which individual problems and situations readily connect with the broader social structure and its processes. The workers are not in a position to oppose the company's unsafe environmental practices. This is essentially a class conflict. What does that say about industrial pollution on a larger scale?

The other way of interpreting workplace illness is to keep it individual and personal, reflecting the individual choices and physical constitution of the person afflicted. Far from being symptomatic of broader social processes, a worker's disease is viewed as a result of personal choices taken by the individual worker: smoking, drinking, lack of exercise, and poor lifestyle choices in general. Injuries happen at the job site because workers are careless (a viewpoint that was reflected in early commercials promoting workplace safety as an individual responsibility). It would be wrong to say that the individual is powerless to play a role in workplace safety; however, this second view, we feel, leans too far in the direction of William Ryan's notion of **blaming the victim**. It's a recurring theme—watch for it in the sections that follow.

What do YOU think?

1. Consider a common workplace setting, such as a warehouse, and a common workplace injury, such as lower back pain. Who should be more responsible for worker safety in this context: the employer or the employee? Now apply the same question to carpal-tunnel syndrome suffered by secretaries whose jobs consist mainly of keyboarding. Is your answer the same?

2. What does Tataryn mean when he calls people who work in or live near polluting industries "human canaries"?

The Asbestos Industry: Dying for a Living

It has long been known that asbestos is hazardous to human health. Roman writers in the second century CE noted that those who spun its threads into valuable robes often became sick. By the early twentieth century, some North American insurance companies were refusing to insure asbestos workers, recognizing that these employees had relatively low chances of long-term survival at the job. In 2012, a consortium of **epidemiology** organizations from around the world issued a position statement on asbestos, declaring their opinion that "all types of asbestos fibre are causally implicated in the development of various diseases and premature death" (JPC-SE 2012: 2). These diseases include lung cancer, mesothelioma, and asbestosis.

Canada became a major producer of asbestos in 1879, when the fibrous mineral was first mined in Thetford Mines in Quebec. But while people in other jurisdictions began to observe standards of what was considered "acceptable" risk of exposure—a figure first set at 35 fibres per cubic centimetre in 1938, before falling, with further study, to 12, then 5, then 2— the world's largest producer of asbestos, Thetford Mines, observed no such standard until 1978, when it bowed to media and public pressure by adopting limits of "acceptable" exposure. In the mid-1970s, Paul Formby—a Canadian who significantly raised the profile of the dangers of asbestos, both for miners and for other workers (such as builders) exposed to the deadly material—discovered levels ranging from 30 to 50 fibres per cubic centimetre in the mines there.

It is not just the miners who have been exposed to the environmental hazards of asbestos:

> Towering over the town of Thetford Mines are massive grey piles of asbestos tailings. These tailings poke their way like giant fingers into sections of the town, spilling asbestos waste into the yards of many of the homes. Positioned on top of the tailings are machines called swivel pilers, constantly spraying out clouds of asbestos waste, a practice that Mount Sinai's doctors say would be illegal in the United States. Thetford's tailings daily grow higher and higher, leaving the town covered in grey dust. (Tataryn 1979: 23)

The prevailing attitude in a one-industry town like Thetford Mines is often one that defends the business that brings food to the table, even in the face of

Rising majestically behind this row of houses in Thetford Mines is a large tailings pile from the town's asbestos quarry. How comfortable would you feel living in one of these houses? Describe the social profile of the typical resident of this street.

environmental health studies with grave conclusions about the health risks to the town's citizens. In a 2007 article, one retired miner, who worked in the mines for 38 years, stated the following:

> Those people who had their houses tested [for asbestos] are just whiners, looking for compensation. . . . We made a very good living in the mines, and I don't regret it for a minute. . . . It's paranoia. It's just like smoking. I know lots of people who smoke and live to be 80 or 90 years old. (as cited in Lalonde 2007)

While some of his colleagues had died of asbestos-caused illnesses, the miner, according to the article, believed the deaths were owing to "a vulnerability on their part" (Lalonde 2007).

Studies of the health risks of asbestos exposure are still being done and debated. Meanwhile, the provincial government of Quebec and the federal government have been involved in promoting the use of asbestos products, particularly in developing countries, the destination for 90 per cent of the 150,000 tonnes of asbestos produced in Canada. It was not until September 2012 that the federal Conservative government announced it would no longer oppose global rules restricting the use and shipment of asbestos (CBC News 2012a).

Industrial Communities and the Disposable People of Pollution

The story of Thetford Mines and Asbestos, Quebec—towns whose names are synonymous with the industry they revolve around—underline the fact that it is not just workers who are exposed to the hazardous pollutants produced by environmentally unfriendly companies. Also affected are the communities surrounding these dangerous enterprises. Again, we find the social ecology approach useful in examining how the poor and marginalized communities are usually the ones most powerfully affected. An illustrative case is that of the chemical giant Monsanto and the tiny city of Anniston, Alabama.

The Industrial Contamination of Anniston, Alabama

A little background is necessary. Monsanto has, since its origin in 1901, manufactured and distributed some of the most toxic chemicals ever produced. Specifically, the company was involved in the production and sale of polychlorinated biphenyls, or PCBs, from 1929 until the early 1980s, when the substance was effectively banned through a series of regulations. What are PCBs? In the words of journalist Marie-Monique Robin, "for half a century they colonized the planet; they were used as coolants in electric transformers and industrial hydraulic machines, but also as lubricants in applications as varied as plastics, paint, ink, and paper" (Robin 2010: 11).

Monsanto has also produced the deadly chemical dioxin, which was used as an ingredient in Agent Orange, the notorious broad-based plant killer and defoliant that was dumped in massive quantities on the jungles and people of Vietnam by the US during the Vietnam War to deprive the enemy fighters of cover. So powerful was Agent Orange that plants still do not grow around an airport in western Newfoundland where the chemical was tested during the 1970s. Then there are the other deadly D's, including 2-4-D (a component of Agent Orange, used for a time in household weed killers) and the environmentally toxic insecticide DDT. Monsanto also produces the controversial artificial sweetener aspartame. If you try to research aspartame to see whether or not it is carcinogenic, you will get two different kinds of responses: one from its sellers and those friendly to Monsanto, and the other is from neutral scientists (see, for example, a 2010 article in the *American Journal of Industrial Medicine*, which presents a link between aspartame and cancers of the lung and liver in male mice: Soffritti et al. 2010).

And now for the story of the small city of Anniston.

Situated in Calhoun County, Alabama, Anniston was home to a Monsanto production facility for PCBs beginning in 1929. Most of the workers at Monsanto's plant in Anniston were black. Many of them lived in the neighbourhoods surrounding the plant, which were likewise predominantly black. During the 1930s, Monsanto was already receiving and documenting warnings about the deadly nature of PCBs to anyone in close contact with the toxic compound, and the company continued to acquire and file away such information until they stopped producing PCBs in 1971. During this time, they did nothing to warn or protect either their workers or their neighbours in the community of Anniston.

The truth of Anniston's PCB contamination began to emerge in a series of news items in 2002. By 2005, the US Environmental Protection Agency (EPA) was reporting that 60 million pounds of PCBs that been emitted into the atmosphere surrounding Anniston.

Our Stories

Shooting the Messenger: The Case of Dr John O'Connor, Whistle-Blower

John O'Connor has served as a physician in northern Alberta since 1993, spending much of this time in the oil sands boomtown of Fort McMurray. In 2001 he started working with the Aboriginal community of Fort Chipewyan, population 1,200, located a little way downriver from the sands. Shortly after beginning to work with the Fort Chipewyan community, whose elders told O'Connor about new deformities they were seeing in fish—a staple of their diet—along with a peculiar oily taste, the doctor began to notice evidence of health problems he hadn't seen in Fort McMurray. Specifically, he observed new cases of cholangiocarcinoma, a rare bile duct cancer that had killed his father, and that often showed up in bile ducts of fish swimming in oil-infested water. He also found a high incidence of liver cancers.

When Dr O'Connor began publicly articulating his concerns, Canada's federal agency, Health Canada, approached the community for its medical files. One government representative even made a very public visit to declare the water fit for consumption. He demonstrated this with a rather unscientific gesture: at the local nursing station, he filled his mouth with water from a tap and announced to an attending *Globe and Mail* reporter: "There's nothing wrong with the water in Fort Chip."

Health Canada presented the findings of their report to the Alberta Energy and Utilities Board in Fort McMurray one week *before* they spoke with members of the Fort Chipewyan community about their experience. After a quick analysis of the data set, which mysteriously omitted statistics from 2004 and 2005, the agency gave the community a clean bill of health.

The agency's work didn't end there, as O'Connor, in a statement given in the House of Commons in June 2009, explained:

> In 2007 I got a large envelope in the mail from the College of Physicians and Surgeons in Edmonton. . . . It was a list of complaints that Health Canada had laid about my activities in Fort Chip. They accused me of blocking access to files, billing irregularities, engendering a sense of mistrust in government in Fort Chip, and causing undue alarm in the community. (Canada 2009)

A nearly equivalent amount—68 million pounds—of PCB-contaminated waste had been dumped at a disposal site in Anniston, while 1.8 million pounds of PCBs had been dumped into local streams, where the locals sometimes fished for food. The reported effects on the health of Anniston's residents included rare cancers, brain tumours, miscarriages, and brain damage to infants and children caused by contaminated breast milk.

Monsanto had taken steps to limit the legal damage it knew could result from any discovery of the extent of contamination. They had begun to buy up homes surrounding the disposal site, offering "good money" in exchange for a written promise from any seller not to sue the company. In 1997, Monsanto sold its industrial chemical division, which included the factory at Anniston, to another company, Solutia Inc., in a move widely seen as an attempt to evade financial liability in lawsuits the company was anticipating.

Nevertheless, in 2002, Monsanto and Solutia were successfully sued in a class action suit by former employees and the citizens of the city of Anniston. Money was awarded to the individual plaintiffs based on the quantities of PCB in their blood, with the cutoff being 20 parts per million (ppm)—10 times the acceptable rate. Under these conditions, only 15 per cent of the plaintiffs qualified for compensation, up to a maximum of $500,000. One of the leaders of the lawsuit, David Barker, whose brother had died of cancer at 17, had a bloodstream PCB level of 341 ppm—170 times the acceptable level—and was awarded $33,000.

It was the first time that a Canadian government agency had ever used a patient complaint process to attack a physician in this way. The charges were serious and could have led to the suspension—temporary or permanent—of O'Connor's licence to practise medicine. The first three charges were dismissed relatively quickly. The people of Fort Chipewyan, who hadn't been consulted concerning whether they felt "undue alarm," supported him, and in fact requested the dismissal of Health Canada's senior physician. Members of the Alberta Medical Association were unanimous in their support.

In 2008 the Alberta Cancer Board engaged in a more comprehensive study of the community, releasing their findings in February 2009. In their report, the board stated that while the number of cases of cholangiocarcinoma and colon cancer were "within the expected range" during the period of investigation,

[t]he number of cancer cases overall was higher than expected. In particular, increases of observed over expected were found for biliary tract cancers as a group and cancers of the blood and lymphatic system. These increases were based on a small number of cases and could be due to chance or increased detection. The possibility that the increased rate is due to increased risk in the community, however, cannot be ruled out. (Alberta Cancer Board 2009: 10)

The board concluded that further study was warranted to see if there was any risk associated with living in Fort Chipewyan. In November 2009, the charge against O'Connor of "causing undue alarm" was dropped.

What do YOU think?

1. Whose interests was Health Canada best serving?
2. What effect might the O'Connor case have on other doctors who had made similar discoveries?

As Marie-Monique Robin reports, the jury's decision was unequivocally condemning:

The legal grounds for the verdict were "negligence, wantonness, fraud, trespass, nuisance, and outrage," and it included a harsh judgment of Monsanto's conduct, which was "so outrageous in character and extreme in degree as to go beyond all possible bounds of decency, so as to be regarded as atrocious and utterly intolerable in civilized society. (Robin 2010: 27)

How could a company conduct business in this way? Is it arrogance, cynicism, or plain greed? We believe that the answer runs deeper. A sociologist might look at the **organizational culture** of such a huge corporate entity, whereby the company and the work it does become a part of the individual identity of the employees working there. We might even draw on Durkheim's study of religions, drawing on his notion of a **moral community**, where individuals have shared mutual identities and a commitment to a common purpose. It's a situation that fosters group loyalty—the kind that is strengthened when the group with which you identify is threatened by outsiders. In war your first loyalty is to with those beside you in the trenches. But the situation can also be viewed as a reflection of prevailing class and "race" relations, where the majority of those in positions of power—the scientists and administrators who directed company policy—were white, while the non-corporate members, the "other," were predominantly black and without power, and therefore more disposable.

Vernon Powell and his wife received about US$20,000 between them from the settlement of the lawsuit against Monsanto. He still owes thousands in medical bills (remember, this is the US—no publicly funded healthcare system), and his stomach bears the scars of surgeries he says were necessary because of PCBs. Looking at the community of Anniston, why do you think that Monsanto thought it was "safe" to pollute there?

The Environment and "Race"

Pollution is racialized. The waters off of poor coastal countries in Africa are often used to dump toxic waste by ships whose deadly cargo originates among developed nations. Thetford Mines, as we saw earlier, ships most of its asbestos to developing nations, where the lethal health risks of the substance are not as widely understood. The City of Halifax, before demolishing the Africville neighbourhood in the mid-1960s, located several major polluters and a dump site right beside the black community. And oil companies observe different environmental guidelines in Africa than they do in Europe and North America. Oil companies frequently do business with dictatorships that can readily oppress Africans who resist Western pollution. The story of Ken Saro-Wiwa is instructive in this regard.

Ken Saro-Wiwa: Resisting Pollution

It has been more than 15 years since Ken Saro-Wiwa was hanged in Nigeria. He was a journalist, a publisher, the writer/producer of a popular Nigerian sitcom, and a successful entrepreneur. More than anything else, however, he was a man of his people, the Ogoni, for whom he was killed.

His story exemplifies the greatest ills of European colonialism in Nigeria specifically and Africa in general. Nigeria was artificially created in the twentieth century, when the British brought together into one massive country three large and very distinct peoples: the Muslim Hausa-Fulani in the north; the Yoruba, rooted in great kingdoms past, in the west; and the Igbo, who tried to separate as Biafra, in the east. Imagine forcing together under the roof of one nation Germany, France, and England. With a population of close to 160 million, Nigeria is the largest country in Africa.

Numbering about 500,000, the Ogoni are a minority people of the once biologically diverse and still oil-rich Niger Delta. Since Nigeria became independent their territory has been dominated by the Igbo. After oil was discovered on the delta, the Ogoni territory was worked by the multinational oil producer Royal Dutch Shell. We could say that Shell's environmental practices in various countries are as different as black

QUICK HITS

Eight Questions About the Environment of the Workplace

At the end of his chapter on the dangers of working with asbestos, Lloyd Tataryn poses 10 questions applicable to all potentially unsafe workplace and living environments (Tataryn 1979: 58–60). We have cut the list down to eight and adapted the questions for our purposes here.

1. Is it important to prevent panic among people exposed or even possibly exposed to a health hazard? (Think of the "undue alarm" charge against Dr John O'Connor.)
2. How do you balance an employer's obligation to provide a safe working environment with a worker's willingness to accept certain risks (and "danger pay") for reasonably well-paying jobs?
3. Whose primary responsibility is it to oversee working conditions to ensure their safety? Does responsibility rest with the company, the industry, government protection agencies at the municipal, provincial, and/or federal level, the union, or an outside watchdog group? How might such groups work together?
4. What responsibility does the industry have regarding the health of those who do not work for the company but who live and work nearby?
5. As a city or town, how do you balance the benefits of hosting a large company that employs local citizens and pays salaries that are spent in the community with the need to guarantee safe working and living conditions by ensuring the company is environmentally responsible?
6. Economic risk is often presented as a reason that owners and executives receive much higher pay than ordinary workers. Should health risk be part of that equation?
7. Should decisions about what constitutes an "acceptable" level of health risk require the approval of those placed in situations of greatest risk?
8. How can it be guaranteed that industry-hired "experts" are objective and trustworthy in compiling and presenting their observations on a particular company's environmental practices?

and white: where the population is black, so is the soil; where the population is white, so is Shell's environmental reputation. Their work on the Niger Delta was characterized by gas flaring, oil spills, and irresponsible dumping of wastewater, which greatly affected the traditional way of life of the Ogoni, who depend on agriculture and fishing.

Oppressed under a succession of military dictatorships that were friendly to the oil companies, the Ogoni had no voice, no ability to express their concerns, until Ken Saro-Wiwa created one. In October 1990, he helped launch the Movement for the Survival of the Ogoni People (MOSOP), and shortly afterwards he composed the Ogoni Bill of Rights. Inspired by what he had read of Gandhi's non-violent protests, he led the Ogoni in peaceful protest to halt oil exploration and production on their land until something was done to improve the deteriorating living conditions of his people. Shell had soldiers brought in to protect their interests from "hostile villagers," with predictable results. Saro-Wiwa took his people's struggles to the United Nations and caught the fickle attention of the world's press. Shell armed itself with high-priced

public relations firms, which, unable to attack his ideas, resorted to character assassination. Saro-Wiwa, along with eight other MOSOP members, was charged with inciting the mob killing of four conservative Ogoni chiefs; he was arrested, jailed for over a year, and found guilty and sentenced to death in a hasty trial. Shell had an opportunity to save Saro-Wiwa from execution. Strategically, however the biggest oil company operating in Nigeria and in the world stated that they would not interfere with the politics of a host country. Ken Saro-Wiwa was hanged on 10 November 1995.

The poverty rate in Nigeria is growing, with almost 100 million of the country's population of 160 million living on less than a dollar a day (Brock & Cocks 2012). Western oil workers, including Canadians, continue to reap economic benefits from the oppression of the Ogoni and other Nigerians. Shell promotes itself as a good corporate citizen, with website testimonials about its positive environmental practices and cooperation with communities affected by their work. In 2009, the company agreed to an out-of-court settlement of US$15 million to end lawsuits brought against it for alleged human rights violations. They denied any wrongdoing, calling the settlement a "humanitarian gesture" while suggesting that part of the sum be put into an educational trust fund for the Ogoni (Mouwad 2009).

The Environment and Gender

Ecofeminism is a social, political, and spiritual movement that aims to bring about a post-industrial culture. The term was coined in 1974 by French writer **Françoise d'Eaubonne** (1920–2005) to refer to the linking of environmental concerns with feminism. Ecofeminists argue that there is a strong parallel between the subordination of women and the degradation of nature through male domination and control. Ecofeminists also explore the intersections between sexism, the domination of nature, racism, animal rights, and other forms of social inequality. Contemporary ecofeminists argue that the capitalist and patriarchal systems that predominate throughout the world create a triple domination of women, nature, and the developing world.

Ecofeminism argues that the connection between women and nature is based on their shared history of oppression in patriarchal societies. Culturally, there is a common symbolism in the idea of "man" being pitted against nature, wherein nature is feminized and women are assumed to have a profound affinity with the natural world. There are linguistic links between the oppression of women and the oppression of land in such phrases as "raping the land" and "claiming virgin territory." Many ecofeminists argue that the European witch hunts of the seventeenth century represented a patriarchal triumph of "male knowledge" over the nature-based wisdom of female herbalists and midwives. Physicist and environmental activist Vandana Shiva (1988) argues that, globally, women have a special connection to the environment through the simple actions of their daily lives, like making and washing clothes, and buying or growing foods.

Members of Nigeria's Ogoni community rally outside the courthouse in New York in advance of the trial of Royal Dutch Shell, charged with complicity in the death of Ken Saro-Wiwa and human rights abuses in Nigeria. Do you think the eventual settlement was really a humanitarian gesture?

Irene Diamond and Gloria Orenstein (1990) identify three strands in ecofeminism. One strand emphasizes that social justice has to be achieved in concert with the well-being of the environment, since all human life is dependent on the earth. Another emphasizes the need to maintain a balance between using the earth as a resource and respecting the earth's needs. The third strand is spiritual and emphasizes the idea that the planet is sacred unto itself. The desire to recover female "pagan" wisdom, typically identified with pre-Christian Europe, as a means of liberating women and nature from patriarchal destruction was the basis for a spiritual revival. Central to this revival is the belief that spirituality is the life force in everything, connecting women to each other, to other life forms, and to the elements. Thinkers in this school of thought have drawn from Hinduism, Buddhism, and Christianity to develop their ideas.

Janet Biehl (1991) criticized this relatively early form of ecofeminism as focusing too much on the idea of a mystical connection with nature and not enough on the actual social and material conditions of women. Her thinking, which reflects the approach of more recent feminists, is typical of the social ecology school of thought. Biehl in fact worked with Murray Bookchin, whose explanation of social ecology was presented earlier in the chapter.

The Environment and Class

As we have seen already in this chapter, there is a fairly clear relationship between class and the environment. People from the lower classes are more likely than those of the upper classes to live and work in conditions characterized by high levels of pollution or environmental hazards. People from the higher socioeconomic classes can also better afford to eat foods that are healthier and less affected by pollution. The following sections provide two more illustrations of the way that environmental issues intersect with class.

Women carry placards at a rally for the Sierra Club, an American environmental organization. Why do you think there is a natural affinity between feminism and environmentalism?

Our Stories

The Canadian Case of Grassy Narrows

In *A Poison Stronger Than Love: The Destruction of an Ojibwa Community* (1985), Anastasia Shkilnyk presents an often cited case study of how pollution is racialized. But while it is a sympathetic study of the plight of the Anishinabe, or Ojibwa, people of Grassy Narrows in northwest Ontario, it is flawed in being entrenched in **victimology** by portraying the people only as hapless victims of an industrial attack on the environment, rather than as agents and leaders in the fight against such an attack. For this reason, the incident and Shkilnyk's role in reporting on it are worth studying as an example both of how environmental issues intersect with "race" and of how knowledge is produced.

In the mid-twentieth century, fishing was vitally important to the community of Grassy Narrows, both as a source of food and as a source of income (largely through tourism). Between 1962 and 1970, the Reed Paper Company, a British-owned multinational, began dumping huge amounts of mercury—about 20,000 pounds—into the English–Wabigoon river system, about 170 kilometres upstream from Grassy Narrows. In 1970, significantly high amounts of the deadly element were detected in the area's fish. Two years later came the first human casualty, a 42-year-old fishing guide.

The people of Grassy Narrows knew that mercury was making fish and the people who depended on them sick, but the provincial government, with significant financial interests at stake, downplayed the problem. The pulp and paper industry, which was the source of the mercury pollution, was a major employer in northwestern Ontario—so much so, in fact, that the government was supporting Reed Paper with tax rebates. Local tourism, another important industry, stood to suffer if concerns about mercury contamination of the river system became public. There, again, the Ontario government was a stakeholder, having invested large sums in Minaki Lodge, just 45 kilometres west of Grassy Narrows. In 1977 it was revealed that the government had spent about $7.5 million in its acquisition and renovation of the lodge.

The people of Grassy Narrows, led by Chief Andy Keewatin, were not afraid to pursue their case against the company and the government's negligence. In 1975, they contacted the people of Minimata, Japan, a fishing community whose name is now synonymous with the motor and nervous disorder resulting from mercury poisoning (Minimata disease). They paid to have experts from Japan come to assess their situation, and armed with evidence of the river's contamination, they took their fight to the courts. In December of that year, the chiefs and councillors of Grassy Narrows, along with those of neighbouring Whitedog, threatened

Walkerton and the Social Politics of Water

In May 2000, the town of Walkerton, Ontario, was hit by an epidemic of the bacterium *Escherichia coli*, commonly known as E. coli, that came from their main water supply. In total, an estimated 2,300 people were affected by the outbreak; just over half of them were residents of the town itself, meaning that roughly one-quarter of Walkerton's population became ill. Seven people died as a consequence of the infection.

The tragedy raised questions about whom to trust when it comes to the social management of pollution. The province's Conservative government had been pursuing a policy of privatizing public-sector government departments, including the one responsible for inspecting the water supply. As a result of granting contracts for testing the water to private companies, the province had drastically reduced its funding to the Ministry of the Environment. Journalist Colin Perkel, in his thorough investigation into the Walkerton tragedy, cites this as evidence of a lack of social responsibility, to deliver poisoned fish to the homes of Ontario's premier, the ministers of natural resources and of health, the attorney general, the leaders of the opposition parties, and the president of Reed. In a letter sent to these individuals, the representatives of Grassy Narrows clearly articulated their determination not to be victims:

> We know that the fish are poisonous. We know that eating the fish can destroy the mind and health and take the life of Indians and whites. This cannot fail to be known by anybody who, for five long years, has watched the growing violence, the deteriorating health, and the declining morale of our people. . . .
>
> For five years, we have fought the bias, indifference and hostility of your minister of natural resources.
>
> It is long enough. Enough have died. Enough people have died. Enough of our people have been destroyed. Enough lack of understanding. Enough pro-polluter bias. Enough indifference. (cited in Hutchison & Wallace 1977:140)

In 1976, Anastasia Shkilnyk was hired by the Department of Indian Affairs and Northern Development (DIAND) to study the community of Grassy Narrows, which she did over the next two years, returning for follow-up research in 1981 and 1983. She had a genuine interest in helping the people, and her work produced some valuable insights. However, she failed to question seriously the destructive role of the multinational company then fighting the community in the courts and the weak response and motives of both the federal government (her employer) and the provincial government. Further, she failed to accurately represent the active role taken by the people in their effort to resolve the crisis. In her work, the people neither understand their situation nor mount any resistance to the large corporate and governmental players. They are merely victims. There is little Aboriginal voice in this book, making it a prime example of one-sided knowledge production.

Sociology textbooks addressing the circumstances of Grassy Narrows typically give equal weight to two other factors, abuse and alcoholism. They do not mention that the people eventually were able to win $8.7 million in an out-of-court settlement from Reed Pulp and Paper in 1985. They do not talk about the community's fight since 1993 against the environmental impact of the logging practices of Abitibi Consolidated Corporations. They are locked into a time zone of perpetual environmental victimhood.

both on the part of the government and on the part of the American firm, A & L Canada Laboratories East, that filled the government-created vacuum:

> Although A & L Canada Laboratories East, a US-based franchise operation, had never tested for bacteria and was not accredited to do so, it nevertheless accepted water samples from Walkerton. In the absence of updated guidelines or regulations the provincial government felt no need to implement, A & L followed private industry practice in deeming test results to be confidential, to be shared only with the client [i.e. the town workers responsible for monitoring the pollution levels of the water]. (Perkel 2002: 35)

One social product of having a private company do this work is a breakdown in the chain of communication and responsibility between the town and Ministry of the Environment.

When the story hit the news, the media followed two main storylines. One focused on the personal incompetence and lack of responsibility shown by the Walkerton employee who was primarily responsible for monitoring the water and notifying the Ministry of the Environment of any problems. We can call this the **rotten apple approach**, which aims to argue that the fault lies not with the system but with the individuals who make it up. This non-sociological line of inquiry, which is typical of tabloid-style reporting, dominated certain parts of the media coverage. A bumbling rural official is an easy target for big-city reporters.

Sociologists tend to believe that there are no rotten apples, just a bad orchard—the social system surrounding the situation. The second main storyline, exhibited in the work of journalists such as Perkel, took this view, arguing that the E. coli epidemic was an inevitable result of the Ministry of the Environment's loss of influence over water testing. The less oversight shown by a large and authoritative social body, the greater the chance that something important will go unnoticed—with tragic consequences, in the case of Walkerton.

What do YOU think?

What are the arguments that governments use to justify outsourcing public-sector responsibilities like water testing to private firms? What are the risks? Can they be overcome?

The China Price: The True Cost of Chinese Competitive Advantage

Does it seem like everything you buy is "Made in China"?

The phenomenon is happening not just in Canada but in the United States and in the rest of the world. In 2007, China exported US\$1,218 billion worth of goods, making it the third-largest exporter in the world, not far behind the United States and Germany (Harney 2009: 4). The US alone imported slightly more than one-third of those exports, valued at \$321.5 billion (with at least \$18 billion in merchandise imported by retail giant Walmart), while they exported only \$65.2 billion in goods to China, resulting in a trade deficit of over \$250 billion for the Americans (Harney 2009: 5).

Canada is in a similar situation, albeit on a much smaller scale. In 2006, Canadians imported \$34.5 billion worth of goods from China, with consumer electronics and industrial machines (reactors, boilers, and so on) each representing roughly 20 per cent of the imports (www.statcan.gc.ca/pub65-508-x/2007001/tf/4129847-eng.htm). Only \$7.7 billion worth of Canadian exports went the other way to China, with the top four trade items being wood pulp, organic chemicals, nickel articles, and metal ores (www.statcan.gc.ca/pub65-508-x/2007001/tf/4129845-eng.htm). As a result, there was in 2006 a China–Canada trade imbalance of some \$26.8 billion.

So why is China becoming the "workshop of the world"? Much of it has to do with what is often called the **China price**. China has a huge competitive advantage in the manufacture and assembly of just about any kind of goods, as it is incredibly cheap to have work done in China. This cheapness comes as the expense of exploited Chinese workers and the environment. Alexandra Harney (another journalist who appears to have a good background in sociology) used the concept of the China price and turned it around to consider it as the price that China is paying for its manufacturing success—a price too dear, as Harney showed.

The mechanism has been called the "survival of the cheapest" (Harney 2009: 40). It has been estimated that the average wage for Chinese manufacturing workers in 2002 was 57 cents an hour. There are literally millions of migrant workers competing for these jobs. Tens of millions of them are from farming areas that have made their former villagers **environmental refugees** and the villages themselves "cancer villages" or "widow towns." The few health benefits that workers can draw on are controlled by the household register, or *hukou*, who typically favour those from cities over those from villages.

The importance of health benefits to Chinese workers cannot be overestimated, since the workplace in China is a major source of pollution. Work-related lung diseases such as silicosis (producing scar tissue in the lungs, and often leading to tuberculosis) claim as many as 1 million new cases every year (Hanrey 2009: 57), many of them found in industries relating to jewellery manufacture. Perhaps the greatest environmental villain is coal, used to provide power to the ever-growing number of Chinese industries (not to mention supplying fuel for heat and cooking in people's homes). China is the world's largest producer and consumer of coal, and because of that it emits more carbon dioxide and sulphur dioxide than any other country (Harney 2009: 89). Corrosive acid rain soaks the ground in nearly all parts of the country.

The last decade seems to have brought a proliferation of dollar stores to large urban centres. What do you think is the environmental impact of so many cheaply made, cheaply bought goods?

It is not just the burning of coal but its extraction that makes it an environmental hazard. In 2006, 4,746 people were killed in Chinese coal mines, according to official statistics (Harney 2009: 90). However, since much of the coal is produced in relatively small, private, often "illegal" mines, the actual number is probably higher. Think of how in 2010 a handful of Chilean miners who escaped death drew media attention and public support from around the world, yet we in the West hear little of the daily deaths occurring in Chinese mines. This is the case in part because of China's famously tightly controlled state news media, acutely aware that Western businesses with interests in the country, as well as their customers, might not want to know this aspect of the China price. Owning a coal mine is a lucrative enterprise in China, making it one of the best sources of millionaires in the country. While China still retains some of the political mechanisms of its earlier communist period, it is now very much a free-wheeling capitalist economy, with the free hand of the market wielding more power in some ways that in most countries of the West.

Shanxi province is the largest coal-producing area in China. Four of the world's 20 most polluted cities are in this province, including its capital, Taiyuan, which in 1998 was the city with the most polluted air in the world. A 2002 survey reported that 64 per cent of children tested in the city had what could be called "excessively high levels of lead" in the blood of their young veins. After a much publicized attempt by municipal officials to clean up the city's image, the title of city with the most polluted air was taken over by nearby Linfen.

Officially, China takes strong measures to control the pollution, and as the country demonstrated during the 2008 Summer Olympics in Beijing, it does not lack the resources to improve its air quality when it is sufficiently motivated to do so. Too often, though, this is not the case, as there are huge financial benefits tied to the lack of effective supervision, both in terms of corporate profits and in personal gain for environmental regulators who take bribes to look the other way. It is easy to blame the Chinese government, but the truth is that Western companies that invest in profitable Chinese businesses regardless of their environmental record make it easy to justify lax oversight of environmental policies. Harney interviewed two women whose husbands (Feng Xingzhong and Deng Wenping) were victims of silicosis. When she asked them why it was that Chinese factories killed young, strong men they answered:

"Isn't it because you Americans have brought all your bad factories to China?" Feng's wife asks me.

"I heard it's because China has so much corruption, and it needs the money so it wants foreign investment," Tang [Deng's widow] offers." (Harney 2009: 86)

What do YOU think?

1. How well does the brief exchange of the two Chinese widows capture the issues involved in China's poor record of meeting reasonable standards on environmental protection?

2. In terms of the environment, what is the China price?

3. Are there environmental refugees in Canada?

WRAP IT UP

Summary

It is easy to find discouraging evidence concerning the state of the environment, but in this chapter we have tried to find some hope to balance any feelings of despair you might be feeling. Human action is the main cause of environmental degradation, but human action can play the most important role in reversing the process. Natural disasters typically bring about uneven results to different social groups, but they can, in theory, provide opportunities for development that will benefit different social groups equally.

It would take an entire book to provide a comprehensive account of the environmental issues of concern to sociologists today. "The environment" is a hot-button topic, with daily news items about the food we eat and where it comes from, about global warming and climate change, about environmental disasters and cleanup, all backed by the latest research and statistics. What we hope we have provided you with here are some sociological tools with which you can assess the issues surrounding the interaction between groups in society and the fate of the environment. These tools include the concepts of social ecology, vested interests, the tobacco strategy, and, as well, the example of people like Ken Saro-Wiwa, demonstrating what individuals can do in the fight against socially powerful opponents.

THINK BACK

Questions for Critical Review

1. Discuss how pollution is a lot like poverty in terms of operational definitions.

2. What is wrong with the "rotten apple approach" to dealing with issues of pollution? Why does it not make for good sociology?

3. What is the tobacco strategy, and how does it affect social policy concerning the environment?

4. Why do you think that major polluting companies work so hard to deny the environmental impact of their products?

5. What is meant by the claim that there is no such thing as a (purely) natural disaster?

READ ON

ONLINE

Stanford Research into the Impact of Tobacco Advertising (SRITA)

http://tobacco.stanford.edu/tobacco_main/index.php

This interdisciplinary research project draws contributions from Stanford faculty and students in the departments of medicine, history, and anthropology, all looking at the effects of advertising. If you've grown up in the age where tobacco advertising is absent from Canadian magazines and television, you'll likely be astonished by this site's gallery of print and TV ads—particularly those featuring doctor endorsements and those unabashedly targeting teens.

Environmental Sociology Research Cluster

www.csa-scs.ca/files/webapps/csapress/environment/

The Canadian Sociological Association's environmental sociology website aims to provide information on research, events, and news to a varied audience that includes "academics, students, the media, policymakers, and non-governmental organizations."

"Theoretical Trends in Environmental Sociology: Implications for Resource Management in the Modern World" (Steven Picou)

www.boem.gov [type "Picou" in the search pane]

Steven Picou's article, found on the website of the Bureau of Ocean Energy Management, provides a close look at theories developing in environmental sociology, and how they relate to some practical applications.

IN PRINT

Murray Bookchin (1996), *The Philosophy of Social Ecology Essays on Dialectical Naturalism* **(Montreal: Black Rose Books).**

This work contains the essential ideas of Bookchin's social ecology.

Andrew Nikiforuk (2009), *Tar Sands: Dirty Oil and the Future of a Continent* **(Vancouver: Greystone Books).**

A prominent Canadian journalist tells a rarely heard story about the devastating social and environmental effects of the Alberta tar sands.

Ike Okonta & Oronto Douglas (2001), *Where Vultures Feast: Shell, Human Rights and Oil* **(San Francisco: Sierra Club Books).**

Written by Nigerian authors, this book tells the story of Royal Dutch Shell's involvement in environmental and socioeconomic disasters that have taken place in the African country.

Naomi Oreskes & Erik M. Conway (2010), *Merchants of Doubt: How a Handful of Scientists Obscured the Truth on Issues from Tobacco Smoke to Global Warming* **(New York: Bloomsbury Press).**

This book outlines how a few politically well-connected scientists assist polluting companies in resisting environmental policies.

Colin N. Perkel (2002), *Well of Lies: The Walkerton Water Tragedy* **(Toronto: McClelland & Stewart).**

This book describes in great detail how the Walkerton tragedy was allowed to occur, and how the drama played out.

Lloyd Tataryn (1979), *Dying for a Living* **(Ottawa: Deneau and Greenberg).**

Despite its age, this is still an important work detailing the social situation surrounding the lethal effects of asbestos on people who work in the industry.

22 Social Change and the Future

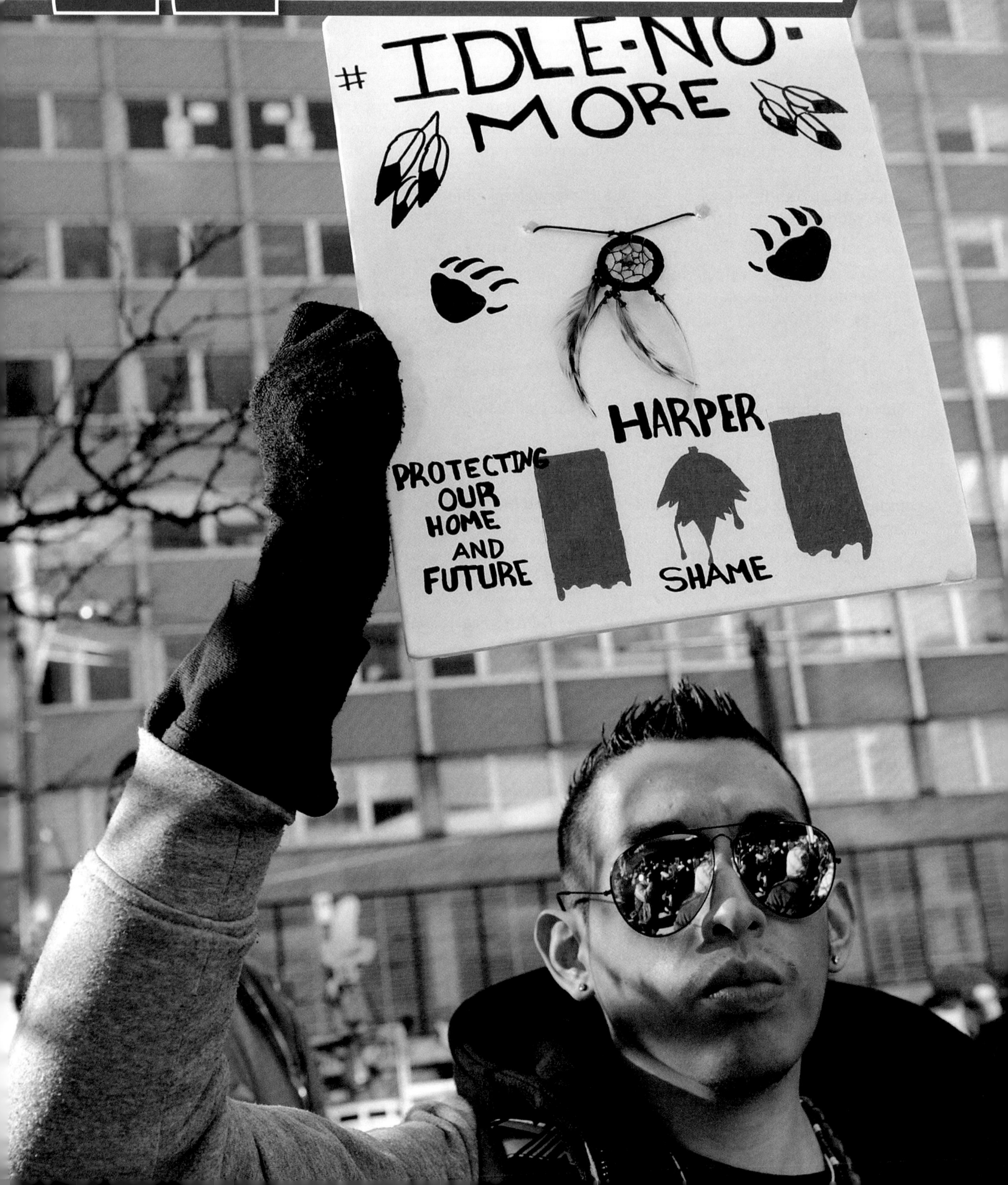

Learning Objectives

After reading this chapter, you should be able to

- outline and contrast five different models of social change

- apply the cycle of civilization to the United States and comment on its applicability

- summarize the social changes to which the Luddites were

- reacting and draw connections to contemporary society

- outline Arthur Kroker's idea of the virtual class and discuss its relevance today.

Key Terms

- barbarism
- civilization
- conservatism
- cycle of civilization
- democracy
- digital divide
- evolution
- fashion
- Luddites

- manufacturing of need
- modernism
- narrow vision
- neoliberalism
- oligarchy
- polyarchy
- postmodernism
- reference group

- relative deprivation
- savagery
- slippery slope
- social change
- social Darwinism
- survival of the fittest
- virtual class

Names to Know

- August Comte
- Robert A. Dahl

- George Grant
- Arthur Kroker

- Lewis Henry Morgan
- Herbert Spencer

Raging against the Machine

The following words were used in 1802 by an English cropper (an independent producer of woollen cloth) to describe the desperate straits of people in his position, and what he wanted to do to the machines that were, in part, the cause of their difficulty:

> The burning of Factorys or setting fire to the property of People we know is not right but Starvation forces Nature to do that which he would not, nor would it reach his Thoughts had he sufficient Employ. We have tried every Effort to live by Pawning our Cloaths and Chattles so we are now on the brink for the last struggle. (as cited in Sale 1996: 71)

People sharing this view would later be known as Luddites, a term that has become synonymous with an opposition to industrialization or technology. But the Luddites weren't really raging against technology as much as they were raging against the social and political machinery of their time—the "system," in other words. To use an expression we will return to later, they knew that technology was not *socially neutral*, that it produces winners and losers.

In this sense, the Luddites have much in common with those fighting to change the system today, from those who have taken part in the Quebec student protests since 2012 or the worldwide Occupy protests that began a year earlier, to the millions engaged in ongoing Arab Spring demonstrations across the Middle East. These are the people bringing about social change in our time—maybe you're one of them.

Introduction: Why Predicting the Future Is a Fool's Game

So what do we mean by **social change**? We mean that a group of people has experienced dramatic change in one part of their lives, and must make adjustments in other areas of their lives in order to adapt. The central fact about society today is that it is changing. Things are not what they used to be, even just a few years ago. Think just of personal technology change: we only have to look back a few years to remember a time before smartphones and tablets, e-readers and Bluetooth headsets—and any of a number of items that first seemed gimmicky and are now indispensable. Some of us can even remember life before touching a computer keyboard.

Throughout much of this textbook we've reviewed trends and events that triggered, exemplified, or proceeded from social change. We've tried to show that these trends and events are subject to different and often equally valid interpretations by groups examining them from different standpoints, depending on such factors as gender, ethnicity, class, and so on. In other words, examining social change in the past is no straightforward exercise. Imagine, then, the difficulty of predicting social change in the future!

Ultimately, we concede, it's a fool's game. In 1987, no one could have predicted that the divorce rate would peak that year, and then decline over the next 25 years. (For that matter, 18 years ago, I could not have predicted that I would get married for a third time—and have that marriage last.) At the start of the twenty-first century, no "futurist" (a consultant who studies trends and gets paid a lot of money to present predictions that generally don't come true) predicted that within 10 years there would be a black president of the United States, that General Motors would crash, that the Canadian and American governments would bail out and impose tight conditions on the automotive industry (once thought to be the ultimate capitalist industry), and that Ontario would become one of Canada's "have-not" provinces. Of course, no one on New Year's Day 2001 could have foreseen the extraordinary set of social changes that would be set in motion by the events of that now infamous date just eight months and eleven days later.

Another cautionary note concerning any discussion of social change: it is important to recognize that as rapid as change is today, it would be wrong to say that earlier society was primarily static, sitting still. Think, for instance, of the Austronesian-speaking people, perhaps as far back as 2,000 years ago, who travelled from mainland Southeast Asia to the far-flung islands of Taiwan, Malaysia, Indonesia, Hawaii, Easter Island, New Zealand, and even Madagascar, hundreds of years before the era of modern travel—all in relatively small outrigger canoes. Think, too, of fourteenth-century China, Africa, and Europe, whose populations, recovering from the devastating effects of the Black Plague, saw their cultures change on a large scale. In Europe, surviving labourers of the plague-ravished workforce were able to charge more for their work. Dramatic social change, certainly a defining feature of our present age, is nevertheless not unique to it.

Five Interpretations of Social Change

Any one instance of social change may be interpreted in a number of different ways. No single model of interpretation is the "right" one all the time. The five we are considering here have varying degrees of applicability to different situations. They are:

1. modernism
2. conservatism
3. postmodernism
4. evolution
5. fashion.

As we present each one, we will point out situations where it is and is not likely to apply. First, though, we offer a disclaimer concerning sociological models based on analogy. It comes from American sociologist Robert A. Nisbet, in *Social Change and History: Aspects of the Western Theory of Development*:

> No one has ever seen a civilization die, and it is unimaginable, short of cosmic disaster or thermonuclear holocaust, that anyone ever will. Nor has anyone ever seen a civilization—or culture or institution—in literal process of decay and degeneration, though there is a rich profusion of these words and their synonyms in Western thought. . . . Nor, finally, has anyone ever seen—actually, empirically seen, as we see these things in the world of plants and animals—growth and development in civilizations and societies and cultures, with all

that is clearly implied by these words: change proceeding gradually, cumulatively, and irreversibly, through a kind of unfolding of internal potentiality, the whole moving toward some end that is presumably contained in the process from the start. We see none of these in culture: death, degeneration, development, birth. (Nisbet 1969: 3)

1. Modernism

Modernism and the discipline of sociology have long been connected. **Modernism** holds that change equals progress, that what is modern or new will automatically be better than the older thing it replaces. It views society as advancing along a straight path from primitive to more sophisticated, from out-of-date to up-to-date, from worse to better. This change is usually portrayed as a single, straight line, one that is not very open to different paths of development.

Seen in its best light, the modernist view is the view of the future long envisioned by Gene Roddenberry, creator of *Star Trek*, and captured in the fictional space

crew's stated mission "to boldly go where no man has gone before." Seen in a more sinister light, modernism reduces progress to a formula that equates "new" with "better" and simultaneously "more expensive." Education technology has co-opted the term "advanced learning" without even having to demonstrate that it is in any way more "advanced" or "better" than traditional methods of instruction. Teachers using older methods are portrayed as educational dinosaurs, even though they may be more effective educators than their pyrotechnically inclined colleagues (known by such nicknames as "Twitter Tutor" and "Blackboard Blogger").

French thinker **August Comte** (1798–1857), often identified as the father of sociology, was a cheerleader for modernism, as we can see in the following:

The true general spirit of social dynamics [i.e. sociology] then consists of each . . . social [state] as the necessary result of the preceding, and the indispensable mover of the following. . . . [T]he present is big [i.e. pregnant] with the future. In this

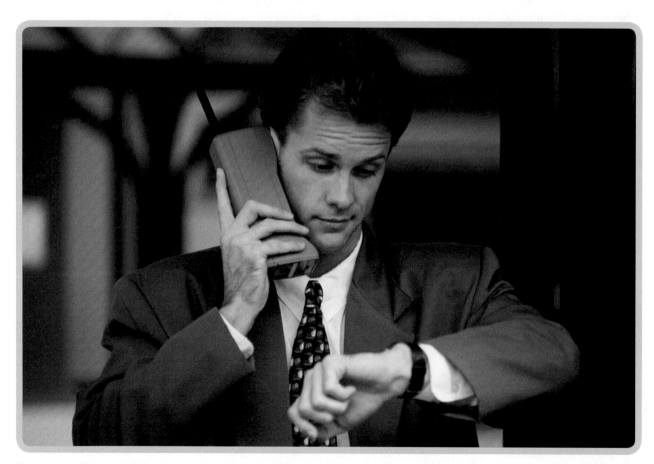

Do you think this businessman looks as cool as he must have thought he did when his mobile phone was the model of convenience and technological sophistication?

view the object of science is to discover the laws which govern that continuity. (Comte 1853)

Positivism, which characterized Comte's view and dominated much of the early history of sociology, is an aspect of modernism. Positivism, as defined in Chapter 3, involves a belief that the rules, methods, and presumed objectivity of the natural sciences can be applied to the social sciences with no accommodation made for the biases, or subjectivity, of the social scientist. This is why Comte, in the passage quoted above, feels it's within the sociologist's abilities to examine the course of social history to find the secrets behind the seemingly "inevitable" progress from one period to the next.

Along with Charles Darwin's theory of evolution came the idea, often referred to as **social Darwinism**, that societies naturally proceed from simple (and inferior) to complex (and superior), and that only the strongest societies triumph. This notion of progress was articulated by **Herbert Spencer** (1820–1903), who coined the expression **survival of the fittest** (later borrowed by Darwin, in a solely biological sense) to refer to societies. The idea that society progresses through distinct stages was developed and put forward by anthropologist **Lewis Henry Morgan** (1818–1881), who identified the three stages of **savagery**, **barbarism**, and **civilization** (Morgan 1964 [1877]: 12). The following passage from his study of human society lays the groundwork for his argument:

> The latest investigations respecting the early condition of the human race are tending to the conclusion that mankind commenced their career at the bottom of the scale and slowly worked their way up from savagery to civilization through the slow accumulations of experimental knowledge.
>
> As it is undeniable that portions of the human family have existed in a state of savagery, other portions in a state of barbarism, and still other portions in a state of civilization, it seems equally so that these three distinct conditions are connected with each other in a natural as well as necessary sequence of progress. . . .
>
> An attempt will be made in the following pages to bring forward additional evidence of the rudeness of the early condition of mankind, of the gradual evolution of their mental and moral powers through experience, and of their protracted struggle with obstacles while winning their way

to civilization. It will be drawn, in part, from the great sequence of inventions and discoveries which stretches along the entire pathway of human progress; but chiefly from domestic institutions, which express the growth of certain ideas and passions. (Morgan 1964 [1877]: 11)

The influence of Morgan's three-tiered view of human development lasted well into the twentieth century. Vestiges of it can be seen in Émile Durkheim's *Elementary Forms of Religious Life* (1912) and in the writings of American sociologist Talcott Parsons, who, in *Societies: Evolutionary and Comparative Perspectives* (1966) divided societies into the supposedly less judgemental but nevertheless still misleading "primitive," "intermediate," and "modern."

Up until the mid-twentieth century, a key aspect of modernism was the belief that science and technology would combine to create a material heaven on earth. Science would become a rational, hard evidence–based religion to supersede the traditional religions built on faith. Technology would free people from having to perform hard physical labour on the job and at home. Thus liberated from drudgery and tedious labour, humans would have abundant leisure time for more worthwhile pursuits. It's easy to smirk at the idealism of the 1950s and early 1960s, but how different is that from the message we hear in TV and radio ads today about how new time-saving technology will keep us more "connected" with the world?

Modernist theories of politics incorporate the idea that societies are constantly improving *politically*. According to this view, societies are becoming more democratic, with respect for human rights on the rise and barriers between societies falling, all of which will help to eradicate the threat of war. Indeed, this was the optimistic premise behind the founding of the United Nations after World War II. A glimpse into that postwar feeling comes from the general introduction to a series of philosophical and religious works that was put together by liberal, religious-minded Oxford scholars during the 1950s:

> Read and pondered with a desire to learn, [these readings] will help men and women to find "fullness of life," and peoples to live together in greater understanding and harmony. Today the earth is beautiful, but men are disillusioned and afraid. But there may come a day, perhaps not a distant day, when there will be a renaissance of man's spirit:

when men will be innocent and happy amid the beauty of the world, or their eyes will be opened to see that egoism and strife are folly, that the universe is fundamentally spiritual, and that men are the sons of God. (The Editors, "Introduction," in Kaizuka 2002: 8)

It is easy for the leaders of developing empires to use modernist principles to justify their decisions on the grounds that their latest achievement represents the culmination of progress and that whatever is in the best interests of their country is in the best interests of humankind. Public intellectual Noam Chomsky has expressed his concern that his country's presidents and policy-makers, and their supporters, have taken this approach, wrapping American policy in the flag of modernism. In *Hegemony or Survival: America's Quest for Global Dominance*, he describes the modernist thinking of the American power elite:

[T]here is a guiding principle that "defines the parameters within which the policy debate occurs," a consensus so broad as to exclude only "tattered remains" on the right and left and "so authoritative as to be virtually immune to challenge." The principle is "*America as historical vanguard*": "History has a discernible direction and destination. Uniquely among all the nations of the world, the United States comprehends and manifests history's purpose." Accordingly, US hegemony is the realization of history's purpose, and what it achieves is for common good, the merest truism, so that empirical evaluation is unnecessary, if not faintly ridiculous. (Chomsky 2004: 42–3)

Chomsky here identifies one of the flaws of the modernist model, namely its **narrow vision**, roughly cast as "Whatever innovation benefits the dominant class is justifiable on the grounds of progress." Today, many are skeptical of modernism. Science and technology have enabled us to create problems of pollution that we need to solve more by how we live than by adding more technology. Commercials for SUVs promise personal freedom, yet if we in North America did not manufacture vehicles with such poor fuel efficiency, if we depended less on automobiles and more on bikes and public transit to commute to work and to school, our demands for oil and the damage to our environment would be less.

Meanwhile, human leisure time is not increasing. People with jobs seem to be working longer hours than in decades past in spite of labour-saving technology. The office is now a virtual space, as advances in telecommunications make it more difficult for people to leave their work at the office. Smartphones enable employers to stay in touch with their staff on weekends. In politics, governments with little respect for democracy, human rights, or peace abound in countries that talk of protecting those ideals.

So where might the modernist view be valid? When asked this question in the classroom, students typically point to medical technology. Certainly diagnostic and life-saving technology has become more sophisticated, and in this sense it validates a modernist view of progress. At the same time, we must accept that reliance on this technology as an alternative to adopting preventative social practices is not a social improvement. The old saying "an ounce of prevention is worth a pound of cure" seems valid.

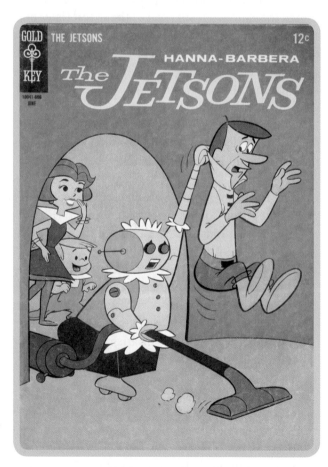

Rosie the Robot gets her hands dirty on the cover of a *Jetsons* comic book from 1963. Do you think the artist expected that by now every home would have its own domestic robot?

2. Conservatism

Conservative thinkers see social change as potentially more destructive than constructive, especially in emotionally charged areas of life such as family, gender roles, sexuality, and the environment.

It would be easy to dismiss conservatism as an "unrealistic" interpretation of social change held by old-timers or religious fanatics romanticizing the past, by red-necked reactionaries gazing down the gun barrel at anyone attempting to interfere with their rights, or by anti-business, tree-hugging nature "freaks." But it would be wrong to do so. Some values and

The Point Is...

The Spread of Democracy

Around the time of the US-led invasion of Iraq in 2003, there was a joke going around that George W. Bush was trying to bring **democracy** to Iraq—and if it worked there, he was going to try to bring it to Florida (the state whose contentious election results decided the outcome of the 2000 presidential election, even as they became the focus of allegations of voter fraud). The joke raises an interesting question: When do we have democracy? A typical definition of democracy involves some notion of government by citizens. Note the Greek root of the word, *demos–*, meaning "the people." But the ancient Greeks, who coined the term, can hardly be said to have had democracy themselves. Women and the large class of slaves were excluded from having a voice.

What are the analytical alternatives to "democracy" when describing a society? In *A Preface to Democratic Theory* (1956), American political scientist and sociologist **Robert A. Dahl** (b. 1915) suggested that modern industrial states were really governed by **polyarchies**, shifting coalitions of powerful interest groups. In *Power Elite*, published that same year, C. Wright Mills disagreed, arguing that the power elite, who ran the big companies and had the most significant say in government, was governing, and

that its governance was relatively stable. In essence, he claimed that there was an **oligarchy**, rule by a few powerful individuals or groups. Kirkpatrick Sale (1980) has argued that democracy cannot exist in a population over 10,000, so that we can only have relative degrees of democracy in state-level societies. While the actual number can be debated, the basic premise seems sound.

customs, such as community and "neighbourliness," need to be preserved. Their loss is neither inevitable nor desirable.

Conservatism as it relates to social change should not be confused with the political principles of right-wing, large-C Conservative parties in Canada, Britain, Australia, and New Zealand. An excellent example of small-c conservatism is found in the nationalist sentiment of **George Grant** (1918–1988), one of Canada's foremost conservative public intellectuals. Grant taught philosophy at McMaster, Dalhousie, and Queen's, and his *Lament for a Nation* (1965) is recognized as a landmark of Canadian writing. His concern, as expressed in *Lament* and in *Technology and Empire* (1969), was that the technology, culture, and sense of progress emanating from the US would lead to the destruction of Canada as a place that cultivated and cherished an alternative to the American vision. A man of deep religious convictions, he inspired Canadian nationalists from the political left to the political right.

We mentioned earlier the modernist belief that science will ultimately replace traditional religion. So far this has not happened, and we cast our bets on the side of its not happening. Humans, it would appear, have spiritual needs, however they might be defined, that science cannot completely address. We see, in the growing strength of conservative religion in the United States and in the battles that proponents of "intelligent design" or "scientific creationism" are mounting against the scientific fact of evolution, that the modernist vision of the new religion of science has not overcome the old religions of faith.

One of the ideas closely associated with conservatism is that of the **cycle of civilization**. This is the belief that civilizations rise and fall in a somewhat predictable cycle. It is an old idea, one that was

The Big Valley Creation Science Museum opened its doors in central Alberta in 2008. Exhibits such as this one claim to provide "considerable evidence that not only did dinosaurs exist recently, but that humans existed with them" (www.bvcsm.com/). How do you account for the recent establishment of galleries like this one and the Creation Museum in Petersburg, Kentucky (where "Children play and dinosaurs roam near Eden's Rivers"—http://creationmuseum.org/), which use "scientific evidence" to support the biblical account of creation? How much do you think it is a rejection of the change to our worldview brought about by science?

articulated, for example, by Greek historian Polybius (*c.* 200–*c.* 118 BCE) in explaining to his fellow Greeks how the Roman Empire came to have dominance over them, while warning the Romans about the potential for their collapse. In his words:

> [T]he destruction of the human race, as tradition tells us, has more than once happened, and as we must believe will often happen again, all arts and crafts perishing at the same time, then in the course of time, when springing from the survivors as from seeds men have again increased in numbers. (Quoted in Nisbet 1969: 34)

Historian Oswald Spengler, in *The Decline of the West* (1918–22), took a similar view when he wrote that civilization was passing "through the age-phases of the individual man. It has its childhood, youth, manhood, and old age" (quoted in Nisbet 1969: 8). Adherents of conservatism are sometimes guilty of the logical fallacy known as **slippery-slope** reasoning. This occurs when they cite one instance of social change—say, for example, gay marriage—as evidence of the imminent collapse of the entire social order (including, to keep with this particular example, polygamy and bestiality). It amounts to an overreaction.

Another pitfall of the conservative position is a tendency to project backwards an idealized picture of social life from which the modern world is said to have fallen. For instance, people who bemoan what they consider the rampant sexual promiscuity occurring today speak in idealized terms of a time when couples would not engage in sex before marriage. They are misinformed. British social historian Peter Laslett wrote about how it was common in the late sixteenth century for couples to contract marriage (like our engagement) and then immediately live together for months, with full sexual benefits. In his conclusion to a discussion of the county of Leicester, Laslett observes that "Brides in Leicestershire at this time must normally have gone to their weddings in the early, and sometimes in the late, stages of pregnancy" (Laslett 1971: 150).

The modernist view of society's continued improvement is countered in popular culture by the popularity of post-apocalyptic dystopias presenting a whole range of future worlds that are much worse than the one we currently inhabit. From vampires, zombies, and aliens to survival tournaments fought to the death, why do you think we take so much pleasure in imagining society's eventual demise?

Sometimes modernism and conservatism combine in theories that view signs of decline as indications that progress is on the horizon. In Marx's thinking, the worse capitalism got, with the shrinking of the bourgeoisie and the growth of the proletariat to include a falling middle class, the more likely capitalism would collapse altogether, leading to the ultimate social change, the communist revolution. With a similar perspective, albeit from a very different position, conservative Americans who believe in fundamentalist Christianity often look upon environmental, economic, political, and social (i.e. moral) decline in their country as a sign that the world is on the verge of the apocalypse. American movies and TV shows often reflect an apocalyptic view. Kirkpatrick Sale

(2005) cites a survey, commissioned by conservative media *Time* and CNN, that indicates 59 per cent of Americans polled believed the apocalypse was just around the corner.

A Case Study in Social Change and Conservatism: The Luddites

From 1811 to 1813, beginning in the English industrializing area of Nottinghamshire and spreading to Yorkshire and Manchester, a group of independent textile workers took desperate measures into their hands by destroying what would today amount to millions of dollars' worth of property. In the words of American writer Kirkpatrick Sale, they were "rebels against the future" (Sale 1996). Part of a larger movement occurring at the time in Britain, France, Germany, and the United States, they made nighttime raids to destroy machinery, sent anonymous threatening letters to known industrialists, stockpiled weapons, and participated in food riots in the marketplace.

They were called **Luddites**, after a mythical, Robin Hood–like figure, Edward (Ned) Ludd, whose precise origin is not known. They were skilled tradesmen—croppers (finishers of wool cloth), wool combers, handloom wool weavers—who in the late eighteenth century worked out of their homes and made good wages. They had leisure time probably similar to that of most Canadians today, and were part of strongly linked small communities.

But the work of the Luddites was becoming obsolete. While in 1812, in Yorkshire, there were about 5,000 croppers, within a generation there were virtually none. New kinds of machinery, owned by the rising class of factory owners, combined with new business practices were changing the working and social world. Even with the earliest generation of machines, one person could do the work of five or six. It is important to note that contrary to the tradition surrounding the old-fashioned machine-hating Luddites, the social practices accompanying the machines were just as much the enemy. A typical workday in the new factories averaged 12 to 14 hours in length, sometimes as many as 16 to 18, and people worked six days a week. Children as young as four and women were hired in preference to men, and these two groups—children and women—made up a great majority of the workforce (80 per cent, according to Sale). And yet they received about a third of a man's wages, and were thought to be less likely than men to resist oppression by the owners.

QUICK HITS

The Impending Collapse of the American Empire?

A good example of modern conservatist thinking appears in Sale's essay "Imperial Entropy: Collapse of the American Empire" (2005). Sale regards the United States as an empire, and therefore subject to what he believes is the inevitable fate of all empires: collapse.

Sale points to four things that could help to bring about the collapse of the American empire, like all empires, in his thinking:

- environmental degradation
- economic meltdown (through excessive resource exploitation)
- military overstretch
- domestic dissent and upheaval.

What do YOU think?

1. Do you think that the United States can be considered an empire akin to earlier Greek, Roman, Mongol, Ottoman, British, and Soviet empires?

2. Do you agree with Sale that the decline or collapse of the United States as an empire is inevitable? Given the country's ongoing economic woes, and the lack of creativity in their movies and television, could it be occurring right now?

Desperate poverty for millions of people was the result. Life expectancy dropped drastically. In the rough statistics for 1830, it was reckoned that 57 per cent of the people of Manchester died before the age of five. While the life expectancy at birth for people throughout England and Wales was 40, for labourers in the textile manufacturing cities of Manchester and Leeds, it was reckoned to be about 18 (Sale 1995: 48).

Working conditions were not the only social change the Luddites were rebelling against. They also opposed the **manufacturing of need**. One of the most profound social changes accompanying the Industrial Revolution and the manufacture of consumer goods was the sudden creation of a need where people had once been mostly self-sufficient. Food and clothing, for instance, now had to be purchased rather than produced at home. The social change this brought about was neatly summed up by nineteenth-century British writer Thomas Carlyle in *The Gospel of Mammonism* (1843): "We have profoundly forgotten everywhere that *Cash-payment* is not the sole relation of human beings" (quoted in Sale 1995: 39). This trend, described by French historian Fernand Braudel as "a revolution in demand," extended from Britain to the colonies—particularly India, where millions of consumers were created by the dumping of manufactured cloth from Britain. It was not until the 1930s and 1940s, when Gandhi and the lesser-known Muslim Pathan Badshah Khan (leader of the non-violent protest movement the Khudai Khidmatgar) intervened, that the people of India began to boycott British cloth and make their own, as had been their tradition.

A remarkable aspect of the Luddite social movement was its solidarity. Despite the rich rewards paid to those who would tell on their neighbours, despite the torture alleged to have been used on those who were caught, there were few informers. In all, 24 Luddites were hanged, and about an equal number died in the raids; a similar number were put in prison, while at least 37 were sent to Australia.

What did they ultimately achieve? There were a few short-term gains for the Luddites. Wages were raised slightly in areas where the Luddites had been the most active. Social reform got on the political agenda, although it would be a long time before significant changes were made. And the "poor laws," which administered what we might today call social welfare, received more attention and greater funding, although charities continued to carry the greater part of the welfare load.

Perhaps the main accomplishment of the Luddites lies in what they can teach us today about social change and what Sale calls the "machine question." We need to realize that machines are not socially neutral, and may be more likely to destroy than to create jobs. The Luddites were not backward-looking "loonies" refusing to face the inevitability of technological "progress." They wanted an alternative future, an alternative modern. That progress can take many forms is perhaps the most important lesson of the Luddite movement.

What do YOU think?

1. Why can it be said that technology is not neutral in terms of social change?

2. Why do you think the Luddites are typically cast as people who destroyed machines simply because they could neither face nor understand "progress"? Is this an accurate view?

3. Do you think that assembly line workers in the automotive industry are in a position like that of the Luddites?

3. Postmodernism

Postmodernism, as a social theory, relates largely to voice. It challenges the notion that, for example, researchers can speak for peoples that they study without letting the people studied have a voice in some way. Postmodernism challenges the notion that anyone can, with any authority, talk of "progress" or "decline" across all society. Instead, a sociologist with a postmodernist perspective on social change might ask, Progress *for which group(s)*? or Decline *for which group(s)*? The same sociologist, hearing conservatives complain about how Canadian values are eroding, might wonder if what they really mean is that *their* ethnic group with *its* set of values is no longer as dominant as it once was.

Think of how modernist media usually present computers and computer-related products and services as bringing about benefits to everyone. But how often do you hear or read the opinions of those, even within Canada, who cannot afford a (decent) computer or the education necessary to make use of one? This is creating a situation that has been called the **digital divide**, a socioeconomic gap separating those who are "haves" from those who are "have-nots" where modern computer technology and reliable Internet

612   Part V | Global Perspectives

access are concerned. One person known for thinking this way is Arthur Kroker.

Arthur Kroker and the Virtual Class

Arthur Kroker, of the University of Victoria's political science department, is a Canadian "futurist" who advanced the notion of the **virtual class** in the mid-1990s as part of his conservativist position. His writing combines Marxist views on class with a lot of postmodernist wordplay (which can make him hard to read). His work is difficult to summarize in an introductory textbook because it depends on a great deal of jargon that would need to be explained in order for any summary to be intelligible. However, we can give you a taste of what Kroker has to say.

The virtual class, according to Kroker, is a class of visionary capitalists or, as he calls them:

> visionless-cynical-business capitalists, and the perhaps visionary, perhaps skill-oriented, perhaps indifferent techno-intelligentsia of cognitive scientists, engineers, computer scientists, video-game developers, and all the other communication specialists, ranged in hierarchies, but all dependent for their economic support on the drive to virtualization. (Kroker & Weinstein 1995: 15–16)

We will briefly outline three ways in which this diverse group acts like a class.

First, says Kroker, this class is responsible for the loss of jobs by those who do not belong to the class. This group supports the goals of a **neoliberalism** that promotes the interests of big business. This is how Kroker accounts for the corporate downsizing that became a widespread cost-saving strategy among North American businesses during the early 1990s:

> Against economic justice, the virtual class practices a mixture of predatory capitalism and gung-ho technical rationalizations for laying waste to social

A public school student in Nicaragua looks at his new laptop, courtesy of a local investment group, the Fundacion Zamora Teran, in partnership with the international non-profit group One Laptop Per Child, which strives to provide affordable educational devices to schoolchildren in the developing world. The program has received some criticism from those who think the funds could be better spent on schools or on children's public health (e.g. providing food, clean water, and public health nurses), as well as from those who think that sending older, recycled computers to developing countries is a more cost-effective (and environmentally friendly) solution. Are these petty complaints about a well-meaning initiative to bridge the digital divide? Or are these students being locked into the "after three years it breaks, and the parts to repair it aren't available" cycle?

concerns for employment, with insistent demands for "restructuring economies," "public policies of labor adjustment," and "deficit cutting," all aimed at maximal profitability. (Kroker & Weinstein 1995: 5)

Another example of the virtual class's move for power has to do with its role in the way the Internet, once democratic and freely accessible, became restricted by the authoritarian "digital superhighway" ever more controlled by what Kroker calls "privileged corporate codes." To use an example close to my own heart, online access to sociological journals is being more and more limited to those who possess expensive memberships and those who are affiliated with universities and not community colleges. Another example: several online newspapers have begun erecting paywalls to charge for content that was once free. *The Globe and Mail*, a source of information for sociology instructors and textbook writers, not to mention students, is one of those that has recently ended the free availability of articles online.

The third defining characteristic of the virtual class is the way this group, according to Kroker, restricts the freedom of creativity, promoting instead "the value of pattern-maintenance (of its own choosing)" (Kroker & Weinstein 1995: 5). Have you ever noticed how computer-generated zombies, ghosts, and aliens all look remarkably alike? How often have you seen black smoke issuing from people possessed by demons? This is an example of "pattern maintenance": the tools of the trade are controlled by a few companies. Compare that with the situation faced by the Luddites.

What do YOU think?

1. How does Kroker portray the virtual class as a class in the Marxist sense?

2. Do you think that Kroker leans a little too far towards conspiracy theory in his worldview?

4. Evolution

Evolution is perhaps the most misused of all scientific concepts. The biological term does not refer to general progress or improvement of a species. What it really means is adapting well to particular circumstances. Darwin's use of Spencer's phrase "survival of the fittest"

is best interpreted as "survival of the *best fit*"—the one best suited to the environment. It was never about the biggest, the meanest, the fastest, and so on.

Jonathan Weiner, in *The Beak of the Finch: A Story of Evolution in Our Time* (1995), provides an example of evolution when he explains that guppies swimming in the rivers of Venezuela come in two basic colour patterns. High in the hills, where the rivers are little more than streams, the guppies are brightly coloured. They compete in terms of sexual selection, with the most colourful having the greatest chance of attracting a mate. The bright colours are the result of the competition. In the waters down in the valleys, the guppies swim where predators feed upon those guppies that are easily seen. Not surprisingly, the guppies there are less brightly coloured. The competition has less to do with attracting a mate, and more to do with not being seen by predators. Neither colour pattern represents an improvement in the species. Each is a better fit in the local environment.

How does this apply to social change? We can look at the history of the family structure in Canada as an example. At different times, the number of children born to parents has varied. In times and places where agriculture is the primary source of income, the number of children is relatively high, since children grow up to be good unpaid help to work the land. During the 1950s and early 1960s, the number of children went up, going against the trend of previous decades, because it was a time of prosperity. People could afford to have more children. Today, with increasing urbanization, Canadian families are less likely to require children as labour; well-paying jobs require more post-secondary education, delaying the point at which young families are in a comfortable position to start having children, and it's generally more expensive to raise children today. Hence, the birth rate has declined. The "ideal" number of children changes with the circumstances—just like the colours of the Venezuelan guppies.

5. Fashion

Sometimes a change is just change solely for its own sake. We seek novelty, and the result is neither an improvement nor a turn for the worse. And it does not reflect some deeper meaning, or a value shift. In this case, we have the **fashion** model of change. Montreal-born, American-raised sociologist Stanley Lieberson argues that the change in North American baby names

QUICK HITS

Most Popular Boys' and Girls' Names, by Decade

	1950s	1960s	1970s	1980s	1990s	2000s	2010s
BOYS							
1.	James	David	Michael	Michael	Michael	Michael	Aiden
2.	Robert	Michael	James	Christopher	Christopher	Jacob	Jacob
3.	John	James	David	Jason	Matthew	Matthew	Jackson
4.	Michael	John	John	David	Joshua	Nicholas	Ethan
5.	David	Robert	Robert	James	Daniel	Christopher	Jayden
GIRLS							
1.	Linda	Mary	Jennifer	Jennifer	Jessica	Hannah	Sophia
2.	Mary	Susan	Lisa	Amanda	Ashley	Emily	Isabella
3.	Patricia	Linda	Kimberly	Jessica	Brittany	Sarah	Olivia
4.	Barbara	Karen	Michelle	Melissa	Amanda	Madison	Emma
5.	Susan	Donna	Amy	Sarah	Samantha	Brianna	Chloe

Note: Data are based on a 1 per cent sample of social security card number applications in the US.

Source: babycenter.com

What do YOU think?

1. Are there factors apart from fashion that could account for the popularity of boys' and girls' names over time? If so, what could these factors tell a sociologist about social change over this time? Do they purely reflect what singers, actors and other celebrities are popular at the time, or is there a sense of "seeking the exotic" (e.g. Irish)?

2. What do you notice when you compare the way that boys' and girls' names have changed since the 1950s? What do these differences suggest about fashion as it relates to baby names?

falls into the category of fashion. Consumer companies likewise profit from this desire for the new, and it's not just clothing companies, either. Tweaking an automotive design, or the "look" of a team uniform can help a company make money on people's desire for the new.

Education involves fashion changes as well. Buzzwords like "whole language," "collaborative learning," and "advanced learning" are used to promote new styles in education, but they merely reflect people's need to feel they have a fresh approach to an ages-old problem. Education fashions come and go, but

real improvement or decline is hard to measure. The culture around education changes and has an impact on the scores that quantify educational "excellence." Declining marks in North American literacy tests may reflect educational changes, but they might also reflect an increase in the number of students whose first language is not English, and a decrease in reading as a leisure activity.

The narrative in the box on page 615 is a look at a social change that separates generations. When you read it, we want you to consider whether this follows a fashion model or has deeper sociological meaning.

Telling It Like It Is

Four-Letter Words and Social Change, or How I Learned to Love the F-Bomb

I don't remember the first time I heard the "f-word" used, but I do recall that in the suburban, middle-class junior high school that I attended in the early 1960s, there was one real tough guy, feared by everyone, who seemed to use it in every sentence he spoke. He was eventually expelled for hitting a teacher.

The first movie I heard the f-word uttered in was the 1970 film *Joe*. It was carefully and deliberately used for shock effect by Peter Boyle's character, a working-class guy who stuns his polite upper-middle-class companions by shouting, "Fucking right!"

The one and only time I heard the word spoken in a university classroom was when a very well-spoken classmate of mine used it (with implied quotation marks around it) after the words *total* and *mind* to describe an incident in which her perception of the situation shifted suddenly and dramatically in a way she did not anticipate. Her male classmates were dumbstruck.

As far as I can remember, the mores, or customs, surrounding the use of the word as I was growing up in my middle-class neighbourhood were these: I could, as a teenage boy, use the word (but not too frequently) with my buddies, but never with my parents or teachers (no matter how tempted I was on occasion to tell them all to f— off). I would not use the word in front of a girl or woman, ever. Generally, use of the f-word in front of a woman was considered a vile offence committed by a man too drunk, too stoned, or too angry to realize what he was doing. Use of the word *by* a woman would normally elicit shock and disgust.

That was a different time. Now, and in the Toronto college where I teach, use of the word seems to depend on social location. It was in the general concourse that I first started hearing the word regularly, between 10 and 15 years ago, and it is where I still hear it used most often. True, it is on the premises of the college, but it isn't really a site of education; it is more of a public place. Recently I've begun to hear the f-word in the halls between classrooms. Five years ago I heard the word spoken for the first time in my classroom. It wasn't spoken in anger, but it was used for effect by someone with a reputation for brash attention-seeking behaviour.

Over the past five years, I've found that the f-word is relatively commonplace in the concourse and still not infrequent in the halls, used with no apparent concern that "the teacher walking past might hear." I have heard it in the classroom in general conversation during breaks, and used about as often by women as by men.

What do YOU think?

1. How have the rules, or mores, surrounding use of the f-word changed, according to this narrative? What changes have you noticed?

2. What would it take for these mores to change back? Could they change back?

3. Could this kind of language use be considered a verbal "fashion statement"?

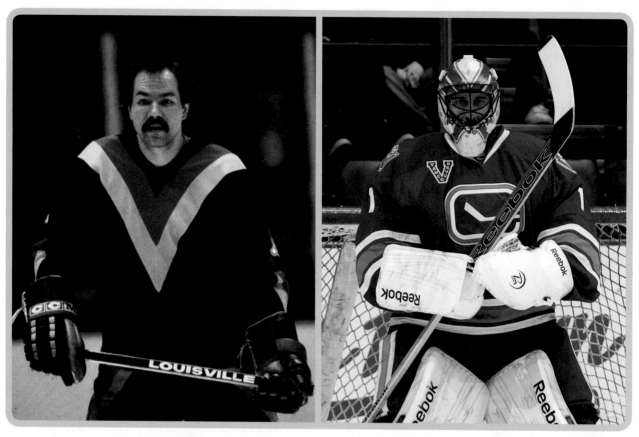

In 1978 the NHL's Vancouver Canucks replaced their conservative blue-and-green sweaters with a new colour scheme meant to look more aggressive and intimidating. The unconventional and widely derided fashion was scrapped in the mid-1980s. After a series of new designs, the team has returned to its "vintage" jersey, sporting the same logo and colour scheme as the sweaters the team wore in its inaugural season (1970–1). Once considered plain and simplistic, the "new look" is popular among fans as well as consumers. How do you think sports merchandisers play to the fan's desire for fashion change?

What do YOU think?

We often hear these days of a video or picture "going viral." What does that mean? Does it have relevance only for the moment, before it is quickly forgotten? Does it have significance in terms of long-term social change? A similar term is "trending," with reference to the prevailing but fleeting patterns in the Twitterverse. Do "trending" issues ever have long-term significance?

Relative Deprivation, Absolute Deprivation, and Movements for Social Change

What we can learn from the Luddites, and from George Grant and Arthur Kroker, is that it would be misleading to regard technology as socially neutral. A change in technology always benefits some, and places others at a disadvantage. Imagine, for example, that you have been running printing presses for a major newspaper for 30 years and have developed an expertise with your machinery that is highly valued and (hopefully) well rewarded. One day your newspaper changes over to computer-run presses, contracting a new company to do that work. Suddenly all of your expertise, knowledge, and seniority mean nothing. Either you are replaced by someone younger who is paid less, or else you accept a lower salary to start over.

Situations like this tend to create in one group—the disadvantaged group—a feeling of **relative deprivation**, a sense of having less or enjoying fewer benefits than another group. Relative deprivation refers to negative feelings experienced when individuals compare themselves with others. They lack something others have, and that lack is meaningful to them, as the ones they are comparing themselves with are significant others seen as equals or betters; they constitute an important **reference group**.

As Marshall (1998: 152) explains, the depth of a person's sense of relative deprivation will always depend on the reference group to which it compares itself. If the reference group is seen as comparatively quite well off, the person experiencing relative deprivation may be moved to protest. This is what happened with the Luddites, who watched the rising class of factory owners thrive under conditions that greatly threatened their own livelihoods.

The concept of relative deprivation is a useful framework for looking at the way people experience poverty. If you are a teenager living in a relatively well-to-do bedroom community on the margins of a big city, it is easy for you to feel poor if your parents' income is less than that of many others in your town. Your reference group includes your peers at high school who have greater access to desired goods (for instance, consumer electronics, or snowboarding gear and associated brand-name clothing). With these peers as your reference group, you may well feel relatively deprived, and therefore "poor." But think of this: others living in a poorer part of town, attending a different high school, might see you as part of a reference group that leaves them feeling their own sense of relative deprivation.

Social Change in China during the 1980s and 1990s

We can apply the theory of relative deprivation to China, which experienced significant social change during the 1980s and 1990s. As Joshua Harman (1998) explains, the country's rapid social change made Chinese workers aware of a new reference group, whose existence sparked feelings of relative deprivation that eventually led to the 1989 Tiananmen Square protests:

Recent high-profile rapes committed against women in India have drawn attention to the startlingly high incidence of sexual violence in that country. It has provoked demonstrations about the way Indian authorities have long been handling sex crimes and alleged offenders. Is this a case of relative deprivation—of rights, rather than material wealth—sparking protest? If so, who makes up the reference group? Why do you think Indian women are now coming to realize that they hold fewer rights before the law than women in other countries do?

In order to understand how and why Chinese workers reached a state of relative deprivation, one must first examine Deng Xiaoping's rise to political preeminence. Deng's rise brought with it the promise of a better material life for the general population as well as the potential for economic discord. Both of these aspects of the reform movement were recognized during the 1980s and the 1990s, and both are primary reasons for the Chinese workers' relative deprivation and political unrest.

Deng's reform coalition used a three-pronged approach to shore up its claim to legitimacy. First, it actively sought to increase the people's awareness of their own relative backwardness. Second, the coalition raised demand for new consumer goods and services. Finally, as it sought to raise consumer demand, it also promised to deliver these goods to the people. (Harman 1998)

Before the 1980s, there were few televisions and few foreign shows available in China. Most programming featured documentaries about the country's supposed economic progress. In 1979, the Chinese government loosened cultural restrictions on programming, and North American and British television programs were suddenly let loose on the Chinese airwaves. By 1991, 12 per cent of total air time and more than 25 per cent of air time for entertainment (rather than news) was taken up by foreign shows. At the same time and at about the same pace, television ownership in China was growing. In 1979, there was 1 television set for every 240 people in the cities, and only 1 per 1,000 in rural areas. By 1988, 1 in every 2.6 city dwellers and 1 in every 15.2 rural citizens owned a TV. A new, foreign reference group had been created, with print media helping to promote this new reference group through increased advertising for Western consumer goods.

As workers' pay increased, there was a dramatic increase in consumer spending on relatively "big ticket" items (see Table 22.1). But the late 1980s brought layoffs and growing job insecurity. The cost of living went up. On 20 April 1989, the Beijing Workers' Autonomous Union declared:

The entire population of China now faces an intolerable situation. Long accustomed to bureaucratic–dictatorial forms of control, they now live with uncontrolled inflation and declining living standards. . . . We earnestly demand the following: a wage increase, price stabilization, and a publication of the incomes and possessions of government officials and their families. (cited in Harman 1998)

In the spring of 1989, crowds of protesters gathered in Tiananmen Square, many of them college and university students and urban workers. The protest ended with a military show of force; it is possible that as many as 2,600 protesters were shot and killed. Despite the clampdown on worker protest, strikes and slowdowns occurred in previously unheard-of numbers throughout the early 1990s. Significant numbers of Chinese citizens now had reference groups that made them feel relatively deprived: their wealthier fellow citizens, themselves in earlier times, and the supposedly typical Westerners they watched on imported TV sitcoms.

Table 22.1 Increase in possession of durable consumer goods among Chinese urban households, 1981–9 (per 100 households)

	1981	1989
refrigerators	0.2	36.5
washing machines	6.3	76.2
electric fans	42.6	128.7
tape recorders	13.0	67.1
cameras	4.3	17.3
bicycles	135.9	184.7
watches	240.9	290.1
sofas	89.3	150.0
wardrobes	86.1	100.0

Source: Based on Harman 1998.

What do YOU think?

The Chinese government restricts the websites its country's users have access to. This effectively limits the exposure of Chinese citizens to other reference groups. What effect do you think this might have on the people of China? Can you compare the situation to that of pre-1980s China, when foreign television programs weren't available?

The Apple Store in Shanghai. Over the past decade, China has thrown its doors open to retailers from Europe and North America. Do you think the presence of Western business has increased or diminished the relative deprivation experienced by the average Chinese citizen?

Weaknesses in the Relative Deprivation Theory

One weakness in the theory of relative deprivation lies in the issue of how to distinguish, in practice, between *absolute* deprivation (however that is established) and *relative* deprivation. Take the earlier example of the suburban teenager. Say the teenager's only computer access is to an outmoded PC with low-speed Internet connections giving slow, intermittent access to the Web. Having an up-to-date computer and reliable Internet access is important, even essential, for achieving success in high school. Achieving good marks in high school might, in turn, determine whether or not she goes to college or university. Who is then to determine whether the teenager merely *feels* poor because the other kids have better computers or genuinely *is* poor because access to goods and services that enhance educational opportunities is part of determining class status in Canada?

Social Change in Canada: Two Case Studies

Canadians have been and are experiencing social change in many forms. In earlier chapters we have looked at how social change is playing out in all aspects of life, from the family and education to health and culture. In the following sections, we examine two striking, and very different, examples of recent social change in Canada.

Social Change and the Decline of the Cod Fishery in Newfoundland and Labrador

One of the most devastating social changes to hit any part of Canada in recent decades is the loss of the cod fishery in Newfoundland and Labrador. Sociologists Lawrence Hamilton and Cynthia Duncan together with biologist Richard Haedrich wrote a fascinating article describing how that change has affected communities along the province's Northern Peninsula (2004).

The most fisheries-dependent part of the province, the Northern Peninsula, was hardest hit by the closure of the cod fishery, which had sustained the region for centuries. The first signs of trouble appeared in the 1970s, when it became apparent that cod stocks were diminishing, owing largely to over-fishing by foreign (mostly Russian and Portuguese) vessels and mismanagement of the resource. When, in 1976, the 200-mile economic exclusion zone was declared, reserving waters within 200 nautical miles of the shore for Canadian fishers, many in the province thought that the troubles were over. People who had left returned, and the fishing population grew.

Sociologically and technologically, there were two different cod fisheries in Newfoundland: the dragger, or long-liner, fishery, and the in-shore fishery. The first made use of larger boats, more technology, and longer trips. Traditionally, both were profitable, and the fishing community overall was very egalitarian. And in the "glory years" following the establishment of the 200-mile line, the dragger fleet increased, as did the catch, which reached unprecedented levels. Dragger captains made huge profits, some as much as $350,000–600,000 a year, and even sharemen (often the teenaged sons of dragger boat owners) could earn $50,000 a year. But the in-shore fishery started to suffer. In the words of one interviewed fisher, "Guys were makin' big bucks and the other guys were just survivin'. Just livin' from day to day, where the other guys were drivin' fancy ski-doos and two vehicles" (quoted in Hamilton, Duncan, & Haedrich 2004). The community was more financially divided than ever before.

Eventually, the cod fishery crashed. In 1992, the federal government declared a two-year moratorium on the fishery from the Labrador coast to the south-eastern tip of Newfoundland, temporarily suspending cod fishing in this part of the province; the following year the closure area was expanded to include the southern shore of the island. Although it was supposed to be in effect for just two years, the moratorium has yet to be lifted.

It was not just fishers and their families who were hit by the moratorium but others along the chain of the fishing industry. At a local fish-processing plant on the Northern Peninsula, 400 workers were laid off. Different adaptations were made by the people in the area. For instance, the birth rate went down, from one of the highest in Canada to just slightly above the national average. Some of the dragger captains were well placed to shift their prey species from fish to invertebrates, such as snow crab, northern shrimp, and the more traditional lobster. Fortunately for them, government money was available to make the transition easier. This new fishery brought revenues comparable to those of the glory days of the cod fishery, but these were distributed across a much smaller segment of the local population. Many, forced out of their livelihood, had to leave the province to look for a new line of work. Young people, especially, travelled west to find work on Alberta's oil fields, and you can see the oil field money in some parts of the province, where earnings made outside of the province have been returned to family members left behind. Others who remained could not afford to become involved in the new fishery, yet refused to move off the island because they didn't feel they could leave their home. The province invested heavily in its own offshore oil industry, but a growing percentage of the local income came from government transfer payments in the form of employment insurance and welfare. The most recent hope, at least for the provincial government, lies with Muskrat Falls, a huge energy project to harvest hydroelectric power in the lower Churchill River in Labrador.

What do YOU think?

What adaptations did the people of Newfoundland and Labrador make with the loss of the cod fishery? What social change did these adaptations bring about?

Religious Change: Islam as a Canadian Religion

According to statistics from 2001 (the last year for which we have data on the subject from Statistics Canada), Islam is Canada's fastest-growing organized religion. From 1991 to 2001, the number of Canadian Muslims rose by 128.9 per cent—more than twice the increase for the period 1981–91. In 2001, Canada's 579,640 Muslims made up 2 per cent of the country's total population. Most of them (352,525) were living in Ontario, where the province's Muslim population had grown by 142.2 per cent over the same 10-year period. Islam was the sixth largest religion in the country, just a little behind the Baptist and Lutheran churches, and way behind the "big three"—the Catholic Church, the United Church, and the Anglican Church. But in contrast to these, Islam was the religion with the youngest median age: its followers averaged just 28.1 years. Muslims come from a broad variety of ethnic backgrounds and countries, including Iran, Iraq, Pakistan, India, Afghanistan, Turkey, Somalia, Bosnia, and Indonesia.

While there isn't what could be called a "Muslim tradition" in Canada, the faith is not entirely new to the country. In 1871, according to that year's census,

What do YOU think?

1. Canada's Muslim population represents a variety of ethnic backgrounds. Do you think this will lead to the development of "Canadianized" multicultural mosques?

2. Canadian introductory sociology textbooks often present Muslims, even those living in Canada, as "them," an "other." What do you think is the effect among non-Muslim Canadians of reading this treatment of Muslim Canadians?

Mombasa is an amateur boxer and PhD candidate. Does she fit your idea of a young Canadian Muslim woman? What do you think it will take for Canada to be considered, at least in part, a "Muslim country"?

there were 13 Muslims living in Canada. The first mosque in Canada—in all of North America, in fact—was Al Rashid, built in Edmonton in 1938, funded by local Muslims, Arab Christians, and Jews.

Social Change and Sociology in Canada

Like all academic disciplines, sociology must change, and it must do so in a way that involves all five of the models of change discussed above. It needs to improve, to get better, in a modernist sense. Perhaps some of this improvement will come in the way sociology is presented to students of the discipline, just as we've tried to fashion something a little different with this

textbook. But sociology also needs a touch of conservatism to ensure that it does not stray too far from the early vision that gave it perception; otherwise, it will diminish. It must constantly have postmodern eyes, using fly-like, multi-dimensional perception to look at who has benefited and who hasn't from sociology as it has been traditionally practised and written about. And it must adapt, evolve.

Concerning that last point, sociology in Canada is facing some serious challenges. In 2003, in *The Canadian Journal of Sociology*, Robert Brym remarked on the fact that while the Canadian Sociology and Anthropology Association (CSAA) was the official organization of Anglo-Canadian sociology, it was losing members, even while the number of faculty members in

Telling It Like It Is

An Expert POV

Irshad Manji on the Gender Challenge for Canadian Muslim Women

A few years ago, the Ontario government considered allowing Islamic *sharia* law to be applied in family law cases involving Muslims. It was strongly opposed by most Muslim women as well as by more liberal Muslim groups. The Canadianization of Islam poses a considerable gender challenge, as the Muslim writer of the excerpt below, Irshad Manji, explains. Born in Uganda in 1972, Manji and her family emigrated to Canada when she was four, during the expulsion of Uganda's South Asian population under Idi Amin. As an activist and a lesbian, Manji has faced considerable opposition from within her Muslim community. In her provocative book *The Trouble with Islam: A Wake-Up Call for Honesty and Change* (2003), Manji describes how she discovered, at the madressa (the Muslim school she attended on weekends), that the separation and inequality of the genders found in strict Muslim countries were being reproduced in Canada. That this situation was not being challenged but obeyed without question conflicted with what she was learning about the importance of individuality and equality taught to her in the regular school system. In the following, she describes the conflict that led her to leaving the madressa:

> The trouble began with *Know Your Islam*, the primer that I packed in my madressa bag every week. After reading it, I needed

to know more about "my" Islam. Why must girls observe the essentials, such as praying five times a day, at an earlier age than boys? Because, Mr Khaki [her nickname for her teacher] told me, girls mature sooner. They reach the "obligatory age" of practice at nine compared to thirteen for boys.

> "Then why not reward girls for our maturity by letting us lead prayer?" I asked.
> "Girls can't lead prayer."
> "What do you mean?"
> "Girls aren't permitted."
> "Why not?"
> "Allah says so."
> "What's His reason."
> "Read the Koran." (Manji 2003: 13–14)

She did not find an answer there that satisfied her Western-trained (and somewhat Western-biased) mind. Still, she remains a Muslim. Later in the book, she writes the following:

> Had I grown up in a Muslim country, I'd probably be an atheist in my heart. It's because I live in this corner of the world, where I can think, dispute, and delve further into any topic, that I've learned why I shouldn't give up on Islam just yet. (Manji 2003: 228)

---

sociology and anthropology was growing. Membership had peaked at 1,165 in 1993 and within 10 years had dropped by 39 per cent. Brym has his explanations for this phenomenon, including (1) external competition from American sociological organizations, (2) internal competition from the *Canadian Journal of Sociology*, (3) a changing organizational environment, and (4) unprofessionalism. On the second-to-last point, he notes reform movements that are "left-leaning" and "feminist." Those he names might argue that they left or never even joined because the organization had become an old boys' club that failed to represent their

interests. Whichever way you interpret it, Canadian sociology needs to change. In the personal narrative that ends our introduction to the discipline, we suggest one way we'd like to see sociology change.

Concluding Narrative: Where Does Sociology Go from Here?

In a book that emphasizes the importance of personal narratives that highlight unique perspectives on our social world, it is only fitting that we should end with a narrative.

In the conclusion to my doctoral dissertation on how Canadian introductory sociology textbooks present information about Aboriginal people, I argued that in order for textbook writers to present the information in a way that is worthy of the best aims and works of the discipline, they must engage in what can be called "Aboriginal sociology." We could generalize this approach to a broader category of "minorities sociology," but here I will speak in terms of the minority I know best.

This Aboriginal sociology, as I envisioned it, must begin by recognizing the inadequacy of traditional methods of producing sociological knowledge concerning Aboriginal people. The voices of the people need to be heard. I warned that if the writers of these textbooks continued to ignore Aboriginal voices in their knowledge production, they would continue to be complicit in the colonialist practices of governments. They were not being neutral, objective, or distanced. They were taking a side.

Equally important is the related recognition that the non-Aboriginal cultural background of the writers of introductory sociology textbooks permits them but a limited perspective, one that, as Dorothy Smith (1990) informs us, will miss core concepts that are intrinsically important to understanding Aboriginal people from an Aboriginal standpoint. The important place of elders in Aboriginal society is one of these core concepts. Elders are involved in all the social institutions of Aboriginal life—education, justice, religion, and politics, for example—and anyone in any way involved in Aboriginal society is aware of their significance. But people coming from other cultures that diminish the role of the elderly could easily miss this important point. Indeed, they *have* missed it. Spirituality is another core concept, one that tends to be erased in sociology textbooks. The reserve is a spiritual centre, often (one can probably say *usually*) the location of a number of sacred sites of significance, and yet in sociology textbooks it is only a site for sorry statistics and horror stories.

More generally, the development of an Aboriginal sociology entails the recognition that non-sociologists have authority in talking about Aboriginal life. There are very few Aboriginal sociologists, something that the discipline should note and rectify. For the Aboriginal standpoint to be represented, the knowledge production of Aboriginal journalists, educators, filmmakers, elders, and literary writers should be sought out and respected. All of them have voices that are valued in Aboriginal society. That alone should guarantee their inclusion in introductory sociology textbooks.

In my first year of university, sociology opened my eyes to a world of understanding that changed my perception forever. Every semester that I teach introductory sociology, I tell my students that my goal in teaching the course is to change how they think. I quote, with pride, a former sociology student of mine—a Brazilian nun—who said that my course had "ruined her" by forcing her (enabling her?) to question her previous perception of society.

I am a believer in the discipline. But I strongly believe that it needs to change its textual presentation of Aboriginal people, as well as its presentation of other groups that do not belong to the dominant culture, in ways as radical as how the discipline itself altered my viewpoint. It requires more voices to thrive in Canada in the twenty-first century.

THINK BACK

Questions for Critical Review

1. Compare and contrast the five different models of social change presented in this chapter.

2. Outline the features of the cycle of civilization, and discuss the degree to which it might apply to the United States.

3. Explain who the Luddites were, and outline the social changes to which they were reacting.

4. Outline Arthur Kroker's idea of the virtual class.

5. How can sociology be made to appeal to Aboriginal students, to encourage the growth of Aboriginal sociology in Canada?

READ ON

ONLINE

Canadian Centre for Policy Alternatives: Commentary and Fact Sheets

www.policyalternatives.ca/publications/commentary

The CCPA is a liberal think tank headquartered in Ottawa. This page provides commentaries on a range of current issues that reflect the centre's approach to influencing social policy in an attempt to make Canada more democratic.

Gay Marriage Plan: Sign of Sweeping Social Change in Canada

www.nytimes.com/2003/06/19/world/gay-marriage-plan-sign-of-sweeping-social
-change-in-Canada.html

This *New York Times* article by Clifford Krauss may seem a little out of date, having been published in 2003, when the legalization of gay marriage was still a hot topic here in Canada. But gay marriage is just a point of departure for a look at the pace and scale of social change taking place in Canada, in comparison with the US.

Interview: Kirkpatrick Sale

www.primitivism.com/sale/htm

This site presents an interview with Kirkpatrick Sale, who discusses his views on social change, the Luddites, and the future.

Occupy Together

www.occupy.together.org

This is the primary site for news and position statements relating to the Occupy movement.

The Luddites — Spartacus Education

www.spartacus.schoolnet.co.uk

This website discusses the Luddite movement, and provides some interesting primary documents of the time.

IN PRINT

George Grant (1965), *Lament for a Nation* (Toronto: McClelland & Stewart).

A classic Canadian work "lamenting" the changes taking place in mid-twentieth-century Canadian society.

Arthur Kroker & Michael A. Weinstein (1995), *Data Trash: Theory of the Virtual Class* (Montreal: New World Perspectives).

It is in this now classic work that the Canadian technology and cultural theorist Arthur Kroker expounds his theory of the virtual class.

Kirkpatrick Sale (1996), *Rebels Against the Future: the Luddites and Their War on the Industrial Revolution—Lessons for the Computer Age* (Cambridge, MA: Perseus).

An elegant case study of an epic fight against the destruction of a social class by technology.

John Steckley (2003), *Aboriginal Voices and the Politics of Representation in Canadian Sociology Textbooks* (Toronto: Canadian Scholars Press).

Shamelessly plugging my own works—this is my doctoral dissertation made readable. It argues for the need to develop a stronger Aboriginal sociology in Canada.

Glossary

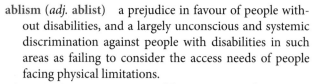

ablism (*adj.* **ablist**) a prejudice in favour of people without disabilities, and a largely unconscious and systemic discrimination against people with disabilities in such areas as failing to consider the access needs of people facing physical limitations.

Aboriginal visions meaningful inspirations, often experienced during a **vision quest** or dream, by an individual who may hear a song or chant in his or her head, see an animal that might take on a role as spiritual guardian, or in some other way perceive something that enables the individual to better understand his or her life and future.

Abrahamic religions the three major religions that trace their origin to the biblical patriarch Abraham: Judaism, Christianity, and Islam.

absolute poverty poverty calculated in absolute material terms. To exist in absolute poverty is to be without sufficient nutritious food, clean and safe shelter, access to education, etc. *Compare* **relative poverty**.

absolutist holding or having to do with the view that certain things are always right, good, moral, modern, or beautiful. Ethnocentrism is a negative example of an absolutist position.

access (without mobility) a buzzword in post-secondary education referring to such things as the availability of online courses to those who would not otherwise be able to attend a college or university because of factors such as cost and family situation. "Without mobility" is my own addition to the buzzword, referring to access that does not bring all of the opportunities required for a student to succeed.

achieved denoting a **status** that a person has earned but was not born into. Professional titles are an example. *Compare* **ascribed**.

adjunct professor a college or university professor who is employed on a contract basis and who does not enjoy the benefits and job security of a full-time member of staff.

affluence generally, wealth. Applied to individuals, affluence usually refers to having a comfortably large **disposable income**. Nations may be considered affluent if the majority of their citizens are affluent.

affluence hypothesis the belief that during times of economic prosperity, people will take a greater interest in social issues (e.g. the environment, global inequality) and will, as a result, make purchasing decisions that are more socially responsible (e.g. paying more for fair-trade coffee).

age group a group composed of people of a particular age (e.g. teenagers, "tweens," twentysomethings), studied over time.

ageism a prejudice against someone based on his or her age.

agency the capacity to influence what happens in one's life. *Compare* **victimology**.

agent a person who takes or is capable of taking an active role in the events and circumstances that shape her or his life.

agents of socialization the groups that have a significant influence on a person's **socialization**. Examples include family, **peer group**, community, school, mass media, the legal system, and culture generally.

age set a cohort of people of similar age who experience different stages of life together.

aid evangelism the practice of sending religious missionaries into developing countries in need of financial assistance, and using their need as a tool for trying to convert them.

Algonquian the largest family of Aboriginal languages in Canada, including Abenaki, Algonquin, Blackfoot, Cree, Delaware, Maliseet, Mi'kmaq, and Ojibwa.

alienation (in Marxist theory) a condition experienced by workers in a capitalist economy when they feel a lack of identity with the products of their labour and a sense of being controlled or exploited.

alternative medicine any medical treatment or remedy that falls outside of conventional Western medical practices. Examples include traditional Chinese medicine, healing techniques such as acupuncture and massage therapy, and herbal remedies. *See* **biomedicine**, **complementary medicine**.

amalgamated union a union made up of workers engaged in different crafts or trades. In Canada, the Amalgamated Transit Union represents workers involved in all areas of public transportation, from drivers and mechanics to ticket agents.

American dream the mostly unrealistic belief that one can become rich and successful through hard work and determination alone. A naive belief in the American dream is sometimes used to justify punishing others for being poor (the "American nightmare"; *see* **blaming the victim**).

androcentrism from *andro*, meaning "man": a form of sexism that views men as central and more important than women.

anomie Durkheim's term for a societal state of breakdown or confusion, or a more personal one based on an individual's lack of connection or contact with society.

anti-colonialism a theoretical framework developed by Fanon and Memmi to analyze the destructive impact colonialism has on both the colonizer and the colonized. *Also called* **post-colonialism**.

archaeology of knowledge Foucault's term for the process of "digging down" to find out how a piece of information was constructed, typically in order to discover or expose flaws in the way supposed facts or truths were established.

Arctic hysteria a **cultural syndrome** that was conjured up by white colonizers of the Arctic to explain behaviour that might better be explained as resulting from colonialism. *Also called **pibloktuq**.*

aristocrats (in Marxist theory) the landowner class of feudal times, who owned the land worked on by the class of **peasants**.

ascribed denoting a **status** that a person is born into (female, daughter, older sister) or has entered involuntarily (adult, diabetic). *Compare **achieved**.*

assimilation (*verb* **assimilate**) the process by which minorities, indigenous peoples, and immigrants lose their distinctive cultural characteristics to become like members of the dominant culture. It is a key principle of **melting pot** societies.

authenticity the quality of being true to the traditions of a people. Authenticity is often **contested** by the modern representatives of the people themselves and "experts" from outside the community.

baby boom generation the generation of people born after the Second World War, roughly between 1946 and 1964.

back stage (in Goffman's **dramaturgical approach**) the site of private, personal, or intimate encounters between individuals. *Compare **front stage**.*

bar mitzvah a Jewish **rite of passage** in which a boy becomes a man.

barbarism (as described by L.H. Morgan in the nineteenth century) the second stage of social evolution on the way to modern civilization. It was identified as one of a series of stages all societies were thought to pass through in their natural development. *Compare **civilization**, **savagery**.*

bat mitzvah a Jewish **rite of passage** in which a girl becomes a woman.

behaviourism a school of thought in psychology which emphasizes that behaviour can be studied and explained scientifically, not in terms of internal mental states (unlike **psychoanalysis**) but through observing how people's actions are supposedly conditioned by earlier actions and reactions.

behaviour modification an approach to changing someone's behaviour by giving rewards or positive sanctions for behaviour that one wishes to encourage and, sometimes, issuing negative sanctions for behaviour one wishes to discourage. *See **law of effect**.*

best practices strategies with a demonstrated history of achieving desired results more effectively or consistently than similar methods used either in the past by a particular organization or currently by other organizations in the same industry.

Big Pharma the pharmaceutical or drug manufacturing industry, especially when viewed as a large, lucrative industry ultimately more concerned with generating corporate profits than with improving public health.

binaries either/or distinctions used to separate people into supposedly discrete categories, such as male/female or able-bodied/disabled, typically when applied to social factors (gender, ability) that are better viewed in terms of a spectrum of possibilities.

biomedicine the application of standard principles of Western scientific disciplines (particularly biology) in the diagnosis and treatment of symptoms of illness. *Compare **alternative medicine**.*

bisexual a person who is sexually attracted to people of both sexes.

blaming the victim W. Ryan's term for the process of assigning individuals responsibility for harmful events or circumstances that have broader social causes.

bodily stigma *see* **stigma**.

bopi (in Mbuti culture) a playground that is almost exclusively the territory of children.

border crossers Henry Giroux's term for people who do not belong to a particular social group (e.g. the blind) but who are sympathetic to the goals of the group and act in a supportive way without claiming to speak for the group. *Compare **honourary members**.*

bourgeoisie Marx's term for **capitalists**, the social class made up of those who own and control the means of production in a capitalist society. Outside of Marxism it is commonly used (unkindly) to refer the middle class, viewed as conventional and conformist, and concerned with acquiring possessions that show off their upper-class tastes and aspirations.

boyah (*plural* **boyat**) a woman living in an Arab country of the Middle East who adopts a masculine style of dress and appearance (e.g. by cutting her hair short) as a way of defying gender expectations.

boycott a ban on buying or using particular goods or services as a form of protest, for ethical reasons.

Brahmin a member of the highest Hindu caste, that of priesthood.

brain drain the exodus of scientists, doctors, and other skilled professionals from a country.

brand bullies (as described by N. Klein) big companies that take advantage of the desire of young people to find belonging in a social group by aggressively marketing their products (esp. clothing) as essential to achieving membership within that group.

branding the corporate use of marketing as an instrument of **socialization**, to encourage teens and younger children to covet brand-name products linked, via advertising, to the cool or fashionable identity of the day.

broad socialization **socialization** in which individualism and independence are promoted. *Compare* **narrow socialization**.

capital Marx's term for the funds and properties necessary for the large-scale manufacture and trade of goods.

capitalists Marx's term for the owners of the means of

production (or **capital**, as these were known during the industrial era). *Also called* **bourgeoisie**.

carbon footprint   a measure of individual human impact on the environment based on the total amount of greenhouse gas emissions a person has caused, directly or indirectly, through reliance on transportation and industrial activities that require carbon-based fuels such as wood, coal, oil, and natural gas.

case study approach   a research design that explores a social entity or phenomenon by examining a single representative case or a few selected examples.

caste   each of the hereditary classes of Hindu society, distinguished by relative degrees of ritual purity and social status. Members of different castes are traditionally born into the unequal possession of specific occupations, dharma (duty in life), rights to foods, colours in clothing, religious practices, and imputed personal qualities. *Also called* **varnas**.

catharsis   emotional relief through the release of built-up energy or tension.

cathedrals of consumption   shopping malls and other venues established solely for the purpose of getting people to buy products.

Catholic-Traditionalists   Angela Robinson's term for Mi'kmaq who adopted Catholicism but incorporated non-Christian elements into their religious practices.

causation   the relationship between cause and effect.

China price   the true cost of China's competitive advantage in manufacturing, which takes into account the harm done to exploited workers and damage caused to the environment.

civilization   (as described by L.H. Morgan in the nineteenth century) the third and final stage of social evolution of all societies, viewed by European and North American thinkers as best exemplified by European and North American culture. *Compare* **barbarism, savagery**.

class   Marx's term for a socioeconomic group defined either relationally—that is, in Marxist terms, with respect to their relationship to the **means of production** (e.g. owner, worker)—or absolutely, in terms of access to socially valued goods such as money, education, and respect (e.g. lower class, middle class, upper class).

class consciousness   Marx's term for the awareness of what is in the best interests of one's class.

class reductionism   the intellectual fallacy that all forms of oppression are just about class, a view that wrongly downplays the role of factors such as "race," ethnicity, gender, and age.

clinical iatrogenesis   Illich's term for the ways in which diagnosis and cure cause problems that are equal to or greater than the health problems they are meant to resolve. An example would be catching a virus while in hospital for minor surgery.

closed shop   a workplace where, as a condition of employment, all workers must belong to the union that represents the workers. Anyone who aspires to teach at a public school in Canada must belong to the teacher's union, making public schools "closed shops." *Compare* **open shop**.

cluttered nest   a situation in which adult children continue to live at home with their parents. *Compare* **empty nest**.

cohabiting union (*or* **couple**)   *see* **common-law union**.

cohort   a group of people with a common statistical characteristic. Examples include baby boomers, who were born during the same period, and the frosh of 2013, who entered college or university in the same year.

collective   *another term for* **small group**.

collective bargaining   negotiations over wages and other working conditions, conducted by a union with an employer.

collective consciousness   Durkheim's term for shared feeling and understanding among people belonging to a particular religion, fostered by group experiences and rituals.

colonialism   the policy or practice of acquiring full or partial control over another country, occupying it with settlers, and exploiting it economically and/or culturally.

commodification   the tendency to treat something as though it were an object to be bought or sold. For example, the commodification of medicine involves identifying certain conditions that might be normal (though slightly regrettable) as diseases that may be treated with "commodity cures" (such as drugs or surgical procedures).

common-law union (*or* **couple**)   two people of the same or opposite sex who are living together as a couple but who are not legally married to each other. *Also called* **cohabiting union**.

communism   a model of social organization in which all property is vested in the community and each person contributes and receives according to their ability and needs.

community of scholars   the people associated with a particular academic discipline, including researchers and instructors.

companionate roles   the overlapping **conjugal roles** of partners in a marriage who both work outside the home and do work around the house. *Compare* **complementary roles**.

complementary medicine   alternative medicine practised in conjunction with conventional medicine. *See* **alternative medicine, biomedicine**.

complementary roles   the **conjugal roles** of partners in a marriage when one (traditionally the husband) does paid work, while the other (traditionally the wife) does the unpaid work of childcare and housework. *Compare* **companionate roles**.

complex household   a household in which there are two or more adults who are related but not married to each other.

complicit masculinity   forms of masculinity that do not contribute to or embody male hegemony yet still benefit from it.

confirmation a Christian **rite of passage** in which an adult who was baptized as a child or an infant affirms Christian belief and is admitted as a full member of the church.

conflict deviance behaviour that is subject to debate over whether or not it is deviant. Examples of conflict deviance include marijuana use and "creative accounting" on tax returns.

conflict theory (*or* **approach**) a sociological perspective espousing the view that complex societies are made up of groups in conflict, with one or more groups dominating or oppressing the others.

conjugal roles the distinctive roles of spouses that result from the division of labour within the family. Conjugal roles can be either **companionate** (**joint**) or **complementary** (**segregated**). Also called **marital roles**.

conservatism a view of social change as potentially more destructive than constructive, especially in emotionally charged areas of life such as family, gender roles, sexuality, and the environment.

conspicuous consumption (as described by Veblen) the purchase and use of goods and services primarily to demonstrate wealth and status.

consumer activism practices aimed at protecting the rights of consumers, such as the right to have ingredients and nutritional information listed on food packaging, and the right to protection from false advertising.

consumerism either (1) the societal promotion of the need to buy goods and services in ever increasing quantities, or (2) *another term for* **consumer activism**.

consumption the purchase and use of goods and services.

consumption as communication thesis the belief, which falls within the **symbolic-interactionist** school, that acts of consumption have socially significant symbolic meanings.

consumption-based society a society whose members are typically defined by how they spend their money and their free time. *Compare* **production-based society**.

consumption reductionism the practice of reducing the study of people to the study of their consumption patterns, while failing to take into account such social factors as class, "race," gender, and age.

content analysis a study of a set of cultural artifacts (e.g. children's books, newspaper articles) or events by systematically counting them and interpreting the themes they reflect.

contested describing a practice whose moral goodness or badness, normalcy or deviance, or general predominance is disputed by some members of society.

contextual objectivity (as described by El-Nawawy & Iskandar) the notion that objectivity in the media is served when there are biased and opposing views that are articulated.

control one of four main elements of Weber's model of **formal rationalization**, having to do with the use of rules, regulations, and a hierarchical structure to keep workers in line. *See* **efficiency**, **predictability**, **quantification**.

cool media (as described by McLuhan) media forms that place a greater demand on the audience in interpreting and consuming the material presented; books and comics are considered cool because they place demands on the reader to fill in missing details. *Compare* **hot media**.

corporate crimes (as described by Clinard and Quinney) (1) offences committed by corporate officials on behalf of the corporation they represent, or (2) the offences of the corporation itself. *Compare* **occupational crimes**.

corporate identity the shared sense of common membership and common purpose that a social group can have. *Also called* **organic identity**.

correlation a mutual relationship or interdependence among **variables**.

cosmology an account of the origin and ruling principles of the universe, especially the role of humans in relationship to non-humans (living and divine).

countercultures groups that reject selected elements of the dominant culture, such as clothing styles or sexual norms. *Compare* **subculture**.

counter-ideology a set of beliefs that challenges or contests the **dominant ideology** put forward by the dominant culture and the ruling classes.

counter-narrative a narrative that presents a viewpoint that opposes the perspective of the mainstream.

covert characteristics (of deviance) the unstated qualities that might make a particular group a target for sanctions. *Compare* **overt characteristics (of deviance)**.

craft union the earliest form of union (still existing today), representing workers who share a craft or trade.

credentialism a bias in favour of job candidates with academic degrees, diplomas, or certificates over those without, regardless of their demonstrated knowledge, ability, and experience.

critical disability theory a social constructionist theory that distinguishes between natural impairment (e.g. paralysis of the legs) and disability, which occurs when society sets up barriers to dealing with impairment (e.g. building stairs without wheelchair-accessible ramps).

critical education an education model that involves the analysis and discussion of ideas. *Compare* **instrumental education**.

critical sociology sociology that challenges both established sociological theories and the research that sociologists do.

crude marriage rate the number of marriages per 1,000 people in a population.

crusade originally, any of several military expeditions waged between the eleventh and thirteenth centuries by European Christians to claim land seen as holy by Christians, Jews, and Muslims. Today, the term is often applied broadly, esp. by militant **Islamists**, to any peacekeeping or military campaign undertaken by Western countries; this use is comparable to the (mis)use, mostly by Westerners, of the term **jihad**.

cultural capital　(as described by Bourdieu) the knowledge and skills required to develop the sophisticated tastes that mark someone as a person of high culture and upper class.

cultural globalization　(as described by M. Steger) the intensification and expansion of the flow of culture across the world in a process that involves media and patterns of consumption.

cultural iatrogenesis　(as described by Illich) a situation in which the knowledge and abilities of health professionals have become so mythologized that individuals lose the capacity to heal themselves.

cultural mosaic　a metaphor for any society in which individual ethnic groups are able to maintain distinctive identities. *Compare* **melting pot**.

cultural norms　generally expected or explicitly stated rules of behaviour. These may reflect the **ideal culture** more than they do the **real culture**.

cultural relativism　the view that any aspect of a culture, including its practices and beliefs, is best explained within the context of the culture itself, not by the standard or ways of another culture.

cultural reproduction theory　the theory that the education system reproduces and reinforces the inequality of the surrounding society.

cultural studies　a field of study drawing on both the social sciences (primarily sociology) and the humanities (primarily literature and media studies) to cast academic light on the meanings expressed in popular culture and their significance.

cultural syndromes　disorders thought to afflict people of only certain ethnicities. They are often invented to psychologize problems brought on by Western colonial control. *See* **Arctic hysteria**.

culture　a social system (sometimes **contested**) comprising behaviour, beliefs, knowledge, practices, values, and material such as buildings, tools, and sacred items.

culture and personality　(as described by R. Benedict) a now discredited school of thought that argued that every culture has a distinct personality that is encouraged by cultural practices and beliefs.

culture industry　an industry that produces commodities and services that in some way express a way of life (such as the film and TV industry) or that occupy a special place in the social communications system (such as advertising or the media).

cultures of education　the attitudes towards education and educational practices associated with different cultural groups (e.g. European, Aboriginal, black).

cultures of medicine　the recognition that different cultures have different ways of practising medicine, including different **social courses of disease**, different techniques, and different physical remedies.

cyber-bullying　the use of social media to publicly shame, embarrass, or denigrate someone.

cycle of civilization　the supposed rise and fall of **civilizations** in somewhat predictable cycles. The term has been applied to the Roman empire, the Mongol empire, the Ottoman (Turkish) empire, and the American empire.

Dalits　the lowest and most discriminated against group in the traditional Hindu **caste** system. *Also called* **Untouchables**.

Deaf culture　the cultural community of deaf people, characterized by shared history, customs, and institutions, including schools, social groups and organizations, and language.

debt-to-income ratio　a measure of a household's debt (from mortgages, lines of credit, credit cards, and other loans) expressed as a percentage of total household after-tax income.

deciles　ranked groups each making up 10 per cent of a total population, used for statistical analysis of such things as household income.

decipherment　the process of examining a text to discover its true meaning, which often involves looking beyond the explicit message to discover the intent (conscious or unconscious) of the individual or organization that produced it.

definition of the situation　a concept related to symbolic interactionism, which states that given a particular situation, different individuals will interpret the circumstances differently, based on their own subjective experiences.

degradation ceremony　a **rite of passage** designed to strip a person of his or her individuality. Hazing rituals typically serve as degradation ceremonies.

delayed life transitions　the experience of major life transitions—getting a full-time job, moving out on one's own, getting married, etc.—at a later stage in life.

delinquent subculture　(as described by A. Cohen) the **subordinate culture** of teenage gangs. *See* **subcultural theory**.

democracy　a political system that involves a broad-based voting electorate, an opposition that is free to criticize the group in power without fear, freedom of the press and of speech, protection of the rights of minorities, and relative equality of men and women.

demotic turn　(as defined by G. Turner) the ability of ordinary people to achieve celebrity status through media exposure, which has the result of making fame a goal that people unrealistically believe they can attain.

density threshold　a measure of the amount of human development that can occur in a particular habitat before a given population will fall into decline.

dependent variable　a **variable** that is assumed to be affected by an **independent variable**.

desensitization theory　the idea that increased exposure to media violence (e.g. from television, movies, and video games) blunts, or desensitizes, natural feelings of revulsion at the sight or thought of violence.

determinism　the belief that personal characteristics, including behaviour and attitudes, are shaped by forces beyond the control, or **agency**, of the individual. Such determinism can be biological or social.

détournement   a media event carried out by members of the Situationist International movement to undermine or oppose mainstream media culture. The legacy of the détournement is the modern-day tactic known as *culture jamming*, practised notably by the Vancouver-based anti-consumerism group Adbusters (see p. 62).

developed nations   the wealthier nations of the world, typically including the United States, Canada, the western European nations, and the more financially successful countries of Asia, Africa, and the Americas.

developing nations   the world's poorer nations that are seeking to become more advanced economically and socially. The label is **contested** by some critics of globalization, who prefer the term "underdeveloping nations" to better reflect the status of these countries as they become poorer as a result of exploitation by **developed nations**.

deviance   straying from or different to what is considered usual or normal.

dialect   a version of a language, usually with a unique set of features (in terms of vocabulary, grammar, and pronunciation) and a socially identifiable group of speakers. Newfoundland English is an example of a dialect (even though technically there are several Newfoundland dialects).

dictatorship of the proletariat   Marx's term for the democratic social order that would prevail once the workers (the **proletariat**) revolted against the control of the owners (the **bourgeoisie**).

digital divide   the situation in which citizens of the world's wealthier nations, as well as richer citizens of the poorer nations, have an access to computers and related technology that gives them an enormous social, economic, and political advantage over the poorer citizens of the richer nations and most people in the poorer countries.

direct correlation   a relationship between two **variables** in which an increase (or decrease) in one causes a corresponding increase (or decrease) in the other. *Compare* **inverse correlation**.

disability   any condition—physical or mental, permanent or temporary—that limits a person's ability to participate in regular activities in the home, at work, at school, or in recreational pursuits.

disability oppression   (as described by M. Oliver) the sum of all the forms of mistreatment, prejudice, and discrimination that people with disabilities face.

disabled   having or living with a disability.

disabled family   the family of a person with a disability. As noted by W. Hower, the disability of an individual can become a kind of **ascribed status** for the individual's entire family, which may lead to discrimination against all family members by others within the community.

discourse   a conceptual framework with its own internal logic and underlying assumptions. Different disciplines, such as sociology and psychology, have their own discourses.

discourse analysis   an approach to analyzing a conversation, a speech, or a written text. More recently the scope of discourse analysis has broadened, with **discourse** now taken to mean such things as entire academic disciplines, like sociology and political philosophy.

discrimination   acts by which individuals are differentially rewarded or punished based on their membership in a social group defined by class, sexual orientation, ethnicity, and so on.

disinformation   (as described by N. Postman) superficial or irrelevant information that, while not necessarily designed to be deliberately misleading, nevertheless distracts media consumers and prevents them from becoming informed about matters of far greater social significance. *See also* **junk food news**.

disjuncture   a gap between knowledges produced from two or more different perspectives (e.g. those of management and employees).

disposable income   the amount of after-tax income remaining to an individual once he or she has paid for all basic living expenses (food, shelter, clothing, transportation, etc.), available to be spent (or "thrown away") however the individual wishes.

disposable workers   temporary migrant workers who are allowed to remain in the host country for only as long as there is work available; once the supply of work runs out, they are sent back to their countries of origin. The term can also apply to unskilled non-unionized workers in their own country.

disqualified knowledges   Foucault's term for knowledge that is discredited on the grounds that it lacks the trained, objective, scientific basis of knowledges considered superior. The exclusion of Aboriginal voices from the coverage of First Nation history in Canadian sociology textbooks can be considered a case of disqualified knowledges.

division of labour   the way that work is divided in a society. Marx, for example, saw a division of labour that featured the owners of machines and factories on the one hand, and on the other, the people who worked for these owners.

docile body   Foucault's term for a group that has been conditioned, through a specific set of procedures and practices, to behave in a particular, pre-programmed way.

dominant capitalist class   the social class composed primarily of those who own or control the **means of production**.

dominant culture   the culture that through its political and economic power is able to impose its values, language, and ways of behaving and interpreting behaviour on a given society.

dominant ideology   a set of beliefs put forward by and in support of the dominant culture and/or ruling classes within a society, to help them to justify their dominant position and dominating practices.

dominants   the group within a society that has the most political and social power, whose culture or subculture is seen as "the" culture of a country.

double burden (*or double ghetto*)   a term used to characterize the imbalance in gender roles in situations where a married woman works a paid job during the day but when she comes home is still expected to perform the unpaid domestic work (cleaning house, preparing meals, looking after children, etc.) traditionally associated with women. *Also called* **second shift**.

Dragon Lady (as described by Tajima & Das Gupta) a stereotype of East Asian women as tough, ruthless, and mercenary. The stereotype is seen in film and TV portrayals of hardened prostitutes and madams, and women who fight with nasty, angry facial expressions. *Compare* **Lotus Blossom Baby**.

dramaturgical approach (as described by Goffman) a way of approaching sociological research as if everyday life were taking place on the stage of a theatre.

dual colonialism a situation that occurs when the most oppressed groups (e.g. Rwanda's Hutu) are colonized both by the colonizing outsider group (the Belgians) and by a local group that is given privilege and power by the outsider group (the Tutsi).

dynamic denoting a social situation in which groups are subject to change.

dystopian set in or having to do with an imagined world in which everything is unpleasant or bad.

ecofeminism a philosophical and political movement that combines ecological concerns with feminist ones, viewing both as resulting from male domination of society.

economic globalization the processes that enable goods to be produced, marketed, and sold anywhere around the world, without the hindrance of government-established barriers designed to protect local production and distribution

economic model (of disability) a way of understanding and representing disabled people in terms of their contribution to or drain on the economy. *Compare* **medical model (of disability)**.

efficiency one of four main elements of Weber's model of **formal rationalization**, having to do with the streamlined movement of people and things. *See* **control**, **predictability**, **quantification**.

egalitarianism (*adj.* egalitarian) the principle that all people are equal and deserve equal rights and opportunities.

ego (as described by Freud) the conscious aspect of the individual personality. *Compare* **id**, **superego**.

elder a person of advanced age, recognized as a leader within society or a particular social group.

elder abuse violence toward or neglect or mistreatment of seniors.

elite consumption the purchase of goods and services attainable only by the wealthiest members of society. *Compare* **mass consumption**.

embedded journalist a journalist who travels with and is protected by the military, but who is, in turn, authorized or encouraged to express views sympathetic to the military's purposes.

embourgeoisement thesis the theory when the working class begins to adopt the consumption patterns and tastes of the bourgeois middle class, it will also adopt middle-class societal goals, resulting in a loss of **class consciousness** and a loss of Marxist revolutionary potential.

empty nest a situation in which the children of an older couple have grown up and moved out of the family home. *Compare* **cluttered nest**.

endogamy the practice of marrying within one's class, "race," or ethnic group. *Compare* **exogamy**.

environmental refugees people forced to leave their home region owing to sudden changes to the local environment (e.g. drought, melting land ice, polluted water) that pose a threat to their livelihood or survival.

epidemiology the study of public health, specifically the incidence and spread of diseases in a population.

epiphenomenal denoting a factor of secondary significance to a more significant cause. For Marx, "race" and ethnicity were epiphenomenal to economic structure.

equal pay the pay received by women and men alike for performing the same job. As a policy, it is one of two ways of addressing the imbalance in men's and women's wages. *Compare* **pay equity**.

eros (as described by Freud) the "sexual" or "life" instinct within the **id**.

essentialism the view that every ethnic group is made up of a set of readily identifiable traits that have been passed down from the past to the present with little or no change. *Also called* **primordialism**.

ethical consumption the purchase of goods and services made judiciously according to deeply held moral or ethical principles, such as concern for the environment or for exploited workers in developing countries. **Fair trade** is a form of ethical consumption.

ethic of consumption a set of moral principles affirming or celebrating the purchase of goods and services without moderation.

ethnic (*or* racial) industry an industry dominated by a particular ethnic group. Occasionally these develop businesses entered into by immigrants working for themselves after they have been unable to find employment working for others because of discriminatory hiring practices.

ethnic class (as described by Dofny & Rioux) the situation that exists when members of different ethnic groups adopt occupations that are ranked differently (e.g. administration versus labourers). An ethnic class system existed in Quebec for most of the twentieth century.

ethnic entrepreneurs individuals who manipulate symbols with strong meaning to their ethnic group in order to gain and wield personal power. Examples include Adolf Hitler and Slobodan Milošević.

ethnocentrism the belief that one culture (often one's own, occasionally another considered more powerful or respectable) is the absolute standard by which other cultures should be judged.

ethnography a research method, shared by sociology and social anthropology, in which communities or groups are studied through extensive fieldwork. Ethnography requires the researcher to participate daily in the lives of the subjects, observing their actions and asking questions. *See* **institutional ethnography**.

eugenics the science of improving a population by controlled breeding. The idea was especially popular in the early twentieth century, when people believed that "good traits" and "bad traits" were inherited, and that the poor, the colonized, and other marginalized people should be sterilized to prevent them from reproducing.

Eurocentrism generally, the belief that "European" (i.e. western and northern European, plus North American) culture is superior to other cultures; more specifically in sociology, the use of a European viewpoint to address others, often with the assumption that the audience shares (or would like to share) that viewpoint.

evolution (as described by Darwin) a model of **social change** in which change is seen as an adaptation to a set of particular circumstances, an idea captured by the expression **survival of the fittest**. *See* **social Darwinism**.

examination a form of disciplinary control that combines the methods of **hierarchical observation** and **normalizing judgement** to condition group behaviour; it is part of a set of tactics used to produce what Foucault called a **docile body**.

exogamy the practice of marrying outside of one's class, "race," or ethnic group. *Compare* **endogamy**.

exoticism the process of making peoples from other cultures seem more exotic or "strange," more different from one's own culture than they actually are or were.

extended family the family beyond mother, father, and children. Use of this term reflects the user's belief that the **nuclear family** is the model of a "normal" family.

fact something that has been observed, and that as far as can be proven is believed to be true.

fair trade a movement that claims to support workers and entrepreneurs in developing countries by promoting fair wages and safe working conditions for marginalized workers, equality for women, the elimination of child labour, and fair market opportunities for small-scale independent farms and businesses. *See also* **ethical consumption**.

false consciousness (as described by Marx) the belief that something is in the best interests of one's class (e.g. religion, racism) when it is not.

farming culture a culture that practises sophisticated forms of agriculture (i.e. involving such practices as irrigation, ploughing, and fertilization), growing and harvesting food crops and raising livestock either for subsistence or for commercial sale.

fashion a model of **social change** that promotes change for its own sake, not for better (**modernism**), not for worse (**conservatism**), nor even for adaptation (**evolution**). Fashion change may occur because a manufacturer wants consumers to believe a product has been improved (though it hasn't), or it may occur because people desire something different.

fecundity a woman's ability to conceive, which changes with age.

feminist essentialism a feminist approach that involves looking at differences between the way women and men think while arguing for the equality—and sometimes female superiority—in that difference. *Also called* **essentialist feminism**.

feminist liberalism a feminist approach that typically involves working towards **pay equity** for women. This form of feminism is criticized as reflecting more the concerns of white middle-class Western women than the women of different ethnicities and classes. *Also called* **liberal feminism**.

feminist organization an organizational form based on principles different to those underlying more patriarchal organizational structures, including inclusiveness, an absence of hierarchy, and a more equitable distribution of power.

feminist postmodernism a feminist approach that involves looking at women more as subjects (i.e. people with **voices** and **standpoints** of interpretation) who guide research, rather than as objects being researched. *Also called* **postmodernist feminism**.

feminist socialism a feminist approach that involves looking at the intersections of oppression between class and gender, focusing mainly on the struggles faced by lower-class women. *Also called* **socialist feminism**.

feminist theory the set of sociological theories and approaches designed to correct centuries of discrimination and male-dominated conceptions of gender roles in order to present an accurate view of the social condition of women.

feminization the process whereby an occupational sphere becomes dominated by and associated with women (e.g. secretarial work, clerical work). Feminized occupations are usually rewarded with lower salaries and fewer benefits.

fertility rate see **total fertility rate**.

filial piety (among Chinese cultures) lifelong respect and reverence for one's parents and ancestors, seen as a virtue.

first law of petropolitics (as described by T. Friedman) the idea that there is an inverse correlation between the global price of oil and the amount of democracy shown by a government of a given oil-producing nation.

First World a term used prior to the collapse of the USSR in the late twentieth century to refer to the world's rich, capitalist countries.

focus group a diverse group of people assembled to participate in a guided discussion about a product, a political campaign, a commercial, etc.

folk society (as described by R. Redfield) a rural, small-scale, homogeneous society imbued with a strong sense of the sacred and the personal, usually in contrast to an urban society.

folkways (as described by W. Sumner) **norms** that in the usual course of events one *should* not (rather than *must* not) violate. They are the least respected and most weakly sanctioned norms.

food bank   a central clearing house run by a non-profit organization to collect, store, and distribute food free of charge to the poor.

forager culture   *another term for* **hunter-and-gatherer culture**.

formal equality   (in critical disability theory) a model according to which everyone faces and must adapt to the same social driven architecture that gives advantages to people without disabilities. The term is also used in studies of gender and ethnicity, where it refers to the criteria set for job application when these criteria give advantage to applicants who are male and white. This situation existed with the RCMP, where minimum height and weight requirements favoured white, male applicants before minimum strength requirements were put into place. *Compare* **substantive equality**.

formal rationalization (*or* **rationality**)   (as described by Weber) a model of improving the effectiveness of an organization or process based on four elements: (1) efficiency, (2) quantification, (3) predictability, and (4) control. Weber was critical of the concept, believing that it led to disenchantment and alienation of the individuals involved in the rationalized process or organization.

formal social movement organization   (as described by C. Mueller) a type of **feminist organization** characterized as professionalized, bureaucratic, and inclusive.

Frankfurt school   a school of social philosophers (including Adorno, Horkheimer, and Marcuse) who, beginning in the 1920s, applied the insights of Nietzsche, Marx, and Freud to their critical writing on fascism, communism, and capitalism.

free-floating statistic   a statistic created in a particular context of time and place that is repeated outside of that context.

friendly racism   (as described by H. Codjoe) a form of racism that is subtle and seemingly (to the perpetrator) harmless.

front stage   (in Goffman's **dramaturgical approach**) the site of social interactions designed for public display. (*Compare* **back stage**.)

functionalism   a sociological approach that involves explaining social structures in terms of their functions, i.e. what they do for society.

game stage   (as described by Mead) the third stage of intellectual development, in which the child considers simultaneously the perspective of several roles. *Compare* **play stage**, **role taking**.

gay   an informal term for someone (male or female) who is sexually attracted to people of the same sex.

geisha   a traditional occupation for Japanese women. Geishas are expected to be well trained in the arts and capable of intelligent conversation so that they can entertain well-to-do customers in the geisha house. *Compare* **Lotus Blossom Baby**.

gender   (as described by A. Oakley) the socially constructed and socially unequal division of masculinity and femininity, as opposed to the biological division of **sex**.

gendered   denoting occupations or post-secondary programs dominated either by men or by women. Examples include early childhood education and interior design for women, fire fighting and industrial design for men.

gender role   the role that a culture or society assigns as "normal" for boys/men and girls/women.

gender strategy   (as described by A. Hochschild) a way of dealing with situations in different areas of life (work, family, etc.) based on culturally defined **gender roles**. For example, in a dual-income household, the typical gender strategy for caring for sick children is for the mother to take time off of work.

genealogy   a form of **discourse analysis** that involves tracing the origin and history of modern **discourses** (e.g. the importance of light-coloured skin in South Asian culture). The term is sometimes considered interchangeable with the **archaeology of knowledge**.

general intelligence   the largely mistaken idea that people have a single intelligence level that applies to many areas of life, skills, and abilities. Belief in general intelligence would lead one to conclude that a boy or girl who does not earn high marks at school, but who has other skills, is stupid.

general strike   a large-scale job action that occurs when one union's strike is joined by other unions sympathetic to the cause. The most famous general strike in Canadian history took place in Winnipeg in 1919.

generalized others   (as described by Mead) the attitudes, viewpoints, and general expectations of the society that a child is socialized into.

generation gap   significant cultural and social differences that produce a lack of understanding between members of different generations.

genetically modified   denoting a plant, animal, or micro-organism whose genetic material has been artificially manipulated in order to produce a desired characteristic. Genetically modified varieties of certain food crops have been produced that are more resistant to plant diseases and insects, but that may exhibit unplanned features that cause yet unknown problems among consumers. *Compare* **transgenic**.

genocide   a set of social practices designed to eliminate or exterminate a people. These practices include warfare, displacement from a homeland, enforced sexual sterilization, separation of family members, and banning languages and other culturally identifiable features, all of which were committed against Aboriginal people in Canada.

globalism   (as described by M. Steger) an ideology that links **globalization** with **neoliberalism**. A proponent of this ideology is a **globalist**.

globality   (as described by M. Steger) a set of social conditions of globalization at a particular time and place.

globalization the worldwide process or policy of making the realms of communication and commerce more international in scope.

globalization from above M. Steger's term for processes of globalization that operate in the best interests of transnational corporations and the power elite of the North.

globalization from below globalization processes that operate in the interests of global equality and the more marginalized peoples of the world.

global village (as described by M. McLuhan) the world made small through mass media and telecommunications technology.

glocalization (as described by R. Robertson) the process of tailoring globalization to local needs and tastes. Glocalization is done either by **transnational corporations** bent on increasing their globalized sales and influence, or by the local culture filtering the effects of globalization.

government terrorism a form of terrorism in which the government of one country sponsors (by providing funding, military training, or a covert military presence) acts of terrorism to destabilize and change the political regime of another country.

group formation effect (as described by M. Ross) one of three components of the **rentier effect**, this is about an oil-rich government's ability to use its oil revenues to prevent opposition groups from forming. *Compare* **spending effect, taxation effect**.

guild an association of craftsmen or merchants, banded together in the pursuit of common interests.

habitus Bourdieu's term for a set of class-affected or culturally affected and socially acquired characteristics (e.g. opinions, definitions of "manners" and "good taste," leisure pursuits).

hallucination an image of something that is not considered to be "objectively" there (not to be confused with an **Aboriginal vision**).

haram forbidden or proscribed under Islamic law.

hegemonic masculinity (as described by R. Connell) practices and beliefs that normalize and naturalize men's dominance and women's subordination.

hegemony (as described by A. Gramsci) a set of relatively non-coercive methods of maintaining power used by the dominant class (e.g. through the various media and the legal system). Often the terms *hegemony* and *hegemonic* are used to refer just to the possession and exercise of power (see, for instance, **hegemonic masculinity**).

heteronormative denoting or relating to the norms, mores, rules, and laws that uphold heterosexual standards of identity and behaviour and heterosexuality as natural and universal.

heterosexual a person who is sexually attracted to people of the opposite sex.

hidden curriculum typically, the unstated, unofficial agenda of school system authorities, including such elements as obedience and ranking.

hierarchical observation a form of disciplinary control in which group behaviour is conditioned through observation and surveillance; it is one of three tactics used to produce what Foucault called a **docile body**. *Compare* **examination, normalizing judgement**.

high culture the culture within a society that is deemed to be sophisticated, civilized, and possessing great taste.

Highland Clearances the eviction by land-owning aristocrats of tenant farmers in Scotland in the late eighteenth and early nineteenth centuries. The clearances, which were carried out to make room for sheep, helped aristocrats capitalize on the rapidly growing textile industry.

hijab an Arabic word for the veil or headscarf worn by Muslim women for religious and cultural reasons.

homosexual a person (male or female) who is sexually attracted to people of the same sex.

honorary members (in Deaf culture) people outside the Deaf community who are sympathetic to the community's goals and who act in a supportive way without claiming to speak for Deaf people. *Compare* **border crossers**.

honorifics terms of respect used in addressing others, esp. others who are older than oneself.

horticultural denoting cultures involved in small-scale subsistence agriculture.

hot media (as described by McLuhan) forms of media that demand less of the audience in interpreting and consuming the material presented; movies are considered hot. *Compare* **cool media**.

human capital thesis the theory that marginalized groups earn less money than dominant groups because they possess less human capital in the form of education, skill, and experience.

hunter-and-gatherer culture a culture that depends for survival on fishing, hunting, and harvesting wild crops, typically while moving from place to place according to the migration patterns of prey and the availability of seasonal crops. *Also called* **forager culture**.

hurried child syndrome a situation in which a child, pushed to high levels of accomplishment in school and in after-school activities (such as extracurricular sports and clubs), experiences adult-like levels of stress and guilt.

hyperglobalizers people who are uncritical of globalization and dismissive of its negative effects; they champion the process of globalization as good for everyone.

hyperreal (as described by Baudrillard) denoting ideas and images that people view as being more real than the actual things they represent. Television's idealized view of family life is hyperreal.

hypothesis a statement that is verifiable/falsifiable (i.e. that can be proven true or false) and that proposes a specific relationship between or among variables. An example of a hypothesis: "Playing violent video games makes a person more violent or antisocial."

iatrogenesis (as described by Illich) health problems that are supposedly caused by health professionals. See **clinical iatrogenesis, cultural iatrogenesis, social iatrogenesis**.

id (as described by Freud) the instinctive part of the subconscious. (Remember it by the term **i**nner **d**emons.)

ideal culture social life and institutions as they actually exist. *Compare* **real culture**.

identity formation the ongoing process by which an individual develops a sense of him- or herself as a unique human being.

ideology (*adj.* **ideological**) a relatively coherent set of beliefs about society and the people in it. Examples include **dominant ideology**, **counter-ideology**, and **liberal ideology**.

ideology of fag (as described by G. Smith) the use of such label as "gay" and "lesbian" pejoratively as a way to make people conform to strictly proscribed gender roles (e.g. telling a young man who expresses interest in poetry, interior design, or figure skating, "You're so gay").

image of limited good (as described by G. Foster) the idea that the resources on which a community depends are limited, so that if one community member is successful in obtaining a large share of these resources, others in the community necessarily lose out.

impression management (as described by Goffman) the ways in which people present themselves publicly in specific roles and social circumstances. Goffman first used the term to discuss the differences between how restaurant staff presented themselves to customers and how they presented themselves to one another behind the kitchen door.

independent variable a **variable** that is believed to have some effect on another variable. *Compare* **dependent variable**.

Indian Princess an Aboriginal woman portrayed or seen as beautiful, submissive to white men, and ready to betray her nation for the love of a European man. The classic example is Disney's Pocahontas. *Compare* **squaw**.

indirect rule a colonial policy in which a European nation uses members of a particular ethnic group as its intermediaries in ruling an area. The policy often leads to **dual colonialism** and **internal colonialism**.

Indo-European (1) a language family that includes almost every language spoken in Europe, as well as the languages of Iran, Afghanistan, Pakistan, and India. (2) the prehistoric peoples that swept from a presumed location in Ukraine to where these languages are spoken today.

industrial culture a city-based culture that depends on large-scale manufacturing and the conversion of natural resources into commercial goods.

industrial union a union representing an entire industry, rather than a specialized individual craft or trade.

infant mortality rate the rate of death among newborns, typically under the age of one.

info-elites countries of the developed North, which have greater access to information technology and the Internet.

informant a person knowledgeable in his or her own culture who provides his or her views of the culture to an outside researcher (a sociologist, an anthropologist, or another ethnographer).

insider perspective the viewpoint(s) of those who experience the subject being studied or written about. *Compare* **outsider perspective**. *See also* **standpoint theory**, **subjective**.

institution an enduring set of ideas, established by law, custom, or practice, about how to accomplish goals that are deemed important within a society or culture. Marriage is an institution, as are education and religion.

institutional ethnography a form of ethnography that challenges the need for a neutral stance in sociological research, claiming instead that any institution or organization can be seen as having two sides: one representing the **ruling interests** of the organization, one representing the interests of those working for the organization (typically in a non-administrative capacity).

institutional racism *another term for* **systemic racism**.

instrumental education an education model in which courses are narrowly directed to particular sets of tasks or outcomes, and do not involve challenging or being critical of information received. *Compare* **critical education**.

instrumentalism a sociological approach that focuses on situations in which ethnic leaders mobilize groups in order to develop the groups' political and social strength.

intellectual property intangible property items such as ideas or artistic works (e.g. literary products, music, films, videos, photographs, drawings, and sculptures) that are the result of a person's creativity.

intelligences a term that expresses the idea that we have different levels of intelligence in different areas of life (e.g. mathematical, computer-related, literary, musical, artistic, culinary, building, etc.).

interlocking matrix of domination the effect on an individual or group of gender-based stereotypes when combined with other minoritizing social factors, such as class, "race," or ethnicity.

internal colonialism a situation that occurs when people within a country are colonized or put in a subordinate position (e.g. Aboriginal people in Canada; the Karen in Myanmar).

internalize incorporate the norms and values that one observes.

intersectionality theory the theory that the experience of a group that is minoritized because of one social factor (e.g. "race") is shaped by the way that factor combines, or "intersects," with other social factors (e.g. sex, class, age, etc.).

intersex a person with both male and female sexual characteristics, as a result of a biological condition that produces either an atypical combination of male and female chromosomes or both male and female genitals/secondary sexual characteristics.

Inuit (*singular* **Inuk**) a people indigenous to Canada, Alaska, Greenland, and Siberia, who have been in Canada for a shorter time (between 5,000 and 10,000 years) than earlier indigenous people. They speak related languages and share various aspects of an Arctic-adapted culture.

inverse care law   the theory, articulated by J.T. Hart, that good medical care is most available in populations where it is needed the least, and least available in populations where it is needed the most.

inverse (*or negative*) correlation   a relationship between two **variables** in which an increase in one variable causes a decrease in the other, or vice versa. *Compare* **direct correlation.**

Islamists   people who oppose globalization and Western culture generally with narrow-minded and distorted fundamentalist notions of Islam.

Islamophobia   fear or hatred of Muslims or of Islam, especially when viewed as a political or social force.

jihad   a term generated from an Arabic word meaning "to struggle, strive"; it has several different forms and interpretations. *See* **jihad-i-akbar, jihad-i-asghar,** and **ummaic jihad.**

jihad-i-akbar   the personal **jihad,** which represents the perpetual struggle to purge oneself of baser instincts such as greed, racism, hedonism, jealousy, revenge, hypocrisy, lying, and cheating.

jihad-i-asghar   (*literally* "the smaller, lower, or lesser jihad") the struggle against aggressors who are not practising Muslims. **Islamists** practise a distorted version of this.

joint conjugal roles   **conjugal roles** in which many tasks, interests, and activities are shared. *Compare* **segregated conjugal roles.**

junk food news   media items, reported as news, that do not inform consumers in any meaningful way and that distract them from understanding events and situations of far greater socio-political significance. Celebrity gossip is an example.

Kshatriya   a member of the second-highest of the Hindu castes, the military caste.

labelling theory   (as described by Becker) the theory that individuals and groups outside the mainstream internalize the labels applied to them by the dominant class. For example, an Aboriginal person who repeatedly hears that "all Indians are drunks" might begin seeing himself or herself this way with respect to alcohol, and so becoming either a strict abstainer from drinking or a binge drinker.

latent function   (as described by Merton) the largely unintended and unrecognized positive function of a social process or institution. A **latent dysfunction** produces socially negative consequences. *Compare* **manifest function.**

law of effect   (as described by E. Thorndike) the principle that the likelihood of a person's repeating an action increases if the action is rewarded, while the likelihood decreases if the action is punished or ignored. The law of effect is central to **behaviour modification.**

left-wing   denoting views or ideas consistent with a socialist or even communist political ideology. *Compare* **right-wing.**

legitimization of inequality   (in cultural reproduction theory) the validation of streaming that occurs when students accept their categorization as, say, "basic" or "advanced" (a judgement that may reflect that person's class or "race"), thereby reproducing social inequality within the school system.

leisure   free time, esp. seen as something available to the very rich, whose wealth frees them from having to do work.

lesbian   a woman who is sexually attracted to other women.

LGBT   an abbreviation for *lesbian, gay, bisexual, transgender*, serving as an all-encompassing term for anyone who is not heterosexual.

liberal ideology   a set of beliefs that focuses on the individual as an independent player in society, not as a member of a class or an ethnic group. Components of this set include a strong belief in the potential for **social mobility** in the individual (as seen in the **American dream**) and a tendency towards **blaming the victim.**

liberalism   (as described by A. Smith) the belief that "the market" should be completely free to expand and grow without any governmental interference. In the writing of nineteenth-century thinker J.S. Mill, it referred to a belief in the freedom of the individual from both government and the dominant culture (the "tyranny of the majority").

liberation theology   a political movement based on a progressive school of Christian thought, rooted in the Catholic church in Latin America, that advocates social justice for the poor, especially in the developing world.

life course   the sequence of socially defined stages of life through which people pass between birth and death.

life expectancy at birth   the average number of years a newborn infant could be expected to live, should prevailing patterns of mortality continue throughout his or her life.

linguistic determinism (*or* causation)   the theory that the way an individual understands the world is shaped by the language he or she speaks.

living wage   a wage or salary on which an individual can live, maintaining a reasonable standard of living while supporting a family, without suffering from poverty.

lockout   a tactic used in collective bargaining in which the management or owner of a unionized workplace prevents employees from going to work and collecting pay, in order to pressure the workers into accepting a contract offer.

longitudinal study   a study that continues over time to track changes in the subjects as they get older.

looking-glass self   (as described by C.H. Cooley) the self as defined and reinforced through interactions with others.

Lotus Blossom Baby   (as described by Tajima & Das Gupta) a stereotype of East Asian women as childlike, sexually available, and respectful of men. Evidence of this stereotype may be found in the China doll and in Western notions of the Japanese **geisha.** *Compare* **Dragon Lady.**

Low Income Cut-Offs (LICOs)   a measure of poverty derived by calculating the percentage of a family's income spent on food, clothing, and shelter.

Low Income Measure (LIM-IAT)   a measure of poverty calculated by identifying those households with total incomes (after taxes) half that of the median income in Canada (with some adjustments made for family size and composition).

Luddites   British members of an early anti-industrial movement in Europe, in which craftspeople who had lost their work with the introduction of labour-saving machines protested by destroying the new machinery. The term is used today to refer to people who resist new technology.

lumpenproletariat   (as described by Marx) the group of people in capitalist society who neither own capital nor participate in wage labour. For the most part they get by with casual/occasional labour, scavenging for food and articles to sell, and crime.

macrosociology   an approach to sociological inquiry that involves looking at the large-scale structure and dynamics of society as a whole.

manifest function   (as described by Merton) the intended and widely recognized function of a social process or institution. *Compare* **latent function**.

manufacturing of need   the creation of consumer demand for (1) items that were once produced in the home, or (2) products that were once considered inessential.

marginalization   the experience of being treated as insignificant or of being moved beyond the margin of mainstream society.

marginalized masculinity   (as described by R. Connell) those forms of masculinity that, owing to class, "race," sexual orientation, and ethnicity, are accorded less respect than other forms of masculinity.

marital roles   *another term for* **conjugal roles**.

marked term   a term with a qualifying or distinguishing label added to it (e.g. *field hockey* or *lite beer*), showing that it is not the usual form. *Compare* **unmarked term**.

Market Basket Measure (MBM)   an estimate of the cost of a specific basket of goods and services for a given year, assuming that all items in the basket were entirely provided for out of the spending of the household. Having an income lower than the MBM constitutes low income or poverty.

Marxist   denoting a way of thinking influenced by the theories of Karl Marx and Friedrich Engels. Generally speaking, Marxism considers social change and inequality in terms of economic factors and class.

mass consumption   the purchase of goods and services that are available to nearly anyone in society. *Compare* **elite consumption**.

mass culture   the **culture** of the majority, when that culture is produced by big companies and powerful governments.

master narrative   a story that a nation or a people constructs about itself. A master narrative typically makes one group (the group that produced it) look heroic while casting other peoples, including minorities within the group, as bad or invisible.

master status   the **status** of an individual that dominates all of his or her other statuses in most social contexts, and plays the greatest role in defining the individual's social identity.

matrilineal   denoting kinship determined along the mother's line.

matrilocal   denoting a situation in which a man and a woman live together in or near the mother's family residence(s).

McDonaldization   (as described by Ritzer) the application of principles of formal rationalization seen in the fast-food industry to other sectors of society.

McJob   a low-paying, unskilled job in the service industry (e.g. at a store or fast-food restaurant).

means of consumption   the main social means by which people consume what is produced.

means of production   (as described by Marx) the social means required for producing wealth (e.g. land in feudal times; capital—wealth, machinery—during the industrial period).

mechanical solidarity   (as described by Durkheim) the social cohesion that exists in a society in which people do the same kind of work as each other, creating a sense of kinship through common experience. *Compare* **organic solidarity**.

media spectacle   a large event that dominates the media, strongly affecting or changing the way people envision the world. The death of Princess Diana and, more recently, the manhunt for suspects in the Boston Marathon bombing are examples.

medicalization   the process by which certain behaviours or conditions are defined as medical problems (rather than, say, social problems), and medical intervention becomes the focus of remedy and social control.

medical model (of disability)   a positivist view of disability, representing the perspective of doctors, researchers, and others who believe that science can and should be used to determine treatments, policies, and programs for people living with disabilities. Compare **economic model (of disability)**.

medical sociology   the use of sociological research and data to analyze and improve public health, focusing primarily on how healthcare is administered and whether the medical system adequately supports both the providers and the recipients of healthcare and health services.

melting pot   a metaphor for a country in which immigrants are believed or expected to lose their cultural distinctiveness and assimilate into the dominant society. *Compare* **cultural mosaic**.

menarche   the first menstruation of an adolescent girl.

menopause   the period in a woman's life, usually between the ages of 45 and 50, when she stops menstruating.

meritocratic   awarding power or rewards to people based on their demonstrated ability or achievements.

Métis a people of mixed Aboriginal and European ethnicity (usually Cree or Saulteaux and French) that developed in the late eighteenth century and grew to take on a sense of nationality as well as a distinct legal status.

metrosexual a term used to describe a man (usually a heterosexual man) whose lifestyle, spending habits, and concern for personal appearance are likened to those considered typical of a fashionable, urban, homosexual man.

microsociology an approach to sociology that focuses not on the grand scale of society but on the plans, motivations, and actions of the individual or a specific group. *Compare* **macrosociology**.

middle class the social class made up primarily of small-scale businesspeople, educated professionals, and salaried employees possessing certifiable credentials.

midlife crisis an emotional crisis occurring in early middle age, which may cause an individual (male or female) to experience restlessness, anxiety, depression, a desire for new challenges, or simply an impulse to "take stock" and re-evaluate life goals and personal priorities.

minimum wage the lowest hourly wage that an employer is permitted by law to pay an employee.

minoritized denoting an identifiable social group that is discriminated against by mainstream society or the **dominants**.

misogyny (*adj.* **misogynous**) practices or beliefs in a patriarchal culture that show contempt for women.

mobility sports sports such as soccer and boxing that provide access to socioeconomic mobility for the poorest groups in society. These sports do not require significant funds or access to resources, but can be played with little or no equipment.

modernism an optimistic view of **social change** that envisions change as producing a world better than what preceded it.

monoculturalism the promotion of just one culture. *Compare* **multiculturalism**.

moral community (as described by Durkheim) a group of individuals sharing a commitment to a common moral (usually religious) worldview. Durkheim differed from his contemporaries in viewing religion as a communal rather than individual experience.

moral entrepreneur someone who tries to convince others of the existence of a particular social problem that he or she has defined.

moral stigma *see* **stigma**.

mores (as described by W. Sumner) rules that one "must not" violate. Some of these are enshrined in the criminal code as laws; violation of mores often results in shock, severe disapproval, or punishment.

multiculturalism the set of policies and practices directed towards the respect for cultural differences in a country.

myth of the liberal media the false notion that the media are dominated by people holding a left-of-centre political and social perspective.

narratives stories that reflect the lives and views of the tellers.

narrow socialization **socialization** in which obedience and conformity to the standards and expectations of the community are emphasized, and punishment for deviation is practised. *Compare* **broad socialization**.

narrow vision (as described by Chomsky) a short-sighted view, held by those who believe in **modernism**, that whatever innovation benefits the dominant class is justifiable on the grounds of progress.

national character a now discredited belief, belonging to the **culture and personality** school of thought, that people of different countries have distinct personalities unique to their country (e.g. Italians are passionate, Germans are cold).

negative correlation *see* **inverse correlation**.

negative sanctions ways of punishing people who contravene cultural norms. Examples of negative sanctions include laughing at or isolating an individual.

neoliberalism policies that involve shrinking the public sector (through privatization of public enterprises, tax cuts, the reduction of public spending, and the downsizing of government) and increasing freedom for big business (through deregulation of the economy, control of organized labour, the expansion of international markets, and the removal of controls on global financial flows). *Also called* **neoconservativism**.

neo-traditionalism (among some Aboriginal peoples) a religious movement that involves the reinterpretation of traditional beliefs and practices in ways that incorporate elements unique to one's own culture and others borrowed from Native cultures elsewhere.

noble savage the romantic belief that indigenous people, or "savages," are superior in outlook and lifestyle because they don't live in the industrialized and urbanized environment of the person invoking the image.

non-utilitarian denoting actions that are not designed to gain financial rewards or desired possessions.

normalized made to seem "normal," "right," and "good."

normalizing judgement a form of disciplinary control in which group behaviour is conditioned through a judging system that ranks individual performance in relation to the performance of others, rather than on its intrinsic merits; it is one of three tactics used to produce what Foucault called a **docile body**. *Compare* **examination**, **hierarchical observation**.

norms rules or standards of behaviour that are expected of a group, society, or culture.

North, the the wealthiest nations of the world, previously termed the **First World** or the **developed nations**. It refers to the fact that the majority of rich countries are located in the northern hemisphere.

nuclear family a family comprising a mother, a father, and children. The term is used to describe what is typically considered a "normal" family.

objectivity (*adj.* **objective**) a supposed quality of scientific research that is not influenced by emotions, personality, or particular life experiences of the individual scientist. It better applies to the physical sciences—physics, chemistry, biology, etc.—than to the social sciences.

observational learning theory the theory that children acquire "aggressive scripts" for solving social problems through watching violence on television.

occupational crimes (as described by Clinard & Quinney) offences committed by individuals for themselves in the course of their occupations, or by employers against their employees. *Compare* **corporate crimes**.

occupational segregation (as described by R. Beaujot) the situation in which women choose (or end up in) occupations that afford them some flexibility and greater tolerance of childcare-related **work interruptions**.

oligarchy rule of a country by a few powerful individuals or groups.

open shop a workplace where membership in the union representing the workplace is optional. *Compare* **closed shop**.

operational definition the definition of an abstract quality (e.g. poverty, pollution) in such a way that it can be counted for statistical purposes.

oralist a bias in favour of those who communicate using speech. Some deaf people object to lip-reading on the grounds it reflects an oralist bias, forcing deaf people to conform to the communication method favoured by those who are not deaf instead of using their own communication (sign language).

organic identity *see* **corporate identity**.

organic solidarity (as described by Durkheim) the kind of social cohesion that exists in a society in which people specialize in different kinds of work and, as a result, recognize their dependence on one another. *Compare* **mechanical solidarity**.

organizational behaviour the study of organizations in terms of the way the individuals within organizations interact.

organizational culture the dynamics of an organization studied in terms of the ritual and symbolic acts carried out by its members.

organizational theory the study of the way organizations operate.

Orientalism (as described by Said) a **discourse** about the Middle East and the Far East constructed by outsider "experts" from the West.

original affluent society (as described by M. Sahlins) hunter-and-gatherer cultures, which are not engaged in farming or industrial manufacturing, and whose few material needs can be met without many hours of labour.

other, the an exotic, often fearful image conjured up by the dominant culture of a racialized subordinate culture, or by a colonizing nation of the colonized.

outsider perspective the viewpoint(s) of those outside of the group or culture being studied. The outsider perspective was once considered a privileged position,

with the outsider viewed as an expert. *Compare* **insider perspective**.

outsourcing the practice of sending work to companies or individuals outside of the organization, and sometimes outside of the country.

oversharing the tendency to divulge excessive amounts of personal information, esp. to a mass media audience.

oversocialized (as described by D. Wrong) a misleading conception of humans as passive recipients of **socialization**.

overt characteristics (of deviance) actions or qualities taken as explicitly violating the cultural norm. *Compare* **covert characteristics**.

owners *another term for* **bourgeoisie**.

packaged rebel an appearance of individuality and counter-cultural sentiment that is conveyed by clothing and accessories that are, paradoxically, marketed by and purchased from large multinational clothing manufacturers and retailers capitalizing on the desire of consumers to want to appear rebellious.

paid work work performed for pay; the term is often used to distinguish what we call *employment* from **unpaid work**.

participant observation a form of research in sociology and anthropology that entails both observing people as an outsider would and actively participating in the various activities of the studied people's lives. It is usually employed in undertaking an **ethnography**.

particularist protectionist a person who favours policies designed to protect the culture, politics, and economy of his or her own country from foreign competition and the forces of globalization in general. *Compare* **universalist protectionist**.

passing the practice of downplaying or disowning an ascribed status (typically "race") by claiming a dominant status. Aboriginal people, for example, may try to pass for white to avoid discrimination.

patriarchal construct a set of social conditions structured in a way that favours men and boys over women and girls.

patriarchy a social system in which men hold political, cultural, and social power. Patriarchy is visible in societies where only male political leaders are elected and where the media and the arts are dominated by male views.

patrilineal kinship determined along the father's line.

patriotism love and vigorous support of one's country.

pay equity compensation paid to women in traditionally female-dominated industries (e.g. childcare, library science, nursing, and secretarial work) where salaries and benefits have been lower than those given to employees in comparable (in terms of educational qualifications, hours worked, and social value) professions dominated by men. As a policy, it is one of two ways of addressing the imbalance in men's and women's pay. *Compare* **equal pay**.

peasants (in Marxist thinking) the people who in feudal times worked the land but did not own it.

pecuniary emulation   (as described by Veblen) the practice of copying the buying and spending habits of others, typically wealthier, trendsetting members of society's "leisure class." Pecuniary emulation is a byproduct of **conspicuous consumption**.

peep culture   (as described by H. Niedziviecki) the fascination with observing the often mundane behaviour of people in unguarded moments, caught on film and then broadcast via the Internet, television, etc.

peer group   the social group to which one belongs, or to which one wishes to belong, as a more-or-less equal.

peer pressure   the social pressure put on an individual to conform to the ways of a particular group that the individual belongs to or wishes to belong to.

peer-review process   the rigorous assessment by academic experts of the draft of a scholarly article or book to ensure that it is suitable for publication.

petty (or *petite*) **bourgeoisie**   (as described by Marx) the sub-class made up of small-time owners with little capital.

phantom aid   *see* **tied aid**.

pibloktuq   *another term for* **Arctic hysteria**.

pin money   a small amount of money for spending on inessentials. The term was originally used for the allowance that women received from their husbands to spend on personal items (such as hair pins). During the early twentieth century, women who were joining the workforce in growing numbers had to fight the notion they were content to work for pin money, when in fact many needed to earn a **living wage**.

plagiarism   a form of academic misconduct in which another person's ideas are presented as one's own, whether knowingly or unknowingly.

planned obsolescence   a strategy used especially by manufacturers of consumer electronics in which a product is designed *not* to last so that consumers will constantly crave the newest version.

playing child model   (as described by Wyness) a contemporary Western model of childhood that equates childhood with play and the absence of work and adult responsibility. Wyness proposed the model—which is not universal across all cultures and all times—to show that childhood is a largely social construction.

play stage   (as described by Mead) the second developmental sequence for child **socialization**, in which pretending is involved. *See* **game stage**, **role taking**.

policy sociology   the use of sociological research and data to produce social change, especially through government or corporate policy.

polite racism   *another term for* **friendly racism**.

political correctness   the avoidance of terms or expressions perceived to exclude, marginalize, or insult people or groups that are social disadvantaged or discriminated against.

political economy   an interdisciplinary approach that involves sociology, political science, economics, law, anthropology, and history. It looks primarily at the relationship between politics and the economics surrounding the production, distribution, and consumption of goods.

political globalization   (as described by M. Steger) the intensification and expansion of political connections across the world.

polyarchy   literally, government by many people. As described by R. Dahl, this refers to government by changing coalitions of powerful interest groups.

polygamy   the practice of having more than one husband or wife at the same time. A situation in which a woman has more than one husband at the same time is **polyandry**; the analogous situation in which a man has more than one wife at the same time is **polygyny**.

popular culture   commercial culture based on popular taste.

positive correlation   *another word for* **direct correlation**.

positive sanctions   ways of rewarding people for following the norms of a society (e.g. inclusion into a desired group, career success).

positivism (*adj.* **positivist**)   the belief that every rational assertion can be verified by scientific proof.

post-colonialism   *another term for* **anti-colonialism**.

post-industrial   denoting a culture or an era in which the service sector produces more wealth than the industrial or manufacturing sector, and in which manufacturing is done in a manner that is much less damaging to the environment.

postmodernism (*adj. & n.* **postmodernist**)   (1) a model of **social change** that recognizes that change can benefit some while harming others (e.g. a **digital divide**); also called **postmodern theory**. (2) a model of social theory that, among other things, discourages the application of **binaries** to the interpretation of social categories such as gender, "race," and ability. Also called postmodern theory. *See also* **feminist postmodernism**.

posttraumatic stress disorder (PTSD)   a condition in which the sufferer experiences serious psychobiological symptoms stemming from his or her experience of harrowing events, such as warfare, political oppression, or crime. The condition is often medicalized, so that treatment focuses on the pathology of the individual rather than the pathology of the social environment that provides the context for the event the sufferer experienced. *See* **medicalization**.

potlatch   any of various traditional ceremonies of Aboriginal groups of the Northwest Coast. It involves reaffirming traditional values and stories through speaking, acting, dancing, and singing important stories, and reflecting the traditional value of generosity through large-scale giveaway of cherished items.

poverty   a state of doing or being without what are considered essentials.

poverty line   the arbitrary dividing point, usually based on household income, that separates the poor from the rest of society. It can differ according to the cost of living in the studied environment, and it may differ for urban and rural communities. It can also vary according to the political biases of the person drawing the line.

power elite   Mills' term for the people wielding significant economic and political power.

Powley test   a set of questions used to determine whether Métis and other Native people can lawfully hunt without a licence.

predictability   one of four main elements of Weber's model of **formal rationalization**, having to do with setting clear expectations for both the employee and the consumer. *See* **control, efficiency, quantification.**

prejudice   the pre-judging of people based on their membership in a particular social group.

preparatory stage   (as described by Mead) the first developmental sequence of child **socialization**, which involves pure imitation.

present-centred   denoting a media source, such as television, that constantly supplies information as new without requiring the consumer to have the background information necessary to understanding it.

preventive war   a military campaign justified on the grounds of preventing an attack on one's own country.

primary socialization   the earliest **socialization** that a child receives.

primordialism (*or* **primordiality**)   *another term for* **essentialism.**

production-based society   a society whose members are defined by their work, specifically their role in producing and selling commodities. *Compare* **consumption-based society.**

profane   not sacred or concerned with religion. *Compare* **sacred.**

professional sociology   sociology that involves research typically designed to generate highly specific information, often with the aim of applying it to a particular problem or intellectual question. Its usual audience is the academic world of sociology departments, academic journals, professional associations, and conferences.

professionalization   the process of turning work done by volunteers into paid work.

proletariat   *see* **workers.**

propaganda model   (as described by Herman & Chomsky) the theory that six factors, or "filters," are chiefly responsible for the way the media are controlled by powerful commercial and political interests; these include (1) the concentration of media ownership, (2) the dependence of media companies on advertisers, (3) the mutual interests of media barons and corporate and political figures, (4) the pressure wielded on the media by powerful groups when they feel that stories are being reported unfairly, (5) the ready supply of "experts" available to appear on or in the media to articulate a government- or corporate-friendly view, and (6) the ability of controlling media interests to maintain the status quo.

Protestant (work) ethic   (as described by Weber) a set of values embodied in early Protestantism, believed to have led to the development of modern capitalism.

psychoanalysis   (as described by Freud) an approach to psychological study that involves hypothesized stages of development and components of the self (*see* **id, ego, eros, superego,** and **thanatos**). It is used by sociologists to look at individual relationships to society and at cultural expression.

psychoneuroimmunology   the study of the effect of the mind on health and resistance to disease.

public sociology   (as described by H. Gans) sociology that addresses an audience outside of the academy. It is presented in a language that can be understood by the college-educated reader, without the dense style of the academic paper or journal, and expresses concern for a breadth of sociological subjects.

public sphere   the places—physical and virtual—where citizens can participate in debate and discussion of matters of social and political importance.

qualitative research   the close examination of characteristics that cannot be counted or measured.

quantification   one of four main elements of Weber's model of **formal rationalization**, having to do with breaking a process down into a number of quantifiable tasks that can be easily measured to gauge success. *See* **control, efficiency, predictability.**

quantitative research   the close examination of social elements that can be counted or measured, and therefore used to generate statistics.

queer   an informal term for someone (male or female) who is sexually attracted to people of the same sex.

queer theory   (as described by J. Butler) an approach that rejects the idea that gender identity is connected to some biological essence, proposing instead that gender reflects social performance on a continuum, with "male" and "female" at opposite poles.

quintile   each of five ranked groups making up 20 per cent of a total population, used for statistical analysis of such things as household income.

racial bigotry   the open, conscious expression of racist views by an individual.

racial profiling   actions undertaken supposedly for reasons of safety, security, or public protection, based on racial stereotypes, rather than on reasonable suspicion.

racialization (*adj.* **racialized**)   a social process in which groups of people are viewed and judged as essentially different in terms of their intellect, morality, values, and innate worth because of differences of physical type or cultural heritage.

racializing deviance   the creation of a connection, through various media (television, movies, textbooks), between a racialized group and a form of deviance or crime (e.g. Latinos and drug dealing, black people and prostitution).

radical monopoly   (as described by Illich) a situation in which professional control work is deemed socially important (e.g. teachers in education; doctors/nurses in healthcare).

reading   the process of analyzing or interpreting narrative texts produced by the culture industry, often in ways not necessarily intended by the creators of the text.

real culture   social life and institutions as they ought to exist based on our social norms, values, and goals. *Compare* **ideal culture**.

reductionist   denoting any unrealistic statement or theory that attempts to explain a set of phenomena by referring to a single cause. In sociology, this includes **class reductionism**, or reducing all inequality to gender, "race," or ethnicity.

reference group   a group perceived by another group to be equal but better off.

registered Indian   an Aboriginal person who bears federal government recognition of his or her legal right to the benefits (and penalties) of being "legally Indian." *Formerly called* **status Indian**.

reincorporation   (as described by Van Gennep) the third and final phase of a rite of passage, in which initiates rejoin society to have their new status recognized. Compare separation, transition.

relational   denoting the relationship between a class and the means of producing wealth.

relational accountability   an approach that balances the social portrayal of a people so that both strengths and weaknesses, problems and successes are seen.

relations of ruling   (as described by D. Smith) the dominance of the individual or group by large government and large business. Smith argues that these are reinforced by uncritical sociological analysis.

relative deprivation   a situation in which an individual or the members of a group feel deprived compared to a **reference group** that they see as having no greater entitlement to their relatively better situation.

relative poverty   a state of poverty based on a comparison with others in the immediate area or country. *Compare* **absolute poverty**.

relativism (*adj.* **relativist**)   the doctrine that concepts such as knowledge, truth, and morality are not absolute but must be understood in terms of their social, cultural, and historical context. *Compare* **universalist**.

rentier effect   (as described by M. Ross) one of the factors that explains the hypothesis that the more dependent a country is on oil, the less democracy exists there. *Rentier* comes from a French word for one who lives on income from property and investments, and the rentier effect has to do with the ways a government appeases its critics through three related effects: the **taxation effect**, the **spending effect**, and the **group formation effect**. *Compare* **repression effect**.

replacement rate   the rate at which children must be born in order to replace the generation before them.

repression effect   (as described by M. Ross) one of the factors that explains the hypothesis that the more dependent a country is on oil, the less democracy exists there. The repression effect is about how a government builds internal security forces in order to dampen criticism. *Compare* **rentier effect**.

reproduction   (as described by Bourdieu) the means by which classes, particularly the upper or dominant class, preserve status differences between classes.

research methodology   the system of strategies a researcher uses to gather data on a particular question.

residential schools   a system of educating Aboriginal children that involved removing them from their homes and communities, isolating them from their culture, and often abusing them physically, emotionally, and sexually. Underfunded by the federal government, the schools were run by a number of church groups, primarily the Roman Catholic, Anglican, and Presbyterian churches. The system, which began in the late nineteenth century and was formalized in 1910, ended slowly between the 1960s and the 1980s.

resocialization   the process of unlearning old ways and learning new ways upon moving into a significantly different social environment.

reverse ethnocentrism   a situation in which individuals set up a culture other than their own as the absolute standard by which to judge their own culture. *Compare* **ethnocentrism**.

rhetoric   the study of how people use language to persuade others or to put together an argument.

right-wing   denoting views or ideas consistent with a conservative political ideology. *Compare* **left-wing**.

right-to-work law   a law that makes it illegal to force employees to join a union, essentially outlawing the **closed shop**. Business owners favour right-to-work laws because they erode the strength and bargaining powers of unions.

risk behaviour   behaviour with a relatively high chance of harming an individual. Examples include driving at unsafe speeds, practising unsafe sexual activities, and abusing drugs and alcohol.

rite of passage   (as described by Van Gennep) a ceremonial or ritualized passage from one stage of life to another. Examples include Christian **confirmation** and the Aboriginal **vision quest**.

ritual degradation   a rite of passage in which the person is stripped of his or her individuality (e.g. hazing).

role   the function assumed or the part played by a person holding a particular status.

role conflict   the tension that occurs when a person is forced to meet the incompatible demands of two or more statuses, such as those of a business professional expected to reply to client e-mails 24/7 who is also a parent to young children.

role exit   the process of disengaging from a role that has been central to one's identity and establishing a new role. Role exit occurs, for example, when a person leaves a long-held job or a marriage.

role model   an influential person whose patterns of behaviour are observed and imitated by others.

role set   all of the roles attached to a particular **status**. For example, attached to the status of "professor" are the roles of educator, colleague, and employee.

role strain   a situation that occurs when two or more roles associated with one **status** come into conflict. A nurse may experience role strain when his duty to his employer (the hospital) comes into conflict with his obligations to a patient (for example, if he feels the therapy recommended for a patient is more cost-efficient than effective).

role-playing game   a game that allows players to experiment with roles outside of their usual experience by adopting fictitious **statuses**.

role-taking   (as described by Mead) the stage at which children assume the perspective of **significant others**, imagining what they are thinking as they act the way they do. *Compare* **game stage**, **play stage**.

rotten apple approach   an attempt to downplay the systemic problems in a process or an organization by placing the blame on individuals.

ruling interests   the interests of the organization, particularly its administration, or the interests of those who are dominant in society.

ruling relations   the conformity of workers to the rules and practices of the organization they work for; ruling relations are activated when workers fulfill the organization's **ruling interests**.

sacred   denoting an act or experience that is positively regarded and deemed worthy of respect and veneration, being associated with religion and set apart from ordinary acts and experiences. *Compare* **profane**.

sanctions   *see* **negative sanctions**, **positive sanctions**.

Sapir-Whorf hypothesis   the theory that the structure of a language determines a person's perception of experience. A milder version argues for linguistic relativity, the view that language and culture have a unique relationship in each society.

savagery   (as described by L.H. Morgan) the supposed first stage of social evolution toward modern civilization. *Compare* **barbarism**, **civilization**.

scientific classism   the use of flawed, pseudoscientific ideas (e.g. eugenics) to justify discriminatory actions against poor people.

scientific management   efforts to find and implement the one best way of doing any job. These typically involve studying the time, methods, and tools required for a proficient worker to complete a particular task, and looking for ways to improve his or her efficiency. *Also called* **Taylorism**.

scientific racism   the use of flawed, pseudoscientific ideas (e.g. eugenics, measuring brain sizes) to justify discriminatory actions against certain racialized groups.

scrips   certificates issued to Métis in the latter part of the nineteenth century, which declared that the bearer could receive payment in land, cash, or goods. The legal status of these certificates was abused by government officials and land speculators.

second shift   *another term for* **double burden**.

secondary socialization   any **socialization** that occurs later than the **primary socialization** in the life of a child.

Second World   (prior to the collapse of the USSR in the late 1980s) a term used to refer to the Soviet Union and the eastern European countries under its power.

secularism   attitudes and activities with no basis in religion.

segregated conjugal roles   **conjugal roles** in which tasks, interests, and activities are clearly different. *Compare* **joint conjugal roles**.

semiotics   the study of signs, symbols, and signifying practices.

semi-structured interview   an informal, face-to-face interview designed to cover specific topics without the rigid structure of a questionnaire but with more structure than an open interview.

separation   (as described by Van Gennep) the first phase of a rite of passage, in which initiates are taken from the place (the physical location and social location) that they've grown accustomed to. *Compare* **reincorporation**, **transition**.

service-provider organization   (as described by C. Mueller) a type of **feminist organization** that combines elements of **formal social movement organizations** and **small groups**.

sex   the biological differences between boys/men and girls/women, as opposed to the sociological differences (which come under the term **gender**).

sick (*or patient*) role   (as described by Parsons) the set of expectations that surround a sick person and the experience of being sick.

sign   communication made up of a **signifier**, which carries meaning, and a **signified**, the meaning that is carried.

significant others   (as described by Mead) those key individuals—primarily parents, to a lesser degree older siblings and close friends—whom young children imitate and model themselves after.

simple household   a household consisting of unmarried, unrelated adults with or without children.

simulacra   (as described by J. Baudrillard) cultural images, often in the form of stereotypes, that are produced and reproduced like material goods or commodities by the media and sometimes by academics.

situationists   members of the Situationist International movement of artists, intellectuals, and Marxists, who, from 1957 to 1972 attempted to present a counter-narrative to advanced capitalism and the mainstream media. *See also* **détournement**.

Sixties Scoop   the removal, between the 1960s and the early 1980s, of thousands of Aboriginal children from their families, their communities, their home provinces (particularly Manitoba), and sometimes their home country, to place them in non-Aboriginal homes.

skeptical globalizers   those who see globalization as a process that is potentially dangerous to the environment and to the economies and social welfare of the "have-not" countries.

slippery slope   the logical fallacy that one small change will automatically snowball into the collapse of the entire social order. Slippery-slope arguments are often voiced by adherents of **conservativism**.

small group   (as described by C. Mueller) a type of **feminist organization** with an informal structure, which typically requires large commitments of time and resources from its members. *Also called* **collective**.

smiling racism   *another term for* **friendly racism**.

social change   the set of adjustments or adaptations made by a group of people in response to a dramatic change experienced in at least one aspect of their lives.

social constructionism   the idea that social identities such as gender, ethnicity, and "race" do not exist naturally but are constructed by individuals or groups for different social purposes. **Instrumentalism** is an example of social constructionism.

social constructionist model   a sociological framework based on the idea that any human social category—"race," gender, ability, etc.—is not a strictly natural category but a category with an important social component.

social course of disease   the social interactions that a sick person goes through in the process of being treated.

social Darwinism   the application, in the late nineteenth and early twentieth centuries, of the principle of **survival of the fittest** to human groups, used to justify the power held by Europeans and the upper classes on the grounds that they were the strongest and the best.

social distance   a lack of personal familiarity that exists when individuals do not have face-to-face interactions, or any interaction at all. Social distance may exist between students of online courses and their instructors.

social ecology   a school of thought, founded by Bookchin, that recognizes the link between environmental issues and social problems, including economic, cultural, ethnic, and gender conflicts.

social fact   Durkheim's term for a patterned way of acting, thinking, and feeling that exists outside of the individual but that exerts control over all people.

social gospel movement   a movement in the late nineteenth and early twentieth centuries in Canada, the United States, and various European countries to apply the human welfare principles of Christianity to the social, medical, and psychological ills brought on by industrialization and uncontrolled capitalism.

social iatrogenesis   (as described by Illich) the deliberate obscuring of political conditions that render society unhealthy.

social inequality   the long-term existence of significant differences in access to goods and services among social groups defined by class, ethnicity, etc.

socialization   the process of learning or being taught the values and standards of behaviour of the social group of which one is a member. *See* **broad socialization, narrow socialization, primary socialization, secondary socialization**.

social location   the important social aspects of an individual, including class, "race," age, gender, sexual orientation, and degree of ability, that inform the individual's perspective and shape his or her experience.

social media   all of the means that enable people to interact with one another within a virtual community supported by the Internet.

social mobility   the movement from one class into another (usually higher) class.

social movement   a group of people organized and working together to achieve a common social goal, through activism, protest, volunteer work, etc.

social organization   the social and cultural principles around which things are structured, ordered, and categorized.

social resources   the knowledge and ability required to get what one needs from the system. In the context of law, for example, social resources include knowledge of the legal system, the ability to pay for legal advice, and the ability to present oneself as respectable in a courtroom.

social segregation   either a deliberate strategy to separate groups of individuals based on social characteristics such as sex, ethnicity, and class, or the outcome of feeling marginalized as a result of this strategy.

society   the community of people living together in a particular country or region, having shared customs, laws, and values, and common systems of social organization.

sociolinguistics   (as described by W. Labov) the study of language (particularly **dialect**) as a social marker of status or general distinctiveness, or the study of how different languages conceptualize the world (e.g. the **Sapir-Whorf Hypothesis**).

sociological imagination   (as described by Mills) the capacity to shift from the perspective of the personal experience to the grander, societal scale that has caused or influenced that personal experience.

sociological poetry   (as described by Mills) the writing of sociology in such a way that it is beautifully crafted and readily understood. *Compare* **public sociology**.

sociology   the social science that studies the development, structure, and functioning of human society.

solidarity   the unity shown by workers in the face of opposition, whether by employers, the media, or society. *See* **mechanical solidarity, organic solidarity**.

South, the   the poorer nations of the world, previously known either as the **Third World** or the **developing nations**.

special interest (group)   a group or organization that seeks or receives special privileges based on its unique circumstances. The term is sometimes used derogatorily for a group trying to express its collective rights.

spending effect   (as described by M. Ross) one of three components of the **rentier effect**, this is about an oil-rich government's ability to appease political opponents by providing them with well-paying jobs and positions of authority. *Compare* **group formation effect, taxation effect**.

spurious reasoning   the perception of a correlation between two factors that are wrongly seen as cause and effect.

squaw   a stereotype of the Aboriginal woman as lazy, drunken, and abused by Aboriginal men. *Compare* **Indian Princess.**

standpoint   the unique perspective of an individual based on a set of sociological characteristics including age, sex and gender, social class, "race" or ethnic background, employment status, family situation, degree of physical ability, etc.

standpoint theory   (as described by D. Smith) the view that knowledge is developed from a particular lived position, or "standpoint," making **objectivity** impossible.

staples   (as described by Innis) natural resources such as fish, fur, minerals, and crops, upon which countries such as Canada built their economy.

statistical norms   **norms** that reflect, statistically, what people actually do, in distinction to **cultural norms**, which are what people claim to do.

statistics   a science that, in sociology, involves the use of numbers to map social behaviour and beliefs.

status   a recognized social position that a person occupies, which comes with a set of responsibilities and expectations. People hold more than one status (husband, stepfather, pet owner, sociology professor, ball fan, garage band drummer, small-town resident), and a person's statuses can and do change over time. More generally, **status** refers to the relative social standing of a person or group, typically when it is highly regarded.

status consistency   *see* **status inconsistency.**

status frustration   (as described by A. Cohen) a feeling of failure to succeed in middle-class terms or institutions, leading to participation in **delinquent subculture**. *See* **subcultural theory.**

status hierarchy   the ranking of **statuses** within the categories of ethnicity, class, age, etc., based on the degree to which they are favoured by society generally. Heterosexuality, for example, is generally ranked above homosexuality and bisexuality in the status hierarchy associated with sexual preference.

status inconsistency   a situation in which the **statuses** a person holds do not align in terms of how they are generally ranked by society. A successful First Nation businessman may experience status inconsistency because his racialized status is not favoured the way his professional and economic statuses are. When an individual's statuses do align, the result is **status consistency.**

status Indian   *a former term for* **registered Indian.**

status set   the complete set of **statuses** held by an individual.

status symbol   an item purchased or used to show off the owner's high social and economic standing.

stigma (*plural* **stigmata**)   (as described by Goffman) a human attribute that is seen to discredit an individual's social identity. **Bodily stigmata** are any of various physical deformities. **Moral stigmata** are perceived flaws in the character of an individual. **Tribal stigmata** relate to being of a particular lineage or family that has been stigmatized (e.g. the family of a murderer or gang member).

strain theory   (as described by Merton) the theory that individuals are drawn to crime because of the frustration they feel at being prevented by their real-life circumstances from attaining society's culturally defined goals (expressed as the **American dream**).

strata (*singular* **stratum**)   social classes in ranked layers, with no specific relationship to the means of producing wealth.

streaming   *another term for* **tracking.**

strike   a form of labour action in which unionized employees withdraw their services entirely in order to force the management or owner of a business to engage in collective bargaining.

structural functionalism   a sociological approach that examines the way social systems operate by viewing those systems in terms of the various parts or structures of which they are made. The structural-functionalist approach views society as being like a human body, made up of different structures, with each having a vital function in ensuring the survival of the whole body.

subcultural theory   (as described by Cohen) the theory that youths drawn to crime are those who, having failed to succeed in middle-class institutions (specifically school), become socialized into a **delinquent subculture** in which the values of middle-class institutions are inverted. Cohen's theory builds on Merton's **strain theory.**

subculture   a group that is organized around occupations or hobbies differing from those of the dominant culture but that is not engaged in any significant opposition to the dominant culture.

subjective   denoting theories, beliefs, and opinions influenced by emotions, personality, and particular life experiences of the individual. The term is used in opposing ways: some sociologists discredit observation that is "merely subjective" rather than "objective fact"; others argue that all "facts" are to some degree subjective but hide behind the mask of objectivity.

subordinate cultures   groups that feel the power of the dominant culture and exist in opposition to it.

subordinate masculinity   (as described by R. Connell) behaviours and presentations of self that can threaten the legitimacy of hegemonic masculinity. The usual examples given are gay or effeminate men, and those whose lives and beliefs challenge traditional definitions of male success.

substantive equality   (in critical disability theory) a model according to which architectural modifications guarantee people with physical limitations equal accessibility to and within buildings. More generally, the term applies to situations in which social disadvantages are reduced or eliminated so that all groups have access to a valued good. *Compare* **formal equality.**

substantive rationalization (*or* **rationality**)   a model of corporate rationality that emphasizes values and ethical norms, rather than the efficiency of business practices. *Compare* **formal rationality.**

Sudra a member of the fourth of the Hindu castes, the worker caste.

superego (as described by Freud) the human conscience or moral sense.

survival of the fittest (as described by Spencer) the principle, wrongly attributed to Darwin, that only the biggest and strongest survive, both in nature and in human society.

swaddling hypothesis (as described by Richman & Gorer) a hypothesis that attributed the presumed "moodiness" of Russian citizens to their having been too tightly swaddled or wrapped up as infants.

symbol an aspect of a culture that has many strings of meaning that are unique to that culture. Examples include the flag for Americans, hockey for Canadians, songs of the early fourteenth century for Scots.

symbolic interactionism a view of social behaviour that looks at the meaning of daily social interactions, including the words and gestures we use and how these are interpreted by others.

systemic racism racist practices, rules, and laws that have become institutionalized or made "part of the system." People who benefit from this type of racism tend to be blind to its existence. *Also called* **institutional racism**.

taboo a **norm** so deeply ingrained that the mere thought or mention of it is enough to arouse disgust or revulsion. An example is incest.

tabula rasa the idea that every human is born as a "blank slate" upon which the culture writes or inscribes a personality, values, and/or a set of abilities.

taxation effect (as described by M. Ross) one of three components of the **rentier effect**, this is about an oil-rich government's ability to appease it citizens by keeping taxes low (or nonexistent) thanks to oil revenues. *Compare* **group formation effect**, **spending effect**.

Taylorism *another word for* **scientific management**.

team approach a business approach that encourages workers to feel greater involvement in the operation of the company by inviting their ideas and input.

technological determinist a person how believes that our ways of acting and behaving are greatly influenced by technology.

technological fetishism a tendency on the part of either consumers or advertisers to make new technological innovations (smartphones, tablets, etc.) objects of uncritical adoration.

terrorism the intentional use or threat of violence against civilians in order to attain political objectives (e.g. freeing political prisoners, establishing an independent country, or destabilizing a political regime in another country in order to produce a regime change).

thanatos (as described by Freud) the violent death instinct within the **id**.

the medium is the message (as articulated by McLuhan) the idea that media (television, print, radio, etc.) have a causative effect on the way human groups think, act, and organize socially, regardless of their actual content.

theocracy a system of government in which the leaders rule in the name of a god or gods.

theorizing an attempt to explain what has been observed.

theory an attempt to explain something that has been observed.

third variable a variable that causes two more variables to correlate.

Third World a twentieth-century term used to refer to the poorer nations of the world. *Compare* **First World**, **Second World**.

Thomas theorem the notion that individuals interpret shared experiences differently, and that an individual's view of a particular situation will influence the way she reacts to it.

tied aid financial assistance given to a developing country with conditions attached (e.g. that the developing country must spend a portion of the money on products purchased from the donor country). This is sometimes called **phantom aid**, which captures the idea that the aid is not real but rather a form of investment.

tobacco strategy a marketing strategy in which a medical professional or other scientific "expert" is paid by a company to endorse the company's product on scientific grounds. The tactic was first used by tobacco producers, who hired medical researchers to combat public concerns about the health risks of cigarettes.

tokenism a symbolic gesture in which a candidate for an award or position is selected from a marginalized or underrepresented group in order to create the impression of equality and inclusiveness.

total fertility rate an estimate of the average number of children that a woman between the ages of 15 and 49 will have in her lifetime if current age-specific fertility rates remain constant during her reproductive years.

total institutions (as described by Goffman) institutions such as the military, hospitals, and asylums that regulate all aspects of an individual's life.

totalitarian discourse any **discourse** that makes a universal claim about how all knowledge and understanding can be achieved.

totem from an Ojibwa word, *ndotem*, meaning "my clan," an animal or natural object that has spiritual significance for a group and is adopted as its emblem. Durkheim viewed the totem as symbolic both of a particular society and of its god, leading him to conclude that *god = society*.

tracking the process in which students are assigned to different groups according to their aptitude (based on marks) and projected outcomes (e.g. whether they are expected to pursue post-secondary education). *Also called* **streaming**.

transgender a person (male or female) who either (a) does not conform to the gender role associated with his or her biological sex, or (b) does not self-identity with the biological sex assigned to him or her at birth.

transgenic denoting a plant or animal that has been engineered by having genes from one species inserted into another. Transgenic plants include flowers that have been genetically modified to alter or "improve" their colour. Transgenic animals have been used in biomedical research. *See* **genetically modified**.

transition   (as described by Van Gennep) the second phase of a rite of passage, in which initiates experience new things and discover things about themselves in the process. *Compare* **reincorporation, separation**.

transnational corporation   a company operating in countries around the world, typically based in the United States, Europe, or Japan.

transsexual   a person who either (a) has the physical characteristics of one sex and a persistent desire to belong to the other, or (b) has had surgery (or who is undergoing surgery) to have his or her sex changed surgically.

triangulation   the use of at least three narratives, theoretical perspectives, or investigators to examine the same phenomenon.

tribalism   a movement to promote the cause of a small nation that is usually not represented as having a country of its own.

tribal stigma   *see* **stigma**.

trickle-down theory   the misleading social theory that if the rich are free to earn as much money as they can, the benefits will "trickle down" to society's poorer citizens.

ummaic jihad   the non-violent struggle for freedom, justice, and truth within the Muslim community.

underemployment   a situation in which a person does not have enough paid work or else has paid work that does not make full use of the person's abilities and experience. A person with a medical degree earned outside of North America who earns a living as a cab driver because he or she has not been licensed to practise medicine in Canada may be considered underemployed. (It does make a taxicab a good place to give birth.)

undifferentiated accessibility   (as described by N. Postman) a media format that can be experienced equally by any viewer, regardless of age. Television, for example, provides undifferentiated accessibility, while books, because they contain words and sentences that some younger readers may not understand, do not.

union density   a measure of the proportion of unionized workers within the overall population of workers.

universal architecture   the design of homes, buildings, and other aspects of the built environment that takes into account the needs of people living with disabilities.

universalist   having to do with the notion that certain things happen to all people at roughly the same time or in roughly the same way, that human experiences are universal. Some developmental psychologists took a universalist view of childhood, arguing that biology ensures that all children go through the same periods of development according to the same basic schedule. This view downplays the role of social forces in influencing childhood development. *Compare* **relativist**.

universalist protectionist   a person who favours policies that shield the domestic culture, politics, and economy of poorer countries from foreign competition and the processes of globalization in general. Universalist protectionists are motivated to promote the interests of poor and other marginalized groups and greater social, economic, environmental, political, and cultural equality worldwide. *Compare* **particularist protectionist**.

unmarked term   a term without any distinguishing or delimiting term added; the usual form, as opposed to a **marked term**. Examples include *hockey* (versus ice *hockey*, field *hockey*, table *hockey*, etc.).

unpaid work   any work performed without the expectation of receiving a salary or pay, typically including the vast amount of household work, such as housekeeping, laundry, and caring for children and elderly parents living at home.

Untouchables   *another term for* **Dalits**.

urban reserve   a parcel of land within an urban area reserved for Aboriginal-run businesses and services.

Vaishya   a member of the third of five Hindu castes, the merchant and farmer caste.

value-free   free of bias; objective.

values   those features held up by a culture as good, right, desirable, and admirable. Values are typically **contested**.

variable   a factor or element that is likely to vary or change according to the circumstances governing it.

varna   *another term for* **caste**.

verstehen   (as described by M. Weber) an empathic understanding of human behaviour; it is the desire to walk a mile in another person's shoes in order to better understand their perspective, their interpretation of the world and events they experience.

vertical mosaic   (as described by J. Porter) a metaphor used to describe a society or nation in which there is a hierarchy of higher and lower ethnic groups.

vested interest   a personal interest in a situation from which an individual or group stands to gain in some way. A vested interest can contribute to bias if it is strong enough to override an individual's interest in learning and presenting the truth.

victimology   generally, the study of victims of crime and psychological effects on them of their experience; in sociology, it often refers to the way a person is portrayed as the victim of some event or situation, in a way that downplays or denies the person's **agency**, the ability to control his or her circumstances.

virtual class   (as described by A. Kroker) a **class** of people who control and are dependent for their jobs and economic well-being on digital technologies and the Internet.

vision quest   (in traditional North American Aboriginal culture) a **rite of passage** in which an adolescent leaves the community for a brief period and goes without eating or sleeping in order to have a vision (*see* **Aboriginal vision**) that will teach him or her such things as what guardian spirit he or she may have and what songs he or she would have as personal songs.

voice the expression of *a* (not *the*) viewpoint that comes from occupying a particular **social location**.

white collar crime (as described by E. Sutherland) non-violent crime committed by a person of the middle or upper middle class in the course of his or her job. Examples include embezzlement and fraud. *See* **corporate crimes, occupational crimes**.

wildcat strike a labour action in which workers go on strike without the (official) support or authorization of the union executive.

workers (as described by Marx) the people who work for wages and do not own capital, the means of production, in an industrial, capitalist society. *Also called* **proletariat**.

working class the social class made up primarily of those who lack resources or skills apart from their own labour power.

working poor working people and their families whose household income is below the poverty line.

work interruptions (as described by Baudrillard) time taken off work, typically by a woman, to care for an infant (i.e. during maternity or paternity leave) or a child who is sick.

work limitations an inability to perform certain kinds of labour owing to a disability.

xenocentrism a preference for foreign goods and tastes based on the belief that anything foreign must be better than the same thing produced domestically.

XYY males men and boys who differ from the "normal" XY chromosome pattern. They are associated with above-average height, a tendency to have acne, and somewhat more impulsive and antisocial behaviour and slightly lower intelligence than "normal" men and boys.

References

Abdo, Nahla, ed. (1996). *Sociological Thought: Beyond Eurocentric Theory*. Toronto: Canadian Scholars' Press.

Abraham, L., M. Morn, & A. Vollman (2010). "Women on the Web: How Women Are Shaping the Internet." Retrieved: www.comscore.com/Press_Events/Presentations_Whitepapers/2010/Women_on_the_Web_How_Women_are_Shaping_the_Internet

Abu-Laban, Yasmeen (1986). "The Vertical Mosaic in Later Life: Ethnicity and Retirement in Canada." *The Journal of Gerontology* 41 (5), pp. 662–71.

Acuna, Kirsten (2012). "Age Discrimination on TV: 10 Anchors Who Were Replaced by Younger Women." *Business Insider* (8 Aug.). Retrieved: www.businessinsider.com/age-discrimination-on-tv-10-anchors-who-were-replaced-by-younger-women-2012-8

Adachi, Ken (1976). *The Enemy That Never Was: A History of Japanese Canadians*. Toronto: McClelland & Stewart.

Adams, Carol, ed. (1993). *Ecofeminism and the Sacred*. New York: The Continuum Pub. Co.

Adams, Howard (1975). *Prison of Grass: Canada from the Native Point of View*. Toronto: New Press.

Adams, Michael (2003). *Fire and Ice: The United States and the Myth of Converging Values*. Toronto: Penguin Canada.

Aguiar, Luis (2001). "'Whiteness' in White Academia." In Carl James & Adrienne Shadd (eds), *Talking About Identity: Encounters in Race, Ethnicity and Language*, 2nd edn, pp. 177–92. Toronto: Between the Lines.

"A Journey into Womanhood: The Berry Fast" (2005). *Wawatay News Online* (27 January). Retrieved: www.wawataynews.ca/node/613

Akard, Patrick J. (1992). "Corporate Mobilization and Political Power: The Transformation of US Economic Policy in the 1970s." *American Sociological Review* 57 (Oct.), pp. 597–615.

Alberta Advanced Education & Career Development (AAECD) (1993). *Adult Learning in Alberta: Budget Roundtable Workbook*. Edmonton: Alberta Dept. of Advanced Education and Career Development (Nov.).

Alberta Cancer Board (2009). *Cancer Incidence in Fort Chipewyan, Alberta, 1995–2006*. Alberta Cancer Board: Division of Population Health and Information Surveillance. Retrieved: www.albertahealthservices.ca/rls/ne-rls-2009-02-06-fort-chipewyan-study.pdf

Allen, Michael Patrick (1978). "Economic Interest Groups and the Corporate Elite Structure." *Social Science Quarterly* 58 (4), pp. 597–615.

Allen, Peter M. (1994). "Evolution, Sustainability and Industrial Metabolism." In R.U. Ayres & U. Simonis (eds), *Industrial Metabolism: Restructuring for Sustainable Development*. Tokyo: United Nations UP.

Allen, Richard (1971). *The Social Passion: Religion and Social Reform in Canada 1914–28*. Toronto: University of Toronto.

Ames, Herbert Brown (1972 [1897]). *The City Below the Hill*. Toronto: University of Toronto.

Anderson, Karen (1996). *Sociology: A Critical Introduction*. Toronto: Nelson.

Anderson, Karen L. (1991). *Chain Her by One Foot: The Subjugation of Women in Seventeenth-Century New France*. London: Routledge.

"A New McDefinition?" (2007). *The Guardian* (24 May). Retrieved: www.guardian.co.uk/commentisfree/2007/may/24/anewmcdefinition

Anyon, Jean (1980). "Social Class and the Hidden Curriculum of Work." *Journal of Education* 162 (1), pp. 67–92.

Ariès, Philippe (1962). *Centuries of Childhood: A Social History*. Trans. Robert Baldick. New York: Knopf.

Aristotle (2000). *Politics*. Mineola, NY: Dover Publications.

Armstrong, Karen (2005 [1982]). *Through the Narrow Gate: A Memoir of Life In and Out of the Convent*. Toronto: Vintage Canada.

Armstrong, Pat, & Hugh Armstrong (1978). *The Double Ghetto: Canadian Women and Their Segregated Work*. Toronto: McClelland & Stewart.

Arnett, Jeffrey (1995). "Broad and Narrow Socialization: The Family in the Context of a Cultural Theory." *Journal of Marriage and the Family* 57 (3), pp. 617–28.

Arnett, Jeffrey, & Lene Balle-Jensen (1993). "Cultural Bases of Risk Behavior: Danish Adolescents." *Child Development* 64, pp. 1842–55.

Arnquist, Sarah (2009). "How Old Do You Feel? It Depends on Your Age." *The New York Times* (30 June). Retrieved: www.nytimes.com/2009/06/30/health/30aging.html?_r=0

Aujla, Angela (1998). "The Colour Bar of Beauty." *The Peak* 1 (99), pp. 1–5.

Axelrod, Paul (1982a). "Businessmen and the Building of Canadian Universities." *Canadian Historical Review* 63, pp. 202–22.

——— (1982b). *Scholars and Dollars: Politics, Economics, and the Universities of Ontario, 1945–1980*. Toronto: University of Toronto.

Backhouse, Constance (1999). *Colour-Coded: A Legal History of Racism in Canada, 1900–1950*. Toronto: University of Toronto.

Bagdikian, Ben H. (2000 [1992]). *The Media Monopoly*. Boston: Beacon.

Banerjee, Mukulika (2000). *The Pathan Unarmed*. Karachi & New Delhi: Oxford.

Barber, Benjamin (1992). "Jihad vs McWorld." *The Atlantic Monthly* (March).

Barnouw, Victor (1987). *An Introduction to Anthropology: Ethnology*, vol. 2, 5th edn. Chicago, IL: Dorsey.

Barrowcliffe, Mark (2008). *The Elfish Gene: Dungeons, Dragons and Growing Up Strange—A Memoir*. London: Soho.

Bartels, E.M., L. Dreyer, S. Jacobsen, A. Jespersen, H. Bliddal, & B. Danneskiold-Samsøe (2009). "Fibromyalgia, Diagnosis and Prevalence. Are Gender Differences Explainable?" *Ugeskr Laeger* 171 (49), pp. 3588–92.

Barthes, Roland (1957). *Mythologies*. London: Paladin/HarperCollins.

Baskin, Cyndy (2003). "Structural Social Work as Seen from an Aboriginal Perspective." In W. Shera (ed.), *Emerging Perspectives on Anti-Oppressive Practice*. Toronto: Canadian Scholars' Press.

Battiste, Marie (1997). "Mi'kmaq Socialization Patterns." In L. Choyce & R. Joe (eds), *Anthology of Mi'kmaq Writers*. East Lawrencetown, NS: Pottersfield.

Baudrillard, Jean (1981). *For a Critique of the Political Economy of the Sign*. Trans. Charles Levin. Telos.

—— (1983). *Simulations*. Trans. Paul Foss, Paul Patton, & Philip Beitchman. New York: Semiotext[e].

Beaujot, Rod (2000). *Earning and Caring in Canadian Families*. Peterborough: Broadview.

—— (2002). "Earning and Caring: Demographic Change and Policy Implications." *Canadian Studies in Population* 29 (2): 195–225.

—— (2004). "Delayed Life Transitions: Trends and Implications." *Vanier Institute of the Family* (15 June). Retrieved: www.vifamily.ca/library/cft/delayed_life.html

Becker, Howard (1963). *Outsiders: Studies in the Sociology of Deviance*. New York: The Free Press.

Bellegarde-Smith, Patrick (2004). *Haiti: The Breached Citadel*. Toronto: Canadian Scholars' Press.

Benedict, Ruth (1946). *The Chrysanthemum and the Sword*. Boston: Houghton Mifflin.

Benton-Banai, Edward (1988). *The Mishomis Book: The Voice of the Ojibway*. St Paul, MN: Red School House, Indian Country Communications.

Berry, Wendell (1992). *Sex, Economy, Freedom & Community*. New York: Pantheon.

Best, Joel (2001). *Damned Lies and Statistics: Untangling Numbers from the Media, Politicians, and Activists*. Berkeley and Los Angeles: University of California.

Beverly, J. (1978). "Higher Education and Capitalist Crisis." *Socialist Review* 8 (6), pp. 67–91.

Bezlova, Antoaneta (2002). "Young Workers Toil to Churn Out Santa's Toys." *Inter Press Service* 19 (23 Dec.). Retrieved: www.commondreams.org/headlines02/1223-01.htm

Bibby, Reginald Wayne (1995). *The Bibby Report: Social Trends Canadian Style*. Toronto: Stoddard.

Biehl, Janet (1991). *Rethinking Ecofeminist Politics*. Boston: South End.

Billy Talent (2002). "Surprise, Surprise." *Dead Silence*. Burbank, CA: Warner Bros Records/Roadrunner.

Birket-Smith, Kaj (1929). *The Caribou Eskimos: Material and Social Life and Their Cultural Position*. Copenhagen: Gyldendalske Boghandel, Nordisk Forlag.

Bissell, Tom (2003). *Chasing the Sea: Lost Among the Ghosts of Empire in Central Asia*. New York: Pantheon.

Blackford, Karen (1996). "Families and Parental Disability." In Marion Lynn (Ed.), *Voices: Essays on Canadian Families*. Scarborough, ON: Nelson.

Blatchford, Christie (2010). "OPP on Remote Reserve Chased Out by Rock-Throwing Mob." *The Globe and Mail* (5 Aug.).

Bloom, Allan (1988). *The Closing of the American Mind*. New York: Simon & Schuster.

Blumer, Herbert (1969). *Symbolic Interactionism: Perspective and Method*. Englewood Cliffs, NJ: Prentice-Hall.

Bohannan, Laura (1966). "Shakespeare in the Bush." *Natural History* (Aug./Sept.). Reprinted in E. Angeloni (ed.), *Annual Editions Anthropology, 1995/1996*, pp. 65–9.

Bolaria, B. Singh, & Peter S. Li (1985). *Racial Oppression in Canada*. Toronto: Garamond.

Bookchin, Murray (1996). *The Philosophy of Social Ecology: Essays on Dialectical Naturalism*. Montreal: Black Rose.

Bott, Elizabeth (1957). *Family and Social Networks: Roles, Norms, and External Relationships in Ordinary Urban Families*. London: Tavistock.

Bourdieu, Pierre (1970). *La reproduction: Eléments pour une théorie d'enseignement*. Paris: Éditions de Minuit.

—— (1979). *La distinction. Critique sociale de jugement*. Paris: Éditions de Minuit.

—— (1984). *Distinction: A Social Critique of the Judgement of Taste*. Trans. Richard Nice. Cambridge, MA: Harvard.

—— (1988). *Homo Academicus*. Trans. P. Collier. Stanford, CA: Stanford.

—— (1996). *On Television*. New York: New.

Bourdieu, Pierre, & Jean-Claude Passeron (1977). *Reproduction in Education, Society and Culture*. Trans. Richard Nice. London: Sage.

Bowles, S., & H. Gintis (1976). *Schooling in Capitalist America: Educational Reform and Contradictions of Economic Life*. New York: Basic.

boyd, danah (2011). "White Flight in Networked Publics? How Race and Class Shaped American Teen Engagement with MySpace and Facebook." In Lisa Nakamura & Peter Chow (Eds), *Race After the Internet*. London: Routledge.

Boyd, Monica, & Doug Norris (1995). "Leaving the Nest? Impact of Family Structure." *Canadian Social Trends* 38, pp. 14–17.

Bradbury, Ray (1953). *Fahrenheit 451*. New York: Ballantine.

Briggs, Jean (1970). *Never in Anger: Portrait of an Eskimo Family*. Cambridge: Harvard.

—— (1998). *Inuit Morality Play: The Emotional Education of a Three-Year-Old*. New Haven, CT: Yale.

Brill, A.A. (1913). "Piblockto or Hysteria among Peary's Eskimos." *Journal of Nervous and Mental Disease* 40, pp. 514–20.

Brock, Joe, & Tim Cocks (2012). "Nigeria Oil Corruption Highlighted by Audits." *Reuters*. Retrieved: www.reuters.com/article/2012/03/08/nigeria-corruption-oil-idUSL5E8E84LV20120308

Broesterhuizen, Marcel, & K.U. Leuven (2008). "Worlds of Difference: An Ethical Analysis of Choices in the Field of Deafness." *Ethical Perspectives: Journal of the European Centre for Ethics* 15 (1), pp. 103–31.

Brookes, Martin (2004). *Extreme Measures: The Dark Visions and Bright Ideas of Francis Galton*. London: Bloomsbury.

Brown, Ian (2009). *The Boy in the Moon: A Father's Search for His Disabled Son*. Toronto: Random House.

Bruemmer, René, & Kevin Dougherty (2012). "CLASSE Student Group Presents Counter Proposal to End Boycott." *The Gazette* (3 May).

Brym, Robert J., ed. (1985). *The Structure of the Canadian Capitalist Class*. Toronto: Garamond.

—— (2000). "Note on the Discipline: The Decline of the Canadian Sociology and Anthropology Association." *The Canadian Journal of Sociology* 28 (3), pp. 411–26.

—— (2008). *Sociology as a Life or Death Issue*. Toronto: Nelson.

Buchbinder, Howard & Janice Newson (1985). "Corporate–University Linkages and the Scientific-Technical Revolution." *Interchange* 16 (3), pp. 37–53.

Budgell, Janet (1999). *Our Way Home: A Report to the Aboriginal Healing and Wellness Strategy: Repatriation of Aboriginal People Removed by the Child Welfare System: Final Report.* Prepared by Native Child and Family Services of Toronto, Sevenato and Associates. Toronto: Native Child and Family Services of Toronto.

Bullivant, Brian (1981). *The Pluralist Dilemma in Education: Six Case Studies.* Sydney: Allen & Unwin.

Burawoy, Michael (2004). "The World Needs Public Sociology." *Sosiologisk tidsskrift (Journal of Sociology, Norway)* 3.

Burnet Jean R., & Howard Palmer (1988). *"Coming Canadians." An Introduction to a History of Canada's Peoples.* Ottawa: Ministry of Supply and Services.

Burton, Kirsteen R., & Ian K. Wong (2004). "A Force to Contend With: The Gender Gap Closes in Canadian Medical Schools." *Canadian Medical Association Journal* 170 (9) (17 April).

Bushman, Brad J., & L. Rowell Huesmann (2001). "Effects of Televised Violence on Aggression." In D. Singer & J. Singer (eds), *Handbook of Children and the Media*, pp. 223–54. Thousand Oaks, CA: Sage.

Butler, Judith (1990). *Gender Trouble: Feminism and the Subversion of Identity.* London: Routledge.

Buttel, Frederick, & Kenneth Gould (2004). "Global Social Movement(s) at the Crossroads: Some Observation on the Trajectory of the Anti-corporate Globalization Movement." *Journal of World Systems Research* 10 (1), pp. 51–2.

Cameron, Linda, & Lee Bartel (2008). *Homework Realities: A Canadian Study of Parental Opinions and Attitudes.* Technical Report. Toronto: University of Toronto, Ontario Institute for Studies in Education.

Campbell, Colin (1997). "When the Meaning Is Not the Message: A Critique of the Consumption as Communication Thesis." In Mica Nava, Andrew Blake, Iain MacRury, & Barry Richards (Eds), *Buy this Book: Studies in Advertising and Consumptions.* New York: Routledge.

Campbell, Marie, & Frances Gregor (2002). *Mapping Social Relations: A Primer in Doing Institutional Ethnography.* Aurora, ON: Garamond.

Campion-Smith, B., & A. Woods (2010). "The Hidden Face of Our Injured Soldiers." *The Star* (Toronto, 7 Nov.).

Canada (1884). An Act to Further Amend the Indian Act 1880. *Statutes of Canada*, 47 Vict. c 27.

Canada, 40th Parliament, 2nd Session (2009). Standing Committee on Environment and Sustainable Development: Evidence (11 June). Retrieved: www.parl.gc.ca/HousePublications/Publication.aspx?DocId=3983714&Language=E&Mode=1

"Canada's Top CEOs Leave the 99% in Their Gold Dust" (2012). *The Star* (Toronto, 3 January), p. A1.

Canadian Association of the Deaf (CAD) (2012a). Issues & Positions: Terminology. Retrieved: www.cad.ca/terminology_deafness.php

——— (2012b). Issues & Positions: Deaf Culture vs. Medicalization. Retrieved: www.cad.ca/deaf_culture_vs._medicalization.php

Canadian Association of Food Banks (2004). *Poverty in a Land of Plenty: Towards a Hunger-Free Canada.* Toronto.

Canadian Press (2012a). "Canada Urged to 'Get Act Together' as National Debt to Hit $600-Billion Saturday." *Financial Post* (23 Nov.). Retrieved: http://business.financialpost.com/2012/11/23/canada-urged-to-get-act-together-as-national-debt-to-hit-600-billion-saturday/

——— (2012b). "Girls in Ontario More Likely to Be Bullied than Boys." CBCNews (24 July). Retrieved: www.cbc.ca/news/canada/toronto/story/2012/07/24/toronto-bullying-boys-girls-cyber.html

Carbin, Clifton F., & Dorothy L. Smith (2012). "Deaf Culture." *The Canadian Encyclopedia.* Historica-Dominion Institute. Retrieved: www.thecanadianencyclopedia.com/articles/deaf-culture

Cardinal, Harold (1969). *The Unjust Society: The Tragedy of Canada's Indians.* Edmonton: New Press.

——— (1977). *The Rebirth of Canada's Indians.* Toronto: New.

Carroll, William (1982). "The Canadian Corporate Elite: Financiers or Finance Capitalists." *Studies in Political Economy* 8, pp. 89–114.

Casey, Catherine (1992). "Restructuring Work: New Work and New Workers in Post-Industrial Production." In R.P. Coulter & I.F. Goodson (eds), *Rethinking Vocationalism: Whose Work Life Is It?* Toronto: Our Schools, Our Selves.

Cavan, Ruth (1965 [1928]). *Suicide.* New York: Russell and Russell.

CBCNews (2011). "By the Numbers: The Decline of Smoking in Canada" (29 July). Retrieved: www.cbc.ca/news/canada/story/2011/07/29/f-smoking-statistics.html

——— (2012a). "Canada Won't Oppose Asbestos Limits. Federal Tories Reverse Course and Won't Veto Substance's Listing in Rotterdam Convention" (14 Sept.). Retrieved: www.cbc.ca/news/canada/montreal/story/2012/09/14/montreal-canada-thetford-mines-asbestos.html

——— (2012b). "Non-Christian Prison Chaplains Chopped by Ottawa." (4 Oct.). Retrieved: www.cbc.ca/news/canada/british-columbia/story/2012/10/04/bc-non-christian-prison-chaplains-cancelled.html

Center for Labor Education & Research (2012). "Union Density in the U.S.: 2012." Center for Labor Education & Research, University of Hawai'i – West O'ahu. Retrieved: http://homepages.uhwo.hawaii.edu/clear/density.html

Centre for Communicable Diseases and Infection Control (CCDIC) (2012). "Tuberculosis in Canada 2010, Pre-Release" (updated 30 April 2012). Retrieved: www.phac-aspc.gc.ca/tbpc-latb/pubs/tbcan10pre/index-eng.php

Chaitin, Gilbert (1996). *Rhetoric and Culture in Lacan.* Cambridge: Cambridge.

Chang, Virginia, & Nicholas Christakis (2002). "Medical Modelling of Obesity: A Transition from Action to Experience in a 20th Century American Medical Textbook." *Sociology of Health and Illness* 24 (2), pp. 151–77.

Chase, Stuart (1934). Foreword. In Thorstein Veblen, *The Theory of the Leisure Class: An Economic Study of Institutions.* New York: Modern.

Chen, Anita Beltran (1998). *From Sunbelt to Snowbelt: Filipinos in Canada.* Calgary: Canadian Ethnic Studies Association.

Chodrow, Nancy (1978). *The Reproduction of Mothering: Psychoanalysis and the Sociology of Gender.* Berkeley: University of California.

——— (1994). *Femininities, Masculinities, Sexualities: Freud and Beyond.* Lexington, KY: University of Kentucky.

Chomsky, Noam (2004). *Hegemony or Survival: America's Quest for Global Dominance.* New York: Henry Holt.

Chretien, Jean-Pierre (1967). *Le Burundi.* Paris: Secretaria general du Gouvernement.

Clark, S.D. (1962). *The Developing Canadian Community*. Toronto: University of Toronto.

—— (1976). *Canadian Society in Historical Perspective*. Toronto: McGraw-Hill.

Clinard, M., & R. Quinney (1973). *Criminal Behavior Systems: A Typology*, 2nd edn. New York: Holt, Rinehart, and Winston.

Codjoe, Henry M. (2001). "Can Blacks Be Racist? Further Reflections on Being 'Too Black and African.'" In Carl James & Adrienne Shadd (eds), *Talking About Identity: Encounters in Race, Ethnicity and Language*, pp. 277–90. Toronto: Between The Lines.

Cohen, Albert K. (1955). *Delinquent Boys: The Culture of the Gang*. Glencoe, IL: Free Press.

Colapinto, John (2000). *As Nature Made Him: The Boy Who Was Raised as a Girl*. New York: HarperCollins.

Comaskey, Brenda, & Anne McGillivray (1999). *Black Eyes All of the Time: Intimate Violence, Aboriginal Women, and the Justice System*. Toronto: University of Toronto.

Comte, Auguste (1830–42). *Cours de Philosophie Positive*. Paris: Librairie Larousse.

—— (1851–4). *Système de Politique Positive*.

—— (1853). *The Positive Philosophy of August Comte*. Trans. & ed. Harriet Martineau.

—— (1877). *The System of Positive Polity*. London: Longmans, Green.

Connell, R.W. (1995). *Masculinities*. Berkeley: University of California.

Conrad, Margaret R., & James K. Hiller (2001). *Atlantic Canada: A Region in the Making*. Don Mills, ON: Oxford.

Contenta, Sandro, & Jim Rankin (2009). "Suspended Sentences: Forging a School-to-Prison Pipeline?" *The Star* (Toronto, 6 Jun.).

Contenta, Sandro, & Laurie Monsebraaten (2009a). "How We're Creating an Illegal Workforce." *The Star* (Toronto, 1 Nov.). Retrieved: www.thestar.com/news/investigations/2009/11/01/how_were_creating_an_illegal_workforce.html

—— & —— (2009b). "A Temporary Worker's Catch-22: Temporary Permits Leave Foreigners Open to Exploitation." *The Star* (Toronto, 2 Nov.). Retrieved: www.thestar.com/news/investigations/2009/11/02/part_2_a_temporary_wodrkers_catch22.html

Cooper, Celeste, & Jeff Miller (2010). *Integrative Therapies for Fibromyalgia, Chronic Fatigue Syndrome, and Myofascial Pain: The Mind–Body Connection*. Vermont: Healing Arts Press.

Cordell, Arthur J. (1993). "The Perils of an Information Age." In P. Elliot (ed.), *Rethinking the Future*. Saskatoon: Fifth House.

Côté, James, & Anton Allahar (2007). *Ivory Tower Blues: A University System in Crisis*. Toronto: University of Toronto.

Coupland, Douglas (1991). *Generation X: Tales for an Accelerated Culture*. New York: St Martin's Press.

Court Brown, W. Michael (1968). "Males with an XYY Sex Chromosome Complement." *Journal of Medical Genetics* 5 (4), pp. 341–59.

Craib, Ian (1989). *Psychoanalysis and Social Theory: The Limits of Sociology*. Amherst, MA: University of Massachusetts.

Crehan, Kate (2002). *Gramsci, Culture and Anthropology*. Berkeley: University of California.

"Cross about Cross-Dressing: Is It a Wicked Western Habit that Should Be Stopped?" (2010). *The Economist* (28 Jan.). Retrieved: www.economist.com/node/15403091

Crozier, Michel (1964). *The Bureaucratic Phenomenon*. Chicago: University of Chicago.

Curtis, James, Edward Grabb, & Neil Guppy, eds (1999). *Social Inequality in Canada: Patterns, Problems and Policies*, 3rd edn. Scarborough, ON: Prentice Hall.

Cushing, Pamela J. (1998). "Completing the Cycle of Transformation: Lessons from the Rites of Passage Model." *Pathways: The Ontario Journal of Experiential Education* 9 (5), pp. 7–12

Dahl, Robert A. (1956). *A Preface to Democratic Theory: How Does Popular Sovereignty Function in America?* Chicago: University of Chicago.

Daily Bread Food Bank (2012). *Who's Hungry: Faces of Hunger. 2012 Profile of Hunger in the GTA*. Retrieved: www.dailybread.ca/wp-content/uploads/2012/09/WhosHungryReport2012LowRes.pdf

Dasgupta, Sathi (1992). "Conjugal Roles and Social Network in Indian Immigrant Families: Bott Revisited." *The Journal of Comparative Family Studies* 23 (3), p. 465.

Das Gupta, Tania (1996). *Racism and Paid Work*. Toronto: Garamond.

Davies, Charles (2009). "Canada Taking Only Baby Steps on White Collar Crime." *Metro News* (8 Dec.). Retrieved: http://metronews.ca/news/174221/canada-taking-only-baby-steps-on-white-collar-crime/

Davis, Lennard J. (2006). "Constructing Normalcy: The Bell Curve, the Novel, and the Invention of the Disabled Body in the Nineteenth Century." In Lennard J. Davis (ed.), *The Disability Studies Reader*, 2nd edn, pp. 3–16. New York: Routledge.

Dawson, Carl A., & Warren E. Getty (1948). *An Introduction to Sociology*, 3rd edn. New York: Ronald.

d'Eaubonne, Françoise (1974). *Le féminisme ou la mort (Feminism or Death)*. Paris: P. Horay.

Debord, Guy (1995 [1967]). *The Society of the Spectacle*. New York: Zone.

de Certeau, Michel (1984). *The Practice of Everyday Life*. Trans. S. Rendell. Berkeley, CA: University of California.

"Defying Gender Expectations through Gender Performance: Boyat in the UAE" (2009). *The Globe and Mail*, (23 Feb.).

Dei, George (1996). *Anti-Racism Education: Theory and Practice*. Halifax: Fernwood.

Dei, George, & Agnes Calliste (2000). *Power Knowledge and Anti-Racism Education: A Critical Reader*. Halifax: Fernwood.

Dei, George, Irma James, L. Karumanchery, S. James-Wilson, & J. Zine (2000). *Aboriginal Margins: The Challenges and Possibilities of Inclusive Schooling*, Toronto: Canadian Scholars' Press.

Dei, George, M. James, S. James-Wilson, L. Karumanchery, & J. Zine (2000). *Removing the Margins: The Challenges and Possibilities of Inclusive Schooling*. Toronto: Canadian Scholar's Press.

Demerson, Velma (2004). *Incorrigible*. Waterloo: Wilfrid Laurier.

Dempsey, L. James (1995). "Alberta's Indians in WWII." In Ken Tingley (ed.), *King and Country, Alberta in the Second World War*. Edmonton: Provincial Museum of Alberta.

Dewling, Michael (2013). "Social Media: Who Uses Them?" Pub. no. 2010-05-E. Ottawa: Library of Parliament, Social Affairs Division. Retrieved: www.parl.gc.ca/Content/LOP/ResearchPublications/2010-05-e.pdf

Diamond, Irene, & Gloria Feman Orenstein, eds (1990). *Reweaving the World: The Emergence of Ecofeminism.* San Francisco: Sierra Club.

Diamond, Jared (2005). *Collapse: How Societies Choose to Fail or Survive.* New York: Viking.

Diamond, Sondra (1981). "Growing up with Parents of a Handicapped Child: A Handicapped Person's Perspective." In James L. Paul (Ed.), *Understanding and Working with Parents of Children with Special Needs.* New York: Holt, Rinehart and Winston.

Dick, Lyle (1995). "'Pibloktoq' (Arctic Hysteria): A Construction of European–Inuit Relations?" *Arctic Anthropology* 32 (2), pp. 1–42.

Dickason, Olive (2002). *Canada's First Nations: A History of Founding Peoples from Earliest Times,* 3rd edn. Don Mills, ON: Oxford.

Dimiero, Ben (2010). "FOXLEAKS: Fox Boss Ordered Staff to Cast Doubt on Climate Science." Retrieved from Media Matters for America [blog], http://mediamatters.org/blog/2010/12/15/foxleaks-fox-boss-ordered-staff-to-cast-doubt-o/174317

Dobbin, Murray (2009). "As the World Turns . . . and the Bubble Expands." Rabble.ca (14 Dec.). Retrieved: http://rabble.ca/blogs/bloggers/murray-dobbin/2009/12/world-turns%80%A6and-bubble-expands

Dofny, Jacques, & Marcel Rioux (1962). "Les classes sociales au Canada français." *Revue français de sociologie* 111 (3), pp. 290–303.

Dollard, John (1937). *Caste and Class in a Southern Town.* New Haven, CT: Yale.

Dosman, Edgar J. (1972). *Indians: An Urban Dilemma.* Toronto: McClelland & Stewart.

Drolet, Marie (2011). "Why Has the Gender Age Gap Narrowed?" *Perspectives on Labour and Income* (Spring). Statistics Canada. Retrieved: www.statcan.gc.ca/pub/75-001-x/2011001/pdf/11394-eng.pdf

Du Bois, W.E.B. (1896). *The Suppression of the African Slave Trade in America.* New York: Longmans, Green.

—— (1903). *The Souls of Black Folk.* Chicago: A.C. McClurg.

—— (1935). *Black Reconstruction: An Essay toward a History of the Part which Black Folk Played in the Attempt to Re-construct Democracy in America.* New York: Harcourt Brace.

—— (1940). *Dusk of Dawn.* New York: Harcourt, Brace & World.

—— (1967 [1899]). *The Philadelphia Negro: A Social Study.* New York: Schocken Books.

Dubson, Michael, ed. (2001). *Ghosts in the Classroom: Stories of College Adjunct Faculty—and the Price We All Pay.* Boston: Camel's Back.

Dumas, Jean, & Alain Bélanger (1996). *Report on the Demographic Situation in Canada, 1995.* Cat. no. 91-209. Ottawa: Statistics Canada.

Dunfield, Allison (2005). "Why Do Women Always Pay More?" *The Globe and Mail* (15 March).

Dupuy, Alex (1997). *Haiti in the New World Order: The Limits of the Democratic Revolution.* Boulder, CO: Westview.

Durkheim, Émile (1938 [1895]). *Rules of the Sociological Method.* Chicago: University of Chicago.

—— (1951 [1897]). *Suicide: A Study in Sociology.* Trans. John A. Spaulding & George Simpson. New York: The Free Press of Glencoe.

—— (1965 [1912]). *The Elementary Forms of the Religious Life.* New York: Free Press.

—— (1995 [1912]). *The Elementary Forms of the Religious Life.* Trans. Karen Fields. New York: Simon & Schuster.

Dusenberry, Verne (1998). *The Montana Cree: A Study in Religious Persistence.* Norman, OK: University of Oklahoma.

Ebaugh, Helen Rose Fuchs (1988). *Becoming an EX: The Process of Role Exit.* Chicago: University of Chicago.

"Editorial: The Loss of Spontaneous Play from Childhood" (2012). *The Globe and Mail* (1 June).

Eichler, Margrit (2001). "Women Pioneers in Canadian Sociology: The Effects of a Politics of Gender and a Politics of Knowledge." *Canadian Journal of Sociology* 26 (3) (Summer), pp. 375–404.

Elder Advocates of Alberta Society (EAAS) (n.d.). "Nelson Struk: Arrested and Detained without Cause." Retrieved: http://elderadvocates.ca/senior-arrested-and-detained-without-cause/

Elkind, David (2001 [1981/1988]). *The Hurried Child: Growing Up Too Fast Too Soon,* 3rd edn. Cambridge, MA: Perseus.

—— (2003). "The Reality of Virtual Stress." *CIO* (fall/winter). Retrieved: www.cio.com/archive/092203/elkind

Emke, Ivan (2002). "Patients in the New Economy: The 'Sick Role' in a Time of Economic Discipline." *Animus: A Philosophical Journal for Our Time* 7.

Endicott, Stephen L. (2002). *Bienfait: The Saskatchewan Miners' Struggle of '31.* Toronto: University of Toronto Press.

Erlick, Larry (2004). Untitled speech to the Economic Club of Toronto. Retrieved: www.oma.org/pcomm/pressrel/economicspeech04.htm

Esar, Evan (1943). *Esar's Comic Dictionary of Wit and Humour.* New York: Horizon.

Etzioni, Amitai (1964). *Modern Organizations.* Englewood Cliffs, NJ: Prentice-Hall.

—— (1986). "The Fast-Food Factories: McJobs are Bad for Kids." *The Washington Post* (24 August).

Fadiman, Anne (1997). *The Spirit Catches You and You Fall Down. A Hmong Child, Her American Doctors, and the Collision of Two Cultures.* New York: Farrar, Straus and Giroux.

Fanon, Franz (1965 [1961]). *The Wretched of the Earth.* New York: Grove.

—— (1967 [1952]). *Black Skin, White Masks.* New York: Grove.

Fields, Karen (1995). Introduction. In Karen Fields (trans.), *The Elementary Forms of the Religious Life,* by Émile Durkheim. New York: Simon & Schuster.

Fine, M., & A. Asch (1988). *Women with Disabilities: Essays in Psychology, Culture and Politics.* Philadelphia: Temple University Press.

Fiske, John (1989). *Understanding Popular Culture.* London: Routledge.

Flavelle, Dana (2003). "Canada's 0.01%." *The Star* (Toronto, 3 Jan.), pp. B1–B3.

—— (2013). "Richest one per cent of Canadians earn one tenth of all income." *The Star* (Toronto, 28 Jan.).

Fleras, Augie, & Jean Elliott (1999). *Unequal Relations: An Introduction to Race, Ethnic, and Aboriginal Dynamics in Canada,* 3rd edn. Scarborough, ON: Prentice-Hall, Allyn & Bacon.

Fletcher, S.D. (2000). "Molded Images: First Nations People, Representation and the Ontario School Curriculum." In T. Goldstein & D. Selby (eds), *Weaving Connections: Educating for Peace, Social and Environmental Justice.* Toronto: Sumach.

Fleury, Dominique, & Myriam Fortin (2006). "When Working Is Not Enough to Escape Poverty: An Analysis of Canada's Working Poor." Working Paper. Cat. no. SP-630-06-06E. Ottawa: Human Resources and Social Development Canada. Retrieved: http://tamarackcommunity.ca/downloads/vc/When_Work_Not_Enough.pdf

Flint, David (1975). *The Hutterites: A Study in Prejudice.* Don Mills, ON: Oxford.

Food Banks Canada (2009). "HungerCount 2009: A Comprehensive Report on Hunger and Food Bank Use in Canada, and Recommendations for Change." Retrieved: http://foodbankscanada.ca/documents/HungerCount2009NOV16.pdf

Foster, George M. (1965). "Peasant Society and the Image of Limited Good." *American Anthropologist* 67 (2), pp. 293–315.

Foucault, Michel (1961). *Madness and Civilisation: A History of Insanity in the Age of Reason.* New York: Vintage.

—— (1975). *Discipline and Punish: The Birth of the Prison.* New York: Vintage.

—— (1977). *Discipline and Punish: The Birth of the Prison.* New York: Pantheon.

—— (1978). *The History of Sexuality. Vol. 1: An Introduction.* New York: Pantheon.

—— (1980). "Two Lectures." In Colin Gordon (ed.), *Power/Knowledge*, pp. 78–108. New York: Pantheon.

—— (1994 [1972]). *The Archaeology of Knowledge.* London: Routledge.

Fournier, S., & E. Crey (1997). *Stolen from Our Embrace.* Vancouver: Douglas & McIntyre.

Fowles, Jib (1999). *The Case for Television Violence.* London: Sage.

—— (2001). "The Whipping Boy: The Hidden Conflicts Underlying the Campaign against TV." *Reason* (March).

Francis, S., R. Anderson, & S. Dyer (2002). "Development of a Threshold Approach to Assessing Industrial Impacts on Woodland Caribou in Yukon." Presentation provided at the Assessment and Management of Cumulative Effects Workshop, Whitehorse, Yukon, 25–26 March 2002.

Frank, David, & Nolan Reilly (1979). "The Emergence of the Socialist Movement in the Maritimes, 1899–1916." In Robert J. Brym & R. James Sacouman (eds), *Underdevelopment and Social Movements in Atlantic Canada*, pp. 81–106. Toronto: New Hogtown.

Frazier, E. Franklin (1939). *The Negro Family in the United States.* Chicago: University of Chicago.

Freeman, Derek (1983). *Margaret Mead and Samoa: The Making and Unmaking of an Anthropological Myth.* Cambridge: Cambridge University Press.

—— (1998). *The Fateful Hoaxing of Margaret Mead: A Historical Analysis of Her Samoan Research.* Boulder, CO: Westview.

Freud, Sigmund (1977 [1916–17]). *On Sexuality*, vol. 7. London: Penguin.

Friedman, Thomas L. (2000). *The Lexus and the Olive Tree: Understanding Globalization.* New York: Anchor.

—— (2006). "The First Law of Petropolitics." *Foreign Policy* (1 May). Retrieved: www.foreignpolicy.com/articles/2006/04/25/the_first_law_of_petropolitics

Galanoy, Terry (1980). *Charge It: Inside the Credit Card Conspiracy.* New York: Putnam.

Galarneau, Diane, & Marian Radulescu (2009). "Employment among the Disabled." *Perspectives on Labour and Income* (May), pp. 5–15. Statistics Canada cat. no. 75-001-X. Retrieved: www.statcan.gc.ca/pub/75-001-x/2009105/pdf/10865-eng.pdf

Gallagher, James E., & Ronald D. Lambert, eds (1971). *Social Process and Institution: The Canadian Case.* Toronto: Holt, Rinehart and Winston.

Gans, Herbert (1989). "Sociology in America: The Discipline and the Public." *American Sociological Review* 54 (Feb.), pp. 1–16.

Garigue, Philippe (1964). "French Canada: A Case-Study in Sociological Analysis." *Canadian Review of Sociology and Anthropology* 1 (4), pp. 186–92.

Gephart, Robert (1988). *Ethnostatistics: Qualitative Foundations for Quantitative Research.* London: Sage.

Gerth, Hans, & C. Wright Mills (1958 [1946]). *The Sociology of Max Weber.* New York: Vintage Books.

Gianotti, Timothy J. (2011). *In the Light of a Blessed Tree: Illuminations of Islamic Belief, Practice, and History.* Eugene, OR: Wipf and Stock.

Giele, Janet Z., & Glen H. Elder, Jr (1998). "Life Course Research: Development of a Field." In Janet Giele & Glen Elder, Jr (Eds), *Methods of Life Course Research: Qualitative and Quantitative Approaches*, pp. 5–27. Thousand Oaks, CA: Sage.

Gilbert, Dennis (1988). *Sandinistas: The Party and the Revolution.* Oxford: Basil Blackwell.

Giles, Philip (2004). "Low Income Measurement in Canada." Retrieved: www.statcan.ca/english/research/75F0002MIE/75F0002MIE2004011.pdf

Gilligan, Carol (1982). *In a Different Voice: Psychological Theory and Women's Development.* Cambridge, MA: Harvard.

—— (1990). *Making Connections: The Relational Worlds of Adolescent Girls at Emma Willard School.* Cambridge, MA: Harvard.

Giroux, Henry A. (2004). *The Terror of Neoliberalism: Authoritarianism and the Eclipse of Democracy.* Boulder, CO: Paradigm.

—— (2005). *Against the New Authoritarianism: Politics After Abu Ghraib.* Winnipeg: Arbeiter Ring.

—— (2006). *Beyond the Spectacle of Terrorism: Global Uncertainty and the Challenge of the New Media.* Boulder, CO: Paradigm.

—— (2007). *The University in Chains: Confronting the Military-Industrial-Academic Complex.* Boulder, CO: Paradigm.

—— (2008). *Against the Terror of Neoliberalism: Politics Beyond the Age of Greed.* Boulder, CO: Paradigm.

Goddard, Henry H. (1911). "Heredity of Feeble-Mindedness." *American Breeders Magazine* 1 (3).

—— (1912). *The Kallikak Family: A Study in the Heredity of Feeble-Mindedness.* New York: Macmillan.

Goffman, Erving (1959). *The Presentation of Self in Everyday Life.* New York: Anchor.

—— (1961). *Asylums: Essays on the Social Situation of Mental Patients and Other Inmates.* New York: Anchor.

—— (1963). *Stigma: Notes on the Management of Spoiled Identity.* Englewood Cliffs, NJ: Prentice-Hall.

—— (1976). *Gender Advertisements.* New York: Harper Torch.

Goldscheider, Frances, & Regina Bures (2003). "The Racial Crossover in Family Complexity in the United States." *Demography* 40 (3), pp. 569–87.

Goldthorpe, John H., David Lockwood, Frank Benchhofer, & Jennifer Platt (1967). "The Affluent Worker and the Thesis of Embourgeoisement: Some Preliminary Research Findings." *Sociology* 1 (1), pp. 11–31.

Gomm, Roger, & Patrick McNeill (1982). *Handbook for Sociology Teachers*. London: Heineman.

Gorer, Geoffrey, & John Rickman (1949). *The People of Great Russia: A Psychological Study*. New York: Norton.

Gramsci, Antonio (1992). *Prison Notebooks*, vol. 1. Ed. Joseph A. Buttligieg. New York: Columbia.

Granatstein, J.L. (1990). *Nation: Canada since Confederation*, 3rd edn. Toronto: McGraw-Hill Ryerson.

Grant, George (1965). *Lament for a Nation: The Defeat of Canadian Nationalism*. Toronto: McClelland & Stewart.

—— (1969). *Technology and Empire: Perspectives on North America*. Toronto: House of Anansi.

Grattan, E. (2003). "Social Inequality and Stratification in Canada." In Paul Angelini (ed.), *Our Society: Human Diversity in Canada*, 2nd edn, pp. 61–86. Scarborough, ON: Thompson-Nelson.

Griffith, Alison, & L. Andre-Bechely (2008). "Standardizing Parents' Educational Work." In Marjorie DeVault (ed.), *Embodied Workers*. New York: NYU Press.

Griswold, Wendy (1994). *Cultures and Societies in a Changing World*. London: Sage.

Groce, Nora E. (1999). "Disability in a Cross-Cultural Perspective: Rethinking Disability." *The Lancet* 354 (9180), pp. 756–7.

Gross, Bertram (1980). *Friendly Fascism: The New Face of Power in America*. Montreal: Black Rose.

Grover, Sonja (2004). "Why Won't They Listen to Us? On Giving Power and Voice to Children Participating in Social Research." *Childhood* 11 (1), pp. 81–93. DOI:10.1177/0907568204040186

Grygier, Pat (1994). *A Long Way from Home: The Tuberculosis Epidemic among the Inuit*. Montreal: McGill–Queen's.

Haedrich, Richard L., & Cynthia M. Duncan (2004). "Above and Below the Water: Social/Ecological Transformation in Northwest Newfoundland." *Population and Environment* 25 (3), pp. 195–215.

Hafez, Kai (2007). "The Case of al-Jazeera: An 'Arab CNN'?" In *The Myth of Media Globalization*. London: Polity.

Hale, Sylvia (1992). "Facticity and Dogma in Introductory Sociology Texts: The Need for Alternative Methods." In William K. Carroll, Linda Christiansen-Ruffman, Raymond F. Currie, & Deborah Harrison (eds), *Fragile Truths: 25 Years of Sociology and Anthropology in Canada*, pp. 135–53. Ottawa, ON: Carleton.

Hall, Elaine J. (1988). "One Week for Women? The Structure of Inclusion of Gender Issues in Introductory Textbooks." *Teaching Sociology* 16 (4), pp. 431–2.

Hamilton, Lawrence, Cynthia Duncan, & Richard Haedrich (2004). "Social/Ecological Transformation in Northwest Newfoundland." *Population and Environment* 25 (3), pp. 195–215.

Hamilton, Roberta (1996). *Gendering the Vertical Mosaic: Feminist Perspectives on Canadian Society*. Toronto: Pearson.

Hanna, William R., & Clive Cockerton (1990). *Humanities: A Course in General Education*. Toronto: Thomson.

Hansen, Rick, & Jim Taylor (2011 [1987]). *Rick Hansen: Man In Motion. 40,000 km, 34 Countries and One Man's Dream to Change the World*. Vancouver: Douglas & McIntyre.

Hanson, Glen R., Peter J. Hanson, Peter J. Venturelli, & Annette E. Fleckenstein (2009). *Drugs and Society*, 10th edn. New York: Jones and Bartlett.

Harley, David (n.d.). "Witchcraft and the Occult, 1400–1700: Gender and Witchcraft." Retrieved: www.nd.edu/~harley/witchcraft/homepage.html

Harman, Joshua (1998). "Relative Deprivation and Worker Unrest in China." 1998 Esterline Prize Winner, Asian Studies on the Pacific Coast.

Harney, Alexandra (2009). *The China Price: The True Cost of Chinese Competitive Advantage*. New York: Penguin.

Harris, Marvin (1987). *Cultural Anthropology*, 2nd edn. New York: Harper & Row.

Harrison, Deborah (1999). "The Limits of Liberalism in Canadian Sociology: Some Notes on S.D. Clark." In Dennis W. Magill & William Michelson (eds), *Images of Change*. Toronto: Canadian Scholars' Press.

Hart, Julian Tudor (1971). "The Inverse Care Law." *The Lancet* 27 (Feb.), pp. 405–12.

Hasenfratz, Linda (2012). "Let's Embrace Michigan's 'Right to Work' Law." *The Globe and Mail* (20 Dec.). Retrieved: www.theglobeandmail.com/commentary/lets-embrace-michigans-right-to-work-law/article6581742/

Hatfield, Leonard Fraser (1990). *Sammy the Prince: The Story of Samuel Henry Prince*. Hantsport, NS: Lancelot.

Hawkes, Ernest (1916). *The Labrador Eskimo*. Ottawa: Government Printing Bureau.

Hegel, Georg Wilhelm Friedrich (1956). *The Philosophy of History*. Trans. J. Sibree. New York: Dover.

Helmes-Hayes, Rick (2010). *Measuring the Mosaic: An Intellectual Biography of John Porter*. Toronto: University of Toronto.

Helmes-Hayes, Rick, & James Curtis, eds (1998). *The Vertical Mosaic Revisited*. Toronto: University of Toronto.

Henry, Frances, & Carol Tator (2006). *The Colour of Democracy: Racism in Canada*. Toronto: Nelson Thomson.

Herman, Edward S., & Noam Chomsky (2002 [1988]). *Manufacturing Consent: The Political Economy of the Mass Media*. New York: Pantheon.

Hill, Daniel (1960). *Negroes in Toronto: A Sociological Study of a Minority Group*. Unpublished doctoral dissertation.

—— (1981). *The Freedom Seekers: Blacks in Early Canada*. Agincourt, ON: Book Society of Canada.

Hiller, Harry H., & Linda Di Luzio (2001). "Text and Context: Another 'Chapter' in the Evolution of Sociology in Canada." *Canadian Journal of Sociology* 26 (3), pp. 487–512.

Hiller, Harry H., & Simon Langlois (2001). "The Most Important Books/Articles in Canadian Sociology in the Twentieth Century: A Report." *Canadian Journal of Sociology / Cahiers canadiens de sociologie* 26 (3), pp. 513–16.

Hing, Julianne (2012). "Asian Americans Respond to Pew: We're Not Your Model Minority." *Color Lines* (21 June). Retrieved: http://colorlines.com/archives/2012/06/pew_asian_american_study.html

Hitchcock, John T., & Leigh Minturn (1963). "The Rajputs of Khalapur." In B. Whiting (ed.), *Six Cultures: Studies of Child Rearing*, pp. 203–362. New York: John Wiley & Sons.

Hitt, Jack (1999a). "Spent." *Saturday Night* 114 (2), pp. 62–72.

—— (1999b). "The Hidden Life of SUVs." *Mother Jones* (July/Aug.). Retrieved: www.motherjones.com/politics/1999/07/hidden-life-suvs

Hochschild, Arlie Russell, & Anne Machung (1989). *The Second Shift: Working Parents and the Revolution at Home*. New York: Viking Penguin.

Hodges, Leah (2005). "Written Testimony for the Record." Washington, DC: Select Bipartisan Committee to Investigate the Preparation and Response to Hurricane Katrina. Retrieved: http://katrina.house.gov/hearings/12_06_05/hodges_120605.rtf

Hoebel, E. Adamson (1965 [1954]). *The Law of Primitive Man, A Study in Comparative Legal Dynamics*. Cambridge, MA: Harvard.

Hofley, John R. (1992). "Canadianization: A Journey Completed?." In William K. Carroll, et al. (eds), *Fragile Truths: 25 Years of Sociology and Anthropology in Canada*, pp. 102–22. Ottawa: Carleton.

Hoodfar, Homa (2003). "More Than Clothing: Veiling as an Adaptive Strategy." In Sajida Alvi, H. Hoodfar, & Sheila McDonough (eds), *The Muslim Veil in North America: Issues and Debates*, pp. 3–40. Toronto: Women's Press.

Horowitz, Irving Louis, ed. (1971). *People, Power and Politics: The Collected Essays of C. Wright Mills*. New York: Oxford.

Hower, Wayne (2006). *Does a Disabled Child = A Disabled Family?* Bloomington, IN: AuthorHouse.

Hubert, Nadine (1985). "Sterilization and the Mentally Retarded." *The Interim* (14 August). Retrieved: www.theinterim.com/issues/bioethics/sterilization-and-the-mentally-retarded/

Huesmann, L. Rowell, & L.D. Eron (1986). *Television and the Aggressive Child: A Cross-national Comparison*. Lawrence Erlbaum.

Huesmann, L. Rowell, & L. Miller (1994). "Long Term Effects of Repeated Exposure to Media Violence in Children." In L.R. Huesmann (ed.), *Aggressive Behavior: Current Perspective*, pp. 153–86. New York: Plenum.

Huesmann, L. Rowell, J. Moise, C.P. Podolski, & L.D. Eron (2003). "Longitudinal Relations between Childhood Exposure to Media Violence and Adult Aggression and Violence: 1977–1992." *Developmental Psychology* 39 (2), pp. 201–21.

Huff, Mickey, & Frances A. Capell (2010). "Infotainment Society: Junk Food News and News Abuse for 2008–2009." In Peter Phillips, Mickey Huff, & Project Censored (Eds), *Censored 2010: The Top Censored Stories and Media Analysis of 2008–2009*, pp. 147–74. New York: Seven Stories

Huff, Mickey, & Project Censored (Eds) (2012). *Censored 2012: The Top Censored Stories and Media Analysis of 2010–2011*. New York: Seven Stories.

Hughes, Everett C. (1945). "Dilemmas and Contractions of Status." *American Journal of Sociology* 50 (5), pp. 353–9.

——— (1963 [1943]). *French Canada in Transition*. Chicago: University of Chicago.

Human Resources and Skills Development Canada (HRSDC) (2003). "Market Basket Measure Report." Retrieved: www.hrsdc.gc.ca/eng/cs/comm/news/2003/030527.shtml

Human Rights Watch (1999). *Broken People: Caste Violence against India's "Untouchables"* (1 April). Retrieved: www.unhcr.org/refworld/docid/3ae6a83f0.html

Humphreys, Margaret (1995). *Empty Cradles*. London: Transworld.

Hurtig, Mel (1992). *A New and Better Canada: Principles and Polices of a New Canadian Political Party*. Toronto: Stoddart.

Husain, Mir Zohair (1995). *Global Islamic Politics*. New York: HarperCollins.

Hutchison, George, & Dick Wallace (1977). *Grassy Narrows*. Toronto: Van Nostrand Rinehold.

Hutton, Samuel K. (1912). *Among the Eskimos of Labrador: A Record of Five Years' Close Intercourse with the Eskimo Tribes of Labrador*. Toronto: Musson.

Ibn Khaldûn (1981). *The Muqaddimah: An Introduction to History*. Trans. F. Rosenthal, ed. N.J. Dawood. Princeton, NJ: Princeton.

Iker, Jack (2003). "A Church's Choice." WCNY Online NewsHour (1 Aug.). Retrieved: www.pbs.org/newshour/bb/religion/july-dec03/episcopalian_8-1.html

Illich, Ivan (1976). *Medical Nemesis: The Limits of Medicine*. London: Penguin.

Inglehart, Ronald (1977). *The Silent Revolution: Changing Values and Political Styles among Western Publics*. Princeton, NJ: Princeton.

Ingstad, B. (1988). "Coping Behavior of Disabled Persons and Their Families: Cross-Cultural Perspectives from Norway and Botswana." *International Journal of Rehabilitation Research* 11, pp. 351–9.

Irish, Paul (2012). "Bullying Debate Erupts after TV Anchor Jennifer Livingston Responds to Viewer's Rude Email." *The Star* (4 Oct.). Retrieved: www.thestar.com/life/parent/2012/10/04/bullying_debate_erupts_after_tv_anchor_jennifer_livingston_responds_to_viewers_rude_email.html

Isajiw, Wsevolod W. (1999). *Understanding Diversity: Ethnicity and Race in the Canadian Context*. Toronto: Thomson.

Islam, Gazi, & Michael J. Zyphur (2009). "Rituals in Organizations: A Review and Expansion of Current Theory." *Group Organization Management* 34 (114): pp. 114–39.

Iwasaki, Mineko (2002). *Geisha: A Life*. New York: Washington Square.

Jacobs, Patricia A., Muriel Brunton, Marie M. Melville, Robert P. Brittain, & William F. McClemont (1965). "Aggressive Behaviour, Mental Sub-normality and the XYY male." *Nature* 208 (5017), pp. 1351–2.

Jaques, Elliott (1965). "Death and the Mid-life Crisis." *International Journal of Psycho-Analysis* 46, pp. 502–14.

Jenkins, Richard (1992). *Pierre Bourdieu*. London: Routledge.

Jenness, Diamond (1932). *Indians of Canada*. Ottawa: King's Printer.

Jenness, Stuart (1991). *Arctic Odyssey: The Diary of Diamond Jenness, 1913–1916*. Ottawa: Canadian Museum of Civilization.

Jhally, Sut (1990). *The Codes of Advertising: Fetishism and the Political Economy of Meaning in the Consumer Society*. New York: Routledge.

Jocas, Yves de, & Guy Rocher (1957). "Inter-generation Occupational Mobility in the Province of Quebec." *The Canadian Journal of Economics and Political Science* 25 (1), pp. 57–68.

Johnson, Kirk A., Mark K. Dolan, & John Sonnett (2011). "Speaking of Looting: An Analysis of Racial Propaganda in National Television Coverage of Hurricane Katrina." *The Howard Journal of Communications* 22, pp. 302–18.

Johnston, Basil (1999). *Crazy Dave*. Toronto: Key Porter.

Johnston, Hugh (1989). *The Voyage of the Komagata Maru: The Sikh Challenge to Canada's Colour Bar*. Vancouver: University of British Columbia.

Joint Policy Committee of the Societies of Epidemiology (JPC-SE) (2012). "Position Statement on Asbestos" (4 June). Retrieved: www.jpc-se.org/documents/01.JPC-SE-Position_Statement_on_Asbestos-June_4_2012-Summary_and_Appendix_A_English.pdf

Journalism.org (2003). "Embedded Reporters: What Are Americans Getting?" Pew Research Center's Project for Excellence in Journalism (3 April). Retrieved: www .journalism.org/node/211

Kachuck, Beatrice (2003 [1995]). "Feminist Social Theories: Themes and Variations." In Sharmila Rege (ed.), *Sociology of Gender: The Challenge of Feminist Sociological Knowledge*. New Delhi: Sage.

Kahn, Jeffery (2004). "Postmortem: Iraq War Media Coverage Dazzled but It Also Obscured." UC Berkeley News (18 March). Retrieved: www.berkeley.edu/news/media/ releases/2004/03/18_iraqmedia.shtml

Kaizuka, Shigeki (2002 [1956]). *Confucius: His Life and Thought*. Mineola, NY: Dover.

Kane, P.R., & A.J. Orsini (2003). "The Need for Teachers of Color in Independent Schools." In P.R. Kane & A.J. Orsini (eds), *The Colors of Excellence: Hiring and Keeping Teachers of Color in Independent Schools*, pp. 7–28. New York: Teachers College.

Keay, John (2000). *India: A History*. London: HarperCollins.

Kehoe, Alice (1995). "Blackfoot Persons." In L. Klein & L. Ackerman, *Women and Power in Native North America*. Norman, OK: University of Oklahoma.

Kellner, Douglas (2005). *Media Spectacle and the Crisis of Democracy*. Boulder, CO: Paradigm.

Kelly, Mary Bess (2012). "Divorce Cases in Civil Court, 2010/2011." *Juristat* (Statistics Canada cat. no. 85-002-X). Ottawa: Minister of Industry.

Kempe, C. Henry, Frederic N. Silverman, Brandt F. Steele, William Droegemueller, & Henry K. Silver (1962). "The Battered Child Syndrome." *The Journal of the American Medical Association* 181 (1), pp. 17–24.

Kimelman, Edwin C. (1985). *No Quiet Place: Review Committee on Indian and Metis Adoption and Placements*. Manitoba Community Services.

King, Alan, Wendy Warren, & Sharon Miklas (2004). "Study of Accessibility to Ontario Law Schools." Executive Summary of the Report Submitted to Deans of Law at Osgood Hall, York University; University of Ottawa; Queen's University; University of Western Ontario; University of Windsor. Queen's University: Social Program Evaluation Group.

Kinsman, Gary (1995 [1987]). *The Regulation of Desire: Homo and Hetero Sexualities*. Montreal & New York: Black Rose.

Kirkby, Mary-Ann (2007). *I Am Hutterite*. Prince Albert SK: Polka Dot.

Kitossa, Tamari (2012). "Criminology and Colonialism: Counter Colonial Criminology and the Canadian Context." *The Journal of Pan African Studies* 4 (10), pp. 204–26.

Klein, Naomi (2000). *No Logo: Taking Aim at the Brand Bullies*. Toronto: Vintage.

——— (2002). *Fences and Windows: Dispatches from the Frontlines of the Globalization Debate*. Toronto: Vintage.

Kleinman, Arthur (1995). *Writing at the Margin: Discourse Between Anthropology and Medicine*. Berkeley: University of California.

Klopfenstein, Kristin (2005). "Beyond Test Scores: The Impact of Black Teacher Role Models on Rigorous Math-Taking." *Contemporary Economic Policy* 23, pp. 416–28.

Knockwood, Isabelle (1992). *Out of the Depths: The Experiences of Mi'kmaw Children at the Indian Residential School at Shubenacadie*. Lockeport, NS: Roseway.

Koos, E.L. (1954). *The Health of Regionsville: What the People Thought and Did About It*. New York: Columbia.

Kral, Andrej, & Gerard M. O'Donoghue (2010). "Profound Deafness in Childhood." *New England Journal of Medicine* 363, pp. 1439–50. DOI:10.1056/NEJMra0911225

Kramer, Reinhold, & Tom Mitchell (2010). *When the State Trembled: How A.J. Andrews and the Citizens' Committee Broke the Winnipeg General Strike*. Toronto: University of Toronto Press.

Krause, Elliott (1980). *Why Study Sociology?* New York: Random House.

Kroker, Arthur, & Michael A. Weinstein (1995). *Data Trash: The Theory of the Virtual Class*. Montreal: New World Perspectives.

Kruijver, F.P.M., J.-N. Zhou, C.W. Pool, M.A. Hofman, L.J.G. Gooren, & D.F. Swaab (2000). "Male-to-Female Transsexuals Have Female Neuron Numbers in a Limbic Nucleus." *Journal of Clinical Endocrinology & Metabolism* 85 (5), pp. 2034–41.

Kwong, J.C., I.A. Dhalla, D.L. Streiner, R.E. Baddour, A.E. Waddell, & I.L. Johnson (2002). "Effects of Rising Tuition Fees on Medical School Class Composition and Financial Outlook." *Canadian Medical Association Journal* 166 (8), pp. 1023–8.

Lafrance, Amélie, & Sébastien LaRochelle-Côté (2011). "Consumption Patterns among Aging Canadians." In *Perspectives on Labour and Income*, Statistics Canada cat. no. 75-001-X. Retrieved: www.statcan.gc.ca/pub/ 75-001-x/2011002/pdf/11417-eng.pdf

Lalonde, Michelle (2007). "Town Built on Asbestos Downplays Health Risks." Montreal *Gazette* (9 Nov.).

Lane, Harlan L. (1992). *The Mask of Benevolence: Disabling the Deaf Community*. New York: Alfred A. Knopf.

——— (1993). "The Medicalisation of Cultural Deafness in Historical Perspective." In Renate Fischer & Harlan L. Lane (Eds), *Looking Back: A Reader on the History of Deaf Communities and Their Sign Languages*, pp. 479–94. International Studies on Sign Language and Communication of the Deaf. Hamburg: Signum.

Langlois, Simon (1999). "Empirical Studies on Social Stratification in Quebec and Canada." In Y. Lemel & N. Noll (eds), *New Structures of Inequality*. Montreal: McGill–Queen's.

LaRocque, Emma (1975). *Defeathering the Indian*. Agincourt, ON: Book Society of Canada.

——— (1993). "Three Conventional Approaches to Native People." In Brett Balon & Peter Resch (eds), *Survival of the Imagination: the Mary Donaldson Memorial Lectures*, pp. 209–18. Regina: Coteau.

Laslett, Peter (1971). *The World We Have Lost*. London: Methuen.

Lawrence, Bonita (2004). *"Real" Indians and Others: Mixed-Blood Urban Native Peoples and Indigenous Nationhood*. Vancouver: University of British Columbia.

Leah, Ronnie, & Gwen Morgan (1979). "Immigrant Women Fight Back: The Case of the Seven Jamaican Women." *Resources for Feminist Research* 7 (3), pp. 23–4.

Lebkowsky, J. (1997). "It's Better to be Inspired than Wired: An Interview with R.U. Sirius." In A. Kroker & M. Kroker (eds), *Digital Delirium*. Montreal: New World Perspectives.

Le Bourdais, C., & N. Marcil-Gratton (1996). "Family Transformations Across the Canadian/American Border: When the Laggard Becomes the Leader." *Journal of Comparative Family Studies* 27 (3) (Fall), pp. 417–36.

Ledbetter, James (1997). *Made Possible By . . . : The Death of Public Broadcasting in the United States*. London: Verso.

Lee, Richard B. (1993). *The Dobe Ju/'hoansi*, 2nd edn. Fort Worth, TX: Harcourt Brace.

Leffingwell, William (1925). *Office Management: Principles and Practice*. Chicago: A.W. Shaw.

Leiss, William, Stephen Kline, & Sut Jhally (1988). *Social Communication in Advertising: Persons, Products, and Images of Well-Being*. Toronto: Nelson.

Lemaistre, Joann (1985). "Parenting." In Susan E. Brownie, Debra Conners, & Nanci Stern (Eds), *With the Power of Each Breath: A Disabled Women's Anthology*, pp. 284–91. San Francisco: Cleiss.

Leung, Carrianne, & Jian Guan (2004). "Yellow Peril Revisited: Impact of SARS on the Chinese and Southeast Asian Canadian Communities." Toronto: Canadian National Council, www.ccnc.ca

Lichenstein, Nelson (2001). Introduction. In C. Wright Mills, *The New Men of Power: America's Labor Leaders*. New York: Harcourt, Brace.

Lieberson, Stanley (2000). *A Matter of Taste: How Names, Fashions and Cultures Change*. New Haven, CT: Yale.

Lipset, Seymour Martin (1990). *Continental Divide: Values and Institutions of the United States and Canada*. New York: Routledge.

Livingstone, David W. (2004). *The Education–Jobs Gap: Underemployment or Economic Democracy* (2nd edn). Toronto: Garamond.

Lockhart, Alexander (1979). "Educational Opportunities and Economic Opportunities—The 'New' Liberal Equality Syndrome." In J. Allan Fry (ed.), *Economy, Class and Social Reality: Issues in Contemporary Canadian Society*, pp. 224–37. Toronto: Butterworths.

Love, John F. (1986). *McDonald's: Behind the Arches*. Toronto: Bantam.

Lowe, Kevin, Stan Fischler, & Shirley Fischler (1988). *Champions: The Making of the Edmonton Oilers*. Scarborough, ON: Prentice-Hall.

Lundy, Katherina, & Barbara Warme (1990 [1986]). *Sociology: A Window on the World*. Toronto: Methuen.

Lyotard, Jean-Francois (1984). *The Postmodern Condition: A Report on Knowledge*. Minneapolis, MN: University of Minnesota.

McChesney, Robert W. (2003). *Rich Media, Poor Democracy: Communication Politics in Dubious Times*. Champaign, IL: University of Illinois.

McClintock, Walter (1910). *The Old North Trail. Life, Legends, and Religion of the Blackfeet Indians*. London: Macmillan.

McCourt, Frank (1996). *Angela's Ashes*. New York: Scribner.

Macdonald, David (2011). "The Shadow Public Service: The Swelling Ranks of Federal Government Outsourced Workers." Canadian Centre for Policy Alternatives (3 March). Retrieved: www.policyalternatives.ca/publications/reports/shadow-public-service

McGillivray, Anne & Brenda Comaskey (1999). *Black Eyes All of the Time: Intimate Violence, Aboriginal Women and the Justice System*. Toronto: University of Toronto.

MacGregor, Roy (2012). "High Price, Fewer Players." *The Globe and Mail* (1 Dec.), p. S2.993

McKay, Ian (1998). "Changing the Subject(s) of the 'History of Canadian Sociology': The Case of Colin McKay and Spencerian Marxism, 1890–1940." *Canadian Journal of Sociology* 23 (4).

MacKrael, Kim, & Ian Bailey (2013). "Ottawa Changes Tack after Report; Backs Committee on Slain Women." *The Globe and Mail* (15 Feb.). Retrieved: www.theglobeandmail.com/news/politics/ottawa-changes-tack-after-report-backs-committee-on-slain-women/article8710765/

MacLean, Annie Marion (1897–8). "Factory Legislation for Women in the United States." *American Journal of Sociology* 3, pp. 183–205.

——— (1898). "Two Weeks in a Department Store." *American Journal of Sociology* 4, pp. 721–41.

——— (1899–1900). "Faculty Legislation for Women in Canada." *American Journal of Sociology* 5, pp. 172–81.

——— (1903–4). "The Sweat Shop Summer." *American Journal of Sociology* 9, pp. 289–309.

——— (1908–9). "Life in the Pennsylvania Coal Fields." *American Journal of Sociology* 14, pp. 329–51.

——— (1909–10). "With the Oregon Hop Pickers." *American Journal of Sociology* 15, pp. 83–95.

——— (1910). *Wage-Earning Women*. New York: Macmillan.

——— (1916). *Women Workers and Society*. Chicago: A.C. McClurg.

——— (1923). "Four Months in a Model Factory." *Century* 106 (July), pp. 436–44.

Maclean, John (1970 [1889]). *The Indians of Canada: Their Manners and Customs*. Toronto: Coles.

Macleans.ca (2010). "How Much Does Medical School Cost? First-Year Tuition for Academic Year 2010–2011." Macleans.ca (16 Sept.). Retrieved: www2.macleans.ca/2010/09/16/how-much-they-pay-for-it/

MacLeod, Linda (1980). *Wife Battering in Canada: The Vicious Circle*. Hull, QC: Canadian Government Publishing Centre.

McKenna, Cara (2013). "'Heartbreaking' Case of Continued Abuse, Says Minister." *Windspeaker* 30 (12). Retrieved: www.windspeaker.com/

McLuhan, Marshall (1962). *The Gutenberg Galaxy: The Making of Typographic Man*. Toronto: University of Toronto.

——— (1964). *Understanding Media: The Extensions of Man*. New York: Signet.

MacNeil, Robert (1982). *The Right Place at the Right Time*. Boston: Little Brown.

McQuaig, Linda (2004). "Closed Shop Gives Doc the Hammer in New Brunswick Strike." *Straight Goods*. Retrieved: www.straightgoods.com/McQuaig/010122.shtml

Madiros, M. (1989). "Conception of Childhood Disability among Mexican-American Parents." *Medical Anthropology* 12, pp. 55–68.

Maines, D.R. (1993). "Narrative's Moment and Sociology's Phenomena—Toward a Narrative Sociology." *Sociological Quarterly* 34 (1), pp. 17–37.

Maioni, Antonia (2004). "New Century, New Risks: The Marsh Report and the Post-War Welfare State in Canada." *Policy Options* (Aug.), pp. 20–3.

Mairs, Nancy (1986). "On Being a Cripple." In Nancy Mairs, *Plaintext: Essays*, pp. 9–21. Tucson, AZ: University of Arizona Press.

Mandell, Nancy, & Ann Duffy (1995). *Canadian Families: Diversity, Conflict and Change*. Toronto: Harcourt, Brace.

Manji, Irshad (2003). *The Trouble with Islam: A Wake Up Call for Honesty and Change*. Toronto: Random House.

Maracle, Brian (1996). *Back on the Rez: Finding The Way Home*. Toronto: Viking Penguin.

Maracle, Lee (1992). *Sundogs*. Penticton, BC: Theytus.

Marcuse, Herbert (1964). *One Dimensional Man*. Boston: Beacon.

Marshall, Gordon (1998). *Oxford Dictionary of Sociology*. New York: Oxford.

Martineau, Harriet (1848). *Eastern Life Past and Present*. London: Moxon.

—— (1962 [1837]). *Society in America*. Garden City, NY: Doubleday.

—— (2005 [1838]). *Retrospect of Western Travel*. Honolulu: University Press of the Pacific.

Martos, Joseph (2000). "What Difference Does Confirmation Make?" newsletter. Retrieved: www.americancatholic.org/newsletters/yu/ay0385.asp

Marx, Karl (1967 [1867]). *Capital: A Critique of Political Economy*. Ed. F. Engels. New York: International.

Marx, Karl, & Friedrich Engels (1967 [1848]). *The Communist Manifesto*. New York: Pantheon.

—— (1970 [1845–6]). *The German Ideology*, part 1. Ed. C.J. Arthur. New York: International.

Mazón, Mauricio (1984). *The Zoot-Suit Riots: The Psychology of Symbolic Annihilation*. Austin, TX: University of Texas.

Mead, George Herbert (1934). *Mind, Self, and Society*. Chicago: University of Chicago.

Mead, Margaret (1928). *Coming of Age in Samoa: A Psychological Study of Primitive Youth for Western Civilization*. New York: William Morrow & Company.

—— (1970). *Culture and Commitment: A Study of the Generation Gap*. Garden City, NY: Natural History Press.

Medicine, Beatrice (1986). "My Elders Tell Me." In Jean Barman, Yvonne M. Hébert, & Don N. McCaskill (Eds), *Indian Education in Canada: The Challenge*, vol. 2, pp. 142–52. Vancouver: UBC.

Memmi, Albert (1991 [1957]). *The Colonizer and the Colonized*. Boston: Beacon.

Menon, Usha (2001). "Middle Adulthood in Cultural Perspective: The Imagined and the Experienced in Three Cultures." In Margie E. Lachman (Ed.), *Handbook of Midlife Development*, pp. 40–74. New York: Wiley.

Mercurio, Antoinette (2013). "First National Blind Hockey Tournament to Be Held at Mattamy Athletic Centre." Ryerson University *News & Events* (13 Feb.). Retrieved: www.ryerson.ca/news/news/General_Public/20130213_blind.html

Merton, Robert K. (1938). "Social Structure and Anomie." *American Sociological Review* 3 (5), pp. 672–82.

—— (1968 [1949]). *Social Theory and Social Structure*. New York: Free Press.

Michaels, Eric (1986). *The Aboriginal Invention of Television in Central Australia, 1982–6*. Canberra: Australian Institute of Aborigine Studies.

Mies, Maria, & Vandana Shiva (1993). *Ecofeminism*. Halifax: Fernwood.

Milan, Anne, Hélène Maheux, & Tina Chui (2010). *A Portrait of Couples in Mixed Unions* (Statistics Canada cat. no. 11-008-X). Ottawa: Statistics Canada.

Milan, Anne, & Kelly Tran (2004). "Blacks in Canada: A Long History." *Canadian Social Trends* (spring), pp. 2–7.

Miller, J.R. (1996). *Shingwauk's Vision: A History of Native Residential Schools*. Toronto: University of Toronto.

Mills, Albert J., & Tony Simmons (1995). *Reading Organization Theory: A Critical Approach*. Toronto: Garamond.

Mills, C. Wright (1948). *The New Men of Power: America's Labor Leaders*. New York: Harcourt, Brace.

—— (1951). *White Collar: The American Middle Classes*. New York: Oxford.

—— (1956). *The Power Elite*. New York: Oxford.

—— (1958). *The Causes of World War Three*. London: Secker & Warburg.

—— (1959). *The Sociological Imagination*. New York: Oxford.

—— (1960). *Listen Yankee: The Revolution in Cuba*. New York: Ballantine Books.

—— (1962). *The Marxists*. New York: Dell Publishing.

—— (2000). *Letters and Writings by C. Wright Mills*. Ed. Kathryn Mills and Pamela Mills. Berkeley and Los Angeles: University of California.

—— (2001 [1948]). *The New Men of Power: America's Labor Leaders*. Ed. Nelson Lichtenstein. Urbana & Chicago: University of Illinois Press.

Miner, Horace (1963 [1939]). *St Denis: A French Canadian Parish*. Chicago: University of Chicago.

Montagu, Ashley (1942). *Man's Most Dangerous Myth: The Fallacy of Race*. New York: Columbia.

Monture-Angus, Patricia (1995). *Thunder in My Soul: A Mohawk Woman Speaks*. Halifax: Fernwood.

Moore, Riley D. (1923). "Social Life of the Eskimo of St Lawrence Island." *American Anthropologist* 25 (3), pp. 339–75.

Morehead Phillip, & Albert Morehead (1981). *Roget's College Dictionary*. New York: Penguin.

Morgan, Lewis Henry (1964 [1877]). *Ancient Society or Researches in the Lines of Human Progress from Savagery through Barbarism to Civilization*. Cambridge, MA: Harvard.

Morin, Rich, & Paul Taylor (2009). "Luxury or Necessity? The Public Makes a U-Turn." *Pew Social and Demographic Trends* (23 April). Pew Research Center. Retrieved: www.pewsocialtrends.org/2009/04/23/luxury-or-necessity-the-public-makes-a-u-turn/

Morrison, David (2010). "Should Disability Be Considered a Master Status?" Blog post (1 February), retrieved: http://disabilities.blogs.starnewsonline.com/10988/should-disability-be-considered-a-master-status/

Mouwad, Jad (2009). "Shell to Pay $15.5 Million to Settle Nigerian Case." *The New York Times* (8 June). Retrieved: www.nytimes.com/2009/06/09/business/global/09shell.html?_r=2&partner=rss&emc=rss&

Mueller, Carol (1995). "The Organizational Basis of Conflict in Contemporary Feminism." In Myra Marx Ferree & Patricia Yancey Martin (eds), *Feminist Organizations*, pp. 263–75. Philadelphia: Temple University.

Murdoch, Michelle, (2005). *Women with Disabilities and Adaptive Technology in the Workplace: Participatory Action Research and Applied Principles of Independent Living*. St John's, NL: Independent Living Resource Centre.

Murphy, Emily (1973 [1922]). *The Black Candle*. Toronto: Coles.

Mussolum, Erin (2009). "Social Media Creates Anxiety, Says TWU Professor." Trinity Western University (22 July). Retrieved: https://twu.ca/about/news/general/2009/the-dangers-of-social-media.html

Muzzin, Linda J. (2001). "Powder Puff Brigades: Professional Caring vs Industry Research in the Pharmaceutical Sciences Curriculum." In Eric Margolis (ed.), *The Hidden Curriculum in Higher Education*, pp. 135–54. London: Routledge.

Myers, S.A., trans. (1862). *Martin's Natural History,* first series. New York: Blackeman & Mason.

Naidoo, Amelia (2011). "Shedding Light on the 'Boyat' Phenomenon." GulfNews.com (21 April). Retrieved: http://gulfnews.com/news/gulf/uae/general/shedding-light-on-the-boyat-phenomenon-1.796816

Nakhaie, M. Reza (1995). "Housework in Canada: The National Picture." *Journal of Comparative Family Studies* 23 (3), pp. 409–25.

Nanda, Serena (1994). *Cultural Anthropology,* 5th edn. Belmont, CA: Wadsworth.

Nebenzahl, Donna (2011). "Working Women: Don't Take It Personally." *The Star* (Toronto; 26 Feb.): p. B5.

Nelson, Joyce (2012). "Enbridge Spills." *Watershed Sentinel: Environmental News from BC and the World* 22 (2). Retrieved: www.watershedsentinel.ca/content/enbridge-spills

Neustadter, Roger (2009). *The Obvious Child: Studies in the Significance of Childhood.* New York: University Press of America.

Newbury, Catharine (1993 [1988]). *The Cohesion of Oppression.* New York: Columbia.

Newson, Janice, & Howard Buchbinder (1988). *The University Means Business: Universities, Corporations and Academic Work.* Toronto: Garamond.

Niedzviecki, Hal (2009). *The Peep Diaries: How We're Learning to Love Watching Ourselves and Our Neighbours.* San Francisco: City Lights.

Nietzsche, Frederick (1968 [1901]). *Will to Power.* Trans. Walter Kaufmann. New York: Vintage.

—— (1996 [1878]). *Human, All Too Human.* Trans. Marion Faber & Stephen Lehmann. Cambridge, MA: Cambridge.

—— (2003 [1887]). *The Genealogy of Morals.* New York: Dover.

—— (2006 [1882]). *The Gay Science.* New York: Dover.

Nihmey, John (1998). *Fireworks and Folly: How We Killed Minnie Sutherland.* Ottawa: Phillip Diamond.

Nikiforuk, Andrew (2009). *The Tar Sands: Dirty Oil and the Future of the Continent.* Vancouver: Greystone.

Niosi, Jorge (1981). *Canadian Capitalism: A Study of Power in the Canadian Business Establishment.* Trans. R. Chodos. Toronto: James Lorimer.

—— (1985). *Canadian Multinationals.* Trans. R. Chodos. Toronto: Between the Lines.

Nisbet, Robert A. (1969). *Social Change and History: Aspects of the Western Theory of Development.* Oxford: Oxford.

Noble, David (1998). "Digital Diploma Mills: The Automation of Higher Education." *Science as Culture* 7 (3), pp. 355–68.

—— (2002). *Digital Diploma Mills: The Automation of Higher Education.* Toronto: Between the Lines.

Nock, David. A. (1993). *"Star Wars in Canadian Sociology": Exploring the Social Construction of Knowledge.* Halifax: Fernwood.

—— (2001). "Careers in Print: Canadian Sociological Books and Their Wider Impact, 1975–1992." *Canadian Journal of Sociology / Cahiers canadiens de sociologie* 26 (3), pp. 469–85.

Nonaka, K., T. Miura, & K. Peter (1993). "Low Twinning Rate and Seasonal Effects on Twinning in a Fertile Population, the Hutterites." *International Journal of Biometeorology* 37 (3), pp. 145–50.

Oakes, Jeannie (2005). *Keeping Track: How Schools Structure Inequality,* 2nd edn. New Haven: Yale.

Oakley, Ann (1972). *Sex, Gender and Society.* London: Temple Smith.

Office of the Auditor General of Canada (2012). *Fall 2012 Report of the Auditor General of Canada to the House of Commons.* Ottawa: Minister of Public Works and Government Services.

Okonta, Ike, & Oronto Douglas (2001). *Where Vultures Feast: Shell, Human Rights and Oil.* San Francisco: Sierra Club.

Onley, David C. (2007). Installation Speech, Hon. David C. Onley, Lieutenant Governor of Ontario (5 Sept.). Retrieved: www.lt.gov.on.ca/en/Speeches/installationSpeech.asp?mav=7&din=1

Ontario Federation of Labour (1992). "Education and Training: A Policy Adopted at the 33rd Annual Convention of the Ontario Federation of Labour, November, 1989." *Our Schools, Our Selves* 4 (2), pp. 87–103.

Ontario Human Rights Commission (OHRC) (2003). *Paying the Price: The Human Cost of Racial Profiling.* Inquiry Report. Toronto: OHRC. Retrieved: www.ohrc.on.ca/sites/default/files/attachments/Paying_the_price%3A_The_human_cost_of_racial_profiling.pdf

Ontario Medical Association (2002). "Position Paper on Physician Workforce Policy and Planning." Document addressing concerns of the Ontario Medical Association (OMA).

Oreskes, Naomi, & Erik M. Conway (2010). *Merchants of Doubt: How a Handful of Scientists Obscured the Truth on Issues from Tobacco Smoke to Global Warming.* New York: Bloomsbury.

Ormsby, Mary (2007). "Why Gear Is Dear." *The Star* (Toronto, 8 Dec.), pp. S1, S6.

Ornstein, Michael (1984). "Interlocking Directorates in Canada: Intercorporate or Class Alliance?" *Administrative Science Quarterly* 29, pp. 210–31.

—— (1988). "Corporate Involvement in Canadian Hospital and University Boards, 1946–1977." *Canadian Review of Sociology and Anthropology* 25 (3) pp. 365–88.

Park, Robert, & Ernest Burgess (1921). *Introduction to the Science of Sociology.* Chicago: University of Chicago.

—— (1967 [1925]). *The City.* Chicago: University of Chicago.

Parry, Tom (2012). "Ottawa Won't Intervene after CRTC Rejects BCE–Astral Deal. Regulator Says Deal Would Have Given BCE Too Much Power." CBC News (18 Oct.). Retrieved: www.cbc.ca/news/politics/story/2012/10/18/pol-parry-crtc-bell.html

Parsons, Talcott (1940). "An analytical approach to the Theory of Social Stratification." *American Journal of Sociology* 45 (6), pp. 841–62.

—— (1951). *The Social System.* New York: Free Press.

—— (1966). *Societies: Evolutionary and Comparative Perspectives.* Englewood Cliffs, NJ: Prentice-Hall.

Patai, Raphael (2002). *The Arab Mind.* New York: Random House.

Payer, Lynn (1992). *Disease-Mongers: How Doctors, Drug Companies, and Insurers Are Making You Feel Sick.* New York: Wiley.

Perkel, Colin N. (2002). *Well of Lies: The Walkerton Tragedy.* Toronto: McClelland & Stewart.

Perreault, Samuel, & Shannon Brennan (2009). "Criminal Victimization in Canada, 2009." *Juristat* (Summer). Statistics Canada cat. no. 85-002-X. Retrieved: www.statcan.gc.ca/pub/85-002-x/2010002/article/11340-eng.htm

Pew Research Center (2012). "The Rise of Asian Americans." *Pew Social and Demographic Trends* (19 June). Pew Research Center. Retrieved: www.pewsocialtrends.org/files/2013/01/SDT_Rise_of_Asian_Americans.pdf

Philip, Margaret (2006). "Cancer in the Mind's Eye." *The Globe and Mail* (9 Dec.). Retrieved: www.theglobeandmail.com/servlet/story/RTGAM.20061208.cover09/BNStory/cancer/home

Phillips, Peter, & Mickey Huff, eds (2009). *Censored 2010: The Top 25 Censored Stories of 2008–09.* New York: Seven Stories.

Phillips, Peter, & Mickey Huff (2010). "Analysis of Project Censored: Are We a Left-Leaning, Conspiracy-Oriented Organization?" Project Censored: Media Democracy in Action (9 June). Retrieved: www.projectcensored.org/top-stories/articles/analysis-of-project-censored-are-we-a-left-leaning-conspiracy-oriented-organization/

"Plural Wife Describes Life in Bountiful Commune" (2011). Canadian Press (27 Jan.). Retrieved: www.ctvnews.ca/plural-wife-describes-life-in-bountiful-commune-1.600642

Pohlmann, Lisa (2002). "Inequality is Bad for your Health." Retrieved: www.mecep.or/MEChoices02/ch_029.htm

Porter, John (1965). *The Vertical Mosaic: An Analysis of Social Class and Power in Canada.* Toronto: University of Toronto.

Postman, Neil (1982). *The Disappearance of Childhood.* New York: Delacorte.

—— (1985). *Amusing Ourselves to Death: Public Discourse in the Age of Show Business.* New York: Penguin.

Powers, Michael (2006). "A Matter of Choice: Historical Lessons for Disaster Recovery." In C. Harman & G.D. Squires (eds), *There Is No Such Thing as a Natural Disaster: Race, Class, and Hurricane Katrina*, pp. 13–35. New York: Routledge.

Price, William H., & Peter B. Whatmore (1967), "Behaviour Disorders and Pattern of Crime among XYY Males Identified at a Maximum Security Hospital." *British Medical Journal* 2 (5601), pp. 533–6.

Prince, Samuel Henry (1920). *Catastrophe and Social Change: Based Upon a Sociological Study of the Halifax Disaster.* New York: Columbia.

Qvortrup, Jens (1990). "A Voice for Children in Statistical and Social Accounting: A Plea for Children's Right to Be Heard." In Allison James & Alan Prout (Eds), *Constructing and Reconstructing Childhood: Contemporary Issues in the Sociological Study of Childhood*, pp. 78–98. New York: Falmer.

Rajulton, Fernando, T.R. Balakrishnan, & Zenaida R. Ravanera (1990). "Measuring Infertility in Contracepting Populations." Presentation, Canadian Population Society Meetings (Victoria, BC, June 1990).

Ransome, Paul (2005). *Work, Consumption and Culture: Affluence and Social Change in the Twenty-First Century.* London: Sage.

Rege, Sharmila (2003). "Feminist Challenge to Sociology: Disenchanting Sociology or 'For Sociology'?" In S. Rege (ed.), *Sociology of Gender: The Challenge of Feminist Sociological Knowledge*, pp. 1–49. London: Sage.

Reid, Anna (2002). *The Shaman's Coat: A Native History of Siberia.* London: Weidenfeld & Nicolson.

Reiman, Jeffrey (1998). *The Rich Get Richer and the Poor Get Prison: Ideology, Class and Criminal Justice.* Boston: Allyn & Bacon.

Reinharz, Shulamit (1992). *Feminist Methods in Social Research.* New York: Oxford .

Rennie, Steve (2012). "Boomerang Kids Mean Empty Nests Not Quite So Empty." *The Globe and Mail* (19 Sept.).

Reynolds, Neil (2010). "Beware the Coming Credit Card Hit on Canadian Families." *The Globe and Mail* (19 May). Retrieved: www.theglobeandmail.com/report-on-business/rob-commentary/beware-the-coming-credit-card-hit-on-Canadian-familiesarticle4320324/

Richards, John, Jennifer Hove, & Kemi Afolabi (2008). *Understanding the Aboriginal/Non-Aboriginal Gap in Student Performance: Lessons from British Columbia.* Commentary 276 (December). Toronto: C.D. Howe Institute.

Richardson, Jack R. (1992). "Free Trade: Why Did It Happen?" *Canadian Review of Sociology and Anthropology* 29 (3), pp. 307–28.

Riesman, David (1950). *The Lonely Crowd: A Study of the Changing American Character.* New Haven, CT: Yale.

Ritzer, George (2001). *Explorations in the Sociology of Consumption: Fast Food, Credit Cards and Casinos.* London: Sage.

—— (2004). *The McDonaldization of Society*, rev. edn. Newbury Park, CA: Pine Forge Press.

—— (2008). *The Sociological Theory* (7th edn). New York: McGraw-Hill.

Robertson, Heather (1970). *Reservations Are for Indians.* Toronto: Lorimer.

Robertson, Roland (1997). "Comments on the 'Global Triad' and 'Glocalization.'" In Inoue Nobutaka (ed.), *Globalization and Indigenous Culture.* Institute for Japanese Culture and Classics, Kokugakuin University.

Robin, Marie-Monique (2010). *The World According to Monsanto: Pollution, Politics, and Power; An Investigation into One of the World's Most Controversial Companies.* Melbourne: Spinifex.

Robinson, Angela (2002). "Ta'n Teli-ktlamsitasit ('Ways of Believing'): Mi'kmaw Religion in Eskasoni, Nova Scotia." *Open Access Dissertations and Theses,* Paper 1477. Retrieved: http://digitalcommons.mcmaster.ca/opendissertations/1477

—— (2005). *Ta'n Teli-ktlamsitasit (Ways of Believing): Mi'kmaw Religion in Eskasoni, Nova Scotia.* Toronto: Pearson.

Rochelau, Dianne, Barbara Thomas-Slayter, & Esther Wangari, eds. (1996). *Feminist Political Ecology: Global Issues and Local Experiences.* London: Routledge.

Rosario, M., E. Scrimshaw, J. Hunter, & L. Braun (2006). "Sexual Identity Development among Lesbian, Gay, and Bisexual Youths: Consistency and Change Over Time." *Journal of Sex Research* 43 (1), pp. 46–58.

Roscoe, Will (1998). *Changing Ones: Third and Fourth Genders in Native North America.* Palgrave/St Martin's Press.

Ross, Aileen (1962). *The Hindu Family in Its Urban Setting.* Toronto: University of Toronto.

—— (1976). "Changing Aspirations and Roles: Middle and Upper Class Indian Women Enter the Business World." In Giri Raj Gupta (ed.), *Main Currents in Indian Sociology*, 103–32. Bombay: Vikas.

—— (1977). "Some Comments on the Home Roles of Businesswomen in India, Australia and Canada." *Journal of Comparative Family Studies* 8 (3), pp. 327–40.

—— (1979). "Businesswomen and Business Cliques in Three Cities: Delhi, Sydney, and Montreal." *Canadian Review of Sociology and Anthropology* 16 (4), pp. 425–35.

—— (1982). *The Lost and the Lonely: Homeless Women in Montreal.* Montreal: Canadian Human Rights Commission.

Ross, Michael L. (2001). "Does Oil Hinder Democracy?" *World Politics* 53 (3), pp. 325–61.

Ruddick, Sara (1989). *Maternal Thinking: Toward a Politics of Peace.* Boston: Beacon.

Ruether, Rosemary Radford (1993). "Ecofeminism: Symbolic and Social Connections of the Oppression of Women and the Domination of Nature." In Carol Adams (ed.), *Ecofeminism and the Sacred.* New York: Continuum.

Runciman, W.G. (Ed.) (1991). *Weber Selections in Translation.* Cambridge: Cambridge University Press.

Russell, George (2001). "Cover Stories Taming the Liberation Theologians." *Time Magazine World* (24 June). Retrieved: www.time.com/time/magazine/article/0,0171,141037,00.html

Ryan, William (1976 [1971]). *Blaming the Victim.* New York: Pantheon.

Said, Edward (1979). *Orientalism.* New York: Pantheon.

Saint-Cyr, Yosie (2010). "Alcoholism and Drug Addiction Are Disabilities—Government Benefits Can't Be Denied." *Slaw: Canada's Online Legal Magazine* (23 Sept.). Retrieved: www.slaw.ca/2010/09/23/alcoholism-and-drug-addiction-are-disabilities-%E2%80%95-government-benefits-can%E2%80%99t-be-denied/

Saitoti, Tepilit Ole (1988). *The Worlds of a Maasai Warrior: An Autobiography.* Berkeley: University of California Press.

Sale, Kirkpatrick (1980). *Human Scale.* New York: Coward, McCann & Geoghegan.

——— (1996). *Rebels Against the Future: The Luddites and Their War on the Industrial Revolution—Lessons for the Computer Age.* Cambridge, MA: Perseus.

——— (2005). "Imperial Entropy: Collapse of the American Empire." *CounterPunch* 22 (Feb.).

Salmo Consulting Inc. & Diversified Environmental Services (2003). *Cumulative Effects Indicators, Thresholds, and Case Studies: Final.* Retrieved: http://scek.ca/documents/scek/Final_Reports/CEAMF%20Final%20Report2.pdf

Sargent, Paul (2005). "The Gendering of Men in Early Childhood Education." *Sex Roles: A Journal of Research* (Feb.).

Sata, T.K. Nonaka, T. Miura, & K. Peter (1994). "Trends in Cohort Fertility of the Dariusleut Hutterite Population." *Human Biology* 66 (3) pp. 421–32.

Saussure, Ferdinand de (1966). *Course in General Linguistics.* New York: McGraw-Hill.

Schecter, Stephen (1977). "Capitalism, Class, and Educational Reform in Canada." In L. Panitch (ed.), *The Canadian State: Political Economy and Political Power.* Toronto: University of Toronto.

Scoffield, Heather (2011). "Locals Disagree on Who's to Blame for Attawapiskat Crisis." Canada Press (29 Nov.).

Seeley, John, R. Alexander Sim, & E.W. Loosely (1956). *Crestwood Heights: A Study of the Culture of Suburban Life.* Toronto: University of Toronto.

Shaw, David (2004). "News as Entertainment Is Sadly Becoming the Norm." *Los Angeles Times* (11 July). Retrieved: http://articles.latimes.com/2004/jul/11/entertainment/ca-shaw11

Shiva, Vandana (1988). *Staying Alive: Women, Ecology and Development.* London: Zed Books.

Shkilnyk, Anastasia M. (1985). *A Poison Stronger Than Love: The Destruction of an Ojibwa Community.* New Haven, CT: Yale

Shrimpton, Gordon (1987). "The Crisis in Canadian Universities." In T. Wotherspoon (ed.), *The Political Economy of Canadian Schooling.* Toronto: Methuen.

Siddiqui, Haroon (2006). *Being Muslim.* Toronto: Groundwood Books.

Simmel, Georg (1890). *On Social Differentiation.* Leipzig: Duncker & Humbolt.

——— (1990 [1900]). *The Philosophy of Money.* Ed. David Frisby. New York: Routledge.

——— (1908). *Sociology: Investigations on the Forms of Socialization.* Lepizig: Duncker & Humbolt.

Singh, Sundar. "The Sikhs in Canada. An Address Delivered before the Empire Club of Canada" (25 Jan. 1912). Retrieved: http://speeches.empireclub.org/62324/data?n=15

Slaughter, Sheila (1990). *The Higher the Learning & Higher Technology: Dynamics of Higher Education Policy Formation.* New York: State University of New York.

Smith, Dorothy (1987). *The Everyday World as Problematic: A Feminist Sociology.* Boston: Northeastern University.

——— (1990). *The Conceptual Practices of Power: A Feminist Sociology of Knowledge.* Toronto: University of Toronto.

Smith, George W. (1998). "The Ideology of 'Fag': The School Experience of Gay Students." *The Sociological Quarterly* 39 (2), pp. 309–35.

Smith, James M. (2007). *Ireland's Magdalen Laundries and the Nation's Architecture of Containment.* Notre Dame, IN: University of Notre Dame.

Smits, David D. (1982). "The 'Squaw Drudge': A Prime Index of Savagism." *Ethnohistory* 29 (4), pp. 281–306.

Soffritti, Morando, Fiorella Belpoggi, Marco Manservigi, Eva Tibaldi, Michelina Lauriola, Laura Falcioni, & Luciano Bua (2010). "Aspartame Administered in Feed, Beginning Prenatally Through Life Span, Induces Cancers of the Liver and Lung in Male Swiss Mice." *American Journal of Industrial Medicine* (30 July). DOI:10.1002/ajim.20896

Song, Miri (1996). "'Helping Out': Young People's Labour Participation in Chinese Take-Away Businesses in Britain." In J. Brannen & M. O'Brien (Eds), *Children in Families,* pp. 101–13. London: Falmer.

Span, Paula (2011). "In China, a More Western Approach to Elder Care." *The New York Times* (27 July).

Speck, Frank (1935). *Naskapi: The Savage Hunters of the Labrador Peninsula.* Norman, OK: University of Oklahoma Press.

Spencer, Herbert (1862). *First Principles.* Retrieved: http://praexology.net/HS-SP-FP-pref1.htm

——— (1896). *Social Statics, Abridged & Revised Together with Man Versus the State.* New York: D. Appleton.

——— (1896 [1880]). *The Study of Sociology.* New York: D. Appleton.

Spengler, Oswald (1918–22). *The Decline of the West.* New York: Alfred A. Knopf.

Starhawk (1979). *The Spiral Dance: A Rebirth of the Ancient Religion of the Great Goddess.* San Francisco: Harper.

——— (1982). *Dreaming the Dark: Magic, Sex, and Politics.* Boston: Beacon.

——— (2002). *Webs of Power: Notes from the Global Uprising.* Victoria: New Society.

Statistics Canada (1992). *Marriage and Conjugal Life in Canada* (cat. no. 91-534E). Ottawa: Statistics Canada.

——— (2001). "Religions in Canada: Highlight Table, 2001 Census" (cat. no. 97F0024XIE2001015). Retrieved: www12.statcan.gc.ca/English/census01/products/highlight/religion/Index.cfm?Lang=E.

——— (2004). "Performance of Canada's Youth in Mathematics, Reading, Science, and Problem Solving." *The Daily* (7 Dec.). Retrieved: www.statcan.gc.ca/daily-quotidien/041207/dq041207a-eng.htm

——— (2007a). "The Haitian Community in Canada" (28 Aug.). Retrieved: www.statcan.gc.ca/pub/89-621-x/89-621-x2007011-eng.htm

——— (2007b). *Participation and Activity Limitation Survey 2006: Analytical Report* (cat. no. 89-628-XIE). Ottawa: Minister of

Industry. Retrieved: www.statcan.gc.ca/pub/89-628-x/89-628-x2007002-eng.pdf

———— (2007c). *Participation and Activity Limitation Survey 2006: Tables* (cat. no. 89-628-XIE, no. 003). Ottawa: Minister of Industry.

———— (2007d). "Seniors as Victims of Crime." *The Daily* (6 March). Retrieved: www.statcan.gc.ca/daily-quotidien/070306/dq070306b-eng.htm

———— (2008). *Mean Age and Median Age of Males and Females, by Type of Marriage and Marital Status, Provinces and Territories, Annual* (CANSIM Table 101-1002). Ottawa: Statistics Canada, Demography Division.

———— (2009). "Household Size Declining." *Canada Year Book Overview. 2008.* Retrieved: www41.statcan.gc.ca/2008/40000/ceb40000_000-eng.htm

———— (2010). "Study: The Financial Impact of Student Loans." *The Daily* (29 Jan.). Retrieved: www.statcan.gc.ca/daily-quotidien/100129/dq100129c-eng.htm

———— (2011a). "Low Income Cut-Offs." *Low Income Lines, 2009–2010. Income Research Paper Series.* Retrieved: www.statcan.gc.ca/pub/75f0002m/75f0002m2011002-eng.htm

———— (2011b). Canadian Vital Statistics, Marriage Database and Demography Division (population estimates). Ottawa: Statistics Canada.

———— (2011c). "Access to a Regular Medical Doctor, 2010." Retrieved: www.statcan.gc.ca/pub/82-625-x/2011001/article/11456-eng.htm

———— (2011d). "Study: Delayed Retirement." *The Daily* (26 Oct.). Retrieved: www.statcan.gc.ca/daily-quotidien/111026/dq111026b-eng.htm

———— (2012a). *Portrait of Families and Living Arrangements in Canada: Families, Households, and Marital Status, 2011 Census of Population* (cat. no. 98-312-X2011001). Ottawa: Minister of Industry.

———— (2012b). *The Canadian Population in 2011: Age and Sex* (cat. no. 98-311-X2011001). Ottawa: Minster of Industry.

———— (2012c). Health Fact Sheet: Smoking, 2011. Retrieved: www.statcan.gc.ca/pub/82-625-x/2012001/article/11668-eng.htm

Steckley, John L. (1999). *Beyond Their Years: Five Native Women's Stories.* Toronto: Canadian Scholars' Press.

———— (2003). *Aboriginal Voices and the Politics of Representation in Canadian Sociology Textbooks.* Toronto: Canadian Scholars' Press.

Steckley, John, & Bryan Cummins (2001). *Full Circle: Canada's First Nations.* Toronto: Prentice-Hall.

———— & ———— (2008). *Full Circle: Canada's First Nations* (2nd edn). Toronto: Pearson.

Steckley, John, & Brian Rice (1997). "Lifelong Learning and Cultural Identity: A Lesson from Canada's Native People." In Michael Hatton (ed.), *Lifelong Learning: Policies, Programs & Practices*, pp. 216–29. Toronto: APEC.

Steger, Manfred B. (2003). *Globalization: A Very Short Introduction.* Oxford: Oxford.

Stewart, Susan (1996). "A Day in the Life of Two Community Police Officers: The Aboriginal Police Directorate Takes a Look at the First Nations Policing Policy in Action." *First Nations Policing Update* 4 (March). Retrieved: www.sgc.gc.ca/whoweare/aboriginal/newsletter/no4/no43.htm

Stewart, Walter (2003). *The Life and Political Times of Tommy Douglas.* Toronto: McArthur.

Stiegelbauer, S.M. (1996). "What Is an Elder? What Do Elders Do? First Nation Elders as Teachers in Culture-Based Urban Organizations." *The Canadian Journal of Native Studies* 16 (1), pp. 37–66.

Stiglitz, Joseph E. (2003). *Globalization and Its Discontents.* New York: Norton.

Sutherland, Edwin (1940). "White Collar Criminality." *American Sociological Review* 5 (1), pp. 1–12.

———— (1949). *White Collar Crime.* New York: Holt, Rinehart and Winston.

Tajima, E. Renee (1989). "Lotus Blossoms Don't Bleed: Images of Asian Women." In Asian Women United of California (ed.), *Making Waves: An Anthology of Writings by and About Asian American Women*, pp. 305–9. Boston: Beacon.

Talbot, Yves, E. Fuller-Thomson, F. Tudiver, Y. Habib, & W.J. McIsaac (2001). "Canadians Without Regular Medical Doctors: Who are They?" *Canadian Family Physician* 47 (Jan.), pp. 58–64.

Tataryn, Lloyd (1979). *Dying for a Living.* Ottawa: Deneau and Greenberg

Tatum, Beverly Daniel (2003). *"Why Are All the Black Kids Sitting Together in the Cafeteria?" and Other Conversations about Race*, rev. edn. New York: Basic.

Taylor, Steven J., & Robert Bogdan (1984). *Introduction to Qualitative Research Methods: The Search for Meaning.* New York: Wiley.

Telfer, Mary A. (1968). "Are Some Criminals Born That Way?" *Think* 34 (6), pp. 24–8.

Tepperman, Lorne, & Michael Rosenberg (1998). *Macro/Micro: A Brief Introduction to Sociology*, 3rd edn. Scarborough, ON: Prentice Hall, Allyn & Bacon.

"The Spectrum of Disability" (1999). *The Lancet* 354 (28 Aug.), p. 693.

Thiessen, Victor, & Christy Nickerson (1999). *Canadian Gender Trends in Education and Work.* Ottawa: Human Resources and Development Canada, Applied Research Branch.

"This Should Not Have Happened [Editorial]" (2011). *Windspeaker* 29 (2). Retrieved: www.windspeaker.com/

Thomas, W.I. (1966). *W.I. Thomas on Social Organization and Social Personality. Selected Papers.* Ed. Morris Janowitz. Chicago: University of Chicago.

Thomas, W.I., & Florian Znaniecki (1996 [1918–20]). *The Polish Peasant in Europe and America.* Urbana: University of Illinois.

Thompson, A.C. (2008). "Katrina's Hidden Race War." *The Nation* (17 Dec.). Retrieved: www.thenation.com/article/katrinas-hidden-race-war#

Thompson, Carol (2006). "Unintended Lessons: Plagiarism and the University." *Teachers College Record* 108 (12), pp. 2439–49.

Thorndike, Edward (1999 [1911]). *Animal Intelligence: Experimental Studies.* Piscataway, NJ: Transaction.

Thrasher, Frederic M. (1927). *The Gang: A Study of 1,313 Gangs in Chicago.* Chicago: University of Chicago.

TransUnion (2012). "Personal Debt Levels Balloon to Highest Levels Ever; Debt Levels Growing at Fastest Rate Since 2010" (14 Nov.). Retrieved: http://newsroom-en.transunion.ca/manual-releases/2012/TransUnion--Personal-Debt-Levels-Balloon-to-Highes

Tuchman, Barbara (1978). *A Distant Mirror: The Calamitous 14th Century*. New York: Knopf.

Tuhiwai Smith, Linda (1999). *Decolonizing Methodologies: Research and Indigenous Peoples*. London: Zed Books.

Turcotte, Martin (2010). "Working at Home: An Update." *Canadian Social Trends* (7 Dec.). Statistics Canada cat. no. 11-008-X. Retrieved: www.statcan.gc.ca/pub/11-008-x/2011001/article/11366-eng.pdf

Turnbull, Colin (1961). *The Forest People*. New York: Simon & Schuster.

Turner, Graeme (2010). *Ordinary People and the Media*. London: Sage.

Turner, Lucien M. (2001 [1894]). *Ethnology of the Ungava District, Hudson Bay Territory*. Montreal: McGill–Queen's University Press.

Urmetzer, Peter, & Neil Guppy (1999). "Changing Income Inequality in Canada." In J. Curtis, et al. (eds), *Social Inequality in Canada*, pp. 56–65. Scarborough, ON: Prentice Hall.

Useem, Michael (1979). "The Social Organization of the American Business Elite and Participation of Corporation Directors in the Governance of American Institutions." *American Sociological Review* 44 (Aug.), pp. 553–72.

—— (1981). "Business Segments and Corporate Relations with US Universities." *Social Problems* 29 (2), pp. 129–41.

Varadarajan, Dhulasi Birundha (2002). "Women and Environment Eco-feminists' Perspectives." In A. Ranga Reddy (ed.), *Empowerment of Women and Ecological Development*. New Delhi: Serials.

Veblen, Thorstein (1904). *The Theory of Business Enterprise*. New York: Charles Scribner's Sons.

—— (1912 [1899]). *The Theory of the Leisure Class: An Economic Study of Institutions*, 2nd edn. New York: Macmillan.

—— (1934 [1899]). *The Theory of the Leisure Class: An Economic Study of Institutions*. Fwd. Stuart Chase. New York: Modern.

Waldrop, M. Mitchell (1992). *Complexity*. New York: Simon & Schuster.

Walla, Harsha (2008). "*Komagata Maru* and the Politics of Apologies." *The Dominion: News from the Grassroots* (11 Sept.). Retrieved: www.dominionpaper.ca/articles/2014

Walton, John (1984). *Reluctant Rebels: Comparative Studies of Revolution and Underdevelopment*. New York: Columbia.

Warner, Jessica (2002). *Craze: Gin and Debauchery in an Age of Reason*. New York: Basic.

wa'Thiong'o, Ngũgĩ (2012). *In the House of the Interpreter: A Memoir*. New York: Pantheon.

Watkins, Mel (1992). *Madness and Ruin: Politics and the Economy in the Neoconservative Age*. Toronto: Between the Lines.

Watson, John B. (1925). *Behaviorism*. New York: Norton.

Watson, John B., & R. Rayner. (1920). "Conditioned Emotional Reactions." *Journal of Experimental Psychology* 3, pp. 1–14.

Weatherford, Jack (2004). *Genghis Khan and the Making of the Modern World*. New York: Crown.

Weber, Max. (1930 [1904]). *The Protestant Ethic and the Spirit of Capitalism*. Trans. Talcott Parsons. New York: Charles Scribner's Sons.

—— (1958 [1946]). "Essays in Sociology." In M. Weber, H. Gerth, & C.W. Mills (eds), *From Max Weber*. New York: Oxford.

—— (1968 [1914]). *Economy and Society: An Outline of Interpretive Sociology*. New York: Bedminster.

Weiner, Jonathan (1995). *The Beak of the Finch: A Story of Evolution in Our Time*. New York: Alfred A. Knopf.

Weir, Ruth (1994). "Attacking the Deck: The Streaming of Working Class Kids in Ontario Schools." *The Spark* (Feb.), pp. 11–12.

Weisbrot, Mark (2011). "Haiti and the International Aid Scam." *The Guardian* (22 April). Retrieved: www.guardian.co.uk/commentisfree/cifamerica/2011/apr/22/haiti-aid

Weyer, Edward M. (1962 [1932]). *The Eskimos: Their Environment and Folkways*. Hamden, CT: Archon Books.

White, Nancy (2007). "Home Sweet Home." *The Star* (Toronto, 20 October), p. L1.

Whiting, Beatrice B. (1963). *Six Cultures: Studies of Child Rearing*. New York: John Wiley.

Whyte. William F. (1955). *Street-Corner Society: The Social Structure of an Italian Slum*, 2nd edn. Chicago: University of Chicago.

Williamson, Judith (1978). *Decoding Advertisements: Ideology and Meaning in Advertising*. London: Marion Boyars.

Willis, Paul E. (1977). *Learning to Labour: How Working Class Kids Get Working Class Jobs*. New York: Columbia.

Wilson, John K. (2008). *Patriotic Correctness: Academic Freedom and Its Enemies*. St Paul, MN: Paradigm.

Wilson, Stan, & Peggy Wilson (1998). "Relational Accountability to All Our Relations." *Canadian Journal of Native Education* (July).

Winn, Conrad (1988). "The Socio-economic Attainment of Visible Minorities: Facts and Policy Implications." In J. Curtis, et al. (eds), *Social Inequality in Canada: Patterns, Problems, Policies*, pp. 195–213. Scarborough, ON: Prentice-Hall.

Wolfe, Frederick (2009). "Fibromyalgia Wars." *The Journal of Rheumatology* 36 (4), pp. 671–8. DOI:10.3899/jrheum.081180

Woolf, H. Bosley (1974). *The Merriam-Webster Dictionary*. New York: G & C Merriam Company.

Wrong, Dennis (1961). "The Oversocialized Conception of Man in Modern Sociology." *American Sociological Review* 26 (2), pp. 183–93.

Wyness, Michael (2006). *Childhood and Society: An Introduction to the Sociology of Childhood*. London: Palgrave Macmillan.

Yalnizyan, Armine (1998). *The Growing Gap: A Report on Growing Inequality between the Rich and Poor in Canada*. Toronto: Centre for Social Justice.

Yellen, John (1985). "Bushmen." *Science 85* (May).

York, Geoffrey (1990). *The Dispossessed: Life and Death in Native Canada*. Toronto: Lester & Orpen Dennys.

Young, Egerton R. (1974 [1893]). *Stories from Indian Wigwams and Northern Campfires*. Toronto: Coles.

Zola, Irving K. (2003 [1982]). *Missing Pieces: A Chronicle of Living with a Disability*, rev. edn. Philadelphia: Temple University Press.

Zweig, Ferdynand (1961). *The Worker in an Affluent Society: Family Life and Industry*. London: Heinemann.

Credits

The author gratefully acknowledges the use of the following material:

Table 3.5: Reprinted with the permission of Simon & Schuster Publishing Group from the Free Press edition of *Suicide: A Study in Sociology* by Emile Durkheim, translated by John A. Spaulding and George Simpson. Edited by George Simpson. Copyright © 1951, copyright © renewed 1979 by the Free Press. All rights reserved.

Excerpts, p. 86 and 304 from Anderson. *Sociology* 1e. © 1996 Nelson Education Ltd. Reproduced by permission.

Excerpt, p. 123 from *Through the Narrow Gate* by Karen Armstrong. Copyright © 2005 Karen Armstrong. Reprinted by permission of Knopf Canada.

Excerpt, p. 126 from Demerson, Velma (2004). *Incorrigible*. Waterloo: Wilfrid Laurier University Press, p. 5. By permission of Velma Demerson.

Excerpt, p. 165 from West Edmonton Mall website at http://www.wem.ca/#/shop/theme-streets/europa-boulevard. Used with permission.

Excerpts, pp. 303, 311, 321 from *Rick Hansen: Man in Motion* by Rick Hansen and Jim Taylor, published in 2011 by Douglas & McIntyre. Reprinted with permission from the publisher.

Excerpt, p. 306-7 from the Installation Speech of David C. Onley at http://www.lgontario.ca/en/events/pages/speeches.aspx

Excerpt, p. 319-320 from *The Boy in the Moon: A Father's Search for His Disabled Son*, by Ian Brown. Copyright © 2009 Ian Brown. Reprinted by permission of Random House Canada.

Excerpt, p. 319 adapted from: Bruce Campion-Smith and Allan Woods, "The Hidden Face of Our Injured Soldiers," *Toronto Star*, November 7th 2010 at http://www.thestar.com/news/canada/woundedwarriors/article/886771--the-hidden-face-of-our-injured-soldiers

Excerpt, p. 367 from pp. 159–60 of Seeley, John R., R. Alexander Sim, and Elizabeth W. Loosely, in collaboration with Norman W. Bell and D.F. Fleming, *Crestwood Heights: A North American Suburb*, © University of Toronto Press 1956. Reprinted with permission of the publisher.

Table 14.2: For 1921 to 1976, source is Wayne McVey & Warren Kalbach (1995), *Canadian Population* (Toronto: Nelson): 270. For 1981 to 2006, the source is Statistics Canada, Fertility: Overview, 2008, Table 2: http://www.statcan.gc.ca/pub/91-209-x/2011001/article/11513/tbl/tbl-eng.htm#a2

Excerpt, page 392, from Gianotti, Timothy J., 2011, *In the Light of a Blessed Tree: Illuminations of Islamic Belief, Practice, and History*. Eugene, Oregon: Wipf & Stock, pp. 14–15. Used by permission of Wipf and Stock Publishers. www.wipfandstock.com

Excerpts, p. 395 and 396, reprinted with the permission of Simon & Schuster Publishing Group from the Free Press edition of *Suicide: A Study in Sociology* by Emile Durkheim, translated by John A. Spaulding and George Simpson. Edited by George Simpson. Copyright © 1951, copyright © renewed 1979 by the Free Press. All rights reserved.

Excerpt, p. 456–7 used by permission of the Douglas Coldwell Foundation.

Excerpt, p. 460 used by permission of Linda Hasenfratz.

Excerpt, pp. 467–9 reproduced with the permission of the Minister of Public Works and Government Services Canada, 2013.

Excerpts, p. 513, from McLuhan, Marshall, *The Gutenberg Galaxy: The Making of Typographic Man*, © University of Toronto Press, 1962; 2011 edition © Estate of Corinne McLuhan. Reprinted with permission of the publisher.

Excerpts, p. 548 and 567 from *The Lexus and the Olive Tree: Understanding Globalization* by Thomas L. Friedman. Copyright © 1999, 2000 by Thomas L. Friedman. Reprinted by permission of Farrar, Straus and Giroux, LLC.

Excerpts, pp 549, 550 and 552 by permission of Oxford University Press.

Excerpt, p. 562 from Husain, Mir Zohair, *Global Islamic Politics*, 1st edition © 1995, pp. 37–8. Reprinted by permission of Pearson Education, Inc., Upper Saddle River, NJ.

Excerpts, p. 622 from *The Trouble with Islam Today: A Wake-up Call for Honesty and Change* by Irshad Manji. Copyright © 2003 Irshad Manji. Reprinted by permission of Random House Canada.

Photos

page iii (from top): Guy Letts; dmvphotos/Shutterstock; AP Photo/Manish Swarup; iStockphoto/Bonnie Jacobs; © jcarillet/iStockphoto; **page iv:** © Sophia Fortier; **page v (top):** John Lehmann/*The Globe and Mail*; **page v (bottom):** iStockphoto/Zhang Bo; **page vi (top):** The Canadian Press/Troy Fleece; **page vi (bottom):** CP/AP Photo/Chris O'Meara; **page vii (top):** Michael Blann/Thinkstock; **page vii (bottom):** iStockphoto / MorePixels; **page viii:** © Myszolow/Dreamstime.com; **page ix (top):** © LL28/iStockphoto; **page ix (bottom):** Julie Oliver/*Ottawa Citizen*, reprinted by permission; **page x (top):** © Paul Lovichi Photography/Alamy; **page x (bottom):** Photo by Natalie Behring/Getty Images; **page xi (top):** xflickrx/Flickr - http://www.flickr.com/photos/environment/2167097486/; **page xi (bottom):** © Sophia Fortier; **page xii (top):** iStockphoto/Thinkstock; **page xii (bottom):** CP Photo/Andrew Tolson; **page xiii:** iStockphoto/Mark Bowden; **page xiv (top):** © Richard Levine / Alamy; **page xiv (bottom):** Dmitry Berkut/Shutterstock; **page xv (top):** iStockphoto/tirc83; **page xv (bottom):** Moe Doiron/*The Globe and Mail*; **page xvi:** photo © Asif Rehman; **page 1:** © Lisa Stokes/Flikr Open/Getty; **page 2:** © David Pearson/Alamy; **page 4:** © Kathy deWitt/Alamy; **page 6:** iStockphoto/Ann Worthy; **page 8:** Ted Jacob/Postmedia News files; **page 10:** © Yaroslava Mills; **page 11:** Mary Evans Picture Library; **page 18:** © McCord Museum; **page 20:** © Nathan Benn/Alamy; **page 24:** © LOOK Die Bildagentur der Fotografen GmbH/Alamy; **page 26:** © pbpvision/Alamy; **page 29:** The Canadian Press/Jonathan Hayward; **page 30:** iStockphoto/Bonnie Jacobs; **page 32:** New York Daily News/Getty; **page 35:** iStockphoto/Zhang Bo; **page 36:** © Richard Baker/In Pictures/Corbis; **page 39:** © Stephanie

Sinclair/VII; **page 41:** John Lehmann/*The Globe and Mail*; **page 44:** © Photos 12/Alamy; **page 48:** Chris Schmidt/Getty Images; **page 50:** iStockphoto.com/Mad Circles; **page 50:** Tyler Anderson/*National Post*; **page 54:** Library and Archives Canada/PA-168131; **page 55:** © David K. Hoffman/Alamy; **page 59:** Keith Beaty/GetStock.com; **page 62:** Courtesy of Adbusters Media Foundation; **page 63:** © Mary Evans/Grenville Collins Postcard Collection; **page 65:** Blend Images/Alamy; **page 69:** © PNC; **page 75:** © Frank and Helena/cultura/Corbis; **page 76:** © Associated Press/Rex Features; **page 78:** Joseph Sohm/Getty Images; **page 80:** foodpix/Alamy; **page 82:** The Canadian Press/Troy Fleece; **page 83:** Shane Danaher, used with permission; **page 84:** Dustin Glick, used with permission; **page 85:** © Canadian Club/Beam Global;**page 87:** Andre Ringuette/NHL1 via Getty Images; **page 91:** © iStockphoto/michael koehl; **page 94:** CP/AP Photo/Andy Wong; **page 95:** © Brian Jungen and Catriona Jeffries Gallery; **page 98:** © Nippon Animation Co, Ltd 1979; **page 104:** © Tim Pannell/Corbis; **page 106:** © Photofusion Picture Library/Alamy; **page 108:** © Joe Cicak/iStockphoto; **page 111:** Bambu Productions/Getty; **page 112:** CP/AP Photo/Leanne Italie; **page 115:** © Angela Hampton Picture Library/Alamy; **page 117:** Andrew Wallace/GetStock.com; **page 118:** Ron Bull/GetStock.com; **page 120:** © David Pearson/Alamy; **page 125:** Copyright © Sisters of Charity, Halifax. Congregational Archives image #1693B; **page 126:** CP/AP Photo/Chris O'Meara; **page 130:** © Jose Fuste Raga/Corbis; **page 132:** A. Steckley; **page 135:** © Chris Schmidt/iStockphoto; **page 136:** Rob Cottingham, used with permission; **page 137:** © Kathy de Witt/Alamy; **page 141:** MorganLane studios/iStockphoto.com; **page 142:** CP/AP Photo/Mike Roemer; **page 143:** © Marianne Helm; **page 145:** NBC-TV/The Kobal Collection at Art Resource, NY; **page 149:** © Ricardo Azoury/iStockphoto; **page 150:** © ITAR-TASS Photo Agency/Alamy; **page 156:** Kobby Dagan/Shutterstock; **page 158:** © ClassicStock/Alamy; **page 161:** wrangler/Shutterstock; **page 163:** iStockphoto / MorePixels; **page 164:** © Danita Delimont/Alamy; **page 172:** iStockphoto/Jose Juan Garcia; **page 177:** iStockphoto/Thinkstock; **page 179:** Photo by Mark Venema/Getty Images; **page 180:** dmvphotos/Shutterstock; **page 182:** © Richard Levine/Alamy; **page 185:** © AF archive/Alamy; **page 188:** © Tim Gainey/Alamy; **page 190:** © John Steckley; **page 191:** © Myszolow/Dreamstime.com; **page 193:** Pawel Dwulit/GetStock.com; **page 195:** © Kim Sidwell/Campaign to Regulate Marijuana Like Alcohol; **page 196:** © Capp Enterprises, Inc. Used by permission; **page 197:** © Corbis; **page 198:** © Debra Wiseberg/iStockphoto; **page 202:** © Asia Photopress/Alamy; **page 207:** G. Letts; **page 208:** © Paul Lovichi Photography/Alamy; **page 210:** Aspen Photo/Shutterstock; **page 213:** Lisa S./Shutterstock; **page 214:** © Tim Gainey/Alamy; **page 216:** The Canadian Press/Adrian Wyld; **page 218:** Kazuyoshi Nomachi/Corbis; **page 220:** © LL28/iStockphoto; **page 221:** © Ricki Rosen/Corbis Saba; **page 223:** © McCord Museum; **page 224:** Photo by Josh Hedges/Zuffa LLC/Zuffa LLC via Getty Images; **page 227:** © jcarillet/iStockphoto; **page 229:** Josh Redler/5days.ca; **page 231:** © JeremyRichards/iStockphoto; **page 236:** © track5/iStockphoto; **page 239:** Rick Eglinton/GetStock.com; **page 242:** © David Norton Photography/Alamy; **page 244:** © Paul Sampson/Concepts/Alamy; **page 245:** Ann Ronan Picture Library/HIP/The Image Works; **page 249:** Nova Scotia Archives; **page 250:** © Sergeibach/Dreamstime.com; **page 254:** Vancouver Public Library, Special Collections, Accession Number: 6231;

page 257: Library and Archives Canada/C-063254; **page 259:** Goran Bogicevic/Shutterstock; **page 264:** Special Collections Department, W.E.B. Du Bois Library, University of Massachusetts-Amherst; **page 265 (left):** Daniel G. Hill fonds, Archives of Ontario, F 2130-4-4, At your service, ca. 1984–1988, Barcode B444348; **page 265 (right):** Al Dunlop/GetStock.com; **page 267:** Julie Oliver / Ottawa Citizen, reprinted by permission; **page 270:** Education Images/UIG/Getty; **page 272 (left):** 12/Alamy; **page 272 (right):** © John Steckley ; **page 275 (left):** Photo by Cameron Spencer/Getty Images; **page 275 (right):** The Canadian Press/Chris Young; **page 277:** Steve Russell/GetStock.com; **page 279:** © PCN Photography/Alamy; **page 284:** AMC/The Kobal Collection at Art Resource, NY; **page 286:** Library and Archives Canada, PA-030212; **page 289:** © lostinbids/iStockphoto; **page 291:** Wisky / Dreamstime.com; **page 292:** Photo by John H. Fouch, 1877. Courtesy of Dr. James Brust; **page 296:** © Blend Images/Alamy; **page 298:** Hemera/Thinkstock; **page 302:** iStockphoto/Thinkstock; **page 306:** *Toronto Star*/GetStock.com; **page 307:** CP Photo/Nathan Denette; **page 308:** Fox Searchlight/The Kobal Collection/Newcomb, Deana; **page 313:** © ZUMA Press, Inc./Alamy; **page 315:** AP Photo/Manish Swarup; **page 318:** Nick Beatty/Courage Canada, used with permission; **page 320:** Photo by Natalie Behring/Getty Images; **page 322:** © Patrick Byrd/Science Faction/Corbis; **page 325:** CP Photo/Nathan Denette; **page 330:** WIN-Initiative/Getty Images; **page 332:** © Sue Cunningham Photographic/Alamy; **page 336:** Image provided courtesy of Canadian Foundation for Healthcare Improvement; **page 337:** John Lehmann/*The Globe and Mail*; **page 340:** AMC-TV/The Kobal Collection at Art Resource, NY; **page 342:** http://lloydminstersportsxpress.ca/2011/05/18/timbits-on-the-soccer-pitches/. Used by permission of Lloydminster Drillers Soccer Club; **page 345:** A Mckeone Carolyn/Getty Images;**page 347:** Michael Blann/Thinkstock; **page 351:** iStockphoto/Thinkstock; **page 352 (left):** Ralph Hagen/Cartoonstock; **page 352 (right):** © Wiley Ink, inc./Distributed by Universal Uclick via Cartoonstock; **page 355:** xflickrx/Flickr — http://www.flickr.com/photos/environment/2167097486/; **page 361:** © Mick House/Alamy; **page 362:** © Sophia Fortier; **page 364:** ABC-TV/The Kobal Collection/Perez, Mario; **page 366:** Catherine Yeulet/iStockphoto; **page 369:** © Image Source/Alamy; **page 373:** Arne9001/Dreamstime.com; **page 374:** © Sophia Fortier; **page 377:** © Simon Jarratt/Corbis; **page 378:** © Blen Images/Alamy; **page 383:** Eamon Mac Mahon © 2005; **page 383:** CP/AP Photo/Joe Sales; **page 386:** © Joseph Tisiga; **page 390:** iStockphoto/Thinkstock; **page 392:** © Narges K. Kalantarian; **page 396:** © Baburns | Dreamstime.com; **page 397:** © Mhryciw/Dreamstime; **page 398 (top):** Dmitry Rukhlenko/iStockphoto; **page 398 (bottom):** Jeremy Richards/iStockphoto; **page 399:** Odd Andersen/AFP/Getty Images; **page 403:** AP Photo/Anthony S. Bush; **page 406:** CP Photo/Moose Jaw Times-Herald/Mark Taylor; **page 408:** AP Photo/Pier Paolo Cito; **page 411:** Deborah Baic/*The Globe and Mail*; **page 414:** Mike Goldwater/Alamy; **page 418:** © Image Source/Alamy; **page 420:** Radius/All Canada Photos; **page 423:** Bill Ivy Images; **page 425:** Tara Walton/GetStock.com; **page 427:** Dave Kendal Elementary School at http://davekandalelementary.weebly.com/dress-code.html, by permission of the Abbotsford School District; **page 429:** AP Photo/Tina Fineberg; **page 434:** © David Leadbitter/Alamy; **page 436:** Ron Bull/GetStock.com; **page 439:** Hogan Wong/The Ubyssey; **page 441:** CP Photo/

Index

Note: Page numbers in italic type indicate illustrations, figures or captions.